THE ORIGINS
OF THE
REPUBLICAN PARTY
1852–1856

WILLIAM E. GIENAPP

OXFORD UNIVERSITY PRESS
New York   Oxford

Oxford University Press

Oxford   New York   Toronto
Delhi   Bombay   Calcutta   Madras   Karachi
Petaling Jaya   Singapore   Hong Kong   Tokyo
Nairobi   Dar es Salaam   Cape Town
Melbourne   Auckland

and associated companies in
Beirut   Berlin   Ibadan   Nicosia

Copyright © 1987 by William E. Gienapp

First published 1987 by Oxford University Press, Inc.,
200 Madison Avenue, New York, New York 10016

First issued as an Oxford University Press paperback, 1988

Oxford is a registered trademark of Oxford University Press

Library of Congress Cataloging-in-Publication Data
Gienapp, William E.
The origins of the Republican party, 1852–1856
Bibliography: p.   Includes index.
1. Republican Party (U.S.: 1854–   )—History
2. Political parties—United States—History—19th century.
3. Elections—United States—History—19th century.
4. United States—Politics and government—1853–1857.
I. Title
JK2357 1852   324.273'04'09   86-8399
ISBN 0-19-504100-3
ISBN 0-19-505501-2 (pbk.)

Quotations from the Adams Family Papers are from the microfilm edition,
by permission of the Massachusetts Historical Society.

2   4   6   8   10   9   7   5   3   1
Printed in the United States of America

The Origins of the Republican Party
1852–1856

For Erica

Preface

Although historians have devoted considerable effort to analyzing the causes of the Civil War, they have given substantially less attention to the process of party realignment in the 1850s. There are no studies of the Whig, Republican, American, or Constitutional Union parties in this decade to complement Roy Nichols's magisterial multivolume analysis of the disruption of the Democratic party. Similarly, the related but not identical questions of party disintegration and party formation are just beginning to receive the attention they merit for the antebellum era. And much less work has been done on voting behavior before the Civil War than has been done, for example, on the realignments of the 1890s and 1930s. Realignments are rare in American history and inevitably produce significant changes in the nation's politics, but none has had consequences as profound as that of the 1850s. A few short years after the Republican party replaced the Whig party in the two-party system—in itself a rare occurrence—the nation fought a tragic civil war in response to the Republicans' national triumph in 1860.

During the last fifteen years, there has been a resurgence of interest in antebellum political history, and a number of important studies have appeared that from varying perspectives analyze different aspects of the political crisis of the 1850s. Much work still remains to be done, however, before we understand fully the process by which the earlier Jacksonian party system gave way to a new sectional alignment. The relationship between the Republican party and the political realignment of mid-decade in the North is a subject of particularly sharp controversy. Little agreement prevails concerning the nature of Republicanism before the Civil War, the party's appeal, or the reasons for its eventual triumph. In this book, I have sought to answer some of the significant questions concerning the party's first years of existence. This study focuses on the complex process by which the Republican party came into being, the political obstacles that it confronted and how it overcame them, and the reasons why it had become by the end of 1856 the most powerful party in the North.

The rise of the Republican party occurred in two separate chronological stages. Each phase, while crucial to the party's ultimate success, posed distinctly different problems. In the first stage, which extended from the party's beginning through the presidential election of 1856, the Republicans waged a desperate and at first seemingly hopeless battle with the rival American party to replace the defunct Whig organization as the primary opponent of the Democratic party in the country. The Republicans' amazing showing in that election sealed the doom of the American party and established the Republican party as the second party in the two-party system. During the second stage, which extended from the party's defeat in 1856 through the 1860 campaign, party leaders sought to broaden the Republican coalition by moderating and expanding its appeal and by bringing additional groups into the party's ranks. Further conversions would occur after 1860, but Lincoln's victory represented the culmination of the Republican party's rapid rise to national power. This volume explores the first—and in many ways more critical—phase of the party's history. It seeks to explain not only why the Republican party organized, but, more important, why it survived and why within a few short years it was the strongest party in the free states. A second volume will carry the story forward to Lincoln's election in November 1860.

In examining the early history of the Republican party, I have combined the traditional methods and sources of political history with a statistical analysis of voting returns in the free states. Too much recent political history, it seems to me, has exploited only one of these methods, yet both add to our knowledge, often in significantly different ways. Political history is more than solely the actions and decisions of party leaders, the behavior of voters, or the structure of party organizations. Rather, the interrelationship of each of these elements forms the core of political history, and a sound understanding of these relationships requires the use of a wide variety of sources, both quantitative and nonquantitative.

In addition to utilizing traditional and statistical sources, I have also integrated developments on the state and local levels with those on the national scene. Most of the work that has been done on politics in the Civil War era has focused primarily on a particular state or on national affairs. Although this approach has obvious advantages, it also has limitations. Parties competed, sometimes simultaneously, at all levels of government, and it is important to have some sense of both the unity and disunity of antebellum politics under the federal system. In this study I have attempted to show how events on one level affected those on another and how together they produced some of the important political changes that occurred in this decade. By this approach, I have endeavored to restate the significance of state politics in the antebellum period and to remind readers that, organizationally, national parties in these years were only loose coalitions of state parties. A satisfactory explanation of the coming of the Civil War cannot be framed entirely within the context of national politics but must also take into account state and local developments; consequently, I believe that the methodology of this study offers a more fruitful approach to unraveling the central event of American history than one limited to national politics.

My discussion of state developments and especially my analysis of voting behavior concentrates on nine states: Connecticut, Massachusetts, and Maine of the New England states; New York and Pennsylvania from the middle states; Ohio, Indiana, and Illinois from the Old Northwest; and Iowa from the Trans-Mississippi West. A number of considerations in addition to geographic distribution prompted this selection. I included New York, Pennsylvania, Ohio, Indiana, and Illinois because of their obvious impor-tance. As the most heavily populated of the northern states, they had great political significance, both nationally and within the Republican organization; indeed, from the beginning Republican leaders confronted the stark political reality that a northern sectional party had little chance of winning national power unless it controlled these states with their large bloc of electoral votes. In addition, Ohio and New York played particularly critical roles in the movement to organize a new party, while in the other three states the party experienced considerable difficulty and was correspondingly much weaker. I chose Iowa because I wanted to examine the party's formation in a predominantly rural state and because of the availability of a detailed state census for 1856. Massachusetts lacked the electoral strength of some of the other northern states, but its importance as the foremost exemplar of New England values and traditions, coupled with the excellent quality of its manuscript sources, led me to give it considerable attention. Maine had several attractions. For one thing, the prohibition movement won its first statewide triumph there, and the liquor question remained an important political issue in the state for an extended period of time. In addition, the outcome of realignment in Maine was particularly dramatic, as the political upheaval of the decade transformed it from a banner Democratic state to a stronghold of Republicanism. I decided to examine Connecticut because it was and remained politically competitive and because the number of townships was small enough to be manageable in terms of data collection and analysis. I have discussed political developments in the other northern states whenever they were important to my analysis.

When quoting from primary sources, I have minimized the use of *sic* except in those cases when confusion might arise, and I have omitted ellipses at the beginning and end of quotations. I have endeavored to quote the sources exactly as they were written, except that I have lowered raised letters and changed terminal dashes to periods. Otherwise, I have let the remarks of men and women of this period stand as they originally wrote them.

The research of this book was made possible in part by financial assistance from several sources. I am particularly grateful to the Mabelle McLeod Lewis Memorial Fund, Stanford, California, which during the early stages of this project awarded me a grant that enabled me to spend more than a year doing research in libraries across the country. In addition, both the University of California, Berkeley, and the University of Wyoming provided essential computer funds, and the Department of History at the latter institution also made available funds for keypunching. I also wish to express my appreciation to Peter Iverson, former Chairman of the Department of History at Wyoming, who obtained money for the drawing of the maps, and who has been a good friend during the past six years. Support for the book's publication came from the Office of the Vice President for Research and the Dean of the College of Arts and Sciences at the University of Wyoming.

Portions of this book were published previously in a different form in *Civil War History*, the *Journal of American History, Ohio History*, and the *Pennsylvania Magazine of History and Biography*, as well as in chapters in books published by Texas A&M University Press and the University Press of Kentucky. I wish to thank the editors of these journals and presses for permission to reproduce this material.

In completing this project, I received assistance from many individuals. A number of friends opened their homes to me, a kindness for which I would like to thank Bob and Peggy Benson, Jack and Maxene Benson, Gena Blythe, Walt and Helen Gienapp, Rich and Lana Kruse, Glenn May and Caitriona Bolster, Mark and Sylvia Neely, Francis and Margery Southern, Dick Southern, and Marc and Susan Trachtenberg. During the course of my research, I visited a large number of repositories and wrote to others for copies of material and information, and I wish to acknowledge the assistance of the staffs of all of them. I would particularly like to express my gratitude for exceptional courtesies extended by Father Thomas Blantz, Roger Bridges, Laura Chace, Billie Gammon, Frances Macdonald, Archie Motley, Karl Kabelac, and Alice Vestal. John McDonough of the

Library of Congress's Manuscript Division deserves special mention for his help and the thoroughness with which he has answered my inquiries over the years. I am also indebted to Donald Williams and the staff of the inter-library loan office of the library of the University of California, Berkeley, and Janet Carlton and the staff of the same division in the University of Wyoming library for indefatigably locating and securing countless items for my use. The research was made less burdensome by the pleasant atmosphere created by JoAnne Brock and the staff of the newspaper and microfilm room at the Berkeley library, particularly Frances Finn, Lyla Eckart, and the late Lisa Layton. I would also like to thank Forbes Rockwell for allowing me to examine the papers of Julius Rockwell and for searching for additional material among his family's holdings.

Margaret Baker of the Survey Research Center at Berkeley, Tom Price, formerly of the University of Wyoming computer center, Bill Burns, and John Schnor provided invaluable assistance with computer programs and the statistical computations used in this study. In addition, John J. Kushma, Allan Lichtman, and William G. Shade all took time to answer, sometimes at considerable length, my queries concerning statistical techniques and to offer advice based on their own research. Ellen Leroe and George Ainslie both sent me election returns that were otherwise inaccessible to me, and Joel H. Silbey, Paul Goodman, Ken Kann, and Carl Abbott generously made available voting returns and other statistical data that they had collected. Grace O'Connell typed the first draft of the manuscript with great efficiency and saved me from several errors. Diane Alexander accurately typed more drafts than either of us care to remember and through it all remained extraordinarily gracious and never lost her sense of humor. In a unique way, Bill and Janet Hermann helped by forming a very special friendship with my family that significantly hastened completion of the first draft of this manuscript.

A number of friends and colleagues read all or parts of the manuscript and made suggestions for its improvement. I wish to thank Richard Carwardine, James W. Davidson, Eric Foner, John Kushma, Robert Middlekauff, Peggy Mooney, Mark E. Neely, Jr., Steven J. Novak, William J. Rorabaugh, and Richard H. Sewell for many helpful comments. Parts of this study incorporate work that I did in seminars directed by Howard R. Lamar and William Stanton, both of whom offered valuable direction as I first began to investigate the origins of the Republican party. At an important point in my graduate education, Edmund S. Morgan extended some much needed support, which has meant a great deal to me ever since. Without Robert Middlekauff's intervention to obtain sufficient funds that enabled me to finish my initial statistical work, the scope of this project would have been severely curtailed and my progress seriously impeded. I very much appreciate the contributions of Stephen E. Maizlish, a specialist in this period as well as a long-time friend, who shared with me material on Ohio politics, and who read the manuscript closely and was always good-natured in voicing his disagreements. Paul Goodman and Joel Silbey both gave the manuscript a searching reading, called my attention to sources that I might otherwise have missed, and offered good advice and friendly encouragement. From the beginning Michael F. Holt, who sparked my interest initially in the early Republican party, has taken a keen interest in my work and has been unfailing in his concern and encouragement. He read the manuscript with great care and special insight, and his probing comments caused me to rethink a number of my arguments. To all these individuals and others I have not mentioned, I offer my sincere thanks.

It was my good fortune to have Sheldon Meyer as my editor at Oxford University Press. Throughout our association, he retained his enthusiasm for this project, and he never wavered in his commitment to see a long manuscript published in the proper form. I also had an outstanding copy editor in Dorothy Z. Seymour, who went over the manuscript a number of times with scrupulous care and immeasurably improved its style and clarity. In addition, Rachel Toor at Oxford was exceedingly helpful on several matters of production, and Leona Capeless oversaw the final editing with great skill and wonderful good humor.

Kenneth M. Stampp has influenced my life in more ways than is usual for a dissertation chairman. It was under his guidance that I first developed my interest in the Civil War, and from the beginning he has been a stimulating teacher, a thoughtful critic, and a concerned adviser. Over the years he has provided encouragement and support, offered good counsel when I needed it, and always allowed me to present my own views, even when he strongly dissented from them. For all this and much more I am extremely grateful. I should also like to extend a special thank you to Isabel Stampp for her hospitality and thoughtfulness during the past decade and a half.

None of these individuals, of course, are responsible for what I have said. They have improved the manuscript in numerous ways, but I wish to exonerate them in advance for whatever errors of fact and stubborn misjudgments remain.

Last but not least, I would like to acknowledge the contribution of my family. In countless ways, large and small, my parents, June and the late Bill Gienapp, and my wife's parents, Frank and the late Dorothy Kilian, rendered valuable assistance for which I am very thankful. The constant interruptions (delightful or otherwise) of my two sons, Billy and Jonathan, did little to speed completion of this work but nevertheless helped me to keep it in perspective. The deepest debt of gratitude, which I can never adequately express, I owe to my wife Erica. She supported me during much of my graduate career, accompanied me on my cross country travels and helped with the research, assumed additional duties in order to give me time to work, served as my most severe critic, and voiced only minimal complaints as our house was increasingly taken over by notes, computer cards, microfilm, and computer printout. Most of all, I want to thank her for sharing her life with me. This book is for her, with love.

W. E. G.

Contents

Abbreviations Used in Footnotes

AHR	*American Historical Review*
APSR	*American Political Science Review*
BECHS	Buffalo and Erie County Historical Society
ChicHS	Chicago Historical Society
CinHS	Cincinnati Historical Society
ConnHS	Connecticut Historical Society
CWH	*Civil War History*
DAB	*Dictionary of American Biography*
DarC	Dartmouth College
HEH	Henry E. Huntington Library
HSDC	Historical Society of Dauphin County
HSPa	Historical Society of Pennsylvania
HU	Harvard University
IaSDHA	Iowa State Department of History and Achives
IllSHL	Illinois State Historical Library
IndHS	Indiana Historical Society
IndSL	Indiana State Library
IndU	Indiana University
JAH	*Journal of American History*
JSH	*Journal of Southern History*
KSHS	Kansas State Historical Society
LC	Library of Congress
MassHS	Massachusetts Historical Society
MVHR	*Mississippi Valley Historical Review*
NEQ	*New England Quarterly*
NHHS	New Hampshire Historical Society
NIHS	Northern Indiana Historical Society
NYHS	New-York Historical Society
NYPL	New York Public Library
NYSL	New York State Library
OHS	Ohio Historical Society
SUNY	State University of New York, Oswego
UChic	University of Chicago
UMe	University of Maine
UR	University of Rochester
WiscSHS	State Historical Society of Wisconsin
WRHS	Western Reserve Historical Society

The Origins of the Republican Party
1852–1856

Introduction

Few political leaders have understood as clearly as Teddy Roosevelt the difficulties inherent in launching a new party. As the candidate of the Bull Moose party, the former president headed one of the most important third-party movements since the Civil War. In fact, the Progressives' second-place finish in the 1912 presidential election surpassed that of any new party since the Republicans' performance in 1856. Yet in spite of the euphoria that burst forth following his great popular showing, Roosevelt dismissed the idea that the two parties' situations were analogous. He observed pointedly that after its first national campaign the Republican party, unlike the Progressive, controlled a number of states, had elected a sizable contingent of congressmen, and, most important, was "overwhelmingly the second party in the nation." Because a disaffected voter's support for another party was usually only temporary, third parties that did not quickly become the second party had no long-term prospects, the defeated Progressive leader argued. "When we failed to establish ourselves at the very outset as the second party," he continued, "it became overwhelmingly probable that politics would soon sink back . . . into a two-party system, the Republicans and Democrats alternating in the first and second place."[1] As Roosevelt well understood, any new party had to confront the reality that the two-party system was a fundamental fact of American politics.[2]

The formation of another political party is a common occurrence in American politics. Beginning with the establishment of national parties in the 1790s, new parties have come and gone with regularity. Like the Progressive party, some have, at least temporarily, won substantial popular support, and a few have exerted significant political influence. Since the organization of the Republican party, however, no new party has carried a national election or even survived very long as a competitive organization. None has matched, even briefly, the power that the Republican party wielded within a few years of its birth. These facts, more than any other, highlight the magnitude of the Republicans' achievement.

The Republican party is one of the most striking success stories in American political annals. A formidable political organization after only a few short years, the party elected its first president in just its second national campaign. Holding power during the greatest

---

1. Theodore Roosevelt to William Allen White, November 7, 1914, Elting E. Morison, ed., *The Letters of Theodore Roosevelt* (8 vols.: Cambridge, 1951–1954), v. 8, 835. I would like to thank Jules Karlin for calling this letter to my attention.

2. A classic discussion of this aspect of American politics is E. E. Schattschneider, *Party Government* (New York, 1942), especially 65–98. For a contemporary assertion of this point, see the *Illinois State Journal*, July 27, 1854.

crisis the Republic ever confronted, it preserved the Union, abolished slavery, and enacted one of the most significant and far-reaching legislative programs in the nation's history. For over a century now, it has been a fixture of the two-party system.[3]

The party's accomplishments and longevity, however, have tended to obscure its precarious early existence. In much of the historiography of the pre-Civil War period, the rise of the Republican party takes on an almost inexorable quality, and as a result the problems of forming a new party and its subsequent emergence as a nationally competitive political organization have received only passing attention. Yet it was not obvious at the outset that the Republican party would become either powerful or permanent, and its continued existence was anything but inevitable. Even to the most loyal supporter the party's national triumph in 1860, when juxtaposed with its early career, must have seemed almost miraculous: Less than five years earlier, defeated almost everywhere and barely organized in half the northern states, the Republican movement seemed destined, like every antislavery party before it, for an early death. Indeed, in view of the fate that befell these previous parties, its survival was in many ways even more remarkable than its eventual success.

The formation of the Republican party must be understood within the context of the antebellum political system, certain basic features of which need to be noted at the outset.[4] Central to political life during these years was the universal acceptance of the ideology of republicanism. Since the Revolution, all major political parties had portrayed themselves as defenders of this heritage. As was true in the eighteenth century, republican thought in the 1850s continued to extoll the values of individual liberty, legal equality, and government restrained by law, while it stressed the existence of internal conspiracies designed to overthrow republican government and eradicate liberty. Furthermore, the strident egalitarian rhetoric so prevalent throughout American society after 1815 strengthened the belief in majority rule as well as the existing popular hatred of aristocracy and its trappings. Republicanism was not a static ideology, however. The democratic reforms enacted during the Jacksonian era incorporated white manhood suffrage and the opening of officeholding to ordinary citizens into the republican creed, while the accompanying breakdown of the system of deference created a new, more familiar relationship between politicians and the masses. In addition, the commitment to safeguard basic civil liberties occupied a more critical place in republican thought than had been true earlier. To mid-century Americans, the continuing survival of republican society depended upon the preservation of liberty and equality, against which aristocratic privilege and concentrated power were the principal threats.[5]

---

3. A recent general history is George H. Mayer, *The Republican Party, 1854–1966*, 2nd ed. (New York, 1967).

4. For a more extended analysis of the antebellum political system, see my essay, " 'Politics Seem to Enter into Everything': Political Culture in the North, 1840–1860," Stephen E. Maizlish and John J. Kushma, eds., *Essays on American Antebellum Politics, 1840–1860* (College Station, Texas, 1982), 14–69. Portions of the following pages have been adapted from this article, which provides fuller documentation for many of these points. Important discussions of this problem are presented in Joel H. Silbey, *A Respectable Minority: The Democratic Party in the Civil War Era, 1860–1868* (New York, 1977), 3–29; Ronald P. Formisano, *The Birth of Mass Political Parties: Michigan, 1827–1861* (Princeton, 1971), 3–14; and Paul Kleppner, *The Third Electoral System, 1853–1892: Parties, Voters, and Political Cultures* (Chapel Hill, 1979), 3–15, 357–82.

5. Michael F. Holt, *The Political Crisis of the 1850s* (New York, 1978) is the best discussion of the significance of republicanism in the politics of this period. Important insights pertaining to this general problem are contained in Daniel Walker Howe, *The Political Culture of the American Whigs* (Chicago, 1979); Rush

Another important change in republican thought since the Revolution was the acceptance of the legitimacy of political parties. By the last decade before the Civil War, anti-partyism was, at least in its traditional form, a dying tradition.[6] Instead of being viewed as threats to republican government, parties were now considered both inevitable and good. "Party is the great engine of human progress," one northerner wrote in 1852. "A world without party would be incapable of progress." Two years later a New England paper forcefully defended the utility of parties. "Under our system of government there will always be parties of some kind," it asserted, "and the interests of the people will be better subserved, and their rights more securely maintained with the checks and balances afforded by two great permanent opposing parties, than by the substitution of numberless smaller factions," which would "inevitably lead to greater abuse and corruption than has yet been witnessed under . . . the old parties."[7] This shift in attitude reflected, more than anything else, the accumulated political experience of the Republic's first half century of existence.

Reflective of the intense popular involvement that characterized political life, voter turnout during these years was remarkably high. Even for off-year elections, average turnout during the 1850s in the free states generally exceeded that for presidential contests in the modern era. Ordinary citizens manifested a greater interest in political affairs and a stronger attachment to the party system than prevails today. At the same time, variations in turnout provide significant clues to voters' values and motivations. As one New York paper observed, weakly politicized voters comprised "the 'stay-at-home party,'" which comes out only in times of great exigency."[8] Analysis of the conditions and issues that mobilize large numbers of voters, particularly those tied only marginally to the existing party system, is essential for an understanding of mass political behavior in this period. Non-voting represented much more a conscious decision than it did more mundane factors, such as inconvenience.[9] The simple act of not voting, the shift from one party to another at a particular time, the rigid adherence to a given party—all these actions are significant indicators of the contours of mass public opinion.

The antebellum voter's political world was not confined to national affairs and presidential contests but extended to state and local politics as well. Preoccupied with national politics, historians analyzing nineteenth century politics have slighted this basic characteristic by concentrating excessively on presidential elections.[10] They have shared

Welter, *The Mind of America, 1820–1860* (New York, 1975); George B. Forgie, *Patricide in the House Divided: A Psychological Interpretation of Lincoln and His Age* (New York, 1979).

6. Richard Hofstadter, *The Idea of a Party System: The Rise of Legitimate Opposition in the United States, 1780–1840* (Berkeley, 1969). For earlier manifestations of anti-partyism, see Ronald P. Formisano, "Political Character, Antipartyism and the Second Party System," *American Quarterly*, v. 21 (Winter, 1969), 683–709.

7. Nahum Capen, *The History of Democracy in the United States*, quoted in Silbey, *A Respectable Minority*, 7; [Augusta] *Kennebec Journal*, April 28, 1854.

8. Rochester *Daily American*, November 22, 1855.

9. The countervailing argument that non-voting was primarily a function of distance from the polls has only limited validity. For one thing, participation in the countryside regularly exceeded that in cities, where the polls obviously were much more conveniently located and where public or party transportation was frequently available. In addition, fluctuations in turnout for urban and rural areas usually paralleled one another, thereby indicating that more general forces were operative. For an emphasis on geographic factors, see Kenneth J. Winkle, "A Social Analysis of Voter Turnout in Ohio, 1850–1860," *Journal of Interdisciplinary History*, v. 13 (Winter, 1983), 411–35.

10. Thomas C. Cochran, "The Presidential Synthesis in American History," *American Historical Review*, v. 53 (July, 1948), 748–59, presents a different approach to this problem.

the view of James Russell Lowell in 1860 that "the next Presidential Election looms always in advance, so that we seem never to have an actual Chief Magistrate, but a prospective one."[11] Such an approach seriously distorts the reality of politics before the Civil War. It also greatly exaggerates the cohesion and unity of national parties, which in actuality were only loose coalitions of state parties, each of which functioned to a large extent independently of the others. As a result, party leaders enjoyed considerable discretion in the manipulation of issues. Certainly there were limits to such diversity, as the disruption of the Democratic national organization in 1860 revealed, but then as now success rather than consistency was the first rule of American politics. "He who engages in political labor, must not be nice and scrupulous about means and ends," a rural New York paper acknowledged unhappily. "Success is the only really serious consideration."[12] This decentralization also reflected the priorities of party leaders. Whatever their hopes of winning a national election, politicians, even those with national aspirations, were tied to state organizations, and controlling the state government took precedence.

In his comparison of the Republican and Progressive parties, Roosevelt emphasized another fundamental characteristic of the political system when he observed, "The average American . . . wishes to vote with his own party and the name has an enormous influence over him." Since the creation of modern parties, the resilient strength of mass partisan loyalties has been one of the most important and persistent aspects of American politics. Studies of popular voting behavior in recent times have revealed party identities to be the single most important influence on an individual's political behavior. The psychological bond between a voter and his party and the mental images that accompany it provide the basic foundation of the modern party system.[13]

Party identities were even stronger in the antebellum period. As a western Republican leader testified, in the Civil War era "party zeal ran higher than it has since." Fashioned in a time of sharp party conflict and intense voter involvement, the party identities of many pre-war Americans were remarkably impervious to change. New crises, different issues, and fresh political faces normally had little impact on most voters' partisan loyalties. An English clergyman traveling in the United States during a presidential campaign was surprised by the strength of Americans' attachment to parties. "Unflinching adherence to party is principle with them," he commented, "and to forsake a party is regarded as an act of greatest dishonour." The Cincinnati *Gazette* affirmed that "there are few stronger feelings in the American heart than that of party fealty."[14]

For many antebellum Americans a party identity, once formed, established a lifelong loyalty that became more powerful with age. The act of voting repeatedly for a party over a period of time invariably reinforced the emotional links between a voter and that party. One shrewd political observer who recognized the tendency for party identifications, once made, to grow stronger with time was former president Martin Van Buren. He warned that disgruntled Democrats who thought of joining the Republican party temporarily to rebuke

---

11. James Russell Lowell, "The Election in November," *Political Essays* (Cambridge, 1904), 25–26.

12. Jamestown *Journal*, January 21, 1859.

13. The most extended discussion of the nature and importance of party identities in the modern electorate is Angus Campbell, Philip E. Converse, Warren E. Miller, and Donald E. Stokes, *The American Voter* (New York, 1960). Also see Norman H. Nie, Sidney Verba, and John R. Petrocik, *The Changing American Voter*, enlarged ed. (Cambridge, 1979).

14. Cornelius Cole, *Memoirs of Cornelius Cole* (New York, 1908), 109; Frederick J. Jobson, *America, and American Methodism* (New York, 1857), 117; Cincinnati *Gazette*, August 21, 1854.

the Pierce administration and then returning to their old party made a serious miscalculation, for an opposing party "has always been a bourne from whence very few Democratic travellers have ever returned."[15]

Because it necessarily entailed the disruption of old friendships and associations, changing one's party was almost always a difficult and uncomfortable decision. Thurlow Weed and Washington Hunt, prominent New York Whigs who followed different political paths in the 1850s, both betrayed a deep sense of personal loss over the severing of former social connections. "In the confusion and breaking of parties," Hunt confided to a fellow conservative, "it is really a painful thing to be obliged to separate from old comrades, towards whom we cherish kindly feelings and recollections."[16] Democrats experienced equally wrenching emotions. Gustave Koerner of Illinois, who reluctantly abandoned the Democratic party in 1856, recorded in his memoirs, "I left my old party not without many pangs, and . . . it cost me much to burn my bridges."[17]

Even members disgruntled with a party's principles or nominees found it difficult to discard their partisan identity. Frequently, party members torn between their loyalty and a dislike of their party's principles eliminated the cross-pressures they felt by gradually forming new opinions rather than leaving their party. Others, paralyzed by conflicting emotions, abstained, at least on a short-term basis. In a related fashion, third parties often served as a temporary way station for voters in the process of changing their partisan identities who initially could not bring themselves to support a party they had opposed during most or all of their adult lives. For some men, voting for a minority party constituted the first step in the abandonment of their previous political affiliation. Even among third-party supporters, however, a surprising number eventally returned to their old allegiance after a temporary absence. A classic example was that of the New York Barnburners, who, after fostering the Free Soil revolt in 1848, drifted back into the regular Democratic fold over the course of the next four years.[18]

State and local issues played a significant role in the formation of antebellum party identities. In traditional treatments of the 1850s, the dramatic nature of national issues combined with the looming specter of civil war tend to overshadow state and local concerns. An exclusive emphasis on national developments, however, seriously distorts the political perspective of the typical voter as well as the sources of mass behavior.[19] Most partisan combat in these years did not occur at the national level, and voting studies have established beyond challenge the critical influence of state and local issues on mass voting patterns.[20] Because political parties before the Civil War—both at the leadership

15. Martin Van Buren to Moses Tilden, September 1, 1856, in John Bigelow, ed., *Letters and Literary Memorials of Samuel J. Tilden* (2 vols.: New York, 1908), v. 1, 121.

16. Washington Hunt to Hamilton Fish, October 7, 1855, Thurlow Weed to Hamilton Fish, November 11, 13, [1855], Hamilton Fish Papers, LC.

17. Thomas J. McCormack, ed., *Memoirs of Gustave Koerner, 1809–1896* (Cedar Rapids, Iowa, 2 vols., 1909), v. 1, 617–18.

18. Walter L. Ferree, "The New York Democracy: Division and Reunion, 1847–1852" (unpublished Ph.D. dissertation, University of Pennsylvania, 1953).

19. An article that has attained the status of a classic and that bears on these points is Joel H. Silbey, "The Civil War Synthesis in American Political History," *CWH*, v. 10 (June, 1964), 130–40.

20. Voting studies for various northern localities include Michael F. Holt, *Forging a Majority: The Formation of the Republican Party in Pittsburgh, 1848–1860* (New Haven, 1969); Formisano, *Mass Political Parties*; Kleppner, *Third Electoral System*; Stephen L. Hansen, *The Making of the Third Party System: Voters and Parties in Illinois, 1850–1876* (Ann Arbor, 1980); Dale Baum, *The Civil War Party System: The Case of Massachusetts, 1848–1876* (Chapel Hill, 1984); Roger D. Petersen, "The Reaction to a Heterogeneous Society:

level and among the rank-and-file—were much more state oriented than is the case today, a party's state and local activities shaped its popular image and constituency as much as did its national campaigns.

In much the same way as today, party identities were an important means by which antebellum voters made sense of their political world. Men were held together in parties "by the force of association and organization," the Cincinnati *Commercial* declared, and thus "under ordinary circumstances . . . mere habit is sufficient to control their acts and to supply the place of opinions which they have not time nor inclination to form."[21] Individuals viewed events, facts, and observations through the prism of party identity. Senator James A. Bayard of Delaware maintained that the "spirit of party operates unconsciously on the minds of even moderate and reflecting men, and warps and perverts their judgment. With the mass of partisans its sway is overwhelming." Through this unconscious filtering, a voter's values and ideals became integrated thoroughly with his partisan loyalty, and parties thus came to represent in the popular mind certain fundamental attitudes independent of specific campaigns. To the average voter, party labels, in other words, were important psychological symbols. As a nonpartisan paper in New England explained, party names become "invested . . . forever in our minds with certain attributes, and it matters little that . . . circumstances change, the *name* still stands, the representative of what is pleasant or hateful." Parties might alter their public positions and policies, it continued, yet "there still seems to be some magical influence about the mere names, which . . . controls our political action."[22]

Political commentators provided widely varying assessments of the extent to which the average voter in the antebellum era was motivated by ideological considerations or understood the fundamental principles at stake in party battles. The Boston *Herald* contended in 1856 that "everybody has read the newspapers lately and almost everybody is pretty well posted up on the facts and issues of the coming campaign." In contrast, the *Atlantic Monthly*, published in the same city, asserted after the 1860 election that only a small minority of voters "had seriously thought out for themselves the real issue of the contest." A much larger number, it insisted, responded to "party names," "party catchwords," and "material interests."[23] Such comments suggest that, as is the case with the modern electorate, voter perception in this period extended over a wide spectrum from a sound grasp of ideology at one extreme to only the dimmest comprehension of the issues involved at the other. It is likely, however, in view of the intense popular interest in politics, the much more important role it occupied in men's lives, and the greater strength of party identities, that the politically aware constituted a larger proportion of the antebellum electorate than they do today.

That ideology played a greater role in politics before the Civil War does not mean that party members shared the same level of comprehension of public issues as the leaders or possessed an equally sophisticated belief system. Political elites—party officials, office holders, and party workers—were more actively involved in politics and had access to

A Behavioral and Quantitative Analysis of Northern Voting Behavior, 1845–1870, Pennsylvania a Test Case" (unpublished Ph.D. dissertation, University of Pittsburgh, 1970); and Thomas W. Kremm, "The Rise of the Republican Party in Cleveland, 1848–1860" (unpublished Ph.D. dissertation, Kent State University, 1974).

   21. Cincinnati *Commercial*, September 21, 1852.
   22. Bayard is quoted in Silbey, *Respectable Minority*, 10–11; Brunswick *Telegraph*, August 19, 1854.
   23. Boston *Herald* quoted in the Brunswick *Telegraph*, June 28, 1856; "The Reign of King Cotton," *Atlantic Monthly*, v. 7 (April, 1861), 453.

more extensive and specific information. The skillful integration of a wide variety of attitudes into a comprehensive and comprehensible world view was restricted largely to the articulate minority. The majority of voters simply did not function on this intellectual level. Mass belief systems, as Paul Kleppner has emphasized, encompassed fewer ideas, were less constrained, and were less abstract than those of political leaders.[24] Nevertheless, it is not true that antebellum voters lacked meaningful political beliefs. A high level of abstraction was unnecessary for making intelligible political decisions, and voters generally shared the fundamental values that underpinned party ideologies in pre-Civil War America, even if they could not explain all the ramifications of their beliefs.

The relationship between antebellum political leaders and voters was complex and multifaceted. Certainly some concerns of politicians, as for example patronage, which often provoked bitter and long-lived disputes at the leadership level, held little importance for the populace. On issues of greater popular interest some historians have argued that the values and behavior of the masses placed definite limits on the attitudes and policies that party leaders could adopt. Other historians view politicians as playing a more dynamic role in shaping voters' responses. In reality, no single relationship linked leaders and voters at all times and under all circumstances. Instead, each of these conceptions describes an important facet of the political system.

At one level, leaders certainly sought to mold public opinion to their own purposes. Their access to and control of the major means of communication, through which they could articulate issues, structure partisan debate, and screen information, were of inestimable importance. Much of the undeniable power of journalists stemmed from their influence on public opinion. Most newspapers of this period were avowedly partisan, and they shaped their coverage accordingly. In discussing the power of the party press, the Toledo *Blade* commented: "Not only does it supply the nation with all its information on public topics, but it supplies it with its notions and opinions in addition. It furnishes not only the materials upon which our conclusions are founded, but it supplies the conclusions themselves, cut and dried, coined, stamped and polished. It enquires, reflects, and decides for us."[25] The self-selective nature of newspaper readership, as well as the fact that the bulk of the audience at a gathering already sympathized with the speaker's point of view, further enhanced the power of party influentials to move opinion among the faithful in a particular direction.

At the same time, politicians had less than a completely free hand in formulating policy or enunciating principles. There were always limits beyond which they could not venture without risking loss of their influence. In analyzing the relationship between party leaders and the masses, Carl Schurz noted that a political argument was effective only if it developed "ideas which lie already, although perhaps in a crude and dormant state, in the minds of those who receive it." Similarly, Preston King, a prominent New York politician, warned that deep-seated feelings in the electorate could not be overborne at will. "Circumstances and events and popular tides are stronger . . . than men," he wrote during the 1854 campaign.[26] To be effective a political impulse required a party focus, but, as King recognized, politicians were not always able to dictate the course of

---

24. Kleppner, *Third Electoral System*, 8.

25. Toledo *Blade*, December 13, 1855.

26. Carl Schurz, *The Speeches of Carl Schurz* (Philadelphia, 1865), ix; Preston King to Francis P. Blair, Sr., October 14, 1854, Blair-Lee Papers, Princeton University.

popular feeling. In times of political upheaval, the initiative clearly shifted to the rank-and-file.

With the establishment of modern parties, stability rather than change has been the hallmark of the American party system. To be sure, a party's popular support inevitably fluctuates to some extent, and even minor shifts can determine the outcome in a close election; still, these changes tend to be limited in amplitude and of relatively short duration. At infrequent intervals, however, the massive inertia of voters' partisan loyalties has broken down and a new alignment has emerged. During such periods, an unusual number of regular partisans adopt new party loyalties, normally apathetic individuals are suddenly mobilized, and new voters often disproportionately favor one party. Although the process of realignment may produce new parties and destroy existing ones, its defining characteristic is that the underlying division of party loyalties among the electorate is fundamentally and durably altered.[27] Such periods have been rare in American politics. The decade of the 1850s was one such era.

These years witnessed not only the death of the Whig party and the rise of the new Republican party but also the temporary ascendancy of a competing third party, the Know Nothings, and the stillborn attempt to form yet another alternative party, the Constitutional Union party. By definition, the disappearance of the Whig party forced its members, or at least those who remained politically active, to form new party identities. Simultaneously, many of the same forces that destroyed the Whig party caused numerous Democrats to abandon their traditional affiliation. Some of these defectors eventually returned to the ranks of the Democracy (as the Democratic party was then called), but others formed a new party identity to which they clung as strongly as they previously had to their old allegiance.

Statewide voting returns provide convincing evidence of this underlying realignment. By 1860 several states, such as Maine and New Hampshire, which at the beginning of the decade had been among the strongest Democratic states in the nation, were firmly Republican. Other states, such as Illinois, which earlier had been solidly Democratic, were by 1860 battleground states. The shift was not always as dramatic. New York, a competitive, fiercely contested state in the Jacksonian period remained so in the new party system; Massachusetts and Vermont continued to be one-party states, shifting from the Whig to the Republican column. Yet even in these last two states realignment was not a simple process, because the nativist Know Nothing party enjoyed momentary power in each.

Evidencing not one but several different patterns, the northern pre-war realignment varied significantly from state to state.[28] It began earlier in some states than others, it

---

27. The concept of political realignment was first proposed by V. O. Key, Jr., in "A Theory of Critical Elections," *Journal of Politics*, v. 17 (February, 1955), 3–18. The concept has since been refined by a number of scholars. See especially Walter Dean Burnham, *Critical Elections and the Mainsprings of American Politics* (New York, 1970); James L. Sundquist, *Dynamics of the Party System: Alignment and Realignment of Political Parties in the United States*, rev. ed. (Washington, D.C., 1983); and Jerome M. Clubb, William H. Flanigan, and Nancy H. Zingale, *Partisan Realignment: Voters, Parties, and Government in American History* (Beverly Hills, 1980). For two recent critical discussions of the literature on political realignment, see Richard L. McCormick, "The Realignment Synthesis in American History," *Journal of Interdisciplinary History*, v. 13 (Summer, 1982), 85–105; and Allan J. Lichtman, "The End of Realignment Theory? Toward a New Research Program for American Political History," *Historical Methods*, v. 15 (Fall, 1982), 170–88.

28. Realignment in the southern states during this decade raises a distinctly separate set of questions that are not examined in this study, but see the important discussions of this problem in Holt, *Political Crisis*; and William J. Cooper, Jr., *The South and the Politics of Slavery, 1828–1856* (Baton Rouge, 1978), 269–374.

followed different courses in various states, and in some it extended over a longer period of time. Whatever the pattern, by the end of the decade the basic outline of a new party system had taken shape throughout the North. Following Lincoln's election in 1860, the Republican party came to national power, and the Civil War quickly ensued. Such a cataclysmic event had been difficult to imagine as long as the Whig and Democratic parties remained dominant, for both were national organizations committed to sectional harmony, and each enjoyed widespread popular support in the North and the South. The collapse of the Whig party heralded the onslaught of a realignment era in American politics from which the Republican party ultimately emerged. This realignment in turn precipitated a crisis that eventually would test the mettle of not just the party system, but the Union itself.

1

The Presidential
Election of 1852

Election night 1852 began with eager anticipation of victory. In Washington a small group of Whig leaders joined General Winfield Scott, the party's presidential nominee, to await the returns and celebrate his impending triumph. Their buoyant hopes were quickly deflated, however, when the first totals, from Baltimore, indicated a shocking Democratic surge. As the evening wore on, each telegraphic dispatch seemed more unbelievable than the last: "a Waterloo defeat—a perfect hurricane that has upturned every thing," was how Secretary of the Navy John Pendleton Kennedy described it. Suddenly, unexpectedly, those present began laughing in spite of themselves—it was simply ludicrous how badly they had been routed. No one bore it better than the candidate himself. After supper Scott mixed a pitcher of whiskey punch, and in good humor he and his colleagues made the best of their misfortunes, joking gaily until midnight about their miscalculations.[1]

Such humor was of course defensive, for Whigs felt acutely the sting of their defeat. In analyzing the significance of the election, historians traditionally emphasize the growing differences between northern and southern Whigs over the slavery issue; they argue that the electoral disaster of the Scott campaign left the party on its deathbed, awaiting its final destruction two years later in the crisis over the Kansas-Nebraska Act.[2] An emphasis on sectional issues, however, misconstrues the difficulties the party faced and the reasons it failed to surmount them. Actually, the party's long-range problems stemmed less from the slavery question than from the rise of ethnocultural issues. These concerns had roots deep in the American experience, but, for reasons not fully foreseen by politicians at the time, the Scott campaign brought them to the forefront. The political revitalization of these issues marked the beginning of a series of complex events that resulted ultimately in the formation of the Republican party.

Note: Unless otherwise indicated, the year for newspaper and manuscript citations in this chapter is 1852.

1. John Pendleton Kennedy Diary, November 2, John Pendleton Kennedy Papers, Enoch Pratt Free Library.

2. A good example of this interpretation is Allan Nevins, *Ordeal of the Union* (2 vols.: New York, 1947), v. 2, 36–43.

I

The Compromise of 1850, which was in reality a series of related laws, passed Congress in September after a nine-month struggle. Although the sectional settlement enjoyed widespread popular support, the fight over its passage scarred the major parties. Factions in both organizations rejected the view that the Compromise was, as President Millard Fillmore declared in his annual message in December, "in its character final and irrevocable" and should be sustained as "a final settlement."[3] Over the long run controversy focused on the fugitive slave law of 1850, which antislavery men abhorred while southerners increasingly considered it the main test of northern compliance.[4] Among Democrats, states' rights men in the deep South, who had called for secession during the crisis of 1850, and the free soil wing, led by some of Andrew Jackson's closest associates, such men as Martin Van Buren and Francis P. Blair, opposed any approbation of the Compromise in the national platform. The Whig party was even more sharply divided, since southern Whigs believed that their political survival depended on the party's acceptance of the Compromise, whereas anti-Compromise advocates were probably a majority in every northern state.[5]

In the aftermath of the passage of the Compromise, some observers looked for a realignment of parties, and Union movements uniting pro-Compromise Whigs and Democrats appeared in the South and in certain parts of the North, but everywhere these alliances proved transitory, their impact fleeting. Party lines emerged substantially intact from the battle over the Compromise, a struggle that primarily reinforced already existing divisions. As a result, the hopes of antislavery agitators that this issue would greatly strengthen their cause were quickly dampened. Reflecting the gloom and despair that pervaded the Free Soil ranks, Charles Sumner, the antislavery senator from Massachusetts, admitted in 1852 that "this is the darkest day of our cause."[6]

With both parties badly factionalized, politicians looked to the approaching presidential election to vindicate their past actions, repudiate their opponents, and end party quarrels. When Congress convened in December 1851, observers recognized that the session would be dominated by president-making. "The political cauldron is beginning to warm," Hamilton Fish, the Whig senator from New York, reported, "& the ingredients which Macbeth's witches used for their Hell broth were not more various or infernal, than those which are being thrown into the mess now preparing." The presidential game was "being played *deeply*," he explained, and to follow events one had to be able to "make the pirouettes, the chassees, and the counter-movements, with sufficient quickness, or skill, to keep up with the dance."[7]

This flux inevitably fired men's ambitions and renewed their hopes. Francis P. Blair thought the existing uncertainty offered the long-awaited chance for the Van Buren wing of the Democratic party to regain its former prominence. Once dominant in the party, Van Buren and his supporters had been eclipsed during the administration of James K. Polk.

---

3. James D. Richardson, ed., *A Compilation of the Messages and Papers of the Presidents, 1789–1902* (10 vols.: Washington, D.C., 1896–1903), v. 5, 93.

4. For the fugitive slave law and the reaction to it, see Stanley W. Campbell, *The Slave Catchers: Enforcement of the Fugitive Slave Law, 1850–1860* (Chapel Hill, 1970).

5. Cooper, *Politics of Slavery*, 269–336; Holt, *Political Crisis*, 67–99.

6. Charles Sumner to Charles Francis Adams, June 21, Adams Family Papers, MassHS.

7. Hamilton Fish to Washington Hunt, December 20, 1851 (Strictly Confidential), Fish to Alvah Hunt, February 23 (copies), Fish Papers, LC.

Alienated from the party's leadership, they bolted in 1848 and helped organize the Free Soil party in order to defeat Lewis Cass, the Democratic presidential candidate who had helped block Van Buren's nomination in 1844—a step that substantially weakened their already waning influence within the Democratic organization. Accustomed to power and prestige, the Van Buren Democrats, or old Jacksonians as they called themselves, smarted at their lack of influence in national party councils. They were particularly jealous of southern political power, in both the party and the nation.

Blair had been an intimate adviser of Jackson and Van Buren. He was a man of passionate loves and hates, and ever since Polk removed him as editor of the party's organ in 1845 because of his loyalty to Van Buren, he had become obsessed with the idea that corruptionists and Calhounites, whose power Jackson had curbed, had taken control of the party. The Democracy had to be restored to the great principles of Jackson, Blair repeated constantly as he brooded about the Van Burenites' situation. Corruption had to be rooted out, just as Jackson had done earlier. Southern state's rights leaders, at heart nullifiers and secessionists, had to be purged from power.

While pondering the future, "Old Bla-ar," as Jackson had called him, began casting about for a suitable presidential candidate. Rebuffed by Thomas Hart Benton, the imperious Jacksonian leader in Missouri who was his first choice, Blair promoted Supreme Court Justice Levi Woodbury and then General William O. Butler, only to see these movements collapse abruptly. After two false starts, the Old Jacksonian clique could not be mobilized again with any enthusiasm, and in reaction members scattered their support among the various leading contenders. A number followed the lead of John Van Buren, the former president's son, who backed fellow New Yorker William Marcy as a means to gain readmission into the party's national councils as well as strengthen the Van Buren faction, or Barnburners, in the state. Wielding power within the Democratic party was a supreme motivation for the Prince, as the younger Van Buren was called, and to him the lesson of 1848 was clear: The Barnburners could not remain isolated from the party.[8] Blair, however, stood apart from the growing strife. Explaining that his efforts were always "abortive," the former editor told the elder Van Buren that he had given up president-making for good.[9]

As several observers had predicted before the Democratic convention assembled, none of the leading candidates was able to muster the requisite two-thirds vote for the presidential nomination. Once the convention deadlocked, several less prominent men were brought forward as possible compromise choices, including Franklin Pierce of New Hampshire, a handsome, charming man with an acceptable but undistinguished military record in the Mexican War. Amid great confusion, his managers assiduously circulated among the various delegations, assuring them that Pierce was sound on the Compromise and would distribute the patronage fairly. On the forty-ninth ballot North Carolina initiated the rush to him, and the little-known Concord lawyer was nominated with an avalanche of support.[10]

With the national ticket finally selected, the exhausted delegates quickly and without debate approved a platform. Democratic managers discovered that the rift over the Compromise of 1850 was too wide to make an explicit declaration feasible, so they settled

---

8. Roy F. Nichols, *The Democratic Machine, 1850–1854* (New York, 1923), 80–98; Ivor D. Spencer, *The Victor and the Spoils: A Life of William L. Marcy* (Providence, 1959), 196–204.

9. Francis P. Blair, Sr., to Martin Van Buren, February 22, Martin Van Buren Papers, LC.

10. Nichols, *Democratic Machine*, 121–28.

for a statement that the party would "abide by" the Compromise measures and faithfully execute them, including the fugitive slave law. Finality was not endorsed specifically, but the platform pledged resistance to all efforts to revive agitation over slavery "in congress or out of it." For the sake of party harmony and victory, all factions acquiesced in this ambiguous declaration and rallied behind the ticket. But the bitter factional rivalry within the party persisted, and the Barnburners and states' rights men in particular continued to eye each other warily. In spite of all the pre-convention rhetoric about purging the party of dissidents, all factions were welcomed into the Democratic camp.

II

The fight over the Compromise of 1850 badly fractured Whig unity as well. The leaders of the pro-Compromise forces were Millard Fillmore, who had assumed the presidency in the summer of 1850, and his secretary of state, Daniel Webster. The anti-Compromise Whigs did not have a leader in the way that Fillmore and Webster headed their opponents, but increasingly Senator William Henry Seward of New York, long the rival of Fillmore, assumed that role. By 1852 personal animosities had become so entangled with policy differences that it was impossible to separate them. Fillmore's and Webster's policy of removing from federal office those Whigs who opposed the Compromise greatly widened the existing breach.[11] Also involved was the question whether the party should insist on uniformity of opinion on the slavery issue or whether it should sustain the traditional Whig position of tolerating diverse sentiments. Inevitably, however, the struggle for control of the party centered on the 1852 presidential nomination. Joining Webster and Fillmore as a leading contender for the nomination was Major General Winfield Scott.[12]

Maintaining outwardly friendly relations, Webster and Fillmore each took as his platform the Union and the finality of the Compromise. But Webster, despite his advanced age, zealously sought the nomination, while Fillmore, as befit his cautious temperament, was plagued with doubts and was consequently a hesitant candidate. The self-centered Webster believed that Fillmore should defer to his claim for the honor, but it was the president who was the principal beneficiary of pro-Compromise sentiment in the party. Even with his ardent courtship of southerners, Webster was never able to expand his popular base of support beyond New England and the large eastern cities.[13] Fillmore, on the other hand, won a large number of delegates and was overwhelmingly the choice of southern Whigs.

Scott was the only other important competitor for the nomination. During the preceding two years, more and more Whig leaders, aware that their party had succeeded in presidential elections only with military candidates, concluded that Scott was the most available man. His distinguished career in the army made him a popular hero whose appeal, it was thought, extended beyond the narrow ranks of party. A few southern leaders endorsed Scott, as did some northern Compromise men, but the bulk of his

---

11. Robert F. Dalzell, Jr., *Daniel Webster and the Trial of American Nationalism, 1843–1852* (Boston, 1973), 196–258.

12. I have presented a fuller analysis of the struggle for the Whig nomination in "The Whig Party, the Compromise of 1850, and the Nomination of Winfield Scott," *Presidential Studies Quarterly*, v. 14 (Summer, 1984), 399–415.

13. Henry A. Wise to Edward Everett, January 18, Millard Fillmore to Everett, February 16, *Private*, Edward Everett Papers, MassHS. For Webster's campaign for the nomination, see Dalzell, *Webster*, 241–58.

support came from northern Whigs who opposed the Compromise measures, or at least wanted no endorsement of them in the platform.[14] Included in this last group was Seward, who saw in the General the only possibility to end the bitterly resented proscription of his friends. The Senator decided to back Scott without the counsel of his close associate Thurlow Weed, the editor of the Albany *Evening Journal* and closest to being the boss of the New York Whig party as anyone came, who had gone to Europe and would not return until after the Whig convention.[15] Almost immediately, public opinion viewed Scott as completely under Seward's control.

Scott's advisers devised a campaign strategy predicated on the candidate's maintaining a perfect silence on the issues of the day. In particular, they insisted that he in no way endorse the Compromise, despite his private support for it in 1850, and extracted a promise that he would, in Senator Benjamin F. Wade's words, "keep his mouth shut." At the same time, the general's northern supporters also opposed the adoption of any Compromise resolutions by the national convention, particularly any endorsement of the fugitive slave law or of finality.[16] With Scott as an unpledged candidate, the party could conduct separate campaigns north and south of the Mason-Dixon line, just as it had done in 1848.

The critical consideration in the minds of Scott's advisers was the strength of the Free Soil party in the North. The party held the balance of power in several crucial northern states, and Whig chances in 1852 depended upon securing a large proportion of this vote.[17] The Scott organizers invested much time and energy wooing Free Soil leaders in Washington, and several seemed ready to lend their support if Scott were not pledged to the Compromise. At the same time, his advisers were confident that Scott could carry at least the traditional Whig border states with or without a platform. Other southern states might be lost by this strategy, but the anticipated gains in the North would more than offset these potential losses. With Scott and no resolutions or letter, Charles A. Dana of the New York *Tribune* predicted, "we shall put this election through with an awful majority at the North." A pro-Compromise platform gave no promise of such strength. To his fellow Ohio Whig John Sherman, Congressman Lewis D. Campbell outlined the situation as perceived by Scott's Washington managers: *"Scott as he is, without weights, and success*—otherwise *invevitable & disastrous defeat."*[18]

While Whig politicians debated the wisdom of this strategy, Scott won the support of most northern delegates, but even with this strength he still lacked a majority. The Scott inner circle remained confident as the convention drew near, however, that the few additional votes needed to nominate him could be found among the Webster and Fillmore

---

14. Charles Winslow Elliott, *Winfield Scott, The Soldier and the Man* (New York, 1937), 606; Fish to George N. Franklin, May 6 (copy), Fish Papers, LC.

15. Thurlow Weed, "Recollections of Horace Greeley," *The Galaxy*, v. 15 (March, 1873), 377; Schuyler Colfax to William H. Seward, April 2, William H. Seward Papers, UR.

16. Benjamin F. Wade to Caroline Wade, December 10, 1851, February 8, 1852, Benjamin F. Wade Papers, LC; Lewis D. Campbell to John Sherman, April 5 (private), John Sherman Papers, LC; Seth Hawley to Seward, June 4, Seward Papers, UR.

17. Philip Greely, Jr., to James Shepherd Pike, January 30, Charles A. Dana to Pike, May 1, James Shepherd Pike Papers, UMe. Fluctuating support made it difficult to determine party strength precisely, but the Free Soilers potentially held the balance of power in Maine, Massachusetts, New Hampshire, New York, Pennsylvania, Ohio, Indiana, Illinois, Iowa, Michigan, and Wisconsin.

18. Charles A. Dana to Pike, n.d. [ca. May 1], Pike Papers, UMe; Campbell to Sherman, April 5 (private), John Sherman Papers.

delegates. At the same time, Scott's advisers reluctantly concluded in the face of intense southern pressure that to prevent a breakup of the convention some concession was necessary, and they therefore decided that after his nomination the candidate would issue a letter. With several proposed versions, drafted by supporters, in circulation, they began deliberating exactly what the promised letter should say.[19] Certain that Scott would be nominated, one northern congressman insisted that the battle at the convention was instead "to be lost or won . . . on the question of finality resolutions."[20]

"*We* are to have a pretty stormy time," commented William Pitt Fessenden, a prominent Maine Whig and national delegate, prior to the opening of the convention.[21] It was clear immediately that the Fillmore and Webster forces were in control. Early in its deliberations, the convention made a critical decision when, breaking with tradition, it endorsed a southern demand that a platform be adopted before making nominations. The platform committee reported a set of resolutions declaring that the Whig party acquiesced in the Compromise measures of 1850, including the fugitive slave law, promised to maintain them "until time and experience shall demonstrate the necessity of further legislation to guard against the evasion of the law on the one hand, and the abuse of their powers on the other, not impairing their present efficiency," and deprecated further sectional agitation.[22] With about half the Scott delegates opposed, the convention approved this platform easily, but some of the minority could be held in line only with the assurance that Scott's forthcoming letter would dissent from the doctrine of making the Compromise a party test.[23]

Once the platform had been adopted, voting began for the presidential nomination. Fillmore and Scott displayed virtually identical strength, with Webster a very distant third. All attempts to unite the anti-Scott majority failed, and on Saturday evening, after forty-six ballots produced almost no change in the totals, the convention adjourned until Monday. During the recess, Senator James Jones of Tennessee, one of Scott's southern backers, conferred with the general in Washington and secured a written pledge that Scott would endorse the national platform.[24] Armed with this commitment, Jones and his allies procured the necessary southern votes, and on the fifty-third ballot Scott was nominated.

For Scott's managers, the outcome of the convention was a mixed blessing. They had nominated their candidate but with a pro-Compromise platform that they had claimed beforehand would be fatal. To make matters worse, Scott, without consulting his political advisers, impetuously dispatched a message to the delegates announcing that he would accept the nomination "with the platform of principles which the convention has laid down."[25] In its different versions, Scott's proposed letter to be issued after his nomination

---

19. Frederick Seward, *Seward at Washington as Senator and Secretary of State* (2 vols.: New York, 1891), v. 2, 183–87; James Shepherd Pike, *First Blows of Civil War* (New York, 1879), 139–41.

20. Israel Washburn, Jr., to William Schouler, May 5, William Schouler Papers, MassHS.

21. William Pitt Fessenden to Ellen Fessenden, June 14, Fessenden Family Papers, Bowdoin College.

22. Neither party endorsed the Compromise directly: The Democrats promised to "adhere" to the settlement, the Whigs "acquiesced" in it. Both straddled the issue of future reform as well, although the Whigs more clearly held out this possibility. Public opinion, however, deemed these statements to be, in effect, an endorsement of finality.

23. Pike, *First Blows*, 151–53; Pike to Seward, Wednesday P.M. [June 16], Seward Papers, UR.

24. Washington *Daily Union*, July 27; *National Intelligencer*, August 6.

25. *Political Letters and Writings of General Scott* (n.p., 1852), 13. The exact provenance of this message is unclear. It may have been a telegram dispatched by Scott upon receipt of the news of his nomination. More likely it was, as some commentators later asserted, the written pledge that James Jones had secured on Sunday,

was equivocal and designed to free him in the North from the stigma of the Compromise without destroying his chances in the South.[26] In the excitement following his selection, however, the candidate ignored his earlier promises to be guided by his advisers. It is difficult to believe that anyone as long-winded as Scott could have remained silent very long in any case, but his pledge lasted less than an hour after his nomination. Seeking to repair some of the damage done by his impulsive declaration, Scott's subsequent formal letter, in which he accepted the nomination "with the resolutions annexed," was more restrained.

Understandably, neither faction was entirely happy with the outcome of the convention. Southern and Fillmore Whigs grumbled about the candidate's meager endorsement of the platform. Some anti-Compromise Whigs, on the other hand, wished that Scott had said nothing, and Horace Greeley, in a widely quoted editorial, scornfully rejected the platform.[27] Nevertheless, despite scattered complaints, the majority of Whigs rallied behind the national ticket, although at times with a noticeable lack of enthusiasm. More critical was the response of the Free Soilers; for, with Scott's acceptance of the platform, Whig prospects for an alliance with the Free Soil party vanished.

III

Prior to the Whig convention there was considerable opposition among Free Soil leaders to making any independent nominations.[28] Once the Whig meeting had adjourned, however, their resistance quickly dissolved, and Free Soil party leaders scheduled a national convention. The contest for the presidential nomination lay between John P. Hale of New Hampshire and Salmon P. Chase of Ohio. Given this choice, Whig leaders greatly preferred Chase, whose policy of allying with the Democrats in Ohio made him unpopular with Whig Free Soilers, and hence they believed he would be much the weaker candidate.[29] Contrary to their wish, it was Hale who received the Free Soil designation. Recognizing the danger that a third-party ticket posed, Weed, who had returned from Europe, and Seward both strongly urged Hale to decline the nomination, but without success.[30]

Hale's nomination and acceptance seriously impaired the original Scott plan of appealing to Free Soilers. With Hale in the field and Scott saddled with a platform despised by Free Soilers, this strategy seemed unlikely to pay the dividends expected earlier. Nevertheless,

---

for it concluded, "Please show this to G. B. Duncan," who was a Louisiana delegate. In the excitement following the nomination, these observers concluded, Jones could not restrain himself and read this private communication. See the telegraphic report from the convention, New York *Herald*, June 22. Be that as it may, Scott had disregarded his earlier promise to write nothing. For a thorough discussion of the conflicting evidence concerning this matter, see the Washington *Daily Union*, July 24, 27, and the *National Intelligencer*, August 6.

26. Philip Greely, Jr., to Pike, May 15, 27, Horace Greeley to Pike, May 29, Pike Papers, UMe; Pike, *First Blows*, 140–42.

27. Greeley said of the platform: "We defy it, execrate it, spit upon it." New York *Tribune*, June 21.

28. Sumner to Henry Wilson, January 10, Henry Wilson Papers, LC; John A. Andrew to Sumner, May 17, Adams to Sumner, February 5, Charles Sumner Papers, HU; Gamaliel Bailey to Adams, March 30, Sumner to Adams, Sunday [June], Adams Family Papers.

29. Seward to Colfax, August 7, Schuyler Colfax Papers, LC; Colfax to Seward, August 2, Seward Papers, UR; Campbell to Sherman, July 12, John Sherman Papers; Weed to Schouler, August 7, Schouler Papers.

30. Sumner to Adams, August 25, Adams Family Papers; Fish to Weed, August 18, Thurlow Weed Papers, UR. For Hale's nomination and the 1852 Free Soil campaign, see Frederick J. Blue, *The Free Soilers: Third Party Politics, 1848–1854* (Urbana, 1973), 232–68.

such third-party leaders as Chase, Charles Sumner, and Henry Wilson claimed to be eager to aid Scott's election. Even Hale expressed hope that his candidacy would elect Scott by taking votes from the Democrats. Such comments may not have been entirely sincere, but Free Soil leaders were probably willing to help Scott if they could do so without appearing to abandon their principles. Sumner outlined the conflicting motivations of many Free Soil leaders when he explained to a political ally: "My hope is to have a third candidate, by whose support we may openly declare our principles, but of democratic inclinings so as to draw from Democrats rather than Whigs, & thus, so far as we can, consistently with our principles, discriminate in favor of Scott."[31]

That Whigs still looked for Free Soil help, even indirectly, testified to their desperation. Whatever realism the idea of a Free Soil alliance contained had long since disappeared; indeed, by July its premises had been rendered obsolete. Some politicians, it is true, desperately sought reassurance in the argument that Hale would take many more Democratic Free Soil votes than Whig and thus help Scott, but Charles Francis Adams more astutely contended that any third-party nomination meant that Pierce would gain an easy victory. In Ohio, where the Free Soilers were predominantly former Whigs and where this strategy should have been most effective, leaders of the other parties were not misled. The Whigs "think we have killed them in Ohio," a concerned Henry Wilson reported, adding, "The Democrats seem of the same opinion."[32]

IV

From the start, the Whig campaign was obviously in serious trouble. The party platform dictated abandonment of sectional issues, and, equally disconcerting, politicians everywhere reported a lack of enthusiasm for either candidate and a general apathy among the electorate. For the Whigs in particular, who had placed so much weight on Scott's alleged popularity, such reports were ominous. At the same time, two additional developments, neither entirely unexpected, made it critically important that Scott gain additional votes in the North. First, a group of southern Whig congressmen, headed by Alexander H. Stephens and Robert Toombs of Georgia, repudiated Scott because of his failure to subscribe wholeheartedly to the Compromise. In the face of this hostility, the Whig high command in Washington, under the management of FitzHenry Warren and Truman Smith, decided to concede the deep South.[33] The second development was the refusal of a mortified Daniel Webster to support Scott. Nursing his disappointment, Webster pronounced the Whig party disbanded and indicated privately that he intended to vote for Pierce. When some diehard supporters nominated him as an independent candidate for

31. Sumner to Samuel Gridley Howe, July 4, Wilson to Sumner, June 23, Sumner Papers, HU; John W. Latson to Seward, July 27, Seward Papers, UR; John P. Hale to O. B. Matteson, September 27, Weed Papers, UR; O. Bowe to John A. King, August 17, John A. King Papers, NYHS.

32. Adams to Hale, August 15, Austin Willey to Hale, August 19, John P. Hale Papers, DarC; John G. Whittier to Sumner, August 10 (copy), Whittier-Pickard Papers, HU; Wilson to Joshua R. Giddings, August 21, Joshua R. Giddings Papers, OHS.

33. Truman Smith to Willie Mangum, October 9, Henry Thomas Shanks, ed., *The Papers of Willie Person Mangum* (5 vols.: Raleigh, 1950–56), v. 5, 247; John M. Berrien to Fillmore, September 21, Millard Fillmore Papers, BECHS. For Whig problems in the South in 1852, see Cooper, *Politics of Slavery*, 322–41.

president, Webster stubbornly resisted pressure to disavow this movement and continued to do so until his death near the end of the campaign.[34]

More worrisome to Whig campaign directors than Webster's candidacy was the disaffection it symbolized. They feared that conservative Whigs would sit on their hands during the campaign and then not vote. Sensitive to the necessity for maintaining his position within the party, Fillmore endorsed Scott and urged his followers to support the choice of the convention.[35] Still, fears of significant conservative abstentions persisted. The Scott managers, already resentful over the platform, refused to make any further concessions. In fact, by now the animosity between the two factions was so intense that some Whigs on both sides did not even wish to see the schism healed. Let the conservative pro-Fillmore Silver Grey Whigs defect to the Democrats, one Sewardite advised: "They are sure death to any man or any party that takes them into their confidence." Such expressions revealed the depth of the Whig division, but they gave little promise of securing the votes Scott needed to win. "The whigs were never in more confusion and disorder," one of Pierce's close associates commented with much truth in August.[36] Not even confident of the normal Whig vote, party leaders realized that they had to look elsewhere to make up these losses. A new campaign strategy was needed.

In the summer of 1852, as these problems became manifest, Whig politicians directed their thoughts toward the burgeoning Roman Catholic and immigrant vote in the North. Beginning in the mid-1840s, vast numbers of German and Irish immigrants, a large proportion of them Catholic, had come to the United States, and this influx was growing steadily. As more and more of these newcomers became citizens, they began to make their impact felt in politics. Charmed by the name *Democrat* and repelled by the nativist wing of the Whig party, immigrants—and especially the Catholics—decisively favored the Democratic party. If this trend continued, the Whig party would be a hopeless minority in many northern states and nationally could not expect to elect a president. To Whig leaders, averting this outcome seemed imperative. Some, led by Seward, had long expressed sympathy for the foreign-born and had urged that a vigorous effort be made to gain their support. Confronted with the continuing growth of Democratic strength among immigrants, Seward and his friends were convinced that their program was not only right in principle but wise politically. With their Free Soil strategy now in ruins, Scott's advisers concluded that naturalized voters represented the most likely source of additional votes.[37]

The belief of Whig strategists that Catholics might be induced to support Scott was not without some basis. For one thing, Democratic leaders in Congress had been especially conspicuous in lavishing praise on Louis Kossuth when he visited the United States at the end of 1851; their enthusiasm irritated the Catholic hierarchy, who viewed the Hungarian

---

34. Peter Harvey, *Reminiscences and Anecdotes of Daniel Webster* (Boston, 1884), 195–203; Dalzell, *Webster*, 290–304.

35. Fillmore to [William D. Lewis], July 19, Frank M. Severance, ed., *The Millard Fillmore Papers, Publications of the Buffalo Historical Society*, v. 11 (Buffalo, 1907), 330. This letter was published in the Philadelphia *Aurora* after the national convention. A copy is in the Lewis-Neilson Papers, HSPa.

36. John Friend to Seward, February 8, Seward Papers, UR; Charles H. Peaslee to John H. George, August 15, John H. George Papers, NHHS. For examples of Whig disaffection, see Gilbert Davis to Fillmore, July 5, W. Channing Gibbs to Fillmore, June 30, October 17, Fillmore Papers, BECHS; Weed to Fish, August 16, Fish Papers, LC.

37. Schouler to Seward, February 14, E. Peshine Smith to Seward, July 4, Seward Papers, UR. Michael Holt advances a similar interpretation of the Whigs' 1852 campaign strategy in *Political Crisis*, 123–27.

revolutionary as an enemy of the church.[38] Whig managers saw other grounds as well on which to bid for the Catholic vote. The fact that Scott's eldest daughter had converted to Catholicism and entered a nunnery might exert some influence. So might his conduct in Mexico, where as military commander he had taken great pains to court the Catholic clergy and protect church property. Of greatest importance, however, was the New Hampshire constitution's ban on Catholics' holding certain state offices. Catholics naturally were sensitive to such discrimination, and it seemed likely that Pierce could be tarred with his state's action. Connecticut Whigs had already used this issue to appeal to immigrant voters in the 1851 state election. Immediately following Pierce's unexpected nomination, a Cincinnati Whig wrote Thomas Corwin asking about the Democratic candidate's role in the adoption of the New Hampshire test. If reports that Pierce had supported this provision were correct, Corwin's correspondent wrote, he was " 'a dead cock in the pit.' "[39]

On the other hand, the Catholic strategy involved certain difficulties. Most notably, the party contained a powerful nativist wing that would be displeased by any overt appeal to immigrants or Catholics. Indeed, Scott himself had in the 1840s made several nativist statements that might prove embarrassing. Party leaders undoubtedly hoped that his repudiation in 1848 of these earlier statements would be sufficient. "I admit the past, and plead repentance," Horace Greeley said of Scott's earlier anti-immigrant pronouncements.[40]

William E. Robinson, an Irish-born correspondent for Greeley's New York *Tribune,* played a leading role in the party's new campaign tactic. Robinson was the recipient of Scott's 1848 letter renouncing his nativist sentiments. Continued reflection, and the brave patriotism of foreign-born soldiers who served under him in Mexico, Scott declared, had modified his views, and he opposed "any measure intended to exclude" naturalized citizens "from a just and full participation in all civil and political rights now secured to them by our republican laws and institutions." During the campaign Robinson prepared a pamphlet setting forth the claims of Scott for Catholic support, while tying Pierce to the New Hampshire constitution's discriminatory clause. The Whigs scattered his pamphlet and similar documents wherever they would serve the cause.[41] "*We will use* it to the best advantage," a Chicago Whig editor said of the constitution's anti-Catholic provision. Similarly, a Democrat reported that Whigs were "making more noise about our religious test than anything else."[42]

---

38. Caleb Cushing to Stephen A. Douglas, February 1, Confidential, Stephen A. Douglas Papers, University of Illinois.

39. Robert D. Parmet, "The Know-Nothings in Connecticut" (unpublished Ph.D. dissertation, Columbia University, 1966), 41; Lowe [?] O. Edwards to Thomas Corwin, June 7 (Private & Confidential), Thomas Corwin Papers, LC. Even prior to Scott's nomination, Whigs raised the Catholic test issue. New York *Tribune*, June 15.

40. Horace Greeley to Colfax, July 15, Greeley-Colfax Papers, NYPL. For Scott's nativist letters, see *Political Letters of Scott*, 9, 16; *National Intelligencer*, November 17, 1844.

41. *Political Letters of Scott*, 11–12; *Speech of William E. Robinson in Exposition of the New Hampshire Democracy in its Relation to Catholic Emancipation, Including a Scrutiny of the Part Taken with Reference Thereto, by Gen. Franklin Pierce* (New York, 1852); *Franklin Pierce and Catholic Persecution in New Hampshire* (New York, 1852).

42. Richard L. Wilson to Seward, June 21, Seward Papers, UR; S. W. Draeborn to John H. George, October 7, George Papers. For Whig use of this issue, see Samuel Sevasey to George, September 26, James B. Allen to George, September 27, George Papers; William Bailhache to John Bailhache, July 4, Bailhache-Brayman Papers, IllSHL; Portland *Advertiser*, October 29.

Accustomed to taking the Catholic vote for granted, Democrats were alarmed. From Washington, Charles H. Peaslee, a leading member of the so-called Concord Clique and one of Pierce's closest advisers, urged that a tract on Pierce and the New Hampshire test be issued immediately for distribution to Catholic voters. Democrats also solicited unsuccessfully Archbishop John Hughes of New York's endorsement of Pierce.[43] The Democratic press reprinted Scott's previous nativist declarations, party committees actively disseminated pamphlets defending Pierce from the charge of anti-Catholicism, and speakers transmitted this message to immigrant audiences.[44]

While appealing to the Germans and Irish, Democratic leaders simultaneously sought the aid of the nativists in Pennsylvania. During the 1840s overtly nativist parties had existed in several cities, and, although most of these parties quickly withered away, in Philadelphia nativists maintained a rudimentary organization and continued to run candidates. The Native American party accounted for only a few thousand votes in the state, but in a close election its support could be crucial. Nativists were furious at Scott because of his reversal on the immigrant question. He was, in the words of their organ, the Philadelphia *Sun*, "a weak demagogue, who trims his sail to catch every breeze of popular favor." Now that Scott was bidding expediently for the Catholic vote, they were adamantly hostile.[45] Since an open alliance might alienate naturalized voters, Democratic managers, after first clearing it with Catholic politicians, covertly cooperated with the Native American party. In October Lewis C. Levin, one of the most prominent nativist leaders in Philadelphia, promised that their "whole force" would rally to Pierce: "The feeling among my friends is intense—intense hostility to the Whigs."[46]

Whig leaders meanwhile received optimistic information concerning the Catholic vote. From a number of localities, party regulars wrote that the Irish and Germans were coming over to Scott.[47] Also encouraging was the report quietly circulating that Archbishop Hughes preferred Scott over Pierce. Surely this was a sign, Whigs believed, that the Catholic clergy would rally to Scott and influence its flock to do likewise. In response to rumors that the Catholic bishops and clergy were either working for Scott or would publicly announce their preference as the election approached, Bishop Louis Rappe of Cleveland released a statement denying that the clergy would in any way participate in the election.[48] Whig hopes nevertheless remained high.

Indeed, Whig perceptions of the Catholic church as a closely knit, tightly controlled

---

43. J. S. Barber to Franklin Pierce, September 15, Pierce Papers, NHHS; Peaslee to George, July 27, George Papers; New York *Herald*, September 27.

44. *The Whig Charge of Intolerance Against the New Hampshire Democracy and Pierce* (n.p., 1852); *The New Hampshire Test* (n.p., [1852]); *Illinois State Register*, August 13, 18, 24. For the Democratic national campaign, see Roy F. Nichols, *Democratic Machine*, 147–68; and Nichols, *Franklin Pierce: Young Hickory of the Granite Hills*, 2nd ed. revised (Philadelphia, 1958), 205–15.

45. Clipping from the Philadelphia *Sun*, enclosed in Jno. H. Bryant to Fillmore, March 18, John W. Ashmead to Fillmore, February 27, March 25 (*Confidential*), 26, *Private and Confidential*, Fillmore Papers, BECHS; E. A. Penniman to Pierce, October 17, Private, Franklin Pierce Papers, NHHS.

46. William J. Crans to William Bigler, September 29, Private and Confidential, William Bigler Papers, HSPa; Lewis C. Levin to William L. Marcy, October 15, William L. Marcy Papers, LC.

47. Henry C. Carey to Thomas H. Dudley, October 9, Thomas H. Dudley Papers, HEH; L. to Dear Charles [Peaslee?], September 23, George Papers; Samuel Galloway to Corwin, August 10, Corwin Papers; William Bailhache to John Bailhache, July 4, Bailhache-Brayman Papers; David Brier to John Dowling, July 2, John Dowling Papers, IndHS.

48. R. S. Holt to Joseph Holt, June 24, Joseph Holt Papers, LC; Cincinnati *Gazette*, November 1; F. H. Davidge to Mangum, September 15, Shanks, ed., *Mangum Papers*, v. 5, 238–39.

organization that moved en masse on election day led Whigs to put excessive faith in gaining the Catholic vote by courting the Catholic clergy. Elihu B. Washburne, a Whig candidate for Congress in an Illinois district with a large Irish Catholic population, asked Greeley for assistance during the campaign. The *Tribune's* editor, after assuring him that the Catholics were going to vote for Scott, urged Washburne to also obtain their support. Washburne in turn wrote to Seward and asked him to get an endorsement from Hughes. Such a recommendation, Washburne assured his Whig colleague, "would help me vastly and probably secure my election."[49] Seward explained that the request was impossible. "I am quite sure," he replied, "that Arch Bishop Hughes has never done any such thing as to write a letter of the nature you suppose possible, and that he would not feel at liberty to do so." Reports that he had done so in the past were "quite groundless. No man guards more carefully the proprieties of the Clerical character," insisted the Senator.[50]

At virtually the same time that Washburne wrote to Seward, Schuyler Colfax of Indiana conferred with Truman Smith, one of the Whig national campaign managers. Colfax warned Smith that the enfranchisement of some 10,000 to 15,000 Germans under the new state constitution made Indiana doubtful for the Whigs, and that German votes also threatened to defeat the Whigs in Ohio and the rest of the Northwest. After talking to Colfax, Smith wrote to Weed that both he and Colfax agreed that "you must devote your whole time to bringing the Catholic element into full play. No one can do this as well as you can & in short *you can* do it & *must*. Therefore we want you to arrange instantly for the conduct of your paper & to devote yourself exclusively to this work." Stressing that time was of the essence, Smith relayed Colfax's information that Archbishop John Purcell of Cincinnati was politically sympathetic and could deliver the Catholic vote in the Northwest to Scott. Smith urged Weed to go immediately to Cincinnati to see Purcell, and, if he proved willing to cooperate, agree on some "scheme of operations." In addition, Smith importuned the New York boss to take care of Connecticut through Bishop Bernard O'Reily. The election promised to be close, and Weed could tip the scales.[51]

Weed had already met with Hughes in New York. Apparently, the Archbishop affirmed his personal support for Scott but declined to use his position openly to influence others. Whatever transpired during the interview, Weed was not entirely discouraged. He showed Smith's letter to his confidant, Congressman John Schoolcraft, who advised him to go to Cincinnati.[52] Whether Weed did, in fact, go to see Purcell is unknown, but no public endorsement was forthcoming. Whig attempts to gain the Catholic vote through the church hierarchy proved abortive.

Whig campaign managers also devised plans to send Scott on a good will tour through the Ohio valley. To entrust the candidate with so sensitive an assignment was risky, for Scott, despite his dignified bearing, was excessively vain and completely devoid of political skill. Moreover, his unfortunate gaffes in the past, coupled with his fussy personality, made him an easy target for ridicule.[53] By this time, however, Whig leaders

---

49. Greeley to Elihu B. Washburne, September 15, Elihu B. Washburne Papers, LC; Washburne to Seward, September 17, Seward Papers, UR.

50. Seward to Washburne, September 22, Elihu B. Washburne Papers, LC.

51. Truman Smith to Weed, September 19, Weed Papers, UR; Colfax to Seward, July 24, Seward Papers, UR.

52. Notation by John Schoolcraft on the back of Truman Smith to Weed, September 19, Weed Papers, UR.

53. Scott's well-publicized statements about fearing "a fire in my rear" from the Polk administration, and

were desperate, and they thus grasped at any straw that offered hope of success.

In September Scott left Washington, ostensibly to examine sites in Kentucky for soldiers' asylums, but so circuitous was his itinerary that the New York *Herald* lampooned the journey as "the Iliad of the Nineteenth Century." At each stop, Whig workers arranged enthusiastic receptions, and Scott responded with a brief, general speech. The motivation of his unusual tour soon became transparent. When interrupted in Cleveland by an Irishman, Scott as if on cue gushed, "I love that Irish brogue—I have heard it before on many battle fields, and I wish to hear it many times more." In another speech, he clumsily referred to the Germans' "mellifluous accent." Elsewhere he made similar remarks, and in Indiana the Whig candidate, who was an Episcopalian, ostentatiously attended a Catholic service on Sunday morning and a Protestant one in the afternoon.[54]

Whigs' reaction to the tour was mixed. From Cincinnati, Rutherford B. Hayes wrote that the Democrats could fume all they wanted, Scott's activities had won him votes. A Whig newspaper correspondent in Pennsylvania reached the same conclusion. "Gen. Scott's presence in the West," he declared, had "created a revolution" in his favor.[55] Other Whigs, however, offered a quite different assessment. Terming the Ohio tour a "blunder," one mortified party member implored Seward:

> For God's sake . . . Keep Scott at home. One more Cleveland speech and "we are ruined." . . . "Oh! that rich brogue! I love to hear it." Just write him some speeches and forward [them] as soon as possible. dont trust him a single minute *alone*. if You do the game is up.

And a thoroughly appalled Michigan Whig dismissed Scott afterwards as "a d——d old fool—a brainless bundle of wind & vanity."[56] Not surprisingly, Democrats claimed that Scott's trip had hurt his chances. Such observations were not disinterested, but perhaps Joseph Lane hit nearest the mark when he told Pierce's campaign manager, "Scotts person and personal appearance is doing something for him, when he says nothing, but when he talks he is sure to be . . . a damn fool."[57]

Whatever its overall impact, Scott's campaign swing, along with the party's pandering to immigrant and Catholic voters, galled nativist Whigs beyond measure. Reports of Whig

---

his partaking "a hasty plate of soup" when Secretary of War Marcy visited his camp unannounced (thereby earning him the designation Marshal Tureen), were endlessly satirized. One Democrat said of the Whig nominee: "He is of all men, the subject for caricature." A. Campbell to Marcy, September 21, Marcy Papers, LC.

54. New York *Herald*, October 26; Cleveland *Plain Dealer*, September 21; Cincinnati *Gazette*, October 6; unidentified clipping enclosed in Nelson J. Waterbury to George, October 16, George Papers; James Ford Rhodes, *History of the United States from the Compromise of 1850* (7 vols.: New York, 1892–1906), v. 1, 276.

55. Rutherford B. Hayes to Sardis Birchard, October 2, Charles R. Williams, ed., *Diary and Letters of Rutherford Birchard Hayes* (5 vols.: Columbus, 1922–1926), v. 1, 424; James E. Harvey to William A. Graham, October 9, J. G. de Roulhac Hamilton, ed., *The Papers of William Alexander Graham* (6 vols.: Raleigh, 1957–1976), v. 4, 421.

56. P. C. H. Harris to Seward, September 24, Seward Papers, UR; Abner Pratt to Henry Waldron, October 29, Waldron Family Papers, Michigan State University; Allan Nevins and Milton Halsey Thomas, eds., *The Diary of George Templeton Strong* (4 vols.: New York, 1952), v. 2, 106.

57. Peaslee to Pierce, September 24, Pierce Papers, NHHS; Henry B. Stanton to George, October 18, George Papers; *Democratic Review*, v. 2 (New Series) (October, 1852), 290–91; Joseph Lane to George, October 5, George Papers.

discontent, especially among Presbyterians and Methodists, two denominations noted for anti-Catholicism, gained widespread currency. "Our Whigs are bidding so openly for Catholic votes, that they are arousing some of the Protestant Whigs particularly amongst the Presbyterians," one Pennsylvania Democrat reported after conferring with a clergyman of that denomination. He added that a number of Whig Presbyterians were intent on not voting. Another Democrat assured Pierce that these Whig overtures would backfire because "many of the members of other denominations opposed to the Catholics have become alarmed and some will not go to the election & others will vote against Scott." From Pennsylvania yet another Democrat indicated: "The naturalized vote has been sought with an ardor that has awakened a Protestant feeling, especially among Methodists and Presbyterians . . . the latter [are] particularly jealous of any thing wearing the appearance of Catholicism." He confirmed that "many Whigs of these sects will vote against Scott."[58]

Democrats were not alone in this assessment. A prominent New York Whig warned Hamilton Fish that the Democrats were trying to make "our good Presbyterians" believe that Scott was a Catholic because his daughter was in a convent. "We have to head [off] this insinuation," he wrote in alarm. Inquiries from concerned Whigs as to whether Scott was a Catholic emphasized further the degree of uneasiness among the party's rank-and-file.[59] Also damaging was the charge that Scott had curried favor openly with Catholics in Mexico. One Whig told Seward that there was great prejudice against Scott "on account of Reports circulated that he compelled Protestant Soldiers to kneel before the Host in Mexico." In a letter to Justice John McLean of the Supreme Court, another disgusted Whig characterized Scott as a "*Sapheaded roman Catholic*," who "compelled the American Armies to prostrate themselves in the Mud whenever a *crucifix*, or an Adolatrous [*sic*] *Doll Baby* passed a long."[60] Scott's fawning over Catholics and immigrants during the presidential campaign reinforced and multiplied the suspicions of nativist Whigs. Such disaffection was particularly strong in New York and Pennsylvania, where nativism exerted a powerful influence in the Whig party, but even many Whigs who were not as strongly anti-Catholic were disgruntled with Scott's blatant expediency.

The October state elections in Indiana, Ohio, and Pennsylvania went against the Whigs. The Democrats carried all three states with majorities of about 15,000 votes in Pennsylvania and Indiana and a plurality of approximately 17,000 in Ohio.[61] Outwardly, most Whigs maintained a brave front, but one admitted privately that these elections

---

58. P. Frazer Smith to J. Alexander Fulton, August 24, John B. Bratton to Fulton, August 7, J. Alexander Fulton Papers, Pennsylvania Historical and Museum Commission; John Davis to Pierce, October 18 (quotation), John Hill Brinton to Pierce, October 6, Pierce Papers, NHHS. Fulton's papers are invaluable on this subject, since he systematically wrote to Democratic leaders throughout Pennsylvania inquiring about the impact of the Catholic issue in their counties.

59. Alvah Hunt to Fish, August 28, Fish Papers, LC; Charles Coburn to Seward, June 14, 30, Seward Papers, UR; John Bell to My Dear Sir, July 13, Draft, John Bell Papers, LC; New York *Tribune*, June 10.

60. Ralph R. Gurley to Seward, June 22, Seward Papers, UR; S. C. Stevens to John McLean, April 19, John McLean Papers, LC; Silas Bruce to Fillmore, April 7, Fillmore Papers, BECHS.

61. The official vote for governor in Indiana was: Whig, 73,545 (43.2 percent); Democrat, 93,576 (54.9 percent); Free Soil, 3,303 (1.9 percent); for Supreme Court judge in Ohio: Whig, 130,507 (43.4 percent); Democrat, 147,936 (49.2 percent); Free Soil, 22,524 (7.5 percent); and for canal commissioner in Pennsylvania: Whig, 151,600 (45.2 percent); Democrat, 171,548 (51.2 percent); Free Soil 3,843 (1.1 percent); Native American, 8,187 (2.4 percent). For an analysis of voting patterns in these elections, see William E. Gienapp, "The Origins of the Republican Party, 1852–1856" (unpublished Ph.D. dissertation, University of California, Berkeley, 1980), 107–9.

were "a stunning blow" to the party command in Washington. The situation in Indiana seemed particularly desperate. Some party leaders, headed by Weed, had previously written off that state as hopeless, and after the October setback the national Whig leadership decided not to expend further effort there. They were not ready, however, to concede Ohio or Pennsylvania. Warren, noting that Taylor had overcome an adverse majority in the 1848 state election in Pennsylvania, urged party workers to intensify their efforts. As for Ohio, the October returns showed that, combined, the Whig-Free Soil vote was sufficient to carry the state. Whig hopes continued to rest on the dubious contention that Hale would draw many more votes from Pierce than he would from Scott.[62]

Shaken by these defeats, Whig managers almost frantically discounted the significance of the October results. They continued to cling to the hope that Scott's reputed popularity with the masses would somehow carry the party through in November.[63] There was little evidence to justify this attitude. The Free Soil strategy had failed; the Catholic clergy had refrained from openly endorsing Scott, although some supported him privately; the Catholic press was generally hostile; reports about Scott's tour and the Catholic and immigrant vote were at best mixed; and statements of widespread apathy were common. Perhaps Whig leaders, with their memories of the 1840 and 1848 campaigns, counted on military glory to solve all their problems.[64] Some of their colleagues were not deceived. Weed, who had been working hard for Scott and had hitherto been optimistic, gave up hope after the October state elections. Similarly, Postmaster General Nathan Hall told Fillmore that he now doubted that any Whig could have been elected. Ohio was gone beyond redemption, he asserted, and in New York and Pennsylvania Whig chances were poor.[65]

V

"Till the day when Babylon the Great shall be cast down into the sea as a millstone, there will not be such another smash and collapse and catastrophe as yesterday befell the Whig party." So George Templeton Strong, the famous New York City diarist, characterized the outcome of the 1852 presidential election. Outwardly at least, Scott's reaction was more restrained. "I admit that I experienced the day after my defeat, both surprise & mortification," he wrote afterwards in a classic bit of understatement.[66] The final returns brutally revealed how misplaced his pre-election confidence had been. Instead of achieving the great triumph he anticipated, Scott managed to carry only Massachusetts and Vermont in the North and Kentucky and Tennessee in the South, the four most faithful Whig states in the nation. All the rest, including New York, Pennsylvania, and Ohio, had gone for Pierce. He lost even Maryland and Delaware, which no Whig candidate had ever failed to carry. The electoral vote was crushing: 254 for Pierce, a mere 42 for Scott. The sheer magnitude of the defeat stunned the Whigs. One of Weed's trusted

---

62. Nathan Sargent to Thomas H. Dudley, October 19, Dudley Papers; FitzHenry Warren to [Henry Waldron?], October 18, Waldron Family Papers.

63. Israel Washburn, Jr., to Charles P. Chandler, July 14, Charles P. Chandler Papers, Maine Historical Society; Warren to Seward, September 28, Seward Papers, UR; Truman Smith to John Wilson, October 7, John Wilson Papers, University of California, Berkeley.

64. A good example of this reasoning is John Teesdale to John McLean, November 19, McLean Papers, LC.

65. Weed to Fish, April 16, August 22, Fish Papers, LC; Weed to Seward, September 25, Seward Papers, UR; Nathan Hall to Fillmore, October 15, 26, Fillmore Papers, BECHS.

66. Nevins and Thomas, eds., *Strong Diary*, v. 2, 108, 104–5; Scott to Fish, November 16, Fish Papers, LC.

lieutenants probably summarized the feeling of the majority when he confessed, "Nobody looked for such a sweeping result." Even Hall admitted that the extent of the party's defeat was worse than he expected. It was, in the words of one Whig governor, a "political deluge."[67]

By focusing on the totals in the Electoral College, Whigs magnified the extent of their loss. Pierce's margin in the popular vote—slightly more than 200,000 votes out of more than three million cast—was not nearly as overwhelming.[68] Although the 1852 turnout in the North was the lowest of any presidential election between 1840 and 1860, thereby substantiating earlier reports of voter apathy, participation was only slightly less than that of 1848. In the face of all the difficulties that afflicted the Whig campaign, Scott ran a creditable race. He lost Connecticut and several southern states by narrow margins, and he made a respectable showing in New York, Pennsylvania, New Jersey, and Ohio.[69]

Throughout the North, Whigs enjoyed varying success in retaining their 1848 supporters (Tables 1.1 through 1.8).[70] They did very well in Pennsylvania, Ohio, and Indiana, but they were less successful in Maine, Massachusetts, and Connecticut. After several rather dispirited state campaigns, the Ohio Whigs embarked on an energetic program to rebuild the party's organization, and their concerted effort did much to restore the party's earlier strength. Such was not the case in Massachusetts, Connecticut, and Illinois. More than one out of ten of Zachary Taylor's adherents in 1848 failed to vote in Illinois or Connecticut in 1852, and in the Bay State the rate of Whig abstentions was staggering as approximately a third of those who backed Taylor sat out the 1852 election. Adverse results in the earlier state elections and low party morale undoubtedly kept many Whigs home. So, too, did factional strife, which had created enmities that continued to fester. "Jealousies in the Whig party had a great deal to do with Genl Scott's defeat," concluded Illinois Whig leader David Davis.[71]

Also critical to the outcome was the failure of the Whigs' Free Soil strategy. Except in Illinois and Maine, Scott received substantial Free Soil support, but in some states, such as Pennsylvania and especially New York, a larger proportion of Free Soilers voted for Pierce, and in others, most notably Massachusetts and Ohio, the number who remained loyal to Hale far exceeded those who defected to Scott. Scott's share of the Free Soil vote was simply too small to bring victory. In addition, in Maine and Illinois a significant proportion of Free Soilers, perhaps because of conflicting feelings, abstained.

The Whigs were hurt especially by the course of the Free Soilers in the three key states of Ohio, Pennsylvania, and New York. In New York and Pennsylvania, the 1848 Free Soil ranks disintegrated, but the return of these voters to the two major parties benefited the Democrats. This result is hardly surprising. In both states Van Buren's strength had come primarily from Democrats, not Whigs; many of these Free Soil Democrats,

---

67. Vivus W. Smith to Weed, November 7, Weed Papers, UR; Hall to Graham, January 5, 1853, Hamilton, ed., *Graham Papers*, v. 4, 447; Washington Hunt to Seward, November 4, Seward Papers, UR.

68. The popular vote was: for Pierce, 1,601,117 (51.0 percent); for Scott, 1,385,453 (44.1 percent); and for Hale, 155,316 (4.9 percent). Hale's total represented a 47 percent decline from Van Buren's vote in 1848; the return of the Barnburners in New York to their former allegiance accounted for over half of this decrease.

69. In 1852, an estimated 75.3 percent of the eligible electorate cast ballots in the North, compared to 77.1 percent in 1848. The drop in participation was more dramatic in the South. See Holt, *Political Crisis*, 127–29.

70. These and other tables in this study are based on the statistical technique of ecological regression. For a discussion of this method, along with related problems in analyzing voter behavior, see the Appendix.

71. David Davis to John F. Henry, December 27, David Davis Papers, ChicHS.

following their national leadership, simply returned to their old party allegiance.[72] In Ohio, however, where the Free Soilers were overwhelmingly former Whigs, efforts to break up the third-party coalition made little headway. There the continuing strength of the Free Soil party destroyed Scott's chances. After the election one Ohio Whig noted that the party had done well in the southern counties, but he observed despondently that it was hopeless to carry the state "in the face of a full Hale vote."[73] The once-powerful Ohio Whig party had since 1848 experienced a series of defeats, and in the aftermath of Scott's loss many despairing party members concluded that, in view of the unrelenting hostility of the Free Soilers, their party was permanently wrecked and could never again carry the state. The failure of their strenuous campaign for Scott enervated Ohio Whigs, and as a result sentiment to abandon the party was stronger in that state, both among the masses and the leaders, than in either New York or Pennsylvania.

In addition, Whig defections to the Democrats weakened the party in Ohio, Indiana, Connecticut, Massachusetts, and New York particularly. In the last two states the abstention of a number of party members also hurt the Whigs. A closer examination of the situation in New York clarifies the dynamics involved in these losses.

The Whig party in New York entered the 1852 campaign badly distracted by the Seward-Fillmore feud, which had intensified during the previous two years.[74] Attempts during the campaign to heal the breach were to a large extent unsuccessful. Some of Seward's prominent associates, vexed over their proscription by the national administration, announced shrilly that the situation would be reversed under Scott. It was hard to yield any support to Scott, one Fillmore Whig explained, "when we are publicly told . . . that [']*every friend of the Administration had their graves allready* [sic] *prepared & their epitath* [sic] *written.*'"[75] Seward Whigs labored zealously for Scott, despite their disappointment over the platform, but the Fillmore faction evidenced no consistent behavior. Some, like Solomon G. Haven, worked very hard for the ticket; others, like the New York collector, Hugh Maxwell, refused to contribute any assistance. Maxwell, in fact, did not even vote.

Many New York Whigs followed the Collector's example. It is difficult to determine statewide which Whigs either declined to vote or defected to the Democrats, for no prior election provides a clear test of Silver Grey strength. In 1850 conservatives nominated a pro-Compromise Union ticket, composed of nominees from the Whig and Democratic tickets, but in many counties the presence of a separate Anti-Renter coalition ticket thoroughly muddled the results. The large rate of Whig abstentions in 1850 confused matters further. The situation in New York City, however, where the Union movement was strong relative to the state as a whole, and where the Anti-Rent crusade was of no importance, is suggestive. In the metropolis in 1852, Silver Greys made up a large portion

72. Regression estimates for 1848 between the October gubernatorial vote and the Free Soil vote for president in November indicate that about 40 percent of the Pennsylvania Free Soilers were ex-Democrats and the rest were new voters. Free Soil strength in the state was concentrated in David Wilmot's congressional district along the New York border. It had previously been a heavily Democratic district.

73. P. B. Ewing to Thomas Ewing, November 9 (quotation), Ewing Family Papers, LC; Eben Newton to Elisha Whittlesey, October 14, 20, Elisha Whittlesey Papers, WRHS.

74. Harry J. Carman and Reinhard H. Luthin, "The Seward-Fillmore Feud and the Crisis of 1850," and "The Seward-Fillmore Feud and the Disruption of the Whig Party," *New York History*, v. 24 (April, July, 1943), 163–84, 335–57; Lee H. Warner, "The Perpetual Crisis of Conservative Whigs: New York's Silver Grays," *New-York Historical Society Quarterly*, v. 57 (July, 1973), 213–36.

75. R. J. Everett to Fillmore, June 28, Fillmore Papers, BECHS.

of the non-voting and bolting Whigs. The day after the election the New York *Tribune* complained: "We hoped the men who have been defeating the Whig party for two or three years past in order to 'kill Seward,' must have finished their job by this time, but they were at it as hard yesterday as if they had just begun."[76]

A similar situation presumably prevailed elsewhere. In Massachusetts, most of the Whig abstainers undoubtedly were Webster loyalists upset by Scott's nomination and disheartened by their leader's recent death. Whig defections and abstentions were so large, in fact, that Pierce won a plurality in Boston—an unheard-of occurrence in that bastion of commercial Whiggery. The assertions of observers in different communities that Union Whigs took little interest in the election and generally stayed away from the polls or refused to support Scott, whom they regarded as a mere pawn of Seward, were probably accurate. One regular Whig who voted for Pierce explained that while he had nothing against Scott personally, he feared that the Whig nominee "would be under abolition influences if elected, and that anti-compromise whigs would be placed in office."[77]

More significant for the future than the defection of these conservatives was the loss of many of the party's traditional Protestant supporters, especially among Presbyterians and Methodists, angry over the Whigs' bid for the Catholic vote. In New York, support for the Whigs among Presbyterians in particular showed a dramatic decline between 1848 and 1852.[78] One Ohio Whig acknowledged that his party's attention to the Irish vote caused many native-born Whigs to vote for Pierce; in like manner, an important Whig officeholder in Philadelphia traced the party's overthrow to its Catholic strategy, which "caused the ultra whig protestants to vote for Pierce . . . as antagonistic to the candidate who made the 'rich Irish brogue' and 'pleasant German accent' such a staple in his harangues."[79] To compound Whig problems in Pennsylvania, Native American party members, who traditionally allied with the Whigs, deserted Scott, the apostate nativist. In Philadelphia, where the vast majority of these nativists were located, more than half the Native American party's supporters either voted for Pierce or Webster or sat out the election in a direct rebuke of Scott.[80]

---

76. New York *Tribune*, November 3; New York *Herald*, November 2; Fish to Daniel D. Barnard, November 24, Daniel D. Barnard Papers, NYSL. Regression estimates indicate that virtually all 1850 Union voters in New York City abstained in 1852. The small number (4 percent) who bothered to go to the polls threw away their vote by casting Webster ballots; significantly, none voted for Scott.

77. George S. Hillard to Francis Lieber, November 2, Francis Lieber Papers, HEH; Moses Kimball to Henry L. Dawes, November 3, Henry L. Dawes Papers, LC; John Davis to William Schouler, November 4, Schouler Papers; Hayes to Sardis Birchard, November 10, Williams, ed., *Hayes Diary and Letters*, v. 1, 432. The quotation is from a letter signed "A Liberal Whig," Portland *Advertiser*, September 6, 1853.

78. Regression estimates for New York suggest that about a third of the Presbyterian Whigs refused to vote for Scott (Whig strength among them fell from roughly 90 percent in 1848 to about 64 percent in 1852), although negative proportions in some categories mean that these figures should be interpreted cautiously. Some of these defectors voted for Pierce (8 percent), but most simply abstained (37 percent). The Whigs had little strength among Methodist voters in New York.

79. John Barr to Seward, November 8, Seward Papers, UR; William D. Lewis Diary, November 3, Lewis-Neilson Papers. For claims that Methodist and Presbyterian Whigs in Pennsylvania deserted Scott, see Miller N. Everly to Fillmore, February 1, 1853, Private, Isaac Newton to Fillmore, November 13, Fillmore Papers, BECHS; James Johnston to Edward McPherson, December 3, Edward McPherson Papers, LC.

80. Scott received the support of about 45 percent of those voters who cast Native American ballots in the October state election, compared to 23 percent for Pierce and 11 percent for Webster. In contrast to Scott's showing, an estimated two-thirds of these voters had a year earlier backed William F. Johnston, the Whig candidate for governor.

At the same time, as many party workers noted, the Whigs had little to show for their efforts among immigrants and Catholics (Table 1.9). One Indiana Whig attributed the loss of his county to "wild, bogtrotting railroad Irishmen," a view in accord with that of another western Whig who asserted that the party was "overwhelmed by the Foreign vote." Thomas Corwin, a prominent party leader in Ohio, declared that everywhere the Catholic vote was solidly against Scott, while a Pennsylvania Whig reported that even Catholics who had hitherto voted Whig went for Pierce.[81] Such reports were not without foundation. In New York, Whig support among both Germans and Irish plummeted, an outcome that suggests that despite exploitation of the religious issue, the party failed to capture a significant share of the Catholic vote (Table 1.10). The increase of non-voting among the Irish in New York may have reflected suspicion of both candidates.[82] Greeley admitted that the results of Whig efforts to win immigrant voters were disappointing. "The cry about Gen. Scott's former Nativism, the citations from Whig papers of former years against Foreigners, Popery, &c., proved too powerful." Well could one New Jersey Whig conclude that Scott fell "between the Catholics and Protestants—each believing him their opponent."[83]

Scott's managers had expected little from the South, but the party's performance in the North demonstrated how badly they had miscalculated in formulating their campaign strategy. The Sewardites' assumption that conservatives would eventually support the ticket was, although not without some validity, excessively optimistic, since in many localities a larger than normal proportion of Whigs defected or abstained. Moreover, Hale's candidacy hurt the party in some states, and, where Hale did poorly compared to Van Buren in 1848, Pierce rather than Scott was the beneficiary. Finally, the Whig emphasis on the religious issue backfired: It not only alienated nativist Whigs, but it also failed to gain Scott much support among Catholics and immigrants. Astutely predicting that Whigs would lose two Protestant votes for every Catholic vote gained, the New York *Herald* aptly characterized the party's campaign tactics as "blundering mismanagement."[84] These difficulties, coupled with the return of the Barnburners to the Democratic fold, proved too much for the Whigs to overcome. The result, at least in the Electoral College, was an overwhelming Whig defeat.

VI

The Seward and Fillmore factions lost no time in blaming each other for the election's outcome. For their part, pro-Compromise Whigs emphasized Scott's failure to endorse the platform with any enthusiasm and his association with "abolition fanaticism."[85] Their opponents, on the other hand, accused Silver Greys of weighing Scott down with a

---

81. David McDonald to George Dunn, November 3, George Dunn Papers, IndU; John Teesdale to McLean, November 19, McLean Papers, LC; Corwin to James A. Pearce, October 20, 1854, James A. Pearce Papers, Maryland Historical Society; James Johnston to McPherson, December 3, McPherson Papers; John Davis to Schouler, November 4, Schouler Papers; Cincinnati *Gazette*, November 25.

82. Regression estimates show that slightly fewer than half the Irish voters abstained in New York in 1852, an increase of almost 10 percent over those abstaining in 1848.

83. New York *Tribune*, November 3; Charles Perrin Smith to Dudley, November 3, Dudley Papers.

84. New York *Herald*, October 6.

85. Henry M. Brackenridge to Peter Force, November 5 (quotation), Henry M. Brackenridge Papers, University of Pittsburgh; Benjamin F. Johnson to John Dean Caton, November 22, John Dean Caton Papers, LC; N. W. Davis to Daniel Ullmann, November 6, Daniel Ullmann Papers, NYHS.

platform obnoxious to the majority and then refusing to support the ticket. "That cursed platform . . . drove from us the anti-slavery Whigs & free Soilers," Lewis D. Campbell exclaimed angrily, "whilst Webster & Fillmore drove their stiletto into us from the rear!"[86] Not allied with either faction, Fish believed that the leaders of both groups shared responsibility for Scott's defeat. "There was much of passion & of personal resentment within our ranks," he conceded. "We were divided by personal attachments, & were weakened by personal jealousies." The 1852 results were a sobering reminder of the consequences of personal feuds among the party leadership. Early in the year Charles Francis Adams had observed that a Whig defeat seemed inevitable because both factions of the party "prefer the success of the enemy to that of the other portion."[87]

With defeat further aggravating these wounds, each faction called for the removal of the other from party leadership. Fillmore's close advisers were quick to argue that Seward and his friends had led the party to defeat, so they should reap the consequences. They "have received a death blow from which they can never recover," one Silver Grey journal exulted.[88] Equally prompt to call for a purge of Silver Greys, Seward Whigs considered the result of the election "a happy expedient for ridding ourselves forever from their dead weight."[89] Amid these recriminations, a number of despondent Whigs shared the view of some Democrats that the Whig party was beyond resurrection. Fessenden, Smith, Campbell, and Henry J. Raymond, for example, all momentarily pronounced the Whig party defunct. "We are slayed—the party is dead—dead—dead!" Campbell proclaimed with his usual vehemence.[90] Some conservative Whigs concurred. "I am sick of the Whig party," one announced.[91]

In the wake of Scott's rout, deeply disillusioned Whigs looked for a realignment of parties. They argued that without a powerful opposition, the Democratic party could not long remain united; soon it would begin to disintegrate, and then new alliances could be formed. The recent defeat rendered a new organization "inevitable," the Philadelphia collector William Lewis told Senator John Clayton. "The Whigs are out of heart," another Pennsylvania Whig declared, "and I think that many will seek new party connexions."[92] A number of conservative Whigs spoke favorably of a new Silver Grey-conservative Democratic coalition; other Whigs called for an antislavery party that

86. Campbell to Israel Washburn, Jr., November 4, Israel Washburn, Jr., Papers, LC; New York *Tribune*, November 3.

87. Fish to Lewis Kingsley, December 30 (copy), Washington Hunt to Fish, November 10, Fish Papers, LC; Adams to Sumner, April 7 (copy), Adams Family Papers.

88. Solomon G. Haven to Fillmore, November 11, Fillmore Papers, BECHS; Albany *State Register*, quoted in the New York *Tribune*, November 15.

89. O. Bowe to John A. King, November 5 (quotation), John A. King Papers; George W. Ball to Seward, November 6, Lyman A. Spalding to Seward, November 6, Seward Papers, UR; Auburn *Weekly Journal*, November 17.

90. Fessenden to Hannibal Hamlin, November 17, Hannibal Hamlin Papers, UMe; Henry J. Raymond to Seward, November 6, Seward Papers, UR; Truman Smith to Weed, November 15, Weed Papers; Campbell to Isaac Strohm, November 4, Isaac Strohm Papers, OHS.

91. N. W. Davis to Ullmann, November 6, Ullmann Papers, NYHS. For other examples, see William Kellogg to Richard Yates, December 16, Yates-Pickering Collection, IllSHL; E. S. Terry to Richard W. Thompson, November 13, Richard W. Thompson Papers, IndSL.

92. William D. Lewis to John M. Clayton, November 13, John M. Clayton Papers, LC; James Johnson to McPherson, December 3, McPherson Papers.

would unite the anti-Compromise Whigs with the Free Soil Democrats. Predicting the formation of such a northern party, one of Seward's associates confessed that he considered the downfall of the Whig party "providential."[93] In fact, conservatives were convinced that the party's destruction had been Seward's goal all along.[94]

Eagerly, almost desperately, Free Soilers joined in the refrain of impending realignment. "Now is the time for a new organization," Charles Sumner informed Seward. "Out of this chaos the party of freedom must arise." Even the usually pessimistic Adams was encouraged. With the Whigs' crushing defeat "one great obstacle is removed from us," he noted in his diary. In a letter to Sumner written at the end of the year, he stressed the need for Free Soil action that would make it impossible to reorganize the Whig party on its old basis. Wendell Phillips, the famous Garrisonian abolitionist who shunned political action, also took heart. "The recent & total annihilation of the National Whig party," he observed, "is, probably, destined to result in the formation very soon, of two great parties northern & southern." It was, he thought, "the beginning of the end."[95]

Calls for a new party did not, however, represent the views of the majority of Whigs—north or south. Such sentiment was a natural outgrowth of the Whigs' humiliating defeat, but for the most part it proved remarkably short-lived. In general, Whig journals firmly, even scornfully, rejected the claim that the party was dead.[96] Weed oscillated between despair and hope, yet at no time during this period did he seriously consider abandoning the Whig organization. "Though we have been very hardly used in our late conflict," one New York City Whig wrote to Weed, "it still appears to me that our wounds are not necessarily mortal & that a good course of treatment under skillful hands will or may restore us to our pristine strength & power."[97] Nor were most of the Fillmore Whigs ready to leave the party; indeed, they believed that the adverse result in 1852 would strengthen their influence in its councils.[98] The proper strategy, Seward urged, was to remain temporarily in the background. Prominent Whig editors agreed. "Now is the time to lie low, stand by your guns, & wait for developments," Samuel Bowles of the Springfield *Republican* advised, and Horace Greeley echoed that "I mean now to lie quiet awhile, and see how the world moves on." Seward dismissed the idea of an imminent political

---

93. E. S. Terry to Thompson, November 13, Thompson Papers, IndSL; John M. Bradford to Seward, November 9 (quotation), Leander Reddy to Seward, November 9, Seward Papers, UR.

94. Daniel Lee to Fillmore, November 5, Nathan Hall to Fillmore, November 3, Gilbert Hall to Fillmore, November 10, Fillmore Papers, BECHS; John Staats to William C. Bouck, February 2, 1853, William C. Bouck Papers, Cornell University. In endorsing this interpretation, Robert J. Rayback relies exclusively on the testimony of Seward's enemies and men who did not share his confidence: *Millard Fillmore: Biography of a President* (Buffalo, 1959) 254–67, 352–54.

95. Sumner to Seward, November 6, Seward Papers, UR; Adams Diary, November 3, Adams to Sumner, December 22 (copy), Adams Family Papers; Wendell Phillips to Elizabeth Pease, November 21, William Lloyd Garrison Papers, Boston Public Library. For a more mixed assessment, see George W. Julian, *Political Recollections, 1840–1872* (Chicago, 1884), 129–31.

96. South Bend *Register*, November 4, quoted in Ovando J. Hollister, *Life of Schuyler Colfax* (New York, 1886), 69; Buffalo *Commercial Advertiser*, quoted in New York *Tribune*, November 15; *Ohio State Journal*, November 5; Portland *Advertiser*, November 4; New York *Times*, December 28; Hartford *Courant*, February 16, 1853, quoted in Parmet, "Know-Nothings in Connecticut," 51.

97. Seward to Frances A. Seward, November 19, Seward Papers, UR; Albany *Evening Journal*, November 10; Weed to Jonathan Nathan, November 11, Typescript, Fish Papers, LC; Nathan to Weed, November 10, Weed Papers, UR.

98. A. L. Linn to Fillmore, December 24, Haven to Fillmore, November 11, Fillmore Papers, BECHS; Albany *State Register* quoted in the Rochester *Democrat*, November 8.

reorganization with the confident prediction, "No new party will arise, nor will any old one fall."[99]

Despite such optimism, it is clear in retrospect that the 1852 defeat dealt the Whig party a severe psychological blow. In effect, many Whigs, including some influential leaders, gave up hope that nationally the party could again seriously challenge the Democrats. The reasons for this despair are subtle. They stem, in part, from the Whig view of the past. Envisioning their party as the representative of talent and respectability, Whigs were frustrated by their failure to dominate national politics, all the more so because they believed that the Democratic party was led by demagogues offering no responsible policies to deal with the problems confronting the nation. The party of negativism had repeatedly vanquished the best the Whigs could offer. Henry Clay's loss in 1844 to James K. Polk, a much less distinguished candidate, especially devastated their self-confidence. Even the victories of William Henry Harrison and Zachary Taylor occasioned misgivings, since they were both military men with at best weak ties to the party, and their untimely deaths further reinforced this uneasiness. The party seemed able to win only through expediency, and when triumphant it seemed almost fated to lose the fruits of its victory. These considerations combined to produce a sense of malaise before the 1852 election. When the last avenue of victory—military popularity—was lost, a number of Whigs were overcome by a profound sense of hopelessness. The party appeared destined to be a permanent minority, and some at least were ready to find a new political home. "For more than a quarter of a century we, as a party, have met with nothing but defeats and disasters, both in our elections and measures," wrote one disheartened Whig who believed that it was "folly" to attempt to keep up the party's organization.[100]

Although the 1852 election strengthened anti-southern feeling among some northern Whigs, such sentiment was surprisingly weak among party leaders, the great majority of whom wished to maintain a national organization. Seward and Weed, in particular, had no interest in abandoning the Whig party for some new, untried coalition. Seward believed that the party could continue to act together as it had in the previous decade by allowing a divergence of opinion on the slavery issue. Neither section would impose its views as a party test. Whether this policy succeeded would depend in part on future events, but four years remained before the party would again have to conduct a national campaign. Until then, each section could look out for its own interests. The passage of time, a common hostility to the Democrats, and a growing recognition that success depended on a policy of toleration would reunite and revitalize the party, Seward insisted. This program represented, as Adams remarked, a continuation of the old system of "a double headed party."[101]

This strategy had proved at least reasonably successful in the 1840s and it might do so again, especially if, as all seemed to agree, the slavery issue was losing its power. The major parties' endorsement of the Compromise removed sectional issues from the political arena. The fugitive slave law might prove an irritant, but so few slaves were arrested under its provisions that it could never be a major problem. If nothing else, the Whigs'

99. Seward to Schouler, December 25, Schouler Papers; Samuel Bowles to Dawes, November 13, Dawes Papers; Horace Greeley to Mrs. G. B. Kirby, December 6, Horace Greeley Papers, NYPL; Seward to Sumner, November 9 (quotation), Sumner Papers, HU.

100. E. S. Terry to Thompson, November 13, Thompson Papers, IndSL.

101. Seward to Sumner, November 9, Sumner Papers, HU; Adams Diary, December 4, 13 (quotation), Adams Family Papers.

experiences during the past twelve months had demonstrated the political bankruptcy of sectional questions.

A more difficult question, which Whig and Democratic spokesmen failed to confront, was what issues would separate the parties in the future. Whigs in particular were rapidly losing much of their traditional appeal. Prudence dictated scrapping the national bank issue; the tariff excited little popular interest outside a few areas; and many Democrats, especially in the West, enthusiastically supported federally financed internal improvements, thus depriving Whigs of another distinctive issue. Democrats and Whigs alike observed that old Jacksonian questions were now obsolete. "In truth the acknowledged issues between the two parties are now of no . . . practical bearing. Neither party present[s] any striking & high principle which the other disclaimed," Fish wrote after the 1852 election. "We lack . . . for issues," Democratic leader Charles Peaslee admitted during the campaign, "since the whigs have come over to many of our leading principles & measure[s] & dare not make [a] fight upon them."[102] With equal justice he could have noted that the Democrats had also adopted many of the traditional Whig positions. As the contest raged about him, Rutherford B. Hayes, then a young Whig lawyer in Cincinnati, perceptively reflected: "The real grounds of difference upon important political questions no longer correspond with party lines. The progressive Whig is nearer in sentiment to the radical Democrat than the radical Democrat is to the 'fogy' of his own party; *vice versa.*"[103]

Not only did the earlier Jacksonian issues seem obsolete, but two other traditional sources of Whig support in the North—nativism and antislavery—had been seriously jeopardized as a result of the 1852 presidential contest. The Scott campaign, by blatantly catering to the foreign vote, stimulated anti-Catholicism while simultaneously alienating nativist party members. The destruction of nativists' faith in Whiggery was a major component of the popular revolt that would soon engulf the party. In addition, national considerations precluded agitation of sectional issues, or at least dampened such agitation, and the slavery issue seemed in any case to be losing force. These trends had been under way in muted form for some time, but the 1852 presidential contest brought them to the crisis stage. The national Whig party lost its traditional issues at a time when it was already severely crippled by the increasingly bitter hatreds among its leaders. For all their problems, however, Whig leaders were not ready to forsake their party's battered organization. Instead, as they surveyed the political horizon in the wake of Scott's defeat, northern Whigs concluded that their salvation lay in state issues.

---

102. Fish to Barnard, November 24, Barnard Papers; Peaslee to Gideon Welles, July 17, Welles Papers, LC. For other assertions to this effect from a wide variety of political perspectives, see William V. Pettit to Welles, July 22, Welles Papers, LC; W. F. M. to his brother [Justin S. Morrill?], September 11, Justin S. Morrill Papers, Vermont Historical Society; Hugh Maxwell to Fillmore, November 10, Fillmore Papers, BECHS; Theodore C. Pease and James G. Randall, eds., *The Diary of Orville Hickman Browning* (2 vols.: Springfield, 1927–1933), v. 1, 68–69, 74; Cincinnati *Commercial*, November 9.

103. Hayes Diary, September 24, Williams, ed., *Hayes Diary and Letters*, v. 1, 421–22.

2

The Collapse of the Second Party System

"Never since Washingtons has an Administration commenced with the hearty g[oo]d will of so large a portion of the country," Amos A. Lawrence, a prominent Massachusetts Whig, commented at the opening of Franklin Pierce's presidency. With the country experiencing heady prosperity and with sectional antagonisms subsiding after a long period of weary strife, Americans looked forward confidently to an era of political tranquility. Some Democrats believed that with the Whigs in disarray the new president had a unique opportunity to reunite and revitalize his party. Others serenely foresaw the decline of partisanship. Even the usually pungent James Shepherd Pike of the New York *Tribune* anticipated that Pierce would preside over a "quiet," "unexceptionable" administration "to which nobody will think of making any especial objection or opposition."[1]

Contrary to these predictions, Pierce's policies produced sharp partisan conflict and unprecedented party turmoil. Denied renomination, he left office in 1857, repudiated by both his party and public opinion and with his influence at an end, a casualty of the political realignment of the mid-decade. By the close of Pierce's presidency, the second party system had disappeared, and a new alignment, the Civil War party system, had begun to crystallize.

The disintegration of the second party system poses several perplexing problems that need to be noted at the outset. One difficulty is the variation in the timing of party decay from state to state. In some states the Jacksonian system was close to death by the end of 1852; in others it retained its vitality for several more years. Another complication lies in the contrasting fates of the Whig and Democratic parties. Although weakened by the realignment of the 1850s, the Democracy remained competitive, whereas the Whig party suffered such extensive desertions among its traditional supporters that it ceased to exist.

---

1. Amos A. Lawrence to Mrs. Robert Means, March 1, 1853, Amos A. Lawrence Papers, MassHS; New York *Tribune*, April 30, 1853, quoted in Glyndon G. Van Deusen, *Horace Greeley, Nineteenth-Century Crusader* (Philadelphia, 1953), 178.

Any analysis of the dissolution of the second party system must not only determine those forces that undermined it in various states but also explain why these forces had such a devastating impact on the Whig party. Finally, because parties competed simultaneously at all levels of the federal system, the relative influence of state and local issues compared with national issues is a further complicating factor. Reflective of the national orientation of most antebellum political history, discussions of the demise of the Jacksonian party system in general, and the Whig party in particular, normally emphasize sectionalism and the slavery issue. As Michael Holt points out, this approach concentrates on periods of heightened sectional tensions and jumps from 1850 to 1852 to 1854 with little if any attention devoted to intervening years. Yet some of the most crucial political developments occurred in state and local contests in years when sectional concerns were distinctly dampened. Nor did antislavery Whigs take the lead in abandoning their party; in many states, they sought new connections only after the defection of other groups had depleted the party's popular strength. In reality, events at the state and local level rather than national questions caused the breakup of the Jacksonian party system.[2]

The distinction between party collapse and party realignment is central to an explanation of the transition from the second to the third party system. Although political realignment inevitably follows party collapse, the two phenomena, as the period after the War of 1812 demonstrates, need not occur simultaneously. In the 1850s these two processes overlapped in time, and consequently there is a strong tendency to view them as identical and to assume that the forces producing the death of the Whig party were also responsible for the creation of the new party alignment. In several critical features, however, the realignment of the mid-nineteenth century more closely resembled that of the 1820s than those after the Civil War, for the disintegration of the party system was well under way before realignment began.

The concept of party decomposition is useful in distinguishing between these two related but not identical developments.[3] Party decomposition results from the weakening of the ties that bind voters to the existing parties. It reflects a decline in the importance of partisanship in determining electoral behavior. Once party disaggregation begins, realignment is possible, since the opportunity then presents itself to detach from their traditional affiliations large numbers of weakly identified voters. Several aggregate indices, including the extent of voter apathy, the proportion of voters switching parties, the instability of party loyalties, and the number and strength of third-party movements measure the degree of party decomposition in the antebellum period.[4] This concept, in turn, provides a framework with which to analyze the collapse of the second party system.

I

When the new administration took office, few observers believed that political realignment was at hand. Many Free Soilers talked as if it were, as they had for years, and a few well-known Whigs joined them, but most politicans, including virtually all Democrats, were convinced that although the issues might change, the Jacksonian party system would

---

2. For a discussion of the problems noted in this introductory section, see Holt, *Political Crisis*, 101–5.

3. In *Critical Elections* (pp. 71–134), Walter Dean Burnham attaches a somewhat different meaning to the term *party decomposition* than the one used in this chapter.

4. Clubb, Flanigan, and Zingale, *Partisan Realignment*, 133–38, present a penetrating discussion of the preconditions for realignment.

continue to flourish. The task of directing the Democratic party's future lay in Pierce's hands. The New Hampshire leader was only forty-four years old and had not held public office for some time, yet party regulars convinced themselves that he had the character and experience necessary to restore harmony to the national party.

Pierce was, in fact, totally unsuited for the task that awaited him. A handsome, slightly built man with a generous head of hair and more than a touch of vanity, he carried himself with a graceful manner that imparted an imposing presence. Preeminently a social person, he was blessed with great personal charm and easily assumed a familiar air with callers, often throwing an arm around their shoulders. Such behavior betrayed the shallowness of his character. Wanting intensely to be liked and uncomfortable with confrontation, Pierce appeared to agree affably with whomever he was conversing, even when he had no intention of accepting the proffered advice; later, when he adopted a different policy, men naturally felt deceived. Politicians in Washington came to see how little his protestations of friendship really meant, how completely undependable he actually was. Pierce's weakness and vacillation, his total lack of will, led one commentator to characterize him as "a weak, imaginative, almost brilliant, undetermined man, who said in the morning that he would do something, and when he said it meant it, but who changed his mind in the afternoon if the smallest obstacle interfered with his purpose." Forceful politicians quickly realized that this unsteady and irresolute president could be intimidated.[5]

Pierce organized his administration on the basis that past opinions and behavior were irrelevant, that all who endorsed the 1852 national platform were entitled to full acceptance. Believing that this policy would restore party concord with a minimum of dissension, he recognized all factions when distributing the patronage. To the contrary, Pierce's policy engendered widespread discontent, and in less than six months the president and his advisers had sacrificed much of their influence and prestige. Throughout the North, factional rivalries rent the party while the administration, under mounting attack for allegedly coddling free soilers, seemed powerless to maintain party discipline. In the words of the closest student of his presidency, "Pierce had carried out his original policy of treating all factions equally with the result that all were now equally disgruntled."[6]

The most significant—and in the long run most portentous—dissatisfaction occurred in New York, where the feuds that had plagued the party in the past continued unabated. Following the rupture of 1848, William L. Marcy, who became Pierce's secretary of state, joined by his younger ally Horatio Seymour, led a movement to reunite the party by forgetting past differences. Their efforts precipitated a further schism between the Softshells and the Hardshells. The Softs, led by Marcy and Seymour, advocated reconciliation with the Barnburners; the Hards, guided by former senator Daniel S. Dickinson, demanded that the Van Burenites be punished for their party irregularity by being proscribed from holding state or federal office. The Softs and Barnburners formed a loose coalition in opposition to the Hards, who were a distinct minority in the party.[7]

---

5. Maunsell B. Field, *Memories of Many Men and Some Women* (New York, 1875), 162; John Slidell to James Buchanan, June 17, 1854, Buchanan Papers, HSPa; Franklin S. Burr to [Gideon Welles], September 15, 1853, Welles Papers, LC. See the sketch in Nevins, *Ordeal of the Union*, v. 2, 41–42; and for a more favorable interpretation, Nichols, *Pierce*, 533–46.

6. Nichols, *Pierce*, 289. Nichols carefully analyzes Pierce's patronage policy and the disputes it produced, 247–93 and passim.

7. The factional quarrels among New York Democrats are outlined in Spencer, *Victor and the Spoils*,

Forced to retreat from his original plan to include the Van Burenites in the cabinet, Pierce still attempted to balance federal appointments in the state among the three factions. It quickly became apparent, however, that almost a decade of strife among New York Democrats could not be papered over by the administration's patronage policy. To make matters worse, the Hards, after unsuccessfully trying to seize control of the 1853 state convention, bolted and nominated a separate ticket. Responsibility for the disruption rested squarely with the patronage-minded Hards, who sensed the waning support for the administration and were determined at all costs to oust the Barnburners from positions of party leadership. In retaliation, the national administration removed Greene Bronson, the collector of the Port of New York and a Hard, and replaced him with a Soft. Once again, the New York Democracy had split in twain.[8]

II

Whig leaders saw in this new outburst of Democratic factionalism, of which the New York situation was only the most glaring manifestation, the opportunity to rescue their party's fortunes, at such low ebb just a few months earlier, if the right issues were taken up and if their own fragile unity could be maintained. Finding a new issue or set of issues, however, with which to rally the party faithful was no easy task. Because of the declining power of sectional concerns and the growing partisan consensus on economic questions, Whig politicians considered their traditional issues bankrupt. "Now is the time to start [a]new," Samuel Bowles declared in mid-1853. "The old issues are gone, we can't live under them, we are beaten out." Unless new issues were found, an Ohio man warned William H. Seward, many Whigs "will be wandering off into other organizations or become permanently disgusted with any attention to public affairs."[9] The lack of burning national issues, the fact that Congress was in recess most of the year, and the decentralization of the national Whig organization allowed each state party to conduct the 1853 campaign as it saw fit.

Whig political fortunes varied considerably in these elections. In some states, the party experienced disillusionment and decay; in others, through skillful leadership and an opportune exploitation of state issues, it managed to remain competitive. A good example of the latter situation was New York, where, thanks to the Democratic breach and shrewd utilization of the canal issue, the Whigs regained control of the state.

The presence of a separate Hard ticket assured the Whigs of an easy victory provided they remained united. Animosity between the Fillmore and Seward wings of the party, however, was as intense as that between the Hards and the Softs. Several Union Whigs favored the policy of forming, with the Hards, a new national conservative party. From Washington, William L. Hodge, a former member of Millard Fillmore's administration, pressed upon the ex-president the desirability of such a step. "There is but a shade if *even*

175–93, and Stewart Mitchell, *Horatio Seymour of New York* (Cambridge, 1938). The William L. Marcy Papers, LC, and the Horatio Seymour Papers, NYHS, contain considerable material on this schism.

8. Samuel Tilden to My Dear Sir, September 17, 1853, [Tilden] to Marcy, September 10, 1853 (copy), Samuel J. Tilden Papers, NYPL; J. M. Hatch to Francis P. Blair, Sr., September 27, 1853, Blair-Lee Papers; J. P. Beekman to Martin Van Buren, August 2, 1853, Martin Van Buren Papers, MassHS.

9. Samuel Bowles to Henry L. Dawes, May 13, 1853, Dawes Papers; George Olmsted to William H. Seward, February 28, 1853, Seward Papers, UR. Holt presents an excellent discussion of the way changes in the economy undermined the old Jacksonian economic issues in *Political Crisis*, 110–13.

a shade of difference" between the Hards and the Silver Grey Whigs in New York, he asserted, adding that many observers thought that rank-and-file conservative Whigs would go over to the Hards even without official sanction. He preferred joining the pro-Compromise Hards instead of the Seward Whigs in any case. "I am morally convinced that there is no *national success for us unless we can clear our skirts of Sewardism,* which will ruin us at the South." In like manner, the Albany *State Register,* a leading Silver Grey organ, called openly for union with the Hards.[10]

In some counties such a coalition came about. On the state level, however, the Silver Greys and Sewardites remained nominally allied. The cautious, slow-moving Fillmore shrank instinctively from rash action, while the crafty Thurlow Weed was in no frame of mind to wreck the party and jeopardize the opportunity presented by the continuing Democratic split.[11] Controlled firmly by Weed and his allies, the state convention put no leading Silver Greys on the state ticket, but the Seward wing tried to minimize conservative discontent by silently passing over the divisive issues raised by the Compromise of 1850. The party leadership also ignored the volatile issue of temperance, hoping thereby to confine it to local contests. Instead, the Whigs conducted the 1853 campaign on the issue of enlarging the state canals.

The canal issue was ideal for Weed's purposes, for it not only avoided the slavery question, which divided the Whig party, but it gave prominence to a matter over which the Democrats had been wrangling for more than a decade. The Whig appeal had always been linked to the state's canal system, and although the party's two factions fought for control of the vast patronage dispensed by the canal board, they agreed on the importance of the canals to the state's economic well-being. Democrats, in contrast, were plagued by wide disagreement over canal policy. The Hards were strong proponents of the canals, while the economically unbending Barnburners had never been completely reconciled to the state's financing or operating a canal system.[12]

Weed had followed a similar strategy in 1851, when the Whigs authorized the floating of a nine-million-dollar bond issue to finance the enlargement of the outmoded Erie Canal, only to have the state court of appeals declare the law unconstitutional. To overcome the court's objections, the Whigs, under Weed's leadership, proposed in 1853 a constitutional amendment, which the legislature eventually approved, to appropriate the necessary funds to enlarge the canals. During the legislative session "canals, canalling and canallers, are all that is talked of," commented the New York *Evening Post.* "This subject governs all the policies of the state."[13] Although Seymour, who had been elected governor in 1852, urged passage of the amendment and the Soft convention adopted a resolution supporting enlargement, in the fall election the Whigs effectively capitalized on the issue. They were aided by the Hards, who charged throughout the campaign that the Softs had shifted positions so many times on the canal question that their belated endorsement of enlargement meant nothing. To emphasize that they were the true friends of the canals,

10. William Hodge to Millard Fillmore, September 26 (quotation), 30, 1853, J. C. Spencer to Fillmore, September 5, Millard Fillmore Papers, SUNY; Albany *State Register* quoted in the Rochester *Daily Union,* October 23, 1853.

11. Hodge to Fillmore, October 6, 1853, Fillmore Papers, SUNY; D. H. Abell to Thurlow Weed, September 24, 1853, Weed Papers, UR.

12. The canal issue in New York politics is treated fully in Ronald E. Shaw, *Erie Water West: A History of the Erie Canal, 1792–1854* (Lexington, 1966). For a discussion of the Barnburners' position, see Tilden to [George W. Newell?], January 15, 1853, Bigelow, ed., *Tilden Letters and Memorials,* v. 1, 92–93.

13. New York *Evening Post,* February 22, 1853.

the Hards nominated to head their ticket George W. Clinton, the son of DeWitt Clinton, whose vision had originally led to construction of the Erie Canal.[14]

To no one's surprise, the Whig ticket overwhelmed each of the Democratic slates.[15] The strength displayed by the Hards, on the other hand, was totally unexpected. With the federal patronage denied them and the administration openly hostile, they polled a vote virtually equal to that of the Softs. The Hards' tally shocked Pierce and his advisers. "The administration are thunderstruck with the New York Elections," an unfriendly journalist reported from Washington, and no less a personage than Marcy confessed that "the result of the election bewilders every one."[16] Soft leaders, who had not expected a close contest from the Hards, hastened to explain away their poor performance. Some pointed to popular disgust over the continuing bickering among party leaders, others noted the lingering bitterness from the 1848 split, and still others emphasized the canal issue.[17] The most common explanation, however, was that a large number of Whigs supported the Hard ticket. Seymour in fact estimated that at least 40,000 Whigs voted for Clinton.[18]

Seymour's emphasis on Whig defections to the Hards was not without foundation. The Softs won a decided majority of the regular Democratic vote, but an estimated fifth of Scott's supporters crossed over to Clinton. In addition, the Hards were the only party to gain significant support from 1852 non-voters, a group that presumably included many disgruntled Fillmore Whigs (Table 2.1). The contemporary belief that these defecting Whigs were predominantly Silver Greys was doubtless correct. Conservative sentiment in the Whig party was strongest in the cities, and the fall-off in the Whig vote was especially marked in urban centers. After the state convention, a leading Silver Grey editor wrote to Fillmore that "the mass of our friends will vote against" the Whig state ticket. Intimating that their alliance with the Hards might not be temporary, Silver Grey leaders spoke of the election as laying the groundwork for a full-scale revolt in 1854 if Weed and his associates remained in control of the party.[19]

The Whigs' easy triumph concealed the loss of an estimated third of the party's 1852 supporters. With victory certain, many Whigs, as party leaders had predicted, did not feel the usual incentive to vote. Nettled by Whig apathy, the New York *Tribune* chided that

---

14. See the Albany *Evening Journal* and the Albany *Argus*, September-November, 1853, for the Whigs' and Hards' use of the canal issue. Daniel S. Dickinson blasted the Softs' endorsement of enlargement as insincere: "No longer ago than last winter, when such [pro-canal] resolutions as the [Soft] platform embodies were introduced into the Assembly, if a cholera patient . . . had been placed in their midst, there could not have been a more effectual scattering of these very men." New York *Tribune*, September 27, 1853.

15. The official vote for secretary of state was Leavenworth (Whig), 160,553 (43.2 percent); Verplank (Soft), 96,137 (25.9 percent); Clinton (Hard), 99,835 (26.9 percent); and Sedgwick (Free Democrat), 14,985 (4.0 percent). Turnout was only 59 percent, compared to 84 percent in 1852. Clinton outpolled his Soft opponent, but the average Soft vote for all state contests slightly exceeded the Hard tally, 96,698 to 95,529.

16. Francis J. Grund to Simon Cameron, November 13, 1853, Simon Cameron Papers, HSDC; Marcy to Herman Redfield, November 14, 1853, Marcy Papers, LC.

17. John Beekman to Martin Van Buren, December 2, 1853, Van Buren Papers, LC; Horatio Seymour to Marcy, November 15, 1853, D. A. Ogden to Marcy, November 3, 1853, J. W. Franklin to Marcy, November 11, 1853, James G. Dickie to Marcy, December 25, 1853, Marcy Papers, LC.

18. Horatio Seymour to Marcy, November 11, 13, 24, 1853, Herman Redfield to Marcy, November 17, 1853, Marcy Papers, LC.

19. John J. Bush to Fillmore, October 6, [1853] (quotation), J. C. Spencer to Fillmore, September 5, 1853, Fillmore Papers, SUNY; Nathan G. King to Daniel Ullmann, September 29, 1853, *Private*, Ullmann Papers, NYHS. Because township returns for the Free Democratic (Free Soil) ticket are unavailable for most counties, county-level returns have been used instead for Tables 2.1 and 2.2

"no party was ever lazier or seemed more indifferent to the result." It fretted that "if there had been a chance for them to throw away the State, they would have done it." More ominous for the party's future, however, was the desertion to the Hards of a significant number of conservatives, who were estranged by the state party's growing identification with various reform movements, including antislavery, and its efforts to attract immigrant and Catholic voters. "Almost every where," the *Tribune* charged, "the Silver Grays were in open revolt or secretly leagued with the adversary."[20]

The plight of the Democrats was more obvious. Voting patterns in the 1853 election demonstrated that the 1848 schism in the New York party had never completely healed: Lewis Cass's supporters backed the Hards by a thin margin, while Martin Van Buren's followers strongly preferred the Soft ticket (Table 2.2). Elated by their showing, Hard leaders vowed to continue their struggle for party dominance. "Every thing here indicates that the division in the party is not only one of the most decisive kind, but that a war full of bitterness and personality, and looking to extermination of one or the other of the parties, has sprung up," a New York Democrat informed Stephen A. Douglas after the election.[21]

Its 1853 sweep enabled the Whig party to survive longer in New York than in most states. Outwardly the second party system in the state remained intact, yet signs of impending collapse were clearly visible. The high degree of voter apathy in 1853, which at least in part reflected substantial disillusionment with the existing parties, and the serious decay of each party's voting base were evidence of ongoing party decomposition. This deterioration was especially apparent in local contests. "The city election returns are a hodge-podge," the New York *Herald* commented after the balloting. Not only was there an unprecedented number of splinter tickets, but "almost every voter added to the confusion, by scratching off names and polling a mixed ticket." The results revealed "the general breaking up of parties."[22]

Massachusetts provides another example of the successful exploitation of a state issue by the Whig party. In 1853 Free Soilers and Democrats drafted a new constitution designed to undermine Whig hegemony in the state and submitted it to the voters for approval. Recognizing the threat it posed, Whig leaders rallied party members against the proposed new state charter.[23] The rejection of the constitution sounded the death knell of its patron, the Coalition, whose effectiveness had already been impaired when the national administration, seeking to disarm the accusation that it was tainted with free soilism, opposed continuation of the Democrats' state alliance with the Free Soil party.[24]

Despite its victory, the Whig party in Massachusetts had not surmounted its problems.

---

20. New York *Tribune*, November 9, 10, 1853. A two-way analysis of variance indicates that statewide the Whigs ran 9.4 percent below the normal non-Democratic vote between 1840 and 1860.

21. Edward C. West to Stephen A. Douglas, November 15, 1853, Stephen A. Douglas Papers, UChic; New York *Times*, November 10, 1853.

22. New York *Herald*, November 9, 1853.

23. Kevin Sweeney, "Rum, Romanism, Representation and Reform: Coalition Politics in Massachusetts, 1847–1853," *CWH*, v. 22 (June, 1976), 128–36; Samuel Shapiro, "The Conservative Dilemma: The Massachusetts Constitutional Convention of 1853," *NEQ*, v. 33 (June, 1960), 207–24. The vote was 62,183 for the constitution, 67,105 against. Of Scott and Webster voters in 1852, some 97 percent opposed the new constitution. Baum, *Civil War Party System*, 30.

24. Nichols, *Democratic Machine*, 214–17. Attorney General Caleb Cushing's "ukase" promulgating the administration's opposition to the Coalition in Massachusetts is printed in Claude M. Feuss, *The Life of Caleb Cushing* (2 vols.: New York, 1923), v. 2, 139–40.

For one thing, opposition to the constitution provided only a temporary means to power; it offered no long-term solution to the party's difficulties, for the very act of defeating the constitution removed it as a state issue. In addition, if the Whig legislature again turned its back on the promise of reform it would alienate party members who sincerely desired change. Richard Henry Dana, Jr., warned that if the Whigs refused to heed the popular demand for reform, they would raise "a storm" after which "there will not be a stick left standing."[25]

Elsewhere Whig efforts to use state issues were less successful. In Pennsylvania the party's strategy of pushing the sale of the state-owned Mainline Canal system proved abortive when the Democrats, long supporters of the system (in contrast to the position of the party in New York), did not oppose the sale. Lacking any statewide rallying point, Whigs agitated a variety of local issues, such as city-county consolidation in Philadelphia, but, as one editor noted, "indifference and apathy have taken possession of the public mind."[26] Aided by the Whigs' spiritless campaign, the Democrats scored a decisive victory.[27]

In the state contest, party lines in Pennsylvania held tightly among 1852 voters who went to the polls in 1853 (Table 2.3).[28] As significant, however, was the number of Whigs and Democrats who failed to vote. In part, this apathy reflected the lackluster campaign, but the decline also indicated popular disillusionment with the parties. "There is a good deal of dissatisfaction among all parties at the present time," a Democratic leader noted during the campaign. The presence in local contests of a number of splinter and independent tickets provided additional evidence of popular discontent. From Philadelphia one politician reported that there were so many local issues and tickets, "no man could '*guess his own allegiance.*'" Summarizing the situation, a Whig paper in Pittsburgh remarked that "party lines are measurably weakened, and partially broken."[29]

III

In the 1853 elections in New York, Pennsylvania, and Massachusetts, temperance was a local question. In other places, however, it had become an issue in state politics. Churches had played a major role in the temperance impulse, with the Methodists leading the way.[30]

---

25. Robert F. Lucid, ed., *The Journal of Richard Henry Dana, Jr.* (3 vols.: Cambridge, 1968), v. 2, 602–3; Edward Everett Diary, November 14, 1853, Everett Papers.

26. Pittsburgh *Gazette*, May 25, 1853, quoted in Holt, *Forging a Majority*, 117; John F. Coleman, *The Disruption of the Pennsylvania Democracy, 1848–1860* (Harrisburg, 1975), 61–63; Holt, *Political Crisis*, 114–15, 130.

27. The vote for canal commissioner was Whig, 118,112 (42.4 percent); Democrat, 153,003 (54.9 percent). The Native American ticket received 7,764 votes (2.8 percent). Turnout was only 51.4 percent.

28. The estimates in Table 2.3 undoubtedly understate Whig non-voting, especially compared to the 1852 state election, and at the same time probably exaggerate Democratic non-voting. Nevertheless, in 1853 both parties clearly suffered from significant apathy.

29. Thomas Forsythe to Henry A. Muhlenberg, II, August 27, 1853, Henry A. Muhlenberg Papers, American Philosophical Society; James G. Blaine to Thomas Ewing, Jr., October 12, 1853, Ewing Family Papers; Pittsburgh *Gazette*, May 25, 1853, quoted in Holt, *Forging a Majority*, 117.

30. For the temperance movement, see Alice Felt Tyler, *Freedom's Ferment: Phases of American Social History from the Colonial Period to the Outbreak of the Civil War* (Minneapolis, 1944), 308–50; W. J. Rorabaugh, *The Alcoholic Republic: An American Tradition* (New York, 1979), 187–222; Ian R. Tyrrell, *Sobering Up: From Temperance to Prohibition in Antebellum America, 1800–1860* (Westport, Conn., 1979); and Jed Dannenbaum, *Drink and Disorder: Temperance Reform in Cincinnati from the Washingtonian Revival*

Since the anti-drinking movement increasingly defined the liquor traffic as sinful, when voluntary reform failed many of its supporters turned to political action. In 1851 in Maine temperance advocates won a significant victory when, under the leadership of Neal Dow, an uncompromising zealot, they induced the state legislature to pass a law—popularly dubbed the Maine Law—prohibiting the sale of spirituous liquors in the state. The law, which allowed wide latitude for searches and seizures, provided for fines and even imprisonment for violators.[31] Inspired by this triumph, anti-liquor crusaders in other states entered the political arena to achieve their goals.

Support for outlawing drink drew on several concerns, but one of the most important was the cluster of social problems critics traced to intemperance. With alcohol consumption at unprecedented levels, more and more Americans became gravely alarmed over the prevalence of drunkenness and its undeniable social costs. Disease, broken families, premature death, crime, and pauperism were some of the social evils temperance reformers pointed to as the consequences of unbridled drinking in America. To its advocates, prohibition was the only effective means of checking social abuses and preserving the moral values of hard work, economic independence, and proper behavior.[32]

Closely connected to the temperance movement was a growing hostility to immigrants. For the Irish and Germans, the two largest immigrant groups, drinking was an integral part of socializing; striving to maintain their separate cultures, they were unwilling to give up their whiskey and lager beer to conform to American conceptions of proper social behavior. Riotous tippling among the foreign-born mocked the social values of reformers, who in reaction often demanded enactment of sabbatarian laws (or enforcement of existing laws) to eradicate public drinking and disorderly behavior on Sundays. At the same time, immigrants' political opposition to prohibition greatly stimulated the nativist feeling that was already part of the anti-liquor movement. Heavy alcoholic consumption among Protestant as well as Catholic immigrants initially prevented a strong emphasis on anti-Catholicism, but when the Catholic church launched a vigorous campaign in the 1850s against prohibition on the grounds that it violated personal liberty, anti-Catholicism became a prominent theme in temperance rhetoric. A letter from a moralistic student to his sister in Illinois illustrated the popular linkage of immigrants, Catholics, and irreligious behavior with the consumption of alcohol. "Most of the people about here are Catholic German and they go to church at the Beer shop and go home drunk at night," he declared. "They attend that kind of church pretty regularly but as to any others they are perfectly ignorant."[33] For a good number of reformers, anti-immigrant, anti-Catholic, and anti-liquor sentiments were fused in the temperance crusade.

---

to the WCTU (Urbana, 1984). Although they eventually came to designate different attitudes, I have used the terms *temperance* and *prohibition* interchangeably (as did contemporaries in the antebellum period) to refer to the drive to eliminate the sale and consumption of alcoholic beverages.

31. For passage of the law, see Frank L. Byrne, *Prophet of Prohibition: Neal Dow and His Crusade* (Madison, 1961), 43–47; Tyrrell, *Sobering Up*, 257–60.

32. Cincinnati *Gazette*, July 7, August 6, 1853. Cf. Jed Dannenbaum, "Immigrants and Temperance: Ethnocultural Conflict in Cincinnati, 1845–1860," *Ohio History*, v. 87 (Spring, 1978), 125–39.

33. John J. Dickey to his sister, April 31 [May 1?], 1855, Wallace-Dickey Papers, IllSHL. Note in particular the pronounced support for prohibition among Know Nothings discussed in Chapters 3 and 5. Tyrrell, *Sobering Up*, 264–69, greatly understates the significance of nativism in the temperance movement. For the foreign-born, see William J. Rorabaugh, "Rising Democratic Spirits: Immigrants, Temperance, and Tammany Hall, 1854–1860," *CWH*, v. 22 (June, 1976), 144–52.

Many Whigs sympathized with the drive to ban liquor, and, encouraged by the movement's mushrooming strength, they urged that prohibition be incorporated into the party's creed. Party members, on the other hand, were far from unanimous in their sentiments, and Whig politicians feared that those hostile to prohibition would bolt if the party took such a stand (Table 2.4). With party ties already weak, embracing a principle that promised to disorganize party coalitions to an even greater extent entailed considerable risk. A fellow Whig cautioned Massachusetts governor John H. Clifford, who had maintained a prudent silence on the Maine Law, that "taking ground either way would break up the party at the next election." Similarly, former Whig governor Washington Hunt of New York advised Weed that many party members were "ready to sacrifice party, country and every thing, sooner than be deprived" of spirits.[34] Seward and his associates were also concerned that endorsing temperance would drive foreign-born voters back into the Democratic fold. Other considerations, however, had to be balanced against these objections. To start with, there was considerable support for temperance among the electorate, and the agitation was steadily mounting. One Massachusetts minister, reporting that "the churches here are totally absorbed" in the movement, proclaimed: "Temperance! *temperance!* TEMPERANCE! is heard in every store—over every work bench, on the high way—and around the hearth stone. It . . . [is] the all absorbing theme for all our meetings of whatever name and nature."[35] In addition, temperance reformers, who manifested a growing impatience with the major parties, adopted the strategy of demanding from candidates pledges that they would support prohibitory bills. If the regularly nominated candidates declined to give satisfactory assurances, Maine Law advocates often made independent nominations, especially for the legislature, and appealed to temperance men in both parties for support. Finally, if Whig leaders feared the impact of anti-rum agitation on their unity, they recognized that it also seriously divided the Democrats (Table 2.4). The Whig Cincinnati *Gazette* asserted that "the people are not divided according to their old political affinities" over the Maine Law, which explained why, as one Indiana Democrat testified, "the temperance question is playing havock in the old party lines."[36] In deciding whether to endorse prohibition, Whig politicians had to weigh losses from their ranks against potential gains from the Democrats. That evangelical Protestants had never united politically complicated the situation.[37] In many regions, Democrats enjoyed significant support among Baptists and Methodists in particular. Because Jacksonian party divisions did not follow religious lines, the injection into politics of an issue with powerful religious overtones, such as temperance, threatened to disturb the major parties' coalitions by dissolving traditional partisan loyalties.

---

34. R. A. Chapman to John Clifford, December 23, 1852, John Clifford Papers, MassHS; Washington Hunt to Weed, October 21, 1854, Weed Papers, UR.

35. E. T. Fletcher to Calvin Fletcher, November 4, 1852, Calvin Fletcher Papers, IndHS; J. A. Chestnut to Richard Yates, December 6, 1852, Richard Yates Papers, IllSHL.

36. Cincinnati *Gazette*, September 30, 1853; A. D. Billingsley to John G. Davis, May 13, 1854, John G. Davis Papers, IndHS; William B. Fairchild to Isaac Strohm, March 21, 1852, Strohm Papers, CinHS; John Chambers to William Bigler, November 6, 1852, Bigler Papers. Also suggestive are the indexes of party disagreement in state legislatures for four northern states 1847–1854, given in Holt, *Political Crisis*, 116. Party disagreement varied from state to state and also over time, but Holt's statistics demonstrate that temperance was not invariably a party issue.

37. Robert Kelley, *The Cultural Pattern of American Politics: The First Century* (New York, 1979), 160–84, summarizes much of the recent relevant literature.

An Indiana voter expressed well the dilemma politicians confronted when he commented, "This prohibition or Maine Law question is one hard for political aspirants to meet not knowing which is the popular horn or side of the question." Some Whigs argued that taking up prohibition would help the party. "Intoxicating drink has long been one of the most formidable engines of the Democratic party," one enthusiastic dry Whig wrote in mid-1853. "Destroy it and the spell of Democracy is half broken." He was convinced that the party had nothing to lose by agitating the issue. Other Whigs disagreed. Wherever temperance had become a party question, one Ohio Whig insisted, "the Whig party has always lost ground."[38]

If both Whig and Democratic leaders were reluctant to embrace this issue, Free Soilers displayed no such hesitancy. Although the antislavery and anti-liquor crusades focused on different social evils and the leadership of the two movements was not identical, the crusades sprang from similar moral impulses. Both were outgrowths of revivalistic religion, both had extensive support among evangelical Protestant denominations, and both worked through associated religious reform organizations. A Presbyterian clergyman in western New York maintained that "Temperance and Freedom are as inseperably [sic] connected as Intemperance and Slavery." In emphasizing the affinity between the two movements, long-time antislavery leader Austin Willey noted that in Maine "all Free Soil men were Maine Law men." Thus the basic dilemma of the two major parties—the wide difference of opinion among party members over the rum question—was not a problem for Free Soilers (Table 2.4). Some third-party leaders, such as Salmon P. Chase, opposed adopting temperance as a party principle, fearing that it would divert attention from the slavery issue, but anti-liquor sentiment among antislavery men was too pervasive to be ignored. Endorsement of prohibition by the Free Soil party was essential for retaining the loyalty of its members.[39]

IV

Politics in Maine amply demonstrated the difficulty of exploiting the temperance issue politically. By the end of the 1840s the state's long-dominant Democratic party contained two rival factions, the so-called Woolheads and Wildcats. The Woolheads, led by Senator Hannibal Hamlin, one of the small circle of Van Burenite congressmen who had initially introduced the Wilmot Proviso, and Governor John Hubbard, were loosely identified with antislavery and temperance. Factional divisions on these issues were not clear-cut, however, and to a great extent personal rivalries lay at the heart of this split.[40]

The passage of the Maine Law in 1851 brought this factionalism to open rupture. The vote in the legislature approving the nation's first statewide prohibitory statute made clear

---

38. A. D. Billingsley to Davis, May 13, 1854, John G. Davis Papers, IndHS; J. A. Chestnut to Yates, June 18, 1853, Yates Papers; William B. Fairchild to Strohm, March 21, 1852, Typescript, Strohm Papers, CinHS; Robert Morris to Hamilton Fish, February 10, 1852, Fish Papers, LC.

39. James T. Henry to Ullmann, December 21, 1854, Ullmann Papers, NYHS; Austin Willey, *The History of the Antislavery Cause in State and Nation* (Portland, 1886), 380; R. W. P. Muse to Salmon P. Chase, July 12, 1853, Chase to [?], August 1, 1851, *Private*, Chase Papers, LC; George W. Julian, *Political Recollections*, 139–40.

40. For Maine politics during these years, see Richard R. Wescott, "A History of Maine Politics, 1840–1856: The Formation of the Republican Party" (unpublished Ph.D. dissertation, University of Maine, 1966); Byrne, *Prophet of Prohibition* 35–69; H. Draper Hunt, *Hannibal Hamlin of Maine: Lincoln's First Vice President* (Syracuse, 1969), 43–79.

the two major parties' lack of unity on the question. Democrats divided 56–35 and Whigs 34–15 in favor of the bill, while all nine Free Soilers supported it. A non-teetotaler, Governor Hubbard hesitated to approve the proposed law. Confronted with a difficult fight to be renominated in 1852, and believing that public opinion favored the new law, he finally signed the bill. With an eye to securing prohibitionist support for his reelection, the opportunistic chief executive subsequently lost no time in placing himself on the right side of the issue. Conveniently ignoring his own use of spirits, Hubbard took the lead in founding a Legislative Temperance Society, and in 1852 he presided at the state temperance convention.[41]

The passage of the Maine Law began a reorientation in Maine's politics. There was no state election in 1851. The following year, when a Democratic legislative caucus renominated Hubbard, the Wildcats, raising the cry that this procedure was undemocratic, called a state convention that put forward a separate ticket, headed by Anson G. Chandler for governor, and approved a platform condemning the prohibitory law.[42] More than principled opposition to the Maine Law was involved in the Wildcat bolt. With considerable justice, one Maine Democrat assured Pierce in 1852 that the questions dividing the state's Democratic party "have mainly been whether one set of men or another should *rule* & this is the 'plain english' of the whole matter. The 'liquor law' has been called in as an *auxiliary* to promote or defeat certain views."[43] Both groups hoped to benefit from the Maine Law controversy in their quest for state power. The Wildcats were confident that the majority of Maine Democrats opposed the law, while Hubbard and his allies staked their political prospects on the assumption that if they converted the campaign into a referendum on the new law, accessions from pro-temperance men in other parties would more than compensate for expected losses from the Democratic ranks.

Although the Whig nominee, William G. Crosby, and the Free Soil candidate, Ezekiel Holmes, both endorsed prohibition, Hubbard was the leading Maine Law candidate. The Whigs played down the issue, and Crosby coupled his support for Neal Dow's law with the announcement that he would accept changes in it, while disagreement arose in the Free Soil convention over whether even to make a nomination (a minority wanted to endorse Hubbard). Moreover, of the three pro-temperance candidates, Hubbard had the best chance to win. Much of the organized anti-liquor movement, including the Maine Temperance Union and the Sons of Temperance, rallied behind the governor, and Dow, who was nominally a Whig, campaigned actively for him.[44] Most politicians did not like the fanatical Dow, and Whig leaders in particular were infuriated over his course. With the Democrats openly split, Whigs believed that at last after years of defeat they had an excellent chance to gain control of the state. The injection of the temperance controversy into the contest and its prominent identification with Democratic factional lines doomed these hopes, for, as the *Kennebec Journal* conceded, "The safety of the Maine Liquor

41. Byrne, *Prophet of Prohibition*, 46; Portland *Advertiser*, June 23, 1852.

42. Actually, the Wildcats had determined beforehand to bolt if Hubbard was nominated. Barnabus Palmer to Shepard Cary, March 20, 1852, *Private*, Shepard Cary Papers, Maine Historical Society; Hannibal Hamlin to John Hubbard, January 16, 1852, Hubbard Family Papers, Bowdoin College.

43. [William H.] Codman to Franklin Pierce, October 23, 1852, Pierce Papers, NHHS; A. B. Caswell to Hubbard, January 15, 1852, Hubbard Family Papers.

44. Portland *Advertiser*, July 16, 27, August 16, 1852; Frederick N. Dow, ed., *The Reminiscences of Neal Dow: Recollections of Eighty Years* (Portland, Maine, 1898), 435–36, 447–48.

Law, in the minds of many Whigs, depends upon the re-election of Governor Hubbard.''[45]

The election occurred in September, two months before the presidential contest. Hubbard received a plurality, easily outdistancing Crosby, who finished second. The Free Soil vote declined drastically from previous years.[46] The large vote confirmed how intensely the liquor issue stirred the interests and emotions of the Maine electorate. An estimated 24,000 new voters (men who had not voted in the state election two years earlier) inundated the polls; in fact, the September turnout actually exceeded that in the ensuing presidential canvass by almost 12,000 votes. The total number of votes cast eclipsed that of any previous election in the state's history.

The relationship between the 1852 gubernatorial vote and that of the preceding state election documents the extent to which traditional party loyalties had been disordered (Table 2.5). Of those who voted in 1850, approximately 30 percent of the Whigs, 50 percent of the Democrats, and more than 80 percent of the Free Soilers either voted for a different party in 1852 or did not vote. In addition, a quarter of the non-voters in 1850 went to the polls in 1852. Political observers uniformly attributed the scrambling of party lines to the controversy over the Maine Law. ''The liquor law has played the mischief with this election all round, and got things badly mixed up,'' the political humorist Major Jack Downing commented. ''A good many temperance Whigs voted for Hubbard and a good many rum Whigs voted for Chandler.''[47] As Downing's remarks suggest, Hubbard owed his victory to the new voters his candidacy attracted, and to temperance Whigs and Free Soilers who abandoned their traditional allegiance to vote for him. Hubbard received sizable support from all three groups, especially the Whigs and, most notably, new voters and former non-voters.[48] The statewide totals obscured the fact that among traditional Democrats, however, Chandler ran almost even with Hubbard. The governor's margin of victory came entirely from men normally unaffiliated with the party.

The other striking phenomenon of the election was the large number of 1850 Whigs who abstained. Their motivation is not entirely clear. Some may have concluded that Crosby's election was an impossibility and therefore did not bother to vote. Others undoubtedly were anti-temperance men who disliked voting for any Democrat and stayed home rather than support Chandler. Balancing this loss were the non-voters of 1850 who supported Crosby.[49]

The remarkable number of new voters brought to the polls and the extraordinarily high proportion of voters switching parties point to this election as particularly crucial in initiating party decomposition in Maine. Despite the prominence of the temperance issue

---

45. *Kennebec Journal*, September 2, 1852.

46. The official vote was Hubbard, 42,132 (44.4 percent); Crosby, 29,347 (30.9 percent); Chandler, 21,804 (23.0 percent); and Holmes, 1,630 (1.7 percent). Turnout was 64.8 percent, compared to 56.7 percent for the presidential election in November.

47. *Kennebec Journal*, October 7, 1852; Portland *Advertiser*, September 14, 16, 1852; William P. Haines to Hannibal Hamlin, August 13, 1852, Hamlin Papers.

48. Augusta *Age* quoted in Portland *Advertiser*, September 17, 1852. These regression estimates no doubt inflate the amount of Free Soil support for the Wildcat ticket.

49. A Democrat reported that in his county, where the Whig and Democratic candidates for state senator had taken opposite stands on the Maine Law, disenchanted Democrats nevertheless were unwilling to vote for a Whig, and consequently many would abstain. William P. Haines to Hannibal Hamlin, August 13, 1852, Hamlin Papers. The same phenomenon undoubtedly operated among disaffected Whigs at the state level, although the regression estimates indicate that even so a number voted for Hubbard.

in the campaign and the effort of such men as Dow to make it paramount, the extent to which attitudes on prohibition motivated the voters cannot be determined precisely. Certainly some men were indifferent to the Maine Law, and undoubtedly many voters, regardless of their sentiments, maintained their customary party identity out of longstanding loyalty. In this respect, Hubbard had an incalculable advantage in being the regular Democratic nominee. Yet even with these qualifications the assessment of contemporaries that it was the temperance issue more than any other factor that disrupted Maine's traditional voting patterns appears accurate.[50] For a significant number of Maine voters, it was the prohibition issue that initially detached them from their traditional party allegiance. Austin Willey, a veteran antislavery agitator, admitted that temperance had completely overshadowed all other issues in the state's politics, while the leading Whig paper in the state attributed the utter "derangement of parties" in the gubernatorial election to "the 'Maine-Law' question."[51]

The Democratic schism continued to widen in 1853. Because no candidate had a popular majority, the legislature had to elect the new governor. In order to defeat Hubbard, the Wildcats joined with the Whigs to elect Crosby. Crosby's triumph over Hubbard, the clear popular choice, caused a worsening of relations between the two Democratic factions, and Pierce's attempt to heal the rift with his state appointments was completely unsuccessful. As a result, in the 1853 state election both factions again ran separate candidates for governor. This time, however, the Wildcats enjoyed the advantage of regularity. Gaining control of the Democratic state convention, they named a ticket headed by Albert G. Pillsbury, a moderate opponent of the Maine Law, for governor. The party platform emphasized traditional Democratic issues and said nothing about the liquor question or the Compromise of 1850. Disaffected Democratic leaders, many of whom were prominent in the prohibition movement, soon published a call for a separate convention. Insisting that they represented the true Democracy in the state, these bolters adopted a platform that endorsed the Maine Law and nominated for governor Anson P. Morrill, who had presided over the state temperance convention in February and was an ally of Hubbard. "Each wing of the party has adopted the rule or ruin motto, and the division would be extensive . . . if there were no Maine Law question put in issue," but the liquor controversy "tended materially to aggravate the troubles," one paper commented after Morrill's selection.[52] The Whigs again chose Crosby as their standard bearer, and the Free Soilers once more selected Holmes.

The Free Soilers, however, had absorbed the lesson of the 1852 election. Believing that they could combine the temperance men from the three parties and "sweep the state," they emphasized the liquor issue rather than the slavery question.[53] Indeed, Holmes, who called for strengthening the Maine Law, was the most thoroughgoing temperance candidate in the field. In a bid to hold most of the regular Democrats, Pillsbury made no official statement concerning prohibition, despite charges by Democratic critics that he

---

50. In a history of the liquor controversy, the *Kennebec Journal*, May 26, 1854, said of the 1852 gubernatorial election: "Party lines were in a great measure obliterated, and the Maine law was the controlling element."

51. Willey to Charles Francis Adams, October 5, 1852, Adams Family Papers; Portland *Advertiser*, September 14, 1852.

52. *Kennebec Journal*, August 25, 1853. The *Clarion*, an organ of the Morrill Democrats, insisted that "there is no possibility of compromise whereby the two wings of the party can ever again be united in one harmonious whole." Quoted in the *Kennebec Journal*, October 6, 1853.

53. Willey to Owen Lovejoy, October 17, 1853, Owen Lovejoy Papers, Texas Tech University.

had given private pledges to opponents of the Maine Law and at the state convention had kept an open bar to entertain delegates.[54] Pillsbury's silence failed to prevent the temperance issue from dominating the campaign. After the election, a leading paper in the state commented: "It cannot be denied that the liquor law question entered largely into our recent election. It was, in fact, the only question or issue of principle upon which there was any considerable feeling."[55]

The results in 1853 were a dramatic reversal of the previous year's outcome.[56] With the prestige of the regular Democratic nomination to buttress his candidacy, Pillsbury won a plurality. Morrill's total of 11,000 votes (less than a third that of Pillsbury's) represented the hardcore Woolhead strength. The Free Soilers, on the other hand, made striking gains over their poor performance in 1853, as presumably many Maine Law men who voted for Hubbard in 1852 returned to the fold. The majority of the 1852 voters who did not cast ballots in 1853 most likely were usual non-voters mobilized temporarily the previous year by the divisive campaign over the Maine Law (Table 2.6).

The deterioration of party loyalties, so apparent in the 1852 state election, continued in the 1853 contest (Tables 2.6 and 2.7). Nearly a third of the electors who backed Pierce in 1852 did not vote the regular Democratic ticket in 1853. Pillsbury suffered an even greater rate of defection among Hubbard's 1852 supporters, almost three-quarters of whom voted for another candidate or abstained. Much more than was the case with Hubbard, Morrill's support came primarily from Democrats. Morrill did not run as well as expected, but his showing demonstrated that the bitter estrangement between the two Democratic factions persisted. The results confounded experienced political observers. A Whig paper commented that "as a general thing, party attachments were weak," while one Democratic journal, noting the prevalence of bolting in the election, declared: "A regular nomination had very little influence, comparatively, over the voters. Like the Kentucky rifleman in the revolutionary war, each man fought 'on his own hook.' "[57]

The Whigs, however, were unable to take advantage of the Democratic split, in part because the party's own voting base was rapidly disintegrating as a growing number of Whigs declined to vote, and in part because the candidacy of a temperance Democrat prevented them from uniting the Maine Law men behind their ticket. Whigs were as confused as their opponents by the rapidly emerging political instability. Immediately after the election one of William Pitt Fessenden's correspondents exclaimed: "What a fog-bank we are in politically! Do you see any head-land or light—or can you get an observation—or soundings?"[58] In spite of their success in twice electing Crosby governor (he was again elected by the legislature in 1854), Whigs fell short in their bid to form an electoral majority. Crosby's victories in the legislature were not translated into Whig

---

54. Speech of Anson P. Morrill, *Kennebec Journal*, September 8, 1853.

55. Portland *Advertiser*, September 23, 1853; Rowland Howard to O. O. Howard, September 8, 1853, Oliver O. Howard Papers, Bowdoin College.

56. The vote was Pillsbury, 36,127 (43.3 percent); Crosby, 27,259 (32.7 percent); Morrill, 11,012 (13.2 percent); and Holmes, 9,039 (10.8 percent). Turnout was 56.9 percent, which equalled that of the presidential election the previous year.

57. Portland *Advertiser*, September 23, 1853; Portland *Eastern Argus*, September 14, 1853. Another paper attributed the confusing results to the fact that "there were so many candidates in the field and *bolting* was so much the order of the day." Brunswick *Telegraph*, September 17, 1853.

58. George Evans to William Pitt Fessenden, September 18, [1853], William Pitt Fessenden Papers, WRHS. The Whigs did not have a majority in the legislature that reelected Crosby governor, but a few anti-Maine Law Democrats backed Crosby in order to block Morrill.

strength in the electorate, and the party was weaker at the end of 1853 than at any time since 1840.

Once the temperance issue had been thrust into Maine's politics, neither party had succeeded in reestablishing its traditional voting base. More than anything else, the extensive deterioration of traditional party loyalties signaled the end of the Jacksonian system. It is easy to date the beginning of this disintegration. Following the passage of the Maine Law in 1851, there was a dramatic increase in the number of voters switching parties (Table 2.8). What made the liquor controversy so disruptive politically was the fact that the division in the electorate on this question cut across previous party and factional lines. Because prohibition produced a fundamental cleavage in society not rooted in existing party divisions, politicians were unable to channel this reform impulse within the prevailing party system. Furthermore, by bringing thousands of new or infrequent voters into the political process—voters with at best only weak party loyalties—the temperance issue amplified the volatility of the Maine electorate. By the end of 1853, party decomposition in Maine had proceeded to the point that it could not be reversed, and the second party system had effectively collapsed.[59]

V

Connecticut politics followed a different path to the same result.[60] As in Maine, by 1850 the prohibition movement wielded significant strength in Connecticut. The state's Democratic party, however, generally opposed temperance, or at least avoided officially embracing it. A major consideration in this decision was the state's significant immigrant vote, which was predominantly Democratic. The earlier defection of a number of Democrats to the Free Soilers served further to reduce pro-temperance sentiment in the Democratic ranks. Democratic leaders hoped that party loyalty or other considerations would hold Maine Law men in the fold, and that any defections would be counterbalanced by accessions of anti-temperance Whigs.[61]

Unhappy with the hesitant response of Connecticut politicians, anti-liquor leaders decided in 1851 to endorse state candidates. Aware of the movement's growing power and anxious to downplay the slavery issue that fragmented the party, the Whig state convention endorsed prohibition, as did the Whig candidate for governor. By virtue of Democratic nominee Thomas Seymour's silence on prohibition, Whigs hoped to attract Maine Law Democrats and also Free Soilers, who as in Maine were strongly pro-temperance.

---

59. The most convincing evidence that by the end of 1853 the process was irreversible is that even after the repeal of the Missouri Compromise, which gave them an issue of extraordinary power and popularity, the Whigs were unable to halt their downward course. Indeed, despite the shift in issues, party disintegration continued unchecked in Maine in 1854. For testimony concerning the power of the rum issue to mobilize men who were normally politically indifferent, see the *Kennebec Journal*, September 14, 1855.

60. For Connecticut's politics during this period, see Parmet, "Know-Nothings in Connecticut"; J. Carroll Noonan, *Nativism in Connecticut, 1829–1860* (Washington, D.C., 1938); and John Niven, *Gideon Welles, Lincoln's Secretary of the Navy* (New York, 1973), 234–52.

61. Noonan, *Nativism in Connecticut*, 130–31. In 1850 the foreign-born constituted 10.4 percent of Connecticut's population, compared to 5.5 percent in Maine. Moreover, in contrast to the situation in Maine, the proportion of foreign-born in Connecticut increased over the decade; in 1860, 4.5 percent of the white males in Maine were foreign-born, compared to 17.8 percent in Connecticut. Most of the immigrants in Connecticut were Irish (68 percent in 1860).

The Whigs' promotion of prohibition yielded indecisive results, since no candidate won a popular majority and the selection, therefore, devolved on the legislature. Whig divisions over the Compromise of 1850 clouded the impact of the temperance controversy on the outcome, but the party's organ, the Hartford *Courant,* attributed the defeat to both issues.[62] That party lines in the legislature were equally chaotic was indicated by the fact that Seymour was elected governor along with the Whig candidate for lieutenant-governor.

Continuing Whig factionalism over the Compromise, as well as Governor Seymour's pocket veto of a bill providing for a popular referendum on prohibition and the strong endorsement of temperance by the Free Soil state convention, induced the Whigs to give greater emphasis to the rum question in the 1852 state election. In response to inquiries from temperance men, both the Whig and Free Soil gubernatorial candidates strongly upheld prohibition, while Seymour, who was running for reelection, again made no reply. The Democratic platform also avoided the subject. In the face of Seymour's hostility, the state temperance convention endorsed the Whig candidate. When some Whig leaders criticized the party's identification with the Maine Law, the editor of the New Haven *Palladium* replied that " 'circumstances beyond our control' have forced the issue upon us."[63] As the *Palladium* admitted, the Whigs were compelled to adopt temperance, since otherwise the Free Soil party's vigorous support of prohibition threatened to detach committed anti-liquor Whigs. During the election one observer commented aptly, "Politics run wild, the cart is a head of the team." A correspondent of the Democratic leader Gideon Welles agreed with the assessment of Whig senator Roger S. Baldwin, who believed that his party would be hurt by the liquor question. "The Whigs generally suffer from all side issues," this Democrat observed. "On the old platform they can always make a good fight, but the addition of any new plank embarrasses them."[64]

The election results confirmed these predictions.[65] Not only did a larger proportion of Whigs than Free Soilers or Democrats not vote in April, but Whig gains from temperance Democrats were more than offset by defections from their ranks (Table 2.9). In addition, the 1852 Whig campaign also failed to attract Free Soil voters. Consequently the battered Whigs suffered their most decisive defeat in more than a decade. Taking up the temperance issue had badly hurt their cause, as party leaders readily recognized. Baldwin, for example, maintained that this question cost the Whigs "all the *cider towns & counties.*" The *Courant* also blamed the result on the liquor issue: "The temperance Democrats who may have acted with us have been wholly out-numbered by the Whigs who have left their ranks, for the first time for many years, and have joined the enemies of their political principles."[66]

Their defeat in the 1852 state election led Connecticut Whigs to demand that prohibition be deleted from the party platform and that former candidates identified with the issue be dropped. According to the *Palladium,* the conviction was widespread that

---

62. Hartford *Courant,* April 11, 1851, quoted in Parmet, "Know-Nothings in Connecticut," 42.

63. New Haven *Palladium,* March 20, 1852, quoted in Noonan, *Nativism in Connecticut,* 153.

64. John S. Peters to William Jarvis, March 13, 1852, quoted in Parmet, "Know-Nothings in Connecticut," 47; Roger S. Baldwin to Roger S. Baldwin, Jr., March 19, 1852, Baldwin Family Papers, Yale University; Charles Chapman to Welles, March 25, 1852, Welles Papers, LC.

65. The vote was Green Kendrick (Whig), 28,241 (45.0 percent); Seymour (Democrat), 31,624 (50.4 percent); and Francis Gillette (Free Soil), 2,923 (4.7 percent).

66. Roger S. Baldwin to Emily Baldwin, April 10, 1852, Baldwin Family Papers; Hartford *Courant,* April 7, 1852.

"pledges and promises from candidates have already disgusted many of our best friends, and it is time that the business was stopped at all hazards." Adopting this view, the 1853 Whig state convention nominated an entirely new ticket and decreed further that no state candidate should commit himself on the temperance question.[67]

The Free Soilers, in contrast, continued to endorse the Maine Law movement. Seeking to capitalize on anti-liquor sentiment in the state, Francis Gillette, the Free Soil nominee for governor, firmly supported prohibition; because the other candidates took no position, he received the state temperance convention's endorsement. Some third-party members expressed concern that by appealing to voters on the liquor question alone the slavery issue would be lost sight of, but advocates of this policy responded that it was more important to attract a large number of voters from the other parties in order to break down their normal partisan loyalties. After the election Moses Pierce, a prominent Free Soil politician, underscored this point in advocating the formation of an independent temperance party under Free Soil leadership. "A . . . very large majority of Whigs & Democrats who leave their parties to support a temperance organization," he insisted, "will never go back but will be found in the ranks of [the] Free Democracy hereafter."[68]

Apathy and despair characterized the 1853 Whig campaign. Prior to the election a Democrat informed Seymour that "the whigs here seem disposed to let the election go pretty much by default."[69] The results demonstrated not only the devasting impact of the temperance issue on Whig strength but the accelerating destruction of the party's electoral base. The Whigs' share of the vote in the gubernatorial contest fell fully ten percent from that in the prior state election, which had represented the poorest Whig showing since 1840.[70] With almost a fifth of Scott's supporters sitting out the election, the party also lost all congressional races. "The Whigs have been routed—horse, foot, dragoons, camp-followers, and all," the *Courant* commented ruefully and without exaggeration.[71]

Accompanying the Whigs' debacle was a marked increase in the Free Soil vote; the party tripled its vote over that in the 1852 state and presidential elections, largely at the expense of the Whigs (Table 2.10). In addition, previous non-voters disproportionately cast Free Soil ballots. Of the three parties, the Whigs were the least successful in retaining their customary supporters, they garnered no Free Soil converts (as would be expected following their renunciation of temperance), and they lost twice as many votes to the Democrats as they gained. Although the Whigs' strength declined everywhere, this decrease was unevenly distributed throughout the state. Whig losses in the western counties, which were more urban and more economically developed, were less severe, particularly in Hartford County. The greatest defections were in Tolland, Windham, and New London Counties in the more rural and isolated eastern section, and in central Middlesex County. Middlesex and Tolland had the highest proportion of Congregationalists in the state, with Windham only slightly behind, while Baptists were strong in all these counties except Tolland. Since Baptist and Congregational churches were prominent

---

67. New Haven *Palladium*, February 12, 1853, quoted in Noonan, *Nativism in Connecticut*, 175–76.

68. F. R. Stewart to Joseph R. Hawley, March 6, 1853, Moses Pierce to Hawley, September 12, 1853, David Lyman to Hawley, October 17, 1853, Joseph R. Hawley Papers, LC. Free Democracy was another name for the Free Soil party.

69. J. C. Comstock to Thomas Seymour, March 23, 1853, Thomas Seymour Papers, ConnHS; Welles Diary, April 4, 1853, Welles Papers, LC.

70. The vote was Dutton (Whig), 20,671 (34.2 percent); Seymour (Democrat), 30,814 (51.0 percent); and Gillette (Free Soil), 8,926 (14.8 percent).

71. Hartford *Courant*, April 6, 1853.

in agitating for a Maine Law, it seems likely that defecting Whigs were especially numerous among these denominations.

As long as the temperance issue remained salient, Connecticut Whigs were caught in an insoluble dilemma: They could not form a majority coalition by endorsing the Maine Law, and they were even weaker when they tried to sidestep the liquor controversy. The 1853 results left party leaders glum and despondent. The Whig coalition seemed to be disintegrating, morale was low, many members were openly willing to abandon the party for a new organization, and no issue was available with which to resurrect the party. In fact, following the 1853 defeat Senator Truman Smith, the most prominent Whig officeholder in the state, pronounced the party dead.[72] So shattered was the Whig organization after its disastrous showing in 1853 that even in 1854, when the party attempted to exploit the issue of the Nebraska bill then pending in Congress, its strength continued to plummet.

Calculation of the year effect—that is, how well a party did in a given year relative to a long series of elections—clarifies the situation of the two parties in Connecticut (Table 2.11).[73] Before 1850 Whig losses were accompanied by Democratic losses, but once temperance became an issue, the decline of the Whigs' strength became more pronounced with each succeeding year, while the Democrats' appeal was enhanced. These figures illuminate the debilitating impact of the 1853 election. The party's loss that year, compared to its long-term performance, was four times larger than that for any other election. Since the Democratic vote was more than 3 percent higher than normal, the net Whig drop in 1853 was almost 19 percent. This steep decrease continued the following year, when the party experienced a net reduction of over 16 percent.

The particular problems afflicting the Whigs in Connecticut are highlighted further by a comparison of both parties' success in retaining their previous members (Table 2.12). Except in the 1851 state election, the Whigs were less successful than the Democrats in holding earlier loyalists. Until 1851, however, gains from other parties compensated for these losses. Desertions among traditional Whigs were especially marked in the 1852 and 1853 state elections—precisely when the temperance issue was most salient. High rates of abstention also plagued the Whigs. Between 1848 and 1853, in every election other than the 1852 presidential contest a greater proportion of Whigs than Democrats did not go to the polls. This development probably reflected several considerations: the greater anti-party feeling among Whigs, their growing sense of hopelessness, and disaffection over their party's policies—including the endorsement of the Compromise of 1850, the appeal to the Catholic vote, and the adoption of temperance. For many of these cross-pressured Whigs, not voting was preferable to supporting their political adversaries. The deterioration of Whig participation peaked in 1853, when 17 percent of Scott's supporters abstained. A similar though less extensive erosion occurred in the Democratic party's traditional base of support, but accessions from past supporters of other parties more than balanced this loss.

By the end of 1853 the second party system had broken down in Connecticut. Beginning in 1851, the temperance issue precipitated a serious shrinkage of the Whigs'

---

72. Truman Smith to John Wilson, August 28, 1853, John Wilson Papers; Smith to Weed, August 29, 1853, *Private*, Weed Papers, UR.

73. For a discussion of the statistical procedure of two-way analysis of variance, see John L. McCarthy and John W. Tukey, "Exploratory Analysis of Aggregate Voting Behavior: Presidential Elections in New Hampshire, 1896–1972," *Social Science History*, v. 2 (Spring, 1978), 292–331.

share of the electorate, a reduction that continued over a series of elections and finally left the party in complete disarray and near death. The combined effect of significant desertions to other parties, the failure to win many converts, and a substantial increase in non-voting among former supporters destroyed the Connecticut Whig party's vitality.

VI

Ohio Whigs faced a similar problem.[74] By 1850 the temperance movement, promoted by many Protestant denominations and finding a natural constituency among the reform-oriented counties of the Western Reserve, had amassed considerable support. In a special election in June 1851 to ratify a new state constitution, Ohio voters narrowly approved a clause declaring that no licenses to sell intoxicating liquors were to be granted and empowering the legislature to act against this traffic.[75] Whigs and Democrats displayed decisively opposite tendencies on this question. Of those who cast ballots, a substantial majority of Whigs voted against issuing licenses while an even larger proportion of Democrats favored continuing the system. Displaying greater unity on the matter than the other parties, the Free Democrats (the name adopted by the Free Soil party in Ohio after 1849) who participated voted unanimously for no licenses (Table 2.4).

Approval of the anti-license clause had no immediate effect on the consumption of liquor in Ohio, since the legislature still had to take action against its sale. Its passage, however, thrust the question directly into state politics, and in February 1852 a state temperance convention in Columbus called for enactment of a Maine Law. "Everybody is now talking about the 'Maine Law,' " one Whig reported after the convention, "and pretty much everybody is petitioning for it."[76] Despite heavy pressure, two successive Democratic-controlled legislatures rejected the reformers' demands. Democratic leaders were sensitive to the general opposition to any state action on the subject among party members, particularly the Germans, who vehemently opposed any interference with their right to enjoy lager beer. Because the legislature refused to take strong action against the liquor traffic, temperance reformers decided to mount a vigorous campaign in the 1853 state election.

Ohio Whiggery was in an unfavorable position to blunt the impact of the temperance issue. So demoralized were the Whigs after the 1852 presidential election that their leaders saw little hope in the foreseeable future of restoring the party to its once dominant position. To compound the state party's problems, Thomas Corwin and Thomas Ewing, its two most influential leaders, retired after the election from active involvement in politics. There was really no one to replace them. Neither Lewis D. Campbell nor Benjamin F. Wade, the only other Ohio Whigs with any national reputation, was a suitable party leader. Campbell had genuine political skills, but he was easily excitable and overly sensitive, and he was prone to nurse grudges and to view any opposition as a personal attack. The coarse, plainspoken Wade, on the other hand, was far too tactless

---

74. Ohio politics in these years are covered in Eugene H. Roseboom, *The Civil War Era, 1850–1873* (Columbus, 1944); and Stephen E. Maizlish, *The Triumph of Sectionalism: The Transformation of Ohio Politics, 1844–1860* (Kent, 1983).

75. For an explanation of the license clause and the popular vote on it, see the Cincinnati *Enquirer*, June 17, 20, July 16, 1851. The vote was 113,796 against licenses (51.8 percent), and 105,944 for licenses (48.2 percent). Turnout in the special election was 66.9 percent.

76. William B. Fairchild to Strohm, February 29, 1852, Strohm Papers, CinHS.

and too radical on the slavery question to wield influence over a conglomerate party. Members of the state central committee also lacked the talent to fill this void. Indeed, there was considerable discontent with this committee, under whose leadership, one discontented party member grumbled, any ticket "must . . . go down."[77]

The disappearance of its old issues coupled with the inability to find new ones added to the party's difficulties.[78] At the state convention in February, the delegates nominated a ticket headed by Nelson Barrere, a congressman from the southern part of the state, and, taking the name National Conservative party, they approved a brief platform that pledged to stand by the Union and oppose the Democratic state administration. Neither the platform nor the candidate took a stand on the liquor question; Whig leaders saw little in the experience of their eastern brethren to encourage the adoption of temperance as a party position. When Horace Greeley urged in the New York *Tribune* that Ohio Whigs and Free Soilers combine on the basis of a Maine Law platform, the Cincinnati *Gazette* replied that whereas the Whig party would gain few votes from other parties on the issue, a significant minority of party members who opposed prohibition would certainly go over to the Democrats. Whig leaders therefore tried to minimize the impact of the issue by taking no position statewide, and allowing local organizations to adopt the stance they deemed most expedient. The Whigs found themselves in the unenviable situation that whatever course they followed, they seemed destined to lose. In condemning the Whigs for attempting to dodge the rum issue, the *Ohio Columbian,* the Free Soil state organ, declared succinctly, "They must take one side or the other, or lose by the [temperance] cause at any rate."[79]

The course of the Free Democrats foiled the Whigs' attempt to finesse the issue. Cognizant of the lethargy of the Whigs and aware that agitation of the Maine Law issue had helped Free Soilers in other states, third-party leaders saw an opportunity to deliver a crippling blow to the Whig organization. At the same time, they believed that their cause had been hurt in the past by concentrating too narrowly on the slavery issue, and they were therefore receptive to including in the platform a strongly worded endorsement of prohibition. For governor the Free Democratic delegates nominated Samuel Lewis, a long-time antislavery agitator, who called unhesitatingly for passage of the Maine Law.[80] Since the Democratic platform and the party's gubernatorial nominee, William Medill, avoided taking a position on the liquor controversy, the Free Democrats were the only party in the 1853 contest that officially favored temperance.[81]

Although the *Ohio Organ of Temperance Reform,* the leading Maine Law paper in the state, backed Lewis strongly, the state temperance convention made no endorsement for state offices. Instead, it focused attention on winning control of the legislature (the governor in Ohio lacked the veto, so he could not block a prohibitory law). Announcing its intention to support Maine Law candidates regardless of party affiliation, the convention urged that, where necessary, temperance men form fusion tickets. Good will between pro-temperance Whigs and Free Soilers was enhanced when the Free Democratic

---

77. William B. Thrall to Strohm, February 25, March 15 (quotation), 1853, Strohm Papers, CinHS.

78. *Cincinnati Gazette* quoted in *National Era,* June 23, 1853; George Olmsted to Seward, February 28, 1853, John Barr to Seward, April 13, 1853, Seward Papers, UR.

79. New York *Tribune,* July 1, 1853; Cincinnati *Gazette,* July 7, 1853; *Ohio Columbian,* October 12, 1853.

80. Theodore Clarke Smith, *The Liberty and Free Soil Parties in the Northwest* (New York, 1897), 267–70; Blue, *Free Soilers,* 271–72.

81. The Democratic state organ, the *Ohio Statesman,* warned candidates and local committees against adding a temperance plank to the party platform. Roseboom, *Civil War Era,* 223.

candidate for lieutenant governor withdrew in favor of the Whig nominee, a well-known temperance supporter, after the latter endorsed the 1852 national Free Soil platform. In response to popular support for union, a number of People's conventions were held throughout the summer, although in some localities fusion did not proceed smoothly and in several places it broke down completely. Even Salmon P. Chase, who had long promoted a Free Soil alliance with the Democrats, lent tepid support to the movement.[82] Some Free Democrats, however, worried about the prominence given in the fusion movement to temperance rather than slavery. Noting that "nearly every Free Soiler is a Maine Law man," one party member fretted that "if they are not careful they will throw away the *stack* to clinch at a straw."[83]

The temperance issue excited what interest there was in the election. Campbell reported that "there is a good deal of *steam* up on the Maine Law," and a Free Democrat indicated that "the great excitement here is about the *Maine Law*." From Cincinnati, another observer disclosed that "the cry of 'banks' is lost in that of 'rum-shops'; of 'tariff,' in that of 'fanaticism,' " so that "party traces have lost their power . . . [and] old division lines are lost in the brilliancy of the new one."[84]

Neither major party expended much energy on the campaign. Democrats were confident of victory and made only the most limited canvass. Whigs displayed even less fervor: Lacking any issues with which to galvanize the electorate and paralyzed by a pervasive sense of hopelessness, they were resigned to defeat. From all parts of the state came reports of Whig indifference. "There is prevailing generally a sort of 'don't care a damn' spirit," Campbell said of the Whigs in his district in the center of the state. The Whig ticket had no chance of victory, one party regular conceded, adding, "*and who cares?*"[85] On the eve of the election, the independent Cincinnati *Commercial* observed that "probably at no time within the last twenty years has there been so little interest felt in the success of any party, or set of candidates." Apathy afflicted all parties, but it was especially ominous for the Whigs, who already faced the prospect of large-scale defection to the Free Soilers. The Cincinnati *Enquirer,* the city's Democratic organ, commented that Whiggery had "fallen into such an apathetic and disorganized State as to threaten its extinction as a regular party."[86]

In contrast to the listless Whigs, the Free Soilers launched an energetic campaign. Third-party speakers, hoping to broaden their base of support and weaken the Whigs, emphasized the issue of temperance over slavery. Prospects were "as good as could be expected," Chase informed Charles Sumner after an extensive state speaking tour. "We hope to cast a vote as will—if not elect our Candidate—at least put an end to triangular contest[s]."[87]

The results were a staggering setback for the Whig party. Medill was triumphantly

82. The People's fusion movement can be followed in the *Ohio Columbian* for 1853. Also see Chase to E. S. Hamlin, July 21, 1853, Chase Papers, LC; John Barr to Seward, July 19, 1853, Seward Papers, UR.

83. R. W. P. Muse to Chase, July 12, 1853, Chase Papers, LC.

84. Lewis D. Campbell to Strohm, August 15, 1853, Strohm Papers, OHS; R. W. P. Muse to Chase, July 12, 1853, Chase Papers, LC; Cincinnati *Times*, October 7, 1853, quoted in Dannenbaum, "Immigrants and Temperance," 139.

85. Benjamin F. Wade to Campbell, June 27, 1853, Lewis D. Campbell Papers, OHS; Campbell to Strohm, June 28, 1853, Strohm Papers, OHS; William B. Thrall to Strohm, March 15, 1853, Strohm Papers, CinHS.

86. Cincinnati *Commercial*, October 11, 1853; Cincinnati *Enquirer*, October 8, 1853.

87. Chase to Charles Sumner, September 3, 1853, Sumner Papers, HU; Chase to Joshua R. Giddings, July 4, 1853, Chase Papers, LC.

elected, but, what is more significant, Barrere received the smallest vote of any Whig gubernatorial candidate since the party had organized in the state. Reflective of the prevailing disinterest, turnout was the lowest of any state election in the decade.[88] The Whig share of the total vote plunged from 43 percent in November 1852 to a mere 30 percent in 1853. The Free Soil vote, on the other hand, was over 60 percent greater than Hale's total in 1852 and nearly three times as large as the party's vote in 1851, when Lewis had also headed its state ticket.

"It is not to be disguised that the recent election . . . over the State, turned on this temperance issue," the *Ohio State Journal,* the Whig state organ, asserted in seeking to explain the party's rout. The Whigs lost, it continued, because many party members did not vote and because thousands of anti-temperance Whigs "deserted us" and "joined hands with their Locofoco [Democratic] opponents to uphold and sustain the free and unrestricted traffic in ardent spirits."[89] However persuasive this explanation may have been to Whig readers, it did not accurately identify the causes of the party's debacle, since a substantial proportion of the 1852 adherents of all three parties, not just the Whigs, failed to vote in the 1853 election (Table 2.13).

The disastrous Whig showing was attributable not to widespread abstentions of party regulars but to the defection of temperance Whigs to the Free Soilers, and to the strength of the Free Soilers and especially the Democrats among earlier non-voters (Tables 2.13 and 2.14).[90] In short, although the *State Journal* was probably correct in attributing Whig desertions to the temperance issue, these defections went to the Free Soil and not the Democratic ticket. The Free Soil coalition was overwhelmingly opposed to the sale of alcohol (Table 2.14). Newly politicized voters were apparently also motivated primarily by the liquor controversy, since for the most part they divided between the parties representing the extremes on the temperance issue. Long-term loyalty still held a majority of Whigs to their party, but the number that abandoned the party was sufficient to shatter its electoral base. The statewide totals obscured the fact that the Free Democrats had a disproportionately high rate of non-voting among their 1852 supporters. Only accessions from the Whigs, coupled with a pervasive decline in turnout, enabled the party to do well relative to the Whigs. The party's performance in 1853 appeared stronger than it really was.

In analyzing the results of the election, the *State Journal* argued that the returns demonstrated that a majority of Ohio voters opposed temperance. This argument could provide little comfort to Whigs. The rise of the temperance issue had sapped what remaining vitality the party possessed, and Ohio Whiggery dissolved in the wake of the 1853 defeat. Even before the votes were counted, a member of the Whig state central committee pronounced the party "hopelessly dead for the present." After the election, one Whig editor, Joseph Medill of Cleveland, began actively promoting the idea of

---

88. The official vote was Medill, 147,663 (52.0 percent); Barrere, 85,820 (30.2 percent); Lewis, 50,346 (17.7 percent). Turnout was 70.3 percent, down 6 percent from the state election the previous year.

89. *Ohio State Journal,* October 14, 1853; Cincinnati *Commercial,* September 26, 1853.

90. Not only did contemporary observers attribute these Whig defections to the temperance issue (for example, Cincinnati correspondence, New York *Tribune,* October 15, 1853; *Ohio Columbian,* October 12, 19, 1853), but it is also suggestive that the estimated proportion of anti-liquor license voters in 1851 who voted Whig declined from 74 percent in the 1852 state election to 50 percent in the 1853 gubernatorial contest. At the same time, the Free Soil share of this pro-temperance vote rose dramatically from 1 to 28 percent. In view of both sources of evidence, it seems likely that the temperance issue accounted for the bulk of the Whig losses.

forming a new party.[91] More and more Whigs looked to an alliance with the Free Soilers. Such an alliance offered hope for victory, but on what basis could it be accomplished?

The results of the 1853 state elections in Maine, Connecticut, and Ohio demonstrated the key role of the temperance issue in breaking down the old party structures.[92] In each state, the Whigs dealt with this question differently. In Maine they endorsed temperance from the beginning; in Connecticut they first adopted and then purged it from their platform; in Ohio they never recognized it as a party principle. In all three states, however, the Free Soil party, because it was firmly united on the issue, outbid the Whigs for the support of ardent drys. At precisely the time that the Whigs needed to shore up their base of support, they suffered extensive defections. The dissolution of many voters' normal party identities, in which temperance played so formidable a role, denoted the end of the Jacksonian alignment. By the end of 1853 the second party system was moribund in these states. With ample justification, Neal Dow characterized the Maine Law movement as the "breaking-up plow" for the realignment of the 1850s.[93]

VII

Temperance reformers were not the only group dissatisfied by the failure of the political parties to respond to their demands who turned to independent political action. Anti-Catholic nativists were also increasingly alienated from the existing parties. With roots deep in the American tradition, anti-Catholicism pervaded popular values and beliefs, and several recent developments had greatly stimulated this feeling. The influx of large numbers of Catholics beginning in the mid-1840s, the new-found assertiveness of the Catholic hierarchy, the growing power of the Catholic vote, and the assiduous courting of this vote by leaders of both parties (as evidenced by the 1852 Whig presidential campaign) all aroused nativists' anger and fears. Political nativism had flared briefly in some eastern cities in the 1840s, yet it remained local in nature and soon receded. But in 1853 the Catholic hierarchy committed a blunder that infused nativism with new life and produced dramatic examples of its potential political power. Following the meeting in 1852 of the first Plenary Council of Baltimore, which condemned public schools as irreligious, the Catholic bishops mounted a concerted campaign against the common school system. In particular, they petitioned state legislatures for public funds to finance parochial schools.[94]

Nativists immediately raised the cry that the Catholic church was trying to destroy the common school system. To comprehend the depth of this outcry, one must appreciate the intensity of anti-Catholic feeling among Protestants, as well as recognize that native-born

---

91. A. F. Perry to Alphonso Taft, October 4, 1853, William Howard Taft Papers, LC; obituary of Joseph Medill, Chicago *Tribune*, March 17, 1899, Joseph Medill Papers, Chicago *Tribune* Archives.

92. The temperance issue disrupted the party system elsewhere as well. For Michigan, see Formisano, *Mass Political Parties*, 229–38; for New Hampshire, Thomas R. Bright, "The Anti-Nebraska Coalition and the Emergence of the Republican Party in New Hampshire, 1853–1857," *Historical New Hampshire*, v. 27 (Summer, 1972), 57–88; and for Vermont, Edward P. Brynn, "Vermont's Political Vacuum of 1845–1856 and the Emergence of the Republican Party," *Vermont History*, v. 28 (Spring, 1970), 113–23.

93. Dow, *Reminiscences*, 444–45.

94. Ray Billington, *The Protestant Crusade, 1800–1860* (New York, 1938), 292–95; Vincent P. Lannie, "Alienation in America: The Immigrant Catholic and Public Education in Pre-Civil War America," *Review of Politics*, v. 32 (October, 1970), 503–21. Robert Francis Heuston, *The Catholic Press and Nativism, 1840–1860* (New York, 1976), 168–79, provides many quotations from Catholic papers condemning the common schools.

northerners viewed the common school system, which preserved and inculcated American values, traditions, and ideals, as the cornerstone of republican society. Northerners valued a society in which men rose because of their merit, and in which hard work and education were rewarded.[95] The common school served both as a symbol and a guardian of this society of opportunity, they believed; providing a free public education to all (white) children was one of the country's surest protections against degenerating into a privileged society similar to those in Europe so abhorred by Americans. "The free schools . . . are the foundation on which our Republican institutions rest," affirmed an Ohio citizen.[96] When Catholics denounced public education and sought to reduce the common schools' financial support, many northerners reacted in alarm. To them, the very fabric of the American social order seemed under attack. In their eyes, the church's criticism of this bastion of republicanism was little short of subversive.

One of the cherished values that the common school system reinforced was Protestantism. Lessons, textbooks, and teachers extolled Protestantism and often made derogatory remarks about the Catholic religion and Catholic countries.[97] Usually, only the Protestant version of the Bible was used in the classroom. To Protestants, this situation seemed entirely appropriate, but Catholic parents and clergy understandably took offense. Attempts to allow pupils to use the Catholic Bible, or to ban religious instruction in the schools altogether, aroused the ire of Protestants.[98] If a school board was receptive to Catholic demands, popular indignation soared as the non-Catholic population, often under the lead of Protestant ministers, rallied to the defense of the common schools. As an integral part of the defense of Protestantism and republicanism, the public school issue touched the lives of ordinary citizens in a way few issues could. "Romanism . . . cannot grow except on the soil of ignorance," contended a Cincinnati resident. "I see in the preservation of common schools . . . a fatal barrier against the influence of Rome."[99]

Eventually despairing of any hope of reforming the public schools, Catholics shifted their efforts to securing tax monies for parochial schools. To most Protestants, the use of public funds to support private religious schools was a wanton violation of the constitutional principle of separation of church and state. Worse still, it seemed a flagrant grab for power by the Catholic church.[100] Nativists were enraged when in many states Democratic legislators introduced and supported church-sponsored school legislation, while the Whigs, despite opposing the church's proposals, refused to launch a strident anti-Catholic crusade. When the major parties proved unresponsive, nativists formed independent anti-Catholic parties on the school issue.

---

95. These values are skillfully analyzed in Eric Foner, *Free Soil, Free Labor, Free Men: The Ideology of the Republican Party before the Civil War* (New York, 1970), 11–39.

96. Letter signed "Ohio," Cincinnati *Gazette*, March 7, 1853 (quotation); letter signed "Quevedo," *Ohio Columbian*, March 31, 1853; A. M. Gow to Richard Henry Dana, Jr., September 3, 1854, Dana Family Papers, MassHS. For a good overview, see Carl F. Kaestle, *Pillars of the Republic: Common Schools and American Society, 1780–1860* (New York, 1983).

97. Ruth M. Elson, *Guardians of Tradition: American Schoolbooks of the Nineteenth Century* (Lincoln, 1964), 47–58. Elson asserts that "no theme in these schoolbooks before 1870 is more universal than anti-Catholicism" (p. 53).

98. Billington, *Protestant Crusade*, 292–93; L. D. Barrow to Horace Mann, December 8, 1854, Horace Mann Papers, MassHS; New York *Tribune*, October 28, 1853.

99. Quoted in William A. Baughin, "Nativism in Cincinnati before 1860" (unpublished M.A. thesis, University of Cincinnati, 1963), 157.

100. Cincinnati *Gazette*, March 12, 1853; *Ohio Columbian*, March 31, 1853.

In Detroit in the spring of 1853 the Catholic bishop petitioned for a share of the school fund. When Democratic leaders tried to ignore the school issue, furious anti-Catholic Democrats formed an Independent ticket for the 1853 city election. The Whig Detroit *Tribune,* sensing the popular current and seeking to worsen the Democratic rift, supported the Independent movement. The election resulted in a sweeping victory for the Independent ticket and a thunderous endorsement of public schools. A number of native-born Protestant Democrats joined Whigs and Protestant immigrants in supporting the anti-Catholic slate. When William H. Seward and his associates criticized the *Tribune* for not taking the side of the Catholics, Joseph Warren, its editor, rejoined that such a course would have destroyed the paper. "The man who takes a stand against free schools, has in my opinion, politically killed himself, judging from the feeling every where shown thus far," he bluntly informed Seward.[101]

The most spectacular popular uprising in 1853 against the Catholic threat to the schools—and also against the traditional parties—occurred in Cincinnati. By the early 1850s the Democratic party controlled the city's politics by means of its strength among naturalized voters, a majority of whom were German.[102] Animosities within the German community among Protestants, Catholics, and free thinkers, as well as rivalry between long-time residents and more recent arrivals, further complicated the city's Democratic politics. Whigs naturally resented the Democrats' hold on the foreign vote, but more significant was the opposition to German influence among native-born Democrats, who, in order to control the party's city and county nominations and thereby exclude Germans from public office, organized a secret society known as the Miami Tribe. When existence of this society was uncovered in 1852, a group of German Protestants and radical free thinkers joined by their native-born allies bolted the local Democratic ticket in the fall election. Although these dissidents voted for Pierce in November, they remained estranged from local party leadership.[103]

A turning point in the city's politics occurred in February 1853 when Archbishop John Purcell of Cincinnati presented to the state legislature a petition requesting a share of the state education fund. The archbishop's organ, the *Catholic Telegraph,* backed his action with a thinly veiled threat of retribution against politicians who thwarted Catholic wishes on this matter.[104] Opponents quickly cited these editorials as proof that the city harbored a Catholic party bent on achieving political supremacy.[105]

Purcell's petition threw the city's politics into turmoil, and the school issue dominated the April city election. Whereas the Democrats, who were sensitive to the importance of the Catholic vote, took no stand on the issue, Whigs accused the Archbishop and his flock of plotting to overthrow the city's public school system. The regular Whig organization, with the *Gazette* as its organ, brought forth a so-called Independent city ticket. Although the ticket's candidates were hostile to Catholic influence in the schools, they found

---

101. Joseph Warren to Seward, March 15, May 7 (quotation), 1853, Seward Papers, UR; Formisano, *Mass Political Parties,* 223–29.

102. In 1850 of Cincinnati's 115,435 residents, 54,541 were foreign-born, including 33,374 Germans and 14,393 Irish. Immigrants constituted an even larger percentage of the voting age population because of the higher proportion of adult males among the foreign-born.

103. The Anti-Miami revolt is covered fully in the city's leading newspapers, the *Gazette,* the *Enquirer,* and the *Commercial,* for the period July–November 1852. The regression estimate is that Germans constituted two-thirds of the Anti-Miami voters, a figure that is probably below the actual proportion.

104. *Catholic Telegraph,* February 26, March 26, 1853.

105. Cincinnati *Gazette,* March 28, 1853; Cincinnati *Commercial,* April 4, 1853.

demagogic appeals to prejudice distasteful and were too moderate to suit extreme nativists in the Queen City.

Disgusted with the Whigs' half-hearted response, zealots who desired a stridently anti-Catholic ticket held a mass meeting, and in the middle of much confusion the assembled throng eventually nominated an Independent Free School ticket, headed by James D. Taylor, the editor of the virulently anti-Catholic, anti-immigrant Cincinnati *Times*, as its candidate for mayor. Defense of the public schools and a rebuke of the machinations of the Catholic church constituted the platform of the Free School movement. Although Taylor was a Whig, he had never attained real power within the party's power structure; his rabble-rousing nativism repelled party leaders, and the *Gazette* flatly proclaimed him unfit to be a mayor. Taylor's rabid nativism, however, had brought him a sizable following among the native-born Protestant workers in the city, many of whom were not only hostile to Catholics but also disgusted with both established parties. Denunciations of the Whig and Democratic organizations as corrupt and unrepresentative of the public will resounded at the Market Street mass meeting, and in the columns of his paper Taylor appealed to voters "to bury for once, all party animosities," and come to the polls "in solid phalanx" to rebuke "the efforts of the Pope of Rome to . . . influence and control your domestic affairs."[106] The city's temperance journal, the *Ohio Organ of Temperance Reform*, warmly backed the Free School slate.

The emergence of the public school issue also solidified the alienation of the Anti-Miami Germans from the Democratic party. Their leaders included several prominent refugees from the abortive revolution of 1848; these men bitterly hated the Catholic church, which they viewed as the enemy of liberty in Europe and the United States. When Taylor's refusal to withdraw undermined attempts to unite the anti-Catholic factions on a single ticket, these dissident Germans nominated their own slate. Despite their intense anti-Catholicism, they were all too aware of Taylor's anti-immigrant sentiments, and not surprisingly they were unwilling to support a man who made no distinction in his attacks on immigrants between Protestants and Catholics.

Four tickets thus contested the Cincinnati mayoral election. Democratic efforts to downplay the school issue were futile. "The Common School question is the all-absorbing topic of the day," the *Commercial* remarked during the campaign, while one speaker at the mass meeting that named the Free School ticket declared (in the words of one reporter) that "the old points of issue between the whigs and democrats, had grown obsolete, and . . . the free school question was the only one of moment before the people." Purcell was shaken by the animosity his actions had unleashed. "We are in the midst of all manner of threats from all manner of Sects & infidels," he wrote with obvious concern during the campaign. "No one knows how soon they may ripen into open, violent and prolonged persecution."[107]

With the opposition vote divided, the Democrats were victorious, but in combination the three opposition factions tallied no less than 60 percent of the vote, led by the Free

---

106. Cincinnati *Gazette*, April 2, 4, 1853; Cincinnati *Times*, March 21, 1853. For accounts of Taylor's nomination, see the Cincinnati *Commercial*, March 26, 29, 1853; Cincinnati *Gazette*, March 23, 28, 1853.

107. Cincinnati *Commercial*, March 22, 26, 1853; John Purcell to Anthony Blanc, March 22, 1853, Archdiocese of New Orleans Records, University of Notre Dame.

School ticket, which finished second with 35 percent.[108] In the contests for city council and for school visitor, where greater unity among the anti-Democratic groups prevailed, every victorious candidate was an avowed friend of the common schools. The *Catholic Telegraph's* contention during the campaign that "hatred of the Catholic Church is deep seated and strong, in the hearts of the masses" was amply borne out by the election returns. The extraordinary number of votes cast—despite a heavy rain that fell throughout election day, the total vote exceeded that in the hotly contested 1852 state election—revealed how deeply the school issue touched the electorate.[109] Taylor's strength among supporters of prohibition documented the close ties between the anti-Catholic and temperance movements. Almost two-thirds of the anti-liquor voters in the city backed the Free School ticket—more than double the share won by the Whig candidate; in addition, the overwhelming majority (85 percent) of Free School voters had opposed authorizing liquor licenses in the 1851 referendum. Also strikingly apparent was the power of anti-Catholicism to break down Democratic hegemony, even in a party stronghold like Cincinnati. The party's organ, the *Enquirer,* estimated that as many as 2,000 Democrats had bolted the party ticket, and it inferred correctly that the bulk of these defectors voted for the Free School candidates (Table 2.15).[110] The Democracy suffered a net loss of approximately a fifth of its previous members.

At the same time, the Whig party in Cincinnati had not benefited from the public school controversy. On the contrary, its share of the popular vote in the 1853 mayoral election fell sharply from 47 percent in 1852 to only 19 percent, as a large majority of the party's traditional supporters went over to the Free School nominees (Table 2.15). The growing popular hostility to the Whig and Democratic parties was too evident to be ignored. "We never have known an election in this city at which old party lines were so much disregarded," the *Commercial* commented afterwards. "The people appear to have become their own judges, and voted for those they supposed the best men, irrespective of the dictation of conventions, cliques or would-be party leaders."[111]

The withering of party loyalties quickened in the October election, when the temperance issue further fragmented the city's politics. So badly had party lines deteriorated that no fewer than seven tickets competed in the legislative and county contests. By the end of 1853 the second party system in Cincinnati had crumbled. Hampered by a forlorn cause in the state and an even weaker position in the city, Whigs were eager for a new organization to oppose the Democrats. At the same time, nativists in both parties were in open rebellion. Also ominous for the Democratic party was the continuing alienation of a number of non-Catholic Germans. Even the temperance issue, which Democrats took up in an attempt to restore their strength in the immigrant wards, failed to bring disaffected Germans back into the party fold.[112] Politics in the Queen City were ripe for realignment.

---

108. The official returns were Democrat, 5,943 (39.6 percent); Independent (Whig), 2,881 (19.2 percent); Free School, 5,187 (34.6 percent); and Anti-Miami, 990 (6.6 percent).

109. *Catholic Telegraph*, March 5, 1853. Turnout increased most markedly in the immigrant wards (where, of course, the majority of the Catholic voters lived), in the normally Whig working-class Fourteenth and Fifteenth Wards, and the closely contested working-class Sixteenth Ward.

110. Cincinnati *Enquirer*, April 8, 1853.

111. Cincinnati *Commercial*, April 7, 1853.

112. The Pearson Product-Moment coefficient of correlation between the Anti-Miami vote in the April mayoral election and the defection from the Democratic county ticket that fall is $+0.54$.

VIII

The 1853 municipal elections in Detroit and Cincinnati provided particularly dramatic examples of the welling popular revolt against the old organizations. In these cities and elsewhere, the formation of new independent parties at the local and state levels was further evidence of waning mass confidence in the party system.[113] As the traditional issues declined in salience, many voters came to think of the old parties as little more than engines of plunder and corruption; politicians seemed to stand for nothing beyond self-interest and holding public office. "I cannot for the life of me see by what rule of principle any man claiming to be *national* can find his bearings," a discontented New Yorker confessed during the 1853 state election. "It's to my faint vision a scramble for the spoils & a fight about Men rather than measures." An article in the *North American Review* made a similar observation. "These party names of Whig and Democrat now mean nothing and point to nothing," the writer argued. "The contest between them, in respect to principles and measures, has virtually ceased, and the opposition is only kept alive as a means of political intrigue and an avenue for the attainment of office." Similarly, a Philadelphia resident who voted for an independent ticket in 1853 declared, "Without any present questions of political importance to preserve the old lines of parties, parties yet preserve the old names which prove convenient vehicles to convey certain individuals to places of trust and distinction and emolument."[114]

Accompanying these assertions was the belief that parties were unresponsive to the popular will. A Vermont Whig typically claimed that the party's past victories had served only "to keep a lot of 'old Fogies' in office who have not cast the first thought for the wellfare [*sic*] of the American people or the Honor of their Country." Everywhere, dissatisfied citizens complained that parties were controlled by cliques and wire-pullers rather than by the people. Such allegations are a common tactic of political outs, but in the twilight of the Jacksonian party system they produced an unusual popular response.[115] In Cincinnati, to take one example, the Anti-Miami protest against control of the Democratic party by a small circle of politicians forced adoption of a direct primary system for making local nominations. Equally damning was both parties' unreceptiveness to new issues. For the most part, neither party was willing to endorse temperance wholeheartedly; indeed, Whig and Democratic leaders alike, fearing the issue's effect on party cohesion, were eager to remove it from the political arena as quickly as possible.[116] Nor was either party disposed to satisfy nativist demands. A frustrated Ohio voter contended that "men placed in power are often too far removed from the people—are not easily approached, seldom comply with the expressed wishes of the people, but on the

---

113. In Boston's municipal election in December 1853, two independent reform parties challenged the regular party slates; both outpolled the Whig and Democratic tickets combined. See James W. Stone to Sumner, December 22, 31, 1853, Sumner Papers, HU.

114. J. S. McLaury to Ansel J. McCall, September 26, 1853, McCall Family Papers, Cornell University; *North American Review*, v. 76 (April, 1853), 498; William V. Pettit to John M. Niles, December 8, 1853, Welles Papers, LC.

115. John Dewey to Justin S. Morrill, July 12, 1853, Justin S. Morrill Papers, LC; Francis P. Blair, Sr., to Franklin Pierce, November 25, 1852, Blair Family Papers, LC; Roger S. Baldwin, Jr., to Emily Baldwin, October 21, 1852, Baldwin Family Papers. For other examples, see Michael F. Holt, "The Politics of Impatience: The Origins of Know Nothingism," *JAH*, v. 60 (September, 1973), 316–18.

116. The *Ohio Columbian*, October 12, 1853, asserted that the lesson of the 1853 election for temperance men was that they could not rely on either of the old parties.

contrary repulse them." A Philadelphia Whig protested similarly against "the high handed attempt" by office holders to "frown down an expression of public opinion."[117]

Although the ties that bound men to parties had been slackening for some time, the events of 1853 severed them for an unprecedented number of voters. Many men switched parties, and others lost interest and no longer bothered to vote. In some states, such as Maine, Connecticut, and Ohio, party loyalties were enfeebled to the point that by the end of the year the second party system was on the brink of extinction. In other states, such as New York and Massachusetts, the debilitated party system still clung to what Horace Greeley aptly termed a "dead-alive state."[118] Everywhere, party loyalties were weaker than at any time since 1840.

The most striking feature of the 1853 elections was a precipitous decrease in the Whig share of the electorate. The party's strength varied from state to state, and it also oscillated over time, but overall the party suffered a sharp reduction in support in 1853. Despite Scott's defeat, the Whigs had done reasonably well in 1852 compared to their performance in immediately preceding elections; their improved showing underscored their decline the following year. Compounding the Whigs' problems was the fact that although the Democratic party also suffered a falling-off in 1853, it was not nearly as steep. Consequently, the percentage difference between the two parties' strength notably increased in 1853 over that of previous years (Table 2.16). Apathy and defections combined to undermine the Whig party's electoral base in 1853: A greater proportion of Whigs than Democrats did not vote, and of those who voted an unprecedented number bolted to other parties.

More than any other factor, the rise of ethnocultural issues destroyed the second party system. In this regard, no issue had a greater impact than temperance. By detaching a significant number of voters from their customary party moorings and by causing additional cross-pressured party members to refrain from voting, the anti-liquor crusade fragmented party lines. As the repository of moral uplift, the Whigs in particular suffered extensive defections to the Free Soilers, since the latter invariably assumed a more extreme stance in favor of prohibition. At the same time, some anti-temperance Whigs voted Democratic, and still more abstained from voting. Crippled by these defections and haunted by a deepening sense of futility, the Whigs proved unable to stay their party's expiration, whereas the Democrats, who in general suffered fewer defections and who also won more converts and new voters, were sufficiently strong to survive. A similar pattern prevailed on the public school issue, which heralded the emergence of nativism as a potent force in American politics after almost a decade of relative quiescence. Both parties suffered desertions to independent nativist parties, as the municipal elections in Detroit and Cincinnati demonstrated, but again the Whigs were more severely weakened precisely because extreme nativists were predominantly Whig. The death of the Whig party stemmed less from a consensus on old controversies than from an inability to handle the new issues that arose after 1850.[119]

---

117. Thomas J. McGarry to Thomas Corwin, November 4, 1852, William Mason to Corwin, May 27, 1851, quoted in Holt, *Political Crisis*, 137.

118. New York *Tribune*, October 3, 1853.

119. In his recent book, Michael Holt argues that the second party system fell apart because the parties lost their old issues and could not find new ones to reinvigorate the system; an emerging consensus destroyed the Whig party as voters, impatient with the old parties, deserted them for new, more responsive organizations. Although Holt's point about the need for sources of party conflict is well made, this interpretation encounters

In contradistinction to the usual emphasis on sectionalism, the Jacksonian party alignment disintegrated at the time when the slavery issue was less significant politically than it had been for years. Historians who point to the Free Soilers' improved showing in 1853 as evidence of the growing power of the slavery issue misperceive totally the reasons for the party's expanded support. Anti-liquor sentiment rather than antislavery feeling was responsible for the party's surge. Ironically, the Free Soil party did best when it downplayed its traditional sectional appeal and stressed ethnocultural concerns instead.

By the end of 1853, *before* the Kansas-Nebraska bill had been introduced, ethnocultural issues, by powerfully stimulating party decomposition, had already precipitated the beginning of realignment in a number of northern states.[120] Even in states where the old parties remained viable, the wearing away of their traditional electoral bases was well advanced by the end of 1853, and when divisive new issues arose in 1854, the party alignment toppled. So badly had the emergence of these ethnocultural issues disrupted the northern Whig organization that in 1854, when party leaders attempted to reverse this downward slide by again agitating the slavery issue, the disintegration of the party's popular base not only continued but accelerated. The inability of the Whigs to revive their strength when sectional issues again became prominent demonstrated forcefully that the damage the party had suffered earlier was too extensive to overcome.

By the end of 1853, both parties were in serious disorder, and in several states the Whigs seemed moribund. Some men saw realignment at hand. In the fall of that year, Fillmore prophesied the imminent dissolution of the two national parties. "Parties are broken up by local causes," he maintained, but national parties could be formed only "by the magnet of some great national and centripetal force at Washington." Less than two months before the fateful Thirty-third Congress convened, he asked his fellow conservative, John Pendleton Kennedy, "Will any question present such a magnet at the ensuing session of Congress?"[121]

---

serious difficulties as an explanation of the Whigs' death and the Democrats' survival. Holt gives insufficient attention to the controversies that arose after 1850 and the reasons they were especially destructive of Whig strength: *Political Crisis*, 101–38.

120. Clubb, Flanigan, and Zingale, *Partisan Realignment*, 133, list as the "necessary preconditions" for realignment the "growth in the pool of voters, particularly new voters, without firm partisan attachments; a weakening in the intensity of the loyalty of partisans to their party . . . in behavior at the polls; the appearance of short-term issues independent of traditional party stands; and a general malaise affecting attitudes toward political leaders and institutions."

121. Fillmore to John P. Kennedy, October 14, 1853, Kennedy Papers.

3

Nebraska and Nativism

The events of 1854 amply confirmed Millard Fillmore's prediction of impending political realignment. Party decomposition, already well advanced in the North, accelerated as the destruction of the Jacksonian party system now rushed to its culmination, while new controversies simultaneously provided additional dimensions to the ongoing process of realignment. In this regard two developments were particularly critical: the passage in May by the Democratic-controlled Congress of the Kansas-Nebraska Act; and the rapid expansion of the secret American party, which exploited the burgeoning nativist hostility to immigrants and Catholics. Competing for ascendancy in northern politics, the Nebraska and nativist impulses would each play a critical role in the party transformation of mid-decade and contribute decisively to its ultimate outcome, the formation of a Republican majority in the free states.

I

When Fillmore wrote to John Pendleton Kennedy speculating on the future course of national politics, Stephen A. Douglas was crossing the Atlantic after a six-month tour of Europe. Upon his return to Washington, the Little Giant quickly reimmersed himself in political affairs. Initially voicing confidence in Franklin Pierce, he soon discovered that discontent in the party over the president and his policies was much deeper and more widespread than he had thought. In explaining political developments during his absence, Douglas's close associate Charles Lanphier, the editor of the *Illinois State Register* in Springfield, expressed particular anxiety about the "everlasting, never-to-be ended New York quarrel," and other informants pointed with concern to internecine conflict elsewhere.[1] By the time Congress convened in December, Douglas had concluded that more forceful leadership was needed to restore party unity, on which he placed a high premium, and he therefore intended to bring forward his long-stalled program of western development.

Note: Unless otherwise indicated, the year for newspaper and manuscript citations in this chapter is 1854.

1. Charles Lanphier to Stephen A. Douglas, November 21, 1853, quoted in Robert W. Johannsen, *Stephen A. Douglas* (New York, 1973), 387; Edward C. West to Douglas, November 15, 1853, Douglas Papers, UChic.

Central features of his program were the organization of the western territories and the construction of a transcontinental railroad. As chairman of the Senate's Committee on Territories, he was determined to organize the region directly west of Iowa and Missouri, in part because of the pressure of westward migration, but also because until this territory was organized the proposed Chicago route for the Pacific railroad, which he enthusiastically advocated, was not feasible. In the previous Congress, strong southern opposition in the Senate had defeated a bill to organize the Nebraska territory, and since then David Rice Atchison of Missouri, who faced a difficult reelection fight, had announced publicly that he would refuse to support any bill that failed to open to slavery the land west of Missouri. Under terms of the Missouri Compromise of 1820, this region had been guaranteed to freedom, but, in a conversation with Douglas, Atchison now insisted that its prohibition on slavery be circumvented.[2] Joining Atchison, the Senate pro tempore, in this demand were three important southern senators with whom he lived in the capital, James Mason and Robert M. T. Hunter of Virginia and Andrew P. Butler of South Carolina. As representatives of radical proslavery opinion, these four messmates undertook to impose new principles on the Democratic party and make it more favorable to southern interests. Convinced that no bill on Nebraska could pass without offering something to the South, Douglas reluctantly agreed to bypass the Missouri Compromise.[3]

The Illinois senator hoped to satisfy southern leaders while avoiding the outright repeal of the 1820 statute. On January 4 he therefore reported a bill that was silent on the Missouri Compromise and merely asserted, in the language of the Utah and New Mexico territorial acts of 1850, that the territory would be admitted as a state or states with or without slavery as their constitutions prescribed. A subsequently added explanatory section upheld the principle of popular sovereignty by stipulating that the residents of the territory would decide the question of slavery.

In the meantime, William H. Seward suggested shrewdly to Whig senator Archibald Dixon of Kentucky that he offer an amendment explicitly repealing the slavery prohibition of the Missouri Compromise. By championing its repeal, southern Whigs could argue that they were the more faithful defenders of slavery and the South's interests. Seward hoped that this move would strengthen southern Whigs at home. At the same time, he wanted to make the bill as obnoxious as possible to northern interests. He knew that the Missouri Compromise enjoyed widespread bipartisan support in the North, and he recognized that Douglas and other northern Democrats shrank from a forthright repeal of the time-honored Compromise. Perhaps the best of both worlds was possible: Southern Whigs could take credit for proposing the repeal, while the bill, freighted with this provision, could then be defeated in the

---

2. Douglas's western program and his earlier attempt to organize the Nebraska territory are covered fully in Johannsen, *Douglas*, 390–400, and passim.

3. For the origins of the Kansas-Nebraska Act and the struggle over its wording, see Roy F. Nichols, "The Kansas-Nebraska Act: A Century of Historiography," *MVHR*, v. 43 (September, 1956), 187–212; Johannsen, *Douglas*, 401–34; and David M. Potter, *The Impending Crisis, 1848–1861* (New York, 1976), 145–76. Two particularly important recollections are Philip Phillips, "A Summary of the Principal Events of My Life," Philip Phillips Papers, LC; and John A. Parker, "Secret History of the Kansas-Nebraska Bill," *National Quarterly Review*, v. 41 (July, 1880), 105–18.

House, where the free states held a decided majority.[4] On January 16, Dixon introduced his amendment.

Dixon's move caught Douglas off guard. Nevertheless, faced with mounting southern criticism, he reluctantly agreed to an explicit repeal of the 1820 Compromise. Intent on shoring up support for this action, Douglas and other party leaders induced a hesitant President Pierce to concur in this step on the grounds that the Missouri Compromise had been superseded by the settlement of 1850. A series of bipartisan conferences of the bill's supporters modified the language further. In its final form the Kansas-Nebraska Act declared the Missouri Compromise "void" and divided the southern section directly west of Missouri into the Kansas Territory and the much larger northern portion, west of Iowa and Minnesota, into the Nebraska Territory. In these caucus deliberations, proponents rejected attempts to define the exact meaning of popular sovereignty: The stage at which settlers of a territory could decide the question of slavery was left unspecified. Northern supporters generally held that the territorial legislature could act on this question—a doctrine opponents derisively dubbed "squatter sovereignty." Southerners even more generally asserted that only when applying for statehood could a territory decide the status of slavery. Unable to agree, the bill's authors left this potentially divisive question to the courts.[5]

On January 24, while these developments were still unfolding, a manifesto entitled "The Appeal of the Independent Democrats in Congress to the People of the United States" appeared in several newspapers, including the *National Era*. Signed by six Free Soil senators and representatives—Salmon P. Chase, Edward Wade, and Joshua R. Giddings of Ohio, Charles Sumner and Alexander DeWitt of Massachusetts, and Gerrit Smith of New York—it lashed both Douglas and the Nebraska bill. Written by Chase from a draft by Giddings, and then polished by Smith and Sumner, this document denounced the bill as "a gross violation of a sacred pledge; as a criminal betrayal of precious rights; as part and parcel of an atrocious plot" to make Nebraska, pledged forever to freedom by the Missouri Compromise, a "dreary region of despotism, inhabited by masters and slaves." Characterizing the bill as a "bold scheme against American liberty," it asked: "Shall a plot against humanity and democracy, so monstrous, and so dangerous to the interests of liberty throughout the world, be permitted to succeed?" If the bill passed, the signers pledged, they would raise the standard of freedom "and call on the people to come to the rescue of the country from the domination of slavery."[6]

---

4. William H. Seward to Thurlow Weed, January 7, 8, Weed Papers, UR; Charles Francis Adams Diary, September 19, 1860, Adams Family Papers; Montgomery Blair to Gideon Welles, May 17, 1873, *Galaxy*, v. 16 (November, 1873), 692. Allan Nevins, completely misunderstanding Seward's purpose, dismisses as "preposterous" his claim to have influenced Dixon: *Ordeal of the Union*, v. 2, 40n.

5. Nichols, "Kansas-Nebraska Act," 207–8. For a contrary interpretation of the bill and popular sovereignty, see Robert R. Russel, "The Issues in the Congressional Struggle over the Kansas-Nebraska Bill, 1854," *JSH*, v. 29 (May, 1963), 203–5.

6. George W. Julian, *The Life of Joshua Giddings* (Chicago, 1892), 311; Joshua R. Giddings, *History of the Rebellion: Its Authors and Causes* (New York, 1864), 366n. In the haste and confusion, several versions appeared, variously dated, titled, and signed. Benjamin F. Wade, Moses Corwin, and possibly Lewis D. Campbell, all Ohio Whigs, signed and then withdrew their names. Giddings claimed afterwards that Seward did likewise, but Chase was undoubtedly correct in denying this, for Seward was not in Washington when the Appeal was drafted and issued. Memo, "Mr. Seward & the Repeal of the Missouri Compromise," Chase Papers, HSPa; New York *Weekly Tribune*, February 11; *Ashtabula Sentinel*, March 29, 1855. Other Whigs were

The Appeal of the Independent Democrats, which Chase later termed "the *most valuable* of my works," was a brilliant piece of antislavery propaganda.[7] Invoking the idea of a conspiracy to subvert republicanism, which had been a staple of American politics since the Revolution, it emphasized the concept of an aggressive Slave Power determined to rule the country without challenge and bent on overriding all compromises and compacts that stood athwart its goals. Thoroughly unprepared for recent developments, a number of northerners found this idea a persuasive explanation of the origins of the Nebraska bill. How else could one account for the suddenly announced intention to repeal a compromise that had been on the statute books for more than thirty years?

To Free Soilers like Chase and Sumner, Douglas's bill offered renewed hope that the party system could at last be reoriented along sectional lines. When the session opened, they spoke for only a small minority in the country and were without influence in Congress. Their long-range political prospects were bleak at best. As a consequence of the Democratic victory in Ohio in 1853, Chase faced certain retirement to private life after this Congress. Sumner's ineffective course in the Senate had sorely disappointed even his friends and, lacking any real personal popularity in his state, he was further weakened by the disintegration of the Coalition that had elected him.[8] Having built political careers on the constant agitation of the slavery question, these men exploited to the fullest the opportunity offered by the Nebraska issue.

Chase, in particular, sought to assume leadership of the opposition to the Nebraska bill. The sincerity of his hatred of slavery is beyond challenge. The Ohio Free Soil leader had committed himself to the antislavery movement in the 1830s when it was not respectable; he had braved anti-abolitionist mobs; he had waged a long legal struggle for black rights; and he had labored diligently for many years to form a powerful antislavery third party. As his commitment to political activity grew, however, so, too, did his ambition; he was, in the words of one Ohio politician, "as ambitious as Julius Caesar." Chase was one of the Senate's handsomest members, over six feet tall and of sturdy build. He was also unbearably self-righteous and on occasion decidedly duplicitous in his political dealings— his enemies called him "a political vampire" and "a sort of moral bull-bitch."[9] Pontificating ceaselessly about his disinterested commitment to the antislavery cause, he displayed (like many politicians) an increasing inability to distinguish between his own political fortunes and the advancement of his party. The Ohio senator was genuinely outraged by Douglas's bill, but he also grasped at the chance to enhance his popularity and strengthen his future political prospects.

Chase always maintained afterwards that the Appeal of the Independent Democrats, of which he claimed at least 500,000 copies were circulated, was responsible for rallying the

---

willing to sign it only if verbal changes were made. The Appeal was finally put forth as an address of the Independent Democrats, but several papers carried it with additional signatures, or asserted incorrectly that a majority of Ohio representatives had signed it. Salmon P. Chase to Ichabod Codding, April 22, Ichabod Codding Papers, Swarthmore College; *Cong. Globe*, 33 Cong., 1st sess., 280–82.

7. Chase to Edward L. Pierce, August 5, Sumner Papers, HU.

8. For Sumner's political situation, see David Donald, *Charles Sumner and the Coming of the Civil War* (New York, 1960), 238–42, 249–50.

9. Albert G. Riddle quoted in David H. Bradford, "The Background and Formation of the Republican Party in Ohio, 1844–1861" (unpublished Ph.D. dissertation, University of Chicago, 1947), 85; Robert Warden, *Private Life and Public Services of Salmon P. Chase* (Cincinnati, 1874), 329; Roeliff Brinkerhoff, *Recollections of a Lifetime* (Cincinnati, 1900), 118. Maizlish, *Triumph of Sectionalism*, presents considerable evidence of Chase's duplicity; see, for example, his account of Chase's election to the Senate in 1849 (pp. 125–44).

North against the Nebraska bill.[10] Without question the Appeal deserves a featured place in any account of the protest against the repeal of the Missouri Compromise. Even so, many opponents of the Nebraska scheme were dismayed and exasperated by the rashness of the small coterie of antislavery agitators who issued the Appeal. The conspicuous position assumed at the beginning by antislavery radicals and their harsh arraignment of the bill dealt a serious blow to the drive to unite against the measure moderates and conservatives from both parties and sections. While the bill was still pending in the House, Oran Follett, an influential Ohio Whig editor who was trying desperately to mobilize sentiment against the bill, complained that the address of Chase and company "came near swamping us altogether."[11] The thin-skinned Boston patrician, Robert C. Winthrop, was equally critical. When the Nebraska bill was introduced, he later asserted, a "handful" of Free Soilers

> precipitated themselves into the front ranks of the opposition, in a way to drive off the only persons who could have prevented its consummation. Half-a-dozen of them, under the style of Independent Democrats, got up a flaming manifesto in such hot haste that it was said to have been dated on Sunday, and put it forth, cock-a-hoop, half-signed, to the utter discomfiture of all who hoped to prevent the bill from passing. They usurped a lead which belonged to others, and gave an odor of abolition to the whole movement.[12]

Whatever the Appeal accomplished toward arousing northern public opinion, it did nothing to secure the necessary votes in Congress to defeat the bill.

The taint of abolitionism that Chase's document gave opposition to the bill, the belief that the repeal of the Compromise stood no chance of passage, and the unrelenting suspicion among Whigs, Democrats, and Free Soilers, all initially hindered the anti-Nebraska protest. A growing sense of crisis, however, helped to overcome these obstacles, and before long mass meetings throughout the North condemned the bill roundly. Both the depth of emotion against the bill and its pervasiveness impressed observers.[13] By mid-February Seward wrote home that remonstrances against the bill were "coming down upon us as if a steady but strong North wind was rattling through the country."[14] Northern anti-Democratic newspapers of all persuasions strongly opposed the bill, as did a surprising number of Democratic papers, led by the New York *Evening Post,* which was free soil in its sympathies. The response of the northern press, the *Evening Post* asserted with some exaggeration after surveying approximately a hundred papers, was "a perfect chorus of condemnation."[15]

Of particular significance for the future course of politics in the North was the political activity of northern clergymen, who, manifesting unusual unity on the issue, threw their

10. Chase to John P. Bigelow, September 23, John P. Bigelow Papers, HU; Chase to Codding, April 22, Codding Papers.

11. Oran Follett to Thomas Ewing, May 1, Ewing Family Papers.

12. Robert C. Winthrop, "The Fusion Parties in Massachusetts: A Letter to the Chairman of the Whig Executive Committee, October 15, 1855," *Addresses and Speeches on Various Occasions* (4 vols.: Boston, 1852–1886), v. 2, 233–34.

13. William D. Wooden to Edwin B. Morgan, February 11, Edwin Barber Morgan Papers, Wells College; William Kent to Hamilton Fish, March 3, Fish Papers, LC; Rhodes, *History of the United States*, v. 1, 467n.

14. Seward to Frances A. Seward, February 19, Seward, *Seward*, v. 2, 222.

15. New York *Evening Post*, February 15. See the summaries of newspaper opinion in Rhodes, *History of the United States*, v. 1, 464n; Nevins, *Ordeal of the Union*, v. 2, 131–32.

considerable influence behind the drive to prevent the Nebraska bill's passage. Anger extended beyond radical antislavery clergymen, as ministers noted for their conservatism and for their reluctance to address political questions brushed aside their usual caution and joined in denouncing the bill.[16] Of the clerical petitions against the bill, the most notable emanated from a committee of Boston ministers; its intention (as Harriet Beecher Stowe explained) was to make every pulpit in New England "a battery against this iniquity." This committee forwarded to Congress in March a memorial signed by 3,050 clergymen of various denominations representing the great majority of their profession in these states. Incensed by its language, Douglas, in particular, assailed the clergy for mixing in politics. Even one of the signers agreed that its wording was not in good taste. "It was drawn up in the iron language of the Beechers & we had no time to alter it, if sent in at all," he explained to Seward afterwards.[17]

A number of Democrats, led by such old Jacksonians as Francis P. Blair and Gideon Welles, and by such younger free soilers as Preston King, denounced Douglas and Pierce for betraying the principles of the party and committing it instead to the expansion of slavery. Democratic congressmen received numerous warnings of a brewing revolt within the party. The reaction of northern Democratic legislatures and state conventions that assembled while the bill was pending provided additional evidence of the direction of public opinion. Almost without exception they refused to endorse the proposed repeal of the Missouri Compromise.[18] David Wilmot, the prominent free soil Democratic leader in Pennsylvania, bluntly warned Democratic governor William Bigler that the Nebraska bill threatened the Democratic party "with annihilation in every free State." Echoing this view, the *Evening Post* proclaimed that its approval "can only result in whittling away the democratic party into shavings."[19]

Northern public opinion condemned the bill on several counts.[20] Many rejected Douglas's assertion that the Compromise of 1850 was intended to supersede that of 1820. Furthermore, opponents of the bill argued that the Missouri Compromise, by virtue of its long history, was more than a statute, that it had taken on the aura of a "sacred compact" between the two sections. Gideon Welles pointed out that since 1820 Congress had several times reaffirmed the Missouri Compromise in various territorial bills:

> In all the legislation of Congress, from the organization of the Constitution, there is not one subject that has by such repeated acts of the government, extending over more than

---

16. Amos A. Lawrence, a leading conservative Bostonian Whig, attested that "the ministers all pray & preach one way" on the Nebraska question. "Pierce & Douglas had better never have been born." Amos A. Lawrence to William Lawrence, June, Lawrence Papers. Also see Edward Everett to Mrs. Charles Eames, March 21, Typescript, Everett Papers.

17. Harriet Beecher Stowe to Charles Sumner, February 23, Sumner Papers, HU; D. Beecher to [Leonard Bacon?], February 16, Bacon Family Papers, Yale University; William A. Hall to John P. Hale, February 13, Hale Papers, NHHS; J. Todd to Seward, July 6, *Private & Confidential*, Seward Papers, UR; Johannsen, *Douglas*, 443–45.

18. Nevins, *Ordeal of the Union*. v. 2, 146–47.

19. David Wilmot to William Bigler, March 3, Bigler Papers; New York *Evening Post*, April 24.

20. In this section, although I speak of northern public opinion, I do not mean to create the impression that the North spoke with one voice. As on all partisan issues, popular sentiment was not unanimous. Nevertheless, northern feeling on this subject displayed greater unity than was normal in political controversies. For an excellent analysis of the northern reaction to the Kansas-Nebraska Act, see Richard H. Sewell, *Ballots for Freedom: Antislavery Politics in the United States, 1837–1860* (New York, 1976), 254–65.

one third of a century, received the sanction, or been considered as so settled a question as this. If the faith of the government is pledged on any one subject it is this.[21]

Angry northerners, noting that southerners demanded the Compromise's repeal only after having obtained all advantages possible under its provisions, charged that the South would not adhere to any agreement longer than served its own self-interest.[22] In addition, northern conservatives, particularly Union Whigs, who had anticipated a long period of tranquility following passage of the Compromise of 1850, were upset over what they considered the needless revival of sectional animosities.[23]

Also critical in producing northern resentment was the widespread belief that the Nebraska bill would permit the further expansion of slavery. Despite Douglas's and many northern Democrats' contention that popular sovereignty would preserve freedom in the new territories, opponents insisted that the real intention of the bill was to extend the peculiar institution into territory that had been pledged forever to freedom. To suspicious northerners the real purpose behind dividing the area into two territories was to create one slave and one free state. Whatever its phraseology, former senator Roger S. Baldwin declared, men both north and south correctly understood that "in its practical bearing" the bill was designed to convert free territory into slave territory. Calling attention to the Senate's rejection of an amendment offered by Chase explicitly providing that the residents of the territory could prohibit slavery, James Shepherd Pike maintained that the true intention of the bill was "to establish a government . . . of such character that the people cannot possibly keep slavery out, let them desire to do so ever so much, and vote to do it ever so often." The principle of popular sovereignty, he scoffed, was "a monstrous fraud."[24] For the most part, the bill's opponents rejected the argument that climate and geography would exclude slavery from Kansas. They pointed to the similarity between the eastern part of the territory and the hemp-growing region of Missouri directly across the Missouri River, which by now was the major slaveholding area in that state.[25] Indeed, whatever their rhetorical professions, most southerners, as Robert M. T. Hunter testified later, were convinced that slavery could expand into Kansas, and John Bell reported that Atchison was quietly assuring southerners that the institution could gain a secure foothold there.[26]

Anti-Nebraska leaders dismissed Douglas's principle of popular sovereignty as a sham and his argument that it would preserve the territories for freedom as a delusion. Focusing on the doctrine's basic ambiguity, they cautioned that the initial decision in the territory would be critical. "The first comer, or the first five hundred, or the first five thousand,

---

21. Welles to [James T. Pratt], March (copy), Welles Papers, LC; Chase to James W. Grimes, November 13, Chase Papers, HSPa. One of Attorney General Caleb Cushing's correspondents maintained that until now the Missouri Compromise "has been deemed almost as sacred as the Constitution itself." William E. Cramer to Cushing, January 26, Caleb Cushing Papers, LC.

22. New York *Evening Post*, January 6; Poughkeepsie *Eagle*, quoted in Sewell, *Ballots for Freedom*, 260; Cincinnati *Gazette*, May 24.

23. New York *Times* quoted in Francis Brown, *Raymond of the Times* (New York, 1951), 130; Welles to Dear Sir, February 17 (copy), Welles Papers, LC; Amos A. Lawrence to Giles Richards, June 1 (copy), Lawrence Papers.

24. Roger S. Baldwin to Bishop Perkins, March 28 (draft), Baldwin Family Papers; Pike, *First Blows*, 206–9.

25. Edward Kent to Israel Washburn, Jr., March 5, Israel Washburn, Jr., Papers, Norlands; New York *Evening Post*, February 28, March 23; Boston *Daily Advertiser* quoted in New York *Evening Post*, March 4.

26. *Cong. Globe*, 33rd Cong., 1st sess., Appendix, 939–40; Nevins, *Ordeal of the Union*, 117 and n.

for nobody says what shall be a quorum, are to have the authority, for all time to come, to decide the immensely important question whether a fine, great country is to be inhabited by free men, or by lords and slaves,'' contended a St. Louis German paper.[27] Moreover, these critics argued that once the decision for slavery was made, it would be impossible to reverse. The *Illinois State Journal,* for example, asserted that in reality Douglas's principle meant that the first few settlers could establish slavery, which "from the nature of things cannot be got rid of in all future time." In his famous Peoria speech in 1854, Abraham Lincoln emphasized that once slavery was established in a territory, any subsequent referendum would favor its continuance.[28]

Northerners opposed the expansion of slavery for a wide variety of reasons: economic self-interest; moral opposition to the institution; a desire to limit the political power of the South; the wish to keep all blacks from the territories; and the need to expand the free labor system and thus preserve the cluster of social values—opportunity, social mobility, economic development—so intimately associated with it.[29] This opposition was more deeply rooted among Whigs and Free Soilers, but northern Democrats were far from indifferent to the issue. With the exception of the Irish, most of them disliked the institution of slavery in the abstract and had no great desire to see it expand. When the slavery extension crisis first arose in the 1840s, northern Democratic politicians, even those who disapproved of the Wilmot Proviso, refused to say that they were not opposed to slavery for, as William L. Marcy admitted, "In truth we all are."[30]

In the view of a number of the Nebraska bill's opponents, the threat of slavery's spread was not confined to the western territories. Many believed, as the Appeal of the Independent Democrats asserted, that the Nebraska bill was part of a larger conspiracy to push slavery throughout the hemisphere and cement the Slave Power's hold on the national government. Prior to this crisis, the concept of a Slave Power—a tightly knit body of slaveholders united in a design to expand slavery and maintain their control of the nation's destiny—did not enjoy wide acceptance outside abolitionist circles, despite efforts for a decade or more by politically oriented antislavery men, led by Chase, to promulgate this idea.[31] Northern skepticism began to weaken in the face of the movement to repeal the Missouri Compromise. The idea of an aggressive slavocracy was especially potent among Van Buren Democrats, who for years had chafed at southern control of their party. Such men as Francis P. Blair, Gideon Welles, and David Wilmot, and such papers as the New York *Evening Post* all warned that the Nebraska bill was merely one step in a larger scheme to extend slavery and make the country a slaveholding republic. In a public letter, Wilmot designated the Nebraska bill "the precursor of a series of measures, destined to give the Slave Oligarchy complete domination . . . and to establish

---

27. St. Louis *Anzeiger*, October 11, quoted in the *Illinois State Journal*, October 24.

28. *Illinois State Journal*, October 30; Abraham Lincoln, speech at Peoria, October 16, Roy P. Basler et al., eds., *The Collected Works of Abraham Lincoln* (8 vols.: New Brunswick, 1953), v. 2, 263; New York *Tribune*, February 1, 1854, December 14, 1853; Pittsburgh *Gazette*, March 24.

29. For a wide-ranging analysis of the sources of northern opposition to slavery and slavery expansion, see Foner, *Free Soil, Free Labor, Free Men.*

30. Marcy quoted in Foner, *Free Soil, Free Labor, Free Men,* 308; J. F. Chamberlain to A. J. McCall, June 8, McCall Family Papers; L. Richmond to John W. Geary, October 26, 1856, John W. Geary Papers, Yale University; Charles Mason Diary, March 16, [1856], Charles Mason Papers, IaSDHA; Newburgh *Telegraph*, October 31, 1856; Portland *Eastern Argus*, April 21, 1851, quoted in Wescott, "History of Maine Politics," 149.

31. Foner, *Free Soil, Free Labor, Free Men,* 73–102.

on the American continent the most powerful and mighty Slave Empire known in the history of the world.''[32] A few observers even claimed that the ultimate goal of the Slave Power was the nationalization of slavery.[33] Citing intemperate southern editorials demanding that the African slave trade be reopened and that slavery be legalized in all territories, the New York *Tribune* alleged that "the Nebraska bill is but the first . . . step in this comprehensive plan of Africanizing the whole of the American hemisphere, and establishing Slavery upon what its advocates regard as an impregnable basis.''[34]

By emphasizing these considerations rather than the immorality of slavery, the anti-Nebraska protest gained a much wider audience than the abolitionist movement had ever enjoyed. Not surprisingly, abolitionists generally were extremely critical of what they perceived as the lower tone of this outcry. "The real conflict is between Liberty and Slavery, not between the North and the South," the *Free West*, an Illinois Free Soil paper, scornfully commented. George W. Julian recalled that many of those who opposed the Nebraska bill "made the sacredness of the bargain of 1820 and the crime of its violation the sole basis of their hostility. Their hatred of slavery was geographical, spending its force north of the Missouri restriction. They talked far more eloquently about the duty of keeping covenants, and the wickedness of reviving sectional agitation than the evils of slavery.''[35] In the long run, these widely differing sources of opposition posed a major difficulty for those who sought to form a new party on the Nebraska issue, but in the struggle to prevent passage of Douglas's measure opponents welcomed support from whatever quarter and for whatever reason.

There was never any doubt, once the southern Whig caucus and the administration endorsed the principle of repeal, that the Kansas-Nebraska bill would pass the Senate. After an extensive debate, the upper house approved it on March 4 by a vote of 37 to 14.[36] The critical struggle occurred in the House. There the measure ran into immediate trouble when a majority of northern Democrats voted to refer the bill not to the Committee on Territories, chaired by Douglas's ally William A. Richardson of Illinois, but to the Committee of the Whole, where more than fifty bills ahead of it on the calendar would have to be laid aside before the Nebraska bill could be considered. Throughout March and April the president and his advisers applied pressure to recalcitrant Democrats, and finally, in May, Richardson was ready to push for passage. After the House voted one by one to table the preceding bills on the calendar, opponents of the Kansas-Nebraska bill resorted to a series of delaying tactics in a desperate effort to block its passage. On

---

32. Charles Buxton Going, *David Wilmot, Free-Soiler* (New York, 1924), 451, 459 (quotation); New York *Evening Post*, January 25, May 23; *Illinois State Journal*, November 7; George W. Julian, *Speeches on Political Questions* (New York, 1872), 108; Pittsburgh *Gazette*, May 11.

33. Welles to My Dear Sir, May (copy), Welles Papers, ConnHS; Enoch Lewis to [Thaddeus Stevens], February 9, Thaddeus Stevens Papers, LC; Jacob Brinkerhoff, speech at Anti-Nebraska state convention, March 22, quoted in Joseph P. Smith, *History of the Republican Party in Ohio* (2 vols.: Chicago, 1898), v. 1, 14; *Daily National Era*, May 22. Sewell properly emphasizes that the Kansas-Nebraska excitement, rather than the later Dred Scott decision, first gave currency to the charge that slavery would expand to the free states. *Ballots for Freedom*, 259.

34. New York *Tribune*, May 15; S. Abel to Mark Howard, March 16, Mark Howard Papers, ConnHS.

35. [Chicago] *Free West*, August 24; Julian, *Political Recollections*, 136–37; Sewell, *Ballots for Freedom*, 257–59.

36. The four negative northern Democratic votes were those of Hannibal Hamlin of Maine, Isaac P. Walker and Henry C. Dodge of Wisconsin, and Charles T. James of Rhode Island. Two southerners, Sam Houston and John Bell, voted against the bill (John Clayton, who was absent, announced his disapproval after considerable indecision).

May 22, following a fierce struggle, the bipartisan majority led by Richardson and Alexander H. Stephens of Georgia approved the bill by a vote of 113 to 100. Northern Democrats divided almost equally, with 44 voting for and 43 against. Five northern Democrats, three of whom were opposed to the bill, did not vote. Only nine congressmen from below the Mason-Dixon line voted against the bill.[37] On May 30, after the Senate concurred quickly in the House's amendments, Pierce signed the bill into law, and the Missouri Compromise had been repealed.

II

Despite strong congressional opposition to the bill, cooperation among northern Whigs, anti-Nebraska Democrats, and Free Soilers was distinctly limited. Retaining their separate identity, Democrats opposed to the bill refused to caucus with northern Whigs. Compounding the opposition's disorganization was the lack of a recognized leader. Several men occupied prominent positions, but none could command the allegiance of the combined anti-Nebraska forces. Thomas Hart Benton enjoyed great prestige in the House, and on May 11 the New York *Tribune* called on him to lead the opposition, but the Missourian lacked both the talent and the will for this role. Finally Gamaliel Bailey, the editor of the antislavery *National Era,* and Preston King, a leading New York Barnburner and former congressman, undertook the task of getting the various opposition groups to cooperate.

The fat, plainspoken King with his common manners and simple attire presented an almost comical contrast to the slightly built, elegant and polished Bailey. Originally educated as a physician, Bailey had converted to abolitionism in the 1830s under the tutelage of Theodore Dwight Weld. Abandoning the medical profession, he began his career as an antislavery editor in Cincinnati, and in 1847 Lewis Tappan brought him to Washington to edit a national antislavery organ, the *National Era.* Much more tolerant and pragmatic than most strong antislavery men, Bailey took the lead in urging that the various anti-Nebraska elements unite, prompting Israel Washburn in retrospect to designate him *"the immediate founder of the Republican party."*[38] King, on the other hand, was originally a devoted follower of Martin Van Buren and Silas Wright. Characterized by Henry Adams as "the most amiable, fat old fanatic that ever existed," he had been the guiding force behind the introduction of the Wilmot Proviso, and, although he had temporarily made his peace with the regular Democratic organization in the early 1850s, he was increasingly restless over what he considered the proslavery orientation of the national party. He and Bailey had become good friends during King's terms in Congress, when the New Yorker was a frequent guest at Bailey's famous soirees, which brought together prominent antislavery figures in the capital. Their talents meshed well. Bailey was more intellectually expansive, while the more ideologically rigid King was a methodical political organizer who left nothing to chance. Earnest yet good-natured, fair minded and honest, they together had a wide network of friends and acquaintances and, more important, knew how to influence others.[39]

---

37. The best account of the passage of the bill in the House is Roy F. Nichols, *American Leviathan* (New York, 1966), 104–21.

38. Israel Washburn, Jr., "Gamaliel Bailey," *Universalist Quarterly,* v. 25 (July, 1868), 298–99. Also see Grace Greenwood, "An American Salon," *Cosmopolitan,* v. 9 (February, 1890), 437–47.

39. Henry Adams to Charles Francis Adams, Jr., January 17, 1861, Worthington Chauncey Ford, ed., *Letters of Henry Adams (1858-1891)* (2 vols.: Boston, 1930), v. 1, 79–80.

From the beginning, Bailey was outspoken in his criticism of the failure of anti-Nebraska men to work together. "For Heaven's sake," he declared in the *National Era* once the bill had been taken up, "let us have . . . a well-planned, well-organized, well-understood plan of operation, to be sustained and carried out by them all, without faltering, distrust of each other, or thought of looking back." King and Bailey faced an uphill struggle, for suspicions among Whigs, Democrats, and Free Soilers remained strong. "Party names & prejudices are the cords that bind the Samson of the North," Bailey cried in frustration. The bill's opponents "could not forget they were Whigs, they were Democrats." On May 21, both groups finally agreed to caucus, but by then it was too late.[40] In order to defeat the bill—if that could have been accomplished at all—the minority had to agree at the outset on tactics. Instead, throughout the struggle the anti-Nebraska men differed over what course to pursue, particularly over whether to use obstructionist tactics, including a filibuster and lack of a quorum, to block passage of the bill. In all probability the minority lacked any real chance of prevailing.[41] Still, the bipartisan outcry against the bill in the North stood in sharp contrast to the crippling divisions among opponents in Congress. Free Soilers, Whigs, and anti-Nebraska Democrats voted together, but they would not work together. This failure provided scant encouragement to those who looked for the Nebraska issue to realign the party system.

Northern protests over the repeal of the Missouri Compromise did not cause Douglas to anticipate any major reshuffling of the parties. The divisions among the bill's opponents seemed to preclude such a possibility, as did continuing party cohesion on other issues during this session of Congress. In addition, he was confident that popular anger would be short-lived, and that the Democracy could retain its strength in the free states on a platform of popular sovereignty, which he believed would make the territories free just as surely as the Missouri Compromise would, and with far less friction and ill will. "The storm will soon spend its fury, and the people of the north will sustain the measure when they come to understand it," he assured Howell Cobb in April. "The great principle of self government is at stake & surely the people of this country are never going to decide that the principle upon which our whole republican system rests is vicious & wrong."[42] His optimism was not wholly without foundation, for a number of observers, especially in the West, began to report growing support for the idea of popular sovereignty.[43] The Illinois leader also counted on party loyalty to preserve the

---

40. *Daily National Era*, March 10, May 10 (quotation), 12; Gamaliel Bailey to James Shepherd Pike, May 21, Pike Papers, UMe; Washington correspondence, New York *Herald*, May 15, 21; Washington correspondence, Philadelphia *North American*, May 19, 21; Pittsburgh *Gazette*, May 23; Washington correspondence, New York *Courier and Enquirer*, quoted in New York *Evening Post*, May 22; Ernest P. Muller, "Preston King: A Political Biography" (unpublished Ph.D. dissertation, Columbia University, 1957), 535–36.

41. Lewis D. Campbell to Pike, May 24, Elihu B. Washburne to Pike, May 8, Pike Papers, UMe; O. B. Matteson to Weed, May 18, 22, Weed Papers, UR; Pike to William Pitt Fessenden, May 15, Pike Papers, LC. For divisions over tactics, see J. Scott Harrison to Benjamin Harrison, May 19, Benjamin Harrison Papers, LC; Pike, *First Blows*, 232; Pittsburgh *Gazette*, May 23; Washington correspondence, Philadelphia *North American*, May 19; Cincinnati *Gazette*, May 15.

42. Douglas to Howell Cobb, April 2, Douglas to Lanphier, February 13 (Private), Robert W. Johannsen, ed., *The Letters of Stephen A. Douglas* (Urbana, 1961), 300, 283–84; Fessenden to Ellen Fessenden, March 29, Fessenden Family Papers. See the analysis of voting in Congress during this session in Gerald W. Wolff, *The Kansas-Nebraska Bill: Party, Section, and the Coming of the Civil War* (New York, 1977).

43. S. N. Johnson to Douglas, March 24, Douglas Papers, UChic; Adam Gurowski to Pike, June 8, Pike

Democrats' electoral strength. The bill "will form the test of Parties," he told Lanphier, and "the only alternative" for Democrats was "either to stand with the Democracy or rally under Seward, John Van Buren & co."[44]

Unlike Douglas, other political commentators concluded that the Nebraska bill had produced a significant change in northern public opinion. They pointed to two developments in particular: a growing determination to resist the aggressions of the Slave Power, and a weakening of northerners' commitment to abide by the Compromise measures of 1850, especially the fugitive slave law. From New Hampshire, an anti-Nebraska Democrat reported that there was "but one feeling here" because of the bill—"a sullen determination to resist the slave power at all hazards in [the] future." The New York *Times* argued that the passage of the Nebraska Act would "root out from the Northern mind the last vestige of confidence in the good faith of the advocates of Slavery, and create a deep-seated, intense and ineradicable hatred of the institution which will crush its political power, at all hazards, and at any cost." Antislavery men reported gleefully that northerners, including many Compromise men of four years ago, would no longer abide by the fugitive slave law, and that the idea of sectional compromise was now completely discredited.[45] The reaction to the rendition of the fugitive slave Anthony Burns in Boston shortly after passage of the Kansas-Nebraska Act underscored the magnitude of change in public opinion. Bostonians who earlier had defended the Compromise now harshly assailed the South, and a petition calling for repeal of the fugitive slave law gathered 3,000 signatures at the Merchants' Exchange. The passage by several northern states of personal liberty laws designed to impede the law's operation, which were precipitated by the Nebraska bill, offered additional evidence of northern animosity toward the South.[46] Into what political channel this anger would flow was not clear in the summer of 1854, but its intensity was unmistakable.

Of more pressing immediate concern to Democratic leaders was restoration of party unity. His fighting fury roused by the vituperative denunciation heaped on him, Douglas was in no mood to temporize with those Democrats who had broken ranks on the Nebraska issue. Southern leaders joined him in insisting that support for the principle of nonintervention be made a touchstone of party regularity. Pierce, however, vacillated over whether to enforce party discipline on this matter. After he had agreed to support the repeal of the 1820 Compromise, the Washington *Union*, which functioned loosely as the administration's organ, declared that the bill was to be considered a standard of Democratic loyalty, only to retreat from this position in early March when it stated that

---

Papers, UMe; John W. Forney to James Buchanan, May 25, Very private, because entirely outspoken, Buchanan Papers, HSPa.

    44. Douglas to Lanphier, February 13 (Private), Johannsen, ed., *Douglas Letters*, 283–84; New York *Tribune*, June 17; Washington correspondence [James Simonton], New York *Times*, May 27. More prescient was the observation of Democratic congressman J. Glancy Jones of Pennsylvania, who declared that Douglas had "made an awful investment" in the Nebraska bill, and that "the North will pursue him with a bitterness, that will always make him unavailable." J. Glancy Jones to Buchanan, March 29, Buchanan Papers, HSPa.

    45. Henry French to Benjamin B. French, June 16, Benjamin Brown French Papers, LC; New York *Times*, January 24; E. A. Stansbury to Sumner, February 23, George Livermore to Sumner, June 1, Sumner Papers, HU; Warsaw [Illinois] *Express*, December 21, quoted in Nevins, *Ordeal of the Union*, v. 2, 153.

    46. George Livermore to Sumner, May [June] 4, John W. Sullivan to Sumner, May 30, Sumner Papers, HU; Lucid, ed., *Dana Journal*, v. 2, 637–38; Edward Everett to Joseph Cottman, June 15 (copy), Everett Papers. Also see Samuel Shapiro, "The Rendition of Anthony Burns," *Journal of Negro History*, v. 44 (January, 1959), 34–51; Thomas D. Morris, *Free Men All: The Personal Liberty Laws of the North, 1780–1861* (Baltimore, 1974).

the president would not oppose Democrats who differed on details of the bill. But in late May, shortly after passage of the bill, the hopes of southern managers were realized. Speaking for the administration, the *Union* announced that approval of the Kansas-Nebraska Act by a majority of Democratic congressmen inexorably established it as "a test of democratic orthodoxy."[47] With the administration's refusal to tolerate dissent, a full-scale referendum in the fall elections on the repeal of the Missouri Compromise seemed assured.

Democratic opponents of the bill complained loudly about the administration's attempt to make support of the measure a party requirement. To do so, they warned, would only further divide the party and strengthen its opponents. "The inference that no one can be recognized as a Democrat who opposed the Nebraska Bill is full of disaster & division," despaired New York governor Horatio Seymour.[48] Confronted with the administration's edict, anti-Nebraska Democrats pursued a variety of courses in 1854. Some, however reluctantly, bowed to the pressures of party regularity and endorsed the law, or at least acquiesced in it as an accomplished fact. This was the response of many beleaguered Softs in New York. Other Democrats, such as Preston King and Oliver P. Morton, were ready to abandon their old party affiliation. Still others clung desperately to the hope that some middle ground could be found between supporting the repeal of the Missouri Compromise and leaving the party. This hope was especially common in Illinois, where such anti-Nebraska leaders as Lyman Trumbull and John M. Palmer continued to think of themselves as Democrats despite their open opposition to the regular party organization. In New York, the *Evening Post* refused to support any gubernatorial candidate in 1854. Still other responses were possible. Francis P. Blair charted a quixotic course. Affirming his willingness to see the Whigs triumph in the 1854 elections, he focused his attention instead on the 1856 presidential contest. He had already started a movement to elect an anti-Nebraska Democrat, preferably Thomas Hart Benton, on an independent ticket.[49] With the party of Jackson deeply divided, a mantle of despondency descended over its leadership in Washington. "To tell you an unwelcome truth," William L. Marcy wrote an American minister in July, "the Nebraska question has sadly shattered our party in all the free states."[50]

The Kansas-Nebraska Act was one of the most fateful measures ever approved by Congress. It weakened the Democratic party throughout the North, disrupted the sectional balance within the parties, gave additional momentum to the ongoing process of party disintegration, and fundamentally altered the nature of the anti-Democratic opposition. It put the Democracy on the defensive in the free states and for the first time precipitated a significant movement to form a northern sectional party. The Democratic party paid a high price for its continuing factional wrangling and for its election of a weak and incompetent president. Seldom was the irresponsibility of politicians more glaring than in

---

47. Washington *Union*, January 12, 24, March 7, May 24; Welles Diary, June 29, 1855, Welles Papers, LC.

48. Horatio Seymour to William L. Marcy, February 21, 1855, Marcy Papers, LC; Marcy to Horatio Seymour, February 14, Seymour Papers, NYHS; *Cong. Globe*, 33rd Cong., 1st sess., Appendix, 156; A. J. Harlan to Douglas, January 18, 1858, quoted in Mildred C. Stoler, "Influence of the Democratic Element in the Republican Party of Illinois and Indiana, 1854–1860" (unpublished Ph.D. dissertation, Indiana University, 1938), 55; A. Loomis to Horatio Seymour, February 6, 1855, Seymour Papers, NYSL.

49. Francis P. Blair, Sr., to Martin Van Buren, August 24, Van Buren Papers, LC.

50. Marcy to John Y. Mason, quoted in James A. Rawley, *Race & Politics: "Bleeding Kansas" and the Coming of the Civil War* (Philadelphia, 1969), 135.

their reckless agitation of this issue, heedless of long-term national consequences, for personal and factional advantages.

As they witnessed the welling popular outcry, many Whig leaders in the free states hailed the Kansas-Nebraska Act as the issue they needed to reunite their party, revive its strength, and make it dominant nationally. The assessment of one of Thurlow Weed's Washington correspondents was blunt and to the point: "The Nebraska Bill Kills *Pierce* and *Douglas* dead as 'Hell.'" Politically the Nebraska bill was "a source of gratification," a western Whig paper declared, "for it raises up the WHIG PARTY from a season of depression and despondency and gloom to action and vigorous life." From Albany the Whig attorney general informed Seward that the Nebraska bill had reunited the state's Whigs because all factions disapproved of the repeal of the Missouri Compromise. A Silver Grey recognized the new strength that the territorial issue had given the Sewardites. "The Nebraska Swindle has driven National & Sectional Whigs into the Same camp where they must mess together," he lamented. "The Whigs will be united . . . and will swallow any thing, on account of Nebraska."[51] Some Democrats feared that the Whigs' expectations would be realized. "I think a mistake has been made in the Nebraska business," a New York Democrat concluded. "The effect will be to consolidate the Whig party at the north, & divide the democrats." In warning a cabinet member of the strength of anti-Nebraska sentiment in the North, another Democrat reported, "I have not seen for a long time such merry politicians as the Seward men." Several observers expressed the belief that the issue would make Seward president, and his traditional adversary, the New York *Evening Post,* predicted that the New York senator would profit most from the Nebraska issue.[52]

Believing that their party would benefit from the Nebraska controversy, many northern Whigs of diverse factional loyalties banished any thought of scrapping their party for some new organization. They reasoned that since Whig congressmen from free states had unanimously opposed the Kansas-Nebraska Act, Whiggery was the most available and legitimate vehicle to represent anti-Nebraska sentiment. With an infrastructure that had taken years to perfect, the Whig party had already proven its fidelity on the slavery extension issue. Why, then, go to the immense trouble of putting together a new organization? Instead, Free Soilers and anti-Nebraska Democrats should support the Whig nominees as the most effective way to oppose Douglas and the Pierce administration.

Foremost among national Whig leaders who held this view were Thurlow Weed and William H. Seward. Privately, Seward advised northern Whigs to keep aloof from the fusion movement in 1854. When Theodore Parker urged that a national antislavery convention be held preparatory to launching a new party, the New York senator rejected the proposal as inappropriate.[53] In the Albany *Evening Journal,* Weed directly confronted the question of disbanding the party. The function of parties was to deal with practical issues, the pragmatic Whig boss wrote in a May editorial, and the only way to do that was

---

51. N. Darling to Weed, February 12, Weed Papers, UR; Chicago *Journal* quoted in the Chicago *Democratic Press,* May 24; Ogden Hoffman to Seward, March 5, Seward Papers, UR; B. Thompson to Daniel Ullmann, May 16, Ullmann Papers, NYHS.

52. T. M. Parmalee to Caleb Cushing, February 15, Charles W. March to Cushing, March 10, Cushing Papers; David Tomlinson to Seward, September 13, Seward Papers, UR; New York *Evening Post,* February 27, May 23.

53. Theodore Parker to Seward, [ca. June], Seward, *Seward,* v. 2, 232; Seward to Parker, June 23 (Private), Seward Papers, UR; Seward to Weed, June 24, Weed Papers, UR.

to vote for candidates who could win and work for organizations that could carry elections. "So far, we have not found freedom *practically* advanced one step except by the Whig Party." On another occasion Weed, who was under increasing pressure from Horace Greeley and others to abandon the party, affirmed: "Having found the Whig Party of the North, on all occasions, and in every emergency, the most efficient and reliable organization both to resist the aggressions of Slavery and to uphold the cause of Freedom, we concur . . . that it is best, now and ever, 'for the Whig Party to stand by its colors.' "[54]

Both state and national considerations influenced Weed's and Seward's attitude. A number of observers, including some of his close advisers, argued that the Kansas-Nebraska crisis had enhanced the New York senator's presidential prospects. Most acknowledged him as the probable choice of northern Whigs, if not a national Whig convention, in 1856. To hazard these prospects by joining a new party, which would necessarily include many former political adversaries, posed great risk. Much more important in the two men's reasoning, however, was the political situation in New York. If his national aspirations were to be viable, Seward had to remain in public office. With his senate term due to expire, Seward's supporters therefore had to control the next legislature—a matter always central to Weed's thoughts anyway—and the Whig state boss judged correctly that, whatever its long-term prospects, a new party faced inevitable defeat in the fall. Divisions among anti-Nebraska factions were too deep, and there was insufficient time to establish an efficient party organization. Moreover, if Weed and his allies left the Whig party, the Silver Greys would seize control of its organization. Weed was determined that if any group bolted the Whig party in 1854, it would be the Silver Greys, not the Sewardites. As he carefully calculated the political probabilities, he concluded that the best chance to retain control of the state government, reelect Seward, and aid the senator's presidential aspirations lay in preserving the Whig party.[55]

Other New York Whigs shared the outlook that the party should not be abandoned. New York *Times* editor Henry J. Raymond, an intimate ally of Seward and Weed, advised William Pitt Fessenden against discarding the party apparatus in Maine. "Nothing would more certainly ruin the general cause than such a formal disbandonment of the Whig party," the New York journalist insisted. If Democrats would not support Whigs on a good antislavery platform, he continued, then no new combination of parties could be permanently successful. "We never stood half so well in the world as we do today. Why then should we not stand still?"[56] To arguments that a new party was needed to fight the present battle, Raymond replied in exasperation in the *Times* that this policy was "very much like that of disbanding a strong, disciplined, and well organized army, on the eve of an engagement, in the hope of raising a better one by calling for volunteers."[57] A number of Silver Greys were equally reluctant to quit the party. Even while opposing the Weed-inspired Whig ticket in the fall, some of them argued, in the hope of purging their adversaries, that the party should be maintained but reorganized.[58]

---

54. Albany *Evening Journal*, May 26, July 13.

55. William E. Cramer to Cushing, January 26, Cushing Papers; Seward, *Seward*, v. 2, 231; Bailey to Pike, May 30, Pike Papers, UMe; Albert G. Browne to Sumner, February 22, Sumner Papers, HU.

56. Henry J. Raymond to Fessenden, June 14, clipping, Fessenden Family Papers; New York *Times*, May 29.

57. New York *Times*, June 10, July 18 (quotation); Poughkeepsie *Eagle*, June 17, quoted in Sewell, *Ballots for Freedom*, 261–62.

58. Washington Hunt to James Watson Webb, July 15, James Watson Webb Papers, Yale University; Robert A. West to Fish, June 27, circular letter of Francis Granger, October 24, Fish Papers, LC; New York

Such sentiments were by no means confined to New York. Massachusetts Whigs generally opposed abandoning the party. Samuel Bowles of the Springfield *Republican,* who called for a fusion of all groups opposed to the Nebraska bill, was a conspicuous exception. Whig leaders in the state generally believed that the party was in a stronger position than it had been for years: The dreaded new constitution had been rejected, the Coalition had collapsed, and Free Soil leaders were feuding and their party's ranks were in turmoil. There was no good reason to scrap the Whig organization when it seemed on the verge of regaining its invincible dominance in the Commonwealth.[59] Most Whigs in Vermont, another party stronghold, also wanted to preserve the party organization. The party was united on the Nebraska question, one Vermont Whig declared, and members would thus gain nothing on this point by dissolving it. He was confident that Whigs could once again be victorious in the state without sacrificing "other articles of their creed which are dear to them." Among party leaders in Pennsylvania, fusion sentiment was even more feeble.[60]

Inasmuch as the Whigs had long been powerful in these states, that party members were wary of an untried fusion movement should occasion little surprise. But this reluctance also characterized Illinois Whigs, particularly outside the more strongly antislavery northern counties. The Whig party had never been competitive in that state, and at first glance its managers' unwillingness to drop what had always been a losing cause appears curious. Several considerations, however, were at work. The party had done better in the 1852 election, especially in the congressional contests, than ever before, and Whig leaders anticipated that the Nebraska issue would further strengthen the party while weakening Douglas and the Democrats. Led by Abraham Lincoln, party spokesmen in central Illinois, where antislavery radicalism had little support, feared that any combination with the extreme Free Soilers of the northern counties would destroy the party's strength in their section. In addition, some conservatives, noting that after the 1848 election the Free Soilers returned quickly to the Democratic fold, doubted that any fusion party would be permanent. If the Whigs gave up their organization and entered a coalition movement, the Springfield *Illinois State Journal* commented, "they might carry the election in this State—but what would be the future of the whigs?" The party's "permanent welfare" required that it be held together.[61] Downstate Whigs remained unyielding in their resistance to the new-party movement.

Critics rejoined that maintaining the Whig organization was shortsighted and futile because anti-Nebraska Democrats would never join the Whig party. "Keep up the old whig party, & the well-disposed democrats in the cause will not unite," asserted one Massachusetts Free Soiler, adding, "There must be a Northern Power, saying nothing

---

Commercial Advertiser, quoted in Nevins, *Ordeal of the Union*, v. 2, 321. Solomon G. Haven was less certain of the proper course. See his letter to Millard Fillmore, February 11, Fillmore Papers, SUNY.

59. Emory Washburn to Julius Rockwell, [June], Private, Walker-Rockwell Papers, NYHS; Robert C. Winthrop to Rockwell, June 2, Julius Rockwell Papers, Lenox Public Library; George S. Merriam, *The Life and Times of Samuel Bowles* (2 vols.: New York, 1885), v. 1, 127; William G. Bean, "The Transformation of Parties in Massachusetts with Special Reference to the Antecedents of Republicanism, from 1848 to 1860" (unpublished Ph.D. dissertation, Harvard University, 1922), 188–90.

60. B. D. Harris to Justin S. Morrill, May 1, Morrill Papers, LC; Pittsburgh *Gazette*, March 24; William Larimer, Jr. to James Pollock, March 28, in the Pittsburgh *Gazette*, May 3.

61. *Illinois State Journal*, July 27; Richard L. Wilson to Abraham Lincoln, October 20, Abraham Lincoln Papers, LC; David Davis to Julius Rockwell, July 15, David Davis Family Papers, IllSHL.

about Whigs or Dems. or Free-soiler."[62] Taking the lead in urging fusion, the *National Era* sternly criticized the course of Seward and his followers. "For the hundredth time, we repeat, . . . that Independent Democrats and Liberal Democrats have no faith in a *National* Whig party, and will not support a *National* Whig party." Henry Wilson, the Massachusetts Free Soil leader, made the same point in calling on the New York senator to leave the Whig party and assume leadership of the fusion movement.[63]

The national strategy of Seward and his party associates remained ill-defined. That they believed they could carry the 1856 presidential election is indisputable, but the amount of southern support they counted on is uncertain. Fessenden declared that Seward was the only experienced Whig leader who had rid himself "of the idea that nothing can be done without Southern aid," yet in a letter to Edward Everett the New York leader professed encouragement about the course of political developments in the South and spoke of a growing repudiation of extremism below the Mason-Dixon line.[64] In contrast to many northern Whigs, he was temperate in his criticism of southern party members. Gamaliel Bailey claimed that Seward, Weed, and their associates hoped to maintain a national Whig organization with strength in the border states and perhaps Louisiana, where support for the repeal of the Missouri Compromise was less pronounced among Whigs, on a platform of restoring the 1820 prohibition of slavery. As an outspoken critic of the Sewardites, Bailey's remarks must be viewed with caution, but the 1854 New York Whig platform, which did not go beyond condemning the Nebraska Act, specifically avoided any reference to the Compromise of 1850, and by implication at least left the door open for possible future cooperation with southern moderates, suggests that he may have been right.[65]

Seward's optimism and that of other Whigs was based in part on the outcome of the Connecticut state election in April, which provided an early test of the ability of the Whigs to revive their party on the Nebraska issue. None of the candidates for governor received a popular majority, but because the anti-Democratic forces won control of the legislature and subsequently elected the Whig nominee, Whigs hailed the election as a great party victory.[66] Closer inspection indicates that they seriously misinterpreted the results.

Connecticut Whigs encountered several serious problems in the campaign. Attendance at the state convention by fewer than half the delegates was further evidence of the ongoing process of party decay. In addition, temperance men, angered by the Whigs' jettisoning of prohibition in 1853, nominated Charles Chapman, a well-known Whig, as an independent temperance candidate for governor. From Washington, Joshua R. Giddings and other antislavery leaders urged that the opposition coalesce on the slavery issue, but little sentiment for fusion materialized, particularly among Whigs, and therefore the Free

---

62. Richard Henry Dana, Sr. to C. Henry, June 5, Dana Family Papers; Springfield *Republican*, November 15.

63. *National Era*, February 16, May 4, July 20, September 28 (quotation); Henry Wilson to Seward, May 28, Seward Papers, UR.

64. Seward to Weed, June 24, Weed Papers, UR; Seward to Everett, June 19, Everett Papers; Fessenden to Ellen Fessenden, April 9, Fessenden Family Papers; Charles W. March to Cushing, March 10, Cushing Papers.

65. *National Era*, February 16, May 4, November 9; New York *Evening Post*, September 22; Hiram Barney to Gerrit Smith, November 8, Gerrit Smith Papers. In rejecting the call for a new party, the New York *Times*, the most nationally prominent Sewardite journal, predicted that southern Whigs would attend the Whig party's 1856 national convention (June 10).

66. New York *Tribune*, April 4, 5; New York *Times*, April 4; Springfield *Republican*, April 5, 6, 11.

Soilers also nominated a candidate.[67] Whig efforts to run on the Nebraska issue were undermined not only by the unremitting agitation of the liquor question but also by the refusal of the Democratic state convention to endorse the bill. The leading Democratic journal in the state, the Hartford *Times,* continued to speak out against the bill, and none of the Democratic state candidates had reputations as Nebraska men.[68]

The belief that the Nebraska issue would restore Whig strength in the state was not substantiated by the results. Although the Democratic share of the eligible electorate declined, Whig losses were only slightly lower. The Free Soil vote, which had risen so markedly in 1853 when that party ran on the liquor issue, now plummeted with a separate Temperance ticket in the field.[69] The large number of 1853 Free Soil voters who defected to the Temperance candidate in 1854, together with the high carryover from 1853 in the Whig and Democratic votes, suggests strongly that dry Whigs and Democrats who voted for the Free Soil ticket in 1853 supported Chapman in 1854 (Table 3.1). In fact, despite the Nebraska controversy the Free Soil party retained fewer than a third of its 1853 supporters. Undoubtedly, a majority of voters in Connecticut opposed the Nebraska bill— the refusal of any party to endorse it is ample testimony to the fact—but there is little evidence that it produced any large shifts in voting allegiances in the statewide contest.[70] Instead, the defection of party members to the Temperance ticket largely accounted for the decline in the Democratic vote. Very few 1853 Democratic voters supported either the Whig or Free Soil candidate in 1854. The failure of the Whigs to maintain even their previous strength, the precipitous decline of the Free Soil vote, and Democratic cross-overs to the Temperance nominee documented the persisting power of the rum issue, as well as the inability of either the Whigs or the Free Soilers to capitalize on hostility to the Kansas-Nebraska bill. The continuing disintegration of both the Whig party's organization and its electoral base in the face of the northern protest over the Nebraska bill illustrated how severely the party had already been weakened. The plight of the Connecticut Whigs was desperate.

All of this was lost on Seward and his circle. Not every northern Whig leader, however, shared his sunny view of the party's future. Three days after the Nebraska bill passed the House, Benjamin F. Wade of Ohio impetuously renounced his allegiance to the party in a speech in the Senate. "We certainly cannot have any further political connection with the Whigs of the South," he stormed. "I am an *Abolitionist* at heart." Few were as vehement as Wade, but other prominent Whigs also criticized the actions of southern Whigs and pronounced the national party dead. The New York *Tribune* proclaimed that

---

67. Giddings to Joseph R. Hawley, March 13, Moses Pierce to Hawley, March 27, H. Hammond to Hawley, March 30, Hawley Papers; Welles to My Dear Sir, September, 1855 (copy), Welles Papers, ConnHS; James Dixon to Alexander H. Holley, March 8, Holley Family Papers, ConnHS.

68. Noonan, *Nativism in Connecticut*, 180–81; Hartford *Times*, October 19; Frank L. Burr to Welles, March 30, Welles Papers, LC.

69. The vote was Dutton (Whig), 19,465 (31.8 percent); Samuel Ingham (Democrat), 28,538 (46.6 pecent); Chapman (Temperance), 10,672 (17.4 percent); and John T. Hooker (Free Soil), 2,560 (4.2 percent). Turnout was 70.9 percent. The Free Soilers' share of the electorate fell from nine percent in 1853 to 2.5 percent in 1854.

70. The Nebraska issue was undoubtedly of more importance in the legislative contests because the next legislature would elect a successor to Truman Smith in the Senate. A bewildering array of coalitions, in which both the Maine Law and Nebraska issues as well as local political considerations entered, was evident in these contests. Cognizant of the confusing nature of these local arrangements, one Democratic editor predicted that the new legislature would be "a ring-streaked & speckled concern, at best." Frank L. Burr to Welles, March 30, Welles Papers, LC.

the Nebraska bill inaugurated sectional parties and placed the blame squarely on the Whigs of the South.[71] Truman Smith also repudiated all further association with southern Whigs. "Further co-operation with them will be impossible," he announced. "I intend to bid them all an eternal farewell." After he resigned his senatorship in disgust, the Connecticut leader muttered: "The Whig party has been killed off effectually by that miserable Nebraska business. . . . We Whigs of the North are unalterably determined never to have any [even?] the slightest political correspondence or connexion" with southern Whigs who voted for the Nebraska bill. "You may depend upon it," he told a fellow Whig, "the break is final. We could not heal it if we would & would not if we could."[72]

III

As the Nebraska crisis unfolded, politicians came to markedly different conclusions about the political future. Some, such as Douglas and Pierce, believed that the anti-Nebraska protest would prove transitory and have little ultimate impact on the party system. Seward and Weed, on the other hand, anticipated that the Nebraska issue would cause a limited but sufficient shift in party strength to establish the Whigs as the nation's dominant party. Nevertheless, Douglas and Seward shared one fundamental assumption: They agreed that the existing two-party alignment would continue.[73] In contrast, a number of political observers predicted that the Nebraska controversy would destroy the Jacksonian party system. The prominent Massachusetts conservative Edward Everett declared in mid-February that the Nebraska issue would unavoidably break down the existing party alignment and "array the Country upon the one question of Slavery." One of Charles Sumner's correspondents wrote that he was "more & more persuaded that things are tending to merge all other parties into two great parties: a Free states party, & a Slavery party." An Indiana Democrat was certain that the Nebraska bill would wreck the Whig and Democratic parties "and establish upon their ruin a No[r]thren and Southren [*sic*] party." On the eve of the passage of the Nebraska bill in the House, Preston King, who was working night and day to unite the opposition, reported that at last men were caucusing without reference to party. "As yet the demolition of party lines here is confined to the repeal of the compromise—but the conversation and opinion is pretty common and general that past lines of party division will be obliterated with the Missouri line—if this bill passes."[74]

---

71. *Cong. Globe*, 33rd Cong., 1st sess., Appendix, 763–65; New York *Tribune*, June 7; Pike, *First Blows*, 223.

72. *Cong. Globe*, 33rd Cong., 1st sess., Appendix, 177; Truman Smith to Leonard Bacon, February 16, Bacon Family Papers; Smith to John Wilson, January 31, March 6, April 27, May 26 (quotation), August 25, John Wilson Papers.

73. In a new interpretation of the origins of the Kansas-Nebraska bill, Holt has argued recently that Douglas was looking for an issue that would revitalize the two-party system—an "issue that Whigs and Democrats could once again fight about on party lines." Although I think he is right that Douglas and Seward were the two most important free-state leaders who believed that the existing party system would continue, there is little evidence, either from Douglas's own words or from men who were in a position to know the origins of the Kansas-Nebraska bill, to support the contention that this was the motivation for Douglas's action: *Political Crisis*, 144–48. For evidence that others shared the view that the anti-Nebraska protest would be channeled within the existing party divisions, see Samuel Tilden to [?], August 26, Bigelow, ed., *Tilden Letters and Memorials*, v. 1, 113.

74. Everett to W. H. Trescot, February 15, Everett Papers; C. S. Henry to Sumner, April 19, Sumner

Sentiment for the formation of a new northern party dedicated to freedom was understandably strongest among the small Free Soil contingent in Congress. Prior to the bill's passage by the Senate, the *National Era* argued that both major parties were tools of slavery, and that the North had the power, if it would use it, to elect the next president. Yet the *Era* stopped short of calling for a new party, and it offered no cogent explanation of the way northern sentiment should to be expressed.[75] In a similar fashion, the Appeal of the Independent Democrats, for all its searing criticism of the Slave Power, did not recommend explicitly that a new party be formed. As the depth of northern excitement became apparent, however, such Free Soil leaders as Sumner and Giddings openly advocated the organization of a new party combining the opponents of Douglas's measure.[76] After the House approved the repeal of the Missouri Compromise, Bailey forthrightly exhorted northerners "to shake off the trammels of old organizations, forget their party differences, and unite in a Party of Freedom, with a fixed purpose to regain possession of the Federal Government, and subvert the Slave Power." The editor of the *National Era* continued throughout the summer to hammer away at this theme. The earlier issues had passed, he argued, and the old parties had died with them. "New and important issues must be met by new organizations." When mutual suspicions and rivalries continued to divide the opposition, he declared (with affected innocence) that it was unimportant who led the movement as long as a union on right principles was achieved.[77]

A number of the leaders of the fight against the Nebraska bill joined in urging the formation of a northern fusion party. Bailey reported that Preston King was "anxious for a general break-up of old organizations" and was advocating a Benton-Seward ticket for 1856. Once the Kansas-Nebraska Act had been approved, James Simonton, the widely respected Washington correspondent of the New York *Times,* counseled that a party of freedom be organized without delay. Such sentiment was stronger in the House, where such Whigs as Israel and Elihu Washburn and John Z. Goodrich and such Democrats as Reuben Fenton and Galusha Grow espoused abandoning the old organizations. In the Senate, the presence of fewer anti-Nebraska men and more especially Seward's unrelenting hostility weakened the movement for a new party, although Wade and Smith were outspoken in its support.[78]

Surprisingly, one prominent antislavery leader who was not wholeheartedly committed to the new party movement was Salmon P. Chase. The anti-Nebraska outcry stoked the Ohioan's ambition, yet he wavered over whether Independent Democrats should

Papers, HU; William R. Nofsinger to John G. Davis, April 14, John G. Davis Papers, IndHS; Preston King to Azariah C. Flagg, May 20, Azariah C. Flagg Papers, Columbia University.

75. *National Era*, February 16; *Daily National Era*, March 24, 28. Prior to approval of the repeal of the Missouri Compromise, Bailey waffled on whether northern Whigs, Democrats, and Free Soilers should form a new party or just cooperate temporarily. *Daily National Era*, April 6, 10.

76. Sumner to John Bigelow, June 13, John Bigelow, *Retrospections of an Active Life* (5 vols.: New York, 1910–1913), v. 1, 135; Giddings to Hawley, March 13, Hawley Papers. Most Free Soilers were ready to abandon their party for a new fusion movement. Blue, *Free Soilers*, 285; Sewell, *Ballots for Freedom*, 261. Henry Wilson went to Washington in May to lobby against the Nebraska bill and for a new party. Elias Nason, *The Life and Public Services of Henry Wilson* (Boston, 1876), 117.

77. *National Era*, May 25, June 1 (quotation), 22, July 20 (quotation); Bailey to Pike, May 30, Pike Papers, UMe.

78. Bailey to Pike, May 30, Pike Papers, UMe.; New York *Times*, May 27; James T. DuBois and Gertrude S. Mathews, *Galusha A. Grow, Father of the Homestead Law* (New York, 1917), 146. Elihu added an *e* to his last name when he went west, whereas his brothers Israel and Cadwallader retained the traditional family spelling of *Washburn*.

surrender their organization. He insisted that any new party must incorporate Democratic principles and even adopt the name, which he believed would increase its popularity. Wary of any organization in which his Whig adversaries would be a large majority, Chase pursued a complex and contradictory course in 1854. He simultaneously encouraged Free Soilers to maintain their party organization, Whigs to unite in a new liberal party, and anti-Nebraska Democrats to aid in the fight to ensure that any fusion party would have a sound Democratic foundation. These objectives were irreconcilable, and the Ohio senator seemed to be preparing for several contingencies. If a new party took shape, he was ready to force himself to the front of its ranks, yet he was not irrevocably committed to a specific plan of action, and even after the Nebraska bill passed he remained ambivalent about discarding the old Free Soil organization.[79]

The movement for a new party commenced in Washington. The first formal step in this direction occurred in May at a meeting of a group of anti-Nebraska representatives, the origins, membership, and details of which are largely lost to history. It was apparently held shortly after the House passed the Nebraska bill, in the rooms of Representatives Thomas D. Eliot and Edward Dickinson of Massachusetts. About thirty members of the House, including anti-Nebraska Whigs, Democrats, and Free Soilers, came together to consult about their future political course. Israel Washburn, the perennially optimistic leader of the Washburn clan in Congress who was in close consultation with Gamaliel Bailey, took the leading role in the meeting and called for a political union of all anti-Nebraska men. He suggested that the new party take the name *Republican* and that its platform focus on opposition to the extension of slavery. Washburn's call for a fusion party was endorsed by virtually all in attendance.[80] Despite the importance of some of those present, nothing came of this meeting directly, because its participants neither issued an address to their constituents nor established a central committee in Washington to direct a fusion movement.

Subsequently a second, apparently larger group of anti-Nebraska congressmen convened to adopt an address. The idea for such a pronouncement apparently originated with Bailey, who told James Shepherd Pike that as soon as the Nebraska bill passed, a protest should be published "invoking the People . . . to rise in their might, and redress the insult & injury thus inflicted on them." He thought that such a document would "lay the foundation of a real Party of Freedom." A meeting of northern Whig congressmen also resolved to issue a declaration, and Benton lent his prestige to the proposal. When anti-Nebraska Democrats agreed to participate, the task of writing it fell to the bipartisan group that had served as an opposition steering committee during the Nebraska contest. Evidently, two drafts were circulated, one by Lewis D. Campbell of Ohio that was decidedly antislavery in its sentiments and a more moderate version by Joseph Chandler,

---

79. For Chase's conflicting views, see Chase to Codding, April 15, 22, Codding Papers; Chase to Edward L. Pierce, September 13, 20, Edward L. Pierce Papers, HU; Chase to James W. Grimes, April 29, Chase to N. S. Townsend, February 10, March 9, Chase Papers, HSPa; Chase to John Greiner, May 10, Private & Confidential, L. Belle Hamlin, ed., "Selections from the Follett Papers," Ohio Historical and Philosophical Society *Quarterly Publications*, v. 13 (April–June, 1918), 56. Sewell is one of the few historians to recognize Chase's ambivalence toward the fusion movement: *Ballots for Freedom*, 261.

80. Israel Washburn, Jr., "Gamaliel Bailey," 300; Henry Wilson, *History of the Rise and Fall of the Slave Power in America* (3 vols.: Boston, 1872–1877), v. 2, 410–11; John Wentworth, *Congressional Reminiscences* (Chicago, 1882), 52. Some historians assert that this meeting was held on May 9, but Washburn implies that it met on May 23. Washburn's call for a new party was fully in accord with Bailey's views, but whether the antislavery editor attended this meeting is not indicated.

a conservative Whig from Philadelphia, neither of them being entirely satisfactory.[81] Finally, a group representing all shades of opinion in opposition to the repeal of the Missouri Compromise met at the National Hotel to consider the document. Senator Solomon Foot of Vermont, a Whig, acted as chairman while Democratic congressmen Reuben Fenton and Daniel Mace served as secretaries. A committee of seven Democrats and six Whigs reported an address, which after further discussion and amendment the meeting adopted unanimously. On June 22 the address appeared in the *National Intelligencer* and other papers. Expressed, as Seward noted, "with the utmost modera-tion" in order to win wide support among anti-Nebraska men, it condemned the Nebraska bill but stopped short of concluding, as Horace Greeley for one had wanted, with a ringing call for a new party.[82]

Bailey, too, was disappointed. "It is unexceptionable, but hath not the trumpet tone. It will not come up to our mark," he confessed to Pike. Chase, who had not been consulted on its wording, was also dissatisfied but conceded that "it goes a step or two in the right direction." Still, as one of Sumner's correspondents warned beforehand, unless "some *simple, well defined form* of action" were presented, "our friends all over the country will use up months, & months in deciding *in what way* to proceed." Even worse than the "rather tame" tone, a Maine Whig told Israel Washburn, was the failure to print the names of the individual members who approved it. This omission made the address "comparatively powerless . . . it rather looks like timidity & hesitation & unwillingness to appear on the record. It don't look like the declaration of *independence*." In this case, he concluded correctly, names were "*every* thing."[83]

The official report gave no hint of any division, and some versions of the address included the statement that it was "indorsed by all the Anti-Nebraska members of Congress." Evidently all northern Whigs and most if not all anti-Nebraska Democrats subscribed to it. In view of its moderation and its failure to recommend specific action, such widespread concurrence was far from remarkable. This unity, however, was only a surface manifestation. Suspicions between anti-Nebraska Democrats and northern Whigs, which had been reinforced by disagreements over tactics during the Nebraska struggle, persisted.[84] The emphasis in the address on unanimity rather than on recommending a definite course of action was a further setback to the new-party movement.

The formation of the Union Emigration Society represented a different attempt to give direction from Washington to the anti-Nebraska movement. Truman Smith was its moving spirit. The society's goals were outlined in a lithographed letter circulated by Whig congressman John Z. Goodrich of Massachusetts. While urging the necessity of concerted action among those who opposed the designs of the Slave Power, the letter

81. Bailey to Pike, May 21, June 6, Pike Papers, UMe; *Daily National Era*, May 22; Pittsburgh *Post*, May 31, June 3; Washington correspondence, Philadelphia *North American*, May 26; *Ashtabula Sentinel*, July 6; Pittsburgh *Gazette*, May 30, June 26, 27.

82. Seward to Horace Greeley, June 22, Greeley Papers, NYPL; Seward to Frances A. Seward, June 22, Seward, *Seward*, v. 2, 234; Seward to Weed, June 24, Weed Papers, UR; Washington correspondence, New York *Courier and Enquirer*, quoted in *National Intelligencer*, June 26; DuBois and Mathews, *Grow*, 146.

83. Bailey to Pike, June 6, Pike Papers, UMe; Chase to John Jay, June 24, Jay Family Papers, Columbia University; J. R. Basham to Sumner, May 28, Sumner Papers, HU; Edward Kent to Washburn, June, 25, Private, Israel Washburn, Jr., Papers, Norlands.

84. Pittsburgh *Gazette*, June 24, 26; Springfield *Republican*, June 26; Washington correspondence, Philadelphia *North American*, June 24; *Daily National Era*, June 24. For evidence of continuing animosity between anti-Nebraska Whigs and Democrats, see Bailey to Pike, May 30, Pike Papers, UMe.

added the significant qualification that "the interests of Freedom may not infrequently be best promoted by means of existing local and political organizations. When this is the case, such organizations should be preserved and used for this purpose." Privately, Goodrich informed Weed that the primary purpose of the society was to organize the North for political action. The Massachusetts congressman also promoted the society at a meeting of political leaders in Boston in July called to explore the possibility of forming a fusion party in his state. Whatever the intention of its founders, the Union Emigration Society never provided national political leadership and was quickly forgotten.[85]

Because of the failure of Washburn's meeting, the mild tone of the anti-Nebraska address, and the ambiguous course recommended by the Union Emigration Society, the fusion movement received no effective direction from Congress. The absence of central control, the opposition of influential Whigs, the continuing salience of the temperance issue in many states, as well as differences over the platform of the proposed new organization all slowed the drive to launch a new party. These difficulties gave added force to Weed's admonition that "the business of reconstructing Parties and Platforms is a difficult and delicate one."[86]

Even those who called for a new party displayed no consensus on what its platform should include beyond the restoration of the Missouri Compromise. Among these sources of disagreement, perhaps the most fundamental was whether to establish a frankly sectional antislavery party, or one that would oppose the repeal of the Missouri Compromise and yet somehow attract support in the South. Advanced antislavery men wanted a platform that demanded the exclusion of slavery from all the territories, opposed the admission of any new slave states, and advocated the repeal of the fugitive slave law. George W. Julian, for example, excoriated the Indiana fusion convention's call for the restoration of the Missouri Compromise as a "halting, half-way, equivocal" issue.[87] On the other hand, Thomas Ewing, a conservative Ohio Whig who recoiled from the idea of a completely sectional party, advised that "we should frame our opposition so that wise and conservative southern men could unite with us in it." Ewing's concern was shared by Francis P. Blair, who, although a southerner and a slaveholder, opposed the Nebraska bill. To his old confidant Martin Van Buren, then traveling in Europe, Blair complained that "the anti-slave force in the north seems incapable of concert on any principle which will make it possible for any Southern man to get a vote in the South." He singled out for criticism the demand that no more slave states be admitted. On this point Blair differed with his old allies William Cullen Bryant and John Bigelow at the New York *Evening Post,* who, in an editorial entitled "Freedom's Battle—the Only Way to Win It," rejected as unattainable the more restricted demand of restoring the Missouri Compromise and proposed instead that the North unite on a platform opposing the admission of any new slave states.[88]

---

85. John Z. Goodrich to Weed, July 14, Weed Papers, UR; Springfield *Republican*, July 12; Adams Diary, July 7, Adams Family Papers; Chase to John Jay, June 24, Jay Family Papers. A copy of Goodrich's circular letter, dated June 29, is in the Webb Papers. Directors of the society included John Z. Goodrich (president), Francis P. Blair (vice-president), Truman Smith, Gamaliel Bailey, Lewis D. Campbell, Daniel Mace, and Preston King, all of whom were active in the new-party movement.

86. Albany *Evening Journal*, June 7.

87. [Julian], "A Voice from Indiana," *National Era*, October 5 (quotation); Julian, *Political Recollections*, 138; Adams to Sumner, March 17, Adams Family Papers; *National Era*, November 16.

88. Ewing to Follett, May 2, Hamlin, ed., "Follett Papers," 54–55; Francis P. Blair, Sr. to Martin Van Buren, August 24, Van Buren Papers, LC; New York *Evening Post*, August 8.

IV

The sudden expansion of the anti-Catholic, anti-foreign American party jolted the plans of all northern political factions in the summer of 1854. Dubbed the Know Nothings because members were instructed if questioned to say that they knew nothing about it, this secret organization, whose official name was the Order of the Star Spangled Banner, had been formed in New York City in 1850 by a small group of nativist zealots. It slumbered in insignificance until 1853, when the party expanded under new leadership, increasing its membership in New York City as well as upstate and in other states. By the end of the year, there were chapters in New Jersey, Vermont, Connecticut, Massachusetts, Pennsylvania, and Ohio.[89] The order's growth quickened the following year under the direction of James W. Barker, a conservative New York City merchant, who became president of the reorganized New York Grand Council in May 1854 and of the newly formed national council the following month. Barker had a flair for organization, undeniable political ability, and a vision of the order as a national political force. He launched a vigorous expansion program throughout the country, and the society grew at an astounding rate. Because membership in the order was secret, claims of its size must be viewed with caution, but by the end of 1854 state councils had been established in every northern state, and the party's national secretary reported privately that there were 10,000 local lodges with an aggregate membership of a million voters.[90]

Membership was limited to adult native-born males who were unconnected with Catholicism, either personally or by family ties. Like many secret organizations, the order utilized passwords, codes, and elaborate rituals, but its goals were strictly political. Members were divided into three categories, or degrees, with only third-degree members eligible to hold public office. The order had a tight, hierarchical organization. At the base of this structure were the local lodges or councils. The size of these councils varied considerably; those in large cities often had several hundred members while those in rural areas sometimes contained as few as nine. All the lodges in a state were organized into a grand council, to which they elected delegates. A national council in turn transacted the national business of the society.

Know Nothing leaders defended this hierarchical structure as responsive to the wishes of the rank-and-file; they portrayed it as a type of primary system that gave members a direct say in the nomination of candidates. In some states, such as Pennsylvania, even statewide nominations were made initially by a direct vote of the members. In general, however, except for local nominations, delegate conventions selected candidates. At these conventions each council, regardless of its size, had equal representation, and this rule coupled with the considerable discretionary power granted to state presidents enabled a small group of leaders to control the order. Nevertheless, it is probably true that

---

89. For the origins of the Know Nothing order, see Charles Deshler to R. M. Guilford, January 20, 1855 (copy), Charles Deshler Papers, Rutgers University; New York *Tribune*, May 29, 1855; New York *Herald*, December 20; Thomas R. Whitney, *A Defence of the American Policy* (New York, 1856), 280–85; and Louis Dow Scisco, *Political Nativism in New York State* (New York, 1901), 65–108.

90. For membership figures, see Deshler to James A. Henry, January 26, 1855 (copy), Deshler Papers; and Whitney, *Defence of American Policy*, 284–85. Deshler was the secretary of the national council. For James W. Barker's claims concerning the society's growth under his leadership, see the New York *Times*, March 8, 1855, and a reply by "Vindex," March 16, 1855.

individuals had a greater voice in the affairs of the order, particularly at the local level, than they did in the conduct of a regular political party.[91]

A number of factors accounted for the sudden growth of the Know Nothings. The novelty of the movement, its rituals, and a love of mystery attracted the curious. Ambitious politicians and disappointed office seekers joined the order as a means of fostering their political careers. In many eastern states, Silver Greys, despairing of ever gaining control of the Whig party from their rivals, saw the society as a conservative Unionist alternative to the existing parties. Job competition from immigrants and other economic grievances upset native-born workers. But these considerations, while helping to increase the order's strength, were subordinate to the major causes of its growth in the North: religious bigotry, a growing fear that Catholics and immigrants threatened republicanism, and a pervasive disgust with politicians and existing parties. The Know Nothings' appeal combined bigotry with a sincere desire for reform.[92]

In evaluating the anxiety, even hysteria, manifested by Americans in this period, the magnitude of immigration after 1845 must be kept in mind. Relative to the nation's total population, this influx was the largest in American history; in the decade 1845–1854, 2,939,000 newcomers arrived, a number that represented 14.5 percent of the population in 1845.[93] In addition, many of these immigrants were Catholics, and for the first time in the country's history American Protestants had to deal with a sizable Catholic population. The deeply rooted, intensely felt antipathy between Protestants and Catholics was an important cause of the sudden upsurge in nativist feeling.

Know Nothings had an ambivalent attitude toward Protestant immigrants, many of whom were imbued with hatred of Catholics. Some members were willing to ally politically with Protestant foreigners, while the more extreme nativists wished to proscribe all immigrants. At first, although the order refused admission to all foreign-born, it cooperated politically with Protestant immigrant groups. Following the party's initial success, its leaders divided over this matter, with a minority urging that anti-immigrant sentiment be dropped completely in favor of anti-Catholicism. Nevertheless, from the party's founding its major antagonism was to Catholics, and its supporters despised no group so thoroughly as Irish Catholics.[94]

Several developments in the early 1850s gave a powerful stimulus to the sudden outbreak in anti-foreign and particularly anti-Catholic feeling. Two important events—the Whigs' blatant appeal to the Catholic and immigrant vote in the 1852 presidential campaign, and the concerted Catholic attack on the public school system in 1853—have already been discussed. Two other occurrences were also significant in this regard:

---

91. Letter signed "Fideliter," New York *Times*, May 22, 1855; Scisco, *Political Nativism in New York*, 101–7. The machinery of the Know Nothings was in constant evolution after 1854 and increasingly approximated that of a regular party organization.

92. See especially the perceptive discussion in the New York *Times*, December 6. Also see the New York *Evening Post*, November 15; New York *Herald*, June 27, 1856; Hartford *Courant* quoted in the Hartford *Times*, November 6, 1855. The best analysis of the Know Nothings' appeal is in Holt, *Political Crisis*, 159–70, to which I am heavily indebted.

93. Potter, *Impending Crisis*, 241.

94. Letter from "WCR," Troy *Daily Times*, December 13; New York *Tribune*, August 26; Chicago *Literary Budget*, January 20, 1855, quoted in Thomas M. Keefe, "Chicago's Flirtation with Political Nativism, 1854–1856," *Records of the American Catholic Historical Society*, v. 82 (September, 1971), 137. For anti-Catholic sentiment among Germans, see the letter signed "Horwitz," New York *Times*, June 20; Henry Roedter to G. A. Neumann, October 18, Henry Roedter Papers, University of Illinois.

Pierce's appointment of James Campbell, a Catholic, as postmaster general; and the visit from June 1853 to February 1854 of Archbishop Gaetano Bedini as a personal emissary of the Pope.

Whereas Bedini's official mission was to adjudicate a local dispute over control of church property, hysterical nativists, joined by European refugees from the abortive 1848 revolutions, charged that the nuncio's visit represented the vanguard of a papal invasion to subvert American liberty.[95] Unnerved, the United States attorney in Pittsburgh reported that Catholics were boasting that "the visit of the Nuncio Bedini . . . is intended to form amongst them an organization so perfect that they will act as a unit in all coming operations. In short, the fraternity of Jesuits, is established and is intended . . . to bring the whole Catholic Body . . . into one scale in all our future elections." Once he disposed of his church business, the archbishop embarked on a good will tour of the country that at its conclusion one Catholic bishop accurately termed "a blunder in every point of view."[96] It hardened the popular image of the church as an enemy of republicanism; it stimulated anxieties about the concentration of church property in the hands of the Catholic clergy and led to laws designed to counteract this situation; and it provoked hostile and sometimes violent demonstrations. Mobs threatened the nuncio in Boston, Pittsburgh, and Cincinnati, while feeling ran so high in New York City that he had to go into hiding and be smuggled aboard a ship for his return voyage. Far from creating the good will Archbishop John Hughes naively foresaw, Bedini's visit left a legacy of virulent anti-Catholicism.[97]

Because of its symbolic importance, nativists gave particular emphasis to Pierce's appointment of James Campbell, a Catholic leader from Philadelphia, as postmaster general. When Campbell lost his bid in 1851 to be elected to the state supreme court and was the only Democratic candidate to be defeated, supporters attributed the outcome to nativist bigotry. Seeking to placate Campbell's partisans, Governor William Bigler subsequently appointed him attorney general, and Pierce then tapped him, at James Buchanan's urging, for the cabinet. Nativists, including many Democrats, were outraged. These appointments seemed to ignore the expressed popular will, and critics charged that Campbell's sole credential was his Catholicism. One Philadelphia Democrat denied that the postmaster possessed either the talent or the experience for his position, and even a Catholic leader ridiculed him (unfairly) as "a legal *imbecile and ignoramus.*"[98] In travelling about the state, Francis Grund, the German-born journalist, was impressed by the great discontent he found among Pennsylvania Germans over Campbell's elevation. An angry Philadelphia Democrat warned Bigler that if the policy of rewarding Catholics continued, "the Party . . . as large, as it is . . . *will cave in.* This

---

95. Bedini's visit is covered in Peter Guilday, "Gaetano Bedini," United States Catholic Historical Society, *Historical Records and Studies*, v. 23 (1933), 87–170; Reverend James F. Connelly, *The Visit of Archbishop Gaetano Bedini to the United States of America (June 1853–February 1854)* (Rome, 1960).

96. Charles Shaler to Marcy, January 7, Marcy Papers, LC; Peter Kenrick to John Purcell, February 9, Archdiocese of Cincinnati Records, University of Notre Dame.

97. For specific assertions linking Bedini's visit to the rise of Know Nothingism, see Henry Slicer to Buchanan, June 10, Buchanan Papers, HSPa; New York *Times*, December 6; Marcellus Ells to Fish, February 14, Fish Papers, LC.

98. Henry W. Phillips to Bigler, June 11, John Campbell to Bigler, June 26 (quotation), Bigler Papers. For Campbell's career, see John F. Coleman, "The Public Career of James Campbell," *Pennsylvania History*, v. 29 (January, 1962), 24–39.

Irish influence must & will be put down.''[99] Indignation over Campbell's new prominence, though most vociferous in Pennsylvania, was by no means confined to that state.[100]

Part of the Know Nothings' hostility to Catholics stemmed from unvarnished bigotry. Both friends and foes of the order concurred in the assessment of a leading Know Nothing that "the Protestant feeling is our great element of strength, as soon as you go out of the cities." A Connecticut Free Soiler conceded the honest bigotry of rank-and-file Know Nothings "& hence their holy horror & unusual zeal against the Roman Catholics." "At the bottom of all this is a deep seated religious question—prejudice if you please, which nothing can withstand," insisted a Philadelphia Democrat. The New York *Times,* in discussing the growth of the secret society, spoke of "the old ineradicable Saxon bigotry, which periodically likes a crusade against the Pope," while in the same vein a Massachusetts Republican wrote after a Know Nothing victory, "The feeling against the subtle working of Cathol[ic]ism & Jesuitism is as old as the days of Cromwell & pervades the whole mass of people."[101] As representatives of Protestant feeling, clergymen, particularly Methodists and Baptists, were especially conspicuous in the order and constituted a much larger proportion of its nominees than was the case with other parties. Indeed, as Everett noted, ministers represented the one professional group that joined the secret party in large numbers.[102]

Anti-immigrant sentiment, stimulated by clashes between native-born Americans and foreigners over a number of social issues, also fueled the Know Nothings' growth. Differing conceptions of Sabbath decorum on the part of immigrants, their use of liquor, and their disproportionate contribution to rowdyism, crime, and pauperism all added to the Know Nothings' appeal. Under the impact of recurring waves of new immigrants, traditional American social values appeared to be eroding. Nativists singled out for particular condemnation the failure of these immigrants to assimilate—a situation the Catholic hierarchy consciously promoted. "It is the prevailing and besetting sin of Irishmen," the nativist Chicago *Tribune* railed, "that when they come to America, they will not become *Americans,* but persist in remaining *Irishmen,* with all the crotchets and absurdities which their national education has given them." The New York *Times* maintained that "bigotry and hostility to foreigners *as such* have had much to do" with the rise of the Know Nothings. These feelings "have mingled with its tide and given strength to its swell and its sweep."[103]

---

99. Francis Grund to Edmund Burke, August 17, 1853, Edmund Burke Papers, LC; Peter Mager to Bigler, June 17, 1853, Bigler Papers; Harrisburg *Telegraph*, July 12. For examples of anti-Catholic sentiment among Democrats, see Lynde Eliot to Bigler, September 20, 1852 (Private & Confidential), G. G. Westcott to Bigler, June, Bigler Papers.

100. Sidney D. Maxwell Diary, ca. September 24, CinHS; Marcellus Ells to Fish, February 14, Fish Papers, LC. For evidence that Campbell's appointment greatly aided the Know Nothing cause, see James Burnside to Bigler, June 12, W. L. Rogers to Bigler, August 21, Bigler Papers; Alexander K. McClure, *Old Time Notes of Pennsylvania* (2 vols.: Philadelphia, 1905), v. 1, 205.

101. Kenneth Rayner to Ullmann, February 17, 1855, Ullmann Papers, NYHS; Edward Prentiss to Francis Gillette, January 5, 1855 (copy), Hawley Papers; E. A. Penniman to Bigler, June 8, Bigler Papers; New York *Times*, December 6; Edward Winston to Adams, January 25, 1855, Adams Family Papers.

102. Joseph Wright to Matthew Simpson, October 23, Matthew Simpson Papers, LC; Everett to Fillmore, December 16 (copy), Everett Papers. For the social bases of Know Nothingism, see Gienapp, "Origins of the Republican Party," 338–39, 348–51; Holt, *Forging a Majority*, 149–53; George Haynes, "A Chapter from the Local History of Knownothingism," *New England Magazine*, v. 15 (September, 1896), 82–96.

103. Chicago *Tribune*, February 2; New York *Times*, December 6; Thurlow Weed Barnes, *Memoir of*

Despite these very real social tensions, nativists' primary objection to both Catholics and immigrants was their political power. The Know Nothings advocated reform of the naturalization laws by lengthening the residency requirement (a number of party spokesmen urged that it be set at twenty-one years). Because of the prevailing liberal naturalization laws, nativists feared that unassimilated foreign-born voters—men professing values different from and even hostile to traditional American values—would soon rule the country. "The simple fact that foreigners arrive upon our shores and walk at once to the ballot box, should decide every man in the land to put an end to the outrage," asserted a Chicago nativist paper. Know Nothings denounced immigrants' political clannishness, their support for demagogues, their bloc voting, and their flouting of the legal suffrage requirements. They attacked priests' alleged control of the Catholic vote, and they readily blamed foreign-born voters for the growing corruption of American politics. While acknowledging that other influences were at work, the New York *Times* perceptively attributed the rise of the Know Nothings "to the conviction that the liberty we grant to aliens of becoming American citizens has been grossly abused," and that "the Roman Catholic vote has been held in a compact, disciplined mass, under the immediate and supreme control" of the church hierarchy.[104]

Appealing to widespread fears among the electorate, Know Nothing spokesmen argued that there was a papal plot to destroy republicanism in America. Just as some antislavery men saw the Slave Power as a threat to the survival of the Republic, Know Nothings pointed to the Catholic church. In 1854 the idea of an internal threat to republicanism was more pervasive in nativist than in antislavery rhetoric, in part because fear of Catholicism had such deep roots in the American tradition, in part because the church was a foreign institution, and in part because this analysis offered a trenchant explanation of the reason national, state, and local government was so unresponsive to the popular will.[105] The object of the American order, one member succinctly declared, was "*to preserve the Republic.*" A sincere and thoughtful Ohio Know Nothing, who was uneasy about religious proscription, insisted nevertheless that it was "equally & more dangerous to permit our government to fall into the hands of romanists whose religion stands paramount to all other considerations and who make government and every thing else subserve the interests of the church." Denouncing officeholding by Catholics, he concluded: "It is this state of things in face of the fact the doctrine of the Catholic church is in direct opposition to principles of republicanism that has aroused the American people to a sense of danger."[106]

Undoubtedly, political adventurers who joined the order merely exploited such fears for

---

Thurlow Weed (2 vols.: Boston, 1884), v. 2, 224; Samuel S. Busey, *Immigration: Its Evils and Consequences* (New York, 1969 reprint; originally published in 1856), 108, 117, 121. Despite its opposition to Know Nothingism, the New York *Tribune*, August 26, conceded the validity of many of the complaints against immigrants, especially the Irish.

104. *American Crusader*, [February, 1855], quoted in Sister Evangeline Thomas, *Nativism in the Old Northwest, 1850–1860* (Washington, 1936), 141; New York *Times*, December 6; letter signed "An American Citizen," Pittsburgh *Gazette*, July 7; Cincinnati *Gazette*, August 21, 31; George W. Morton to Fish, February 27, Fish Papers, LC.

105. See Holt, *Political Crisis*, 162–63, for an excellent discussion of Know Nothingism and fears for republicanism.

106. Letter signed "***," New York *Tribune*, August 12; Sidney D. Maxwell Diary, ca. September 24. Whitney asserted that the Know Nothing movement had "as its cardinal object, the maintenance of the institutions of American Republicanism." *Defence of American Policy*, 299.

their own purposes, but a number of leaders, and a much larger proportion of the rank-and-file, were genuinely alarmed. Former New York governor Washington Hunt, for example, reported that one usually level-headed associate who joined the oath-bound fraternity was "almost delirious" and "beyond the reach of argument" concerning the Catholic threat to liberty.[107] Fears for the safety of the Republic and for America's Protestant heritage gripped many rural as well as urban Americans, and grossly exaggerated stories of Catholic power in the cities inflamed these fears and conjured up an alien threat. Citing the history of Catholicism in countries where it was dominant, one rural correspondent attacked the notion that it was not a danger in America. "When we see our magnificent school system tottering from the influence of Romish power, demagogues and politicians seeking the Roman vote, and obtaining it—struck off to the highest bidder—what are we to believe?" "In my judgment," a Vermont resident solemnly insisted, "our liberties are in greater danger from the political influence of catholicism than from any other cause whatever."[108]

In their attacks on the Catholic church, Know Nothing leaders and newspapers sought to distinguish between Catholicism as a religion and as a political power. Denying that the order interfered with Catholics' religious freedom, the Albany *Express,* a leading Know Nothing journal, asserted that it objected instead "to the political Roman power, and all the alien and anti-republican influence that cluster around it." The American movement opposed only "political Romanism," a New York council declared in 1855. "With the principles and doctrines of the faith we have no concern." If there had been no "banding together" of Catholics "under the lead of priests and bishops" to gain political favors, the Chicago *Tribune* proclaimed, there would have been no Know Nothing movement even had immigration been double what it was. "It is not the foreign element of which the . . . Americans complain. It is the papist portion of that element, consolidated, organized, and drilled under skilful [*sic*] leaders for purely political purposes." Dissatisfied with the privileges of other sects, the Catholic church had always striven for power, the *Tribune* contended. The church "tried to overturn the system of schools and education to which the liberties of the country are due, and has so artfully played its game that to all political intents and purposes it is now the established religion of the nation."[109]

Closely linked to resentment of immigrant bloc voting and officeholding was a growing hostility to politicians who courted this vote. From Philadelphia one of Senator John Clayton's correspondents wrote that

> the native citizens of the Northern Middle & Western States are so completely disgusted with the conduct of our leading politicians in bidding for the foreign vote and also in filling so many of our offices with foreigners, that they are determined to make

---

107. Washington Hunt to Fish, March 4, Fish Papers, LC; Edward Prentiss to Francis Gillette, January 5, 1855 (copy), Hawley Papers.

108. Letter signed "C. R.," *National Era,* November 2; George P. Marsh to Erastus Fairbanks, April 19, 1855, *Private,* Erastus Fairbanks Papers, Vermont Historical Society.

109. Albany *Express* quoted in the Buffalo *Commercial Advertiser,* November 6; *Principles and Objects of the American Party,* quoted in Thomas Curran, "Know Nothings of New York State" (unpublished Ph.D. dissertation, Columbia University, 1963), 225; Chicago *Tribune,* February 4, 1856, June 29, 1855; *Chenango American,* October 25, 1855; Harrisburg *Morning Herald,* August 26.

a strong effort to place the government of the country in the hands of those to whom it rightfully belongs.[110]

Know Nothings attributed the corruption of American politics and the unresponsiveness of the parties to selfish wire-pullers who cared nothing about the public good. A Know Nothing paper, in explaining the rise of the party, declared that the people "saw parties without any apparent difference contending for power, for *the sake of power.* They saw politics made a profession, and public plunder an employment. . . . They beheld our public works the plaything of a rotten dynasty, enriching gamblers, and purchasing power at our expense." The New York *Times* stressed that the Know Nothings arose at a time when the old parties had lost the confidence of the public: "Their machinery of intrigue, their shuffling evasions, the dodges, the chicanery and the deception of their leaders have excited universal disgust, and have created a general readiness in the public mind for any new organization that shall promise to shun their vices."[111]

Know Nothing leaders singled out William H. Seward and Thurlow Weed for special censure. "In this state Know-Nothingism is notoriously a conspiracy to overthrow 'Seward, Weed and Greeley,' and particularly to defeat Gov. Seward's re-election to the Senate," Horace Greeley complained with good reason. Wanting to end Weed's and Seward's power, Silver Greys greeted this new movement as a "god send," the means by which, one predicted, "we shall Sweep Sewardism & Political Catholicism off the face of the Earth." Also evident was the continuing resentment of Scott's fawning over immigrants during his 1852 campaign tour, a strategy popularly identified with Seward. An editor sympathetic to the Know Nothing movement thus announced that one of its purposes was "to teach American Demagogues that the time has come for them to cease their everlasting and stereotype prattle of 'the rich Irish brogue and sweet German accent.' "[112]

In analyzing the emergence of Know Nothingism, historians have noted the role of ethnocultural conflict and a growing distrust of parties and politicians as unresponsive to the popular will. Less attention has been given the connection between the Know Nothing movement and the temperance crusade. In part, this neglect stems from the Know Nothings' incomplete unity on the liquor question. Especially in cities, the American party gained the support of many native-born workers who liked to drink, and for this reason it sometimes downplayed the issue. Nevertheless, in general, members of the secret order, especially in rural areas, favored prohibition. This linkage grew naturally out of the Know Nothings' strident appeal to Protestant values and to the religious element of the population, and out of the anti-liquor movement's hostility to immigrants and Catholics. For both Know Nothings and temperance crusaders, besotted Irish Catholics functioned as their primary negative reference group. Neal Dow neatly symbolized the connection between the two movements. As a member of the nativist

110. D. Rodney King to John M. Clayton, [July–August], Private, Clayton Papers, LC; Ross Wilkins to John McLean, January 11, 1855, McLean Papers, LC.

111. *Livingston Republican*, October 11, 1855; New York *Times*, December 6; Buffalo *Republic*, November 16; New York *Evening Post*, November 20.

112. Greeley to Schuyler Colfax, August 24 (quotation), September 7, Greeley-Colfax Papers; James R. Thompson to Ullmann, March 15, 24, Confidential, 1855, Ullmann Papers, NYHS; Sag Harbor *Corrector*, November 4. Also see the Rochester *Daily Union*, October 30; letter signed "Whig But No MAN Worshiper," Rochester *Daily American*, November 2; Oliver B. Pierce to Weed, November 26, 1855, Weed Papers, UR; Seward, *Seward*, v. 2, 257.

society, the famous Maine Law leader, while Mayor of Portland, manifested unreserved hostility to immigrants, particularly the Irish. Likewise James Barker, the order's national president, first became acquainted with the American organization through his temperance activities. In 1854 in Pennsylvania, Indiana, Maine, Massachusetts, and elsewhere, the Know Nothings supported state candidates who endorsed prohibition, and several political commentators noted that the secret society enjoyed great strength among temperance men. From Philadelphia one of Buchanan's informants reported that the Know Nothings had "nearly all the Temperence [*sic*] men on their side." Similarly a veteran New York politician observed that their ticket "carried every strong temperance town" in his county.[113]

Voting patterns in two states that held advisory referendums on prohibition in this decade—Ohio and Pennsylvania—provide further evidence of the affinity between Know Nothingism and the Maine Law movement (Tables 3.2 and 3.3). In Ohio more than two-thirds of the Know Nothing members endorsed prohibition in the 1851 referendum. When Pennsylvania held a plebiscite on the Maine Law as part of its 1854 state election, almost three-fourths of those casting Know Nothing ballots favored enactment of a strict anti-liquor law and virtually none opposed it. In fact, although a majority of Whigs also favored a Maine Law, the preponderance of supporting votes came not from Whigs but from Know Nothings. In addition, a much larger proportion of Whigs than Know Nothings voted against prohibition. A Pennsylvania nativist organ promised, "If the American party . . . succeed[s], the prohibition . . . of the liquor traffic is inevitable."[114]

Although Know Nothings in the free states emphasized the Catholic menace over that of the slaveholder, they joined readily in the outcry over the repeal of the Missouri Compromise. Ultimately, the sectional controversy would divide the order, whose members held a wide variety of viewpoints on the slavery issue. In 1854, however, its free-state recruits united easily behind anti-Nebraskaism, for there was virtually no dissent on this point within the northern lodges, and the order had not yet attempted to devise a national position on the territorial controversy. Silver Grey Know Nothings united with Free Soil nativists in condemning Douglas's bill. Even the *National Era,* which waged an unrelenting campaign against the Know Nothings, conceded that "many Anti-Slavery men, many even of those who have hitherto acted with the Free Democracy, have joined the new party." The idea that the movement could be easily converted into a conservative Union party was a "delusion," insisted the New York *Evening Post,* which was also highly critical of the nativist organization. The men it had elected to state and national office, "on the great question of the non-extension of slavery, adopt, to the full extent, the prevalent northern view."[115]

Much more than the anti-Nebraska movement, the Know Nothing impulse capitalized on the forces that destroyed the Jacksonian party system. Its appeal integrated a virulent nativism with pro-temperance overtones and an abiding hostility to the existing parties as

---

113. Daniel T. Jenks to Buchanan, August 18, Buchanan Papers, HSPa; Francis Granger to Ullmann, November 14, Ullmann Papers, NYHS; Milwaukee *Daily News,* March 31, 1855, quoted in Thomas, *Nativism in the Old Northwest,* 129–30; Samuel Downer to Horace Mann, November 13, Mann Papers.

114. Harrisburg *Morning Herald,* August 16. Tyrrell, *Sobering Up,* 265–69, argues that nativism and temperance appealed to different social groups, but the voting patterns revealed in Tables 3.2 and 3.3 establish the strong links between the two movements.

115. *National Era,* November 23; New York *Evening Post,* November 20. Also see Samuel Downer to Mann, November 13, Mann Papers; A. R. Crikfield to Seward, April 4, 1855, Seward Papers, UR; letter signed "Know Nothing," *Free West,* March 15, 1855.

corrupt and unresponsive. At the same time, voters who sympathized with these policies and yet also wished to rebuke the repeal of the Missouri Compromise had no need to turn elsewhere. Moving with the political tide, the Know Nothings were in a position to benefit most from the looming popular upheaval. Politicians who based their strategies on exploiting the anti-Nebraska issue alone ignored other—and potentially more powerful— forces at work in northern politics. Marcellus Ells, a prominent New York City nativist, informed Hamilton Fish as early as March that "there is a mighty power that has began [*sic*] to feel its strength in the country—and you may rest assured that it will not be the Nebraska bill that will decide the next State election." Promising that nativism would prove more important, he added, "I know you will say that I am wild—but time will show if I am mistaken."[116]

<h1 style="text-align:center">V</h1>

Despite the farsighted prediction of the *Evening Post* that the order would "perplex and often disappoint our shrewdest political calculators" in 1854, experienced politicians initially discounted its importance. For one thing, in the past the society had eschewed separate nominations, a policy that, along with its secrecy prevented an accurate estimate of its strength. Those in the inner circle of leadership, however, advised outsiders that membership in the nativist organization was multiplying rapidly.[117] Brushing aside these warnings, political prognosticators remained skeptical in the spring when the Know Nothings scored victories in several local elections. It was the Philadelphia municipal election in June that finally alerted politicians to the magnitude of this new threat.

The city and county of Philadelphia had recently been consolidated, and Democrats were confident of their power in the reorganized municipality. The Whigs nominated Robert T. Conrad, a literary dilettante and notable conservative who was also a Know Nothing, while the Democrats selected Richard Vaux. The Democrats attempted to keep the Nebraska issue out of the canvass by taking no position on it at their city convention and by denying that it had any relevance to a local contest. More damaging to Vaux was his close association with Catholics and immigrants. He won the three-way primary contest in large part because William L. Hirst, a notorious Catholic leader and close friend of Postmaster General Campbell, delivered a large portion of the Catholic vote for him. In turn, Hirst secured the nomination for city solicitor. One indignant Democrat, who claimed that Vaux had been nominated by illegal votes, dismissed the Democratic mayoral candidate as "really an ass of the first water."[118]

The results were a rude shock for Democrats. Conrad won with a majority of more than 8,000 votes, and Hirst went down to defeat by an even larger margin. The entire Know Nothing ticket was elected. The returns left no doubt that Know Nothingism had made extensive inroads into the traditional Democratic vote. Whereas in the old city limits, Conrad received only the usual Whig majority, in the county towns, which were heavily Democratic before consolidation, he ran almost 6,000 votes ahead of Scott's 1852

---

116. Marcellus Ells to Fish, March 21, Fish Papers, LC.

117. New York *Evening Post*, July 19; L. R. Shepard to Marcy, January 28, Marcy Papers, LC.

118. Robert Tyler to Cushing, April 20, *Private*, Cushing Papers.

showing. New voters undoubtedly swelled Conrad's total, but clearly large numbers of Democrats voted for the Whig-Know Nothing nominee.[119]

Deeming the election an "*earthquake shake*," panicky Democrats easily grasped its significance. Know Nothingism was a force to be reckoned with, and all previous calculations for the fall election were invalid.[120] Although resentment over the Nebraska Act had played a part in the result, observers realized that nativism had been more potent. "I take it for granted that hereafter, no foreigner or *Catholic* can be elected to any office in this city," a Philadelphia Democrat emphasized. Noting that even foreigners voted against the Democratic ticket, he lamented that "our party is made to bear the sin of *catholicism* and every other evil sentiment promulgated in the country."[121] All agreed that it was a sharp rebuke to the Pierce administration. More than any other issue, Democrats singled out Campbell's appointment to the cabinet in accounting for the popular revolution in the city's politics. "The fight was religious and the victory sectarian," one of Bigler's correspondents wrote from the city. "In my opinion, this is the direct result of Campbell-ism." With an eye to the gubernatorial election that fall, he told the governor, who was running for reelection: "If you are not alarmed, you must have very strong nerves."[122]

Throughout the summer, northern political leaders received disturbing reports of unexpected Know Nothing strength. After members of the secret society, who were not even known to be candidates until election day, were victorious in Lancaster, an agitated Democrat commented: "These 'Know nothings' act in perfect concert, it would seem; but where they meet, or how they are organized, no one can tell." Democrats were stunned by the number of party associates who suddenly affiliated with the new party. "There are too many of our young men in it, sons of Democrats, that dont care, have no idea of the rong [*sic*] that they are doing," cried another Democrat. Worse still, party leaders could not even be certain whom they could trust. "They mix with us talk against themselves and denounce the order," a loyal Democrat complained of the Know Nothings. "Ever[y] body suspects everybody," he wailed; "We cannot trust our brothers."[123] Defections

---

119. The official vote was Conrad, 29,421 (58.4 percent), and Vaux, 20,993 (41.6 percent). The majority against Hirst was 11,843. Conrad's majority in the old city was 3,423 compared to Scott's 3,539, but he ran 5,627 votes ahead of the Whig presidential candidate in the county townships. For a discussion of Democratic support for Conrad, see Eli K. Price to Bigler, June 7, Bigler Papers; Cincinnati *Gazette*, July 27. Because consolidation altered the ward boundaries, it is impossible to link voting patterns in 1854 with those of previous years.

120. Daniel T. Jenks to Buchanan, June 9, Henry Slicer to Buchanan, June 10, Buchanan Papers, HSPa; Samuel W. Black to Simon Cameron, June 11, Thomas Koss to Cameron, June 15, Cameron Papers, HSDC.

121. E. A. Penniman to Bigler, June 8, Bigler Papers; Daniel T. Jenks to Buchanan, June 9, Buchanan Papers, HSPa; Joseph Sill Diary, June 7, HSPa. Although the Nebraska question cannot be dismissed as a factor in the election, there are good reasons for believing that experienced political analysts were right when they attributed greater weight to the nativist issue. Not only had nativism long been strong in the city, but Vaux criticized the repeal of the Missouri Compromise. The most persuasive evidence of the importance of nativism, however, was the resounding vote against Hirst, a well-known Catholic politico considered to be Campbell's right-hand man in the city. The majority against Hirst was "a demonstration of peculiar significance," one Democrat told Cameron, and "must be attributed to something else than a mere coalition of the old enemies of the democratic party." Thomas Koss to Cameron, June 15, Cameron Papers, HSDC.

122. Henry W. Phillips to Bigler, June 11, Bigler Papers; Philadelphia *Evening Bulletin*, June 7, quoted in Henry R. Mueller, *The Whig Party in Pennsylvania* (New York, 1922), 212n.

123. A. L. Hayes to Buchanan, May 8 (quotation), Daniel T. Jenks to Buchanan, October 3 (quotation), Buchanan Papers, HSPa; R. M. DeFrance to Simon Cameron, October 12 (quotation), Cameron Papers, HSDC; Jeremiah S. Black to Bigler, July 1, Bigler Papers.

were not limited to Democrats, since the Know Nothings held even greater attraction for Whig voters incensed by their party's performance over the past few years. From the Burned Over District in western New York, normally a stronghold of Whiggery and antislavery sentiment, a faithful Weed lieutenant disclosed that the Know Nothings were rushing in and controlling the primary meetings of all parties. Explaining that nativism and temperance had disrupted the Whig organization in his county, another of Weed's correspondents reported that these ''new questions have destroyed everything like party discipline, and many staunch old Whigs are floating off they dont know where.''[124]

The optimism of the Sewardites in the spring turned to gloom as the extent of the Know Nothings' power became apparent. The great referendum on Nebraska, anticipated for different reasons by such men as Seward and Chase, was now hopelessly clouded by the emergence of an organized nativist movement. The unexpected strength of nativism represented a major obstacle to their plans to capitalize on the popular discontent over the repeal of the Missouri Compromise. At the same time, rivalries among the various factions of the opposition—Whigs, Anti-Nebraska Democrats, Free Soilers, and Know Nothings—meant that politics would vary considerably from state to state. To appeals that he and other congressional leaders provide direction to recent political events, Seward expressed the view of many of his colleagues when he advised that the people should ''look away from Washington and settle these things practically at home.''[125]

---

124. Vivus W. Smith to Seward, September 4, Seward Papers, UR; Washington Hunt to Weed, October 21 (quotation), Lyman Spalding to Weed, August 3, 1853 [1854], Private, Weed Papers, UR; New York *Evening Post*, September 20; G. Westcott to My Dear Sir, September 7, Bigler Papers. Significantly, in his rather lengthy discussion of the breakup of the Whig ranks, Hunt avoided any mention of the Nebraska bill or the slavery question.

125. Seward to Weed, June 24, Weed Papers, UR.

4

The Confusion of Fusion

Following his retirement from Congress, George W. Julian, the famous Indiana Republican, wrote a memoir of his political career, which spanned almost three decades. To some extent time and retirement had softened the outlook of the once fiery antislavery radical, yet he remained intensely proud of his role in the organization of the Republican party. While celebrating its ultimate national triumph, he retained a keen appreciation of the difficulties the party confronted in its early existence. The problem of forming a new party "was exceedingly difficult, and could not be solved in a day," the Hoosier Republican observed in recalling the political events of 1854. "The dispersion of the old parties was one thing," he emphasized, "but the organization of their fragments into a new one on a just basis was quite a different thing."[1]

Historians have not always been as careful as Julian in distinguishing between the collapse of the Jacksonian party system and the establishment of the new Civil War party system. In much historical writing on the politics of the 1850s, the formation of the Republican party and its subsequent rise to national power seem almost the fulfillment of destiny. Attributing the antebellum realignment to the repeal of the Missouri Compromise, the standard account portrays indignant northerners in 1854 as rushing into the new Republican party, which almost immediately in this version emerges as the principal anti-Democratic party in the nation. Without question, the slavery expansion issue was crucial to the formation of a northern sectional party. But emphasis on the Kansas-Nebraska Act has obscured the importance of other factors in the antebellum realignment, and consequently historians have underestimated the extent to which the Republican party's organization was a lengthy and difficult process.[2] In reality, the interaction of the slavery issue with other concerns, particularly nativism, in the 1854 state elections produced a complex and at times bewildering set of developments that represented only the first faltering steps toward the formation of the Republican party.

The drive to combine the various anti-Democratic groups into a single party achieved

---

1. Julian, *Political Recollections*, 143–44.

2. Holt, *Forging a Majority* and *Political Crisis*, and Formisano, *Mass Political Parties*, call attention to the importance of other issues in politics before the Civil War.

greater success initially in the western states than in the East.[3] In general, however, even where the opposition united in 1854, the fusion movement resulted in only a temporary alliance with no clear ideological focus. The comment of an Illinois Democratic paper concerning local politics that ''there will be less of fusion than of confusion'' was applicable to the region as a whole.[4]

I

The first successful attempt at fusion occurred in Michigan. The main difficulty was getting the Free Soilers to withdraw their ticket, which had been nominated in late February. Informal consultations between Whig and Free Soil leaders could not overcome suspicions between the two groups, and a meeting at the office of the Detroit *Tribune* in March broke up in discord.[5] At this point Joseph Warren, the editor of the *Tribune*, took the lead by publicly calling on the Whigs to give up their party for a new fusion organization. Noting that the Whig party had ''suffered defeat after defeat of the most overwhelming and hopeless character for the last 14 years,'' he castigated party members for letting ''their love for an empty name'' override the present opportunity to achieve victory. In early June the *Tribune* proposed that a convention be called ''irrespective of the old party organizations, for the purpose of agreeing upon some plan of action that shall combine the whole anti-Nebraska, anti-slavery sentiment of the State, upon one ticket.''[6]

Despite the efforts of Warren and of Isaac Christiancy, who, though a candidate on the Free Democratic state ticket, was lobbying for its withdrawal, the opposition remained divided because most Free Democratic leaders, according to Christiancy, still clung ''to the idea that we could bring to *our* organization all the anti-slavery sentiment in both the Whig and Democratic parties, and thus carry the State under *our organization*.'' Whig leader Zachariah Chandler reported that the Free Soilers ''*insist* upon our nameing their platform & taking their nominations *just as they are*.'' Asserting that any attempt to transfer the Whigs to the Free Soil party would fail, he countered that any fusion ticket had to be an independent one, not simply a ratification of the Free Soil slate.[7] Finally, at a meeting in Detroit, Whig and Free Soil leaders agreed on the wording of the call for a mass convention on July 6 at Jackson ''to take such measures as shall be thought best to concentrate the popular sentiment of this state against the aggression of the slave power.''[8] With the Free Democrats' grudging abandonment of their attempt to control the fusion movement, the efforts of those opposition leaders who favored union were at last to bear fruit.

---

3. The New York *Evening Post*, September 15, noting the widespread use of the term *fusion*, provided a succinct definition: Fusion occurred ''when two or more parties are melted into one.''

4. Rock River *Democrat*, August 8, Arthur C. Cole Notes, Illinois Historical Survey, University of Illinois.

5. New York *Tribune*, June 17; Fred B. Porter Diary, March 23, University of Michigan; William Stocking, ed., *Under the Oaks* (Detroit, 1904); Charles V. DeLand, *DeLand's History of Jackson County* (Jackson, 1903), 166–72.

6. Detroit *Tribune* quoted in William Stocking, ''Little Journeys in Journalism: Joseph Warren,'' *Michigan History*, v. 22 (Autumn, 1938), 209; Detroit *Tribune* quoted in Floyd B. Streeter, *Political Parties in Michigan, 1837–1860* (Lansing, 1918), 188.

7. Letter of Isaac P. Christiancy, April 11, 1885, in Frank A. Flower, *History of the Republican Party* (Springfield, Ill., 1884), 170–74; Zachariah Chandler to James F. Joy, May 30 (quotation), June 2, James F. Joy Papers, Detroit Public Library.

8. Smith, *Liberty and Free Soil Parties*, 293; *National Era*, July 6; Stocking, *Under the Oaks*, 8–12.

The Jackson convention has often been characterized as a grass roots phenomenon, but as an historian of the convention observes aptly, "there was never anything in this state that was more carefully planned and nursed and fostered than that movement."[9] Because of the unwieldy size of the gathering, most of its business was conducted in small committees controlled tightly by experienced politicians. With great enthusiasm the assembly nominated a carefully balanced ticket headed by Kinsley S. Bingham, the erstwhile Free Democratic nominee for governor, and took the name *Republican* "until the contest be terminated." Later, several men associated with the Jackson convention claimed responsibility for the name, but in fact, as one participant recalled, it was very much in the air at the time as a natural complement to the term *Democrat*. Experience had taught Whigs the value of a party name that could be linked directly to Jefferson and his original Republican party. Prior to the Jackson convention, which was the first state convention to adopt the designation *Republican*, Horace Greeley had already begun to advocate the name as suitable for a new party, and indeed he urged fusion leaders in Michigan to adopt it. Many local fusion conventions in the state, however, avoided the name and invoked the simple title *Independent*.[10] In the existing political confusion, voters could not be certain that a permanent party had been formed.

Whigs and Free Soilers had agreed previously on the main antislavery planks of the platform.[11] Drafted largely by Jacob M. Howard, the chairman of the committee on resolutions, the platform dealt almost entirely with the slavery issue. Censuring the institution as "a great moral, social, and political evil," it opposed slavery's extension and called for its abolition in the District of Columbia. In demanding the repeal of the Kansas-Nebraska Act, the Republicans contended that the law's purpose was to "give to the slave States such a decided and practical preponderance in all the measures of government as shall reduce the North . . . to the mere province of a few slaveholding oligarchs of the South," and therefore advocated reducing the South's political power. Although two resolutions dealt with state issues, the platform omitted any reference to temperance, despite strong support locally among fusionists for the Maine Law. Presumably, party leaders believed that they could carry the state without adopting prohibition and possibly alienating potential supporters. Men who felt strongly on this issue were unlikely to support the Democrats, who were closely identified with immigrants and liquor.[12]

The election in Michigan was a two-way contest between the new Republican party and the Democrats. In October a Whig state convention, with pro-fusion elements firmly in control, defeated an attempt by conservatives to make separate nominations. In addition, although the Know Nothings commenced organizing in the state during the summer, they apparently made no independent nominations and worked within the fusion ranks. With only two tickets competing, Chandler predicted that the new party would "make a *clean Sweep*," and indeed the entire Republican state ticket was triumphantly elected.[13] While not overpowering, the Republican margin was still impressive in view of the party's

---

9. [William R. Stocking] to James O'Donnall, November 2, 1903, William R. Stocking Papers, Detroit Public Library.

10. Jacob Howard to Charles Lanman, April 27, 1864, Charles Lanman Papers, Detroit Public Library; Horace Hunt to Mrs. Richardson, October 31, 1904, Detroit Public Library; DeLand, *Jackson County*, 181; Michigan Pioneer and Historical Society, *Historical Collections*, v. 17 (1910), 265–66; Van Deusen, *Greeley*, 183.

11. Chandler to Joy, May 30, Joy Papers.

12. Resolutions and proceedings are in New York *Tribune*, July 11.

13. Chandler to Henry Waldron, October 14, Waldron Family Papers. The anti-Nebraska congressional

pronounced antislavery platform and the state's longstanding loyalty to the Democratic party.

That Michigan took the lead in the movement to form a northern party was entirely an accident of timing. Fusion conventions had already been called in several other states to meet at a later date, and the success of the movement in Michigan exerted limited influence elsewhere. The Michigan Republican platform was, as Greeley noted, "too steep" to be tenable in other states, and the American party, which was just being organized, was weaker there than in most states.[14]

The only other state where the opposition united and took the name *Republican* was Wisconsin.[15] In the previous two state contests, Whigs and Free Soilers had maintained a loose alliance, and after some hesitancy both groups endorsed a state fusion convention at Madison on July 13. The official call, directed to all who opposed "the repeal of the Missouri Compromise, the extension of slavery, and the rule of the slave power," stipulated that the purpose of the convention was "to take such measures as may be deemed necessary to prevent the future encroachments of the slave power, to repeal all compromises in favor of slavery, and to establish the principle of freedom as the rule of the State and National governments."[16]

The convention was well attended, with Whigs, Free Soilers, and anti-Nebraska Democrats present. Since no state offices were at stake, the meeting made no nominations, but it formalized the organization of the Republican party by appointing a state central committee. The resolutions were fully in keeping with the objectives announced in the convention call. In order to appeal to Germans and other immigrants, who were a significant minority of the state's electorate, Republicans attempted to play down two divisive issues, temperance and nativism.[17] Instead, except for the last resolution, which appealed to foreign-born voters for support, the platform was devoted entirely to the slavery issue. Decidedly radical in its principles, it called for repeal of the Kansas-Nebraska Act, the restriction of slavery to states where it already existed, the admission of no new slave states, the exclusion of slavery from all territories including any acquired hereafter, and "the repeal and entire abrogation" of the fugitive slave law.[18] Despite the state platform's emphasis on the slavery controversy, other issues, especially nativism and temperance, were also important in the legislative races. For a number of voters, these issues were intertwined. One Republican thus characterized the Wisconsin Democracy as *"founded upon niggerology, liquor and Romanism."*[19] The absence of a statewide contest made it difficult to measure Republican strength in the state, but as in Michigan the Democrats managed to retain only one seat in Congress.

----

candidates were all Know Nothings, although this was not known at the time. The vote was Bingham (Republican), 43,652 (53.0 percent), and Barry (Democrat), 38,675 (47.0 percent).

14. Horace Greeley to Schuyler Colfax, July 26, Greeley-Colfax Papers.

15. For Wisconsin politics in this period, see Richard N. Current, *The Civil War Era, 1848–1873* (Madison, 1976), 214–23; Frank L. Byrne, "Maine Law versus Lager Beer: A Dilemma of Wisconsin's Young Republican Party," *Wisconsin Magazine of History*, v. 42 (Winter, 1958–1959), 115–20.

16. The call appears in Flower, *Republican Party*, 183n.

17. Byrne, "Maine Law versus Lager Beer," 116–17. In 1850 foreign-born whites in Wisconsin totaled 110,471, or 36.2 percent of the white population. Their political influence was enhanced by the provision of the state constitution allowing aliens to vote.

18. The platform is printed in Flower, *Republican Party*, 184.

19. J. C. Carey to Horace A. Tenney, December 4, Horace A. Tenney Papers, WiscSHS. For evidence of the salience of the nativist and temperance issues, see George Hyer to Elisha Keyes, [September], *Private*, S. S. Keyes to Elisha Keyes, August 18, William T. Butler to Keyes, September 11, Elisha W. Keyes Papers, WiscSHS; J. R. Sharpstein to George H. Paul, September 6, George H. Paul Papers, WiscSHS.

II

Elsewhere in the West, the fusion movement was less successful. The movement to organize a new party in Indiana drew not only on opposition to the Kansas-Nebraska Act but also on the closely linked temperance and nativist crusades. Sentiment in favor of the Maine Law had been gaining strength in the state for some time and cut across party lines, as a significant minority of Democrats, especially among various evangelical denominations, favored prohibition. In 1853 the Democratic-controlled legislature had tried to undercut the temperance movement by enacting a local option law, but the state Supreme Court soon nullified this approach by declaring the law unconstitutional. In response to this decision, a large and enthusiastic temperance convention met in Indianapolis in January 1854. With a number of Democrats as conspicuous participants, the assemblage renewed the demand for a strict prohibitory law and vowed to vote only for candidates pledged to support such a statute.[20]

Besides temperance, Democrats were also concerned about the Nebraska controversy. Generally in agreement on these issues, Whigs and Free Soilers were eager to exploit both in the fall election. More ominous for the Democrats, however, was the fact that a number of party members who favored a stringent liquor law were also anti-Nebraska, a stance that was especially apparent among Democrats who were Methodists. The chairman of the state temperance convention, Methodist bishop Edward R. Ames, was a well-known Democrat. Indeed, according to that sect's organ, the *Western Christian Advocate,* the whole Methodist church seemed to be present at this convention. Subsequently, Methodist conferences in the state resolved to support only candidates who both favored temperance and opposed the Nebraska bill.[21]

The dominant leader of the Hoosier Democracy was Jesse Bright, the authoritarian United States senator. Hateful and extraordinarily ambitious, the paunchy Bright began his career as a bully, and as he rose in the ranks of the party he retained much of his earlier pugilistic makeup and tolerated no opposition among associates. Despite his belligerent personality, the senator often dodged controversial issues until it was clear which way the political winds were blowing, and his pro-southern sympathies (he owned a plantation and slaves in Kentucky) would ultimately subvert his leadership of the state party, but at mid-decade he was at the zenith of his power, the boss of a tightly organized political machine.[22]

In the existing political confusion, Bright saw an opportunity to tighten his grip on the party.[23] He laid plans to commit the party firmly to the principle of nonintervention and force his adversaries, headed by the urbane governor Joseph A. Wright, to submit or bolt. The senator's enemies in the party rallied around Wright and urged him to wage

---

20. Emma Lou Thornbrough, *Indiana in the Civil War, 1850–1880* (Indianapolis, 1965), 58–59; Charles E. Canup, "Temperence [*sic*] Movement and Legislation in Indiana," *Indiana Magazine of History,* v. 16 (March, 1920), 14–24.

21. Roger H. Van Bolt, "Fusion Out of Confusion, 1854," *Indiana Magazine of History,* v. 49 (December, 1953), 356; Mildred C. Stoler, "Insurgent Democrats of Indiana and Illinois in 1854," *Indiana Magazine of History,* v. 33 (March, 1937), 23.

22. Kenneth M. Stampp, *Indiana Politics During the Civil War* (Indianapolis, 1949), 15–16.

23. Bright's enemies included four talented Democratic editors, Michael C. Garber of the Madison *Courier,* Jacob Page Chapman of *Chapman's Chanticleer,* and two brothers, William R. Ellis of the Lafayette *Courier* and E. W. H. Ellis of the Goshen *Democrat,* whose earlier clashes with the imperious senator had resulted in their political ostracism. All were ready for open revolt. Van Bolt, "Fusion Out of Confusion," 364–66, 373–75.

unrelenting war on the would-be dictator, but, convinced that the national administration would silence all dissent against the Nebraska bill, the governor fatally hesitated. When the Democratic state convention met in May, Bright's subordinates rammed through a resolution endorsing the repeal of the Missouri Compromise, along with another that, while terming intemperance an evil, opposed any liquor law that allowed searches or seizures of private property. Bright's victory was an outgrowth of his many years of attention to the details of party organization, combined with his use of steamroller tactics and the presence of a number of informally appointed delegates under the close supervision of United States Marshall John L. Robinson, a key member of the Bright faction.[24] Contemporary accounts fail to substantiate the claim made in later years that a minority of delegates, led by Oliver P. Morton, walked out of the hall after passage of the Nebraska resolution, or that the convention passed a resolution expelling anti-Nebraska members; but district and county conventions that summer generally ostracized party members who refused to support the state platform. Almost immediately Bright was boasting within party circles that he had his foot firmly on Wright's neck.[25]

The fissure in the Democratic ranks offered the Whigs a chance at last to end the Democrats' long control of the state. Because of their party's weakness, Whig leaders were interested in a fusion movement that combined Whigs, Free Soilers, and dissident Democrats. As early as March Horace Greeley had specified the grounds for this union: Anti-rum and anti-Nebraska, he assured Schuyler Colfax, would unite the Whigs and Free Soilers and revolutionize the state.[26] To attract Democratic support, Whig leaders were anxious that anti-Nebraska Democrats appear to lead the drive for a fusion convention. John D. Defrees, editor of the Indianapolis *Journal* and chairman of the Whig state committee, told Colfax privately, "I have been prevailing on others to make the move for a State Convention, preferring that it should come from Democrats, if possible. Had the *Journal* been first to move, it would have been set down as a Whig movement."[27] Several anti-Nebraska Democratic editors, including Michael C. Garber and Jacob Page Chapman, were foremost in urging union, and in mid-June *Chapman's Chanticleer* printed a call for a fusion convention at Indianapolis on July 13. Similar calls, signed largely by Democrats, soon appeared.[28] Meanwhile, Whigs stayed discreetly in the background. Nevertheless, Whig leader Godlove Orth emphasized to Colfax: *"The Whigs must control that convention—without SEEMING to do so."*[29] During the campaign, when conservative Whigs attacked Defrees for opposing a separate Whig convention, his response hinted at the motivation of many Whigs in backing fusion in Indiana: "Should we divide the

---

24. Gayle Thornbrough et al., eds., *The Diary of Calvin Fletcher* (9 vols.: Indianapolis, 1972–1983), v. 5, 276; W. Wick to William H. English, June 5, English Papers, IndHS; Joseph A. Wright to John G. Davis, May 25, *Private*, John G. Davis Papers, IndHS. The Democratic platform is in William E. Henry, ed., *State Platforms of the Two Dominant Political Parties in Indiana, 1850–1900* (Indianapolis, 1902), 9.

25. Thornbrough, *Indiana in the Civil War Era*, 57n; John Hunt to Wright, June 3, July 22, Joseph A. Wright Papers, IndSL.

26. Greeley to Colfax, March 12, June 5, July 7, Greeley-Colfax Papers.

27. John W. Defrees to Colfax, June 16, quoted in Hollister, *Colfax*, 73.

28. An earlier call for a state anti-Nebraska convention issued by the Free Democratic state convention, which met on May 25, was largely ignored because of its disreputable origin. See the *National Era*, June 15.

29. Godlove S. Orth to Colfax, July 4, J. Herman Schauinger, ed., "The Letters of Godlove S. Orth, Hoosier American," *Indiana Magazine of History*, v. 40 (March, 1944), 54.

Democracy, any fool ought to see that it will inure to our benefit hereafter. The *game* will go into our net. It will have no where else to go."[30]

The organization that controlled the July 13 convention, however, was not the Whigs but the Know Nothings. First organized in Indiana in February, the secret society had spread rapidly throughout the state, especially in the southern and central counties. By June it claimed to have 60,000 Hoosier members and by fall more than 80,000. Even allowing for exaggeration, there is no question that the order was unusually strong, especially for a western state. "I never saw such a *ground swell* in Indiana as at the present time," a Methodist clergyman wrote that summer. Predicting that a great political revolution was at hand, he noted that "the *'Know nothings'* are as thick as the Locusts in Egypt."[31] Despite the state's relatively small foreign-born population, the Know Nothings successfully exploited resentment against Catholics, immigrants, and politicians.[32] In addition, both the party's members and its leaders disapproved of the Kansas-Nebraska Act and generally supported temperance.[33] With their own party disintegrating, Whigs flocked to the new organization and supplied a majority of its members, as well as most of its leaders, including Orth, Colfax, and the notable conservative Richard W. Thompson. Even so, a significant number of Democrats also joined the secret society, as alarmed party members testified. Reporting that nativist lodges were cropping up throughout the district, a constituent of Democratic congressman John G. Davis warned, "You would be startled by the number of Democrats who have joined."[34]

Two days before the state fusion convention, the first Know Nothing state council convened in Indianapolis. The council tried to keep its deliberations secret, but eventually they leaked out. The delegates devoted part of their time to organizing the state council and adopting a ritual, after which they turned their attention to the coming fusion convention. They secretly nominated a slate of candidates and resolved to present this ticket to the mass convention on the thirteenth.[35]

A large crowd, representing a wide variety of anti-Democratic groups, gathered in Indianapolis on this date, but the Know Nothings surreptitiously controlled the proceedings. The fusionists nominated the entire Know Nothing ticket secretly selected beforehand. Reflecting both its disparate composition and its conservatism, as well as opposition to politicians and questionable party practices, the movement took the name *People's party*. Its conservative platform opposed the further extension of slavery, called for the restoration of the Missouri Compromise, favored passage of a "judicious" and "efficient" prohibitory law, and rebuked attacks on Protestant ministers. The platform was artfully written. Although it did not call specifically for a temperance law that

---

30. Defrees to Samuel Judah, September 21, Samuel Judah Papers, IndU.

31. Carl F. Brand, "The History of the Know Nothing Party in Indiana," *Indiana Magazine of History*, v. 17 (March, 1922), 58–66; E. R. Ames to Matthew Simpson, June 24, Simpson Papers.

32. In 1850, of Indiana's 977,154 white inhabitants only 55,537 were foreign-born. The political power of immigrants was inflated, however, by the fact that the 1851 state constitution did not require voters to be citizens. Germans were the largest immigrant group throughout the 1850s, representing slightly over half the state's foreign-born population.

33. Mark E. Neely, Jr., "Richard W. Thompson: The Persistent Know Nothing," *Indiana Magazine of History*, v. 72 (June, 1976), 99–104, 120, emphasizes the anti-Catholic basis of the movement in Indiana.

34. A. Bussey to English, July 13, English Papers, IndHS; "D———" to Davis, August 24 (quotation), A. W. Lowdermilk to Davis, September 18, Daniel A. Farley to Davis, September 24, John G. Davis Papers, IndHS.

35. Brand, "Know Nothing Party in Indiana," 62–64.

provided for searches and seizures, it could be so interpreted. The final plank, while phrased in the most general terms, could be read as a nativist declaration. The slavery resolutions were so narrow, however, that George W. Julian introduced a minority platform calling for the denationalization of slavery and declaring that the repeal of the Missouri Compromise absolved the North from obeying the Compromise of 1850 (which, in effect, repudiated the fugitive slave law). The convention tabled his report by a voice vote.[36] "The new movement is thus harnessed to a narrow and false issue," Julian recorded in his journal in disgust. "Every Doughface in Indiana can demand the restoration of this compromise." With much justice, he characterized the fusion movement as essentially a Know Nothing venture.[37]

The order's control of the fusion movement extended to the congressional contests as well. After some false starts, the anti-Democratic forces managed to combine on a single candidate in each of the state's eleven congressional districts. Every one of these nominees was a member of the American organization. They included such former Whigs as Colfax and Samuel Brenton as well as ex-Democrats like Daniel Mace, who had taken a leading role in the congressional fight against the Nebraska bill, and Will Cumback. In no other state did the Know Nothings assume such a dominant position in the fusion movement.

Given the heterogeneous make-up of the People's party, few politicians believed it would survive. Morton, for example, despite endorsing the People's ticket, continued to describe himself as a Democrat. A number of Whigs were also far from certain what shape the anti-Democratic party would finally assume. Although he campaigned for the fusion nominees, Julian was outspoken in his criticism. Terming the People's party "merely a political combination" whose members were hopelessly divided, he dismissed as laughable the idea that it would long endure.[38] His assessment represented more than mere grumbling. Although the July 13 convention appointed a central committee, chaired by Michael Garber, in reality little had been accomplished either at the state convention or in the ensuing canvass to establish a permanent party organization. In addition, motivated by a general desire to defeat the Democrats, the People's party suppressed basic policy disagreements. With some validity, Democrats sarcastically dubbed the new organization "The Abolition Free-Soil Maine-Law Native-American Anti-Catholic Anti-Nebraska Party of Indiana." One Hoosier Democrat, who denoted the opposition as "a combination of all the *isms*," said of the fusion convention: "a more inco[n]gruous set, never gathered under Peter the Hermit, during the Crusades." The party's identification with ethnocultural issues posed a particular dilemma for the state's German voters. The Germans "are between hawk & buzzard," one observer reported during the summer. "They abhor the Nebraska bill, but still more abhor to have their whiskey and lager beer stopped."[39] The significance of such divisions, however, can be exaggerated. Fusion

36. The proceedings of the fusion convention are given in the Indianapolis *Daily Journal*, July 18; Cincinnati *Gazette*, July 15. For Julian's minority report, see his Scrapbook 1854–1857, George W. Julian Papers, IndSL. Julian's platform also contained a stronger temperance plank, which called for a law to suppress the manufacture and sale of intoxicating drinks.

37. Julian Diary, August 5, quoted in Grace Julian Clarke, *George W. Julian* (Indianapolis, 1923), 151–52; [Julian], "A Voice from Indiana," *National Era*, October 5; Julian, *Political Recollections*, 144.

38. Julian, "The Death-Struggle of the Republican Party," *North American Review*, v. 126 (March-April, 1878), 266; [Julian], "A Voice from Indiana," *National Era*, October 5; William D. Foulke, *Life of Oliver P. Morton* (2 vols.: Indianapolis, 1899), v. 1, 39–40.

39. Hollister, *Colfax*, 74; John Law to William L. Marcy, September 3, Marcy Papers, LC; W. Wick to

supporters differed on specific policies, but they were generally united in their opposition to the Nebraska bill, Catholics, and (less completely) liquor. Even those fusion leaders who opposed the Know Nothings for the most part endorsed the demand for reform of the naturalization laws without embracing wholesale proscription of Catholics and immigrants.[40] Subsequently Lew Wallace, the famous novelist and a pre-war Democrat, when discussing the diverse elements that fought under the People's party banner in 1854, compared the Indiana Democracy to "a whale assailed at the same time by many boats harpooning it from every direction."[41]

No group more effectively symbolized the union of these reform impulses in the Indiana fusion movement than the Protestant clergy, particularly the Methodists. Governor Joseph A. Wright, himself a Methodist, claimed that two-thirds of that sect's ministers had joined the Know Nothings, along with many clergymen from other Protestant denominations. He alleged that more than a hundred Methodist preachers were delegates to the fusion state convention, while another Democrat added that at least twenty-seven were Presbyterians.[42] Democrats were increasingly angered by the clergy's political activity on behalf of the opposition. At the Democratic state convention John Robinson, the presiding officer, intemperately referred to Methodist ministers as "non-tax-paying itinerant vagabonds." Robinson ignored the rebuke of some party members that such denunciations hurt the party, which was already on the defensive, and renewed his attack from the stump.[43] From the southern part of the state a Democrat reported while the contest was in full swing that "nearly all the protestant clergy" were aiding the People's ticket:

> I have myself *on a butchers block,* in our *market House* in one night, seen—a *D.D.* of the presbyterian Church—and the Methodist Presiding Elder in this District— harranguing a mixed assembly of men, boys, and rowdies . . . on those peculiarly *solemn—theological—pious* and *clerical* subjects—the Nebraska and Kansas bill—the Maine Liquor Law bill—and the beauties of "Know Nothingism." If this is following out the commands of their Lord and Master—I have read the Bible but with little advantage.[44]

Opposition spokesmen, noting the strength of the Methodist Church in the state and the "immense influence" its preachers exercised, quite naturally were delighted with the action of the clergy.[45]

With so many elements involved in the election, experienced politicians were uncertain

---

English, June 5, English Papers, IndHS; Rockport *Democrat*, October 17, quoted in Charles Zimmerman, "The Origin and Rise of the Republican Party in Indiana from 1854 to 1860," *Indiana Magazine of History*, v. 13 (September, 1917), 245.

40. Indianapolis *Journal*, October 21, quoted in Brand, "Know Nothing Party in Indiana," 73–74; Foulke, *Morton*, v. 1, 43–44; Stoler, "Influence of the Democratic Element," 121; Thornbrough, ed., *Fletcher Diary*, v. 5, 268.

41. Lew Wallace, *Lew Wallace: An Autobiography* (2 vols.: New York, 1906), v. 1, 237–38.

42. Wright to Simpson, October 23, Simpson Papers; William P. Bryant to Davis, July 19, John G. Davis Papers, IndHS. Bryant affirmed, "I think the Methodist clergy are expected to make an open square Political fight."

43. Van Bolt, "Fusion Out of Confusion," 373 (quotation), 365; M. F. Cullom to English, July 24, English Papers, IndHS; Scott Noel to Davis, April 27, Abraham Cutter to Davis, May 16, John G. Davis Papers, IndHS.

44. John Law to Marcy, September 25, Marcy Papers, LC.

45. Indianapolis correspondence, New York *Tribune*, October 5 (quotation); Thornbrough, ed., *Fletcher Diary*, v. 5, 282; Indianapolis correspondence, Cincinnati *Gazette*, July 17.

about the probable outcome. "The recent union of all the *isms* against us will give us a fight just sufficiently warm to be interesting," predicted one overly confident member of Bright's inner circle. More prescient, Wright counseled that the campaign had to be conducted with considerable skill. The attitude of Michael Bright, Jesse's brother and close adviser, probably was that of many Old Line Democrats. "He seems dreadfully puzzled as to the results of the next election," an acquaintance disclosed during the summer, "and to have an idea that the undercurrents are so mixed and complicated as to baffle the most prophetic foresight as to results."[46]

The returns verified Democrats' fears. The People's state ticket triumphed in a moderately close election, while only two Democratic congressmen, representing the southernmost districts, survived the opposition surge (Map 1).[47] Anti-Nebraska Know Nothings overwhelmingly dominated the new Indiana congressional delegation. The analysis of a Democratic leader conveyed the sense of shock party members experienced at the magnitude of the October defeat: "A tidal wave of great force and rapidity had swept over our former constituencies. It had submerged the highest and dryest places in the political reserves." The party met defeat everywhere, he observed, "and if there had been anything else to lose we should have lost it."[48]

The People's party's state candidates received the overwhelming backing of former Whig voters as well as solid support from Free Soilers. Democratic defections were larger than the normal shifting between parties common to every election, but not as extensive as fusionists had hoped (Table 4.1). Whereas native-born voters preferred the People's ticket by a clear margin, the opposition, with its ties to the temperance and nativist movements, had only limited success in attracting foreign-born voters. Germans, the state's largest immigrant voting bloc, strongly backed the Democratic ticket (Table 4.2.)[49] In addition, Democrats did much better among 1852 abstainers. The majority of these new Democratic voters probably were immigrants responding to the threats posed by nativism and temperance.

Experienced political observers grasped that Nebraska, nativism, temperance, and discontent with the older parties had combined to overthrow the Indiana Democracy. Because they united all these sentiments in their popular appeal, the Know Nothings played the dominant role in the fusion victory. Democrats were astounded by the nativist society's unexpected strength at the polls.[50] The *Indiana State Journal,* the fusionist state organ, promptly attributed the outcome to the secret order. "There can be little doubt," it commented afterwards, "that a vast majority of all native born citizens of the State are unchangeably hostile to the subserviency to foreigners, which for years has been the disgrace of the country." Its Democratic counterpart, the *Indiana State Sentinel,* in explaining the party's electoral setback, complained: "We had to fight the church, the

---

46. Graham N. Fitch to English, July 18, English Papers, IndHS; Wright to John G. Davis, May 18, John G. Davis Papers, IndHS; John Lyle King Diary, June 26, IndHS.

47. The vote for secretary of state: Collins (People's party), 99,636 (53.4 percent), and Hayden (Democrat), 87,027 (46.6 percent).

48. David S. Turpie, *Sketches of My Own Times* (Indianapolis, 1903), 154.

49. Dubois County, often looked to as a barometer of German political behavior because it had the heaviest concentration of Germans of any county in the state, rolled up heavy Democratic majorities in 1854, with the Democratic state and congressional tickets polling over 76 percent of the vote in the county.

50. Stoler, "Insurgent Democrats," 30; H. W. Daniels to John G. Davis, October 12, John G. Davis Papers, IndHS; John C. Sivey to Daniel R. Bearss, October 19, Daniel R. Bearss Papers, IndHS.

flesh, and the devil; the church in the temperance question; the flesh in the Old Whigs and the Devil in the Know-Nothings."[51]

III

The movement to unite the opposition in Ohio also capitalized on widespread resentment over the Kansas-Nebraska Act. Previous elections had demonstrated that between them the Whigs and Free Soilers controlled a majority of the state's voters; moreover, German protests against the Nebraska bill induced opposition leaders to hope that a significant proportion of Germans as well as anti-Nebraska Democrats could be brought into a fusion movement.[52]

To get these groups to cooperate, however, was not easy, despite the broad appeal of the Nebraska issue. The major difficulty was not the natural distrust between Whigs and Democrats but the intense antagonism that divided Whigs and Free Soilers. Blaming the third party for the political setbacks they had suffered in recent years, Ohio Whigs viewed these antislavery men as reckless, irrational extremists. One Whig attributed this animosity to the fact that the Free Soil party "long ago adopted the resolution of the early settlers of Connecticut, viz. 'The earth is the Lord's and belongs to his saints. We are his saints, etc.' They have heretofore and will unquestionably hereafter claim the offices on the ground that they are the only *pure* men in the field—all others being untrustworthy." With equal distrust a Free Soiler voiced trepidation that the leaders of the fusion movement would "take a kind of halfway course from fear of driving off a few blue conservatives" and thereby jeopardize success.[53] The rise of the Know Nothings seriously compounded the problems confronting opposition leaders, for Germans and nativists eyed each other with deep-seated suspicion.

Their party's weakness and disarray made many Whigs, particularly in the northern counties, eager for fusion. But in the central and southern portions of the state, party members maintained a cautious attitude toward the movement. The two leading Whig newspapers in the state, the Columbus *Ohio State Journal* and the Cincinnati *Gazette,* both under new editorial management, played a critical role in overcoming Whig hesitancy. The *Journal,* under the direction of Oran Follett, and the *Gazette,* edited by William Schouler, were far more interested in forming a winning coalition than in preserving a faltering party. Attacked by Free Soilers as "an incorrigible hunker," Follett, although suspicious of antislavery agitators, sincerely opposed the expansion of slavery, and he was not only a skilled journalist but was also extremely adept at behind-the-scenes political management. Less conservative than his mid-state colleague, the good-natured Schouler was allied loosely with William H. Seward and Thurlow Weed. As a party editor in Boston, he had broken with Daniel Webster over the

---

51. *Indiana State Journal*, October 14, quoted in Brand, "Know Nothing Party in Indiana," 77; *Indiana State Sentinel*, quoted in Canup, "Temperance Movement in Indiana," 24. See Chapter 5 below (p. 162) for a discussion of religion and voting in Indiana in the 1854 election.

52. Joseph Medill to the editors of the *Ohio State Journal,* May 29, Hamlin, ed., "Follett Papers," 59; Salmon P. Chase to Edward L. Pierce, March 12, Sumner Papers, HU; Chase to Sidney H. Gay, March 14 (Private), Jay Family Papers. For evidence of the opposition of Ohio Germans to the Nebraska bill, see the Cincinnati *Gazette*, February 27, April 7, July 13; *Ohio Columbian*, September 6; *Illinois State Journal*, August 14.

53. William Fairchild to Isaac Strohm, July 2, Typescript, Strohm Papers, CinHS; Adams Jewitt to Charles Sumner, July 9, Sumner Papers, HU.

Compromise of 1850—a step that led conservatives to boycott his paper and eventually ruined him financially. Seeking to restore his fortunes in the West, he assumed control of the *Gazette* at the end of 1853 with Weed's assistance.[54] Follett and Schouler believed that the protest over the Kansas-Nebraska bill offered a chance to form a majority coalition in the state, and therefore they counseled against attempting to preserve the Whig organization on either the state or local level. The *Gazette* proclaimed that a united opposition could carry the state in the fall and pushed openly for independent state nominations.[55]

In the meantime Salmon P. Chase, now a lame duck in the Senate, searched anxiously for a chance to revive his political career. Shortly after the *Gazette* endorsed the nomination of an independent state ticket, the Ohio antislavery leader penned a remarkable letter to former senator William Allen, the old hard money leader of the Ohio Democracy, whose organ, the *Ohio State Democrat,* had criticized the Nebraska bill. Assuming a greater air of confidence than he in fact felt, Chase declared that political realignment was at hand and predicted that once it had run its course "there must be as heretofore a Democratic Party & a Conservative Party under some name." Baldly remarking that he and Allen agreed on all points except slavery, Chase wrote with dubious sincerity, "It would give me the greatest pleasure to acknowledge you as a leader, in a really progressive & earnestly resolute democracy, suited to the times."[56] An untiring calculator, Chase carefully masked his motives for writing this letter behind ingratiating compliments and pious self-denials. Yet he could not fail to recognize that his future political aspirations would best be served in a Democratic-oriented fusion party rather than one dominated by former Whigs, many of whom were still incensed over his bargain with the Democrats that had originally sent him to the Senate in 1849. His bid to Allen was part of his effort to assure significant Democratic participation in the fusion movement. Indeed, he was already encouraging German Democratic leaders Stephen Molitor and Friedrich Hassaurek of Cincinnati to leave the party.[57] Allen, however, refused the bait and steadfastly adhered to the Democratic organization.

The failure of Allen, or any other Democratic leader of the first rank in the state, to lead a party bolt on the Nebraska issue was a disappointment to Chase, but, undaunted, he continued to urge the necessity of organizing a new Democratic party even as this possibility became increasingly remote. In May he privately informed an associate editor of the *State Journal* that he was ready to join a new political organization that united Whigs and liberal Democrats—provided it took the name Democrat. Barring this, he continued, "the Independent Democrats must of necessity maintain their distinct organization," although they would be willing to cooperate with all opponents of slavery's extension.[58]

---

54. Roseboom, *Civil War Era*, 283; Mrs. William S. Robinson, *"Warrington" Pen-Portraits* (Boston, 1877), 529; Henry L. Dawes Diary, June 8, [1853], Dawes Papers. Schouler's ties to Seward and Weed are amply documented in his personal papers.

55. Cincinnati *Gazette*, April 5, 22.

56. Chase to William Allen, April 8, *Private*, William Allen Papers, LC. Earlier, Francis P. Blair had also urged Allen to assume leadership of the anti-Nebraska Democrats in the state. Francis P. Blair, Sr., to Allen, February 10, Private, Allen Papers.

57. Chase to Edward L. Pierce, March 12, Sumner Papers, HU; Chase to Norton S. Townshend, March 9, Chase Papers, HSPa. Free Soilers held the balance of power in the 1849 legislature and eventually reached an agreement with the Democrats, giving the latter control of the legislature in exchange for Chase's election to the U.S. Senate. Outraged Whigs accused Chase of making a corrupt bargain for his own advancement. Whigs never forgot or forgave Chase. The Free Soil leader's moral sanctimoniousness made it rankle all the more. See Maizlish, *Triumph of Sectionalism*, 124–43.

58. Chase to John Griener, May 10, Private & Confidential, Hamlin, ed., "Follett Papers," 55–56.

Chase gained unexpected support from his senatorial colleague, Benjamin F. Wade. A decided antislavery man, Wade until now had remained loyal to the Whig party, but southern Whigs' support for the Nebraska bill, following so closely upon their apostasy in the 1852 national campaign, finally snapped his party ties. In early February, before the Nebraska bill had even passed the Senate, Chase reported that Wade was willing to join in the organization of "a new Democratic Party." Wade soon told Follett, "I hope we of the north will drop all party contentions and make common cause against the arrogance of the south until we have humbled them," adding that he did not care what name the new organization adopted. To a close political associate the outspoken senator confided, "I go for the death of slavery whether the Union survives it or not."[59]

The radical views of Chase and Wade were precisely what conservative Whigs feared most. As the fusion movement gathered momentum, the retired conservative Whig Thomas Ewing warned Follett that the Democrats would attempt to tar any new party with the fatal charge of abolitionism, and it was therefore "exceedingly important" that the Nebraska question be kept "entirely clear of any association beyond its strictly defined limits." Follett wholeheartedly concurred in this assessment, and conservatives began to call for a platform confined to the Nebraska issue.[60]

Alarmed by the conservatism represented by the *Journal* and the *Gazette,* Chase, in conjunction with other members of the state's congressional delegation, undertook to direct the Ohio fusion movement from Washington. Consultations among prominent members, most notably Chase, Wade, Lewis D. Campbell, and Joshua R. Giddings, produced a proposed call for a state convention. That Chase was the principal author of this document was transparent. Asserting that the repeal of the Missouri Compromise was "part and parcel" of a scheme to extend slavery and establish the Slave Power's dominance over the North American continent, the call advocated the total withdrawal of federal support for slavery, including the exclusion of slavery from all the territories, the repeal of the fugitive slave law, and a foreign policy that favored universal liberty. Alluding to several state issues as well, it called on Ohioans without regard to former party affiliation to meet in Columbus on July 13 to organize "a Democracy of the People" and adopt an appropriate platform.[61] Chase sent a copy to Schouler with the explanation that it was being sent to the various counties for signatures. He expressed confidence that the call would be "acceptable to all the opponents of the Nebraska Outrage."[62]

The call did not, however, meet with the wide approval its authors anticipated. It did not coincide with the views of the pro-fusion leaders in the state and apparently was used only in areas of pronounced antislavery feeling.[63] Instead, state leaders substituted a new, less radical version for the one drafted in Washington. The congressional call provided for

59. Chase to Norton S. Townshend, February 10, Chase Papers, HSPa; Benjamin F. Wade to Oran Follett, March 27, Hamlin, ed., "Follett Papers," 47; Wade to Milton Sutliff, April 21, Milton Sutliff Papers, WRHS.

60. Thomas Ewing to Follett, April 28 (Private), Hamlin, ed., "Follett Papers," 51; Follett to Ewing, May 1, Ewing Family Papers; Cincinnati *Gazette,* July 10; Cleveland *Herald,* June 10, quoted in the *Ohio Columbian,* June 14.

61. *National Era,* June 15, 22; *Ohio Columbian,* June 7. In places the Ohio call's language was very similar to the Appeal of the Independent Democrats, which Chase had written, and its discussion of slavery and the Constitution paralleled Chase's theories.

62. Chase to William Schouler, May 28, *Private,* Schouler Papers; Chase to My Dear Friend, May 30, Chase Papers, HSPa.

63. Cincinnati *Gazette,* May 31. Neither the *Gazette* nor the *Ohio State Journal* published the call. It circulated briefly in Ashtabula County in the Western Reserve, and probably in other strongly antislavery counties as well. *Ashtabula Sentinel,* June 22.

the organization of a new party, but, as Chase explained later, "a movement for a similar Convention less definite in object, originated in Columbus & . . . superceded that which we proposed."[64] This development involved two significant points: leadership of the fusion movement shifted from Washington to the state, and the idea of forming a permanent party, rather than uniting temporarily for the 1854 campaign, was dropped. Officially issued by a three-man committee representing Whigs, Democrats, and Free Soilers, the revised call for the July 13 convention was addressed to all who opposed the repeal of the Missouri Compromise and the extension of slavery. The "ONE QUESTION" involved in the present crisis, it declared, was whether the country would be ruled by freedom or by slavery. Nothing was said of forming a new party or even of making nominations.[65]

Despite the call's ambiguity, most political observers expected that an independent state ticket would be nominated. Whether a new party was to be launched provoked less agreement, although third-party men generally assumed that this would occur. Before the convention assembled, the platform was the major source of disagreement. The Cleveland *Herald,* seconded by the *Gazette,* argued that the Nebraska Act was the only subject before the meeting and that nothing else should be considered. Condemning such efforts to "whittle down" the platform, the Cleveland *Leader* countered that the platform should advocate the complete denationalization of slavery. Among Free Soil journals, the *Ohio Columbian,* the party's state organ, announced that the minimally acceptable platform would include the restoration of the Missouri Compromise, a ban on the further expansion of slavery, the repeal of the fugitive slave law, the admission of no additional slave states, and the "ENTIRE DENATIONALIZATION" of slavery. An even more comprehensive platform appeared in Giddings's paper, the *Ashtabula Sentinel,* which proposed, in addition to the *Columbian's* suggestions, planks calling for the abolition of slavery in the District of Columbia, prohibition of the interstate slave trade, and a homestead law. Both the *Columbian* and the *Sentinel,* however, stopped short of asserting that they would refuse to support the convention's nominees if a less advanced platform was approved.[66]

A large throng of delegates and unofficial participants, including Whigs of varying persuasions, anti-Nebraska Democrats, Free Soilers, Know Nothings, and Germans, came together at Columbus on July 13.[67] The moderates were in firm control. With none of the state's congressional leaders in attendance, leadership fell to lesser state politicians. A number of Democrats were present, but Benjamin F. Leiter, a former speaker of the assembly, was virtually the only one who had a statewide reputation. Among the Germans, Hassaurek was the best-known participant.

In spite of the convention's heterogeneous composition, remarkable harmony prevailed, as speakers emphasized the need for cooperation. Joseph M. Root, a Free Soiler,

64. Chase Diary, 1854, Chase Papers, LC. This entry, which Chase dated only 1854, is not contemporaneous. The alteration of the call for the convention is totally ignored by Ohio historians.

65. The revised call is in the *Ohio State Journal,* June 26.

66. Cleveland *Herald,* June 10, quoted in the *Ohio State Journal,* June 12; Cleveland *Leader,* July 6, *Annals of Cleveland,* v. 37, 273; *Ohio Columbian,* May 31, June 28, July 12 (quotation); *Ashtabula Sentinel,* June 15; Cincinnati *Gazette,* July 10.

67. For the convention proceedings, see the *Ohio State Journal,* July 13, 14. The Cincinnati delegation illustrated this diverse mixture. It contained such Whigs as William Schouler, anti-Nebraska Democrats the most prominent of whom was future congressman Timothy C. Day, Germans led by Friedrich Hassaurek and Stephen Molitor, such Free Soilers as George Hoadley, Know Nothings headed by Thomas Spooner, the future president of the state order, and James D. Taylor, who was the Free School candidate for mayor in 1853, and even abolitionists like Levi Coffin.

set the tone for the gathering in the opening speech when he said: "We must all be practical. There are things to forget, as well as things to hope for." He balanced his advocacy of adopting a platform that encompassed more than the Nebraska issue with an exhortation to Free Soilers to be satisfied with whatever they could get. For the two state offices being contested in October, the assembled crowd nominated with almost no dissent an anti-Nebraska Democrat and a Whig. In addition to endorsing the restoration of the Missouri Compromise, the resolutions opposed the extension of slavery and the admission of any new slave states. The fugitive slave law and other controversial points stipulated by third-party men before the convention met remained unmentioned (the resolutions referred vaguely to unspecified "encroachments of slavery"). No state issues and no collateral issues, such as temperance, were touched. Although the convention appointed a state central committee, it did not announce the formation of a new party and did not even adopt a name. The *Ohio State Journal* labeled the ticket "Republican Nominations," but there was no uniformity, and the terms *People's Ticket* and *Anti-Nebraska Ticket* were used more frequently. The failure to establish a new party reflected the attitude of both Whigs and Democrats, neither of whom were ready to give up their old party loyalties and both of whom desired only a temporary coalition to meet the present crisis. Because of this opposition, antislavery leaders concluded that any attempt to organize a permanent party was premature.

The Free Democrats also suffered a substantial defeat over the platform, on which they had placed such emphasis beforehand. Except for the plank opposing any additional slave states, only the most conservative antislavery principles had been promulgated. Voicing the general disappointment of third-party men, Chase observed somewhat meekly that the convention "took rather low ground." To a close supporter he commented with a noticeable lack of enthusiasm: "It seems that nothing remains except to make the best of what was done."[68] Several factors contributed to this outcome. First, the Free Soilers were misled by the composition of the committee on resolutions, which contained several third-party men of repute, including Rufus P. Spalding, the chairman. Many Free Democratic delegates undoubtedly assumed that his position ensured that their principles would be endorsed. In reality, Spalding, who was gradually moving away from Chase and the Free Soilers, was a leading voice of moderation in the committee. Moreover, other third-party members of the committee were exceedingly anxious not to weaken the movement in areas less advanced on the slavery question. Despite widespread opposition to the fugitive slave law among the committee members, they concluded that incorporating a plank on this issue would seriously harm the ticket in southern Ohio without bringing any additional strength to it in the northern counties. Second, the convention adopted a rule referring all proposed resolutions to this committee without debate. Whether intended or not, this decision, according to one antislavery delegate, "strangled every radical resolution in its incipiency" and effectively throttled whatever discontent there was on the floor among antislavery men.[69] Finally, from the beginning, control of the convention rested in the hands of a group of experienced politicians,

---

68. Chase to John Jay, July 16, Jay Family Papers; Chase to Norton S. Townshend, July 22 (quotation), Chase Papers, HSPa; Chase to E. S. Hamlin, July 21, Chase Papers, LC.

69. For the deliberations of the committee on resolutions, see the letters of D. Worth, W. G. Kephart, and especially James Elliott, *Ohio Columbian*, July 19, August 2. Also see the *Ohio State Journal* quoted in the *Ohio Columbian*, July 19. A desire to form a broad coalition also dictated avoidance of the Maine Law question, despite strong anti-liquor sentiment in the Free Soil ranks. After their 1853 electoral debacle, Whigs understandably did not wish to raise this issue, and Germans were adamantly hostile to prohibition.

including a few Free Soil leaders, who were unwilling to imperil what they believed was a rare opportunity to crush the Ohio Democracy and significantly alter the state's politics. For third-party leaders, the chance to be part of a major party without sacrificing their principles completely was irresistible.

Contemporaries were uncertain of the role the Know Nothings played in the Columbus convention. The order began full-scale organizing efforts in Ohio in March and quickly spread throughout the state, garnering particular strength in the southern counties. Campbell joined the society while in Washington and almost certainly was a member when negotiating with Chase, Wade, and others concerning the wording of the abortive convention call. A number of delegates to the fusion state convention were Know Nothings, but it seems unlikely, given the absence of complaints later, that they operated in any organized way. The American party's statewide organization had not yet been perfected, and with most of its growth still in the future, nativist leaders acted cautiously and endorsed the anti-Nebraska state ticket.[70]

Their action was entirely understandable. Not only were members of the order generally opposed to the repeal of the Missouri Compromise, but most fusionist newspapers were friendly to the nativist organization, while Democratic journals were scorching in their denunciations. The Cincinnati *Gazette* was openly nativist—despite his Scottish birth, Schouler was sympathetic to the American movement—while the *Ohio State Journal* upheld hostility to "politico-religionists" led by Jesuit priests who were strongly attached to the "Slave Democracy," but it refused to approve indiscriminate opposition to the foreign-born. Unlike the leaders in Indiana, Ohio's anti-Democratic politicians were unwilling to write off the much more sizable foreign vote there. Hoping to appeal to non-Catholic German voters as well as Know Nothings, opposition papers in general distinguished between anti-Catholicism, which they supported, and anti-immigrant sentiment, which they disapproved. Even the intensely nativist Cincinnati *Times* momentarily adopted this distinction. "It should never be lost sight of," it declared during the contest, "that Romanism is the head and front and that native Americanism is secondary and contingent."[71] Anti-Catholicism had a wide appeal not only to the nativists but to the German fusionists as well, most of whom were Protestants or free thinkers. Pronouncing "the political influence of Popery" as the most dangerous threat to the nation's liberties, a German meeting in Cincinnati to select delegates to the Columbus convention announced that "any movement, whose aim is opposition to Popery and Jesuitism, will have our warmest sympathies and heartiest support."[72] Along with the Nebraska issue, nativism contributed greatly to the strength of the anti-Democratic opposition.

Confronted with the challenge of the fusion movement, Democrats tried to downplay

---

70. Eugene H. Roseboom, "Salmon P. Chase and the Know Nothings," *MVHR*, v. 25 (December, 1938), 335–39; William E. Van Horne, "Lewis D. Campbell and the Know Nothing Party in Ohio," *Ohio History*, v. 76 (Autumn, 1967), 205; New York *Times*, October 20.

71. *Ohio State Journal*, July 8, June 8, 19; Cincinnati *Times*, August 3, quoted in Roseboom, *Civil War Era*, 293. For other examples of fusionist anti-Catholic rhetoric, see the Cincinnati *Gazette*, July 27, August 21, 31, September 19, 30; and the Cleveland *Leader*, October 10, December 15, *Annals of Cleveland*, v. 37, 94, 229. In his desire to establish the slavery issue as paramount in Ohio politics, Stephen Maizlish dismisses the role of nativism in the 1854 campaign. His argument that the election was a referendum on whether the voters considered slavery or nativism the pressing issue is unpersuasive: *Triumph of Sectionalism*, 202–6.

72. Cincinnati *Gazette*, July 13. For another example of German anti-Catholicism, see the resolutions of the Américan Protestant Association, Cincinnati *Gazette*, October 10.

the Nebraska issue in the campaign. The party's state convention met in early January and passed over the Kansas-Nebraska bill in silence. Caught between public opinion in the state on the one hand and the stance of the national party on the other, the Democratic-controlled legislature took no action on resolutions opposing the repeal of the Missouri Compromise. In addition, the party's state and congressional candidates minimized the Nebraska issue in their campaigns, and its county conventions adopted a variety of positions on the territorial controversy. Hoping to hold antislavery party members in line and to appeal to immigrant voters, Democrats instead directed their campaign against the Know Nothings. The party's basic strategy, which made sense in view of popular sentiment against the Kansas-Nebraska Act, was to identify the fusion movement with Know Nothingism.

More a conglomeration of opposition factions than a tightly knit, smoothly functioning political party, the Ohio People's organization nevertheless displayed unusual harmony. Contrary to the fears of some politicians that the county conventions would be disruptive, a spirit of enthusiastic cooperation pervaded the opposition ranks.[73] Setting the tone for the campaign, the *State Journal* urged that "prejudices should be forgotten." "Whatever errors in policy our Freesoil friends may have committed (and we believe they are many)," it asserted, "it is clear that on the issue now tendered by the South *they are right.* And, being right, shall Whigs and Democrats refuse their association?" In Cincinnati, the *Gazette* endorsed the Know Nothing county ticket and successfully opposed the nomination of a separate Whig slate. Even the Know Nothings and anti-Nebraska Germans managed to bury their animosity for the time being behind the anti-Catholic and slavery expansion issues. In each of the state's twenty-one congressional districts, the anti-Nebraska forces ultimately united on a single candidate. By the end of the campaign, opposition papers glowed with the confidence of victory. Indeed, a few days before the balloting the Cleveland *Leader* predicted that the anti-Nebraska majority in the state might be as high as 40,000 votes.[74]

When Ohio voters went to the polls in October, the People's party scored an astounding triumph. Exceeding even the most optimistic expectations of its supporters, the People's ticket swamped the Democracy by an unprecedented majority of almost 70,000 votes.[75] The Democrats carried only eight counties, and the opposition gained its largest majority in usually solidly Democratic Hamilton County (Cincinnati) (Map 2). Democratic losses were even greater in the congressional races. Ohio, in fact, returned an unbroken anti-Nebraska delegation: Every Democratic district had been lost, and although the state's delegation was a conglomeration of Know Nothings, anti-Nebraska Democrats, and antislavery fusionists, its members were united in their opposition to Pierce and the Kansas-Nebraska Act.

As in Indiana, Whigs and Free Soilers in Ohio strongly supported the People's party. The number of Democrats who defected to the opposition, however, was considerably

---

73. Joseph Medill to the editors of the *Ohio State Journal*, May 29, Hamlin, ed., "Follett Papers," 58; *Ohio Columbian*, September 6.

74. *Ohio State Journal*, July 17; Cincinnati *Gazette*, July 17; Cleveland *Leader*, October 10, *Annals of Cleveland*, v. 37, 94.

75. The totals in the contest for Board of Public Works were Blickensderfer (People's party), 183,452 (62.6 percent), and Miller (Democrat), 109,685 (37.4 percent). The Cleveland *Leader* admitted that the election outcome "astonished the friends and foes" of the People's party. Quoted in the *Kennebec Journal*, November 3. In the contest for Supreme Court justice, the People's party candidate won by an even larger margin.

Note: Numbers are the People's percentage of the votes cast.

1. Indiana Vote for Secretary of State, 1854

Note: Numbers are the People's percentage of the votes cast.

2. Ohio Vote for Board of Public Works, 1854

higher in the Buckeye state. Somewhat fewer than a third of the regular Democratic voters cast opposition ballots in 1854. In addition, the People's party received the support of a number of men who had not voted in the earlier state election (Table 4.3).[76] Although the fusion campaign did not emphasize the temperance issue, there was a strong tendency for anti-liquor men to support the People's slate—further evidence that, among native-born voters at least, antislavery and prohibition often flowed in intersecting channels (Table 4.4). Significant support for the People's ticket among German voters, however, weakened the relationship somewhat.[77]

There were several reasons for the greater defection rate among Ohio Democrats. Although the Nebraska and nativist issues were involved in the canvasses in both states, the identification of the People's party with the Know Nothings was much stronger in Indiana. In addition, the Hoosier fusion platform contained an anti-liquor plank while in Ohio party leaders, cognizant of the results of the 1853 election when the temperance controversy demolished the Whig party, carefully kept the liquor question out of the contest. Presumably, both considerations deterred some anti-Nebraska Democrats in Indiana from deserting their party. More important, however, was the more powerful antislavery tradition of the Ohio Democracy. With the party's leaders, this tradition had largely ceased to be anything but rhetoric, but among the rank-and-file resistance to the expansion of slavery remained strong. Upset by the Kansas-Nebraska Act, many of these Democrats manifested their anger by voting for the People's ticket. Political commentators were uncertain whether these Democratic defections represented a permanent disruption of partisan affiliation or only a temporary protest against the party's policy. At least one observer feared that in Ohio and elsewhere before long "the Democrats who discarded the Nebraska pill will go a whoring after the euphorious name again and lapse into the old ranks."[78]

Because the Ohio Know Nothings did not run a separate ticket, the election provided no direct test of the order's voting strength. Antislavery men, especially later, sought to downplay the society's significance in the 1854 election, and in general historians minimize its importance in the western states, particularly Ohio. From admittedly imprecise county membership figures for Ohio, it appears that contemporary claims that the Know Nothings strongly backed the anti-Democratic state ticket and played a major part in its victory were accurate (Table 4.5).[79] Members apparently also voted at a much higher rate than did outsiders. Possibly, the order's emphasis on political action and its close scrutiny of members' behavior at the polls produced a high turnout.

Cincinnati provides an excellent example of the connection between anti-Catholic

---

76. Table 4.3 undoubtedly exaggerates the extent of non-voting among Free Soilers but not the one-sided direction of their partisanship.

77. A regression analysis for 49 of the state's 88 counties estimates that 52 percent of the German voters cast People's party ballots. The remainder voted Democratic, with few abstentions.

78. J. P. Charles to Strohm, October 26, Strohm Papers, OHS. Maizlish, *Triumph of Sectionalism*, 121–205, carefully traces the maneuvering between the Democrats and Free Soilers in Ohio during the years 1849–1854.

79. These totals, representing the order's reported strength in October 1854, are given in the *Ohio Statesman*, March 8, 1855. Because of their uncertain accuracy, the estimates in Table 4.5 should be viewed with caution. For conflicting assertions of the Know Nothings' importance in the 1854 election, see the *Ashtabula Sentinel*, April 12, May 17, 1855; Cincinnati *Commercial*, October 1, 1855; Sidney D. Maxwell Diary, January 10, 1855; G. W. Lewis to Cyrus Carpenter, October 1, Cyrus Carpenter Papers, Iowa State Historical Society; and the New York *Times*, October 20.

sentiment and the People's party's victory in October. With anti-Catholic feeling already inflamed by the recent struggle over the public schools, the city became a Know Nothing stronghold, and the nativist society easily dominated the local opposition to the Democrats. Appealing to anti-Catholic and anti-Nebraska sentiment, the People's party carried the city by almost a two-to-one margin. The relationship between the political divisions arising out of the school controversy the previous year and the opposition victory in October demonstrated the degree to which anti-Catholicism had disrupted the city's politics. The supporters of all three anti-Catholic candidates in the 1853 mayoral contest, including the heavily German Anti-Miamis, overwhelmingly backed the People's ticket (Table 4.6). German cooperation with the Know Nothings was obvious, and both the *Enquirer* and the *Gazette* agreed that a significant proportion of immigrants voted for the anti-Democratic candidates. In the four most heavily German wards, the Democrats polled 53 percent of the vote in 1854; by way of contrast, in the state election a year earlier, when temperance was the major issue, the party's share had been fully 88 percent.[80] The contention of a writer to the *Enquirer* that defections among the foreign-born from the Democratic party were confined largely to non-Catholics was probably true. Anti-Catholic German leaders were especially prominent in the opposition movement, and a German Democratic leader asserted that his countrymen had voted the anti-Democratic ticket "upon the false pretense of rebuking the pope of Rome."[81] As long as the opposition focused on anti-Catholicism rather than anti-foreignism or temperance, a substantial number of Germans were ready to support its ticket.

The overwhelming victory of the Cincinnati fusion movement, attracting as it did former Whigs, virulent nativists, anti-Nebraska Democrats, and non-Catholic immigrants, rested on the twin pillars of anti-Nebraskaism and anti-Catholicism. Rutherford B. Hayes understood how fundamentally important the latter issue was. Attributing the outcome in the city to "Anti-Nebraska, Know-Nothings, and a general disgust with the powers that be," he concluded: "How people do hate Catholics, and what a happiness it was to thousands to have a chance to show it in what seemed a lawful and patriotic manner."[82]

IV

In no other state did the opposition unite by means of a state convention, although in Iowa a single anti-Nebraska ticket evolved from negotiations among opposition leaders when the Free Soilers eventually endorsed the Whig nominee, James W. Grimes, an earnest

---

80. Regression estimates are that 54 percent of the Cincinnati Germans who went to the polls cast Democratic ballots in the state contest, but approximately half the German voters abstained. This figure probably overstates German non-voting, but it still seems clear that a number of Germans felt cross-pressured. Presumably, they were unhappy with the Democratic party while at the same time they were reluctant to support a ticket backed by the Know Nothings. The Know Nothings' power in the local opposition party no doubt also contributed to Germans' concern.

81. Letter signed "American Democrat," Cincinnati *Enquirer*, October 15; Henry Roedter to G. A. Neumann, October 18 (quotation), Henry Roedter Papers, University of Illinois; letter from James Elliott, Cincinnati correspondence, "P.," *National Era*, August 3, 24; letter of Cincinnati Germans to congressional candidate Timothy C. Day, Cincinnati *Commercial*, October 5; J. Scott Harrison to Benjamin Harrison, September 30, Benjamin Harrison Papers.

82. Rutherford B. Hayes to Sardis Birchard, October 13, Williams, ed., *Hayes Diary and Letters*, v. 1, 470.

prohibitionist who only recently had avowed himself a committed antislavery man. Designating himself the opposition candidate, Grimes undertook to combine a variety of dissimilar groups, including Whigs, anti-Nebraska Democrats, Germans, temperance advocates, and ardent antislavery men. So skillful was Grimes at fusing these various elements behind his candidacy that one historian has observed that by the end of the canvass Grimes himself "probably could not have said what political designation he deserved."[83]

In August Grimes was elected as a general opposition candidate. His advantage was not great, but Iowa had previously been a Democratic state, and politicians recognized the importance of this result.[84] In winning the governorship, Grimes put together a successful coalition of Whigs and Free Soilers (Table 4.7). He attracted very little support from traditional Democratic voters, and his substantial strength among non-voters in 1852 and new voters was for the most part offset by somewhat smaller Democratic gains with the same groups. Democratic strength among previous non-voters suggests that the liquor question, which the party stressed in an attempt to neutralize the damage of the Nebraska bill, was important along with the Nebraska controversy in bringing these voters to the polls (Grimes's appeal to earlier non-voters probably reflected both considerations). Grimes won some support among naturalized voters, although a majority remained loyal to the Democracy (Table 4.2). Apparently conservative Whigs who were unhappy over Grimes's open alliance with the Free Soilers refused to vote.[85]

Among the states of the Old Northwest, fusionists encountered the greatest resistance in Illinois. There, although a number of reputable Democrats as well as Whigs and Free Soilers opposed the repeal of the Missouri Compromise, the attempt to form a fusion party failed to get off the ground. The call for a new party gained little support except in the northern counties, where two years earlier Whigs and Free Soilers had cooperated in local and congressional contests. The most noteworthy Whig paper that endorsed fusion was the Chicago *Tribune*, which announced that it was "sick and tired of party organizations which are dead and lifeless." After some hesitation, the *Free West*, the organ of the Free Soilers, also called for formation of a new party.[86] In the central counties, however, where the Whigs were strong, fusion sparked little enthusiasm. Whig hostility, the lack of interest on the part of anti-Nebraska Democrats, and the radicalism of some of the local fusion conventions, as well as discord over the nativist and liquor questions, frustrated new-party promoters. Interest focused less on the state election, where only the office of state treasurer was to be filled, than on the contests for Congress and the legislature.

---

83. For Iowa politics in this decade, see Morton M. Rosenberg, *Iowa on the Eve of the Civil War* (Norman, 1972); and two articles by David S. Sparks: "The Decline of the Democratic Party in Iowa, 1850–1860," *Iowa Journal of History*, v. 53 (January, 1955), 1–30, and "The Birth of the Republican Party in Iowa, 1854–1856." ibid., v. 54 (January, 1956), 1–34 (quotation, p. 1).

84. Jesse Bright to Robert M. T. Hunter, September 12, Charles H. Ambler, ed., *Correspondence of Robert M. T. Hunter, 1826–1876, Annual Report of the American Historical Association for the Year 1916* (Washington, 1918), v. 2, 159. The vote was Grimes 23,040 (52.9 percent), and Bates (Democrat), 20,554 (47.1 percent).

85. "Anti Nebraska and Anti Whiskey was the issue here." J. P. Charles to Strohm, August 13, Strohm Papers, OHS. For evidence of conservative Whig opposition to Grimes, see John F. Henry to [David Davis], March 2, David Davis Family Papers; James W. Grimes to Chase, October 3, in William Salter, *Life of James W. Grimes* (New York, 1876), 54.

86. Chicago *Tribune* quoted in *National Era*, June 1; *Free West*, May 4, August 31, September 7. At first the *Free West* urged only cooperation rather than union, but its reserve melted as the campaign approached.

Because the next legislature would elect a successor to Senator James Shields, politicians, including those with an eye on his seat, preferred to maintain the existing party organizations with which to mobilize old associates rather than plunge headlong into a new party.

The unwillingness of Whigs and anti-Nebraska Democrats to act forced Free Soil leaders to undertake management of the fusion movement. In early September, a notice appeared in the *Free West* for a convention "of all citizens of . . . Illinois who are opposed to the repeal of the Missouri Compromise and to the future extension and consolidation of the slave power" to be held in Springfield on October 5, in order to organize "a party which shall put the Government on a Republican tack."[87] In the capital the Whig *Illinois State Journal* remained coldly aloof from the movement, and an attempt by Owen Lovejoy to recruit Abraham Lincoln was unavailing. One important downstate figure who endorsed the meeting was George Brown, editor of the Alton *Courier* and a leading anti-Nebraska Democrat.

When delegates to the convention arrived in Springfield, they discovered that no local arrangements had been made: No notice of the meeting had been given, no hall had been reserved, and confusion prevailed over whether the date had been changed to the fourth. Because only a handful of men gathered shortly after noon on that day, fusion leaders decided to postpone the session until the following day and in the meantime distribute announcements of the meeting. To compound these problems, poor planning resulted in the convention's being scheduled for eight o'clock in the morning, the only time the statehouse was available.[88]

Attendance at this early morning session was more respectable, with the bulk of the delegates representing the northern counties. Committed antislavery men, led by Lovejoy and Ichabod Codding, dominated its deliberations; yet, contrary to the expectations of those Whigs and Democrats who declined to participate, the convention adopted a moderate statement of principles. Lovejoy, whose antislavery principles were tinctured with a large measure of political pragmatism, was probably influential in formulating this broad appeal. The resolutions declared it the "right and the duty of the General Government" to prohibit slavery in all territories, including any acquired in the future. They called for federal aid to internal improvements and included a vague declaration upholding the rights of trial by jury and the writ of habeas corpus, which could be interpreted as a call for modification of the fugitive slave law. The convention announced the formation of the Republican party and appointed a state central committee. For state treasurer, the delegates endorsed the Whig nominee unanimously.[89]

Members of the Republican state central committee represented various shades of opinion. They included three Whigs (among them Lincoln), three Free Soilers, one Know Nothing, and two Democrats. Fearing the party's radicalism, Lincoln had not participated

---

87. *Free West*, September 7.

88. Chicago *Democrat*, November 6, 1860.

89. Chicago *Democrat*, November 6, 1860; Paul Selby, "Genesis of the Republican Party in Illinois," Illinois State Historical Society *Transactions* (1906), 270–83; Selby, "The Republican State Convention, Springfield, Ill., October 4–5, 1854," *Transactions of the McLean County Historical Society*, v. 3 (1900), 43–47. The best account of the convention is Victor B. Howard, "The Illinois Republican Party," *Journal of the Illinois State Historical Society*, v. 64 (Summer, 1971), 146–52. The Republican platform is given in the Freeport *Journal*, October 12, which also includes a full report of the convention's proceedings.

in any of its deliberations, and he subsequently declined the appointment.[90] His action symbolized the failure of the fusion movement to enlist the support of downstate Whigs, a development that doomed it to ineffectiveness. Actually, the Illinois Republican party existed only on paper in 1854: Its state committee never met, its nominee declined, and the party conducted no campaign.

Not only was the attempt to form a state Republican party stillborn in Illinois, the nomination there of an anti-Nebraska candidate for state treasurer was highly irregular. Initially, Whig and anti-Nebraska papers recommended John E. McClun of McLean County, and he also received the endorsement of the Lovejoy-Codding convention. When McClun declined to run, an informal committee from McLean County substituted James Miller, a relatively unknown anti-Nebraska pro-temperance Whig who was also a Know Nothing. For the most part Whig papers endorsed Miller's candidacy, but he had been selected by a small group in a single county and was in no sense the nominee of a party convention. Miller's informal nomination testified to the absence of any effective opposition state organization.

In the congressional contests, only in the northern districts was a serious attempt made to unite opponents of the regular Democracy into a new party. Even so, in the end there were three anti-Douglas candidates in the Second District and two in the First. In the Second District, Democratic congressman John Wentworth's bid for renomination badly fragmented the anti-Nebraska forces. Despite his vote against the Nebraska bill, Wentworth had roused the ire of many of its opponents by his hesitant course during the struggle in the House. He was an extraordinarily talented political manipulator, but his ambition and demagoguery spawned strenuous opposition, not only among Whigs and Free Soilers but among Democrats as well.[91] Elsewhere Whig congressman Elihu B. Washburne in the First District and Jesse Norton in the Bloomington District both actively promoted the Republican movement as a means to strengthen themselves. Despite receiving the Republican nomination, Washburne was not totally committed to the new party; he distanced himself from the state fusion movement and preserved ties to the Whig organization, as his active support of Lincoln's senatorial bid in the winter demonstrated. Norton's commitment was also qualified, since he was a Know Nothing. He finally managed to secure the Republican nomination, but not until after, in the words of one observer, "a most stormy time." The nativist order was a shadowy presence in these congressional contests. At least two anti-Nebraska congressional candidates, Norton and Thomas Knox, were members of the secret society, and several others, including William R. Archer (who subsequently joined) and James Woodworth, definitely received Know Nothing backing.[92]

The continuing disunity among anti-Nebraska men in the Illinois congressional contests contrasted with the harmony that prevailed, at least by the time of the election,

---

90. Ichabod Codding to Abraham Lincoln, November 13, Lincoln Papers, LC; Lincoln to Codding, November 27, Basler, ed., *Lincoln Collected Works*, v. 2, 288.

91. R. L. Wilson to Elihu B. Washburne, September 29, Elihu B. Washburne Papers, LC; *Free West*, September 21, Aurora *Guardian*, October 5, Cole Notes; Don E. Fehrenbacher, *Chicago Giant: A Biography of "Long John" Wentworth* (Madison, 1957), 130–34; Chicago *Democratic Press*, September 19, 22, Cole Notes.

92. Elihu B. Washburne to Zebina Eastman, June 11, July 5, James F. Aldrich Papers, ChicHS; John S. Wright, "The Background and Formation of the Republican Party in Illinois, 1846–1860" (unpublished Ph.D. dissertation, University of Chicago, 1947), 148–54; Joliet *Signal*, September 5, Cole Notes; R. L. Wilson to Washburne, September 19 (quotation), Elihu B. Washburne Papers, LC.

in other western states. In part this situation reflected the presence of such diverse figures as Wentworth, but additional factors were involved as well. For one thing, the unity in other states reflected the strength of the Know Nothings, who secretly controlled many of these nominations. In Illinois the nativist society, although certainly not without influence, had less time to organize and did not operate as effectively. In addition, the radicalism of the local fusion conventions, which were not tempered by an active state organization, caused conservative Whigs and Democrats to hold back. More important, however, was the unwillingness of both Whigs and Democrats to abandon their old loyalties. Many Whigs viewed the fusion movement as an adjunct of the Whig party, and they were reluctant to concede positions of influence to longtime Democrats. The prestige of the leaders of the anti-Nebraska Democrats also contributed to the lack of cooperation. In contrast to those in Indiana and especially Ohio, a number of important Illinois Democratic leaders bolted their party over the Nebraska issue. Skilled political operators, they were naturally suspicious of the close ties between Whiggery and Republicanism, and they were unwilling to take a back seat in a Whig-controlled fusion movement. Nor did disaffected Democrats always share the views of fellow opponents of the Nebraska bill on other questions. As one of their number stipulated, anti-Nebraska Democrats were "not willing to forsake every principle of the Democratic party" for a one-idea party.[93] Old antagonisms and rivalries mingled with aspirations for the future to keep apart the anti-Douglas forces. The result was discord and, in some districts, competing opposition tickets. In spite of the Nebraska issue, the opposition in Illinois remained hopelessly divided.

Only in Illinois of the northwestern states did the Democrats win a statewide victory.[94] In the congressional and legislative contests, where the anti-Douglas men concentrated their efforts, the opposition's strength was more apparent (Maps 3 and 4). Anti-Nebraska candidates for Congress outpolled their opponents by a significant margin and carried five of the nine districts, including a seat in Egypt (southern Illinois) where Lyman Trumbull was victorious as an independent anti-Nebraska Democrat. The only points of Democratic solace were the reelection of William A. Richardson, the House floor manager of the Nebraska bill, after a fierce contest, and Thomas Harris's upset victory over Richard Yates in the Springfield District. Yates was one of the few anti-Nebraska congressmen defeated by a Nebraska Democrat in 1854. His loss turned not on the Nebraska issue, however, but on nativism, when a number of foreign-born Whigs deserted Yates because of rumors he was a Know Nothing. (These rumors were apparently false, but Yates was close to the order's local leaders.) Nevertheless, Harris campaigned forthrightly on the doctrine of popular sovereignty, and his victory gave Douglas men heart that they could survive in the North on this issue.[95] As important as

93. C. G. Holbrook to Washburne, December 30, Elihu B. Washburne Papers, LC; Rock River *Democrat*, September 12, quoted in Hansen, *Third Party System*, 54. For evidence of Democratic suspicions, see the Aurora *Guardian*, August 24, Cole Notes.

94. The result in the treasurer's race stood: Miller (Anti-Nebraska), 65,477 (48.9 percent), and Moore (Democrat), 68,392 (51.1 percent). Because of the lack of anti-Democratic ballots, Miller received no votes in a number of counties in the southern part of the state, thus providing further evidence of the opposition's organizational disarray. In the congressional contests, anti-Nebraska candidates polled a combined total of 78,064 votes compared to 60,451 for pro-Douglas nominees.

95. Lincoln to Richard Yates, October 30, November 1 [October 31], Lincoln to Orville W. Browning, November 12, Basler, ed., *Lincoln Collected Works*, v. 2, 284–87; Browning to John McLean, December 5, McLean Papers, LC. It is difficult to know whether Lincoln's explanation of Yates's defeat was sound. Yates

Miller (Anti-Nebraska)

Democrat

Note: Numbers are Miller's percentage of the votes cast.

3. Illinois Vote for Treasurer, 1854

Legend:

☐ Anti-Nebraska Majority

▨ Regular Democrat Majority

4. Illinois Vote for Congress, 1854

the Democrats' congressional losses was the composition of the next legislature. Even with Democratic holdovers, the anti-Nebraska and Whig members were a majority, and it appeared that no Nebraska man could be elected senator.

Despite his designation as the anti-Nebraska nominee for treasurer, James Miller received virtually no Democratic support. Instead, his candidacy represented a strictly Whig-Free Soil coalition reinforced by some new voters (Table 4.8). The rate of non-voting among Democrats suggests that discontented party members, including those who disliked the repeal of the Missouri Compromise, abstained on the state contest rather than support a Whig-Know Nothing. In the congressional elections, a different pattern took shape: Opposition candidates still received strong support from Whigs and Free Soilers, but they also won some traditional Democratic votes along with a larger share of new and previous non-voters (Table 4.9). Although they were not numerous, a slightly higher number of Whigs defected in these races than in the treasurer's contest. These defectors were probably immigrants nervous about nativism and, more especially, conservatives uneasy over the growing Whig ties in some districts to the radical Republican movement. The lower rate of non-voting among Democrats in these contests presumably indicates that a number of anti-Nebraska Democrats who abstained on the treasurer's race cast ballots in the congressional elections—a decision no doubt made easier by the fact that some of the opposition candidates were former Democrats rather than Whigs. The results in the Eighth District, where Trumbull was victorious, furnish a case in point. The number of votes cast in the congressional contest exceeded that in the state contest by more than 1,000 votes. Moreover, Trumbull ran almost 3,000 votes ahead of Miller in this heavily Democratic district. In addition to traditional party animosities, fear of nativism among foreign-born voters, which Democrats stimulated, also had an effect. In St. Clair County, which had a sizable German population, Trumbull polled 1,619 votes compared to only 687 for Miller. In the neighboring Ninth District, Edwards County, long an English Whig stronghold, voted 73 percent Democratic in the treasurer's contest.[96]

Accustomed to unchallenged dominance in the state, Democrats could not hide their chagrin at the results of the election. "Never before have the democracy of Illinois been so completely vanquished," mourned one Democratic editor. Led by Douglas, some party leaders tried to minimize the importance of the Kansas-Nebraska Act in the outcome by pointing to other factors that undeniably had been important, including nativism, temperance sentiment, and the adverse effect on Democratic morale of the party's setbacks in other states. More forthright, James Shields concluded that the Democratic

---

ran ahead of his ticket in every county in his district, including Morgan County, where the disaffection supposedly existed. William A. Richardson had expected to be defeated because of the strength of the Know Nothings in his district and the large number of Democrats who had enrolled in the secret lodges. Richardson to Stephen A. Douglas, November 5, Douglas Papers, UChic.

96. The vote in the Eighth District for congressman was: Trumbull, 7,917 (58.2 percent), and Foulke (Nebraska Democrat), 5,306 (39.0 percent); for treasurer, Miller (Anti-Nebraska), 4,876 (38.9 percent), and Moore (Democrat), 7,671 (61.1 percent). A Whig candidate for Congress polled 388 votes. The rate of Democratic defection to opposition candidates for Congress was not constant throughout the state. Estimates of 1852 Democratic voters casting opposition ballots for Congress in 1854 were zero percent for the northern third of the counties, 16 percent for the central counties, and 4 percent for the southern counties. The estimate for the northern part of the state undoubtedly understates the true proportion there. In addition, the process of rounding obscures the differences in the proportions of Whigs and Democrats switching parties in the state and congressional contests.

party had been hurt by the establishment of the Nebraska Act as a party test and by the popular belief that the purpose of the law was to make Kansas a slave state. After stumping in the central and southern parts of the state, he told Lanphier, "The Anti Nebraska feeling is too deep—more than I thought it was."[97] Voicing Whig elation after years of frustration, the impulsive William H. Herndon crowed: "Douglas can no more control Illinois than a Hottentot Chief can."[98]

V

The 1854 elections in the western states were a serious setback for the Democratic party.[99] Besides the defeats the party suffered in the state contests, its strength in the western congressional delegations was virtually wiped out. Yet so many forces had been at work in these elections that, beyond the repudiation of Douglas and his party, their meaning was unclear. Bewildered by the conglomerate nature of the opposition, an Illinois paper commented aptly that "the Democratic banner has gone down before a torrent of abolitionism, Whigism, freesoilism, religious bigotry and intolerance."[100] Politicians disagreed on the relative contribution of the various impulses to the popular revolt against the old parties.

Equally baffling was the future course of realignment. The opposition had managed to unite, at least temporarily, in all these states save Illinois, yet the new Republican party had been organized in only two relatively unimportant states. In addition, the rapid growth of the Know Nothings disconcerted opposition leaders outside the secret society. Generally encouraged by the outcome of the elections in the West, they were concerned about the course the order would follow in the future, particularly whether it would continue to cooperate with other anti-Democratic groups or operate as an independent political party. Antislavery men like George W. Julian feared that the order would undermine the popular movement against the expansion of slavery by emphasizing nativism instead. In the West, fusion was at best an uncertain movement in 1854, and even where victorious its future direction was yet to be determined. When anti-Democratic leaders studied political developments that year in the eastern states, however, they found even less to make them hopeful. If the fusion movement was confused in the West, in the East it was a resounding failure.

---

97. Joliet *Signal*, November 14, quoted in Arthur C. Cole, *Era of the Civil War, 1848–1860* (Chicago, 1922), 133; Richardson to Douglas, November 5, Douglas Papers, UChi; James Shields to Lanphier, October 25, Confidential, Charles Lanphier Papers, IllSHL; R. W. English to William H. English, October 30, William H. English Papers, IndHS; H. L. Breese to Sidney Breese, September 26, Sidney Breese Papers, IllSHL.

98. William H. Herndon to Theodore Parker, February 13, 1855 (copy), Theodore Parker Papers, MassHS.

99. In California the Democratic vote was split between the Broderick and Gwin factions, yet the party managed to win both congressional seats (voting was at-large rather than by district). The Whigs narrowly elected the clerk of the Supreme Court, although the combined Democratic vote was almost 60 percent.

100. Joliet *Signal*, November 14, quoted in Albert J. Beveridge, *Abraham Lincoln, 1809–1858* (2 vols.: Boston, 1928), v. 2, 273–74.

5

The Failure of Fusion

The fusion movement made little headway in the East. Only in Vermont, where the Whigs and most Free Soilers eventually agreed on a common ticket while preserving their separate organizations, did the opposition form even a temporary coalition in 1854. Elsewhere, not even this degree of unity was achieved. "We doubt if there has ever been . . . so much confusion . . . both among whigs and democrats, as there is at the present time," a Democratic paper in western New York commented. Sharing a similar sense of bewilderment, a Whig editor in Maine conceded that "the political elements are in a state of commotion that baffles all calculation and all foresight." Former governor Washington Hunt of New York sounded the keynote for the 1854 elections in the eastern states when he surmised that "we are to have political chaos—'confusion worse confounded.' "[1]

I

In Maine, the liquor controversy continued to divide both parties, especially the Democrats. "Parties in Maine have been so disorganized by the Temperance Question," the *National Era* noted in June, "that it requires considerable circumlocution to define them." Encouraged by the widespread condemnation of the repeal of the Missouri Compromise, Free Soilers were particularly anxious to organize a new party on the twin planks of anti-Nebraska and the Maine Law, but Whig resistance effectively blocked fusion.[2] Whigs' confidence had soared at the beginning of the year when the legislature, ignoring Anson Morrill's popular strength in the 1853 general election, reelected William Crosby governor and selected William Pitt Fessenden, a moderate antislavery and temperance Whig, for United States senator. The vote for governor demonstrated the extent to which party lines had collapsed. Whigs in the legislature split evenly between Crosby and Morrill, while more Democrats actually voted for the Whig candidate, since

---

Note: Unless otherwise indicated, the year for newspaper and manuscript citations in this chapter is 1854.

1. Buffalo *Courier*, November 6; *Kennebec Journal*, June 23; Washington Hunt to Hamilton Fish, August 2, Fish Papers, LC.

2. *Daily National Era*, June 29. Resolutions opposing the repeal of the Missouri Compromise passed the state legislature by a vote of ninety-six to six in the Assembly and twenty-four to one in the Senate.

anti-Morrill Democrats preferred to let Crosby serve another term rather than see the office go to their hated party rivals. "The Whigs have . . . obtained a large dividend on a small capital," one party leader aptly observed.[3] After years of impotence, Whiggery seemed on the threshold of becoming a powerful entity in the state's politics, and Fessenden, anxious not to let this opportunity slip by, urged Crosby to use his patronage to conciliate the Morrill Democrats.[4]

Whigs were also heartened by the steadily worsening division of the Democratic party in the state. "Maine is in a very bad condition," one Democrat admitted early in the year, "& nothing but a complete re-organization, and regeneration, will restore the democracy to power there."[5] The Morrill faction remained defiantly outside the regular Democratic organization, and, hoping to unite the opposition under its lead, renominated Morrill on a platform that condemned the overthrow of the Missouri Compromise, strongly endorsed the Maine Law, and called for the repeal of the fugitive slave law. The rival Wildcat Democrats, on the other hand, again in control of the party machinery, took a new tack. Having lost the last two state contests on the liquor issue and now confronted with the embarrassing Nebraska question as well, they passed over all leading aspirants and nominated for governor Albion K. Parris, a temperance Democrat who had defeated Neal Dow for mayor of Portland. The convention refused to adopt any platform. "Let us take care of the Democracy of Maine," one delegate advised, "and let the parties in the other sections of the Union take care of themselves." Pointing to Parris's checkered political past, a leading Whig journal jibed that the Democratic candidate was "a blank mummy."[6]

Such a policy was unacceptable to the diehard anti-Maine Law Democrats led by Shepard Cary. The most vociferous legislative opponent of Dow's statute when it passed in 1851, Cary had surrendered neither his position as its leading critic nor his battle against the law. Angered by his failure to receive the nomination at the last two party conventions, he decided to run as an independent Democrat. The Liberal platform ignored the Nebraska question and other national issues, even though most members of this faction supported the repeal of the Missouri Compromise, and concentrated its fire on the Maine Law. Cary's popular designation as the Rum candidate succinctly summarized his faction's public image.

Meanwhile, Free Soil leaders were determined to bring about a fusion of the opposition. They therefore engineered Morrill's endorsement by the Free Soil state convention, despite some resistance among the delegates, and in effect disbanded the party. Attempts to induce the Whig party to take up Morrill, however, were unavailing. Several Whig leaders, most notably Israel Washburn and Edward Kent and to a lesser extent William Pitt Fessenden, urged Whigs to unite with the Morrill Democrats. They pointed out that both groups agreed on major principles and that therefore nothing blocked fusion but the ambitions of rival leaders.[7] This consideration was more than sufficient. As

3. Isaac Reed to Israel Washburn, Jr., February 10, Edward Kent to Washburn, March 5 (quotation), Israel Washburn, Jr., Papers, Norlands. For Crosby's election, see Wescott, "Maine Politics," 201–11; Dow, *Reminiscences*, 488–95.

4. Israel Washburn, Jr., to William Pitt Fessenden, January 30, Fessenden Papers, WRHS; Fessenden to William G. Crosby, February 11, Private (copy), Fessenden Papers, LC.

5. C. G. Greene to Caleb Cushing, March 3, Cushing Papers; *Kennebec Journal*, May 19.

6. Lewis C. Hatch, ed., *Maine: A History* (3 vols.: New York, 1919), v. 2, 378–79; *Kennebec Journal*, June 23.

7. Fessenden to Henry Carter, June 16, clipping, Fessenden Family Papers; Edward Kent to Israel Washburn, Jr., June 21, Israel Washburn, Jr., Papers, Norlands.

far as offices were concerned, the Whigs had greatly benefited from the political confusion of the past few years, and ambitious party members were unwilling to sacrifice their chances now. Past experience demonstrated that both Democratic factions preferred the success of a Whig to that of their party enemies. Whig leaders assumed that they could continue to exploit this situation, and Cary's independent candidacy promised to weaken the Democrats still further. Thus the Whig convention nominated a full ticket headed by Isaac Reed and adopted a platform confined almost entirely to the slavery issue (one plank endorsed a prohibitory law). The Whig statement of principles condemned the Nebraska Act, opposed the expansion of slavery to any territory or the admission of any new slave states, and called for the modification of the fugitive slave law to secure the rights of the accused. The only concession that the convention made to fusion sentiment was to recommend that anti-Nebraska men lay aside party differences "for the time" to elect men opposed to the Kansas-Nebraska Act to Congress.[8]

Discouraged by the continuing division of the opposition, Kent vented his frustration on "tender toed & impractical" Whigs. "These men seem to think more & care more for some little paltry county election, than the great issues before us & to care more about their village splits & strifes than about the extension of slavery & the success of the most ultra democracy." Fusion failed in most counties as well. As Kent complained, "A portion of the Whigs are not disposed to do more than to *accept* help where they can't get along without it, and to 'neither borrow nor lend' where they are strong enough without borrowing." He was disgusted at the Whigs' unwillingness to make any concessions. "They wanted every thing to be whig & nothing but old whig." On most congressional races the opposition managed to unite, although in two districts Whig intransigence undermined all attempts at union. "Is it not provoking that with men enough to sweep the State clean," Fessenden exclaimed, "we should be beaten by the utter folly of men calling themselves *Whigs!*"[9]

The multiplicity of tickets made it impossible to forecast the results of the fall election, which presented three candidates claiming the name Democrat and two contestants (Morrill and Reed) running on virtually identical platforms. Still, Morrill was clearly the popular choice of the fusionists. In addition to the endorsement of the now disbanded Free Soil party, he also received the sanction of the state temperance convention with Dow presiding, and of the Know Nothing party, which had recently begun organizing in the state. Some discontent over this last decision surfaced among committed nativists, who charged that Morrill men had rushed into the order at the last minute and diverted it from its true principles. The prohibitionists' support for Morrill, on the other hand, occasioned no surprise. From the beginning temperance men had actively promoted fusion; indeed, they had earlier assumed the lead in the legislature in an abortive attempt to form a fusion coalition, and Morrill had long been identified with the anti-liquor cause.[10]

The Nebraska issue, like the liquor question before it, could not bring the opposition in Maine to support a common ticket, let alone combine into a single organization. Even so, the popular desire for fusion was stronger than the events of 1854 indicated. Fusion failed primarily because Whigs believed that they could again take advantage of existing

---

8. Bangor *Whig and Courier*, July 3; *Kennebec Journal*, May 19, June 16.

9. Kent to Israel Washburn, Jr., June 25, July 27, Israel Washburn, Jr., Papers, Norlands; Fessenden to James Shepherd Pike, August 14, Pike Papers, UMe; Wescott, "Maine Politics," 238–39.

10. Portland *Eastern Argus*, September 8; Bangor *Whig and Courier*, June 10, July 10; Dow, *Reminiscences*, 502–3, 509, 514; Wescott, "Maine Politics," 216–18.

Democratic divisions. Despite this setback, Free Soil leader Austin Willey nevertheless remained hopeful. The important thing, he told Fessenden, was to outpoll the Whigs in the fall and thus "induce reasonable action hereafter" among anti-fusion Whigs. "Nothing but party *depletion*," he added, "will produce the right state of mind in that class of whigs."[11]

Prior to the election, Maine Whigs believed that their party was on the verge of supremacy. When the votes were tallied, they discovered instead that it had completely collapsed. Morrill led all candidates, and although he narrowly missed gaining a majority, his election by the legislature was a foregone conclusion. Political commentators were astonished at Morrill's popular showing, which far surpassed pre-election prognostications. Most impressive was the fact that he polled more than three times as many votes as Reed, the Whig nominee.[12] The results left no doubt as to the fatal impact of previous controversies on the party's vitality. So weakened was Maine Whiggery before 1854 that even the Nebraska issue could not revive it. Instead, thousands of voters, anxious for a new party and distrustful of the old organizations, supported Morrill as a man independent of party. The Whig *Kennebec Journal* attributed Morrill's showing in part to the popular desire "to DISCARD THE OLD BLOOD-SUCKERS who have grown fat and corrupt by holding office all their lives, and who have long since lost the confidence of the community." The results sustained its observation at the beginning of the campaign that "party ties, names and adhesions were never so weak . . . regular nominations and *regular* everything else have lost their power."[13]

As an independent candidate, Morrill drew votes from all previous political parties (Tables 5.1 and 5.2). In addition to his own faction, which backed him strongly, he received overwhelming support from the Free Soilers and won a majority of Whigs along with a significant number of earlier non-voters. Neither the Whig nor Democratic candidates had much appeal to those who previously abstained from voting. By contrast, almost a quarter of Morrill's supporters had not gone to the polls in 1853. Cary's vote came largely from Democrats, and (as would be expected) he did poorly among Morrill's prior adherents. Although divisions in the state's politics stemming from the prohibition issue were a crucial element in the 1854 voting alignment, other factors were also at work. It is difficult to account for Morrill's strength among non-voters on the basis of the liquor issue, which had been the primary focus of the previous two state elections and had brought out a full vote, especially in 1852. It also seems significant that few of this group voted for Cary, the only candidate running on an anti-Maine Law platform. Although precise evidence is lacking, many of these newly mobilized voters who cast Morrill ballots were probably Know Nothings.[14]

Contemporaries were undoubtedly correct in emphasizing the importance of the

---

11. Austin Willey to Fessenden, July 12, Fessenden Papers, WRHS.

12. The results were Morrill, 44,852 (49.5 percent); Reed (Whig), 14,017 (15.5 percent); Parris (Democrat), 28,396 (31.3 percent); and Cary (Liberal), 3,424 (3.8 percent).

13. *Kennebec Journal*, October 6, June 23; Bangor *Whig and Courier*, September 12. Popular discontent with the existing parties was also evident in the two congressional contests in which there was more than one opposition candidate. In both districts, voters thrust aside the regular politicians and elected clergymen running as independents.

14. In other states the Know Nothings displayed unusual strength among new voters, and this was presumably the case in Maine as well. The Nebraska issue may have been more crucial in bringing previously indifferent voters to the polls, but, in that case Reed, the Whig nominee who was as sound on the slavery extension question as Morrill, should have won a much larger proportion of previous non-voters than he did.

Nebraska and nativist issues as well as temperance in producing Morrill's victory.[15] Comparison of Morrill's support with the divisions in the 1852 state election, when Governor John Hubbard won reelection on the anti-liquor issue, further substantiates this analysis. As would be expected, Morrill, who had assumed leadership of Hubbard's Democratic faction, won by far the largest share of the latter's followers (Table 5.2). But Morrill did as well as Cary among the supporters of Albert Pillsbury, who had run in 1852 as an anti-Maine Law candidate. The Nebraska issue probably was crucial to Morrill's strength among these Democrats. By exploiting the Nebraska issue and the growing disenchantment with the old parties, Morrill significantly expanded as well as gave new direction to Hubbard's earlier anti-rum coalition. At the same time, Morrill benefited from his endorsement by the Know Nothings. Some analysts flatly attributed his victory to the workings of the secret order, and the *Kennebec Journal* asserted that, as was true in other New England states, a large proportion of the Free Soilers who backed Morrill were members of nativist lodges. The role of the Know Nothings in the 1854 election cannot be charted precisely, but James G. Blaine, an extraordinarily well-informed observer, tabulated that Americans constituted more than half the membership of the next legislature.[16] With just cause a Democratic journal, noting the disparate nature of Morrill's support, concluded: "However easy it may be to understand who has been beaten in the election, it is impossible to determine, as yet who has been victorious. . . . If the union of *isms* has obtained success, it remains to be seen how far the same *isms* can agree in the management of what they have won."[17]

Despite the storm over the Nebraska bill, the Whig party, which had adopted the most pronounced antislavery platform of any of the state's parties, suffered a decisive defeat at the hands of a broad-based independent party. After the election, the *Kennebec Journal*, which had retreated earlier from its endorsement of fusion in the face of Whig opposition, argued that it was hopeless to maintain the Whig organization any longer. It noted that the Whig vote had been reduced from 46,000 in 1840 to a mere 14,000 in 1854, and it estimated that at least half the remaining Whigs sympathized with Morrill but voted for Reed out of party loyalty and would now leave the party as well. Calling for the various factions in the state that "think alike" to act under a common name, it announced its allegiance to the Republican movement rather than "hug the fossil remains of dead issues."[18]

II

Whig resistance also blocked fusion in nearby Massachusetts, where the power of the Know Nothings greatly complicated matters. The defeat of the new constitution, the breakup of the Coalition, and continuing internecine feuds left the Massachusetts Free Soilers desperate. Party leaders hailed the Nebraska bill as the issue needed to revive their

15. Neal Dow to Gerrit Smith, September 20, Smith Family Papers, NYPL; letter from George H. Witherlee, October 30, *National Era*, November 9.

16. For assertions that the Know Nothings voted for Morrill, see the Bangor *Whig and Courier*, September 12; Portland *Transcript*, September 16; Portland *Eastern Argus*, September 11, 13; *Kennebec Journal*, October 6, December 1. James G. Blaine pegged Know Nothing strength in the legislature at between eighty and ninety representatives out of a total of 151 members. *Kennebec Journal*, October 6.

17. Portland *Eastern Argus*, September 13.

18. *Kennebec Journal*, September 29, October 6, November 10 (quotation).

faltering cause, but subsequent events would reveal the extent of their misperception. One of Charles Sumner's correspondents observed that the Free Soil party had "destroyed its influence with such large portions of the Whigs & Democrats by its *party alliances* & maneuvres" that it could never capitalize on the strong popular desire for a northern party.[19] Furthermore, anti-Nebraska sentiment was so pervasive it was an ineffective issue with which to distinguish the various opposition parties.[20] Nor did Whigs concede leadership of this protest to their long-time rivals. They claimed that their party, and not a fusion organization, offered the most effective vehicle for anti-Nebraska sentiment. But the jolt that most enfeebled fusion was the rise of the Know Nothing party. Embracing not only the issue of anti-Nebraska but also the general desire for reform, this new organization contested the fall election as an independent party, thus further fragmenting Bay State politics.

Passage of the Kansas-Nebraska Act rekindled antislavery men's dreams of forming a new party. In calling for "a complete dissolution of the old party organizations," the Boston *Commonwealth*, the Free Soil organ, urged the masses to override party leaders and establish a new party. Free Soilers, however, split over the fusion movement, with one faction led by Henry Wilson in favor, while their opponents, typified by Charles Francis Adams, dismissed the idea of a new party as a mere "scheme" to save former Coalitionists from their impending political demise and refused to aid the movement.[21]

Confident of their power, Whigs disdainfully rejected all overtures for union, nominated a full state ticket, and rejected cooperation even in the congressional contests. Nor would Whigs forget the past. An address of the Whig state central committee repudiating fusion renewed the party's condemnation of past Free Soil participation in the Coalition. Furthermore, as many opponents had predicted, the Whigs, despite their earlier pledges, enacted few reforms in the 1854 legislative session. Whig leaders thus flouted arrogantly not only the desire for fusion but also the much stronger demand for reform. They mistook the narrow rejection of an extreme constitution in 1853 for a thundering endorsement of the Whig party and its policies.[22]

Despite the persistence of widespread opposition, Free Soil Coalitionists led by Wilson plunged ahead and called a fusion convention to meet in Worcester on September 6. Although members of other parties attended, the convention was, as the Springfield *Republican* acknowledged, "a thoroughly . . . free soil gathering," which adoption of the name *Republican* could not camouflage. The delegates nominated a ticket headed by Wilson for governor and approved an extreme platform that specified the repeal of the fugitive slave law, no more slave states, prohibition of slavery in all the territories, the acquisition of Cuba only without slavery, and the abolition of slavery in the District of Columbia. Such sentiments far outstripped public opinion in the state. The Free Soil party had merely changed names without garnering any significant support from other parties. Adams, noting that even most former Free Soilers stayed out of the

---

19. C. G. Loring to Charles Sumner, March 14, Sumner Papers, HU.

20. For the unanimity of Massachusetts public opinion on the Nebraska bill, see Henry Wilson's remarks, *Cong. Globe*, 33rd Cong., 2nd sess., Appendix, 216.

21. Boston *Commonwealth* quoted in the *National Era*, June 1; Charles Francis Adams Diary, June 1, July 22 (quotation), Adams Family Papers.

22. T. D. Eliot to Sumner, September 13, Sumner Papers, HU; Emory Washburn to Julius Rockwell, [June], Private, Walker-Rockwell Papers; Bean, "Transformation of Parties," 188–90. The Whig address is in the Boston *Daily Advertiser*, June 26. The Springfield *Republican* was the most important Whig paper to endorse fusion; for example, July 10, 15.

Republican movement, scorned the party as "a drum and fife [corps] without followers."[23] In the absence of a genuine fusion in the state, the "Republican" party existed in name only.

At the center of this abortive fusion movement stood Henry Wilson, one of the most remarkable politicians of his generation. Born Jeremiah Colbath in a rude New Hampshire shack, he had by talent and hard work overcome poverty and a severely limited education to become a successful shoe manufacturer and powerful party leader. Prior to the commencement of his public career he had taken a new name in a symbolic break with his past. Genial and even-tempered, he remained a peacemaker and harmonizer in the face of scathing criticism. Wilson also had a knack for assessing public opinion and was a master at political intrigue—he displayed, in the words of one Massachusetts journalist, "an incurable propensity to manage and to manoeuvre"—yet throughout his career he remained a sincere opponent of slavery. The Free Soil leader was, according to no less an authority than Salmon P. Chase, "hot shot from [an] abolition cannon." Blessed with more fortunate origins, less charitable critics like Charles Francis Adams refused to acknowledge his talents or concede him any sincerity of purpose. More than disagreement over policies and distrust of Wilson's hunger for office separated Adams and his class from the coarse Natick cobbler. "I could wish Wilson had more polish & dignity," one fair-minded political associate wrote, "but he is a good honest fellow, & deserves kinder treatment than he has received at the hands of these men. . . . Considering what he was, & what he *has made himself*, he is worthy of great praise."[24]

Far from disarming his critics, Wilson's course in 1854 provided them with additional ammunition. The existing political chaos offered a shrewd and not overly scrupulous manipulator like Wilson an ideal situation in which to strike for personal advantage. Early on, his wide network of political contacts alerted him to the rapidly growing power of the Know Nothings. Although he lacked deep nativist convictions, early in the spring he joined a lodge in Boston after being rejected in his home town of Natick. Rumors of his membership spread throughout the state that summer. Robert C. Winthrop, for one, recognized that if the rumors were true the Know Nothings were likely to be a power in Massachusetts, for Wilson was "far too shrewd to allow himself to be made a catspaw."[25]

As a result, Wilson was not even in hearty accord with the party whose ticket he headed. Redirecting his ambition from the long-sought governorship to the United States Senate, he secretly conducted negotiations within the Know Nothing ranks while still the "Republican" nominee for governor; as a result of these discussions, he eventually agreed to support Henry J. Gardner for governor in exchange for the remaining portion of Edward Everett's Senate term to be filled by the next legislature. The wily Wilson withdrew from the gubernatorial race on the eve of the election, deliberately leaving the "Republican" central committee insufficient time to name a new candidate, thus further

23. Springfield *Republican*, September 8; Adams to Francis Bird, October 16 (copy) (quotation), Diary, September 7, Adams Family Papers; George F. Hoar, *Autobiography of Seventy Years* (2 vols.: New York, 1903), v. 1, 30–31.

24. Charles T. Congdon, *Reminiscences of a Journalist* (Boston, 1880), 87, 132 (quotation); Chase quoted in Sewell, *Ballots for Freedom*, 271; Albert G. Browne to Sumner, February 22, Sumner Papers, HU. For Wilson's career, see Richard H. Abbott, *Cobbler in Congress: The Life of Henry Wilson, 1812–1875* (Lexington, Ky., 1972); and Ernest McKay, *Henry Wilson: Practical Radical* (Port Washington, N.Y., 1971).

25. Robert C. Winthrop, Jr., *A Memoir of Robert C. Winthrop* (Boston, 1897), 168; Boston *Daily Bee*, September 15; Congdon, *Reminiscences*, 146; Abbott, *Cobbler in Congress*, 58.

crippling a rapidly disintegrating Free Soil movement. The angered committee had no choice but to leave Wilson's name on the ticket.[26]

The new party that organized in Massachusetts in 1854 was not the Republican but the American. As it expanded throughout the state, the Know Nothing order absorbed a great number of Whig and Democrat voters as well as men who previously belonged to no party. It was especially strong among the Free Soilers, in part because the new party was anti-Nebraska and called for state reform, and in part because many Free Soilers blamed Catholics for the defeat of the 1853 constitution. A Boston observer, noting that many Free Soilers were joining the secret society, attributed these gains to anti-Catholicism. The nativist party's identification with temperance in the campaign also strengthened it with antislavery men. Because of these Free Soil accessions, some men predicted that the society would be converted into an antislavery organization. Others were not so sure. The Boston correspondent of the New York *Tribune*, who reported that many Free Soilers had gone into the order with the expectation that they could control it, added: "I am inclined to believe that those that went out to shear will come back shorn."[27] From the beginning the Massachusetts Know Nothing organization, especially at the leadership level, was divided between a Free Soil wing, headed by Wilson and Congressman Nathaniel Banks, and a rival, largely Whig faction led by Henry J. Gardner.

Aided by Wilson and Anson Burlingame, another Free Soil leader who joined the order, Gardner obtained the American party's gubernatorial nomination. A wool merchant who was politically unknown outside Boston, Gardner experienced in 1854 a remarkable change in his political views. Although he had never displayed any anti-foreign principles, and indeed had warmly recommended the appointment of an Irishman as justice of the peace, Gardner suddenly converted to nativism. An ultra Webster Whig who had ardently backed the federal authorities in an earlier fugitive slave case, he now portrayed himself as an antislavery man and commenced denouncing the fugitive slave law. Formerly an opponent of the Maine Law and well-known for serving alcoholic refreshments, he abruptly endorsed prohibition. Disgusted at Gardner's opportunistic course, Everett described the Know Nothing leader somewhat lamely as "a man of some cleverness, but no solidity of character."[28] As his subsequent career demonstrated, Gardner possessed considerable political ability, which he directed to the single-minded purpose of gaining and retaining power.

The result in the Bay State confounded the most astute political observers: The Know Nothings scored a wholly unanticipated and completely unprecedented sweep. In the gubernatorial contest, with more than 63 percent of the vote, Gardner won a clear majority over his three rivals.[29] All but a handful of the members of the next legislature belonged to the order. The secret society carried all the state's congressional districts; among its victims were four Whigs who had opposed the Nebraska bill, including John Z. Goodrich, one of the most prominent leaders of the anti-Nebraska forces in the House. Even in

---

26. D. W. Alvord to Bird, November 8, Simeon Merrit to Bird, October 20, Bird Papers; Abbott, *Cobbler in Congress*, 59; George S. Merriam, *The Life and Times of Samuel Bowles* (2 vols.: New York, 1885), v. 1, 125; Adams Diary, October 25, Adams Family Papers.

27. E. Winslow to Sumner, May 5, Sumner Papers, HU; New York *Tribune*, September 27; William C. Whitcomb to Sumner, January 16, 1855, Sumner Papers, HU.

28. Bean, "Transformation of Parties," 250–54; Edward Everett to Millard Fillmore, December 16, Private (copy), Everett Papers; New York *Evening Post*, November 20; *National Era*, November 2.

29. The vote was Washburn (Whig), 27,279 (21.1 percent); Bishop (Democrat), 13,742 (10.7 percent); Wilson (Free Soil), 6,483 (5.0 percent); and Gardner (Know Nothing), 81,503 (63.2 percent).

the traditional Whig district in Boston, Burlingame, who received the Know Nothing nomination in exchange for backing Gardner, triumphed over William Appleton, the representative of State Street Whiggery. In a result pregnant with significance for the eventual formation of a national Republican organization, Nathaniel P. Banks easily won reelection to Congress once he belatedly got the American party nomination after the original Know Nothing candidate withdrew. Seven of the eleven Know Nothing congressmen elected were former Free Soilers—an indication of the strong overlap between the antislavery and nativist movements.

"There has been no revolution so complete since the organization of the government," commented Adams, who concurred with Samuel Bowles's simplistic assessment that this result was attributable to the failure to form a fusion party in the state. The tally of votes exposed the depth of popular impatience with all the old parties and the deep-seated yearning for reform. One keen-sighted observer commented that "having become wearied of the follies of what are called 'leaders,' the people took the matter into their own hands, and decided the contest in a manner that has astounded all, not even excepting themselves."[30] No one outside the order was prepared for the outcome of the election, and Whigs in particular expressed amazement at the utter collapse of their party. Confident beforehand of victory, one Whig journalist recalled, "I no more suspected the impending result than I looked for an earthquake which would level the State House and reduce Faneuil Hall to a heap of ruins." Likewise, Winthrop exclaimed in dismay, "Poor old Massachusetts! . . . Who could have believed the old Whig party would have been so thoroughly demoralized in so short a space of time?"[31]

The Know Nothing majority in the state rested on a solid bipartisan base (Table 5.3). The new party won a large proportion of Whigs and a majority of both Democrats and Free Soilers. If Adams's assertion that "four fifths of our organization has left the standard of freedom to enlist itself against a shadow" exaggerated Free Soil defections to the Know Nothings, nevertheless a clear majority of Free Soilers followed Wilson into the nativist camp, and of those remaining, almost as many did not vote as cast "Republican" ballots. Gardner also attracted the support of many more previous non-voters than did Emory Washburn, the Whig nominee. The contention of one Massachusetts observer that the Know Nothing movement "embraces men from all the old political parties, as well as those from *no* political party" was accurate.[32]

The behavior of the Massachusetts Free Soilers stemmed from several causes. The endorsement of the Know Nothing movement by a number of prominent third-party leaders carried weight.[33] Gardner's strong identification with temperance, which contrasted with Washburn's lukewarm support, appealed to antislavery men, who as in other states were strongly opposed to spirits. Earlier, the Massachusetts Supreme Court had struck down the search-and-seizures clause of the state's 1852 prohibitory statute, and

---

30. Adams Diary, November 14, Adams Family Papers; Springfield *Republican*, November 15; Massachusetts correspondence, November 14, New York *Evening Post*, November 15.

31. Congdon, *Reminiscences*, 142–44; Robert C. Winthrop to John Clifford, November 16 (copy), Robert C. Winthrop Papers, MassHS; Everett Diary, November 14; Everett Papers; Samuel Gridley Howe to Horace Mann, November 14, Howe Papers, HU.

32. Adams Diary, November 14, Adams Family Papers; S. A. Bradbury to Amos A. Lawrence, November 27, Lawrence Papers.

33. Although the order's membership was secret, the affiliation of many Free Soil leaders was well-advertised. Besides Wilson, other prominent Free Soilers who became Know Nothings included Anson Burlingame, E. L. Keyes, John L. Swift, James W. Stone, and A. F. Alvord.

when the two houses of the legislature could not agree on how to amend the law to meet the court's objections, the rum issue was thrust into the state election. Unduly slighted by historians, Gardner's exploitation of the liquor issue was a crucial aspect of his popular success.[34] In addition, antagonism between Catholics and antislavery men intensified following the defeat in 1853 of the new constitution, and conspicuous Irish support for the fugitive slave law further inflamed this feeling. The Boston *Evening Telegraph* probably expressed the view of many voters when it declared, "Slavery and Catholicism are essentially one."[35] Also important was the Free Soilers' hatred of Whiggery. Adams believed that many of his former associates went into the nativist order out of "their eager zeal to beat the Whigs." Angered by the Whigs' arrogant refusal to participate in the fusion movement and by their continuing denunciation of Free Soilers' past involvement in the Coalition, third-party voters strongly backed the American party.[36] In so doing, they did not sacrifice their antislavery principles, for the Know Nothings opposed the Nebraska Act, and Gardner also denounced the fugitive slave law. The subsequent behavior of the overwhelmingly nativist state legislature in 1855, which passed the state's first personal liberty law, demonstrated that the Know Nothings' antislavery pronouncements were not solely opportunistic. At the same time, the Free Soil–Know Nothings were far from indifferent to the order's anti-Catholic and anti-immigrant principles.[37] To former Free Soil voters, the American party movement offered a chance to express hostility to both Catholics and slaveowners and to achieve state reform, while at the same time opposing the hated Whigs. As one Free Soil officeholder observed succinctly, the issues

---

34. Samuel Downer to Mann, November 13, Mann Papers; New York *Evening Post*, November 20. A Massachusetts correspondent reported that the Know Nothings were "remarkable . . . for their aversion to stimulants." Brunswick *Telegraph*, November 18. Sweeney, "Rum, Romanism, Representation, and Reform," 128–33, 135–37, demonstrates strong Free Soil support for prohibition.

35. Boston *Evening Telegraph*, July 20, quoted in Bean, "Transformation of Parties," 242. John G. Whittier emphasized that "wherever you found a Catholic you found a noisy Fugitive Slave Law advocate." *National Era*, November 24. Bean amply documents hostility among Free Soilers to the Irish over the defeat of the constitution (pp. 174–78). Desirous of separating the crusade against slavery from less attractive causes, historians generally have ignored the strength of anti-Catholic feeling within the antislavery movement, while at the same time they have exaggerated its tolerance and its defense of cultural pluralism. A good example is Gilbert Osofsky, "Abolitionists, Irish Immigrants, and the Dilemma of Romantic Nationalism," *AHR*, v. 80 (October, 1975), 889–912.

36. Adams to Stephen C. Phillips, November 16 (copy), Adams Family Papers; Howe to Mann, September 21, Howe Papers, HU; Clifford to Richard Henry Dana, Jr., June 10, Dana Family Papers.

37. For evidence of anti-Catholic sentiment among Free Soilers, see James Lodge to Sumner, n.d. [May–June], Sumner Papers, HU; Boston *Pilot*, February 11, Worcester *Spy*, July 29, both quoted in Bean, "Transformation of Parties," 237, 243. Dale Baum argues that Free Soilers who voted Know Nothing had no interest in nativism and supported the order purely out of expediency because it offered the best chance to carry the state: "Know-Nothingism and the Republican Majority in Massachusetts: The Political Realignment of the 1850s," *JAH*, v. 64 (March, 1973), 964–68. In reality, even experienced politicians with a wide network of informants were completely unprepared for the Know Nothings' popular showing in the election. The assumption that ordinary voters, with far more limited sources of information, foresaw the secret order's commanding power prior to the election is not credible. Furthermore, the contention that those Free Soilers who went into the Know Nothing lodges were indifferent to issues other than slavery is difficult to reconcile with their contribution to the defeat of four congressmen who had voted against the Kansas-Nebraska bill (the largest number of such congressmen rejected in any northern state in 1854). A Free Soil leader who tried to stem the order's inroads into the third party's ranks by "talking pretty plainly to them on the matter" provided a strikingly different assessment of his colleagues' attitudes. "They seemed altogether infatuated," he said of his former associates, "& ready to vote for any kind of cloven-foot provided he was the nominee of the 'Order.'" D. A. Wasson to Samuel Johnson, December 2, Samuel Johnson Papers, Essex Institute.

involved in the election were "freedom, temperance and Protestantism against slavery, rum, and Romanism."[38]

III

The most important states where fusion was thwarted were Pennsylvania and New York, which controlled the two largest blocs of electoral votes in the Union. For a northern sectional party to carry a national election, it had to win New York, and to have a realistic chance of victory, it really needed both states.[39] The failure of the fusion movement in the nation's two most populous states was therefore particularly significant.

The interest of Pennsylvania politicians during the first part of 1854 focused on the course of David Wilmot, the famous leader of the free soil Democrats. The Nebraska issue prompted Whigs to hope that they could detach Wilmot and other anti-Nebraska men from the Democratic party, as well as obtain the backing of the third-party Free Democrats.[40] Maneuvering during the summer of 1854 between the Whigs and Free Soilers represented the first stage of the movement to form a Republican party in Pennsylvania.[41]

For several years Wilmot had been only loosely contained within any party. A loyal disciple of Martin Van Buren, he followed his chieftain in 1848 into the Free Soil party, but, like many of the former president's supporters, he soon returned to the Democratic fold. Although he was subsequently elected to the bench on the Democratic ticket, his party allegiance remained perceptibly shaky. Jealously guarding his antislavery reputation gained as the result of his chance authorship of the famed proviso that bore his name, he was acutely sensitive to anything that appeared to ally him with slavery. Although he had become increasingly stout and lazy, the former congressman still exerted great influence in his old district along the state's northern border, which normally rolled up heavy Democratic majorities and where under his leadership the party was identified with opposition to the expansion of slavery. Despite his influence in his home region, Wilmot was unpopular with the state's Democratic leaders. They did not trust his party loyalty, and they viewed him as a dangerous agitator. Even so, he was a force to be reckoned with.

Democrats disagreed over the merits of the repeal of the Missouri Compromise, with the free soil wing led by Wilmot vehement in its opposition. Governor William Bigler, who intended to seek reelection, was particularly anxious not to alienate Wilmot and his associates. At the same time, the Pierce administration, worried about the growing northern opposition to the Nebraska bill, lobbied vigorously for its endorsement by the

---

38. Boston *Daily Advertiser*, November 6.

39. New York and Pennsylvania had thirty-five and twenty-seven electoral votes respectively in this decade. Because the free states cast a majority of the electoral votes, a northern sectional party could elect a president without any southern support. To do so, however, the party had to carry New York, and without Pennsylvania it needed to win every other free state—a difficult task.

40. The terminology is somewhat confusing. As was true in other states, the Free Soil party took the name Free Democratic party, but by this time many of the original Free Soilers, of whom David Wilmot was the most conspicuous example, had returned to their traditional allegiance. Even though Wilmot was no longer a member of the Free Democratic organization, he enjoyed a wide following among its members, and many still looked to him for guidance. Going, *Wilmot*, covers his career adequately.

41. For a more extensive analysis of the 1854 Pennsylvania election, see my article, "Nebraska, Nativism, and Rum: The Failure of Fusion in Pennsylvania, 1854," *Pennsylvania Magazine of History and Biography*, v. 109 (October, 1985), 425–71.

state convention. A man of limited talents, Bigler was far too timid to take a forthright stand on so controversial an issue as the Kansas-Nebraska bill; instead, once he had been renominated, his allies in the convention pushed through a platform that made no mention of the repeal of the Missouri Compromise. The Pierce men were mortified by the outcome, but the governor believed that he had successfully finessed the issue and would score an easy victory in the fall.[42]

By contrast, the Whig convention took a clear stand against the destruction of the Missouri Compromise, yet proposed no remedy. Pennsylvania Whigs looked to the Nebraska controversy to revive their party's strength. One prominent Whig politician assured James Pollock, the party's gubernatorial candidate, that the Whig party "is, this day, stronger than at any former period," and that the policies of the Pierce administration, including the Nebraska bill, would render Whiggery "*invincible.*" Confident that their party could garner the support of the bulk of the state's anti-Nebraska voters, Whig leaders saw little need to make concessions to the weak Free Democratic party or to form a new fusion party.[43]

Whig tacticians, joined by some third-party men, hoped that rather than making separate nominations the Free Democratic state convention would endorse the Whig nominees. The delegates, however, selected David Potts, Jr., an obscure antislavery man, to head their ticket as the gubernatorial candidate.[44] Potts was merely a conveniently insignificant temporary choice, who could easily be removed from the track if the hoped-for contingencies arose. Encouraged by Gamaliel Bailey of the *National Era*, who presumably spoke for the party's national leadership, Free Democratic managers in Pennsylvania hoped to bring Wilmot forth at the appropriate time as an anti-Nebraska candidate and force Pollock from the race. The *Era* contended that as the Whig nominee, Pollock would run on the old issues, and his election would thus represent nothing but a party victory. An independent nomination was necessary in order to make a distinct issue of the Nebraska bill, and the *National Era* advocated Wilmot as the strongest candidate on whom the opposition could unite. The antislavery journal also had harsh words for the Whig platform, which it criticized as inadequate for the present crisis. Nor was Bailey reassured by Pollock's letter of acceptance, which avoided any mention of even the platform's limited Nebraska resolution.[45]

Hoping to rally the Free Democrats to Pollock's standard, a Pittsburgh correspondent (probably Russell Errett, an assistant editor of the *Gazette*) publicly criticized Bailey's position. Pollock was as reliable on the slavery question as Wilmot, this writer asserted, and, equally to the point, because of his well-known free trade principles Wilmot could

42. James C. Van Dyke to James Buchanan, March 22, James Campbell to Buchanan, March 14, Buchanan Papers, HSPa; Lewis S. Coryell to William Bigler, June 5, Bigler to Dear Sir, March 27, Bigler Papers; *Keystone*, March 15.

43. William Larimer, Jr., to James Pollock, March 28, in the Pittsburgh *Gazette*, May 3; Pittsburgh *Gazette*, March 24. The Whig platform is given in the Harrisburg *Telegraph*, March 22.

44. The convention proceedings are in the *National Era*, May 25. Perhaps because he was never far from Free Democrats' thoughts, the myth has arisen in the historical literature that Wilmot was the party's gubernatorial candidate in 1854. Although he was widely talked of for the nomination and could have been nominated easily at the May convention if party leaders had decided to push him, the former Free Soiler was not a candidate for any political office in 1854. Coleman, *Disruption of the Pennsylvania Democracy*, 69, is only the latest of a number of studies that mistakenly asserts Wilmot was nominated.

45. *National Era*, May 18, June 8.

not win the entire Whig vote, whereas antislavery men could readily vote for Pollock.[46] Nevertheless, the idea of running Wilmot as an anti-Nebraska candidate was endorsed by several Whig papers, headed by the *Gazette*'s rival, the Pittsburgh *Journal*.[47]

Despite scattered defections, Whig papers as a group showed little interest in the fusion movement. Even in the western part of the state, where antislavery sentiment was most pronounced among Whigs, support for a new party was weak. The Pittsburgh *Gazette*, while counseling union of the opposition, advocated only a temporary coalition of Whigs and anti-Nebraska Democrats for the 1854 campaign. Looking ahead to 1856, the paper believed that shorn of its southern wing Whiggery would survive as a northern party. Calling on the Free Soilers to back Pollock, it announced, apparently on authority, that the Whig standard bearer would not withdraw. In addition, conservative Whigs, who, one Free Democrat complained, "cannot be brought to see that the world moves," adamantly opposed making any concessions to the Free Soilers.[48]

Meanwhile, Bailey privately asked James Shepherd Pike of the New York *Tribune* to get Pollock to write "a stiff anti-slavery letter." The *Era*'s editor hinted strongly that this action would bring the Free Democrats to his banner.[49] The Whig candidate responded with a letter, obviously intended for publication, in which he not only called for the restoration of the Missouri Compromise but also advanced the far more radical principle that Congress had no authority to establish slavery in any territory. Furthermore, in his campaign speeches—at least in areas where free soil sentiment was strong—he called for the repeal of the fugitive slave law. In order to attract free soil support, the Whig state committee issued an address that demanded the repeal of the Nebraska Act, vaguely recommended the protection of northern rights, and (without specifically referring to the fugitive slave law) declared that the rights of habeas corpus and trial by jury should be granted to all persons.[50] On interrogation by a committee of antislavery men, Pollock endorsed the principles of the address and went even further, unqualifiedly favoring the abolition of slavery in all present and future territories. His support of prohibition no doubt also helped, since the Free Democratic platform included a strong anti-liquor plank. Third-party leaders, under national pressure not to divide the opposition vote, seized these statements eagerly as sufficient pretext for cooperation, and in short order a second Free Democratic convention withdrew the party's ticket and endorsed Pollock and the remainder of the Whig nominees. The *National Era* promptly pronounced Pollock the People's candidate and urged his election.[51]

Wilmot's course, however, was still subject to speculation. Following the passage of

---

46. *National Era*, May 25. There are several reasons for attributing this letter, which was signed "E.," to Errett. For one thing, as a delegate to the Free Democratic convention, Errett led the unsuccessful fight to endorse Pollock. For another, the fact that the letter appeared in the *Gazette* on May 24, after the *Era* delayed publication in its weekly edition, probably purposefully, until after the convention's deliberations, suggests a close tie between the *Gazette*'s editors and the author of the letter.

47. Pittsburgh *Journal*, April 18, quoted in the *National Era*, May 18; Harrisburg *Telegraph*, April 29.

48. Pittsburgh *Gazette*, May 3, 25, 29, June 13, 15, 17, 20, 21, 23, July 12, August 2, September 27; William Birney to James G. Birney, June 19, James G. Birney Papers, University of Michigan.

49. Gamaliel Bailey to Pike, June 6, Pike Papers, UMe.

50. Pollock to Gentlemen, June 19, Harrisburg *Telegraph*, July 12. The Whig address is in the Pittsburgh *Gazette*, July 20.

51. Philadelphia *Register* quoted in the Pittsburgh *Gazette*, July 27; letter signed "Mac.," Pittsburgh *Gazette*, July 26; *National Era*, September 14. Pollock's reply to the committee is in the New York *Tribune*, September 5.

the Kansas-Nebraska Act in May, he began to have second thoughts about Bigler's policy of silence. "Wilmot wants a fuss," John Forney feared, "and won't stand silence." Throughout the summer the ex-congressman delivered in his district and elsewhere a series of speeches in which he advocated the overthrow of the national administration and its allies.[52] Still, he stopped short of publicly opposing Bigler. Wilmot's hesitancy is understandable. He had done nothing to discourage the movement to unite the opponents of the Nebraska Act behind him rather than Pollock. Moreover, if he bolted the Democratic party a second time there would be no going back, and thus any decision was not to be made lightly. Bigler, too, was carefully weighing his options.[53] Under heavy pressure from Washington, the governor finally announced in late August, albeit in a less than decisive tone, his support for the repeal of the Missouri Compromise. Wilmot now found himself in the untenable position of being associated with a ticket identified on both the national and state levels with the odious Nebraska measure. In response the free soil leader openly endorsed Pollock.[54] With this act, Wilmot completed the process he had begun in 1848 when he backed Martin Van Buren over Lewis Cass. He had burned all his bridges to the Democratic party.

Wilmot's decision to sever his connection with the Pennsylvania Democracy had important consequences for the future, because he soon became a prominent leader of the movement to form a Republican party in the state. Its immediate impact, however, was more limited. Whig journals, led by the Pittsburgh *Gazette*, commenced referring to Pollock as the fusion anti-Nebraska candidate, but in reality no new party had been formed. Despite an alliance with the Free Democrats, the Whigs maintained their separate organization and fully expected to continue as a viable party. Following the agreement of Whigs and Free Soilers on a common ticket, Horace Greeley perceptively observed that this arrangement "was very different from having one ticket at the start, and that nominated on the distinct anti-Nebraska platform."[55]

Wilmot likewise viewed his support of Pollock as only a temporary alliance. Whether he understood that his action would propel him into the movement to form a new antislavery party is not entirely clear but seems quite likely. In his speeches Wilmot was unspecific about his future political course, although he implied that he expected a realignment of the party system. In private he was less guarded. After an exchange of ideas with Wilmot, a former political colleague reported that the free soil leader was ready for any movement necessary "in order that the organization of the [Democratic] party may be destroyed by '56 when he lays out for a desperate struggle."[56]

The temperance issue also contributed to the breakdown of party loyalties in the state. No question absorbed more of the legislature's attention in its 1854 session, and members finally agreed to submit the volatile issue to the voters in the October election. The electorate was not presented with a specific law to approve or reject; instead, voters were simply to indicate (in what was essentially an opinion poll) whether they wanted a rigorous prohibition statute enacted. Frustrated temperance supporters angrily criticized

---

52. John W. Forney to Buchanan, May 25, Very private, because entirely out spoken, Buchanan Papers, HSPa; Going, *Wilmot*, 460.

53. Bigler continued to receive alarming reports from the Wilmot district. See E. B. Chase to Bigler, May 15, June 14, John C. Knox to Bigler, July 6, Bigler Papers.

54. Pittsburgh *Gazette*, September 1, October 10; Harrisburg *Morning Herald*, September 21.

55. Pittsburgh *Gazette*, August 31, September 1, and passim; New York *Tribune*, October 16.

56. E. B. Chase to Bigler, May 24, J. Lowrey to Bigler, August 14, Bigler Papers; Going, *Wilmot*, 260.

the legislature's action, but they nevertheless were determined to bring their influence into full sway in the fall canvass. After interrogating both Bigler and Pollock on the subject, the state temperance convention, although not entirely satisfied with the latter's reply, for all practical purposes endorsed the Whig candidate. Bigler's characteristically evasive response, coupled with his reputation as a hard drinker and his conspicuous support by the Irish, threw the weight of the organized temperance movement against him.[57]

By the end of the campaign, despite their resistance to demands for a new party, Whigs had finally managed to unite the anti-Nebraska forces, represented by the Wilmot Democrats and the Free Soilers, as well as the organized prohibition movement, behind Pollock's candidacy. The ultimate failure of the anti-Democratic elements to combine in Pennsylvania stemmed not from the slavery or liquor controversies but from the issue of nativism and the course of the Know Nothings. Indeed, by the time of Wilmot's defection, Democratic strategists were no longer principally concerned with the free soilers. By early summer, party managers realized that the most serious threat to their power came not from the Nebraska issue but from the Know Nothings.[58] Reports of the order's mushrooming strength poured in to Democratic headquarters. Uncertain whom to trust, Chief Justice Jeremiah S. Black, who was seeking reelection, warned his fellow nominee Bigler: "Remember that you are compassed round about with spies and so am I. Men who are your most confidential friends are betraying you hourly."[59]

Because of his close identification with Postmaster James Campbell, Bigler was a special target for the Know Nothings' wrath. Not only had he appointed the Catholic leader attorney general, but men commonly charged that the governor had been instrumental in Campell's subsequent advancement to the cabinet. Several commentators emphasized the great popular resentment over Campbell's appointments as a major force behind the rise of the Know Nothings; in fact, one party loyalist maintained that Bigler's alleged intimacy with the postmaster would "cause more democrats to join the Know Nothings than any thing else."[60] Sensing the drift of public opinion, Whig journals hammered away at this issue. Bigler was "in reality the Catholic candidate," the *Gazette* declared, and his election would be "considered the triumph of the Campbell and Romanist party."[61] As nativism swept over the state carrying off countless Democrats, dejected party managers concluded that Bigler faced almost certain defeat.[62]

The reaction of Pennsylvania Whigs to the nativist movement varied. A number of party leaders, believing that they could use the order for their own purposes, supported it, while others, particularly in areas where anti-Masonry had been strong in the 1820s, opposed the society because of its secrecy. Antislavery Whigs, whose mouthpiece was

---

57. Harrisburg *Telegraph*, June 14; Asa Earl Martin, "The Temperance Movement in Pennsylvania Prior to the Civil War," *Pennsylvania Magazine of History and Biography*, v. 49 (July, 1925), 219–23.

58. Henry Slicer to Buchanan, June 10, J. Franklin Reigart to Buchanan, July 28, Buchanan Papers, HSPa.

59. Jeremiah S. Black to Bigler, [July 1], Campbell to Bigler, August 23, Bigler Papers.

60. James Burnside to Bigler, June 12 (quotation), Charles Frailey to Bigler, June 14, W. L. Rogers to Bigler, August 21, John H. Nigley to Bigler, July 13 (Private), Bigler Papers; O. Watson to Simon Cameron, July 20, Cameron Papers, HSDC. Actually, Bigler advised against Campbell's cabinet appointment. See Samuel Tilden to Franklin Pierce, February 23, 1853 (Confidential) (copy), Tilden Papers.

61. Pittsburgh *Gazette*, September 4, 12 (quotation), 14, 28; Easton *Whig*, September 13, quoted in Coleman, *Disruption of the Pennsylvania Democracy*, 71n.

62. Daniel T. Jenks to Buchanan, October 3, J. Glancy Jones to Buchanan, July 9, Buchanan Papers, HSPa; G. G. Westcott to Bigler, June, *Confidential*, James Gilleland to Bigler, June 27, Bigler Papers; John M. Cauley to Cameron, September 26, Cameron Papers, HSDC.

the Pittsburgh *Gazette*, criticized the movement for distracting attention from the slavery issue and for crippling efforts to bring together the anti-Nebraska opposition behind a single ticket, and minimized the movement's importance.[63] The actions of the party's high command, however, indicated otherwise. Andrew G. Curtin, the Whig state chairman and a Know Nothing, opened negotiations with American party leaders in hopes of securing endorsement of the Whig state ticket. In addition, immediately after the Philadelphia election, Pollock's advisers sent him to that city where, sponsored by Mayor Robert Conrad, he joined the secret society. In his campaign speeches Pollock was careful to oppose any sharing of the common school fund and, while denying any desire to interfere with freedom of worship, strongly denounced religious bodies that functioned as political machines.[64]

Aided by Pollock's timely conversion, Curtin's efforts were partly successful. Know Nothing leaders decided against separate nominations and instead continued the order's original policy of selecting candidates from already existing party slates. In the equivalent of a primary system, members in local lodges voted on the various candidates already in the field. In the end, the American party endorsed Pollock along with the Democratic nominee for canal commissioner and the Native American party's choice for supreme court justice. A former member who denounced the order as "a whig trick" testified that when his lodge balloted, the president, a long-time Whig, vigorously urged Pollock's selection because the party was new and defeat would ruin it.[65] Despite their eclectic ticket, by refusing to endorse either major party's nominee in the Supreme Court race the Know Nothings carefully assured that the election would provide a clear test of their strength.

Party lines thus crisscrossed intricately in the 1854 Pennsylvania election. For governor, the opposition had united on one candidate, an antislavery Whig-Know Nothing, but over the other offices disagreement remained. Furthermore, though cooperating, the Whigs and Know Nothings worked at cross purposes. Whigs hoped to keep antislavery and nativism within traditional Whig channels and thus revitalize the party in the state, while the Know Nothings intended to demonstrate their power and lay the groundwork to become a fully independent party in the future. Calling his attention to the fact that "party ties . . . hang very loosely upon men at the present time," one of Bigler's advisers detected a new tone to the state's politics. "Moral questions have much more to do with elections now than formerly. Simple political questions are nearly obsolete, while the development of principles draw after them the religious and moral feelings of the people."[66] As he witnessed the attempt of Whigs, temperance advocates, antislavery men, and nativists to combine, another Democratic regular nervously predicted—with a mixture of astonishment and foreboding—that the state was on the eve of "the most remarkable revolution in Politics since the formation of our Government."[67]

---

63. Pittsburgh *Gazette*, August 5, September 8, October 10.

64. Pittsburgh *Post*, July 12; McClure, *Old Time Notes*, v. 1, 215–17; Pittsburgh *Gazette*, September 6; Tuscarora *Register*, August 17, quoted in Warren F. Hewitt, "The Know Nothing Party in Pennsylvania," *Pennsylvania History*, v. 2 (April, 1935), 76.

65. Pittsburgh *Post*, October 9, 26; J. Ellis Bonham to Jeremiah S. Black, August 29, Jeremiah S. Black Papers, LC; S. Kifenberick to Buchanan, August 13, 1856, Buchanan Papers, HSPa. The *Pennsylvanian*, in a purported report of the proceedings of the state council, gave the result of the balloting. This report is reprinted in the *Post*, October 9. Although parts of this account are highly dubious, the statements concerning selection of a ticket seem plausible.

66. E. A. Penniman to Bigler, June 18, Bigler Papers.

67. J. Franklin Reigart to Buchanan, July 28, Buchanan Papers, HSPa.

Democrats' fears were more than justified. On the defensive on several major issues, the Pennsylvania Democracy suffered a major defeat in the October election. Pollock bested Bigler by more than 30,000 votes, and only four administration Democrats were elected to Congress in the state's twenty-five-man delegation. The power of the Know Nothings was strikingly apparent. In the Supreme Court race, the American party candidate easily outpolled his Whig opponent, leaving no doubt that Pollock owed his election to the endorsement of the order (Map 5).[68] Observers were completely unprepared for this astounding display of nativist strength. The election was "certainly the most extraordinary ever witnessed," a Pennsylvania Democrat remarked, and an influential Democratic paper conceded, "The contest has been fought upon strange and singular issues, and we look to the future with alarm." Equally taken aback, another Pennsylvania Democrat confessed that he hardly knew what to say, "the tornado has been so Stunning and overwhelming."[69]

The source of Know Nothing votes substantiated the basis for Democratic concern. In no other free state was the influx of former Democrats into the order so extensive.[70] The pattern of the returns belied the claims of some observers that the voters attracted by the Know Nothings were primarily former Whigs. Actually, the nativist party drew significant support from both Whigs and Democrats as well as new voters and traditional non-voters (Table 5.4). Indeed, Whigs actually accounted for less than half the total nativist vote. Former Democrats who voted Know Nothing probably included not only native-born voters but also Protestant immigrants angered by the growing power of Catholics in the party, a power that Campbell's career highlighted so clearly. A Democratic paper in Pittsburgh reported that the Know Nothings boasted openly that Protestant Germans and Irish would vote for Pollock, and the support given the Know Nothing ticket by the two dominant German religious groups, the Lutherans and the German Reformed, suggests that such assertions were accurate (Table 5.11).[71] As long as anti-Catholicism remained the focus of the Know Nothing movement, many non-Catholic immigrants were attracted to its ticket, even though they were ineligible for membership in the order.[72] The Free Soil vote, on the other hand, was almost unanimously cast for Pollock and the rest of the Whig candidates; influenced by the Whigs' courtship of Wilmot, only

---

68. The vote for Governor stood as follows: Pollock (Whig and Know Nothing), 204,008 (55.0 percent), and Bigler (Democrat), 167,001 (45.0 percent). For Supreme Court judge the totals were Smyser (Whig), 78,571 (21.5 percent); Black (Democrat), 167,010 (45.6 percent); and Baird (Know Nothing), 120,576 (32.9 percent).

69. George W. Bowman to Black, October 23, Black Papers; *Pennsylvanian*, October 11, quoted in Coleman, *Disruption of the Pennsylvania Democracy*, 77; Daniel T. Jenks to Buchanan, October 13, Buchanan Papers, HSPa.

70. A greater proportion of Democrats voted Know Nothing in Massachusetts in 1854, but because the Democratic party was weak in that state the number switching parties was lower than in Pennsylvania. Regression estimates for Pennsylvania indicate that Know Nothings solidly supported the order's entire state ticket.

71. Pittsburgh *Post*, September 21. Michael F. Holt argues that Protestant immigrants voted Know Nothing in Pittsburgh: *Forging a Majority*, 147–48. The Philadelphia *North American*, October 19, however, asserted that in Philadelphia "the foreign vote irrespective of religious distinctions, was cast solidly for the Democratic ticket." The difference between the behavior of foreign-born voters in the two cities probably stemmed from Robert Conrad's course as mayor in Philadelphia, particularly his ban on foreign-born officeholding and his attempts to end liquor-selling on the Sabbath. New York *Herald*, August 30. See pp. 162–63 for a further discussion of religion and voting behavior in Pennsylvania.

72. Holt's conclusion that the 1854 Know Nothing vote "seems essentially to have been an anti-Catholic rather than a nativist one" appears valid: *Forging a Majority*, 151.

a negligible proportion of the 1852 Hale voters who went to the polls supported either the Democratic or the Know Nothing ticket (Table 5.4). The nativist crusade weakened both major parties, but the Democrats were able to offset their losses to some extent by gaining support from new voters (although in smaller numbers than had the Know Nothings). These new Democratic voters undoubtedly included Catholics frightened by the resurgence of nativism, and native and foreign-born voters who opposed the Maine Law. Know Nothingism "frightens the Irish," one Democratic candidate reported, "and drives them in Schools into my Support."[73]

In the temperance referendum, the voters by a narrow margin came out against the Maine Law.[74] The traditional Whig and Democratic coalitions both split, but not in the same way as in the Supreme Court contest (Table 5.5). Whigs divided evenly on the issue, with a substantial proportion not voting. Democrats were less deeply polarized, as a clear majority opposed prohibition but still more than a quarter voted dry. Free Soilers, on the other hand, as campaign rhetoric suggests, solidly favored the Maine Law. It is also significant that traditional non-voters brought to the polls voted overwhelmingly for temperance. For some, the liquor controversy may have been more important than nativism or anti-Nebraska in overcoming their usual apathy, but since a smaller vote was cast in the referendum than in the state contests this motivation could not have held with all voters. The strongest support for prohibition came from Know Nothings, who voted overwhelmingly to outlaw the sale of alcoholic drink, thereby confirming reports during the campaign that the "majority of Temperance fanatics . . . mostly belong to that infamous secret [Know Nothing] organization" (Table 3.3).[75] Comparison of prohibitionist sentiment among 1852 and 1854 Democratic voters suggests that many of the Democrats who left their party for the nativist movement were pro-temperance. Fully one out of four 1852 Democrats, who included many future Know Nothings, supported prohibition, but when these Know Nothing defectors were excluded, virtually none of the remaining 1854 Democrats favored a Maine Law.

In seeking to explain the election's outcome, analysts pointed to a number of issues, but anti-Nebraska and nativism were easily the most frequently cited. There was no agreement, however, on which had been more important. Understandably, Democrats were eager to deny that the Nebraska issue had anything to do with the result. Instead, a Pittsburgh Democrat contended that Bigler had been sacrificed to the "spirit of religious intolerance and political insanity. . . . It is idle to talk of *causes* for the result," he declared, "there was but one, and that was the momentary supremacy of bigotry and prejudice. It was the power of political frenzy."[76] Even with the impressive showing of the Know Nothings, such assertions dismissed too easily the importance of the slavery expansion issue. Criticizing these administration claims, the Pittsburgh *Gazette* insisted that "Nebraska *had* something to do with the result." George Sanderson, an experienced Democratic politico, acknowledged that in the congressional races the party's losses were "mainly owing to the Nebraska business." In the northern part of the state, including

---

73. J. W. Cake to Cameron, October 9, Cameron Papers, HSDC.

74. The vote was 158,342 (49.3 percent) for and 163,150 (50.7 percent) against enactment of a stringent anti-liquor law.

75. H. G. Seisenring to Bigler, August 8, Bigler Papers.

76. Alfred B. McCalmont to Bigler, October 16, Bigler Papers. Also see the Pittsburgh *Post*, October 16; R. M. DeFrance to Cameron, October 12, Cameron Papers, HSDC; James L. Reynolds to Buchanan, October 23, Daniel T. Jenks to Buchanan, October 17, Buchanan Papers, HSPa.

Wilmot's district, the slavery issue was obviously important.[77] Moreover, a Know Nothing vote was hardly a pro-Nebraska vote, for with only a few exceptions the order backed anti-Nebraska candidates. Pointing to the showing of the Know Nothings in the interior counties, one of Bigler's advisers commented: ''I think however that the feeling of opposition to Nebraska here, helped give the Know Nothings strength. Those who were sour because of that were ready to jump into any organization to defeat us, and the more ready to join them to strike you, because they could do so covertly.''[78]

Still, despite the importance of the Nebraska issue, nativism was the most powerful impulse in the election, as the preference of the strongly antislavery Baptists and Methodists for the Know Nothing ticket demonstrated, and as the collapse of the Whigs' electoral base confirmed (Table 5.11). Acknowledging that various forces were at work in the election, the widely respected Philadelphia *North American* nevertheless concluded that nativism was ''more potent and pervasive in its influence, perhaps, than any or all others combined.''[79] Whig managers had mapped out the wrong campaign strategy, for contrary to their expectations nativism, not Nebraska, dominated the canvass. Thousands of anti-Nebraska voters who wanted also to rebuke Catholics and liquor dealers trooped to the Know Nothings instead. At the same time countless voters less concerned about the slavery issue found a haven in the new party. Nativism, Nebraska, and rum had combined to hand the Pennsylvania Democracy a stinging defeat.

IV

Before 1854 no state had more complicated politics than New York. For years out-of-state observers looked on in amazement at its bewildering array of political factions, divisions, and subdivisions. ''New York had always been distinguished . . . for the number, variety, peculiar nomenclature, and nearly unintelligible distinctions and shades of difference into which her political parties have been split up,'' commented the *National Intelligencer* with ample justification.[80] This situation worsened in 1854 as the issues of Nebraska, nativism, and temperance further disordered the state's already chaotic political alignments.

The rupture of the Democratic party had allowed the Whigs to carry the state in 1853, but the voters' ratification of an amendment in February 1854 to enlarge the state's canal system signaled the final demise of the canal issue in New York politics, thereby depriving the Whigs of an issue they had exploited for years. As they witnessed the widespread protest against the repeal of the Missouri Compromise, Thurlow Weed and William H. Seward acclaimed the Nebraska issue as the means to maintain Whig ascendancy. As Sewardite journals joined Silver Grey organs in attacking Douglas's measure, party leaders envisioned a reestablishment of party unity. From Albany a firm Seward loyalist reported that the Nebraska issue had ''united the Whig Party, & broken down the foolish Partition Wall, which separated one Portion from Another''—an assessment shared by the Albany *Reg-*

---

77. Pittsburgh *Gazette*, October 17; George Sanderson to Buchanan, October 24, Buchanan Papers, HSPa; Philadelphia *North American*, October 11; Daniel Sheffer to Cameron, October 14, Cameron Papers, HSDC. Roger D. Petersen, ''The Reaction to a Heterogeneous Society: A Behavioral and Quantitative Analysis of Northern Voting Behavior 1845–1870, Pennsylvania a Test Case'' (unpublished Ph.D. dissertation, University of Pittsburgh, 1970), 55, 250, too readily dismisses the slavery extension issue.

78. E. B. Chase to Bigler, October 10, Bigler Papers; Philadelphia *Evening Bulletin*, October 11, quoted in the New York *Evening Post*, October 12. See the careful discussion in Holt, *Forging a Majority*, 142.

79. Philadelphia *North American*, October 11.

80. *National Intelligencer*, September 30.

ister, a leading Silver Grey paper, which pronounced the Whig party stronger in the state than it had been in years. This development disheartened Fillmore Whigs, who were looking for an issue with which to build a conservative Union party, for they believed that the slavery extension question would revitalize the Whig party and strengthen their party adversaries. In high spirits, Seward reached the same conclusion.[81]

Whig strategists encountered major difficulties, however, in making the Nebraska bill the primary focus of the fall campaign. Other issues, most notably temperance, competed for the voters' attention. In 1853, thanks in part to Democratic factionalism, anti-liquor forces captured control of the legislature. Led by state senator Myron H. Clark, a former cabinetmaker who had become a prosperous merchant, prohibitionists won approval in both houses of a stringent prohibitory measure. Clark was a Whig, as were a majority of Maine Law enthusiasts, but the party's high command, led by Weed, was wary of embracing prohibition as Whig doctrine. Weed had no love for the drys (he once termed them "queer chaps"), and he realized that too close an identification with the anti-liquor crusade would drive wet Whigs from the party.[82] Governor Horatio Seymour's unexpected veto of Clark's bill destroyed Weed's strategy of downplaying the issue. When attempts to override the veto failed, prohibitionists refused to accept the Whig boss's scheme for a referendum and instead gave top priority to the election of a reliable Maine Law governor in the fall. Weed fully grasped the impact of this turn of events: Temperance would inevitably divert attention from the Nebraska question and be a significant issue in the approaching election.[83]

Whig plans to exploit the slavery expansion controversy were also hindered by the action of the state's Democratic factions, particularly that of the Softs. The Nebraska bill presented a dilemma to both Democratic groups as they maneuvered in the complex maze of national and state politics. Ultimately, the anti-Pierce, pro-southern Hards adhered to the Janus-faced policy of endorsing the Nebraska Act while denouncing the president. For governor, their state convention nominated Greene Bronson, the recalcitrant former collector whom Franklin Pierce had removed the previous year.

The Softs were also in a difficult position. Of particular concern to the administration was the course of John Van Buren, the leader of the Barnburners. An extraordinarily effective public speaker, the ex-president's son relished political combat, and some Softs expressed fear that once again, as in 1848, he would lead an anti-slavery-extension crusade. But, as Gideon Welles complained, politics to the prince (as he was called) had increasingly become "mere play, a game of mere personal cunning and intriguing." His standing already seriously weakened by his desertion of the party in 1848, Van Buren had no desire to destroy it completely. So he made perhaps the most critical decision of his career: He intimated to William L. Marcy that, despite his dislike for the bill, he had no intention of leading another party bolt. With this decision, leadership of the more militant free soil Democrats passed from Van Buren's hands. Henry Wilson later

---

81. Ogden Hoffman to William H. Seward, March 5, Seward Papers, UR; Albany *Register* quoted in the Pittsburgh *Gazette*, March 24; Seward to Theodore Parker, June 23 (Private), Seward Papers, UR.

82. Thurlow Weed to George W. Patterson, May 10, July 24 (quotation), George W. Patterson Papers, UR; Albany *Evening Journal*, March 31, quoted in Richard L. Watson, Jr., "Thurlow Weed, Political Leader, 1848–1855" (unpublished Ph.D. dissertation, Yale University, 1939), 234; Bradford Wood to Hannibal Hamlin, March 11, Hamlin Papers. For a general discussion, see John A. Krout, "The Maine Law in New York Politics," *New York History*, v. 17 (July, 1936), 260–72.

83. Weed to Patterson, May 10, July 24, Patterson Papers; Patterson to Weed, April 3, May 8, 20, Weed Papers, UR.

maintained that had Van Buren remained faithful to free soil principles, "he would unquestionably have been one of the foremost men of the Republican party, if not its accepted leader."[84]

Confronted with the administration's decree that the bill was party doctrine, Soft leaders, who had pontificated for years about free soil principles, sought desperately to devise a face-saving position. One group, led by men close to Marcy and Seymour and including Pierce's appointees as well as John Van Buren, favored the approach of acquiescing in rather than endorsing the Kansas-Nebraska Act. Another group, led by Preston King, who had replaced the younger Van Buren as the leader of the free soil Democrats, and the *Evening Post* clique, wanted the platform to condemn the territorial law outright.[85] At the Soft convention, King led an unsuccessful floor fight against acceptance of the Nebraska Act, bluntly telling the delegates, many of whom had backed Martin Van Buren in 1848, that the proposed platform would wed the party to the cause of slavery's expansion. When the convention refused to condemn the repeal of the Missouri Compromise, King, followed by a number of delegates, walked out of the hall in protest.[86] Those who remained easily renominated Seymour for governor.

Because King and his followers were unprepared to support a new party movement, their bolt had only limited immediate impact. But King's desertion of the Democratic party, which would prove to be permanent, was particularly significant for the future course of the state's politics. It represented the first of a series of secessions that the party would suffer in the next few years. Although its significance was unclear to all observers at the time, the decision of this Soft convention ended the era of free soil influence within the New York Democratic party. Greeley was one contemporary observer who sensed that the Softs' acceptance of the Nebraska Act represented a genuine turning point. The Softs had lost "their golden moment," he declared after their convention adjourned. Had they rejected the leadership of the government officeholders and nominated King on an anti-Nebraska platform, they would have been invincible. Instead, he maintained, they sealed their doom.[87]

In seeking to account for the Softs' action, critics pointed to the influence of government officers at the convention. Hard leader Daniel S. Dickinson (Scripture Dick), for example, jeered that control of the convention rested with "tenants of the New York custom house, who were there crammed like Christmas turkeys with Government bread and butter to sing hosannas to the wisdom of the Administration who fed them." Undoubtedly, such men exerted considerable influence on the gathering's deliberations, and certainly the desire to retain the administration's favor loomed large in their thoughts. Other considerations, however, must have swayed the rest of the delegates. Some no doubt convinced themselves that under popular sovereignty Kansas and Nebraska would be free states anyway; others had only reluctantly left the party in 1848, and most had no

---

84. Gideon Welles to Preston King, November 25 (copy), Welles Papers, LC; John Van Buren to William L. Marcy, February 12, Marcy Papers, LC; Wilson, *Slave Power*, v. 2, 142.

85. Herman J. Redfield to Marcy, July 13 (Private), Marcy Papers, LC; Marcy to Horatio Seymour, February 14, Typescript, Seymour Papers, NYHS; New York *Evening Post*, June 26; John Bigelow to Francis P. Blair, Sr., August 30, Blair-Lee Papers.

86. New York *Evening Post*, September 7, 8, 11; Preston King to Welles, October 21, Welles Papers, LC; Seymour to Marcy, September 9, 18, Marcy Papers, LC. While labeling the repeal of the Missouri Compromise "inexpedient and unnecessary," the Soft platform opposed any agitation for its restoration and hailed the measure's anticipated "beneficial" results for the territories.

87. New York *Tribune*, September 8.

stomach for independent action again. Samuel J. Tilden, the New York lawyer and future presidential candidate who had in 1848 participated in the Barnburner revolt, explained that, despite dissatisfaction with the course of affairs in Washington, very little sentiment for organized, independent action existed among former Free Soilers. "They expect the Democratic party to be broken down for the time," he wrote, but "most . . . expect the Democratic party to rise again, purified, and [look] to resuming relations with it." He believed that no more than a quarter of those who followed Van Buren six years earlier would support a new party movement.[88]

By dodging the Nebraska issue and renominating Seymour on a platform upholding his temperance veto, Soft strategists intended to shift the focus of the campaign from slavery to rum. Seymour's renomination inevitably linked their party with the liquor issue, a development they welcomed as a means of holding their ranks together. It was important to poll the full Soft vote, one Democratic politician explained, and with Seymour as the party's candidate "we shall have a sharp, fiery, exciting canvass, on account of the 'liquor question' . . . & all the votes will be out."[89] Given their immediate situation, the Softs' strategy made sense: There was a better chance of carrying the state on the liquor question than on the Nebraska issue. For the Whigs, however, the Softs' failure to take an unambiguous stand made it difficult to exploit the territorial issue.

Whig attempts to monopolize popular indignation over the Kansas-Nebraska Act also encountered opposition from anti-Nebraska men intent on organizing a new party. Early in the summer, committees appointed by two anti-Nebraska meetings, one in New York and the other in Albany, issued a joint call for a mass anti-Nebraska state convention to meet at Saratoga Springs in mid-August. The call said nothing about forming a new party, but this was the intention of many of its supporters, including third-party Free Democrats, who were particularly active in sponsoring the meeting. They gained a powerful ally in Horace Greeley, who used the columns of the New York *Tribune* to promote the Saratoga convention and a union of Whigs and Free Democrats in a new party. He castigated Whig leaders who opposed the Saratoga meeting and wished to retain their old party organization. During the summer, the New York City editor's ambition boiled over. Convinced that anti-Nebraska and anti-rum, two movements to which he had given conspicuous support, would be the main issues of the fall campaign, Greeley decided that he was the logical nominee for governor on a fusion ticket.[90]

Whig boss Thurlow Weed realized that if antislavery nominations were made at Saratoga, the Silver Greys and Know Nothings, by arguing that antislavery Whigs had deserted the party for the fusion movement, would dominate the Whig convention. Only by preventing nominations could he block a Know Nothing takeover of the Whig organization, control of which brought not only prestige but also countless votes of party loyalists. If instead the Know Nothings entered the campaign as a new party, they would be hampered by severe disadvantages. "Weed is apprehensive that the Know nothings & Silver Grays will control our State Convention," former governor Washington Hunt

---

88. New York *Tribune*, October 9; Tilden to [?], August 26, Bigelow, ed., *Tilden Letters and Memorials*, v. 1, 113.

89. Henry S. Randall to Marcy, June 24, Marcy Papers, LC.

90. New York *Tribune*, June 28, July 18; Horace Greeley to Colfax, March 12, July 7, Greeley-Colfax Papers. See the excellent discussion in Jeter Isely, *Horace Greeley and the Republican Party* (Princeton, 1947), 86–91.

informed Hamilton Fish. "This will be so if nominations are made at Saratoga—not otherwise."[91]

Greeley's growing ambition also worried Weed. A brilliant editorial writer, Greeley was not a profound thinker, and he was more a dabbler in and publicist for reform causes than a true reformer. Still, he thrived on controversy, and having already witnessed the *Tribune* editor's brief but disastrous service in Congress, Weed was in no humor to place Greeley in so sensitive a position as governor. Greeley was too apt to take up idiosyncratic crusades, was too dictatorial and dogmatic, was too enamored of his own political infallibility to be a reliable member of any party machine or to work smoothly with party leaders in Albany. "I shall never comprehend Greeley, for I can never discern the personal considerations which sway and govern him," Weed once exclaimed in a moment of exasperation. He was hardly alone in his distrust of his editorial colleague. The usually restrained Hamilton Fish, for example, wrote on one occasion: "I confess however that I cannot be inspired with confidence in any movement that Greeley controls. With all his ability he has a crack across his brain that amounts to little short of derangement & will destroy anything which he may be allowed to lead." Prior to the 1854 Whig convention one of Weed's political cronies, perhaps with Greeley in mind, pleaded for a ticket made up of men "whom we can call on and pass those long winter evenings at C[ongress] Hall [,] willing that we should take a trifle of that old rum and *a* oyster—and men finally who have no idea that office confers any spiritual power."[92]

Alert to these dangers, Weed moved to block fusion. Widely recognized as one of the most skilled political operators of his generation, the New York boss was now in his mid-fifties and at the pinnacle of his power. Tall and dark-complexioned, with a large, long head and stooped shoulders, he was readily recognizable in his familiar haunts of power. Contemporaries were struck by his secretive manner: He always spoke in low tones, almost in a whisper, as if he feared being overheard. His benevolent countenance and mild manner masked his ruthless political realism and intellectual vigor, which he applied single-mindedly to pragmatic political ends. Few men were his equal in reading the shifting public mood in the state. "When a political battle is to be fought on practical issues," one admiring editorial notice declared, "he has no superior in surveying the field and executing and planning whatever is necessary to secure a triumph." His social affability, financial generosity, and personal loyalty brought him a wide body of friends; in palmier days Greeley observed that Weed had "probably a larger personal acquaintance, and can call more men by name, than any other living American, and is not surpassed by any man living in the number of his devoted, enthusiastic friends." The Albany leader welded his friends into a powerful political machine, yet he had no desire for office, and not until late in life did he become avaricious. Disdaining the trappings of power, the "Lord of the Lobby," as he was sometimes called, was content to manage others, and in his editorial office in Albany, in legislative corridors, and in backroom caucuses he wielded the real power within the Whig organization. "He was more deferred to than the Whig Governors, for he created . . . them," one paper commented after his

---

91. Washington Hunt to Fish, August 2, Fish Papers, LC; Washington Hunt to Weed, July 30, Weed Papers, UR.

92. Weed to Seward, May 11, [1856], Seward Papers, UR; Fish to Weed, March 22, 1856, Weed Papers, UR; D. H. Abell to Weed, September 10, quoted in Isely, *Greeley and the Republican Party*, 90–91. Congress Hall was a famous Albany tavern.

death. "They remained in Albany for two or four years, as he might desire, but Mr. Weed remained there always."[93] Intensely loved by his friends, he was as fiercely hated by his enemies, but over the years the Whig dictator had successfully turned back every challenge to his party leadership.

Throughout the summer, Weed plied Greeley, whom he had taken under his wing years before as a poor young editor, with his captivating charm. In late July at his famous Room No. 11 in the Astor House in New York City he conferred with the *Tribune*'s editor, whose cherubic face and proverbial Pickwickian appearance gave no hint of his petulant jealousy and his sensitivity to personal slights, real or imagined. Weed reminded Greeley of the importance to the antislavery cause of Seward's reelection, and he emphasized the threat that both the Know Nothings and the fusion movement posed to Whig hegemony. Deftly turning aside his colleague's desire for the gubernatorial nomination, Weed reiterated that it was critical no nomination be made at Saratoga. When at a subsequent conference Greeley broached the subject of running for lieutenant governor, Weed again demurred, and when they parted, he was under the impression that Greeley concurred fully with his views.[94]

Weed's legendary powers of persuasion finally converted the at-times-imperceptive Greeley, who agreed to work against naming a separate ticket at Saratoga. Before the end of July, the *Tribune*, while still hailing the Republican movement in other states, announced in a sudden about-face that the formation of a new party was not the object of the Saratoga convention. To his confidant Colfax, Greeley wrote candidly, "We shall have no nomination at Saratoga, and, alas! no fusion at all, which will do harm in all the 'fusion' States. It will tell heavily against us that we carry all the States Whig that we can, and go 'fusion' where we can do no better . . . this won't work." The *Tribune* did not return to the subject of nominations until the day before the Saratoga convention, when it asserted that the people of New York were not yet prepared to abandon their old loyalties for a new party.[95]

The call for the Saratoga convention was directed to men of all parties who opposed the Nebraska Act. Perhaps as many as five hundred delegates representing a variety of viewpoints attended, but Seward Whigs dominated its tumultuous proceedings, for Weed had spurred his lieutenants to get the right kind of men selected as delegates.[96] Greeley was chairman of the critical committee on resolutions, and he and Henry J. Raymond of the New York *Times* (a firm Weed ally) performed most of the committee's work. When Greeley reported a set of resolutions that omitted any mention of state nominations, protests arose from the floor. In the ensuing uproar, Preston King came to the rescue of

93. Portland *Advertiser*, n.d., clipping, [Greeley], MS biography of Weed, [1852], Weed Papers, UR; New York *World*, November 23, 1882, quoted in Watson, "Weed," 262. See Glyndon G. Van Deusen, *Thurlow Weed: Wizard of the Lobby* (Boston, 1947).

94. Horace Greeley, *Recollections of a Busy Life* (New York, 1868), 311–22; Barnes, *Memoir of Weed*, v. 2, 225–26, 282–89; Greeley to Seward, October 25, Seward Papers, UR.

95. Greeley to Colfax, July 26, Greeley-Colfax Papers; New York *Tribune*, July 24, August 15; Isely, *Greeley and the Republican Party*, 96.

96. Weed to Patterson, July 11, Patterson Papers; Elbridge G. Spaulding to Weed, August 8, Henry J. Raymond to Weed, August 8, Orson Nicholson to Weed, August 11, Confidential, Greeley to Weed, August 10, Weed Papers, UR; Greeley to Weed, August 13, Thomas Madigan Collection, NYPL. Greeley even sent Weed, for approval, a draft of the resolutions he intended to introduce at Saratoga. For the convention proceedings, see the New York *Tribune*, August 17–19; New York *Times*, August 17; New York *Evening Post*, August 17.

the Sewardites. Addressing the convention, King opposed launching a new party, and his remarks deflated the spirits of the new-party men. Afterwards he explained that the voters were not ready for such nominations, and it was necessary first to let party disorganization run its course. "I think we shall [then] . . . be in a better condition for future action," he told John Bigelow of the *Evening Post*, "than by a premature attempt to bring order out of chaos." In the end, the delegates agreed to make no nominations, but to reassemble at Auburn after the other conventions had met and then decide on a course of action. This decision in effect meant that no independent nominations would be made, for the Whigs were certain to name an anti-Nebraska ticket. Disappointed by this turn of events, Bigelow fumed that the convention had been a waste of time.[97]

Having warded off the threat of a new party, Weed turned his attention to the approaching Whig convention, where he faced a serious challenge from both temperance advocates and Know Nothings. Once Seymour vetoed the prohibitory law, Weed, always a realist, realized that the Whigs had to placate the temperance men, who in their frustration threatened to make a separate nomination. "We've got to have that law & we may just as well face the music now as ever," one of his most trusted advisers wrote that summer, no doubt closely mirroring Weed's own thoughts. "The People must have it tried & we may as well make use of it as not. We must take that side. Seymour has already occupied the other."[98] Besides, the Maine Law men were not the most serious threat; Weed feared the Know Nothings much more. Whatever the nature of the order's popular appeal, the Whig dictator was fully aware that the intention of its leaders was "to kill Seward and his friends." By September, his worst apprehensions seemed confirmed, as Know Nothing leaders whispered confidently that a majority of the Whig delegates were members of the secret society. "I don't see how we are to get through the Convention safely," Weed confessed shortly before it assembled.[99]

For once, Weed was not firmly in command of a Whig convention. Actually, no group was able to control its proceedings, and in the resulting disorder the Albany editor scrambled for best advantage. The temperance lobby vetoed his personal choices, and he lacked the votes to force them through, so in the end Weed settled on Myron Clark, who was nominated for governor. The Maine Law reformer was no favorite of Weed, but he had the advantage of being a member of a Know Nothing lodge, and indeed was the choice of a caucus of the Know Nothing delegates held the evening before the convention.[100] Furthermore, once his personal preferences had been eliminated, the party boss was determined to get a pliable nominee, and Clark, an incompetent who was an admirer of Seward and willing to follow directions from Weed, filled the bill sufficiently. In a bitter blow to Greeley, the nomination for lieutenant governor, which he had sought,

97. Preston King to John Bigelow, September 16, quoted in Muller, "Preston King," 546–47; John Bigelow to Francis P. Blair, Sr., August 30, Blair-Lee Papers.

98. Edward C. Delavan to Seward, May 16, Seward Papers, UR; Weed to Patterson, May 10, July 24, Patterson Papers; John M. Bradford to Weed, June 24 (quotation), David H. Abell to Weed, September 10, Weed Papers, UR.

99. Weed to Patterson, May 10, July 24, September 17 (quotation), 23, Patterson Papers; D. L. Pattee [?] to Daniel Ullmann, September 18, S. S. Parsons to Ullmann, September 16, A. Perry to Robert C. Wetmore, August 2, Ullmann Papers, NYHS.

100. Benjamin F. Bunce to Patterson, September 21, Weed to Patterson, September 23, Patterson Papers; Whitney, *Defence of the American Policy*, 290; letter signed "Fideliter," New York *Times*, May 22, 1855. Weed was fully informed concerning Clark's Know Nothing membership. See Elbridge G. Spaulding to Weed, August 20, Weed Papers, UR.

went to his hated rival (whom he referred to as the "little villain"), Henry J. Raymond, heretofore a wet. The cautious Whig platform was designed to placate nervous conservatives. Focusing primarily on the Nebraska issue, it proposed no specific future action, and the delegates hissed down a resolution calling for repeal of the fugitive slave law. The platform was silent on the Maine Law, but Clark's nomination was sufficient on that point. Antislavery critics seized on the party's declaration of principles as further evidence that New York leaders were intent on keeping the door open for future cooperation with southern Whigs.

In late September, after the Whig and Democratic conventions had adjourned, the Saratoga convention reassembled in Seward's home town of Auburn. A state temperance convention and the Free Democratic convention met there at the same time. Some sentiment had developed in Democratic circles to nominate Preston King, but the free soil leader made clear his opposition. In fact, in a move signaling his growing alliance with Seward and Weed, King asked the New York senator to prevent his nomination.[101] Only about two hundred delegates attended the Auburn convention, and Whig influence was readily apparent. A number of Whig outsiders swarmed over the delegates, while a small knot of party leaders, including Seward, Raymond, Congressman Edwin B. Morgan, and future governor Edwin D. Morgan of New York City, surreptitiously directed its deliberations. Following an alteration in the method of voting that gave the Whigs greater strength, the meeting ratified the Whig ticket, as did the temperance convention. A group of bolters from the anti-Nebraska convention, who wanted a genuine fusion ticket, defiantly nominated Bradford Wood, a Free Soil Democrat, for lieutenant governor; they were joined in this step by the Free Democratic meeting, but Wood eventually withdrew.[102] Although both the anti-Nebraska and Free Democratic conventions adopted resolutions proclaiming themselves the Republican party and jointly established a Republican state central committee, these were paper organizations only. Weed had achieved his goal. He had prevented the formation of the Republican party and obtained the endorsement of the Whig ticket by the splinter organizations. Fusion had failed in New York.

He reckoned, however, without the Silver Greys. The unexpected rise of Know Nothingism, which seemed to offer the long-sought means to challenge Weed's power, dispelled these conservatives' earlier gloom. Rapidly taking control of the society in New York, they decided to make separate nominations. In October, only a month before the election, the state council of the society assembled for this purpose in New York City.[103] Once Myron Clark's lodge had been declared spurious and the Whig nominee unceremoniously expelled from the order, the delegates proceeded to nominate a ticket headed by Daniel Ullmann, a leading conservative Whig and perpetual office-seeker (he had been

---

101. Letter signed "Freeman," New York *Evening Post*, September 20; Preston King to Seward, September 19, Seward Papers, UR; Preston King to Weed, October 4, Weed Papers, UR.

102. New York *Times*, September 26, 27; New York *Tribune*, September 26, 27; letter signed "A Free Democrat," New York *Evening Post*, September 29. Some squabbling also occurred over the endorsement of Raymond.

103. For accounts of the state council, see New York *Times*, October 6, 7, 26, December 4; New York *Tribune*, October 9; letters signed "United Forever," New York *Times*, October 10, 23; letter signed "Fideliter," New York *Times*, May 22, 1855.

a candidate for the Whig gubernatorial nomination the previous month).[104] All parties were represented on the ticket.

Ullmann ran on no official platform. He was known to be an opponent of the Nebraska Act, and at the last minute he wrote a private letter for use at the Whig convention signifying his willingness to sign a temperance law. This pledge was not made public, however, and outside the order his position on prohibition was unclear. Ullmann was inundated with pleas that he openly announce his support for temperance, but he accepted the advice of one friend "not to write any letters, to keep dark and 'Know Nothing.'" Within the lodges of the secret society, in areas where Maine Law sentiment was powerful, Know Nothing leaders pledged that he was sound on the rum issue.[105] Furthermore, in order to retain the support of the general membership, which was less conservative on the question of slavery than was the leadership, those in control of the secret society deliberately played down Silver Grey support for Ullmann, and plans for a separate meeting of conservatives to endorse him were quietly shelved.[106]

Weed now faced the fight of his life. The nomination of a separate Know Nothing ticket with a strong Silver Grey taint completely wrecked his plans. Whigs' earlier optimism, generated by the outcry over the repeal of the Missouri Compromise, abruptly evaporated. Ullmann's opposition to the bill and the Softs' careful avoidance of the issue negated the Whigs' strategy to run as the anti-Nebraska party. With no clear-cut choice on the slavery extension issue, nativism and especially temperance seemed to many voters more directly at issue in the canvass. In its final edition before the election, a Buffalo paper affirmed:

> Every person of common understanding knows that the election tomorrow in this State, turns about as much upon the Nebraska issue as upon the opium trade in China, and that one will be about as much affected as the other by the result. Ninety-nine out of every hundred voters will think about as much of Nebraska when they go to the polls as of Timbuctoo.

From the countryside another political observer emphasized that temperance and nativism absorbed most of the voters' attention. "The Nebraska-Kansas bill is obsolete, or in the language of its famous Author 'is superceded & inoperative' in comparison with these immediate & practical questions." A discouraged Sewardite provided a similar assess-

---

104. Know Nothing leaders claimed that Clark, who had been rejected by the lodge in his home town, got some Sewardite members to come from Albany and establish a second lodge—something they had no authority to do. See the printed circular from J. P. Faurot, September 26, Ullmann Papers, NYHS; letter signed "O.K.," New York *Herald*, September 27; Whitney, *Defence of American Policy*, 289–90. This account is partly substantiated in Elbridge G. Spaulding to Weed, August 20, Weed Papers, UR. Yet prior to the Whig convention, others privy to the secrets of the order declared that Clark was a legitimate member. See S. S. Parsons to Ullmann, September 16, 27, Ullmann Papers, NYHS; letter signed "Fideliter," New York *Times*, May 22, 1855.

105. Ullmann to Dear Sir, September 16 (copy), Ullmann Papers, NYHS; Henry Sherman to Ullmann, October 9, quoted in Mark L. Berger, *The Revolution in the New York Party Systems, 1840–1860* (Port Washington, N.Y., 1973), 61.

106. E. R. Jewett to Fillmore, October 24, Fillmore Papers, SUNY; L. L. Pratt to Ullmann, October 19, *Private*, Ullmann Papers, NYHS; Buffalo *Republic*, November 1; New York *Times*, November 1.

ment: "In our state the Nebraska issue is pretty much lost sight of—being overlaid and smothered by the Liquor & know nothing distractions."[107]

In mapping their campaign strategy, Weed and his advisers miscalculated. Rum, not Nebraska, was the dominant issue of the contest. Here the division was clear-cut for, much to Weed's dislike, the Whigs were saddled with a pronounced anti-liquor standard bearer, while Seymour, though personally a teetotaler, was popularly viewed as the wet candidate. Ullmann, who took a hesitant pro-temperance position very late, also misread the political current. "The truth is that this temperance question is the main issue ostensibly before the people," Fillmore wrote at the end of the campaign; likewise a strict antislavery man complained that the primary issue involved in the election was "*Rum or No Rum.*"[108] On the defensive concerning the slavery issue, Soft spokesmen encouraged this emphasis, and Seymour rallies focused almost exclusively on the liquor question. The Softs "skulk behind whiskey barrels, and talk of nothing but two-penny rum," the Albany *Argus*, the Hards' organ, charged, while the New York *Tribune* complained that Seymour's "organs and his spouters electioneer on toddy, and hardly anything else." With his usual biting wit, Daniel S. Dickinson, the Hards' leading spokesman, characterized the issue of the campaign as "Bronson and good liquor, Seymour and bad liquor and Clark and no liquor at all."[109]

In order to neutralize some of the damage produced by the nativist issue, Whigs charged that Ullmann was not a native-born citizen but had been born in Calcutta. The origin of this story, which was intended to make the Know Nothings look patently ridiculous, is unknown, but one suspects that the skillful hand of Weed was involved. Whatever its source, Whig papers devoted increasing attention to Ullmann's mysterious birthplace (actually, he had been born in Wilmington, Delaware) and put the Know Nothings, whom opponents promptly nicknamed the Hindoos, on the defensive. So widely was the charge circulated and believed that leaders of the order found it necessary to issue to the membership a circular attesting to Ullmann's native birth. "This is just the most scoundrelly canvass that I was ever engaged in," Greeley wrote in disgust near its close. "I feel a crawling all over on account of it."[110] Two years later in the 1856 presidential election, Know Nothing leaders would remember the Hindoo story and seek to even the score.

As the campaign neared its conclusion, Weed received ever more disheartening reports. From the central and western sections of the state especially, his lieutenants reported that normally safe Whig districts could not be relied on, and that the Know Nothings were expanding at an incredible pace. "There never was a time when party ties seemed of so little account," former governor Washington Hunt wrote with obvious concern. A

107. Buffalo *Commercial Advertiser*, November 6; Samuel Jellitts to Robert C. Wetmore, August 12, Ullmann Papers, NYHS; E. Peshine Smith to Henry C. Carey, October 21, Henry C. Carey Papers, HSPa.

108. Fillmore to John Pendleton Kennedy, November 1, Kennedy Papers; letter from P. Osterhaut, Jr., November 7, *National Era*, November 16; E. Peshine Smith to Carey, October 21, Carey Papers; Fish to John M. Bradford, December 16 (copy), Fish Papers, LC; *National Era*, November 23. Weed admitted that the Nebraska question had been thrust aside by the nativist and temperance issues. Albany *Evening Journal*, November 7.

109. Albany *Argus*, November 1; New York *Tribune*, October 21; Dickinson quoted in Krout, "Maine Law in New York Politics," 268.

110. Greeley to Colfax, November 6, Greeley-Colfax Papers. For evidence that the Hindoo story hurt Ullmann's candidacy, see Francis Granger to Ullmann, October 17, Stephen Sammons to Ullmann, October 28, Ullmann Papers, NYHS.

Whig congressional candidate conceded that it was "out of my power to accurately calculate results." Greeley became despondent as he watched the Whig campaign become entangled in these difficulties. On election eve he dashed off a blunt analysis of the situation. Ullmann looked unexpectedly strong, Bronson appeared quite weak, and Seymour would receive a huge vote in this rum-soaked metropolis, he moaned to Colfax. "It looks infernally black to-night."[111]

The New York gubernatorial election was a cliffhanger, because Ullmann displayed entirely unexpected strength. Before the election, normally perceptive observers dismissed Know Nothing claims of 60,000 members, but Ullmann polled more than twice that total. The Hard vote declined precipitously as a number of previous supporters voted Know Nothing and many others rallied to Seymour, who represented the only hope for a Democratic victory. In an outcome that was unknown for over a month, Clark finally defeated Seymour by a mere 309 votes out of more than 450,000 cast.[112] The new legislature was decidedly pro-temperance. The state's congressional delegation was overwhelmingly anti-Nebraska, and it contained not a single Hard and only two Softs (one a firm ally of Preston King). As in other states, Know Nothings constituted a significant proportion of the New York delegation, and, beyond the fact that it was strongly anti-administration, little could be predicted of its future course.

The results heralded a new era in the state's politics. "Nothing can be assumed from *former* Elections," the Albany *Evening Journal* remarked the day after the election. "Nearly all the old political landmarks are obliterated. Of all parties there has been a regular 'smash-up'" in the face of "a complete 'Know Nothing' stampede." As Weed's words indicated, the most striking feature about the election was not Clark's narrow victory or the vastly enlarged Soft vote, but the Know Nothings' strength. The new party had "completely defeated the calculations of political leaders," commented a Buffalo paper. Labeling the present situation "an anomaly in the history of politics," it noted that the party's growth had been "accomplished by means altogether without precedent in political tactics. The Know-Nothings have no authorized press, have held no public discussions, but by mysterious processes" had succeeded in tallying almost as many votes as the two major parties.[113]

Weed's gamble on the Maine Law issue had narrowly paid off in the state contest. More important in his eyes, however, was the legislature. Greeley complained tellingly that Weed was willing to bargain away anything during the campaign to get Seward men elected to the legislature.[114] Both houses had a majority of Whigs of all stripes, but whether Seward could gain a majority was very uncertain because of the Know Nothings' strength. American leaders were elated. The election "crushes the hopes of Weed Seward & Company," one wrote enthusiastically. "Certainly the back of Weed is broken & we stand erect."[115] With the Whig majority badly factionalized and with such an intense

---

111. Washington Hunt to Weed, October 21, *Private*, Edward Dodd to Weed, October 30, Weed Papers, UR; Greeley to Colfax, November 6, Greeley-Colfax Papers.

112. The official tally was Clark (Whig), 156,804 (33.4 percent); Seymour (Soft), 156,495 (33.3 percent); Bronson (Hard), 33,850 (7.2 percent); and Ullmann (Know Nothing), 122,282 (26.0 percent). Raymond ran slightly ahead of Clark and was elected lieutenant governor.

113. Albany *Evening Journal*, November 8; Buffalo *Daily Courier*, November 11.

114. Greeley to Colfax, November 6, Greeley-Colfax Papers; Andrew B. Dickinson to Seward, November 4, Seward Papers, UR; George W. Newell to Marcy, October 28, Marcy Papers, LC.

115. S. S. Parsons to Ullmann, November 11, Ullmann Papers, NYHS.

animus toward Seward prevalent among Know Nothing leaders, a desperate struggle to save Seward's political career loomed before Weed.

In temporarily salvaging his party's fortunes, Weed permanently lost his political alliance with Greeley. Near the close of the campaign, Greeley complained privately to Seward about his treatment: "Weed likes me, and always did—I don't think he ever had a dog about his house that he liked better—but he thinks I know nothing about politics. . . . I won't try any more to overcome his fixed prepossessions on this point." Shortly after the election, Greeley, in a caustic editorial, excoriated Whig leaders for blocking the formation of a Republican party in the state. Two days later, with the late-arriving returns still discouraging, he again blasted Whig leaders for conducting such a spiritless campaign. "One would hardly have supposed that Freedom and Slavery were at issue at all," he fumed. "It was the play of Hamlet, with Hamlet not only omitted, but forgotten." The editor of the *Tribune* sank into deep despondency as he mulled over the likely prospect of a Seymour victory and the utter loss of any hope for a prohibitory law. He poured out his resentment to Seward, denouncing Weed for opposing fusion, for rebuffing his desire to run for office, and for thrusting forward a mediocrity and bogus Know Nothing like Clark. He announced the dissolution of "the political firm of Seward Weed & Greeley." Henceforth, he told the New York senator, he would be an independent man and would no longer fight under the direction of others.[116] Greeley's estrangement from Seward and Weed had important repercussions for the movement to organize a national Republican party and, ultimately, for Seward's bid for the Republican nomination in 1860.

There was probably little Weed could have done to prevent Greeley's break. The latter's insatiable appetite for public recognition, his growing delusion that he was a brilliant political strategist, his erratic course on many issues of the day, all doomed his relationship with Weed. Greeley simply never understood the political situation in New York in 1854. In reality, Weed had pursued the best available strategy. Had he favored the Republican movement, his enemies would have captured control of the Whig party and thereby been considerably stronger; furthermore, there was no realistic chance the Republican party could carry the state. Wherever fusion had been victorious, the Know Nothings had supported its ticket. Where they opposed it, as they without question would have done in New York, fusion went down to ignominious defeat. Greeley's strategy was a prescription for certain failure. Weed still faced serious problems, but he operated from a position of greater strength than he would have as the leader in 1854 of a weak Republican party.

As in Massachusetts, the Know Nothings in New York received support from members of all parties and from earlier non-voters (Table 5.6). In New York, however, the nativist vote came primarily from former Whigs and earlier non-voters; a smaller proportion of Democrats cast Know Nothing ballots than in either Massachusetts or Pennsylvania. One of the striking features of the election was an increase over the previous year of more than 100,000 votes. New participants distributed their allegiance among the Whigs, Softs, and Know Nothings, with the largest proportion supporting the nativist ticket. As in other states, one of the important consequences of the Know Nothing upheaval was to politicize

---

116. New York *Tribune*, November 9, 11 (quotation); Greeley to Seward, October 25 (quotation), November 11, 24, Seward Papers, UR; Seward to Weed, November 21, December 2, Weed Papers, UR. Van Deusen, *Greeley*, 190–91, provides an excellent analysis of the various pressures weighing on Greeley's mind.

a number of previously apathetic citizens. The liquor question also undoubtedly mobilized many men, as Seymour's and Clark's gains suggest.

Seymour's vote came largely from Democrats; even a majority of the 1853 Hard voters supported him. Contemporary analysts most commonly emphasized the Hards' sympathy for Know Nothingism, yet even Dickinson hesitated to cast his lot unreservedly with the American party, and in fact almost as many Softs as Hards voted for Ullmann. The previous year a significant proportion of Silver Grey Whigs had cast Hard ballots, and they probably represented the bulk of these nativist defections. The Hard vote plummeted in 1854 less because former loyalists joined the Know Nothings than because they voted for Seymour. The results verified the belief of Soft leaders that by exploiting the temperance controversy they could make substantial inroads into the Hards' ranks. Many of these Hard voters who cast Seymour ballots were probably foreign-born. In 1853 the Hard ticket had drawn disproportionate support from immigrant voters, most of whom now rallied behind Seymour's banner in response to the liquor and nativist issues. Seymour ran particularly well among both the Irish and Germans (Table 5.8).[117] Overwhelming Catholic preference for the Soft ticket, coupled with Presbyterian and some Lutheran support for the Know Nothings, makes it quite probable that Irish and German voters divided roughly along religious lines, with Catholics voting for Seymour and Protestants for Ullmann. In addition, a sizable minority of English voters, who were normally Whig but who strongly opposed prohibition and hated Irish Catholics, apparently also cast American ballots. The contention of several political observers that large numbers of Protestant immigrants voted Know Nothing appears accurate (Tables 5.8 and 5.9).[118] Soft desertions to Clark, whether caused by the slavery or rum issue, were few (what defections occurred were probably Hale men who had voted Soft in 1853). Anti-slavery-extension sentiment in the Softs' ranks was stronger than these limited crossovers imply, but by emphasizing the liquor question the Softs were able to minimize the impact of the Nebraska issue and retain the support of the bulk of their followers.[119]

Clark's support drew substantially on Whigs and men who voted for Hale in 1852 (Table 5.7). Compared to these groups, his proportional strength among Democrats was slight. Free Democrats, in fact, voted as a bloc for the Whig nominee. They gave virtually no support to any of the other three candidates. Despite Clark's narrow victory, the traditional Whig electoral base had been thoroughly disrupted, since as many Whigs voted for Ullmann as for Clark. The Whig nominee suffered massive losses among native-born voters, and in fact he ran behind Ullmann in a number of Whig strongholds in the western part of the state. Chautauqua County was a good example. Long a banner Whig county, it suddenly switched in 1854 to the American party. At the same time, Clark picked up unexpected support in the northern counties, no doubt in part because the Know Nothings had not yet extensively recruited in that area, but also in response to the Whig candidate's anti-liquor and anti-Nebraska positions. St. Lawrence County, Preston King's bailiwick,

---

117. One letter-writer criticized Germans for supporting the Softs out of the belief that it was more important to rebuke Know Nothingism and the Maine Law than to protest the Nebraska perfidy. Letter signed "Hans," New York *Tribune*, November 4.

118. Charles D. Irish, Jr., to Ullmann, October 16, J. A. Scroggs to Ullmann, October 14, 30, Ullmann Papers, NYHS; New York *Tribune*, November 8; Rochester *Daily Union*, November 9; Hartford *Times*, November 9.

119. Henry S. Randall to Marcy, June 24, Marcy Papers, LC; New York *Herald*, November 10.

led the way and voted Whig after being solidly Democratic for years, much to King's satisfaction (Map 6).[120]

The temperance issue definitely aided Seymour, in part by attracting new voters but primarily by bringing the majority of the Hards to his support. Its impact on Clark's vote, however, is less easily determined. The Whig nominee did not gain substantial backing from either Democratic faction, and although his prohibitionist principles certainly appealed to Free Democrats, his opposition to the Nebraska bill was more important in securing their endorsement. Several commentators, in fact, claimed that many temperance men voted for Ullmann, and his strength in the Burned Over District, where revivalist Protestantism was especially strong, suggests that such assertions may well have been true.[121] Few temperance Democrats seem to have voted for Clark, although the liquor issue was probably responsible for his strength among earlier non-voters.

In analyzing the outcome of the New York election, commentators generally agreed that the temperance and nativist issues exerted greater influence than the Kansas-Nebraska Act. Hamilton Fish, for one, blamed Maine Law fanatics for the eclipse of the territorial question. The issue should have been Nebraska, he wrote in exasperation, but the results demonstrated that "the advocacy & the antagonism of the Liquor Bill were more efficient, if not more natural questions in a Political canvas[s] than the Slavery question." The New York correspondent of an out-of-state paper reported that the Nebraska issue "was overshadowed by the more pressing issues between the various parties on the liquor question. . . . Both the Temperance question and Know Nothingism exerted more influence upon the result than did the Nebraska question." With the Nebraska issue swallowed by the forces of ethnocultural conflict, the major parties in turmoil, and a powerful new party having arisen almost overnight ("as if by magic," one paper claimed), even experienced politicians were at a loss as to what the future would bring. "Parties are now in a state of disorganization—rather of utter anarchy," a veteran New York Democratic leader observed at the end of the year. "What is to come out of it, no one can foresee."[122]

V

The 1854 elections, while they gave added impetus to the process of realignment, did not establish a new party system. Rather, they represented only the first phase in a series of

120. Preston King to Welles, April 14, 1855, Welles Papers, LC. For evidence of the lack of a Know Nothing organization in many counties in 1854, see S. H. Lathrop to Ullmann, November 15, *Private*, E. M. Holbrook to Ullmann, December 21, S. S. Parsons to Ullmann, November 11, Ullmann Papers, NYHS; Buffalo *Commercial Advertiser*, October 29; Elmira *Gazette*, November 9. Whitney, who was part of the order's inner leadership, claimed that only a quarter of the towns in the state had been organized before the election: *Defence of American Policy*, 291. With sufficient time to organize, the Know Nothings would unquestionably have carried the election, since a number of the counties neglected by nativist organizers in 1854 swung sharply to the American party in 1855.

121. Granger to Ullmann, November 14, Ullmann Papers, NYHS; New York *Herald*, November 10. New York City observers, on the other hand, believed that the temperance issue hurt the Know Nothings in the metropolis. New York *Herald*, November 9; Nevins and Thomas, eds., *Strong Diary*, v. 2, 196.

122. Fish to John M. Bradford, December 16 (copy) (quotation), Fish to James Springsteed, November 8 (copy), Fish Papers, LC; New York correspondent "Ion," Baltimore *Sun*, quoted in the *National Era*, November 23; Sag Harbor *Corrector*, November 4; Benjamin F. Butler to Martin Van Buren, December 2, Van Buren Papers, LC.

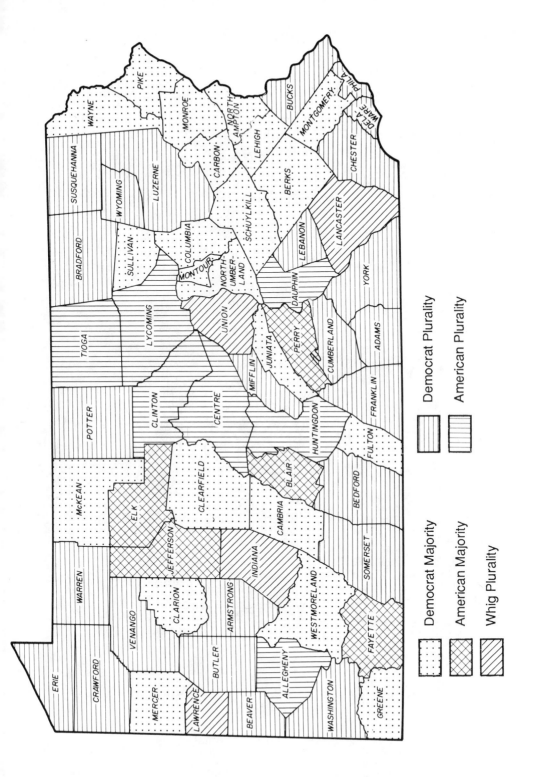

5. Pennsylvania Vote for Supreme Court Justice, 1854

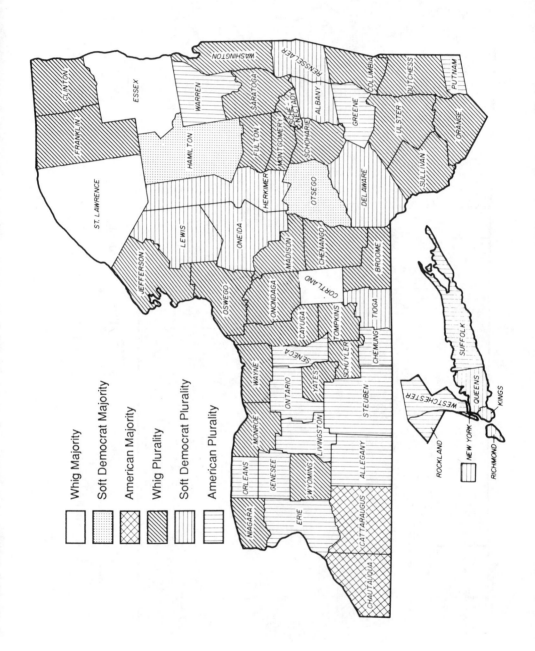

6. New York Vote for Governor, 1854

Whig Majority

Soft Democrat Majority

American Majority

Whig Plurality

Soft Democrat Plurality

American Plurality

elections that would ultimately result in the creation of a new party alignment.[123] Already weakened by the events of the last few years, the party system crumbled in 1854. "We see the work finished in the North—the destruction of the two old party organizations" that had ruled the country for a quarter of a century, a Philadelphia resident observed in the wake of these elections. While critical of the Know Nothings, John Gorham Palfrey nevertheless was thankful "for the 'eternal smash' into which they have brought the two corrupt old parties in Massachusetts." Neither, he believed, could be revived. In much the same fashion a Michigan politician characterized the Know Nothing movement as "a great political sledge hammer to break to pieces old parties, & old discipline"—an assessment that paralleled Bowles's analysis in Massachusetts.[124] Two distinct phenomena overlapped in this year: The Jacksonian party system was in the final throes of disintegration while a new party system was in the first stages of formation.

There were two clear casualties of the 1854 elections, the Pierce administration and the Whig party. The elections delivered a blow from which the president would never recover politically. Two-thirds of the northern Democratic seats in Congress had been lost and with them the party's control of the House. Pierce's leadership had been thoroughly discredited, and party managers began to think a new man was needed in 1856.[125] At the same time, the Whig party's decline, apparent in a number of states in 1852 and 1853, climaxed in 1854. Almost everywhere the party met defeat as vast numbers of former supporters deserted for new connections. "Of the Whig party there is not left even a monumental remembrance," Howell Cobb wrote once the northern elections were over. The election had left "the old Whig Organization a mass of ruins," a Whig paper in upstate New York commented ruefully. "We are utterly wrecked. It is altogether idle to think of a reconstruction of the Whig Party. It is past all surgery, past all medicine." Whether the party could have survived under the strategy Seward and Weed had devised earlier was now academic. Nativism had sealed the party's fate. The Know Nothings, as one New York politician remarked, had "torn the Whig strength to pieces."[126]

Yet if the magnitude of the political upheaval of 1854 is clear, the causes of the popular revolt that engulfed northern politics were the subjects of controversy. Certainly Democrats lost no time in blaming the Protestant clergy for their troubles. "Our defeat was owing to the Secret Conclave [Know Nothings] & the Methodist Church," one indignant Indiana Democrat complained. Voicing a common refrain, a party member in

---

123. Examination of a factor analysis of party percentages in Illinois, Indiana, Ohio, New York, and Pennsylvania confirms that 1854 marked the final overthrow of the second party system. In Illinois, Ohio, and New York, the 1854 election represents a sharp break with the previous voting patterns. New York provides the most striking example of this pattern. The 1854 vote does not align with any previous or subsequent elections; it was unique, constituting merely the first stage of the realignment process. In Indiana and Pennsylvania, on the other hand, the 1854 vote aligns with both the old and the new party systems. In both states it represented a transition stage from the Jacksonian to the Civil War party system.

124. Robert J. Arundel to John McLean, October 14, John McLean Papers, LC; John Gorham Palfrey to Joshua R. Giddings, December 2, Giddings Papers; Charles H. Stewart to S. R. Treadwell, January 22, 1855, Treadwell Family Papers, University of Michigan; Springfield *Republican*, November 15.

125. Nathaniel G. Upham to Buchanan, April 9, 1855, *Private*, Buchanan Papers, HSPa; C. M. Ingersoll to Thomas H. Seymour, January 8, 1855, Thomas H. Seymour Papers; George M. Dallas to Richard Rush, January 1, 1855, quoted in Rawley, *Race & Politics*, 92.

126. Howell Cobb to Buchanan, December 5, Ulrich B. Phillips, ed., *The Correspondence of Robert Toombs, Alexander H. Stephens, and Howell Cobb, Annual Report of the American Historical Association for the Year 1911* (Washington, D.C., 1913), v. 2, 348; Buffalo *Democrat* quoted in Buffalo *Daily Republican*, November 11; John Kelley to Horatio Seymour, November 15, Horatio Seymour Papers, NYSL.

Pennsylvania alleged, "We owe our defeat more to the *Protestant Ministry*, and the professed religious *press*, than to any other Cause."[127] An analysis of religion and voting in three states—New York, Pennsylvania, and Indiana—suggests that such assertions were exaggerated.

In Indiana, Democrats overstated the unanimity of Protestant opposition.[128] Among Presbyterians, Baptists, and Methodists—three denominations closely associated with temperance agitation—the Democrats retained their traditional support among Baptists and Methodists (Table 5.10). The most significant switch occurred among Presbyterians, a majority of whom voted Democratic in 1852 but who backed the People's ticket in 1854. Despite the prominent role played by Methodist ministers in the anti-Democratic campaign, voters in this denomination seemingly split more or less evenly, an outcome that represented at best only a slight increase in opposition strength. Furthermore, Democrats improved their showing among Lutherans, presumably because of the People's party endorsement of prohibition.

An examination of the relationship between religion and voting in Pennsylvania in 1854 highlights the connection between the anti-Catholic and anti-rum crusades. As in Indiana, the Protestant clergy in Pennsylvania was especially conspicuous in the agitation for a Maine Law, and Methodists, Baptists, and Presbyterians were all well-known for their anti-liquor principles. These three denominations were also stridently anti-Catholic, and contemporaries stressed Methodist and Baptist support for the Know Nothing movement in Pennsylvania. These assertions appear well-founded. Methodists, Baptists, and Presbyterians voted solidly dry, and, of these three church groups, Baptists and Methodists both shifted to Know Nothingism in 1854.[129] Of these evangelical denominations only the Presbyterians largely rejected the Know Nothings (Table 5.11). Among Baptists, apparently about an equal number of both Whigs and Democrats went into the nativist movement, for the decline in each party's percentage in 1854 was almost identical. Methodists behaved in a strikingly different manner. Democratic losses among Methodists were less severe than among Baptists. Although Methodist Whigs seem to have defected to the Know Nothings in 1854, the dramatic change in Methodist voting behavior occurred not so much among prior voters as among those who previously had not voted. This group apparently backed the Know Nothings overwhelmingly, and it probably accounts for the bulk of the Methodist support for the nativist ticket.[130]

Also noteworthy was the support for the Know Nothing ticket among German Reformed and, to a lesser extent, Lutheran voters, most of whom were not foreign-born but descendants of earlier German immigrants. These church groups probably experienced conflicting pressures: Their anti-Catholicism and hostility to the Irish drew them toward the secret order while their opposition to temperance (especially among

---

127. R. S. Staunton to John G. Davis, October 21, Davis Papers, IndHS; George W. Bowman to Bigler, October 23, Bigler Papers. Also see H. B. Pickett to John G. Davis, October 25, Davis Papers, IndHS; John Law to Marcy, September 25, Marcy Papers, LC; Thornbrough, ed., *Fletcher Diary*, v. 5, 282; E. W. Fairley to William H. English, October 2, English Papers, IndHS.

128. See the appendix for a discussion of the way these estimates were derived.

129. Of those who went to the polls, members of these three denominations were almost unanimous in support of prohibition, and only among the Methodists was there a significant rate of non-voting.

130. The number of previous non-voters among Methodists who cast Know Nothing ballots cannot be determined, but Democratic support among this church group declined only slightly, and the rate of non-voting among Methodists dropped in 1854, a change suggesting that Know Nothing accessions came predominantly from Whigs and non-voters.

Lutherans), their dislike of Yankee moral reformers, and their fear of an upsurge in anti-foreignism repelled them from Know Nothingism. In the end, they divided their ballots among all three parties, with the Lutherans more favorable to the Democrats than the more evangelical German Reformed.

In New York the relationship between religion and partisan preference was much different. Of the three largest Protestant denominations, Baptists seem to have voted solidly Whig and Presbyterians almost as solidly Know Nothing, and Methodists seem to have given support to both the Whig and Democratic tickets (Table 5.9). Presbyterians, who in New York were predominantly Yankees, were especially outspoken in denouncing Seward's proposal when he was governor to give tax money to parochial schools, an animosity that probably accounts for their strong affinity for the Know Nothing ticket. Baptists and Methodists were presumably attracted to Clark on the liquor issue, and Whigs registered substantial gains among the latter, but their weak support for the Know Nothing ticket is perplexing in view of their intense anti-Catholicism. Whig losses among their traditional Presbyterian supporters were counterbalanced by gains among usually Democratic Methodists. Catholics, on the other hand, voted overwhelmingly for Seymour.[131]

The variation of Protestant voting behavior in these states raises serious questions concerning interpretation of northern politics before the Civil War in terms of a pietist-nonpietist dichotomy. It has been too readily assumed that religious values were so fundamental in determining political attitudes that the voting of church groups evidenced only minor variation between states. In reality, the connection between religion and politics was not as direct and invariant as sometimes pictured.[132] Antebellum political behavior reflected much more than the basic religious cleavages in American society, as the quite different political behavior of northern and southern Methodists, Baptists, and Presbyterians in this period demonstrated. The partisan preferences of religious denominations took shape within the context of a state's political history, and once established these preferences proved difficult to disrupt.

Given the bewildering array of factions, alliances, issues, and movements involved, contemporaries, not surprisingly, had difficulty interpreting the significance of the 1854 results. During the next congressional session a sharp exchange ensued between Benjamin F. Wade and Stephen A. Douglas over the meaning of the 1854 elections. When the Ohio senator asserted that the northern electorate had rebuked the doctrine of popular sovereignty, Douglas retorted furiously that in the recent elections the Know Nothings had dominated the opposition. Know Nothingism, he charged, was "a crucible into which they poured Abolitionism, Maine liquor law-ism, and what there was left of northern Whigism, and then the Protestant feeling against the Catholic, and the native feeling

---

131. E. Peshine Smith to Carey, June 14, Carey Papers.

132. Recently, some historians have interpreted northern voting in this period in terms of the religious split between evangelicals, such as Methodists, Baptists, Congregationalists, and Presbyterians, who rallied behind the temperance, antislavery, and anti-Catholic crusades and voted Republican, and pietists, such as Catholics, Lutherans, and Episcopalians, who opposed state regulation of moral behavior and were Democrats. The most extended statement of this interpretation is Kleppner, *Third Electoral System*. Formisano, *Mass Political Parties*, Petersen, "Reaction to a Heterogeneous Society," and (with qualifications) Hansen, *Third Party System*, advance a similar interpretation. For a penetrating critique of this view, see Allan J. Lichtman, "Political Realignment and 'Ethnocultural' Voting in Late Nineteenth Century America," *Journal of Social History*, v. 16 (Spring, 1983), 55–82.

against the foreigner. All these elements were melted down in that crucible," he continued, "and the result was what was called the Fusion party."[133]

Historians have traditionally deemed Wade's assessment the more accurate. They point to the number of anti-Nebraska candidates elected to Congress and to the almost unbroken anti-Democratic triumphs in the state elections. Yet the Nebraska issue was not solely responsible for these victories. Indeed, the salience of other issues explains why the Whig party did not benefit from the revival of the slavery question. It was even more a casualty of the 1854 upheaval than the Democracy, even though northern Whig congressmen unanimously opposed the Nebraska bill.[134] While several issues, most notably Nebraska, nativism, and temperance, contributed to the overthrow of the Democrats, nativism represented the most powerful impulse in the 1854 northern elections. The Know Nothings dominated the fusion movement in Indiana, played a major role in the anti-Democratic victory in Maine and Ohio, and swamped the Whigs in Pennsylvania and Massachusetts. Even in New York, where the Whig party polled more votes than its upstart rival, the Know Nothings were clearly on the rise. "This Catholic power is felt to be at the north a more dangerous power than the Slave Power & therefore absorbs all other considerations," grieved one of Charles Sumner's correspondents. After the election a despondent New York Whig drew the same conclusion: "This election has demonstrated that, by a majority, Roman Catholicism is feared more than American slavery."[135]

The strength of the nativist movement was the major reason that the Nebraska issue failed to precipitate the formation of a new sectional party. Capitalizing on the forces that had undermined the Whig party *before* the reopening of the slavery controversy— temperance, nativism, and a growing impatience with the existing parties—the Know Nothing revolt proved too powerful to be deflected by the anti-Nebraska movement. The American party, not the antislavery Republicans, benefited from the popular desire in 1854 for a new party. By opposing the expansion of slavery as well as taking a nativist stance, the Know Nothing party blunted the anti-Nebraska impulse and prevented either the Whigs or a fusion party from monopolizing this issue, thus further undermining the new-party movement. Antislavery men complained bitterly that the nativist movement barred a clear vote on the Nebraska issue. Charles Francis Adams, who had earlier hoped for a decisive condemnation of the repeal of the Missouri Compromise, was dismayed by the course of events in Massachusetts. "At this moment . . . when the people of the State are more united in sentiment than they have been for twenty years," he lamented before the election, "circumstances would make it appear that it was never so distracted in an election." After the popular verdict was known, another Massachusetts man wailed that

---

133. *Cong. Globe*, 33rd Cong., 2nd sess., Appendix, 216.

134. Those historians who emphasize the role of the Kansas-Nebraska Act in the onset of realignment and the destruction of the second party system must explain why the Whig party, despite the unbroken opposition of its northern members in Congress to the repeal of the Missouri Compromise, disintegrated in the North while the pro-Nebraska Democratic party survived; why the Know Nothings were so strong in 1854 compared to the Whigs, even though the latter gave greater emphasis to the slavery issue in their state platforms and campaigns; why the attempt to form a Republican party on the Nebraska issue failed almost everywhere in 1854; and why the antislavery Republican party was so weak initially (the reason cannot be that the party was new, since the Know Nothings were also new). Proponents of the traditional view have not addressed any of these questions satisfactorily.

135. E. Winslow to Sumner, May 5, Sumner Papers, HU; J. W. Taylor to Fish, November 11, Fish Papers, LC.

"Know-nothingism has come in most inopportunely to drown out all the enthusiasm which had been aroused in the northern states by the Nebraska perfidy."[136]

Whig opposition, especially in the East, was the other major reason for the failure of the Republican movement in 1854. Disregarding the depth of hostility in the electorate to the old party organizations, Whig leaders mistakenly believed that they would benefit from the existing popular discontent. Gamaliel Bailey placed the blame for the outcome of the fall elections squarely on Whig politicians: "Their ill-judged policy, while subverting their own Party, gave power to another, which now threatens to check, if not paralyze the Republican movement." With passage of the Kansas-Nebraska Act fusion was an "imperative necessity," Samuel Bowles declared in the Springfield *Republican*, but instead party managers judged that Whigs could monopolize the offices by exploiting this issue, only to see the rank-and-file desert to the Know Nothings and destroy the party.[137] The results of the 1854 elections gave convincing evidence that the erosion of the Whig voting base prior to the Nebraska crisis was irreversible. Even when the Democratic administration blundered and handed its northern opponents an unusually popular issue, the Whigs were unable to halt their decline.

Two factors—the attitude of the Whigs and the response of the Know Nothings—were critical in determining the success or failure of fusion. Wherever the Whigs opposed the new party movement, it made little progress. Wherever the Whigs encouraged it *and* the Know Nothings also lent their support, fusion was victorious. In the West, fusion made greater headway in 1854 not because, as is sometimes asserted, westerners cared more about the territorial issue, but because the Know Nothings had less time to organize, and because in several states the Whig organization was already in shambles from other causes.

For fusionists the 1854 elections constituted a severe setback. Their expectation of forming a new antislavery party on the Nebraska issue had been largely disappointed. The Republican movement had barely gotten under way, and the party had organized in only two minor states. Moreover, the strength of the Know Nothings in a number of key states erected a major roadblock to the establishment of a powerful Republican party, and the order's national leaders, buoyed by the recent results, immediately embarked on an expansion drive in states and regions where previous organizing efforts had been limited. The ethnocultural forces that disrupted the second party system had spawned a powerful nativist party that threatened to overwhelm the political system.

For hard-headed antislavery men, the administration's defeat offered scant cause for rejoicing. "What is to come out of the conglomeration of elements that have brought about this revolution?" Gamaliel Bailey asked pointedly. Shocked by the Know Nothings' commanding power, he pronounced the country "demoralized." Similarly, Charles Francis Adams maintained that the election results were "disastrous" for the antislavery cause, "notwithstanding the appearance of triumph which they give at this moment. . . . It is plain that the victory which seemed almost in our hands is slipping out of it." To Sumner he mourned that "the prospect of success is dimmed for years." Less radical than these men, Hamilton Fish nonetheless concurred with their analysis. Noting that thousands of Whigs, to say nothing of free soil Democrats, had opposed Clark in New

---

136. Adams Diary, October 21, Adams Family Papers; T. M. Brewer to Israel Washburn, Jr., January 27, 1855 (quotation), Israel Washburn, Jr., Papers, Norlands; D. A. Wasson to Samuel Johnson, October 30, Johnson Papers; Pittsburgh *Gazette*, October 10.

137. *National Era*, November 23; Springfield *Republican*, November 15 (quotation), 27.

York "while the Nebraska issue was still blistering," he saw little hope that a new antislavery party could be organized. "The time for 'fusion' is in my opinion past," he proclaimed. "Fire will not burn a second time over the same field."[138] Dismayed by this turn of events, experienced politicians concluded that the unprecedented opportunity offered by the Nebraska controversy to organize a northern antislavery party had been irretrievably lost.

---

138. Bailey to Gerrit Smith, November 15, Gerrit Smith Papers, Syracuse University; Adams to Francis Bird, October 16, Adams Diary, November 14 (quotation), 15, Adams Family Papers; Fish to John M. Bradford, December 16 (copy), Fish Papers, LC.

6

New Issues, New Leaders, New Organizations

"Public sentiment in this country is in a transition state so far as the principle of party organization is concerned," Alexander H. Stephens reflected as the year 1854 drew to a close. "Old parties, old names, old issues, and old organizations are passing away. A day of new things, new issues, new leaders, and new organizations is at hand."[1] Many of Stephens's congressional colleagues shared his sense of an impending shift in the country's politics. Yet few if any saw clearly the ultimate outcome of realignment. "We are all very much in the dark as to the political future," Elihu B. Washburne of Illinois confessed after Congress reassembled. "Nobody can begin to *guess* even, as to what shape things will eventually assume." With the political future so murky, "almost all" party leaders were "looking over their shoulders," another observer at the capital reported, "to discern from what quarter the breeze is coming."[2]

In the opening months of 1855, the predominant breeze seemed to be in the direction of the Know Nothings. But the nativist organization had yet to consolidate its strength nationally, despite the national council's recent adoption of a new third or Union degree, which pledged its candidates to support the Union. Widely varying interpretations of the degree's meaning rendered it uncertain whether the northern and southern branches could remain united.[3] Nevertheless, in view of the Know Nothings' obvious power throughout the free states, many politicians harbored grave doubts about the Republican party's potential. When the Thirty-third Congress finally concluded its labors, the outlook for a

---

Note: Unless otherwise indicated, the year for newspaper and manuscript citations in this chapter is 1855.

1. Alexander H. Stephens to [Linton Stephens?], December 31, 1854, in Richard M. Johnson and William H. Browne, *Life of Alexander H. Stephens*, rev. ed. (Philadelphia, 1883), 286.

2. Elihu B. Washburne to Israel Washburn, Sr., February 18, Elihu B. Washburne Papers, Norlands Library; Benjamin R. Curtis to George Ticknor, February 6, Benjamin R. Curtis, ed., *A Memoir of Benjamin Robbins Curtis* (2 vols.: Boston, 1879), v. 1, 176–77.

3. For the Union degree, see Scisco, *Political Nativism in New York*, 133–38.

northern sectional party remained bleak. A series of events in the spring and summer of 1855, however, provided a new opportunity to organize an antislavery party and formed the background for the launching of the Republican party.

I

Developments in the far-off territory of Kansas were of fundamental importance in strengthening the nascent Republican movement. Americans always looked to the West for opportunity, and Kansas was no exception. Much research has demonstrated the overriding importance of traditional frontier concerns, particularly the ownership of land, in the affairs of that troubled territory. Making a fortune, speculating in land, developing towns, and starting a farm dominated the outlook of the first inhabitants from both sections. "We went to Kansas to better our condition," a settler from New England later explained, "incidently expecting to make it a free state." Furthermore, much of the violence in the territory arose out of the problems in settling any frontier region and had little to do with sectional tensions.[4] Yet if these facts are clear in hindsight, they were less obvious to contemporaries. Before long, the strife in Kansas was transformed in the popular mind into a fierce struggle over slavery. In the North, newspapers that eventually affiliated with the Republican party played a critical role in creating the symbol of Bleeding Kansas, which first became a significant issue in the 1855 state elections.[5]

Even before the Kansas-Nebraska Act became law, the idea gained currency that the two sections would contest for control of Kansas. Eventually, a number of Kansas aid societies were organized in the North, but from the beginning the New England Emigrant Aid Company was the most important and attracted the most publicity. The company's purpose, as outlined by its founder, Eli Thayer, was to encourage settlement of Kansas from the northern states while making a profit for its shareholders by investing in land and improvements. Despite Thayer's grandiose plans, the company's role in Kansas was distinctly limited. It sent few settlers to the territory—in 1854 and 1855 only 1,240 settlers went there under its auspices, of whom perhaps a third did not stay—and its investments were never profitable. After two fruitless years, Amos A. Lawrence, a wealthy Boston businessman and prominent conservative who quickly assumed active leadership of the company's affairs, admitted that its settlement efforts were a dismal failure and that it was bankrupt.[6]

Despite these modest accomplishments, the company played an important role in stimulating northern concern over affairs in Kansas. One of its directors' first acts was to finance the establishment of a free soil newspaper, the *Herald of Freedom*, edited by G. W. Brown in Lawrence. The paper was far too partisan and extreme to wield much influence in the territory, yet it had a significant impact on public opinion in the free states. Widely distributed throughout the North by the company, it was the only Kansas

---

4. William H. Carruth, "The New England Emigrant Aid Company as an Investment Society," *Kansas Historical Collections*, v. 6 (1897–1900), 93. For a fuller discussion of the situation in Kansas, see Gienapp, "Origins of the Republican Party," 561–83, which provides extensive citations. The most important works on the Kansas Territory are Paul Wallace Gates, *Fifty Million Acres: Conflicts over Kansas Land Policy, 1854–1890* (Ithaca, 1954), and James C. Malin, *John Brown and the Legend of Fifty-Six* (Philadelphia, 1942).

5. Bernard Weisberger, "The Newspaper Reporter and the Kansas Imbroglio," *MVHR*, v. 36 (March, 1950), 633–56.

6. Samuel A. Johnson, *The Battle Cry of Freedom: The New England Emigrant Aid Company in the Kansas Crusade* (Lawrence, 1954), is a full and complete account of the company's history.

paper that enjoyed a sizable circulation outside the territory, and as a result it was quoted extensively in the northern press. It was a powerful propaganda vehicle in exciting northern indignation.[7]

Also important was the effect on public opinion in Missouri's border region of Eli Thayer's widely publicized "Plan of Operations," which announced the incorporation of the company with a capitalization of five million dollars and referred to arrangements to pour 20,000 free-state emigrants into Kansas. Taking these wildly exaggerated statements at face value, western Missourians were frantic. They viewed the Massachusetts organization as an attempt to cheat them out of neighboring lands that were rightfully theirs, and they considered it a serious threat to the security of slavery in Missouri. Future Kansas governor John W. Geary did not exaggerate when he spoke of "a virulent spirit of dogged determination to *force* slavery into this Territory" as rampant in the western counties. Senator David Rice Atchison of Missouri quickly assumed leadership of the movement to save Kansas for slavery. Atchison's motives were mixed. Still seeking reelection to the Senate, he saw a chance to promote his political aspirations, yet he also was genuinely convinced that the survival of southern institutions was connected intimately with the fate of Kansas. At a series of meetings along the western border that summer, Atchison advocated using whatever force necessary to prevent abolitionists from seizing control of the territory.[8] In the brawling society of western Missouri such rhetoric was like sparks in a tinderbox.

Despite surface calm, therefore, the situation in Kansas was deeply unsettled when territorial governor Andrew Reeder of Pennsylvania took up his post in October 1854. The forty-seven-year-old Reeder was a lawyer and prominent local Democratic politician, but he had never held public office before and lacked administrative experience. Cautious and deliberate, yet at the same time paradoxically lacking in tact, he had an impressive demeanor that belied his hesitancy and indecision under pressure. After his appointment, he visited Washington and assured southern leaders that he had no scruples against slavery and would as soon buy a slave as a horse. He intended that popular sovereignty be given a fair trial, yet like most others he thought of Kansas primarily in terms of the economic opportunities it offered, and before long he was enmeshed in a web of land speculations, including some of questionable legality.

The first election in Kansas was a complete fiasco. Prior to the voting, Atchison recklessly inflamed public feeling by urging the residents of Missouri's border counties to cross the river and vote in order to safeguard their interests. The poorly drafted Kansas-Nebraska Act complicated matters by failing to specify any term of residence for voters. What would have been a chaotic situation in any case was made hopelessly so by the invasion of hundreds of Missourians under Atchison's lead. If election judges rejected their votes, the invaders promptly thrust the judges aside. As a result, John Whitfield, a proslavery man nominated by a meeting in Missouri, was overwhelmingly elected

7. For the company's ties with the *Herald of Freedom*, see Johnson, *Battle Cry of Freedom*, 90.

8. John W. Geary to Franklin Pierce, December 22, 1856, *Confidential*, Pierce Papers, LC; William E. Parrish, *David Rice Atchison of Missouri, Border Politician* (Columbia, Mo., 1961), 162–65, 187; David Rice Atchison to Jefferson Davis, September 24, 1854, David Rice Atchison Papers, University of Missouri. Amos A. Lawrence aptly termed Thayer's published plan a "harum scarum paper." Quoted in Johnson, *Battle Cry of Freedom*, 95.

congressional delegate for Kansas.[9] More important, the action of Atchison and his compatriots tarnished popular sovereignty from the very outset.

Of much greater concern to both sides was the election of the territorial legislature, scheduled for March 1855. Men assumed that the action of the first legislature, particularly on the subject of slavery, would be decisive. Forewarned, Reeder this time made a legitimate effort to guarantee a fair election. He ordered the legal authorities to prevent disorder at the polls, and he stipulated, much to the anger of proslavery leaders, that voters had to be actual residents of the territory without homes in other states. Once again, however, Missourians poured across the border as the election approached. They were carefully dispatched to all districts to assure a proslavery majority in the legislature. "There are eleven hundred coming over from Platte County to vote," Atchison allegedly boasted as he led one group into Kansas, "and if that ain't enough we can send five thousand— enough to kill every God-damned abolitionist in the Territory." Election day was a repeat of the scenes in October. Massive illegal voting allowed proslavery candidates to sweep the field. Whether this blatant provocation of northern public opinion served any purpose is questionable. With southerners constituting more than 60 percent of the legal voters in the territory, proslavery forces would probably have triumphed in a fair election. Heedless of these considerations, the Leavenworth *Herald* could not resist exulting, "Abolitionism is rebuked, her fortress stormed, her flag is dragging in the dust."[10]

This massive show of force was a much more serious political miscalculation than the illegal voting the previous October. It set the stage for the repudiation of the territorial authorities by the free-state men and prepared the way for the outbreak of violence between the two contending factions in the territory. It strengthened the image in the North of an aggressive slavocracy willing to trample northern rights to achieve its goals. And it gave added credence to the popular image of the Missourians as "border ruffians"—"Cossacks of civilization," James Shepherd Pike termed them—violent half-civilized men bent on terrorizing innocent Kansas settlers. The election frauds, accompanied by threats of force and backed by an approving chorus from southern newspapers and leaders, greatly exacerbated anti-southern feeling in the free states. "An inevitable collision is before us, between the North and the South, on the question of Slavery Extension," warned the New York *Tribune* after the territorial election.[11]

Badly shaken by this turn of events, Reeder capitulated to blustering proslavery claimants and certified the election results. He then summoned the legislature to meet at Pawnee City, a collection of shacks miles from the settled portion of the territory, but where—coincidentally—he had invested heavily in land and owned the only hotel. When the legislature convened, its members ousted all free-state representatives but one (he subsequently resigned) and gave the vacated seats to proslavery men. Then, over the governor's veto, they moved from Pawnee City to Shawnee Mission, just over the border from Missouri, which was a much more convenient location since most members

---

9. A subsequent investigation estimated that of the 2,871 votes cast, only 1,114 were legal. House Report No. 220, 34th Cong., 1st sess. [hereafter referred to as *Howard Report*], 3–100.

10. Atchison quoted in Nevins, *Ordeal of the Union*, v. 2, 385; Leavenworth *Herald* quoted in Alice Nichols, *Bleeding Kansas* (New York, 1954), 29. For the election, see the testimony in the *Howard Report*, and the colorful description in William Phillips, *The Conquest of Kansas by Missouri and Her Allies* (Boston, 1856), 63–82. A later congressional investigation concluded that 4,908 illegal votes had been cast compared to only 1,410 legal ones.

11. New York *Tribune*, April 13 (quotation), 17. For examples of the southern press's reaction, see Rhodes, *History of the United States*, v. 2, 40.

were residents of that state. At this point relations between Reeder, who had expected to get rich once Pawnee City became the capital, and the legislators collapsed completely. He now denounced the legislature as illegal and began systematically vetoing its acts. The members in turn repeatedly overrode his vetoes and petitioned Franklin Pierce for the governor's dismissal. Under mounting southern pressure, the pliant president finally removed Reeder. Almost overnight the Republican press ludicrously transformed the former governor into a northern hero and a champion of the anti-southern cause.

In providing a legal code for the territory, the legislators enacted what were basically the existing laws of Missouri. Only on the question of slavery and its protection did they diverge significantly from this model by passing a set of Draconian measures directed against the free-state men. Its more stringent features made it a felony to maintain that slavery did not legally exist in the territory, or to circulate any printed material containing such an argument; disqualified all antislavery men from serving as jurors; prohibited opponents of slavery from holding office; and provided the death penalty for anyone who assisted fugitive slaves. In order to assure continued proslavery dominance, the legislature also enacted a thoroughly unfair election law. Lewis Cass, anything but a radical on the slavery question, expressed northern sentiment when he said in the Senate: "There is no doubt that some of the statutes passed by the Legislature of Kansas are a disgrace to the age and the country."[12]

Adoption of this legal code was another costly victory for the South. The legislators intended to intimidate the free-state men in Kansas, and they wanted to encourage slaveowners to move there. They accomplished neither objective. At the same time, their action aroused public opinion in the North and gave opponents of slavery renewed hope that the troubles in Kansas would lead to the formation of a northern antislavery party. The extensive vote frauds in the spring election, followed by the aggressive behavior of the legislature, significantly affected Kansas affairs as well by precipitating the formation of a rival free-state "government." Before the March election, organized free-state sentiment had been confined to the area around Lawrence, where the New England Emigrant Aid Company settlers were concentrated. In the wake of that election and the subsequent conduct of the legislature, many settlers previously indifferent to the slavery question now joined the free-state movement in order to defend their rights and liberties. Denying the legality of the existing territorial government and defying its authority, the free-state men drafted a state constitution, elected state officers, headed by Charles Robinson, an agent of the New England Emigrant Aid Company, as "governor," and petitioned Congress for admission as a free state. Reeder, who was now a prominent free-state leader, won the extralegal election for congressional delegate conducted by the free-state "government" headquartered in Topeka.

By the end of the year Pierce's new governor, Wilson Shannon, yet another mediocrity, confronted a potentially explosive situation in Kansas. Two governments were in existence, and the slavery issue intensified the conflict. Two different processes intertwined: Northern journalists in Kansas interpreted the continuing violence almost exclusively in terms of the sectional conflict, while simultaneously lawless elements began to cloak their criminal activity behind the slavery issue. "There are too many men here of all parties who care nothing for the final result," one Kansas resident wrote at the height of the turmoil in the territory, "but take advantage of the excitement to commit acts

---

12. Cass quoted in Rawley, *Race & Politics*, 91–92.

of rapine plunder and murder and then attribute it to one or [the] other of the contending political parties.''[13] With the escalation of violence, proponents of the Republican movement discerned a potentially powerful issue that could be used to build a sectional antislavery party. Equally significant, many northern politicians still uncertain of their course began to think that such a party might indeed attract great popular support.

II

Republican organizers also drew encouragement from the results of the 1855 senatorial elections in the northern states. In none of these contests did a Nebraska man win. The only solace for the Pierce administration was that in Indiana and Pennsylvania no senator was named. In Indiana Democratic holdovers prevented any choice when the Senate, narrowly under Democratic control, refused to join the House in an election. The deadlock in Pennsylvania was more ominous for the future of the opposition. Unlike their counterparts in Indiana, the anti-administration forces had solid majorities in both houses of the Pennsylvania legislature. In the 1854 contest, sixty-one legislators had been elected as Whigs and fifty-nine as Democrats, yet ninety-one members, easily a majority, participated in the American caucus to select a nominee. Despite the Know Nothings' preponderance, the diversity of anti-Democratic elements united loosely under their banner made effective control difficult. As one local leader explained to Simon Cameron, the leading aspirant for the senatorship, ''We have such a hotch potch delgation [*sic*] in our next Legislature that there is no telling'' what the outcome would be.[14]

A maverick Democrat and successful businessman and financier, Cameron was a perpetual aspirant to return to the Senate, where he had served one term in the 1840s. He was a political adventurer who had marshaled his political talents and considerable wealth to build a personal following throughout the state. During the 1854 campaign, he gave Governor William Bigler restrained support, but, never a man to miss an opportunity to strengthen himself politically, Cameron made haste following the governor's defeat to join the Know Nothings. In doing so, he conveniently overlooked the repeated attacks on the order by his personal organ, the Harrisburg *Union*, during the just-completed campaign. Cameron's nativist affiliation represented naked opportunism. In similar fashion, the former senator suddenly discovered that he was an opponent of the Nebraska Act, even though his associates had led the fight in the 1854 convention to endorse the then-pending repeal of the Missouri Compromise, and the Dauphin County Democratic convention, which he firmly controlled, adopted resolutions denouncing the Know Nothings and endorsing Pierce and the Kansas-Nebraska Act (opponents charged, probably with truth, that Cameron had drafted these resolutions personally).[15] In an effort to gain additional votes in the senatorial contest, he publicly endorsed a set of nativist and

---

13. William J. Osborne to William L. Marcy, September 26, 1856, Marcy Papers, LC; Thomas Wentworth Higginson to his mother, September 24, 1856, Thomas Wentworth Higginson Papers, HU. The most famous example of this phenomenon was that psychopathic ne'er-do-well, John Brown.

14. Philadelphia *Public Ledger*, February 10; Daniel Sheffer to Simon Cameron, November 1, 1854, Simon Cameron Papers, LC.

15. Alexander K. McClure, *Abraham Lincoln and Men of War-Times*, 4th ed. (Philadelphia, 1892), 149; clipping from the Philadelphia *North American*, enclosed in Daniel T. Jenks to James Buchanan, March 6, Buchanan Papers, HSPa. See the untitled Know Nothing circular discussing Cameron's political conversion in the Society Collection, HSPa.

anti-Nebraska principles, including a twenty-one-year residence requirement for natural-ized voters.[16]

After several ballots, Cameron won the nomination of the American caucus. When it was discovered that one more vote had been cast than there were members present, indignant anti-Cameron men stormed out of the meeting crying fraud. These American bolters issued a circular, written secretly by Thaddeus Stevens, who two years later would mastermind Cameron's election to the Senate, charging that Cameron's nomination had been accomplished by "shameless and wholesale private bribery."[17] The result was a hopeless deadlock. Cameron led all contenders, but his unsavory reputation, his frequent shifts in party allegiance, and his alienation during the contest of his leading rival, Andrew G. Curtin, the Whig state chairman and a prominent Know Nothing, made it impossible for him to secure a majority. In the end, after a number of fruitless ballots, the legislature put the election over until 1856.

Despite its inconclusive outcome, the 1855 Pennsylvania senatorial contest had several very important consequences for the future course of politics in the state. With Cameron's decision to cast his lot with the American movement, the opposition gained a powerful and skillful leader. Not all Cameron's personal followers left the Democratic camp with him, but many did. Most of these men were influential county politicians, and they brought vital leadership experience to the anti-Democratic forces. Still nurturing senato-rial ambitions, Cameron actively promoted union among the various opposition factions in order to enhance his prospects for office. In addition, the personal feud between Cameron and Curtin, which would play a crucial role in the 1856 campaign and which would seriously factionalize the state's Republican party in the future, grew out of this senatorial contest.[18]

Elsewhere the Pierce administration encountered an unbroken chain of setbacks. Iowa and Wisconsin both elected anti-Nebraska men to the Senate. In Pierce's native state of New Hampshire, the outcome of the June senatorial election was especially mortifying to the president. With both senatorships to be filled, the legislature elected two staunch anti-Nebraska men, James Bell, a Know Nothing Whig, to the full term, and John P. Hale, the long-time Free Soil leader, to the short term. Hale's election in particular was humiliating to Pierce, who as head of the Democratic party in New Hampshire in the 1840s had waged a bitter, unceasing struggle to remove Hale from public life. Solid Know Nothing support contributed significantly to Hale's victory, and he maintained suspi-ciously close ties with the order, yet his triumphant return to the Senate undeniably constituted an antislavery victory.[19] One New Hampshire politician believed, prema-

---

16. Cameron to J. M. Kirkpatrick, February 9, Draft, Cameron to Howell Powell, February 20, Draft, Cameron Papers, LC.

17. A copy of the bolters' protest (misfiled under 1854) is in the Cameron Papers, LC. Also see the circular in the same collection issued by those who remained in the caucus defending their action. For Thaddeus Stevens's authorship, see Jeremiah S. Black to Buchanan, February 17, Buchanan Papers, HSPa.

18. The exact origin of the Cameron-Curtin feud was never revealed. In a letter to an ally, Cameron accused Curtin of attempting to blackmail him but provided no specifics. Without offering any details, McClure attributed their falling-out to a "personal reproach" by Cameron. See Cameron to A. L. Mackey, August 27, Cameron Papers, LC; McClure, *Old Time Notes*, v. 1, 387; Erwin S. Bradley, *Simon Cameron, Lincoln's Secretary of War* (Philadelphia, 1966), 101–2.

19. Richard H. Sewell, *John P. Hale and the Politics of Abolition* (Cambridge, 1965), 154–62, contains a careful discussion of the senatorial contest. Hale denied membership in the secret order, but opponents charged that he had been inducted into the Dover lodge in a private ceremony, and those inside the secret society asserted

turely, as it turned out, that Bell's and Hale's victories cleared the way for the formation of a new anti-Democratic party in the state "upon just and liberal Anti-Slavery grounds, that cannot be beat."[20]

Because of Stephen A. Douglas's national prominence, the Illinois senatorial contest was watched closely in Washington. Anti-Douglas forces held a narrow majority in the legislature, but anti-Nebraska members could reach no consensus on a candidate to replace James Shields. A number of politicians carefully nurtured aspirations for the position. One observer, musing that there were as many senatorial candidates "as black berries in July," reported that "it seems as tho' the subject becomes each day more and more involved in obscurity."[21] The reluctance of anti-Nebraska Democrats to cooperate with the Whigs made precise calculations impossible, and the defection of several conservative downstate Whigs to the Douglas forces further muddied the waters.

Still smarting over the 1854 results, Douglas contemptuously rejected any suggestion that he make peace with his adversaries in the state party. He placed Thomas Harris, congressman-elect from the Springfield District, and Charles H. Lanphier, editor of the party's organ, the *Illinois State Register*, in command of the senatorial contest, and instructed them that the Democrats should nominate Shields, "nail his flag to the mast, and never haul it down under any circumstances nor for any body." More than gratitude for Shields's faithful support motivated Douglas in this decision. Anticipating that the opposition could never unite on a candidate, he hoped to prevent an election altogether in expectation that the next legislature would be Democratic. Moreover, he was anxious to make Know Nothingism rather than Nebraska the dividing issue in the state's politics, and, because Shields was an Irish-born Catholic, his candidacy offered the best opportunity to exploit this strategy. "Our friends should stand by Shields and throw the responsibility on the Whigs of beating him *because he was born in Ireland*," Douglas exhorted Lanphier. "Let this be made the issue in the Newspapers & in the Legislature & everywhere; and with reference to this issue let us rise or fall with Shields."[22]

Of the anti-Nebraska aspirants, Abraham Lincoln was far and away the strongest candidate, having collected pledges of support from most of the Whig members. But some staunch antislavery men from the North, who disliked his continuing adherence to the Whig party, and a coterie of five anti-Nebraska Democrats, four of whom vowed that they would never vote for a Whig, opposed his candidacy. This latter group, which included Norman B. Judd and John M. Palmer, both future leaders of the Republican party, supported Lyman Trumbull, who had been elected to Congress in 1854 as an independent anti-Nebraska Democrat. Lincoln conceded before the balloting began that he did not see where he would get the additional votes necessary for a majority.[23]

The secret candidacy of Democratic governor Joel Matteson, who was nominally uncommitted on the Nebraska question, complicated the situation. From the beginning

that he had joined. See Schuyler Colfax to Rev. E. W. Jackson, March 15, *Confidential*, Colfax Papers, IndU; Albert G. Browne to Charles Sumner, January 3, Sumner Papers; George Bradburn to Salmon P. Chase, May 10, Chase Papers, LC; [Concord] *New Hampshire Patriot*, January 3.

20. Aaron H. Cragin to Thurlow Weed, June 15, Seward Papers, UR.

21. Churchill Coffing to Washburne, February 8, Elihu B. Washburne Papers, LC.

22. Stephen A. Douglas to Charles Lanphier, December 18, 1854 (*Confidential*), Douglas to James W. Sheahan, February 6 (Confidential), Johannsen, ed., *Douglas Letters*, 333–34.

23. Abraham Lincoln to Richard Yates, January 14, Basler, ed., *Lincoln Collected Works Supplement*, 25–26; Lincoln to Elihu B. Washburne, February 9, Basler, *Lincoln Collected Works*, v. 2, 304–6; James Shields to Lanphier, January 19, Charles H. Lanphier Papers, IllSHL.

Matteson played what Lincoln termed a "double game," assuring Douglas's associates of his fidelity while telling the anti-Nebraska Democrats that he opposed the repeal of the Missouri Compromise. Not wishing to sever their ties with the party, some anti-Nebraska Democrats grasped eagerly at the reed Matteson offered. Even Palmer, who sincerely opposed the Kansas-Nebraska Act, was attracted to Matteson's candidacy and believed that in the end he would be taken up by both wings of the party and be elected.[24]

Lincoln led on the first ballot, but on subsequent tallies failed to muster a majority. After six fruitless ballots, the Democratic managers, contrary to Douglas's wishes, dropped Shields and took up Matteson. By the ninth ballot the governor was within three votes of election, and rumors circulated that he would be elected on the next ballot. At this point Lincoln took matters decisively into his own hands. Wishing to see a genuine anti-Nebraska man sent to the Senate, he instructed his remaining supporters to vote for Trumbull, and on the next ballot, much to the Democrats' astonishment, the latter was elected. Long a minority in the state, Whigs were understandably disheartened at the outcome. Lincoln's close associate David Davis conceded that Trumbull was sincerely anti-Nebraska, but added that he did not trust Trumbull because "he has been a Democrat all his life—dyed in the wool—as ultra as he could be." Lincoln was disappointed as well, but in a letter to Elihu Washburne, who had worked ardently for his election, he reflected, "On the whole, it is perhaps as well for our general cause that Trumbull is elected. The Neb. men confess that they hate it worse than any thing that could have happened."[25]

Trumbull's election was an important preliminary step in the formation of the Illinois Republican party. Like most anti-Nebraska Democrats in Illinois, the new senator was slow to abandon his old party ties, but his election inevitably widened the gap between the two Democratic factions. For once William Herndon understood the situation when, contending that the outcome was a significant blow to Douglas, he predicted that Trumbull would prove a "great thorn, rough and poisonous" in the Democratic leader's heart.[26] Douglas had misread the situation. Granted, Lincoln was a formidable opponent, and it is easy to see why Douglas did not relish the idea of confronting him in the Senate, but the combative Trumbull, who was unwilling to make any concessions on the slavery expansion issue, would prove a dogged adversary who relentlessly hounded Douglas. Furthermore, Trumbull's untainted Democratic career enabled him to influence dissident Democrats much more easily than could a lifelong Whig like Lincoln. Trumbull's election gave anti-Douglas Democrats a national leader, something they had previously lacked, as well as renewed dedication. Within a year the new senator would exert significant influence on the formation of the Republican party in Illinois.

The election in the Massachusetts legislature to fill the remaining portion of Edward Everett's term also received widespread notice because of the candidacy of Henry Wilson. Wilson had withdrawn from the 1854 gubernatorial contest and backed Henry J. Gardner on the understanding that he, Wilson, would receive the senatorship. As soon as the fall

24. Lincoln to Elihu B. Washburne, February 9, Basler, ed., *Lincoln Collected Works*, v. 2, 304–6; Paul Selby to Yates, February 15, Yates Papers; John M. Palmer to Malinda A. Palmer, January 31, John M. Palmer Papers, IllSHL; Sheahan to Lanphier, February 17, Lanphier Papers; Thomas L. Harris to Douglas, January 25, Douglas Papers, UChic.

25. David Davis to Julius Rockwell, March 4, Julius Rockwell Papers, Lenox Public Library; Lincoln to Elihu B. Washburne, February 9, Basler, ed., *Lincoln Collected Works*, v. 2, 304–6.

26. William H. Herndon to Theodore Parker, February 13 (copy), Theodore Parker Papers, MassHS; James Sheahan to Douglas, February 8, Douglas Papers, UChic.

election was over, the crafty former Free Soil leader began canvassing for votes in the new legislature. The major opposition to Wilson among Americans came from those who distrusted his commitment to nativism and from conservatives who feared that his antislavery principles would destroy the American party's national harmony. In order to overcome this opposition, Wilson penned a public letter which, in obvious deference to the rampant anti-Catholic sentiment in the state, condemned "the insidious and malign tendencies of that sectarian power that instinctively sympathizes with oppression in the Old World and the New."[27] In the meantime, Gardner had second thoughts about elevating so talented a rival to national prominence and began working quietly against Wilson's election. The order's national leadership also threw its influence behind the effort to stymie Wilson's selection.[28] Nor did his candidacy receive the endorsement of his former Free Soil colleagues outside the Know Nothing organization, one of whom chided that "when the freedom of an empire is at issue, Wilson runs off to chase a paddy."[29]

Despite this mixed bag of opponents, Wilson easily won the election in the House. The contest in the Senate was much closer, but Wilson's skill as a tactician, coupled with his popularity stemming from his careful blending of free soil and nativist sentiment, eventually put him through. Amos A. Lawrence, who actively opposed Wilson's election, conceded that the new senator represented "a vast majority of our people at the present time." Lawrence attributed the result to "super-human" management, and a Boston paper charged afterwards that Wilson had been elected "by intrigue, by duplicity, by bargain and sale of his party, by denying his own language, and ignoring his own sentiments."[30] Certainly Wilson could be accused of playing fast and loose with his views on nativism in order to win the senatorship. Still, once in Washington Wilson preserved his ties with the Know Nothings, and he actively sought grounds of accommodation with southern nativists. Yet he never lost sight of his goal to form in the North a united opposition party that would oppose the extension of slavery. When Theodore Parker criticized his professed nativist principles, the new senator pledged that "I shall give no votes here that shall infringe upon the rights of any man black or white, native or foreign." Although he was hardly as free from nativist feelings as some historians have claimed, Wilson harbored no deep nativist principles, and before long he would more than justify Lawrence's earlier prediction that if Wilson were elected senator, "the American party from wh. we expected much good, will go to pieces."[31]

New York's senatorial contest attracted the most national attention, since William H. Seward's political career was at stake. Unlike the case in Massachusetts, where the struggle over Wilson's candidacy took place strictly within the Know Nothing ranks, the situation in New York was much more complex. The disintegration of anything like party

---

27. Abbott, *Cobbler in Congress*, 60–62.

28. Lawrence Diary, January 14, Lawrence Papers; Edward Everett to Millard Fillmore, April 11 (copy), Everett Papers; Bean, "Transformation of Parties," 268–72; Charles D. Deshler to Dear Warren, January 14 (copy), Deshler Papers; Solomon G. Haven to Fillmore, December 22, 1854, Fillmore Papers, SUNY.

29. Edward L. Pierce to Horace Mann, January 18, Mann Papers.

30. Lawrence Diary, January 26, Lawrence to Sarah Lawrence, January 30 (copy), Lawrence Papers; Boston *Atlas* quoted in Abbott, *Cobbler in Congress*, 63.

31. Parker to Henry Wilson, February 15, Wilson Papers, LC; Wilson to Parker, February 28 (copy), Parker Papers, MassHS; Lawrence to J. M. Williams, January 20 (copy), Lawrence Papers. Late in 1855, after he had left the Know Nothing party and had no need to cater to nativist sentiment, Wilson was considering introducing a bill in the Senate to extend to ten years the waiting period for naturalization. Wilson to Salmon P. Chase, November 17, Chase Papers, HSPa.

regularity in the chaotic four-party election of 1854 made it impossible to forecast the party breakdown in the new legislature. In listing the composition of the new legislature, the *Whig Almanac* noted that "Know-Nothings are sprinkled miscellaneously among Whigs, Hards and Softs; and exactly how many there are of these gentry in the Assembly Nobody knows." As nearly as can be determined, eleven members of the thirty-three-man Senate and forty members of the 129-man Assembly were Know Nothings. By cooperating with the Hards, their most likely allies, the Know Nothings would have a majority of both houses.[32]

Prior pledges on the senatorial question by many Know Nothing legislators confused the situation further. Wherever possible Sewardites had in advance exacted a pledge requiring that Whig nominees support Seward's reelection. In addition, a number of the senator's friends had infiltrated the order surreptitiously. James Simonton, the New York *Times'* Washington correspondent, guessed correctly that a number of the Know Nothing legislators were secretly supporters of Seward, while Hamilton Fish observed that with many of these men "this new alliance was a matter of convenience assumed for the purposes of their own election, & that obligations then assumed, like the drop of water on a ducks back, is easily shaken off."[33] Nevertheless, after carefully canvassing the legislature, several Know Nothing managers relayed word that it contained an anti-Seward majority.[34]

Meanwhile, Thurlow Weed scrambled frantically to round up the necessary votes. Besides his unmatched tactical ability, Weed had two major advantages. The first was Seward's great popularity, which the Nebraska controversy had enhanced. Many Know Nothing members of the legislature represented western districts where antislavery sentiment was powerful, and they knew that opposing Seward would be unpopular with their constituents. In addition, a number of traditional adversaries led by Preston King actively promoted his reelection on anti-Nebraska grounds, and several Democratic legislators promised Weed privately that they would vote for Seward if needed.[35] Weed's second advantage was his control of the state patronage, which no one knew how to use to better purpose. Subservient to Weed's direction, Governor Myron Clark delayed all appointments until after the senatorial election. At the height of the struggle, a Silver Grey complained: "The State creeps all over, like an old cheese, & swarms of maggots are out hopping & skipping about all the avenues to the Legislature. . . . Gross corruption appears to be the order of the day."[36] Anti-Seward strategists countered with pressure of their own on wavering members of the order, and the national council also intervened in an attempt

---

32. *Whig Almanac* (1855), 54; Thomas J. Curran, "Seward and the Know-Nothings," *New-York Historical Society Quarterly*, v. 51 (April, 1967), 146. Slightly different totals appear in John T. Bush to Fillmore, November 16, 1854, E. R. Jewett to Fillmore, December 28, 1854 (Private), Fillmore Papers, SUNY; Stephen Sammons to Daniel Ullmann, December 15, 1854, Ullmann Papers, NYHS. There were eight Hard senators; estimates of Hard strength in the Assembly ran as high as twenty-eight.

33. James Simonton to William H. Seward, November 9, 1854, Seward Papers, UR; Hamilton Fish to D. B. St. John, December 22, 1854 (copy), Fish Papers, LC; Horace Greeley to Colfax, November 6, 1854, Greeley-Colfax Papers.

34. E. R. Jewett to Ullmann, December 10, 1854, Francis S. Edwards to Ullmann, December 10, 1854, Ullmann Papers, NYHS; E. R. Jewett to Fillmore, December 28, 1854 (Private), John T. Bush to Fillmore, November 16, 1854, Fillmore Papers, SUNY.

35. Haven to Fillmore, January 29, Fillmore Papers, SUNY; Preston King to Gideon Welles, April 14, Welles Papers, LC; Trumbull Cary to Weed, November 11, 1854, Weed Papers, UR.

36. Daniel D. Barnard to Fish, January 30 (quotation), Fish Papers, LC; E. R. Jewett to Fillmore, February 4, Fillmore Papers, SUNY.

to defeat Seward. As a leading nativist from western New York conceded, neither side held all the trumps, "and the best player will be the winner."[37]

The contest for speaker demonstrated that Weed was still a master of political maneuver. Deciding that he had to support a Know Nothing, the Whig boss selected DeWitt C. Littlejohn, a political opportunist who had joined the secret society early in 1854. Littlejohn was a good friend of Governor Clark, and he was allied with the leaders of the Choctaws, a group of dissident pro-Seward Know Nothings who had bolted Daniel Ullmann's nomination and backed Clark. Once Littlejohn was in the speaker's chair, Weed reached an understanding with a group of nativists and with the temperance men, many of whom were also Know Nothings. In exchange for Seward's reelection, Weed agreed not to hinder passage of a temperance law and of an anti-Catholic church property law designed to prevent clerical control of ecclesiastical property.[38] Know Nothings from the western part of the state could thus get two key pieces of reform legislation while endorsing Seward's antislavery principles, which their constituents also approved. Their inability to agree on an alternative candidate further crippled the anti-Seward forces, who seemed more intent on defeating Seward than electing anyone else.[39]

In the end, despite the Know Nothings' strength in the legislature, Seward won reelection. His victory was testimony not only to Weed's political skill but also to the power of anti-Nebraska sentiment among rural Know Nothings. In fact, a majority of the American party members voted for the senator, a development that caused the *Evening Post* to scoff that "one need not be surprised if the vote of the Know-Nothings is cast for Pope Pius at the next election."[40] Shortly thereafter, the legislature approved and Clark signed both a temperance law and a church property law.

Weed's associates marveled at his victory, and even Horace Greeley, who was still brimming with resentment over his treatment the previous year, exclaimed, "Weed is a giant." From Washington a beaming Seward expressed to Weed his "amazement at the magnitude and complexity of the dangers through which you have conducted our shattered bark and the sagacity and skill with which you have saved us all from so imminent a wreck."[41] Know Nothing leaders, on the other hand, were mortified: Not only had they been defeated, but, even worse, Seward undeniably owed his election to American votes. In retrospect one prominent nativist faulted the order's 1854 campaign strategy. The party should have put first priority on electing an anti-Seward legislature, he concluded, but instead it had sacrificed everything to gain votes for Ullmann for governor, and the result was defeat in both contests.[42]

---

37. C. D. Deshler to George W. Moore, January 17 (copy), Deshler Papers; Kenneth Rayner to Ullmann, January 22, Roswell Hart to Ullmann, January 25 (quotation), Ullmann Papers, NYHS; Curran, "Seward and the Know-Nothings," 153.

38. Barnard to Fish, January 30, Barnard Papers; Curran, "Seward and the Know-Nothings," 156–58; John McCloskey to John Hughes, March 28, 29, Archbishop John Hughes Papers, St. Joseph's Seminary.

39. In announcing his withdrawal from the order, one antislavery nativist charged that the American party "seems to have withdrawn its forces from their assaults on the Papal power, to direct them against William H. Seward." Quoted in Curran, "Seward and the Know-Nothings," 160.

40. New York *Evening Post*, February 3, quoted in Foner, *Free Soil, Free Labor, Free Men*, 235n. Of the Know Nothing legislators, seven of eleven senators and twenty-five of forty assemblymen voted for Seward. *The Know-Nothing Almanac; or True American's Manual, for 1855* (Philadelphia, 1855), 53–54.

41. Greeley to George B. Baker, February 8, Barnes, *Memoir of Weed*, v. 2, 232; Seward to Weed, February 7, Weed Papers, UR.

42. James R. Thompson to Fillmore, March 8, Fillmore Papers, SUNY.

Even in those senatorial elections that resulted in an anti-administration triumph, the degree of cooperation among anti-Nebraska men can easily be exaggerated. Almost as impressive was the lingering power of old party loyalties. For example, in Massachusetts Wilson's nucleus of supporters were Know Nothings who were former Free Soilers. New York and Illinois provided even more striking manifestations of this phenomenon. Anti-Nebraska Democrats made up the core of Trumbull's partisans, while the preponderant majority of Whig members backed Lincoln. Nothing short of Lincoln's active intervention could have persuaded the remaining portion of his original supporters to vote for a Democrat. Likewise, in New York, Seward received the votes of the bulk of the Whigs and those of very few Democrats. Even among the Know Nothing members, former party ties prevailed to a remarkable degree, since virtually all the nativists who voted for Seward were former Whigs.

None of these men—Wilson, Seward, Hale, or Trumbull—was a Republican when elected to the Senate in 1855. Nor did the victory of any one of them magically create harmony in the opposition ranks. Even in Illinois, where Lincoln's magnanimous gesture in backing Trumbull and his gracious acceptance of defeat should have encouraged unity among anti-Nebraska men, suspicions between Whigs and anti-Nebraska Democrats remained strong. The significance of these senatorial contests was less in promoting unity among anti-Democratic factions than in providing the opposition with national leaders. Of the four, only Seward (and to a lesser extent Hale) previously enjoyed a national forum from which to propound his views. Bolstered by newly won national prestige, these men strengthened the anti-Nebraska forces in the Senate to a greater degree than their numbers would suggest.[43] In the long run these senatorial elections were crucial to the Republican movement, as would be clear in the 1856 congressional session, when Hale, Seward, Trumbull, and Wilson would be important leaders of the new party.

III

If the Kansas situation and the senatorial elections encouraged Republican organizers, the continuing strength of the Know Nothings dampened their spirits. Stimulated by the victories of 1854, the nativist society's growth continued in the first half of 1855. In January the national secretary reported privately that the order was "flourishing," with more than 10,000 councils in the country and an aggregate membership exceeding a million. When the next national council met in June, the New York *Herald* estimated the Know Nothings' membership at 1,375,000, and Henry Wilson placed it at not less than 1,250,000.[44] With councils now organized in every state, the party was without question a national power.

The strength of the American party posed the greatest obstacle to the formation of a sectional party on the slavery extension issue. Creating a majority party in the North required substantial Know Nothing support. Advocates of the Republican movement coalesced into two camps: those who wanted to find some common ground of union with the northern Know Nothings and those who wanted to form a new party without making

---

43. Chase to E. S. Hamlin, February 9, Chase Papers, LC. Hale had been the 1852 Free Soil presidential candidate, but following this futile race he retired from politics to pursue a legal career in New York City (while still retaining his New Hampshire residence). His election to the Senate in 1855 again gave him national prominence, which he had lacked for the previous couple of years.

44. Charles Deshler to James A. Henry, January 26 (copy), Deshler Papers; Wilson, *Slave Power*, v. 2, 423.

any concessions to the nativists. Temperance, which enjoyed strong support among nativists but which also alienated antislavery foreign-born voters, most notably lager beer-drinking Germans, posed a related difficulty for the Republican party.

The organization in early 1855 of a competing secret society, the Know Somethings, represented a movement to unite the anti-Nebraska forces. This new society sought to alleviate some of the objections raised against the Know Nothings. Its platform emphasized antislavery and anti-Catholicism, but it specifically renounced indiscriminate proscription of the foreign-born, and Protestant immigrants were eligible for membership. In some states, it endorsed the Maine Law, while in others it termed intemperance an evil but did not call specifically for enactment of a prohibitory law. The organization spread throughout the North and was especially strong in Ohio and Massachusetts, northern Indiana and Illinois, and in New York. In reality the Know Somethings represented a covert attempt by antislavery leaders in Ohio to undermine the Know Nothings by getting nativists to leave the order and join the new society. The mastermind of this movement was Joseph Medill, the future editor of the Chicago *Tribune*. He worked in close collaboration with his associate at the Cleveland *Leader*, John Vaughn, who served as president of the new society. Soon the Know Somethings received the nickname Jonathans, in contrast to the Know Nothings, who were popularly called Sams.[45]

Medill launched the organization in January 1855. Its main purpose was to provide a basis on which nativists and antislavery men could cooperate. The Know Nothings could never unite the anti-Democratic elements in the North, the Ohio editor argued, as long as they proscribed Protestant immigrants and ignored the slavery issue. Apparently, the Know Something society was intended only as a temporary organization until a permanent fusion party came into being. "It works as a *wheel within a wheel*," Medill said in defending the secret association. "It is the best that can be done to keep K. N'ism from doing mischief until the fever for secret societies is past."[46]

The expansion of the Know Somethings drew attention to the growing demand for reform within the Know Nothing organization. A number of leaders urged that the order drop its secrecy and function like an open party. Others advocated that Protestant foreigners, who had backed the nativist ticket in many localities in 1854, be eligible for membership. Schuyler Colfax was a leading proponent of admitting "Protestant foreigners, who are thoroughly Americanized." They were anxious to join the order, he argued, and had generally voted the People's ticket in Indiana last fall, "but every canvass that we push them off, & keep them at arm's length, tends to alienate them more & more."[47] The Louisiana state council, on the other hand, urged that Catholics, who were numerous in that state, be allowed to join the society; the result of this step, the prominent southern

---

45. Ichabod Codding to Marie Codding, April 14, Codding Family Papers, IllSHL; Samuel Gridley Howe to Sumner, February 9, Howe Papers, HU; Henry Morgan to Edwin B. Morgan, March 1, Edwin Barber Morgan Papers; Know Something Initiation, Fairbanks Papers; Cleveland correspondence, New York *Tribune*, January 17, March 24; letter signed "Wide-Awake," New York *Tribune*, March 7; B. Wadleigh to Stillman S. Davis, April 5, Misc. MSS, NHHS.

46. Joseph Medill to Oran Follett, January 27, April 18 (quotation), Hamlin, ed., "Follett Papers," 63, 72; Medill to John Klippart, October 17, 1854, John Klippart Papers, OHS. The growth of the Know Somethings in Ohio is documented in the Joel Wilson Papers, HEH.

47. Colfax to William Cumback, April 16, William Cumback Papers, IndU; Godlove S. Orth to Colfax, February 14, Schauinger, ed., "Letters of Godlove Orth," 64–65; James Pollock to John M. Clayton, October 30, 1854, Clayton Papers, LC.

politician Kenneth Rayner was certain, would be that in less than two years "Jesuits will control our order."[48] For intense nativists, these proposals were rankest heresy.

But it was the slavery expansion issue that loomed as the most divisive question within the American party. The new third degree, which had been adopted in December 1854 at the urging of southern moderates, was obviously meaningless, although some party leaders still clung to it in the desperate hope that it would check sectionalism. Mason Tappan, a former New Hampshire Free Soiler who had joined the order, assured Hale that the degree was harmless. Noting that it "says nothing about ignoring the slavery question, but goes in for *saving the Union*," he observed, "the design is apparent enough, but still it leaves every man to judge for himself, of the best course to prevent a dissolution of the Union." Indeed, at the state council in New Hampshire, Tappan introduced a series of antislavery resolutions that, he argued, constituted "the *true* construction" of the third degree and that won easy approval.[49]

A number of Know Nothing leaders wanted the order to ignore the slavery question altogether. Such was certainly the spirit of Rayner's Union degree. Support for this approach came from moderates in both the North and the South, including New York's Silver Greys, who preferred to emphasize nativism and reform.[50] The actions of the *American Organ* in Washington, however, which became repeatedly embroiled in controversies with northern antislavery journals like the New York *Tribune*, interfered with this strategy. Rayner, chastising the editor of the *American Organ* for being too violently proslavery, contended that the proper course was to disregard the slavery issue "and not to hazard the integrity of the Union, by discussing or agitating the question, either at the North or the South." Charles Deshler, the secretary of the national council, was also exasperated by the *Organ*'s conduct. Public sentiment "is so pre-eminently and morbidly sensitive on the subject, and it is a question so intrinsically difficult," he wrote, that the best policy was to "preserve utter silence" on the slavery question.[51]

A minority of American leaders in the free states, on the other hand, recognizing that the party had appealed successfully to anti-slavery-extension sentiment in the 1854 elections, demanded that the coming national council adopt an acceptable anti-Nebraska platform. "The American party cannot stand an instant in New England," maintained one New Hampshire man, "after its anti-slavery principles are gone." Sensitive to the widespread indignation in the free states over the frauds in Kansas, Lewis Campbell of Ohio believed it was imperative that the American party assume an antislavery stance. "The Pro-slavery 'higher law' of Atchison in Kanzas cant get a corporals guard N[orth]. of [the] M[ason]. & Dixon" line, he warned. Schuyler Colfax also urged that northern delegates to the national council insist that an antislavery plank be included in the national platform. "I *cannot* give up my hostility to the extension or encouragement of Slavery, & if the Order requires *that*, I cannot submit." The "monstrous outrages in Kansas that they call 'elections'" made it impossible to ignore the slavery issue, he told a fellow nativist. "They have been driving us to the wall for 10 years past, & we can't cry Peace when there is really no peace." Godlove Orth, the president of the Indiana state council,

48. Rayner to Ullmann, May 4, Ullmann Papers, NYHS.

49. Mason W. Tappan to Hale, May 2, Hale Papers, NHHS.

50. James R. Thompson to Ullmann, March 24, Confidential, Stephen Sammons to Ullmann, June 16, Ullmann Papers, NYHS.

51. Rayner to Ullmann, January 22, Ullmann Papers, NYHS; Deshler to Jno. M. McCalla, January 20 (copy), Deshler Papers.

agreed with Colfax that an antislavery position was needed, but cautioned: "While there is a strong Anti-Slavery feeling in the State, there is also a strong American feeling—and both must be preserved & united if possible, else both go by the board."[52]

Southern leaders believed that any antislavery platform, even one as mild as demanding the restoration of the Missouri Compromise, would destroy the movement in their section. The defeat suffered by the American party in the Virginia gubernatorial election intensified their opposition to any concessions to northern antislavery feeling. By exploiting Know Nothing support for Seward and Wilson in the recent senatorial contests, as well as the action of the Massachusetts legislature in passing a personal liberty law, Henry Wise, the Democratic nominee, successfully tarred the American party in the Old Dominion with the fatal charge of abolitionism. Virginia nativists were all but unanimous in blaming their loss on the antislavery record of northern Know Nothings. In a typical assessment, one prominent southern conservative attributed the outcome to "the fools & fanatics in the Legislature of Massachusetts who unfortunately were in session & running riot during the Canvass. All their proceedings were harped upon daily in the Press & on the stump with the grossest exaggerations." In retrospect, it seems clear that American party leaders overreacted to this setback. Virginia, after all, had been safely Democratic for years, and the 1855 election was the new party's first campaign in the state. But these leaders' earlier overconfidence led them to conclude that this defeat seriously impaired the American party's future prospects. As a result, southern Know Nothings looked to the national council to purge the stigma of abolitionism from the party. In fact, in an attempt to mitigate the force of this accusation, the national organization sent a representative to New Hampshire to prevent Hale's election to the Senate, but he arrived too late.[53]

The national council was scheduled to convene on June 5 in Philadelphia. Keeping a close watch on these developments was Charles A. Dana of the New York *Tribune*. When Horace Greeley sailed for Europe in April, he left Dana and James Shepherd Pike in charge of the paper. Like Greeley, both men were firmly committed to the Republican movement. Unlike their editorial colleague, however, they believed that in order to build a powerful Republican party, concessions had to be made to the antislavery Know Nothings. "Pike is disposed to make terms with Satan," one of Seward's followers wrote with alarm. "He says, *combined*, K. Nism & Anti Slavery can sweep the country." To Salmon P. Chase, Pike expressed his willingness to support a Know Nothing for president in 1856 on an anti-Nebraska platform. As part of their political strategy, Dana and Pike laid plans to disrupt the national council by stiffening the resolve of the northern delegates to demand an antislavery platform. There could be no neutrality on the slavery question, the *Tribune* declared on the eve of the Know Nothing conclave. "The moment the new party begins to act in the domain of National politics it must be on one side or the other."[54] Anxious to publicize the council's secret deliberations, Dana now made a crucial decision. He hired Samuel Bowles, the well-respected editor of the Springfield

52. Aaron H. Cragin to Weed, June 15, Seward Papers, UR; Lewis D. Campbell to Isaac Strohm, May 24 (private) Strohm Papers, OHS; Colfax to Rev. E. W. Jackson, March 15, *Confidential*, Colfax Papers, IndU; Colfax to Cumback, April 16, Cumback Papers; Orth to Colfax, June 23, Schauinger, ed., "Letters of Godlove Orth," 66.

53. William L. Hodge to Fillmore, June 25 (quotation), Fillmore Papers, SUNY; D. Timberlake to Ullmann, May 8, 24, 30, Rayner to Ullmann, May 8, Ullmann Papers, NYHS; John Pendleton Kennedy to Fillmore, November 18, Fillmore Papers, SUNY; Kennedy to Robert C. Winthrop, June 18, Winthrop Papers.

54. George E. Baker to Seward, April 19, Seward Papers, UR; James Shepherd Pike to Chase, April 3, Chase Papers, HSPa; New York *Tribune*, June 2 (quotation), 4.

Republican, to report on the proceedings in Philadelphia. As events would confirm, Bowles was a most fortunate choice.

Although Bowles was not a Know Nothing and thus could not attend the council meetings, he had a number of friends and contacts among the northern delegates. As a Whig, he had called for a union of the opposition in 1854, and he went to Philadelphia specifically to promote the fusion movement. The intense, hard-working Massachusetts editor brought several important capabilities to this task. Moody and nervous, irritable at times, he could also be charming when he wanted—a quality that helped him obtain the cooperation of those he sought to influence. Moreover, Bowles was a good newspaperman. He combined a keen ear for information with a love of gossip, and he was at his best coaxing delegates to give him confidential information.

Bowles undoubtedly received information, divulged both intentionally and inadvertently, from a number of indiscreet delegates, but his main source was Henry Wilson. Following his election to the Senate, Wilson had temporarily muffled his antislavery beliefs in an attempt to promote party harmony, but once Congress adjourned, he delivered a series of speeches in the North in which he called on the American party to drop its secrecy and renounce its bigotry against foreign-born citizens. He also proclaimed that any party that avoided the slavery issue deserved to die and promised to "do what little I can to make it die." He therefore went to the national council in Philadelphia determined either to secure a moderate antislavery platform or, as he put it, to "blow their party to hell." To Theodore Parker, he outlined three possible outcomes of the Know Nothing meeting: "that the Anti Slavery men must ignore their principles to make a national party—or they must fight for the supremacy of their principles and impose them upon the organization which would drive off the Southern men, or they must break up the party."[55] With these possibilities in mind, Wilson formed a close alliance with Bowles, steadily leaking information to him on the secret proceedings.

Wilson and Bowles set themselves no easy task, for most northern delegates wanted to preserve the nationality of the American party and were anxious to find common ground with their southern brethren on the slavery issue. When the council opened, a large number of northern delegates were willing to accept a platform that was silent on the slavery issue. Such a platform would allow them to maintain an anti-Nebraska stance back home without endangering the party's national unity. Even as staunch an antislavery man as William Howard of Michigan, when speaking of the national American platform, asserted that the slavery issue "had no more business there than the fly in amber." Another sizable segment of the free-state representatives favored some kind of mild compromise plank concerning slavery—what Bowles scorned as a "milk and water" statement—on which both sections could unite. The Ohio Know Nothing leader Lewis D. Campbell, though not a delegate to the Philadelphia convention, drafted one such pronouncement. Campbell's proposed platform deprecated geographical parties, affirmed Congress's authority on the question of slave representation and the reclamation of fugitive slaves, declared that the power of Congress to legislate on slavery in the territories was a judicial question and that the expediency of its exercise was a matter for the people to decide, and asserted that all other questions pertaining to slavery belonged exclusively to the states. A number of other compromise proposals circulated at

---

55. Abbott, *Cobbler in Congress*, 72; Robinson, *"Warrington" Pen-Portraits*, 542; Wilson to Parker, July 23 (copy), Parker Papers, MassHS; Wilson to William Schouler, April 16, Schouler Papers; Wilson to Samuel Bowles, June 23, Samuel Bowles Papers, Yale University.

Philadelphia. Together, these two groups—those who favored a policy of silence on the issue and those who wanted a compromise bisectional declaration—represented a substantial majority of representatives from the North. Campbell's proposed plank, and others like it, were precisely what Bowles and Wilson sought to guard against. Backed by a handful of delegates numbering fewer than twenty, the two Massachusetts leaders set out to impress on the free-state delegates the importance of insisting that the national council adopt a firm anti-Nebraska position.[56]

They were aided by the course of the southern delegates, still reeling from Wise's victory in Virginia. John P. Hale's election while the council was in session intensified their alarm and hardened their position. No sooner had the council convened than angry southerners commenced denouncing the Massachusetts delegation in general and Wilson in particular on the slavery issue. Wilson hurled back the challenge. "We wish you men of the South distinctly to understand that we have the power to prohibit slavery in the Territories and to abolish it in the District of Columbia, and we mean to do it," he retorted defiantly. "We intend to repeal the Fugitive Slave Act, and we mean that Kansas shall never come into the Union as a slave State—no, never." The verbal battle between the southern delegates and a minority of the northern delegates continued for eight days. The major point of controversy was the slavery plank in the platform. Finally, the resolutions committee reported two statements of principles. The majority report, which reflected the dominant southern viewpoint, pronounced the existing laws on slavery "a final and conclusive settlement . . . in spirit and in substance." It denied specifically that Congress had the right to refuse to admit any state into the Union because its constitution recognized or prohibited slavery, condemned any interference by Congress with slavery in the District of Columbia, and declared that Congress ought not to legislate on the subject of slavery in the territories. The minority report, which Bowles secretly wrote, called for the restoration of the Missouri Compromise, protection of actual settlers in Kansas, and the admission of Kansas and Nebraska as free states. Although this platform fell far short of Wilson's fiery pronouncements from the floor, it was unacceptable to a majority of delegates from the South. Rumors were rife that if the majority platform were approved, northern representatives would bolt, but most of the southern delegates refused to budge. Fearful that the disruption of the party was imminent, Kenneth Rayner introduced an alternate set of resolutions declaring that the slavery question did not come within the purview of the order.[57]

In the ensuing debate, Wilson argued that adoption of the majority platform would commit "the American party unconditionally to the policy of slavery, [and] to the iron dominion of the black power." He announced that he would support no man who endorsed it. Denouncing as doughfaces those who failed to oppose the majority platform, Bowles and his allies sought to rouse popular feeling against these men in order to pressure them into supporting the minority platform. One reluctant convert was Governor

---

56. William Howard to Henry Waldron, December 8, Waldron Family Papers; Edward L. Pierce to Chase, June 4, Chase Papers, LC; Campbell to Schouler, June 26, Schouler Papers; Bowles's account of the convention in the New York *Tribune*, October 31. Campbell's proposed plank is given in the *Ohio State Journal*, March 28, 1856.

57. The council's proceedings can best be followed in Bowles's dispatches in the New York *Tribune*, June 6–16. Also see Wilson's account in *Slave Power*, v. 2, 423–33. For rumors of a northern bolt, see N. Darling to Weed, May 30, Weed Papers, UR. For the reaction to Hale's election, see Darling to Hale, June 21, Hale Papers, NHHS. Darling was a Weed operative at the Philadelphia meeting.

Henry J. Gardner of Massachusetts, who up to this point had taken no part in the struggle against the majority report. Once he lost his bid to become the order's national president, however, Gardner moved to solidify his standing at home by belatedly opposing the majority platform. In a widely quoted statement, he proclaimed that the American party could not carry a single township in Massachusetts on this platform. In the end, the convention rejected both Rayner's compromise statement and Bowles's minority report. Then, by a vote of eighty to fifty-nine, it adopted the majority platform with the controversial Twelfth Section on slavery, which in substance endorsed the Kansas-Nebraska Act, intact. From the beginning, Wilson, working closely with Bowles, led the northern opposition to this platform. By the time the vote occurred, the large majority of northern delegates voted with the Massachusetts senator.

Of the northern delegates, only the representatives from New York, under the tight leadership of James W. Barker, who was completing his term as the president of the national council, gave no support to the minority platform. Their accommodating posture towards the South arose out of the rival candidacies of two New Yorkers, Millard Fillmore and George Law, for the 1856 American presidential nomination. Promoters of each man were anxious not to offend southerners, whose support would be necessary to win the nomination. Law, a wealthy New York City contractor and steamboat entrepreneur, had a number of friends in the New York delegation, headed by Barker, one of his most important managers. The presidential election was more than a year distant, yet the Law-Fillmore rivalry already divided the order's leadership in New York. Although not a member of Fillmore's inner circle of advisers, Daniel Ullmann, the party's 1854 gubernatorial nominee, was a prominent anti-Barker leader. This schism would have important repercussions in 1856, but its main significance in 1855 was in encouraging the New York delegates to ally with the South on the platform. Barker even helped close off debate to prevent a moderate substitute platform from being considered.[58]

The next morning a meeting of the northern delegates opposed to the American party platform convened in a parlor of the Girard House.[59] Wilson introduced a proposed address to the people, which Bowles and he had written earlier in anticipation of this contingency. The address declared slavery was a local institution which Congress had no power to establish, that the Missouri Compromise should be restored, that actual settlers in Kansas needed protection, and that Kansas and Nebraska should at the proper time be admitted as free states. It concluded by calling on all opponents of slavery expansion to combine in one party. At this point Gardner objected strenuously to Wilson's statement. Striking his fist on the table, he protested that he "*would be d——d if he would be abolitionized, any how.*" He was adamant that the address also emphasize nativist principles. Wishing to preserve unity, the assembled delegates eventually issued a more limited appeal, drafted for the most part by Gardner, which called for the restoration of the Missouri Compromise but said nothing about a new party, and which reaffirmed the

58. Rayner to Ullmann, August 21, Stephen Sammons to Ullmann, June 16, James R. Thompson to Ullmann, September 12, Ullmann Papers, NYHS; Scisco, *Political Nativism in New York*, 144–48. Barker had other motives as well: He unsuccessfully sought reelection as national president and was courting southern votes. Unlike Gardner, after his defeat he adhered to his position on the platform.

59. A full account of the deliberations among northern delegates is given in Bowles's history of the convention, New York *Tribune*, October 31. Also see the New York *Tribune*, June 16; New York *Times*, June 15.

order's nativist doctrines. Fifty-three members signed this address.[60] As they left for home, Bowles reported that these northern delegates, although they still retained their nativist principles, had agreed to "throw up the American organization as an organization in order to unite the North in an all-powerful and effective party against the aggressiveness of Slavery." In accord with this sentiment, one of the seceding Ohio delegates sent a telegram to the national Know Something convention then in session in Cleveland, affirming that the bolters "are with you heart and soul. May God eternally d——n Slavery and Doughfaceism." The American party had split in two.[61]

The outcome of the national council sessions represented a sharp defeat for party moderates. Rayner, their leading spokesman at the meeting, criticized ultras in both sections for being inflexible. He feared that the order had become "the mere stalking-horse of politicians . . . the mere instrument by which sectional rivalry and ambition are to carry out their selfish ends." In retrospect, the North Carolina leader dated the downfall of the American party from the Philadelphia meeting. In like manner, a Kentucky delegate who had struggled in vain to devise an acceptable compromise on the slavery issue denounced the council's members as "fools & demagogues" who sacrificed national principles in order to "make a little miserable personal popularity at home." The debate over the platform, the uncompromising stand taken by Wilson and his circle, and Bowles's efforts to rally northern opinion against those delegates who spoke for moderation and conciliation hardened sectional lines in the council and destroyed its national unity. Rayner saw that outside influences had been critical in fragmenting the order, and "these same enemies are now laughing and cajoling over our troubles."[62]

In contrast to the despair felt by such men as Rayner, northern leaders were elated. Colfax, for example, wrote home from Philadelphia, "I am satisfied I did more good for freedom than I ever did before in my whole life." Bowles, too, was pleased. "We have had a good deal of excitement here, and much fun," he chuckled as the council deliberations neared their conclusion. He felt that he had done "some good to the right side of the political questions of the day." Lavishing praise on Wilson, he announced: "Thank God! *There is a North* at last." Bolstered by reports of popular support for his course, Wilson stated in a conference with Bowles and another Massachusetts Whig that he was ready to enter the Republican movement. In a letter to Bowles written after his return home, Wilson attested: "To your efforts are we indebted in a great degree for the

---

60. The lack of an official list of delegates prevents a precise calculation of the northern dissidents' strength. But using the roll call on the majority and minority platforms, given in the New York *Times*, June 16, supplemented by the imperfect list of delegates in the New York *Herald*, June 8, the northern bolters apparently included all the representatives from Maine, Vermont, New Hampshire, Massachusetts, Rhode Island, Ohio, Indiana, Michigan, Wisconsin, and Iowa, a majority of those of Connecticut, Pennsylvania, and Illinois, and a minority from New Jersey. New York and California stood apart in their unanimous hostility. Furthermore, the one Illinois delegate whose name does not appear among the signers voted for the minority platform and in all likelihood sympathized with the walkout, and the two Connecticut delegates who are not listed also did not vote on the platform and presumably had left the convention. Included in these figures are those delegates, principally from Pennsylvania and New Jersey, who issued a separate protest that largely reflected the influence of former governor William F. Johnston of Pennsylvania, who was angling for a presidential nomination. James A. Dean to Cameron, June 22, Cameron Papers, LC.

61. New York *Tribune*, June 16, October 31 (quotation); New York *Times*, June 15 (quotation).

62. Rayner to Ullmann, August 21, 1855, June 2, 1856, Ullmann Papers, NYHS; Albert T. Burnley to John J. Crittenden, Saturday evening [June 2], June 12 (quotation), John J. Crittenden Papers, LC.

results. . . . In private I have told all my friends that no one accomplished more for our cause."[63]

Wilson had been the most conspicuous figure at the council, while Bowles had been only a shadowy presence (although suspected of being the *Tribune*'s reporter, his identity had not been uncovered). Together they had masterminded a strategy to force the Know Nothings to either adopt an acceptable platform that would provide a basis for fusion with other opponents of the Pierce administration in the North or else be shorn of its northern wing. Bowles attributed the outcome to the determination of a small group of northern delegates, the extreme demands of the South, and his reports in the *Tribune*, which publicized any defections among the representatives from the free states.[64] How many northern Know Nothings would follow Wilson out of the American ranks was impossible to predict, but Robert C. Winthrop, for one, feared that the bolters were "a vast majority" in Massachusetts. In a similar vein a New Hampshire politician asserted that a candidate running on the national American platform could not poll 500 votes in that state. He was confident that three-fourths of the Know Nothings would support a party "that shall fairly and truly represent Northern principles."[65]

The breach of the American national council encouraged antislavery men inside and outside the order. From Iowa, Governor James Grimes, who had been pushing for a union of the anti-Nebraska forces, rejoiced over the breakup of the Know Nothings' national organization. "It has gone overboard sooner than I expected, and I can see nothing now to obstruct a perfect anti-Nebraska and antislavery triumph." A Massachusetts man concurred that the rupture of the American party "seems to leave the ground clear for a strong Anti Nebraska movement in all the Northern States." With the Know Nothings encumbered in the free states with an unpopular national platform, the prospects for a new attempt to organize the Republican party seemed bright. "The results [of the Philadelphia convention] cannot fail to be propitious to the cause of Freedom," Colfax assured Hale. Ultimate victory was certain, "& may be won, after all, even as early as 1856." Immediately following adoption of the majority platform, the New York *Tribune* urged that a new attempt at fusion be made. Calling on Northerners to "postpone all minor interests" in order to rescue Kansas and Nebraska for freedom and roll back slavery "within its proper bounds," it stressed the necessity of forgetting political antecedents and ignoring opinions on other subjects.[66] Time would reveal that the national American organization had received a blow from which it would never recover. With much justice Bowles, in discussing the significance of the northern Know Nothing secession led by Wilson, maintained subsequently that "the great Republican party of the Free States has received its chief impetus from the action of these men at Philadelphia."[67]

---

63. Hollister, *Colfax*, 80; Bowles to [Mary S. Bowles?], Monday Evening [June 11], Merriam, *Bowles*, v. 1, 167; Wilson to Bowles, June 23, Bowles Papers; Bowles's dispatch, New York *Tribune*, June 15. Also see Boston correspondence, "Oliver," New York *Tribune*, June 9.

64. Bowles to Mary S. Bowles, Friday night [June 8], Merriam, *Bowles*, v. 1, 166; Parker to Wilson, July 7 (copy), Henry Wilson Papers, LC; New York *Tribune*, October 31.

65. Winthrop to Kennedy, June 20, Kennedy Papers; Aaron Cragin to Weed, June 15, Seward Papers, UR; N. Darling to Weed, June 20, Weed Papers, UR; J. D. Colver to Ullmann, July 21, William T. Minor to Ullmann, July 14, Ullmann Papers, NYHS.

66. James W. Grimes to Elizabeth S. Grimes, June 17, Salter, *Grimes*, 71–72; Increase Tarbox to Alphonso Taft, July 13, Taft Papers; Colfax to John P. Hale, June 21, Hale Papers, DarC; New York *Tribune*, June 15.

67. New York *Tribune*, October 31.

7

Launching the Republican Party

The disruption of the national American organization and the steadily deteriorating situation in Kansas offered a new opportunity to organize the Republican party. With the Whig party dead and the American party's ranks splintered, a growing number of anti-Democratic politicians in the North concluded that aided by rising sectional tensions the Republican party might well emerge as the dominant opposition party in the country. "The continued imprisonment of Passmore Williamson [in a fugitive slave case], the daily repeated outrages of the Slavedrivers in Kansas, and the insulting and defiant attitude of the Administration, all seem especially ordained to make our success certain," one Republican organizer wrote confidently. Solomon G. Haven, a prominent New York Know Nothing, made a similar assessment. Events in Kansas and elsewhere "concur in keeping the northern sentiment much excited & very uneasy," he told Millard Fillmore. "Every thing," he lamented, "seems conspiring to favor the Republican movement."[1]

I

The response of Republican leaders to the situation in Kansas exposed wide disagreement about the party's program and purpose. To conservatives, it was sufficient to demand the restoration of the Missouri Compromise, but already there were signs of a hardening of attitudes. Horace Greeley, for example, who had previously endorsed this limited platform, after the 1854 elections pronounced it inadequate and called instead for the prohibition of slavery in all the territories. This more advanced position, along with the demand that no more slave states be admitted, gained support in reaction to the unfolding crisis in Kansas. Another group of party leaders wanted a more extensive antislavery program, including repeal of the fugitive slave law and a severing of the federal government's ties to the peculiar institution.[2] To be successful, the party needed

---

Note: Unless otherwise indicated, the year for manuscript and newspaper citations in this chapter is 1855.

1. Edward A. Stansbury to Salmon P. Chase, August 23, Chase Papers, HSPa; Solomon G. Haven to Millard Fillmore, August 15, Fillmore Papers, SUNY. Passmore Williamson assisted some slaves who fled a ship docked in Philadelphia in 1855. When he failed to produce these runaways, he was jailed for contempt for more than four months in a case that attracted national publicity. Campbell, *Slave Catchers*, 142–43.

2. Pike, *First Blows*, 283–85; New York *Tribune*, December 16, 1854.

an appeal satisfactory to all these viewpoints, and party spokesmen, aware of conservatives' fears of a sectional party, recognized the delicacy of their situation.

In addition to differences on the slavery issue, Republicans clashed over what Lyman Trumbull termed the "side issues" of nativism and temperance. The bolt of the northern Know Nothings at Philadelphia strengthened the hand of Republican managers who stressed the necessity of uniting with the antislavery nativists. Nevertheless, influential leaders persisted in denouncing the order and, though willing to accept American party support, adamantly opposed any endorsement of nativist principles. The liquor issue proved equally troubling. One New York man colorfully described the threat the anti-liquor crusade posed to the Republican cause. No sooner had a significant portion of the foreign vote finally broken with the Democratic party in 1854, he complained, than "the Puritan intolerants, Greely at their head, cold water, Vegetable diet & sabath observances on their banners, ran amuck with their Maine Law," and if unchecked they threatened to drive anti-temperance immigrants "back, body & soul" into the Democratic ranks. In order to build a heterogeneous coalition, Republicans had to handle both issues with great care. As Preston King observed, one important result of the Republican campaigns in 1855 would be to "know who & what we are for in the future."[3]

The party's 1855 platform varied from state to state, but everywhere Republicans focused on the slavery extension issue and the situation in Kansas. Exploiting the welling anger in the North over alleged proslavery outrages in that territory, Republican speakers and editors stressed the need for a northern sectional party that would limit southern political power and bring Kansas into the Union as a free state. The 1855 campaigns in the free states marked the emergence of Kansas as an emotion-laden partisan issue. Misled by reports from the territory, always ready to assume the worst about the Missourians in Kansas, and failing to scrutinize with any detachment the motives and activities of the free-state men, Republican propagandists greatly exaggerated both the amount of violence there and the degree to which slavery lay at the core of these difficulties. Whether conscious or unconscious, this distortion inflamed northern public opinion and widened the gulf between the two sections.[4]

During this formative period, William Henry Seward took the lead in placing the Kansas issue within a larger context. Henry Adams etched a memorable description of the blue-eyed, red-haired New York leader: "A slouching, slender figure; a head like a wise macaw; a beaked nose; shaggy eyebrows; unorderly hair and clothes; hoarse voice; offhand manner; free talk, and perpetual cigar."[5] Quiet in demeanor and short in stature, he lacked a commanding presence, and while adept and charming socially where he sparkled in private conversation, he was a poor public speaker. His voice was harsh and unpleasant, his words often almost indistinct and his manner awkward, and yet, with all these faults, he exerted an undeniable magnetism over his audience. Simple, direct, and devoid of pomp, Seward's remarks created the impression of candor, an appearance that, along with his irrefutable intellectual gifts and his philosophical bent, earned him the reputation of a statesman.

---

3. Lyman Trumbull to Owen Lovejoy, August 20, Trumbull Family Papers; H. Forbes to Charles Sumner, June 1, Sumner Papers, HU; Preston King to John Bigelow, October 13, quoted in Muller, "Preston King," 563.

4. Republicans' distortion of the Kansas situation is analyzed in Weisberger, "Newspaper Reporter and Kansas," and Isely, *Greeley and the Republican Party*, 131–37.

5. Henry Adams, *The Education of Henry Adams* (Boston, 1918), 104.

In spite of his obvious influence, Seward never comprehended fully the power of his words. Basically a conciliator, he overestimated his ability to mitigate in private the intensity of his public remarks, and he failed to foresee the impact that some of his speeches would have on his public image. Indeed, his undeserved reputation as a radical derived largely from his invocation of such extreme-sounding phrases as "the higher law" and later "the irrepressible conflict." Although identified with a number of reform causes, the New Yorker was fundamentally a conservative who believed that change, while necessary, should "not be hastily or convulsively made." He was genuinely antislavery (even as harsh a critic as Greeley conceded that he "hated Slavery and all its belongings"), yet his opposition, as one acquaintance observed, "was based entirely upon his intellectual processes, and not upon his heart."[6] For all his abilities, the New York senator generated distrust among many of his colleagues. Conservatives like William Pitt Fessenden were suspicious of his obvious ambition and his tendency to ride every popular hobby that came along, while pronounced antislavery men regarded his opposition to the institution as self-interested and insincere. Earnest reformers were also put off by his at least partly affected cynicism, which was particularly apparent in his contention that politics was substantially a game of intrigue at which he overrated his talent. A complex personality, Seward attempted to be both the statesman and the politician, the bold thinker and the cautious conservative, the forceful spokesman and the quiet conciliator. For all these contradictions, Seward was a leader of the first rank, and few politicians had greater impact on this generation.

Seward offered the most important statement in 1855 of the Republican party's purposes and goals. In a bid to assume leadership of the party after considerable foot dragging, he delivered two major speeches during the 1855 campaign, one in Albany on "The Advent of the Republican Party: The Privileged Class," and another in Buffalo a week later entitled "The Contest and the Crisis."[7] In his Albany address, Seward brought together a number of themes floating about loosely and incorporated them into a coherent argument; his fundamental contribution was in defining the nature of the crisis that confronted the nation. He directed his hostility not at slavery or southerners but at the small group of slaveowners—"the privileged class"—who ruled their section strictly in their own self-interest and threatened to transform the Republic into an aristocracy. Only one percent of the population, this class, he alleged, controlled the president, Congress, and the judiciary, and federal policy followed its dictates both at home and abroad.

In his Buffalo speech Seward sharpened and refined his basic argument. The liberties of the free whites of the North were under attack, he declared, and he asked pointedly whether the interests of twenty-five million whites were to be sacrificed for the convenience of 350,000 slaveowners. Attempting to rouse northern public opinion to the impending danger, he discarded his habitual optimism:

> The Republican party is sounding throughout all our borders a deep-toned alarum for
> the safety of the Constitution, of union, and of liberty. Do you hear it? The Republican
> party declares that, by means of recent treacherous measures adopted by Congress and
> the President . . . the constitutional safeguards of citizens, identical with the rights of

6. William H. Seward to Theodore Parker, December 13, 1855, June 23, 1854 (Private) (copies), Parker Papers, MassHS; Horace Greeley, *Recollections*, 311; Donn Piatt, *Memories of the Men Who Saved the Union* (New York, 1887), 138 (quotation), 149.

7. George E. Baker (ed.), *The Works of William H. Seward* (5 vols.: Boston, 1853–1884), v. 4, 225–52.

human nature itself, hitherto a fortress of republicanism, will pass into the hands of an insidious aristocracy, and its batteries be turned against the cause which it was reared to defend.

This appeal, by defining a powerful threat to republicanism and hinting at a well-laid conspiracy to subvert liberty, invoked a fundamental political mechanism by which parties since the 1790s had sought to rally public support.[8] He deflected concern brilliantly from the plight of the black slave to the fear that the liberties of all white northerners, not just those in Kansas, were threatened with extinction by the expansion of slavery. Richard Henry Dana, Jr., a thoughtful political observer sensitive to the power of ideas, designated Seward's Albany speech "the key note of the New [Republican] Party."[9]

II

The Republican movement grew out of national developments, but the party first took shape at the state level. With Congress out of session throughout most of 1855, decisions concerning the formation of the party and the nature of its electoral appeal were made within the context of each state's politics. The drive to organize the Republican party made little headway in states that held elections in the spring, before the disruption of the Know Nothings at Philadelphia, and in states that had no statewide contest during the year. Uncertain of the future, leaders in these states could without risk wait for further developments.[10] In states with important fall elections, however, politicians could not indulge in this luxury. These elections provided the impetus to launch the Republican party and constituted the first critical test of its strength.

Political developments in Ohio were particularly significant for the organization of the Republican party.[11] No sooner was the 1854 election over than Salmon P. Chase, who was due to retire from the Senate in March, cast his eyes on the 1855 gubernatorial race, and at a secret meeting chaired by James M. Ashley a group of prominent antislavery politicians decided to promote Chase's candidacy.[12] Indeed, in the dizzying political atmosphere that prevailed following the 1854 elections, Chase's overweening ambition extended far beyond the Ohio governorship. He began to formulate plans to organize under his leadership an antislavery party that would nominate him for president in 1856. In the long run, no individual made a more significant contribution to the formation of the Republican party than did Chase.

After some initial indecision, Chase and his advisers concluded that the Republican movement represented the best chance of uniting the opposition forces under their leadership.[13] The major obstacle to Chase's blossoming gubernatorial ambitions was the

---

8. This theme is more fully developed in Holt, *Political Crisis.*

9. Lucid, ed., *Dana Journal*, v. 2, 681; James Ashley to Chase, October 21, Chase Papers, LC.

10. California was the one state with a statewide fall contest where the Republican party did not organize in 1855. For a discussion of political developments during this year in Connecticut, Indiana, Illinois, and Iowa, see Chapter 9.

11. For a more extensive analysis of Ohio politics in 1855, see my article, "Salmon P. Chase, Nativism, and the Formation of the Republican Party in Ohio," *Ohio History*, v. 93 (Winter-Spring, 1984), 5–39.

12. James M. Ashley, MS Memoir, Chapter 10, University of Toledo Library.

13. Adoption of the name *Republican* to designate the Ohio fusion movement occurred gradually, but Chase indicated his sensitivity to the importance of the opposition's employing a common terminology throughout the

power of the Ohio Know Nothings. He hoped that the cooperation that the People's party had brought about between the nativists and other anti-Democratic groups would continue. In contrast, Know Nothing leaders increasingly spoke of nominating their own ticket. Since the October election, the nativist society had more than doubled its membership in the state and was still expanding. By February reliable sources placed its strength at 120,000 voters, and even opponents conceded that a majority of the 1854 anti-Nebraska voters had joined the American party.[14] "I am very, very sorry that the K.N. trouble has come upon us," a worried Chase told Oran Follett, the editor of the *Ohio State Journal*. "But for this the sky of the future would be clear." The taunt of the Cleveland *Express*, a Know Nothing organ, in reply to antislavery critics concisely summarized the situation in the state: "Why, gentlemen, you can't select enough prominent 'Republicans' in Ohio, to act as delegates to the convention, without having in it a majority of Know Nothings."[15]

Confronted with the reality of Know Nothing strength, the former Ohio senator tried to carve a middle course between either repudiating or joining the nativist order. He was chagrined when the *Ohio Columbian*, the leading Free Democratic paper that was widely regarded as his personal organ, commenced denouncing the Know Nothings. On several occasions Chase, with an eye to promoting harmony among the opposition, urged its editor, E. S. Hamlin, to cease his assaults on the order. "It seems to me you have said enough agst the Kns, and had better hold up," he advised in February. "My idea is fight nobody who does not fight us." In another letter, Chase expressed fear that Hamlin's repeated denunciations of the Know Nothings as proslavery would weaken the influence of antislavery men in the organization and "make the members of the order less disposed than they would be otherwise to cooperate with outsiders on the Slavery issue." The Ohio senator assured Follett that attacks on the Know Nothings by Hamlin and other associates did not meet with his approval.[16]

In addition, Chase undertook to devise a common set of principles upon which the two groups could come together. He insisted that antislavery must be kept "paramount," but at the same time he was willing to trim on nativism in order to preserve the unity of the opposition. "It would be better if you admitted that there was some ground for the uprising of the people against papal influences & organized foreignism," he suggested to Hamlin, "while you might condemn the secret organization & indiscriminate proscription on account of origin or creed." He was particularly anxious not to alienate the foreign-born voters. Senator Benjamin F. Wade, an equally staunch antislavery man, also

---

North when he remarked to George W. Julian, "A party with half a dozen names must necessarily be a party without clearly apprehended principles & cannot make itself respected." Nevertheless, Chase hoped that eventually the label *Democratic* would be added to the party's name, so much so that Joseph Medill recalled that Chase grumbled off and on for years about its being discarded. Chase to Julian, January 20, Giddings-Julian Papers, LC; Chase to Gideon Welles, October 26, Welles Papers, LC; Chase to [James W. Grimes], October 17, Chase Papers, HSPa; Clipping, Chicago *Tribune*, March 17, 1899, Joseph Medill Papers.

14. *Ohio Columbian*, June 13; Toledo *Blade*, June 8. In mid-January, the order's national secretary reported that there were 830 councils in Ohio. By June, according to the official report of Thomas Spooner, president of the order in Ohio, the state had 1,195 councils with a membership of 130,000. Charles D. Deshler to H. Crane, January 15 (copy), Deshler Papers; Spooner's report, dated June 3, is in the Cincinnati *Commercial*, June 8.

15. Chase to Oran Follett, January 1, Hamlin, ed., "Follett Papers," 62; Cleveland *Express* quoted in *Ohio Columbian*, May 30.

16. Chase to E. S. Hamlin, November 21, 1854, *Private*, February 9 (quotation), Chase to A. M. Gangewer, February 15, Chase Papers, LC; Chase to Follett, January 1, February 14, Hamlin, ed., "Follett Papers," 62, 64.

endorsed a policy of conciliating the Know Nothings without embracing proscription of all immigrants or shunting "hostility to slavery" from the political forefront. "Every intelligent man knows full well that our country has suffered much from the too great influence of foreigners, ignorant of our institutions & that their power for evil ought to be abridged," he told William Schouler of the Cincinnati *Gazette*.[17]

Although some pronounced antislavery men, led by Joshua R. Giddings and his organ, the *Ashtabula Sentinel*, opposed any union with the Know Nothings, Free Soilers generally rallied behind Chase's candidacy. So did a number of Germans, whom he had long courted and who were frightened by nativism, and antislavery Whigs, particularly in the Western Reserve, headed by Wade. Backed by this coalition, Chase was by early spring the only serious candidate of the antislavery forces.

Other elements of the opposition, however, were less than ecstatic at the prospect of Chase's heading the anti-Democratic ticket. Almost simultaneously with the commencement of the Chase movement, another group of opposition leaders began promoting the candidacy of Jacob Brinkerhoff, a Know Nothing. As a Democratic congressman, Brinkerhoff had played a leading role in the original introduction of the Wilmot Proviso, and, whatever the validity of his later claim to have been the real author of the Proviso, he enjoyed a reputation as a notable antislavery leader and had taken a leading part in the opposition to the repeal of the Missouri Compromise.

Brinkerhoff gained valuable support from men outside the order, including Congressman-elect John Sherman, who was a resident of his home town, Follett, who lent private assistance, and Joseph Medill of the Cleveland *Leader*, who feared Chase's nomination would imperil the chances for victory. Nevertheless, Brinkerhoff's candidacy was tied closely to Know Nothingism. Early in 1855 Lewis D. Campbell, the most influential Know Nothing in the state, undertook to marshal support for Brinkerhoff's nomination, and at a subsequent secret meeting American party leaders designated the former congressman the nativist candidate.[18] Long before a fusion convention had even been called, the struggle for its gubernatorial nomination had narrowed to Chase and Brinkerhoff.

After considerable bickering, all factions agreed to hold the fusion convention in Columbus on July 13, the same date as the anti-Nebraska state convention the previous year. The convention call was worded to include all opposition elements. It directed the "independent anti-Nebraska voters of Ohio, who participated in the glorious triumph of last year, and such others as may sympathize with them" to elect delegates to a convention that would nominate candidates for governor and the other state offices to be filled in the fall. Its circulation signified the agreement of the Free Soilers, following Chase's lead, to join the Know Nothings in a fusion convention.

Neither side, however, was unqualifiedly committed to fusion, even after the call appeared. Several Free Soilers urged that, as a guarantee that the convention would act

---

17. Chase to E. S. Hamlin, January 22, Chase Papers, LC; Benjamin F. Wade to William Schouler, May 3, *Confidential*, Schouler Papers. In another letter, which was eventually published, Chase asserted that in the activities of some Catholic priests and foreigners "there has been something justly censurable & calculated to provoke the hostility which has embodied itself in the Know Nothing organization." Chase to John Paul, December 27, 1854, Draft, Chase Papers, HSPa.

18. R. P. L. Baber to John Sherman, October 16, 1854, Confidential, May 5, June 28, 1855, John Sherman Papers; *Ohio State Journal*, May 10, 18; E. S. Hamlin to Chase, November 10, 1854, Chase Papers, HSPa; Joseph Medill to Follett, December 20, 1854, *Confidential*, Hamlin, ed., "Follett Papers," 77–78; Lewis D. Campbell to Schouler, February 15, Schouler Papers.

properly, a mass meeting also assemble in Columbus on the same day. If the regular convention nominated Chase, this mass gathering could ratify his selection; if, on the other hand, the Know Nothings controlled matters, then this meeting could, in the words of one third-party leader, "proceed at once to an independent organization and action."[19] Chase did not interfere with this plan, but he recognized that his best chance to be elected was as head of a united opposition party. When Ashley, Hamlin, and others proposed to advance the date of the mass meeting to precede the Republican convention, therefore, he quickly quashed their suggestion. Yet Chase attached significant qualifications to his cooperation with the Know Nothings as well. He insisted that nativism could not be made a test of nomination and, in effect, specified that only his selection would indicate that the convention's proceedings were fair; any other result would be irrefutable evidence of unfair dealing by the Know Nothings, and consequently the antislavery men would not be bound to support the ticket.[20]

Chase's opponents readily perceived the implications of these terms. Brinkerhoff, for example, commented that "the peculiar friends of Mr. C. have about made up their minds to 'rule or ruin.'" Follett was equally critical. Warning that the position of the Free Soilers, if persisted in, ended all chance for fusion, he condemned Chase's friends, who "object to *secret* dictation, and fall into [the] mistake of *open* dictation!" Angry at the threat of the antislavery men to bolt the convention if Chase were not nominated, the Columbus editor momentarily declared in exasperation that he would no longer work for fusion with "such impractical materials." The "course of your friends is *open*," he reprimanded Chase, "but it is not free and fair."[21]

While Chase scotched plans for independent action within the Free Soil ranks, he relied on Campbell to prevent any similar move by the Know Nothings. The two men had never been close personally, but both realized that at this juncture each was in a position to render valuable service to the other. For almost a year now, Campbell had been running for speaker of the next House of Representatives, which would assemble in December. Chase skillfully exploited his fellow Ohioan's well-known ambition in order to further the Republican movement in the state. Subtly implying that Campbell's assistance would secure Free Soil backing in the speakership contest, Chase in a rather acrimonious correspondence pressed Campbell hard to block any nominations at the state council in Cleveland, and the latter finally agreed to attend and work against any independent action. After some heated debate, the state council made no nominations and resolved to go into the July 13 convention. The Know Nothings did not commit themselves to supporting Chase, however, and the Cincinnati *Commercial* charged that at the July convention nativist delegates intended to sustain the ticket that a group of Know Nothing leaders and some outsiders had devised at a secret meeting in Cincinnati. The state council decided to reassemble in August, after the Republican candidates were chosen.[22]

----

19. Letter signed "G." [Joshua R. Giddings], *Ashtabula Sentinel*, May 17; Giddings to Chase, May 1, J. H. Coulter to Chase, May 27 (quotation), Ashley to Chase, May 29, June 16, P. Bliss to Chase, June 6, Chase Papers, LC; N. S. Townshend to Chase, June 9, Chase Papers, HSPa; Richard Mott to Giddings, June 2, Giddings Papers.

20. Chase to James Shepherd Pike, March 22, Pike Papers, UMe; Chase to Campbell, May 25 (copy), June 2, Chase Papers, LC.

21. Jacob Brinkerhoff to Follett, May 21, Hamlin, ed., "Follett Papers," 75; Follett to Chase, May 2, *Private*, Chase Papers, LC.

22. Chase to Campbell, May 29, June 2 (copy), Campbell to Chase, May 28, 31, June 15, Chase Papers, LC; Chase to Campbell, November 8, Campbell Papers; Campbell to Schouler, June 26 (private), Schouler Papers;

The state council also adopted a platform that enunciated several cardinal nativist doctrines. It called for a twenty-one-year residency requirement for naturalization and the abolition of foreign military companies, lauded the public school system, and denounced all attempts to exclude the Bible from the public schools. At the same time it endorsed "unlimited *Freedom of Religion* disconnected with politics," "hostility to ecclesiastical influences upon the affairs of Government," and equal rights for all foreign-born who were thoroughly Americanized and owed no temporal allegiance because of their religion to an authority higher than the Constitution. In a circular to the local councils before the state council met, Thomas Spooner, the president of the Ohio order, urged that foreign-born Protestants be allowed to join the society. "It is not men of Foreign birth that we war against," he claimed. "Our arms are, and should only be, directed against Foreignism and Romanism—those who should subvert our Institutions, and place our country under the yoke of Rome." The state council did not adopt this change, although it urged its delegates to the national council to work for this reform. One plank dealt with the slavery issue. Declaring slavery a local and not a national institution, the Ohio American platform opposed slavery's extension into any territory or the admission of any more slave states, and demanded the "immediate redress" of the great wrongs of the repeal of the Missouri Compromise and the election frauds in Kansas. "We see no barrier to a full and cordial union of all the true anti-Nebraska friends of Reform in Ohio," the *Ohio State Journal* announced after the state council concluded its work.[23]

The Cleveland meeting proved the critical turning point in the drive to merge the opposition in Ohio into a new party. For several months beforehand, each side had attempted to intimidate the other. One purpose of the Chase faction's talk of a bolt and a new convention was to coerce the Know Nothings into adopting an acceptable course.[24] This strategy succeeded brilliantly. The Know Nothings suffered a failure of nerve.

Why did the Ohio American party leaders, who earlier had been confident and even arrogant, abandon their plan to dictate the fusion ticket? One important factor was the influence of Campbell, whose personal ambition led him to oppose separate nominations. He received valuable aid from Spooner, who, though not a supporter of Chase, was personally friendly with the Free Soil leader. A sincere nativist, Spooner was also a long-time antislavery man who desired the formation of a united opposition party on a platform that was—in part at least—antislavery. Prior to the convening of state council, Spooner warned his fellow nativists that a split in the anti-Democratic forces assured a Democratic victory in the fall.

But the most critical reason for the change in attitude among the Know Nothings was the outcome of the Cincinnati municipal election in April. Confident of their power, the Know Nothings nominated a disreputable ticket headed by James Taylor, the rabble-rousing editor of the Cincinnati *Times* and the anti-Catholic Free School candidate for mayor in 1853. Taylor's indiscriminate attacks on the foreign-born greatly exacerbated tensions in the city. On election day fighting broke out between immigrants and nativists, and the next night a Know Nothing mob attacked the German section of the city. The

---

letter signed "An American," *Ohio State Journal*, October 5; William Gibson to Samuel Galloway, April 23, Samuel Galloway Papers, OHS. The ticket named by the Cincinnati meeting is given in the Cincinnati *Commercial*, May 12.

23. *Ohio State Journal*, June 7. Spooner's address before the state council appears in the Cincinnati *Commercial*, June 8.

24. Giddings to Chase, April 10, Chase Papers, HSPa; J. H. Coulter to Chase, May 27, Chase Papers, LC.

rioting left several men dead. In addition, Know Nothings destroyed the ballots in two German wards to prevent them from being tallied. With both sides claiming victory and issuing threats, election officials finally declared the Democratic mayoral candidate victorious.[25] Republican editor Joseph Medill, long an advocate of using the Catholic issue to gain the support of Protestant immigrants, looked on in dismay as the city's Germans were driven back into the arms of the Democrats. He angrily denounced the Cincinnati Know Nothing leaders as "knaves and asses."[26] For the state American party, the rioting was an even more serious blow than was Taylor's defeat. It made a mockery of the party's reform image and discredited it with an important segment of the public. Know Nothing leaders' confidence in their ability to carry the state without antislavery allies evaporated after this election. Giddings's informants reported that the order's state leaders viewed the Cincinnati election as a disaster to the nativist cause, and that as a result they had given up the idea of making separate nominations.[27]

Hard on the heels of the Cleveland meeting came the disruption of the national council in Philadelphia. The national schism further sapped the Know Nothings' confidence while simultaneously producing a more favorable attitude toward reaching agreement with the antislavery forces. In the aftermath of the Cleveland and Philadelphia meetings, Chase informed James Shepherd Pike that "the political atmosphere has cleared somewhat," and he predicted that he would receive the July 13 nomination and that Know Nothingism in Ohio would "gracefully give itself up to die." Most members were "honest men" who "sincerely opposed" slavery, he asserted, and "adhere but slightly to their order," especially since the adoption of the Philadelphia platform.[28]

Nevertheless, the Republican delegate elections in the first week of July disquieted the Free Soilers. In spite of all the difficulties the American party had experienced recently, it exercised remarkable strength in the selection of delegates. When the July 13 convention assembled, all sides agreed that a majority of the delegates were Know Nothings.[29] Any triumph by Chase and the antislavery forces could be achieved only with nativist votes.

Although they did not control a majority of the delegates, the Chase forces had several advantages. One was their unshakable commitment to Chase's candidacy. Led by Giddings, antislavery men argued that Chase's nomination would make the "issue of Slavery and freedom more distinctly the question" in the election, and they refused to consider suggestions that Chase and Brinkerhoff yield to someone else.[30] The Know Nothings' resolve was weakened by the defection of some northern delegates to Chase and

---

25. The riot is covered fully in the Cincinnati *Gazette*, *Commercial*, and *Enquirer*, April 3, 4, 5, 6. Also see William A. Baughin, "Bullets and Ballots: The Election Day Riots of 1855," *Bulletin of the Historical and Philosophical Society of Ohio*, v. 21 (October, 1963), 267–73.

26. Joseph Medill to Follett, April 18, Follett Papers. The ecological regression estimates indicate that whereas 20 percent of the Germans supported the People's ticket in 1854, none voted for Taylor in the 1855 city election. In the two elections Democratic strength among German voters increased from 31 percent to 48 percent.

27. Letter signed "G." [Giddings], *Ashtabula Sentinel*, June 21; *Ashtabula Sentinel*, June 7.

28. Chase to Pike, June 20, Pike Papers, UMe; Chase to Grimes, June 27, Chase to [Norton S. Townshend?], June 21 (quotation), Chase Papers, HSPa.

29. *Ohio State Journal*, July 13, 14; R. B. Pullan, *Origin of the Republican Party*, Pamphlet Collection, OHS; letter signed "An American," *Ohio State Journal*, October 5; Address of Thomas Spooner, July 23, Cincinnati *Commercial*, July 24.

30. *Ashtabula Sentinel*, April 19.

by the desire of some leaders, particularly Spooner and Campbell, to promote harmony at the convention. The composition of the Cincinnati delegation, in which Chase had disproportionate strength stemming from local considerations, also gave his candidacy an unexpected boost. The greatest advantage of the Chase forces at Columbus, however, was the determination of his more ultra supporters to bolt if their favorite were rejected. To reinforce this threat. the old Free Soil state central committee, which had been moribund since 1853, issued a call for a mass convention on July 13 to ratify the nominations or take appropriate action. On the day of the fusion convention, perhaps as many as 400 outsiders were present, ready to give Chase an independent nomination if he failed to receive the Republican designation.[31] Opposition leaders, aware that Chase and his followers had bolted parties a number of times in the past, knew that this was no idle threat.

On the morning of Friday the thirteenth, the Ohio Republican convention convened amid great excitement in the Town Street Methodist Church.[32] While the delegates listened to speeches, party managers labored assiduously behind the scenes to preserve the fragile spirit of good will on the convention floor. Follett, in particular, worked to formulate an acceptable compromise. The Columbus editor had been lukewarm toward Chase's candidacy, but he recognized that the Free Soilers were unbending. Believing that Chase's rejection would precipitate a third ticket and thus ensure defeat, Follett urged Brinkerhoff to withdraw from the gubernatorial contest and accept the nomination for supreme court justice instead. Somewhat unexpectedly, Brinkerhoff, who apparently saw that his cause was hopeless, agreed to this proposal.[33]

Brinkerhoff's acceptance of Follett's terms climaxed the struggle between the Americans and the Free Soilers for control of the Ohio Republican party. With this impediment eliminated, the proceedings were for the most part harmonious. The committee on resolutions reported a platform that opposed the extension of slavery, rejected the addition of new slave states, and condemned the violence in Kansas. Another plank made a vague reference to states' rights, and a section on state issues called for retrenchment, a just taxation system, and the election of legislators from single districts. Giddings was the only committee member who criticized these resolutions. He argued that they did not go far enough, but he nevertheless called for their adoption. Campbell spoke in their favor, and they were unanimously approved.

Once the platform had been adopted, the anti-Chase forces made one last attempt to forestall his nomination by urging that both Chase and Brinkerhoff withdraw. Chase's supporters shouted their disapproval, and some threatened to retire from the hall. Finally, the delegates laid the motion on the table. At this point Campbell withdrew Brinkerhoff's name as per arrangement, and Chase was nominated with 225 votes compared to 144 votes cast for two last-minute candidates. Know Nothings were named for all eight

---

31. *Ashtabula Sentinel*, June 28, July 12; Giddings to Chase, May 1, Chase Papers, HSPa; R. P. L. Baber to John Sherman, June 28, John Sherman Papers. Chase was secretly involved in preparing plans for independent action if the July 13 convention did not nominate him. See J. H. Coulter to Chase, June 1, Chase Papers, LC.

32. The convention proceedings are in the *Ohio State Journal*, July 13, 14. Also see Giddings's report in the *Ashtabula Sentinel*, July 19, and the account of the Cincinnati *Commercial*'s reporter (probably Murat Halstead), July 14.

33. Follett, "The Coalition of 1855," Alfred E. Lee, ed., *History of the City of Columbus* (2 vols.: New York, 1892), v. 2, 432–33; Kinsley S. Bingham to Chase, July 7, Chase Papers, LC; Roeliff Brinkerhoff, *Recollections*, 92. An earlier attempt to induce Jacob Brinkerhoff to retire had failed. C. K. Watson to Chase, June 25, Chase Papers, LC.

remaining positions on the state ticket. Most prominent of these nominees were Brinkerhoff, who was unanimously selected for Supreme Court justice, and Thomas Ford, whose widely publicized speech at the recent Philadelphia convention in opposition to the majority platform helped him win the nomination for lieutenant governor. When the nominations were completed, Spooner urged support for the entire ticket, and the convention adjourned. Afterwards Chase praised his fellow nominees, but more perceptive was the comment of one observer that, other than Chase, the ticket was a group of mediocrities and "very weak." In particular, future events would amply justify his dismissal of Ford as "nothing but a monteback [*sic*]."[34]

Historians have traditionally cited Chase's nomination as a great victory over nativism.[35] In one sense, of course, it was. Chase was not a member of the order, and the Know Nothings had expended considerable energy trying to prevent his nomination. Moreover, the Republican platform contained no nativist plank. But the results of the convention hardly represented a series of unbroken defeats for the Know Nothings. For one thing, the Republican and American state platforms exhibited no significant differences on the slavery issue.[36] The demand for the repeal of the fugitive slave law, long a key issue among Free Soilers, found no place in the Republican platform, and, in addition, the desire of some anti-Know Nothing leaders to place a foreigner on the ticket was totally ignored. Furthermore, the order obtained eight out of nine nominations— certainly a significant accomplishment. If Chase could go before the electorate unhindered by a nativist platform, he was also running on a preponderantly Know Nothing ticket. Despite Chase's triumph, the Republican party in Ohio rested on a substantial Know Nothing foundation.

Much the more numerous faction, the Know Nothings were confident that in the future they would dominate the Republican party. Time revealed, however, how serious was their miscalculation. Support for Chase and the Republican platform made it impossible for the Know Nothings to maintain their distinctive political identity. At its August meeting the state council freed each member to vote as he wished; with this decision it was inevitable that most nativists would be absorbed into the Republican ranks. The intimidation tactics of the Chase forces, who were willing to see the Democrats triumph rather than tolerate Know Nothing domination of the Republican party, reaped handsome dividends. The failure to defy the Free Soilers doomed the American party in Ohio to a rapid death. In the final analysis, Know Nothing leaders sacrificed their party's future for entirely modest immediate gains. Their ineptness contrasted sharply with the performance of the Chase managers, who, by a dazzling mixture of conciliation and intimidation, forced the nativist majority to abandon its organization and accept the nomination of one of the least popular politicians in the state.

Not all Know Nothings, however, were willing to acquiesce in Chase's nomination. Immediately following the Republican convention, the American executive council

---

34. Chase to Kinsley S. Bingham, October 19 (copy), Chase Papers, HSPa; William B. Fairchild to Isaac Strohm, October 12, Typescript, Strohm Papers, CinHS. One exception to this analysis might be Brinkerhoff, who had political ability, although his legal attainments were modest.

35. Roseboom, "Chase and the Know Nothings," 349–50. This idea is also implicit in Maizlish's analysis, although he views nativism as ultimately untenable because of America's liberal tradition: *Triumph of Sectionalism*, 214–17.

36. The doctrine of barring any more slave states might be considered radical, although it enjoyed considerable support in the North and was becoming standard Republican dogma in many states. The address of the bolters at Philadelphia did not endorse the principle, although the Ohio American platform did.

considered a motion to expel Spooner, who was accused by diehard anti-Chase elements of double-dealing. After long and bitter debate, the motion lost and Spooner, now solidly in Chase's camp, remained president of the order in Ohio.[37] Rebuffed in this effort, dissident American party men eventually joined dissatisfied conservative Whigs and nominated former governor Allen Trimble, who was over seventy years old and no longer politically active, to oppose Chase. The delegates approved a platform that denounced sectional parties, called for restoration of the Missouri Compromise, upheld unspecified American principles, and endorsed reform of the state's banking and tax systems. The meeting designated itself the American party of Ohio, but in reality it represented only a small fraction of the Know Nothings, and in fact Trimble had never been a member of the order.[38] That the intent of this group was solely to defeat Chase was transparent, since the convention made no other nominations. Thus of the Republican nominees, only Chase faced a third-party challenge.

With Chase the symbol of the Republican party, the gubernatorial election was unusually hard-fought. The Democrats, who had earlier renominated Governor William Medill on a platform that avoided any direct reference to the Kansas-Nebraska Act, made Chase the focus of the campaign. Recognizing the Republican leader's vulnerability, Democrats concentrated on his alleged abolitionism and on nativist influence in the Republican party. The Republican standard bearer found himself damned from both sides: Germans denounced his association with Know Nothings on the state ticket while hard-core nativists refused to support him because of his tempered opposition to Know Nothingism. The center of the greatest disaffection was Cincinnati. Here conservative businessmen fearful of Chase's radicalism, American party members angry over what they believed to be the sellout of the order in Columbus, Germans alarmed by the widely circulated charge that he was a Know Nothing, and old-line Whigs still indignant about the 1849 senatorial election—all unleashed their hostility on the Republican nominee. Assailed from all directions, Chase took to the stump and waged a strenuous campaign, delivering fifty-seven major addresses in forty-nine counties. His leading theme was always Kansas, although in Cincinnati and other conservative strongholds he was also careful to identify himself with preservation of the Union. He received loyal support from Campbell, Ford, Spooner, and other American leaders, who endeavored to keep Know Nothings and former Whigs from voting for Trimble. As summer slipped into fall, Chase held firm to his earlier prediction that he would have a majority of 40,000 votes.[39]

When the ballots were counted, the entire Republican ticket had triumphed, but Chase's margin hardly equaled his expectations. Although he defeated his Democratic opponent by 15,000 votes, he obtained only a plurality because Trimble polled more than 24,000 votes. In the remaining state contests in which the Republican candidates were also Know Nothings, the margin of victory was more substantial. Ford, for example, won the lieutenant governorship by a clear majority of almost 36,000 votes, as virtually all the

---

37. Pullan, *Origin of the Republican Party*, 10–11.

38. The proceedings of the Trimble convention are in the Cincinnati *Commercial*, August 10. For conservative Whig opposition to Chase, see William Johnson to A. Banning Norton and others, August 18 (copy), Lincoln Papers, LC; *Ohio State Journal* quoted in *Ashtabula Sentinel*, August 2; T. G. Jones to Thomas Ewing, July 28, R. P. L. Baber to Ewing, August 16, Ewing Family Papers; letter signed "Federalist," Cincinnati *Commercial*, July 27.

39. Chase to Schouler, September 3, Schouler Papers; Chase to E. S. Hamlin, August 27, Follett to Chase, September 9, Chase Papers, LC; Hermann Kreismann to Sumner, September 18, Sumner Papers, HU. Republican strategists felt it necessary to publish a letter from Chase declaring that he was not a Know Nothing. See Chase to Homer Goodwin, August 24, Cincinnati *Commercial*, September 12.

Trimble voters supported him and the rest of the Republican nominees (Table 7.1).[40] Chase was hurt badly by Trimble's candidacy, which appealed primarily to old-line Whigs and nativists who would not support a radical like Chase and yet voted for the rest of his Republican running mates. Although very few traditional Whigs defected to the Democracy even in the face of Chase's candidacy, his weakness among them was obvious. Substantially fewer than half those who supported the Whig ticket in the 1852 state election, the last such contest in which the Whig party mustered respectable strength, voted for Chase in 1855 (Table 7.2). He performed even more poorly among Scott voters, two-thirds of whom either voted for Trimble (24 percent) or abstained (44 percent). Even conservatives who voted for Chase found him a bitter dose.[41] The Republican gubernatorial candidate's unpopularity was most apparent in Hamilton County, where Chase finished a distant third with only 19 percent of the vote. He received fewer than half the votes Scott polled in the county in 1852, and his fall-off was especially noteworthy compared to the vote in 1854, when Hamilton provided the largest anti-Nebraska majority in the state. Counterbalancing to a great extent his huge majority in the Western Reserve, Chase's abysmal showing in Cincinnati and its environs almost cost him the governorship (Map 7).[42]

Chase admitted that he had a difficult canvass. "Never was such an effort made to kill off a man as to kill off me," he complained to Governor James Grimes of Iowa. The Democrats combined with the "proscriptive & proslavery Kns to annihilate me, & I was favored with a vigor & ferocity of detraction and vituperation almost without parallel." He believed that he lost "on both sides—on the American because not a member of the order & the naturalized because connected with the Kns on the ticket." Conveniently overlooking earlier predictions of his strength, Chase angrily criticized the assertion of the New York *Tribune* that a more suitable candidate would have scored a decisive victory. To Pike he boasted that "no other man could have carried the State at all under existing circumstances." More detached observers, however, provided a rather different assessment. Immensely pleased by the result, Wade nevertheless conceded that "we were . . . forced into the canvass with the most unpopular candidate, probably, that could have been started . . . because of prejudices growing out of old conflicts."[43]

Chase's problems resulted fundamentally from his weakness among anti-Nebraska voters. Only about half the voters who supported the People's state ticket in 1854 backed Chase in 1855 (Table 7.3). The return of some Democrats to their traditional loyalty was expected in Republican circles, yet fully a sixth of the anti-Nebraska force voted for Trimble in preference to Chase, and an even larger group sat out the election. Bolstered by his Know Nothing ties, Ford, in contrast, garnered two-thirds of the anti-Nebraska vote and did slightly better than Chase among earlier non-voters (Table 7.4). Trimble's strength came exclusively from traditional non-voters, new voters, and former Whigs (Tables 7.2 and 7.3). Chase's coalition, on the other hand, contained numerous voters from all three parties. As would be expected, the Free Soil vote was cast solidly in his

---

40. The official vote was Chase, 146,641 (48.5 percent); Medill, 131,091 (43.4 percent); and Trimble, 24,310 (8.0 percent). In the lieutenant governor's race, Ford polled 169,439 votes (55.9 percent) to his Democratic opponent's 133,485 votes (44.1 percent).

41. John McLean to John Teesdale, November 2, John McLean Papers, OHS.

42. The official tally in Hamilton County was Chase, 4,516 votes (19.4 percent); Medill, 12,226 votes (52.5 percent); and Trimble, 6,538 votes (28.1 percent).

43. Chase to Sumner, October 15, Sumner Papers, HU; Chase to [Grimes], October 17, Chase Papers, HSPa; Chase to Edward L. Pierce, October 20, Edward L. Pierce Papers, HU; Chase to Pike, October 18, Pike Papers, UMe; Wade to Israel Washburn, Jr., October 13, Israel Washburn, Jr., Papers, LC.

favor. More surprising, however, was his showing among men who voted Democratic in 1852. In fact, he did only slightly better among 1852 Whigs (Table 7.2). Perhaps no development revealed so clearly the devastating impact of nativism and the slavery issue on the Ohio Democracy and the continuing deterioration of its electoral base than the loss to the Republican party of more than a third of its traditional loyalists. At least some Democratic leaders understood that nativism cut both ways, and that this issue kept some anti-Nebraska Democrats, who otherwise would have bolted, loyal to the party. "The Nebraska question was the real rock of danger here," one Democrat conceded after the election, "and if we had not had Know nothingism to fight, [we] would have been beaten badly."[44]

After the balloting Chase acknowledged the significant assistance of "the liberal Americans" who fought "with us like brothers." He paid particular tribute to Campbell, who had placed heavy emphasis on nativism in his campaign speeches. Some of Chase's supporters, however, minimized the contribution of the Know Nothings to the Republican triumph, an attitude that infuriated at least one American party leader who contended flatly that the order furnished the votes that elected Chase.[45] The only figures available for Know Nothing membership are for October 1854, and they vastly underestimate the order's strength a year later. Nevertheless, confining the analysis to those counties where the order was organized in 1854, it appears that the largest proportion of the American vote went to Chase. At the same time, Trimble's vote represented more than proscriptive nativists, since a larger share came from men who were not Know Nothings in 1854 (how many joined the order afterwards is unknown). Not surprisingly, Ford ran better among nativist voters than did Chase (Table 7.5).[46]

Contemporaries generally agreed that Chase failed to win the foreign vote. Cincinnati German leader Stephen Molitor, who endorsed Chase while opposing the rest of the Republican nominees, reported that German-born voters in general opposed Chase because of the presence of Know Nothings on the rest of the ticket. He pleaded for understanding. "That they are anxious not to act treacherously against themselves, is I trust not an unpardonable sin." Several Chase managers, including Ashley in Toledo, expressed disappointment that the bulk of the naturalized voters in their locality went against the Republicans.[47] In Cincinnati, approximately 10 percent of the German voters supported Chase; virtually none backed Ford in the lieutenant governor's contest. Another example of the failure of the Republican campaign to overcome German suspicions of nativist influence in the party was the vote in the heavily German Fifth Ward in Columbus, where Medill routed Chase by a count of 451 to 67 (Trimble polled a meager twenty votes). Most likely those Germans who did vote for Chase were overwhelmingly non-Catholics. The Cleveland *Leader* charged that "the Roman Catholics in Ohio, voted

44. Jonathan M. Cornell to William Medill, November 28, William Medill Papers, LC.

45. Chase to [Grimes], October 17 (quotation), Chase Papers, HSPa; Chase to Pike, October 18, Pike Papers, UMe; W. C. Howells to Chase, November 5, Chase Papers, LC; John Paul to Chase, October 24, Chase Papers, HSPa; O. F. Fishback to Campbell, October 30, Campbell Papers.

46. Some of the Know Nothings' growth since the 1854 election represented expansion into counties that in October 1854 had no lodges and are thus excluded from the analysis, but an indeterminate proportion constituted additional recruits in counties included in the analysis.

47. Stephen Molitor to Chase, February 25, 1856, Ashley to Chase, October 21, J. Walkap to Chase, November 8, Chase Papers, LC; Toledo *Blade*, October 12.

the Locofoco [Democratic] ticket in an undivided body,'' an assertion unchallenged by other leading Republican journals.[48]

The disastrous Republican performance in Cincinnati, which almost cost the party the election, merits closer inspection. The Republican campaign in the metropolis encountered the difficult task of minimizing Trimble's strength among nativists and conservative Whigs while at the same time appealing to German voters with a largely Know Nothing ticket. In the end, the Republicans failed to win any of these groups. Not just Chase but the entire state and local ticket went down to defeat, as nativists refused to support Chase but voted for the rest of the ticket while a minority of Germans backed Chase but deserted the remaining Republican nominees. Chase won only weak support from the rabid nativists who rallied behind Free School candidate James Taylor in the 1853 mayoral election, and he did only slightly better among the conservative Whigs, who generally backed Joseph Ross, the regular Whig nominee, in that contest (Table 7.6). Moreover, Trimble outdistanced Chase among 1854 anti-Nebraska voters by a margin of better than two to one.[49] Despite their opposition to the Nebraska bill, the majority of American party members and conservative Whigs refused to support so advanced an antislavery man as the Republican gubernatorial nominee.

Spurred by Chase's victory, slender as it was, Ohio Republicans were optimistic about the future. To have carried the state in the party's first campaign with so unpopular a candidate was a remarkable achievement. Giddings, who declared that the Know Nothings' prestige was gone "forever," discounted Campbell's assertion that the Americans would rally next year as a distinct and independent party. Another Chase supporter belived that the Trimble clique would now break up, with some going into each of the two major parties. Already looking ahead to 1856, Chase contended that Republicanism in Ohio had been put "on a solid basis." He was certain that the liberal Know Nothings would remain within the Republican ranks, and he anticipated additional Democratic defections. In the future, he predicted, "we shall be stronger than ever."[50]

Without question Chase's election was a great Republican victory. But the returns also confirmed the accuracy of his opponents' preconvention accusation that the inflexible course of Chase's supporters seriously endangered the chances for a Republican triumph. The disparity between Chase's vote and that for the other Republican nominees provided strong evidence that an antislavery candidate fully acceptable to the Know Nothings would have scored a much more impressive victory. Chase and his circle had risked their future power in the state party in a bold bid for control, yet their audacity had been rewarded. They had killed the American party in Ohio.

III

As in Ohio, anti-Democratic politicians in Maine hoped to form a new party that would combine Whigs, anti-Nebraska Democrats, Free Soilers, and Know Nothings. The

---

48. Cincinnati *Enquirer* quoted in *Illinois State Register*, June 25, 1856; *Ohio State Journal*, October 13, 15; Cleveland *Leader* quoted in *Ashtabula Sentinel*, November 1. Ford polled less than one percent of the German vote in Cincinnati. Virtually all Chase's German supporters switched to the Democratic candidate in the lieutenant governor's race.

49. Only an estimated 21 percent of the 1854 People's party voters in Cincinnati supported Chase compared to 54 percent who preferred Trimble (less than 2 percent voted Democratic and the rest abstained).

50. Giddings to Chase, October 16, F. D. Parish to Chase, November 5, Chase to [Grimes], October 17 (quotation), Chase Papers, HSPa; Sidney D. Maxwell Diary, ca. November 1; Chase to Welles, October 26, Welles Papers, LC; Toledo *Blade*, October 12.

process of party formation was much easier in the latter state, however, because Governor Anson P. Morrill's independent candidacy in 1854 had laid the foundation for a broad-based fusion movement. Subsequently elected by the legislature, Morrill had routed his rivals in the popular vote as the candidate of the anti-Nebraska Democrats, temperance men, Free Soilers, and Know Nothings. Whig resistance blocked the formation of the Republican party in 1854, but fusion organizers were convinced that the Whigs' poor showing in Maine and other states that year had eliminated this problem.

If Morrill had won the previous year backed by an ad hoc coalition, he realized that the backing of a well-organized party was essential for continued political success. Any hopes he entertained for gaining Democratic support were dashed by the unremitting hostility of the regular Democrats and the Pierce administration. Party factionalism, which had grown out of personal rivalries and the liquor issue, reinforced to some extent by the Nebraska controversy, had by now evolved to the point that a reunion of the Maine Democracy was impossible. Whatever his intentions during the previous campaign, the new governor was a political realist, and by early 1855 he had discarded his Democratic affiliation and was actively encouraging the formation of a Republican party.

Morrill was in a strategic position to promote a union of the opposition. To dispel Whig suspicions of fusion, he and his advisers courted the party's leaders in an effort to bring the bulk of its membership into the Republican ranks. Central to this strategy was Morrill's retention in office of most of the Whig appointees of his predecessor, Governor William Crosby. A letter from an ostensible Morrill Democrat complained with some exaggeration that Whigs "hold office all over the State," and that no Democrat exerted any influence with the governor. The extremely close ties between Morrill and leaders of the Know Nothing order in the state were also crucial in promoting fusion.[51]

The fusionist-controlled legislature, which enacted several reforms desired by Know Nothings, temperance crusaders, and antislavery men, played an important role in conciliating the various anti-Democratic factions. The legislature's sympathy with the nativist movement was understandable, since Know Nothings constituted the largest bloc in it, and other anti-Democratic politicians were sensitive to the powerful nativist sentiment in the state.[52] The legislature passed a law forbidding state courts from naturalizing anyone, and another preventing naturalized citizens from voting unless they presented their citizenship papers to the proper authorities, for enrollment on a registration roll, at least three months before an election. Members were also receptive to the wishes of Neal Dow and the Maine Law crusaders. They approved, and the governor signed, an "Intensified Maine Law" that Dow had drafted to make the state's anti-liquor law even more stringent. Slavery also occupied the attention of the fusionist leaders in Augusta. The legislature passed a series of bold resolutions that deprecated slavery as a moral evil, declared the fugitive slave law unconstitutional and called for its repeal, condemned the overthrow of the Missouri Compromise, endorsed the abolition of slavery in the District of Columbia and its exclusion from all the territories, and opposed the admission of any

---

51. Letter signed "An original Morrill Democrat," Portland *Eastern Argus*, quoted in Hatch, ed., *Maine*, v. 2, 382. Whether Morrill was a Know Nothing is unclear, although the evidence leans in that direction; at the minimum, he strongly sympathized with the movement and maintained a firm political alliance with it.

52. William Pitt Fessenden's brother warned that the Know Nothings "constitute a power in this state just now" and were "not to be handled unceremoniously." Samuel C. Fessenden to William Pitt Fessenden, February 28, Fessenden Papers, LC. Also see Israel Washburn, Sr., to Elihu B. Washburne, April 3, Elihu B. Washburne Papers, Norlands.

more slave states. To reinforce its antislavery commitment, this body passed a personal liberty law designed to hinder enforcement of the fugitive slave law in the state. Cooperation on these matters among anti-Democratic groups in the legislature smoothed the way for fusion.

A caucus of pro-fusion members of the legislature called a convention for February 22 in Augusta to organize a Republican party in the state. The call was directed to men without distinction of former party ties "who are in favor of a prohibitory Liquor Law, and opposed to the further extension of Slavery and the encroachments of the Slave Power." Relatively inexperienced politicians were especially prominent at the gathering, which nominated Morrill for reelection and approved a platform that was antislavery, anti-liquor, and anti-immigrant. The liquor resolution declared that "the existence and execution of the Maine Temperance Law is a vital element in the organization and life of the Republican Party of this state, and is one of the chief safe guards [sic] of the lives, reputation, property and homes of our people." Another plank, which characterized the "debasement of the right of suffrage" by naturalized voters as "an alarming evil," urged strict enforcement or modification of the existing naturalization laws. Most of the document, however, dealt with the slavery issue. Maine Republicans adopted the most radical antislavery platform of any Republican state organization in 1855. Asserting that the question of human freedom was "paramount to all other questions now agitating the country," the platform advocated the abolition of slavery in the District of Columbia, declared that it was "the right and the duty" of Congress to prohibit it from all territories, denounced the fugitive slave law as "inhuman" and "unconstitutional" and demanded it be "immediately and unconditionally" repealed, condemned the destruction of the Missouri Compromise, called for the admission of no more slave states, and affirmed that all persons regardless of color were entitled to due process of law.[53] To no one's surprise, the American organization endorsed Morrill, and by the end of the campaign Know Nothingism in Maine had been substantially absorbed into the Republican party. Aiding this process was the disruption of the national council in June; in fact, all the state's delegates who signed the northern protest were Republicans.

While Republicans concentrated on the slavery issue, Democratic strategists strove as much as possible to avoid sectional questions. The Kansas-Nebraska Act was unpopular in the state, but pressure from the national administration made it impossible to oppose the law. Consequently, the state convention endorsed the Pierce administration but took no position on the repeal of the Missouri Compromise. Democratic managers intended to emphasize the nativist and liquor issues in the campaign. In a deliberately vague plank, the state platform called for a "suitable" prohibitory law and condemned secret political organizations. Samuel Wells received the Democratic nomination for governor.

Ignoring the party's dwindling base of support, those Whigs unwilling to join a sectional party or ally with their old adversaries, the Democrats, held a separate state convention. With only nine counties represented, the delegates nominated the Whig candidate of the previous year, Isaac Reed, for governor on a platform that condemned nativism, denounced the repeal of the Missouri Compromise, and called for an extensive revision of the stringent Maine Law. As the action of the fusionist legislature and

---

53. *Kennebec Journal*, March 2. Of the fifteen vice presidents, nine had not been politically prominent before 1854. Equally revealing was the composition of the state central committee, which had charge of the campaign; twelve of its fifteen members had no political record before 1852. In no other state were so many inexperienced men in top positions of Republican leadership. Wescott, "Maine Politics," 264–65.

Republican convention demonstrated, nativist and temperance Whigs had gone largely into the Republican ranks. For the first time since Neal Dow's moral crusade had disorganized the state's traditional partisan loyalties, a Maine Whig state convention failed to pass a strong resolution in favor of prohibition. Anti-liquor sentiment, at least in party platforms, was confined to the Republicans. While rejecting statewide coalition with the Democrats, straight Whigs nevertheless directed their chief hostility toward the Republican party, which they denounced as "the offspring of a corrupt fusion of men of opposite political opinions, and associations aided recently by a secret political organization of the most dangerous character." On legislative and county tickets, these Whigs for the most part united with the Democrats.[54]

Despite their endorsement of nativism and prohibition, Republicans intended to emphasize the Kansas issue in the 1855 contest. "The Kansas outrages give us a great opportunity to revive & keep alive the great issue of Slavery," Edward Kent counseled. "This is the true rallying point & ought to be kept prominent." A Democratic paper complained that the speeches at a Republican meeting at Portland were "Nebraska! Nebraska, and nothing else." Kent was confident of a Republican victory if the campaign were properly conducted. Exuding even greater self-confidence, one Republican editor divulged: "We, privately, regard the victory as already won."[55]

The Republican campaign sustained two major setbacks, however. First, all attempts to secure the allegiance of Senator Hannibal Hamlin, the state's leading anti-Nebraska Democrat, were unsuccessful. Morrill devoted considerable effort to wooing his former Democratic ally. Assuring the senator that he had many friends in the Republican party, the governor exhorted, "Old friends who feel alike on the questions and issues before the country should act together and not be separated by dead issues or organizations." On another occasion the Republican nominee intimated to Hamlin that Republicans would do almost anything to gratify him. Professing confidence in his reelection, Morrill nevertheless maintained that Hamlin's endorsement of the Republican cause would annihilate any chance for a Democratic victory. But the future Republican vice-president continued to avoid any affiliation with the new party. Bereaved by the recent death of his wife and uncertain of his proper political course, the cautious Hamlin took no part in the state campaign.[56]

The second major difficulty Republicans encountered was the Portland riot in June. Desirous of vindication after his defeat in 1852, Neal Dow ran for mayor of Portland in April 1855 and scored a narrow victory over what one of his chief supporters termed "Rum, Hunkerism, Catholicism and Corruption." Dow's anti-liquor crusade had earned him many enemies, both among the city's merchants and its Irish population, and his vigorous enforcement as mayor of the Intensified Maine Law increased tensions in the city. Violence finally erupted on June 2 when a mob, inflamed by a report that Dow had violated his own law in purchasing liquor for the city, and encouraged by some of the mayor's most conspicuous political enemies, attacked the police guarding city hall, where the allegedly illegal liquor was stored. Eager to demonstrate his authority and believing

54. Portland *Advertiser*, March 17; Edward Kent to Fessenden, June 6, George Ingersoll to Noah Smith, June 12, Israel Washburn, Jr., to Fessenden, June 29, Fessenden Papers, WRHS.

55. Kent to Fessenden, May 21, Fessenden Papers, WRHS; Portland *Eastern Argus*, August 15; J. Bartlett to Charles Hamlin, June 28, Hannibal Hamlin Papers.

56. Morrill to Hannibal Hamlin, April 3, *Confidential* (quotation), June 18, August 6, Charles J. Gilman to Hamlin, June 28, Hamlin to Charles Hamlin, July 1, September 7, October 13, 14, Hannibal Hamlin Papers.

the mob to be composed primarily of ignorant Irish rabble, Dow ordered the state militia to fire on the crowd without warning. In the ensuing gunfire, one man was killed and several wounded. Dow's Democratic opponents brought him to trial on charges of having illegally purchased the liquor, but he was acquitted, and attempts to indict him for manslaughter came to naught.[57] Even so, the fanatical Dow, unwilling to tolerate any opposition and confident of his own rectitude, had greatly overreacted, and in the process he handed the Democrats the issue they needed.

For the Democrats, the Portland riot was an ideal issue, since it enabled the party to focus attention on temperance rather than on the slavery question. The party responded by mounting an all-out campaign to discredit Dow and the prohibitionists. *"Dow ought to be hanged, and if we succeed this fall, he will be hanged,"* a leading Democrat thundered at one rally. At the same time, the Democrats had no difficulty linking Dow with the Republican party, of which he was a prominent member. Proclaimed one Democratic paper, *"A vote for Morrill is a vote for Neal Dow."* Democrats pictured the Republican party as a party of fanaticism, be it abolitionism and disunion, nativism, or Dowism. As the campaign continued, Republican leaders were increasingly wary of Dow and the extreme Maine Law men, but they remained confident, despite this unanticipated turn.[58] After all, in the last three state contests Maine voters had elected pro-temperance governors. Even in the face of Dow's overzealousness, why should they now repudiate the state's great moral experiment?

In the most startling Republican setback of the year, Morrill lost his bid for reelection, even though he received a slight plurality.[59] Because the straight Whigs and Democrats had for the most part united on legislative tickets, the anti-Morrill forces were a majority in the new legislature, thus assuring that Samuel Wells, the Democratic nominee, would be the next governor. Turnout was very heavy, with almost 20,000 more votes cast than in 1854. Morrill received 6,636 more votes than he had in 1854, but Wells increased the Democratic tally by an astonishing 19,977 votes (even counting Liberal candidate Shepard Cary's votes in 1854 as part of the Democratic total, the Democratic surge was still 16,553 votes). One of Wells's correspondents assured him that his victory represented "the spontaneous up-rising of the people."[60]

A remarkable amount of shifting occurred between the 1854 and 1855 elections. Morrill won important support from 1854 Whigs and Democrats, as well as previous non-voters, but at the same time suffered extensive defections of his 1854 backers to the two opposing candidates (Table 7.7). The 1855 election disturbed partisan affiliations to a much greater extent than had the 1854 balloting. Except for the small Liberal faction that backed Cary earlier, every party in 1854 experienced significant losses of past members in 1855. Morrill's major problem was the presence of a separate Whig candidate, and in fact he won only a minority of the traditional Whig vote (Table 7.8). Kent maintained subsequently that a number of these Whig voters "are with us in feeling and desire more or less earnestly to act against the slave power & its outrages—but . . . are frightened by the cry of sectionalism and disunion." Conservative Whigs' reluctance to support a sectional party, a reluctance that the Republicans' extreme platform reinforced, prevented

---

57. Byrne, *Prophet of Prohibition*, 62–66.

58. *Ibid.*, 66; Giddings, "Letter from Away Down East," August 20, *Ashtabula Sentinel*, August 30.

59. The official result was Morrill (Republican), 51,488 votes (46.6 percent); Wells (Democrat), 48,373 votes (43.8 percent); and Reed (Whig), 10,645 votes (9.6 percent). The turnout was an estimated 73.7 percent.

60. M. L. Appleton to Samuel Wells, September 17, Appleton Family Papers, MassHS.

Morrill from scoring a clear victory. "We are beaten . . . by the folly of our friends," mourned William Pitt Fessenden.[61]

Earlier divisions over the Maine Law played a crucial role in the formation of the Republican coalition in Maine. The supporters of Governor John Hubbard, who won reelection in 1852 after signing the state's anti-liquor law, made up the core of the Republican vote in 1855, and Morrill consistently ran well among voters who had in the past backed pro-temperance candidates (Tables 7.7, 7.9, and 7.10). Yet Morrill's appeal transcended the liquor question. The Republican nominee won votes from supporters of anti-temperance candidates as well (though, to be sure, at a significantly lower rate than among drys).[62] No doubt other issues, and especially those relating to slavery and nativism, brought additional voters into the Republican camp and at the same time reinforced the commitment of anti-liquor men to the party's cause.

In seeking to account for their unexpected defeat, Republican strategists generally affixed responsibility on Dow and the Maine Law zealots along with ultra antislavery men. Benjamin F. Wade and Joshua R. Giddings, both of whom stumped the state, blamed the liquor issue for the party's setback. Giddings believed that the Republican party should never have made the Maine Law an issue, and added that he hoped it would never do so again in Maine or any other state. The fatal error of making rum an issue, he argued, was that it allowed the Democrats to avoid the territorial controversy.[63] The party's stridently antislavery plaform also weakened Morrill by scaring off nervous conservatives. In the aftermath of the election, Republican leaders moved to tone down the party's radical antislavery image, as well as to check the influence of Dow and his followers by inducing them to lay the rum issue aside during the 1856 presidential election. In a frank letter to Hannibal Hamlin, one Republican organizer discussed the party's past difficulties and future prospects. "The Republican party, in this State, for the past year, has been too much under the control of *ultra* and *extreme* men," he conceded. "Its late *temporary* defeat, is attributable to that fact alone." He singled out for particular censure temperance reformers and men "tinctured with old-fashioned abolitionism" and stressed that the party had to recognize that "the free soil sentiment, (not abolitionism,) is the prevailing sentiment in the State." Declaring that new leaders were needed, he urged Hamlin to join the Republican party and accept its gubernatorial nomination in 1856.[64]

IV

The 1854 election left Pennsylvania's politics badly factionalized, and as a result the task of bringing together the opposition to the Democrats proved extraordinarily complex and difficult. The failure of the legislature to elect a senator despite its heavy anti-Democratic

---

61. Kent to Seward, October 20, Private, Seward Papers, UR; Fessenden to Elizabeth C. Wariner, September 23, Fessenden Family Papers; Portland *Eastern Argus*, September 11.

62. Pro-temperance candidates in the previous three state contests included John Hubbard, the Democratic nominee in 1852, Anson P. Morrill in 1853 and 1854, the Whig candidate in all three elections, and the Free Soil nominee in 1852 and 1853. The remaining candidates were popularly perceived as anti-prohibition. Not every supporter of any of these candidates, of course, was motivated solely or even principally by the liquor question.

63. Wade to Israel Washburn, Jr., October 13, Israel Washburn, Jr., Papers, LC; Giddings to Lincoln, September 18, *Private*, Herndon-Weik Collection, LC.

64. Nehemiah Abbot to Hannibal Hamlin, November 2, Hamlin Papers; Dow, *Reminiscences*, 551–52.

majority demonstrated how much at odds and lacking in effective leadership the opposition forces were. The only state office to be filled in the 1855 election was canal commissioner, and although this position was not of much importance, observers viewed the contest as a test of the relative strength between the Democrats and their opponents. It would also show whether the anti-Democratic majority could unite on a common platform and ticket.

Eventually, no fewer than four anti-Democratic candidates were in the field. Despite their obviously shrinking base of support, the Whigs nominated a candidate for canal commissioner. Alexander McClure, who was a delegate to the Whig state convention, described it as "an assembly of leaders without rank and file." With reports from all sections of the state uniformly despondent, he observed wryly that the party's only remaining adherents were "a few old Scotch-Irish Whigs, most of whom would have been compelled to lie awake at night to decide whether they most hated Know Nothingism or Democracy." Democratic leader Jeremiah S. Black, who pronounced the Whigs "gone hook & line," discerned correctly that inducing those members "who stand obstinately on the old platform" to act with any other party would prove quite difficult. The Native Americans also nominated a candidate for canal commissioner, but, like the Whig choice, he stood absolutely no chance of election.[65]

More significant was the action of the Know Nothing state council, which met at the beginning of July after the schism of the national organization in Philadelphia. Upholding the action of its delegates at this meeting, the council refused to endorse the national platform and, in a bid to carve out a middle position, it called for restoration of the Missouri Compromise while at the same time asserting that "the question of Slavery should not be introduced into the Platform of the American Party." Former governor William F. Johnston was the leading spirit at the state council. The American state platform reiterated the position Johnston had taken earlier at the national council when he had declined to sign the northern bolters' address and, joined by a handful of colleagues, had issued a separate declaration. Critics in and out of the secret order charged that Johnston was aiming for a presidential nomination in 1856 on this platform. For canal commissioner the state council named a close ally of Simon Cameron, the most influential American leader in the state.[66]

Members of the opposition who refused to support the Know Nothings looked increasingly to the Republican movement, which had demonstrated strength in some western states, as an alternative anti-Democratic party. A leading spokesman for this viewpoint was the Pittsburgh *Gazette*, which though anti-Catholic condemned the secrecy of the American party and called for the formation of a Republican party that would give precedence to the slavery issue. Anti-Masonic and foreign-born Whigs were leery of the American party, and in both the Philadelphia and Pittsburgh municipal elections in the spring of 1855 anti-Know Nothing Whigs formed coalitions with the Democrats. In addition, a number of antislavery Whigs, typified by the *Gazette*, expressed strong doubts about the order's commitment to the cause against slavery. Promoters of the Republican party anticipated that by emphasizing sectional issues, the new party could undermine the order's position as an antislavery party and detach anti-Nebraska nativists from its ranks,

65. McClure, *Old Time Notes*, v. 1, 235–36; Jeremiah S. Black to James Buchanan, February 17, Buchanan Papers, HSPa.

66. New York *Tribune*, July 6; Harrisburg *Telegraph*, July 11; James A. Dean to Simon Cameron, June 22, W. R. Wilson to Cameron, July 12, Cameron Papers, LC.

with a resulting loss that would seriously weaken the American party. The Democratic Pittsburgh *Post* agreed with the *Gazette's* contention that many antislavery Know Nothings would join a Republican party. "Thousands" of the order's members throughout the state "with whom antislavery sentiment is stronger than all other political purposes," the former paper predicted, "will leave the ranks of the K.N.'s for the more congenial fellowship" of the Republican party.[67]

The renewed attempt to form a fusion party in Pennsylvania began in Bradford County, home of David Wilmot, after the 1854 election. Eventually, a gathering in Reading in which ten counties were represented issued a call without regard to former party ties for a mass meeting in Pittsburgh on September 5 "to organize a republican party whose object shall be to place all branches of government actively on the side of Liberty." The same day a similar call, signed by leaders from a dozen counties, was published in Pittsburgh. Undoubtedly, Republican organizers selected Pittsburgh because the stronger antislavery sentiment in the western counties made it a more favorable setting than either Harrisburg or Philadelphia.

On the appointed day a large number of men assembled at the city hall in Pittsburgh for the first Pennsylvania Republican state convention.[68] To lend encouragement, its organizers imported Joshua R. Giddings, Lewis D. Campbell, and John Bingham, all prominent Ohio Republicans, to address the assembly. Indicative of the party's rocky beginning was that fewer than a third of the state's counties were represented, with the majority of those in attendance from the west. As chairman of the resolutions committee, Alexander McClure reported a platform devoted entirely to the slavery issue, which, the opening resolution asserted, "overshadows all others in a national point of view." Proclaiming the principle "FREEDOM IS NATIONAL AND SLAVERY SECTIONAL" as the foundation of the party's political faith, the resolutions condemned the repeal of the Missouri Compromise and the subsequent Kansas election frauds as part of a "conspiracy against Freedom." Careful to deny any desire to interfere with slavery in the states where it already existed, the Republican platform advocated that the federal government be relieved from all connection with the peculiar institution, opposed its extension to any territory and the admission of any additional slave states, and called for the repeal of the fugitive slave law.

Republican strategists had beforehand discussed nominating Kansas ex-governor Andrew Reeder as a means to exploit the Kansas issue and win over Democrats unhappy with Pierce's increasingly pro-southern policies. Reeder, however, was uninterested and remained allied with the Democratic party despite his collision with Pierce. His refusal to run deprived Republicans of an excellent chance to capitalize on the Kansas imbroglio. Moderates were anxious to unite the opposition behind a single candidate, and after a series of conferences the resolutions committee proposed that the convention endorse the American candidate. This plan was unacceptable to staunch antislavery men, who believed that such a step would signify the party's absorption by the Know Nothings. At this point, one antislavery delegate delivered an emotional speech advocating the nomination of Passmore Williamson, an antislavery martyr currently in jail on a contempt

67. Pittsburgh *Post*, August 4, quoted in Holt, *Forging a Majority*, 160n.

68. This account of the Republican convention is based on Russell Errett to Chase, November 16, Chase Papers, LC; New York *Tribune*, September 8; McClure, *Old Time Notes*, v. 1, 236–38; and C. Maxwell Myers, "The Rise of the Republican Party in Pennsylvania, 1854–1860" (unpublished Ph.D. dissertation, University of Pittsburgh, 1940), 62–64.

charge stemming from a fugitive slave case. "A torch applied to a powder magazine could not have been more explosive," McClure recalled, and in "a tempest of enthusiasm" Williamson received the Republican nomination for canal commissioner.[69]

Whatever hope remained of uniting the other anti-Democratic factions on the Republican ticket disappeared in the wake of Williamson's selection. The Republican nominee was, as McClure noted, "an impossible candidate." His radicalism hardly appealed to old-line Whigs or Americans, and to conduct the campaign on the issue of the court's authority to cite citizens for contempt or on the validity of the fugitive slave law would be the height of folly. The hostile Philadelphia *News* accused the Republican party of "rushing into a wild abolition crusade against the South," while McClure, whose pleas for conciliation and concession had been overridden, asserted that the party, instead of representing hope for the future, "started out with such revolutionary radicalism that it appeared only as a political suicide."[70]

Having made one blunder, the delegates then compounded their mistake by leaving the appointment of the state central committee to the convention chairman, Judge William Jessup, who afterwards revealed that he was a Know Nothing not in sympathy with the Republican movement. Jessup delayed organizing the state committee for almost a month, and when two weeks before the election he finally appointed its members, he packed it with Know Nothings. The Republican state committee contained six Republicans, two old-line Whigs, and seventeen Know Nothings, including David Wilmot, the chairman. Several members were notoriously and intensely antagonistic to Republicanism. Jessup selected the committee with a view to force Williamson, whose nomination he had opposed, out of the race and to name a new candidate in conjunction with the Whigs and Know Nothings. With ample reason, the Pittsburgh *Gazette* complained that the new party had been "thrown into the hands of its enemy."[71]

Getting the opposition to agree on one candidate offered the only hope of defeating the Democrats. Probably, the aggressive free soil elements who controlled the Republican convention would never have consented to Williamson's withdrawal in favor of a less-advanced antislavery candidate, but because of Jessup's chicanery they had very little power in the state central committee. After consultations, the Whig, American, and Republican state chairmen agreed that the three state committees would meet in Harrisburg on September 27 to discuss fusion. Republicans distrusted this movement, which, they correctly suspected, represented a Know Nothing scheme to dominate the opposition. Because of these fears, along with the very short notice given, only eleven of the twenty-five members of the Republican state committee appeared at the Harrisburg conference. To facilitate discussion, each party designated a three-man subcommittee to confer about union; those present agreed that any arrangement had to be acceptable to a majority of each party's representatives. The Whig, American, and Republican candidates had already authorized their withdrawal if necessary. Cameron headed the American

---

69. McClure, *Old Time Notes*, v. 1, 237. Williamson was not released from jail until after the election. McClure probably overstated the impact of the speeches in the convention, since Williamson's nomination had been suggested prior to the convention. New York *Tribune*, August 29.

70. McClure, *Old Time Notes*, v. 1, 237–38; Philadelphia *Daily News*, November 10, quoted in Mueller, *Whig Party in Pennsylvania*, 223n. McClure contended that without the backing of Whigs and Americans the Republican party could not carry a township in the state. McClure, *Our Presidents and How We Make Them*, 3rd ed. (New York, 1909), 136. For an attack on Williamson as a radical, see the *Keystone*, September 19.

71. Errett to Chase, November 16, Chase Papers, LC; Pittsburgh *Gazette*, October 1.

subcommittee and McClure the Whig; the Republican delegates were of lesser note. Still sustaining senatorial ambitions, Cameron was especially anxious to promote cooperation, since a new legislature was to be elected in the fall. Though an outsider, Governor James Pollock also took an active role in encouraging harmony, as did Thaddeus Stevens, who like the governor was a Whig-Know Nothing. Finally, after hours of contentious deliberations, the three parties agreed on Thomas Nicholson, the chief clerk in the state treasurer's office, as a union candidate for canal commissioner. The American, Whig, and Republican candidates were all withdrawn.[72]

At this point, less than two weeks remained until the election—far too little time to get all opposition factions to work in harness. Indeed, a number of Republicans disavowed the action of their state committee, with the Pittsburgh *Gazette* particularly vehement in its denunciations. Republicans were deeply suspicious of Nicholson's true relationship to the Know Nothings. Despite strong denials at the Harrisburg meeting that he was a member of the order, their qualms were well grounded, for after the election his nativist affiliation was confirmed.[73] In its first campaign, therefore, the Republican party in Pennsylvania found itself in the unenviable position of having a Know Nothing for its state chairman and for its only state candidate, along with a state committee two-thirds of whom were members of the American order. Not surprisingly, little progress was made toward perfecting a Republican organization or in generating any enthusiasm for the party. Thanks to Know Nothing subterfuge and the dominance of antislavery zealots at the state convention, the attempt to organize the Republican party in Pennsylvania in 1855 was stillborn.

As expected, the Republicans' worst showing in 1855 occurred in the Keystone State. As the fusion candidate, Nicholson lost the election by about 13,000 votes. Williamson polled slightly more than 7,000 votes on the Republican ticket, mostly in the western counties (Map 8).[74] The last-minute agreement among Americans, Republicans, and Whigs prevented a clear-cut test of the Republican party's strength, but considering that Nicholson was a Know Nothing and the bulk of his support came from the nativist order, the Republican total was extremely discouraging. The few votes Williamson received came primarily from Whigs and men who did not vote in 1854 (Table 7.11). He displayed no appeal to Democrats or Americans. Both the Whigs and Know Nothings voted solidly for the fusion ticket. The defection of a number of American party men to the Democrats was substantially negated by a similar movement from the Democrats to the fusionists. These defecting Americans were probably former Democrats returning to their old loyalty. Democrats exulted over the victory, particularly because they carried the legislature, thereby assuring that the new senator would be a Democrat (the opposition, by failing to agree in the 1855 session, had squandered its opportunity). Yet Democrats

72. *Pennsylvania Telegraph*, October 3; McClure, *Old Time Notes*, v. 1, 239–40; Myers, ''Republican Party in Pennsylvania,'' 70. No overtures were made to the Native Americans, in part because they were so weak, but also because of the animosity between them and the Know Nothings, whom they viewed as upstarts. See Kimber Cleaver to Cameron, October 4, Cameron Papers, LC.

73. Pittsburgh *Gazette*, October 1, 2, 8, 9; B. G. David to Eli Slifer, October 23, Slifer-Dill Papers, Dickinson College; William Birney to Sumner, November 9, Sumner Papers, HU.

74. The official results were: Nicholson (Fusion), 149,745 votes (46.0 percent); Plumer (Democrat), 161,281 votes (49.6 percent); Williamson (Republican), 7,226 votes (2.2 percent); Martin (American), 678 votes (0.2 percent); Henderson (Whig), 2,293 votes (0.7 percent); and Cleaver (Native American), 4,056 votes (1.2 percent). Of all the opposition parties, the Know Nothings were by far the most successful at transferring their strength to Nicholson.

Republican Majority

Democrat Majority

Republican Plurality

Democrat Plurality

Trimble Plurality

Note: Numbers are the Republican percentage of the votes cast.

7. Ohio Vote for Governor, 1855

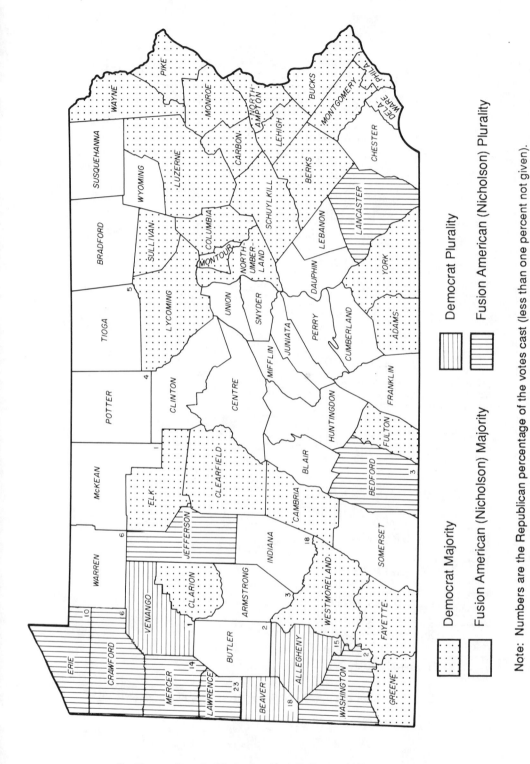

Note: Numbers are the Republican percentage of the votes cast (less than one percent not given).

Democrat Plurality

Fusion American (Nicholson) Plurality

Democrat Majority

Fusion American (Nicholson) Majority

8. Pennsylvania Vote for Canal Commissioner, 1855

could not overlook that they were a minority and had won only because their adversaries were divided.

Opposition leaders advanced various explanations for the loss after their impressive victory a year previously. Probably no issue was cited as frequently as the recently enacted so-called jug law, which prohibited the sale of liquor in quantities of less than a quart. The law was strongly denounced on the ground that it impinged only on the lower class and left the rich free to drink at home; in response to its passage, liquor interests in the state waged an intensive campaign against the fusionists.[75] The main difficulty for the anti-Democratic forces, however, appears to have been the loss of Protestant immigrant supporters and the refusal of many Scotch-Irish voters, a number of whom were former anti-Masons, to vote for a member of a secret society. This latter group accounted substantially for what little strength the Republican party had.[76] From Pittsburgh, a Democrat explained that the Democratic victory in that city was "mainly owing to the strong foreign vote, to the catholic vote, to the liquor movement and the fact that a Republican ticket was in the field." All these factors were needed to break down the anti-Democratic majority in the county. A Philadelphia German leader also emphasized the defection of naturalized voters:

> Had it not been for the ill-advised surrender of the Republicans in this state to the Know-Nothing party, shortly before the last election, thousands of Germans in this city would have voted the Republican ticket, but were driven back into the ranks of their old party, as they thought they would forge their own chains, were they to vote for the K.N. candidate. Hundreds of Germans who formerly always voted the whig ticket went over to the Sham Democracy in order to kill their common enemy Know-Nothingism.[77]

By agitating the nativist and liquor questions, Democrats successfully deflected attention from the slavery issue, which seemed less relevant in state and local contests. Ethnocultural issues still were more potent in Pennsylvania politics.

The opposition in Pennsylvania remained fragmented, its previous majority was largely dissipated, and it lacked a common vision of the future. For Republicans, with their party mired in Know Nothing intrigues and overwhelmed at the polls, a completely new start seemed necessary. Reviewing the party's difficulties in the late contest, Russell Errett of the Pittsburgh *Gazette* confessed, "The short and the long of the matter is that, as things now are, I have no hope of Pennsylvania. I cannot see how all parties can co-operate here without a sacrifice of principle or a loss of votes sufficient to ensure defeat." He saw no alternative but to repudiate the existing Republican organization and begin anew.[78]

---

75. Edward McPherson to his father, October 12, McPherson Papers; Jonathan M. Kirkpatrick to Cameron, October 31, Cameron Papers, LC; J. Glancy Jones to Buchanan, October 12, Private, Josiah Randall to Buchanan, November 5 (Confidential), Buchanan Papers, HSPa.

76. Regression estimates for eighteen of the state's counties indicate that Scotch-Irish voters provided more than three-fourths of the Republican party's small total. Voters of German descent, in contrast, gave no support to the Republican party. Moreover, the opposition's strength among German voters fell from 39 percent in 1854 to less than 25 percent in 1855. Most of these defectors apparently abstained rather than switching to the Democrats, since the Democratic proportion showed only a slight variation in the two elections (41 and 37 percent respectively).

77. A. B. McCalmont to William Bigler, October 10, Bigler Papers; Charles Dunning to Chase, November 4, Chase Papers, LC; letter from George Orr, October 13, *National Era*, October 18; Holt, *Forging a Majority*, 167–71.

78. Errett to Chase, November 16, Chase Papers, LC.

V

"Politics is in a perfect *muss*," one keen-eyed observer said of the situation in Massachusetts in 1855. He offered the following assessment: "Whig party nowhere. Demo. very small. Free Soil small[,] Repu[b]lic[an]. small. Anti Pope & anti slavery large. Rum party pretty large, very active, Temperance pretty large, & doubtfull [*sic*]— pure Native American small & active, Catholic perfectly quiet." Conceding that there was "material to work upon," he nonetheless cautioned, "Nobody now know[s] what will come out of it." Another experienced Bay State politician, Charles Francis Adams, shared this uncertain outlook. He was almost contemptuous when Charles Sumner predicted that the antislavery elements would unite in the fall campaign. On the contrary, Adams foresaw only continuing division ahead. Massachusetts was "now afloat and at the mercy of winds and waves," and he feared that the state "had only storms in store for some time."[79]

Earlier in the year, Adams had been instrumental in an attempt to reorganize the Free Soil party on an antislavery, anti-Know Nothing basis. Hesitation, procrastination, and difference of opinion among party leaders eventually undermined this effort, and its collapse marked the end of the Free Soil party in the state.[80] Those leaders who had not gone over to the Know Nothings recognized that a new organization was needed. Some were attracted to the Know Something organization, which was stronger in Massachusetts than in any other state except perhaps Ohio. Coalitionists dominated the new secret society, and contemporary claims that it recruited most of its members among antislavery Know Nothings were no doubt correct. By summer, however, it was apparent that the Know Something movement was only temporary, and indeed by that time its leaders were actively promoting fusion of the various opposition parties.[81]

Despite growing hostility to the Know Nothings sparked by the severely criticized performance of the 1855 legislature, the fusion movement in Massachusetts remained stalled until summer. The disruption of the national American party, in which the Massachusetts delegates played such a decisive role, gave new momentum to the drive in the state for fusion. "The recent *events* at Phila affords the true anti-slavery men of Massachusetts an opportunity of laying the foundation of a great republican party," maintained John W. Foster, one of Henry Wilson's closest associates at the national council. "It behooves all of us to lay aside past differences on minor points, and unite with entire cordiality on the great questions" now before the country. Not surprisingly, Wilson and Samuel Bowles, his collaborator at Philadelphia, were in the forefront in advocating union. "All that can be done must be to make a fusion of parties," Wilson told Bowles after returning home. "I shall do all I can to unite all who feel and think as we do. Not one day must be lost. . . . We must . . . do all we can to conciliate and harmonise." Likewise, Bowles affirmed that he had "an abiding faith in fusion, . . . &

---

79. Samuel Downer to Horace Mann, August 25, Mann Papers; Charles Francis Adams Diary, May 24 (quotation), Adams to Gamaliel Bailey, April 15 (copy), Adams Family Papers.

80. This abortive attempt to reorganize the Free Soil party can be traced in Adams's Diary, January 10, 13, 17, April 14, 19, 21, Adams to Bailey, January 20, April 15 (copies), Adams Family Papers; Samuel Gridley Howe to Sumner, January 19, Howe Papers, HU; James M. Stone to Sir, April 17, Circular, Robert Carter Papers, HU.

81. Adams Diary, April 14, Adams to Bailey, April 15 (copy), Adams Family Papers; Howe to Sumner, February 9, Laura E. Richards, ed., *Letters and Journal of Samuel Gridley Howe* (2 vols.: Boston, 1909), v.1, 409; James W. Stone to Sumner, February 3, Sumner Papers, HU.

the means by which it shall be achieved are matter of little moment to me, so that they succeed.'' Still, he acknowledged that it was hard to get men to work together; the state was "reaping in the harvest of ill feeling, bitter prejudice, & unconquerable aversion, the evils of coalitionism, Know nothingism, & hunker whiggery.''[82]

Know Nothingism posed the major stumbling block to union. A number of pro-fusion politicians opposed any new party movement that recognized the secret order or made concessions to nativist principles. Some who held this view, most notably Adams, were motivated to a much greater extent by personal antagonism to Wilson and other American party leaders than they cared to admit, but whatever its cause, this hostility had to be blunted, since no fusion party could be successful without a significant infusion of Know Nothings, who were dominant in the state. Equally critical was the resistance of certain of the Americans to fusion. Wilson and Foster, the president of the state council, masterminded the effort within the order to induce the Know Nothings to participate in a fusion movement. Conceding that the secret order could remain supreme on the northern platform adopted by the bolters at Philadelphia, Foster nevertheless announced that he was "in favor of grounding arms." He was less than frank, however, in his contention that the Know Nothings "ask no undue participation in the direction of affairs.''[83]

The struggle within the American organization between the antislavery forces, led by Foster and Wilson, and the ardent nativists, led by Alfred E. Ely and A. C. Carey, culminated at the state council in Springfield on August 7. Anxious to affiliate with the Republican movement in other states, the Wilson clique demanded an end to proscription and abandonment of the proposed amendment passed by the recent legislature that lengthened the residence requirement for naturalized voters to twenty-one years. Under the influence of Governor Henry J. Gardner, the council rebuffed the Wilson forces and approved the proposed amendment as well as several other nativist planks. The American platform was a moderate antislavery document, which called for a restoration of the Missouri Compromise, a ban on any slave states created from the region covered by the 1820 prohibition, and protection of the elective franchise in the territories. Another resolution endorsed fusion with groups that agreed with these principles. Since the Republicans would not accept all the planks of the Springfield platform, the Know Nothings in effect had given themselves a loophole to oppose the party if they failed to control it. The order's attitude toward fusion remained deliberately ambiguous.[84]

When Wilson disclosed at Philadelphia that he was in favor of organizing the Republican party in Massachusetts, he suggested to Samuel Bowles and Ezra Lincoln, a prominent Boston Whig, that Robert C. Winthrop be its candidate for governor. Winthrop would bring prestige to the party, and his antislavery record was stronger than that of some of the party's founders. When approached, however, the aristocratic Winthrop declined to enter the new party. He feared its radicalism, he was disturbed by the rising tide of sectionalism in the country, and he could never forget or forgive the criticism he

---

82. John W. Foster to Julius Rockwell, June 16, Rockwell Papers; Henry Wilson to Samuel Bowles, June 23, Bowles Papers; Bowles to Henry L. Dawes, August 6, [?] Stowe to Dawes, July 30, Dawes Papers.

83. Foster to Rockwell, June 16, Rockwell Papers; Albert G. Browne to Sumner, January 3 [?], Sumner Papers, HU; Adams Diary, August 27, Adams Family Papers.

84. Boston *Daily Bee*, August 8, 9, 16; Bean, "Transformation of Parties," 303–09. The Wilsonites included John W. Foster, Anson Burlingame, James M. Stone, John S. Swift, Daniel Alvord, and Charles W. Slack. Wilson, who asserted that "we have a class of fools in the party who have already disgraced the state and the party," lobbied against the 21-year amendment. Wilson to Schouler, April 16, Schouler Papers.

had been subjected to, particularly from the Free Soilers. Nor could he be comfortable with the party's leadership, especially Sumner, whom he abhorred, and Wilson, whom he held in contempt. Not all Whigs were so fastidious or shortsighted. The eminent jurist E. Rockwood Hoar, for one, urged that his Whig colleagues support fusion. He explained to Amos A. Lawrence, who despite his Kansas aid activities opposed the Republican movement, that "if our house gets on fire we must not wait for clear water but put it out with dirty water if that is nearest." He bluntly warned conservatives that "if they remain so squeamish about their company, Henry Wilson will carry Massachusetts politics in his breeches pocket these 5 years." Winthrop, who persisted in his opposition to the Republican party despite such level-headed advice, preferred to believe that he had traveled the high road of principle, but in actuality he had fumbled his brightest opportunity to return to public life, moderate the antislavery movement, and help shape the destiny of his country.[85]

A new attempt to unite the opposition to the Democrats commenced nominally under the direction of the Know Somethings. In the middle of August a circular appeared, signed by generally lesser men from all parties, which announced a meeting on August 16 at Chapman Hall in Boston to promote fusion. Richard Henry Dana, Jr., expressed the fear of many that the Know Nothings would try to control this meeting for their purposes. "There is so much juggle in politics that one cannot trust to, & has no right even, to act upon the mere outer form of things." Even so, he concluded that "the risk must be run" and decided to participate. "The demand for fusion was great," he explained, and "there might not be another opportunity" to combine the anti-Democratic factions. The meeting was well attended, although most present were veterans of the Free Soil party, led by Stephen C. Phillips, Charles Allen, Dana, and Adams. Still, a few prominent politicians of other parties showed up, including Wilson and Foster from the Know Nothings, ex-governor George Boutwell, the only Democrat of any importance in attendance, Peleg E. Aldrich, the head of the Know Somethings, along with Samuel Bowles, ex-governor George Bliss, and former congressman John Z. Goodrich representing the Whigs. Since Whig opposition had blocked fusion the previous year, party members were assigned key positions: Goodrich served as president and Bowles was chairman of the committee on business. Laying down antislavery as the common basis of action, the assembly appointed a committee to consult with other parties to arrange a mass convention to organize a Republican party. Prior to meeting with committees representing the other anti-Democratic parties, the Chapman Hall committee, acting on a private warning that the Know Nothings were preparing a trap, decided to welcome individual recruits from other parties but avoid cooperating with existing organizations. In effect, the committee demanded that the Know Nothings disband if they wanted to take part in the Republican movement—a position intended to demolish the pro-fusion pretensions of Governor Gardner.[86]

On August 22 at the United States Hotel the Chapman Hall committee met with the representatives of the Know Nothings, the Know Somethings, and the Free Soilers. The conference, which lasted all day and into the evening, did not go smoothly. The main stumbling block was the determination of the Know Nothings to control the fusion

85. Wilson, *Slave Power*, v. 2, 433; Amos A. Lawrence Diary, August 29, Lawrence Papers.

86. Lucid, ed., *Dana Journal*, v. 2, 677–79; Richard Henry Dana, Jr. to Adams, August 14 (quotation), Adams Diary, August 15, 16, 17, 20, 23, Adams Family Papers; Springfield *Republican*, August 17; Boston *Daily Bee*, August 17. The call appears in the Springfield *Republican*, August 13.

movement. Declaring that he was willing to fuse but not to be swallowed up, one member of the Chapman Hall committee criticized those Americans who intended to maintain their separate party organization while insisting that the fusionists nominate Gardner. Dominated by anti-Know Nothings, the Chapman Hall committee wanted to call a mass convention to adopt a platform and appoint a state central committee, to be followed by a delegate convention to nominate a state ticket. The committee's intention was to prevent the Know Nothings from controlling the new party. The Americans, in contrast, wanted only a delegate convention held, since they would have a good chance of electing a majority of delegates by virtue of the order's superior organization. The discussions broke up in discord, and a second meeting of the various opposition factions was eventually scheduled to arrange for a state convention. The main points of controversy were whether the call should exclude men who did not surrender their previous affiliations and whether the convention should be a delegate meeting or mass assembly. Finally, after another week of wrangling, all parties agreed to a Know Nothing compromise to hold two conventions, one a mass meeting and one a delegate convention (the latter to make nominations), both to meet in Worcester on September 20 to organize the Republican party. To promote harmony, the resulting call for the Worcester convention was directed simply to men "opposed to the extension of slavery."[87]

The key uncertainty remained whether the Know Nothings would control this convention and foist Gardner on the Republicans as their candidate for governor. Following the appearance of the Worcester convention call, the struggle between the anti-Know Nothings and the Gardnerites centered on election of delegates to the Worcester convention. Confident that with both the Republican and American nominations he would be invincible, Gardner avidly courted the fusionists, pledging his fidelity to the Republican party and warmly denying that his commitment to fusion was contingent on his renomination. Before long both groups were trading accusations of bad faith. The fusionists charged that, contrary to previous pledges, the Know Nothings were making arrangements in their lodges to swamp the delegate meetings and thereby control of the convention. Almost immediately one member of the Chapman Hall committee complained of the participation in fusion meetings of "men who want to prevent the formation of a new party—who mean to keep the power which their dishonest and jesuitical practices have temporarily gained and would be glad to make this movement tend to their own personal uses."[88] In reply, Gardner accused his enemies of using the same tactics they attributed to his friends. He was particularly irked with Bowles, who was waging a fierce battle in the columns of the Springfield *Republican* against the incumbent. Protesting his sincere support for fusion, the governor blamed Bowles for producing jealousies among antislavery men and causing them to expend their energies fighting one another. Not only would "a desperate battle" for the nomination be disastrous for the fusion movement in the coming election, Gardner warned, but its consequences "would last bitter and sweltering thro' the Presidential campaign." Gardner had devoted

87. New York *Tribune*, August 25; Boston *Daily Bee*, August 23, 30; Adams Diary, August 22, 25, 29, Adams to Bailey, September 2 (copy), Adams Family Papers; Homer Bartlett to George Bliss, September 18, George Bliss Papers, MassHS; Bean, "Transformation of Parties," 314–17; Lucid, ed., *Dana Journal*, v. 2, 679–80; Richard Henry Dana, Jr., to Richard Henry Dana, Sr., August 30, Dana Family Papers. The address of the Chapman Hall committee is given in the Springfield *Republican*, August 23.

88. T. D. Eliot to Richard Henry Dana, Jr., August 24, September 1 (quotation), Dana Family Papers; Adams Diary, September 3, 11, Adams Family Papers.

much time and effort to winning Bowles over, but the former's timid, self-serving course at the Philadelphia convention damned him forever in the eyes of the Massachusetts journalist. Gardner's protestations of support for fusion were insincere, Bowles claimed, and it would thus be "fatal" for the Republicans to nominate him. On the morning of the Worcester convention, the Springfield *Republican* argued that the governor was the only man who stood in the way of the successful inauguration of the Republican party in the state. "With him withdrawn all would be peace, confidence, faith, success."[89]

Afraid that no other candidate could carry the state, some fusionists were willing to acquiesce in Gardner's nomination on an antislavery platform that had no nativist plank. Most, however, were unwilling to accept his selection on any terms. Gardner's nomination "would be death to the movement," one fusion leader declared; another argued that it inevitably would be considered "not only as the indorsement but the continuance of the present administration and order of things."[90] To defeat the governor's well-organized campaign for the Republican nomination, the anti-Gardner forces needed a strong candidate, and after canvassing various possibilities they rallied behind former Whig senator Julius Rockwell. As late as the beginning of August, Rockwell had opposed fusion and stated that he expected to remain a Whig. But sometime during the ensuing weeks, he decided to go over to the Republicans. Before the convention, Moses Kimball and Richard Henry Dana secured Rockwell's endorsement in writing of the Republican movement and, so armed, formulated plans to block Gardner's takeover bid. Bowles denied later that there had been any prior coordination, but informed observers agreed that a Gardner triumph would precipitate a significant walk-out from the Republican convention.[91]

Despite contrasting views on the relative importance of nativism and antislavery, Gardner and Chase nevertheless occupied similar positions in the movement to organize a Republican party in their respective states. Both men made their nomination a condition for their support of the party; both defined their selection as the only test of the convention's ultimate fairness; and both intended to run on another ticket if denied the Republican nomination. Gardner was handicapped, however, by the fact that the Know Nothings were not united behind his candidacy. Distrustful of the sincerity of the governor's antislavery professions, Wilson and his circle, including Anson Burlingame and Foster, strongly opposed his renomination. Chase, by contrast, had very early driven from the field all antislavery candidates outside the American order. Furthermore, Gardner was unable to use the pre-convention threat of a bolt as effectively as did Chase. The opposition to Gardner stemmed from his shallow antislavery principles, his blatant opportunism, and the recognition that his nomination would be regarded as a nativist triumph. But his enemies did not find it easy to exploit these objections, because

89. Gardner to Bowles, June 26, August 17, *Strictly & honorably Confidential*, August 20, September 17, *Private & Confidential*, Tuesday morning [August–September] (quotation), Bowles Papers; Bowles to Richard Henry Dana, Jr., September 15, Dana Family Papers; Springfield *Republican*, September 20.

90. Moses Kimball to Bliss, September 6, 17 (quotation), Homer Bartlett to Bliss, September 18 (quotation), Bliss Papers; Richard Henry Dana, Jr., to Rockwell, September 5, Rockwell Papers.

91. Bowles to Richard Henry Dana, Jr., September 15, Dana Family Papers; Dana to Rockwell, September 5, 13, Kimball and William Bingham to Rockwell, September 11, Rockwell to Bingham and Kimball, September 12 (private) (copy), Rockwell Papers; Winthrop to Clifford, August 2, September 24 (copies), Winthrop Papers; Rockwell to Dana, September 11, Dana Family Papers; Bowles to Dawes, October 10, Dawes Papers.

Gardner's support of the northern bolt at Philadelphia bolstered his antislavery image, and any severe arraignment of nativism threatened to drive antislavery Know Nothings from the Republican camp. As a result, Gardner's enemies resorted to the strategy of questioning the sincerity of his allegiance to the fusion movement. In the face of this assault, the incumbent could hardly adopt the strategy Chase employed and let it be known that if he were denied the Republican nomination he would accept another. Such action would have destroyed any chance he had to head the Republican ticket. The logic of the situation forced the Gardnerites to be much more circumspect in their demands, and consequently they were much less effective at intimidating their opponents.

When the two conventions assembled in Worcester on September 20, all of Nathaniel Banks's great skill as a presiding officer was required to maintain even a semblance of order.[92] Convention managers decided to draft a platform before making nominations so as to bind the candidates to the platform. Largely written by Dana, the Republican platform concentrated exclusively on the issue of slavery, which it denoted "the paramount practical question in the politics of the country." Unlike the American state platform, which merely called for the restoration of the Missouri Compromise, the Republican platform opposed (in somewhat indirect language) the admission of new slave states. Although it contained no nativist plank, the platform did not demand "conformity of opinion on other subjects of national or state policy." State and local issues received no attention.

Once the platform had been approved, the delegates turned their attention to the gubernatorial nomination. Wilson and a number of his associates lobbied against Gardner, but for tactical reasons they took no leading role. Bowles and Goodrich also toiled unceasingly to unite the anti-Know Nothing forces. The most prominent leader, however, was Dana. In a bid for support, one of Gardner's lieutenants read a letter from the governor that seemed to pledge that he would accept the results of the convention and not be the candidate of another party against the Republican nominee. On an informal ballot, Gardner led all challengers and was within twenty-four votes of a majority. For antislavery men, their worst fears were on the verge of fulfillment. At this point debate broke out anew over the governor's relationship to the Republican movement. Dana, the principal spokesman for the anti-Gardner forces, questioned the sincerity of Gardner's support for the party and, referring to Rockwell's letter endorsing fusion, urged the latter's nomination instead. Observers believed that Dana's forceful speech turned the tide. On a subsequent, formal ballot, Rockwell won the nomination over the badly disappointed incumbent. "We have passed a day of the most intense excitement, running on the verge of defeat all the while, but ending in the most entire & triumphant success," Dana wrote ecstatically that evening. With much justice Gardner characterized Dana as the "master spirit" of the anti-Know Nothing forces and sneered at the Worcester meeting as "Mr. Dana's Convention."[93]

---

92. For the convention's proceedings, see the Springfield *Republican*, September 21; Boston *Daily Bee*, September 21.

93. Kimball to Bliss, September 17, Richard Henry Dana, Jr., to Bliss, September 25, Bliss Papers; Dana to Sarah Dana, September 20, Dana Family Papers; Thomas D. Eliot to Rockwell, September 22, Rockwell Papers; Samuel Shapiro, *Richard Henry Dana, Jr., 1815–1882* (East Lansing, 1961), 102, 104. Several prominent future Republican leaders, including Adams, George Boutwell, and Sumner, who displayed something less than the rigid backbone he so often called for in his speeches, lent no aid to the struggle against Gardner and were conspicuous by their absence at Worcester. After the convention, Bowles unmercifully scored Sumner, "whose backbone," he acidly remarked, "was not strong enough to bring him to Worcester, & who

Because of Rockwell's former Whig affiliation and his continued good relations with many of that party's leaders, Republicans feared that the Whigs would also nominate him, thus destroying the Republican party's distinctiveness. Some Whigs openly advocated precisely this course. As a result, the Republican nominee was flooded with letters warning him against accepting the Whig nomination if tendered. Dana, in particular, was emphatic on this point, since in the convention debate he had specifically denied the possibility Rockwell would retain any ties to the Whigs. Another supporter thought Rockwell should "explicitly" sever his connection with the Whig party and declare himself "in politics, a Republican & nothing else." Hostility to the Whig dynasty was powerful among many Republicans, particularly those who were former Democrats and Free Soilers; these last two groups would not countenance any action that might resurrect Whiggery. In response to this pressure, Rockwell declined to be considered for the Whig nomination.[94] In the end, those Whigs who were unwilling to support a sectional party nominated conservative Samuel Walley in an irregular convention on a platform that denounced the Republican party without even rebuking the Kansas-Nebraska Act. In the words of one indignant former Whig, the party represented "the Hunker clique alone . . . men of the most illiberal & old foggish [fogyish] sentiments."[95]

While others were imploring Rockwell to avoid any further ties with Whiggery, Bowles correctly warned that the Know Nothings were the real danger. He feared that once rejected by the Republicans Gardner would seek a separate Know Nothing nomination, and indeed three weeks later at the Know Nothing state convention, a number of Gardner men who attended the Worcester convention joined hard-line nativists who always opposed fusion and nominated the governor for reelection.[96] Many moderate antislavery men who were unwilling to sacrifice their nativist principles remained faithful to Gardner and the American party. Defending the party's antislavery record in the 1855 legislature, they saw no legitimate reason for the formation of the Republican party. Gardner's acceptance of the American nomination left no doubt that his professed fusionist sentiments were, as his adversaries charged, a total sham.

Even so, the incumbent was a formidable foe. Skillfully blending moderate antislavery declarations with ardent nativist sentiments, Gardner had a great popular following

---

has had no part in this preparatory & most severe fight." Bowles to Dana, September 24, Dana Family Papers; Donald, *Sumner*, 227, 272–74. It should be noted that the vaunted Bird Club, which Baum credits with leading the struggle against nativist influence in the Massachusetts Republican party, played no significant role in Gardner's defeat at Worcester; indeed, leadership of the anti-Gardner forces rested in the hands of men at odds with the Bird faction. At the party's birth, as throughout the decade, the radical Bird Club was not a dominant element in Republican state politics. The large vote for Gardner in the Republican convention also calls into serious question Baum's argument that at its founding the Massachusetts Republican party was made up of hard-core antislavery men who were inflexibly hostile to nativism: *Civil War Party System*, 34–35.

94. Richard Henry Dana, Jr., to Rockwell, September 21, Robert Carter to Rockwell, September 22, Private, Bowles to Rockwell, September 25, Foster to Rockwell, September 22, D. W. Alvord to Rockwell, September 24, Seth Webb, Jr., to Rockwell, September 24 (Private), W. Bingham to Rockwell, September 25 (Confidential), Elizur Wright to Rockwell, September 21, T. D. Eliot to Rockwell, September 22, Rockwell Papers.

95. Springfield *Republican*, October 3; Henry H. Crapo to William W. Crapo, October 2, Henry W. Crapo Papers, University of Michigan; Israel D. Andrews to Hale, October 29, *Private*, Hale Papers, DarC.

96. Bowles to Rockwell, September 25, Rockwell Papers. For the proceedings of the Know Nothing convention, see the Boston *Daily Bee*, October 4. Bowles conceded that many "honest antislavery men" in the order saw no reason to repudiate the Springfield platform and join the Republican party. Bowles to Richard Henry Dana, Jr., October 15, Dana Family Papers. After the election, Greeley acknowledged that the Know Nothings' platform was "at least as Anti-Slavery as the Republican." New York *Tribune*, November 21.

backed by a well-organized personal machine both within and outside the Know Nothing lodges that extended to every part of the state. He remained confident of reelection, despite the desertion to the Republican cause of a number of former allies led by Wilson and Foster. The regular Americans particularly censured Wilson, whom they accused of betrayal after pledging to support Gardner for the fusion nomination, and of seeking to destroy the party that had elevated him to the Senate. They were less indignant with the more cautious Banks, who supported Rockwell, but who also needed nativist backing in his bid for the speakership and therefore curbed his campaigning in the state election and strove to keep on good personal terms with Gardner.[97]

Encouraged by the rupture of the Know Nothings, Bowles projected a Republican victory, as did Wilson. Another Republican manager, however, contrasted the party's disorganized condition with the smooth operation of the Know Nothing machine. "*We have a big fight before us*," he warned in cautioning against overconfidence. Even Bowles admitted that the popular mind was unusually unsettled. "Gardner's partizans are spending money, traversing the state, waking up the Council fires, poisoning the public mind, misrepresenting the Worcester Convention, & playing the deuce generally," he reported.[98] Gardner and his supporters pursued a dual strategy. Defending their own antislavery principles, they portrayed the Republican party as a fanatical abolitionist crusade—a theme the Whig campaign also emphasized. At the same time, Gardner carefully kept nativism before the voters. Some Republicans, most notably Bowles, stressed the importance of meeting this issue. From the western part of the state, a Republican editor reported that, in the absence of any assurance that Rockwell favored American principles, a large number of electors in that section would vote for Gardner. Republicans, however, found themselves in an impossible situation. Not only was a vocal section of the party adamantly opposed to any accommodation with nativism, realistically the party could never outbid Gardner for nativist support.[99]

Although the Republican party made a respectable showing in its first state campaign, Gardner won reelection, leading Rockwell by a count of 51,674 to 36,521 votes. Rockwell finished second, ahead of the Democratic nominee Edward Beach, who polled 34,920 votes, and Samuel Walley, who was a distant fourth on the straight Whig ticket with only 14,454 votes. Unlike his showing in the previous year, in 1855 Gardner failed to win a majority, as the Know Nothing total declined by 29,829 votes from 1854. Rockwell's strength was concentrated in two areas, the old Free Soil stronghold around Worcester and the Connecticut River valley, which had been strongly Whig in the past and had opposed Know Nothingism.

Wilson, a perceptive analyst, believed that the Republicans had committed two critical

97. Lawrence Diary, September 21, Lawrence Papers; Bean, "Transformation of Parties," 321–22, 324–25; Boston *Daily Bee*, October 4, 9; McKay, *Wilson*, 101–2; Fred H. Harrington, *Fighting Politician: Major General N. P. Banks* (Philadelphia, 1948), 24–25. Prior to the Worcester convention, Banks refused to endorse fusion openly until Gardner also pledged support, and as chairman of the convention the congressman stayed safely out of the fray.

98. Adams Diary, October 3, Adams Family Papers; Bowles to Richard Henry Dana, Jr., October 15 (quotation), Dana Family Papers; Bowles to Dawes, October 10, Seth Webb, Jr., to Bowles, October 9 (quotation), Dawes Papers.

99. C. Jillison to Rockwell, October 13, Bowles to Rockwell, September 25, Rockwell Papers; E. L. G. Green to Robert Carter, October 18, Carter Papers; New York *Tribune*, October 29. For Gardner's emphasis on nativism in his campaign, see Charles Delano to Rockwell, October 22, Rockwell Papers; Henry H. Crapo to William W. Crapo, October 2, Crapo Papers.

errors. First, they had been too hostile to the Know Nothings. He particularly deprecated the course of Dana, who believed that the nativist organization was in dissolution and consequently argued against making any concessions to the Americans. "He and all of us overestimated the power of the Anti Slavery sentiment and underestimated the power of old organizations," was Wilson's assessment. Second, once the ticket had been selected, Republican leaders dawdled before taking the field and wasted precious time that could have been used to perfect the party's organization and bring the issues before the electorate. For special criticism he singled out Sumner, who hesitated to challenge Gardner's power and would not speak until eleven days before the election when "we were beaten beyond the hope of recovery."[100] Other Republicans pointed to additional causes: the "malignant opposition" of the straight Whigs, the failure to get out the full Republican vote, the continuing power of nativism, the difficulty of exploiting national issues in a state contest, and the fact that Gardner ran on a moderate free soil platform and thus prevented a clear choice on the slavery issue. Goodrich regretted that the election "ran largely into a more personal fight, & in it we lost many who ought to have been & were at heart with us."[101]

In many ways, the election was a personal triumph for Gardner. He was opposed not only by Wilson but also by the president of the state council, every state officer elected with him in 1854, and most of the Know Nothing congressmen, and yet he still managed to win. Characteristically, Gardner was immodest about his achievement, and he took special pleasure in Wilson's mortification, recalling the senator's earlier threat to blow the American party to hell. Designating Wilson "the grand leader of 'fusion,' its chief fugleman," the governor rejoiced, "He is down here deeper than he ever was before."[102]

Massachusetts political alignments shifted considerably in 1855. Only the 1854 Free Soilers voted as a unit, and even the Democrats suffered defections (Table 7.12). Rockwell, in fact, received support from members of all the 1854 parties, with former Americans constituting the largest bloc in the Republican coalition. Gardner retained only about half his original 1854 supporters, as a significant number went over to the Democrats (these were probably former party members disillusioned with the Know Nothings), and a slightly larger group followed Wilson into the Republican ranks. The governor's strength among new and previously apathetic voters partly compensated for these losses; adding to his margin of victory was Rockwell's failure to make any inroads with these two groups. Gardner's gains among members of the major parties, on the other hand, were limited and, as a number of observers concluded, came entirely at the expense of the dying Whig organization.

The old Whig coalition in Massachusetts shattered completely in the 1855 election. Only somewhat more than a third of the 1854 Whigs (who in turn represented only a portion of the usual Whig strength) remained loyal to the party, and only a slightly smaller proportion voted for either Rockwell or Beach (Table 7.12). Whig losses were even more

---

100. Wilson to Chase, December 17, Chase Papers, HSPa. John Z. Goodrich, another able Republican manager, also stressed the importance of the Republican attacks on Gardner and the Know Nothings in producing the overall result. Goodrich to Rockwell, November 8, Rockwell Papers.

101. T. D. Eliot to Rockwell, November 6 (quotation), Rockwell Papers; Sumner to Seward, November 11, Seward Papers, UR; Edward L. Pierce to Chase, November 9, Goodrich to Chase, November 17, Chase Papers, LC.

102. Gardner to George R. Morton, November 17 (quotation), George R. Morton Papers, Hayes Memorial Library; Gardner to Daniel Ullmann, November 12, Ullmann Papers, NYHS.

startling compared to Scott's performance in 1852; no fewer than nine out of ten of the general's supporters voted for another party or abstained in 1855 (Table 7.13). Contemporaries were probably correct in surmising that those who voted for Walley or Beach came largely from the conservative wing of the party while those who backed Rockwell or Gardner were more antislavery in their sentiments. Edward Everett claimed that had the Democratic party not endorsed the Nebraska bill, the conservative Whigs would have voted for Beach "almost *en masse*" in order to rebuke Gardner's unprincipled course and the pretensions of the fusionists.[103]

As a result of these electoral shifts, the Massachusetts Republican coalition in 1855 was significantly different from that of the American party (Tables 7.12 and 7.13). One-time Whigs and Free Soilers, many of whom had voted Know Nothing in 1854, accounted for virtually all the Republican votes in the 1855 gubernatorial election. At the same time, Rockwell attracted only a limited number of Democrats. Gardner's support, in contrast, was more broadly based, with almost as many former Democrats as Whigs voting for him, along with a substantial number of new and previous non-voters and a small minority of Free Soilers. Former Whigs and especially Free Soilers seem to have accounted for most of the desertions from the American order to the Republicans, whereas Democratic-Americans generally withheld their support from the Republican movement. Apparently, those ex-Democrats who abandoned the American party for the most part returned to their earlier loyalty or did not vote. Even with Rockwell's strong showing among Whigs, approximately a quarter of those who voted for Scott remained in the American organization.

At a well-attended meeting in Boston after the election, Massachusetts Republicans manifested a determination to perfect the party's organization and continue the battle. Looking for a silver lining, Dana proclaimed that the election sealed the fate of the Whig party, and that its remaining members would have to choose in the future between the Republicans and the Democrats, or else be defiled with Know Nothingism.[104] Still, the major roadblock to the formation of a Republican majority remained the power of the American party. The election returns left no doubt that nativism retained its potency in the Commonwealth. Rockwell's failure to gain a larger share of the Know Nothing vote doomed his candidacy, and for Republicans to carry the state, they had to win additional nativist support. "The people will not confront the issues we present," wrote one despondent Republican in summarizing the election's significance. "They want a Paddy hunt & on a Paddy hunt they will go."[105]

VI

In contrast to the tactics of their brethren in other states, New York Republicans took decided ground against the proscriptive principles of the Know Nothings. In part, this divergent response arose from the sincere opposition to nativism of the Seward Whigs and

---

103. Edward Everett to Mrs. Charles Eames, November 7, Typescript, Everett Papers; Boston *Telegraph*, November 7, quoted in Bean, "Transformation of Parties," 327.

104. Adams Diary, November 16, Adams Family Papers; Seth Webb, Jr., to Rockwell, November 17, Goodrich to Rockwell, November 8, Dana to Rockwell, November 18, Rockwell Papers; Goodrich to Seth Webb, Jr., November 9, Miscellaneous MSS, Boston Public Library.

105. Edward L. Pierce to Chase, November 9 (quotation), Chase Papers, LC; J. P. Gould to Nathaniel P. Banks, Jr., n.d. [in December 1–15, 1855 folder], Nathaniel P. Banks, Jr., Papers, LC.

free soil Democrats. It also reflected the prevailing reality of New York politics. The vitriolic hatred of William H. Seward and Thurlow Weed among the Silver Greys, many of whom had gone into the American order, made impossible any cooperation between Republican and Know Nothing leaders. Consequently, Weed wanted to organize a Republican party that attracted support from antislavery nativists but avoided any collaboration with the order. In Ohio and Massachusetts, Republican organizers also avowed such an intention, but in reality they negotiated with the Know Nothings as a separate entity. Because the New York Know Nothings were "a different breed from those in other Northern states," one Sewardite argued that "we can do nothing with them so profitable as to knock them in the head & bury them deep under ground as fast as possible."[106] Presenting contrasting modes of party formation, New York and Ohio Republicanism offered alternative visions of the way to build a powerful Republican party.

Fusion had failed in New York in 1854 because of the resistance of Thurlow Weed. Throughout the early months of 1855 the Whig dictator kept his counsel as to his future intentions so as not to endanger William H. Seward's reelection to the Senate. But once the dust from the 1854 election had settled, the Whig boss recognized that the party was dead. With the Whig organization in shambles in so many states, it could not be rallied for the 1856 presidential campaign even if it remained strong in New York—something that was far from certain in any case. The 1854 election had demonstrated that free soil Democrats would not support a Whig ticket even on the Nebraska issue. Citing the course of the Whigs in 1854, Barnburner leader Henry B. Stanton complained that instead of embracing fusion Seward and his associates wanted everybody to become a Whig. A number of antislavery Democrats were "ready to fuse," he asserted, "but not to become Whigs." Furthermore, if the Whig party were sustained, New York would be out of step with the other northern states, where the opposition was uniting under the Republican banner. "The necessity for getting in line with other states is imperative," Weed told Seward, looking ahead to 1856. "National parties depend upon national needs," the Albany leader contended in an editorial. "No permanent organization can be created by skillful management, or maintained by prolonged intrigue, unless there exists in public affairs a necessity, and in the public mind a demand, for such an organization to meet some actual and present emergency."[107]

Once Seward had been reelected, Weed gravitated toward the Republican movement. Although he did not specifically call for abandoning the Whig organization, his hopes for a harmonious fusion were clear. Other Whigs concurred in this decision. Horace Greeley, who had wanted to organize a fusion anti-Nebraska party in 1854, continued to advocate the Republican cause. Governor Myron H. Clark reported that there was a "rage for some new organization," and another Weed follower announced that "the time for fusion has now come." Encouraged by the rupture of the national American party, one of Weed's correspondents, in urging that a fusion antislavery party be organized, emphasized: "This is, if not the last, at least the best opportunity that will occur for many years."[108]

Despite his close ties to Weed, Seward conspicuously refrained from any active role in

---

106. E. Peshine Smith to Henry C. Carey, June 8, Carey Papers.

107. Henry B. Stanton to Sumner, May 31, Sumner Papers, HU; Weed to Seward, July 23, Seward Papers, UR; Albany *Evening Journal*, September 22; Hiram Barney to Henry Wilson, June 26 (copy), Hiram Barney Papers, HEH.

108. Myron H. Clark to Seward, February 15, Seward Papers, UR; E. Peshine Smith to Carey, February 10, Carey Papers; Henry W. Taylor to Weed, June 30, Weed Papers, UR.

the formation of the Republican party in New York. Aware of the negotiations under way to organize the party, he declared as late as May that he would die a Whig and showed no enthusiasm for the Republican movement. He derived little comfort from the thought of joining a new party that included a number of lifelong adversaries, and prior to the organization of the New York Republican party he did not publicly endorse fusion. Only when the campaign commenced did Weed pressure the senator to assume leadership of the Republican cause. Whatever his later services to the party, Seward was at its beginning a reluctant convert at best, one whose hesitancy stood in stark contrast to the boldness of his rival Chase.

While Weed sought to rally Whig opinion, the most important Democrat who pushed fusion was Preston King. The former congressman's dramatic exit from the 1854 Soft convention propelled him to the forefront of those anti-Nebraska Democrats who could not stomach their party's equivocal stand on the expansion of slavery. King inherited leadership of these Democrats virtually by default. Most of the old Free Soilers, such as Martin Van Buren and Benjamin F. Butler, were no longer politically active, whereas of the younger leaders John Van Buren's primary concern remained national party recognition of the Softs, Samuel Tilden displayed no interest in another party bolt, and John A. Dix, after a futile attempt to obtain a place in the Pierce administration, had largely withdrawn from public life. Moreover, the New York *Evening Post* clung to the independent course it had adopted in 1854 when it endorsed no candidate for governor and remained deeply suspicious that any fusion movement in New York would come under Whig control. Still, after consulting with other leaders in Albany, King reported optimistically that "the vague idea of the necessity for those who agree in principles and measures to come together and to act together . . . is gradually developing itself and growing more clear to the minds of all."[109]

The fears of the Democrats that the new party would be Whiggery in disguise had to be allayed. A Republican leader firmly rejected the suggestion of John Schoolcraft, Weed's top lieutenant, that the Republican convention be postponed until after the Whig state convention in order to prepare the way for fusion. Such a step, he argued, "would make us subject to the charge of being a mere tender to the Whig party, a charge which was made to tell against us last fall, and certain to deprive us of the support" of the free soil Democrats. After consulting with New York Democratic leaders, Montgomery Blair disclosed that King and John Bigelow intended to unite with the Seward Whigs. He predicted that this decision would prove "a mistake," because Democrats "always come off second best in these 'fusions.'" At this time Blair believed that remaining in the Democratic party and fighting for antislavery principles was preferable to "an alliance with Seward."[110]

By July Weed was optimistic that a Republican party could be formed that would include free soil Democrats and yet be dominated by Whigs. Apparently, he toyed with the idea of a People's convention, which would obviate the impression that fusion represented a bargain among party leaders, but probably because of the difficulty of controlling such an arrangement discarded this plan. Eventually, fusion leaders decided to call two state conventions, one Whig and the other Republican, to meet in Syracuse on

109. King to Azariah C. Flagg, March 5 (quotation), Flagg Papers; King to Hannibal Hamlin, January 6, April 12, Hamlin Papers; Welles to King, November 25, 1854, April 23, 1855 (copies), Welles Papers, LC.
110. Joseph J. Chambers to Clark, July 12, Myron H. Clark Papers, NYSL; Montgomery Blair to Francis P. Blair, Sr., June 27, Blair-Lee Papers; Haven to Fillmore, June 29, Fillmore Papers, SUNY.

September 26. The two conventions were scheduled late in the political season, after the Softs and Know Nothings had selected their state tickets, in order to lure any dissenters from these earlier meetings. Although fusion of the two gatherings was not specified, the Albany *Evening Journal* carried notices of both conventions at its masthead, thus making the intent of the dual call readily apparent. When one delegate, perplexed about which meeting to attend, asked for advice, Seward replied that it made no difference: The delegates would go in by two doors, he explained, but they would all come out through one.[111]

It was important that the so-called Republican convention be well attended, but, in the absence of any efficient organizational apparatus, the New York *Tribune* announced that "the rank and file will have to manage for themselves." It recommended that local meetings select delegates "of diverse by-gone politics, if that be feasible." To provide badly needed leadership, particularly in areas where anti-Nebraska Democrats were not active, Whigs who had participated in the 1854 Saratoga convention assumed control of the Republican movement. In addition, a number of pro-fusion Whigs attended the Republican convention to ensure that it would be a respectable gathering and that there would be no problem with union.[112]

Prior to the Whig and Republican conventions, the Know Somethings and the Choctaws (the pro-Seward Know Nothings who had bolted in 1854) held conventions, agreed to combine the two organizations, and then adjourned until after the two major conventions met. This action signaled the end of both societies, which intended to merge with the Republicans once that party had organized.

The Whig and Republican conventions assembled separately on the twenty-sixth.[113] Sentiment for fusion was almost unanimous in both bodies, and each convention appointed a committee to discuss a union of the two groups. This conference recommended that each convention name a resolutions committee and a nominating committee to confer jointly with its counterpart. By requiring agreement on a ticket before fusion was consummated, the conferees gave each side a veto over its composition. This rather cumbersome procedure was probably adopted to allay Democratic fears of being overwhelmed by the Whigs. The excessive size of the nominating committee—it had sixty-four members—militated against any quick agreement, as did party jealousies and rival personal ambitions, which lay beneath the surface of outward harmony. As the deliberations of the nominating committee dragged on into the evening, both conventions finally adjourned until the next day.

Late that day the committee formulated an acceptable compromise. The nominations were apportioned carefully between the parties, with Preston King's nomination for secretary of state counterbalanced by the selection of James M. Cook, a Whig, for comptroller. Free Soil leader Abijah Mann, the Republican choice for this latter office, agreed instead to accept the nomination for attorney general. Mann assured Weed that he appreciated that Democrats could not receive the two most important spots on the ticket, but removing Mann from the comptrollership represented more than a desire to balance the ticket. As members of the canal board, the secretary of state and comptroller wielded critical power over the management of the state canal system, including the enlargement

---

111. Weed to Seward, July 12, Seward Papers, UR; Barnes, *Memoir of Weed*, v. 2, 233; James C. Hopkins to Weed, July 17, Weed Papers, UR; Seward, *Seward*, v. 2, 254; J. J. Chambers to Clark, July 10, Clark Papers.

112. New York *Tribune*, August 24; N. Darling to Weed, September 2, Weed Papers, UR.

113. The convention proceedings are in the New York *Tribune* and New York *Times*, September 27, 28.

program currently under way. To put guidance of enlargement, so dear to former Whigs, in the hands of King and Mann, who had been its conspicuous opponents, was more than Whigs could have borne.[114]

The joint resolutions committee had less difficulty reaching agreement. Devoted largely to the slavery issue, the platform demanded the exclusion of slavery from all territories, denounced the proslavery frauds in Kansas and Reeder's removal, and opposed the admission of new slave states. One plank was devoted to Know Nothingism. Terming secret political organizations as "inconsistent with the liberal principles of our free Government," it declared, "we repudiate and condemn the proscriptive and anti-republican doctrines of the order of Know-Nothings, and all their secret constitutions, oaths, rituals, and organizations." The New York platform was the only 1855 Republican state platform explicitly to condemn the Know Nothings. Another resolution dealt with the canal question. It upheld enlargement as a "settled" policy (thus pleasing the Whigs), but insisted upon an honest application of the enlargement fund and called for a system of strict accountability in its expenditure (thus appealing to the fiscally conservative Barnburners).

The Whig convention adopted the platform without dissent. In the Republican proceedings, however, a snag developed when a group of delegates sought to incorporate a pro-temperance resolution into the platform. Determined to sidestep the issue that had done so much to wreck their party, Whigs were immovable in their opposition. The Republicans finally agreed to accept the resolution as expressing the sense of the meeting, rather than including it in the party's formal declaration of principles. As one observer commented, it was no small matter to get two distinct bodies, containing some 400 men, "many of them presumptively impracticable," to agree on a common platform and ticket.[115]

Following adoption of the platform, the Whig convention adjourned, and the delegates rose and marched to Wieting Hall, where the Republicans were assembled. Led by Weed, they entered to tremendous applause. The combined convention, with the two chairmen, Reuben E. Fenton, a pro-fusion Soft, and John A. King, a Weed lieutenant, jointly presiding, ratified the platform and ticket; reaching out to disgruntled Democrats, the delegates also adopted two antislavery resolutions rejected by the Soft state convention. Before adjourning, the convention took the name *Republican* and appointed a state committee. The New York Republican party had been born.

Somewhat unexpectedly, prohibition had been a serious stumbling block to fusion. Surprisingly, Greeley, inspired by the possibility of forming the antislavery party he had called for during the Nebraska crisis, played a critical role in smothering the floor revolt over the platform's deliberate silence on the rum question. Speaking as chairman of the Republican resolutions committee, he opposed insertion of a prohibition plank in the platform, and afterwards he worked to prevent any independent temperance nominations. Little short of amazed at the change in the *Tribune* editor's attitude, one political observer remarked, "Greely [*sic*] acted in reference to temperance & other matters with a degree of wisdom that was not to be expected from him." The major concession the Republicans made to the anti-liquor forces was the nomination of Bradford Wood, a well-known dry, for the state Court of Appeals, which would decide the constitutionality of the new

---

114. Abijah Mann, Jr., to Weed, September 27, Weed Papers, UR.
115. E. Peshine Smith to Carey, October 3, Carey Papers.

temperance law.[116] The state temperance convention endorsed most of the Republican state ticket.

A number of conservative Whigs, however, led by former governor Washington Hunt and Senator Hamilton Fish, refused to countenance a sectional party. While reaffirming his opposition to the expansion of slavery, Hunt pronounced the Republican party a threat to the Union and declared, "I could not join such a movement without committing a crime against my country." Fish also criticized the Republican movement despite his continued opposition to the repeal of the Missouri Compromise. He proposed to unite with Whigs who were untainted with Silver Greyism or Know Nothingism and indicate their "unwillingness to make the Slavery question the 'be-all & end all' of political organization, & of political strife." Hunt and Fish no doubt spoke for many conservative Whigs when they intimated that they had no faith in those Democrats who had joined the Republican party. When criticized by a past associate, Fish responded that he could not support men whose political principles he had resisted his entire life, and with whom he had "at most but one, & probably not one political sentiment in common."[117]

A straight Whig convention assembled in New York City in late October. Although slightly more than half the state's counties were represented, fully a quarter of the delegates were from New York City, and the upstate representatives generally gave discouraging reports. The delegates approved a set of resolutions that denounced the Republican party and urged Whigs to vote against the Republican ticket.[118] The rapid course of events, the desertion of the Silver Greys to the Know Nothings, and the movement of the Sewardites into the Republican ranks made ridiculous this attempt to resurrect the Whig party.

Under Daniel S. Dickinson's guidance, the Hards continued their pro-southern policies in order to gain recognition at the 1856 national convention. Their platform reaffirmed support for the Nebraska Act; pointedly missing was any condemnation of the Missouri frauds or any praise for the Pierce administration. Seeking to silence Democratic criticism of the Hards' well-documented affinity for the Know Nothings, the convention also passed a resolution condemning all secret societies that proscribed men on account of religion or nationality. Despite this public stance, the surreptitious ties between the two groups continued. Dickinson played a double game: Publicly he continued to avow his Democratic loyalty, while privately he favored the Know Nothings.[119]

For the Softs, events in Kansas posed a much greater difficulty, because unlike the Hards the preservation of a strong state electoral base was a primary consideration with them, and therefore they had to steer a careful course so as not to offend either New York public opinion, which generally disapproved the Kansas frauds, or the president, who had showered them with federal appointments. At the Soft state convention those platform

---

116. New York *Tribune*, August 24; E. Peshine Smith to Carey, October 3 (quotation), September 21, Carey Papers; John Jay to Hale, September 16, Hale Papers, NHHS; N. Darling to Weed, September 20, Weed Papers, UR.

117. Washington Hunt to Fish, October 7 (quotation), Fish Papers, LC; Hunt to Weed, August 10, Weed Papers, UR; Hunt to Samuel B. Ruggles, October 7, Washington Hunt Papers, NYSL; Fish to Robert E. West, October 22 (copy), Fish to Hunt, October 6 (Confidential) (quotation), Fish to Edgar Ketcham, October 17 (quotation) (copies), Fish Papers, LC.

118. New York *Tribune*, October 24.

119. New York *Tribune*, August 24, 25; William Cassidy to Horatio Seymour, August 18, Horatio Seymour Papers, NYSL; John Slidell to Buchanan, October 11, Buchanan Papers, HSPa; Berger, *New York Party Systems*, 88.

planks that attacked the Whig state policies as profligate, denounced the Know Nothings, and called for repeal of the state's new prohibitory liquor law caused no problems.[120] But the convention erupted into a bitter fight over the slavery issue. A large contingent of rural free soilers resisted the leadership of federal officeholders and demanded approval of resolutions that condemned the repeal of the Missouri Compromise and the proslavery frauds in Kansas. They warned that without an anti-Nebraska platform the party stood no chance in the coming election. After wrangling most of the day, the delegates accepted a compromise declaration that acquiesced in the Kansas-Nebraska Act as an accomplished fact but demanded it be strictly enforced and, while silent on Pierce's conduct, criticized interference with free elections in the territory. With the potentially explosive slavery issue apparently thus disposed of, John Van Buren startled the convention managers by introducing the so-called Corner Stone resolution, adopted by the 1848 Barnburner convention, which had heralded the beginning of the Free Soil movement. This resolution, while it pledged to adhere to all compromises of the Constitution, also proclaimed "fixed hostility to the extension of slavery into free territory." Emotions ran high on the floor as the exhausted delegates finally approved the platform with Van Buren's amendment attached. When party leaders expressed considerable anger with Van Buren, he rejoined that without the resolution Democratic-Republicans, led by Preston King, would destroy his influence with the Barnburners. As was true in 1854, national and state considerations forced the Softs to follow a policy of expediency and equivocation on the territorial controversy.[121]

The Know Nothings also had great difficulty with the Kansas issue. At the national council meeting in Philadelphia, the New York delegates, under the tight leadership of James W. Barker, endorsed the pro-southern majority platform, and none participated in the northern bolt. Almost immediately state party leaders, especially in the western counties, denounced the controversial Twelfth Section upholding the repeal of the Missouri Compromise. Some wanted the slavery issue omitted entirely from the American platform, but those more in tune with popular sentiment demanded that the offending section be repudiated by the state council. Even the Buffalo *Commercial Advertiser*, which was Millard Fillmore's unofficial organ, took ground against the platform. One Know Nothing warned Daniel Ullmann that in voting for the national platform the New York delegates to the national council "entirely mistook & misrepresented four fifths of the voters of this State." The Twelfth Section, he declared, mincing no words, "must come out forthwith in this state or we are lost!" A nativist congressman was equally frank: "With the Slavery clause in the platform I very much doubt whether a single County in the State can be carried." Desirous of preserving the party's nationality, Know Nothing leaders nonetheless were unwilling to jeopardize their state power. As one Silver Grey advised, "We must look out for ourselves."[122]

As had been true in every other northern state, the New York state council, which

120. Convention proceedings are in the New York *Tribune*, New York *Times*, and Albany *Argus*, August 31, September 1.

121. John J. Taylor to William L. Marcy, November 2, John Van Buren to Marcy, September 20, Marcy Papers, LC; Slidell to Buchanan, October 11, Buchanan Papers, HSPa; Daniel S. Dickinson to Edmund Burke, September 2, Burke Papers. Disgusted with the Softs' waffling on the territorial controversy, the New York *Evening Post*, which had up to now resisted fusion out of fear of Whig dominance, endorsed the Republican movement following the Soft convention: September 2, 8.

122. J. D. Colver to Ullmann, July 21 (quotation), Killian Miller to Ullmann, June 24 (quotation), James R. Thompson to Ullmann, June 23, 28, August 14, Ullmann Papers, NYHS.

convened in Binghamton on August 18, rejected the Twelfth Section. Asserting that differences of opinion over slavery should be tolerated in the order, the American state platform condemned the Kansas-Nebraska Act and, although it did not call for restoration of the Missouri Compromise, declared vaguely that its repeal should not lead to the further expansion of slavery.[123] In effect, Silver Grey leaders, who were willing to make substantial concessions to the South, were forced to confront the fact that the party could not retain its rural supporters, particularly in the Burned Over District, with a platform upholding the Kansas-Nebraska Act. Members of the order had not necessarily lessened their commitment to nativist principles, but it was evident that a significant proportion—indeed, a majority outside the large urban centers—would not accept the repeal of the Missouri Compromise.

Early in the summer as the campaign got under way Weed was optimistic. "It is possible that the state may be carried this fall. There are elements enough, if combined, to effect it." Before long, however, the Republican campaign became mired in serious difficulties. Perhaps the most obvious problem was lack of an efficient organization. The Republican party did not simply take over the Whig machine. The disintegration of the Whig party left its organizational apparatus in complete disorder, and thus a Republican party structure had to be created in a very short time. With obvious concern Henry B. Stanton, a Barnburner who joined the Republican party, informed Weed: "Everything in the shape of *organization* is in utter chaos—I mean the kind of minute & detailed organization having for its chief object the bringing of voters to the polls. All old *whig* committees are of course dissolved—& their substitutes are to a large extent yet to be appointed."[124] Furthermore, a number of traditional Whig contributors declined to join the Republican party, and consequently raising funds for the campaign was very difficult. Chastened by these troubles, a political colleague conceded to Seward, "I now see what you saw long ago, how hard it is to break up an old party and organise a new one."[125]

The basic Republican strategy in the campaign was to emphasize the slavery extension issue, particularly the situation in Kansas, and avoid the nativist and liquor controversies as much as possible. "Weed & others hope to drown out all other questions by an agitation of the Slavery issue," Horatio Seymour predicted accurately. Despite the Republicans' quasi-rejection of the prohibition plank, the Softs devoted considerable effort to linking the Republican party with temperance. The liquor issue hurt the Republicans, one antislavery man reported, because Gemans who were free soil in their sentiments refused to support a ticket that they felt represented a temperance party in disguise. As in 1854, the Softs hoped to make rum the dominant issue in the state election. At the same time, the Know Nothings continued to exploit the nativist issue by linking Weed, Seward, and Republicanism to Catholicism.[126]

Republicans were frustrated in their attempt to take advantage of the Kansas issue, since both the Soft and the Know Nothing platforms deferred to anti-Nebraska sentiment

123. New York *Tribune*, New York *Times*, August 29, 30, 31.

124. Weed to Seward, July 23, Seward Papers, UR; Stanton to Weed, October 15, Henry B. Stanton Papers, NYHS; New York *Tribune*, October 20, 31; George E. Baker to Seward, August 3, Seward Papers, UR; Charles W. Elliott to Weed, September 27, 1856, Weed Papers, UR; letter signed "B.," *National Era*, October 11.

125. DeWitt Littlejohn to Weed, October 15, Weed Papers, UR; George E. Baker to Seward, October 17 (quotation), Seward Papers, UR.

126. Horatio Seymour to Marcy, July 31, Marcy Papers, LC; Jay to Sumner, October 13, Sumner Papers, HU; E G S [Elbridge G. Spaulding] to Dear Sir, October 14, Weed Papers, UR; E. Peshine Smith to Carey, September 4, Carey Papers.

in the state. Weed conceded that the Softs "by their half-way Resolutions prevent a general out-break" from their ranks, while another New York Republican complained that the Softs' pretended free soil principles caused many Democrats who inclined to the Republican cause to remain loyal to their party.[127] Requests for speakers who could influence wavering Democrats poured into Republican headquarters. Republican managers were uncertain how many Democrats would follow King and Mann into the new party, but they recognized that such accessions were crucial, especially in view of the obvious disaffection of a portion of the former Whig vote.

Heightening the difficulties the Republicans labored under was the continuing strength of the Know Nothings. American leaders reported a membership of 178,000 in May, and two months later the New York *Herald* placed the order's strength at 185,000 voters. How many members had defected to the Know Somethings, and how many intended to join the Republican party because of the American national platform, were imponderables. Still, Charles A. Dana was clearly premature in his assessment that "the K Ns, thank God, are in their graves." Without question the Americans were far better organized than the struggling Republicans. The primary cause of the order's loss in 1854 had been lack of time to organize interior towns and the northern part of the state. During the preceding twelve months, nativist leaders had devoted considerable attention to this matter. The Buffalo *Commercial Advertiser*, which acknowledged the inadequate organization the previous year, boasted at the conclusion of the 1855 contest that "the Order has put forth innumerable new branches, and their offshoots extend to every village and hamlet in the State."[128]

Although Republican leaders in New York were cautious in predicting victory, most thought the party stood a good chance of carrying the state. In fact, the Know Nothings were victorious, but the Republican party did reasonably well in its first campaign.[129] King polled only about 20,000 votes fewer than Myron Clark had received in 1854, and Republicans took solace in the fact that they outpolled both the Hards and the Softs to finish second. Some Democrats, on the other hand, preferred to point out that with the Hard and Soft totals added together the Democrats had a very slight advantage over the other two parties. In reality, however, the results offered little encouragement to Democrats, for the combined Hard-Soft vote declined some 40,000 votes compared to that of 1854. At the same time, the Know Nothings had managed to increase their total by only 26,000 votes—not a very impressive showing, considering the order's earlier organizational shortcomings. Furthermore, a large number of voters, as the high abstention rate indicated, lacked firm party loyalties in the existing political turmoil. "Many persons whom the dissolution of old parties had left afloat upon the sea of politics," the New York *Times* maintained, "have declined to vote until they see clearly pronounced the future course of those with whom they feel inclined to identify their fortunes."[130] Actually, the election revealed that none of the state parties was even close to achieving a majority.

---

127. Weed to Hale, September 6, Hale Papers, DarC; Hiram Barney to Chase, October 11, Chase Papers, HSPa; E. Peshine Smith to Carey, September 4, Carey Papers.

128. Charles A. Dana to Pike, August 23, Pike Papers, UMe; New York *Herald*, July 29; Buffalo *Commercial Advertiser*, October 29; Rochester *Daily Union*, October 26.

129. The final result was King (Republican), 136,698 votes (31.4 percent); Headley (American), 148,557 votes (34.1 percent); Hatch (Soft), 91,336 votes (21.0 percent); and Ward (Hard), 59,353 votes (13.6 percent).

130. New York *Times*, November 22. The total vote was some 33,000 votes below that of 1854, a decline of more than 7 percent.

One of the striking features of the returns was the weak relationship between the American vote in 1854 and that of 1855. Only about three-fifths of Ullmann's 1854 supporters cast Know Nothing ballots in 1855. In addition to significant abstentions, the Know Nothings suffered moderate defections to both the Republicans and the Softs (Table 7.14). The party's accessions since 1854 came largely from Whigs. During the campaign political observers emphasized the affinity of the Hardshell Democrats for the American cause, and indeed approximately one out of six Hard voters in 1853, when the party had run neck and neck with the Softs, voted Know Nothing (Table 7.16). Whig defectors probably were primarily conservatives who remained loyal to their party as long as it ran candidates and Whigs who lived in areas that nativist organizers had not penetrated the year before. Presumably, a large contingent of these latter Whigs would have voted for the Know Nothing ticket in 1854 had they been able to obtain ballots.

The Republican coalition, on the other hand, was overwhelmingly composed of former Whigs (Tables 7.14, 7.15, and 7.16). Not surprisingly, the party displayed no attraction to Hards, and what Democratic votes it received came from the Softs. The party actually did somewhat better at winning converts from the American ranks than from the Soft column. The Republican belief that a large number of rank-and-file Softs would bolt despite the refusal of most Soft leaders to support the new party proved unfounded. The Soft vote declined from the previous election not because former supporters went over to the Republicans, but because a large number of Hards who voted for Seymour in 1854 when prohibition was distinctly the issue now returned to their old allegiance. Many of these Democrats were probably Irish immigrants who had no sympathy with the Softs' antislavery pretensions, yet rallied behind Seymour after his veto of the prohibitory bill (Table 7.18). Less hostile to free soil principles, Germans, including apparently the non-Catholics, remained loyal to the Softs. In the Yankee-settled Burned Over District, where Know Nothing losses were especially severe, the Republican party made marked gains over the Whig showing the previous year. Weed, in particular, hailed Republican strength in the western counties as the foundation for a powerful party, but while the Republicans had generally run well in the rural districts, they had little strength in the large urban centers and had done poorly in the conservative, Yorker-dominated Hudson River valley (Map 9).[131]

Republican strategists preferred to overlook the party's lack of success at attracting Softs and its failure to secure a greater proportion of antislavery Know Nothings. Instead, they attributed the party's setback to poor organization. Greeley, for example, claimed that the true strength of the parties was such that there were 20,000 more Republican voters than Know Nothings, "but our active men for the polls had nearly all 'seen Sam [were Know Nothings],' and we could not get our votes to the polls. That is the whole story." Contrasting the party's poor organization with the Know Nothings' well-oiled machine, another Republican argued that under these circumstances the party did well to

---

131. Seward, *Seward*, v. 2, 258; Frederick Seward to William H. Seward, November 11, Seward Papers, UR; Albany *Evening Journal*, November 8. Yorkers were descendants of the Dutch settlers in New York. See Dixon Ryan Fox, *Yankees and Yorkers* (New York, 1940). New York City, where King finished last with less than twelve percent of the vote, was particularly hostile to Republicanism. The Know Nothing tally in the metropolis was more than three times his total, and the combined Democratic vote represented four times his strength. For an analysis of the Republican party's troubles in New York City, see Hendrik Booraem, V, *The Formation of the Republican Party in New York: Politics and Conscience in the Antebellum North* (New York, 1983), 156–63.

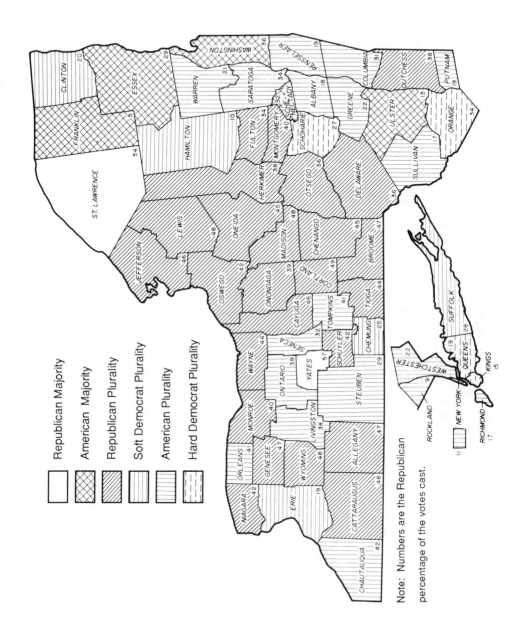

Note: Numbers are the Republican percentage of the votes cast.

9. New York Vote for Secretary of State, 1855

poll almost as many votes as the Americans. "The Hindoo [Know Nothing] organization is magnificent because it reaches every little nook, marshalling & drilling its forces in every school district almost," a Seward ally marveled. "We, on the other hand, formed the Republican party so late, that Whigs & Democrats had not finished looking at each others faces & wondering what company they had got into, when they were called to the polls." The New York *Evening Post* well expressed the prevailing point of view: "Considering that the Republican party was a sort of improvisation, an extempore affair, a spontaneous association of men not accustomed to act together, who came together reluctantly, and had no proper organization, it has done wonders." Even Seward, who admitted that the party had "rather a rough beginning," was confident that "it will work effectually in the end."[132]

The impossibility of creating an effective party organization in just six weeks obviously hindered the Republican performance, but it does not adequately account for the party's weakness. The party was also hurt by the moderate antislavery images of both the Know Nothings and the Softs. The American state council was careful to avoid any identification with the Nebraska Act, and the Softs' endorsement of the unpopular measure was mitigated by their denunciation of the proslavery frauds in Kansas and more especially by Van Buren's Corner Stone resolution. The results gave force to Van Buren's claim that such a declaration would hold the bulk of the Barnburners in the Soft ranks. In the end, Soft defections to the Republicans were significantly less than had been anticipated; those Softs who voted Republican were probably largely former Free Soilers (Table 7.17).[133]

In addition, the election returns revealed the unabated power of nativism in the state. Astonished by the Know Nothing victory, George Templeton Strong termed it "a resurrection from the dead," and commented, "Our antipathy to the Pope and to Paddy is a pretty deep-seated feeling." Republicans mistakenly assumed that most of the anti-Nebraska men had left the order, and they thus refused to make any concessions to the Americans—indeed, they had specifically denounced the nativist order in their platform. Overly confident, Greeley was particularly severe on the Know Nothings during the campaign. After visiting one county where antislavery Whigs had largely joined the nativist lodges and voted the American ticket, a Sewardite confessed that he had failed to give sufficient importance to the Binghamton platform, which, along with the adoption of strong antislavery resolutions by local councils, "blind the masses" to the order's true proslavery character. The outcome of the election also demonstrated that there were definite limits to the potency of the Kansas issue. Insisting that more issues were at stake

132. Greeley to Schuyler Colfax, November 13, Greeley-Colfax Papers; Hiram Barney to Chase, November 14, Chase Papers, HSPa; E. Peshine Smith to Carey, November 13 (quotation), Carey Papers; New York *Evening Post,* November 9, quoted in Berger, *New York Party Systems,* 97; Seward to W. McKinstry, November 8, Seward Papers, UR. "Hindoo" was a nickname for the Know Nothings in New York; it derived from the false accusation by Whigs in 1854 that Daniel Ullmann, the Know Nothing gubernatorial candidate, had been born in Calcutta.

133. William S. Cornwell to Fish, December 15, Fish Papers, LC; New York *Tribune,* November 3; letter signed "B.," *National Era,* November 22. One New York Democrat maintained that many Soft non-voters were 1848 Free Soilers who were unhappy with the Softs' recent course on the territorial controversy. Henry D. Rich to John Van Buren, November 21, Tilden Papers. Table 7.17 probably understates Whig strength in the Republican coalition; Tables 7.14 and 7.15 suggest that many of the 1848 Free Soilers who joined the New York Republican party in 1855 were ex-Whigs rather than the much-emphasized Barnburners. Not surprisingly, the overwhelming majority (80 percent) of the radical antislavery men who remained loyal to the Free Democratic party in 1853 voted Republican in 1855, with the remainder not voting rather than supporting any of the other parties.

than just slavery, conservatives rejoiced over the Republican defeat. The people of the North, the Know Nothing New York *Express* proclaimed, "do not mean to sacrifice all to Kansas."[134]

Also critical to the party's defeat was its weakness among immigrant voters (Table 7.18). The Republicans did well among native-born voters, but they had almost no strength among the Germans and Irish despite devoting substantial attention to the foreign-born. The liquor issue, which the Republican party could not entirely avoid, undoubtedly hurt it with foreign-born voters. Weed conceded that the Democrats received the liquor vote and "most of the votes of the adopted citizens." At the same time, he believed that the temperance voters had largely favored the Know Nothings. The Democrats carried Buffalo, which had previously contained a decisive Whig majority, thanks in part to solid support from immigrants, who, according to one paper, "gave an emphatic verdict against the prohibitory liquor law and the intolerant doctrines of the know-nothings."[135]

One consequence of the 1855 defeat was a surge of anti-Catholicism in several important Republican newspapers. On all sides there was substantial agreement that the Catholic vote had been cast solidly for the Democrats. A good example of this burgeoning anti-Catholic sentiment in the Republican party was the Buffalo *Express*, a leading Sewardite journal in western New York. Angered by the endorsement of the Soft ticket by the bishop's newspaper in Buffalo, the *Express* could not contain its resentment once the results were known. It charged that the Catholics voted "*en masse*" for the Democrats, "and the impression has obtained generally that they did so under instructions from their Priesthood." The Catholic church was nothing short of "a political institution" and "an auxilliary of the Democratic party."[136]

This failure to confront directly the causes of the Republican defeat, together with the party's respectable showing, fostered excessive optimism among New York party leaders. Seward argued that the Know Nothings would fall as rapidly as a balloon losing gas. "It is apparent that we could not, all at once, get the whole public mind engaged," he maintained. Republicans also believed that prohibition would no longer be a major issue, a circumstance that would enable the party to win a large share of foreign-born voters. In addition, party leaders were confident that the coming presidential election, by focusing attention on national issues, would aid their cause. They counted on the pressure of waging a national campaign to undermine both the Know Nothings' and the Softs' antislavery posture in the state. Next year "we shall be the only real party of Freedom," one of Seward's correspondents declared, and as a result "we shall attract to our side, thousands of Free Soil Democrats, and nearly all the Foreign vote."[137] Left unspoken was the election's most significant lesson: that combined, anti-slavery-extension and anti-Catholicism remained the most powerful political program in the state.

---

134. Nevins and Thomas, eds., *Strong Diary*, v. 2, 240–41; E. Peshine Smith to Carey, November 13, Carey Papers; New York *Express*, quoted in the *Chenango American*, November 15; *Chenango American*, November 8; William S. Cornwell to Fish, December 15, Fish Papers, LC.

135. Albany *Evening Journal*, November 6 (quotation), 7; Poughkeepsie *Eagle*, November 10; Buffalo *Express*, November 10; Buffalo *Daily Republic*, November 12 (quotation).

136. Buffalo *Express*, November 7 (quotation), 10, 11, 12, 13 (quotation), 14, 20.

137. King to Welles, November 17, quoted in Muller, "Preston King," 564; Seward to George Baker, quoted in Seward, *Seward*, v. 2, 259; E. Peshine Smith to Carey, November 13, Carey Papers; Amos W. Muzzy to Seward, November 20 (quotation), George M. Grier to Seward, November 12, Seward Papers, UR; Reuben Fenton to T. Napoleon Cheny, December 14, Miscellaneous MSS, NYSL.

VII

Contrary to rather strained professions of optimism among Republicans in New York and elsewhere, taken together the 1855 state elections represented an inauspicious beginning for the sectional party. In direct confrontations with the Know Nothings in New York and Massachusetts, the Republicans, despite the deteriorating situation in Kansas, went down to defeat, and in Pennsylvania Americanism was so powerful that the Republican party had been subverted by nativist subterfuge and was barely established.[138] In several other critical states, divisions among anti-Democratic factions were so deep that the Republican party still had not even organized. In the face of these numerous setbacks, Chase's election in Ohio, which Governor Kinsley S. Bingham of Michigan termed "the only real Anti Slavery victory that has been achieved this fall," took on added importance. Henry Wilson voiced a similar viewpoint when he told Chase after all the state contests were concluded, "Your election is the only bright spot in the political sky of this autumn."[139] The Ohio result, by encouraging Republicans in other states and intensifying the drive already inaugurated under Chase's direction to establish a national Republican organization, ensured that a serious effort would be made to field a Republican presidential ticket in 1856.

For Republicans, the 1855 elections offered several important insights. One was the necessity of minimizing the party's identification with the Maine Law. The most prescient Republican leaders had struggled against making prohibition a party doctrine, but in some states, most notably Maine and to a lesser extent New York, the prevailing political situation dictated Republican identification with temperance. In most states, either through popular referenda or by court decisions striking down prohibitory statutes, the liquor controversy was gradually losing its force, and elsewhere Republicans pointed to the 1855 results as demonstrating the necessity of excluding the question from the party's platform.

More important was the Republican party's inability to ride to victory on the Kansas issue alone. Indignation over Kansas affairs did not prove as powerful politically as party strategists had anticipated. Furthermore, the American party's refusal in the free states to adopt the pro-southern national platform seriously hampered Republicans' use of the Kansas controversy. By denouncing the situation in Kansas and agitating their traditional nativist issues, the Know Nothings retained a majority of their supporters, gained new converts to counterbalance their losses, and demonstrated that their appeal was more effective with the northern electorate. A perceptive Massachusetts Republican, who ascribed the defeat of the party in that state to the fact that "*it* is based upon an idea of *National* Policy while the officers to be chosen at this election were all [of] them *State* and local," emphasized: "You cannot bring the principles of national Politics *fully* to bear on State elections."[140]

The most important omen of these elections, however, was the continuing power of nativism in northern politics. The fundamental dilemma for Republicans was what policy

---

138. Referring to the results of the 1855 state elections, one Ohio nativist asked pointedly of the Republicans, "Where is their boasted strengh [*sic*] divested of that support which the Americans accorded to the Republican party in 1854?" Sidney D. Maxwell Diary, ca. December 2.

139. Bingham to Chase, November 16, Chase Papers, LC; Wilson to Chase, November 17, Chase Papers, HSPa; *National Era*, October 18.

140. Artemas Carter to Sumner, November 16, Sumner Papers, HU.

to adopt toward the Know Nothings. One group of Republicans, typified by the unlikely combination of Seward and Gamaliel Bailey, advocated unremitting hostility to the order's principles and leaders. Bailey was particularly severe on his old ally Chase, who he believed had made shameful concessions to the Americans in Ohio. John C. Vaughn, the president of the Know Somethings, who hoped to use that organization to destroy the American movement, likewise endorsed the policy of cutting loose from the Know Nothings. "Fight them, we must. Kill them we must, or else they will kill us," he warned Chase. Another of Chase's correspondents emphasized that "K Nism must be crushed out of the Republican Party, *now* henceforth, and forever."[141]

Other Republicans advocated the opposite policy of conciliating the nativists. A few urged endorsement of nativist principles. "Our Republican movement will best succeed if there be admitted a clause into the Platform expressing the general doctrine of Native Americanism," a Massachusetts man concluded. Most Republicans who urged a conciliatory approach were reluctant to go this far for fear of alienating the foreign vote, but they opposed vehement denunciations of the Know Nothings. One of Seward's western correspondents, who believed that the great mass of the American party could be brought into the Republican coalition, criticized the New York *Tribune*'s attacks on the Know Nothings during the recent election as "folly and blind suicide." "You can easily drive men from you by abuse," he declared, "but by such means you can never get them into the converts fold. Who ever knew bitterness and vituperation . . . to create any thing other than negative action?" Chase was a foremost advocate of the policy of conciliation. Pointing to his election as proof, he argued that the rank-and-file Know Nothings were more committed to antislavery than to nativist principles and that the Republicans, by not needlessly alienating them, could detach them from the order and win their support. One of Simon Cameron's associates advised, "I would step on two planks of a new platform and carry the state with a rush viz Americanism & antislavery."[142]

A convention of northern Americans in Cincinnati in November further unsettled the relationship between Republicans and the seceding Know Nothings at Philadelphia. As many Republicans had feared, the meeting undertook to lay the basis for reuniting the national American organization. The delegates approved a platform that merely called for the restoration of the Missouri Compromise, and they agreed to attend a national council meeting, scheduled for Philadelphia in mid-February, a few days before the American nominating convention, in order to devise an acceptable national platform. If the Twelfth Section were discarded, the majority of northern Know Nothings seemed ready to return to the party and support the American ticket in 1856. The regular national American organization also endorsed the plan to consult in February concerning a new platform. Campbell, who was already circulating a proposed platform, predicted that the alliance of the Know Nothings and Republicans in Ohio and elsewhere would not continue. To Republicans, these developments were ominous.[143]

Republican leaders looked to the coming national election to clarify the party's political

---

141. Bailey to Chase, November 27, Chase Papers, HSPa; Adams Diary, December 26, Adams Family Papers; John C. Vaughn to Chase, November 8, Chase Papers, HSPa; T. M. Tweed to Chase, October 25, Chase Papers, LC.

142. J. P. Gould to Banks, n.d. [in December 1–15, 1855 folder], Banks Papers, LC; Wilson N. Brown to Seward, November 15. Seward Papers, UR; Chase to Bingham, October 19 (copy), Chase Papers, HSPa; James A. Dean to Cameron, June 22, Cameron Papers, LC.

143. Cincinnati *Commercial*, November 22, 23, 24; Cincinnati *Gazette*, November 22, 23.

situation, sharpen its ideological focus, and broaden its base of support. Because they intended to exploit the Kansas issue in the 1856 presidential campaign, Republican strategists were especially sensitive to the critical importance of controlling the House of Representatives in the new Congress, which was due to convene in early December. In order to organize the House, however, Republicans and northern Know Nothings would have to cooperate, and many Americans, encouraged by the 1855 elections, saw no reason to defer to the Republicans. For Greeley, the fall elections had been a rude shock. Confident beforehand that the House could be organized without Know Nothing votes, the New York editor suddenly realized that a nativist alliance offered the only chance of victory. Reflecting this new outlook, the *Tribune* abruptly dropped its attacks on the Know Nothings and began ardently courting rank-and-file Americans.[144] More insightful Republican leaders had reached this conclusion some months earlier. Indicative of the importance of the struggle rapidly taking shape over organization of the House was that a number of prominent Republican operators, including Weed, Greeley, Preston King, Follett, and Schouler, made plans to go to Washington to help marshal the opposition forces in Congress under Republican leadership. Supporters and opponents alike perceived that developments in Washington would exercise a critical influence on the movement to organize a national Republican party.

---

144. Greeley to Colfax, November 13, September 7, Greeley-Colfax Papers. "So that the new Speaker and Clerk are clearly hostile to Atchison, Stringfellow and Whitfield, we do not care to ask what they [members of the House of Representatives] think of 'Sam.'" New York *Tribune*, November 21.

8

The Formation of a National Party Organization

The 1855 elections left Gamaliel Bailey deeply discouraged. An outspoken critic of nativism, the long-time antislavery editor believed that the strength of the Know Nothings, so manifest in the recent elections, rendered the outlook for the Republican party decidedly bleak. "There is just now little prospect for a respectable fight next year," he concluded. He was certain that the Know Nothings would "keep up their organization, and utterly divide the North." Forecasting that there would be two northern candidates in the next presidential election, "one Republican, one Know Nothing," Theodore Parker, another committed antislavery man, harbored no doubt that "the latter will get the most votes."[1]

When the Thirty-fourth Congress opened in December 1855, the Republican party faced an uphill struggle for survival. Former governor Washington Hunt of New York, a diehard Whig, thought the party would hardly outlive the 1856 presidential election. John Pendleton Kennedy, another conservative Whig, manifested a similar outlook. "The American party has disclosed a predominant strength in the Country," he informed Millard Fillmore in November, "and is regarded now as in a position to determine the issue of 1856." In pointing out to Francis P. Blair the folly of embracing the Republican cause, John Van Buren was direct and to the point. "The Presl. contest must be between the Democrats & the Know Nothings," he warned his old Free Soil ally. The Albany *Argus*, in an assessment endorsed by the *Illinois State Journal*, the future Republican state organ, expressed the dominant viewpoint when it declared, "Nobody believes that this Republican movement can prove the basis of a permanent party."[2]

Note: Unless otherwise indicated, the year for newspaper and manuscript citations in this chapter is 1856.

1. Gamaliel Bailey to Salmon P. Chase, November 27, 1855, Chase Papers, HSPa; Theodore Parker to William Herndon, November 30, 1855 (copy), Parker Papers, MassHS. For similar assessments by antislavery men, see Julian, *Political Recollections*, 145–46; Solomon Foot to Lewis D. Campbell, November 1, 1855, Campbell Papers.

2. Washington Hunt to Samuel B. Ruggles, December 23, 1855, Washington Hunt Papers; John P. Kennedy to Millard Fillmore, November 18, 1855, Fillmore Papers, SUNY; John Van Buren to [Francis P.

Some anti-Republican leaders, however, remained uneasy about the political future. Cheered by the 1855 results, Edward Everett nevertheless cautioned that "the greatest danger to be apprehended is, that the events of the impending [congressional] session may be such as to invigorate the Republican [party], . . . split the K.N.'s into a northern and southern wing,—and break up what little nationality we have left."[3] Everett's fears represented Republican hopes, and by the time Congress adjourned, the Massachusetts conservative would prove a reluctant prophet.

I

Republican leaders looked to developments in Congress to strengthen their cause and weaken the Know Nothings. In particular, they intended to use the session to develop what they considered their main issue: the situation in Kansas. In order to raise this issue effectively, however, Republicans needed to control the organization of the House, particularly the speakership. Joshua R. Giddings, who had been the target of several speakers' hostility during his long congressional career, maintained that the speaker "exerts more influence upon the destinies of the nation than any other member of the government except the President." The speaker exercised one extremely important prerogative, since under the rules of the House he appointed the members of all committees. Naturally, a speaker traditionally arranged the committees so as to advance the interests of his party. To a significant extent, therefore, control of the speakership included the power to determine legislation and shape political issues. Consequently, once the 1855 state elections had concluded, Washington observers, both in and out of Congress, quickly turned their attention to the contest to organize the new House.[4]

As a result of the political upheaval of 1854, administration supporters were a distinct minority in the new House. After a careful survey, Congressman Thomas L. Harris of Illinois, a key Douglas lieutenant, concluded that even under the most optimistic circumstances, with the entire southern bloc, including a good number of Whigs and Know Nothings, voting with the Democrats, the opposition would still have a majority of ten.[5] It was clear that if the various opposition factions cooperated, they would control the House. But the question was: Could the anti-administration factions unite?

A precise party breakdown of the House membership was impossible. The major imponderable was the strength of the Know Nothings. When elected, almost two-thirds of the anti-Nebraska members were also affiliated with the secret order, but, with the elapse of more than a year since their election, which competing allegiance took precedence was in many cases unclear. The *Tribune Almanac*, in a heroic effort to sort out these factions, placed the anti-Nebraska strength at 118 Representatives, including Republicans, anti-

Blair, Sr.], December 26, 1855, Blair Family Papers; Albany *Argus*, October 20, 1855; *Illinois State Journal*, November 15, 1855.

3. Edward Everett to James A. Hamilton, November 10, December 3, 1855 (quotation) (copies), Everett Papers.

4. Joshua R. Giddings quoted in Nevins, *Ordeal of the Union*, v. 1, 170; Edwin B. Morgan to Dear Brothers, December 22, 1855, Temple R. Hollcroft, ed., "A Congressman's Letters on the Speaker Election in the Thirty-fourth Congress," *MVHR*, v. 43 (December, 1956), 451.

5. Thomas Harris to Howell Cobb, October 15, 1855, Phillips, ed., *Correspondence of Toombs, Stephens, and Cobb*, 355.

Nebraska Democrats, and antislavery Know Nothings. This total represented a small majority of the House.[6]

Maneuvering to organize the House commenced shortly after the 1854 elections. In the wake of the Democrats' repudiation, opposition leaders realized that the man who could combine the anti-Nebraska and nativist strength would be elected speaker in the next Congress. When queried about the 1856 presidential election, Schuyler Colfax told William Schouler in October 1854, "Our first rock to look out for is the organization of the next Congress." According to Solomon G. Haven, Fillmore's former law partner and a congressman from Buffalo, William H. Seward and a number of close associates spent much of their time during the lame duck session that began in December 1854 "constantly caucusing to keep control of the next house."[7]

Haven himself was a candidate for the speakership and was likewise promoting his chances. He looked for a deadlock, from which he would emerge as a compromise choice, and he hoped then to triumph by putting together a diverse coalition of northern and southern Know Nothings, anti-Nebraska men, and regular Democrats. When the balloting began, he remained out of the fray, waiting for the right opportunity.[8] There was no potential speaker whom the Republicans feared more. Haven's close ties to Fillmore would have sufficed to damn him with Republicans, but he had also proved notoriously unreliable in the fight over the Nebraska bill, and he was a leading spokesman for the creation of a national Union party uniting conservative Whigs and Democrats. Republican leaders foresaw that he would use the speaker's power to promote Fillmore's well-known presidential aspirations. "We need praying for," Colfax asserted after Horace Greeley wrote in alarm detailing Haven's growing strength.[9]

The major difficulty for the anti-administration men was to agree on a candidate. "There are about thirty *modest* men who think the country needs their services in the Speaker's chair," Cincinnati Congressman Timothy C. Day commented sarcastically once the session opened, and "to get rid of this swarm of patriots will take time."[10] Northern opposition members bandied about many names, but in the end there were three serious anti-administration candidates for speaker: Lewis D. Campbell of Ohio, Nathaniel P. Banks, Jr., of Massachusetts, and Alexander C. M. Pennington of New Jersey. All three were anti-Nebraska Know Nothings who hoped to combine the Republican and northern Know Nothing strength in the House. Campbell and Pennington were ex-Whigs while Banks was a former Democrat. Campbell and Banks were the frontrunners, with Pennington as a compromise choice should they falter.

---

6. *Tribune Almanac* (1856), 4; *Cong. Globe*, 34th Cong., 1st sess., Appendix, 352–53. Hereafter, unless specified, all citations in the chapter are to this Congress and session. The *Almanac* mistakenly listed Francis E. Spinner of New York, a close associate of Preston King and a determined opponent of the Nebraska bill, with the Democrats. Counting him with the anti-Nebraska forces produces the totals given in the text. Somewhat different totals are given in Isely, *Greeley and the Republican Party*, 143.

7. Schuyler Colfax to William Schouler, October 23, 1854, Schouler Papers; Solomon G. Haven to Fillmore, February 22, 1855, Fillmore Papers, SUNY.

8. Haven's campaign for the speakership can be followed in Campbell to Samuel Galloway, May 16, 22, 1855, Galloway Papers; Campbell to Isaac Strohm, May 24, 1855 (private), Strohm Papers, OHS; Nathan K. Hall to Fillmore, December 2, 1855, Fillmore Papers, SUNY.

9. Colfax to Henry Waldron, November 17, 1855, Waldron Family Papers; Charles A. Dana to James Shepherd Pike, September 15, 1855 (misfiled as part of a July 14, [1855] letter from Dana), Pike Papers, UMe.

10. Timothy C. Day to his uncle, December 6, 1855, quoted in Sarah J. Day, *The Man on a Hill Top* (Philadelphia, 1931), 140.

A four-term veteran, Campbell had gained widespread publicity for his leadership in the fight over the Kansas-Nebraska bill in the House in 1854. He had been running hard for the speaker's post for more than a year.[11] Campbell was the most strongly antislavery of the three anti-Nebraska candidates, and he was also the most committed nativist of the group. The egotistical Ohio representative, his ambition stimulated by political developments during the previous two years, even dreamed of being president, much to the merriment of his opponents and many of his supporters. In promoting his candidacy, Campbell argued that he could best appeal to former Whigs, who constituted the majority of the opposition, and that he was the only serious anti-administration contender who could secure the votes of southern Whigs and Know Nothings. "The Anti Nebraska sentiment of the House & Country being found so overwhelmingly with old Whigs rather than old Locos [Democrats]," one of Campbell's advocates declared, "other things . . . equal—the speaker should be *Whig*."[12]

Campbell's candidacy suffered from several handicaps. In addition to the hostility of anti-Nebraska Democrats, his erratic political course in 1855 badly undermined his support in antislavery circles. The American leader had scandalized antislavery men when he drafted a compromise slavery plank for consideration by the national council in Philadelphia in June. He further alarmed his old antislavery associates when, following the Ohio election, he spoke favorably of reuniting the national American party and making independent nominations for the 1856 presidential election. His appeals to southern nativists for support in the speakership contest convinced Republicans that Campbell was unwilling to subordinate nativism in any national fusion organization and was thus unreliable.[13] The Ohio congressman's contentious personality, which kept him embroiled in an endless series of feuds, also drove away potential supporters. Even many of his political friends believed that he was "too impetuous and imperious" to be a good speaker.[14] Despite these objections, Campbell, thanks in large part to his former Whig ties, started as the strongest opposition candidate. He had several influential backers, including Colfax, Schouler, and Thurlow Weed. Schouler, in fact, went to Washington in part to help manage Campbell's bid for the speakership. One defector, however, was Salmon P. Chase. Campbell quickly learned how sincere the new Ohio governor's professions of friendship were. Safely elected with Campbell's aid, Chase refused to honor his inferred commitment made earlier to back the Ohio congressman for speaker. Chase's opposition helped fragment the Ohio delegation and seriously damaged Campbell's prospects.[15]

Campbell's chief rival was Banks. Whereas Campbell was a sincere nativist, Banks was a blatant opportunist who joined the secret society in 1854 in order, as his biographer

---

11. Campbell to Schouler, December 23, 26, 1854, Schouler Papers; Campbell to Galloway, May 22, 1855 (private), Galloway Papers.

12. Campbell to Galloway, May 22, 1855 (private), S. W. Parker to Galloway, May 16, 1855 (quotation), Galloway Papers. One correspondent warned Campbell that he would probably not receive a single southern vote. Solomon Foot to Campbell, November 1, 1855, Campbell Papers.

13. Charles A. Dana to Pike, September 15, 1855, Pike Papers, UMe; Campbell to Schouler, June 26, 1855, Schouler Papers; New York *Tribune*, November 17, 1855.

14. Cincinnati *Commercial*, December 10, 1855 (quotation); Henry Wilson to Schouler, April 16, 1855, Schouler Papers.

15. [?] Greene to Schouler, September 1, 1855 (Strictly Confidential), Schouler Papers; Cincinnati *Gazette*, April 18; Campbell to Chase, October 11, 16, November 5, 1855, Chase Papers, LC; Chase to Campbell, November 8, 1855, Campbell Papers; Van Horne, "Campbell and the Know-Nothing Party," 212–19.

so aptly puts it, to "save his political skin." Banks's antislavery principles were equally shallow. Prior to 1854 his position on the slavery issue fluctuated widely as he assumed whatever stance he believed would best promote his political career. Evidencing an "utter unconcern for principles," Banks's record was one of "shifting stands and exploitation of anti-slavery feeling for personal gain." He was, he once confessed to a friend, "neither . . . pro-slavery nor anti-slavery."[16] Slow to oppose the Nebraska bill and deserting his colleagues on one very crucial vote, the Massachusetts representative became a leading tactician of the anti-Nebraska forces during the last stages of the struggle in the House. The publicity he received gave him a largely undeserved reputation as a firm opponent of the extension of slavery, which he exploited along with his well-advertised nativist affiliation in order to gain the speakership. Those who knew him perceived his true character. Acknowledging that personally he liked Banks, a former congressional associate added that "he is very ambitious & has always left the impression on my mind that he was not 'nice' as to how he 'stayed himself up'—so [long as] he stood. I deem him cold-hearted—& inclined to be scheming & sinister."[17] Banks's close association with Israel D. Andrews of Massachusetts and Colonel Charles James of Wisconsin, lobbyists with well-deserved reputations for shady dealings, also disturbed many members.

For all this well-aimed criticism, Banks enjoyed several advantages in the speakership contest. Exceptionally personable, he was well liked even by his adversaries, and as a one-time actor the handsome Bay State politician possessed a fine speaking voice and a dignified manner, and displayed, in the words of a hostile journalist, "a genius for being looked at." In addition, he was a skillful parliamentary tactician and an experienced presiding officer.[18] As a former Democrat, he was particularly strong among anti-Nebraska Democrats in the House, and he could obtain votes that were unavailable to Campbell or any other former Whig. The difficulty was to transfer Campbell's Whig supporters to Banks, for many resented taking an ex-Democrat.[19] Confident that he could in the end muster a larger vote than any other anti-administration member, Banks encapsulated his basic appeal with the comment: "I think our only inquiry should be, 'what *sure* man can be elected.' "[20]

Fearful that the northern and southern Americans would patch up their differences and cooperate, Republican strategists worked to drive a wedge between the two groups by emphasizing the slavery issue and thereby prevent the House from being organized on a national, nativist basis.[21] The course of the administration's supporters aided their

---

16. Fred Harvey Harrington, "Nathaniel Prentiss Banks: A Study in Anti-Slavery Politics," *NEQ*, v. 9 (December, 1936), 638, 630, 626.

17. S. W. Parker to Galloway, May 16, 1855, Galloway Papers. Everett was scathing in his assessment of the self-made Banks, who had risen from the textile factories of Massachusetts to a seat in Congress. "No person now on the stage has given so gross an example of the most bare-faced tergiversation," the patrician Whig leader charged, "old line democrat—coalitionist—Know-Nothing—fusionist—all in 6 years with one or two accessory changes." Diary, February 4, Everett Papers.

18. Robinson, *"Warrington" Pen Portraits*, 437–38 (quotation); Congdon, *Reminiscences*, 151–52.

19. David Davis to Julius Rockwell, December 27, 1855, David Davis Papers, IllSHL. One former Democrat in the Ohio delegation intimated that he would not vote for Campbell, for "nothing should induce me to consent to a *Whig* organization." M. H. Nichols to Chase, December 11, 1855, Chase Papers, LC. Also see Colfax to Charles M. Heaton, Sr., December 3, 1855, Schuyler Colfax Papers, NIHS.

20. Nathaniel P. Banks, Jr., to C. Farran, November 21, 1855, Whittier-Pickard Papers.

21. Joshua R. Giddings to Bailey, *Private*, November 11, 1855, Giddings-Julian Papers; Richard Mott to Chase, November 11, 1855, Chase Papers, LC; Timothy C. Day to his uncle, December 6, 1855, quoted in Day, *Man on a Hill Top*, 140–41.

efforts. Any possibility of a Democratic-national Know Nothing alliance was destroyed when the Democratic caucus adopted resolutions that strongly denounced nativism. The caucus named William A. Richardson of Illinois, a heavy-set, tobacco-chewing ally of Douglas and the floor manager of the Nebraska bill, as the Democratic candidate for speaker. By this action, party leaders not only threw down the gauntlet to anti-Nebraska Democrats but made the Kansas-Nebraska Act the central issue separating Richardson from the anti-administration hopefuls. "It is just what we wanted," a New York Republican congressman wrote in reference to the Democrats' action. Republicans, he chortled, "could not fix it any better."[22]

Attempts to concentrate northern opposition members on a candidate or to agree on a strategy prior to the convening of Congress failed. Nor was there any general agreement among Republicans concerning the wording of a call for a caucus. In the end, a simple announcement circulated that a meeting for consultation would be held Friday morning, November 30, at the Republican rooms. Only about twenty-five representatives, mostly new members, appeared, and their spirit was noticeably timid. A subsequent meeting that evening attracted about forty members, who spent most of their time wrangling over the comparative merits of the Republican and American organizations. Attendance improved the next day. The seventy or so members present unanimously approved a resolution, introduced by Giddings, which pledged to support any candidate who could unite a majority of those present and who agreed to organize the standing committees "by placing on each a majority of the friends of freedom." No decision was made on a candidate.[23]

John W. Forney, the clerk of the previous House, called the representatives to order at noon on Monday, December 3.[24] The initial ballot for speaker revealed how deep the divisions among the anti-Nebraska forces ran. In all, seventeen anti-Nebraska members received votes, with not one polling as much as a quarter of the House membership. Campbell was the strongest anti-Democratic candidate, with fifty-three votes, but he trailed Richardson by twenty-one votes. After two days of fruitless balloting, a caucus of the anti-Nebraska members decided to close ranks behind Campbell, and, if he could not win a majority, then to try Banks or Pennington. Accordingly, Campbell's total reached eighty-one on the third day, but he could go no higher and was nowhere near a majority. The Ohioan's candidacy collapsed and, after a conference with Colfax and Schouler that lasted all night, he withdrew from the race with bad grace and in obvious ill humor.[25]

With Campbell's candidacy obviously untenable, Republicans decided to mobilize their

22. Edwin B. Morgan to Dear Brothers, December 2, 1855, Hollcroft, ed., "A Congressman's Letters," 449.

23. The fullest account of these meetings appears in Giddings's correspondence, December 6, 1855, in the *Ashtabula Sentinel*, December 13, 27, 1855.

24. The speakership contest can best be followed in the Washington dispatches of the New York newspapers and in the correspondence of the participants, supplemented by the following sources: Greeley, *Recollections*, 345–51; William B. Parker, *The Life and Public Services of Justin Smith Morrill* (Boston, 1924), 64–68; and William Schouler's history in the Cincinnati *Gazette*, February 16, 18, 19. One important source usually overlooked by historians is Giddings's series of letters in the *Ashtabula Sentinel*, December 1855–February 1856. A perceptive historical analysis is Fred Harvey Harrington, "'The First Northern Victory,'" *JSH*, v. 5 (May, 1939), 186–205.

25. Colfax to Charles M. Heaton, Sr., December 11, 1855, Colfax Papers, NIHS; letter signed "G." [Giddings], December 6, 1855, *Ashtabula Sentinel*, December 27, 1855; *Cong. Globe*, 11; Cincinnati *Gazette*, April 18, 1856; Harrington, "'First Northern Victory,'" 192–93.

efforts behind Banks. By December 8 his total stood at 100 votes; two days later he gained seven more, which brought him within six votes of a majority. But try as they might, Republican strategists could not enlist the necessary additional votes, and in fact on subsequent ballots Banks suffered some defections. Pennington's advocates argued that he should now be taken up, but Republican leaders, afraid that national Know Nothings would also adopt him and thereby impair Republican attempts to weaken nativism, voted the Pennington men down. At this point Republican managers made a crucial decision: They resolved to stick with Banks throughout the contest and hazard everything on electing him. As a result, a caucus in mid-December officially named the Massachusetts congressman the anti-Nebraska nominee.[26] Without renouncing his nativist affiliation, Banks became the candidate of those antislavery men, including a number of Know Nothings, who wanted nativism subordinated to the slavery issue in the 1856 presidential campaign.[27]

In the ensuing struggle, a small group of congressmen of diverse past political loyalties and viewpoints took over management of Banks's candidacy. Among them were antislavery Know Nothings including Schuyler Colfax and Anson Burlingame, such anti-Nebraska Democrats as Francis E. Spinner, Free Soilers like Galusha A. Grow, and former Whigs led by the three Washburn brothers and Edwin B. Morgan, a close associate of Weed and Seward. As the contest dragged on week after week, this steering committee used constituent pressure to hold waverers in line.[28] Working in close cooperation with this directory was a group of Banks's original supporters, led by Henry Wilson and Russell Sage, an antislavery Know Nothing congressman from New York, as well as a handful of powerful Republican outsiders including Weed, Schouler, and Preston King. Schouler had originally backed Campbell but went over to Banks after he concluded that his fellow Ohioan stood no chance. Not as closely tied to the inner Banks leadership were Giddings, who nonetheless worked valiantly for the choice of the anti-Nebraska caucus, and Greeley, whose intemperate denunciations of northern representatives who refused to support Banks did more harm than good. "If Greeley and I had paired from the beginning it would have been better," Weed sighed as the contest wore on.[29]

Throughout December and January the House remained deadlocked, with Banks stalled at around 105 votes. All attempts to break the impasse failed. The House endured an all-night session in a futile attempt to select a speaker; a day devoted to questioning the candidates, which was intended to weaken Banks, produced no change; the Democrats

---

26. Giddings to Gerrit Smith, January 21, 1856, Gerrit Smith Papers; letter signed "G." [Giddings], December 6, 17, 1855, *Ashtabula Sentinel*, December 27, 1855, January 3, 1856; New York *Tribune*, December 15, 1855; Colfax to Charles M. Heaton, Sr., December 25, 1855, Colfax Papers, NIHS; Harrington, "'First Northern Victory,'" 192–93.

27. The exact relationship of the Know Nothings in this group to the American order was ambiguous. Even Schuyler Colfax, who announced his intention to act with the Republican party in the 1856 campaign, nonetheless continued to attend lodge meetings in Washington. Colfax to Charles M. Heaton, Sr., December 25, 1855, Colfax Papers, NIHS.

28. Colfax, "Anson Burlingame," *Independent*, v. 22 (April 7, 1870), 3. In addition to himself, Colfax listed as members of the Banks steering committee Galusha A. Grow, Benjamin Stanton, William A. Howard, Justin S. Morrill, Francis E. Spinner, Aaron Cragin, Mason W. Tappan, the three Washburns (Israel, Elihu, and Cadwallader), Edwin B. Morgan, and Anson Burlingame.

29. Thurlow Weed to William H. Seward, January 24, Seward Papers, UR; Hamilton Fish to Robert A. West, January 12, 30 (copies), Fish Papers, LC; Isaac Sherman to Banks, December 4, 1855, Banks Papers, LC; Giddings to [Grotius R. Giddings], December 12, 1855, Giddings Papers; Indianapolis *State Journal*, quoted in the New York *Tribune*, February 6.

finally replaced Richardson with James Orr of South Carolina in hopes of picking up southern Know Nothing votes without success; even the fact that members could not be paid until the House organized was insufficient to end the stalemate. Proposals to adopt a plurality rule as had been done in the 1849 speakership contest were rejected repeatedly by the House in hopes that Republicans would finally abandon Banks. Convinced that any deviation would spell certain defeat, Republican leaders held firm behind the Massachusetts representative.[30]

Eventually, Alexander H. Stephens devised a strategy for Democrats to allow adoption of a plurality rule and then switch from Orr to another South Carolinian, William Aiken, who party leaders hoped could attract enough southern American votes to defeat Banks. Therefore, on Saturday, February 2, the House agreed that if no choice occurred on the next three ballots, the speaker would be chosen by a plurality on the fourth tally. When the three additional ballots failed to produce a majority, the House took the 133rd and final ballot. After nine weeks of voting, Banks was elected by a margin of 103 votes to 100 for Aiken, with eleven scattered. Graciously escorted by Aiken to the speaker's desk, Banks took the oath of office, and the struggle was over. "By science, by engineering, by industry and wholesome discipline, we managed to beat them all," Greeley crowed.[31]

One casualty of the battle, both from a personal and party standpoint, was Campbell. Mortified by his failure, resentful of being cast aside, and convinced that Banks's friends had been false to him, Campbell sulked throughout the balance of the speakership contest. What little remaining faith Republicans had in the erratic Ohio representative had been all but obliterated by the time of Banks's victory. Nevertheless, Banks magnanimously appointed Campbell chairman of the Ways and Means Committee, a key position that carried with it the Republican floor leadership. Given an opportunity to redeem himself and demonstrate his ability for party leadership, Campbell failed miserably. He engaged in an unseemly controversy with William Schouler of the Cincinnati *Gazette* and Oran Follett of the *Ohio State Journal*, charging that they had sold him out in the speaker's race in an abortive attempt to win the House printing; he spoke at an American rally held to endorse the nomination of Millard Fillmore; and by the end of the congressional session he was at odds with the vast majority of Republican members on several vital issues.[32] Campbell, who had been one of the leaders in the fight in the House against the Nebraska bill, and who had made such a critical contribution to Chase's nomination and election as governor, had no future place in the Republican party.

Banks's victory was of crucial importance in the drive to organize a national Republican party. Not only did the long stalemate in the House arouse great popular interest throughout the North, but the Banks managers were very skillful in portraying the contest in sectional terms. As Fred Harvey Harrington notes, what was essentially a squabble among anti-Nebraska men became in Republican propaganda a conflict between freedom and slavery. From the beginning, Republicans stigmatized Banks's northern opponents as doughfaces and charged that only their obstinate opposition prevented the organization of the House on a northern, antislavery basis. Consequently, Banks's

---

30. Colfax to Henry J. Raymond, January 23, Confidential, Henry J. Raymond Papers, NYPL; Washington correspondence, "T.," New York *Evening Post*, January 18.

31. Horace Greeley to O. A. Bowe, February 9, Greeley Papers, NYPL.

32. Campbell to Schouler, February 16 (Private), March 10, Schouler Papers; Colfax to Francis Stebbins, April 29, Francis Stebbins Papers, University of Michigan. Campbell's difficulties in 1856 are fully discussed in Van Horne, "Campbell and the Know-Nothing Party," 214–20.

supporters termed his election "the first victory of the North . . . since 1787." From this moment, another northerner insisted, "the South can date the downfall of the slave power."[33] The protracted contest heightened sectional tensions and helped make the controversy between the North and the South paramount in Congress.

The outcome had other significant ramifications as well, not the least of which was that it badly weakened the American party. Banks's triumph prevented the northern and southern Know Nothings, who together were the largest bloc in the House, from controlling its organization or exercising effective leadership. By the end of the contest the American ranks in Congress were in total disorder, with the northern and southern wings more antagonistic than ever. Haven complained that members of the order "sink so far, every other consideration in the Nebraska issue" that they had "become as essentially allied to Republicanism as if they were its lone [?] heirs and sole representatives." The Americans in Washington, he lamented, "are disunited[,] broken up—fragmentary." The speakership fight served to submerge nativism within the halls of Congress. "The lines of demarcation which seperate [*sic*] us from the South Americans, and from the democrats are becoming more and more distinctly marked and more and more impossible for our men to go to them," Giddings noted with approval.[34]

Another important consequence of the long struggle was that it welded the Banks forces into a more coherent party. Preston King maintained beforehand that Banks's election would "consolidate the union of our friends"; indeed, he professed that "it is possible that his Election is indispensible for Union." From Massachusetts a prominent former Free Soiler observed perceptively: "The more votes for the speaker the better. The lines between the Parties will be more firmly consolidated." Giddings agreed. "We have got our party formed consolidated and established," he announced at the end of the contest.[35]

Most important of all, the speakership struggle gave new strength and impetus to the Republican movement nationally. The clear-sighted Samuel Bowles wrote Colfax during the contest, "You are making a great fight, and one of more importance and of vaster consequence than most people imagine. It is settling the next Presidential election and the new order of things, politically, for the next generation." Banks's victory was, according to another prominent Massachusetts politician, the Republican party's "first and most important triumph." Thurlow Weed penned the most concise statement of the importance of the speakership contest. "This triumph is worth all it cost in time, toil, and solicitude," he assured Banks. "The Republican party is now Inaugurated. We can now work 'with a will.'"[36]

---

33. Theodore Parker to Charles Sumner, February 16, Sumner Papers, HU; Richard Morgan to Edwin B. Morgan, February 6, Edwin Barber Morgan Papers. For other examples, see the New York *Evening Post*, February 4; Samuel S. Billings to Justin S. Morrill, January 20, Morrill Papers, LC; Colfax to D. D. Pratt, February 4, Confidential, Colfax Papers, IndHS; Allen Payne to George W. Patterson, February 20, Patterson Papers; Cincinnati *Commercial*, February 4; George W. Patterson to Banks, February 4, Andrew L. Allen to Banks, March 3, William M. Stone to Banks, February 4, William Kendrick to Banks, February 4, Banks Papers, LC.

34. Haven to Daniel Ullmann, December 12, 1855, *Confidential*, Ullmann Papers, NYHS; Giddings to Gerrit Smith, January 21, Gerrit Smith Papers.

35. Preston King to Francis P. Blair, Sr., January 3, Blair-Lee Papers; James W. Stone to Banks, January 25, Banks Papers, LC; Giddings to Lura M. Giddings, February 1, Giddings-Julian Papers.

36. Samuel Bowles to Colfax, December 26, 1855, quoted in Hollister, *Colfax*, 87; Levi Lincoln to Banks, February 5, Weed to Banks, February 3, Banks Papers, LC; Greeley to Mark Howard, January 20, Mark Howard Papers. The Washington correspondent of the New York *Evening Post*, February 8, assured his readers that Banks's victory was "the key and precursor to a perpetual supremacy over the national government. It is

Analysis of the votes for Banks underlines the magnitude of the Republican accomplishment and the corresponding failure of the Know Nothings. After the contest, Greeley conceded that a majority of those who voted for Banks were currently members of Know Nothing councils, and "some twenty or thirty of them," he scoffed, "actually believe in the swindle." Gamaliel Bailey disclosed that from thirty to thirty-five of Banks's supporters had never been Know Nothings and were "simply" Republicans. "All others have been and with few exceptions are now Know Nothings." Of this remaining group of about seventy-five representatives, the editor of the *National Era* estimated that about thirty-five had committed themselves to the Republican movement, wished to discard their Know Nothingism, and would go with the Republican party in the presidential campaign. The remainder were "Know Nothings of all grades." Some were anxious to promote both the Nebraska and nativist issues, some were "nearly Republicans," some were leery of Republicanism, and some wished to dampen all sectional agitation. Combining the first two groups, he estimated the true Republican strength in the House to be somewhere between sixty-five and seventy out of a total membership of 224. Bailey believed that by careful management additional members who voted for Banks could eventually be brought into the Republican camp, but with the current makeup of the House, he warned, "Expect nothing from this Congress, except agitation. In the House, it is chaos."[37]

Bailey's figures made it clear that despite Banks's election, the Republicans were a decided minority in the House and could not, as a matter of course, pass legislation. Even so, a group of about seventy-five congressmen, constituting only a third of the members, had managed to gain control of the speaker's office, organize the committees under Republican direction, and deal a severe blow to nativist dreams of reuniting the national American party.[38] Prospects brightened for a national Republican organization representing a fusion of the antislavery and nativist elements under the general anti-Nebraska banner. As William Pitt Fessenden accurately noted, "Events are fast bringing the Republicans and Americans from the free States to the conviction that neither can do without the other."[39]

II

The drive to establish a national Republican organization was under way before Congress assembled in December. The call for an organizing convention at Pittsburgh in February grew out of two separate initiatives, one from Ohio under Salmon P. Chase's tutelage and the other from Washington that was closely tied to Gamaliel Bailey and the staff of the *National Era*. Not without difficulty did the two groups eventually agree to cooperate and merge their efforts.

---

not one victory, but a thousand victories which it has thus gained." Also see John Bigelow, *Retrospections*, v. 1, 141.

37. Greeley to Charles A. Dana, February 9, Joel Benton (ed.), *Greeley on Lincoln with Mr. Greeley's Letters to Charles A. Dana* (New York, 1893), 117–18; Bailey to Charles Francis Adams, January 20, Adams Family Papers; Bailey to Chase, February 21 (quotation), Chase Papers, LC.

38. "With the Speaker & the Committees ag[ain]st us, we should be totally powerless. With them, we may effect a little & but little, but we can *resist* & that will be something, even if we could do nothing affirmatively." Colfax to Charles M. Heaton, Sr., January 27, Colfax Papers, NIHS.

39. William Pitt Fessenden to his son, December 1855, quoted in Francis Fessenden, *Life and Public Services of William Pitt Fessenden* (2 vols.: Boston, 1907), v. 1, 70.

The movement to hold a preliminary national convention was a key part of Chase's campaign to win a presidential nomination in 1856. The Ohio leader commenced seeking support for his presidential bid even before he was elected governor in October. In addition to corresponding widely with anti-Democratic leaders throughout the North, he made several trips east in 1855 to solicit support for a new antislavery party.[40] That Chase's national ambitions lay behind this movement was apparent to all. In response, Republican politicians generally encouraged the idea of forming a northern fusion party without committing themselves to a presidential candidate.

The major point of contention between Chase and some of those he sounded out was the role of the Know Nothings in the proposed fusion party. The Ohio governor advocated the union of Republicans and Americans on a liberal, anti-Nebraska platform. He outlined his views in a letter to Governor Kinsley S. Bingham of Michigan. For victory the support of both the "liberal Americans" and the "Anti slavery adopted citizens" was essential, he declared. "Neither . . . can be spared without imminent danger of defeat." In addition, the party needed a large accession of old Democrats. A platform and especially a presidential candidate acceptable to all of these groups were necessary, Chase observed, and he not so subtly pointed out that "the elements required for a Presidential election have been harmonized in my election in Ohio." Chase was not specific concerning the platform he envisioned, although he stipulated that the issue of "Slavery or Freedom" should be paramount.[41] Presumably, he had in mind one similar to the one he had proposed in Ohio, in which the planks might endorse anti-Catholicism and reforms against illegal voting but not significant alteration of the naturalization laws or a ban on foreign-born officeholding. Chase was the foremost spokesman for extensive recognition of American members in the Republican party. He received powerful support from Henry Wilson, who agreed that "we must let it be known that we are ready for union for freedom."[42]

Much of the initial labor enlisting support for a national organizing convention fell to James Ashley and Alfred P. Stone, two of Chase's top lieutenants. Stone was a Know Nothing whereas Ashley was a Know Something. The July 13 convention that nominated Chase for governor instructed the Republican state central committee, of which Stone was chairman, to correspond with leaders in other states concerning formation of a national party in 1856. Ashley in the meantime directed his attention to controlling the national Know Something convention held in Cleveland in June 1855, where he seized every opportunity to promote Chase as the most suitable candidate in 1856. More important, he worked zealously to get a committee appointed under his chairmanship to correspond with the bolting Know Nothings at Philadelphia and all independent organizations opposed to the administration and the Slave Power. To Chase he indicated that he favored a mass meeting in Pittsburgh in early September to make preliminary arrangements for the 1856 campaign. The Toledo leader's goal was to nominate Chase, and therefore he wanted to

40. James W. Grimes to Chase, April 8, 1855, Salter, *Grimes*, 68–69; Chase to Pike, June 20, 1855, Pike, *First Blows*, 296; Adams Diary, July 23, 1855, Adams Family Papers; Giddings to Chase, August 28, 1855 (*Confidential*), Bailey to Chase, June 24, 26, Chase Papers, HSPa; Andrew Wallace Crandall, *The Early History of the Republican Party, 1854–1856* (Boston, 1930), 48.

41. Chase to Kinsley S. Bingham, October 19, 1855 (copy), Chase Papers, HSPa; A. P. Stone to Chase, December 14, 1855, Chase Papers, LC.

42. Wilson to Chase, January 15, Chase Papers, HSPa. Wilson indicated that he concurred "entirely" with Chase about "our future policy."

be in advance of any movement on behalf of William H. Seward, John P. Hale, or any other rival.[43]

Working in loose conjunction with one another, Ashley and Stone opened correspondence that summer with Republicans in other states, but they soon concluded that little could be accomplished until after the Ohio gubernatorial election. This decision necessitated a later date for the proposed convention. Once Chase had been elected, a group of his supporters, including Ashley, held a secret conference in order to lay the groundwork for Chase's presidential bid. They agreed that a preliminary convention to organize a new national party was essential, and shortly thereafter Stone and Ashley resumed their active correspondence and sought support for a meeting in Pittsburgh on February 22.[44] They cast their net widely, in accord with Chase's view that any viable organization must include many diverse factions. Among those Stone contacted, for example, was Francis Preston Blair, who, despite his complete disillusionment with Franklin Pierce and the "rotters" who controlled the Democracy, had not yet abandoned the party to which he had belonged for so many years. In November, Ashley visited Russell Errett of the Pittsburgh *Gazette* in an effort to secure the concurrence of Pennsylvania Republicans for the proposed gathering. Errett explained that the Know Nothings were in complete control of the Republican state central committee and was downcast about the possibility of the Pennsylvania party's officially endorsing the movement. The Pittsburgh journalist recommended to Ashley that Stone write David Wilmot, the party's state chairman, who although a Know Nothing was a committed antislavery man; Errett thought it "barely possible" that Wilmot would sign the call without consulting the committee, which if polled would certainly reject the proposal. If not, Errett could obtain a few signatures, although these would not convey any official sanction. John Z. Goodrich, the Republican chairman in Massachusetts, wrote to Chase on his own initiative and recommended correspondence among the various state committees to bring about a general convention—precisely the course upon which the Chase forces were already embarked. Apparently, the Ohioans also contacted the Republican chairmen in other states where the party had been organized, as well as the chairman of the People's party in Indiana.[45] The Ohio proposal gained support from the Republican press as well. By mid-January, Ashley reported that he had received forty-one replies to his letters and that all but one favored the proposed mass convention in Pittsburgh.[46]

A December gathering at Francis Preston Blair's home in Silver Spring provided an important boost for Chase's plan. The old Jacksonian editor was reluctant to discard his

43. James Ashley to Chase, June 16, 1855, Chase Papers, LC. The proceedings of the Know Something convention are in the Cincinnati *Commercial*, June 16, 19, 1855. Also see Robert F. Horowitz, "James M. Ashley and the Presidential Election of 1856," *Ohio History*, v. 83 (Winter, 1974), 4–16.

44. Ashley, MS Memoirs.

45. A. P. Stone to Francis P. Blair, Sr., December 16, 1855, Blair-Lee Papers; Stone to Cassius Clay, [November-December, 1855], New York *Tribune*, December 25, 1855; Errett to Chase, November 16, 1855, Chase Papers, LC; Chase to John P. Hale, December 10, 1855, Hale Papers, NHHS; John Z. Goodrich to Chase, November 17, 1855, Stone to Chase, December 14, 1855, Ashley to Chase, January 18, Chase Papers, LC; Almon M. Clapp to Seward, December 26, 1855, Seward Papers, UR; James Elliott to Weed, November 27, 1855, Weed Papers, UR.

46. *Ashtabula Sentinel*, December 20, 1855; New York *Tribune*, January 17; Almon M. Clapp to Seward, December 26, 1855, Seward Papers, UR; New York *Evening Post*, January 31; Ashley to Chase, January 18, Chase Papers, LC.

Democratic affiliation, yet he was determined to defeat Pierce and the southern politicians around the president in 1856. Uncertain about his ultimate course, Blair invited a small group of important Republican leaders to exchange political views over Christmas dinner. On his guest list were Chase, Banks, Bailey, Seward, Charles Sumner, and Preston King. Blair stipulated that the purpose of the conference was to organize the anti-Nebraska movement for the presidential election. Of those invited, only Seward declined. When Bailey, at Blair's request, called on the New Yorker to solicit his participation, since he was the only former Whig included in the group, Seward again demurred, lamely giving as his reason that he wished to keep free from "plans or schemes for political action." He confided to Weed that his real motive was an unwillingness to combine with Know Nothings.[47]

Seward's absence was cause for concern, but otherwise Blair's party went smoothly. Those present concurred that Banks's election as speaker was indispensable to the formation of a national fusion party. They also agreed that a nominating convention to meet in June in either Pittsburgh or Cincinnati would be called from Ohio. Afterwards King informed Seward that (in the latter's words) the convention "was to be on the Ohio plan, half Republican and half Know Nothing." The group concluded that the movement would be acquiesced in by every state except perhaps New York. Broad support also existed for the preliminary Pittsburgh meeting, although neither Bailey nor Blair committed themselves firmly to the proposal. Informed of the outcome of these deliberations, Seward declined either to give his endorsement or to pledge New York's support.[48] Recognizing the importance of this meeting for the future of the Republican movement, Weed hastened to make amends for Seward's ill-advised action. He told Blair that New York would participate in the movement to launch a national anti-Nebraska party.[49]

As Chase and his allies moved forward with their plan to hold a convention at the end of February, Gamaliel Bailey became uneasy. The normally mild-mannered journalist had been a good friend of Chase since the 1830s, when Bailey had edited an antislavery journal in Cincinnati. Chase's alliance with the Know Nothings in Ohio, however, had strained their friendship. Telling Chase that he had no faith in the governor's Know Nothing allies, Bailey bluntly declared: "Your position in relation to their detestable organization is not so satisfactory as that of Seward. You temporize with it—he opposes it boldly and outright." Although he assured the Ohio governor of his continued friendship, the Washington editor nevertheless announced, "I cannot go with you into any organization with Republicans *and* Know Nothings."[50] Before long, it was common talk among Republicans in the capital that the two men had had a falling out, and that Bailey was no longer warmly pushing Chase for the 1856 presidential nomination.

Worried that the so-called Ohio plan would give the Know Nothings a prominent place in the national Republican organization, Bailey moved to block Chase's efforts. He concluded that the proposed Pittsburgh gathering could not be prevented, and he therefore undertook to assume control of the convention movement and change its focus. Bowing to the demand for the conference, he told Charles Francis Adams, "The thing now to be

---

47. Seward to Francis P. Blair, Sr., December 29, 1855, Blair-Lee Papers; Seward to Weed, December 31, 1855, January 6, Weed Papers, UR.

48. Seward to Weed, December 31, 1855 (quotation), Weed Papers, UR; King to Welles, January 3, 10, Welles Papers, LC.

49. Weed to Seward, January 3, Seward Papers, UR.

50. Bailey to Chase, November 27, 1855, Chase Papers, HSPa.

done is, to prevent mischief & make the Convention an instrument of good.'' It was important that ''solid & judicious'' men attend to prevent it from promulgating a platform or doing anything that might embarrass the party. Moreover, Bailey insisted that ''there must be no tampering with Know Nothings. I want no mixed issues or mixed ticket—and therefore no mixed Convention.''[51] He drafted a call for the proposed convention that quietly changed the date from February 22 to March 26 with the intention of checking the plans of Chase's circle. He secured the approval of Giddings, Israel Washburn, and other friends in Congress, who sent the call to the chairmen of the Republican committees in their states for signatures. Although they agreed on Know Nothingism, Bailey failed to win Seward's support for the project.[52]

Up until this point Chase, who was actively promoting the Pittsburgh meeting while such rivals as Seward did nothing, had faced little challenge. Convinced that delay would weaken his hold on the party apparatus, Chase rallied his followers in support of the original date. Western Republicans who had endorsed the initial Ohio proposal remained firm that the convention meet on February 22. Richard Mott, an Ohio congressman and close associate of Chase, attempted to mobilize opinion in Washington in favor of the February date. Of those contacted, only Massachusetts chairman John Z. Goodrich and Wilmot joined Bailey in preferring a March meeting. Michigan Republicans announced that they intended to go to Pittsburgh on the twenty-second, even if they were the only ones present.[53]

The reasons for the struggle over the convention date are not immediately obvious. Perhaps first and foremost, Chase preferred the earlier date in order to enhance his chances of controlling the party organization. Travel was difficult in the winter, and nearby Ohio would have an advantage by sending an oversized delegation. The Ohio governor no doubt was also simply anxious to get the Republican movement under way nationally. In view of the difficulties a new party would face in its first national campaign, the sooner it was organized the better. Bailey and others advocated the later date in order to assure a more broadly representative convention. They feared that the lack of time to make adequate preparations and the unfavorable season would severely reduce attendance from more distant states, particularly New England. Ironically, the fact that the Know Nothing national convention was also scheduled to meet on February 22 worked against Chase's plan to include antislavery Americans in the Republican organization, since some of his nativist allies would be otherwise engaged, although the *Ashtabula Sentinel* suspected that the intention was for the two conventions to cooperate. Meeting on Washington's birthday had great symbolic value, and Chase, who had developed an elaborate argument linking the antislavery movement to the goals of the founding fathers, was especially loath to forgo this deliberate association.[54]

---

51. Bailey to Adams, December 25, 1855, Adams Diary, December 26, 1855, Adams Family Papers. The Republican Association of Washington, which Bailey's colleagues at the *National Era* dominated, was already promoting a national Republican organization through the establishment of a network of Republican clubs. As the movement for the Pittsburgh convention gained increasing support, however, Bailey saw that more direct action was required. Lewis Clephane, *Birth of the Republican Party* (Washington, 1889), 8–10, 13, 24–25.

52. Clephane, *Birth of the Republican Party*, 12; Israel Washburn, Jr., to John L. Stevens, December 25, 26, 1855, Israel Washburn, Jr., Papers, LC; Seward to Weed, January 29, Weed Papers, UR.

53. Ashley to Chase, January 18, Chase Papers, LC.

54. Goodrich to George Bliss, February 13, Bliss Papers. Isely's assertion that Chase intended for the Pittsburgh convention to make nominations, only to see this idea stymied by Greeley, is without foundation: *Greeley and the Republican Party*, 152. From the beginning, Chase and his allies were quite explicit that the

While he refused to budge on the date, Chase sought to allay Bailey's apprehensions. Using as a pretext the recent decision of the Ohio Americans to attend the national council in Philadelphia in February, he seemingly reversed himself and agreed with Bailey that the Republicans should avoid all entanglements with Know Nothingism. He argued that by assembling in Pittsburgh on February 22, before the American nominating convention could act, the Republicans would avoid, as Bailey paraphrased their exchange, "the odium of doing anything that looked like waiting upon the motions of the Order." Bailey was completely taken in by Chase's glib assurances. Convinced that the Ohio leader now favored "an uncompromising policy," the Washington editor declared that he was "better satisfied" as to the Pittsburgh convention, and he altered the date in his call to February 22, as originally proposed.[55]

Bailey's call appeared in mid-January. Only five of the eight Republican state chairmen had signed it, but leaders in the national capital felt that time was too short to delay its release any longer. Lack of time for full consultation, rather than disagreement over its language, accounted for the failure of the New York, Michigan, and Maine chairmen to sign. Their names were added later. The call, which was issued in the name of the existing Republican state committees, invited "the Republicans of the Union to meet in an informal convention at Pittsburgh on the 22d of February, 1856, for the purpose of perfecting a national organization and providing for a national delegate convention of the Republican party at some subsequent day, to nominate candidates for the presidency and vice-presidency to be supported in the election in November, 1856." Papers such as the New York *Tribune* and the New York *Evening Post* assured their readers that no nominations would be made—that the Pittsburgh gathering was only a preliminary meeting to prepare for a later nominating convention.[56]

At the same time he was telling Bailey that he had abandoned any idea of an alliance with the Know Nothings, Chase was carefully formulating plans to disrupt the approaching American nominating convention and precipitate a northern bolt. His chief ally in the scheme to prevent a reunion of the two wings of the American party was Thomas Spooner, the president of the Ohio order and by now a firm supporter of the governor. Spooner revealed his hand in November at a convention in Cincinnati of the bolters from the June 1855 national council. As a member of the resolutions committee, Spooner presented a minority report that in essence espoused the merger of the nativist organization with the Republican movement. Spooner's resolutions declared that "proscription on account of birth or creed, is unwarranted by American principles"; their only concessions to nativism were an insistence that naturalized citizens renounce all foreign allegiance and a call to guard against any attempt by an ecclesiastic power to subvert American institutions. On the matter of slavery, Spooner's platform endorsed the exclusion of the institution from all territories while opposing any interference with it in the states where it already existed. His resolutions declared that the question of slavery extension was "at present of paramount importance" and pledged that the order would cooperate with any men ready to unite on such a basis. Spooner's report was rejected by a lopsided margin, since it smacked far too much of Republicanism for most delegates

---

Pittsburgh meeting was to be a preliminary conference, whose sole purpose was to prepare for a nominating convention in the summer. Stone's and Chase's correspondence, cited in note 45, make this amply clear.

55. Bailey to Adams, January 14, 20, Adams Family Papers.

56. New York *Tribune*, January 17; New York *Evening Post*, January 31. The original signatories to the call were Stone, Goodrich, Wilmot, Lawrence Brainerd of Vermont, and William A. White of Wisconsin.

outside Ohio.[57] Nevertheless, Spooner, with the avid encouragement of Chase, resolved to attend the meeting of the national council in Philadelphia in February to renew the fight over his platform and induce northern delegates to secede and join the Republican party. When other Ohio American delegates, who frankly admitted that they intended to join the Republicans, asked Chase for advice, he urged them to attend the Philadelphia meeting. The Ohio governor's ultimate goal had not changed. He still desired a national fusion party made up of anti-Nebraska men and liberal Americans.[58]

III

Republican organizers expended much effort recruiting a respectable attendance at the Pittsburgh convention. Leaders in the western states where the party had already organized had less difficulty getting men to attend than did their counterparts in the eastern states, especially New England. Traveling a great distance in the dead of winter by uncertain train connections to a convention that would make no nominations—indeed, it was not clear what it would do beyond setting up a national committee—was anything but appealing. Charles Francis Adams, who declined to go, confessed, "I have no fancy for another winter journey, particularly to so uninviting a place as Pittsburgh."[59]

The Pittsburgh convention was a mass meeting rather than a delegate convention (although the New York Republican state committee appointed official delegates), which technically meant that anyone so inclined could attend. The largest delegations came from Ohio, which sent almost 200 men, New York, and Pennsylvania. New England was poorly represented because a storm prevented some delegates from departing, and, of the few who undertook the journey, most arrived late. Also present were a handful of men who claimed to represent some southern states. Greeley enthused over the large number present—estimated at between 300 and 400—who had come "in the dead of an inclement Winter, when no nominations were to be made and no dispensers of patronage to be propitiated."[60]

If the size of the Pittsburgh meeting was encouraging, the absence of most of the party's important leaders was disappointing. Congressional representation was especially slim, with only Joshua R. Giddings and John Allison of Pennsylvania figuring prominently in the proceedings. The most influential delegations were from New York and Ohio. Among those from New York were John A. King, Horace Greeley, Preston King, Simeon Draper, Abijah Mann, Edwin D. Morgan, and James W. Nye. Those representing Ohio included Jacob Brinkerhoff, future governor William Dennison, Giddings, Rufus Spald-

57. *Ohio Columbian*, November 28, 1855; *Ashtabula Sentinel*, November 29, 1855. A majority of Ohio's delegates voted for Spooner's report, which the Cincinnati *Commercial* proclaimed took "true Republican ground" on the slavery issue and provided the basis for "a cordial cooperation with Americans entertaining these views, and the Republicans." November 23, 1855.

58. Thomas B. Spooner to Chase, February 5, B. F. Williams to Chase, February 7, Chase Papers, LC; legislative correspondence, *Ashtabula Sentinel*, February 11; Chase to My Dear Cleveland, February 11, March 21, Galloway to Chase, January 10, Confidential, Joseph Medill to Chase, February 14, Chase Papers, HSPa; Israel Washburn, Jr., to James G. Blaine, February 14, James G. Blaine Papers, LC.

59. Adams Diary, December 26, 1855, Adams Family Papers.

60. New York *Tribune*, February 25; New York *Times*, February 22; Israel Washburn, Jr., to Blaine, February 26, Blaine Papers; Jacob Heaton to Chase, February 25, Chase Papers, LC. No official list of delegates was published, so these figures are the estimates of reporters on the scene. Deciding on the size of various state delegations was complicated by the imprecise distinction between participants and spectators.

ing, Charles Reemelin, James Ashley, and Joseph Medill. Other noteworthy delegates included Owen Lovejoy, David Wilmot, Senator Charles Durkee of Wisconsin, former senator John M. Niles from Connecticut, Michigan governor Kinsley Bingham, George W. Julian, Oliver P. Morton, and Zachariah Chandler. But the delegate whose presence elicited the most comment was Francis P. Blair.[61]

Until shortly before the convention, Blair had remained undecided about his political plans. By January he was advocating no fewer than three anti-administration conferences—Republican, anti-Nebraska Democrat, and Know Nothing—to meet simultaneously and work out details for cooperating in the presidential contest. Somewhat earlier, in late 1855, the old Jacksonian leader had been asked to serve as president of the Republican Association of Washington. Blair declined, but by prearrangement he wrote a long letter opposing the extension of slavery and denouncing popular sovereignty as the creed of nullifiers, which the association published as a Republican document. Privately he told Martin Van Buren that, although the Democratic party had become "a rotten organization composed & managed altogether by rotten men," he was uncertain whether to join another party. Thus when Lewis Clephane of the association asked Blair to go to Pittsburgh, the Maryland slaveholder refused. At this point Clephane, who was the business manager of the *National Era*, cleverly arranged for some Quaker merchants in Baltimore to organize a Republican club, endorse the principles of Blair's public letter, and select the former editor as their delegate to the Pittsburgh convention. Fearful that Blair was on the verge of abandoning the Democratic party, Van Buren urged him to refrain from taking so drastic a step. To Blair, however, his duty was at last clear.[62] Unaware of the Baltimore meeting's origins, the former editor of the *Globe* set off for Pittsburgh as the sole representative from the slave state of Maryland.

On the train to Pittsburgh Blair ran into Joshua R. Giddings, also on his way to the convention. Their chance encounter was symbolically appropriate, since the emerging Republican coalition contained a full complement of strange political bedfellows, and a more incongruous pair could hardly be imagined. The small, frail Blair was a southerner, a slaveowner, and a passionate defender of Jacksonianism; his tall, sturdy, heavy-set traveling companion was a Yankee, a former Whig, and a forceful spokesman for the antislavery cause. Yet for all their differences, the two men had a pleasant trip. Indeed, Giddings not only intimated that he had always thought well of Blair even when they had clashed previously but even volunteered that he had always known that Blair was an abolitionist! Blair's thoughts at being so described can be surmised, but the two men continued their journey together, chatting amiably about politics. Despite his restrained antislavery principles, Blair was destined to serve as the presiding officer at the first Republican national convention. The irony of this development was not lost on the abolitionist Lewis Tappan, who scornfully commented: "Think of an anti Slavery

---

61. The list of participants was compiled from the various newspaper reports of the convention proceedings. The most complete list, totaling 131 names, appears in Russell Errett, "Formation of the Republican Party in 1856," *Magazine of Western History*, v. 7 (December, 1887), 183.

62. Francis P. Blair, Sr., to Martin Van Buren, January 25 (quotation), February 13, Van Buren Papers, LC; Martin Van Buren to Blair, November 12, 1855, February 4, May 21, John Van Buren to Blair, December 26, 1855, Blair Family Papers; Clephane, *Birth of the Republican Party*, 9–12; *Letter of Francis P. Blair, Esq., to the Republican Association of Washington, D.C.* (Washington, D.C., 1855); Daniel R. Goodloe to Blair, January 8, Blair-Lee Papers.

Convention being presided over by a slaveholder!''[63]

An informal meeting, chaired by Governor Bingham, assembled on Thursday evening, February 21, in the parlors of the Monongahela House. Attendance was full. The powerful conflicting feelings that burst forth at this conference disquieted party leaders. As one participant recalled, ''It was a difficult matter to harmonize the various party interests . . . each striving for ascendancy in the organization of the convention.'' The meeting broke up with obvious bad feeling. A small knot of Republican leaders who were especially sensitive to the potential for disruption met at eight o'clock the next morning to arrange the convention's organization and formulate plans to control its proceedings. Members of this committee, which numbered less than a dozen, included Owen Lovejoy, William Dennison of Ohio, Edwin D. Morgan, Kinsley S. Bingham, James W. Stone of Massachusetts, M. K. Puleston of New Jersey, and Lewis Clephane. During their discussion, Clephane suggested that Blair be the presiding officer. Until then few men knew that Jackson's adviser sympathized with the Republican cause, or that he was in Pittsburgh. The group agreed readily to Clephane's proposal. When approached by the informal steering committee, Blair hesitated, since he had no gift for public speaking, but when pressed he finally agreed to serve. So smoothly did the work of organizing proceed that those not privy to the inner workings of the committee were unaware that it had all been prearranged.[64]

Lawrence Brainard, Vermont Republican state chairman and one of the signers of the call, gaveled the convention to order at 11 A.M. on Friday, February 22.[65] Probably about half the 700 to 800 people present in Lafayette Hall were delegates. Every free state and eight slave states, plus the Kansas, Nebraska, and Minnesota Territories, were represented. As arranged, Blair was elected permanent president. Amidst wild cheering, Preston King and Jacob Brinkerhoff, two members of the clique of Democratic congressmen that originally drafted and introduced the Wilmot Proviso, escorted the Jacksonian leader to the chair. Thanking the delegates, Blair made a brief speech—the first public speech of his long career—and introduced his ''Address of the Southern Republicans.'' Read that evening, this document presented a very conservative analysis of the crisis confronting the nation. Blair traced at great length the various intrigues of southern nullifiers to overthrow the existing sectional compromises and expand slavery, and he urged that all political differences be subsumed under the single issue of restoring the Missouri Compromise. Blair's address reflected the views of his son, Frank, Jr., the leader of the antislavery forces in Missouri, who contended (unrealistically) that with this cautious platform the party could carry Missouri. The elder Blair's declaration, however, was too conservative for most delegates. Even so, to Republicans, who were very

---

63. Samuel Phillips Lee to Frank Blair, Jr., March 17, Blair Family Papers; Lewis Tappan to John G. Fee, February 29, quoted in Louis Filler, *The Crusade Against Slavery* (New York, 1960), 247.

64. Clephane, *Birth of the Republican Party*, 12–13 (quotation); Brinkerhoff, *Recollections*, 123–25; New York *Times*, February 22. Clephane exaggerated the extent to which Blair's presence was unknown. Both the correspondent for the New York *Times* and Greeley in his dispatch to the New York *Tribune* noted his presence, and Greeley even predicted that he would be made chairman. See these reports, dated February 21, in the February 22 edition of each paper.

65. This discussion is based on accounts in the New York *Tribune*, New York *Times*, and Pittsburgh *Gazette*, February 22, 23, 25; Pittsburgh *Post*, February 23, 25; Errett, ''Formation of the Republican Party''; George W. Julian, ''The First Republican National Convention,'' *AHR*, v. 4 (January, 1899), 313–22; and Leonard H. Bernstein, ''Convention in Pittsburgh: The Story of the National Founding of a New Party,'' *Western Pennsylvania Historical Magazine*, v. 49 (October, 1966), 289–300.

sensitive to the charge of being a sectional party, his address held out the hope that with a moderate, conciliatory program the party would soon develop significant strength in the border South, if not the entire section.[66]

Once the convention had been permanently organized, the delegates approved a committee on the address and resolutions, with one member from each state. Abijah Mann of New York, a former Free Soil Democrat, served as chairman. In its afternoon session, the convention agreed to the appointment of a committee on national organization, chaired by Julian. The establishment of these two committees dispensed with the main purpose of the meeting, and until they reported there was little for the delegates to do but listen to speeches.

Political oratory occupied most of the first day's session and a large portion of the second. The major point of debate was the party's attitude toward Know Nothingism. Greeley opened by emphasizing that Republicans in Washington counseled "extreme caution." He opposed an acrimonious collision with the American party, "for many of that party were good Republicans." Others joined Greeley in urging that the party take a moderate stance. During the afternoon session, an Ohio delegate read a telegram from Thomas Spooner, who was at the American convention in Philadelphia, that announced: "The American Party are no longer united. Raise the Republican banner. Let there be no further extension of slavery. The Americans are with you." The delegates responded with tremendous cheering. Spooner's dispatch gave added urgency to the debate over nativism. The two leading spokesmen for the anti-nativist forces were George W. Julian and the Cincinnati German leader Charles Reemelin, both of whom were in their remarks especially severe on the Know Nothings. Calling for adoption of a plank upholding the rights of immigrants, Julian declared that the Republican party should have nothing to do with Know Nothingism. Because the committee on the address was not ready to report, the convention finally adjourned until the next morning.

The committee on the address considered two drafts that had been prepared beforehand. One, written by Henry J. Raymond and brought by the New York delegation, was a long historical discussion of the aggressions of the Slave Power on the rights of the North. The Ohio delegation introduced a shorter address that focused on the Kansas issue and largely reflected the views of Chase. Evidently, a wide divergence of opinion separated committee members, although the New York *Times* correspondent reported as discussions continued that the majority favored a "temperate and conciliatory" tone. Some delegates opposed the adoption of any platform; others urged the incorporation of specific planks. The inordinate length of Raymond's draft also caused difficulties for the committee, which met until three A.M. and then reassembled at eight to complete its work.

The convention reconvened at nine o'clock on the second day. Following some additional speeches, the two committees presented their reports. Julian's committee on organization recommended the establishment of a national committee with one member from each state and the power to add to its membership. Edwin D. Morgan of New York, a close associate of Weed, was designated the party's interim national chairman. Morgan's appointment was especially significant. It acknowledged the influence of the

---

66. Blair's address is in the New York *Times*, February 25; Frank Blair, Jr., to Chase, February 10, Chase Papers, HSPa; *Oneida Weekly Herald* quoted in the *Cortland County Republican*, March 6. In his summary of the convention, Greeley blathered that the elder Blair's sentiments were those of "a very numerous and most respectable portion" of southerners and contended that adoption of a moderate policy would render the Republican party strong in every southern state. New York *Tribune*, February 25.

Seward-Weed wing of the party, as well as the importance of New York City to the Republicans' national fund-raising, the national committee's most important task. Debate focused on the proposal to hold a national convention at Harrisburg on June 17, the anniversary of the battle of Bunker Hill. Considerable opposition to the choice of Harrisburg was voiced on account of its limited accommodations, yet the delegates were also anxious to encourage the weak Republican movement in Pennsylvania. In the end they changed the location to Philadelphia. Selection of Philadelphia represented a decided defeat for the Chase forces, because they had lobbied hard for Cincinnati instead. Delegates probably felt that the choice of the Queen City was tied too closely to Chase's presidential ambitions.[67] The convention left the exact wording of the call for the national convention to the national committee, with the general understanding that it would consult with Republicans in Congress.

The address of the resolutions committee, which was substantially Raymond's version, took almost two hours to read. Its adoption occasioned no controversy. Three resolutions proposed by the committee at the end of the address were approved. They called for "the repeal of all laws which allow the introduction of Slavery into territories once consecrated to freedom" and pledged (somewhat ambiguously) to "resist, by every Constitutional means, the existence of Slavery in any of the Territories of the United States," demanded the immediate admission of Kansas as a free state, and proclaimed the party's intention to oust the Pierce administration from power. Reemelin expressed keen disappointment that the convention took no stand on nativism, and an attempt by John C. Vaughn of the Chicago *Tribune* to have the convention establish a committee of safety to respond to the crisis in Kansas, which seemed to many a call for violent resistance, was shouted down. After two days of public speeches and behind-the-scenes deliberations, the convention adjourned. Its principal purposes had been achieved: A national committee had been appointed and the time and place for a national nominating convention fixed. The party's principles, particularly on questions other than those arising out of the Kansas crisis, were not delineated. Sharp divisions over these principles, coupled with strong resistance to a mass convention promulgating a platform, dictated that no platform be proposed. Deliberately left unresolved was the role of nativism in the party.[68] At this early stage of the campaign, Republican leaders were careful not to alienate any potential supporters. "Who would have expected such moderation?" asked one amazed anti-Nebraska Democrat in Illinois.[69]

Less successful was the resolutions committee's address, whose length mitigated against wide circulation in Republican papers. "Have we got to surrender a page of [the] next weekly to Raymond's bore of an Address?" Greeley muttered to Charles Dana. "The man who could inflict six columns on a long-suffering public, on such an occasion, cannot possibly know enough to write an Address." Greeley was hardly one to do justice to his hated rival, but his criticism was essentially fair. More blunt was the rebuke of the

---

67. New York *Evening Post*, February 25; convention correspondence, New York *Times*, February 22; Ashley to Chase, June 16, 1855, Chase Papers, LC. An amendment that set each state's number of delegates at three times its congressional representation also passed.

68. Convention correspondence, New York *Times*, February 23; Bailey to Adams, January 14, Adams Family Papers. Julian's contention that the proceedings of the convention constituted a repudiation of Know Nothingism was hardly justified, as the scuttling of his proposed resolution defending the rights of the foreign-born forcefully demonstrated. See his account in the [Columbus] *Independent* quoted in Clarke, *Julian*, 170–71; and that by Charles Reemelin in the Cincinnati *Commercial*, March 22.

69. George T. Brown to Lyman Trumbull, March 29, Lyman Trumbull Papers, LC.

Cincinnati *Commercial*, which remarked that the address "began like an ancient chronicle with the creation" and that it was ten times longer than the Declaration of Independence.[70]

Despite some shortcomings, the Pittsburgh conference gave additional impetus to the Republican cause. Party leaders took heart especially from the obvious and intense enthusiasm of the participants. A veteran of forty years of political conventions insisted that the Pittsburgh convention "was all and more than all that the most enthusiastic member expected or even hoped for." Giddings pronounced the spirit of the people far in advance of their leaders, while Ashley observed that the convention "exced [*sic*] by far my most sanguine anticipations, both in point of numbers and enthusiasm."[71] Critical decisions remained—the wording of the call for the Philadelphia convention, the relationship with the North Americans, the adoption of a platform, and the nomination of a national ticket—but the Republican party had been launched as a national organization. Greeley was not far wrong when he prophesied that the convention's "moral and political effect will be felt for a quarter of a century."[72]

Murat Halstead, who covered the Pittsburgh convention for the Cincinnati *Commercial*, reported that "there was little said about Presidents or Presidential candidates." Although the presidency was not the main focus of the meeting, discussion of possible national candidates inevitably occurred. Greeley, for example, suggested Preston King in response to the overbearing tactics of Chase's backers. At the same time, Rufus Spalding signaled his desertion of Chase's cause by actively promoting Justice John McLean of the Supreme Court. Congressman John Allison of Pennsylvania reinforced Spalding's efforts. The most widely mentioned presidential candidate, however, was Chase. "Had the Pittsburgh convention been a nominating convention," one Ohio delegate assured Chase, "you would have had the nomination for the Presidency by two to one." Cheered by such reports, the Ohio governor believed that, thanks in large part to his efforts, the national Republican party had started on the right track, and he was now in a position to reap his reward for his incessant efforts to promote its formation. Little did he realize that his presidential campaign had peaked.[73]

IV

Simultaneous with the Republican convention in Pittsburgh, the American party met in Philadelphia to draft a national platform and nominate a national ticket. With most states whose delegates had bolted the previous June again represented, the national council assembled on February 18. Spooner was on hand, intent on promoting fusion with the Republicans. Also in Philadelphia buttonholing delegates and circulating in the hotel lobbies was Samuel Bowles, who had played such a critical role in the disruption of the

---

70. Greeley to Charles A. Dana, March 2, Benton, ed., *Greeley on Lincoln*, 126; Cincinnati *Commercial*, March 8; Thomas Bolton to Chase, February 25, Chase Papers, HSPa. Despite Greeley's criticism, the *Weekly Tribune* published the entire address in its March 8 issue.

71. Frank Wadsworth to Benjamin F. Wade, February 25 (quotation), Wade Papers; Giddings to Michael H. Jenks, March 11, Michael H. Jenks Papers, Bucks County Historical Society; Ashley to Chase, February 26, Salmon P. Chase Papers, OHS; New York *Evening Post*, February 25.

72. Julian, "First Republican National Convention," 322.

73. Cincinnati *Commercial*, February 26; F. D. Kimball to Chase, February 28, Jacob Heaton to Chase, February 25, Chase Papers, LC; Thomas Bolton to Chase, February 25 (quotation), Chase Papers, HSPa; Arthur B. Bradford to Gerrit Smith, March 2, Smith Papers; Chase to Hiram Barney, February 25, Hiram Barney Papers. HEH.

national council the previous year. Predicting that the convention would probably be "a dough-face affair," the Springfield editor promised that "if there is any raw material there, we will have some stiffening pumped into it. At any rate, I am up for some fun, though I don't anticipate any such luck as I had in June."[74]

The delegates' major problem was to devise an acceptable position on the slavery issue and end the impasse over the controversial Section Twelve adopted in 1855. After a stormy debate, the delegates agreed to remove the divisive section and adopted a compromise statement on slavery, written by Vespasian Ellis, editor of the *American Organ*. Under the guise of neutrality, the new American platform essentially endorsed the southern position. It called for "the maintenance and enforcement of all laws constitutionally enacted until said laws shall be repealed, or shall be declared null and void by competent judicial authority." Because this provision in effect upheld the Kansas-Nebraska Act, northern delegates were not mollified and vowed to continue their fight in the nominating convention.[75]

The Know Nothing nominating convention, which assembled on February 22, marked the climax of the struggle between the supporters of George Law and those of Millard Fillmore for supremacy in the party. Fillmore had begun pursuing the nomination earnestly as early as 1854. He appealed principally to the Silver Grey element in the order and to southerners who desired the preservation of a national Union party. Although the former president endorsed limited nativist reforms, he had little interest in this aspect of the American movement (indeed, while visiting Rome in January 1856, he had an audience with the Pope). Instead, from the first he envisioned the American party as a conservative, pro-Union replacement for the Whig organization. To enhance his prospects for the American nomination, Fillmore joined the order early in 1855 in a ceremony in the parlor of his home and then departed for Europe, safely isolated from the treacherous shoals of American politics. He left his candidacy in the hands of Solomon G. Haven and John Pendleton Kennedy, both old-line Whigs. Kennedy, in fact, was not even a member of the order.[76]

Fillmore's principal rival for the nomination was George Law, who had risen from hod carrier to celebrated New York City steamship, railroad, and construction magnate. A figure of moderate importance in the New York Democratic party, the aggressive, burly Law longed for greater distinction.[77] Live Oak George, as he was known, was poorly educated and had never held public office, but he had a great deal of money, which he generously dispensed in order to gain support, and not surprisingly he quickly attracted a horde of political hangers-on. Espousing nativist dogmas and projecting himself as a new man untrammeled by past party associations, Law joined the Know Nothings and wrested control of the New York organization from the Fillmore men. He purchased the Albany

74. Bowles to Henry L. Dawes, February 10, Dawes Papers.

75. See the accounts in the New York *Times*, *Tribune*, and *Herald*, February 19–22.

76. Fillmore to Isaac Newton, January 3, 1855, Fillmore to Haven, January 22, Severance, ed., *Fillmore Papers*, 347–49, 356–57; Fillmore to Everett, April 7, 1855, Everett Papers; Haven to Fillmore, June 29, 1854, Fillmore Papers, SUNY; John Pendleton Kennedy Diary, May 3, 1855, Kennedy Papers. Fillmore did not publicly acknowledge his membership in the order, and some historians have mistakenly asserted that the former president was not a member. See, for example, Nevins, *Ordeal of the Union*, v. 2, 467. Fillmore, however, privately admitted his initiation. See Fillmore to Dorothea Dix, October 30, *Private*, Dorothea Dix Papers, HU. Also see Elbridge G. Spaulding to Seward, August 2, Seward Papers, UR.

77. For Law's career, see *A Sketch of the Events in the Life of George Law* (New York, 1855); obituary, New York *Herald*, November 19, 1881.

State Register, which began booming his candidacy, and soon James Gordon Bennett of the New York *Herald*, thinking Law a winner, boarded his bandwagon. The American-controlled Pennsylvania legislature endorsed him in February 1855, which gave his candidacy additional momentum. Aghast, Kennedy charged that the candidate was surrounded by "a band of loafers, gamblers, needy procurers and politicians out at elbow," who flattered him while systematically bilking him of his money. Law's candidacy was, he fairly concluded, "the most open attempt to purchase the Presidency" in the country's history.[78]

As Law continued to gain support, Fillmore's friends proposed in alarm that the American nominations be delayed until summer. Law's advisers pushed for the February convention to make nominations as originally scheduled; indeed, the convention had been set early in the year specifically to aid Law.[79] Once the convention assembled, however, the attitude of each group suddenly reversed. After canvassing the delegates, Fillmore's managers realized that, thanks to his strong southern support, the ex-president would be nominated, while Law's men, under the same impression, desperately tried to postpone the nominations until July. In the end the Fillmore forces carried the day, and the former president, who was still in Europe, received the American party nomination. Halstead jeered that men voted against Law "with his dinners and wine in their stomachs, to say nothing of his money in their pockets."[80] A mortified Law vowed that he would not support the ticket.

More ominous for the party's prospects was the growing alienation of northern antislavery delegates. Debate broke out anew in the convention over the national platform. The result was bitter strife, during which, according to one reporter, the "members ran about the hall as if they were mad, and roared like bulls."[81] On the second day of the convention, before the nominations were made, northern dissidents attempted to substitute an anti-Nebraska platform for the one just approved by the national council. When this new platform was rejected, a group of about thirty northern delegates walked out. After Fillmore received the presidential nomination, another bloc of northerners who sympathized with the initial bolters announced their determination to oppose the American ticket as well. All attempts to reunite the American party, first sundered in June 1855, had failed. Led by such men as Thomas Spooner, who was eager to embrace Republicanism, and Lieutenant Governor Thomas Ford of Ohio, who went to Philadelphia uncertain of his intentions only to find himself the target of vehement southern denunciations, approximately seventy northern representatives again seceded from the party. One Ohio delegate who was a strong Chase ally promised that his departure was permanent. "If I am ever caught in another place such as this," he sheepishly

---

78. Kennedy Diary, February 24, Kennedy Papers; Haven to Fillmore, January 20, Fillmore Papers, SUNY.

79. Haven to Fillmore, January 20, James W. Hale to Fillmore, March 4, Fillmore Papers, SUNY; Vespasian Ellis to Ullmann, October 22, 1855, *Private*, Ullmann Papers, NYHS.

80. Kennedy to Haven, January 29 (copy), Kennedy Papers; Haven to Fillmore, March 2, Kennedy to Fillmore, March 15, D. O. Kellogg to Fillmore, February 29, Fillmore Papers, SUNY; Stephen Sammons to Ullmann, November 26, 1855, Haven to Ullmann, February 29, *Confidential*, Ullmann Papers, NYHS; William B. Hesseltine and Rex G. Fisher, eds., *Trimmers, Trucklers & Temporizers: Notes of Murat Halstead from the Political Conventions of 1856* (Madison, 1961), 5.

81. Full accounts are in the New York *Herald*, *Times*, and *Tribune*, February 23–26. The quotation is given in Potter, *Impending Crisis*, 255.

acknowledged, "I hope as my next friend you will do me the favor to secure a place in the Lunatic Asylum for me."[82]

The Ohio delegates played the crucial role in the final disruption of the American party. "They look only to the republican organization for advice," one of the state's representatives to the national convention wrote afterwards concerning his colleagues. He was confident that "Ohio will be better united in the republican movement than ever before," and that Ford and Spooner "will now go into the fight with us without once looking in any other direction." Cognizant of the sympathies of his state's American delegates, Ohio congressman Richard Mott predicted that these new Republican accessions would aid Chase's presidential ambitions.[83] Chase's hopes had been fulfilled: The national unity of the American organization had shattered once again, and the northern bolters obviously expected to form some kind of alliance with the Republicans in the 1856 presidential contest. The Ohio plan—half Republican, half American—remained viable.

Fillmore's closest advisers generally minimized the importance of the northern walkout at Philadelphia, even after the dissidents, adopting the name North Americans, called a national convention to meet in New York City in early June to nominate candidates for president and vice president.[84] Other political analysts, however, pointed to evidence of widespread northern discontent over Fillmore's selection. Led by Ohio, the American state councils in a number of northern states refused to ratify the national ticket. A New Hampshire resident believed that the former president's selection provided the necessary impetus finally to organize the Republican party in the state. Disaffection also surfaced in Massachusetts, where one observer noted that the national ticket "has divided the K. N.'s in the Legislature down to the very roots, & . . . a goodly number of them . . . only wait the signal to join the Republicans." In response, the order's national president stripped bolting state councils of their charters and reorganized them under reliable leadership. Fillmore's nomination, as one Republican commented, had scattered the Know Nothings "to the four winds."[85]

Fillmore was a weaker candidate than Know Nothing leaders had anticipated. To be sure, he had some appeal to outsiders, particularly conservative old-line Whigs who had refrained from joining the secret society, and he had some popularity in the South. Still, the former president seemed a stale, shopworn candidate, and his obvious emphasis on the Union issue in preference to nativism deprived the party of its principal appeal in the North, where its strength had always been concentrated.[86] A conservative Union

---

82. John Paul to Chase, February 24, Chase Papers, HSPa. The Cincinnati *Commercial*, February 27, said 67 delegates attended the subsequent bolters' meeting at the Merchants' Hotel. The New York *Tribune*, February 27, put the number at 71. Whatever the correct total, the North Americans' strength was greater than attendance at this meeting. The 19 New York representatives who opposed Fillmore's nomination issued a separate protest, as did 19 delegates from Ohio, yet not all members of these two groups attended this meeting, although they clearly sympathized with its purposes. Furthermore, several northern delegates had returned home in disgust before the convention concluded its business and should be included in the total number of seceders.

83. John Paul to Chase, February 24 (quotation), Chase Papers, HSPa; Richard Mott to Chase, February 21, Chase Papers, LC.

84. Kennedy to Fillmore, March 15, Haven to Fillmore, March 2, Fillmore Papers, SUNY; Kennedy Diary, February 25, Kennedy Papers.

85. Henry F. French to Benjamin Brown French, March 23, French Papers; Seth Webb, Jr., to Sumner, March 19 (quotation), Sumner Papers, HU; Richard Morgan to Edwin B. Morgan, March 1 (quotation), Edwin Barber Morgan Papers; Weed to Seward, March 15, Seward Papers, UR; John A. Sanborn to Banks, April 9, Banks Papers, LC.

86. The admission of Catholic delegates from Louisiana, which precipitated an acrimonious dispute on the

campaign was certain to alienate northern anti-Nebraska Know Nothings, who despite the prominence of Silver Greys in the order constituted a large majority of its members in the free states. In the debate over the platform, northern delegates expressed great doubt that the American party could carry a single southern state, regardless of what the platform said, and argued instead that victory could be won only in the free states. Although they underestimated American strength in the South, their basic point—that to have any chance of carrying the election the party had to make some accommodation to the public sentiment in the free states—was valid.[87]

Fillmore's nomination so early in the year, leaving him open to attack from all parties months before any other ticket was in the field, further weakened his candidacy. "The best feature in this Fillmore nomination," Weed noted, "is that it has to stand eight months of wear and tear."[88] Unwilling to risk the outcome of a summer convention, Haven and Kennedy made a serious miscalculation when they reversed themselves and forced through the selection of a national ticket at Philadelphia. Given Fillmore's southern support, delay almost certainly would not have cost him the nomination. Haven defended the decision with the rationale that postponing the nominations "would have broken up the party." He alleged that there was a scheme afoot to call the Republican convention at an earlier date, nominate a conservative like John McLean, "and switch us all off the American [and] on to the Republican track."[89] In reality, the action of the American convention increased rather than lessened the likelihood of a union between northern Know Nothings and Republicans by giving them additional time to reach agreement, time that would be of the utmost importance. Had the nomination been postponed, a majority of the northern bolters would have remained, for the time being at least, in the American ranks. A few like Spooner who were already committed to Republicanism would have departed in any case, but many others, including Law's supporters, would have continued to work within the order in hopes of controlling the nominating convention and rewriting the platform.[90] The most notable example was Law, who, seething at his rejection, intimated to Republicans his willingness to aid in defeating Fillmore. Weeks before the

convention floor, also sapped the American party's nativist appeal. At the instigation of Lieutenant Governor Thomas Ford of Ohio, who claimed that without an anti-Catholic test the North Americans would lose thousands of votes, the bolting northern delegates approved a resolution asserting that the acceptance of the Louisiana delegation "absolved every true American from all obligation to sustain" Fillmore's nomination. New York *Times*, February 26.

87. New York *Tribune*, February 26. See in particular the speeches of Edward Perkins of Connecticut and T. J. Coffey of Pennsylvania.

88. Weed to Seward, March 5, Seward Papers, UR; Pike, *First Blows*, 308.

89. Haven to Fillmore, March 2 (quotation), Fillmore Papers, SUNY; Haven to Ullmann, February 29, *Confidential*, Ullmann Papers, NYHS; Kennedy Diary, February 24, Kennedy Papers; George P. Norris to John Clayton, February 23, Clayton Papers, LC.

90. The strength of these two groups cannot be determined precisely, but it is worth noting that at the subsequent bolters' meeting, forty-one participants signed a call for a North American convention in New York City on June 6 while four affixed their names to a protest against holding a convention. The chief proponent of this protest, which asserted that "the whole North ought to unite in a common organization to resist the aggressions of Slavery," was Thomas B. Spooner, who in a speech urged the seceding members to coalesce with the Republicans. In addition, 12 New York delegates who did not sign the call pledged that their state would participate in the June convention, and they were therefore allotted a member of the committee to arrange for this convention. Not only did those who wanted to maintain an independent organization vastly outnumber Spooner's group, but every signer of Spooner's protest save one was from Ohio. New York *Times*, February 26.

North American convention filled with Law's followers met, Republican leaders like Greeley and Weed were quietly giving assurances that Law was with them.[91]

V

Despite the success of the Pittsburgh convention, the simultaneous disruption of the American convention at Philadelphia, and the lukewarm response to Fillmore's candidacy, the Republican party was still a long way from absorbing the northern anti-administration factions into its ranks. The spring elections, in which the Republicans did poorly, gave added urgency to the necessity of broadening the party. Pragmatic party leaders in Washington, where the speakership contest had done much to consolidate the anti-Nebraska forces, stressed the importance of conciliation and union. So did Edwin D. Morgan, the party's national chairman, who emphasized that success in the presidential election depended "entirely" upon the opposition's capacity "to make a combination."[92] The continuing instability of partisan alignments also encouraged hopes for fusion. With the party's future still precarious, Republican strategists looked principally to three groups for additional recruits: anti-Nebraska Democrats, old-line Whigs, and antislavery Americans.

In the 1855 contests, Republicans had enjoyed modest success at best in winning over anti-Nebraska Democrats. Although increasingly disillusioned with their party's policies, the majority of these Democrats refused to join the Republican party. A prominent example was Lyman Trumbull. His experience in Washington only strengthened the new Illinois senator's animosity toward pro-Nebraska Democrats, and he intimated to a close associate back home that he would not support the nominee of the national Democratic convention, who was certain to be a Nebraska man. He announced his intention to "keep clear of all conventions called by the Nebraskaites," yet he withheld any commitment to the Republican cause, primarily out of apprehension that radical antislavery elements would control it.[93] Nowhere was Republican disappointment over the inability to convert Democrats more evident than in New York, where a majority of Barnburners declined to follow Preston King and renounce their Democratic affiliation. An attempt in 1856 to organize a convention in the state to prepare the way for a full-scale exodus collapsed, and in the end Republican organizers had to settle for an address, written by H. H. Van Dyck, a former editor of the Albany *Atlas*, and signed by a number of reputable Democrats, that pledged to support no pro-Nebraska candidate.[94] Still, members of the Republican national committee wanted to do nothing that might discourage wavering Democrats from deserting their party.

Republican managers were also anxious to attract those old-line Whigs who had not joined the Know Nothing order yet also rejected the Republican party because of its

---

91. Greeley to Charles A. Dana, [March-April], Thomas Madigan Collection, NYPL; Weed to Seward, March 5, Seward Papers, UR; Raymond to Sumner, March 6, Sumner Papers, HU; Albany *State Register*, March 1, clipping, enclosed in Haven to Fillmore, March 2, Fillmore Papers, SUNY.

92. Morgan to James W. Stone, April 10, *Private* (copy), Edwin D. Morgan Papers, NYSL; Weed to Seward, March 5, Seward Papers, UR; Colfax to Alfred Wheeler, April 5, Colfax Papers, LC; A. P. Stone to Chase, March 30, Chase Papers, LC; Bailey to Chase, April 18, Chase Papers. HSPa.

93. Trumbull to John Palmer, January 2 (quotation), 24, Palmer Papers; Trumbull to Julia Trumbull, April 25, Trumbull Family Papers, IllSHL.

94. John Bigelow to Chase, February 26, Chase Papers, LC; Isaac Sherman to Banks, March 5, Banks Papers, LC; Bigelow to Washburn, May 17, Israel Washburn, Jr., Papers, LC.

radical reputation. These men were angered by the repeal of the Missouri Compromise and wanted it restored; they had no sympathy, however, for wide-ranging reform programs, disapproved of intemperate denunciations of the South, and worried about the survival of the Union. One such Whig was Hamilton Fish. Earlier, the New York senator summoned a meeting of conservative Whigs in Washington to explore the possibility of holding a national convention in 1856. Most who attended saw little chance that the Whigs could present a formidable ticket. Discouraged, Fish continued to harbor misgivings about the Republican party and decided to wait and see what course its national committee pursued. A number of Whigs were ready to endorse Fillmore despite their dislike for Know Nothingism, but many others shared Fish's indecision.[95] Included in this latter group was James Watson Webb, the erratic editor of the New York *Courier and Enquirer*, who had reluctantly supported the Republican ticket in 1855 but remained fearful that the party would become tainted with abolitionism and was thus exploring his political options.[96] The desire for success required that Republicans allay the fears of these conservatives.

The largest source of potential Republican converts, however, was the North American party. Reluctant to treat these antislavery nativists as equals, Republicans nonetheless coveted their support. Banks, Wilson, Weed, Elihu and Israel Washburn, Greeley, and Colfax were leading proponents of uniting with the northern seceders from the Philadelphia convention. Bailey and Seward, the most important anti-nativist spokesmen, grew despondent as they witnessed this turn of events. "It is manifest that here, the tone of anti-slavery feeling is becoming daily more and more modified, under the pressure of the 'Know-Nothing' influences," Seward complained from the capital. Censuring the party's congressional leaders as "timid, short-sighted men," Bailey fumed, "They are afraid of Know Nothingism, and are constantly in danger of temporising with it." He praised Seward as the only one who joined him in opposing a coalition with the Americans. "The mania for mere success has seized a majority of the men here," the antislavery journalist observed contemptuously.[97]

The wording of the call for the Republican nominating convention, which had been delegated to the national committee, was a crucial aspect of the party's effort to attract additional supporters. Those members of the national committee who attended the Pittsburgh convention held a brief organizational meeting before returning home. They decided to meet again in Washington on March 27 to draft a call for the Philadelphia convention in consultation with the Republican members of Congress. The decision to leave the wording of the call to the committee rather than to the Pittsburgh convention and to include anti-administration congressmen in the deliberations represented a victory for those who favored fusion with the North Americans. Know Nothing influence was much stronger among the anti-Nebraska members of Congress than it had been at Pittsburgh, and, as Greeley's remarks at the February convention revealed, sentiment for a

---

95. Fish to Washington Hunt, February 13 (copy), Fish Papers, LC; Fish to Weed, March 22, Weed Papers, UR.

96. James Watson Webb to James Buchanan, March 10, April 27, Buchanan Papers. HSPa. It is difficult to know how sincere Webb was in his flirtation with Buchanan, but his uneasiness about the Republican party was quite evident.

97. Seward to Weed, March 13, Seward, *Seward*, v. 2, 267; Bailey to George W. Julian, March 9 (quotation), Giddings-Julian Papers; Weed to Seward, March 5, Seward Papers, UR; Bailey to Chase, April 18, Chase Papers, HSPa.

conciliatory policy was especially pronounced in Washington. Colfax outlined the view of the party's congressional leaders when he declared that "the call should be so broad that no one who resisted the aggressions of Slavery could have any excuse on a/c of party names" from participating in the June convention. Anti-Know Nothing leaders like Bailey privately expressed trepidation over the upcoming meeting of the national committee.[98]

When the national committee assembled in Washington as scheduled, its membership was slightly different from that appointed at Pittsburgh, since several members had declined and the committee designated replacements. Joining the committee in its deliberations were influential Republican managers in Congress, led by Banks, Israel Washburn, and other members of the inner circle that had engineered Banks's election as speaker. No official minutes of the committee's deliberations exist, only the fragmentary reports of Washington reporters and scattered comments in private correspondence. The pragmatists on the committee, along with Republican leaders in Congress, wanted a call that encompassed as many northern opponents of the administration as was feasible. North American sympathizers in Congress reiterated the demand that the call not be restricted to Republicans. Members of the national committee thus faced an interesting challenge: Appointed by a Republican convention and given the task of calling a Republican nominating convention, they had to write a call that was not exclusively Republican.

Harmonizing so many groups was not easy, and the national committee, aided by numerous congressmen, met at least four times at Willard's Hotel between March 27 and March 29. One member testified afterwards that much "distrust and jelousy [*sic*]" existed among members of the committee and extensive "bad feeling" among congressmen. About thirty members of Congress, who represented (according to one committeeman) "all the different shades of divisions, Republicans[,] North Americans proper & Americans who are more Republicans than Americans," aired their views. A number insisted that they be allowed to join in issuing the call—an idea the national committee resisted. In addition, many of the North Americans wanted distinct recognition and proclaimed that they "could not and would not go into it as a Republican movement." A. P. Stone of Ohio rejoined that "it was things not names we were after" and indicated that he was willing to forgo use of the name *Republican* in the call. Wide disagreement was also expressed over the principles that should be endorsed. The Sewardites wanted the admission of Kansas as a free state made a distinct issue, and others specified that the repeal of the Missouri Compromise be mentioned. Another dispute erupted over whether a demand for the restriction of slavery apply to all territories or only to those covered by the Missouri Compromise. At this point Stone, who had agreed to several concessions to make the statement more palatable to other groups, asserted that Ohio Republicans would never consent to the latter interpretation and insisted that slavery be excluded from all territories. He added, however, that he was "willing to say the Teritories [*sic*] and they might construe it as they pleased and we would construe it to suit ourselves."[99] As these

---

98. Colfax to Alfred Wheeler, April 5, Colfax Papers, LC; Bailey to Chase, April 18, Chase Papers, HSPa.

99. A. P. Stone to Chase, March 30 (quotation), Chase Papers, LC; Washington correspondence, New York *Times*, New York *Tribune*, March 29; *National Era*, April 3; "Drafts of Different Members of Committee," Edwin D. Morgan Papers. The last-cited item contains drafts of the proposed call by various Republicans, including some non-committee members.

consultations concluded, the congressional participants voiced the hope that the committee would fix the matter so as to promote unity.[100]

Reassembling the next morning, the committee finally agreed to the wording of the call. The original version was not published, but the Washington correspondents of several New York papers leaked its text. The version approved by the committee was directed to

> the people of the United States, (without regard to past differences or divisions), who are opposed to the repeal of the Missouri Compromise and the policy of the present Administration, who favor the exclusion of Slavery from the Territories and the admission of Kansas as a Free State, and who desire to have the action of the Federal Government restored to the principles of Washington and Jefferson.[101]

The wording of this document, which reflected the points of view of several groups as expressed in the committee's sessions, was undoubtedly a joint effort. It avoided the name *Republican*, and it did not attack the South or southerners. A version submitted by Blair, which was a long denunciation of the political power of slaveholders, was unsatisfactory to a majority of committee members. The committee issued it as a circular a few days after the call appeared. Originally, Morgan intended to hold the call back until most members had signed it, but congressional leaders pressed him to release it promptly.[102]

In the meantime, intense criticism of the proposed call's phraseology descended on Morgan. Leading the outcry was James Watson Webb. He sent a blistering note to Morgan, stating that he would publish the document only with an accompanying protest, and vowing that he would not attend the Philadelphia convention under its provisions. "It commits me to *Abolitionism*. I am opposed to the *extension* of Slavery, but am not in favor of abolishing it. To *exclude* is to *abolish* it; while to oppose its *extension* is quite another matter." The New York editor warned that as the call now read he and others "will be excluded from the Convention by its terms." Those unsatisfied with opposition to the extension of slavery, he advised in conclusion, were "too unreasonable to be entitled to further concessions."[103]

Morgan was obviously shaken by Webb's protest and perhaps others like it. The

---

100. Late in life James Ashley claimed that he tried unsuccessfully to get the national committee to alter the basis of representation at the convention by allotting states an additional delegate for every 8,000 Republican votes polled in the previous state election: Ashley, MS Memoir. Ashley's scheme would have strengthened Chase's chances for the nomination by reducing the power of states where the Republican party was more conservative and where Chase had little support, especially Pennsylvania, Indiana, and Illinois. Whether Ashley did, in fact, make such a proposal is unclear, since there is no contemporary evidence to support his recollection and his account contains factual errors. It may be that Ashley advocated his plan at the initial meeting of the national committee in Pittsburgh rather than at the March conference.

101. Washington correspondence, New York *Times*, New York *Tribune*, March 29. The fact that both papers independently printed identical versions of the call indicates that they were privy to the committee's decisions. Though not a member, Greeley probably attended the meetings, since he submitted a proposed call for consideration.

102. Clephane to Morgan, March 29, Edwin D. Morgan Papers; New York *Evening Post* quoted in New York *Times*, March 29. Blair's circular appears in the New York *Times*, April 12. The version among the various drafts in the Morgan Papers that most clearly resembles the final call is in the handwriting of William C. Chace of Rhode Island, but, since he was the committee's secretary, he probably was delegated to write out the result of the committee's collaborative effort.

103. James Watson Webb to Morgan, March 31, Edwin D. Morgan Papers.

national chairman faced an unenviable decision. Altering the call without the consent of the committee was certain to cause resentment, yet issuing it in the face of Webb's complaints seemed to start the Republican national campaign on the wrong foot. Even worse, party managers in the capital desired immediate publication, but committee members had by now departed and could not be reassembled for some days (how many would return to rehash points they had already spent three days discussing was anyone's guess). Before reaching a decision Morgan no doubt consulted Weed, with whom he had close personal and political ties, and perhaps others as well. In any event, taking full responsibility and acting on his own authority, Morgan altered the call to accommodate conservatives.[104] Instead of endorsing "the exclusion of Slavery from the Territories," the rewritten version expressed opposition to "the extension of Slavery into the Territories." Morgan then released the revised call for publication. It read:

> The People of the United States, without regard to past political differences or divisions, who are opposed to the repeal of the Missouri Compromise, to the policy of the present Administration, to the extension of Slavery into the Territories, in favor of the admission of Kansas as a free State, and of restoring the action of the Federal Government to the principles of Washington and Jefferson, are invited by the National Committee, appointed by the Pittsburgh Convention of the 22d of February, 1856, to send from each State three Delegates from every Congressional District, and six delegates at large, to meet in PHILADELPHIA, *on the seventeenth day of June next*, for the purpose of recommending candidates to be supported for the offices of President and Vice-President of the United States.

It was dated Washington, March 29, 1856, and signed by the members of the Republican national committee, who were simply identified as "National Committee." The name *Republican* appeared nowhere in the call.

Privately, some Republicans accused Morgan of sacrificing one of the party's cardinal principles, the restriction of slavery from the territories, in order to placate conservatives. Chase and his advisers, in particular, were furious over the national chairman's action. The Ohio committeeman, A. P. Stone, immediately dispatched a letter to Morgan demanding to know on whose authority the wording had been changed and the reasons for the alteration. Morgan's reply has not survived, but the Republican chairman told another member of the committee that "some change" in the call had been made "for sufficient reasons." Elsewhere he explained that the "broad" call was designed "to meet the views of many of the members who voted for Banks but who are not yet enrolled as Republicans." He believed that it was popular "with our friends in Congress and elsewhere."[105]

One displeased individual was Bailey, who poured out his frustration to his old friend Chase. He complained that those in control of the Republican party were demoralized by a passion for immediate success. "Conceding and conceding,—diluting and diluting,— they are seeking to trim and weaken our movement so as to secure conservatives" and other groups. The admission of Kansas was merely "a temporary question," not one of

---

104. Morgan to William C. Chace, April 9 (copy), Edwin D. Morgan Papers; Bailey to Chase, May 8, Chase Papers, HSPa; A. P. Stone to Chase, March 31, Chase Papers, LC.

105. A. P. Stone to Morgan, April 3, Morgan to William C. Chace, April 9 (copy) (quotation), Morgan to James M. Bunce, April 17 (copy) (quotation), Morgan to J. W. Stone, April 10, *Private* (copy), Edwin D. Morgan Papers.

principle, and as such should not serve as the foundation for party action. When the Washington journalist learned that the call had been "tampered with," he sent Lewis Clephane to see Israel Washburn, with whom Bailey had worked closely the past two years, to urge restoration of the word *exclusion*. Washburn, however, did not consider the change important, and so Bailey let the matter drop. The antislavery editor soon regretted this decision, and a month later he was growling that "since then . . . I have seen a steady purpose" among Republican leaders "to keep up the dodge." The "real question" was the exclusion of slavery, not its extension, he insisted, for "slavery already exists in all the Territories, from which it is not excluded by positive law—what nonsense to talk about opposing its *extension*." It was nothing less than "lowering the platform." In the columns of the *National Era*, he demanded that the Philadelphia convention endorse the principle that Congress should prohibit slavery by positive law from all the territories.[106]

Morgan and other Republican managers waved aside the new wording as of limited importance. The Philadelphia convention, not the call, would ultimately specify the Republican platform, and most party leaders understood that until then it was more important to bring as many men as possible into the party's ranks. Above all, as practical politicians they were determined to avoid the fate of earlier antislavery parties, whose quest for moral purity took precedence over creation of a powerful (and permanent) political organization. Pragmatists, as Bailey fretted while trying to rally the old guard of the antislavery cause, were firmly in control of the Republican organization. These men had no interest in lost causes.

The all-inclusive nature of the call for the June convention created difficulties for some Republican state organizations. In Connecticut, for example, prior to the appearance of the call, Republicans appointed delegates to the national convention at their state convention in March. A prominent state Republican leader asked Morgan for clarification of the intended meaning of the national committee's summons. He noted that if delegates to the Philadelphia convention were expected to represent all anti-Democratic groups, it would be necessary to begin anew in Connecticut. Morgan responded that each state should decide for itself how delegates were to be selected. Dissension also surfaced in Pennsylvania, where Wilmot, as chairman of the discredited state committee appointed in 1855, initiated a movement to reorganize the state party by summoning a convention to elect national delegates. Some Republicans, who with good cause feared American domination of the Pennsylvania party, protested because the call was not confined to Republicans. As in Connecticut, Morgan declined to intervene. To one Pennsylvania correspondent, he explained that the national committee *"purposely omitted* to designate the manner of choosing Delegates to the Presidential Convention, . . . but left that question to the people of the several States *to act as circumstances, in each, might seem to require."* In the end, selection of delegates in the various states went forward without intractable difficulties. The concern of Republicans in such states as Connecticut and Pennsylvania, however, where the North Americans were powerful, well led, and determined to control any fusion organization, were not without substance, as events during the 1856 campaign would demonstrate.[107]

---

106. Bailey to Chase, April 18 (quotation), May 8 (quotation), Chase Papers, HSPa; *National Era*, April 10, May 1, 15.

107. James M. Bunce to Morgan, April 15, 19, Morgan to Bunce, April 18 (copy), B. D. Pettigill to Morgan, May 8, Morgan to Pettigill, May 8 (copy) (quotation), Stephen I. Johnson to Morgan, April 7, Weed to Morgan, April 22, Morgan to Myron H. Clark, April 23 (copy), Edwin D. Morgan Papers.

Of greater immediate concern for the national committee was an attempt emanating from a group of North American leaders to have the anti-Nebraska members of Congress issue another call for a separate nominating convention. Former governor William F. Johnston of Pennsylvania, who was looking for a new political opening after being rebuffed in his quest for a cabinet post by Fillmore's managers at Philadelphia in February, concocted the scheme. Representative Russell Sage of New York, a Know Nothing and a close adviser to Banks, was particularly active in rallying support in Washington for the proposal. Assisting him was Henry Wilson, who, although no longer identified with the Know Nothings, was a leading advocate of a broad fusion party. The object of this congressional call, which circulated among anti-Nebraska senators and representatives for signatures, was to organize a convention of all opponents of the administration and the Kansas-Nebraska Act to meet at the same time as the Republican convention, so that, in Seward's words, "through that distinct door Americans could enter" the Republican ranks. This nativist plan was similar to that used in New York in 1855, when the Republican and Whig conventions assembled separately and then merged. To Weed, Seward expressed his unwillingness to lend to "Sage and other Know Nothings the use of my fingers to pull their chestnuts out of the Ashes."[108] Because of sharp divisions over its propriety, nothing came of this proposed People's convention. North American leaders therefore went ahead with their plans to hold a convention in New York City in June, a few days before the Republicans were to meet in Philadelphia.

As these plans proceeded, Blair became concerned that the nativists would nominate a candidate before the Republicans met, and he broached with Weed the possibility of moving forward the date of the Republican convention. Blair was not alone in his anxiety, but committee members concluded that they had no authority to change the date set by the Pittsburgh convention. Their reluctance also signified a determination to avoid the appearance that their action in any way hinged on that of the North Americans. Privately, however, party leaders acknowledged that the New York City meeting was fraught with danger. "Our *real* trouble is the K.N. convention on the 12th prox.," Greeley wrote to Colfax with obvious trepidation. "I can't see by that corner."[109]

As the uneasiness of Greeley, Blair, and other Republican managers revealed, the struggle to dominate the opposition had not abated in the wake of the division of the American convention in February. An agreement with the North Americans concerning fusion had yet to be worked out, and the prospects for a successful merger, upon which all chance of defeating the Democrats hinged, were squally at best. While a minority of bolting Know Nothing leaders were ready to enter the Republican party immediately, the majority were determined to exact concessions from the Republicans before abandoning their separate organization. To compound the problem, the more militant North Americans clung to the belief that they could control any fusion party. At the northern bolters' meeting in Philadelphia, Samuel H. Hammond of the Albany *Register* affirmed that he "had no objection to letting Republicans go up with their kite, but it must be in the tail." His remarks produced great applause throughout the hall.[110]

---

108. Seward to Weed, Saturday morning [April], and fragment, n.d. [April], Weed Papers, UR. Frederick Seward published these two items as a single letter, dated April 27, in *Seward*, v. 2, 270–71. From content as well as physical evidence they appear to be two separate letters.

109. Seward to Weed, April 14, Weed Papers, UR; William C. Chace to Morgan, May 8, James M. Bunce to Morgan, May 6, Edwin D. Morgan Papers; Greeley to Colfax, May 6, Greeley-Colfax Papers.

110. New York *Times*, February 26.

The Republican movement had made significant strides since the 1855 fall elections. Under the influence of Banks's election, which had forged the first bonds of cooperation between Republicans and northern Know Nothings, the second disruption in as many years of the national American party over the slavery extension issue, the Pittsburgh convention, and the promulgation of a broad call for the Philadelphia convention in June, a number of diverse groups were slowly coalescing in the Republican organization. Nevertheless, by mid-spring the outlook for the Republican party remained uncertain, its future far from secure. For one thing, the Know Nothings' commanding power coupled with divisions among various opposition factions had blocked the formation of the Republican party in half the northern states in 1855, and thus establishment of a party organization in these states was an urgent priority. In addition, the absorption of the North Americans nationally and in various states, which had yet to be accomplished, was mandatory if the Republican party were to supplant the Know Nothings as the Democrats' principal adversary. With the presidential election only six months away, the Republican party had not yet gained the momentum necessary to mobilize under its banner the anti-Democratic forces in the free states.

9

Spring Breakthrough

More than a century later, it is difficult to appreciate the Republican party's precarious situation in the spring of 1856. Armed with the knowledge of the party's ultimate success, the modern historian is almost irresistibly drawn to the view that by the time the call for the Philadelphia convention appeared, the party's future was secure. Republican leaders, however, harbored no illusions about the inevitability of the party's emergence as a powerful political organization or about its longevity. While cautiously encouraged by developments since the opening of Congress in December, they realized that the party's position as the major anti-Democratic party in the country was far from established, its survival anything but certain. The Republican party's relationship with the Know Nothings at the national level and in states where the party had not organized in 1855 remained unsettled, and, with the June conventions fast approaching, any fusion of the two organizations had to be hammered out in a short space of time.

Any expectations that the North Americans would submit meekly to Republican control were dashed by the results of the 1856 spring elections, in which the Republican party's basic weakness contrasted sharply with the continuing strength of the Know Nothings. In several states, the American party, in spite of the disruption of its national organization, remained sufficiently powerful that the Republicans shrank from even fielding an independent ticket. Even more dismaying was the series of humiliating defeats suffered in a number of cities and states where Republicans for the first time openly challenged the Know Nothings. Outwardly maintaining a brave front, Republican managers were privately despondent. Solomon G. Haven, one of Millard Fillmore's closest advisers, was optimistic that the Republican party's obvious lack of strength would deter North American party members from entering any fusion coalition and even drive them back into the regular American organization. He noted that in the recent elections in Connecticut, Rhode Island, Albany, and Cincinnati, independent Republican candidates polled approximately one vote in eleven—hardly an auspicious performance. The idea that the Republicans could sweep the North, Haven snorted, was absurd.[1]

Note: Unless otherwise indicated, the year for newspaper and manuscript citations in this chapter is 1856.

1. Solomon G. Haven to Millard Fillmore, April 24, Fillmore Papers, SUNY; Haven to Daniel Ullmann, April 23, Ullmann Papers, NYHS; Cincinnati *Enquirer*, April 11.

I

Politics in Connecticut, where the Know Nothings fashioned a popular program that enabled them to retain their ascendancy over the other anti-Democratic groups in the state, illustrated the difficulties that still beset the Republican party. Beginning in the summer of 1854, the secret order had expanded rapidly in the state, and as the 1855 state election approached, the Hartford *Courant* said of the Know Nothings, "They're making sweeping headway just now with the old parties. The wild-fire breaks out everywhere, North, East, South, West."[2] The escalating strength of the nativist movement, the refusal of some Whig leaders to abandon their party organization, and the failure of leading anti-Nebraska Democrats to endorse fusion made futile any attempt that year to organize a Connecticut Republican party.

Encouraged by this expansion, the state's Know Nothing leaders decided to run a separate ticket in 1855. The American state convention nominated William T. Minor for governor over Henry Dutton, the Whig incumbent who joined the nativist society in a calculated move to win reelection. At the Whig state convention Thomas M. Day of the Hartford *Courant* urged that the party unite with the Know Nothings by endorsing Minor, but the delegates instead renominated Dutton. Although the Whigs rejected fusion on the state ticket, for the most part they cooperated with Know Nothings in other contests. The two parties nominated the same candidates in all four of the state's congressional districts and combined in the great majority of the legislative contests as well. Dutton also obtained the nomination of the Free Soil convention after he disclosed that he had left the nativist order following his rejection by the American state convention. After considerable discussion, a separate temperance convention gave a joint endorsement to Minor and Dutton. As they had done the year before, the Democrats nominated Samuel Ingham for governor. The party's platform denounced the state's prohibitory law, and tried to sidestep the slavery issue by declaring that Congress's power in the territories "should be only employed to such an extent as the necessities of the case may require, and for the equal benefit of all the parties to the federal compact."[3]

Minor scored a narrow victory over Ingham in the popular vote, although he lacked a majority. Dutton, running on the Whig and Free Soil tickets and with half the temperance endorsement, trailed far behind; in fact, in only one township in the entire state did he manage to win even a plurality.[4] Minor was especially strong in the more isolated, less economically developed eastern counties where Baptists and Methodists were particularly numerous. Ingham, on the other hand, displayed greater appeal in the more industrialized western counties. In the legislative and congressional contests, the Know Nothings won solid control of the legislature (thus assuring Minor's election) and elected every one of the state's congressmen.

Although he criticized the Democratic platform's weak stance on slavery expansion, the old Jacksonian leader Gideon Welles, now a political independent, maintained that

---

2. Hartford *Courant*, January 4, 1855, quoted in Noonan, *Nativism in Connecticut*, 200; Gideon Welles to My Dear Sir, March, 1855 (copy), John Boyd to Welles, March 23, 1855, Welles Papers, LC. When the state council met in February 1855, it reported that there were 169 local lodges in the state, with a total membership of 22,000. Hartford *Times*, February 17, 1855.

3. Hartford *Times*, February 15, 23, 28, March 2, 1855; Parmet, "Know-Nothings in Connecticut," 106–12;, *Nativism in Connecticut*, 206–07.

4. The official vote was Minor, 28,028 (43.5 percent); Ingham, 27,290 (42.3 percent); and Dutton, 9,162 (14.2 percent).

temperance was "more potent and decisive perhaps than any other" issue in the election. He was apparently on solid ground when he asserted that despite Ingham's strong showing, the Democrats had suffered significant defections of traditional supporters. In fact, the rate of defection to the Know Nothings was similar among former Whigs and Democrats (Table 9.1). In addition, both the 1854 Temperance voters and Free Soilers provided solid support to the Know Nothing ticket—further evidence of the strong nativist feeling in the ranks of these reform movements. A sizable number of 1854 Whigs cast Democratic ballots in 1855, and Welles may well have been right in attributing these defections largely to the rum question. While contemporaries emphasized the prominence of ex-Whigs in the Know Nothing order, approximately a third of the American strength came from former Democrats (Table 9.2). In their first state campaign, Connecticut Know Nothings skillfully exploited the nativist, temperance, and slavery issues to emerge victorious.[5]

Following the 1855 spring election, Know Nothing leaders labored to solidify the party's power in the state. The head of the order in Connecticut was Nehemiah Day Sperry, a twenty-seven-year-old stonemason and Whig alderman from New Haven. Despite his youth and limited political experience, Sperry was a superbly talented political operator, and under his guidance the order's program adroitly blended nativism and antislavery. In a popular move, Governor Minor disbanded foreign-born military companies. In addition, the new legislature enacted a series of nativist reforms including a church property act, a law denying the right of state courts to naturalize aliens, and a constitutional amendment imposing a literacy test on the right of suffrage, which the voters ratified in the fall.[6] It also gave the first approval to a proposed amendment extending to twenty-one years the period of residence in the United States before being eligible to vote.[7] After the 1855 legislative session concluded, the order gave greater emphasis to its antislavery principles, and all the state's delegates walked out of the national council in June of that year in protest over the American platform. In defending this action, Governor Minor declared that "the American party would have been blown to atoms in every Northern state" had the Twelfth Section been accepted, and it could not have been rallied again.[8] The state council subsequently approved a platform that demanded restoration of the Missouri Compromise, opposed the extension of slavery, and called for protection of the right of suffrage in the territories by the federal government. In an effort to disarm critics, the council also abandoned secrecy, abolished oaths, discarded its elaborate ritual, and made Protestant immigrants eligible for membership.[9]

---

5. "State Election 1855—Reasons of Dem[ocratic] defeat," Draft Article (quotation), Welles Papers, LC; James T. Pratt to Thomas H. Seymour, July 17, 1855, J. Olney to Seymour, August 25, 1855, Thomas H. Seymour Papers; Welles to [Preston King], April 23, 1855 (copy), Welles Papers, ConnHS. For claims of Whig influence in the Know Nothing organization, see the Hartford *Times*, February 22, 23, 1855. For Free Soil links to the Know Nothings, see Edward Prentiss to Francis Gillette, December 25, 1854, January 5, 1855 (copies), Joseph Hawley Papers.

6. In October 1855, the literacy amendment was ratified by a popular vote of 17,370 to 12,544. It proved ineffective for, while it specified that voters had to be literate, it failed to stipulate that they be able to read English. Parmet, "Know-Nothings in Connecticut," 130–48; Noonan, *Nativism in Connecticut*, 218.

7. Proposed amendments had to pass both houses of the Connecticut legislature for two successive years (the second time by a two-thirds majority) before being submitted to the electorate for approval. The twenty-one-year residency requirement failed to secure a two-thirds vote in the House in 1856.

8. William T. Minor to Ullmann, July 17, 1855, Ullmann Papers, NYHS.

9. The Connecticut Know Nothing platform is given in the New York *Tribune*, July 2, 1855.

These actions held great significance for the future of Connecticut Republicanism. By the end of 1855, the Americans were the strongest opposition party in the state, and its leaders were determined to control any fusion coalition. Challenged by a powerful nativist movement that had co-opted its program, the Connecticut Republican party faced an uphill struggle.

Early in February 1856, a group of Hartford politicians representing various former party affiliations inaugurated a concerted drive to organize a state Republican party. Especially prominent in the movement were two antislavery Democrats, Gideon Welles, the one-time editor of the party's state organ, the Hartford *Times*, and former United States senator John M. Niles, who had supported Martin Van Buren on the Free Soil ticket in 1848. The less cautious of the pair, Niles headed the state's delegation to the Pittsburgh convention. Welles was a much more circumspect politician, but nudged by Niles, he, too, endorsed the Republican cause. Although he had no wish to see slavery expand, Welles's estrangement from the Democracy grew in large part out of his states' rights conservatism. Convinced that under southern domination the Democratic party had become a great force for centralization, the Connecticut leader outlined the basis of the Republican party as "the rights of man, the rights of the state, a strict construction of the constitution, opposition to the nationality and extension of slavery, and to the aggressive measures and unauthorized assumption of powers by the federal government."[10] Niles undertook to raise the necessary funds to publish in the capital a Republican journal free from the taint of Know Nothingism and unconnected with past partisan divisions. With considerable reluctance Welles agreed to edit the paper, the *Evening Press*. Shortly thereafter a mass meeting in Hartford issued a call for a convention to organize a state Republican party.[11]

The first Republican state convention assembled on March 12 in Hartford with more than 300 delegates from most towns in the state answering the roll. The convention call had not stipulated a strict basis of representation, so all delegates who presented credentials were accredited. The danger Republican leaders feared most was that the Americans would seize control of the new party, a concern greatly stimulated by the nativist society's decision to send delegates to the meeting. Their worst fears seemed on the verge of realization when Know Nothing governor William Minor, who had already been renominated by the Americans, led on an informal ballot for the Republican nomination. One of Minor's supporters in the convention was former governor Chauncey Cleveland, a non-nativist, who argued that taking the incumbent would help conciliate the Americans, adding, "*It is from them that our strength is to come.*" Most Republican managers, however, were convinced that if the new party chose Minor, it would be swallowed up by the Americans and lose its separate identity at its founding. Rallying their supporters, the party's leaders emphasized the peril it was in, and on a second, formal ballot, Welles received the nomination. The Hartford editor had no taste for campaigning, but he agreed to accept the Republican nomination in order to keep the party's organization in safe hands, and also because he knew that, with only three weeks

---

10. "The Repeal of the Missouri Compromise, its Effect on Connecticut," Essay, Typescript, Welles Papers, ConnHS; Niven, *Welles*, 230–31, 259–64.

11. Welles Diary, January 12, 15, 16, 17, February 4, 11, 26, 27, Welles Papers, LC; Francis Gillette to Charles Sumner, February 14, Sumner Papers, HU; Essay, "The Establishing of the Hartford Press," Printed Circular, "Republican Meeting in Hartford," Welles Papers, ConnHS. A printed copy of the call for the Hartford mass meeting is also in this last collection.

until election day, there was no possibility he would win. Rather, the party's goal was, as one Republican put it, to "defeat the Slave Democracy, now, and triumph in the fall."[12]

Whereas Americans desired a coalition with the Republicans, the Democrats' strategy was to induce old-line Whigs to unite with them. In the end, neither strategy came to fruition. The Republicans spurned any coalition with the nativists in the governor's race, while the remaining fragment of the Whig party met in a sparsely attended convention and nominated an independent ticket. With the gubernatorial contest a four-way race, Americans actively wooed Republicans. Thus the Hartford *Courant* insisted that Americans and Republicans were *"brothers"* without any "earthly necessity for the slightest collision," and pronounced that, united, they would be invincible in the free states. Although their rejection of Minor was a calculated rebuke to Know Nothingism, Republicans invited the "more liberal and enlightened" nativists to join their ranks.[13] Republican leaders headed by Niles relayed optimistic reports of the party's strength. "We shall poll a full vote larger than we expected when our movement commenced," a prominent Connecticut Republican assured Edwin Morgan, the party's national chairman.[14]

Juxtaposed against these predictions, the results were a stinging setback for Republicans. The hard-fought campaign produced a heavy turnout, but unexpectedly Samuel Ingham, the Democratic nominee, ran more than 6,500 votes ahead of Minor. Welles finished a dismal third, with a mere 10 percent of the votes cast. Ingham lacked a majority, and, because in the legislative races Republicans and Whigs generally cooperated with the Know Nothings, Minor's reelection by the legislature was inevitable. It was also certain that only an American could be elected to the United States Senate. Disappointed at the Republican party's showing, Chauncey Cleveland conceded that the Americans still dominated the opposition in Connecticut.[15]

The sources of the Republican vote documented the party's failure to make significant inroads into the Know Nothings' strength. The largest share of Welles's vote came from men who voted Whig in 1855. Despite his prominent Democratic past, he polled virtually no votes among 1855 Democrats and did substantially poorer among Know Nothing voters than did even Ingham. Although the American total declined some 2,000 votes in 1856 compared to 1855, the Republicans were not the prime beneficiaries; three times as many of these nativist defectors voted Democratic as Republican (Table 9.3). Most of the bolters were probably former Democrats returning to their earlier allegiance. Accessions from the Americans and Whigs, coupled with the fact that the Democrats were much more successful than their competitors in retaining their traditional supporters, accounted for Ingham's strong showing. The Whig vote, already small in 1855, dwindled to insignificance in 1856, as some three-fourths of the party's 1855 followers went over to either the Republicans or the Americans. The fundamental problem for the Republicans was that

---

12. Noonan, *Nativism in Connecticut*, 239; Parmet, "Know-Nothings in Connecticut," 182–83; James M. Bunce to Edwin D. Morgan, February 12, Edwin D. Morgan Papers; Niven, *Welles*, 269.

13. Hartford *Courant*, March 6; Hartford *Evening Press*, March 18; Welles to [James Babcock], February 20 (copy), Chauncey Cleveland to Welles, March 27, Welles Papers, LC.

14. John Niles to Morgan, March 15, James M. Bunce to Morgan, March 18 (quotation), Edwin D. Morgan Papers.

15. Cleveland to Welles, April 18, Welles Papers, LC; Cleveland to Salmon P. Chase, April 21, Chase Papers, LC. The final tally stood Ingham (Democrat), 32,704 (49.0 percent); Minor (American), 26,108 (39.1 percent); Welles (Republican), 6,740 (10.1 percent); and John A. Rockwell (Whig), 1,251 (1.9 percent).

almost two-thirds of the Americans remained loyal to their party, and few of those who did defect voted for Welles. Moreover, Minor gained new supporters from other parties, a development that to some extent offset his losses among former partisans. The core of Republican strength was, not surprisingly, the old Free Soil vote. Temperance voters, on the other hand, continued to find the American party, with its anti-immigrant, anti-rum, and antislavery appeal, more attractive than the single-issue Republican party (Table 9.4). Nor did the Republican cause disproportionately attract new voters. The expectations of Connecticut Republicans proved grossly unrealistic. Although the rival Americans suffered a decline in strength, they continued to control the state government, and even their reduced vote was almost four times as great as that of the Republicans. Looking ahead to the national election, confident nativist leaders saw little reason to yield to Republican dictation.[16]

II

The formation of a national Republican organization and the call for a nominating convention supplied the thrust necessary to organize the party in those northern states where it had not previously taken shape. At the beginning of 1856 no Republican organization existed in more than half the free states; by June, when the Philadelphia convention assembled, the party had been organized throughout the North. Four states—Iowa, New Hampshire, Indiana, and Illinois—provide examples of the party's formation during these months.

The liquor controversy continued to disorder Iowa's politics following James Grimes's election as governor in 1854. Although his gubernatorial campaign was based on more than the rum question, Grimes was a strong prohibitionist, and when the legislature approved a moderately strict temperance law in January 1855, he unhesitatingly signed the bill. The legislature, however, stipulated that the controversial law would not go into effect until ratified by the electorate, and it scheduled the referendum in April to coincide with the state election. The voters approved the law by a small majority.[17] Whereas Democrats overwhelmingly opposed the anti-liquor statute, Grimes's 1854 supporters voted three to two in favor of prohibition and, unlike the Democrats, turned out in full. In addition, almost all previous non-voters and a majority of new voters who went to the polls endorsed temperance (Table 9.5). Approval of the law meant that the liquor issue would remain salient in Iowa politics, a situation that complicated the movement to organize a state Republican party. Grimes was already advocating creating a Republican coalition that would include both Germans and the Know Nothings, but any endorsement or disapproval of prohibition threatened to alienate one group or the other. Furthermore, although anti-liquor sentiment was dominant in the anti-Nebraska coalition, a very sizable minority opposed outlawing drink. As a result, the task before Grimes and his advisers was anything but easy. The absence of a state election in the fall of 1855, along with

---

16. Hartford *Courant*, April 11.

17. The totals were: for the proposed temperance law, 25,555 (53.0 percent); and against, 22,645 (47.0 percent). The estimated turnout was 61.4 percent. Table 9.5 probably exaggerates anti-temperance sentiment among Grimes's supporters; the large negative number for the not voting category dictates caution in accepting these estimates.

persisting disagreement among anti-Democratic factions in the state, persuaded them to delay any attempt to inaugurate a Republican party until next year.[18]

A convention for that purpose met in Iowa City on February 22, 1856, the same date as the Pittsburgh convention. Grimes, who had for a year been in correspondence with Republican leaders in other states, was the most important and active proponent of this movement. The convention was essentially a mass meeting, with many of the delegates self-appointed, and contained, in the words of one historian, "the full rainbow of Iowa political sentiment" except for administration Democrats. Sensitive to propriety, Grimes remained in the background, leaving direction of the proceedings to trusted associates.[18]

The nomination of a state ticket produced only minor friction, since all officers to be elected in the fall were of limited importance. The real fight occurred over the platform, particularly on the questions of nativism and temperance. German voters in one county appointed their own representatives and threatened to withdraw if the platform were not kept free of what they denoted as "all the isms of the day—such as nativism, abolitionism, religious fanaticism, Maine Lawism, etc." Know Nothings were equally insistent that their doctrines be ratified. Maine Law men made a determined fight to include a prohibition plank in the platform, while Germans demanded that the platform endorse the existing naturalization laws. Aware that no declaration on either issue would satisfy all groups, party managers adopted the expedient position that the platform should be confined to the slavery issue, over which fewer differences emerged. Germans aided in defeating a proposed temperance plank, while the drys helped reject the proposed resolution on naturalization. Proclaiming that "freedom is alone national," the Iowa Republican platform denounced the Slave Power for the repeal of the Missouri Compromise, vowed to oppose the spread of slavery, and demanded that "all national territory *shall be free.*"[19] The convention also named delegates to the Republican national convention, yet to be called.

The Republican party had finally coalesced in Iowa, but whether the strategy of suppressing ethnocultural issues would be successful had yet to be tested. German voters were clearly uneasy, and in fact a few German editors repudiated the party because it dodged the question of nativism. Furthermore, several county conventions grafted these rejected planks onto local Republican platforms. Alienated by the action of the national American convention, nativists, on the other hand, went into the Republican movement with far less friction. A poorly attended state council ratified Fillmore's nomination and the national platform; careful observers, however, believed that most Know Nothings had joined the Republican party. For substantiation, they pointed out that even the pro-Fillmore state organization endorsed the Republican state ticket. By April, Grimes reported that "Know Nothingism *per se* is very weak in this State" and that Fillmore was "universally repudiated." He believed that by election day in November the large majority of Americans would be found in the Republican ranks.[20]

---

18. James Grimes to Chase, April 8, July 16, 1855, Salter, *Grimes*, 69, 76. For a discussion of the liquor issue during this period, see Dan E. Clark, "The History of Liquor Legislation in Iowa, 1846–1861," *Iowa Journal of History and Politics*, v. 6 (January, 1908), 55–87.

18. Sparks, "Republican Party in Iowa," 25. Grimes apparently wrote the call for the Republican state convention. See a memo concerning the call in the William Salter Papers, Ia SDHA.

19. Sparks, "Republican Party in Iowa," 24–27; Rosenberg, *Iowa on the Eve of the Civil War*, 128–30. The Republican platform is given in Herbert S. Fairall, *Manual of Iowa Politics* (Iowa City, 1884), 40–41.

20. Grimes to William Penn Clarke, April 3, *Annals of Iowa*, v. 22 (October, 1940), 475; Sparks, "Republican Party in Iowa," 27–29.

III

Whereas in Iowa the Republican party essentially absorbed the Americans, in New Hampshire precisely the opposite occurred: the Know Nothings went into the Republican organization in force and exercised effective control. From Washington, such leaders as Senator John P. Hale and Congressman Mason W. Tappan urged Americans early on to merge in the Republican movement. So strong was the order in the Granite State, however, that state leaders resisted this step until after the gubernatorial election in March. Only then did they think that a movement to organize the Republican party would be feasible.[22] The nativists renominated Governor Ralph Metcalf, who ran on the rechristened American-Republican ticket. In a move that foreshadowed the future Republican coalition, the former Free Soil organ, the *Independent Democrat*, which had backed an independent ticket in 1855, now endorsed Metcalf. A straight Whig ticket, designed to keep anti-Know Nothing voters out of the Democratic column, was also in the field.[23] Several observers believed that Fillmore's nomination had hurt Metcalf and helped swell the Whig vote beyond all expectations, but in any case the results established the overwhelming dominance of the Americans in the anti-Democratic ranks. Metcalf lacked a majority, so the election devolved on the legislature, where Know Nothing control guaranteed his reelection.[24]

With the state contest out of the way, the movement to organize the Republican party began in earnest. Metcalf's failure to win an absolute majority made the Know Nothing leaders more tractable on the question of union. One of Tappan's correspondents informed him that there was among the opposition a general willingness to make the concessions necessary to unite for the presidential campaign. Occasionally a diehard nativist grumbled about Republicanism, but with careful management he thought even they could be "kept straight." A "Grand Mass Meeting of the People of New Hampshire" was scheduled for June 10 under a call that was almost a verbatim copy of the one promulgated by the national committee. A former Whig journal announced that the mass meeting, which was to select delegates to the Philadelphia convention, was open to all of "the great AMERICAN REPUBLICAN FAMILY" who wished to attend.[25]

The mass assembly brought together a medley of anti-Democratic elements in the state, but despite its disparate make-up, its deliberations were for the most part harmonious and evidenced a general desire for unity. Fusion was facilitated by the emotional reaction to the recent attack on Lawrence, Kansas, and the caning of Charles Sumner, by the strong popular support in the state for nativism and anti-slavery-extension, by the prominence of former Free Soilers in American councils, and by the spirit of mutual cooperation evident

---

22. Mason W. Tappan to John P. Hale, October 20, 1855, Hale Papers, NHHS; Henry F. French to Benjamin B. French, March 16, 23, French Papers; Lucy M. Lowden, "The People's Party: The 'Heirs of Jackson' and the Rise of the Republican Party in New Hampshire, 1845–1860" (unpublished M.A. thesis, Western Illinois University, 1971), 72.

23. Horace Greeley, confirming that the Whig ticket was "got up in our interest," instructed Charles A. Dana not to attack it in the columns of the *Tribune*. Greeley to Dana, February 27, Private Memorandum, Pike Papers, UMe. Also see Henry F. French to Benjamin B. French, March 23, French Papers.

24. A. H. Cragin to Tappan, March 16, Mason W. Tappan Papers, NHHS; Henry French to Benjamin B. French, March 23, French Papers. Metcalf received 32,119 votes (48.3 percent), compared to 32,031 (48.2 percent) for the Democratic nominee and only 2,360 (3.5 percent) for the Whig.

25. Henry F. French to Benjamin B. French, March 16, French Papers; E. H. Rollins to Tappan, April 23, Tappan Papers; *New Hampshire Statesman*, June 14, quoted in Lowden, "People's Party," 75.

in the recent state election. Dominated by ex-Know Nothings, the meeting established the state Republican party and approved a set of resolutions that concentrated on recent events in Kansas and Washington. Out of deference to American sensibilities, the convention did not adopt the name *Republican*, although it signalled the party's identity by selecting delegates to the Philadelphia convention and pledging to support its nominees. Actually, the New Hampshire party used a variety of designations, including American-Republican, during the 1856 campaign, and once the Republican presidential nomination was made, the state committee took the title *Fremont Central Committee* and referred to the Republican national ticket as the People's Candidates.[26] Nevertheless, this nomenclature could not disguise that the New Hampshire Republican party had finally taken shape.

IV

While victorious in the 1854 election, the People's party in Indiana was at best only a loose coalition. Except for passage of a temperance law, the subsequent legislative session was not particularly gratifying to anti-Democratic groups, and suspicions and rivalries among various opposition factions seemed to be worsening. Schuyler Colfax, who went to Indianapolis during the session to promote unity, complained especially of the presence of "outsiders" who "ought to be . . . preaching concord rather than attempting to sow disunity." Consequently, fusion leaders, repeating the scenario of the previous year, called a mass meeting in 1855 to meet in Indianapolis on July 13 in order to perfect the party's organization and consolidate the anti-Democratic forces in the state.[27]

In the spring of that year, prior to the national council meeting in Philadelphia, Know Nothing leaders disagreed over the course to pursue. Although he hoped that the two elements would be able to cooperate, Colfax emerged as the leading spokesman for the view that antislavery should take precedence over nativism. The order's state president, Godlove Orth, wanted the national party to take an antislavery position as well, but he advised Colfax, "We must not lose sight of the fact, that while there is a strong Anti-Slavery feeling in the State, there is also a strong American feeling—and both must be preserved & united if possible, else both go by the board." Orth advocated that the American state organization drop its secrecy but otherwise maintain its present position as an "auxiliary to the Ant[i-Democratic]. Party—directing its public movements."[28]

Both Colfax and Orth were delegates to the national council in June, and despite their somewhat different purposes, each played a leading role in the fight against the platform's Twelfth Section, which upheld the Kansas-Nebraska Act. In fact, Indiana delegates were part of the small group of northerners who from the beginning were determined to secure an antislavery platform. Besides signing the address of the northern bolters, the state's representatives placed their own protest before the national council and announced that the order in Indiana would no longer recognize the national body's

---

26. Lowden, "People's Party," 76. The convention's proceedings are in the *Independent Democrat*, June 12, and the [Concord] *New Hampshire Patriot*, June 18. A few days before the convention, Pierce and Preston S. Brooks, Sumner's assailant, were hanged in effigy in front of the State House.

27. South Bend *Register*, January 18, 1855, quoted in Willard H. Smith, *Schuyler Colfax: The Changing Fortunes of a Political Idol* (Indianapolis, 1952), 55; Lucian Barbour et al. to Thurlow Weed, June 28, 1855, Weed Papers, UR.

28. Godlove Orth to Schuyler Colfax, February 14 (quotation), April 6, June 23 (quotation), 1855, Schauinger, ed., "Letters of Godlove Orth," 64–66; Orth to William Cumback, April 14, 1855, Cumback Papers.

authority. With only a few exceptions in the southern part of the state, local councils, joined by the great majority of Know Nothing newspapers, approved this action. In response to widespread discontent, the state council repudiated the recently adopted Philadelphia platform and seceded from the party's national organization.[29] Analysts concluded that a number of Hoosier Americans were ready to join the Republican party.

All was not harmony within the opposition ranks, however, following the rupture of the national American organization. Denunciations of Know Nothingism by a handful of Free Soilers led by George W. Julian continued to split the fusion movement. From the first, Julian viewed the Know Nothing movement as a plot of southern slaveholders to divide the North and distract northern voters from the true issue of slavery, and he adhered inflexibly to this view in the face of mounting evidence that Indiana Know Nothings genuinely opposed the expansion of slavery. In a widely publicized speech delivered at an antislavery convention in Indianapolis in late June, shortly before the state fusion meeting, the veteran antislavery agitator scorned the anti-Nebraska movement as "the product of political rather than moral causes, of transient influences rather than deep-rooted convictions." While he conceded that the growth of the Catholic church in the country posed some danger, he assailed the Know Nothings for avoiding the real issue of slavery and for their secrecy and bigotry. "An anti-slavery man," he proclaimed, "is, of necessity, the enemy of caste, bigotry, and proscription."[30] Julian's intemperate attack led to a harsh exchange with several former political associates who defended the secret society's antislavery record. Julian found himself in a minority even among Free Democrats, as the Indianapolis meeting decisively rejected his anti-Know Nothing resolution and instead adopted one supporting the People's party. Julian admitted that his opposition to Know Nothingism "has laid me prostrate, & precipitated me out of politics." Fusion leaders had no faith in him.[31]

The American state council assembled in Indianapolis on July 11, 1855, two days before the People's party state convention, in order to formulate plans to control the latter meeting. In addition to upholding the action of the state's delegates at the Philadelphia convention and reaffirming its separation from the national organization, the state council enacted several reforms, including the abolition of secrecy and making Protestant immigrants eligible for membership. It also approved a platform that called for restoration of the Missouri Compromise, opposed the extension of slavery, took ground against any alteration in the state's new temperance law, and disapproved of giving aliens the right to vote. Although a minority of delegates, objecting to the subordination of the order's original nativist principles in the platform, walked out of the council, the great majority supported these changes. Quite clearly, the Indiana American party, which more and more functioned like any other political party, was drawing closer to the Republican.[32]

---

29. Brand, "Know Nothing Party in Indiana," 187–95. The Indiana protest is given on pp. 191–92. Orth was chairman of the corresponding committee established by the seceders' meeting at the Girard Hotel. The prominence of the Indiana delegation at the Philadelphia meeting earned the state the designation as the "Massachusetts of her section." See Samuel Bowles's account in the New York *Tribune*, October 31, 1855.

30. Julian, *Speeches*, 102–25 (quotations 106, 125); Julian, *Political Recollections*, 141.

31. George W. Julian to E. A. Stansbury, September 14, 1855, Giddings-Julian Papers; Indianapolis *Daily Journal*, June 19, 20, 1855; Patrick W. Riddleberger, *George Washington Julian: Radical Republican* (Indianapolis, 1966), 106–07. Among those who criticized Julian's speech was Rawson Vaile, the former editor of the Free Soil state organ, the *Free Democrat*.

32. Indianapolis *Daily Journal*, July 14, 17, 1855; Brand, "Know Nothing Party in Indiana," 197–200. All native and naturalized citizens except Catholics were eligible for membership in the state American party; the

As in 1854, the Know Nothings played the dominant role in the People's convention on the thirteenth. The presiding officer, several of the speakers, and six members of the fifteen-man state central committee were members of the order. Julian was pointedly absent. Appropriately, the main orator at the convention was Henry Wilson, who urged all opposition elements to unite. Reaffirming the very conservative slavery planks of the party's 1854 platform, the meeting also condemned the Kansas policy of the Pierce administration, endorsed prohibition, and called for the abolition of alien suffrage. One Indiana resident fittingly described the gathering as "a mixture of Abolition, Temprance [*sic*] Knownothing & Anti Nebraska feeling." The meeting did not officially take the name *Republican*, even though the Indianapolis *Journal*, the leading fusion paper in the state, had since January been using this designation.[33] Still, it was evident that the elements of such a party were slowly coming together in the state. Considerable progress had been made in 1855 in formulating a satisfactory platform and eliminating discord. The split in the national American party strengthened this movement, but the major hindrance to the formation of a state Republican party remained the insistence of American leaders on maintaining their separate party organization.

The fall elections in the state were purely local and stirred little popular interest. The Democracy regained much of the ground it had lost in 1854, but politicians placed little importance on these results. Julian, however, remained discouraged. "There is so much cheap & shallow antislavery now abounding" in the state, he observed disdainfully, "leading many foolishly to imagine our cause very near its millennium." He argued instead that the emergent Republican movement in Indiana contained "very little soundness" and dismissed it as merely "Whiggery with a change of name reinforced by some office seeking democrats & entirely controled [*sic*] by Nativism."[34]

Julian's unrelenting criticism did not deter fusionists, who before the Pittsburgh convention began formulating plans for the 1856 campaign. A meeting of anti-Democratic editors on December 18, 1855, chaired by Know Nothing Milton Gregg of the New Albany *Tribune*, recommended that a state convention be held in May and affirmed that the 1854 People's party state platform, which had provoked strong protests from antislavery stalwarts, was sufficient for the national contest. Colfax counseled delay. An early convention would be "suicidal," he asserted, for "we don't know yet who is to be our candidate, nor what kind of fight we are to make." Professing that he saw little hope for victory in the fall, he still wanted the party to "make the best fight possible & an early Convention would ruin us." Alfred Wheeler, who was conducting the *Register* in South Bend in Colfax's absence, sounded a similar note of caution. "Political affairs are so mixed up and ticklish," he noted, "that I have not said much, and shall not." He was particularly concerned about what course the Know Nothings would follow in the state. In January the fusion state central committee issued a call for a mass convention to meet on May 1 in Indianapolis. The call was directed to those who were opposed to the repeal of the Missouri Compromise, the efforts to extend slavery into formerly free

---

new platform also refused to support anyone for office who acknowledged the authority of a political-ecclesiastical power superior to the president of the United States.

33. Indianapolis *Journal*, January 3, July 14, 1855; Brand, "Know Nothing Party in Indiana," 200–201; Thornbrough, ed., *Fletcher Diary*, v. 5, 427–28 (quotation).

34. Julian to Gerrit Smith, August 10, 1855 (quotation), Gerrit Smith Papers; Julian to E. A. Stansbury, September 14, 1855 (quotation), Giddings-Julian Papers; Julian to William Lloyd Garrison, August 2, 1855, Garrison Papers.

territory, the nationalization of slavery, threats of disunion, intemperance, and heavy taxation.[35]

Indiana's delegates had assumed a leading role in the disruption of the 1855 American national council, but in November, at a convention of northern Know Nothings in Cincinnati, the state's representatives supported the movement to reunite the party and agreed to attend the national council in February. By the time the council convened, a number of the state's Know Nothing leaders were firmly in the Republican camp. Colfax was a notable example, and others, such as Godlove Orth and William Cumback, both of whom had been especially prominent in the 1855 national council, were now conspicuous by their absence. Indiana sent only three delegates to the 1856 American convention, none of whom withdrew with the northern bolters. Although the American papers in the state widely opposed Fillmore's nomination, the refusal of the Hoosier delegates to join the North American secession left the position of the Indiana organization uncertain. Without question, the past two years had taken their toll on the once-powerful order in the state, but even so, informed observers estimated its membership at about 50,000. If it was apparent that the Know Nothings could not control the fusion movement as in the past, it was also obvious that no anti-Democratic ticket could carry the state without their support. The order's state executive committee met in early April and after some debate voted to take part in the fusion state convention, and William Sheets, the president of the state council, issued a circular urging full American participation.[36]

When the People's state convention assembled in Indianapolis on May 1, various anti-Democratic elements were liberally represented, including Americans, ex-Whigs, Free Soilers, temperance men, and former Democrats. Once the meeting had organized, conflict erupted over a resolution to appoint delegates to the Republican national convention in Philadelphia. The protest of one Know Nothing editor that the convention was not an exclusively Republican meeting and could not properly select delegates provoked cries of disapproval from the floor. Defending the resolution, David Kilgore, another nativist leader, rejoined that while Americanism could be postponed, the Kansas question could not wait. He urged that a delegation be sent to Philadelphia, but that no nomination be made that would "tread upon the toes of the Know Nothings." Approval of Kilgore's resolution marked the transition of the People's party from a loose opposition coalition to a Republican organization. The convention bowed to the sensibilities of Americans and other hesitant groups and did not officially adopt the name *Republican*; nevertheless, its recognition by the Philadelphia convention and the state party's subsequent ratification of the national ticket confirmed its Republican legitimacy. The dominance of the Americans as an organized separate entity within the People's party had been broken—a remarkable accomplishment, since such a large proportion of Indiana Republicans were one-time members of the nativist society.[37]

The convention named a state ticket headed by Oliver P. Morton, then only thirty-two years old, for governor. Several of the party's nominees were former Know Nothings, but only one was presently affiliated with the order, and some American leaders intimated afterwards that the Republicans had violated an earlier agreement concerning the composition of the state ticket. Morton's true relationship to the American order became

---

35. Indianapolis *Daily Journal*, December 19, 1855; Colfax to Alfred Wheeler, January 26, Colfax Papers, LC; Wheeler to Colfax, January 17, Colfax Papers, IndU.

36. Indianapolis *Daily Journal*, April 3; Brand, "Know Nothing Party in Indiana," 267–72.

37. Indianapolis *Daily Journal*, May 2; Brand, "Know Nothing Party in Indiana," 272–75.

a point of controversy during the campaign. The Republican nominee vigorously denied the charge, which was circulated widely even in opposition circles, that he had been a Know Nothing in 1854. Whether the charge was true or not, the ambitious Morton was a political opportunist who had been careful to avoid alienating the Know Nothings, and his nomination brought little comfort to antislavery veterans. Julian, who had clashed repeatedly with Morton over political matters in the past, was especially downcast.[38]

The convention approved a platform that was one of the most conservative adopted by any Republican state organization in 1856. The resolutions expressed uncompromising opposition to the extension of slavery, called for the immediate admission of Kansas as a free state, and pledged to resist the admission of any more slave states "formed out of the Territories secured to freedom by the Missouri Compromise, or otherwise." As antislavery critics disdainfully noted, the phrase "or otherwise" was subject to widely varying interpretations and could easily be taken to mean nothing more than the restoration of the 1820 compromise line. The convention sought to conciliate both the nativists and the foreign-born by endorsing the current naturalization laws while opposing alien suffrage. A leading German editor pronounced the plank satisfactory. The final resolution dealt with temperance and the state Supreme Court's recent decision striking down the stringent 1855 law. It affirmed that the legislature had the power to prohibit the sale of intoxicating beverages and called for enactment of "a constitutional law which will effectively suppress the evils of intemperance." Despite passage of this resolution demanded by anti-liquor forces, Republican leaders were anxious to downplay the liquor question. Colfax argued that until the judges were reformed, no effective prohibitory law was possible, and, this being the case, he queried, "Need we provoke prejudice against us without being able to effect any good?" The party hoped to appeal to a wide spectrum of Hoosier voters by concentrating on the Kansas issue and by assuming a very mild antislavery stance.[39]

Even though the convention accorded them only limited recognition, most Know Nothing leaders supported the People's party state ticket. Fillmore Americans, on the other hand, who were primarily from the southern part of the state, were vexed that the convention had agreed to send delegates to the Republican national convention. One ultra American paper blamed Sheets, the state president, for the outcome of the May 1 convention. "He has sold us to our enemies," it charged angrily, and it demanded a larger share of the nominations before the state council endorsed the ticket. A subsequent ratification meeting left little doubt, however, that the majority of Know Nothings had joined the Republican party. While the Know Nothings remained a basic element in the Republican coalition, they were no longer dominant, and the order's leaders generally agreed to subordinate nativist concerns to the Kansas issue.[40]

The Republican party had finally organized in Indiana, but on an uncertain platform and with a small group of antislavery men still chafing over its leadership and principles. Julian, who with an air of self-inflated importance had earlier boasted that he would compel the Indiana fusionists to "walk up on to a clean Republican platform on the single issue of slavery," could hardly contain his contempt. He characterized the People's party

---

38. Zimmerman, "Republican Party in Indiana," 260; letters from L. R. Johnson and Isaac Julian in the Cincinnati *Commercial*, October 27, 30; Riddleberger, *Julian*, 81–82, 111–13.

39. Colfax to Alfred Wheeler, March 31 (quotation), May 1, Colfax Papers, LC; Stoler, "Influence of the Democratic Element," 124–25. The Republican platform is given in Henry, *State Platforms in Indiana*, 13.

40. Brand, "Know Nothing Party in Indiana," 274–77; Vevay *Reveille* quoted in Brand, 275.

as "a combination of weaknesses instead of a union of forces," and he discerned but one true antislavery man among the party's nominees, electors, and national delegates. "We have a very mean scurvy pack of politicians here in our so-called republican party, doughfaces at heart, whose knavery for the past two years has been greatly facilitated by Know Nothingism," he explained to Chase. Criticizing antislavery men in the state for their past policy of "trimming, temporizing, diluting, and *surrendering*," he condemned the platform adopted by the May 1 meeting, which was almost as conservative as the People's platform two years before, as "the climax of political tergiversation, almost every line of which is stamped with cowardice and a studied purpose to deceive." An antislavery associate who attended the May convention was equally outspoken. The gathering was "a poor miserable truckling concern without either soul or body," he contended, adding: "You will mark the fact that our wise-acres at Indianapolis ignored even the name of Republican as well as all anti-slavery principle." The convention was animated by a desire to placate the nativists and conservative Whigs, groups, he observed caustically, that were "now ready to take office at the hands of the anti-slavery men provided they are not compelled to take more antislavery than they might safely take of *arsenic*."[41]

V

The most important state in which the Republican party organized during the first half of 1856 was Illinois. Previous attempts in 1854 and 1855 to form a fusion anti-Nebraska party in Illinois foundered on the persistence of old party loyalties and widespread suspicion of such ultra antislavery men as Owen Lovejoy and Ichabod Codding, as well as on wide disagreement over nativism and temperance. As he had done the year before, Lovejoy again took the lead in 1855 in trying to bring the anti-Douglas forces together in a single party organization. He wrote to a number of opposition leaders, advocating that a state convention be held early in the fall at Springfield "to consult together & to organize with a view of carrying the State for Freedom in 1856." Seeking to reassure conservatives, he pledged that he and other radicals would accept a moderate antislavery platform, since all "see & acknowledge the necessity of not loading the Middle & Southern portion of the State with too heavy a load."[42]

Although a few newspapers, led by the Chicago *Tribune*, now under new management and no longer as rabidly nativist as before, endorsed the proposed convention, Lovejoy's scheme was doomed from the beginning.[43] Little support for the idea developed outside the northern counties. Joshua R. Giddings toured the state in an effort to generate support for the Republican movement but encountered great resistance among Whigs in central and southern Illinois. He was particularly critical of the *Illinois State Journal* in Springfield, which he pronounced "hesitating, uncertain and timid." Throughout 1855

41. Julian quoted in Riddleberger, *Julian*, 112; Julian, *Political Recollections*, 155 (quotation); Julian to Chase, July 22, Chase Papers, HSPa; letters from Julian, *National Era*, May 22 (quotation), June 12; D. Worth to Julian, May 13, Giddings-Julian Papers; Clarke, *Julian*, 168–69.

42. Owen Lovejoy to Archibald Williams, August 6, 1855, U.S. History MSS, IndU. Lovejoy's co-worker, Ichabod Codding, had been stumping the state since May also promoting the idea of a convention. Howard, "Illinois Republican Party," 289–95.

43. *Illinois State Journal*, September 1, 1855. For other favorable reactions, see Cole, *Era of the Civil War*, 140–41.

the paper clung to the Whig party and opposed the Republican movement on the ground that the latter organization was "so intensely sectional, that its existence could not be continued with safety to the Union." Giddings also tried gently but without success to prod Abraham Lincoln into assuming leadership of the movement to form a Republican party. The Illinois leader cited the continuing power of Know Nothingism in the state as an insuperable barrier to forming a successful fusion party. The American party had not yet completely disintegrated, Lincoln noted, and "until we can get the elements of this organization, there is not sufficient materials to successfully combat the Nebraska democracy with." He judged that as long as the Know Nothings retained hope of victory as an independent party, fusion was infeasible in Illinois.[44]

Lyman Trumbull, the most prominent anti-Nebraska Democrat in the state, also refused to countenance a fusion convention. In the central and southern sections of the state, he told Lovejoy, there was "so great [an] aversion to what is called *fusion*, that very few democrats would be likely to unite in a convention composed of all parties." He believed that any convention that would get a respectable representation from these areas would not be supported in northern Illinois. "In order to carry this State," the recently elected senator explained, "we must keep out of the pro-slavery party a large number of those who are democrats. There would be no difficulty in doing this, were it not for old party associations, & side issues, such as Know Nothingism & the Temperance question." Trumbull recommended waiting for future developments, both in Kansas and the coming congressional session, that he hoped would make the spread of slavery the controlling issue in the 1856 election.[45]

Actually, the gap in Illinois between the Know Nothings and the fusionists was narrowing. For one thing, the order moderated its hostility to non-Catholic immigrants in response to the rise of the Know Something society, which displayed great popularity in the northern counties. Non-Catholic Germans and Irishmen, along with Scots and Englishmen, flocked to the new organization, which opposed Catholics but welcomed Protestant immigrants. A Know Nothing organizer reported that the anti-Catholicism of many of the state's immigrants undercut friction with the native-born population. He singled out Swedes in particular. "They are Lutheran & down on the Pope & where the proper cue is given they are first rate K Ns."[46] The growth of the Know Somethings, along with the national rupture of the American party, also gave greater prominence to the slavery issue. A state council in July in Springfield approved a platform that reflected these changes. The American platform called for the restoration of the Missouri Compromise, affirmed that Congress had full power to legislate on slavery in the territories, denounced the voting frauds in Kansas, condemned the "corrupting influences and aggressive policy of the Roman Church" and upheld the public school system, and advocated the modification of the naturalization laws. Furthermore, the meeting

44. Letter from "G." [Joshua R. Giddings], *Ashtabula Sentinel*, October 11, 1855 (quotation); *Illinois State Journal*, November 15, 1855; Giddings to Abraham Lincoln, September 18, 1855, *Private*, Herndon-Weik Collection; Lincoln to Lovejoy, August 11, 1855, Basler, ed., *Lincoln Collected Works*, v. 2, 316–17.

45. Lyman Trumbull to Lovejoy, August 20, 1855, Trumbull Family Papers. John Wentworth in the Chicago *Democrat* also rejected the movement for a new party. Calling on the Democratic party to return to its old principles, the paper declared, "We want no new party—no new names." Quoted in Hansen, *Third Party System*, 54.

46. Charles H. Ray to Elihu B. Washburne, April 21, 1855, Elihu B. Washburne Papers, LC; Chicago *Democrat*, May 5, 1855; James R. Thompson to Ullmann, August 14, 1855 (quotation), Ullmann Papers, NYHS.

announced that it would "cheerfully co-operate with any party as a national party" whose object was to enact these principles. Unlike its counterpart in Indiana, the Illinois state council did not open the order to non-Catholic immigrants. Still, anti-Catholicism was more potent than anti-immigrant sentiment within the American ranks. Indeed, by the end of the year the party's organ, the Chicago *Native Citizen*, edited by W. W. Danenhower, president of the state council, even spoke favorably of nominating German leader Gustave Koerner for governor.[47]

A separate development in 1855 lessened the importance of prohibition, the other side issue cited by Trumbull. Unable to get a Maine Law through the legislature, temperance supporters settled for a referendum in June on a statewide prohibitory law. After a heated campaign, the state's voters narrowly rejected the proposed law. Support for temperance came overwhelmingly from anti-Nebraska men (Table 9.6), but the hostility of Germans was apparent. Koerner claimed that the Germans "turned out to a man" in the special election, and the Chicago *Tribune*, advancing a similar explanation, complained that "every Irishman and German in the State" went to the polls "to rescue . . . Lager Beer and Mountain Dew."[48] The defeat of prohibition in this referendum curtailed the political force of the anti-liquor movement and thereby decreased the pressure on the Republican movement to take a pro-temperance stand that would alienate potential supporters. Several developments in 1855 thus facilitated the eventual formation of the Republican party in Illinois, but at the end of the year Douglas's opponents still remained divided and without organization.

The failure of Lovejoy's 1855 initiative necessitated a new start for the Illinois fusion movement under different and more conservative leadership. Whigs who had never joined the Know Nothings, along with Americans who wanted to make the territorial issue paramount, were anxious to organize a broad-based party. Having been vanquished for many years, pro-fusion Whigs had no interest in merely reviving the old Whig coalition; Democratic accessions, both foreign and native-born, were required to build a majority coalition. At the beginning of 1856, nativist leader William Jayne observed that the anti-Douglas forces were a majority in the state but wondered, "Can the opposition unite?"[49]

In December 1855, Paul Selby of the *Morgan Journal* in Jacksonville suggested that anti-Nebraska editors consult in order to prepare the way for uniting the opposition for the 1856 campaign. Eventually the editors of twenty-five leading anti-Nebraska journals in the state endorsed the call for a conference at Decatur on February 22 to consider

---

47. *Illinois State Journal*, July 11, 1855; Cole, *Era of the Civil War*, 139. Danenhower was one of the northern bolters at the 1855 national council. Keefe, "Chicago's Flirtation with Political Nativism," discusses his nativist career in Chicago. For the state council meeting, see John P. Senning, "The Know-Nothing Movement in Illinois," *Illinois State Historical Society Journal*, v. 7 (April, 1914), 20–21.

48. Koerner, *Memoirs*, v. 1, 622–23; Chicago *Tribune*, June 21, 1855; Welles Diary, June 27, 1855, Welles Papers, LC. The official vote was: for prohibition, 79,258 (45.9 percent); and against, 93,551 (54.1 percent). Turnout in this special election, scheduled at the height of the farming season, was an estimated 59.7 percent, a figure exceeding that of the previous fall. I have used the 1854 opposition vote in the congressional contests, since a number of Democrats, including many Germans, refused to support the anti-Democratic candidate for state treasurer that year because he was a Whig-Know Nothing. As one would anticipate, anti-Democratic voters in the treasurer's race favored prohibition more strongly (92 percent) than did the supporters of anti-Douglas congressional candidates (80 percent).

49. William Jayne to Trumbull, January 20, Joseph Gillespie to Trumbull, January 8, L. Southern to Trumbull, January 7, Ebenezer Peck to Trumbull, January 7, Trumbull Family Papers.

"arrangements for the organization of the anti-Nebraska forces in the state for the coming contest." Several German papers, headed by the *Staats Zeitung*, supported the Decatur conclave, but two important Chicago papers—the *Democratic Press* and John Wentworth's *Democrat*—ignored it.[50] Abraham Lincoln, who had been chosen as a delegate to the Pittsburgh convention on the same day, made arrangements to go to Decatur instead to help keep the meeting on the right track. Selby urged Richard Yates, another conservative Whig, to attend as an outsider also, but the former congressman declined. He probably joined Lincoln, Selby, and others, however, in urging the editors of the old Whig organ, the *Illinois State Journal*, to be present. In the end, after considerable indecision one of its editors, Edward L. Baker, went to Decatur under instructions to make no commitments.[51]

When the conference began, attendance was disappointingly thin, with only twelve present, but it was subsequently bolstered by late arrivals. The Decatur meeting selected Charles Ray of the Chicago *Tribune* as chairman of the all-important committee on resolutions. Its members worked closely with Lincoln in drafting an acceptable declaration of principles. Conservative on the slavery issue, these resolutions called for the restoration of the Missouri Compromise, denied that Congress had a constitutional obligation to admit new states, pledged noninterference with slavery in states where it already existed, upheld the fugitive slave law, and affirmed that the national government was founded on the principle that freedom was "the *rule*" and slavery "the *exception*." On other matters, the editors tried to avoid offending either the Know Nothings or the foreign-born. The resolutions thus opposed any change in the naturalization laws and advocated religious toleration while expressing determination to "repel all attacks" upon the common school system "by the adherents of any religious body whatever."[52] Fusion leaders in Illinois, like their counterparts in several other states, emphasized anti-Catholicism over anti-foreignism in an attempt to weld mutually suspicious nativists and immigrants into a unified party. The Decatur conference concluded its work by appointing a committee to draft a call and make the necessary arrangements for a state fusion convention at Bloomington on May 29. It was widely understood that the purpose of this convention was to organize the Republican party and nominate a state ticket, although the call avoided the label *Republican*, which the abortive attempt to launch a fusion party in 1854 had helped discredit, and employed the designation *anti-Nebraska* instead.[53]

Between the Decatur and Bloomington conventions, opposition leaders concentrated on

50. Paul Selby, "The Editorial Convention, February 22, 1856." *Transactions of the McLean County Historical Society*, v. 3 (1900), 30–43; *Illinois State Journal*, February 27; Rockford *Republican*, January 30, Belleville *Advocate*, January 30, Cole Notes; Cole, *Era of the Civil War*, 143.

51. Paul Selby to Richard Yates, February 14, Yates Papers; W. H. Bailhache to J. Bailhache, February 22, Bailhache-Brayman Papers; Peck to Trumbull, February 24, Trumbull Family Papers. Since June 1855, when Simeon Francis left the concern, the *Illinois State Journal* had openly sympathized with the Know Nothings while at the same time trying not to alienate its former Whig readership. Francis was angry that Lincoln and John T. Stuart, another Whig leader in the capital, did not come to his aid when the Know Nothings threatened to set up a rival paper in Springfield under the direction of William H. Bailhache and Edward L. Baker. In response, Francis sold his interest to Bailhache and Baker. Simeon Francis to Lincoln, December 26, 1859, Abraham Lincoln Papers, LC. I wish to thank Mark Neely for directing me to this letter.

52. Selby, "Editorial Convention," 36–39; *Illinois State Journal*, February 25, 27; *Illinois State Register*, February 25; Oliver P. Wharton, "Lincoln and the Beginnings of the Republican Party in Illinois," Illinois State Historical Society *Transactions* (1911), 62–63.

53. *Illinois State Register*, April 8; Chicago *Journal* quoted in the *Illinois State Register*, February 25. The call appears in the *Illinois State Journal*, April 9.

securing support from diverse anti-Nebraska groups. Moderates and conservatives feared that radicals would control the convention, while more advanced antislavery men were unhappy at their eclipse. "We can never sail under *that* flag," the Galesburg *Free Democrat* announced after seeing the Decatur resolutions. Whigs in the northern part of the state readily embraced the movement but, as one pro-fusion editor recalled, their brethren in central Illinois, joined by the anti-Nebraska Democrats, were sitting "on the fence like benumbed prairie chickens in winter."[54] In the meantime, a conference of the state's anti-Nebraska congressmen, composed of Lyman Trumbull and James H. Woodworth (representing former Democrats), Jesse Norton and Thomas Knox (both Know Nothings), and Elihu B. Washburne (a former Whig, though hardly a conservative) produced agreement that all elements of the opposition should participate in the convention. "If we do not take hold of this Bloomington convention, what shall we do?" Washburne asked pointedly. "We all think it is the only way. If we cannot come together as opponents of the Nebraska Infamy, how can we?"[55]

Worried about Whig inactivity back home, Washburne emphasized to Yates and probably other Whigs as well the critical importance of the Bloomington convention. Lincoln was already committed firmly to the fusion movement, and Orville H. Browning, a prominent conservative Whig, was also actively promoting the Bloomington meeting. It was essential "to keep the party in this State under the control of moderate men, and Conservative influences," Browning observed. "If rash and ultra counsels prevail," he warned, "all is lost."[56] After much hesitation and not a little inconsistency, the *State Journal* endorsed the Bloomington convention while steadfastly denying any intention of surrendering its Whig principles.[57]

Anti-Nebraska Democrats, as Trumbull's correspondence during these months documented, were even more uncertain about the fusion movement. Some, such as John Reynolds, John A. McClernand, and William H. Underwood, were unable to discard their long-standing party loyalty and reconciled themselves as best they could to the Democracy's territorial policy. Others, such as Lieutenant Governor Gustave Koerner, who ultimately joined the Republicans, came to a final decision only after the Democratic national convention in June.[58] One pro-Nebraska Democrat admonished John M. Palmer that if he deserted the Democracy, "you would be flung among a set of men that worship strange gods, that you nor no man retaining the spirit and heart of a true democrat can bow down to." Another anti-Nebraska Democrat who momentarily wavered over the Bloomington convention was William H. Bissell, the leading contender for the Repub-

---

54. Galesburg *Free Democrat*, February 28, John G. Nicolay to Selby, August 14, 1886, both quoted in Howard, "Illinois Republican Party," 298–99.

55. Elihu B. Washburne to Yates, April 3, Yates Papers.

56. Elihu B. Washburne to Yates, April 3, Yates Papers; Orville H. Browning to Trumbull, May 19, Trumbull Papers; F. A. Arenz to Yates, May 26, in Richard Yates and Catharine Yates Pickering, *Richard Yates, Civil War Governor*, ed. John H. Krenkel (Danville, Ill., [1966]), 118. Also see Elihu B. Washburne to Yates, March 29, Yates-Pickering Collection.

57. *Illinois State Journal*, February 25, 28, May 10; *Illinois State Register*, February 28, March 3, April 10, 11, 16; William Bailhache to John Bailhache, February 26, Bailhache-Brayman Papers. The *State Journal* endorsed the Decatur resolutions while simultaneously praising Fillmore's nomination on a platform that directly contradicted them. The Springfield paper also lauded the resolutions adopted by the Republicans at Pittsburgh, which were more radical still.

58. Koerner, *Memoirs*, v. 2, 3–4; Koerner to the editor of the Belleville *Advocate*, in the Quincy *Whig*, March 14, Cole Notes; Trumbull to John M. Palmer, May 21, Palmer Papers; George T. Brown to Trumbull, June 3, Trumbull Papers.

lican gubernatorial nomination. Earlier the former congressman had authorized Joseph Gillespie, a notable American, and Ebenezer Peck, a prominent anti-Nebraska Democrat, to begin a campaign on his behalf for the nomination. As fellow Democrats continued to hold back, however, Bissell worried that he was caught in an ultra organization. Presumably, political associates reassured him, for he withdrew his objections.[59]

So strong were the fears of anti-Nebraska Democrats that despite his commitment to Washburne and others in Washington, Trumbull was wracked with doubt. Early in the year he told Palmer that he was willing to join the Republicans provided they "abandon[ed] their altruisms" and limited their platform to opposition to the expansion of slavery. Yet less than a month before the Bloomington convention, he confided to his wife that he wanted to wait until after the state and national Democratic conventions before making a final decision.[60] This plan was unrealistic, since the Bloomington convention would assemble before the Democratic national convention met. One of Trumbull's correspondents emphasized the need for an early decision concerning the Republican movement: "If we join that party we should do so soon, and thus have a hand in shaping its course in the coming campaign, and prevent any extreme abolition, or fanatical tests being incorporated into its platform." Admitting that he was reluctant "to join in the ranks of *some* of the leaders of the Republican party," he added that he saw "no escape from it with our principles whole."[61]

The lingering doubts of men like Trumbull, and the more substantial uncertainty of men like Palmer, were largely removed by the action of the state Democratic convention, which met at the beginning of May. With the Douglasites in complete control, the convention enthusiastically endorsed the Nebraska Act and nominated William A. Richardson, Douglas's top lieutenant and the House floor manager of the Nebraska bill, to head the state ticket. Another resolution, adopted by acclamation, censured Trumbull and repudiated his claim to be a Democrat. By these actions, the regular party organization threw down the gauntlet to the anti-Nebraska Democrats.[62]

In the aftermath of the Democratic convention, most anti-Douglas Democrats endorsed the Bloomington convention. "Hurry is now the word," George T. Brown, the editor of the Alton *Courier*, informed Trumbull. He regretted that they had not gone to work before the Democratic state convention. By the middle of May, Norman Judd, one of Trumbull's loyal supporters, reported that "all of our leading Anti Nebraska Democrats are for the Bloomington Convention." Wentworth endorsed the fusion movement, once he decided it had a good chance to carry the state, and, in spite of their strong aversion to the former Chicago congressman, Peck and the *Democratic Press* clique also came out in its favor. Undertaking more active leadership than heretofore, Trumbull urged anti-Nebraska Democrats to attend the convention, which he was now confident would approve "conservative measures avoiding all altruisms."[63]

---

59. Benjamin Baldwin to Palmer, May 5, Palmer Papers; Palmer to Trumbull, February 28, Trumbull Papers; Peck to Trumbull, January 17, February 24, Trumbull Family Papers; William Bissell to Joseph Gillespie, February 17, Bissell to Peck, January 21 (copy), Joseph Gillespie Papers, IllSHL; Bissell to Trumbull, May 5, J. W. Ross to Trumbull, May 20, Trumbull Papers.

60. Trumbull to Palmer, January 24, Palmer Papers; Trumbull to Julia Trumbull, April 25, Trumbull Family Papers.

61. Jeff L. Dugger to Trumbull, February 26, Trumbull Papers.

62. *Illinois State Register*, May 2, 3.

63. George T. Brown to Trumbull, May 12, Norman B. Judd to Trumbull, May 15, Peck to Trumbull, May 26, Trumbull Papers; Trumbull to Palmer, May 21, Palmer Papers; Fehrenbacher, *Chicago Giant*, 137–38.

From the beginning, as the Decatur resolutions made clear, fusionists were concerned about getting the Germans and Know Nothings to cooperate in one party. Charles Ray of the Chicago *Tribune* was particularly anxious that nothing be done to alienate the 20,000 antislavery German voters in the state, without whose support, he warned Trumbull, defeat was inevitable. Afraid that the party would be weighted down with Know Nothing nominees and principles, he urged the senator to enlist Knox's and Norton's aid in inducing the Know Nothings to be reasonable. "We need no denunciation—nothing to excite angry feeling—only a plain and unequivocal declaration that the party do[es] not contemplate any change of the naturalization laws. And that we must have."[64]

The result of the hotly contested Chicago municipal election in March provided a telling demonstration to Republican leaders—if any were needed—of the danger ethnocultural issues posed to the anti-Douglas forces. The defection in 1854 of a considerable number of traditional Democrats, both native- and foreign-born, gave the anti-Douglas forces a majority in the city, but while anti-Nebraska men concurred on the repeal of the Missouri Compromise, they differed strongly over the merits of nativism and temperance. Hostility between the Germans and the Know Nothings was especially marked, and attempts by the nativist city administration to close saloons in 1855 provoked a German-led so-called lager beer riot. Despite the defeat of prohibition in the June 1855 referendum and the subsequent decision by Chicago Republicans to drop the liquor issue, the party was unable to sidestep ethnocultural issues in the 1856 city election. Because the Republican candidate for mayor was also nominated by the Know Nothings, the Democrats raised the cry of nativism and, as one observer reported, rang it "in every saloon and shop of the Germans" in an attempt to recapture the immigrant vote.[65] One Republican alleged that on the Sunday before the election, the Democratic mayoral candidate "visited over eighty grog shops . . . on an electioneering tour, and of course was pretty well 'over the bay' before evening." The symbolism of his activity was not lost on German voters, with their well-known contempt for puritan fanaticism. Election day "was about as noisy and drunken a time as I ever hope to see," this disgusted Republican wrote afterward. "Long wagons with temporary seats with free barrells of whiskey on tap . . . were scouring the City in every direction" for Democratic votes.[66]

In a heavy turnout the Democrats won a resounding victory. The claim of Douglas and his associates that the result was a great Nebraska victory was partisan propaganda. The crucial factor, as at least one close Douglas associate acknowledged, was the return of German voters to the Democratic ranks.[67] The analysis of Norman Judd, a prominent anti-Douglas leader, was compelling. "It was impossible," he declared, "to make the free soil german population distinguish between" the fusion candidate "*being* a know nothing and *being* supported by know nothings." Wentworth, a shrewd observer of the

---

64. Ray to Trumbull, March 21, Trumbull Papers; Ray to Washburne, May 4, Elihu B. Washburne Papers, LC.

65. Letter from Chicago signed "*", *National Era*, March 20; *Illinois State Register*, March 10. I have also relied on Ken Kann's excellent essay, "The Chicago Republican Party, 1854–1861" (unpublished seminar paper, University of California, Berkeley, 1971).

66. George W. Baldwin to Roger S. Baldwin, March 5, Baldwin Family Papers.

67. William F. Snyder to John F. Snyder, May 27, John F. Snyder Papers, IllSHL; Samuel A. Ashton to Stephen A. Douglas, March 5, B. M. Vickar to Douglas, March 5, James W. Sheahan to Douglas, March 16, Douglas Papers, UChi.

Chicago scene, attributed the defeat to the fact that "our friends have acted so foolishly almost every where upon the Liquor laws."[68]

The Chicago result reinforced several conclusions already held by the promoters of the Bloomington convention. The foreign vote and the nativist vote were both needed to form a majority coalition, a fact that necessitated dropping divisive ethnocultural issues in favor of emphasis on the single issue of slavery's extension. Embracing either temperance or nativism would kill the fusion movement as effectively as taking advanced antislavery ground. The true point of union for the Republican party in Illinois, these men argued, was the issue of freedom in Kansas.

Anti-Douglas leaders considered Bissell, a popular former Democrat from the southern part of the state, their strongest potential candidate. His antislavery record in Congress was hardly beyond challenge: He had supported the 1850 Compromise and had privately promised Douglas that he would vote for the Kansas-Nebraska bill, then reversed himself and opposed the controversial measure.[69] Republicans were attracted to Bissell because he appeared to be a winner, because they wanted a Democrat to head their ticket, and because his nomination would reassure nervous conservatives. The major uncertainty was his health—he was still recovering from a stroke that had left him temporarily paralyzed—although one party leader ventured the opinion that if Bissell could make it through the campaign "even sitting down," he would be elected. Democrats recognized that he would be a formidable candidate whose nomination would endanger the party's hold on German voters. "We cannot persuade them that Bissle [sic] is not a Democrat," one of Douglas's correspondents asserted, "and with a Catholic wife Know-Nothingism won't take a good hold upon him."[70]

With preparations for the Bloomington convention under way, Republican managers got wind of a plan for the Know Nothings to nominate Bissell first. Charles Ray charged that William Danenhower, the head of the American order in the state, had entered a plot with the Douglasites to kill Bissell politically by tarring him with nativism, thereby ruining him with the Germans. To block this move, Ray enlisted Joseph Gillespie, who with cool calculation had maintained his American affiliation even though he was one of Bissell's main promoters and was fully committed to the Republican movement. Gillespie attended the American convention in Springfield, where he worked in close collaboration with the editors of the *State Journal*. Unable to accomplish their initial objective of preventing any nominations, Gillespie and his allies shifted tactics and took up the cause of defeated congressional candidate William B. Archer, who after a hard struggle was

---

68. Judd to Trumbull, March 23, Trumbull Family Papers; Chicago letters signed "Insider" and "*", *National Era*, March 13, 20; John Wentworth to Trumbull, March 24, Trumbull Family Papers; J. F. Colby to William H. Seward, March 10, Seward Papers, UR; Chicago correspondence, "Milton," New York *Evening Post*, March 12. The Pearson Product-Moment coefficient of correlation between the percent of foreign-born and the percent of Democratic votes is 0.86 (calculated from data collected by Kann). For a perspective discussion, written as the contest opened, see Peck to Trumbull, February 24, Trumbull Family Papers.

69. Douglas to Ninian W. Edwards, April 13, 1854, Johannsen, ed., *Douglas Letters*, 322; Thomas Harris to Charles Lanphier, February 26 (copy), Lanphier Papers; Ottawa *Free Trader*, quoted in the *Illinois State Register*, June 13. Bissell missed the final vote on the Kansas-Nebraska bill because of illness, but he had John Wentworth announce that he would have voted against it.

70. George T. Brown to Trumbull, March 29, May 12 (quotation), Trumbull Papers; Brown to Trumbull, January 9, Trumbull Family Papers; J. D. Morrison to Douglas, April 16, quoted in Mildred C. Stoler, "The Democratic Element in the New Republican Party in Illinois, 1856–1860," *Papers in Illinois History and Transactions for the Year 1942* (Springfield, 1944), 42.

nominated for governor. Republican intrigues had subverted the American party, for Archer was firmly in the Republican camp and had no intention of accepting the nomination.[71] He withheld his declination, however, until the Bloomington convention met, in order to prevent any further mischief by the Know Nothings. The Americans eventually replaced Archer with a lesser-known candidate, but the withdrawal of virtually its entire original ticket was a crippling setback to the party. Republicans did not achieve the two-way race for the state offices that they had wanted, but they had greatly diminished the threat posed by the American ticket.[72]

A number of important state politicians representing a wide spectrum of anti-Douglas viewpoints gathered in Bloomington on May 29 to organize the Republican party. Moderates and conservatives, such as Lincoln, Yates, David Davis, Browning, Edward Baker, and William Bailhache (the latter two being editors of the *State Journal*), along with more pronounced antislavery men, such as Washburne, headed the Whig contingent. Anti-Nebraska Democrats in attendance included Palmer (who served as president of the convention), Judd, Peck, and "Long John" Wentworth, who towered over the delegates as he urged them to forgo their differences for the sake of union. Also on hand were German leaders George Schneider and Adolph Mayer. Prominent Know Nothings included Gillespie, William Jayne, Jesse O. Norton, Jesse DuBois, and Ozias M. Hatch, the last two destined to win places on the Republican state ticket. Finally, radical Free Soilers, including Lovejoy, Codding, and John H. Bryant (the brother of William Cullen Bryant), mingled among the delegates. Leaders stressed the need for concession and unity, although, if Henry C. Whitney can be believed, only Lincoln's intervention prevented DuBois from going home after he spotted Codding and Lovejoy in town.[73]

When the convention opened at Major's Hall, about 270 delegates were present, a number that, though impressive, was lower than the organizers had hoped for. More than thirty counties, mostly in the southern part of the state, remained unrepresented, while some counties sent more representatives than they were entitled to. Many delegates had been appointed informally and thus the convention became, in essence, a mass meeting. What could have been a chaotic situation was averted because of the sure-handed preparations of party leaders headed by Orville H. Browning. Arriving a day early, Browning learned that no resolutions had been prepared and no organization provided for, so he assembled about twenty influential politicians "of all shades of opinion" to agree upon the convention's organization. Equally important, after a long discussion they drew up a resolution designed to conciliate both the Germans and the Know Nothings.[74]

Aided by these prearrangements and by the willingness of pronounced antislavery men to make concessions in order to promote fusion, the convention's proceedings went

71. Ray to Washburne, May 4, Elihu B. Washburne Papers, LC; Judd to Trumbull, May 15, Trumbull Papers; *Illinois State Register*, May 7.

72. *Illinois State Register*, May 8, 9, 10, 17, 30; William Archer to R. L. Dulaney, May 19, 24, June 5, William B. Archer Papers, IllSHL; Browning to Trumbull, May 19, J. C. Sloo to Trumbull, May 16, Trumbull Papers. Indicative of the true situation was the fact that prior to notifying the American state committee officially of his refusal to run, Archer informed Lincoln that he intended to decline the nomination and authorized him to make prudent use of this information. With but one exception, all the original American nominees declined.

73. J. O. Cunningham, "The Bloomington Convention of 1856 and Those Who Participated in It," Illinois State Historical Society *Transactions* (1905) 104–07; Henry Clay Whitney, *Life on the Circuit with Lincoln*, ed. Paul Angle (Caldwell, Idaho, 1940), 92.

74. Randall and Pease, eds., *Browning Diary*, v. 1, 237–38; Stoler, "Influence of the Democratic Element," 114.

smoothly.[75] Conservatives and moderates controlled all the committees. The committee on resolutions reported a platform with the plank on nativism agreed to the night before; it was adopted without change. As expected, Bissell easily won the nomination for governor. The rest of the ticket was comprised of four former Know Nothings and Francis A. Hoffman, an important German leader, who was nominated for lieutenant governor. Particularly significant was the prominence accorded to former Democrats, who were honored with the chairmanship, the two top spots on the ticket (one of the Know Nothings nominated was also an ex-Democrat), a majority of the state central committee members, and at least four of the eleven presidential electors. When the convention adjourned, all factions expressed satisfaction with its outcome. With so many diverse interests represented, conflict appeared inevitable, one delegate marvelled afterwards, "but I never attended a political convention that seemed more harmonious."[76]

The resolutions, like those adopted at Decatur, were quite conservative, and under the impact of the worsening sectional crisis they emphasized the slavery question. The platform demanded that Congress prohibit the extension of slavery "into territories heretofore free," denounced the repeal of the Missouri Compromise and the attempt to force slavery into Kansas, and advocated the immediate admission of Kansas as a free state. The Illinois party's position on slavery amounted to little more than a call for the restoration of the Missouri Compromise; it left deliberately vague the status of slavery in other territories, and it said nothing about the admission of additional slave states. In an effort to placate the Germans, it ignored temperance altogether and pledged to "proscribe no one, by legislation or otherwise, on account of religious opinions, or in consequence of place of birth." Out of deference to the sensitivity of old-line Whigs and anti-Nebraska Democrats, the convention did not officially take the name *Republican*, but by appointing delegates to the June Republican national convention it left no doubt as to its identity. After several false starts, the Republican party, shorn of its radical image, had finally organized in Illinois.[77]

VI

The existence of a party organization in all the northern states was essential if the Republicans were to have any chance of carrying the presidential election; achievement of this goal, however, did not overcome the party's fundamental weakness. Republican programs had no chance of passing Congress, and the situation in Kansas, the issue party

---

75. The Chicago *Tribune*, an outspoken antislavery paper that had tangled recently with the *State Journal* over the fugitive slave law, pledged beforehand (on May 15) that the more advanced antislavery elements would accept the platform and ticket named at Bloomington. "The republicans . . . consent to be represented there purely as anti-Nebraska men, and if there is anything in their political creed, which points to more radical measures than old-line whigs or anti-Nebraska democrats consent to, they have expressed their willingness, without dissent *to put such things in abeyance*, and unite upon the platform upon which all northern men, who are not avowedly pro-slavery, ought to stand." As for the nominations, the *Tribune* announced that the Republicans "do not demand uniformity of belief." Quoted in the *Illinois State Register*, May 23.

76. *Transactions of the McLean County Historical Society*, v. 3 (1900), 148–79; George W. Baldwin to Roger S. Baldwin, May 31 (quotation), Baldwin Family Papers; *Illinois State Register*, June 12; Stoler, "Democratic Element in the Republican Party in Illinois," 46. Hoffman was withdrawn when it was discovered that he was ineligible to serve, and a substitute was named.

77. *Illinois State Journal*, May 30; letter from John H. Bryant to the New York *Evening Post*, quoted in John S. Wright, *Lincoln and the Politics of Slavery* (Reno, 1970), 91; Thomas Knox to Yates, June 9, Yates Papers.

leaders were banking on for the presidential campaign, had been used in the 1855 elections with only limited success. Republican hopes derived from the presence of a large undecided vote. With party lines "much confused" and the political future "very foggy," many voters were adrift and not firmly tied to any political party. "There are large numbers of men, enough to control the coming contest, who are standing still, awaiting the developement [*sic*] of the outlines of all parties before they take a *slide* in any direction," Haven reported to Fillmore late in April.[78] The success of the Republican party depended on converting the majority of these undecided voters, including old-line Whigs and anti-Nebraska Democrats and especially Know Nothings discontented with Fillmore's nomination and the national American platform. The turning point in the Republican party's struggle for political survival came in late May, when two dramatic events that occurred almost simultaneously at opposite ends of the country suddenly galvanized northern public opinion around sectional issues and combined to give the faltering Republican cause a desperately needed boost.

Congress spent most of the winter wrangling over Kansas affairs. Debate began in the Senate when Douglas introduced a bill to take a census and admit Kansas once it had the requisite population. Speaking for the Republicans, Seward countered with a bill to admit Kansas as a free state under the Topeka constitution. In the House, the rival claims of Andrew Reeder and John Whitfield for the seat of the territory's congressional delegate brought the Kansas controversy directly before that body.[79] While the Senate continued to struggle with the Kansas issue, the House voted to send an investigating committee to the territory to collect evidence concerning past elections and allegations of fraud. On this matter, Republican control of the speakership was critical, since selection of the members of this committee rested with Banks. By tradition, George Dunn, an Indiana congressman who introduced the resolution establishing the committee, should have been designated chairman. Dunn, however, was a conservative Whig-American, one of the handful of northern anti-Nebraska members who steadfastly refused to vote for Banks during the speakership contest. He was constantly alert for any chance to weaken the Republican party and advance the cause of a national conservative party. Unwilling to provide Dunn a forum, Banks ignored custom and appointed William A. Howard of Michigan, a Know Nothing turned Republican, chairman of the committee. The other Republican member of the three-man committee was John Sherman, who bore the brunt of its work. Assembling a small staff, the committee began amassing evidence in late April. Its voluminous report would not be available until the beginning of July, after both the Republican and Democratic national conventions had met.

In the meantime, the prospects for a legislative solution to the territorial impasse were negligible. Any bill passed by the southern-dominated Senate was certain to be rejected by the House. Furthermore, the lower chamber was badly factionalized and without a clear majority, and it was exceedingly doubtful that any bill relating to Kansas could win approval. Greeley accurately assessed the situation in Congress. "We cannot (I fear) admit Reeder; we cannot admit Kansas as a State; we can only make issues on which to go to the people at the Presidential election."[80] So matters stood, in an apparently hopeless deadlock, as spring came to the plains of Kansas.

---

78. Haven to Fillmore, April 24, Fillmore Papers, SUNY; Edwin D. Morgan to William M. Chace, May 10 (copy), Edwin D. Morgan Papers.

79. The Kansas debate is summarized in Nevins, *Ordeal of the Union*, v. 2, 419–28.

80. Greeley to Charles A. Dana, February 16, Benton, ed., *Greeley on Lincoln*, 120.

The unusually severe winter of 1855–56 had largely brought to an end the earlier marauding and violence in the territory, but with the thawing weather men on both sides feared an outbreak of new fighting. Against this uncertain background, the free-state "government" organized in Topeka in early March, although it refrained from taking any action to enforce its putative authority. In a questionable move, a grand jury, influenced by the proslavery chief justice, Samuel Lecompte, indicted the leaders of the free-state party, and a number of the accused, including Charles Robinson, the free state "governor," were arrested. Although reasonably well treated and in no real danger after the first few days of their detention, the prisoners became yet another Republican symbol of proslavery tyranny in Kansas, as well as a great embarrassment to the Pierce administration. The grand jury also recommended that the publication of two free-state newspapers in Lawrence be stopped, and that the Emigrant Aid Company's Free State Hotel in the same town, which more closely resembled a fort than a hotel, be destroyed as a public nuisance.[81] When United States marshal Israel B. Donaldson called for volunteers to put down resistance in Lawrence, proslavery men, believing that the long-awaited opportunity to crush abolitionism in the territory was finally at hand, eagerly joined his posse.

On the morning of May 21 the marshal's army, numbering at least several hundred strong, appeared on the outskirts of Lawrence, the symbol of the free-state cause in the territory. After arresting several residents of the town without incident, Donaldson disbanded the posse. At this point, Sheriff Samuel J. Jones, a swaggering, belligerent man with a flair for provoking trouble in almost any situation, reassembled the motley band under his own authority. Devoid of judgment even under the best of circumstances, he overrode the advice of other proslavery leaders on the scene, who expostulated against unprovoked violence. "Jones was bent on mischief, and I could do nothing with him," David Rice Atchison declared later in detailing his efforts to hold the impulsive sheriff in check. Falsely claiming to be acting under a court order, Jones entered the hated free-state town at the head of the mob, complete with artillery and flying banners with inscriptions like "Southern Rights" and "South Carolina." Deprived of effective leadership by the action of the grand jury, the inhabitants of Lawrence offered no resistance. Members of the proslavery horde wrecked the presses and offices of the two offensive newspapers, finally burned the Free State Hotel after attempts to cannonade it were ineffective, and partly destroyed "Governor" Robinson's home. Confiscating the hotel's liquor supply, they went on a drunken spree, and, over the protests of some of their leaders, committed a limited amount of plundering and vandalism, although for the most part the town's residents were not bothered. The only fatality of the raid was a member of the proslavery army, who was killed when one of the burning hotel's walls suddenly collapsed. Responsibility for the attack rested squarely with the hot-tempered Jones, who was fixed upon teaching the fanatics at Lawrence a lesson, whatever the cost.[82]

81. James C. Malin, "Judge Lecompte and the 'Sack of Lawrence,' May 21, 1856," *Kansas Historical Quarterly*, v. 20 (August, November, 1953), 465–494, 553–97. Using court records long believed lost, Malin demonstrates that the usual claim that the grand jury made a bill of presentment against either the newspapers or the hotel is false.

82. For contemporary accounts, see H. L. Jones to John A. King, May 23, John A. King Papers; St. Louis *Republican* quoted in the *Illinois State Register*, May 28; Samuel W. Eldridge, "Early Days in Kansas," 48–55; James A. Finey to Dear Sister, May 24, University of Kansas; George W. Martin, "The First Two Years of Kansas," *Kansas Historical Collections*, v. 10 (1907–1908), 139; John Sedgwick to My Dear Sister, June 11,

As the members of the conquering army withdrew from Lawrence, little did they realize what a devastating blow they had dealt the cause of the South. Not only did they furnish the Republicans with an emotional campaign issue, but their reckless act ushered in a new round of violence that continued throughout the summer, providing additional ammunition for the Republicans with virtually every new telegraphic dispatch.

In its details the so-called Sack of Lawrence was shocking enough. More important to inflaming northern public opinion, however, was the manner in which Republican journals magnified and distorted the incident. Two papers in particular, the Chicago *Tribune*, which because of its proximity to the scene received news sooner, and the New York *Tribune*, whose weekly edition enjoyed a vast circulation throughout the free states, were especially important in developing the Republican version of events in Kansas. Lending able assistance was the St. Louis *Democrat*, the Benton-Blair organ. Comprehending the political potential of affairs in Kansas, these and other Republican papers sent to the territory a number of talented, blatantly partisan correspondents who relayed back a steady stream of distorted information.[83]

For these reporters, the destruction at Lawrence represented an ideal opportunity to score a decisive propaganda victory by liberally mixing fiction with fact. The first dispatches concerning the raid amounted to nothing more than wild, unsubstantiated rumors. Painting a much blacker picture of events in the town than later reports, these stories were grist for the Republican propaganda mill. It was these reports, and not later corrections, that gave northern readers their impression of the nature of the attack on Lawrence. In its initial account of the affair, the New York *Tribune* set the tone for the Republican exaggerations that followed. Lawrence, the paper declared, had been "devastated and burned to ashes. . . . A few bare and tottering chimneys, a charred and blackened waste, now mark the site hallowed to all eyes as that where the free sons of the North have for two years confronted the myrmidons of Border-Ruffianism, intent on the transformation of Kansas into a breeding-ground and fortress of Human Slavery." The first full treatment in the Chicago *Tribune*, which many Republican journals copied, was a masterpiece of innuendo that carefully masqueraded rumors as facts. It left the impression that there had been a substantial loss of life and that Samuel Pomeroy and other free-state leaders had been lynched. One anti-Republican newspaper, after carefully analyzing this particular report, predicted with some truth that "when the real facts are made public, this excitement in Kansas will be found to be all moonshine."[84]

Atchison's reputed remarks to the assembled throng before it entered Lawrence provided another example of gross distortion in the Republican press. Accounts of his speech were sheer invention. Atchison actually had been a voice of moderation, yet one report circulated widely in Republican journals quoted the former senator as bellowing to the crowd, "If a man or woman dare to stand before you, blow them to he— with a chunk of cold lead." In a more colorful version, the Missouri leader was alleged to have exclaimed, "Ruffians! draw your daggers and bowie-knives, and warm them in the

---

Correspondence of John Sedgwick Major-General (2 vols.: n.p., 1903), v. 2, 78–79. Reports differ as to whether one or two members of the posse were killed. Atchison is quoted in Spring, *Kansas*, 124.

83. Weisberger, "Newspaper Reporter and Kansas," presents an excellent analysis of Kansas propaganda and the Republican press. Also see Isely, *Greeley and the Republican Party*, 131–36, 140–42, 173–84.

84. New York *Tribune*, May 26, 30, June 2, 5; Chicago *Tribune* quoted in the New York *Tribune*, June 9; Chicago *Tribune*, May 25, quoted in New York *Evening Post*, May 27; [Greene, New York] *Chenango American*, May 29.

heart's blood of all those damned dogs that dare defend that dammed [*sic*] breathing hole of hell.''[85]

In exploiting the early accounts of the raid to arouse northern anger, Republican journals quickly shifted the emphasis from the border ruffians to the national administration. Republican editors affixed blame for the violence on Donaldson and Lecompte, both government officials, and through them on Governor Wilson Shannon and President Franklin Pierce. Summarizing reports of destruction in Lawrence, the New York *Tribune* cried: ''All this . . . [has] been performed in the name and by the authority of the Federal Union.'' Jones, who more than anyone else deserved to bear the brunt of the blame for what happened at Lawrence, became in the Republican interpretation a minor pawn, a man who simply did the bidding of his more powerful superiors. Ultimate responsibility, Republicans charged, rested with Pierce. The president, the New York *Tribune* declared in an especially repugnant passage, stood ''sprinkled from head to foot with the blood of the Free-State men of Kansas, and his whole person illuminated and lighted up with the blaze of their burning houses.'' The political implications of this emphasis were obvious. The belief that Pierce and the cabinet sanctioned the violence at Lawrence, one New Yorker told Banks, had produced ''a *tremendous* Excitement.'' After hearing the ''startling intelligence'' of the attack on Lawrence, a particularly thoughtful Ohio nativist, now on his way to becoming a Republican, wrote in his journal: ''How long this ill fated country is to suffer for the black crimes of the Democratic party remains to be seen.''[86]

VII

Before news of the attack on Lawrence arrived, an event in Congress shocked northerners and unleashed an unprecedented wave of indignation throughout the free states. Just as on the plains of Kansas, affairs in Congress hastened to a violent climax. On May 19 and 20, at virtually the same time that the proslavery army was approaching Lawrence, Charles Sumner delivered in the Senate a speech entitled ''The Crime Against Kansas,'' in which he severely criticized the administration, the South, and the proslavery men in Kansas. The Republican leader also made scathing personal attacks on several important Democrats, including Senator Andrew P. Butler of South Carolina, who was then absent. As if to make his words rankle even more, the Massachusetts senator was openly contemptuous when speaking of South Carolina. Sumner's attack on the sixty-year-old Butler, a kindly man of charm and grace, who was widely admired and respected in Washington, produced considerable resentment.[87]

No one was more angered by Sumner's comments than Preston S. Brooks, a proud, aristocratic South Carolina congressman now serving his second term and a distant relative of Butler. Brooks considered Sumner's speech an insult to his aged relative and his state, for which he decided to chastise the Massachusetts senator, as a southern

85. New York *Tribune*, June 5, 19; Chicago *Tribune*, July 15; Parrish, *David Rice Atchison*, 200–01; Weisberger, ''Newspaper Reporter and Kansas,'' 645–46.

86. New York *Tribune*, May 26; S. H. Clarke to Nathaniel Banks, Jr., May 31, Banks Papers, LC; Sidney D. Maxwell Diary, ca. May 26 (quotation); H. S. McCollum to John C. Breckinridge, July 23, Breckinridge Family Papers, LC.

87. For a full discussion of the speech and its aftermath, see Donald, *Sumner*, 278–89. I have analyzed the reaction to the Sumner-Brooks affair and its political ramifications more extensively in ''The Crime Against Sumner: The Caning of Charles Sumner and the Rise of the Republican Party,'' *Civil War History*, v. 25 (September, 1979), 218–45.

gentleman would any inferior. On May 22, after the Senate adjourned, Brooks entered the Senate chamber, went up to Sumner, who was seated at his desk, and after a few brief words began beating Sumner over the head with his cane. Sumner, stunned and blinded by blood, finally wrenched himself free from his desk and staggered forward, his arms vainly trying to ward off blows to his head. Brooks caught him by the lapel of his coat and continued to strike him until seized by a Republican congressman. The assault lasted less than a minute. When it was over, the Massachusetts leader lay on the floor, unconscious and bleeding profusely. After regaining consciousness, he remarked, "I could not believe that a thing like this was possible." It was four years before Sumner returned to his seat in the Senate.[88]

At the insistence of the Republican members, the Senate established a special committee to investigate the incident. Lacking a single Republican member, it promptly decided that it had no jurisdiction over the matter. When the House of Representatives voted to appoint a committee of investigation, only two southern congressmen, both border state men, supported the majority. By a straight party vote, the committee recommended that Brooks be expelled, and after a heated debate the House voted for expulsion by 121 to 95, but the motion fell short of the required two-thirds majority. Only one southern representative voted against Brooks. Following the vote, Brooks resigned and was triumphantly reelected. In the end, the only punishment the South Carolinian received was a fine of $300 for assault, levied by a Washington court.

News of the attack on Sumner electrified the North, and as the reaction in the South, which was generally one of strong approval of Brooks's action, became clear, it heightened the northern sense of outrage. A Boston clergyman declared, "I have experienced more moral misery in thinking on the assault than any other event ever excited in me," while a prominent German leader in Chicago testified that news of the attack "perfectly overwhelmed me with indignation and rage." Horace Mann, the famous educator, expressed northern sentiment eloquently when he wrote the stricken senator: "We are all not only shocked at the outrage committed upon you, but we are wounded in your wounds, & bleed in your bleeding." Richard Henry Dana, Jr., perhaps best described the impact of the assault when he told Sumner, "When Brooks brought his cane in contact with your head, he completed the circuit of electricity to 30 millions!"[89]

The depth of feeling and the level of excitement in the North surpassed anything observers had witnessed. A western correspondent assured Sumner that he had never seen people so aroused before; William H. Furness, the distinguished clergyman, described the same response in Philadelphia. A New York man informed Banks that no event in the history of Congress had produced so much excitement. The greatest indignation, naturally, was felt in Massachusetts, where conservatives were badly shaken by the depth of sectional animosity they observed. "You can have little idea of the depth & intensity of the feeling which has been excited in New England," Robert C. Winthrop warned John

---

88. This summary of the assault is based on the testimony before the House Investigating Committee (*House Report*, No. 182, 34 Cong., 1st sess.) entitled *Alleged Assault upon Senator Sumner*; "Statement by Preston S. Brooks," *Massachusetts Historical Society Proceedings*, v. 61 (June, 1928), 221–23; three memos by Edwin B. Morgan, one written the day of the caning, concerning the assault on Sumner, all in the Edwin Barber Morgan Papers; and Donald, *Sumner*, 290–97 (quotation 297). For a judicious analysis of the nature of Sumner's injuries, see Donald, pp. 312–47.

89. E. P. Whipple to Sumner, June 11, Hermann Kriesmann to Sumner, May 21 [22?], Richard Henry Dana, Jr., to Sumner, July 1, Sumner Papers, HU; Horace Mann to Sumner, May 27, Mann Papers.

Crittenden. Countless meetings throughout the North to protest the caning revealed that northern anger transcended party lines.[90]

It was against this background that news of the so-called Sack of Lawrence arrived. Although the raid on the free-state town actually took place the day before Brooks's assault, word of the event reached the North after that of the Sumner-Brooks incident. Popular emotions in the free states, already greatly aroused, inevitably increased with the intelligence from Lawrence. As the first wildly exaggerated accounts arrived from the territory, Republican newspapers shrilly exclaimed that yet another proslavery outrage had occurred. "Violence reigns in the streets of Washington," the usually restrained New York *Evening Post* proclaimed.

> Violence has now found its way into the Senate chamber. Violence lies in wait on all the navigable rivers and all the railways of Missouri, to obstruct those who pass from the free states to Kansas. Violence overhangs the frontier of that territory like a storm-cloud charged with hail and lightening. Violence has carried election after election in that territory. . . . In short, violence is the order of the day; the North is to be pushed to the wall by it, and this plot will succeed if the people of the free states are as apathetic as the slaveholders are insolent.

The coincidental timing of these two events greatly magnified northern indignation. Winthrop reported in alarm that the "concurrence of the Kansas horrors" with the Sumner caning "has wrought up the masses to a state of fearful exasperation." Winthrop's fellow conservative Bostonian, Amos A. Lawrence, noted that the invasion of Lawrence and the assault on Sumner had excited the people of the country more than he had ever seen.[91]

The continuing "outrages" in Kansas, which began anew following the Lawrence raid, were destined to be the Republicans' main staple in the 1856 presidential campaign. Because of this development, historians have missed the critical importance of the Sumner caning in vitalizing the Republican cause. It was an accident of timing that the Sumner assault precipitated the first outpouring of northern feeling, but as developments continued to unfold, most seasoned political observers agreed that of the two events, the attack on Sumner was more important in producing northern indignation. Meetings to protest the caning dwarfed Kansas meetings in size, they attracted many more non-Republicans both in the audience and as participants, and they revealed more widespread excitement and deeply felt anger. There are several reasons for this. Unlike accounts of the Sumner-Brooks incident, the news from Kansas was invariably fragmentary, uncertain, and contradictory; the deliberate attack on a senator for words spoken in debate seemed an attack on the Constitution, and as such it was much more ominous and threatening than events in a distant, sparsely settled territory. "The Kansas murders are on the border and border men are always represented and known to be often desperate but to see a senator assaulted in the Senate Chamber no one can find any excuse for it," one northerner explained. Men who had listened for more than a year to stories of Kansas atrocities without feeling that drastic action was necessary were suddenly shaken from

---

90. Robert C. Winthrop to John J. Crittenden, June 3, *Private*, Crittenden Papers; Edward Everett to Horace Maynard, October 3, 1857, Everett to Mr. and Mrs. Stanard, June 4 (copies), Everett Papers; Gienapp, "Crime Against Sumner," 224–27, 239–41.

91. New York *Evening Post*, May 23; Winthrop to Crittenden, June 3, Crittenden Papers; Amos A. Lawrence Diary, June 8, Lawrence Papers.

their complacency by the antislavery leader's injuries. "The Northern blood is boiling at the outrage upon you," a New York Republican informed Sumner. "It really sinks Kansas out of sight."[92]

As important as the deeply felt anger spawned by the attack on Sumner was the way the caning enhanced the appeal of the Republicans' main stock in trade, the Kansas issue. Far from viewing the assault on Sumner as competing with the Kansas crisis for public attention, Republicans considered them mutually reinforcing, and they lost no time in linking the two issues. While historians have recognized that Bleeding Sumner and Bleeding Kansas were powerful Republican symbols in the 1856 presidential campaign, they have overlooked the manner in which the Sumner assault gave credence to Bleeding Kansas. "It may seem hard to think but still it is true that the north needed in order to *see* the slave aggression, one of its best men Butchered in Congress, or something else as wicked which could be brought home to them. Had it not been for your poor head, the Kansas outrage would not have been felt at the North," one supporter consoled Sumner. Despite a year of agitation by the Republican press over the problems in Kansas, many northerners remained dubious of Republican claims. "I take it for granted neither you [n]or I will ever live to get at the truth," one New York conservative told John Clayton in 1856 concerning the situation in Kansas. "It lies I apprehend much deeper than the bottom of a well."[93] This skepticism greatly diminished with the Sumner assault. Northerners were now more easily convinced that southern aggression was a fact, that the South was capable of any atrocity to maintain its national power. "Soon men will be convinced Kansas difficulties are real, not stories circulated without foundation, for mere political capital," a correspondent assured New York congressman Edwin B. Morgan after the caning. A Vermont Republican agreed: "*Brooks* has knocked the scales from the eyes of the blind, and they now *see!*"[94]

The Sumner caning and the violence at Lawrence strengthened the Republican party significantly. Both incidents occurred just before the Democratic and Republican nominating conventions were to assemble, when numerous uncommitted voters were beginning to form new (or reaffirm old) party identities. Contemporaries recognized the party's rapid growth as events unfolded in 1856. Edwin D. Morgan observed after the Sumner protest meeting in New York City that "the changes *now taking place* in our city are very great." Similarly, a concerned Indiana Democrat reported that party members, who had been quite confident until the last week of May, were now gripped with "gloom" over the approaching presidential contest. The courthouse in his town had been draped in mourning after the news from Lawrence arrived, and he lamented that "good honest democrats, by scores and hundreds, in this section of the state became deluded, wavered and now, many are against us." The raid on Lawrence, and more especially the attack on Sumner, were critical in driving moderates and conservatives into the Republican camp. "The Straight Whigs and conservatives are fast finding their places,"

---

92. Henry N. Walker to John S. Bagg, June 24 (quotation), John S. Bagg Papers, Detroit Public Library; John P. Jewett to Sumner, May 28, George E. Baker to Sumner, June 7 (quotation), M. S. Perry to Sumner, October 25, Sumner Papers, HU. Julian wrote later that the assault on Sumner "perhaps did more to stir the blood of the people of the Northern States than any of the wholesale outrages thus far perpetrated" in Kansas: *Political Recollections*, 153.

93. F. A. Sumner to Sumner, June 24, Sumner Papers, HU: J. K. Paulding to John Clayton, April 12, Clayton Papers, LC.

94. Henry Morgan to Edwin B. Morgan, May 28, Edwin Barber Morgan Papers; E. P. Walton to Justin S. Morrill, May 28, Morrill Papers, LC.

the Republican national chairman commented at the beginning of June. "The doubtful hesitating men are more excited now—than those who took the right ground early."[95] It was in the spring of 1856 that the Republican party at last emerged as a major political force, and no event was of greater importance in this development than the caning of Charles Sumner. "By great odds," Alexander K. McClure concluded in retrospect, "the most effective deliverance made by any man to advance the Republican party was made by the bludgeon of Preston S. Brooks."[96]

Almost overnight, the entire complexion of the presidential campaign had been transformed. Democrats' confidence of an easy triumph in November evaporated as the extent of northern anger became clear. Conversely, Republican hopes of victory, weak and limited before the events of May, soared in the aftermath of the Sumner beating and the attack on Lawrence. "The feeling here is much better than it was some months ago," Trumbull apprised Lincoln from Washington in mid-June. "The outrage upon Sumner & the occurrences in Kansas have helped us vastly." For the first time, he believed that the Republicans had a chance of carrying the presidential election. After serving as the hostess of a dinner party in early June at which a number of important Republican leaders were present, Elizabeth Blair Lee remarked, "There is a new tone & spirit among our people. . . . They talk confidently."[97] To John McLean, an aspirant for the Republican nomination, one journalist wrote that the Sumner and Kansas outrages had made an issue that, "properly directed, might carry the election by storm." Watching developments from the capital, John Bell reached a similar conclusion. "All that has recently occurred here & in Kansas, strengthened the Republicans," he told a Tennessee associate at the end of May. He thought that if the Republicans made "politic" nominations, they might well "carry every northern state."[98] Evincing a new-found optimism, Republicans prepared to assemble in Philadelphia for the party's first national nominating convention.

95. Edwin D. Morgan to John Bigelow, June 2 (copy), Edwin D. Morgan Papers; H. S. McCollum to Breckinridge, July 23, Breckinridge Family Papers.

96. McClure, *Recollections*, 393. For other examples and citations, see Gienapp, "Crime Against Sumner," 240–44.

97. Trumbull to Lincoln, June 15, Trumbull Family Papers; Elizabeth Blair Lee to Samuel Phillips Lee, June 7, Blair-Lee Papers.

98. James E. Harvey to John McLean, May 30, *Private*, McLean Papers, LC; John Bell to William B. Campbell, May 29, Campbell Family Papers, Duke University; Charles Francis Adams to John Palfrey, July 10, Adams Family Papers; Charles A. Dana to James Shepherd Pike, n.d. [late May or early June], Pike Papers, UMe; Indiana correspondence, "D.B.," New York *Evening Post*, May 30; Israel Washburn, Jr., to John L. Stevens, May 29, Israel Washburn, Jr., Papers, LC. I am indebted to Michael Holt for calling Bell's letter to my attention.

10

The Nomination of Frémont

Three national conventions were scheduled to meet within a two-week period in June 1856. The Republicans and North Americans were to assemble in Philadelphia and New York City respectively, while the Democrats would journey to Cincinnati for the first national nominating convention of a major party to meet west of the Appalachian Mountains. Although Republicans understandably devoted greater attention to the two eastern meetings, the outcome of the Democrats' deliberations held great significance as well, since the Democratic platform and national ticket would strongly influence the type of presidential campaign the Republicans would conduct. Samuel Bowles was fairly close to the mark when he observed, "The secret of the campaign is at Cincinnati. The Republican candidate will really be nominated there."[1]

I

The disastrous events of May left Franklin Pierce's bid for a second term shipwrecked. Even prior to the May violence in Washington and Kansas, Pierce's campaign for renomination was in serious trouble. To a growing number of party leaders he seemed incapable of providing leadership, either in foreign or domestic affairs, and the recent incidents obliterated what slim chance he had for renomination. Pierce "is in rather bad odor, and he will stink worse yet before the 4th of next March," Benjamin B. French, the president's former secretary, wrote from Washington on May 29. "The Kansas outrages are all imputable to him, and if he is not called to answer for them here, 'In Hell they'll roast him like a herring.'"[2] With Pierce's weakness obvious, Democratic strategists realized that he faced almost certain defeat in November.

The most dynamic possibility for new party leadership was Stephen A. Douglas, far and away the most talented candidate for the Democratic nomination. Douglas's greatest handicap was that he, too, was tarnished by the breakdown of law and order in Kansas,

---

Note: Unless otherwise indicated, the year for newspaper and manuscript citations in this chapter is 1856.

1. Samuel Bowles to Henry Dawes, April 19, Merriam, *Bowles*, v. 1, 172.
2. Benjamin B. French to Henry French, May 29, French Papers. For Pierce's bid for renomination, see Nichols, *Pierce*, 425-69.

for which northern public opinion held him partly responsible. Except for Pierce, no Democrat was so closely identified in the public mind with the Kansas crisis, and so party leaders concluded that Douglas could not be elected. In addition, the Illinois Democrat's aggressive rise to national prominence hurt him with many established Democratic professionals, who disliked him personally, were jealous of his ability, and resented his great popular following.[3]

As Democratic politicians searched for a safe candidate unconnected with the policy failures of the past two years, they settled increasingly on James Buchanan, the veteran Pennsylvania politician. As United States minister to England, he had been safely abroad when the Kansas-Nebraska Act passed Congress and the crisis in Kansas subsequently unfolded. Under pressure from his advisers, Buchanan wrote, at the end of 1855, to Senator John Slidell of Louisiana a letter to be used as needed, in which he retreated from his earlier support of the Missouri Compromise and announced that he now accepted the principle of nonintervention as the final settlement of the territorial question. Buchanan had other advantages as well. He was certainly experienced, having served in public life for over four decades, and he came from a doubtful state that Democrats were convinced they had to carry in order to be victorious in the fall. John C. Rives, Francis P. Blair's former associate at the Washington *Globe*, listed Buchanan's strengths as "1st He starts with Penna in his pocket, and 2nd He is not mixed up with the repeal of the Missouri Compromise, the settlement of Kansas, &c &c."[4] Several Buchanan supporters reported that the latest violence in Kansas and Washington immeasurably strengthened his chances for the nomination. "Every blow over Sumner's head, has brought out crowds for your nomination," a confident supporter noted after arriving in Cincinnati.[5]

That he easily had the best personal organization of any presidential aspirant also aided Buchanan's cause in no small measure. In a move of great significance for the ultimate outcome of the election, John W. Forney, the alcoholic but brilliantly talented journalist, deserted Pierce to support his old friend Buchanan. Forney resigned from his post at the Washington *Union* on March 28. In addition, on the eve of the convention a small group of highly skilled political operatives took over management of the Buchanan forces and set up headquarters in Cincinnati, determined to block Pierce and Douglas and nominate Buchanan, the one man they believed could lead the party to victory against the suddenly robust Republicans.[6]

The Democratic convention, both in its membership and deliberations, was not noted for its decorum. The convention opened on June 2 with a near riot, as the Benton delegation, headed by Frank Blair, Jr., forced its way past the doorkeepers and onto the floor. In accrediting delegates, the convention solved its two thorniest problems by excluding the Benton group altogether and by seating both the Hard and Soft delegations from New York. The acceptance of the Hard delegation was a blow to the Fillmore campaign, because the Americans had anticipated sizable Hard accessions if the

3. The Douglas campaign can be followed in the Douglas Papers, UChi, and the Lanphier Papers, and is discussed fully in Johannsen, *Douglas*, 505–20.

4. John Slidell to James Buchanan, January 17, 1855 [1856], January 30, 1856, Buchanan to Slidell, December 28, 1855 (copy), Buchanan Papers, HSPa; John C. Rives to John C. Breckinridge, June 2, quoted in Rawley, *Race & Politics*, 137–38.

5. Jonathan M. Foltz to Buchanan, June 2 (quotation), Fernando Wood to Buchanan, May 26, George N. Sanders to Buchanan, May 24, Buchanan Papers, HSPa; Forney, *Anecdotes*, v. 2, 254.

6. The Buchanan organization is analyzed in Roy F. Nichols, *The Disruption of American Democracy* (New York, 1948), 2–18. See especially Daniel E. Sickles to Buchanan, June 4, Buchanan Papers, HSPa.

Cincinnati gathering rejected them. Democratic leaders in effect served notice to the incessantly squabbling New York factions that union was mandatory in the presidential campaign. By now, both groups had all but exhausted the patience and good will of party members.[7]

Although the debate on the platform produced some dissension, the slavery planks passed unanimously. They destroyed the lingering hopes of some Democrats who opposed the Nebraska bill that it would not be made a test of party regularity. In its national platform the Democratic party upheld the Compromise of 1850 and endorsed the Kansas-Nebraska Act as "the only sound and safe solution of the 'slavery question.'" It did not adjudicate the growing controversy between Douglas and many southerners about exactly when the inhabitants of a territory could decide the legality of slavery. Instead, as J. Glancy Jones feared beforehand, the Democrats once again adopted "an elastic platform susceptible of double reading."[8]

In the balloting for the presidential nomination, Buchanan led from the beginning, but he showed no promise of ever gaining the necessary two-thirds vote. After Pierce's managers transferred the president's support to Douglas, the convention deadlocked, and the party faced the prospect of taking yet another relatively unknown compromise choice. At this point, with the Buchanan managers intimating that Douglas could unite the party and assure himself the nomination in 1860, William A. Richardson withdrew the senator's name, and Buchanan then received the nomination by acclamation. In gratitude for Douglas's magnanimous gesture, the convention, on the recommendation of Richardson, named one of Douglas's supporters, John C. Breckinridge of Kentucky, for the vice-presidency. When the Cincinnati convention adjourned, harmony reigned, outwardly at least, in the party's ranks.

Most Democrats felt, and their opponents certainly agreed, that Buchanan was the strongest candidate they could have nominated. Republicans, who had been eager to run against Pierce or Douglas, recognized that the Pennsylvanian, because he was not directly connected to the Kansas crisis, was a much more formidable opponent and would be difficult to beat.

II

In order to carry the 1856 presidential election, the Republicans had to nominate a man acceptable to the various anti-Democratic factions. Winning the large majority of the Know Nothings was particularly crucial, and in the months before the Philadelphia convention, much of the discussion among Republican leaders concerned which candidate could best appeal to the Americans. Israel Washburn complained that "the quest for as small a modicum of Republicanism as will answer, & as large an infusion of K.N.ism as will be safe," meant that, despite the aspirations of Salmon P. Chase and William H. Seward, only a second- or third-rate man could be selected. Horace Greeley emerged as perhaps the most vocal proponent of taking a candidate with a limited record who could attract a wide range of voters. "I shall go for the man who can secure the most strength

---

7. Hesseltine and Fisher, eds., *Trimmers, Trucklers & Temporizers*, 27–28, 32–35; Nathan K. Hall to Millard Fillmore, March 23, Fillmore Papers, SUNY.

8. J. Glancy Jones to Buchanan, May 30, Buchanan Papers, HSPa. The proceedings of the convention can be followed in the New York papers and the Cincinnati *Enquirer*, June 2–7, and in Hesseltine and Fisher, eds., *Trimmers, Trucklers & Temporizers*, 26–62.

outside our regular ranks," he told a fellow New York editor, "and let earnest Anti Slavery men come in when they get ready."[9] A number of men were proposed as possible candidates and their strengths canvassed, but eventually four major contenders emerged: Salmon P. Chase, William Henry Seward, John McLean, and John C. Frémont.

Chase was the first candidate to actively enter the race for the Republican nomination. Even before he received the party's nomination for governor in Ohio in 1855, he sent out feelers concerning his possible presidential candidacy, but the Ohioan's campaign did not get fully under way until after his election in October. A much more advanced antislavery man than the other men mentioned prominently for the nomination, Chase gained immense prestige from his gubernatorial victory, especially in view of Republican defeats elsewhere. Bolstered by his triumph, Chase and his advisers opened an extensive correspondence with anti-Democratic leaders. In addition, by the end of the year, arrangements had been made for publication of a campaign biography. Governor Kinsley Bingham of Michigan, Governor James Grimes of Iowa, and Senators John P. Hale and Charles Sumner all pledged their support (Grimes and Hale later defected). Charles A. Dana of the New York *Tribune* made no commitment but was definitely friendly. Gamaliel Bailey, on the other hand, who earlier had been one of Chase's strongest supporters, cooled decidedly because of the Ohio leader's advocacy of an alliance with the Americans.[10]

Seeking to assume leadership of the Republican movement, Chase, after his inauguration, issued a special message on Kansas, in which he called for the admission of Kansas under the Topeka constitution and urged the protection of the free-state settlers. He felt even more confident after the Pittsburgh convention, where his subordinates reported that he was the first choice of the delegates.[11] Although the Ohio governor did not realize it, he had no chance for the nomination. Talented political veterans like Israel Washburn, Henry Wilson, Thurlow Weed, and Nathaniel P. Banks let Chase and those around him do much of the work to launch the national organization, then quickly displaced the Ohio group from control once the party's machinery was in place. They had no interest in Chase as a candidate, for he was far too radical on the slavery question to run a strong race; furthermore, men like Weed who were looking ahead to 1860 distrusted his burning ambition.

The Chase movement failed for several reasons. Outside Ohio, except for some scattered support in the West, his candidacy met with little success. He was particularly weak in the East, where no powerful politicians undertook to procure delegates for him. In this section even his old colleagues in the Free Soil party either distrusted him personally or doubted his popularity.[12] The continuing indifference of German leaders

---

9. Israel Washburn, Jr., to James G. Blaine, February 26, Blaine Papers; Horace Greeley to Charles A. Dana, March 10, Benton, ed., *Greeley on Lincoln*, 133; Greeley to Beeman Brockway, June 8 (quotation), Greeley Papers, LC.

10. T. M. Tweed to Salmon P. Chase, October 25, 1855, John P. Jewett to Chase, November 16, 1855, Kinsley S. Bingham to Chase, July 7, 1855, Chase Papers, LC; Chase to James Shepherd Pike, June 20, 1855, Pike, *First Blows*, 296; Chase to John P. Hale, December 10, 1855, Hale Papers, NHHS; Gamaliel Bailey to Chase, June 24, 26, 1855, Chase Papers, HSPa; Charles Francis Adams Diary, December 26, 1855, Adams Family Papers; James W. Grimes to Chase, April 8, 1855, Salter, *Grimes*, 68.

11. Pike, *First Blows*, 302–03; Thomas Bolton to Chase, February 25, Chase Papers, HSPa; Jacob Heaton to Chase, February 25, F. D. Kimball to Chase, February 28, Chase Papers, LC; James M. Ashley to Chase, February 26, Salmon P. Chase Papers, OHS.

12. Adams Diary, July 23, 1855, Adams Family Papers. Chase was particularly bitter about Hale's refusal

outside Ohio, who remained suspicious of him on account of his alliance with the Know Nothings, also damaged Chase's candidacy, which was predicated in part on his alleged ability to appeal to Germans and the liberal Americans.[13] Chase's inability to command the entire Ohio delegation also seriously hurt him.[14] Moreover, his organization was not as effective as it might have been, a lapse that in large part was directly attributable to the candidate. Chase was not a shrewd judge of character—his closest associates agreed on that—and he surrounded himself with a group of younger men, many of whom were sycophants and all of whom lacked sufficient experience to evaluate political intelligence and to conduct a national campaign. As a result, the Ohio governor was consistently over confident about his strength before the Philadelphia convention.[15]

Chase was understandably disturbed by the growing sentiment among Republicans for taking a new man. In reaction, he emphasized the necessity of retaining the enthusiastic support of devoted antislavery men. Acknowledging the need to unite a large number of anti-administration voters, he also stressed that success required a candidate who had "the confidence of the earnest opponents of slavery without which there is no propelling power." This strategy was self-defeating, for it focused attention on his antislavery radicalism, which was his greatest handicap.[16] No one had done more to inaugurate and promote the Republican party, but from the beginning Chase's drive for the nomination labored under too many disadvantages. He felt the nomination to be rightfully his, so much so that he remained blind to the reality of his faltering campaign. A few days before the Philadelphia convention convened, the governor told a close associate that "it seems to me that if the . . . wishes of the people could prevail I should be nominated." More realistic was the analysis of a loyal supporter, who conceded that Chase was the best man, "but those very qualities which entitle you to superior regard, are those which are thought to diminish your availability. Posterity will do justice to the leaders of the anti-slavery enterprise," he continued, "but the men of this generation do not recognize the prophets who are sent unto them."[17]

III

Seward was also quite eager for the nomination. He was the most prominent Republican in the country and had a great popular following, especially among the Whig element of the new party. Although he had recently come out in favor of the abolition of slavery in the District of Columbia, he was not as radical as Chase, and for this and other reasons he was a much stronger candidate. Throughout the early months of 1856, evidence mounted

---

to support him. See Chase to E. S. Hamlin, June 12, *Confidential*, Chase Papers, LC; Chase to Joshua R. Giddings, May 5, Giddings Papers.

13. Charles Reemelin to Chase, April 29, Bailey to Chase, February 21, Chase Papers, LC; Cincinnati *Volksblatt*, April 11, quoted in the New York *Evening Post*, April 16; Hermann Kreismann to Charles Sumner, December 28, 1855, Sumner Papers, HU; Crandall, *Republican Party*, 156.

14. Caleb B. Smith to John McLean, May 30, Richard M.Corwine to McLean, May 16, McLean Papers, LC.

15. James M. Ashley, *Reminiscences of the Great Rebellion* (n.p., 1890), 33; Piatt, *Memories*, 97; Joseph M. Root to Giddings, May 26, 1860, Giddings Papers.

16. Chase to John Bigelow, March 28, *Private*, John Bigelow Papers, NYPL; Chase to My Dear Cleveland, March 21, *Private Strictly* (quotation), Chase Papers, HSPa; Chase to Edward L. Pierce, April 15, Edward L. Pierce Papers, HU; Cincinnati *Commercial*, June 9.

17. Chase to E. S. Hamlin, June 12, *Confidential*, Edward L. Pierce to Chase, May 3, Chase Papers, LC.

of his strength with the masses. Jacob Howard reported that the Michigan delegation was almost solidly for him, and at virtually the same time one of Weed's lieutenants, who was traveling in the West, wrote that Seward enjoyed immense popularity in that section. Even Weed confessed surprise at the feeling manifested at a mass Republican meeting in conservative New York City, where mention of the senator's name was greeted with ''an enthusiasm as universal and vehement as was ever known.'' The New Yorker also picked up support in several unlikely quarters. Banks, originally a Frémont man, wavered and let it be known that he favored Seward if he could be elected. Gamaliel Bailey of the *National Era*, a former opponent, also took up his cause. Advocating the nomination of a man with a clear antislavery record who was untainted with Know Nothingism, he argued that ''Seward is by all odds the strongest man we could run.''[18]

Spurred on by reports of his popularity, Seward was irked that his associates, particularly in New York, displayed considerably less enthusiasm about the possibility of his heading the Republican ticket. His advisers differed over the wisdom of seeking the nomination. Some urged him to run; others, including Weed, counseled him to wait. Unwilling to act without Weed's concurrence, Seward held back, torn between his desire for the nomination and the feeling he might be, as many claimed, unelectable. Even Bailey, one supporter outside Weed's influence, admitted in private that with Seward at the head of the ticket defeat was inevitable. As the convention neared, the senator complained about his position and intimated peevishly to Weed his intention to retire at the end of the present session. Weed had heard this threat before when the two had been at loggerheads and did not take it seriously. A loyal friend, he was determined to pursue the course that best served Seward's long-term interests.[19]

Nothing would have given Weed greater satisfaction than to make Seward president, but his instincts told him that 1856 was not the year. Not one to risk future prospects for no immediate gain, he could never bring himself to believe that the Republicans might win, primarily because Millard Fillmore's candidacy would divide the anti-Democratic vote. Moreover, he was acutely conscious of the hostility to Seward among the nativists stemming from the senator's open denunciations of the Know Nothing order and his pro-Catholic record. Weed was certain that the passage of time would soften this prejudice and that by 1860 it would not be an important consideration, but right now it was an insuperable objection.[20] Representative Henry Waldron of Michigan disclosed that even firm antislavery men acknowledged that Seward ''would not get one-fourth of the votes'' in the key state of Pennsylvania. Confident that a very different man would be needed four years hence, Samuel Wilkeson, Weed's successor at the *Evening Journal*, consoled Seward before the convention, ''The times have not yet caught up with you.''[21]

---

18. Jacob M. Howard to William H. Seward, May 3, Seward Papers, UR; Seth C. Hawley to Thurlow Weed, May 1, Barnes, *Memoir of Weed*, v. 2, 244; Weed to Edwin B. Morgan, May 4 (photostat), Weed Papers, UR; Bowles to Dawes, April 19, Merriam, *Bowles*, v. 1, 172; E. Peshine Smith to Henry C. Carey, May 31, Carey Papers; Bailey to Chase, April 18, Chase Papers, HSPa; Bailey to George W. Julian, March 9, Giddings-Julian Papers.

19. Seward to Weed, April 27, Seward to Frances A. Seward, June 6, 13, 14, Seward, *Seward*, v. 2, 270, 276–78; Seward to Weed, May 4, Weed Papers, UR; Bailey to Chase, April 18, Chase Papers, HSPa; Bailey to Julian, March 9 (quotation), Giddings-Julian Papers.

20. Lewis Benedict to Seward, May 15, John Wilson to Seward, April 1, Seward Papers, UR; Rodney B. Field to Justin S. Morrill, February 18, May 20, Morrill Papers, LC.

21. Samuel Wilkeson to Seward, June 15, Seward Papers, UR; Henry Waldron to Charles S. May, April 26, *Private*, Charles S. May Papers, Detroit Public Library; Bailey to Chase, February 21, Chase Papers, LC.

As the Republican party continued to gain strength, however, Weed began to entertain doubts about his earlier decision to hold Seward's name back.[22] Bombarded with growing demands by Seward's supporters that the senator become a candidate, Weed finally decided in May to wait until the convention to make a final decision. He confessed to Seward that he was uncertain whether to withdraw the latter's name. "It will require all our wisdom and prudence to decide *that* question," the New York boss admitted. A tipoff that Weed could not make up his mind was the sudden reversal in the attitude of the New York *Times*. Henry J. Raymond was close to Weed and certainly knew his thoughts on so significant a matter. In an editorial that appeared on April 18, the *Times* argued that the Republicans would be compelled to "take up a *new name*, one not identified with the political struggles and animosities of the past." Seward, it declared, was disqualified by his anti-nativist principles. "In the western and New England States, the Republican Party owes its strength in a very great degree to its alliance with Americanism," and it could thus not afford to alienate the nativists. By the end of May, however, Raymond changed his tune. The Republican party appeared much more powerful than expected, and the *Times* called upon the New York delegation to present Seward's name at the convention, asserting that he was the "strongest" and "most fitting" candidate. As the June convention neared, Weed was still inclined to keep Seward out of the contest, but his earlier convictions had lost much of their force. Weed did not know yet whether Seward could be elected, one of the senator's supporters reported, "and will not until he sees the convention. You may rely upon it, " he wrote, speaking of Seward's candidacy, "that we do not want him nominated for *fun*."[23]

IV

Unlike Chase and Seward, who appealed to the more advanced antislavery elements in the party, Supreme Court justice John McLean was the favorite of the nativists and conservatives (mostly former Whigs) joined by those party managers, especially in Congress, who believed that he was the strongest man the Republicans could run. His undeniable strength in Pennsylvania, New Jersey, and Illinois, all doubtful states where the party was notably weak, gave added force to his supporters' contention that he was the only man the Republicans could elect. The widely heard assertion that he could carry Pennsylvania, the state that politicians of all parties recognized would be the battleground of the election, lay at the heart of McLean's attractiveness to Republicans. "If McLean is the man for Pennsylvania and New Jersey," Horace Greeley announced, "then I am for McLean."[24]

McLean celebrated his seventy-first birthday in 1856. Originally a Democrat, the Ohio politician had served in the cabinets of both James Monroe and John Quincy Adams, and Andrew Jackson elevated him to the Supreme Court in 1829, after which he eventually became a Whig. During his tenure on the bench, he had issued several important decisions

---

22. Although historians have long known that Weed opposed nominating Seward in 1856, they have not generally recognized the shift in Weed's attitude in May. Some have been perplexed by his behavior at the convention, when he seemed suddenly uncertain of the proper course. In reality, Weed's indecision developed earlier and dominated his thoughts as the convention approached.

23. Weed to Seward, May 11, Seward Papers, UR; New York *Times*, April 18, May 28; E. Peshine Smith to Carey, June 7, Carey Papers.

24. Greeley to Schuyler Colfax, May 6, Greeley-Colfax Papers.

in fugitive slave cases, upholding the constitutionality of both the 1790 and 1850 statutes. In addition, McLean had developed the legal theory that the Constitution granted Congress no power to establish slavery in the territories; since the institution could exist only by virtue of local law, he argued, free territory must remain so until its residents formed a state constitution.[25] He had never indicated, however, whether he believed Congress had the power to prohibit slavery in the territories. Nor had a public word escaped his lips concerning the violence and fraud in Kansas. Whatever his views on the territorial issue, his judicial rulings on the fugitive slave law damned him forever with staunch antislavery men. "He has *no sentiment* or *sympathy* with the *principle of universal Liberty*," contended one of Wade's correspondents in dismissing McLean's candidacy.[26]

In what sense McLean should have been considered a Republican at all was anything but clear. Although he reluctantly voted for Chase in the Ohio gubernatorial election, he had made no open professions of Republicanism. Yet the justice yielded to no one in his ambition to be president. Nearly a quarter of a century earlier, John Quincy Adams commented acidly that McLean "thinks of nothing but the Presidency by day and dreams of nothing else by night." The passing years had done nothing to lessen his zeal. "For more years than we can remember," the Cincinnati *Commercial* observed with much truth in 1856, McLean had been "a floating candidate for the Presidency."[27] For years he had pontificated about the growing political corruption in the country and the degeneracy of political parties. His political creed drew him to the Know Nothings, and when the power of the nativist society became obvious, this attraction blossomed (at least on his part) into an ardent love affair. Greeting the nativist movement with "unmeasured satisfaction" as a much-needed reform movement, he intimated that he would accept the American presidential nomination if offered. Always cautious, McLean declined to join the order while simultaneously endorsing its principles, voting its ticket, and seeking its nomination.[28] When Fillmore's nomination in February 1856 closed this avenue, the judge was more than willing to run on the North American ticket, and a few of his supporters apparently were amenable that he do so even if the Republicans made another choice.[29] With good reason, McLean's critics challenged his Republican credentials.

Despite McLean's weak ties to the party, a number of Republicans rallied behind his candidacy. Nativist Republicans naturally found the prospect of his nomination congenial,

25. Francis Weisenburger, *The Life of John McLean* (Columbus, 1937), 140–41, 194, 122–23; *National Intelligencer*, December 23, 1847, January 14, 1848; McLean to John Teesdale, November 2, 1855, McLean Papers, OHS. For a telling criticism of McLean's legal theory concerning the territories, see a letter from Ohio in the Boston *Atlas*, quoted in the *Illinois State Register*, June 2.

26. M. Smith to Benjamin F. Wade, May 11, *Confidential*, Wade Papers.

27. Charles Francis Adams, ed., *Memoirs of John Quincy Adams* (12 vols.: Philadelphia, 1874–1877), v. 8, 537; Cincinnati *Commercial*, October 23; Welles to Morgan, May 5, Edwin D. Morgan Papers.

28. McLean to [?], September 15, 1846, McLean Papers, LC; McLean to Elijah Whittlesey, August 9, 1845, Whittlesey Papers; McLean to Robert A. Parrish, March 3 (quotation), McLean Papers, LC. Also see McLean to Teesdale, November 2, 1855, McLean Papers, OHS; and McLean's letters cited in the following note. I am indebted to Stephen Maizlish for calling the first two letters to my attention.

29. McLean's courtship of the Know Nothings is detailed in McLean to Hector Orr, November 25, 1854, McLean to John S. Prettyman, November 25, 1854, McLean to Robert A. Parrish, March 3, 1855, Prettyman to McLean, November 21, 1854, Matthew Simpson to McLean, January 13, 1855, Chauncey Shaffer to McLean, May 31, 1855, R. J. Arundel to McLean, March 14, 1855, Thomas H. Ford to McLean, November 27, 1855, Caleb B. Smith and S. Meredith to McLean, October 30, 1855, James E. Harvey to McLean, May 30, *Private*, McLean Papers, LC.

as did conservatives who wished to undercut the influence of the party's vocal antislavery wing. McLean's supporters also maintained, with no confirmation from reliable sources, that Fillmore would decline if McLean were the Republican nominee. This contention was, in fact, extremely dubious. To be sure, no substantial policy differences divided the two men, but Fillmore had been pursuing the presidency almost from the day he vacated the White House, and, convinced that he had a good chance to be elected, he would never renounce his last chance for popular vindication. Even Fillmore's acceptance did not deter McLean's more ardent promoters, who insisted that even if Fillmore remained in the race, McLean would still be the strongest candidate.[30] His prominent affiliation with the Methodist church brought him additional support. "He is a pet of the Methodists & it might help him to a good many votes," one Sewardite acknowledged.[31]

For a number of Republicans, however, the thought of McLean's heading the Republican ticket was repugnant. They viewed him as a candidate of the old fogies, a trimmer on the slavery issue, and not even wholeheartedly a member of the party. As an outspoken critic of the fugitive slave law, Benjamin F. Wade maintained that McLean's nomination would be "fatal" to the Republican movement. "If he is with us at all it is but timidly and feebly," the Ohio senator charged. Other antislavery men joined Wade in expressing alarm over the impact that the nomination of a conservative like McLean would have on the new party. W. C. Howells, the editor of the *Ashtabula Sentinel*, wrote that McLean's election would represent "a total defeat of the Republican party. It would not survive such an event six months."[32] The correspondence of anti-McLean men revealed how much importance antislavery men placed on his fugitive slave law decisions, although some critics—Greeley was a conspicuous example—simply seized on the issue as a means to weaken the justice's candidacy. (As McLean noted with legitimate irritation, the *Tribune*'s editor repudiated him for upholding the law at the same time that Greeley avowed his willingness to support William Bissell of Illinois, who had voted for the law while a member of Congress.) McLean's opponents also doubted his firmness and alleged that he would capitulate to the South at the first crisis. "We have suffered so much from expediency men," wrote one Sewardite, "that I cannot be false to the voice that has warned me always against them."[33] Former Democrats generally sympathized with him on the fugitive slave law, but they were uneasy about his past Whig affinities, while the Germans and foreign-born were intensely hostile because of his flirtation with the Know Nothings. The New York *Abend-Zeitung* asserted that McLean could not win more than one out of every ten German votes. Even keeping exaggerated pre-convention rhetoric in perspective, Republican strategists nonetheless realized that Mclean's nomination would cut both ways.[34]

McLean provided a simple explanation for the opposition to his candidacy. "All the

30. A. C. W. Pennington to McLean, June 12, David Gordon to McLean, June 3, McLean Papers, LC.

31. E. Peshine Smith to Carey, March 17 (quotation), Carey Papers; Greeley to Colfax, May 17, Greeley-Colfax Papers; Victor E. Piollet to Buchanan, n.d. [endorsed March 1856], Buchanan Papers, HSPa.

32. Wade to Chase, May 5 (Confidential) (quotation), Chase Papers, HSPa; W. C. Howells to Giddings, April 29, Giddings Papers; Wade to Milton Sutliff, May 8, Sutliff Papers; Colfax to Alfred Wheeler, May 8, Colfax Papers, LC.

33. Henry Willis to Seward, May 17, Lewis Benedict to Seward, May 15 (quotation), Seward Papers, UR; Wade to Sutliff, May 8, Sutliff Papers; Colfax to Alfred Wheeler, May 8, Colfax Papers, LC; New York *Tribune*, June 6.

34. New York *Tribune*, June 6; Rhodes, *History of the United States*, v. 2, 141n; Blaine to Israel Washburn, Jr., February 12, Israel Washburn, Jr., Papers, Norlands.

politicians are against me,'' he alleged, because of his commitment to political reform.[35] Nothing was further from the truth. Few took McLean's reform platform seriously, and the strongest support for his candidacy was found among Republicans in Congress. Wade, in fact, believed that a majority of the congressional Republicans were in McLean's corner.[36] The speakership struggle and the bonds of unity it forged between North Americans and Republicans did much to promote the disarming belief that McLean's candidacy posed no threat to Republican ideals. Moreover, congressional Republicans were generally practical men, and they knew that victory hinged on nominating a man who could unite the opposition. The judge's backing in the capital was by no means confined to nativists. Elihu and Israel Washburn, for example, concluded that policy dictated McLean's nomination. Lyman Trumbull, partly influenced by Abraham Lincoln, eventually concurred in this judgment. Warning that conservative Whigs were undecided now that Buchanan had been nominated, Lincoln stressed the necessity of making a nomination at Philadelphia that would be acceptable to the Whigs, who represented 90 percent of the anti-Nebraska strength in Illinois. McLean's selection, he declared, would save more Whig votes than any other, and he emphasized that unless the Republicans won the old Whig vote, they could not possibly carry the state. Surely the most surprising converts to McLean's cause were Joshua R. Giddings and Gamaliel Bailey, whose support amply demonstrated that Greeley's assertion that ''all our *old*, earnest anti-slavery men'' disliked McLean was not entirely accurate. After long denouncing the policy of availability, Bailey announced as the convention neared that if the nomination were to be made on this basis, McLean was, in his opinion, the strongest possible candidate.[37]

Thomas Hart Benton once said of McLean that he was ''abolitionist enough for any body outside of a mad house—& his wife is abolitionist enough for all those who ought to be in one.'' Still, for some time McLean's managers had believed that the candidate had to strengthen his standing among antislavery men.[38] The Supreme Court justice's bid for the 1856 nomination was based on a strategy that last-minute developments rendered inoperative. For months McLean had counted on using the case of the slave Dred Scott, which was pending before the Supreme Court, to promote his candidacy. He had written his dissent in the case some time earlier; in it, he enunciated the doctrine that Congress possessed full authority to prohibit slavery in the territories—one of the Republican party's cardinal principles. To make this pronouncement, McLean had carefully chosen the forum that would give him the most publicity. In discussing the pending opinion, one supporter emphasized, ''It is of great consequence to yourself & to your friends, that the repeal of the Missouri Compromise, should be demonstrated to be a breach of faith—both morally & legally.'' While declining to release his opinion in advance, McLean's sense of judicial propriety did not prevent him from divulging to supporters that it would fully

---

35. McLean to John Teesdale, November 2, 1855 (quotation), McLean Papers, OHS; McLean to My Dear Sir, June 12 (copy), James E. Harvey to McLean, May 30, *Private*, McLean Papers, LC.

36. Wade to Sutliff, May 8, Sutliff Papers; Edwin D. Morgan to Gideon Welles, May 1, Welles Papers, LC; Russell Sage to Morgan, June 24, Edwin D. Morgan Papers.

37. Elihu B. Washburne to Abraham Lincoln, June 3, Herndon-Weik Papers; George Bradburn to Adams, June 13, Adams Family Papers; Lincoln to Lyman Trumbull, June 7, Basler, ed., *Lincoln Collected Works*, v. 2, 342–43; Greeley to Washburn, June 13, Israel Washburn, Jr., Papers, LC; Samuel Brenton to Allen Hamilton, March 13, Allen Hamilton Papers, IndSL.

38. Elizabeth Blair Lee to Samuel Phillips Lee, May 12, Blair-Lee Papers; H. H. Emmons to McLean, April 17, C. J. Jack to McLean, April 25, John Teesdale to McLean, October 25, McLean Papers, LC.

satisfy their wishes.[39] Unfortunately for the McLean movement, the court, in a politically motivated step, ordered reargument of the case, a decision that put off any ruling until safely after the election. McLean's plans had been foiled. Not only was he forced to withhold his opinion, but he could not properly even comment on the case. Some other— and a much less effective—means had to be found to bring McLean's antislavery views before the electorate.

An editorial in the New York *Tribune* in early June questioning the extent of McLean's antislavery principles made clear the need for him to elaborate his position, particularly on the repeal of the Missouri Compromise and the violence in Kansas. In May, the *National Intelligencer* published an exchange between Lewis Cass and McLean, in which the latter affirmed Congress's power over slavery in the territories. McLean's congressional supporters, however, judged this letter insufficient. Representative Alexander Pennington of New Jersey, one of McLean's most influential backers, urged him to write a new letter for publication. He warned that many honest men who were personally friendly "have an apprehension that you may not be sufficiently decided firm & earnest for the occasion." It was particularly important that he declare his sympathy with the Republicans on the Kansas issue. Pennington and other boosters in Washington had already drafted a letter asking McLean for his views on various issues in order to provide the judge with an excuse to make another public statement. Following Greeley's attack, these managers stressed that an immediate answer was "absolutely essential."[40] Finally pushed into action, McLean sent the requested letter to Pennington, who, in consultation with Representative John Allison of Pennsylvania, rewrote it to make it more acceptable and then released it to the press for publication.[41]

In his letter as rewritten, McLean termed the troubles in Kansas "the fruits of the ill-advised and mischievous measure—the repeal of the Missouri Compromise," and he called for the admission of Kansas under the Topeka constitution. He stopped short of opposing the admission of any new slave states; nor did he subscribe to the demand that Congress prohibit slavery from all the territories. Only by indirection did McLean even call for the restoration of the Missouri Compromise (that this was his solution, a subsequent draft of a proposed platform made clear).[42] Even this extremely limited position he assumed very late. His new letter did not appear until June 14, only three days before the opening of the Republican convention.

In the last-minute maneuvering before the convention, James Watson Webb of the New York *Courier and Enquirer* devised a scheme to bring the Sewardites to McLean's support and thus ensure his nomination. Webb intimated that the Ohio jurist could draw Seward and Weed into his camp if he wrote a letter promising that their interests would be looked after in the event he was elected. Acting without authorization, Webb also promised Robert Stockton the navy department in the McLean administration in an

39. James E. Harvey to McLean, March 30, McLean Papers; Weisenburger, *McLean*, 197. The best study of the Supreme Court and the Dred Scott case is Don Fehrenbacher, *The Dred Scott Case* (New York, 1978).

40. *National Intelligencer*, May 16; John Allison to McLean, June 2, A. C. W. Pennington to McLean, June 7 (quotation), John A. Bingham to McLean, June 9 (quotation), James E. Harvey to McLean, May 30, *Private*, McLean Papers, LC.

41. A. C. W. Pennington to McLean, June 12, McLean to Pennington, June 6 (copy), McLean Papers, LC. The published letter, dated June 6 and addressed to Joseph Hornblower, the chairman of the New Jersey Republican delegation, appeared in the New York *Evening Post*, June 14.

42. Draft of Platform contained in McLean to My Dear Sir, June 11, McLean Papers, LC. There is another and almost identical draft of a proposed platform, undated, in the same collection.

attempt to obtain the New Jersey leader's influence. When informed of these matters, the candidate immediately composed a letter that Webb pronounced "all I could desire."[43] The New York editor was unquestionably sincere in wishing to see McLean nominated if Seward could not be put on the track, and he undoubtedly concluded, from snatches of conversation with various associates of Weed and Seward, that some pledges on patronage were required. But there is no doubt that he acted on his own and was not fully apprised of Weed's thoughts. The New York boss had no intention of throwing his support to McLean, who he feared would be another Tyler or Fillmore and betray the party. One political associate relayed Weed's scathing private assessment of the Justice as a "'white-liver'd hollow-hearted Janus-faced rascal'. . . I think he prefixed 'd——d.'"[44]

McLean's well-known timidity badly undermined his friends' efforts on his behalf. His failure to speak out until the last minute on Kansas affairs or to endorse congressional power over slavery in the territories weakened the confidence of too many Republicans. The associate justice pleaded his court membership as the reason for his silence, but his position had never in the past prevented him from placing his views before the public. For years his critics had noted his propensity for thrusting his views forward in obvious bids for political preferment in spite of his judicial office. His unwillingness to make an avowal of his Republicanism well before the June convention further crippled his bid for the nomination. McLean wished, in effect, to appeal to both the Republicans and the Americans without committing himself fully to either. Nevertheless, he was a formidable contender for the Republican nomination.

V

McLean's most important rival was John C. Frémont. Only forty-three years old in 1856, Frémont was the youngest, the least experienced, and in many ways the most unlikely of the potential choices to head the Republican national ticket.[45] Although he was a southerner by birth—he had been born in Savannah and raised in South Carolina—he had spent a good portion of his adult life in the army and as a western explorer. Quiet and shy, of middling stature, with black hair and beard, Frémont did not in person loom larger than life. Yet his life was one of romance and adventure as exotic as his name. His wanderlust inherited from his father, his rise from abject poverty to public acclaim, his marriage to the vivacious Jessie Anne Benton in defiance of her father (and at the risk of Old Bullion's legendary wrath), and his subsequent exploits in the West combined to make him a national hero.

Frémont captured the public imagination by successfully crossing the Rocky Mountains on five separate expeditions in the 1840s and 1850s. His third journey placed him opportunely in California at the time of the Bear Flag Revolt. Assuming leadership of the insurgents, Frémont dashed about the countryside, gaining publicity back home while doing little to bring California under American control. His exaggerated efforts, however,

---

43. James Watson Webb to McLean, June 2, 12, James E. Harvey to McLean, June 1, *Private*, McLean Papers, LC; McLean to Webb, June 8, *Confidential*, Webb Papers.

44. Jonathan Nathan to Hamilton Fish, n.d. [received April 17] (quotation), quoted in Berger, *New York Party Systems*, 131; E. Peshine Smith to Carey, May 23, Carey Papers. For Seward's hostility to McLean, see Weisenburger, *McLean*, 131–32.

45. Frémont's career is covered in Allan Nevins, *Frémont, Pathmarker of the West*, new ed. (New York, 1955).

earned him the widely honored if ill-deserved designation as the Conqueror of California, and fully established his image as a daring, romantic figure, a man of force and will. His subsequent privately financed expeditions further enhanced his reputation as an explorer, westward expansionist, and promoter of western development, although his image as the Pathfinder was definitely overstated. He was, as one Ohio Republican recalled, "a half myth alike of history and romance."[46]

In his explorations, Frémont had displayed great courage and resourcefulness in the face of overwhelming adversity. If his successful crossings of the mountains testified to his remarkable tenacity of spirit, his career also provided disturbing evidence of shortcomings in his character. His reserved manner in conversation betrayed none of his well-documented penchant for rash and implusive action. Perhaps because of his illegitimate birth and poverty as a child, he was extremely sensitive to actual or imagined personal slights. Egotistical and self-seeking, he lacked tact, often needlessly provoked disputes, and was unable to work in harmony with superiors or equals. He functioned best in a military command when his authority was unquestioned, but even then he gave ample proof that he did not always possess sound judgment or the ability to assess men's characters accurately.[47]

After resigning from the army, Frémont returned to California and entered politics. His experience was unusually sparse. He served one brief term in the United States Senate but was defeated for reelection and had since been out of political office (critics noted that his actual time of service amounted to seventeen working days). Republicans later created the myth that he had been defeated for reelection because of his antislavery views, but this contention had no substance. His western explorations identified him with the project to construct a Pacific railroad, and he had been a Democrat while active in California politics, but beyond that he was largely a political cypher. His record in California and in the Senate suggested that he was at best a moderate antislavery man, yet his contribution to the cause was negligible. Returning east in 1854, he did not publicly identify with the Republican party for almost two years and made no public pronouncements on any current issues until April 1856. With Frémont having so undistinguished a political career and with his possessing so few claims on the Republican movement, one of McLean's supporters quite understandably expressed bewilderment at Frémont's nomination and demanded "some open, potent, rational *cause* for the sudden, extraordinary uprising of a hitherto politically unknown man."[48]

The New York *Tribune* provided a simple if shopworn explanation of Frémont's rise to political prominence. "As by a spontaneous instinct almost," it intoned, "the People in all quarters seem to have fixed upon *Col. Fremont* as their candidate for the Presidency." As was usually the case in "spontaneous" political movements, the skilled hands of seasoned politicians worked invisibly in the background. More accurate was the

---

46. Albert G. Riddle, *Life of Benjamin F. Wade* (Cleveland, 1886), 216.

47. For Frémont's character, see Colfax to Charles M. Heaton, Sr., August 22, Colfax Papers, NIHS; Carl Schurz, *Reminiscences of Carl Schurz* (3 vols.: New York, 1907–1908), v. 2, 344; letter of S. G. Goodrich, New York *Evening Post*, July 2; Howard K. Beale, ed., *Diary of Gideon Welles* (3 vols.: New York, 1960), v. 2, 42; William Tecumseh Sherman to John Sherman, August 3, William Tecumseh Sherman Papers, LC; Thomas O. Larkin to Alpheus Hardy, August 2, George P. Hammond, ed., *The Larkin Papers* (10 vols.: Berkeley, 1951–68), v. 10, 290.

48. H. H. Emmons to McLean, June 30, McLean Papers, LC. Edward Everett termed Frémont's nomination "one of those freaks of politics which defy all account. Nobody can tell why or by whom he was started." Everett to Mrs. Charles Eames, June 21 (copy), Everett Papers.

contention of Gamaliel Bailey that all the demonstrations for Frémont "have been contrived by Washington management."[49]

Beginning in 1855, several clusters of politicians indulged in loose talk about running Frémont for national office. The first important politician to take an interest was Nathaniel P. Banks, whom George S. Boutwell rightfully called "the discoverer of Fremont as a Presidential Candidate." Banks had first met Frémont in 1853 and, like so many men, was particularly charmed by his wife, Jessie. He apparently first thought of promoting the intrepid explorer for the presidency in mid-1855. Frémont enjoyed a favorable public image, was a former Democrat, and best of all, he had a meager political record that was sufficiently malleable for the times. Some time in October 1855, a group of southern Democratic leaders approached the one-time Californian with a proposal to run him on a national ticket, hoping thus to unite the Democrats and nativists. After conferring with Banks and with his own wife, who was blessed with considerable political talent, Frémont rejected these overtures. Many years later he claimed that he gave as his reason an unwillingness to endorse the repeal of the Missouri Compromise as stipulated.[50] Whether he was, as he later maintained, already contemplating, under Banks's guidance, seeking the Republican nomination seems most unlikely, since Banks was not yet fully committed to the Republican movement, which had exhibited only limited popular strength. Although it was not well-known except to his close friends and advisers, Frémont sympathized strongly with the Know Nothings. Concurring, as he put it, "in the main features of their political faith," he believed that there should be a restriction on unlimited immigration, and he supported a twenty-one year residency-requirement for voting, one of the nativists' most extreme demands. At this time, Frémont most likely was thinking of a possible nomination either by antislavery Americans or by anti-Nebraska Democrats.[51]

Despite Banks's efforts, the Frémont boom did not begin in earnest until late in 1855, when Francis P. Blair also took up the Californian's cause. To a large extent, Frémont's candidacy grew out of the wrecked political hopes of Blair and the old Jacksonians. Four years earlier, in an effort to regain his power in the Democratic party, Blair had trotted out several starcrossed presidential candidates, only to see each boom collapse, and he finally forswore president-making. Blair's festering bitterness at his eclipse in the Democratic party, his hatred for those whom he considered nullifiers, and his morbid fear of Calhounite influence in the party did not diminish after 1852. Indeed, the repeal of the Missouri Compromise two years later brought all of Blair's feelings to a new blaze. Believing that the regular Democracy was corrupt beyond salvation, he found the idea of running a candidate on an independent Democratic ticket compelling. Furthermore, convinced that the will of the people had no chance to be fulfilled at such conclaves, he opposed holding any national nominating convention. Repeated failures at national conventions had soured the Jacksonians on the utility of such gatherings; believing themselves the rightful heirs of Jackson and thus the true guardians of the Democratic

49. New York *Tribune* quoted in William E. Smith, *The Francis Preston Blair Family in Politics* (2 vols.: New York, 1933), v. 1, 355; Bailey to Chase, April 18, Chase Papers, HSPa.

50. George S. Boutwell to Nathaniel P. Banks, Jr., July 1, Banks Papers, LC; Bailey to Chase, April 18, Chase Papers, HSPa; John C. Frémont, MS Memoirs, 192–204, Jessie Benton Frémont, MS Memoirs, 123–24, both in the John C. Frémont Papers, University of California, Berkeley; speech of George C. Bates, New York *Times*, September 3; Elizabeth Benton Frémont, *Recollections of Elizabeth Benton Frémont* (New York, 1912), 75–76.

51. John C. Frémont, MS Memoirs, 192–94, Frémont Papers.

party's future, they were mortified by their lack of power in these assemblages, a situation they attributed simplistically to the power of corrupt influences and wire-pullers. Gideon Welles's attitude was typical. "National Conventions," he maintained, "are mere hot beds of intrigue where unscrupulous & unprincipled men bring out their schemes, and call on the people to sustain the tools that these intriguers select." Blair and his associates proposed that, instead, the people choose their candidate independent of the control of the "rotters," as they had done with Jackson.[52]

During the crisis precipitated by the Nebraska bill, Blair once again took up his old idea of promoting Thomas Hart Benton for president. Blair envisioned running the Missouri leader as a man of the people, independent of all parties, untainted by the intrigues of a nominating convention. This idea had possessed Blair before, and each time it had been abandoned as unrealistic. But Benton's opposition to the Kansas-Nebraska Act, the former *Globe* editor felt, provided the necessary issue with which to galvanize popular support. Benton—faithful ally of Jackson, enemy of Calhoun, and southern statesman who opposed the reckless repeal of the Missouri Compromise—would be invincible.[53]

Beginning in the summer of 1854, a number of members of the old Van Buren clique lined up behind Benton's potential candidacy, and the New York *Evening Post* launched a trial balloon about a "personal party" for Benton that would unite all men who opposed the repeal of the Missouri Compromise. Blair and his circle were confident that opponents of the Nebraska bill, including northern Whigs, would rally to Benton's standard. While in Washington, Preston King advocated a Benton-Seward ticket, with the latter to have the succession in 1860, in order to make the movement more attractive to northern Whigs. "The best plan," the younger Frank Blair instructed, was "for the people to resume the powers so long usurped by party conventions" and nominate Benton "in the primary meetings . . . in the different states, counties, cities towns & villages . . . upon the platform he has built in his thirty years of public service."[54]

The senior Blair's project entailed a number of difficulties, not the least of which was that he had not gotten Benton's consent. The Missouri leader refused to talk to anyone about the presidency, and by the end of 1854 Blair feared that Benton had no interest in the office. Early the next year, Benton forced the issue. Anxious to preserve his power back home and still consumed by the increasingly futile hope of returning to the Senate, he bowed to political reality and announced that he acquiesced in the repeal of the Missouri Compromise. Benton's desertion sent shock waves through the Jacksonian ranks. His support in the North quickly vanished, and even Blair, who was always slow to give up lost causes, eventually had to abandon his long-time ally. As had been true so many times in his career, Old Bullion, as Blair lamented, "kicked over the pail of milk" others had labored to fill.[55]

---

52. Francis P. Blair, Sr., to Frank Blair, Jr., July 21, 1854, Blair Family Papers; Welles to Francis P. Blair, Sr., July 8, 1854 (quotation), Blair-Lee Papers; Welles to [Preston King], April 23, 1855, Welles Papers, LC; Frank Blair, Jr., to Charles H. Ray, December 4, 1854, Charles H. Ray Papers, HEH.

53. Francis P. Blair, Sr. to Frank Blair, Jr., July 21, 1854, Francis P. Blair, Sr., to Montgomery Blair, July 17, 1854, Blair Family Papers.

54. Preston King to Francis P. Blair, Sr., July 16 [1854], October 14, 1854, Blair-Lee Papers; Bailey to Pike, May 30, 1854, Pike Papers, UMe; Preston King to Welles, October 21, 1854, Welles Papers, LC: Frank Blair, Jr., to Charles Ray, December 4, 1854 (quotation), Ray Papers; Ezra Lincoln to Schouler, October 23, 1854, Schouler Papers; Frank Blair, Jr., to J. M. Stone, 1855, Blair Papers, Missouri Historical Society.

55. Francis P. Blair, Sr., to Frank Blair, Jr., December 17, 1854, January 10, 1855, May 21, 1855, Blair Family Papers; Francis P. Blair, Sr., to Martin Van Buren, February 9, 1855 (quotation), Blair-Lee Papers;

With Benton no longer available, Blair decided to push Sam Houston. He urged the Texas senator's selection on the grounds that "he is unstained by corrupt Jobs & is inclined to make Jackson his exemplar especially in regard to the new nullification movements." Eager to be a candidate, Houston attempted to take advantage of his earlier association with Jackson and consciously promoted himself as Jackson's disciple. Censuring national conventions as corrupt, he intimated that he was willing to entrust his candidacy to the people.[56] Houston also had a much broader appeal than had Benton. Some prominent Whigs, including Israel Washburn and William Schouler, were sympathetic, as were a few former Free Soilers led by Charles Sumner. Still deeply suspicious of nominating conventions, the Jacksonians proposed to bring Houston forward at popular gatherings instead. "Let him be taken up in township meetings, crossroads gatherings, and Militia meetings as the popular candidate," exactly as Jackson had been, Gideon Welles advised.[57] By the first months of 1855, a full-fledged Houston boom was under way.

Just as the old Jacksonians seemed agreed that Houston was their strongest man, rumors began to fly that the hero of the Texas Revolution was a Know Nothing. Unwilling to accept this accusation, Blair nevertheless recognized that unless Houston kept his distance from the nativists, the old Jacksonian Democrats would never endorse him. Houston, however, ignored warnings from his long-time associates about identifying too closely with the order. With obvious exasperation, Welles finally delivered a veiled ultimatum: Houston could accept the support of the Americans as an independent candidate, but he could not expect any outside support if first nominated by them. He must be independent of the order. Houston's reply was deliberately ambiguous, but his growing coziness with the Know Nothings was too obvious to be ignored, and in the end the Jacksonians were forced to drop him because of his American affiliation.[58]

By the summer of 1855, the Houston boom, at least outside the American party, was at an end. Abandoning the Texas leader, Blair and the Jacksonians set out to find a more suitable candidate. In less than a year, both Benton and Houston, Blair's top choices, had proved totally unequal to the task he had envisioned. A new man was needed. And time was running out.

Preston King to Welles, April 14, 1855, Welles Papers, LC; Preston King to Hannibal Hamlin, January 6, 1855, Hamlin Papers.

56. Francis P. Blair, Sr., to Martin Van Buren, February 9, 1855 (quotation), Blair-Lee Papers; Frank Blair, Jr., to Montgomery Blair, March 16, 1855, Francis P. Blair, Sr., to Frank Blair, Jr., January 10, 1855, Blair Family Papers; Sam Houston to Welles, January 26, 1853, Philip H. and A. S. W. Rosenbach Foundation; Frank L. Burr to [Welles], n.d. [Summer 1854], Welles Papers, LC; Welles to My Dear Sir, May, 1854 (copy), Welles Papers, ConnHS.

57. Truman Smith to Welles, December 10, 1854, Private, John S. Williams to Welles, July 14, 1854, December 11, 1854, Welles Papers, LC; Weed to William Schouler, June 16, 1854, Schouler Papers; Lot Morrill to Hannibal Hamlin, June 15, 1854, Hamlin Papers; Joshua Leavitt to Chase, March 14, 1855, Chase Papers, HSPa; Israel Washburn, Jr., to Pike, January 19, 1855, Pike, *First Blows*, 263, J. B. Newman to Chase, May 5, 1855, Chase Papers, LC; Welles to Francis P. Blair, Sr., July 8, 1854, (quotation), Blair-Lee Papers.

58. Welles to Preston King, November 25, 1854, April 23, 1855, John S. Williams to Welles, November 25, 1854, January 14, 1855, April 2, 1855, Welles to Houston, February 26, 1855, Typescript, Welles to My Dear Sir, March 1855, Welles to [Williams], December 9, 1854, Welles Papers, LC; Charles D. Deshler to Hugh McIntyre, January 26, 1855, Deshler Papers; Solomon G. Haven to Fillmore, January 10, 1855, Fillmore Papers, SUNY.

VI

As Blair pondered his predicament, his thoughts turned to Frémont. He was young and vigorous, a great popular hero, a Democrat, and had no embarrassing political record. True, he could not be linked directly to Jackson, but his connection with Benton was a decided asset. Blair, with his usual overenthusiasm, was particulary drawn to Frémont's "indomitable will." He even prattled to Wade that the Californian was more like Jackson than any man he knew![59] Moreover, after his past failures at candidate-making, the former editor considered the colonel's limited political experience, which presumably made him amenable to guidance and advice, an important asset. Blair was also comforted by the expectation that he could exercise considerable influence through his daughter, Elizabeth Blair Lee, who was a close friend of Jessie Frémont. (Those who knew the Frémonts quickly perceived that it was Jessie, not John, who possessed the political brains of the marriage.) In addition, the Jacksonian leader was certain that Frémont's candidacy would inevitably bring the obstinate Benton, who was very secretive about his political intentions, into the fold, an accomplishment that had long been one of Blair's primary goals. Some time in the late summer of 1855, Blair decided to mount an all-out effort to elect Frémont president in 1856.

Blair undertook to bring his fellow Jacksonians, still reeling from Houston's apostasy, to Frémont's standard. By the end of the year several important political figures, including John Bigelow at the *Evening Post* and Gideon Welles, had been consulted and were definitely interested. Before long, Preston King declared for the Californian as well. Blair also launched a short-lived movement to win southern support, and his son Frank sent assurances before New Year's Day that the Benton Democracy in Missouri would endorse the Pathfinder. At the Christmas conference at Blair's home, at which Chase, Banks, King, Sumner, and Bailey were present, their host forthrightly avowed his support for Frémont's nomination.[60] At this point, Blair had not yet committed himself to the Republican cause and was still thinking of Frémont as an independent anti-Nebraska candidate. Only gradually, over the next few months, did he drop this idea in favor of winning the Republican nomination. With even greater reluctance he finally abandoned his opposition to holding a nominating convention.

Earlier, when Blair first launched the Frémont movement, he undertook to provide the candidate with a platform. He had a free hand, since the colonel had not declared his sentiments on any of the controversial issues of the day. In September, Blair drafted a letter in which he laid down as Frémont's basic platform the restoration of the Missouri Compromise. The letter endorsed the ordinance of 1787 and the compromises of 1820 and 1850; they were "as obligatory on the good faith of the people of the States and of the federal Government as the Constitution itself." Attributing the difficulties in Kansas to the breach of the Missouri Compromise, it charged that the "banditti of Missouri" had legislated "a code of lynch law" in the territory. In an attempt to assume a national and not a sectional perspective, the statement also criticized northern laws that interfered with

---

59. Wade to Sutliff, May 8, Sutliff Papers.

60. Frank Blair, Jr., to Francis P. Blair, Sr., December 17, 1855, Blair-Lee Papers; Bigelow to Welles, December 27, 1855, Welles Papers, LC; Francis P. Blair, Sr., to Bedford Brown, October 30, 1855 (Private), "Correspondence of Bedford Brown," Historical Society of Trinity College *Historical Papers*, ser. 6 (1906), 86–88; Welles Diary, February 6, Welles Papers, LC.

the rights of southerners (an indirect reference to personal liberty laws).[61] For reasons that are unclear, this letter was never sent; it was a long way, however, from the doctrines of this letter to the first Republican national platform. That Frémont could easily stand on the principles of either document indicates how limited his public record really was. Also gone by the time of his nomination in June was any serious thought of southern support.

Sharing a common goal, Banks and Blair joined forces in late 1855 to promote Frémont's candidacy. Even when Banks had been a Democrat, the two men had not been close politically or personally. The Massachusetts representative was twenty-five years Blair's junior and had never been part of the Van Buren wing of the party. The speakership contest, however, brought the two men together. Shortly after its inception, the Frémont movement gained two additional influential backers: Henry Wilson, who thought the Californian would make a strong candidate, and Thurlow Weed, who John Bigelow reported by the end of the year was satisfied with Frémont, adding (inaccurately), "and if so of course Seward is." Around Christmas, Banks visited several eastern cities and enlisted two anti-Nebraska editors, Bigelow of the *Evening Post* and Charles Congdon of the Boston *Atlas*. Another meeting in New York City in January, which Bigelow organized and Blair attended, won over Edwin D. Morgan, soon to be Republican national chairman. One long-time associate Bigelow approached who had no enthusiasm for the project was Samuel Tilden, who disclosed that he intended to remain in the Democratic party. Banks also brought in former representative Charles W. Upham of Massachusetts, who would later write a campaign biography of the Pathfinder. By the start of the new year, the movement was fully under way.

Several papers, including the Worcester *Spy* and the Cleveland *Herald*, came out for Frémont in the first part of 1856, but until April the colonel's managers made no concerted effort to generate public support. Instead, between January and March they concentrated on courting party leaders and establishing a smoothly functioning organization. Most of the House members who masterminded Banks's election (except for the Washburn brothers) joined the movement. Also prominent in the Frémont organization were several talented political manipulators who were closely associated with Banks, including Isaac Sherman of New York, railroad promoter Charles James of Wisconsin, and Israel D. Andrews, a New England journalist and political "fixer." Dividing their time between Washington and other cities, the Frémont organizers were indefatigable in promoting his cause. Sherman, aided by Bigelow, expended considerable effort in New York and reported good success. In Maine, young James G. Blaine was enthusiastic; he thought that the Californian would be particularly strong with conservative Whigs.[62] One cherished endorsement the Frémont managers failed to acquire was that of Benton, who, contrary to Blair's expectations, refused to countenance the candidacy of his son-in-law.[63]

---

61. Francis P. Blair, Sr., draft of letter by John C. Frémont, September 16, 1855, Blair-Lee Papers. There are two copies of this letter in the collection. One, in Blair's hand, is undated. The other, a copy made by Elizabeth Blair Lee and corrected by Blair, is dated September 16, 1855. In his October 30 letter, Blair suggested that Brown write Frémont requesting his political opinions.

62. John Bigelow to Welles, December 27, 1855 (quotation), Welles Papers, LC; Bigelow, *Retrospections*, v. 1, 141–43; Congdon, *Reminiscences*, 152–53; Weed to Fish, January 6, Fish Papers, LC; Isaac Sherman to Banks, February 9, Private, March 5, *Private*, Israel D. Andrews to Banks, January 5, *Private*, Banks Papers, LC; Blaine to Washburn, February 21, Israel Washburn, Jr., Papers, Norlands; William Pitt Fessenden to Ellen Fessenden, March 9, Fessenden Family Papers.

63. Benton to Richard T. Jacob, n.d. [1856], quoted in William M. Meigs, *The Life of Thomas Hart Benton* (Philadelphia, 1904), 509; Smith, *Blair Family*, v. 1, 342.

By early April, Seward believed that Frémont was the front runner among anti-Nebraska men in Washington. By then the colonel had picked up an impressive list of official and unofficial endorsements. Included in his camp were such nativists as Schuyler Colfax, Wilson, and Banks; ex-Democrats headed by Blair and his faction; antislavery Whigs, most notably Weed and Wade; conservative Whigs like William Pitt Fessenden; and eastern Free Soilers, led by John P. Hale. The Pathfinder also was strong among Germans. Without a political following six months earlier, Frémont was by the onset of spring a formidable candidate.

These endorsements involved a considerable element of faith. Most Republican leaders knew little of Frémont personally and even less of his views on the slavery issue or any other political question. They largely accepted the assurances of close acquaintances like Blair and Banks, who in urging his claims portrayed him as a man of great strength of will and firm antislavery principles. Although the candidate spent part of the congressional session in Washington and became acquainted with at least some Republican leaders, he was singularly unimpressive in private conversation. He was quiet and unassertive, yet men believed that this reserve masked his true nature. His reputation as an explorer predisposed politicians to accept the image of him as a man of force and character. Colfax exuded enthusiasm after he met the colonel; he was confident that as president, Frémont would be "equal to old Hickory in firmness." Another Republican told Banks: "Fremont is the man for the occasion. He is a man of boldness, independence, & capacity; & has a history that inspires admiration. He has many of the qualities of Jackson."[64] The Californian's managers offered similar pledges to worried party members concerning his antislavery sentiments. Wade, for example, informed an undecided Oran Follett that Frémont was "decidedly & enthusiastically right on the great issue." Writing to a close associate back home, Colfax affirmed that the Pathfinder was "sound as a nut on the Slavery question." In like fashion, New Hampshire Republican Amos Tuck was hesitant to commit himself to Frémont until Mason Tappan provided "explicit assurances in regard to his being with us in sentiment."[65]

After analyzing the political situation, many Republicans concluded that Frémont was the party's strongest potential nominee. "Many of us here think that he is the only man who can carry Pennsylvania," Colfax declared—a point Banks stressed repeatedly in conversation. Frémont, the speaker pithily remarked, was "the favorite of those who desire to *win*." Party leaders in Washington were for him, a Michigan representative reported, "not as a matter of choice so much as of policy." A well-known antislavery man, he asserted, could not carry the East, where the recent Connecticut election showed how weak pure Republicanism was. The choice, as he saw it, was between a proven candidate and certain defeat or adapting the candidate and platform "to the times" and hoping public sentiment would come up to the mark.[66]

Frémont possessed several appealing qualities that his supporters believed would give

---

64. Colfax to Alfred Wheeler, April 11, May 1, Colfax Papers, LC; Edward Hamilton to Banks, May 20, Banks Papers, LC; Waldron to Charles S. May, April 26, *Private*, Charles S. May Papers; Wade to Sutliff, May 8, Sutliff Papers; Charles A. Dana to Pike, June 11, Pike Papers, UMe.

65. Wade to Oran Follett, April 13 (*Private*), Oran Follett Papers, CinHS; Colfax to Alfred Wheeler, January 13, *Private*, Colfax Papers, LC; Amos Tuck to Mason Tappan, April 25, Tappan Papers.

66. Colfax to Alfred Wheeler, April 11, *Private*, Colfax Papers, LC; Banks to Bigelow, March 24, quoted in Harrington, *Fighting Politician*, 35; Waldron to Charles S. May, April 26, *Private* (quotation), Charles S. May Papers; Ebenezer Peck to Trumbull, June 10, Trumbull Papers; Charles A. Dana to Pike, June 11, Pike Papers, UMe.

him strength. Finding him quite popular, Indianapolis editor John D. Defrees commented, "We *can* raise a breeze for him."[67] Several observers noted that the youthful Pathfinder was particularly strong with young men. Because of the tenacity of old party loyalties, the new party would gain a great advantage if it could win a substantial share of young, weakly identified voters. As a fresh new face on the political scene, Frémont could appeal to those voters hostile to old leaders. James Grimes of Iowa argued that it was very important "an entirely *new man*" be nominated. The Republicans could not elect any of the old politicians "against whom there are old chronic prejudices, which . . . are so hard to be conquered. To build up & consolidate a new party," he concluded with considerable insight, "we must have men who have not been before the people as politicians." Defrees concurred that "a new man and a new Party will take thousands!"[68]

Frémont's lack of an extensive political career had other advantages as well. Greeley concluded that "a candidate must have a slim record in these times," and as Wade emphasized, the colonel had "no past political sins to answer for." Representative Daniel Mace of Indiana, one of the managers of the anti-Nebraska forces two years before and a Know Nothing, also came aboard. "It will never do to go into the contest and be called upon to defend the acts and speeches of old stagers," he insisted. "We must have a position that will enable us to be the changing party." Furthermore, Frémont had said and done nothing to antagonize either the Americans or the foreign-born, and Republicans thus hoped that with him at the head of their ticket they could appeal successfully to both groups. He also enjoyed the advantage of being a former Democrat. A number of Republican leaders deemed it critical that the party's nominee be an ex-Democrat, not only in order to reassure anti-Nebraska Democrats who had left their party but to encourage still more of their wavering colleagues to do likewise. Bowles was confident that with Frémont as the nominee, the Republicans would "sweep the country beyond peradventure. He will take from 20 to 30 percent of the northern democrats," the Massachusetts editor predicted optimistically, "& come in flying."[69]

A variety of considerations, on the other hand, caused a number of Republicans to resist the Frémont tide. The basic assertion of his managers—that he could make the strongest race—was precisely the claim McLean's advisers made for their candidate. In addition, the Californian's qualifications and experience were dwarfed by those of his rivals. Doubting that he could be relied on, a New Hampshire voter observed, "He has neither experience, knowledge nor the confidence of anybody, except as a fast rider, & hunter." Frémont was "the merest baby in politics," grumbled Greeley. "He don't know the A B Cs, and attributes importance to the most ridiculously insignificant matters and regards the most vital as of no account." One of the leading voices against the policy of nominating a new man was the Cincinnati *Commercial*. The true issue of the campaign was the extension of slavery, but "the discoverers of FREMONT," it charged, were "endeavoring . . . to avoid and obscure the true issue" and thereby make the contest

67. John Defrees to Henry S. Lane, May 19, Henry S. Lane Papers, IndU; Colfax to Alfred Wheeler, January 13, *Private*, Colfax Papers, LC; Wade to Sutliff, May 8, Sutliff Papers; New York *Tribune*, June 6.

68. Grimes to William Penn Clarke, April 3, James W. Grimes Papers, IaSDHA; Defrees to Henry S. Lane, May 19, Lane Papers, IndU.

69. Greeley to Dana, March 10, Benton, ed., *Greeley on Lincoln*, 133; Wade to Sutliff, May 8, Sutliff Papers; Daniel Mace quoted in Rhodes, *History of the United States*, v. 2, 134; Bowles to Dawes, April 19, Dawes Papers; Colfax to Francis Stebbins, April 29, Stebbins Papers; Boston *Atlas*, March 27, quoted in New York *Evening Post*, March 29.

"insignificant." He should serve in the ranks first and give proof of his devotion to the cause of liberty. "A TRIED MAN, and NOT 'a new man,' IS WHAT THE COUNTRY WANTS." Bailey took the identical tack in the *National Era*. To George W. Julian the Washington journalist complained: "The mania for mere success has seized a majority of the men here, and to accomplish it, they are eternally talking about taking up some *new man*—Mr Availability." Victory with a candidate like Frémont, he insisted, would be "almost fruitless."[70]

The immediate cause of the *Commercial*'s attack was the appearance of a letter from Frémont to Charles Robinson, the head of the free-state movement in Kansas. The two had met in California, where they had become friends, and some time in February—on whose initiative is unclear—the Kansas leader wrote renewing their acquaintance. Frémont's advisers saw in this fortuitous relationship a chance to make political capital. Although party leaders could be assured privately of his antislavery principles, converting the Republican masses required a different strategy. Having achieved considerable support in Washington and in certain state organizations, these managers were by April ready to undertake a movement to influence public opinion. Some, at least, decided that the candidate needed a stronger antislavery record before the voters. Reports continued to arrive from Republicans back home that popular uneasiness persisted because the colonel's views were insufficiently known.[71]

Whereas Frémont's advisers agreed on the necessity of appealing openly for mass support, they were divided over the advisability of writing any letter for publication. Recalling the faux pas of Clay in 1844 and of Scott in 1852, many politicians believed that letter-writing was an occupational disease that inevitably turned out badly. Thomas H. Ford expressed the pervasive attitude about candidates' letters when he advised McLean to throw away his pen, put his right hand in a sling, and write no living person a single political sentence. "Just as soon as a man is nominated for the Presidency," the Ohio lieutenant governor observed, "he Generally becomes a fool and sets himself to work writing Political letters to Jackasses Every where." Banks's right hand man, Isaac Sherman, opposed having Frémont write any letter. "As a *veiled prophet* he will have followers from the romance of his life and position but when he enters the arena as a public letter writer, the charm will be broken." If he wrote one, where would it stop? Surely the Know Nothings would demand to know his views on nativism. Thousands of letters would inundate him "on every subject from the question of the Trinity down to his views on cough candy and every writer will think himself insulted if he does not receive an answer."[72]

Blair, on the other hand, was anxious to exploit Frémont's connection with Robinson, and he therefore suggested that Frémont be nominated by the free-state settlers in Kansas as a means of identifying the Californian with their cause.[73] The Frémont managers rejected this strategy out of concern that any nomination prior to the Philadelphia

70. Henry F. French to Benjamin B. French, June 1 (quotation), French Papers; Greeley to Colfax, May 16, Greeley-Colfax Papers; Cincinnati *Commercial*, April 17, 29; Bailey to Julian, March 9 (quotation), Giddings-Julian Papers; Bailey to Chase, April 18 (quotation), Chase Papers, HSPa; Bowles to Dawes, April 19, Dawes Papers.

71. Francis P. Blair, Sr., to Frémont, February 18, Blair-Lee Papers; Thomas Quick to Trumbull, January 24, Trumbull Papers; Israel Washburn, Jr., to Blaine, February 26, Blaine Papers.

72. Thomas H. Ford to McLean, November 27, 1855, McLean Papers, LC; Isaac Sherman to Banks, April 3, *Private,* Banks Papers, LC.

73. Francis P. Blair, Sr., to Frémont, February 18, Blair-Lee Papers.

convention would hurt the candidate and also fear that the Kansas men might place him on an undesirable platform. After some discussion, however, his advisers approved releasing a letter to Robinson in reply to an earlier communication. The author of Frémont's letter is unknown, although some commentators suggested that Banks wrote it. Probably several politicians had a hand in it. In any event, Banks sent it to Robinson along with a covering letter that recommended Frémont's message "should have immediate publication among your people."[74] The Lawrence *Kansas Free State*, on April 7, was the first newspaper to publish the letter, dated March 17. This fact was not immediately known outside the territory, and its initial eastern appearance, in the Boston *Atlas* on April 9, had much greater impact. Robinson was in Boston at the time and may have handed a copy of the document to *Atlas* editor Charles Congdon, although Greeley, for one, suspected that it was sent from Washington. Snatched up eagerly by other Republican journals, Frémont's letter to Robinson received an unusually wide circulation.[75]

Frémont's letter made two important points. First, it pictured the candidate as a martyr to the antislavery cause by implying that he had been defeated for reelection in California because of his opposition to the Slave Power. Second, it identified Frémont—in carefully chosen language—with the free-state cause in Kansas. Reviewing the situation in the territory in general terms, Frémont characterized the existing territorial government as a "usurpation," and he assured Robinson, "I sympathize cordially with you, and that as you stood by me firmly and generously when we were defeated by the nullifiers in California, I have every disposition to stand by you in the same way in your battle with them in Kansas."

The Frémont-Robinson letter marked the opening of the public campaign for the Pathfinder's nomination. It was obviously intended for publication (as Banks's covering letter confirmed), and, despite some criticism, Republican reaction was generally favorable.[76] The New York *Evening Post*, which was uncommitted to any candidate although Bigelow was an early Frémont man, summed up the popular reaction when it declared that the Californian's pronouncement "gives him a high and prominent place in the list" of possible Republican nominees. Almost immediately, Samuel Bowles reported that the Frémont movement was "going like prairie fire" in the West.[77] That this artful letter generated such enthusiasm is little short of astounding. Frémont's statement fell far

---

74. Banks to Charles Robinson, March 19, Charles Robinson Papers, KSHS; Greeley to Charles A. Dana, April 11, Greeley Papers, LC; Colfax to Alfred Wheeler, March 31, Colfax Papers, LC; Congdon, *Reminiscences*, 153. Compare James C. Malin, "Speaker Banks Courts the Free-Soilers: The Frémont-Robinson Letter of 1856,"*NEQ*, v. 12 (March, 1939), 103–12; and Fred Harvey Harrington, "The Reception of the Frémont-Robinson Letter: A Note on the 1856 Campaign," *NEQ*, v. 12 (September, 1939), 545–48. Malin called historians' attention to Banks's accompanying letter, although S. W. Eldridge revealed its existence much earlier and quoted from it briefly in his recollections, "Early Days in Kansas," 67. Colfax, one of the inner circle of congressional leaders, knew in advance about Frémont's letter and may have helped draft it. Its reference to "nullifiers" betrays the presence of Blair's hand as well.

75. Congdon, *Reminiscences*, 153; Amos A. Lawrence Diary, April 6, Lawrence Papers; Malin, "Banks Courts the Free-Soilers," 104; Harrington, "Frémont-Robinson Letter," 547. Ruhl J. Bartlett declares that of approximately a hundred anti-Nebraska newspapers he checked, not one failed to print the letter at least in part. *John C. Frémont and the Republican Party* (Columbus, 1930), 17n.

76. Massachusetts correspondent "Pictor," New York *Evening Post*, April 11; James M. Bunce to Morgan, April 15, Edwin D. Morgan Papers; Daniel W. Alvord to Francis W. Bird, April 17, Bird Papers; Greeley to Charles A. Dana, April 9, Benton, ed., *Greeley on Lincoln*, 148. A sample of editorial comments is given in the New York *Evening Post*, April 11.

77. New York *Evening Post*, April 10; Bowles to Dawes, April 19, Dawes Papers.

short of the private pledges given by his advisers, or even the position McLean assumed in his two letters published in May and June. Nor was it of the vintage that Colfax claimed the western explorer had already written on slavery—"plain as a pike staff & as straight out too."[78] What Frémont did not say was notable: He did not identify himself with the Republican party, he did not take a position on the expansion of slavery, he did not even call except by indirection for the admission of Kansas under the Topeka constitution (he predicted Robinson's ultimate triumph, which could be interpreted to mean the admission of Kansas with its free-state government).

Less surprising was the reaction of apprehensive Republicans who declared that Frémont's avowal of his principles was insufficient and that a further explanation was required. He must "say something spicy, to the point, and adequate for the occasion," Amos Tuck maintained, adding, "Let there be no doubt, or chance to doubt, the material of which the Candidate is made. The times demand a positive character." A well-informed man would search Frémont's career in vain for proof that he adhered to sound Republican principles, an uneasy Sewardite contended after the letter's publication. Welles considered the Robinson letter "very acceptable," but added that "the public . . . crave something more," although the Connecticut leader was willing that the testimonials come from reliable friends rather than from the candidate.[79]

Members of the Frémont high command resisted the call for another public statement, however. The candidate was gaining strength, they reasoned, and additional letters increased the risk of alienating potential supporters. A mass meeting in New York City at the end of April, designed to give the Republican movement an indirect boost, presented a new dilemma, for the party's national chairman, Edwin D. Morgan, on behalf of the organizing committee, invited Frémont to speak. As was traditional with such meetings, its directors intended to publish the replies of those who could not address the gathering in order to bring their views before the public. Cognizant of the opposition of some of his advisers to any more public letters, Frémont was uncertain about whether to respond, but ultimately he—or, more likely, one of his confederates—wrote a very strongly worded letter in which he announced that he "heartily concur[red]" in all movements "'to repair the mischiefs arising from the violation of good faith in the repeal of the Missouri compromise.'" He went even further and declared that he was "opposed to slavery in the abstract and upon principle . . . by long settled convictions." Repudiating any attempt to interfere with the institution in the states where it existed, he also proclaimed, "I am . . . inflexibly opposed to its extension on the Continent beyond its present limits."[80]

In response to criticism for publishing the Robinson letter, Banks had already assured Greeley that he would (in the latter's words) "keep out of such ruts hereafter." When this new letter from the candidate came to its attention, the Banks group vigorously urged the Republican national chairman not to print Frémont's reply. Whether others agreed with the speaker is not entirely clear, but it seems likely, for Morgan laid aside the letter to the New York meeting to be used or not as needed at a later date. Greeley was not convinced that the national chairman had done the best thing, but he agreed that "it is not by

---

78. Colfax to Alfred Wheeler, May 1, Colfax Papers, LC.

79. Tuck to Tappan, May 7, Tappan Papers; Lewis Benedict to Seward, May 15, Seward Papers, UR; Pike, *First Blows*, 322; Welles to My Dear Sir, May (copy) (quotation), Welles Papers, ConnHS; Welles to Morgan, May 5, Edwin D. Morgan Papers.

80. Greeley to Colfax, June 4, Greeley-Colfax Papers; New York *Herald*, June 17.

suppressed but by *published* letters that candidates get knocked over."[81] Bigelow, on the other hand, wanted the letter published before it was "*too late.*" Elizabeth Blair Lee, who knew the innermost details of the Frémont campaign, divulged that the suppressed letter was written to satisfy "the Ultras" and that they were "now for keeping quiet." In response to protests from Banks, Isaac Sherman promised, "No letters will be hereafter written unless first presented to you and at least thirty other friends." A week later he flatly declared that Frémont "will write no letters if all Washington require him to write."[82]

Throughout this period, Greeley carefully watched the course of public opinion without firmly committing himself to any candidate. The New York editor above all wanted to win. Brushing aside complaints of antislavery veterans about ignoring the party's tried and true leaders, he maintained that the Republicans were not strong enough to elect anybody and thus had to take a man who had the best chance of carrying the doubtful northern states. By the end of April, Colfax reported that the editor of the *Tribune* was "moderately" for Frémont, but in May Greeley began to have serious second doubts. "I am afraid he lacks stamina for President, or even for a canvass," he confided to Colfax concerning Frémont. "I am afraid several volumes might be filled with what he don't know about the first elements of Politics. I am afraid we shall be sorry if we get him elected. And I am afraid we can't elect him." Greeley had also heard disturbing rumors about financial misdealings in the sale of Frémont's California Mariposa estate. If the rumors were true, the New York editor was sure they would kill his candidacy. Greeley's inquiry on Wall Street did not completely satisfy him, although he concluded that the rumors were exaggerated. Charles A. Dana, on the other hand, who was Greeley's closest associate at the *Tribune*, was an enthusiastic Frémont man and an equally fervid opponent of McLean. "I tell you Fremont is the man for us to beat with, & the only one," Dana wrote to James Shepherd Pike. "*He is the true metal*, that I'll swear to, and more than that, if he is elected, *his cabinet will be made up of our sort of men*. With McLean we are all at sea & besides he can't be elected."[83]

It was not until June 6 that Greeley, apprehensive about McLean's growing strength, finally swung the *Tribune* behind Frémont. In a long article, the influential New York journal advocated the Californian's nomination because (among other things) he had a natural appeal to young men, was a former Democrat and the choice of the Jacksonians, was "among the first" to sympathize with the free-state movement in Kansas, and was not "obnoxious either to Americans or adopted citizens." The endorsement of the *Tribune*, with its assurances of Frémont's essential soundness on the slavery and Kansas questions, gave a powerful boost to his candidacy. Increasingly, the Frémont movement appeared unstoppable.

The Californian's managers were quite confident by the eve of the Philadelphia convention that, if they could prevent the North Americans from nominating him first, he

---

81. Greeley to Charles A. Dana, April 11 (quotation), Greeley Papers, LC; Isaac Sherman to Banks, April 2, Private, George White to Banks, April 15, George S. Boutwell to Banks, April 9, Banks Papers, LC; Greeley to Colfax, May 11 (quotation), Greeley-Colfax Papers; New York *Tribune*, April 30, May 1.

82. Elizabeth Blair Lee to Samuel Phillips Lee, April 28, May 9, Blair-Lee Papers; Isaac Sherman to Banks, May 4, 12, Banks Papers, LC.

83. Greeley to Beeman Brockway, June 8, Greeley Papers, LC; Colfax to Francis Stebbins, April 29, Stebbins Papers; Greeley to Colfax, May 16, 18 (quotation), 19, n.d. [May], Greeley-Colfax Papers; Charles A. Dana to Pike, June 11, Pike Papers, UMe.

would win the Republican nomination. There were several straws in the wind besides the *Tribune*'s endorsement. The New Hampshire state convention, meeting less than a week before the national convention, instructed the state's delegates to vote for the Pathfinder. The New York state central committee also passed resolutions in his favor. James Gordon Bennett, who enjoyed a reputation for picking winners, threw the weight of the New York *Herald*, which had never evidenced the slightest sympathy for the antislavery crusade, behind the colonel's candidacy. The *Herald*'s endorsement was doubly significant, for Bennett was one of George Law's most important backers. With Law and Bennett joining the Frémont forces, victory at the convention seemed beyond doubt. Indeed, after stopping in New York City for consultations on his way to Philadelphia, Rufus P. Spalding of Ohio, whom McLean had designated his floor manager, was ready to concede defeat.[84]

VII

If Frémont's prospects at Philadelphia were bright, his advisers remained keenly aware that the North American convention could easily demolish all their plans. In the final hectic weeks before the New York City meeting convened, they debated various proposals to prevent it from acting precipitately. Isaac Sherman suggested that the Rhode Island state convention and the Illinois convention at Bloomington nominate Frémont in order "to counteract the effect of a Know Nothing nomination." Colfax, too, feared that the American convention would "give us great trouble, whether it nominates a new man of their own, or Fremont either." He suggested that the colonel be nominated at "spontaneous combustion meetings *before* that time by the people at large, to take off the edge" of any nomination by the New York City convention.[85] Like the earlier idea of a Kansas nomination, these suggestions came to naught.

So did Blair's long-contemplated plan to have Frémont nominated by a convention of bolters from the Cincinnati Democratic convention joined by outsiders. Blair's motives were twofold: Such a nomination would greatly enhance Frémont's appeal to dissident Democrats, and it would considerably lessen the danger of a subsequent Know Nothing nomination. If either Pierce or Douglas were nominated, Republican organizers antici- pated that a large number of delegates would walk out of the convention, followed by a mass meeting under the direction of the pro-Benton Missouri delegation, which would nominate Frémont as an anti-Nebraska Democratic candidate. The plan was abandoned for several reasons. A number of Republicans opposed any action before the June 17 convention, sentiment for a bolt was much weaker at Cincinnati than Blair had anticipated, and Buchanan's nomination further lessened the discontent. The most critical reason, however, was the opposition of Benton, who vowed at one point that he would go to Cincinnati and prevent any such nomination. Any attempt by the Blairs to nominate Frémont over Benton's objections would have ruined all concerned. To provoke Benton

---

84. New York *Herald*, June 10, 11; Rufus P. Spalding to McLean, June 14, McLean Papers, LC. Charles A. Dana, noting that Bennett had taken up Zachary Taylor in 1848, pointed to the *Herald*'s support of Frémont as "a sign that . . . he has great elements of popularity & success." Dana to Pike, June 11, Pike Papers, UMe.

85. Isaac Sherman to Banks, May 12, Ezra Lincoln to Banks, May 8, Banks Papers, LC; Colfax to Alfred Wheeler, May 1, Colfax Papers, LC.

into publicly attacking his son-in-law on the eve of the Republican convention would have been foolhardy in the extreme.[86]

Shortly after the collapse of Blair's Cincinnati scheme, the North American convention assembled in New York City. How to manage this gathering had been the subject of much discussion among Republicans. The initial Republican plan was to have the North Americans adopt a platform, appoint a committee for consultation, and leave the selection of a national ticket to the Philadelphia convention. The New York City meeting would subsequently ratify the Republican ticket. Some nativist leaders approved this idea, and Republicans were for a time optimistic that there would be only a minimal fuss. In order to make the convention more malleable, Wilson and Banks saw to it that the New England states were heavily represented.[87]

A number of delegates, however, proved recalcitrant. They were willing to unite with the Republicans on a national ticket, but they were determined to obtain concessions first. Some, encouraged by the New York *Herald*, a recent but noisy convert to Frémont's cause, believed that they could force the Republicans to accept their nominee and thus wanted to act first. Others were intent on compelling the Republican nominee to endorse the American platform. As Republican politicians recognized, any nominations would be troublesome. "Whether it nominates right or wrong," Greeley said of the June 12 convention, "it will be a bother to us."[88]

Several important Republican leaders were on hand to make sure nothing occurred to destroy Frémont's chances or wreck the contemplated fusion of the two organizations. "Weed is here doing all that is possible," Greeley informed Colfax from the metropolis. The New York boss's efforts were ably seconded by Preston King, Henry Wilson, Edwin D. Morgan, and Isaac Sherman. They and other Republicans circulated unobtrusively among the delegates, smiling amiably while urging that no nominations be made before consulting with the Philadelphia convention. Some participants charged later that the Republicans gained additional power of persuasion from the lavish expenditure of upwards of $30,000. Although this figure was wildly exaggerated, the Republicans definitely had funds at their disposal and made liberal promises of aid. The analysis of the New York *Herald*'s reporter was on the mark. "A large proportion of sharp, hungry and calculating politicians enter into its composition," he said of the convention, and "Thurlow Weed and his set have a pretty long finger in the pie."[89]

On the morning of June 12, Weed held a preliminary meeting at the Astor House to formulate strategy. Keeping his distance from the Apollo Room, where the convention

86. Elizabeth Blair Lee to Samuel Phillips Lee, April 30, May 2, 6, 7, 13, 23, Frank Blair, Jr., to Samuel Phillips Lee, March 17, Blair-Lee Papers; Colfax to Alfred Wheeler, May 1, Colfax Papers, LC; Haven to Daniel Ullmann, April 23, Ullmann Papers, NYHS; Isaac Sherman to Banks, February 24, *Private*, Banks Papers, LC.

87. Greeley to Colfax, June 1, Greeley-Colfax Papers; Colfax to Alfred Wheeler, May 1, Colfax Papers, LC; Isaac Sherman to Banks, June 11, Banks Papers, LC; A. C. W. Pennington to McLean, June 12, McLean Papers, LC; Hesseltine and Fisher, eds., *Trimmers, Trucklers & Temporizers*, 68.

88. Greeley to Colfax, May 6, Greeley-Colfax Papers; James M. Bunce to Morgan, May 17, Edwin D. Morgan Papers; New York *Herald*, June 2; Francis S. Edwards to Banks, June 4, Banks Papers, LC.

89. Greeley to Colfax, June 4, Greeley-Colfax Papers; S. M. Allen to Banks, June 12, 13, Banks Papers, LC; New York *Herald*, June 13 (quotation), 18; A. Oakey Hall to Morgan, August 2, Edwin D. Morgan Papers; Fred Harvey Harrington, "Frémont and the North Americans," *AHR*, v. 49 (July, 1939), 843. Halstead, who was in New York City to cover the convention, reported that Weed and Greeley "have been at work busily as beavers and sly as moles . . . trying to make an arrangement" with the North Americans. Hesseltine and Fisher, eds., *Trimmers, Trucklers & Temporizers*, 69.

met, Weed relied on several nativist allies to direct affairs from the floor. Prominent among these were former governor William F. Johnston of Pennsylvania, desirous of the vice-presidential nomination or, failing that, a cabinet appointment; Lieutenant Governor Thomas H. Ford of Ohio, who let it be known that he wanted a lucrative federal office; one-time mayor Robert Conrad of Philadelphia; and George Law of New York, who had his eye on the Republican gubernatorial nomination and had been basking in the sunshine of Republican flattery since the American convention in February.[90] All were committed to Frémont. By the time the convention adjourned, Weed's appraisal of their usefulness would be amply borne out.

The Republican strategy unfolded initially without a hitch. Seeking to encourage co-operation, national party chairman Edwin D. Morgan sent a letter to the convention inviting its members to confer with the Republican convention. Conrad was elected president of the convention, and Law was named head of a committee to meet with the Republicans. The delegates spent two days doing little more than listening to speeches and debating the Republican overture. But the desire to nominate a ticket was too strong to be resisted. Once the balloting began on the fourteenth, Republican fears multiplied when the Connecticut delegates mustered considerable sentiment on the floor to nominate Frémont. Indeed, one Republican operative believed that a majority of the delegates favored his selection. A rumor—subsequently denied—spread through the hall that in an interview with a group of Massachusetts delegates, Frémont had endorsed American principles and had indicated that he would accept the North American nomination whether he was nominated at Philadelphia or not.[91] In an effort to stem this tide, on the fourteenth the New York *Tribune* warned the North Americans that they must not try to coerce the Philadelphia convention. Fearing Frémont would be brought forth by the New York convention, Republican strategists moved to block this possibility by having him draft a firm letter in which he endorsed the Republican movement and stipulated that he could not accept the nativist nomination "unconditionally." To the candidate's later good fortune, this letter was not sent. Isaac Sherman persuaded him that such an important statement had to be approved by Blair and others laboring on his behalf. The candidate dutifully sent it to Blair for perusal, but the occasion never arose to release it to the New York gathering.[92] Whatever this declaration might have done for his standing at Philadelphia, it certainly would have hurt Frémont's chances of being endorsed by the North Americans.

As Frémont's advisers well knew, his nomination at New York before the Philadelphia convention acted would be fatal to his candidacy. "The Philadelphia convention will not consent that the [North American] convention should dictate a nomination and then the foreigners of Iowa Illinois and Wisconsin will leave us en masse if such a nomination

90. New York *Herald*, June 13; Isaac Sherman to Banks, June 10, Private, M. G. Hart to Banks, June 2, S. M. Allen to Banks, June 13, Banks Papers; Lewis I. Allen to Morgan, April 14, Edwin D. Morgan Papers; Horace H. Day to Fillmore, September 9, Fillmore Papers, SUNY. Law had joined forces with Weed several months earlier. Weed to Seward, March 5, Seward Papers, UR. When Ford deserted McLean for Frémont is unclear.

91. S. M. Allen to Banks, June 12, Banks Papers, LC; Alfred B. Ely to Arch Grand Executive Committee of the Order of the United Americans, July 15, McLean Papers, LC. Without indicating his source of information, Allen reported that Frémont's answers were "quite unsatisfactory" to some members of the committee. The New York *Herald*, June 13–15, 17, 20, 21, contains full coverage of the convention's proceedings.

92. Frémont to Ford, and notation on back by Frémont, June 15, Frémont to Francis P. Blair, Sr., [June] 17, John Bigelow Papers, NYPL.

should be ratified at Philadelphia,'' one of Banks's associates noted.[93] By careful management, Republican leaders had to prevent Frémont's nomination at New York while steering the convention to name someone who would, on the appropriate signal, decline in favor of the Republican nominee. Besides Banks and Frémont, McLean was the only candidate with significant support at the convention, and Republican strategists did not trust the ambitious Supreme Court justice to step aside for Frémont, even if the latter won the Republican nomination. Had they known how contemptuous McLean was of his rival's abilities, they would have had even less confidence in his reliability. The only possible choice was Banks. A consummate politician, the speaker had already given ample evidence that he possessed the requisite qualities to handle such a delicate situation with the necessary finesse.

Isaac Sherman had, in fact, suggested precisely this plan to Banks in May:

> Would it not be well to have the K. Ns nominate you on the 12th of June for President and some Whig like Gov. Johnson [*sic*] of Penn for Vice President and then you decline the moment that the Republican convention at Philadelphia has nominated Fremont? Could we not have an understanding of this kind which would virtually give the K. Ns the nomination of the Vice President?

Banks reluctantly sanctioned the strategy. Two days before the convention assembled, Sherman, after conferring with Law, Ford, and Johnston in New York, told Banks: ''It has been decided that you shall be nominated here. . . . I can see clearly that it has been decreed by the men who have control of the convention.''[94]

By this time, Sherman was no longer certain that his earlier strategy was wise. He became convinced that Banks could be nominated at Philadelphia with Frémont as a running mate, and he warned, ''It is useless to talk of electing you or any other man nominated first as a K.N.'' Russell Sage, another Banks intimate, was likewise of the opinion that Banks could win the Republican presidential nomination.[95] Banks's true intentions are difficult to discern, for he guarded his counsel carefully. The ambitious Massachusetts congressman was not averse to national recognition and, under the right circumstances, would have welcomed the chance for a presidential nomination. He certainly wanted to be in a position to come forward as a compromise choice if the convention deadlocked between Frémont and McLean. Earlier, several congressmen, who did not know Banks's thoughts, decided that he was aiming for a nomination, although, as one aptly remarked, ''Nothing escapes him looking like it, and he will be too shrewd a manager to spring his chance prematurely.''[96] Banks had also been widely mentioned for the Republican vice-presidential nomination, but he had no desire for this honor and declined to be considered. Moreover, if Frémont were the presidential nominee, the vice-presidential choice would inevitably be a former Whig. Before deciding to endorse

---

93. Isaac Sherman to Banks, June 10, Private (quotation), Banks Papers, LC; Seth C. Hawley to Weed, May 1, Barnes, *Memoir of Weed*, v. 2, 144.

94. Isaac Sherman to Banks, May 4, 24, *Private* (quotation), June 10, Private (quotation), Banks to Law, Johnston, and Ford, June 11 (copy), Banks Papers, LC.

95. Isaac Sherman to Banks, June 10, Private (quotation), June 11, Russell Sage to Banks, May 31, 1855 [1856], George White to Banks, June 10, Banks Papers, LC.

96. Richard Mott to Chase, February 21 (quotation), A. P. Stone to Chase, March 30, Chase Papers, LC; E. Dodd to Weed, March 13, Weed Papers, UR; James Harlan to William Penn Clarke, April 21, William Penn Clarke Papers, IaSDHA.

Frémont, Greeley gave serious consideration to supporting Banks despite their strained personal relations. "After all," he told Colfax, "Banks *is* a politician—and won't break down under us, nor run away with us." He thought no one would run a stronger race in the Northeast. Indeed, the New York editor was even willing to trust Banks to write letters.[97]

Banks remained loyal to Frémont and did not forbid the use of his name at New York. His well-earned reputation for duplicity, however, caused some Republicans to believe that the speaker was playing his own game. Not fully informed of the Republicans' strategy, Charles A. Dana, for instance, warned James Shepherd Pike that "Banks has been arranging things in a quiet way to sell us out at the K.N[.] Convention" and "force himself" on the Philadelphia convention.[98] To prevent detection of the Republican strategy, the managers of the New York convention left the apparent direction of the Banks movement to a group of young, inexperienced nativists who sincerely desired his nomination. Most prominent of these men were Stephen M. Allen, who was under the misapprehension that he was Banks's spokesman at the convention, and Horace H. Day, who had made a fortune in the rubber business and was willing to spend large sums of money to gain political influence. Those familiar with the inner workings of the convention intimated afterwards that Day, who agreed to pay the expenses of a number of Banks delegates, had expended $20,000 in promoting Banks's candidacy.[99] In addition, Ford and Johnston voted for McLean on the first ballots in order to further mislead nativists who were suspicious of Republican interference. Banks could have been nominated on Saturday, but, hoping to delay any nomination as long as possible, Republicans told Allen, who was completely taken in, that if the convention adjourned until Monday, the sixteenth, Banks would certainly be nominated at Philadelphia.[100]

The weekend recess was a mistake. Cries of a Republican trick emanated from some restless delegates, and on Monday a group of dissidents bolted and, joined by a number of outsiders, nominated Robert F. Stockton for president. Although this group was not large, its action forced the Republicans' hand, and when the convention reassembled Banks was nominated. Johnston received the vice-presidential designation. The convention then adjourned until June 19 to await the report of Law's committee after it conferred with the Republicans. Thus one day before the Republican national convention opened, a North American ticket was nominally in the field, and the committee appointed in response to Morgan's invitation was preparing to come to Philadelphia for consultations. Republican leaders breathed a sigh of relief, convinced that they had averted the threat

97. Greeley to Colfax, May 6, 18 (quotation), 21, Greeley-Colfax Papers.

98. Charles A. Dana to Pike, June 5, 11 (quotation), Pike Papers, UMe. Banks apparently sent Allen noncommittal instructions, probably hoping to keep the convention from making any nomination. Allen to Banks, June 15 [16], Banks Papers, LC. Elizabeth Blair Lee doubted Banks's intentions, but Jessie Frémont remained confident of his good faith. Elizabeth Blair Lee to Samuel Phillips Lee, June 14, Jessie Frémont to Elizabeth Blair Lee, Thursday [June 12?], Blair-Lee Papers. Samuel Phillips Lee, Elizabeth Blair Lee's husband, erroneously endorsed this last letter "Thursday April 17/56 rcd. Friday 18th." Since Lee was not with his wife in April, his endorsement is not contemporary. Content clearly establishes that it was written in June, before the Republican convention.

99. Also prominent in this group of zealous Banks men was Z. K. Pangborn. Allen's, Day's, and Pangborn's relationships to the Banks boom are fully documented in the Banks Papers, LC, for June. See especially Allen to Banks, June 7, Strictly Confidential, June 11, 14, 15, 15 [16], Day to Banks, June 10, 11, 12, *Private.* For delegates being paid to stay, see the New York *Herald*, June 18.

100. Allen to Banks, June 15, Banks Papers, LC.

posed by the North American convention. They were certain that Banks would decline on cue; indeed, the speaker was already in Philadelphia promoting Frémont's nomination.[101] All that remained was to work out some suitable arrangement on the vice-presidency, and fusion would be a reality.

VIII

The first Republican national nominating convention convened on June 17 in the Musical Fund Hall in Philadelphia. The hall, which seated more than 2,000 people, was full and an air of excitement prevailed when Edwin D. Morgan gaveled the delegates to order. Observers were struck by the assembly's unusual earnestness and sense of purpose. Murat Halstead, in Philadelphia to cover the convention for the Cincinnati *Commercial*, reported that the crowd was "not so noisy" and profane as the one that had gathered earlier in Cincinnati, and "everything is managed with excessive and intense propriety." The delegates' seriousness, their fervor and hopeful expectation created an atmosphere akin to that of an evangelical camp meeting. One participant, struck by the righteous enthusiasm of the delegates, commented that the Philadelphia convention reminded him of a "Methodist conference rather than a political convention."[102]

Attendance was much more substantial than at Pittsburgh in February, not only in sheer numbers but in talent as well. Every northern state sent a full delegation, as did the Republican Association of Washington and several territories. Also present were a small number of delegates claiming to represent slave states. Not unfairly, the Democratic Washington *Union* protested that "the few *exotics* from Maryland, Virginia, and Kentucky, who appeared there as delegates, have no constituencies at home." In all, 565 delegates were present, along with a large number of outsiders and a bevy of scribbling reporters.[103] A group of a hundred free soil Democrats from New York were also given seats on the convention floor, although they had no votes.

The emphasis of commentators on the convention's revivalistic atmosphere could not conceal the large number of experienced politicians on hand, either as delegates or outsiders, to direct affairs. Many more important party leaders attended the June convention than had journeyed to Pittsburgh in February. Among those in evidence at Philadelphia were Weed, Greeley, Morgan, Blair, Trumbull, Banks, Elihu and Israel Washburn, Hannibal Hamlin (who had just joined the party), Wilson, Thaddeus Stevens, Wilmot, Bailey, Giddings, and Welles. Also present were several less well-known men with important party careers ahead of them, such as E. R. Hoar, Zachariah Chandler, James G. Blaine, and William Dennison, Jr. The convention's proximity to Washington, the greater importance of its business, the season, and the party's growth in the past three months all contributed to the increased participation.

Morgan wanted a free soil Democrat of sufficient stature to serve as chairman of the convention, but eventually party leaders abandoned this idea and selected Henry S. Lane

---

101. Hesseltine and Fisher, eds., *Trimmers, Trucklers & Temporizers*, 69; New York *Tribune*, June 18.

102. Hesseltine and Fisher, eds., *Trimmers, Trucklers & Temporizers*, 87; Eldridge, "Early Days in Kansas," 65; Brinkerhoff, *Recollections*, 128; Merriam, *Bowles*, v. 1, 151.

103. Charles W. Johnson, *Proceedings of the First Three Republican National Conventions of 1856, 1860, and 1864* (Minneapolis, 1893), 15–82; Washington *Union* quoted in Rawley, *Race & Politics*, 147. Partial lists of delegates appear in the newspaper reports of the convention; the fullest (though not entirely accurate) list is given in Johnson, 35–42.

of Indiana, a former Whig. His selection was unfortunate. Befuddled by parliamentary rules, Lane was unable to exercise control over the proceedings and eventually turned his duties over to others. More refined easterners found his behavior rather shocking. A representative of western manners, Lane presided with his boots on the table and a large chew of tobacco in his cheek, and he joined in applause by thumping his cane on the platform. Uncertain what to make of this uncouth westerner, Charles Francis Adams sniffed that he spoke "as if he had the dance of St Vitus."[104]

The first critical business was adoption of a platform. In addition to Wilmot, who was chairman, the other important members of the resolution committee were Blair, Welles, Preston King, and Giddings. Former Whigs on the committee were not as notable, perhaps the best-known being Henry Carter, editor of the Portland *Advertiser*, and John D. Defrees of the Indianapolis *Journal*. Giddings, who always magnified his own importance, credited the significant sections of the final document to King and himself.[105]

On the second day Wilmot reported the product of the committee's deliberations. The first Republican national platform was truly a remarkable document. Absent were the earlier evasions of the Pittsburgh resolutions and the call for the nominating convention. Wilmot's habitually smiling countenance seemed strangely inappropriate as he read the party's stern statement of principles. The platform commenced with a general endorsement of the Declaration of Independence, the Constitution, and the perpetuity of the Union. Its most famous and oft-quoted plank affirmed that Congress had "sovereign powers" over the territories, and that it was "both the right and the imperative duty of Congress to prohibit in the Territories those twin relics of barbarism—Polygamy, and Slavery." Without mincing words, the platform thus incorporated one of the cardinal demands of the old Liberty party men. Less noticed was the plank immediately before this statement, although antislavery proponents believed it more important. It began with a brief expostulation of the constitutional theory, popularized by Chase, that the founding fathers had committed the nation to an antislavery policy, and that the purpose of the national government was to secure the right of "life, liberty, and the pursuit of happiness . . . to all persons under its exclusive jurisdiction." The section concluded with the sweeping statement: "We deny the authority of Congress, of a Territorial Legislature, of any individual, or association of individuals, to give legal existence to Slavery in any Territory of the United States" under the Constitution.

The longest section of the platform recited the violations of the rights of the free-state settlers in Kansas and censured the Pierce administration and its supporters for condoning these acts. A separate plank called for the immediate admission of Kansas under the Topeka constitution. Other resolutions condemned the Ostend Manifesto as embodying "the highwayman's plea, that 'might makes right,'" urged the construction of a Pacific railroad "by the most central and practicable route," and endorsed federal aid to internal improvements "of a national character." Except for internal improvements, Jacksonian economic issues, most notably the national bank and the tariff, were carefully omitted

---

104. Adams Diary, June 17, Adams Family Papers; Eldridge, "Early Days in Kansas," 68. Morgan sounded out Blair about getting Martin Van Buren to preside, but Blair replied that the ex-president did not intend to leave the Democratic party. Morgan to Francis P. Blair, Sr., May 14 (copy), Blair to Morgan, May 30, Edwin D. Morgan Papers.

105. Giddings, *History of the Rebellion*, 397–98. The Manuscript Division of the New York Public Library contains drafts of various proposed planks presented to the Republican committee.

from the party's declaration of principles. Divisions among Republicans over these issues necessitated their exclusion.

The carefully crafted final plank, which dealt with the difficult nativist question, was intentionally ambiguous. It was the only resolution that sparked a debate. As slightly amended, the final version called on all those who agreed with the principles of the platform, however they might differ on other questions, to join in support of the national ticket, and opposed any legislation impairing "liberty of conscience and equality of rights among citizens." Historians usually interpret this declaration as an attempt to cater to immigrants, particularly Germans. Actually, as the debate over it revealed, this plank was carefully worded so as not to offend nativists as well, since it spoke of the rights of citizens, not aliens, and it contained no reference to or specific censure of the Know Nothings. The clause was much weaker than the platform recently adopted in Illinois by the Bloomington convention, of which Germans had been loud in their praise. In addition, "liberty of conscience" was a time-honored nativist slogan that referred to an individual's right to read the Bible and its use in schools, and to Catholic interference with these practices. As a concession to the nativists, and largely at the insistence of the New England and Pennsylvania delegates, a declaration in the original draft voicing opposition to "all proscriptive legislation" was dropped.[106]

The slavery planks, which constituted the overwhelming bulk of the platform, represented a clear victory for the resolute antislavery men. The endorsement of the Declaration of Independence, the recapitulation of the theory of the antislavery principles of the founding fathers, the reference to slavery as a relic of barbarism, and the call for Congress to prohibit slavery in all territories were in full accord with the views of antislavery advocates. To be sure, the platform contained no call for a ban on the admission of any new slave states, a position many state organizations had taken previously. Equally noticeable was the lack of any reference to the fugitive slave law. Strategic considerations dictated this latter omission especially, since no question struck a more sensitive nerve among conservatives and former Democrats than resistance to the 1850 law. Also glossed over silently was the abolition of slavery in the District of Columbia. Still, even with these concessions to moderates and conservatives, the platform remained an unusually radical document for a major party with any serious hope of winning a national election.

Giddings could hardly contain his joy. The principles of the platform were "all we have ever contended for," he assured the readers of the *Ashtabula Sentinel*. "I think it ahead of all other platforms ever adopted." Julian, who was normally as pessimistic as Giddings was optimistic, also praised the platform; he was particularly pleased that the doctrine of restoring the Missouri Compromise had been disowned, and that the convention's resolutions considered the Kansas question a "mere incident of the conflict between liberty and slavery." Referring to the platform, he told a colleague: "I think I can stand on it, and *without doing much violence to its language, preach the whole anti-Slavery*

---

106. The debate over the nativist resolution is barely outlined in the official proceedings. For a fuller account, see the New York *Herald*, June 19. Also see Adams Diary, June 18, Adams Family Papers; Hermann Kreismann to Banks, June 9, Banks Papers, LC. Seward reported that the convention's managers had wanted the platform to be completely silent on Americanism. Seward to Frances A. Seward, June 26, Seward, *Seward*, v. 2, 279. Holt, *Political Crisis*, 178–79, notes the platform's ambiguous stance on nativism.

gospel." The document was to be commended for "occupying boldly and unequivocally so much true anti-slavery ground."[107]

In the face of their earlier ambiguous statements, why did the Republicans at Philadelphia embrace such strong antislavery principles in such uncompromising language? No conclusive answer is possible; some suggestions, however, are pertinent. The makeup of the resolutions committee, though obviously important, can be overstressed. Radical antislavery men did not constitute a majority of the committee membership, non-members were undoubtedly consulted, at least unofficially, and in any event the delegates could have rejected or substantially modified the platform had they wished. Chase provided an intriguing explanation. He suspected that the convention "builded wiser than they knew":

> I hardly believe that the majority understood what broad principles they were avowing. The recognition of the constitutional provision, denying to the Government power to deprive any person of life liberty or prop[er]ty without due process of law as a practical & effectual prohibition of slavery in any territory of the United States, is a point gained, which includes, in logical comprehension, all that is most important for us. It includes denationalization of slavery entire.[108]

Chase may have overstated the implications of the platform, especially since its calls for specific action were decidedly limited, but his main point—that the platform could serve as the justification for a wide variety of measures that would weaken slavery—was well taken.

The final version was probably the result of several considerations: the influence of certain members (particularly King, Wilmot, and the other free soil Democrats on the committee), the moralistic fervor that prevailed on the convention floor (tremendous cheering greeted the denunciation of polygamy and slavery, and the audience demanded that the censure of the Ostend Manifesto be read a second time), and the popular excitement arising out of the Sumner and Lawrence incidents.[109] Also a factor was Republican confidence, which had been greatly bolstered by the apparent willingness of the North Americans in the New York convention to unite with the Republicans. In February, when the Pittsburgh convention met, the American party was still a unit, Republican prospects were grim, and the necessity of attracting additional support was painfully apparent. With the party more firmly established, its outlook improved, and the Americans largely willing to fuse, caution was no longer as imperative.

The other important action the convention took before making its nominations was the appointment of a national committee. The committee designated at Pittsburgh had been functioning as an interim organization. Members of the new committee would serve for four years, but their major task would be to supervise and coordinate the 1856 presidential campaign. The committee's membership appointed at Philadelphia was not identical to its

---

107. Letter from Giddings, *Ashtabula Sentinel*, July 3; Giddings to Julian, June 24, Giddings-Julian Papers; Julian, *Political Recollections*, 150; Julian to J. F. Myers, June 23, in Columbus [Indiana] *Independent*, clipping, George W. Julian Papers, IndHS.

108. Chase to Julian, July 17, Giddings-Julian Papers.

109. Preston King's influence was especially apparent. For a decade he had argued that slavery could not exist except by virtue of positive law and that Congress had no power to establish slavery. The call for a congressional ban on slavery in the territories was the substance of the Wilmot Proviso, which King, Blair, and David Wilmot, all members of the committee, had endorsed in the 1840s as Democrats.

predecessor's. Illinois gained a far stronger spokesman in Norman Judd, and, in the most important change, Gideon Welles replaced John Niles, who had recently died, as Connecticut's member. The direction of the committee, however, was in essence the same, since Edwin D. Morgan not only remained New York's representative but was again elected national chairman. Along with Morgan, its most important members were holdovers John Z. Goodrich of Massachusetts and William Chace of Rhode Island, the committee's secretary, joined by newcomer Welles.

IX

Excitement gripped delegates and spectators alike when, following adoption of the platform, the convention turned its attention to the selection of the national ticket. During the previous few days, as the delegates arrived in Philadelphia, the optimism of the Frémont men remained high. Before the convention's first meeting, two perceptive political reporters, James Shepherd Pike and Murat Halstead, both wired their papers that the Pathfinder's nomination was a certainty. On June 17, in a move carefully timed to coincide with the opening of the convention, the committee around Frémont finally published his suppressed April letter to the New York Kansas meeting, which announced his opposition to the extension of slavery beyond its present limits. Although the letter left vague the status of the institution in the territories, including Kansas, it was the strongest public statement on slavery that Frémont had made.[110] His managers' expectation that this newest declaration would carry the convention with a rush proved overly optimistic. Some delegates still harbored grave doubts about his faithfulness to Republican principles. In addition, the McLean forces tried to check the Californian's momentum by proposing a McLean-Frémont ticket, and Halstead, among others, believed that they had made some headway.[111]

The heart of McLean's strength was the Pennsylvania and New Jersey delegations, but he also had significant backing among the delegates from Maine (where Israel Washburn promoted him), Illinois (where Lyman Trumbull and Elihu Washburne headed his advocates), and his home state of Ohio (where, despite Chase's attempts to pack the state's delegation, almost half its members, led by William Schouler, Joshua R. Giddings, Samuel Galloway, and Rufus Spalding, preferred McLean). After surveying various delegations, Chase's managers concluded that he did not have a chance, an assessment that had been reached several months earlier by other party leaders. The governor's failure to hold the entire Ohio delegation was merely the final blow to a dying campaign.[112] With

110. Pike, *First Blows*, 344–45; Hesseltine and Fisher, eds., *Trimmers, Trucklers & Temporizers*, 82, 88–89, 102; Elizabeth Blair Lee to Samuel Phillips Lee, June 7, 14, Blair-Lee Papers; Colfax to Alfred Wheeler, May 1, Colfax Papers, LC; James W. Stone to Banks, June 14, Banks Papers, LC. Frémont's New York letter is printed in the New York *Herald*, June 17.

111. Hesseltine and Fisher, eds., *Trimmers, Trucklers & Temporizers*, 85, 88–90; Joseph Bartlett to Hannibal Hamlin, [June 14], Hamlin Papers; Adams Diary, June 17, Adams Family Papers; John Z. Goodrich to Julius Rockwell, September 9, Rockwell Papers; Hector Orr to McLean, June 20, McLean Papers, LC. In authorizing Blair to present or withdraw his name, Frémont stipulated that he was not to be considered for the vice-presidency. Frémont to Blair, [June] 17, John Bigelow Papers, NYPL.

112. Chase to E. S. Hamlin, June 2, Chase Diary, June [written after June 19], Chase Papers, LC; Noah H. Swayne to Thomas Ewing, June 19, Ewing Family Papers; Hesseltine and Fisher, eds., *Trimmers, Trucklers & Temporizers*, 97. On the informal ballot after Chase's withdrawal, McLean received thirty-nine of Ohio's

Chase's elimination, Seward was the one candidate other than Frémont and McLean who had significant support.

Seward's unexpected strength posed a dilemma for Weed. In the previous few days, delegates had repeatedly asked Weed and his lieutenants why Seward was not a candidate for the nomination. The New York senator enjoyed widespread popularity, as the audience's response to Henry Wilson's speech during the first day's proceedings demonstrated. Seeking to generate enthusiasm, Wilson rhetorically referred to the various candidates for the nomination, and as he named each one, great cheering broke out. He saved Seward's name until the end, when his reference to the New York leader as "the foremost statesman of America" unleashed a spontaneous popular demonstration that was unmatched. The entire assembly rose en masse and, amidst the waving of hats and handkerchiefs, cheered wildly for several minutes. Surprised by this display, Weed was already under heavy pressure from James Watson Webb to allow Seward to be nominated, and he was also mindful that the senator was sulking over what he viewed as the half-hearted commitment of his friends.

On June 16, Webb, with Weed's knowledge, wrote Seward, apprising him of his strength and asking him to telegraph authority to use his name. "One word from you will give the Country its Candidate. . . . I tell you again, you can succeed." If he decided not to seek the nomination, Webb assured him that "*you* can say *who* shall be nominated." The same day Seward received Webb's letter, he opened another from John Schoolcraft, Weed's chief lieutenant. Schoolcraft reiterated the belief of Weed and others that there was no possibility of victory in 1856. Torn between conflicting emotions, Seward reluctantly dispatched a message declining to let his name go before the convention. Afterwards, one of the senator's relatives, who was at Philadelphia, complained that the convention was ready to nominate him, and only with considerable difficulty did Weed, Schoolcraft, Greeley, and Congressman Edwin B. Morgan prevent it.[113] All four remained convinced that victory was impossible and that Seward would be hurt by the Know Nothing issue (Greeley did not have his fellow New Yorker's interests at heart in any case). Had Seward allowed his name to be used, he would unquestionably have been the first Republican standard bearer.

Seward's decision ended all doubt about the outcome. New York had more than ninety votes, the largest bloc in the convention, and, with that total added to Frémont's strength, there was no possibility that he could be defeated. Before the voting for the presidential nomination began, Rufus Spalding read a letter from McLean and withdrew the judge's name. Another Ohio delegate did the same with Chase.[114] Spalding acted, however,

---

sixty-nine votes, but this tally inflated his true strength somewhat, as a few of the delegates who voted for him were Chase men.

113. Webb to Seward, 10 P.M., June 16, Seward Papers, UR; Seward to Frances A. Seward, June 17, Seward, *Seward*, v. 2, 179; note by Webb on the back of Seward to Webb, June 17, Webb Papers; Thomas C. Miller to Frances A. Seward, July 19, Frances A. Seward to Seward, July 27, Seward Papers, UR; Seward to Myron H. Clark, June 11, Boston Public Library; Lizzie Pike to Chase, September 14, Chase Papers, HSPa. Van Deusen questions whether Seward wrote to John Schoolcraft declining to have his name go before the convention. Seward's June 17 letter to Webb leaves no doubt that he did. Whether it arrived before George Patterson withdrew the senator's name is unclear; when Webb protested, Patterson admitted that he had no direct authorization from Seward, and said he was acting on the advice of Seward's friends. See Van Deusen, *Seward*, 177.

114. For the decision to withdraw Chase, see Chase to George Hoadley, June 12 (copy), in Chase Diary, June, Chase Papers, LC; Hiram Barney to Chase, June 21, Chase Papers, HSPa.

without consulting McLean's supporters in other states, and his move caught the Pennsylvania delegates, in particular, by surprise. With considerable agitation, they requested time for consultation. Rising to address the convention, Thaddeus Stevens pleaded for the nomination of McLean, the only man, he passionately insisted, who could carry Pennsylvania. Russell Errett of the Pittsburgh *Gazette*, who was at the convention, said of Stevens's speech: "I do not think he thought success probable (however possible it might be) with McLean; but with any one else it was impossible, in his view."[115] Finally, amid roaring confusion, the convention adjourned until five P.M.

When it reassembled, every seat was taken and all the standing space filled. The day was hot and muggy, with drizzling rain, and the packed, poorly ventilated hall was oppressively hot. In this atmosphere, the convention proceeded to the business of nominating a presidential candidate. During the recess, the Pennsylvania delegates voted to stand by McLean. Taken aback by the bitter condemnation heaped on him by McLean's supporters, Spalding again presented the judge's name to the convention. On an informal ballot, the result stood Frémont 359 votes to McLean's 190. Frémont's support followed a sectional pattern. He was particularly strong in New England (only Maine and New Hampshire gave McLean any votes), carried virtually the entire New York delegation, and swept Iowa, Michigan, Wisconsin, Kansas, and California. He divided the Ohio River valley states and was very weak in New Jersey and especially Pennsylvania. Further resistance was pointless. A formal ballot, which followed after a certain amount of bickering over whether one should even be taken, gave Frémont 520 votes to 37 for McLean. As soon as the vote was made unanimous, an enthusiastic demonstration broke out, although the McLean men, particularly those from Pennsylvania, were obviously despondent. Speaking for this group, Congressman John Allison made a generous speech on behalf of the nominee, but he was unable to hide his disappointment.[116]

In seeking to explain their defeat, some of McLean's most committed delegates angrily denounced Spalding for withdrawing the justice's name. McLean took up this refrain and later characterized Spalding's behavior as "a base betrayal of confidence." Allison, who likewise was angry and charged that Spalding had secretly become a Frémont man, nevertheless concluded correctly, "I do not think that the result would have been much different from what it was." The Supreme Court justice did not lose the nomination because of Spalding's precipitate action. In reality, once New York went for Frémont, McLean had no chance of being nominated, and Spalding had acted on his previously announced intention to avoid bringing McLean forward merely to be rejected.[117] Chase's withdrawal also hurt McLean, since most of the Ohio governor's backers preferred Frémont to McLean. By the conclusion of the convention, a powerful animosity separated the Chase and McLean factions in the Ohio delegation. Reporting that the hostility of Chase's followers was "implacable," one of McLean's supporters charged that they actively spread the impression that the justice was the only candidate who could not carry

---

115. Russell Errett, "The Republican Nominating Conventions of 1856 and 1860," *Magazine of Western History*, v. 10 (July 1889), 261; Elihu B. Washburne, ed., *The Edwards Papers* (Chicago, 1884), 246–47.

116. N. H. Swayne to Ewing, June 19, Ewing Family Papers; Allison to McLean, June 20, McLean Papers, LC; McClure, *Our Presidents*, 136–37; William Bailhache to John Bailhache, June 21, Bailhache-Brayman Papers; William Emmons to Buchanan, June 18, Buchanan Papers, HSPa.

117. Spalding to McLean, June 9, 14, McLean to Spalding, June 14, Spalding to McLean, Telegram, June 18, McLean to Thaddeus Stevens, May 12, 1860 (quotation), Allison to McLean, June 20, July 14 (quotation), McLean Papers, LC.

Ohio. Allison attributed McLean's rejection to the action of the Chase men and to New England's going almost as a unit for Frémont.[118]

Frémont's nomination was a triumph of image over achievement. Few delegates knew anything about his views on any of the major political controversies of the day. They voted for him because they believed he would make a strong race, and because they had confidence in his character. Exasperated by what they considered endless and unjustified southern complaints and by threats of secession, which they dismissed as mere bluster, Republicans wanted a candidate of firm resolution who could be relied on to stand up to the South. The Pathfinder's image was perfectly suited to capitalize on their welling frustration. With a good measure of insight the New York *Evening Post* attributed Frémont's popularity to the fact that the people saw in him the heroic qualities that they felt were required in the present controversy: unshakable courage, steadiness of purpose, ready command of resources. From what they knew of his explorations, they inferred that he was qualified for this new challenge.[119] Many party members, in contrast, viewed McLean, despite his long experience, as indecisive and unreliable.

Most delegates who voted for Frémont did so on little more than faith and the assurance of others. Halstead spoke of "a very deep and solemn conviction" among a majority of the delegates that the Pathfinder was "THE MAN" for the times. He found this faith "very remarkable, and . . . to a great degree unaccountable." Charles Francis Adams was an example of a delegate eventually won over to the Frémont column despite strong misgivings. Adams's first choice was Seward. Unsatisfied as to Frémont's fidelity to the cause, he viewed the Californian as a little-known man "whose reputation has been marvellously made within six months for this emergency." At a caucus of the Massachusetts delegation, Adams stated that he was unwilling to back Frémont without further evidence of his antislavery principles. Three delegates then described private conversations they had with the colonel in which he gave explicit promises on the slavery issue, and apparently another member read a private letter from him. In the end, Adams decided to vote for Frémont as the most eligible candidate.[120] The means by which he was converted were typical.

Others believed Frémont's selection a humiliating spectacle. Intriguers and unprincipled men, Allison charged, betraying his deeply felt disappointment, succeeded in nominating for the nation's highest office "a man who has never shown to the world that he possesses one single qualification for that office." Frémont's selection rankled Chase as well. The Republican party had "committed an act of positive injustice," he told Sumner, "in failing to take as their nominees men who truly personified the great real issue before the country."[121] Swallowing his disappointment, Chase actively campaigned for the Republican ticket. Less creditable was the behavior of Frémont's other principal rivals, Seward and McLean. Complaining that Weed and his friends had betrayed him, Seward pouted throughout the summer and refused to take the stump. Only during the last

---

118. Allison to McLean, July 16, Israel Garrard to McLean, June 21, McLean Papers, LC.

119. New York *Evening Post*, June 19; New York *Tribune* and New York *Times*, quoted in Nevins, *Frémont*, 435–36; McClure, *Our Presidents*, 137. An Illinois voter rallied to Frémont in part because "his California and pioneer experience has shown him to be a man of determination and backbone." George Baldwin to Emily Baldwin, April 17, Baldwin Family Papers.

120. Hesseltine and Fisher, eds., *Trimmers, Trucklers & Temporizers*, 102; Adams Diary, June 14, 16, Adams to Palfrey, July 10 (copy), Adams Family Papers.

121. Allison to McLean, June 20, McLean Papers, LC; Chase to Sumner, May 1, 1857, quoted in Reinhard H. Luthin, "Salmon P. Chase's Career Before the Civil War," *MVHR*, v. 29 (March, 1943), 527.

few weeks of the contest did he finally render any aid to the ticket by delivering several campaign speeches. Already looking ahead to 1860, Weed was privately angry with Seward's behavior, but, aware of the latter's excessive sensitivity, he refrained from direct criticism. Singling out Chase's contrasting behavior for particular praise, Charles A. Dana pronounced the Ohio governor "about ten times as much of a man" as Seward.[122] McLean behaved even worse. Beyond a halfhearted denial of a report that he had endorsed Fillmore, the judge did nothing for the Republican cause. In a private interview with Orville Browning before the election, he bared his deep humiliation. Denouncing Frémont as "not fit to discharge the duties of an auditor," the associate justice alleged that the Republican nominee was in the hands of ultras, and peevishly attributed his nomination to the power of corruption.[123]

Frémont's nomination capped almost a year of political effort by Francis P. Blair. The veteran Jacksonian leader's success in 1856 contrasted sharply with his failure in 1852. One reason Blair was so successful after achieving so little four years earlier was that Frémont was simply a more attractive candidate. But other factors were involved as well. Of considerable importance in the Californian's victory was the aid supplied by a number of talented operators from outside Blair's circle, most notably Banks and Weed. With so much political talent united behind Frémont's candidacy, Blair's shortcomings as a politician were not as serious. The former *Globe* editor also benefited from being something like the man of the hour at the Republican convention. Wanting to attract as many Democratic voters as possible, delegates and party leaders displayed great respect for him and a strong desire to accommodate him. Terming Jackson's old crony "one of the notables" at the convention, Halstead remarked that, despite his slightly absurd appearance, with his short stature, ill-fitting teeth, and large head accented by an oversized hat, Blair was invariably treated with "distinguished consideration."[124] In 1852 his standing in the Democratic party was quite different. Then he had no influence outside the Van Buren ranks, and because his enemies increasingly controlled the party, his future prospects were too bleak to attract anyone of power and importance. But at Philadelphia, after so much frustration, Blair was able for once in his life to assume the guise of kingmaker at a national convention. With much justice, Alexander McClure singled out the Jacksonian leader as the man who did the most to make Frémont the Republican party's first presidential candidate.[125]

In later years, Frémont's nomination was a great embarrassment to Republicans. The distinguished educator Andrew Dickson White, who as a young man had enthusiastically voted for Frémont, conceded that "of all the candidates for the Presidency ever formally nominated by either of the great parties up to that time, Fremont was probably the most unfit." Sobered by the secession of the southern states following Abraham Lincoln's election and four years of civil war, Republicans recognized that Frémont lacked the

---

122. Seward to Frances A. Seward, June 6, 29, Seward, *Seward* v. 2, 276, 279–80; Seward to Weed, May 4, Seward to Samuel Wilkeson, Jr., September 10, Weed Papers, UR; Hiram Barney to Chase, June 21, Chase Papers, HSPa; Weed to Seward, October 5, Frances A. Seward to Seward, July 20, James Bowen to Seward, September 9, Seward Papers, UR; Charles A. Dana to Pike, August 9, Pike Papers, UMe.

123. Randall and Pease, eds., *Browning Diary*, v. 1, 245–46; McLean to John Teesdale, September 3, 1859, Private, McLean Papers, LC.

124. Hesseltine and Fisher, eds., *Trimmers, Trucklers & Temporizers*, 92.

125. McClure, *Recollections*, 45.

requisite qualities to meet such a momentous crisis.[126] In this sense his nomination was an act of grave irresponsibility. In assessing the decision of the Philadelphia convention, however, the circumstances under which he won the nomination should also be considered. In particular, had Weed believed that the Republicans could win in 1856, Seward—and not Frémont—would have been the Republican nominee.[127]

X

Often a perfunctory matter, the selection of a vice-presidential candidate was of more than usual significance for the 1856 Republican campaign. From the start, party leaders like Weed and Morgan intended to use the second spot on the Republican ticket to placate the North Americans still assembled in New York and thereby pave the way for fusion. Weed's strategy had succeeded in New York, but it ran into difficulties in Philadelphia. On the second day, a communication from George Law, as chairman of the North American committee, came before the Republican convention. At this point Joshua R. Giddings, spurred on by Gamaliel Bailey, moved successfully that the subject of conferring with the North Americans be laid on the table.

Astute Republican leaders knew that Giddings's move could spell disaster. To insult the New York committee members after they had responded to Morgan's invitation would certainly work against a merger of the opposition. Weed and others urged Giddings to reconsider his ill-advised action, and the Ohio radical finally agreed, once the presidential nomination had been made without interference from the North Americans. Owen Lovejoy, however, now took up the question and protested against any alliance with the Americans as a separate party, claiming that, armed with such ammunition, Stephen A. Douglas "would tickle the sense of the foreign-born citizens . . . and Illinois would be lost." But a motion to reconsider carried, and the problem was referred to the platform committee.

Meeting on the night of June 18 from nine P.M. until two in the morning, the Republican and North American committees eventually each appointed a subcommittee to continue the negotiations concerning a vice-presidential nominee. The North Americans strongly advocated the claims of William F. Johnston, whom they had already nominated, but Thaddeus Stevens and others from Pennsylvania strenuously opposed his selection, and he was thus unacceptable. Colfax believed that if the Pennsylvania delegation, both in the convention and in Congress, had not been hostile to Johnston, his nomination would have been ratified at Philadelphia, but, as Greeley telegraphed in a dispatch from the convention, the former Pennsylvania governor's selection threatened to revive the old political feuds in that state. Johnston's friends, in turn, would not endorse Wilmot. Banks declined to be considered, and Ford, who was acceptable to the nativists, was unavailable because of the strong opposition to him among Ohio Republicans. In the end, inflexible men in both parties vetoed all possible choices, and when the Republican convention assembled in the morning, Wilmot announced that the two committees had been unable

---

126. Andrew Dickson White, *Autobiography of Andrew Dickson White* (2 vols.: New York, 1906), v. 1, 75; Rhodes, *History of the United States*, v. 2, 192; Nevins, *Frémont*, 457–58.

127. If either Pierce or Douglas had been the Democratic candidate, men whom Republican leaders were confident they could defeat, the Philadelphia convention would have selected Seward as the party's standard bearer. In this sense, Bowles was correct when he said the Cincinnati convention would determine the Republican nominee.

to reach an agreement.[128] With that announcement died the hope of using the vice-presidential nomination to promote fusion.

Even before these negotiations collapsed, a number of names had been suggested for the second spot on the Republican ticket. "Opinions are all afloat about it, no individual concentrating the wishes of all," Charles Francis Adams wrote concerning the vice-presidency. Party leaders were anxious to placate Pennsylvania, which was bitterly disappointed by McLean's rejection; political analysts foresaw that the Keystone State would be the critical state in the upcoming contest. The Pennsylvania opposition was too fragmented, however, to be unified by any vice-presidential nomination. "There is too much faction and clannishness in that State," commented Greeley with some exasperation. Frémont, revealing his complete political naiveté, wanted Simon Cameron as his running mate under the assumption that his nomination would secure Pennsylvania. Cameron had a host of enemies in the state and was an impossible choice. Blair also opposed his selection, since in 1845 the Pennsylvanian, while in the Senate, had supported the former's ouster as the editor of the Democratic party's national organ. Because the Pennsylvanians could not agree on a candidate, the delegates finally nominated William Dayton from neighboring New Jersey, another doubtful state. Dayton was a conservative Whig, was thought to be acceptable to Pennsylvania, and was a McLean man. His nearest competitor was Abraham Lincoln, whom the Illinois delegation took up late in the contest. Concerned lest foreign-born voters be alienated, Greeley took a leading role in promoting Dayton's nomination rather than selecting someone completely amenable to the Know Nothings.[129]

Dayton brought no real strength to the ticket. Because he was not a member of the order, he was not entirely acceptable to the North Americans, and his selection did little if anything to diminish the personal feuds in Pennsylvania. As time would show, the failure of the two committees to agree on a vice-presidential candidate before dispersing had serious consequences. Banks would have been the strongest nominee, but in addition to his categorical refusal to be considered, he would have been required by custom to resign as speaker, and besides, like Frémont, he was an ex-Democrat. The most interesting suggestion was to nominate Charles Sumner in order to capitalize on his injuries. Charles A. Dana took the lead in promoting this idea, but the opposition of the Massachusetts delegation effectively killed the proposal. In the end, Adams probably spoke for many delegates when he concluded, with a noticeable lack of enthusiasm, that Dayton "seems to be the most eligible choice."[130]

When it adjourned, the Philadelphia convention's record concerning fusion with the nativists was basically ambiguous. Hard-headed Republican leaders like Weed favored an open alliance with the North Americans for the 1856 campaign. The New York boss had no love for the nativists, but with the Republicans facing a stiff contest Know Nothing

---

128. Law's report to the North American convention on the negotiations is in the New York *Herald*, June 20. Also see the *Herald* reporter's dispatch from Philadelphia, in the June 19 issue; Colfax to Morgan, July 8, Edwin D. Morgan Papers; convention correspondence, New York *Tribune*, June 18, 21.

129. Adams Diary, June 18, Adams Family Papers; Greeley to Colfax, n.d. [May], Greeley-Colfax Papers; John C. Frémont, MS Memoirs, 198, 204, Frémont Papers; William A. Rust to Seward, May 14, Seward Papers, UR; Seward, *Seward*, v. 2, 283; New York *Tribune*, July 3; Colfax to Francis Stebbins, April 29, Stebbins Papers; Hesseltine and Fisher, eds., *Trimmers, Trucklers & Temporizers*, 98–99; Colfax to Morgan, July 8, Edwin D. Morgan Papers.

130. Adams Diary, June 16, 18 (quotation), Adams Family Papers; James W. Stone to Weed, July 7, Weed Papers, UR.

support was essential, and he was confident that the Americans would be quickly shunted aside in the Republican ranks. Those party members who opposed any coalition with the North Americans were concerned that such a policy would drive off naturalized voters, yet they, too, were anxious to win nativist support. Some of those who were in the forefront of the fight against any separate recognition of the nativists, most notably Giddings and Bailey, simultaneously advocated the nomination of McLean, who had openly courted the Know Nothings, and who did not insist that his American supporters renounce their creed or even abandon the order. Others no doubt shared Greeley's excessively optimistic belief that the North Americans had no alternative but to join the Republican movement and that thus no concessions were required. As the convention demonstrated, most Republican leaders agreed on the necessity of securing Know Nothing support, but they disagreed over the most effective means to accomplish this goal.

Not surprisingly, Dayton's nomination generated hard feelings among the North Americans, and Weed's fear that they would persist in sustaining their own ticket was partially fulfilled. As agreed upon beforehand, Banks declined the North American nomination, but when the New York convention reassembled, the delegates expressed great anger over the Republicans' haughty treatment of Law's committee in Philadelphia, and it took all the soothing the North American leaders could muster to convince the convention to accept Frémont in place of Banks. The fight over Frémont's endorsement was "the hardest run that I have ever seen yet," one of Banks's allies reported. "The way our people were treated at Phila. so disgusted them that up to a late hour yesterday morning it seemed impossible to bring them round." Law expressed regret that a more harmonious fusion had not been achieved, but cautioned against reckless retaliation. On the vice-presidential issue, however, the delegates would not budge. Insisting that since they had accepted Frémont the Republicans should endorse Johnston, the North Americans refused to remove the former Pennsylvania governor from their ticket. Well could one of Banks's supporters, who was not briefed on the Republicans' strategy, write at the convention's conclusion: "This is a strange matter, and has turned out strangely."[131]

An interview after the New York convention reassembled, between Frémont and some North American leaders already smarting over the Republican performance at Philadelphia, spawned additional difficulties. The Republican standard bearer demonstrated his political inexperience by apparently promising that Dayton would be withdrawn in favor of Johnston once the New York convention adjourned. The precise nature of Frémont's pledge is unclear, but the nativists believed that they had received a firm commitment. With less than complete candor, they contended afterwards that the New York convention would never have endorsed the Republican nominee without such a promise. Armed with this apparent understanding, North American leaders managed to calm the more excited delegates. Having designated Frémont and Johnston as its national ticket, the North American convention finally adjourned. In the meantime, Dayton publicly accepted the Republican nomination.[132]

Frémont's pledge to the North American committee was not generally known, and Republicans differed markedly in their reactions to the unsuccessful negotiations with the North Americans. Giddings and Greeley, who had spearheaded the drive to reject fusion,

---

131. S. M. Allen to Banks, fragment, n.d. [June], June 21 (quotation), Law to Banks, June 23, Banks Papers, LC; E. A. Spencer to Jno. J. Brasee, July 20, John Brasee Papers, OHS.

132. Z. K. Pangborn to Banks, June 25, S. M. Allen to Banks, June 21, Banks Papers, LC; Seward to Frances A. Seward, June 26, July 7, Seward, *Seward*, v. 2, 279, 283.

were immensely pleased with the result of the Republican deliberations. Giddings declared after the convention adjourned, "My policy was to say nothing about the Know Nothings but others thrust it into our convention, but [so] others had to thrust it out." He was certain that the Americans would support the Republican ticket. Julian likewise was pleased that the North Americans had been all but denied a hearing. Greeley, too, according to Seward, was "exultant that he has done the very best thing in the rightest way."[133]

More astute party members took a different view. John Jay, as strong an antislavery man as Giddings, expressed fear that the Ohio representative had blundered at the convention, an assessment echoed by John G. Whittier, another pronounced opponent of slavery, who believed that division of the opposition on minor matters spelled defeat.[134] Morgan was also disappointed. The nomination of a vice-president acceptable to the Americans was critical, he emphasized after the convention, but his and Weed's efforts to influence some Republicans were futile. He hoped that early in the campaign the matter would be resolved satisfactorily. Weed believed that the failure of the Republicans to accommodate the North Americans on the vice-presidency dealt a crippling blow to the Frémont campaign. "The first, and as I still think fatal error," he wrote after the election, "was in not taking a Vice-President in whose nomination the North Americans would have concured [*sic*] cordially. . . . The McLean men, aided by Greeley, threw us off the Track."[135] When the two conventions adjourned, fusion, to which Republican strategists had devoted so much attention, had been only partly achieved. The presidential campaign opened with Frémont's supporters divided, and the perplexing problem of the vice-presidency, which had become the symbol for complete fusion, still to be resolved.

---

133. Giddings to Julian, June 24 (quotation), Julian to Giddings, January 29, 1857, Giddings to [Lura M. Giddings], June 18, Giddings to [Laura A. Giddings], June 20, Giddings-Julian Papers; Giddings to [Joseph A. Giddings], July 2, Giddings Papers; letter from Giddings, June 26, in *Ashtabula Sentinel*, July 3; Seward to Frances A. Seward, June 27, *Seward*, v. 2, 279.

134. John Jay to Anson Burlingame, June 26, Anson Burlingame Papers, LC; John G. Whittier to Dear Sir, June 20, Boston Public Library; Olean [New York] *Advertiser*, July 18, clipping, Giddings Papers.

135. Morgan to Russell Sage, June 28, Morgan to Edward Dodd, June 28 (copies), Edwin D. Morgan Papers; Weed to Simon Cameron, November 12, Cameron Papers, LC.

11

Free Soil, Free Labor, Free Speech, Free Men, Frémont

"The signs are thickening fast about us of a most desperate and exciting struggle for the presidency," the New York *Herald* commented after the Republican convention adjourned. It reported that the meeting to ratify the Republican nominations in New York City, anything but a party stronghold, brought out men not normally active in political affairs, and that the overflowing crowd shook the rafters with "frantic cheerings, over and over again, with every mention" of John C. Frémont's name.[1] Similar scenes were repeated in countless northern communities, evidence of the depth of feeling produced by Frémont's nomination and the symbols of Bleeding Kansas and Bleeding Sumner. "My feeling[s] are up the old *40* which I never expected, but I cannot help it," a Michigan Republican asserted. "The outrages in Kansus [*sic*] and the caning of the R[igh]t hon[orable] Senator from Massachusetts has done the Job." George W. Julian recalled later that under the impact of Brooks's assault and the Kansas violence "Republican enthusiasm reached its white heat, borrowing the self-forgetting devotion and dedicated zeal of a religious conversion."[2]

For Democrats, the response to the Republican ticket throughout the free states came as a sobering shock. Their initial reaction to Frémont's nomination was one of ridicule; they deemed it inconceivable that a party with a candidate of such limited experience and questionable qualifications could mount a serious challenge to a well-established organization.[3] Before long, however, reports from all parts of the North began to arrive

---

Note: Unless otherwise indicated, the year for newspaper and manuscript citations in this chapter is 1856.

1. New York *Herald*, June 27.

2. E. A. King to William H. Seward, July 4 (quotation), Seward Papers, UR; George W. Julian, *Political Recollections*, 153; A. Tracey to Justin S. Morrill, July 22, Morrill Papers, LC. See the discussion in Rhodes, *History of the United States*, v. 2, 180–81.

3. One exception was Alexander H. Stephens, who from the beginning believed that the party had a fierce contest on its hands. Stephens to Thomas W. Thomas, June 16, Phillips, ed., *Correspondence of Toombs, Stephens, and Cobb*, 367.

at Buchanan headquarters warning that Frémont showed unexpected strength, and that the Republicans were raising a whirlwind on the Sumner and Kansas issues. Within a month of the Philadelphia convention, the lighthearted attitude displayed earlier by Democrats in Washington had disappeared. One cabinet member warned John C. Breckinridge, the party's vice-presidential nominee: "This nomination of Freemont [*sic*] & Sumner excitement will give the free States against us with few exceptions and we cant afford to loose a state south. . . . N York is gone in the opinion of many of our best Politicians here and the Sumner Beating has done it in this early stage of the Game."[4] Pointing to the popular demonstrations that greeted Frémont's nomination, the New York *Herald* insisted: "This campaign will be no child's play to the administration [D]emocracy."[5]

I

Events in Kansas, which formed a backdrop of escalating violence against which the 1856 presidential campaign played, were crucial in sustaining popular excitement in the North. Sheriff Samuel Jones's ill-considered raid on Lawrence, and more particularly John Brown's butchery of five innocent settlers along Pottawatomie Creek, unleashed a new round of guerrilla warfare in Kansas. Full-scale pitched battles remained nonexistent; as before, the fighting consisted of skirmishes between small bands of raiders. Still, the violence in the summer of 1856 took more lives and resulted in more havoc than the somewhat comical antics of both parties during the previous years.[6] A hooligan element, unchecked by the woefully incompetent governor, Wilson Shannon, operated virtually without interference. From Kansas, Lieutenant Colonel Philip St. George Cooke wrote in mid-June with considerable truth: "The disorders in the Territory have, in fact, changed their character, and consist now of robberies and assassinations, by a set of bandits whom the excitement of the times has attracted hither."[7] Although greatly exaggerated, the claims of free-state men that a reign of terror gripped the territory were evidence that the situation was much more serious and threatening than had previously been the case.

Northern—and more particularly Republican—anger intensified when federal troops under the command of Colonel Edwin V. Sumner dispersed the free-state "legislature" that assembled in Topeka on July 4. With a number of free-state leaders already under arrest and charged with treason, only seventeen members showed up for the scheduled meeting. When the body attempted to organize, Sumner, acting largely for symbolic reasons, intervened, and those few members on hand departed quietly. In the face of the ensuing Republican outcry, the administration made Sumner a convenient scapegoat and summarily replaced him. His action, along with the continued imprisonment of Charles Robinson and other free-state leaders at Lecompton, added fuel to the Republican campaign.

---

4. James Guthrie to John C. Breckinridge, July 18 (quotation), Breckinridge Family Papers; Seward to Frances A. Seward, June 28, Seward, *Seward*, v. 2, 279; Washington correspondence, New York *Evening Post*, July 22; Howell Cobb to James Buchanan, July 14, Phillips, ed., *Correspondence of Toombs, Stephens, and Cobb*, 375; John W. Forney to Buchanan, July 12, Buchanan Papers, HSPa; Henry A. Wise to Edward Everett, July 14, Everett Papers.

5. New York *Herald*, June 27.

6. This warfare and other events in Kansas in this period are described in Spring, *Kansas*, 129–208; Nichols, *Bleeding Kansas*, 120–50; Nevins, *Ordeal of the Union*, v. 2, 476–78, 481–86.

7. Cooke quoted in Burke Davis, *Jeb Stuart, the Last Cavalier* (New York, 1957), 39. "A great trouble is brewing—which, to tell the truth, I like to see. If it wasn't for that I would get out of the Territory as soon as possible." Francis B. Swift to Benjamin Swift, February 28, Francis B. Swift Papers, KSHS.

Reports that Missourians were turning back Kansas-bound free-state settlers further inflamed northern public opinion. Beginning in July, proslavery partisans blockaded river travel through the state; large, heavily armed bands were more or less certain to be detained for questioning, although, apparently, small groups who were discreet and unarmed could travel safely by the Missouri River at any time. In a widely publicized incident, a large free-state party from Chicago, after having its weapons confiscated while on a Missouri River steamboat, was ejected from the territory, transported downriver, and unceremoniously put ashore near Alton, Illinois. In addition, proslavery men illegally seized freight consigned to well-known free-state men and tampered with the mails. Supporters of the free-state movement, led by the officers of the Emigrant Aid Company, charged that a blockade existed, but the federal government took no notice.

By August, the badly unnerved Shannon had had enough. Going to Lawrence to settle yet another dispute between the contending factions in the territory, he found the town fully armed and prepared for battle. Frantically telling officials in Washington that Lecompton, where he made his headquarters, lay open to destruction by the free-state forces, he resigned from office on August 18 and vacated the territory with unseemly haste. "Govern the Kansas of 1855 and '56," he exclaimed years later in recalling his unhappy tenure in office, "you might as well have attempted to govern the devil in hell!"[8] With only two months until the national election, Franklin Pierce's Kansas policy was in ruins.

In response to the steadily worsening Kansas crisis, the Democratic congressional leadership made a serious effort to end the territorial imbroglio by means of a bill that was the handiwork of Alexander H. Stephens of Georgia. Stephens's colleague, Senator Robert Toombs, introduced the proposed legislation. Under terms of the bill, the president was empowered to appoint five commissioners who were to take a census of bona fide citizens, register voters, and conduct an election in November (when residents of neighboring states would be voting in the presidential contest) for delegates to a new constitutional convention. The commissioners were to prevent the fraud and intimidation that had marred past elections. The bill specified that the new convention would assemble in December and, if expedient, draft a state constitution. To answer northern objections, free soil men driven from the territory were given until October first to return and register, and the obnoxious territorial laws were repealed. The intention of the bill's authors was to undercut the Republican agitation on Kansas through the Republican-controlled House's rejection of what seemed to be a fair and reasonable solution to the Kansas difficulties. After the Democratic senatorial caucus approved the measure, Senator William Bigler predicted that it "will utterly prostrate the Republican party. . . . This [bill] will be worth more to you that [than] all the addresses that the wit of man can devise," he advised James Buchanan.[9]

As expected, the bill passed the Senate, but the House rejected it with only scant consideration. Republicans' ingrained suspicions of Pierce, whom they were unwilling to entrust with the naming of the commission (despite assurances from Amos A. Lawrence, after an interview with the president, that its members would be acceptable), and, more

8. Shannon quoted in Spring, *Kansas*, 187. For a scathing indictment by a southerner in Kansas of Shannon as a weakling and a tool of stronger men, see G. J. Park to John J. Crittenden, May 20, Crittenden Papers.

9. William Bigler to Buchanan, June 28, J. Glancy Jones to Buchanan, June 27, Buchanan Papers, HSPa; James M. Mason to David Rice Atchison, September 5, Atchison Papers.

especially, Republicans' unwillingness to relinquish their major campaign staple blocked passage.[10] "All these gentlemen want," Douglas charged angrily, referring to the Republicans, "is to get up murder and bloodshed in Kansas for political effect. They do not mean that there shall be peace until after the presidential election."[11] For all its partisanship, Douglas's assertion was not entirely wide of the mark. Republican leaders were quite ready to let Kansas bleed for partisan purposes until the election was over. When Congress adjourned in August, it had accomplished nothing toward restoring order in the territory. The fate of Kansas, Republicans proclaimed over and over again, was to be determined not in the halls of Congress or on the plains of Kansas, but by the outcome of the presidential election. Placing responsibility for the violence in Kansas squarely on Pierce, his advisers, and the Democratic party, they insisted that the only salvation for the free-state cause was Frémont's election.

As they watched these developments, the Buchanan managers concluded that new policies were urgently needed. Kansas could not remain in turmoil until election day. Many Democrats had already deserted the party over the Kansas issue, and if Pierce continued his policy the party would be reduced to a corporal's guard, a New Yorker warned Buchanan. Former senator John Pettit, another Buchanan supporter, wrote that if the violence continued in Kansas, Indiana and probably every northern state would be lost.[12] Pressure from Buchanan's advisers and congressional Democrats finally swayed Pierce, and the president pursued a more even-handed policy in Kansas. He appointed Brigadier General Persifor F. Smith as commander of the Department of the West in place of Colonel Sumner. Smith was capable, efficient, and nonpartisan. Pierce also moved to release on bail the free-state leaders being held prisoner; eventually, the government dropped the treason prosecutions altogether.[13] Northern Democrats were pleased with the outcome, even those who believed that the arrests were warranted, for they saw evidence daily of the Republicans' effective exploitation of this issue.

Pierce's most important move to defuse the Kansas issue was his appointment of John W. Geary of Pennsylvania as Shannon's successor. Unlike his predecessors Reeder and Shannon, Geary was a fortunate selection. A bearded giant of a man, standing six feet five and a half inches tall, he was not easily intimidated. The energetic new governor had both military experience in the Mexican War and knowledge of the frontier as a former mayor of San Francisco. He was determined to administer fairly in all matters and, as he later explained, be "the governor of the entire people." In doing so, Geary was not blind to the political situation back home; he allegedly remarked, with some justice, that he was "carrying a Presidential candidate on his shoulders."[14]

The new governor arrived in Lecompton on September 11. He promptly disbanded the militia that had been called out, reorganized it to minimize participation by nonresidents, and demonstrated that he would not tolerate lawless behavior. Moving with dispatch, he intercepted various private armies as they plundered the countryside, sent a proslavery

---

10. G. W. Smith et al. to Henry Wilson, July 5, Edward Bumgardner Papers, KSHS; Benjamin F. Wade quoted in Bartlett, *Frémont and the Republican Party*, 33; Nevins, *Ordeal of the Union*, v. 2, 472.

11. Douglas quoted in Johannsen, *Douglas*, 527.

12. Henry Baldwin to Buchanan, September 17, John Pettit to Buchanan, June 27, *Private*, John Slidell to Buchanan, June 17, Bigler to Buchanan, June 23, Buchanan Papers, HSPa.

13. Nichols, *Pierce*, 474–75, 478–79, 483.

14. Geary quoted in Nevins, *Ordeal of the Union*, v. 2, 484–85, 484n. At the time of his appointment, Geary was in Virginia working mines with slave labor. For Nathaniel P. Banks's shrewd assessment of Geary, see Banks to My Dear Sir [Horace Greeley?], August 13, Private, Greeley Papers, LC.

force under former senator David Rice Atchison's command home, and warned southern leaders privately that any repetition of incidents like the attack on Lawrence would defeat the Democratic party in the pending presidential election. Equally important, he rebuked the courts for their dilatory performance in punishing wrongdoers, arrested a number of free-state agitators, and issued warrants for the arrest of Benjamin F. Stringfellow and other southern ringleaders. Soon the governor, who was not averse to self-praise, was sending letters back to Washington reporting that peace reigned in the territory. By establishing some semblance of order, and by repudiating the earlier, one-sided policies of the government, Geary performed an invaluable service for Buchanan and the Democratic party. His success partly checked the momentum of the Republicans. "I labored night and day here" for Buchanan's election, the governor wrote with much truth after the election.[15]

But as David Potter observes, the conflict for control of Kansas did not have ramifications as significant as did the battle to win the propaganda war.[16] With hindsight it is clear that violence was decreasing in Kansas and that affairs there had entered a new phase. To contemporaries, however, the truth about the situation in Kansas remained cloudy. Not only did Geary go to the territory very late in the campaign, but Republicans, recognizing how effective the Kansas issue was, kept up a steady drumbeat of partisan propaganda. Kansas continued to bleed, in political rhetoric if not in fact, until election day. Referring to affairs in the distant territory, Theodore Parker, a militant antislavery man, said in 1856, "I know of no transaction in human history which has been covered up with such abundant lying." Parker spoke more accurately than he realized. The report of the commissioners of the Kansas territory, issued the following year, alleged that "the excitement in the Eastern and Southern States in 1856 was instigated and kept up by garbled and exaggerated accounts of Kansas affairs, published in the Eastern and Southern papers."[17] Democratic journals, which were badly on the defensive, promoted this line of argument, but throughout the summer, as reports of escalating violence filtered out of the territory, more and more doubters in the free states converted to the Republican point of view.[18]

The caning of Charles Sumner was the most important cause of this change in public sentiment. Also crucial was the report presented on July 1 of the House's Kansas investigating committee, detailing many weeks of testimony taken in the territory. Written primarily by John Sherman, the majority report scored a major propaganda victory for the Republicans by presenting evidence of dishonesty, intimidation, and terror. It asserted that invading Missourians had fraudulently controlled all elections held in the territory, that the existing territorial legislature was illegal, and that the Topeka constitution "embodies the will of a majority of the people."[19] Republican members of Congress distributed thousands of copies of the report, and party newspapers printed substantial extracts; the large number of requests to congressmen for copies testified to the public's

---

15. John W. Geary to Bigler, November 28, Bigler Papers.

16. Potter, *Impending Crisis*, 218–24.

17. Parker quoted in Spring, *Kansas*, v–vi; Rhodes, *History of the United States*, v. 2, 174n.

18. Cincinnati *Enquirer*, May 24, 29; Chicago *Times* quoted in the *Illinois State Register*, April 3; Rhodes, *History of the United States*, v. 2, 156. For similar assertions by Fillmore supporters, see the New York *Express* quoted in the *Illinois State Register*, June 23; Henry A. Wise to Everett, June 8, Everett Papers.

19. *Howard Report*, 1–67 (quotation 67); John Sherman to William Tecumseh Sherman, June 29, John Sherman Papers; William Howard to Nathaniel P. Banks, Jr., June 2, Banks Papers, LC.

avid interest. Amos Lawrence, not a Republican, believed that because of the report men "cannot refuse now to give credit to what has heretofore been half believed or disbelieved." An Illinois resident informed Trumbull that the committee's findings had greatly strengthened Frémont by inducing many cautious and wavering voters to back the Republican ticket.[20] Although the report contained much invaluable testimony, it was far from free of partisan bias, yet Ralph Waldo Emerson considered it an effective and telling reply to the argument that stories of Kansas outrages were all abolitionist lies.[21]

"Kansas," in the words of one free-state leader, was "the ward of the Republican party."[22] No theme received greater emphasis from party spokesmen in the 1856 campaign; indeed, approximately four-fifths of the campaign documents issued by the Republican Association in Washington, the party's central distribution agency, dealt with the Kansas question. This matter "cannot be agitated too much," one party member informed Banks. "I wish our friends would pour their red hot shot thick & fast upon the ruffians."[23] When the Kansas prisoners were released on bail, the Republican national committee inquired about the possibility of having them brought East immediately to campaign.[24] Lawrence believed that the Republicans should never have been allowed to take "possession of the Kanzas question on the 'Free State' side," for they were certain to draw strength from this identification.[25]

The Republicans gained an important accession in the midst of the presidential contest when Andrew H. Reeder finally endorsed Frémont. The former Kansas governor wanted to remain in the Democratic party, but he finally concluded that this course was impossible. The demands of party loyalty prevented Democratic leaders from taking his side, either in his dispute with Pierce or in his challenge to John Whitfield as the territory's congressional delegate. That Reeder, as a leader of the free-state cause in Kansas, wielded great influence was not lost on John W. Forney, the mastermind of Buchanan's campaign. "Reeder is troubling us greatly," he wrote after the former governor came out in favor of Frémont. "He must be met and brained."[26]

In the propaganda war over Kansas, the Republicans clearly triumphed. Thrown on the defensive by the constant din about Kansas, supporters of Buchanan and Fillmore complained that the Republicans tried to avoid all issues in the campaign by shouting *Kansas* and *freedom*. "When enquiry was made of them of Fremont's position, the answer was Kansas," one American paper charged. "Ask what you would and the same answer—Kansas! Kansas! was all that was heard." One of William L. Marcy's nephews

---

20. Amos A. Lawrence to Rev. H. A. Wilson, June 27 (copy), Lawrence Papers; A. Ballinger to Lyman Trumbull, July 15, Trumbull Papers.

21. Ralph Waldo Emerson, "Speech on Affairs in Kansas," Edward W. Emerson, ed., *Complete Works of Ralph Waldo Emerson* (12 vols.: Boston, 1903–1904), v. 11, 256; William Edwards to William L. Marcy, September 24, Marcy Papers, LC.

22. Eldridge, "Early Days in Kansas," 65–66.

23. Edward Hamilton to Banks, May 20, Banks Papers, LC.

24. W. F. M. Arny to Edwin D. Morgan, September 18, Edwin D. Morgan Papers. One Republican suggested that in order to heighten the dramatic effect the former Kansas prisoners campaign with their chains. Thomas H. Dudley to Morgan, September 20, Edwin D. Morgan Papers.

25. Lawrence to Solomon G. Haven, April 7 (quotation), Lawrence to William Appleton, May 13 (copies), Lawrence Papers.

26. Andrew Reeder to William Hutchinson, August 25, William Hutchinson Papers, KSHS; Forney to Buchanan, October 5, Thomas J. McCamet to Buchanan, July 19, William H. Hutter to Buchanan, June 9 (Confidential), Buchanan Papers, HSPa; George S. Boutwell to Banks, July 1, Banks Papers, LC. James Lane, another Kansas free-state leader, had earlier been stumping for the Republicans.

offered a similar analysis: "Bleeding Kansas and free Speak [*sic*] and Bully Brooks is all the arg[u]m[en]t the Black Republican[s] rant."[27] The unbroken fire maintained by the Republican press, reinforced by the shocking assault on Sumner, paid handsome dividends as the summer wore on. All but certain that Frémont would sweep New England, Edward Everett reported in dismay that "a constantly increasing excitement is kept up by the intelligence coming every day from Kansas. . . . I have never known political excitement—I ought rather to say exasperation—approach that which now rages."[28]

II

Although the assault on Sumner and the troubles in Kansas provided the material from which the Republicans fashioned their appeal to the northern electorate in the Frémont campaign, the nature of the party's ideology requires further examination.[29] Historians have devoted considerable attention to distilling the essence of the Republican persuasion before the Civil War. A number of ideas have been stressed—moral opposition to slavery, racial fear of blacks, opposition to the extension of slavery, a commitment to a free labor society, and a desire to promote industrial capitalism—and Eric Foner has demonstrated how, once matured, the party's ideology could simultaneously reflect a number of these not-entirely-compatible concepts.[30] While the broad outlines of the Republicans' funda- mental appeal crystallized in the 1856 campaign, it was still in the process of evolution. In the first years of the party's existence, moreover, many voters were motivated more by antagonisms to certain groups or policies than by positive identification with the Republican party. It took time for the voters to develop loyalty to the party and its program, and thus much of the Republican appeal in the 1856 campaign was stated in terms of what the party opposed.[31]

Of the various interpretations of the early Republican party, the view identified with Charles Beard that it represented the forces of emerging industrial capitalism is the least persuasive. The only economic plank in the 1856 Republican national platform called for federal aid for internal improvements—hardly a controversial position—and Republican

---

27. *Chenango American*, September 11; William Edwards to Marcy, September 24, Marcy Papers, LC.

28. Everett to W. H. Trescot, September 12, Private, Everett Papers.

29. I am using the concept of ideology in the sense that a number of historians of early American politics have recently employed it. Lance Banning provides a succinct definition of ideology as "the more or less coherent body of assumptions, values, and ideas that bound [party members] together as it shaped their common understanding of society and politics and lent a common meaning to events." The term refers "to a constellation of ideas—and not a formal 'theory'—which made it possible for members of the party to perceive a pattern in the happenings around them, to define a group identity in terms related to that pattern, and to sketch a course of action that would make the pattern change." *The Jeffersonian Persuasion: Evolution of a Party Ideology* (Ithaca, 1978), 15. Also see Foner, *Free Soil, Free Labor, Free Men*, 4–5. Some historians prefer to use the terms *appeal* and *persuasion* for less-structured beliefs, but I have used these terms interchangeably for what I mean by *ideology*.

30. Foner, *Free Soil, Free Labor, Free Men*, passim; Foner, "Politics, Ideology, and the Origins of the American Civil War," George M. Fredrickson, ed., *A Nation Divided: Problems and Issues of the Civil War and Reconstruction* (Minneapolis, 1975), 15–34. This section on Republican ideology elaborates ideas I presented in "Crime Against Sumner." Since that essay was written, my thinking on the nature of Republican ideology has been stimulated by Holt's analysis in *Political Crisis*, 183–217, and passim.

31. Paul Kleppner makes this point well in *Third Electoral System*.

efforts to exploit this issue were curtailed and of limited importance.[32] Republicans' disagreements over other economic questions, such as the tariff and a national bank, dictated avoidance of these matters in order to promote party unity. Those planks grafted onto the party's platform after 1856, such as the homestead act and a protective tariff, represented attempts to attract specific interest groups in the North, but they did not alter the Republicans' basic appeal. Rather, historians like Beard who have pointed to the impetus given to industrialism by Republican policies after the Civil War have too readily assumed this to be the intention of the party from its origin. Whatever the party became after the war, in the 1850s specific economic issues played only a minor role in its attractiveness to voters.

Most historians view the debate over slavery in these years not as masking an underlying conflict between economic world views but as a substantive issue in itself. In analyzing the nature of the Republicans' opposition to slavery, a few emphasize moral opposition to the peculiar institution.[33] Without question, for some Republicans the moral aspects of the controversy were paramount. Radical antislavery men like George W. Julian and Theodore Parker spoke eloquently against the morality of slavery, and Harriet Beecher Stowe's enormously popular *Uncle Tom's Cabin*, published early in the decade, greatly stimulated this concern. The *Ashtabula Sentinel* argued that Republicans opposed slavery "as a *wrong*, and seek its overthrow as a matter of *principle* and *duty* . . . at all points where they *can* act upon it." Scoring the moral wickedness of slavery, Parker was outspoken in his criticism of Republicans for denying any "intention *ever* to interfere with slavery in the states! It is *my intention* as soon as I can get the power."[34] The presence of a large number of Protestant clergymen in the Frémont campaign gave greater attention to the moral impulse than it would otherwise have received. Yet a number of historians, without denying the existence of the moral aspect of the slavery question, have demonstrated persuasively that concern for the welfare of the slave did not motivate a majority of Republicans.

Equally on the fringe of the main Republican appeal stood racial hatred of blacks.[35] Examples of Republican racism, if not exactly plentiful, are well known. Thus a future Republican congressman from Pennsylvania declared in 1856 that "he cared nothing for the 'nigger' . . . he had a higher mission to preach—deliverance of the white man." The Hartford *Courant* upheld this view when it proclaimed, "The Republicans mean to preserve all of this country that they can from the *pestilence presence of the black man.*"

---

32. The most precise statement of this interpretation is Charles and Mary Beard, *The Rise of American Civilization* (2 vols.: New York, 1933), v. 2, 3–51. A number of historians have criticized this view. Foner, in *Free Soil, Free Labor, Free Men*, presents a good amount of evidence of Republican divisions over economic matters.

33. Examples include Dwight L. Dumond, *Antislavery Origins of the Civil War in the United States* (Ann Arbor, 1939); Rhodes, *History of the United States*; Don E. Fehrenbacher, "The Republican Decision at Chicago," Norman A. Graebner, ed., *Politics and the Crisis of 1860* (Urbana, 1961), 36; and Bruce Collins, "The Ideology of the Ante-bellum Northern Democrats," *Journal of American Studies*, v. 11 (April, 1977), 118–19.

34. *Ashtabula Sentinel*, May 8; Theodore Parker to John P. Hale, December 19 (quotation), Hale Papers, DarC; Parker to Salmon P. Chase, July 25, Chase Papers, HSPa.

35. Examples of this emphasis include Leon Litwack, *North of Slavery: The Negro in the Free States, 1790–1860* (Chicago, 1961), 247–79; Eugene H. Berwanger, *The Frontier Against Slavery: Western Anti-Negro Prejudice and the Slavery Extension Controversy* (Urbana, 1967); Robert F. Durden, "Ambiguities in the Antislavery Crusade of the Republican Party," Martin Duberman, ed., *The Antislavery Vanguard* (Princeton, 1965), 362–94; and Rawley, *Race & Politics*.

At other times, Republican spokesmen were less rabid in their pronouncements, yet made it clear that the plight of the white man, not the black, concerned them. "The real question at issue between the North and the South," the Pittsburgh *Gazette* insisted, "is not a sentimental difference growing out of the oppression of the negro." Similarly, Ohio congressman Samuel Galloway asserted at a rally in New York City that "the great question now before the people of this country is not the emancipation of the negro, but the emancipation of the white man."[36] Despite such statements, the recent emphasis on the racial theme does not capture the essence of Republican ideology. The importance of the race issue before the Civil War has been overstated. What is striking about Republican rhetoric during these years is not how often one encounters racist declarations, but how infrequently. When discussing party strategy in private correspondence, Republicans gave virtually no attention to the problem of race. They ignored the question as much as possible because they could never outbid the Democrats for racist support.[37] As the decade wore on, Democrats attempted to make race a major issue in northern politics, but they had distinctly limited success. Indeed, Democrats' attempt to stir up this issue in the Buchanan campaign was a sign of desperation, for they seized on the race question only *after* events had deprived them of much of their traditional appeal.

Other historians stress the Republicans' commitment to free labor and the protection of its concomitant social values.[38] Republicans appealed to farmers and workingmen with the argument that slavery would inevitably drive free labor out of the territories. In a series of papers written for the Frémont campaign, Francis P. Blair elaborated on the theme that slavery oppressed "the laboring people of *all classes*" and therefore should not be allowed to expand. In an address to his constituents, Ohio congressman Timothy C. Day succinctly summarized the free labor ideal:

> I appeal to the merchant, who knows the value of free trade; to the mechanic, who owns the value of his labor, and enjoys it without contact with Slavery; to the farmer, who tills his own lands, and knows the thrift of *free* labor; to the laborer, who toils but is not owned—to come forward and secure a Territory, large enough in extent to form three States like Ohio, for themselves and their children.[39]

Because the advocates of slavery "look upon and despise all labor as servile and degrading," free and slave labor "cannot exist together," Gideon Welles asserted in a campaign essay. "If slavery is established in Kansas," he continued, "free labor must be expelled. It is not the cause of the negro, but that of the free laboring white man that is involved in this question." Frémont was "the representative man of free labor."[40]

Defining labor broadly to encompass all productive classes, Republicans extolled northern society and the social and economic values associated with it as superior to those

---

36. Holt, *Political Crisis*, 188; Hartford *Courant* quoted in Rawley, *Race & Politics*, 150; New York *Tribune*, June 10.

37. Foner, *Free Soil, Free Labor, Free Men*, 261–300; Sewell, *Ballots for Freedom*, 321–36; and Kenneth M. Stampp, *The Imperiled Union: Essays on the Background of the Civil War* (New York, 1980), 105–35, effectively challenge an unqualified emphasis on Republican racism.

38. Foner's study, *Free Soil, Free Labor, Free Men*, presents the most extended treatment of this theme, and my summary relies heavily on his discussion, especially pp. 11–39.

39. Francis P. Blair, Sr., to Montgomery Blair, September 21, Blair Family Papers; Day, *Man on a Hill Top*, 175 (quotation); Cincinnati *Commercial*, November 3.

40. "Fremont Campaign," Essay, Typescript, Welles Papers, ConnHS.

of the South. They pictured the North as a progressive, fluid society of opportunity where work was honored and enterprising, talented individuals could rise. The South, by contrast, was, Republicans charged, a stagnant, hierarchical society where labor was debased and the workingman, be he farmer or worker, had no chance to improve his lot in life. Because opportunity and social mobility were central to the free labor ideal, Republicans viewed institutions that promoted self-improvement, such as public schools and churches, as essential to the welfare of the community, and they did not neatly separate moral and economic progress. Far from a curse, the God-given duty to labor "has been the parent of improvement, the incentive to progress, the road to happiness," contended a Republican paper in New England. "Whatever tends to elevate labor, elevates the human race. To degrade labor is to deteriorate the great bulk of mankind and to reduce them to the low, debasing condition of slaves."[41]

This ideal incorporated central components of the Protestant ethic and was thus closely attuned to the values and aspirations of the rural and urban northern middle class. Success would come to those who were imbued with the Protestant values of hard work, self-discipline, and sobriety; in the same way, failure sprang from individual character defects, not social causes. Drawing a link between these attitudes and the party's constituency, the Springfield *Republican* maintained that "the great middling-interest class" of the North constituted the backbone of the party:

> Those who work with their hands [it declared], who live and act independently, who hold the stakes of home and family, of farm and workshop, of education and freedom—these, as a mass, are enrolled in the [R]epublican ranks. . . . They form the very heart of the nation, as opposed to the two extremes of aristocracy and ignorance.[42]

Blind to the growing concentration of wealth in the North and the ways in which industrialization was closing off avenues of mobility, Republicans upheld the social ideal of the independent farmer, shopkeeper, and skilled worker.

The concept of free labor had its roots in one of the two main sources of American political thought: Lockeian liberalism, with its emphasis on economic individualism. At the heart of the free labor ideology was the idea that every man, as Abraham Lincoln phrased it, had a right to rise economically and socially to the limit of his ability.[43] At the same time, this ideology manifested a certain complacency about northern society, evidenced by an ingrained belief that this society promoted the interests of all groups within it. Upholding the reality of the American dream, the free labor ideal represented the optimistic side of the Republican appeal.

---

41. Hartford *Courant*, October 24.

42. Springfield *Republican*, November 1.

43. Gabor S. Boritt, "The Right to Rise," Cullom Davis et al., eds., *The Public and the Private Lincoln: Contemporary Perspectives* (Carbondale, 1979), 57–70; Boritt, *Lincoln and the Economics of the American Dream* (Memphis, 1978). Much recent scholarship has challenged the earlier emphasis on liberalism as America's dominant mode of social and political thought, but the transformation of society that occurred in the wake of the rise of a national market after 1815 made certain aspects of liberalism increasingly important. The effort of the Jacksonian and Civil War generations to reconcile the tenets of liberalism with the competing ideology of republicanism, permeated as it was by a strong suspicion of commerce and wealth, is one of the crucial unresolved problems of nineteenth-century American history. For a recent reaffirmation of the importance of liberalism to the founding generation, see Joyce Appleby, *Capitalism and a New Social Order: The Republican Vision of the 1790s* (New York, 1984).

As the decade wore on, the free labor argument assumed increasing significance in Republican thought, particularly following the Panic of 1857, which gave renewed importance to economic issues.[44] In the party's formative period, however, as it groped for its identity, the themes associated with this concept, while present, remained secondary to other aspects of the party's emerging appeal. Furthermore, while the free labor ideology may have distinguished northerners from slaveowners, that it divided Republicans from northern Democrats is questionable. Belief in the values associated with free labor, including a fervent desire to protect and expand northern society, was not confined to Republicans. All northerners shared these values. Indeed, it has been argued that these values were not even exclusively northern, but were held by all Americans, or perhaps (although even this is not clear) by all except slaveowners. Republicans differed from their adversaries not in their views of the good society but in their conception of the way it should be protected.[45]

Other historians, noting the weakness of the moral impulse and questioning the pervasiveness of Republican racism, emphasize instead the view of the Republican party as an anti-slavery-extension party. Certainly, when Republicans addressed themselves to the issue of slavery, they spoke much more frequently about the evils of its expansion than of its existence; indeed, opposition to the extension of slavery was the one policy on which all Republicans could agree.

Yet, as Michael Holt points out, if prevention of the extension of slavery, particularly into Kansas, was the issue Republicans used to publicize their persuasion, it was not their primary motivation. Kansas offered only a convenient issue with which to wage a much larger, more basic struggle. Close inspection of what Republicans said suggests that they were concerned less about slavery than the Slave Power, that it was white slaveholders— not black slaves—whom they hated, and that it was the growing threat to white liberties, not black, that they feared most. For all his hatred of slavery, Charles Sumner contended that the Kansas crisis was incidental to a more fundamental conflict. Writing Henry J. Raymond to congratulate him on his address issued by the Pittsburgh convention, which focused almost exclusively on the aggression of the Slave Power, Sumner declared:

> For a long time my desire has been to make an issue with the Slave Oligarchy; & provided this can be had, I am indifferent to the special point selected. Of course, at this moment Kansas is the inevitable point. In protecting this territory against tyranny we are driven to battle with the tyrants, who are the Oligarchs of Slavery.

The Cincinnati *Commercial* emphasized that the territorial issue "is merely a temporary

---

44. One problem with Foner's analysis is that, despite some attention to events, he presents an essentially static view of the ideology of the Republican party. It should be noted that the bulk of his evidence comes from the years after 1856. Although the outline of the party's appeal could be discerned in the 1856 campaign, the attention given to certain themes like free labor varied over time. The shift by the end of the decade to the more positive aspects of the party's program was a response to developments after 1856 and also a manifestation of the party's growing maturity and stability.

45. Collins, "Ideology of Northern Democrats," 104–05. For a Democratic defense of free labor, see George Duffield to Buchanan, November 17, Buchanan Papers, HSPa; and for Know Nothing identification with free labor, see the Hartford *Courant*, April 1, 4, 6, 7. When the *Courant* switched to the Republican party, it stressed the same themes without modification; for example October 21, 23, 24, 27, 31, November 4. James Oakes, *The Ruling Race: A History of American Slaveholders* (New York, 1982) attributes these values to slaveowners as well; however, more work needs to be done on this question.

form—a single manifestation of one that is infinitely more important.'' The fundamental issue, it argued, was whether the North or the South would exercise political power in the nation. In announcing his conversion to Republicanism, former governor John H. Clifford of Massachusetts identified the central issue as whether the free states or the South would control the federal government. "With the negroes I have nothing to do. But with their masters I propose to try conclusions as to our respective political rights."[46] It was precisely because the extension of slavery was only part of this larger crisis perceived by Republicans that the caning of Sumner was as critical to the party's appeal as the situation in Kansas. In emphasizing this internal threat to liberty, the Republican appeal drew upon the ideology of republicanism, which had been the dominant tradition in American politics since the Revolution.

As the Republicans' master symbol, the concept of a Slave Power united a number of diverse themes in a coherent intellectual construct.[47] Despite its importance to their thought, Republicans were not always consistent in the way they defined the Slave Power. Sometimes they used the term loosely, to refer to the entire South. At other times they employed the concept as a metaphor for southern power. Most frequently, however, they invoked it to designate the slaveholding class in the South—the privileged class, as William H. Seward denoted it, of 350,000 individuals who ruled their section without challenge and now were endeavoring to maintain by any means necessary their national power as well. First propounded by the abolitionists, the notion of a Slave Power expressed northern resentment of the power and privileges of the South and especially slaveowners. At its core was the assumption that the South had long dominated the national government and dictated federal policy at will.

Integrally linked to the Republican idea of the Slave Power was the fear of conspiracy. Republicans charged that there was a conspiracy, of which southern politicians were merely the most visible agents, to protect and enlarge the power and position of slaveowners. To party spokesmen, American history since the adoption of the Constitution was largely an unfolding of this conspiracy. Reciting a long litany of political developments, including the three-fifths clause, the Missouri Compromise, the notorious gag law, the banning of abolitionist literature from the mails, the annexation of Texas and the seizure of lands from Mexico, the Compromise of 1850, and finally the repeal of the Missouri Compromise, Republicans claimed that the South had won an unbroken series of victories over the North. Each demand by southerners had been followed by one even more extreme until finally the rights of the North were in serious jeopardy of being permanently obliterated. Charles A. Dana of the New York *Tribune* was convinced that southern aggression against northern rights provided the Republicans with a winning issue. Neither the Pope nor immigrants could really govern the country or endanger its liberties, he insisted, "but the slave breeders and slave traders *do* govern it, and threaten to put an end to all other government than theirs. Here is something tangible

---

46. Charles Sumner to Henry J. Raymond, March 2, Raymond Papers; Cincinnati *Commercial*, April 11; John Clifford to Robert C. Winthrop, June 10 (copy), Winthrop Papers. Holt, *Political Crisis*, 189, presents a similar analysis.

47. For discussions of the concept of a Slave Power, see Foner, *Free Soil, Free Labor, Free Men*, 73–102; Russel B. Nye, *Fettered Freedom: Civil Liberties and the Slavery Controversy, 1830–1860* (East Lansing, 1948), 282–315; Larry Gara, "Slavery and the Slave Power: A Crucial Distinction," *CWH*, v. 15 (March, 1969), 5–18; and David Brion Davis, *The Slave Power and the Paranoid Style* (Baton Rouge, 1969). I have discussed this theme in more detail in "The Republican Party and The Slave Power," Robert H. Abzug and Stephen E. Maizlish, eds., *New Perspectives on Race and Slavery in America* (Lexington, 1986), 51–78.

to go upon," he continued, "an issue on which we will . . . surely succeed in the long run."[48]

Republicans used the Sumner assault and the incidents in Kansas to support their basic contention that the Slave Power had united in a plan designed to stamp out all liberties of northern white men. Northern liberties, northern manhood, northern equality were all under assault by slaveholders, party spokesmen argued. By such rhetoric, Republicans made the threat posed by the Slave Power seem much more real and personal. They used the slave-master relationship, the essence of everything northerners feared and hated, to describe this threat. The New York *Evening Post* asked after the Sumner caning:

> Has it come to this, that we must speak with bated breath in the presence of our Southern masters . . . ? If we venture to laugh at them, or to question their logic, or dispute their facts, are we to be chastised as they chastise their slaves? Are we too, slaves, slaves for life, a target for their brutal blows, when we do not comport ourselves to please them?

The normally restrained New York *Times* charged that the Slave Power, arrogant and domineering, was determined to rule the country at all costs. The Sumner assault confirmed that "it will stop at no extremity of violence in order to subdue the people of the Free States and force them into a tame subservience to its own domination."[49]

The Kansas "outrages" raised precisely the same issue, for Republicans claimed that freedom of speech and of the press, as well as purity of the ballot box, had been trampled underfoot in that far-off territory. Both in Kansas and in the nation's capital, men seemed to be attacked for what they said and thought. Slavery propagandists, the Cincinnati *Gazette* asserted, "cannot tolerate free speech anywhere, and would stifle it in Washington with the bludgeon and the bowie-knife, as they are now trying to stifle it in Kansas by massacre, rapine and murder." The war on the free-state settlers in Kansas, the *Ashtabula Sentinel* declared, "establishes . . . that from this time forth the slave power will wield the General Government against freedom—not only in Kansas, but every where else." It was only a short step, it exclaimed almost hysterically, from dispersing the Topeka legislature to taking the same action against a national Republican convention. One of the most frequently requested and widely distributed Republican campaign documents in 1856 was a speech by Schuyler Colfax detailing the abridgment of civil liberties by the notorious legal code enacted by the proslavery Kansas legislature. "The issues now before the people," a letter to the religious periodical, the *Independent*, maintained, "are those of Despotism or Freedom. The question has passed on from that of slavery for negro servants, to that of tyranny over free white men."[50]

Along with the violence in Washington and Kansas, Republicans' perception of southern society fanned their fears. When Republicans looked south, they saw a society that seemed to deny some of the most fundamental American values. Party members were acutely aware that freedom of speech, at least on the topic of slavery, had largely disappeared from the South, and they projected that southerners intended to abrogate such

---

48. Charles A. Dana to Henry C. Carey, November 27, [1856], Carey Papers.

49. New York *Evening Post*, May 23; New York *Times*, May 24.

50. Cincinnati *Gazette*, May 24; *Ashtabula Sentinel*, July 17; letter signed "C.," *Independent*, June 5; George Rathbun to Eli Slifer, August 23, Slifer-Dill Papers; Hollister, *Colfax*, 101; N. H. Swayne to Thomas Ewing, June 19, Ewing Family Papers; Jacob M. Howard to Seward, February 18 (Private & Confidential), Seward Papers, UR. On the importance of Colfax's speech, see Gideon Welles to James T. Hale, September 4, Welles Papers, LC; J. M. Bunce to Morgan, May 6, Edwin D. Morgan Papers.

rights in the North as well. Political liberty as well was circumscribed in the South. Republicans noted that John C. Underwood had been forced to leave his home in Virginia because he attended the Republican national convention, that Professor Benjamin S. Hedrick had been driven from North Carolina for expressing a preference for Frémont, and that outside the border states the Republican party was not allowed to contest elections. In a speech on "The Dominant Class in the Republic" delivered during the 1856 campaign, Seward directed attention to the absence of freedom of speech, the press, the ballot box, education, literature, and popular assembly in the South, all of which he traced to the power of the slaveholding class. Reckless demands by southern newspapers after the Sumner caning that other Republican leaders be thrashed, accompanied by assertions that no discussion of slavery could be tolerated, did nothing to alleviate Republican anxieties.[51]

As the proponent of slavery, aristocracy, tyranny, and minority rule, the Slave Power was, in Republican thought, the absolute negation of the country's founding principles. Insolent southern slaveholders threatened the very essence of republican government. A Republican congressman asked in June 1856: "Are we to have a government of the people, a real representative Republican Government? or are the owners of slave property, small in number but with the power now in their hands, and strongly intrenched in every department, to rule us with arbitrary and undisputed sway?" Here was the Republicans' reply to the accusation that they were fomenting trouble by meddling in southern affairs. They reversed the argument. It was southerners who were interfering in northern society by seeking to curtail northern civil liberties. It was slavery that would not leave northern free men alone, cried party leaders. "The Liberties of our country are in tenfold the danger that they were at the commencement of the American Revolution," the Concord *Independent Democrat* declared in a powerful editorial after the assault on Sumner. "We then had a distant foe to contend with. Now the enemy is within our borders."[52]

The image of the Slave Power as a vehicle of aristocracy exerted a powerful influence among northern voters, long nurtured on egalitarian rhetoric. Denunciation of the Slave Power enabled the Republicans to avoid the aristocratic stigma that had so burdened the Whigs. Even the elitist George Templeton Strong, in announcing his conversion to Republicanism, wrote (rather incongruously), "I belong to the insurgent plebeians of the North arming against a two-penny South Carolina aristocracy." In accounting for the Republican party's strength in the 1856 election, a thoughtful Boston Republican told a southern friend that, although the moral question of slavery and its economic inefficiency undoubtedly had some influence, these arguments were insignificant compared to "the aristocratic nature of . . . slavery," and the accompanying issue of whether the small class of slaveholders "shall own half the Senate and shall use the national arm to extend their institution at home and abroad." The masses could be aroused only by appeals to the country's interests and their own prejudices, he continued, "and if there is anything in this country fixed, it is the prejudice against aught which has the appearance even of

---

51. Hopkins R. Smith to H. Miles Moore, June 3, 1855, H. Miles Moore Papers, KSHS; O. B. Matteson to John A. King, June 14, John A. King Papers; New York *Evening Post*, September 11, 23, October 1; Seward, *Works*, v. 4, 258; Gienapp, "Crime Against Sumner," 221–22. Other personal assaults committed by southerners this session, such as Congressman Albert Rust's attack on Horace Greeley on a Washington street, and the murder of an Irish waiter at Willard's Hotel by Congressman Philemon T. Herbert of California, who was from Alabama, gave Republicans additional ammunition.

52. Henry Bennett quoted in Sewell, *Ballots for Freedom*, 305; [Concord] *Independent Democrat*, June 5.

aristocracy." He was convinced that "the aristocratic element of the slave power . . . has made us [Republicans] a hundred votes, where the moral question has given us one."[53] More than any other party spokesman, Seward defined the basic conflict between the two sections as one of aristocracy versus democracy. The issue of the contest was not unreal or imaginary, he insisted in a campaign speech in his home town of Auburn. Instead, it was "a conflict for not merely toleration, but for absolute political sway in the republic, between the system of free labor with equal and universal suffrage, free speech[,] free thought, and free action, and the system of slave labor with unequal franchises secured by arbitrary, oppressive and tyrannical laws." Slaveholders were the country's privileged class.[54]

Socially the agent of aristocracy, the Slave Power politically was the proponent of minority rule. Republicans thus coupled the Slave Power, in both its social pretensions and its political principles, with values utterly repugnant to northern voters. "Stript of its coverings, the true issue is simply one of equal rights," a downstate Indiana Republican journal declared. "Shall the people of the great Northwest have their proper influence in the management of the Federal Government, or will the few men in the South . . . rule, as heretofore, the twenty odd millions of non-slaveholders?" The radical Cincinnati *Commercial* insisted: "If our Government, for the sake of Slavery, is to be perpetually the representative of a minority, it may continue republican in form, but the substance of its republicanism has departed." The *Ohio State Journal*, a much more conservative paper, made the same point. "Majorities rule, or should rule, in this Republican land," it maintained. Despite all the noise they made, the slaveholders were "a contemptible minority . . . an arrogant little Aristocracy." Noting that this class controlled the southern states, the paper concluded:

> If the white population of the Slave States see fit to submit like bondmen to the political chains imposed upon them by this handful of Aristocrats, so be it—that's *their* business. It is *our* business—we of the Free States—to see that we are not brought down to the same humiliating condition.

Control of the nation by "a mere handful of Southerners," contended a newspaper published in southern Illinois, represented the "paradox of a republican government, in which a minority rules the majority."[55]

To the modern reader, these Republican claims, which betray at least a touch of the apocalyptic, seem grossly exaggerated. Yet they struck a responsive chord in the minds of countless northerners, most of whom had no sympathy for a crusade to abolish slavery

53. Nevins and Thomas, eds., *Strong Diary*, v. 2, 281–82; John M. Forbes to J. Hamilton Cowper, December 4, Sarah Forbes Hughes, ed., *Letters and Recollections of John Murray Forbes* (2 vols.: Boston, 1899), v. 1, 156–57; Foner, *Free Soil, Free Labor, Free Men*, 68. Also see the *Cortland County Republican*, May 29; New York *Evening Post*, April 10; Foner, "Politics, Ideology, and the Civil War," 29–30.

54. Seward, *Works*, v. 4, 279–80. In the 1856 campaign Seward delivered two very important speeches that elaborated on the themes he expounded a year earlier in the New York state election: "The Dominant Class in the Republic," at Detroit on October 2, and "The Political Parties of the Day," at Auburn on October 21. These two speeches, along with his 1855 addresses at Buffalo and Albany, constitute the most carefully reasoned statement of Republican principles until after 1856.

55. Madison *Evening Courier*, March 5, quoted in Stoler, "Influence of the Democratic Element," 11; Cincinnati *Commercial*, April 11; *Ohio State Journal*, June 12; *Southern Illinoisian*, September 26, quoted in the *Ashtabula Sentinel*, October 16.

in the South. But from their perspective the South, not the North, was acting aggressively, and northern rights, not southern, were under attack. After the Civil War a Republican journalist argued, with some justice, that the slavery issue would not have been so precipitated "but for the fatuity of the slaveholders, exhibited in their persistent demand that there should be no discussion."[56]

While none of these themes were entirely new in 1856, their powerful hold on northern public opinion was. More than anything else, the events of the previous twelve months had converted thousands of northerners to the Republican viewpoint. If these had been isolated incidents, it would have been impossible to convince northern public opinion that a real threat existed. What made the Republican view compelling was that these latest "outrages" were part of a long series of what were considered to be attacks on northern civil liberties, beginning with the gag rule in the 1830s. Their cumulative effect, coupled with the particularly dramatic nature of the caning of Sumner and the sack of Lawrence, convinced many northerners that these charges were more than political propaganda. The assault on Sumner was "not merely an *incident*, but a *demonstration*," Hannibal Hamlin's father-in-law asserted. Citing the repeal of the Missouri Compromise, the invasions of Kansas, the behavior of southern congressmen, the policy of the administration, and all the acts of violence of the period, he contended that together these developments "furnish a clear demonstration of settled purpose to annihilate freedom. . . . It seems to me the demonstration is as certain as any demonstration in mathematics," he continued. "Incidents are no longer incidents—they are links in the chain of demonstration, infallible, plain, conclusive."[57]

Republican strategists were certainly aware that concern for the welfare of blacks, free or slave, had never been a strong sentiment in the free states, and that arguments based on the immorality of slavery were not calculated to bring political success. The symbols of Bleeding Sumner and Bleeding Kansas allowed Republicans to attack the South without attacking slavery directly. By appropriating the great abolitionist symbol of the Slave Power and linking it with the threat to northern rights, Republicans made a much more powerful appeal to northern sensibilities than they could otherwise have done. As John Van Buren warned Buchanan during the campaign, this argument was especially effective among old Jacksonian Democrats. The acrimonious struggle between the Van Buren Democrats and southern political leaders since the 1840s had made the former very sensitive to charges of southern arrogance and dictation.[58] One rank-and-file Democrat who joined the Republican party after the Sumner caning denied that he had any sympathy for abolitionism, or that his views on the social position of blacks had changed. But he was no longer willing to tolerate the aggressions of the Slave Power in Congress, in Kansas, and in the country generally: "Had the Slave power been less *insolently aggressive*, I would have been content to see it extend . . . but when it seeks to extend its sway by fire & sword . . . I am ready to say hold enough!" "Reserve no place for me," he told a longtime Democratic associate, "*I shall not come back.*"[59]

Republicans skillfully used the Sumner and Kansas incidents to instill a bitter

---

56. Congdon, *Reminiscences*, 131.

57. Stephen Emery to Hannibal Hamlin, May 27, Hamlin Papers.

58. John Van Buren to Buchanan, June 10, Buchanan Papers, HSPa. Also see the excellent discussion in Foner, *Free Soil, Free Labor, Free Men*, 149–85.

59. James F. Chamberlain to Ansel J. McCall, June 21, July 11, 29 (quotation), October 28 (quotation), McCall Family Papers.

antagonism toward the South into countless northerners. "I have never before seen anything at all like the present state of deep, determined, & desperat [*sic*] feelings of hatred, & hostility to the further extension of slavery, & its political power," one man commented to Seward. Democrats were troubled by the intensity of anti-southern feeling they observed in the North. An Illinois Democrat informed Buchanan: "There is a terrible rancor in the public mind against the people and institutions of the south—a rancor utterly uncontrolable [*sic*] and I do not know but it is bound to be perpetual." Supporters of Fillmore made the same observation. Republicans had created "a deep seated and almost vindictive Antipathy . . . over the entire north towards the entire south," the president of the New York state council asserted after the 1856 election.[60]

The Republican picture of the South as a backward, degraded, barbaric society built on brutality and depravity gained added credence in the face of Brooks's attack on Sumner and the alleged border ruffian activities in Kansas. Sneers at southern society and accomplishments and taunts about southern economic backwardness were common themes in Republican speeches and newspapers during the campaign. Robert C. Winthrop was not totally unfair when he characterized the standard Frémont campaign speech as

> one-third part Missouri Compromise Repeal, . . . one-third Kansas Outrages by Border Ruffians, . . . and one-third disjointed facts, and misapplied figures, and great swelling words of vanity, to prove that the South is, upon the whole, the poorest, meanest, least productive and most miserable part of creation, and therefore ought to be continually teased and taunted and reproached and reviled.

Another Massachusetts conservative upbraided Republicans for their unrelenting attacks on the South. "All their artillery is brought to bear in personal abuse against the South," he declared, and he accused the party of having "no other grand primary object, except to make the North hate the South."[61]

Already sensitive to the accusation that the party was a sectional organization that threatened the Union, some Republicans were uneasy about the growing hatred of the South among party members. They urged especially that a distinction be made between the governing power of the South, that is, the Slave Power, and the mass of southern whites, who were as much the victims of the ruling class as northerners were. Horace Greeley, for example, instructed Charles A. Dana, when the latter was temporarily editor of the *Tribune*, "Above all things not to allow anything to get in [the paper] which seems impelled by hatred of the South, or a desire to humiliate that section. On the contrary, ours is the course to renovate and exalt the South, and must so be commended." Francis P. Blair, himself a southerner and slaveowner, wrote several campaign essays arguing that the party's struggle was not against the South but only against one group of southerners, the followers of Calhoun.[62]

At the same time some Republicans glimpsed a new and more ominous threat. Elaborating on an idea first formulated during the Nebraska crisis, they argued that

60. Jeremiah Wilbur to Seward, June 20, Seward Papers, UR; Samuel W. Randall to Buchanan, November 10, Buchanan Papers, HSPa; Stephen Sammons to Millard Fillmore, November 7, Fillmore Papers, SUNY.

61. Winthrop, *Addresses and Speeches*, v. 2, 294; Otis P. Lord, *Fremont's "Principles" Exposed* (np, [1856]), 7.

62. Greeley to Charles A. Dana, April 2, Benton, ed., *Greeley on Lincoln*, 141; Blair, *To My Neighbors* (New York, 1856); Francis P. Blair, Sr., to Montgomery Blair, September 21, Blair Family Papers.

slavery threatened not only Kansas and the territories, but the free states as well. Either freedom or slavery must be national, declared alarmed party members. One Ohioan told John P. Hale, "The time will soon come, when slavery must *be abolished* in *all the states, or prevail in all.*" If the South and its allies "have the right to force slavery upon Kansas," the Cincinnati *Commercial* maintained, "they have the right to force it upon Ohio." Such assertions were by no means limited to pronounced antislavery men. The conservative Philadelphia *North American* alleged that the South sought to make "slavery as wide as the national domain and as lasting as any mere human institution on earth." Slavery, the paper solemnly affirmed, threatened Pennsylvania.[63] Agitated Republicans pointed to the decision by Judge John K. Kane in the Passmore Williamson case, the southern argument that slavery had the same rights as any other property in all the territories, and the demand for the right of indefinite transit of slave property in the free states, as the opening wedge for the announcement of a new doctrine that the Constitution protected slavery everywhere.[64]

No doubt some party spokesmen resorted to this fear simply as a means to get votes, but without question many sincerely believed that the threat was real, despite southern denials of any desire to force slavery north. An earnest, level-headed Cincinnati Republican wrote to his congressman:

> You may think me ridiculously apprehensive, but the time has come in my humble opinion when our own liberty is at stake, and the question is no longer whether the semi-civilized aristocracy that domineers over the people of Virginia and the Carolinas shall be permitted to reduce those fertile states to sterility and waste without interruption, but the blight of slavery threatens Ohio also, and for me I am in for the fight to the end.[65]

Critics North and South ridiculed these fears, yet one of Buchanan's correspondents noted with astonishment that "many honest men believe that if Fremont shall fail in his election, slavery will be established in all the free states."[66] In 1856 this idea was inchoate and not accepted by all—or even most—Republicans, but in the next few years it would become a major Republican theme.

As a heritage of the American Revolution, republicanism exerted great influence in antebellum politics, and Republican spokesmen took great pains to identify their party's cause with this tradition. In reality, however, the ideology of republicanism, which had

---

63. Luther Humphrey to John P. Hale, February 28, Hale Papers, NHHS; Cincinnati *Commercial*, May 22, November 3; Philadelphia *North American* October 14, 30; Cyrus Woodman to Cadwallader C. Washburn, November 27, Cyrus Woodman Papers, Maine Historical Society; [Rome, New York] *Roman Citizen*, October 29; *Long Islander*, October 24; Parker to Edward Desor, [August 9], John Weiss, ed., *Life and Correspondence of Theodore Parker*, (2 vols.: New York, 1864), v. 2, 189; N. C. Deering to Hannibal Hamlin, June 15, Hamlin Papers.

64. Cincinnati *Commercial*, August 30; *Ashtabula Sentinel*, March 6, 13, 20; Charles Miner to John A. King, March 2, John A. King Papers. Southern assertions that slavery should not be restricted to blacks reinforced this theme. For one example, see the Charleston *Standard* quoted in the *Ashtabula Sentinel*, October 9.

65. George Hoadley, Jr., to Timothy C. Day, April 5, Day, *Man on a Hill Top*, 168; J. B. Hubbard to John Hubbard, July 2, Hubbard Family Papers.

66. Ranson H. Gillet to Buchanan, October 2, Buchanan Papers, HSPa; J. Glancy Jones to [Frank Jones?], December 13, 1855, Frank Jones Papers, CinHS; Thomas Corwin to James A. Pearce, May 16, Pearce Papers; [Concord] *New Hampshire Patriot*, November 26.

continued to evolve since the Revolution, was not the same in the 1850s as in 1776 or 1789. It had been shorn of its moral dimensions and its anti-commerical ethos, political parties were now deemed essential to the health of the Republic rather than its bane, and the long-standing connection between ownership of property and full citizenship had been swept away by the democratic reform movement of the Jacksonian era. Only the fading echoes of the idea of virtue, so central to eighteenth-century republicanism, could be heard by mid-century, and by then virtue referred not to a rejection of luxury but instead to the idea that every citizen must be constantly vigilant on behalf of liberty. In some aspects of American political culture, republicanism had been supplanted by democracy, a profoundly different thing, and as a result republican ideology lacked the coherence it had possessed for earlier generations.

Nevertheless, the Republican party's use of this ideology was not empty sloganeering; indeed, certain parts of the Republican appeal were clear outgrowths of this intellectual tradition.[67] These included the fear of concentrated power, now directed less at government than at aristocracy, and the belief that such power was the natural enemy of liberty and if unchecked would eventually destroy it. But the most obvious and important debt the party's appeal owed to republican thought was a deep-seated belief in the existence of conspiracies against liberty. Since 1815, American political parties had viewed the primary danger to the Republic as internal. For Republicans, this threat was the Slave Power conspiracy, with its goal of unchallenged power and the eradication of northern liberty. Americans were so accustomed to thinking in terms of conspiracies that Republicans devoted only limited effort to proving the existence of this conspiracy and focused instead on urging the necessity of concerted action against it. The party's main message in the 1856 campaign—that the slaveholding oligarchy posed a threat of unprecedented magnitude to the survival of the Republic, its values and institutions—was clear and compelling evidence of the continuing significance of the ideology of republicanism in antebellum politics.

III

Although Republican ideology in the 1856 election focused primarily on the Slave Power's threat to northern liberty, party spokesmen raised other issues as well, not all of which were entirely compatible. The relative importance given these secondary concerns varied greatly from locality to locality. Various aspects of the slavery controversy competed for attention, and hatred of Pierce and of the Democratic party both counted for much among Republican voters. So, too, did the party's image as the upholder of reform and the repository of moral righteousness. These and other considerations helped attract voters to the Republican column.

The most important sub-theme of the Republican appeal, however, was anti-Catholicism. The party contained such a powerful nativist wing that some attention to ethnocultural issues was inevitable. Tactical considerations, as well as the opposition

---

67. The argument that, because all parties in this decade expressed their appeal in terms of republicanism this ideology was devoid of meaning and its use was vacuous propaganda, misses the point. That all parties felt compelled to link their cause with this tradition is testimony not to its unimportance but to its significance. While antebellum parties agreed on the necessity of defending republicanism, they exhibited wide disagreement over the nature of the threat to the Republic and the policies required to preserve this heritage—concerns that lay at the heart of party conflict in the 1850s.

of certain vocal factions, made undesirable an emphasis on anti-foreignism. The divisive nature of the temperance issue led party leaders to minimize its agitation, although with so many reformers and nativists having joined the party anti-liquor sentiment was strong in the Republican ranks. But in the present crisis, with sectional feelings running high, Republicans could safely relegate temperance to the background. Anti-Catholicism, on the other hand, entailed little political risk, since the Catholic vote was solidly Democratic. Indeed, anti-Catholicism and anti-southernism were the two principles on which both North Americans and Protestant immigrants could unite. A Republican congressman emphasized to German leader Friedrich Hassaurek that a union of liberal Germans and Know Nothings was possible precisely because the two groups shared an intense "hatred of Jesuitism. . . . Take K. N'ism as now developed at the North," he declared, "and you will find that nine tenths of it will nearly assimilate with your own views."[68]

In some areas Republicans had appealed to animosity toward Catholics in 1855, and they continued to do so in 1856. Charging that "Popery and Slavery . . . [had] banded together for a common object—the attainment of political power," the Chicago *Tribune*, a Republican paper, insisted that "the Republican Party, which is the avowed and mortal enemy of chattel bondage, is not less the opponent of partisan schemes of political Catholicism." State and local party platforms catered to nativists and Protestant immigrants on this issue. The most significant example was the Union party platform in Pennsylvania, which condemned the interference of "foreign influence of every kind" in the American government, denounced "the pandering of any party to foreign influence as fraught with manifold evils to the country," and pledged to defend the common school system from any attempt to pervert it to sectarian uses.[69] Seeking to take advantage of negative reference attitudes in the northern electorate, Republicans strove to identify the Democratic party with Catholics and especially the despised Irish. At the same time, Republican papers lauded Germans and other Protestant immigrants as superior to the "clannish" and "ignorant" Irish who were "blindly controlled by leaders and demagogues."[70] The idea that ethnic and religious tensions, which had been the major force behind the rise of the Know Nothings, suddenly lost political salience in 1856 after several years of great intensity is a serious misperception. Events of the previous year had weakened the nativist impulse and correspondingly strengthened the sectional one, but these events had by no means exorcized ethnoreligious questions from northern politics.

The well-developed image of the Catholic church as an alien, anti-republican institution enabled Republicans to easily incorporate opposition to the political pretensions of the church into the party's discussion of the threat to northern liberties. One of Seward's correspondents stressed that the central plank of the Republican platform should be "Opposition to Despotism—whether the seat of its power be in the papal chair of Rome or on a Cotton Plantation of the South."[71] Solid Catholic support for the Democratic

---

68. Timothy C. Day to Friedrich Hassaurek, March 25, Friedrich Hassaurek Papers, OHS. For a concise statement by a German Republican leader of the absolute necessity that the party avoid the temperance and anti-immigrant issues, see Stephen Molitor to Chase, March 27, Chase Papers, HSPa. This and the following section draw in part on material in my essay, "Nativism and the Creation of a Republican Majority in the North before the Civil War," *JAH*, v. 72 (December, 1985), 529–59.

69. Chicago *Tribune*, February 4, 13; *Ohio State Journal*, November 16; Holt, *Political Crisis*, 178. For other examples of Republican use of anti-Catholicism, see Formisano, *Mass Political Parties*, 271–72; Holt, *Forging a Majority*, 206–09, 243–44, 259–61, 286–88.

70. New York *Times*, November 7.

71. Justin D. Fulton to Seward, May 26, Seward Papers, UR.

party, which was (Republicans charged) the ally of the Slave Power, the church's failure to speak out strongly against slavery, and southern denunciations of such northern institutions as free schools allowed Republicans to link the Slave Power and the Catholic church. The Republican organ in Ohio charged that Frémont was opposed "by a close and perfect combination of two powerful Tyrannies,—that of the slavedrivers, and that of the Roman Catholic church." The mainstay of Buchanan's strength, these two tyrannies, "one of the mind, and the other of the body," were "naturally allies" and would "ever be found acting together."[72] Republicans thus depicted a dual threat to northern liberties—the Slave Power and the papal power—and, although they gave greater emphasis to the former and considered it the more serious danger, they by no means ignored the latter. Ethnocultural issues, particularly anti-Catholicism, were crucial to the party's popular strength.

Republicans attempted to win over former Know Nothings not merely with rhetoric but also by securing the endorsement of notable American party leaders. James W. Barker, former national president of the secret order, George Law, who had been defeated for the party's presidential nomination, Ephraim Marsh, who presided at the convention that nominated Fillmore in February, and Chauncey Shaffer, an important New York American, all wrote public letters endorsing Frémont, which the Republicans issued as campaign documents.[73] Marsh and Shaffer were also especially active on the stump during the campaign and, along with earlier Know Nothing converts to Republicanism, such as Henry Wilson, Nathaniel P. Banks, and Anson Burlingame, were in heavy demand as speakers. The prominence of former Know Nothings in the Frémont campaign further strengthened the Republicans' nativist image. Throughout the 1850s and well beyond, the Republican party projected an anti-Catholic image, a fact readily perceived by nativists and Catholic voters alike. The church organ in Cincinnati defended Catholic hostility to the Republican party on the grounds that "the men who threatened our churches, who burned Archbishop Bedini in effigy, whose papers are filled with calumnies the most atrocious, are now all Freesoilers, Fremonters, and remarkable for the savage animosity which they manifest on all occasions against Roman Catholics."[74] Nor was it necessary for the Republicans to devote great attention to ethnocultural issues. That so many former Know Nothings were now comfortably housed in the Republican party, coupled with overwhelming Irish Catholic support for the Democratic party, was more than sufficient to ensure the continuing relevance of nativism, and provided ample motivation for voters sensitive to such concerns to vote Republican.

IV

Democrats and Fillmore Americans attempted in a variety of ways to counteract the Republicans' appeal. They raised important questions about Frémont's lack of experience

---

72. *Ohio State Journal*, November 14.

73. Ephraim Marsh, *Reasons for Going for Fremont* (np, 1856); *George Law's and Chauncey Shaffer's Reasons for Repudiating Fillmore and Donelson* (New York, 1856). Holt, *Political Crisis*, 176–81, provides the best discussion of the importance of anti-Catholicism to Republican ideology during these years. Holt properly notes that anti-Catholicism was more important on the state and local levels, where the Republicans contested many more elections and ran many more candidates, than on the national level. For a contrary view, see Foner, *Free Soil, Free Labor, Free Men*, 226–60.

74. *Catholic Telegraph*, August 9.

and his questionable financial transactions in California. They made great capital of the Republican party's sectionalism and exploited fears of southern secession in the event of Frémont's election. The Democrats gave some attention to the race issue, although, as with the Republicans, the prevalence of this theme has been overemphasized. Democrats and Fillmore men also indulged liberally in personal assaults on Frémont, indicting him as, among other things, a slaveowner, a swindler, and a drunkard.[75] But the most damaging charge they raised against the Republican candidate was that he was a Catholic. This controversy ideally suited the needs of the Buchanan and Fillmore managers, for it weakened the Republicans' cause with precisely the group they most needed to attract, the Know Nothings. In seeking American support, Republicans had to discredit this accusation, and throughout the presidential campaign the question of Frémont's religion gave Republican strategists more difficulty than any other issue.

While Fillmore's supporters made effective use of the allegation of Frémont's Catholicism, they did not invent it. Even before he was nominated, rumors circulated that the colonel was a Catholic. In a major blunder, the Republican Boston *Atlas* printed a dispatch from its Washington correspondent attesting to this fact, and Benjamin F. Wade was momentarily shaken when he first heard the rumor. Visiting Boston to drum up support for the Pathfinder, Charles James found it necessary to allay the fears arising from the Catholic story, which, he reported with considerable understatement, "somewhat alarmed our people." Henry Wilson and other leaders in Washington felt compelled to provide assurances to constituents that Frémont was a Protestant.[76] The reaction of Nathaniel Banks and Robert B. Hall of Massachusetts, two of Frémont's most ardent congressional supporters, dramatically revealed the power of the accusation. With some merriment, Gamaliel Bailey recorded that they "stretched their eyes 'wide as saucers'" when told he was a Catholic.[77]

Quietly whispered before the Republican convention, Frémont's alleged Catholicism became the subject of public comment as soon as he received the nomination. First to hurl the charge was the Washington *Evening Star*, but it soon gave way in this controversy to Erastus Brooks's New York *Express*. No paper was more zealous in ferreting out new stories and testimony about Frémont's supposed Romanism, and no paper was more unscrupulous in personally abusing the Republican candidate.[78] No one maintained seriously that Brooks actually believed the stories he published; more important, he realized that unless conclusively answered the Catholic accusation would ruin the Republican nominee politically. It must have given the editor of the *Express* satisfaction to see the Republicans attempt to deny these ever more numerous stories in a fashion similar to that forced on the Know Nothings in the 1854 New York gubernatorial election, when the latter had tried futilely to discredit Whig claims that Daniel Ullmann had been born in Calcutta.

Several aspects of Frémont's life made the assertion that he was a Catholic plausible:

75. These charges are discussed in Nevins, *Frémont*, 445–50.

76. Congdon, *Reminiscences*, 154; Wade to Caroline Wade, March 30, Wade Papers; Charles James to Banks, March 5, Banks Papers, LC; Wilson to [Seth?] Webb, March 10, Misc MSS, Boston Public Library. Wade later corrected his report. Wade to Milton Sutliff, May 8, Sutliff Papers.

77. Gamaliel Bailey to Chase, February 21, Chase Papers, LC.

78. For Brooks's role in the controversy, see Greeley to John Stevens and James G. Blaine, November 25, Blaine Papers; Blaine to James Watson Webb, November 24, Webb Papers; New York *Express*, July–November.

His father was French Catholic, the Republican nominee was educated at a Catholic school, he and Jessie Benton were married by a Catholic priest, and their adopted daughter attended a Catholic school. To make matters worse, a number of acquaintances testified that the colonel was a Romanist. The ingenuity of the nativist press in concocting new evidence to establish Frémont's Catholic faith far outstripped the Republicans' ability to muster effective denials. Stories circulated that Frémont had always claimed to be a Catholic, that he had refused an Episcopal Bible, that he attended mass, that he had baptized his children as Catholics, that he had a private chapel in his home, and many more of a similar nature.[79]

As the testimonials multiplied, American leaders collected the more plausible ones in campaign pamphlets. The president of the New York state council urged that the issue of Frémont's Catholic faith be used especially to influence the Methodist and Baptist press, as well as other religious journals. Some more excitable nativists even charged that Thurlow Weed, William H. Seward, and Archbishop John Hughes had entered into a secret conspiracy to elect a Catholic president. Fillmore leaders considered the Catholic issue "the battery which proves most effective in thinning his [Frémont's] ranks." One American concisely stated the rationale for the effort nativist editors devoted to perpetuating and publicizing the story: "We are positive that a great majority" of Protestant voters "when they are convinced of the fact that Fremont is a Catholic, will hold that question of more importance than the false issue of 'Free Kansas.' "[80]

Weed, summarizing the political intelligence received at Republican headquarters, admitted that "the Catholic story is doing much damage." Republicans and Americans alike reported that many antislavery Know Nothings would not vote for Frémont because they were convinced he was a Catholic.[81] One of Seward's friends maintained that "the very idea of his [Frémont] being a Catholic will be the death of him forever, as a Presidential candidate." Another Republican, who originally supported the decision not to have Frémont make any comment on the controversy, admitted that he was "a little staggered" at the defections he witnessed on this issue.[82] Party leaders found themselves inundated with requests for documents that proved the Republican standard bearer was not a Catholic.

Republicans were uncertain how to handle the issue, since the evidence was straightforward: Frémont was an Episcopalian, all his children had been baptized in that church, and although one of his daughters did attend a Catholic school, so too had Fillmore's daughter. Jessie Frémont denied privately that her husband had ever attended

---

79. *Col. Fremont's Religious History* (np, [1856]); *J. C. Fremont's Record. Proof of his Romanism* (np. 1856); *Fremont's Romanism Established* (np, 1856). The Catholic press and clergy generally asserted that Frémont was a Protestant: Boston *Pilot* quoted in *Ashtabula Sentinel*, September 11; letter from S. Straight, September 1, *Ashtabula Sentinel*, September 11. One exception was the New York *Freeman's Journal*, quoted in the *Chenango American*, September 18.

80. Stephen Sammons to Fillmore, July 24, N. Sargent to Fillmore, October 12 (quotation), Fillmore Papers, SUNY; *Chenango American*, August 28 (quotation), September 4, 11; Vespasian Ellis to [J. Scott Harrison], September 3, J. Scott Harrison Papers, LC.

81. Weed to Morgan, August 9, Edwin D. Morgan Papers; *Chenango American*, August 7; J. J. Marlett to Andrew J. Donelson, July 10, Andrew Jackson Donelson Papers, LC; Alexander S. Diven to Weed, August 20, Weed Papers, UR; Edwin H. Tenney to Seward, July 23, Seward Papers, UR; S. C. Johnson to Morgan, September 8, Edwin D. Morgan Papers; Duncan C. Niven to Fillmore, August 13, Fillmore Papers, SUNY; James Walker to Chase, September 22, Chase Papers, LC.

82. Harrison Smith to Seward, October 27, Seward Papers, UR; S. P. Allen to Morgan, July 31, Edwin D. Morgan Papers.

a Catholic service. As for their marriage by a Catholic priest, which Schuyler Colfax contended more than anything else gave "color" to the charge, it was a civil ceremony, and the young lovers turned to a priest only after two Protestant clergymen, fearing Thomas Hart Benton's fury after he had forbidden the marriage, had refused to officiate.[83]

Initially, Republicans relied on counter-testimony from prominent men who personally knew the candidate to discredit these stories and affidavits. Henry Raymond of the New York *Times* authored a denial of the report, as did Henry Ward Beecher, who denounced the accusation as "a lie." A group of Protestant ministers in New York City offered similar testimony after an interview with the candidate.[84] In addition, Colfax published the baptism records for Frémont's children, and he urged Blair to prepare an affidavit based on his own knowledge and especially to obtain a statement from Benton as to the Republican nominee's faith. The attacks continued, however, and finally the Republican state central committee in New York authorized the preparation of a tract setting forth the evidence that Frémont was not a Catholic. National party chairman Edwin D. Morgan, who noted that earlier many Republican leaders wished to ignore the issue, now decided that the document should be issued as quickly as possible, agreeing that "it has been too long delayed."[85] Eventually, a number of pamphlets on both sides of the controversy appeared. Against his better judgment, Greeley capitulated to the continuing clamor and announced that there were two Frémonts, one Protestant and one Catholic, sufficiently similar in appearance and career to be confused! With great glee, Know Nothing journals heaped ridicule on Greeley's "fishy" Frémont, and before long the *Tribune*'s editor was anxious to drop the whole matter.

Frémont's advisers were not of one mind over whether he should respond personally to the Catholic indictment. Some, including the candidate, considered it undignified to answer the charge, and they recognized correctly that no letter, however carefully phrased, would end the attacks. Instead, a public statement would only increase the demand for still further denials. "If Fremont should deny it over his own signature," Morgan maintained, the *Express* "would make some other charge & expect him to deny that, and so on without limit."[86] Other party leaders, however, including Schuyler Colfax, Simon Cameron, and Thurlow Weed, urged that a letter be drafted for Frémont to release. "These Catholic reports must be extinguished," Colfax warned Blair, "or we shall lose Pa, N.J., Inda., Conn. & the Lord knows how many more States." To John Bigelow, one of the Republican campaign directors, the Indiana congressman reported that of "the hundreds of letters" he received from the Northwest, "scarcely any omits a reference to the fact that the Catholic story injures us materially, both in keeping men in the Fillmore ranks who ought to be with us, & in cooling many of our own friends who

---

83. Colfax to Francis P. Blair, Sr., July 17, Francis P. Blair, Sr., to Charles Albright, n.d. [1856], August 11, Jessie Frémont to Elizabeth Blair Lee, July 23, August 14, letter signed J. G. Nelson, clipping, Blair-Lee Papers; Jessie Frémont to Dr. Robertson, June 30, Thomas Hart Benton Papers, Missouri Historical Society; New York *Evening Post*, July 8, 10, 22, August 6, September 2, 5, 6.

84. For testimonials see the *Ashtabula Sentinel*, October 2 (Protestant clergy); New York *Evening Post*, August 6 (Henry J. Raymond), September 2 (Henry Ward Beecher).

85. Edwin D. Morgan to Allen Munroe, October 9 (copy) (quotation), Edwin Barber Morgan to Edwin D. Morgan, September 30, Minutes, Republican State Central Committee, October 2, Edwin D. Morgan Papers.

86. Morgan to S. P. Allen, August 6, Morgan to Thomas B. Carroll, July 30 (quotation) (copies), Edwin D. Morgan Papers; John C. Frémont, MS Memoirs, 199–200, Frémont Papers; Francis P. Blair, Sr., to Charles J. Albright, August 11, Blair-Lee Papers. The New York *Evening Post*, August 6, editorialized against Frémont's issuing any letter.

fear from Col. F's silence & the cloud of rumors on the subject in K.N. papers, that there may be some truth in it.'' Prompted by Thaddeus Stevens, Truman Smith lobbied for an official denial from the candidate himself, claiming that such a statement was absolutely essential for carrying Pennsylvania.[87]

With information supplied by Jessie Frémont, Blair drafted a letter for the colonel to release; this letter attempted to tread the thin line between denying the charge and sanctioning any religious test for office. Despite writing the candidate's prospective letter, Blair still believed that none should be issued, since he assumed naively that few who were sincere countenanced the allegation. Finally, a conference of leading Republican managers convened in the Astor House in New York City. Apparently, there was sharp disagreement, but those present finally decided that Frémont would not issue a letter affirming his Protestantism.[88]

This decision was a mistake. Undoubtedly, no denial, however phrased, would have silenced the nativist press but, as the failure of all other strategies demonstrated, only an unequivocal statement by Frémont had any chance of being effective with voters who were otherwise sympathetic to the party. The concerns of Blair and Greeley about antagonizing the Catholic vote were, as critics noted, pointless. Catholics would overwhelmingly vote for Buchanan in any event, and offending them could not damage the Republican cause. The argument that it would be humiliating for Frémont to make a public profession of his religious belief was also flawed, since in private interviews for weeks the candidate had done exactly that. Greeley, who was obviously irritated by the situation, exaggerated only slightly when he related that in private conversations Frémont had been required to deny that he was a Catholic ''at least three times per day for the last three months.''[89] Politicians had an ingrained suspicion of letters from presidential candidates, however, and as a result Republicans were unable to deal successfully with the religious question. As the campaign drew to a close, large numbers of northern voters remained convinced that the Republican nominee was a Catholic, or at least they were not completely persuaded otherwise. A Methodist minister in Connecticut, after voting for Frémont, confessed that he had ''misgivings,'' for ''I am not fully satisfied that he is not a Catholic.'' Then, as if to emphasize his anxiety, he added, *''I fear he is a Catholic.''* With ample cause, the New York *Mirror* asserted at the end of the campaign that Frémont's supposed Romanism was the most damaging charge brought against him. ''Tens of thousands of the more bigoted Protestants,'' it noted, ''persist in the belief, after all denials, that Col Fremont is a little fishy on the Catholic question.''[90]

Frémont's predicament was not without irony. His nativist sympathies were sufficiently pronounced that in 1855 certain politicians had approached him about seeking a Know Nothing nomination, yet the issue that hurt him most in the 1856 election was the misconception that he was a Catholic. At the same time, he enjoyed an entirely

---

87. Colfax to Francis P. Blair, Sr., August 15, Blair-Lee Papers; Truman Smith to Thaddeus Stevens, August 14, *Private*, Stevens Papers; Greeley to Simon Cameron, September 15, Cameron Papers, LC; Colfax to John Bigelow, August 29, John Bigelow Papers, NYPL; E. Dodd to Weed, September 8, Weed Papers, UR.

88. [Francis P. Blair, Sr.] to Colfax, August 16 (2 drafts), Blair-Lee Papers. Blair's undated draft letter, which is incomplete, is in the Blair-Lee Papers. Although he preferred not to get involved in a public controversy, Frémont was willing to do whatever his advisers concluded was best. Truman Smith to Thaddeus Stevens, August 14, *Private*, Stevens Papers.

89. Greeley to Cameron, September 15, Cameron Papers, LC.

90. Horatio Nelson Weed Diary, November 4, Yale University; New York *Mirror* quoted in Washington *Evening Star*, November 3; E. C. Delavan to Hiram Barney, November 11, Barney Papers.

undeserved reputation as a strong antislavery man, despite his extremely limited record on the slavery issue. Seward saw another irony as well. With a certain self-satisfaction, he noted that "Fremont, who was preferred over me because I was not a bigoted Protestant, is nearly convicted of being a Catholic."[91]

The difficulty Republicans encountered in the controversy over Frémont's religion provided forceful evidence, if any were needed, that anti-Catholicism did not disappear abruptly from American politics in 1856, and that the Sumner and Kansas outrages, if they muted the intensity of religious antagonisms, failed to eradicate them from the political system. Fear and hatred of Catholics continued to motivate many voters, and, as a number of observers commented in 1856, a widespread belief that a presidential candidate was tainted with Catholicism was politically fatal (and would be for more than a century thereafter).

V

Parties that wish to attain national power necessarily phrase their appeal in broad terms, and the early Republican party was no exception. Through its emphasis on the Slave Power and its defense of free labor, the party's ideology, which came together in the 1856 presidential campaign, drew upon the two most important traditions of American politics, republicanism and liberalism. At the same time, it incorporated aspects of the Protestant ethic and exploited ethnoreligous tensions in northern society, particularly the nation's deeply rooted heritage of anti-Catholicism, to project an image of middle-class Protestant respectability. As a blatantly sectional organization, the Republican party had no strength in the South. In the North, on the other hand, except for Catholic immigrants who found little in the party's persuasion to appeal to them, the Republican program was sufficiently inclusive to attract wide support.

A mixture of hope and fear, the ideology of the Republican party juxtaposed a celebration of the blessings of free labor and republicanism with a shrill warning of the dangers that the Slave Power and the Catholic church posed to these cherished American ideals. Like many political ideologies, it looked both forward and backward, lauding the forces of enterprise, innovation, and economic development while simultaneously endorsing certain anachronistic assumptions of republicanism and clinging to a dream of a society that was already vanishing. Yet the emphasis in Republican thought was on the negative rather than the positive, on what the party opposed instead of what it favored. In arousing mass emotions, Republicans stimulated and focused the fears and anxieties of northerners much more than they addressed their hopes. At the heart of the party's ideology was the belief that the Slave Power threatened the existence of republicanism. The Republic confronted its most serious challenge since independence, Republicans cried, and unless disarmed, the slavocracy would soon be so entrenched in power that its rule would be permanent. Adding force to the Republican vision of this crisis was the idea that the continued political ascendancy of slaveholders would be fatal to the liberties of northern white men. The result was a powerful and effective appeal that for the first time mobilized large numbers of northerners beneath the Republican banner.

An editorial in the Cincinnati *Commercial*, published on the eve of the 1856 election, captured the prevailing thrust of the ideology of the Republican party. Blended in this

---

91. Seward to Frances A. Seward, August 17, Seward, *Seward*, v. 2, 287.

final plea were several basic Republican themes intended to rally the voters, but in confronting its readers with the dreaded image of servile dependence, the editorial's dominant tone was one of haunting fear. The present contest, it declared, was

> between those who hold that labor and laboring men are honorable . . . and those who contend that the proper condition of the laboring classes is that of servitude—that the rich should own the poor. . . . What intelligent man, who toils with his own hands, can vote to sustain the overbearing oligarchy that holds such shameful sentiments, and seeks now to consolidate, extend and perpetuate its baleful power . . . ? The question is not, whether the negroes shall be set free . . . but whether poor white men are to be kept out of territories of the United States, and trodden down and shackled in servitude.[92]

Fueled by these emotions, the Republican party's first presidential campaign became in the eyes of its participants a crusade to save freedom.

---

92. Cincinnati *Commercial*, November 3.

12

The Frémont Campaign

The country had seen nothing like it since 1840. The 1856 presidential campaign swept northerners into a state of almost delirious excitement. "The coming campaign promises to be as excited and active as any Presidential Election we have had," the Republican national chairman wrote as the contest opened.[1] Party veterans, who had experienced the rousing exuberance of the legendary Log Cabin campaign, believed that the 1856 contest approached, perhaps even matched, the popular fervor for which 1840 was justly famous. "You never Saw so much Enthusiasms in the People," one of William H. Seward's correspondents asserted typically. Even those normally immune were pulled irresistibly into the vortex of national politics. The usually apolitical Henry Wadsworth Longfellow conceded that "it is difficult to sit still with such excitement in the air."[2]

In making comparisons with 1840, observers differed as to whether the level of mass involvement equaled that of "Tippecanoe and Tyler Too," but all agreed that the 1856 contest exhibited a much more serious tone than its predecessor. Beneath the layer of boisterous excitement typical of antebellum politics lay the realization that serious consequences hung in the balance. "There never has been such enthusiasm manifested since 1840, & then it was much more superficial," a Republican in upstate New York testified. He was especially impressed that almost half those in attendance at Frémont meetings were women. After stumping the state, a veteran Indiana politician and former Whig congressman reported that "Men, Women & Children all seemed to be out, with a kind of fervor, I have never witnessed before in six Pres. Elections in which I have taken an active part. . . . In '40, all was jubilant [*sic*]—Now there is little effervescence—but a *solemn earnestness* that is almost painful." George W. Julian, who had spent the last two years grousing about political affairs, found himself caught up by the popular feeling.

Note: Unless otherwise indicated, the year for newspaper and manuscript citations in this chapter is 1856.

1. Edwin D. Morgan to Cornelius Cole, July 10, Cornelius Cole Papers, University of California, Los Angeles.

2. John B. Dill to William H. Seward, July 5, Seward Papers, UR; Ezra Lincoln to William Schouler, June 30, Schouler Papers; Henry Wadsworth Longfellow quoted in Nevins, *Ordeal of the Union*, v. 2, 487.

No previous presidential contest displayed such a "pervading moral enthusiasm," he remembered. "The canvass had no parallel in the history of American politics."[3]

I

The wild enthusiasm generated by the 1856 Republican campaign was not enough to propel the party to victory, and in some ways it was a decided handicap. According to a Republican editor in Boston, camp followers and zealous volunteers were a particular nuisance in the party's first national campaign; he complained that their involvement "resulted in something like anarchy."[4] The establishment of an efficient, smooth-functioning organization at both the state and national levels was essential, but welding diverse state organizations into a coherent national organization was not easy. The conduct of the party's campaign in each state was largely the province of the state central committee and its affiliated local and county committees. Jealously guarding their prerogatives, state committees resisted any central direction, and thus the Republican organization was at best a loose federation. Any effective organizational structure would necessarily be imposed from the top.

Those Republicans who wanted some national direction given to the party's presidential campaign were forced to look elsewhere than to the head of the ticket. John C. Frémont's role in the conduct of the campaign, as befitted his talents, was negligible. His political activity amounted to receiving callers of political note and making short, innocuous speeches to delegations that visited him. He wrote no public letters and made no important statements during the campaign. The Pennsylvania Republican leader Alexander McClure remembered that when he called on Frémont merely to pay his respects, the candidate, under orders to say nothing, "was so extremely cautious that he evaded the most ordinary expressions relating to the conduct and prospects of the battle."[5] In fact, a committee entrusted with the task of preventing any gaffes by the candidate closely supervised and circumscribed Frémont's activities. Its members included Jessie Frémont, John Bigelow of the *Evening Post*, who wrote a campaign biography with her assistance, and Isaac Sherman and Charles James, two self-seeking wirepullers associated with Nathaniel Banks. Together they carefully guarded the inner sanctum. The presence around Frémont of such men as James stirred Gideon Welles's deepest distrust. The candidate's personal headquarters were at 34 Broadway in the office of John Howard, his California business manager, but the Frémont home at 56 West Ninth Street soon became a branch office, mail station, press clipping bureau, and buffet lunchroom. In all this activity the candidate took little part. He spent his days fencing, riding, and exercising while others directed

3. Seth M. Gates to Charles Francis Adams, September 5 (quotation), Adams Family Papers; Samuel W. Parker to Seward, July 4 (quotation), Seward Papers, UR; George W. Julian, *Political Recollections*, 152–54. On his return from a political speaking tour, Charles A. Dana confessed that he was "astonished at the depth and ardor of the popular sentiment" and contended that "for genuine inspiration 1840 couldn't hold a candle." Dana to James Shepherd Pike, July 24, Pike Papers, UMe.

4. Congdon, *Reminiscences*, 213; Lindley Smyth to Morgan, October 25, Edwin D. Morgan Papers [throughout this chapter, all citations of the Morgan Papers refer to this collection]. Henry B. Stanton described party headquarters in New York City as plagued by "a set of political loafers" who apparently intended to carry the election by shouting "alls well!," "guzzling champagne," and "telling large yarns." Stanton to Horace Greeley, August 5, Greeley Papers, NYPL.

5. McClure, *Our Presidents*, 147–48; John C. Frémont to James Watson Webb, July 3, Webb Papers; James R. Thompson to Millard Fillmore, September 17, Fillmore Papers, SUNY.

affairs. Francis P. Blair and Banks were his closest advisers, but because of Banks's absence in Washington, Blair took the most active role in managing the campaign. So thoroughly isolated was Frémont from the conduct of the campaign that Jessie Frémont and her associates read and censored his mail and even the daily newspapers, and she and Bigelow answered the incoming correspondence.[6]

A disinterested observer might well question the capacity of a man to fill the nation's highest office who could not be trusted to answer his mail and was so sensitive to personal abuse that newspapers had to be screened beforehand. Jessie Benton Frémont's campaign associates, on the other hand, held in high regard her undeniable political ability. She could, as Bigelow remarked, "look into the political cauldron when it was boiling without losing . . . [her] head." Never before had the wife of a presidential candidate participated so actively in a national campaign. The judgment of one Ohio Republican that she "would have been the better candidate" was sound.[7] Political customs denied Jessie Frémont the opportunity to develop her political talents to anywhere near their potential, yet even so she was able to leave her mark on the popular imagination. Banners in Republican processions invariably contained references to the gifted daughter of Thomas Hart Benton.

II

Frémont's ineptitude left a leadership void that the national committee did not entirely fill. Under Edwin D. Morgan's direction, its efforts were concentrated on three principal fields: fund-raising, distribution of documents, and scheduling of speakers. Direction of the committee's affairs rested within a narrow circle. As national chairman, Morgan undertook most of the day-to-day supervision at Republican headquarters in the Trinity Building. Working closely with him was William C. Chace of Rhode Island, the national secretary, and for counsel and advice Morgan drew on Gideon Welles, Connecticut's national committeeman. Welles was a former Democrat, and thus his active participation alleviated fears that ex-Whigs, exclusively, were running the campaign. Together these three men acted as an executive committee, handling problems as they arose without formally conferring with the full membership. Joshua R. Giddings's assumption that New York politicians would henceforth have to consult western party leaders proved incorrect. Morgan's prominent role in the daily operations, the fact that fund-raising focused on Wall Street, and the city's proximity to Philadelphia, where the committee's efforts were mainly directed, inevitably meant that the Republican campaign would be conducted from New York City.[8]

---

6. John C. Frémont, MS Memoirs, 205, Frémont Papers; Elizabeth Benton Frémont, *Recollections*, 76–79; Catherine C. Phillips, *Jessie Benton Frémont* (San Francisco, 1935), 204; Beale, ed., *Welles Diary*, v. 2, 42. Gideon Welles had good reason for uneasiness. For evidence of a scheme by Charles James and Israel Andrews to line their pockets with Maine campaign funds, see Alexander H. Greene to Thurlow Weed, August 26, 27, Weed Papers, UR; Greene to Morgan, August 26 (Private), August 30, Morgan Papers.

7. Frémont, MS Memoirs, 205, Frémont Papers; Charles Reemelin, *Life of Charles Reemelin* (Cincinnati, 1892), 131; William Barnes, *The Origin and Early History of the Republican Party* (Albany, 1906), 34; Ryland Fletcher to Justin S. Morrill, July 8, Morrill Papers, LC.

8. The day-to-day functioning of the campaign is detailed in Morgan's outgoing correspondence and in the letters he received from Welles. John Z. Goodrich, Massachusetts' committeeman, played a major role in the committee's fund-raising activities (to be discussed below), and other members, such as Norman B. Judd, figured prominently in the campaign in their own states, but national policy decisions were largely the province of party leaders separate from the committee.

Policy decisions concerning the Republicans' first national campaign fell substantially to men outside the national committee. A loose, informal campaign structure evolved in which the committee served as a clearinghouse for political intelligence from the various states and handled the official correspondence. Critical decisions, however, were made by a larger, less formal group of seasoned party managers, which included, besides Morgan and Welles, Thurlow Weed, Blair, Banks, Truman Smith, Preston King, Simon Cameron, Schuyler Colfax, and Bigelow. Of this inner circle, only Colfax came from a western state, but otherwise all important party factions were represented. Weed, Morgan, Smith, and Colfax were former Whigs, while the others were ex-Democrats. In addition, Banks, Cameron, and Colfax had been Know Nothings, while Blair, King, and Bigelow were erstwhile Free Soilers. Membership in this steering committee, which met as crises arose, was not rigid, and on occasion a wider selection of party leaders came together to reach some collective decision.

Members of this policy-making group spent the early weeks of the summer sifting political intelligence in order to formulate a sound campaign strategy. Frémont seemed certain to carry six states: Ohio, Wisconsin, and Michigan, where the party had already triumphed; and Vermont, Iowa, and New Hampshire, where the various anti-Democratic factions, including the vast majority of Know Nothings, had fused in the Republican party. Republican managers were also moderately confident of New York and Maine, even though the party had yet to carry either state. In Maine the Republicans fielded an unusually strong state ticket, while, in spite of the reunion of the Hards and the Softs in New York, the continuing erosion of the Know Nothings' electoral base and the defection of a number of Soft leaders to the Republican cause seemed to promise victory. The outcome in Massachusetts and Rhode Island hinged on the cooperation of the North American party. In both states, if the Frémont forces united on a common electoral ticket, victory was assured. That left six northern states that most political analysts put in the doubtful column: Connecticut, New Jersey, Pennsylvania, Indiana, Illinois, and California.[9]

To be victorious, Republicans, in addition to winning all the states they considered reasonably safe, had to carry all the closely contested states except Pennsylvania, or carry Pennsylvania plus two or three (depending on the combination) additional ones that were doubtful.[10] The national committee viewed the party's chances in California as hopeless; Republican leaders in the Far West were told to do the best they could without any aid from national headquarters.[11] The almost certain loss of California meant that the only feasible strategy was to gamble everything on carrying Pennsylvania. This decision made sense from a national perspective, since loss of Pennsylvania meant loss of the election. Still, the national committee's strategy definitely hurt the Republican campaign in Connecticut, Indiana, and Illinois, states where the party had organized only recently

---

9. Every politician had his own list, and prospects in some states ebbed and flowed as the campaign progressed. Blessed with hindsight, historians usually list as doubtful only the states Frémont failed to carry in the North. Most observers, however, viewed Connecticut as questionable, and Maine was uncertain for the party before the state election in September. Several Democrats, including Franklin Pierce, also held out hopes for New Hampshire until the very end, and some doubt existed about New York as well.

10. In 1856, of the 296 electoral votes in the Electoral College, northern states cast 176. Assuming that the Republicans carried all the free states that they were reasonably confident of, they had to win an additional 41 electoral votes by some appropriate combination of Pennsylvania (27), Indiana (13), Illinois (11), New Jersey (7), Connecticut (6), and California (4).

11. Morgan to E. D. Williams, September 19, *Confidential*, Morgan to E. B. Crocker, July 19 (copies), Morgan Papers.

(indeed, in Indiana and Illinois it had never contested a state election), and where state party leaders now faced the challenge of carrying their state virtually without outside aid.

Weed's close ties to Morgan, and Blair's and Bigelow's to Welles, ensured that the larger policy group generally worked in conjunction with the national committee. Nevertheless, the failure to impose a more rigid command structure weakened the party's efforts, for the resulting organization did not function particularly well. It encouraged individual action where coordination was imperative, and at times it led to duplication of activity and unclear designation of authority. Fund-raising was a case in point. In Boston, where the party made a concerted effort to collect contributions, the drive was managed by John Z. Goodrich and George F. Morey, who until very late in the contest operated independently of the national committee, not only in raising funds but in dispensing them. Distribution of documents did not proceed smoothly either. Morgan and others at headquarters tried to oversee this aspect of the campaign, but in order for the party to take advantage of the franking privilege, documents were mailed from Washington under the auspices of the Republican Association. In addition to the inevitable confusion arising from this division of authority, several organizers complained that congressmen did not work closely enough with the committee.[12]

The national committee also experienced problems with its speakers' bureau, which Morgan put under the supervision of Henry B. Stanton, a former New York Democrat.[13] Stanton directed most of his attention to Pennsylvania, but he tried to recruit speakers for other states, particularly doubtful ones, when requested. His efforts produced mixed results. Although he kept a number of men on the stump, he was unable to fill all requests, even from critical states. Illinois, for example, was left largely to its own resources as far as speakers were concerned. Stanton also had trouble getting skillful orators, and he maintained somewhat defensively that the very poorest were "a good deal better (considering the barrenness of the field) than nobody." According to Morgan, some of those sent out under the auspices of the national committee were impervious to instructions and traveled where they pleased.[14] Complaints from state politicians about the allocation of funds and speakers were endemic to any national campaign, as similar protests directed to John W. Forney and those in charge of Buchanan's campaign attest. Still, the criticism of the national committee by some Republicans, particularly in the western states, was legitimate. New York received more top speakers than it warranted, while few were sent to Indiana and Illinois, both closely contested states.[15]

These organizational problems persisted until election day. At the beginning of the

---

12. FitzHenry Warren to Nathaniel P. Banks, Jr., August 14, Banks Papers, LC; Lewis Clephane to Morgan, September 8, Edward Dodd to Morgan, June 26, H. B. Haswell to Morgan, October 9, Morgan Papers; Morgan to Thomas H. Dudley, October 11, Dudley Papers; Henry C. Carey to George G. Fogg, September 14, [1860], George G. Fogg Papers, NHHS. For the difficulties over the Boston funds, see Goodrich's and George F. Morey's correspondence with Morgan, September-November.

13. Morgan to Henry B. Stanton, July 18, August 12, Morgan to Charles Gibbons, July 17 (copies), Morgan Papers; William Chace to Welles, July 17, Welles Papers, LC. Morgan refused to interfere with Stanton's operations. Morgan to William A. Sackett, August 19 (copy), Morgan Papers.

14. Henry B. Stanton to Greeley, August 5, Greeley Papers, NYPL; Morgan to G. G. Cornell, October 8, Morgan to Israel Harris, September 8, Morgan to O. J. Bundy et al., September 8, Morgan Papers.

15. Elihu B. Washburne to John P. Hale, October 5, Hale Papers, NHHS; Judd to Morgan, September 18, Weed Papers, UR; Morgan to Weed, October 4, Morgan to Welles, October 8, *Private*, Morgan to Samuel Wilkeson, October 4 (copies), E. W. Leavenworth to Morgan, October 24, Morgan Papers; C. W. Elliott to Robert Carter, September 22, Carter Papers; Greeley to Washburne, September 26, Elihu B. Washburne Papers, LC.

campaign, one of Banks's associates complained that "the National Committee are scattered, silent and indifferent. Can you conceive of such folly?" The situation did not improve immediately. It took Morgan and William Chace, neither of whom devoted their full attention to the work, several months to get the party's records in any order. As late as September Welles reported that the committee's business was conducted without energy, system, or application. "If we carry this election," Charles A. Dana contended with only slight hyperbole, "it will be in spite of the most defective organization & smallest resources with which any party ever went into a contest."[16]

As Dana's reference to finances indicated, the national committee also experienced difficulty in obtaining money. One of the committee's most important functions was to raise an ample campaign chest.[17] As he looked back on the Frémont campaign, Thurlow Weed reflected, "We suppose it was generally understood that party organizations cost money, and that Presidential elections, especially are expensive." Welles put it somewhat differently and more to the point: "Money is potent in politics, and will command some services that cannot be otherwise secured."[18] The national committee delegated to state organizations the task of raising funds for their own campaigns. Morgan intended to collect a separate national fund to be used selectively in battleground states. In August, at a meeting of the full committee in New York, he outlined an ambitious program to raise $50,000 for Pennsylvania and "as much more as is necessary for any western State or States."[19]

Wild claims about the effectiveness of the Republican financial juggernaut were bandied about during the campaign. Alexander H. Stephens, normally a sober political calculator, asserted that the Republicans had by the end of August spent $500,000 on Pennsylvania alone. In reality, the entire party budget, including all state organizations as well as the national committee, did not approach that figure. At the time Stephens made his statement, Morgan reported that the national commitee had no funds at all in its treasury. The amount raised by the state committees is unknown, but the figures involved were certainly insubstantial. In Illinois, for example, a populous state with an economically booming metropolis in which the party was strong, the Republican state central committee established a goal of raising $15,000. Whether they collected even this modest sum is unclear.[20] At the close of the contest, William M. Chace, who had never before been involved with the management of a presidential campaign, expressed amazement over how small the sums received and dispensed by the national committee actually were.[21]

The national committee concentrated its fund-raising in two northern financial centers, New York and Boston (Philadelphia, which had in the past contributed heavily to the Whig party, was barren soil for Republicanism). Republican fund-raisers received a cool response from the business communities in these cities, since many businessmen who

---

16. "Wales" [Israel D. Andrews] to Banks, July 21, *Private*, Banks Papers, LC; Welles to [William Chace], September 5 (copy), Welles Papers, LC; Charles A. Dana to Carey, June 14, *Private*, Carey Papers.

17. The analysis that follows relies in part on James A. Rawley's careful study, "Financing the Frémont Campaign," *Pennsylvania Magazine of History and Biography*, v. 75 (January, 1951), 25–35. Close scrutiny of the financial records in the Morgan Papers substantiates Rawley's analysis.

18. Albany *Evening Journal*, September 21, 1861, quoted in Rawley, "Financing the Frémont Campaign," 25; Welles to Morgan, September 15, Morgan Papers.

19. Morgan to Weed, August 13, Weed Papers, UR.

20. Alexander H. Stephens to [Linton Stephens?], August 31, Johnston and Browne, *Stephens*, 316; Morgan to Welles, August 27, Welles Papers, LC; Morgan to James W. Nye, August 27 (copy), Morgan Papers; Judd to Morgan, September 18, Weed Papers, UR.

21. William Chace to Morgan, October 26, Morgan Papers.

were former Whig contributors considered the party a radical organization that threatened the Union and hence refused to render financial assistance. The Democrats and Americans had "almost all" the money, Charles A. Dana reported from New York City. "The rich men here, who used to give to the Whigs, are now for Fillmore and Buchanan." Acknowledging that he was having difficulty raising money, Morgan explained that "our monied men are more unwilling to contribute than I have ever known them."[22] Assessments on officeholders in the few states where the government was in Republican hands brought in money for state organizations but none for the national committee.

Morgan and his associates did not commence fund-raising until August. At that point Morgan had received a mere $100, while the Democrats had already amassed $4,000. By September 2, the Republican treasury contained $3,485, still less than the Democrats had a month earlier. Well could Horace Greeley complain to James Shepherd Pike that the Republicans in New York City "have not one dollar where the Fillmoreans and Buchaniers have ten each." He pronounced Pennsylvania and New Jersey, two of the party's target states, "utterly miserable, so far as money is concerned." While contributions increased after the Maine state election, Republicans still lagged behind the Democrats, and the setbacks in the October elections further undermined their fund-raising activities.[23] In the remaining three weeks until the presidential election, some money funneled in to party headquarters, but not nearly enough to meet the demand from Pennsylvania, let alone other states. Eventually, in a desperate attempt to secure the necessary funds, Republicans established a contingency fund of $80,000 payable only if Frémont were elected. By the end of the campaign, excluding this contingency fund, the national committee had raised only $45,966.32. Goodrich and Morey collected some additional money in Boston not included in this figure, but the amount was not large.[24]

The national committee raised most of its money in New York City from individual contributors and spent almost all of it in Pennsylvania. Over two-thirds of the committee's funds, at least $30,635, went to that state. Most states received no money at all from national headquarters, including the critical state of Indiana. Illinois and New Jersey, two other doubtful states, received $700 and $365 respectively, and New Hampshire, inexplicably, was given $400. Excluding Pennsylvania, the largest amount, $2,700, went to Maine, where the party was particularly anxious to begin its campaign with a victory. In retrospect, the Republican party did quite well given its severely limited financial resources. The situation varied from state to state, but almost everywhere Republicans were at a financial disadvantage compared to their opponents.

The Democratic national committee, in comparison, raised a much larger war chest and

22. Charles A. Dana to Carey, June 14, *Private*, Carey Papers; Morgan to Goodrich, September 5, *Private*, Morgan to E. P. Sherman, September 12, Morgan to Lewis Clephane, September 12, Private (copies), Moses Grinnell to Morgan, October 4, Morgan Papers. One month before the Pennsylvania state election Carey disclosed that Republicans had raised only $2,500 in Philadelphia. Carey to George Morey, September 12 (copy), Carey Papers.

23. Greeley to Pike, August 6, Pike Papers, UMe; Morgan to Goodrich, October 15 (copy), Goodrich to Morgan, October 21, Morgan Papers; Rawley, "Financing the Frémont Campaign," 28–33.

24. Morey to Morgan, September 21, 1860, *Private*, Morgan Papers. The collection and dispersal of the contingency fund is fully documented in the Morgan Papers. The fund could be used principally in two ways: to encourage party workers by providing rewards to be paid only in the event of victory, and to get men to advance money in hopes of receiving a larger sum in repayment should Frémont win. See A. Rood to Carey, October 24, Carey Papers.

easily outspent their Republican counterpart, thanks principally to John Slidell's successful efforts on Wall Street. Taking advantage of his close ties to the New York commercial community, Slidell, assisted ably by Augustus Schell, collected a fund, later made notorious by the Covode Committee, that amounted to between $30,000 and $40,000. How much the Democrats spent in Pennsylvania is unknown, but George Plitt, the Democratic campaign treasurer in that state, later estimated his expenditures at $70,000. By the time of the October election, Morgan's account book listed contributions of less than $27,000. An exact comparison of the expenditures of the two national committees is impossible, but Thurlow Weed, who should have known, placed the Democrats' advantage at $50,000. Weed's figure suggests that the Democratic national committee probably spent about twice as much as the Republican.[25]

III

In the crucial opening stages of the campaign, Republican managers were unable to devote full time to eliminating these organizational shortcomings, despite their important bearing on the outcome of the election. They directed much of their attention instead to resolving the imbroglio over the vice-presidency, which they considered their most serious immediate problem. Consultations between Republicans and North Americans began in New York and in Washington as soon as the two June conventions adjourned, but little progress was made initially toward breaking the deadlock.[26] The struggle over the vice-presidency, which Welles termed "the most unimportant office in the country," symbolized a more basic conflict between the nativists and the Republicans.[27] It represented the final phase of the drive by the North Americans to gain separate recognition in the Republican party.

Upset by rumors that William Dayton was to be withdrawn, several prominent western Republicans protested to Morgan against any alteration of the national ticket. Citing the action of the Philadelphia convention, they opposed recognition of the North Americans as a separate body, and they argued that disastrous consequences would result if Dayton were displaced. The masses cared nothing about this silly quarrel, insisted A. P. Stone, Ohio's state party chairman. He was confident that for all their bluster, the North Americans would join the Republicans, for "there is no other place for them to go."[28] Morgan denied that steps were under way to alter the national ticket, or that the national committee had any power to take such action. "The Philadelphia Convention settled those questions, and adjourned and our duty is plain, to show no signs of vacillation," he told Colfax. At the same time, the national chairman confessed that the vice-presidential question was an "embarrassment," and although he expected it to be settled eventually, so far "the precise way, of doing it does not present itself."[29]

25. Rawley, "Financing the Frémont Campaign," 25, 29–30, 33; Nichols, *Disruption of American Democracy*, 45–47; *House Report*, No. 648, 36 Cong., 1st sess., 472–74, 548–50. The Samuel L. M. Barlow Papers, HEH, document Democratic fund-raising activities in New York City in 1856.

26. S. M. Allen to Banks, June 25 [?], Banks Papers, LC; New York *Herald*, June 30; Seward to Frances A. Seward, July 6, Seward, *Seward*, v. 2, 282; Isaac M. Tucker to Morgan, July 26, Morgan Papers.

27. Welles to James T. Babcock, July 23, Gideon Welles Papers, ChicHS; James M. Bunce to Morgan, June 28, Morgan Papers.

28. A. P. Stone to Morgan, July 12, Joshua R. Giddings to Morgan, July 1, *Private*, Schuyler Colfax to Morgan, July 8, Morgan Papers.

29. Morgan to Schuyler Colfax, July 10, Private, Schuyler Colfax Papers, IndU; Morgan to Welles, June

The North Americans, on the other hand, were not ready to concede defeat. Seething over their treatment at Philadelphia and remembering informal Republican promises that Dayton would be withdrawn, the North American national committee, acting through its chairman, Francis H. Ruggles, sent a letter to Morgan demanding that the Republicans reach a decision on the vice-presidency within twenty-four hours. Gravely offended by its tone and angered by its presumptuousness, Morgan ignored the letter, explaining to Welles that "*any* answer would have been unsatisfactory, where so much incorrectness was assumed." Despite the denials of the Republican chairman that he or any Republican had given pledges in this matter, Frémont had earlier led a committee of North Americans to understand that Dayton would be withdrawn, and apparently Republican leaders had whispered similar assurances to trusting North American delegates.[30]

Morgan's failure to answer Ruggles's letter deepened the resentment of North Americans and intensified their determination to force concessions from the Republicans. The action of the Massachusetts state council on July 1, and that of the Rhode Island and Connecticut state councils shortly thereafter, all of which endorsed Frémont and Johnston, heightened Republicans' concern. These endorsements of Johnston did not bode well for Frémont's chances in the three states, none of which the Republicans had ever carried. If the nativists persisted in running a separate electoral ticket, Connecticut would unquestionably be lost, and almost certainly Massachusetts and Rhode Island as well.

In this struggle, the Republicans enjoyed several advantages over their nativist rivals. First, as one Connecticut politician noted, the rank-and-file Know Nothings did not "care one straw about Dayton or Johnson [*sic*], but will have union for Fremont & Freedom."[31] The difficulty sprang entirely from the rival ambitions of various leaders. Second, Johnston's popularity was confined mainly to western Pennsylvania, and forcing the former Pennsylvania governor off the track seemingly did not threaten serious consequences to the fusion movement.[32] Third, Johnston himself was less concerned about remaining in the race than in receiving commitments on patronage should Frémont be elected. For more than a year the Pennsylvania leader had been maneuvering in the swift political currents for the greatest possible personal advantage. A year earlier, he had tested the presidential waters, and at the American convention in Philadelphia in February he tried to exact a promise of a cabinet post from Millard Fillmore's managers as the price for his support of the national ticket. Rebuffed, he thrust himself to the head of the northern bolt over Fillmore's nomination.[33] Republicans knew their man. No sooner had the New York convention adjourned than Russell Errett of the Pittsburgh *Gazette* sent word to Morgan that Johnston was really angling for a cabinet post. "The Ex Governor obviously wants to *sell out*," another Pittsburgh Republican disclosed, "but he has run his capital so low that he would be a poor speculation at any price." Errett believed that the North Americans were indifferent to Johnston's candidacy, but they wanted the bargaining power that recognition as a party would bring to them in the division of the

28, Morgan to Russell Errett, June 28 (quotation), Morgan to Giddings, July 2, Morgan to A. P. Stone, July 17, *Private* (copies), Morgan Papers.

30. Francis H. Ruggles to the Executive Committee of the Republican Party, June 30, Morgan Papers; Morgan to Welles, July 9, Welles Papers, LC; Morgan to James M. Bunce, June 30 (copy), Morgan Papers.

31. James M. Bunce to Morgan, August 1, Morgan Papers.

32. Errett to Morgan, June 21, 25, July 1, Morgan Papers; New York *Evening Post*, August 2; Jno. M. Kirkpatrick to Simon Cameron, August 28, Cameron Papers, HSDC.

33. John Pendleton Kennedy Diary, February 24, Kennedy Papers; Solomon G. Haven to Fillmore, March 2, Fillmore Papers, SUNY.

spoils. As for Johnston's cabinet ambitions, Errett observed diplomatically: "I would not be understood as advising any absolute pledge to that effect; but there is a delicate way of managing such things which I need but refer to."[34]

Whereas Johnston displayed a less than fixed determination to remain in the race, Dayton firmly resisted being forced off the ticket. He irritably advised Morgan that he had been nominated without any solicitation on his part, and that he was in the race "for good or evil, and there I propose to remain." Gentle hints directed at Dayton had no effect, nor did direct demands that he step aside. "A sense of self-respect; the weight of responsibility involved in such an act, as well as ordinary good faith towards the Repn Convention would forbid it," he insisted. Greeley announced "by authority" that the New Jersey leader would not withdraw and advised those going to see the Republican nominee on any such mission to save their carfare.[35]

With matters at a stalemate nationally, North American leaders decided to test their strength on the vice-presidential question in Connecticut, a state where the Know Nothings were particularly powerful compared to the Republicans. For the previous two years, thanks to talented leadership and a popular program, the American party had dominated Connecticut's politics. Arrogant and self-confident, the state's nativist leaders had no intention of taking a back seat to their adversaries in the Republican movement. The American state council met on July 10 and, after endorsing Frémont and Johnston, summoned a state convention for August 6 to select an electoral ticket. The convention call was directed to Americans and "all others opposed to the election of the nominees of the Cincinnati Convention, and to the principles" of the Democratic national platform. Noting that the Republicans commanded only 7,000 votes in the state compared to the Americans' 27,000, one nativist leader expressed the controlling sentiment at the state council when he declared, "The American party is the great dominant party in this State, and *should have precedent over the Republican party, and be allowed to call the Convention to nominate an electoral ticket.* If the Republicans do not like this," he continued, "let them put in nomination an extra ticket, and take responsibility."[36]

After some deliberation, Republicans decided to organize a separate convention. Gideon Welles drafted a call for a People's convention of all the friends of Frémont, also to meet in Hartford on August 6. He shaped the call, which was signed by 151 leading men, including some Americans, to be "attractive to all, gathering in men of every party, and creed, and sect, irrespective of antecedants, or present differences on other questions." It made no reference to the vice-presidency.[37] In providing for a convention that included all of Frémont's supporters, Connecticut Republicans had two goals: to carry

34. Errett to Morgan, June 21, July 1, Thomas Williams to Morgan, June 26, Morgan Papers. Welles saw some good in the fact that Johnston was the nominee and that he did not immediately decline. "If he were to do so now," the Connecticut leader wrote in late July, "there are certain impracticable Know Nothings who would immediately bring out a more objectionable man who would not decline." Welles to James F. Babcock, July 23, Welles Papers, ChicHS.

35. William Dayton to Morgan, June 30, Morgan Papers; Dayton to Morgan, August 15, *Private* (quotation), Welles Papers LC; Dayton to Israel Washburn, Jr., July 12, Israel Washburn, Jr., Papers, LC; Greeley to Thomas Williams, July 7, Burton Alva Konkle, *The Life and Speeches of Thomas Williams* (2 vols.: Philadelphia, 1905), v. 1, 299: New York *Tribune*, July 7.

36. Hartford *Courant*, August 2; Parmet, "Know-Nothings in Connecticut," 225–26.

37. Welles to Morgan, July 22, August 20, Morgan Papers; James F. Babcock to Welles, July 12, Welles Papers, LC; Welles to Babcock, July 23 (quotation), Welles Papers, ChicHS. A copy of the convention call is in the Welles Papers, ConnHS.

the state for Frémont, and to "emancipate ourselves and the public from the insolent and mischievous gang who control the American party and, through the party, the State." The Republicans' August 6 convention, one party member noted anxiously, "is a *crisis* in our Presidential campaign."[38]

Republicans viewed the struggle as one with "a mere clique of office holders" and alleged that "the great body of the Americans" had "no attachment to the Party, as such." Such assertions were too extreme, but James Bunce was essentially correct in his assessment that ordinary Frémont Americans cared nothing about the conflict between Dayton and Johnston.[39] Welles's only concern was that "impracticable men" would control the American convention and attempt to force Johnston down the throats of Republicans. As the date for the two conventions approached, he remained cautiously optimistic. "If we can well get over the 6 of August, we shall have pretty plain sailing thereafter."[40] The vice-presidential nomination had become a pawn in the struggle between leaders of both parties for political ascendancy in the state.

The two conventions that assembled in Hartford on August 6 were well attended—more than 500 delegates were present at the Republican gathering, and more than 400 at the American—but it was clear that the Republicans had the upper hand. The resolve of nativist leaders to force a showdown over control of the anti-Democratic forces melted in the face of the pervasive sentiment among the American delegates for union with the Republicans. One delegate reported that the masses were prepared to set the leaders aside if they persisted in opposing a merger with the Republicans; aware of the brewing revolt, American leaders reluctantly agreed to a joint electoral ticket. Welles assured Morgan that although the electors were unpledged on the vice-presidency, they would vote for Dayton, whereas this course would enable Americans to support Frémont heartily. Over the opposition of Nehemiah Sperry, the head of the Connecticut order, the American convention agreed to consolidate the two campaigns. "We virtually had control of both conventions," Welles boasted afterwards. "It has been a hard & laborious work for a few of us to get things into shape. We had to take the Americans from their leaders."[41]

One Republican leader too optimistically believed that a "cordial union" had been created at Hartford, while even the hardheaded Welles felt that the campaign was "going on harmoniously." The significance of developments in Connecticut was twofold. First, there was no longer any doubt that Johnston would withdraw. If the North Americans could not dominate the Republicans in Connecticut, where could they? Second, the state was now reasonably certain for Frémont. "You may I think safely take Connt. out of your list of doubtful States," a cheerful Republican notified Morgan the day after the two conventions adjourned.[42]

Nationally, matters with the North Americans now came to a head. The erosion of

---

38. [?] to Welles, July 14 (incomplete), Charles L. English to Welles, July 31, Welles Papers, LC.

39. James F. Babcock to Welles, July 12, Private (quotation), Welles to My Dear Sir [Morgan?], July 11 (copy), Welles Papers, LC; Charles L. English to Welles, July 31 (quotation), Welles Papers, LC; James M. Bunce to Morgan, August 1, Morgan Papers.

40. Welles to James F. Babcock, July 23, Welles Papers, ChicHS; Welles to Morgan, July 22 (quotation), Morgan Papers.

41. Charles L. English to Welles, [August-September], Welles Papers, LC; Welles to Morgan, August 20, Morgan Papers. For the proceedings of the two conventions, see the Hartford *Courant* and the Hartford *Times*, August 7.

42. Welles to Morgan, August 20, James M. Bunce to Morgan, August 7, Morgan Papers.

Johnston's support in Connecticut and also in Massachusetts, two states where the North American movement was especially strong, demonstrated that his candidacy was untenable. In early August, members of the North American executive committee tried a new strategy. They proposed that both Johnston and Dayton withdraw and a new convention, representing all the friends of Frémont, be held in September to select a vice-presidential candidate. Morgan summoned a meeting of the Republican executive committee to consider this demand, while intimating to North American leaders that it would be rejected. Some days earlier Weed, after sounding out Johnston, had reported that the Pennsylvanian was amenable to this proposal, but that he would not withdraw unless Dayton also did.[43] Republicans, however, had no interest in a new convention. To remove Dayton from the ticket would be a great embarrassment and a confession of weakness; nor did they wish to be associated in a convention with the North Americans or take any other action that smacked of an open alliance. Republicans were anxious for nativist support, but, with an eye on naturalized voters, they needed to avoid the appearance of having made any deals with the North Americans. The Republicans' inflexible rejection of any compromise took the North Americans aback. Two days after the collapse of their movement in Connecticut, before the Republican committee met, they withdrew their proposal for a new convention.[44]

In the meantime, the Republican national chairman wrote to Johnston and, expressing regret that the Philadelphia convention had not named an American for the second spot on the ticket, affirmed his willingness to exert his influence on behalf of all Frémont's supporters in the event of a Republican national victory. "The past we cannot recall, but, for the future something may be done." Morgan's veiled hint that Johnston and his friends would be fairly treated in patronage matters by a Frémont administration induced the North American vice-presidential nominee to promptly arrange a personal meeting with Frémont. Morgan pronounced the outcome of the meeting "satisfactory," and he informed Welles: "Though I know no promise was made to him, the Col said in case of his election he should give all his friends who participated in it, fair play."[45] Mollified, Johnston wrote a letter, dated August 29, to the North American committee declining the vice-presidential nomination. His letter was made public two weeks later. Perhaps as the final step in this elaborate dance, the Republican national committee paid $300 to Ruggles, the North American chairman, near the end of August, and $500 to Johnston in late October. The exact purpose of these payments was unspecified in the committee's financial records, although word filtered back to headquarters that Johnston was "satisfied."[46] As the campaign entered its final two months, the Frémont forces were at last united on a single national ticket. Fusion, belated and imperfect, had finally been achieved.

---

43. Francis H. Ruggles to Morgan, July 15, Morgan Papers; Morgan to Welles, August 8, Welles Papers, LC; Morgan to Dayton, August 8 (copy), Morgan to Weed, August 3 [8] (copy), Weed to Morgan, July 25, Morgan Papers; N. P. Sawyer to Ruggles, July 7, Nathaniel P. Banks, Jr., Papers, IllSHL.

44. Morgan to Welles, August 8, Welles Papers, LC; Morgan to Dayton, August 8 (copy), Morgan Papers.

45. Morgan to William Johnston, August 6, Confidential (copy), Johnston to Morgan, August 13, *Private & Confidential*, Morgan Papers; Morgan to Welles, September 1, *Private*, Welles Papers, LC.

46. William M. Chace to Morgan, October 24, Morgan Papers. Johnston's letter declining the nomination is in the New York *Evening Post*, September 15. Word that Johnston had resigned leaked prior to publication of this letter. See Horace H. Day to Fillmore, September 8, Fillmore Papers, SUNY.

IV

The Republican and American state organizations also came into conflict in Massachusetts. Here, too, the vice-presidential controversy masked an underlying struggle for state power. The battle in Massachusetts was more prolonged than in Connecticut, however, and was not finally resolved until after Johnston had declined.

As in 1855, the stumbling block for a union of the two anti-Democratic factions was the ambition of Governor Henry J. Gardner. The Massachusetts nativist leader displayed in 1856 the same dazzling skill for political maneuver that had been a hallmark of his career in state office. Eager for the American party's vice-presidential nomination, the governor bid for southern support in his annual message in 1856 by recommending the repeal of the state's personal liberty law. He remained silent about Fillmore's nomination, although the Boston *Bee*, his personal mouthpiece, endorsed the former president. In May the governor's followers prevented the state council from formally repudiating Fillmore's nomination, leaving Massachusetts the only New England state that failed to take this step. The Sumner assault, however, drastically altered the political situation. In the wake of the reaction that swept over the state, Gardner took the lead in denouncing Brooks's action and scrambled into the North American movement. The Springfield *Republican* charged that the governor was aiming for the North American vice-presidential nomination, but his candidacy produced little interest at the New York convention.[47]

His national ambitions bankrupt and his plan to succeed Sumner in the Senate blocked by the latter's martyrdom, Gardner redirected his attention to the governorship, which he had held now for two terms, and let it be known that he was anxious to run again. Cognizant of important Republicans' hatred of him, the governor saw in the Johnston-Dayton difficulty the means by which to force his enemies to concede him another term. He adopted the position, though he did not phrase it so baldly, that unless the Republicans did not oppose him in the state election, the North Americans would run a separate electoral ticket and thereby jeopardize Frémont's chances in the state. In late June, therefore, the governor repudiated Fillmore and took up Frémont, and under his guidance the state council endorsed Frémont and Johnston. The Fillmore Americans established a separate organization and named their own candidate for governor to join Gardner and the Democratic nominee in the race. The Republicans, who had not yet acted, were due to meet in Worcester in September.

Republican strategists outside Massachusetts viewed the possible loss of the state in the presidential election as a calamity. Every electoral vote would be needed, and with several northern states uncertain, throwing away the Commonwealth for local ends seemed foolish. Both Blair and Morgan implored state party leaders to reach some understanding with Gardner. Massachusetts Republicans, however, had different priorities, and they had to weigh state against national concerns. Had they been certain of carrying the state in spite of Gardner's opposition, they would not have hesitated to discard him. But uncertainty over the electoral result and their failure in 1855 sapped their resolve. In addition, the governor's patient work at building up a personal machine was of great value to him in this struggle. The popular chief executive was not to be taken lightly, and the

47. Samuel Gridley Howe to Charles Sumner, June 7, Howe Papers, HU; Robinson, *"Warrington" Pen-Portraits*, 217; Amos A. Lawrence Diary, June 24, Lawrence Papers; Crandall, *Republican Party*, 251–52.

American masses, desiring some recognition from the haughty Republicans, stood firmly behind him.[48]

In the face of this strong outside pressure, Samuel Bowles spoke for those Massachusetts Republicans who opposed any endorsement of the governor. Also prominent in the fight against the incumbent was Julius Rockwell, the 1855 Republican nominee who desired to run again now that some observers believed that he could be elected.[49] Others considered such a course ill-advised. Nathaniel Banks and Henry Wilson both favored making some arrangement with Gardner, and another party member warned that if the Republicans refused to cooperate with the North Americans on the state and national tickets, "you will lose the State and be damned for it." In the end, party leaders decided to make no nomination for governor in 1856. Gardner was satisfied, for without Republican opposition he was certain to triumph, while Republicans were at least consoled that they had not endorsed the governor or his policies. In exchange, Republicans demanded certain concessions in the congressional races, and the two groups agreed on a common Frémont electoral ticket. Under Wilson's guiding hand, the Worcester convention ratified these previously negotiated arrangements.[50]

Afterwards, one disgusted Republican denounced the agreement with the Gardner Americans as "formed by men who threw away the election of 1856 by dabbling in the dirty pool of Know-Nothingism; or, if they did not do this, they pursued a cautious, timid, and time-serving policy."[51] Not all Gardner's inveterate foes were angry, however. Richard Henry Dana, who had led the fight against his nomination in 1855, approved of the convention's course, as did Charles Francis Adams and George Morey. Morey predicted that Frémont would carry the state by a 75,000 majority, while noting that the convention had done nothing to displease nativists or Germans in other states. Men divided not so much on their old affiliations but on their expectation of the future course of the state's politics. Even Bowles acquiesced in the convention's outcome, pleased at least that Gardner had not been formally endorsed. Some of those at Worcester, the Springfield editor declared, had supported Gardner because they had their eye on some office, great or small, but many others who did so "believed it a matter of patriotic duty" in order to elect Frémont and viewed the governor as "a dose of medicine" to be taken to get good results this year. Such men fully expected to be rid of the despised chief executive in another year.[52]

---

48. Morgan to Goodrich, August 25 (copy), Goodrich to Morgan, August 21, Morgan Papers; Francis P. Blair, Sr., to Banks, September 4, Banks Papers, IllSHL; "Wales" [Israel D. Andrews] to Banks, July 26, Banks Papers, LC; James W. Stone to Weed, July 7, Weed Papers, UR. Goodrich claimed that the state was safe for Frémont regardless of the divisions between the North Americans and Republicans, but national leaders were not persuaded.

49. Adams Diary, September 13, Adams Family Papers; Samuel Bowles to Charles Allen, August 26, Merriam, *Bowles*, v. 1, 173; Robinson, *"Warrington" Pen-Portraits*, 472; Julius Rockwell to Richard Henry Dana, Jr., August 6 (Confidential), September 11 (Confidential), Dana Family Papers; Theodore Parker to Robert Carter, September 11, Carter Papers; J. D. Baldwin to Welles, July 11, Welles Papers, LC.

50. C. W. Elliott to Carter, July 13 (quotation), Carter Papers; Goodrich to Morgan, September 3, Morgan Papers; Adams Diary, September 15, Adams Family Papers; Bean, "Transformation of Parties," 343–45. Two-thirds of the Republican delegates were willing to endorse Gardner, but a proportion of the remainder threatened to bolt if this were done, so in the end the convention decided to make no nomination.

51. Robinson, *"Warrington" Pen-Portraits*, 63–64.

52. Richard Henry Dana, Jr., to John Gorham Palfrey, September 23, John Gorham Palfrey Papers, HU; Adams Diary, September 16, Adams Family Papers; Morey to Carey, September 18, Carey Papers; Bowles to [Charles Allen ?], September 17, Merriam, *Bowles*, v. 1, 174–75; Howe to Sumner, September 21, Howe

A handful of Republicans, however, refused to accept this compromise. Francis W. Bird censured the Worcester convention's action and shortly before the election put together the so-called Honest Man's Ticket, with octogenarian Josiah Quincy as its gubernatorial candidate. It represented a protest against any connection, even indirectly, with the opportunistic Gardner and Know Nothingism. The movement attracted little attention and represented few men of political consequence. The most important Republican leaders in the state either heartily supported the policy of not opposing Gardner or at the minimum quietly acquiesced in it. Massachusetts was safe for Frémont.

V

Developments in Connecticut and Massachusetts, along with Johnston's withdrawal, understandably cheered Republican managers. So, too, did the party's triumph in Iowa in August. The real battle was yet to come, and party leaders were especially anxious to score an impressive victory in the Maine state election in September. Republicans had never carried the state, and a triumph there would demonstrate that the party posed a serious challenge to the Democrats, while sending political reverberations far beyond Maine's borders. "Maine going right, our cause will get new accessions, and Penna & N Jersey will be with us," explained Morgan. A Republican paper termed Maine "eminently a *test* State, both from its recent political history, and from the very influential time of its election. Carry Maine either way, and you shall read the clear consequences in thousands of votes in Pennsylvania and other States."[53]

With an all but bare treasury, national Republican leaders had to decide whether to commit any of the party's limited resources to the state. Urging the national committee to provide money, Weed declared that a victory in Maine in September would do as much good as three or four times as much money applied to other states in October. The penurious Welles, who when at headquarters spent much of his time scrutinizing expenditures and advocating fiscal restraint, was the one important party director to recommend against sending national funds. One of Banks's correspondents, noting that the Maine Republicans were in "a hand to hand fight," emphasized that "we must not loose [*sic*] Maine[,] if we do the contest is ended."[54] Unsubstantiated (and vastly inflated) reports concerning the amount of money Democrats were spending in the state increased Republican anxiety. George Morey, for example, claimed that Democrats were "pouring money into the state like water . . . to the tune" of $30–40,000.[55] In reality, Maine was the only northern state where the Republican national committee may have outspent its Democratic counterpart. Morgan sent Hamlin and Fessenden $2,700, and from Boston Goodrich dispatched another $3,000.[56]

Papers, HU. The action of the Massachusetts Republicans constitutes one of the rare examples in this period of politicians putting national concerns ahead of state ascendancy.

53. Morgan to Joseph Bartlett, September 3 (copy), Morgan Papers; Portland *Advertiser*, July 30, quoted in Wescott, "Maine Politics," 313; Morey to Carey, September 10, Carey Papers.

54. Weed to Morgan, July 29, Welles to Morgan, August 26, *Private*, George G. Fogg to Morgan, August 26, Morgan Papers; "H." [Stephen Hoyt] to Banks, August 22, Banks Papers, LC.

55. John L. Stevens to Morgan, July 19, Morgan Papers; Morey to Julius Rockwell, August 10, Rockwell Papers.

56. Republican Account Book, Morgan Papers. Goodrich's and Morey's transactions in Boston must be pieced together from the following letters: Goodrich to Morgan, August 29, September 3, Morey to Morgan, September 4, Morgan Papers; Goodrich to William Pitt Fessenden, August 29, September 3, Fessenden Papers,

In 1855 Anson P. Morrill, the Republican candidate for governor, won a narrow plurality of the popular vote in a three-way race. In the legislative contests, however, the straight Whigs cooperated with the Democrats, thereby giving the anti-Republican forces control of the legislature, which subsequently elected Samuel Wells, the Democratic candidate. While the Republican party's prospects in 1856 were brighter because of the events of the past year, it had to overcome an adverse majority of 7,000 votes. Furthermore, Morrill, after three consecutive races, declined to be a candidate again. More than any other man, he had served as the catalyst for fusion, and Republicans had to find a suitable successor.

To head their state ticket, Maine Republicans turned, almost with a single voice, to Senator Hannibal Hamlin. An anti-Nebraska Democrat, Hamlin abandoned his party with the greatest reluctance, and then not until June, after the Democratic national convention endorsed the doctrine of nonintervention. Although he had long been an opponent of the extension of slavery, Hamlin's last-minute switch in party affiliation was laced with a healthy dose of opportunism. He left the Democracy and joined the Republicans only when he really had no alternative. At odds with the Democratic leadership both at the state and national levels, and representing a state where the party was badly on the decline, Hamlin faced certain retirement the following year unless he became a Republican. As it was, he waited until the last possible moment to do so.[57]

Hamlin's name had been canvassed for the Republican gubernatorial nomination since the beginning of the year, even before he renounced his Democratic affiliation.[58] Republicans believed that he was the strongest candidate they could run. For one thing, they thought he would attract many wavering Democrats to the Republican cause. In addition, Hamlin had not participated in state politics in recent years and thus enjoyed the advantage that, as one Republican put it, he was "not mixed up with the vexed question of the Maine law." He was sufficiently antislavery to keep the focus on Kansas as the main issue, James G. Blaine argued, yet conservative enough to avoid the taint of radicalism that had so badly weakened the party in 1855. "We have a great many men in our party who go off *half cocked. . . . They* must be made to ride in the rear car instead of in the engine or else we are in constant danger of being thrown from the track."[59] With Hamlin out of the way, another party leader wrote, half a dozen candidates with nearly equal claims would seek the nomination, and the result would be a bitter and perhaps protracted struggle that would leave a legacy of hard feelings. Blaine implored Israel Washburn and others in Washington to press Hamlin to run. "It is absolutely essential that he should in order to consolidate the party."[60]

The major difficulty was Hamlin's reluctance to be a candidate. He wished to remain

WRHS. The amount of money sent to Maine Democrats is unknown, but it was at least $2,500. Christopher L. Ward to James Buchanan, August 27, Buchanan Papers, HSPa. John Stevens, Republican state chairman, claimed that the Republicans also raised between $15,000 and $20,000 in Maine—almost certainly a considerable exaggeration. Stevens to Morgan, September 11, Morgan Papers.

57. For Hamlin's decision to leave the Democracy and the ensuing reaction, see Hunt, *Hamlin*, 88–94.

58. James G. Blaine to Washburn, April 2, Israel Washburn, Jr., Papers, Norlands; Anson P. Morrill to Hannibal Hamlin, February 16, Hamlin Papers; Israel Washburn, Jr., to Blaine, February 26, Blaine Papers.

59. John H. Rice to Fessenden, May 15, Fessenden Papers, LC; Josiah H. Drummond to Hannibal Hamlin, April 9 (quotation), C. J. Talbot to Hamlin, May 8, Hamlin Papers; Blaine to Washburn, April 2, Israel Washburn, Jr., Papers, Norlands.

60. A. Nourse to Hannibal Hamlin, May 8, Hamlin Papers; Blaine to Washburn, April 2, Israel Washburn, Jr., Papers, Norlands.

in the Senate, but Republican strategists, eager to poll the largest vote possible in order to influence the presidential election, insisted that Hamlin make the sacrifice. Party leaders finally agreed that if he accepted the nomination, the Republican members of the legislature would reelect him to the Senate in 1857 if they had a majority. A friend bluntly told Hamlin that his refusal to run for governor would end all chance of his being returned to the Senate. To stand back "in the thickest of the fight" would be fatal to his ambitions. "Those who 'beat the bush' will claim to 'catch the bird.' " When Democrats charged during the campaign that such an agreement existed, Republicans brushed the assertion aside. Privately, however, they acknowledged the understanding.[61]

When Hamlin did not positively withdraw, the outcome of the Republican convention was a foregone conclusion. His nomination for governor provoked an outpouring of enthusiasm. The opposition of Hamlin's personal friends, who were aware that the senator was reluctant to be the candidate, proved feeble against the "tornado" of popular sentiment. It was an *"utter impossibility"* to prevent his nomination, one delegate maintained. "We might as well have attempted to dam the Kennebec with a handful of mud as to resist it."[62] Hence the Republicans in Maine entered the campaign with a very popular candidate who enjoyed several advantages, but who did not want to be governor and had no intention of serving more than a few weeks.[63]

Carefully excluded from the Republican platform were the radical antislavery planks of the previous year. Temperance, on the other hand, remained a troublesome issue for Maine Republicans. Blaine expressed the feelings of many party leaders when he characterized prohibition as a "subject . . . which may at any time create trouble & dissension in the party." Many party leaders blamed their defeat in 1855 on the fanaticism of Neal Dow and his followers, and they were thus anxious to minimize the party's identification with Dow's crusade while avoiding an anti-temperance stance. As a result, neither the Republicans' convention call nor their 1856 state platform mentioned prohibition. Instead, the platform declared that all state issues "should be suspended" during the election. By adopting this position, Republicans hoped to appeal to the wet Whigs without losing the support of the Dowites. Even some of Dow's ardent supporters advised caution in 1856, and finally he and the Republicans reached an understanding by which Dow agreed, temporarily and reluctantly, to allow the liquor question to remain quiescent during the coming election in exchange for a Republican promise to promote prohibition the following year.[64] If this arrangement did not entirely remove the liquor question from the state's politics, Republicans had at least minimized its impact on the 1856 election.

To oppose Hamlin, the Democrats renominated Governor Samuel Wells, while the straight Whigs (who increasingly were allied with the Democrats) named a separate candidate for governor as a way to take votes from Hamlin. Despite separate state tickets, the growing alliance between the Whigs and Democrats was readily apparent. The Whig

---

61. C. J. Talbot to Hannibal Hamlin, May 8, 14 (quotation), Nathaniel C. Deering to Hamlin, July 9, Stephen Emery to Hamlin, July 9, S. Cutle [?] to Hamlin, April 1, Confidential, Hamlin Papers.

62. Stephen Emery to Hannibal Hamlin, July 9, Josiah H. Drummond to Hamlin, July 9 (quotation), S. Cutle [?] to Hamlin, July 8, F. H. Morse to Hamlin, July 13, Hamlin Papers.

63. Hannibal Hamlin to J. Knight, July 12, Hamlin to Charles Hamlin, June [July] 9, Hamlin Papers.

64. Blaine to Hannibal Hamlin, December 27, Josiah H. Drummond to Hamlin, November 18, "A Maine Law Man, & a Republican" to Hamlin, August 3, Hamlin Papers; Dow, *Reminiscences*, 558–59; Wescott, "Maine Politics," 293; Byrne, *Prophet of Prohibition*, 68; Hatch, ed., *Maine*, v. 2, 400.

state convention refused to condemn the Pierce administration, the Democratic national platform, or the repeal of the Missouri Compromise. In addition, several prominent Whigs campaigned actively for Buchanan, and four of the six Democratic candidates for Congress were former Whigs. A Maine Democrat informed John C. Breckinridge that the Whigs "are allied and working in concert with us on state issues."[65]

The two major parties pursued vastly different strategies in the hotly contested state election. The Republicans emphasized the Kansas issue while the Democrats stressed state issues, particularly temperance, which divided their adversaries and, they hoped, would keep anti-Maine Law Whigs from voting Republican on the territorial issue.[66] While guardedly confident, Republicans were intent on registering a huge margin of victory. "With ordinary exertion we can carry this State by a large majority this fall," Morrill declared, "but we must not be content with anything short [of] a tornado, a perfect annihilation of the *alliance*" of Whigs and Democrats.[67] Under the direction of John L. Stevens, who devoted full time to the work, the Republican organization functioned much more smoothly than in 1855. To avoid the squabbling over congressional candidates, which had plagued the anti-Democratic forces badly in 1854, the state committee appointed new district committees. Excitement was high as the contest drew to a close. "The fight is monstrously hard—the worst I ever saw," testified William Pitt Fessenden, a veteran of many campaigns. A young lawyer who campaigned for Hamlin recalled that "the excitement buoyed me up. The very air seemed like champagne."[68]

Republicans in other states waited with anticipation as Maine voters trooped to the polls on September 8. Reflecting the deep interest in the election, turnout was almost 80 percent, the highest in the state since 1840; in fact, voter participation in September surpassed that of the November presidential election by more than 7 percent. The result astounded political observers of all parties. Hamlin won a smashing victory, with 69,429 votes to 44,889 for Wells and 6,659 for the Whig nominee. Hamlin's margin of nearly 18,000 votes eclipsed the most hopeful Republican predictions. State chairman John L. Stevens had expected a majority of 4,500 and Morgan looked for at most 8,000, while Edward Kent dismissed talk of a majority of 15,000 as "foolishly extravagant."[69] The Republicans also swept all six congressional districts and carried the legislature. "Nobody anticipated so disastrous [*sic*] a defeat," a stunned Maine Democrat confessed; another party member termed the results "a most unexpected Waterloo defeat."[70] In Washington Democratic leaders were visibly shaken by the outcome.

Hamlin's triumph, and especially the margin by which he won, gave the Frémont

---

65. Wyman B. S. Moor to Breckinridge, July 23, Breckinridge Family Papers; Nathan Clifford to Buchanan, June 19, Buchanan Papers, HSPa; Edward Kent to Hannibal Hamlin, July 12, Hamlin Papers. Rank-and-file resistance prevented the Whig convention from endorsing the Democratic ticket as Whig leaders had intended.

66. Portland *Eastern Argus*, September 8, 10; Dow, *Reminiscences*, 558–59; Charles E. Hamlin, *The Life and Times of Hannibal Hamlin* (Cambridge, 1899), 310; Charles Levi Woodbury to John C. Breckinridge, July 26, Breckinridge Family Papers.

67. Lyndon Oak to Charles P. Chandler, July 16, Charles P. Chandler Papers; Anson P. Morrill to Hannibal Hamlin, June 12, Hamlin Papers.

68. Fessenden to Morgan, September 5, Morgan Papers; Portland *Transcript*, September 13; Wescott, "Maine Politics," 297, 309–312; Hamlin, *Hamlin*, 311–12 (quotation).

69. John L. Stevens to Weed, August 8, *Private*, Weed Papers, UR; Morgan to Isaac Platt, September 6 (copy), Morgan Papers; Edward Kent to Hannibal Hamlin, July 12, Hamlin Papers.

70. James W. Bradbury to Buchanan, September 11, Buchanan Papers, HSPa; T. J. D. Fuller to William H. English, October 3, English Papers, IndHS.

campaign a great psychological boost. Maine, unlike Iowa and Vermont, where the Republicans also won impressive victories in the fall state elections, had not been counted as certain for Frémont prior to the September election, and both parties had conducted vigorous campaigns. Republicians were elated. "Can't you hold an election in Maine once a week till November?" Greeley joked to Pike. "We need it badly." An Illinois Republican reported that the Maine result galvanized the party's members, while George Templeton Strong predicted that countless "cautious gentlemen" would at last decide "to get down from their fence and go for Fremont." Morgan heaved a sigh of relief, since his decision to send precious resources to Maine was more than vindicated.[71] Simultaneously, the Maine returns ended whatever complacency still lingered in the Buchanan camp, and the Democratic national committee exhorted party members to muster their forces for what promised to be a close national election.[72]

Democrats attributed their rout to several causes, including the Republicans' refusal to make the Maine Law an issue, popular anger over the situation in Kansas, the active backing that the clergy of most denominations gave their opponents, and the lavish use of money. Republicans additionally cited the strong support of young men, new or recent voters, for their ticket.[73] Democrats' emphasis on money was overstated. Both parties were well funded, and finances were the least important cause of the result. The importance of Morgan's decision to commit funds to Maine was not that it allowed the Republicans to buy the election, as Democrats charged, but that it prevented the party from suffering any undue disadvantage as far as resources were concerned.

Voting patterns suggest that the Kansas and liquor issues were both important in producing the result, but not in precisely the same way. Hamlin won virtually all the Republican voters of 1855, plus a small proportion of Democrats and about a fifth of the Whigs (Table 12.1). Despite the surge in turnout, his strength among new voters was not significantly greater than that of Wells. Some of these earlier non-voters who supported Wells may have been anti-temperance men less interested in sectional issues, for the Democratic legislature in 1856 had repealed Dow's hated Intensified Maine Law and reinstituted the license system. This dramatic reversal in state policy probably propelled anti-drys to the polls. The straight Whig strength fell almost in half, and nearly all these defections went to Hamlin. Hamlin's gains, in other words, came from Whigs, Democrats, and non-voters alike, and at least in part were evidence of his great popularity with the state's voters.

The motivation of those Whigs who shifted to the Republican party reflected a combination of causes. Certainly the dramatic increase of sectional tensions in the previous twelve months converted to Republicanism a number of former Whigs who were uncomfortable over the idea of a sectional party. Former Democratic governor John Hubbard concluded that "the predominant cause of our defeat was doubtless the Anti Slavery sentiment of our whole community roused from its short slumber to a pitch of

71. Greeley to Pike, September 21, Pike Papers, UMe; Nevins and Thomas, eds., *Strong Diary*, v. 2, 292; John S. Wilson to Abraham Lincoln, September 11, Herndon-Weik Collection; Welles to Morgan, September 13, *Private*, Morgan to Welles, September 11, *Private* (copy), Morgan to A. R. Hollowell [?], September 19 (copy), Fessenden to Weed, September 12, A. H. Greene to Morgan, September 1, Morgan Papers.

72. John W. Forney to John C. Breckinridge, September 30, Breckinridge Family Papers.

73. Israel Chadbourne to Horatio Seymour, September 15, Horatio Seymour Papers, NYSL; James W. Bradbury to Buchanan, September 11, Buchanan Papers, HSPa; Portland *Advertiser*, September 22, quoted in Wescott, "Maine Politics," 315; Joseph Bartlett to Morgan, September 20, Morgan Papers.

fanaticism bordering upon Monomania, by the repeal of the Missouri Compromise.'' The party might have been able to check this sentiment by appealing to the doctrine of nonintervention, he added, but the people had no faith that Pierce or any Democratic administration would administer the Kansas-Nebraska Act fairly. Another Democrat, who conceded that the Kansas reports had made *"a deeper impression* than any one anticipated,'' argued that the voters were ready to believe even the most absurd Kansas stories. At the same time, anti-temperance Whigs, who had refused to support Morrill in 1855 when he ran on a strident Maine Law platform, found the Republican party's 1856 platform much more palatable, and presumably they contributed to Hamlin's gains. Some former Whigs simply recognized the hoplessness of the Whig cause and resented the increasingly pro-Democratic stance of the party's remaining leaders. One Whig, who admitted his great reluctance to leave the party, charged in 1856 that ''the policy of the now called straight Whig Party is not the policy of the old Whig party[.] It is the reverse of this. The *eclipse . . .* is now *total . . .* I cannot follow its direction.''[74] Whatever their reasons for switching parties, virtually none of the rank-and-file Whigs, contrary to the inclination of the party's leaders, voted Democratic. Whigs either retained their party loyalty to the bitter end or they supported Hamlin. Only the Democrats' strength among traditional non-voters prevented an even more humiliating defeat.

Distinguishing the relative influence of the slavery and liquor issues is a difficult problem, since the two reform crusades intertwined too closely in Maine politics to permit an easy distinction. Hamlin received solid support from the 1852 Free Soil voters and won about two-thirds of the Whigs, but about one-third of Pierce's supporters voted for him as well (Table 12.2). Hamlin's Democratic support was not limited to temperance men, but he ran much better among previous supporters of pro-temperance Democratic candidates than he did among those who voted for anti-Maine Law Democrats. Hamlin thus had considerable strength among 1852 Hubbard voters (Democrat) and among Morrill voters in 1853 and 1854. At the same time, his rate of support among Wildcat Democrats in 1852 and regular Democrats in 1853 was substantially below his proportion of Hubbard and Morrill voters in those years, and the followers in 1854 of Liberal candidate Shepard Cary, the leading anti-prohibition Democrat in the state, though not numerous, gave Hamlin almost no votes (Tables 12.3 through 12.5).

The Maine Law controversy disrupted the old party alignment, and agitation of the liquor issue over a series of contests deepened the existing Democratic split. The temperance question alone, however, was an insufficient spur to form a new majority coalition. To some extent, the slavery issue reinforced the divisions produced by temperance, but it also enabled the Republicans to significantly broaden their electoral base by attracting voters either indifferent or hostile to prohibition. Probably a majority of Hamlin's supporters were pro-temperance and also anti-southern and anti-Slave Power. Still, the party's refusal to embrace prohibition was a wise decision. In the foreseeable future, the slavery issue was politically more potent than the liquor question.

VI

Most politicians assumed that the October state elections in Pennsylvania, Ohio, and Indiana would decide the presidential contest. Ohio seemed safely Republican, but the

---

74. John Hubbard to Buchanan, November 15 (copy), Hubbard Family Papers; James W. Bradbury to Buchanan, September 11, Buchanan Papers, HSPa; William Freeman to Washburn, April 11, Israel Washburn, Jr., Papers, Norlands.

other two were battleground states. "The whole canvass depends on Indiana & Pa.," declared Schuyler Colfax in exhorting a vigorous Republican campaign. The loss of Pennsylvania, in particular, would spell doom for Frémont's chances, and Morgan argued that much more could be accomplished by concentrating on the Pennsylvania state election "than by diffusing our strength." The Republican campaign in Indiana, desperately in need of outside assistance, was impaired as a result, but party strategists could see no alternative. "All the force we have is devoted to that State, of necessity," wrote Charles A. Dana in reference to Pennsylvania.[75]

In both Pennsylvania and Indiana, the support of the vast majority of present and former Know Nothings was indispensible if Republicans were to carry these states. Much of the Republican campaign in both states, then, focused on appealing to the nativists and conservative old-line Whigs attracted to Fillmore's candidacy. Republicans refrained from attacking Fillmore or nativism, hoping thereby to foster a climate of good will and cooperation.[76] In Indiana, the opposition elements had for the previous two years worked together in a loose coalition although the Republican organization did not take shape fully until 1856. In Pennsylvania, on the other hand, Know Nothing intrigues had undermined the Republican movement in 1855, and consequently an entirely new start was required.

The North American bolt and subsequent disruption of the state organization drastically altered the nature of the American party in Indiana. Earlier, when led by men like Schuyler Colfax, Daniel Mace, and Godlove Orth, opposition to the extension of slavery had been an important facet of its creed, but their defection to the Republicans severely weakened this sentiment in the Know Nothing order. Under the aegis of Richard W. Thompson, a conservative old-line Whig and the most important American in the state, the party emphasized the Union issue over nativism; besides retaining some nativist support, the Fillmore cause also provided a refuge for conservative Whigs who opposed the sectional Republican party yet did not want to vote for the hated Democrats. The American organization remained strong in the southern counties, but in the central and northern areas of the state its members for the most part had joined the People's party. A sparsely attended American convention did not nominate a state ticket, but its refusal to endorse Oliver P. Morton and the other candidates on the People's ticket seriously hurt its chances. With a separate Fillmore slate of electors in the field, Frémont's prospects seemed even bleaker.[77]

The gubernatorial race between Morton and Ashbel Willard, the Democratic nominee, was the fierce battle party workers had anticipated. The rivals stumped the state together, debating the issues of the canvass. Reflective of the national importance of the election as well as the evenly matched strength of the two parties, popular interest was remarkably high. "I have never in the most exciting of our political contests, witnessed larger audiences, more attentive, or more enthusiastic," one Democrat reported. "They count by thousands, instead of hundreds. There seems to be an upheaving, and uprising, of the people, such as I have never witnessed since I have been in Indiana, now nearly forty

75. Colfax to Charles M. Heaton, Sr., August 15, Colfax Papers, NIHS; Morgan to Welles, September 30 (copy), Morgan Papers; Charles A. Dana to Washburne, September 25, Elihu B. Washburne Papers, LC.

76. For criticism of this strategy, see N. Field to George W. Julian, September 19, Giddings-Julian Papers; Madison *Evening Courier*, November 6, quoted in Stoler, "Democratic Element in Indiana," 189–90; Charles A. Dana to Carey, September 19, Carey Papers.

77. Van Bolt, "Republican Party in Indiana," 210; Brand, "Know Nothing Party in Indiana," 277–79.

years.''[78] In contrast to the poorly financed Republican campaign, the Democrats received substantial outside aid—perhaps as much as $35,000—which they used to distribute large quantities of documents and sustain a number of speakers on the hustings.[79] Notwithstanding their advantage in campaign funds, Democrats were quick to recognize that the contest would be, as one warned, "bitter and close." As the campaign drew to an end, leaders in both parties were uncertain how the old Whigs and remaining Americans, who all agreed held the balance of power, would vote in the state election.[80]

The Republican campaign in Pennsylvania faltered badly from the outset. The party labored under several major difficulties: The American party was strong and well organized while the Republican organization had to be established anew, the party lacked sufficient funds, and personal feuds and jealousies among its leaders rent the state organization. Despite considerable effort, Republican leaders at national headquarters and in the state were unable to cope effectively with these problems.

David Wilmot, who had been appointed state chairman in 1855, assumed leadership of the movement to reorganize the Republican party. Bypassing the existing Know Nothing-dominated Republican central committee, he signed the call for the Pittsburgh convention in his capacity as state chairman without even consulting the committee. Acting again on his own, he summoned a state convention of "the friends of freedom" to meet in Philadelphia on June 16, the day before the opening of the Republican national convention, to select delegates to the Philadelphia convention, perfect a separate organization, and nominate a state ticket. The former Free Soil leader cited as authority for his action his membership on the interim national committee named by the Pittsburgh convention. Before the state convention assembled, Republican managers decided to postpone naming a Republican electoral ticket, so the convention's most important action was the establishment of a new Republican state central committee headed by Charles Gibbons, a former Whig, who was installed as the new party chairman. For the October state election, the convention endorsed the Union party's state ticket, which had been nominated at Harrisburg in March. The impulse for the Union convention came largely from Americans, and, although its ticket represented all important anti-Democratic factions, the movement was most closely identified in the popular mind with the Know Nothings.[81]

The early and relatively harmonious agreement on a single opposition state ticket encouraged the hope that the anti-Democratic forces would eventually combine in the presidential election as well. Republican strategists at party headquarters in New York in conjunction with state leaders like Wilmot, Thaddeus Stevens, and Cameron, wanted to postpone any decision on an electoral ticket until close to or even after the state election. When zealous Frémont men attempted to name an electoral ticket independent of the

---

78. John Law to William L. Marcy, September 12 (quotation), Marcy Papers, LC; William Nye to John, Betsey, and Bink, September 12, William Nye Papers, Vermont Historical Society; Thornbrough, ed., *Fletcher Diary*, v. 5, 567.

79. Nichols, *Disruption of American Democracy*, 47. Nichols calculates that the Democrats raised approximately $70,000 for Pennsylvania.

80. John Law to Stephen A. Douglas, May 17 (quotation), John Pettit to Douglas, June 10, Douglas Papers, UChi; T. M. King [?] to Breckinridge, October 7, Breckinridge Family Papers; James A. Wright to Buchanan, August 28, *Private*, Buchanan Papers, HSPa; E. C. Hibben to Joseph Lane, July 24, Joseph Lane Papers, IndU; John H. Steers et al. to Henry S. Lane, August 15, Henry S. Lane Papers, IndHS.

81. Coleman, *Disruption of the Pennsylvania Democracy*, 89–90; Myers, "Republican Party in Pennsylvania," 91–92; McClure, *Old Time Notes*, v. 1, 248; Russell Errett to Chase, August 2, Chase Papers, LC.

Americans, party managers in both the state and national organizations moved swiftly to block the movement.[82] Republicans looked to a Union triumph in October to smooth the way for a subsequent agreement on a common ticket in the national election.

Because of the critical importance of Pennsylvania to Frémont's chances, the state received virtually all of the national committee's campaign funds. As head of the speakers' bureau, Henry B. Stanton also gave Pennsylvania top priority and attempted to have from one to two dozen men speaking in the state from July until November. Stanton envisioned a systematic canvass that would hold meetings in all the principal towns of a county "& not a mere glancing at county seats." Moreover, he wanted to send only men "competent to deal with the rather peculiar politics of Pa.," men who would pave the way for the formation of a union electoral ticket. Speakers who opposed any recognition of the Know Nothings would be dispatched to other states. Although Stanton secured a number of speakers, the inefficiency of the state committee undermined his efforts. After several frustrating weeks, he decided to entirely ignore the Pennsylvania committee, which was "scattered & slow," and use special committees to arrange meetings. His exasperation with the state's Republican organization was obvious. "We shall probably have to furnish the money to pay men for pri[n]ting the handbills, & for the paste which sticks them to the horsesheds," he declared in disgust. "If we hope to carry Pa we must literally lift it & *carry* it."[83]

Stanton's difficulties with the Republican state committee represented only the tip of the iceberg. Despite the party's reorganization following its disastrous beginning in 1855, its structure remained defective. As late as August, Errett reported that half the counties, including many of the most populous ones, still had no Republican press or county organization. Nowhere was Republican organizational disarray more apparent than in Philadelphia; the situation seemed so desperate that a number of politicians urged Morgan to intervene. "The materials are there however—floating loosely & at large—for a powerful organization," one Republican emphasized, but "they must be drawn together & *massed* before they are too widely dispersed." The national chairman prodded the state committee to act, but he felt it inappropriate to undercut local leadership.[84]

After investigating the situation, Weed advised there were too many committees, a situation that severely hindered management of the Pennsylvania campaign. Indicative of the disorganization was that two separate committees were located in Philadelphia. As state chairman, Gibbons conducted the state campaign from there while a different committee had responsibility for the canvass in the city and county. Additional confusion arose because Henry Carey, who had charge of the party's finances, was a member of neither committee yet was responsible to both. Stanton's decision to bypass the state committee and establish new committees to arrange political meetings only aggravated the problem. Weed, Henry Wilson, FitzHenry Warren, and Truman Smith all went to Philadelphia on several occasions in an attempt to bring order to an increasingly chaotic party structure.[85]

---

82. Morgan to Welles, September 19 (copy), Morgan Papers.

83. Henry B. Stanton to Morgan, n.d. [fragment, late July] (quotation), July 22, Morgan Papers; Stanton to Banks, July 28, *Private* (quotation), Banks Papers, LC; Stanton to Greeley, August 5 (quotation), Greeley Papers, NYPL.

84. Russell Errett to Morgan, June 21, Private & Confidential, Thomas Williams to Morgan, June 26 (quotation), Morgan Papers.

85. Weed to Morgan, October 6, Morgan to Goodrich, October 4 (copy), Morgan to David Wilmot,

The deep-seated personal rivalries among Republican leaders further paralyzed the state party. Welles in despair decried the "cliques, local controversies, and personal rivalries *ad infinitem*" for which the state was notorious. Hostility between former Whigs and Democrats remained quite strong. In particular, Gibbons, an ex-Whig, refused to cooperate with his old adversary Cameron, who openly joined the Republican party in 1856. The result was parallel organizations, since Cameron preserved his personal organization. Recognizing the value of Cameron's assistance, national party leaders pointedly invited him to attend in August the national committee meeting which formulated plans for the campaign in Pennsylvania. Weed and Morgan made special efforts to work with him, Blair ended his personal feud with the Pennsylvanian in order to make common cause against Buchanan, and Cameron became an important member of the inner directory that determined national strategy. Although Gibbons continued to function as state chairman and Morgan funneled funds through his committee, Cameron, who had the ear of Weed and Morgan, wielded far greater influence and authority in matters of strategy and organization.[86]

The multitude of committees, the lack of system in affairs, the scarcity of funds, the personal feuds among leaders, and what Weed termed "a plentiful lack of sense" at Philadelphia all combined to produce chaos. Thaddeus Stevens, who had long been active in Pennsylvania politics, eventually exclaimed that "the State is worse managed this campaign than I ever knew it," and another party worker agreed that he "never saw the state in such a miserable state of disorganization."[87] Charles Francis Adams, who went to Philadelphia to speak, left thoroughly disillusioned. After discussions with party leaders in the city, he reported that "there was an utter absence of system in all their arrangements." Adams complained that inappropriate speakers were sent to meetings, that too much effort was wasted on already converted voters, and that areas where the party was weak were badly neglected.[88] In exasperation, Charles A. Dana castigated the state committee. Gibbons, in particular, he pronounced a major hindrance. "He is a damned fool, and a nasty little office seeker to boot, and does nothing but harm." Equally frustrated, FitzHenry Warren, who was sent to Philadelphia by the national committee to assist the state committee, dismissed the leading politicians of the state as "not worth a pair of old shoes."[89]

Throughout the summer, Morgan resisted the only step that could possibly rectify the deficiencies of the state organization: assumption by the national committee of direction of the campaign. Wilmot intimated that something had to be done about the incompetence of the state committee, but the national chairman, while expressing regret at the disorganization in Philadelphia, hastened to add that he saw "no other way but [to] go

---

October 3 (copy), Charles Gibbons to Morgan, September 19, Morgan Papers; A. Rood to Carey, September 5, Carey to Rood, September 7, Carey Papers; Francis P. Blair, Sr., to Sumner, July 29, Sumner Papers, HU.

86. Welles to Morgan, September 13, *Private*, Welles Papers, LC; Greeley to A. E. Bovay, September 10, Typescript, Greeley Papers, LC; Morgan to Cameron, August 14, 20, Thaddeus Stevens to Cameron, August 16, Cameron Papers, HSDC; Weed to Cameron, August 15, September 19, Cameron Papers, LC. Bradley, *Cameron*, 112; Lee F. Crippen, *Simon Cameron: Ante-bellum Years* (Oxford, Ohio, 1942), 154.

87. Weed to Morgan, September 22, Morgan Papers; Thaddeus Stevens to Carey, September 30, Carey Papers; S. H. Clark to Morgan, October 22 (quotation), Wilmot to Morgan, September 26, Morgan Papers.

88. Adams Diary, October 8 (quotation), 11, Adams Family Papers.

89. Charles A. Dana to Carey, September 11 (quotation), 19, Carey Papers; FitzHenry Warren to Banks, August 14, Banks Papers, LC. For defenses of Gibbons, see William V. Pettit to Welles, August 25, Welles Papers, LC; Gibbons to Morgan, August 8, Lindley Smyth to Morgan, October 25, Morgan Papers.

through'' Gibbon's committee, "accommodating to circumstances as we best can, and getting other friends to act as co-adjutors."[90] Resistance by state organizations to outside interference was understandably strong, but the Pennsylvania committee was particularly vulnerable because for funds it had to depend almost exclusively on the national committee. The state party had almost no money of its own, since conservative former Whig merchants, especially in Philadelphia, refused to contribute. One party organizer in that city lamented that "nearly *all* our monied men are for Buchanan or are wasting their powder on Fillmore. . . . In the old Whig times, we could go out into Market St. and easily get a few thousand dollars, but now of all our Merchants trading with the West and *South*, we can't get a cent, with two or three exceptions."[91] Rejecting calls for drastic action, Morgan followed a policy of periodically sending party leaders, particularly Weed, to Philadelphia to consult and give advice. This approach amounted to part-time supervision of the campaign from national headquarters.

This uneasy relationship between national headquarters and the Pennsylvania committee ended in early October, when the activities of Thomas H. Ford, Ohio's lieutenant governor and a prominent North American leader, precipitated a crisis. Earlier, in a move to promote a union of the Americans and Republicans, the national committee had placed Ford in charge of a project to purchase the support of Fillmore papers in Pennsylvania. Ford was an unfortunate choice, for while he had enjoyed a certain measure of fame as an orator, he was extremely indolent and betrayed a happy-go-lucky disposition. For a month or more, he jaunted about the state, offering payments to nativist editors if they would switch to Frémont. Ford operated with only nominal supervision from New York; Morgan, in fact, confessed ignorance of either the papers Ford had bought or the amount of money he had expended. The state committee, on the other hand, was not even advised of his mission.[92] When Ford finally communicated with Morgan, the chairman was shocked to discover that the Ohio leader, authorized to spend $5,000, had made commitments totaling $9,050, almost all of which was to be paid immediately. "He went too far and ought to have advisd. from time to time as the papers were arranged for," Morgan commented with admirable restraint. Despite Ford's having overstepped his instructions, the chairman felt obliged to pay the drafts, since their repudiation would have caused considerable trouble. On the whole, he approved of Ford's selection of journals, although he allowed that the price paid for some exceeded their value. Others suspected (perhaps with justification) that Ford had profited personally, and Welles concluded, less severely, that he had "no financial talent or capacity, and really needed a man to accompany him who knew the value of a dollar. He does not."[93]

The lieutenant governor's unauthorized expenditures exceeded the funds Morgan had on hand and finally forced a restructuring of the Pennsylvania campaign apparatus. Not informing the state committee of Ford's project was ill-advised, while delegating financial authority to him was certainly a serious error in judgment on Morgan's part. Whatever the

---

90. Morgan to Wilmot, October 3 (copy), Morgan Papers.

91. M. L. Hallowell to Simeon Draper, August 18, quoted in Coleman, *Disruption of the Pennsylvania Democracy*, 92n.

92. Thomas Ford to Dear Sir, September 12, Weed Papers, UR; Morgan to Welles, September 19 (copy), Ford to Morgan, October 6, Gibbons to Morgan, October 19, Morgan Papers; A. Rood to Carey and Mr. Fry, October 9, Carey Papers; Brinkerhoff, *Recollections*, 93.

93. Morgan to Weed, October 7 (quotation), Weed Papers, UR; Morgan to Goodrich, October 13, *Private* (copy), Ford to Morgan, October 6, Welles to Morgan, October 10, Morgan Papers; Morgan to Welles, October 8, Private, Welles Papers, LC.

past mistakes involved, the only way Morgan could cover Ford's drafts was to order Morey and Goodrich, who had been remitting money from Boston directly to Carey in Philadelphia, to send the contributions they collected to New York instead. Party leaders in Philadelphia, desirous of maintaining control of these much-coveted funds, protested Morgan's action and urged the Boston men to defy the chairman. Goodrich, however, acceded to Morgan's request.[94] Ford's drafts provided the national committee with justification for assuming direction of the Pennsylvania campaign by means of its control of the purse strings. This reorganization occurred in the final week before the October election, too late to affect the state contest, but it was an important development for the presidential canvass in November. By the time of the state election, the national committee had in essence taken charge of the campaign in Pennsylvania. The continuing dispute among party leaders in Philadelphia over the dispersal of funds forced the committee to either take control or write off the state. As tactfully as possible, Morgan explained the unprecedented development to Gibbons and his colleagues, but he divulged to Goodrich that he was acting on Weed's recommendation. Only by sending all money through party headquarters could its disposition be monitored.[95] After the state election, Morgan further tightened the national committee's control. "The New York Republicans appear to have taken the party in this State completely into their hands and to have them in leading strings," commented a Philadelphia observer.[96]

In contrast to the Republican organization, which was beset by problems in its campaign, the Democratic organization, under John W. Forney's skillful guidance, performed wonders. Well supplied with funds—where the Democrats "get their money God only knows," one Republican declared, "but they have plenty of it and use it freely"—Forney flooded the state with speakers and documents. He boasted that every home in Philadelphia received at least one Democratic document.[97] A fellow Democrat, who asserted that "every thing has been managed with the most consummate skill and energy," acclaimed Forney as the "Napoleon" of the fight. The hard-drinking journalist drove himself and his associates at a feverish pace. Friends and foes alike marveled at the energetic Democratic canvass. Whatever the final result, "never was there a better organization—and never have men worked more faithfully, actively and *judiciously* than Mr Forney's committee," gasped former Whig leader William B. Reed. "I have never known any thing like it."[98]

The final two weeks before the balloting witnessed frantic efforts on both sides. "The enemy are preparing to give us a h—ll of a chase," one Democrat warned as the parties

---

94. Morgan to Morey, October 7, Private, Morgan to Morey or Goodrich, October 10, *Private*, Morgan to Goodrich, October 9, 11, Morgan to Carey, Telegram, October 10 (copies), Goodrich to Morgan, October 13, Truman Smith to Ezra Lincoln, Telegram, n.d. [October 10 or 11], Weed to Morgan, October 3, Welles to Morgan, August 26, *Private*, Morgan Papers.

95. Morgan to Goodrich, October 9, 11 (copies), Morgan Papers.

96. Philadelphia correspondence, *National Intelligencer*, October 20, The national committee's takeover of the campaign occurred over a period of a week or so, and the movement to do so gained added momentum from the defeat in the state election. But it was Ford's drafts, rather than the result of the state contest, that finally caused the committee to take action.

97. Job G. Patterson to Cameron, September 18 (quotation), Cameron Papers, HSDC; Ford to Morgan, October 6, Morgan Papers; Forney to Buchanan, September 11, Buchanan Papers, HSPa; Forney to George Plitt, June 16, James D. Barbee Papers, LC.

98. William Rice to Breckinridge, October 6, Breckinridge Family Papers; William B. Reed to Buchanan, October 11, Buchanan Papers, HSPa.

threw all available funds and speakers into a last-minute effort to carry the state. "The political cauldron is certainly at boiling point, and is bubbling and foaming in the most exciting manner in this city, and . . . all over the State," a reporter wrote early in October. Excitement seemed at a peak, as interest in the upcoming election gripped the state and nation. "Politics! politics! politics! Nothing but politics!" exclaimed one Philadelphia commentator:

> Flags across the streets meet the eye in every direction; music in open carriages, with placards to announce political gatherings; ward meetings and mass meetings and committee meetings every day and every night, and, as it appears to me, at every hour in the day and night; and discussions and estimates and guesses at the result, with all the other accessories of the highest political excitement, are all you see or hear in this city.[99]

People everywhere recognized that this was no ordinary state election, and that the presidential aspirations of Buchanan and Frémont were inextricably linked to the outcome in October.

VII

The elections passed off peacefully in all three states. In Pennsylvania the day was cold and overcast with a light rain, but the poor weather did not prevent a high turnout. Indiana, where the weather was cold but dry, registered an even greater rate of participation. In many cities and towns throughout the North, crowds gathered to await the returns from both states, but the tallies were so close that it was several days before the outcome was beyond doubt. The October elections all but extinguished Frémont's chances. As expected, the Republican state ticket swept to victory in Ohio, but in Pennsylvania and Indiana, the Union and People's tickets suffered narrow defeats (Maps 10 and 11). Contrary to Forney's prediction of a 10,000 vote majority, the Democratic edge in Pennsylvania was very slender, fewer than 3,000 votes, while in Indiana Morton lost by only 5,000 votes.[100] Democrats knew that they had had a close escape. "Great God what a terrific battle we had in Inda!!" exclaimed one Democratic leader. Three days after the balloting, when it was finally clear that the Democrats had triumphed in Pennsylvania, a relieved Forney, exhausted from lack of sleep, dispatched word to Buchanan that "our poor boys, yesterday so depressed, are now wild with joy."[101]

In Ohio, the Republicans preserved Chase's victorious coalition of 1855 and picked up additional strength from new voters and prior abstainers (Table 12.6). The Democrats, in

99. David R. Porter to Buchanan, September 29 (quotation), Buchanan Papers, HSPa; Philadelphia correspondence, *National Intelligencer*, October 8, 11.

100. The official vote in each state was: in Ohio for supreme court judge, Scott (Republican) 173,618 (49.4 percent), Ramsey (Democrat) 154,238 (43.9 percent), and Peck (American) 23,570 (6.7 percent); in Pennsylvania for canal commissioner, Cochrane (Union) 210,111 (49.7 percent), and Scott (Democrat) 212,886 (50.3 percent); and in Indiana for governor, Morton (People's) 112,039 (48.7 percent), and Willard (Democrat) 117,911 (51.3 percent). Turnout was 81.9 percent in Ohio, 72.7 percent in Pennsylvania, and 86.3 percent in Indiana. As noted below, both the Indiana and Pennsylvania figures were suspiciously high compared to previous elections. For Forney's prediction, see Forney to George Sanders, October 13, quoted in Crippen, *Cameron*, 154–55.

101. John L. Robinson to Breckinridge, October 21, Breckinridge Family Papers; Forney to Buchanan, October 16, Buchanan Papers, HSPa.

Note: Numbers are the People's percentage of the votes cast.

10. Indiana Vote for Governor, 1856

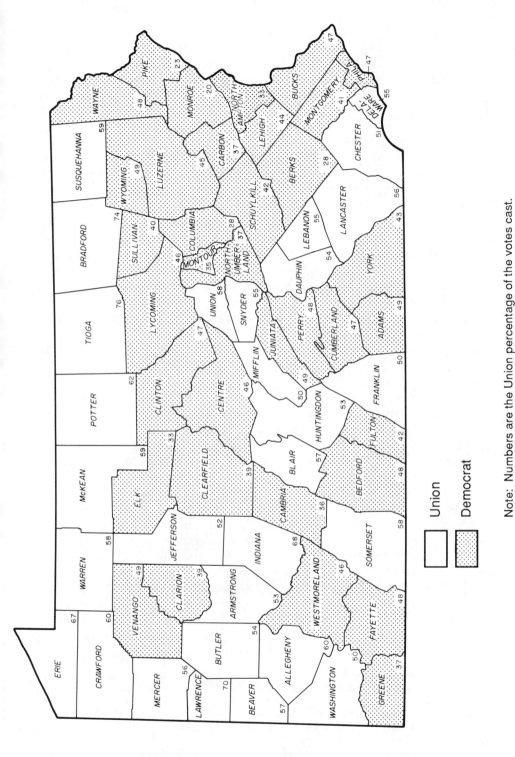

11. Pennsylvania Vote for Canal Commissioner, 1856

contrast, had little appeal to new voters and made no inroads into the ranks of the Trimble men. The Democrats' gains from other parties were more than balanced by the defections they incurred. Conceding the state races, Democrats concentrated on defeating vulnerable Republican congressmen. Their strategy achieved some success, because they won eight seats in the new House. Since the state's entire delegation elected in 1854 was anti-Nebraska, some reduction in strength was inevitable. Even so, the state remained safely under Republican control.[102]

Republicans attributed their defeat in Indiana in part to the loss of former Whig voters, but actually very few of Scott's supporters cast Democratic ballots in 1856, and those disenchanted with the People's ticket were much more likely to sit out the election (Table 12.7). More crucial was the small number of 1854 anti-Nebraska (People's party) voters who backed Willard in 1856; while some of these undoubtedly were conservative Whigs who opposed Republicanism, probably a larger proportion were Democrats returning to their old loyalty after a temporary protest against national party policy (Table 12.8). Despite his Democratic antecedents, Morton displayed no particular appeal to Democrats, but both he and Willard had important strength among new voters and men who failed to vote earlier. Republican analysts could not agree on how the Fillmore men voted. Some claimed that they split more or less evenly, but John Defrees, state party chairman, finally concluded that at least three-fourths had voted for the People's state ticket.[103] Defrees's estimate of Morton's strength among Fillmore men was conservative, as apparently almost all who went to the polls supported the Republican nominee. With good reason, the state chairman moaned that ''we have but a bare chance to carry the State'' in November.[104]

In explaining their setback, Republican spokesmen also charged that the Democrats had imported massive numbers of illegal voters. One overheated Republican politician, for example, insisted that there was ''nothing like it this side of Kansas—Border Ruffians from Ohio, Mich. Ill. & Ky were avalanched upon us by thousands.'' He also made allegations of ''double, tripple [*sic*] & multiplex voting by the same individuals.'' Republicans had for some time worried about illegal voting, particularly by Irish railroad gangs. Democrats were not alone, however, in taking advantage of the state's lax voting laws. The Republican state committee also made plans to import voters, and Calvin Fletcher, a committee member who protested this decision, commented privately that ''Bribery & Corruption seems to be the order of the day.''[105] Republicans provided various estimates of the extent of illegal voting by their adversaries. Some, including the usually judicious Colfax, put the figure at a highly improbable 20,000 votes. Others, while presenting lower estimates, nonetheless insisted that the number of illegal ballots cast exceeded Willard's margin of victory. Republican importations canceled at least some of the fraudulent Democratic votes, and although it is possible that the Democrats carried the election by such means, Morton's biographer struck nearer the truth when he

102. Thomas B. Spooner to Welles, August 6, Welles Papers, ConnHS; Lewis D. Campbell to Banks, September 6, Banks Papers, IllSHL; Ford to John Sherman, July 24, John Sherman Papers.

103. John Defrees to Morgan, October 21, Morgan Papers; ''Steeltrap'' [James R. Thompson] to Fillmore, November 1, Fillmore Papers, SUNY; Stoler, ''Influence of the Democratic Element,'' 139–41.

104. Defrees to Morgan, October 21, Morgan Papers. The regression estimate is that 84 percent of Fillmore's supporters in November voted for Morton, while fewer than 3 percent backed Willard.

105. Samuel W. Parker to Ignatius Brown, October 22, quoted in Van Bolt, ''Republican Party in Indiana,'' 218; Thornbrough, ed., *Fletcher Diary*, v. 5, 568–71, 573–74, 579–81, 591 (quotation 580); Elisha King Diary, October 14, IndHS; Indianapolis *Journal*, October 20, quoted in the Cincinnati *Commercial*, October 22.

declared that despite illegal voting, it was "more than doubtful" that fraud altered the outcome. Republicans who saw the margin of victory in old-line Whig support for Willard advanced a sounder explanation.[106]

In Pennsylvania, the Union ticket won nearly all of the 1854 Whig voters, and compared to the Democrats it gained substantial support from earlier non-voters (Table 12.10). At the same time, as several contemporary observers claimed, a number of 1852 Whigs defected to the Democrats (Table 12.9). In such a close election, their support was crucial.[107] More significant was the sizable minority of Know Nothings who voted Democratic. Before the election, Democratic leaders reported that "the Democrats who went over to the K-N s are mostly coming back." Similarly, Bigler maintained that "scores of . . . violent Know Nothings in 1854" were now supporting the Democratic ticket. These assertions seem partly justified. Approximately a fifth of the 1854 Americans cast Democratic ballots in 1856 (Table 12.10). Although a number of Democrats who deserted the party in 1854 for the Know Nothings remained alienated, others proved to be only temporarily disaffected. Some of the Know Nothing support for the Democrats may have represented Fillmore men who, as one Republican alleged, "feared absorption by the Republican party," but they were probably less numerous than former Democrats returning to their old loyalty. Some, especially those who voted Know Nothing but were not members of the order, may never have considered their defection from the Democracy as permanent. Others no doubt were disillusioned by the nativists' sorry record in office. For still others, the shift in the opposition's appeal from nativism to sectionalism, coupled with earlier vehement denunciations of the Democratic party that rekindled old feelings of party loyalty, drove these former Know Nothings back into the Democratic ranks.[108] Republican accusations that Fillmore men betrayed their pledges and bolted the Union ticket were apparently unjustified. As one would expect, those Americans who favored a joint electoral ticket voted overwhelmingly for the Union slate, but the so-called straight Fillmoreites, who steadfastly rejected all proposals for fusion in the presidential contest, were no less united in their support for the Union state ticket.[109] As Republicans charged repeatedly, American leaders directed their greatest animosity toward the Republican party rather than toward the Democrats.

Republicans pointed as well to other causes of the party's defeat. Several emphasized the damage produced by the charge that Frémont was a Catholic, although this issue was less a factor in the state than in the presidential contest. In some counties the liquor question continued to exact its toll. Carey conceded that Republican organizational shortcomings were also detrimental; lacking sufficient funds, the state committee expended little energy until after the Maine election and then conducted only a "spasmodic" campaign. The well-heeled Democrats, in contrast, made "a steady & regular effort . . . from the day of the adjournment of the Cincinnati convention."

106. Colfax to [?], October 24, Colfax Papers, NIHS; Thornbrough, ed., *Fletcher Diary*, v. 5, 591; Charles James to Morgan, October 27, Morgan Papers; Foulke, *Morton*, v. 1, 58.

107. John B. Guthrie to Buchanan, September 8, Buchanan Papers, HSPa; Philadelphia correspondence, *National Intelligencer*, October 18; Carey to Goodrich, October (copy), Carey Papers.

108. George A. Crawford to Breckinridge, August 20 (quotation), Breckinridge Family Papers; Bigler to Buchanan, September 10, Buchanan Papers, HSPa; Benjamin F. Killer to Cameron, October 19, Cameron Papers, HSDC; William V. Pettit to Welles, October 21 (quotation), Welles Papers, LC. Holt stresses the importance of attacks on the Democratic party in restoring the loyalty of disgruntled party members.

109. The regression estimates are that 97 percent of the Fillmore Union voters and 99 percent of the Fillmore Straight voters in November supported the Union ticket in the October election.

Another Republican denounced the state committee for concentrating almost exclusively on Philadelphia and for failing to get out the vote in the eastern counties.[110]

Republicans had little to show for their heavy expenditures in Philadelphia. The results in the city starkly illuminated the problems that afflicted the party. In the one city contest where the Republicans and Americans ran separate candidates, the results clearly revealed the weakness of the sectional party. The Republican candidate, who was popular and had support outside the party's ranks, polled only 8,000 votes, compared to 26,000 for the American and 33,000 for the Democratic. One careful observer calculated that in a tally of 68,000 votes, no more than 6,000 were Republican. The inept Republican organization in the city, the fear in the business classes of the party's radicalism, and the party's failure to crack the American ranks all contributed to the Republicans' feeble performance.[111]

The most common Republican explanation of their statewide loss was Democratic fraud. Blair, Weed, and Cameron, among others, had expressed fear beforehand that the Democrats would stuff the ballot boxes, particularly in Philadelphia, and afterwards Blair claimed that the Democrats had cast 4,000 illegal votes, more than the state margin of victory, in the city alone.[112] Such charges were not unusual after hotly contested elections in this period, but in this particular case they were more than partisan propaganda. Evidence surfaced later that the Democrats had resorted to large-scale naturalization of illegal voters before the election, had inflated the assessment lists by paying the taxes of political sympathizers, and had colonized a large number of floaters. The New York *Evening Post* pointed to the suspicious discrepancy that whereas statewide the total vote increased only 4 percent over that of 1852, in Philadelphia the increase was fully 30 percent. The Pittsburgh *Gazette* noted indignantly that the vote in Philadelphia changed several times as the results from the rest of the state were received with each change benefiting the Democrats. It proclaimed flatly that the Union ticket had received a majority of the legal votes cast.[113]

Forney persistently denied any wrongdoing. "We spent a great deal of money, but not one cent selfishly or corruptly," he recalled. Yet before the election, Forney hinted at the use of dishonest practices all too traditional in the city's politics. "We have naturalized a vast mass of men," he reported with great satisfaction. "The opposition are appalled. They cry fraud. Our most experienced men say *all is well.*" William L. Hirst, the Catholic leader of Philadelphia, disclosed on the eve of the balloting that the Democratic machine had naturalized 6,000 voters and added 8,700 men to the assessment rolls. Eventually, a clerk of the Philadelphia court of common pleas stood trial for issuing

---

110. William Chace to Welles, October 21, Welles Papers, LC; Carey to E. C. Caner, October 23, Carey to Mr. Smith, October 19 (quotation), Carey to Goodrich, October [ca. 17] (copies), Carey Papers; H. Calkins to D. A. Baldwin, October 18, Weed Papers, UR; New York *Evening Post*, October 21; Morgan to E. D. Williams, October 23, *Private*, Morgan Papers. Although critical of the state committee, Wilmot also pointed out somewhat irksomely that the liberal promises of aid for the state made at the June national convention had remained unfulfilled. Wilmot to Morgan, September 26, Morgan Papers.

111. Philadelphia correspondence, *National Intelligencer*, October 20. William L. Hirst, a prominent Philadelphia Democratic leader, believed that half the city's businessmen would vote Democratic. Hirst to Buchanan, October 12, Buchanan Papers, HSPa.

112. Weed to Morgan, Sunday morning [October 5], Morgan Papers; Francis P. Blair, Sr., to Elizabeth Blair Lee, October 7, Cameron to Francis P. Blair, Sr., October 9, Blair-Lee Papers; Francis P. Blair, Sr., to Montgomery Blair, Friday [October 17?], Blair Family Papers.

113. New York *Evening Post*, October 8, 22, November 6; Pittsburgh *Gazette*, October 18, 20, 21, quoted in Myers, "Republican Party in Pennsylvania," 132. For an example of Republican colonization, see T. Galick to Cameron, October 27, Cameron Papers, HSDC.

fraudulent naturalization papers. He admitted that he helped print 2,700 blank naturalization forms for the Democrats, documents that enabled unnaturalized immigrants to vote.[114] While the Republicans were hardly pristine innocents, had the votes been honestly cast the Union ticket would probably have carried the state.

VIII

The October defeats, while resting on razor-thin margins, understandably hurt Republican morale. "The majorities are small—very small—but they discourage our side," a dejected Rutherford B. Hayes testified. Morgan conceded that "our friends are more disappointed than it is pleasant to talk about." However narrow, the party's defeats in Pennsylvania and Indiana were decisive. "The prestige of our invincibility was destroyed by those elections," Caleb B. Smith noted, "& our friends have been desponding ever since." Realistic Republicans realized that the October elections ended any chance of victory in November. After waiting several days for fuller returns from Pennsylvania, Adams, speaking for most party leaders, reluctantly concluded that Republicans "must bid adieu to any idea of success" this year.[115]

Still, Republicans were not ready to abandon the fight. "The battle is to be fought to the last with all the power we can bring to it," Morgan announced. Sentiment to persevere derived from several considerations. Some party members, encouraged by the narrowness of the Democrats' victory and by extravagant claims of Republican non-voting, sustained hope that the verdict in Pennsylvania could somehow be reversed in November. Others saw nothing to be gained by quitting prematurely. They argued that an outward air of confidence coupled with a strenuous campaign until election day would strengthen the party's cause elsewhere. Weed conceded that all hope for national success was gone, but he maintained that "it was necessary to carry on the war" in Pennsylvania and Indiana in order to save other states.[116]

In the doubtful northern states, a union electoral ticket seemed the last hope for victory. The Fillmore forces had previously rejected all such proposals, while Republicans had counted heavily on victories in the October elections to give impetus to the union movement. Morgan pointed to the Republicans' fundamental handicap: "I am confident that but for Americanism—Victory would be certain."[117] Party leaders in several states, backed by the national committee, undertook a desperate, last-minute attempt to get the opposition to agree on a single electoral ticket. Eventually, Republicans considered proposals for union in New Jersey, Illinois, Indiana, and Pennsylvania. Sentiment for combining with the Fillmore Americans was stronger in Pennsylvania and New Jersey, where Republicans took the lead in proposing a coalition, than in Indiana and Illinois, where they evidenced little enthusiasm for the idea.

---

114. Forney to Buchanan, October 3 (quotation), Hirst to Buchanan, October 12, 16, Buchanan Papers, HSPa; Forney, *Anecdotes*, v. 2, 240; Myers, "Republican Party in Pennsylvania," 133–34. Subsequently one well-placed Philadelphia Democrat acknowledged privately that the party had used fraudulent naturalization papers in the 1856 election. Joseph B. Baker to Buchanan, June 27, July 4, 1857, June 1, 1860, Buchanan Papers, HSPa.

115. Morgan to Welles, October 22, *Private*, Welles Papers, LC; Hayes quoted in Nevins, *Ordeal of the Union*, v. 2, 509; Caleb B. Smith to Schouler, November 2, Schouler Papers; Adams Diary, October 15, 16, 17 (quotation), Adams Family Papers.

116. Morgan to Welles, October 22, *Private*, Welles Papers, LC; Weed to Samuel G. Andrews, November 12, Jane Andrews Espy Papers, CinHS.

117. Morgan to Welles, October 22, *Private*, Welles Papers, LC.

In New Jersey and Illinois, attempts to form a common electoral ticket faltered in the face of the continuing opposition of the Americans. Nativist leaders in New Jersey capitulated to intense outside pressure and rejected an agreement negotiated by the executive committee of the Frémont and Fillmore organizations. Greatly complicating the situation was the complex course of Robert Stockton, who tried to be all things to all parties. He endorsed Fillmore only on condition that no union with the Republicans be made, conducted marathon discussions with the Frémont leaders to arrange for a single slate of electors, and then in the final days of the campaign threw his influence behind Buchanan.[118] Negotiations between the Republicans and Americans in Illinois were much more informal and never very serious, since neither party displayed much interest in the proposal.[119]

In Indiana, the bitter accusations exchanged by Republicans and Americans following the state election destroyed what little chance there was for union. Blaming alleged American desertions for Morton's defeat, one Indiana Republican announced that he was ready to "fight alone for the Republican principles, even though I am beaten at every election." Colfax related that the Republicans rejected an unofficial American proposal to divide the electoral ticket with eight Frémont and five Fillmore electors. "We were satisfied that we should be weaker with this Fusion than without—as it would alienate all the foreign vote & would not bring more than half the Fillmore vote to us at any rate," he explained, adding, "We told them we had a future before us & they had not."[120]

American leaders could not agree on the correct policy to pursue. Armed with letters from Stephen Sammons, president of the New York state council, and E. R. Jewett, chairman of the American campaign committee in the same state, James R. Thompson of Rochester, a second-rank American politician, went to Indiana following the collapse of these negotiations. In separate interviews with John Defrees and Richard W. Thompson, the chairman of the Republican and American parties respectively, James Thompson stressed the imperative necessity of union in the presidential election. While Defrees was amenable, his American counterpart absolutely refused to countenance any such proposal, pleading lack of time to make cooperation effective and declaring that "the breach here was so wide that it could not be healed" in any event. Most American leaders backed the state chairman, and in the end nothing came of the New Yorker's trip. Believing that the obstinacy of Indiana Americans would inevitably elect Buchanan, he angrily termed their course "suecidal [*sic*]."[121]

---

118. Efforts to unite the Republicans and Fillmore Americans in New Jersey can be followed in Charles Deshler to Fillmore, August 8, October 24, 27, Joseph N. Randolph to Fillmore, September 1, October 29, Fillmore Papers, SUNY; William P. Sherman to Morgan, October 24, Private and Confidential, Morgan to Welles, October 27, *Private* (copy), Morgan Papers; J. N. Randolph to James Bishop, September 15, Jonathan R. Ford to Bishop, September 8, James Bishop Papers, Rutgers University; Egbert N. Grandin to Thomas H. Dudley, August 27, Dudley Papers; Alexander Cummings to Weed, October 28, F. S. Evans to Weed, September 10, *Strictly Confidential*, Weed Papers, UR.

119. "Steeltrap" [James R. Thompson] to Fillmore, November 1, Fillmore Papers, SUNY.

120. W. Morrow to S. Straight, October 26, Cincinnati *Commercial*, October 28 (quotation); Colfax to Defrees, October 27, quoted in Van Bolt, "Republican Party in Indiana," 215; Brand, "Know Nothing Party in Indiana," 286.

121. "Steeltrap" [James R. Thompson] to Fillmore, November 1 (quotation), James R. Thompson to Fillmore, October 29, Richard W. Thompson to Fillmore, November 10, Fillmore Papers, SUNY; Thornbrough, ed., *Fletcher Diary*, v. 5, 593–94; Cincinnati *Commercial*, October 17, 20, 21, 23, 24, 25; Charles James to Morgan, November 2, Morgan Papers. For Richard W. Thompson's opposition to the Republicans, see J. B. Jones and J. T. Moffatt to Henry S. Lane, June 25, Henry S. Lane Papers, IndHS.

To what extent James Thompson acted with Fillmore's concurrence is unclear. He tried to meet the former president on his way west, but whether he did so is unknown. On the other hand, he informed Fillmore fully on the progress of his talks. Emphasizing the importance of preventing Buchanan from carrying the state, he apparently advocated that the Americans support the Frémont electoral ticket (no wonder Defrees endorsed the plan!). Richard Thompson retorted that such a course would destroy the American organization in the state. His suspicions were aroused further when he learned that the New Yorker's mission had been secretly funded by Republicans.[122]

The most concerted attempt by Republicans to reach some agreement with the nativists occurred in Pennsylvania. The eventual Republican plan, devised by Blair, Cameron, Weed, and Wilson, was to name twenty-six electors who would run on both the Fillmore and Frémont electoral tickets, with the twenty-seventh elector being Fillmore or Frémont. If victorious, the electors would cast the state's vote (minus the one elector inevitably lost) for Frémont and Fillmore in proportion to each party's share of the combined vote as indicated by the totals for the twenty-seventh elector, or in the event that the state's electoral vote would elect either candidate, then they would cast all twenty-six votes for him. Republican leaders were confident that under this arrangement Frémont would receive a majority of the electors and perhaps all twenty-six. Attempts to agree on a plan before the state election failed, but Republicans and North Americans joined in calling a convention for October 21 to arrange for union. After some prodding even to consider the matter, a majority of the Fillmore state committee members rejected the plan along with five additional proposals offered by the North Americans. The committee then reaffirmed its commitment to the Fillmore ticket already in the field, whereupon a minority of the committee's members announced their support for the union movement and withdrew. At the subsequent October 21 convention the Republicans and North Americans, joined by a group of Fillmore Americans, named a joint electoral ticket.[123] Although the Republicans entered no separate slate of Frémont electors, the union of opposition was only partial at best. Having suffered several earlier bolts, the Americans now confronted another division between the so-called Fillmore Union men, who endorsed the joint ticket, and the Fillmore Straight men, who supported the original Fillmore electoral slate. Disappointed, Morgan accused the Fillmore leaders of keeping their electoral ticket in the field "for the express purpose of giving Buchanan the state."[124] The discovery that John Sanderson, the American

---

Thompson admitted after the election that he overestimated Fillmore's strength but expressed no regret over his action. Richard W. Thompson to Fillmore, November 10, Fillmore Papers, SUNY.

122. Richard W. Thompson to Fillmore, November 10, James R. Thompson to Fillmore, October 27, unsigned telegram from James R. Thompson, dated Rochester, October 28, Fillmore Papers, SUNY. James Thompson's telegram requested that Fillmore meet him at the train station in Buffalo, but Fillmore did not know whom the message was from, for he endorsed it "Anonymous." His confusion arose from an unexplained delay in delivery of Thompson's letter indicating that he was going west; Fillmore's endorsement establishes that he did not receive the letter until the 29th, the day after the requested meeting. Whether Fillmore learned of Thompson's trip by other means and conferred with him is not indicated, although it is clear from Thompson's reports that he believed that he was acting in accord with the former president's wishes.

123. Morgan to Welles, October 15, 18, 22, Welles Papers, LC; McClure, *Recollections*, 45–46; Myers, "Republican Party in Pennsylvania," 134–36. Six members of the twenty-seven-man American committee backed the Union ticket. For efforts of the Fillmore men to block any agreement with the Republicans, see E. R. Jewett to Fillmore, October 12, Fillmore Papers, SUNY.

124. Morgan to Welles, October 18, Welles Papers, LC.

chairman, was working in close collaboration with Forney further excited Republican indignation.[125]

Some Republicans, particularly those prominent in denouncing the Know Nothings, protested against any attempt to form a coalition with the Americans.[126] Republican hostility was more important in Indiana and Illinois than in Pennsylvania and New Jersey, but in each of these states, the anti-Democratic vote failed to unite in the presidential election primarily because of American opposition. Except possibly in Indiana, the Americans' rejection of all Republican offers was in accord with the policy of Fillmore and his advisers. In fact, Christopher L. Ward, the Democratic national chairman, privately informed Buchanan that he had arranged with the Fillmore leaders in New York to block, if necessary, any coalition between the Republicans and Americans in Pennsylvania.[127] Because of ominous warnings from southern supporters, Fillmore and his associates feared that any open alliance with the Republicans would destroy his chances in the South. If Fillmore managed to carry a few southern states, the election would probably be decided by the House; the former president therefore opposed any campaign strategy that might weaken him south of the Mason-Dixon line. Fillmore leaders also argued that uniting with the Republicans would not prevent Buchanan from carrying the doubtful northern states, while it would strengthen the Republicans.[128] Fillmore's conviction that the sectional party threatened the Union, combined with his hatred for many of the party's leaders, most notably Seward and Weed, made him unwilling to do anything that would aid the Republicans. In an interview during the campaign, McClure found the former president "embittered against those whom he regarded as the radical Republicans who supported Fremont. I found the dregs of his great battle for the acceptance of the Compromise measures, and the sting of his defeat in the Whig convention of 1852, pointedly reflected in him, and he was tenfold more hostile to Fremont than he was to Buchanan."[129]

After the October elections, Fillmore hailed the certainty that Frémont could not be elected as "a great point gained." Far shrewder was the assessment of his running mate, Andrew Jackson Donelson. "My idea throughout the canvass," he told Fillmore, "has been that it was our policy first to kill off Buchanan." If the Democratic nominee carried Pennsylvania, Indiana, and Illinois because of divisions among the opposition, the American vice-presidential nominee noted, he would be elected.[130] Taking a far too

---

125. Forney to Buchanan, October 18, Buchanan Papers, HSPa; Myers, "Republican Party in Pennsylvania," 134–36; Crandall, *Republican Party*, 278.

126. The Cincinnati *Commercial* and the *Ashtabula Sentinel* were two papers that spoke out consistently against any coalition with the Know Nothings. See, for example, the *Commercial*, June 10, October 17, 20, 21, 23, 24.

127. Christopher Ward to Buchanan, September 10, Buchanan Papers, HSPa; Morgan to George P. Morgan, October 21, *Private* (copy), Morgan Papers; E. R. Jewett to Fillmore, October 12, Fillmore Papers, SUNY. Jewett and Francis Granger both went to Pennsylvania to work against any joint electoral ticket, and Jewett reported that "a good many letters" opposing the union movement had been written to American leaders in the state.

128. Vespasian Ellis to Alexander H. H. Stuart, October 10, Alexander H. H. Stuart Papers, University of Virginia; Fillmore to Kenneth Rayner, November 14, Fillmore Papers, BECHS; Henry D. Moore to Fillmore, October 31, William R. Wilson to Fillmore, October 14, Henry F. Thomas to Fillmore, July 25, W. A. Glanville to Fillmore, October 21, Fillmore Papers, SUNY.

129. McClure, *Recollections*, 80.

130. Fillmore to Kennedy, October 25, Kennedy Papers; Andrew J. Donelson to Fillmore, October 22 (quotation), 25, Confidential, 29, Fillmore Papers, SUNY. After the election, Stephen Sammons asserted in

optimistic view of his popular strength, an outlook based largely on flattering but unrealistic reports from political associates, Fillmore badly misjudged his situation. To the very end he remained confident that if he failed to win an electoral majority, he would at least carry enough states to send the election into the House, where he believed that his chances were "decidedly the best." He thus saw no advantage in union. He remained immune to the warnings of his most clear-sighted correspondents that by opposing any cooperation with the Republicans, he was throwing away his only chance for victory.[131]

Near the end of the campaign, Fillmore wavered slightly in his opposition to any electoral coalition. In the final days before the election, when American leaders in Pennsylvania inquired whether they should continue to resist any alliance with the Republicans, the ex-president telegraphed characteristically, "Do as our friends there think best."[132] In reality, by this time it was too late to unite the two campaigns. The final chance for meaningful cooperation had passed with the October 21 convention, which his political cronies had labored night and day to sabotage. It was somehow appropriate that Fillmore closed his public life with the habitual indecisiveness that characterized his entire political career.

Following the October setback in Pennsylvania, and especially in view of the less than complete union that had been achieved, Morgan and others at party headquarters had to decide whether to spend any more money on the state. After visiting Pennsylvania, one of Morgan's correspondents reported that Republican leaders there "hardly know whether to make one more bold *vigorous* push—or give up all for lost." Asserting that Pennsylvania "*may* yet be saved," he informed the chairman that "they want men, & *funds*." William Chace, the secretary of the national committee, cautioned against sending any additional money unless the party structure in Philadelphia were reorganized. After inspecting the committee's records, he reported that its finances were in such complete disorder that "what was done with other funds & how much there was of other funds does not appear on their books." With Gibbons and the state committee already under heavy fire, Morgan sent Truman Smith to Philadelphia to investigate the situation and decide whether the expenditure of more funds would be justified. After a hasty survey, Smith concluded that Republicans had a chance to carry the state, and recommended that the national committee allot its remaining resources.[133] Embarking on a final drive for funds, Morgan sent to the state approximately $15,000 in additional money, plus a contingency fund of more than $80,000.[134] To ensure efficient distribution of the committee's money, Morgan delegated to Smith full power over the state

---

hindsight that the Americans should have pursued a policy of "warring directly & unremittingly against the Democracy." Sammons to Fillmore, November 7, Fillmore Papers, SUNY.

131. Fillmore to Kennedy, October 25 (quotation), Kennedy Papers; Fillmore to Edward Everett, October 8, Everett Papers; Fillmore to Donelson, August 7, Andrew Jackson Donelson Papers, LC; Edmund Blanchard to Fillmore, October 22, William R. Wilson to Fillmore, October 14, Fillmore Papers, SUNY.

132. Rayner to Fillmore, Telegram, November 3, Isaac Hazelhurst to Fillmore, October 30, Private (Fillmore's answer by telegraph, November 1, copy on the back of the letter), Fillmore to Rayner, November 24, Fillmore Papers, SUNY; Fillmore to Rayner, November 14, Fillmore Papers, BECHS. Fillmore telegraphed a similar message to Rayner, November 3 (copy on back of Rayner's telegram of the same date).

133. E. D. Culver to Morgan, October 20 (quotation), William Chace to Morgan, October 24, Truman Smith to Morgan, October 20, 27, Morgan Papers.

134. Morgan to John Schoolcraft, October 31, *Private* (copy), Morgan Papers; Rawley, "Financing the Frémont Campaign," 32–33.

committee's finances.[135] In addition, Cameron joined Smith to help oversee the campaign, and, with little more than a week remaining until the presidential election, the Republican campaign committee was reorganized to reflect Cameron's influence. But it was a case of too little, too late. The Republican organization remained slow and inefficient, as local leaders bitterly resented the imposition of outside control.[136]

Even had the national committee moved earlier to deal with the problem of the organizational disarray in Philadelphia, the presence of a separate Fillmore electoral ticket continued to be the major obstacle to a Frémont victory. The Know Nothing vote in Philadelphia, where the nativists were exceptionally strong, was critical. Kenneth Rayner, the prominent North Carolina American, indicated that he was willing to aid the union movement, and Republicans secretly paid him to deliver a series of speeches in the city during the campaign's final days. "He will in fact be the means of saving us if we are saved at all," a Republican editor declared. In his speeches, Rayner advised that Fillmore's supporters unite on a common ticket (which was an indirect endorsement of the union ticket). Looking desperately for some ray of hope, Republicans believed that his speeches had accomplished "great good."[137]

In contrast to the party's difficulties in Pennsylvania, the Republican campaign in New York proceeded smoothly. Not only did the state organization function effectively, but Republicans also gained influential converts from the other parties. George Law, Chauncey Shaffer, and James Barker headed a parade of American leaders who endorsed Frémont, and several Republicans predicted that Fillmore would receive less than half the previous nativist vote.[138] The party picked up new supporters from the Softs as well, including the former editor of the Albany *Atlas*, Henry Van Dyck, who ran for Congress in 1856 as a Republican. The Soft state convention's unqualified support for the Pierce administration, the party's national platform, and the subsequent reunion of the two New York factions alienated a number of free soil Democrats who until now had remained loyal to the party. The Republican state convention was careful to accord former Democrats prominent positions on the ticket. Morgan reported that converts from the Softs were "very numerous" and pronounced the state "eminently safe" for Frémont.[139] Republicans also recruited some notable conservative Whigs. Hamilton Fish was the best known example. Finally abandoning the attempt to maintain the national Whig organization, Fish wrote a carefully argued public letter advocating Frémont's election, which Republicans distributed widely.[140]

---

135. William C. Chace to Morgan, October 26, Lindley Smyth to Morgan, October 29, Truman Smith to Morgan, October 27, Morgan to Smyth, October 25, 24 (copies), Morgan to Welles, October 27, *Private* (copy), Morgan Papers.

136. Alexander Cummings to Weed, October 25, Morgan to Welles, October 27, *Private* (copy), William Chace to Morgan, October 26, Lindley Smyth to Morgan, October 29, Morgan Papers.

137. Alexander Cummings to Weed, October 28, 31 (quotation), Weed Papers, UR; Kenneth Rayner to Fillmore, November 27, Fillmore Papers SUNY.

138. Jesse Segoine to Seward, June 20, Ira Peck to Seward, August 4, Seward Papers, UR; H. W. Vail to Daniel Ullmann, August 20, Ullmann Papers, NYHS; Henry S. Randall to Henry D. Gilpin, June 10, Buchanan Papers, HSPa.

139. Henry Van Dyck to Martin Van Buren, January 14, Van Buren Papers, LC; Samuel Beardsley to Buchanan, July 1, October 18, Buchanan Papers, HSPa; John A. Cooke to Morgan, July 19, Morgan to James Nye, July 7 (copy), Morgan Papers; J. P. Guiteau to [Alpheus Felch], July 31, Alpheus Felch Papers, Detroit Public Library; "Voice from the Radical Democracy of New York," New York *Evening Post*, May 17.

140. Hamilton Fish, *Fremont, the Conservative Candidate* (n.p., [1856]); Weed to Fish, September 27, Fish Papers, LC.

Bolstered by these accessions and by the inability of the Buchanan and Fillmore forces to unite on a common opposition ticket, New York Republicans were confident of victory. A party worker informed Morgan after campaigning in the western counties that "you will be astonished at the majorities which some of them will give for the Republican ticket." Similarly Greeley, after a tour of the state, predicted that Frémont's majority would approach 100,000, an unheard-of margin.[141] Democrats were correspondingly glum. The Democratic party had been "annihilated" in the center of the state, former lieutenant governor Henry S. Randall told Martin Van Buren; he forecast that Frémont's vote in this section would "overwhelm" Buchanan's strength in the cities "by *thousands on thousands.*" Outwardly trying to appear confident, William L. Marcy privately acknowledged that the state was irredeemably lost.[142]

As the long and arduous 1856 presidential campaign finally drew to a close, Republicans manifested a variety of expectations. But dimly aware of political reality, Frémont remained confident to the very end. The would-be president devoted his time to organizing his cabinet. A handful of party strategists, most notably Blair, still believed that victory was possible.[143] Morgan oscillated between hope and despair. The party's most skillful leaders, however—such men as Weed, Cameron, Wilson, and Colfax—considered Frémont's cause hopeless and, already looking to the future, concentrated on polling as large a popular vote and carrying as many states as possible. After the Republican loss in October, Colfax spent a week in Indianapolis trying to rally the state committee, only to conclude that defeat was inevitable. "Our friends are disheartened, and I share it myself, though I say nothing."[144]

141. V. M. Rice to Morgan, November 1, Private (quotation), Morgan Papers; Greeley to Colfax, September 26, Greeley-Colfax Papers; Francis E. Spinner to John C. Underwood, October 9, John C. Underwood Papers, LC; William Cullen Bryant to John Bryant, October 14, Bryant Family Papers, NYPL; James M. Cook to Morgan, October 14, Morgan to D. F. Robinson, September 26 (copy), Morgan Papers.

142. Henry S. Randall to Martin Van Buren, September 5, Van Buren Papers, LC; Marcy to George Newell, October 26, William L. Marcy Papers, NYHS; Charles Mason Diary, August 6, 20, Mason Papers; Amasa J. Parker to Buchanan, September 14, Buchanan Papers, HSPa.

143. Jessie Frémont to Elizabeth Blair Lee, November 2, n.d. [October 15–November 1], Blair-Lee Papers; Smith, *Blair Family*, v. 1, 378–79. For other examples of Republican optimism, see Charles Gibbons to Morgan, November 3, Lindley Smyth to Morgan, October 22, Morgan Papers.

144. Morgan to William Chace, October 29, Morgan to Schoolcraft, November 3, *Private* (copies), Morgan Papers; Hollister, *Colfax*, 105.

13

A Victorious Defeat

Election day of 1856 was cold and overcast throughout much of the North. Despite the disagreeable weather, balloting in the free states on November 4 for the most part proceeded peacefully. In marked contrast to the enthusiasm so evident during the campaign, a mood of quiet seriousness prevailed as northerners stood patiently in what were at times very long lines to vote. At the peak of the crush, New York City voters waited well over two hours to cast their ballots. That evening, in large cities and smaller towns, wherever there were telegraph offices, men and women congregated in anxious anticipation to await first word of the results. "The whole Town is moved—as dispatches arrive," the wife of former senator Roger S. Baldwin wrote from New Haven as the returns clattered in over the wires. "I do not think there will be much quiet sleep through the length and breadth of our Country this night."[1]

I

Turnout in the free states verified reports during the campaign of intense popular interest. An estimated almost 83 percent of the northern electorate went to the polls in 1856, an increase of more than 7 percent compared to the 1852 presidential election. In fact, the rate of voting in the free states exceeded that of all other presidential contests during the period 1848–1860. Five states—California, Indiana, Iowa, Michigan, and Wisconsin—recorded their highest turnout for any election in this period. Of the four northern states that held significant state elections prior to the national election, only in Maine did voter participation drop. Reflecting the intensity of the campaign and the importance placed on the state contests, turnout in Indiana, Ohio, and Pennsylvania was especially high in October, yet in each state it was even greater in November. In Maine, on the other hand, the lopsided verdict in September badly deflated Democrats' confidence, and a significant decline in popular interest occurred in the presidential election.[2]

Note: Unless otherwise indicated, the year for newspaper and manuscript citations in this chapter is 1856.

1. Emily Baldwin to George W. Baldwin, November 4, Baldwin Family Papers; Nevins and Thomas, eds. *Strong Diary*, v. 2, 307; Thornbrough, ed., *Fletcher Diary*, v. 5, 595; New York *Times*, November 5.

2. See the turnout estimates presented in my essay, " 'Politics Seem to Enter into Everything,' " 18–19.

In the electoral vote, Buchanan was an easy victor, with 174 votes to 114 for Frémont and a mere eight for Fillmore. The Democratic nominee carried every southern state except Maryland, which went for Fillmore, along with five states in the North: Pennsylvania, New Jersey, Indiana, Illinois, and California. Frémont carried the remaining free states. Of the doubtful northern states, the Republicans won only Connecticut. In contradistinction to his performance in the Electoral College, where he had a comfortable margin, Buchanan failed to win a majority of the popular vote. Nationwide the Democratic nominee polled 1,832,955 votes (45.3 percent) compared to 1,340,537 for Frémont (33.1 percent) and 871,731 for Fillmore (21.6 percent).[3] The distribution of the vote was badly skewed sectionally. Frémont's strength was overwhelmingly confined to the northern states; he received only a minuscule 1,196 votes in the South (intimidation prevented distribution of Republican ballots in most southern states, but the party had virtually no supporters south of the Mason-Dixon line anyway). Fillmore, in contrast, was much stronger in the South, where he won 43.9 percent of the popular vote, than in the North, where he received only 13.4 percent. In fact, despite the wide disparity in population between the two sections, Fillmore tallied a majority (54.7 percent) of his votes in the slave states (Table 13.1). Fillmore's strength in the South, however, was insufficient to throw the election into the House, as too many of his southern supporters, fearful that Frémont would win, switched late in the contest to Buchanan and thereby cost the former president whatever chance he had to return to the White House.[4]

The Republicans' understanding with Henry Gardner enabled the party's national ticket to roll up a solid majority in Massachusetts, while at the same time the governor, with no substantial opposition, easily won a third term. Illinois also exhibited an unusual result, since Frémont narrowly lost the state (the outcome was unknown for several days) but William Bissell won the governorship, thus registering the Republicans' first statewide triumph in that closely contested state (Map 16). Frémont's performance in New York, where elections had previously been quite close, was especially noteworthy. His plurality over Buchanan exceeded 80,000 votes and was almost twice as large over Fillmore (Map 12).

Fillmore's vote was far below that of the American party in earlier contests, but, as Republican strategists had feared from the beginning, his candidacy, by dividing the opposition vote, assured a Democratic triumph. The combined Frémont-Fillmore totals surpassed Buchanan's vote in New Jersey and Illinois, while in Indiana and Pennsylvania Buchanan had a very slim majority (fewer than 2,000 votes in Indiana and half that in Pennsylvania) (Maps 13 and 15).[5] Though defeated, Frémont won a plurality of the popular

---

3. Election returns are from Walter Dean Burnham, *Presidential Ballots, 1836–1892* (Baltimore, 1955), supplemented by the *Tribune Almanac*, 1857. Gideon Welles thought that the Republicans had done as well as could be expected in all states except Pennsylvania and "probably" Indiana. Welles to Edwin D. Morgan, November 7, Edwin D. Morgan Papers.

4. John Pendleton Kennedy to Millard Fillmore, January 4, 1857 (copy), Kennedy Papers; Andrew J. Donelson to Fillmore, November 6, Blanton Duncan to Fillmore, November 6, Fillmore Papers, SUNY. A change of fewer than 7,700 votes in Kentucky, Tennessee, and Delaware, the three most loyal southern Whig states that Fillmore lost, would have thrown the election into the House. Buchanan's margin was very slender (fewer than 1,500 votes) in Louisiana as well. The Republicans' commanding victory in Maine in September, and the exceedingly close October elections in Indiana and Pennsylvania, exerted a significant impact on southern public opinion by convincing a number of conservatives that Fillmore stood no chance and that Buchanan represented the only hope to defeat Frémont and block the dreaded Republicans.

5. Even had Frémont's and Fillmore's votes been combined, Buchanan still would have been elected, assuming no other change in the distribution of the vote. Republicans countered, however, that a single anti-Democratic ticket would have polled a larger vote, since the October results and the division of the

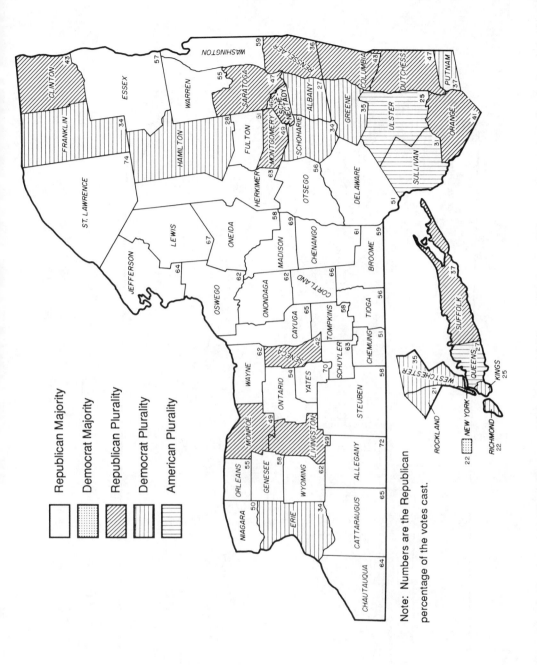

Republican Majority
Democrat Majority
Republican Plurality
Democrat Plurality
American Plurality

Note: Numbers are the Republican
percentage of the votes cast.

12. New York Vote for President, 1856

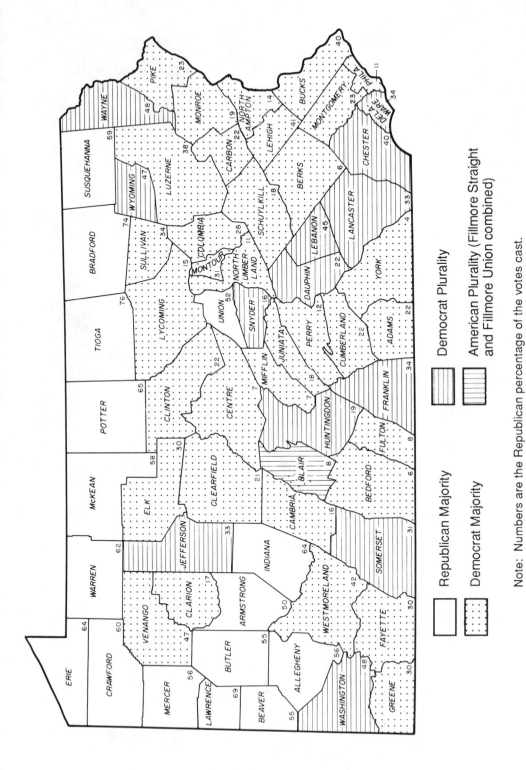

Note: Numbers are the Republican percentage of the votes cast.

Republican Majority

Democrat Majority

Democrat Plurality

American Plurality (Fillmore Straight and Fillmore Union combined)

13. Pennsylvania Vote for President, 1856

WILLIAMS
FULTON 56
LUCAS 41
OTTAWA 48
DEFIANCE 46
HENRY 46
WOOD
SANDUSKY 48
ERIE 60
LORAIN 57
CUYAHOGA
GEAUGA 80
LAKE 78
ASHTABULA 80
TRUMBULL 67
PAULDING 73
PUTNAM 41
HANCOCK
SENECA 48
HURON 66
MEDINA 62
SUMMIT 63
PORTAGE 58
MAHONING 54
VAN WERT 48
ALLEN 46
HARDIN
WYANDOT 47
CRAWFORD 47
RICHLAND 43
ASHLAND
WAYNE 49
STARK 50
COLUMBIANA 57
MERCER 33
AUGLAIZE 35
LOGAN 56
MARION 51
MORROW 47
KNOX 53
HOLMES 37
COSHOCTON 48
TUSCARAWAS 52
CARROLL 56
HARRISON 56
JEFFERSON 51
SHELBY 46
UNION 52
DELAWARE 55
LICKING
GUERNSEY 52
BELMONT 28
DARKE 48
MIAMI 59
CHAMPAIGN 49
CLARK 60
MADISON 46
FRANKLIN 44
MUSKINGUM 44
NOBLE 41
MONROE 23
PREBLE 55
MONTGOMERY 46
GREENE 46
FAYETTE 64
PICKAWAY 41
FAIRFIELD 30
PERRY 37
MORGAN 53
WASHINGTON 52
MONROE 51
BUTLER 37
WARREN 55
CLINTON 60
ROSS 42
HOCKING 41
VINTON 43
ATHENS 60
HAMILTON 33
CLERMONT
HIGHLAND 37
PIKE 25
JACKSON 34
MEIGS 50
BROWN 38
ADAMS 36
SCIOTO 40
GALLIA 19
LAWRENCE 15
26

☐ Republican Majority

▨ Democrat Majority

▨ Republican Plurality

▤ Democrat Plurality

Note: Numbers are the Republican percentage of the votes cast.

14. Ohio Vote for President, 1856

Note: Numbers are the Republican percentage of the votes cast

Republican Majority

Democrat Majority

Republican Plurality

Democrat Plurality

15. Indiana Vote for President, 1856

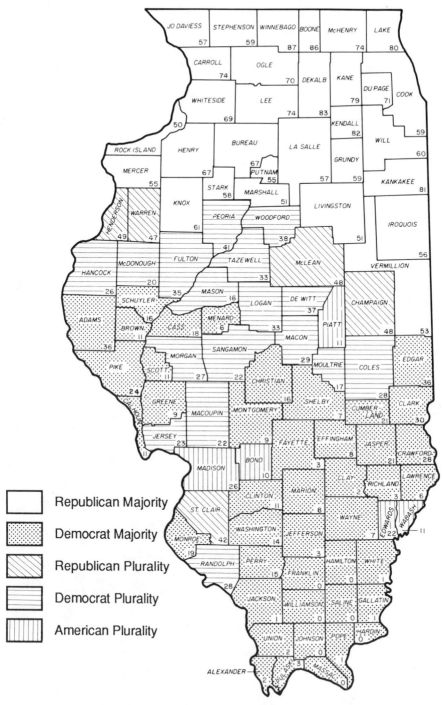

Note: Numbers are the Republican percentage of the votes cast.

16. Illinois Vote for President, 1856

vote in the free states, a performance that was little short of astounding in view of the party's position the year before. In less than twelve months the Republicans had transformed their party from the weakest party in the North to the strongest.

II

"We are beaten, and that is enough," Ohio governor Salmon P. Chase noted despondently. "Every body can tell why; but hardly any dozen men agree in their whys."[6] As Chase's words suggested, the Republican defeat grew out of a number of causes. Governor Geary's efforts to restore peace in Kansas, the Democrats' advantage in campaign funds, the race issue and the inevitable identification of the Republican party with the cause of blacks, Buchanan's image as a safe conservative, and Democratic promises that he would deal fairly with both sides in Kansas all exerted influence. More important was the Republicans' lack of time to establish an effective party organization, particularly in states where they faced stiff competition. In addition to Pennsylvania, where these problems were monumental, organizational difficulties plagued the party in several states where it formed relatively late, especially Indiana, New Jersey, and Connecticut. Following Frémont's defeat, former People's party chairman Michael Garber voiced his disgust over the conduct of the campaign. "The gentlemen who engineered the Republican party in Indiana are clever, estimable men, every one of them," he commented sarcastically, "but as political leaders they are imbeciles." Looking back on the 1856 campaign, a Massachusetts Republican mused that "we were a sort of mob, unorganized, contending with a well drilled and bold enemy. We did wonders because we were enthusiastic and in earnest, but no enthusiasm or earnestness can stand against cold blooded and efficient drill."[7]

Republicans' disorganization was most apparent in Pennsylvania, where repeated efforts by national leaders to coordinate the party's campaign had failed. After the election, Thurlow Weed and Simon Cameron exchanged views on the party's difficulties in the state. Miffed that the state committee had tried to ignore him, Cameron placed responsibility for the chaotic state of affairs squarely on Charles Gibbons and other members of the Andrew Curtin-James Pollock faction of former Whigs: "I saw the error committed in placing the movement in the hands of ignorant and conceited men. The whigs of this state cannot control a campaign; and they would not permit democrats to advise or help them." Weed agreed tactfully that organization "was sadly neglected" in the state and that the party was led by "feeble men in Philadelphia."[8] Less charitable, the *Ashtabula Sentinel* also blamed the Republican defeat on party leaders in Pennsylvania, "as sublime a set of asses as the sun ever shone upon." It dismissed them as "utterly unfit

---

opposition between Frémont and Fillmore caused some men to lose hope and abstain, but this argument did not take into account that a number of Fillmore's supporters would have gone over to the Democrats if the choice were narrowed to Buchanan and Frémont.

6. Salmon P. Chase to E. L. Pierce, December 7, Edward L. Pierce Papers, HU.

7. Madison *Evening Courier*, November 6, quoted in Mildred Stoler, "The Democratic Element in the New Republican Party in Indiana," *Indiana Magazine of History*, v. 36 (September, 1940), 189–90; Charles W. Elliott to Robert Carter, February 6, 1859, Carter Papers, Also see Congdon, *Reminiscences*, 211; Welles to Morgan, June 12, 1857, quoted in Parmet, "Know-Nothings in Connecticut," 237; Philadelphia *North American*, November 7, 8.

8. Simon Cameron to Thurlow Weed, November 9, Weed Papers, UR; Weed to Cameron, November 12, Cameron Papers, LC; James T. Furness to Sumner, November 13, Sumner Papers, HU.

to conduct a spelling match in a log school house.'' By catering to the Fillmore men, they were promptly cheated, and not surprisingly, for ''a more ridiculous contrivance than the union . . . project of Pennsylvania, never was enacted by men outside a mad house.'' In the long run, it may have been wiser, as the *Sentinel* advocated, to attack Fillmore and the Americans openly—something the state central committee refused to do; but there is no doubt that such a policy would have led to defeat in 1856. Critics in other states, as one member of the state committee emphasized, never fully appreciated the special difficulties that the Republican movement in Pennsylvania had to overcome.[9]

The most important cause of the Republican defeat, one these organizational problems merely exacerbated, was the party's failure to win greater support from conservative Whigs and Know Nothings. Fear of disunion, which one Democrat termed ''our strongest argument,'' was especially influential among old-line Whigs, while the bogus charge of Frémont's Catholicism, which Thaddeus Stevens contended ''lost us the Nation,'' particularly hurt among nativists.[10] Of the two, the Catholic accusation was probably more damaging. Horace Greeley's frustration over his and other party leaders' inability to deal effectively with this matter burst forth after the election. ''Thousands'' of free soil men, he exclaimed in exasperation, refused to vote for Frémont out of fear that his election ''would give us all over to the tender mercies of the Pope!'' Weed believed that the loss of a portion of the nativist vote to Fillmore turned the tide; he considered the Republican convention's failure to take a vice-presidential nominee acceptable to the North Americans the major error of the campaign. This refusal not only engendered hard feelings and made fusion less harmonious, but it wasted a good deal of Republican leaders' time in solving the problem, time that could have been spent more profitably on other aspects of the campaign.[11]

Their hopes dashed, a number of Republicans blamed Fillmore for Buchanan's victory. ''Our defeat is clearly not owing to the numerical strength of the Nebraska Bill party, but by [*sic*] a sullen duplicity on the part of Mr. Fillmores small impracticable faction in Penna and other northern States,'' mourned a Kansas free state leader. North American governor Ralph Metcalf of New Hampshire insisted that nine-tenths of Fillmore's supporters in the free states preferred Frémont to Buchanan. Whether, as Metcalf and other Republicans too readily assumed, the vast majority of Fillmore's northern votes would have gone to the Republicans in a two-way race is questionable.[12] Still, analysis of the sources of Frémont's vote indicates that Republicans were correct in identifying the problem they faced if not its solution.

Only in Indiana, Connecticut, and Massachusetts, of the eight states examined, did the Republicans win three-fourths or better of the former Whig vote (Tables 13.2 through

---

9. *Ashtabula Sentinel*, November 13; Lindley Smyth to Morgan, October 25, Edwin D. Morgan Papers. The Cincinnati *Commercial*, November 8, and the New York *Herald*, November 8, were also particularly severe in their criticism.

10. Charles Mason Diary, October 17, Mason Papers; Thaddeus Stevens to Dr. Gazzam, August 24 (copy), Edward McPherson Papers; Wilson, *Slave Power*, v. 2, 522; Philadelphia *North American*, November 7. The *Ohio State Journal*, November 7, after reiterating the many personal accusations levied against Frémont during the campaign, said: ''The Catholic charge, however, was the one most dwelt upon, and it had the most effect. It undoubtedly kept from him many votes, and added thousands to Buchanan and Fillmore, especially the latter.''

11. New York *Tribune*, November 8; Weed to Cameron, November 12, Cameron Papers, LC.

12. M. M. Delahay to Nathaniel P. Banks, Jr., November 8, Banks Papers, IllSHL; Ralph Metcalf to Stilman S. Davis, November 16, NHHS; Chicago *Tribune* quoted in the Springfield *Republican*, November 18.

13.9). [13] In Maine, New York, Ohio, and Illinois, a majority of Scott's supporters backed Frémont, but in Pennsylvania, a critical state that the party lost, apparently fewer than half the 1852 Whigs cast Republican ballots, and Whig opposition to Frémont was also especially marked in the southern counties of Indiana and Illinois. The claim of one Indiana Whig that statewide 20,000 of his fellow party members voted for Buchanan appears exaggerated, but a sizable number, as Schuyler Colfax had foreseen after speaking in the southern portion of the state, obviously voted for Fillmore rather than Frémont.[14] George W. Julian and Michael Garber, an unlikely pair, joined in criticizing the policy of the Republican central committee for abandoning southern Indiana to the Democrats and Americans. These were the very counties, they argued, where the Republicans should have labored vigorously to win votes (Maps 15 and 16).[15]

Republicans' "half victory" in Illinois, as Gustave Koerner termed it, where Bissell was victorious while Buchanan simultaneously carried the state, highlighted Frémont's failure to win the conservative Whig vote. The popular Bissell had a reputation as an antislavery conservative, which his residence in the southern part of the state enhanced, and he enjoyed the additional advantage that he was opposed by only a weak third-party candidate. The difference in the two Republican candidates' totals stemmed almost entirely from former Whigs. Despite his Democratic background, Bissell displayed no special appeal to former Democrats, but among Scott voters he ran significantly better than did Frémont. Three times as many of these men cast American ballots in the presidential as in the state contest (Tables 13.3 and 13.10). Illinois politicians were no doubt correct in identifying these Whigs as mainly conservatives who hated the Democracy yet feared a sectional party. In fact, one Republican initially was apprehensive that conservatives would not support even Bissell, "so tender footed Some did appear on the name of *Black Republican*."[16] Especially in southern Illinois, where the Whigs were much more conservative than their counterparts in the northern part of the state, Bissell ran substantially better than Frémont among former Whigs. By way of contrast, in the northern counties, where Whigs had been gravitating to a coalition with the Free Soilers even before the Nebraska bill passed, Frémont garnered a much greater share of the old Whig vote, and Bissell's advantage was negligible.[17] Immediately after the national convention, Lincoln precisely analyzed the situation confronting the Republican party: "I think we shall elect Bissell, at all events—and, if we can get rid of the Filmore ticket, we

---

13. Because of its large increase in population between 1852 and 1856, Iowa has been excluded from this part of the analysis.

14. E. M. Huntington to John J. Crittenden, March 21, 1858, Crittenden Papers; Colfax to Horace Greeley and [Isaac?] Sherman, October 30, Greeley-Colfax Papers; *Ohio State Journal*, November 18. Whereas in Indiana's northernmost counties 1852 Whig voters almost unanimously backed Frémont, in the southern counties they divided evenly between him and Fillmore (47 and 45 percent respectively). Few traditional Whigs seem to have voted for Buchanan, although the estimates in Table 13.4 probably understate the extent of such defections.

15. Madison *Evening Courier*, November 6, quoted in Stoler, "Democratic Element in Indiana," 189–90; George W. Julian Diary, December 5, quoted in Clarke, *Julian*, 180–81.

16. Parneas Bond to Lyman Trumbull, June 2 (quotation), H. D. Simpson to Trumbull, November 29, Trumbull Papers; H. S. Baldwin to William Breckinridge, November 29, Breckinridge Family Papers.

17. Regression estimates for central and southern Illinois indicate that Bissell won 74 percent of the Scott voters in the central part of the state and 70 percent of these voters in the southern counties compared to 59 and 10 percent respectively who went for Frémont (in the southern counties the majority of old Whigs split their ticket and voted for Fillmore and Bissell). In the northern third of the state, however, among Scott voters Frémont ran only slightly behind Bissell (84 to 82 percent).

shall carry the state for Fremont also.'' Fillmore's strength among old-line Whigs in the central and southern portions of the state kept Illinois in Buchanan's column.[18]

In Illinois and elsewhere, accessions of anti-Nebraska Democrats did not entirely compensate for the loss of these old Whigs. To be sure, contemporaries gave great emphasis to alleged Republican strength among former Democrats. One of Buchanan's correspondents, for example, blamed the party's defeat in New York on the free soil agitation that had disconcerted the party for a decade and finally led ''multitudes'' of Democrats to leave the party.[19] Although defections of Democratic leaders to the Republican party received great publicity, the percentage of 1852 Democrats who voted Republican in Indiana, Illinois, and Pennsylvania was quite small (Tables 13.3, 13.4, and 13.9). The much-publicized conversions of Lyman Trumbull, Gustave Koerner, John Wentworth, John Palmer, and other important Democratic politicians to the Republican cause in Illinois apparently brought no large number of rank-and-file Democrats into the party.[20] Even in New York, where the Democratic party had been badly factionalized for years and where in 1855, and in even larger numbers in 1856, many party leaders joined the Republican party, approximately one in five Pierce voters went over to the Republicans (Table 13.7).[21] In Massachusetts, Connecticut, Maine, and Ohio, in contrast, Democratic losses were more substantial (Tables 13.2, 13.5, 13.6, and 13.8).[22] As this variation implies, the nature and context of past partisan conflict in a state, as well as national issues, were important in shaping the Republican coalition.

Also critical to Republican success or failure in 1856 was the Know Nothing vote. Contemporary observers pointed to the role of the Know Nothing movement in converting Whigs and Democrats, especially the latter, to Republicanism. Although far from being a defender of the secret society, Julian nevertheless called it ''a sort of 'underground railroad' '' by which Whigs and Democrats ''generally made their exodus from their former political masters.'' Vindicating the American party's utility, a New Hampshire politician argued that ''it has drawn many from the Democratic party, anti-slavery men, who could not have been induced to join the Whig or Free Soil parties.'' The Know Nothing movement, an Ohio Republican commented, ''was simply a stepping-stone'' for disaffected Whigs and Democrats on their way to becoming Republicans.[23] Voting patterns in four states—New York, Connecticut, Massachusetts,

---

18. Abraham Lincoln to Lyman Trumbull, June 27, Abraham Lincoln Papers, IllSHL; Chicago *Tribune* quoted in the Springfield *Republican*, November 18.

19. Samuel Beardsley to James Buchanan, November 7, Daniel S. Dickinson to Buchanan, November 11, Buchanan Papers, HSPa; Solomon G. Haven to Fillmore, July 15, Stephen S. Sammons to Fillmore, September 5, Fillmore Papers, SUNY. Hamilton Fish, on the other hand, questioned the extent of Democratic defections to the Republicans. Fish to John M. Bradford, December 20 (copy), Fish Papers, LC.

20. The Illinois tables probably underestimate Republican strength among former Democrats, especially in the northern counties. See Koerner, *Memoirs*, v. 2, 22–23. Nevertheless, contemporary observers seem to have exaggerated the extent of party switching among Illinois Democrats.

21. Table 13.7 probably underestimates Democratic defections to the Republicans, because the township sample overweights Buchanan's strength and underweights Frémont's.

22. From a factor analysis of the party's electoral support, John L. Hammond argues that the realignment of the 1850s ''affected the Democratic party very little in Ohio'': *The Politics of Benevolence: Revival Religion and American Voting Behavior* (Norwood, N. J., 1979), 111. In reality, as Table 13.8 indicates, the Ohio Democrats lost more than a quarter of their earlier supporters to the Republicans, a blow that crippled the state party for the remainder of the century.

23. Julian, ''Death-Struggle of the Republican Party,'' 265; Aaron Cragin to Weed, June 15, Seward Papers, UR; Brinkerhoff, *Recollections*, 91–92.

and Pennsylvania—where the Americans ran separate state tickets before the presidential election, plus Ohio, where a group of nativists promoted a third-party ticket in 1855, demonstrate the fundamental importance of the Know Nothings in the Republican coalition.

Former governor Allan Trimble's independent candidacy almost defeated Chase in the 1855 Ohio gubernatorial election. A year later, strengthened by the sectional events of the past twelve months, as well as by Frémont's much less radical image compared to Chase's, Republicans won a solid though not overwhelming victory (Map 14). Contributing to the increased Republican vote was that approximately one out of five of Trimble's supporters backed Frémont (Table 13.11). The extent of this defection is especially noteworthy, since the bulk of the Know Nothings voted for Chase in 1855, and thus Republican accessions in 1856 came from men who were previously hostile to the party.

Voting patterns in New York illustrate even more clearly the two-step erosion of the American voting base. Of Daniel Ullmann's supporters in 1854, about 40 percent voted for Frémont (Table 13.12). Some of these nativists had joined the Republican party in 1855, but many more did so in 1856. At the same time, a number of Democrats, who were initially attracted to the order, returned to their old allegiance. These desertions left the Fillmore cause a small minority in the state. One of Seward's correspondents was confident before the election that "Fillmore cannot get over one half of the votes of those who have been Know Nothings."[24] Furthermore, Frémont's greater strength among Pierce voters than among 1855 Soft voters (almost no Hards voted Republican) strongly infers that many, probably even a majority, of the former Democrats in the Republican ranks were not of the much-publicized Preston King-Abijah Mann, Jr., Free Soil-Barnburner variety, but entered via the secret American order (Tables 13.7 and 13.13).

Fillmore suffered even greater losses among traditional American voters in Connecticut and Massachusetts, where the American state organization had always taken an antislavery stance and was dominated by North Americans. In Connecticut, the dramatic increase in the Republican vote between April and November came overwhelmingly from Americans (Table 13.14). The diehard Whigs also moved predominantly into the Republican column, but they constituted only a small number of voters. Frémont won the Know Nothing vote in Connecticut by a landslide.[25] In Connecticut as in New York, the American movement seems to have been the means whereby many Democrats were eventually transferred to the Republican column. Whereas more than a third of the 1852 Democrats cast Frémont ballots, a much smaller proportion, only about four percent of those remaining in the party in April 1856 after many members had joined the Know Nothings, voted Republican. It appears, therefore, that well over half the Democratic defections to the Republicans in Connecticut occurred through the agency of Know Nothing lodges (Tables 13.2 and 13.14).[26]

In Massachusetts the Republican party also won substantial Know Nothing support. Of the original 1854 Know Nothings in the state, almost three-fourths voted for Frémont (Table 13.15). A number of these initial members had gone into the Republican party in 1855, but, even among Henry Gardner's 1855 supporters, men who rejected the

---

24. Ira R. Peck to William H. Seward, August 4, Seward Papers, UR.

25. In addition, an estimated 73 percent of the 1855 American voters supported Frémont.

26. Holt's conclusion for Pittsburgh appears much more widely applicable: "The Know-Nothing party, not the anti-Nebraska coalition, was the halfway house through which Democrats passed on their journey into the Republican party." *Forging a Majority*, 158.

blandishments of the Republican party in its first state campaign, an almost identical proportion cast Frémont ballots (Table 13.16). By a decisive margin former Know Nothings constituted the largest single group in the Republican coalition; it is revealing that Frémont ran as well among earlier Know Nothing voters as did Gardner, the most popular and influential American leader in the state. Voting patterns in the 1856 presidential and gubernatorial contests further substantiate the close ties between Know Nothingism and the Bay State Republicanism. Gardner's supporters almost unanimously (95 percent) voted for Frémont in the presidential contest. Fillmore's vote was confined primarily to men who voted for the Whig and the national American candidates in the state election. In addition, although some Frémont voters abstained in the gubernatorial race or voted for the anti-Gardner Honest Man's Independent ticket, an estimated 83 percent supported Gardner (Table 13.17). The significant Know Nothing infusion into the Republican ranks in 1856 and the close carryover in voting between the state and national elections leave no doubt that Know Nothingism played a major role—indeed, numerically the most significant role—in the transition to a Republican majority in Massachusetts.[27]

In the battleground state of Pennsylvania, where Republicans suffered their most crucial defeat, the party performed poorly among Scott's supporters, more than a third of whom went for Fillmore (Table 13.9). The strength of the Fillmore Union ticket was quite apparent. Republicans were correct when they argued during the campaign that the American masses desired some type of union to defeat Buchanan, only to have the Fillmore leaders stubbornly block any agreement. More than 50 percent of the 1854 Know Nothings supported the Fillmore Union ticket compared to only 10 percent who cast straight Fillmore ballots. Indeed, a majority of the original Know Nothings endorsed the Union movement at the polls (Table 13.18). The Republicans' weakness in the state arose directly from their limited success in detaching Americans from their previous affiliation. Even the majority who desired union on the presidential ticket remained loyal to the American party. Comparison of Frémont's strength among 1852 and 1854 Democratic voters reveals that a number of Democratic Know Nothings became Republicans while still others retained their American identification (Tables 13.9 and 13.18).[28] At the same time, because a decisive majority of Americans remained loyal to Fillmore, Frémont actually won fewer Know Nothing votes than did Buchanan. The return of nativist Democrats to their former allegiance probably accounted for the bulk of these desertions. The failure of the Republican party to make more substantial inroads into the American vote was the major reason for its weakness in Pennsylvania. In nearby New York, in

---

27. By a highly selective comparison of elections, Dale Baum, in "Know-Nothingism and the Republican Majority in Massachusetts: The Political Realignment of the 1850s," *JAH*, v. 64 (March, 1978), 969, 985–86, argues that Know Nothings were an unimportant part of the Republican coalition in Massachusetts. Tables 13.15 and 13.16 irrefutably demonstrate precisely the opposite. In making his argument, Baum inexplicably omits any analysis of Frémont's vote (even though Frémont was the first Republican candidate to carry the state), as well as any analysis of the relationship between Gardner's vote in 1854 and 1856 and Lincoln's in 1860. As contemporaries stressed repeatedly, former Know Nothings were a vital part of the Republican coalition in Massachusetts. Furthermore, of those 1855 Republicans participating, a majority (53 percent) voted for Gardner—behavior that is hardly consistent with Baum's view that the initial Republican coalition was made up of hardcore antislavery men unwilling to temporize with nativism. Even at the party's founding, as these figures demonstrate, only a minority of Massachusetts Republicans were unwilling to brook any concessions to nativism, and subsequent accessions from the Know Nothings reduced their strength in the Republican ranks still further.

28. John B. Guthrie to Buchanan, September 8, Buchanan Papers, HSPa.

contrast, over a third of the original 1854 Know Nothings cast Republican ballots in 1856—better than three times the proportion that did so in Pennsylvania. In Ohio, the rate of defection was almost double that of Pennsylvania, and this figure substantially underestimates the movement of Know Nothings into the Ohio Republican party. And in Connecticut, where the Americans moved en masse into the sectional party, and in Massachusetts, where a large majority did, the rate of American defections dwarfed that in Pennsylvania.

In voting for the Republican party, these former Know Nothings had not discarded their nativist sentiments, nor were these attitudes irrelevant to their new partisan identity. No doubt some Americans had never been deeply committed to nativist principles and without much deliberation quickly left the order for the Republican party. For the large majority of one-time Know Nothings, however, both nativism and antislavery remained important values, although many now gave greater priority to the latter without ceasing to care about the former. The argument that former Know Nothings' nativism ceased to have political significance when they voted Republican makes an artificial distinction between cultural and political nativism that is not found in the contemporary sources. For Know Nothing Republicans, as well as some Republicans who had never joined a nativist lodge, a dislike of Catholics remained relevant to their partisanship, since both the Republican party's rhetoric and its membership gave it an anti-Catholic image, even though the party placed first priority on the slavery issue. As long as Catholics were identified overwhelmingly with the Democratic party—an identification Republican spokesmen carefully fostered—and the Republican party recognized former Know Nothings and did not court the Catholic vote, nativists could find ample motivation to support the Republican party. A dislike of Catholics, as much as positive factors, accounts for the heavy nativist influx into the Republican ranks.[29] The New York *Times* wisely cautioned against the view, rooted more in some Republicans' wishful thinking than in hard political reality, that the American party's poor showing signaled the disappearance of nativist feeling from northern politics. "No sentiment, or conviction, which has the power to create such a party in so short a time, can perish or lose its vital force so suddenly," the paper admonished in analyzing the decline of the Know Nothing order. "We have very little doubt that the American sentiment is as strong now as it ever has been. The people of the country at large entertain the same convictions now upon the subject of the foreign vote, as they did a year ago."[30] By the time of the 1856 presidential election, however, a

---

29. For a contrary argument, see Foner, *Free Soil, Free Labor, Free Men,* 260; Baum, *Civil War Party System,* 31–32. Holt, *Political Crisis,* 179, presents a persuasive rebuttal. One might ask why, if nativism was irrelevant to the Republican party's electoral support, Republicans failed to nominate for office Catholics who were soundly antislavery. Unlike the Democrats, who on occasion, selected Catholics, Republicans in Pittsburgh and Cleveland, two cities with large Catholic populations, did not during the period 1855–1860 nominate a single Catholic. Holt, *Forging a Majority,* 354, 365; Kremm, "Republican Party in Cleveland," 289.

30. New York *Times,* November 18. Robert Kelley emphasizes that throughout American history "parties have been shaped by a feeling that their members shared a common enemy. This basic sense of an adversary relationship [is] the strongest force binding parties together and giving them meaning." "Ideology and Political Culture from Jefferson to Nixon," *AHR,* v. 82 (June, 1977), 558–59. Irish Catholics, like southerners and slaveholders, were a negative reference group for Republicans. Those historians who minimize the importance of anti-Catholicism in the formation of the Republican coalition ignore the importance of negative reference attitudes in voting behavior. For examples of these attitudes, see the Cincinnati *Enquirer,* March 29, 1855, November 2, 6.

majority of those who held these sentiments were in the ranks of the Republican party, not the American.

Some Republicans argued afterwards that Frémont's nomination had thrown away all chance for victory, whereas McLean, because he would have been stronger among Whigs and Americans, could have been elected.[31] Yet McLean's gains among these voters may well have been offset by losses among other groups, particularly Democrats. Although Republicans overemphasized their strength among anti-Nebraska Democrats, these votes were nevertheless essential to the party's winning margin in some of the states Frémont carried. One claim of the McLean managers—that Fillmore would withdraw if the judge were the nominee—was patently false. Their other contention—that the mass of Americans would desert the former president in any event—was probably also spurious. All things considered, it is likely that the Republicans would still have lost with McLean at the head of the ticket. The straight Fillmore vote in Pennsylvania was sufficiently large to give the state to Buchanan, and in Indiana, where the two parties had united on the state ticket, the Democrats triumphed anyway. Only in Illinois, where Whig defections cost Frémont the state, might McLean's nomination have made a difference, but he probably would have been much weaker among new and previous non-voters and the foreign-born, and this factor might well have produced defeat. It is difficult to imagine the same popular enthusiasm generated by Frémont's candidacy being manifested for such an elderly, lackluster political hack as McLean. Charles Dana expressed the view of many Republicans when he wrote after the election: "As for his [McLean's] coming within a gunshot of Fremont's vote, it is all gammon. He could not have carried the Northwest." Charles Francis Adams was probably nearest the truth when he commented immediately after the Philadelphia convention that if the Republicans lost, "We shall be told that it was because we rejected McLean. Had we taken McLean with the same result, we should be told that it was because we did not take Fremont."[32]

A comparison between the voting patterns in the anti-Nebraska-Know Nothing upheaval of 1854 with those in the 1856 presidential election further clarifies the process of realignment. In Ohio and Indiana, anti-Nebraska tickets were nominated in 1854, both of which employed the name *People's party* and represented a combined nativist-anti-Nebraska impulse. The large majority of People's party voters in Indiana backed Frémont, but a noteworthy minority voted for Buchanan or Fillmore in the southern portion of the state (Table 13.19). [33] In Ohio, the defection of anti-Nebraska voters to the Democrats was more sizable, and an additional number deserted to the Americans (Table 13.20). A similar pattern existed in Maine, where Anson Morrill's independent candidacy in 1854 had some attributes of a fusion movement, while in Iowa, where James Grimes had united a diverse coalition behind him, a small proportion of his supporters backed Fillmore in 1856 (Tables 13.21 and 13.22). The opposition in Pennsylvania and Illinois, on the other hand, had been unable to unite even in 1854, and these divisions, while less pronounced

---

31. Gamaliel Bailey to John Gorham Palfrey, October 19, Palfrey Papers, HU; Solomon Foot to Henry C. Carey, December 6, Carey Papers.

32. Charles A. Dana to James Shepherd Pike, December 23, *First Blows*, 354; Charles Francis Adams Diary, June 19, Adams Family Papers; Richard Corwine to William Schouler, November 7, Schouler Papers.

33. People's party supporters in northern and central Indiana voted solidly for Frémont, but in the southern part of the state approximately one out of five voted for Buchanan or Fillmore. Table 13.19 undoubtedly understates Fillmore's strength among People's party adherents.

in 1856, continued to undermine the anti-Democratic strength in both states (Tables 13.18 and 13.23). In none of these states was the anti-Nebraska vote cast solidly for Frémont.

The splintering of the 1854 anti-Democratic vote explains why the opposition victory of that year failed to produce a national victory two years later. A substantial number of anti-Nebraska voters were also Know Nothings, and even though the majority of the anti-Nebraska men gravitated to the Republican party, a minority supported Fillmore. Also an important factor was the return of a portion of the anti-Nebraska Democrats to their old partisan loyalty. Many, especially those who did not join the Know Nothings, probably never ceased to think of themselves as Democrats. Their 1854 bolt represented a one-time protest against the party's endorsement of the Kansas-Nebraska bill. Torn between their party identity and a dislike of national party policy, they reconciled themselves by one means or another to remaining Democrats. It is traditional to envision disillusioned party members whose views did not correspond with their party's as solving their internal conflict by forming a new party identity, and such changes did occur, both among nativist and anti-Nebraska Democrats, as the 1856 returns demonstrated. Nonetheless, a number of dissident Democrats eliminated the cross-pressures they felt not by deserting their party but by gradually adopting new opinions. Many Democrats who were angry over the Kansas-Nebraska Act presumably eventually endorsed Douglas's doctrine of popular sovereignty, and others perhaps suppressed their views on this matter in preference to other issues dividing the parties. This process has been amply documented for modern voters, and it seems reasonable to assume that it operated in the nineteenth century as well.[34] Still, even with the return of some earlier bolters, the Democratic majority in the North had shattered, although the anti-Democratic factions had not yet united in a single organization.

III

As with the nativists, Republicans also lavished considerable attention on immigrant voters, again with mixed results. Virtually all observers agreed that the Catholic Irish voted strongly Democratic. "All the Catholic Priests, and all the Irish Catholics [were] against us," one Republican typically reported.[35] In a letter widely ascribed to Archbishop Hughes, a Catholic prelate defended the opposition of Catholic voters to the Republican party. It was not so much that the Democrats particularly appealed to them,

---

34. Philip Converse, "The Nature of Belief Systems in Mass Publics," David Apter, ed., *Ideology and Discontent* (New York, 1964), 206–61, is the most influential exposition of modern findings concerning American voting behavior. Also see his "Public Opinion and Voting Behavior," Fred I. Greenstein and Nelson W. Polsby, eds., *Handbook of Political Science* (8 vols.: Reading, Mass., 1975), v. 4, 75–169. There is a wide and expanding literature on this topic. Among the most important studies are Norman H. Nie and Kristi Andersen, "Mass Belief Systems Revisited: Political Change and Attitude Structure," *Journal of Politics*, v. 36 (August, 1974), 540–87; Gerald M. Pomper, "From Confusion to Clarity: Issues and American Voters, 1956–1968," *APSR*, v. 66 (June, 1972), 415–28; and Michael Margolis, "From Confusion to Confusion: Issues and the American Voter (1956–1972)," *APSR*, v. 71 (March, 1977), 31–43.

35. R. U. Piper to William Cullen Bryant, November 12, Bryant-Godwin Collection, NYPL; Boston *Bee*, January 1, 1857, quoted in Bean, "Transformation of Parties," 367; Pittsburgh *Gazette*, November 11, 18; *Ohio State Journal*, November 7. The New York *Tribune*, November 8, asserted that there were at least 20,000 Catholic votes cast in New York City, and not one in fifty was for Frémont. Multiple regression analysis establishes a consistently negative relationship between Catholicism and Republican strength in New York, Pennsylvania, Ohio, Indiana, and Illinois. Table 13.27 surely exaggerates Catholic support for Fillmore but not Catholic hostility to the Republican party.

the author asserted, but rather that the opponents of the Democrats drove them away. First the Whigs and now the Republicans "have perpetually kept up an alliance with every species of anti-Catholic sympathies, and with the fag ends of every intolerant clique." By voting Republican, Catholics would have been "voting for their own degradation."[36]

Republicans disagreed, on the other hand, over the extent to which non-Catholic immigrants supported Frémont. For the most part, these groups were imbued with a strong hatred of Catholics, and they increasingly identified Catholicism with the Democratic party, yet they were also understandably anxious about nativist influence in the Republican party. In New York and Iowa, it appears that the Republican party held a marked appeal for English, Scottish, and Welsh voters, none of whom had been particular targets of the Know Nothings and indeed had often allied with the American movement. With a well-established tradition of hostility to the Irish Democracy, and less nervous about nativism than more visible foreign groups, the English, Scots, and Welsh seem to have transferred their allegiance largely to the Republicans (Tables 13.24 and 13.26).[37] Political observers were probably correct in claiming that a majority of Scandinavians, who were found primarily in the Northwest, voted Republican as well, while the more conservative Dutch for the most part were Democratic (Table 13.26).[38]

The evidence is less clear for the Scotch-Irish, although contemporaries generally placed them in the Republican column.[39] They were an especially important group in Pennsylvania, where they had tended to be Democratic until the nativist upheaval had shaken them loose from their loyalty. While some had spurned the Know Nothing movement because of its secrecy, many more because of their intense anti-Catholicism were drawn to the order's candidates; relations between the two groups were so intimate in many communities that one German leader referred to the Protestant Irish as "sort of backstairs members of the Know-Nothing lodges." Not all left the American camp in 1856, but the large majority seem to have become Republicans. A letter to the New York *Times*, written in response to an anti-Irish editorial, criticized the paper for failing to distinguish between Catholic and Protestant Irish and protested that while the former

---

36. Letter signed "A Catholic," which originally appeared in the New York *Courier and Enquirer*, reprinted in the *Catholic Telegraph*, December 13; John Hughes to Bernard Smith, November 28, Hughes Papers. For a strongly worded Catholic attack on the Republican party, see the *Catholic Telegraph*, August 9.

37. For claims of similar partisan behavior among the English, Scots, and Welsh in other areas, see Lewis Pughe to Morgan, October 14, Welles to Morgan, October 25, Edwin D. Morgan Papers; Schuyler Fassett to Hendrick B. Wright, August 15, Hendrick B. Wright Papers, Wyoming Historical and Geological Society; Pittsburgh *Gazette*, November 11; *Illinois State Journal*, November 17; *Ohio State Journal*, November 7. In Cincinnati, however, British voters seem to have scattered their support among all three presidential candidates with no clear preference; also note the negative relationship between the English-Welsh population and Frémont's vote in Indiana, and the positive coefficient for the proportion born in Scotland and the Republican vote in Pennsylvania (Table 13.41 and 13.43). Formisano finds that British and Canadian newcomers were strongly Republican in Michigan. "Ethnicity and Party in Michigan, 1854–60," Frederick C. Luebke, ed., *Ethnic Voters and the Election of Lincoln* (Lincoln, Neb., 1971), 193–94.

38. K. J. Fleischer to Seward, November 24, Broadside, Seward Papers, UR; Illinois correspondence signed "Grundy," New York *Evening Post*, August 28; Edward Pierce to Sumner, November 9, Sumner Papers, HU; Henry F. Scholte to Buchanan, November 17, Buchanan Papers, HSPa; Robert F. Swierenga, "The Ethnic Voter and the First Lincoln Election," *Civil War History*, v. 11 (March, 1965), 27–43; Formisano, "Ethnicity and Party," 188–89. Multiple regression analysis establishes that, without exception, in New York, Pennsylvania, Indiana, and Illinois the presence of Dutch Reform churches tended to reduce Frémont's vote.

39. Pittsburgh *Gazette*, November 11; *Ohio State Journal*, November 7.

voted Democratic, the Scotch-Irish "voted the Republican ticket almost without exception."[40]

Republicans devoted the greatest effort among foreign-born voters to the Germans because of their numbers and because there appeared to be a good prospect of making significant inroads into this traditional Democratic constituency. Republican strength among German voters varied greatly from locality to locality. In New York City, Republicans were unable to detach Germans from the Democratic party because of the nativist and temperance issues that earlier divided the city's politics and reinforced the Germans' loyalty to the Democratic party. The *Times* maintained that only a small minority of Germans in the metropolis supported Frémont, and the party seems not to have appealed to Germans throughout the rest of the state either (Table 13.24).[41] German opposition to the Republican ticket was apparently quite strong in Indiana as well (Table 13.25). In Du Bois County, which had the highest concentration of Germans in the state, Frémont received a minuscule twenty-one votes out of a total poll of 1,448, and in Vanderburgh County (Evansville), where about a third of the electorate was German, he ran almost thirty points below his statewide average, with only 12 percent of the vote. Dominated by the Know Nothings from its birth, the Hoosier Republican party had endorsed several nativist demands, and its 1856 state platform also called for enactment of a prohibitory law. All these considerations solidified the Democrats' hold on German voters, who, along with the other immigrant groups in the state, the New York *Tribune* maintained, "have gone in solid mass against the cause of Free Labor."[42] Similarly, in Iowa, where the Republican state convention had rejected German-sponsored resolutions on nativism, Germans do not seem to have voted Republican to any significant degree (Table 13.26).[43] In other states, however, Republicans appear to have done better among German voters. In Ohio, for example, through diligent effort Republicans apparently won only slightly fewer German votes than did the Democrats, and in Illinois, another western state with a significant German population, party managers believed that a majority of Germans voted for Frémont.[44] In these latter two states, the Republicans had actively

---

40. Charles Reemelin quoted in John B. Weaver, "Nativism and the Birth of the Republican Party in Ohio, 1854–1860" (unpublished Ph.D. dissertation, Ohio State University, 1982), 71; letter signed "A North of Ireland Protestant Republican," November 7, New York *Times*, November 11. The partisanship of the Scotch-Irish is especially difficult to determine because neither place of birth nor religion offers a clear index of their strength. An ecological regression analysis for Pennsylvania, based on the ethnic background of heads of households in 1850 in approximately a third (18) of the state's counties, reveals unanimous Scotch-Irish support for Frémont. The low number of cases is troubling, but these figures probably correctly reflect the one-sided partisanship of the Scotch-Irish. Also note the overwhelming support for Frémont among Presbyterians, and among the Irish when religion is controlled, in Pennsylvania (Table 13.28 and 13.41).

41. New York *Times*, November 6, 7. For a good discussion of the reasons for Democratic ascendancy among immigrant voters in New York City, see Rorabaugh, "Rising Democratic Spirits."

42. New York *Tribune*, November 7, Hollister, *Colfax*, 102; William T. Page to Lincoln, June 30, Herndon-Weik Collection; *Ohio State Journal*, November 7.

43. Table 13.26 undoubtedly exaggerates Fillmore's strength among Germans and understates Frémont's support, but nevertheless it seems clear that Buchanan won the bulk of the German vote in Iowa.

44. *Ohio State Journal*, November 7; Edward L. Pierce to Sumner, November 9, Sumner Papers, HU; Edward L. Pierce, *Effect of Proscriptive or Extreme Legislation against Foreigners in Massachusetts* (Boston, 1857); Buffalo *Telegraph* quoted in the New York *Times*, November 25. Regression estimates for Ohio are that German voters backed Buchanan over Frémont, 54 to 46 percent ($N = 49$). None voted for Fillmore. James M. Bergquist estimates that the Republicans won 55 to 60 percent of the German vote in Illinois, with wide variations among communities: "People and Politics in Transition: The Illinois Germans, 1850–60," Luebke, ed., *Ethnic Voters and the Election of Lincoln*, 209–10.

courted the Germans and recognized them within the party organization, had kept the Maine Law out of the party creed, and had sought from the beginning to direct nativist feeling into an anti-Catholic rather than anti-foreign channel.

The division in the German community to some extent followed religious lines, with Protestant Germans more likely to vote Republican while their Catholic countrymen remained Democratic, although German Catholics probably were not as intensely hostile to Republicanism as were their Irish co-religionists. Apparently only the more radical Germans, typified by the Turners, voted solidly for Frémont.[45] William A. Richardson, the Democratic candidate for governor in Illinois, informed Douglas after the 1856 campaign that unless Know Nothingism could be tied to the Republican party "time is thrown away upon any other Germans except Catholics."[46] In Cincinnati, where the Republican party's nativist taint drove many Protestant Germans back into the Democratic party in 1855, some naturalized voters returned to the Republican ranks, but a sufficient proportion remained Democratic, when combined with Fillmore's total, to give the city to Buchanan.[47] From Pittsburgh, a Democratic leader alerted Buchanan in 1856 that "we shall not have that portion of the Irish and German Protestant vote, that came over to us last fall." Likewise, a Michigan correspondent affirmed that "a considerable part of the Protestant Germans will sustain Fremont," an assessment parallel to that offered by Koerner concerning German voters in Illinois.[48] Republicans won many more naturalized votes than the Whigs had and were without question stronger among German voters, but Protestant Germans were far from unanimous in their support for Frémont, as the

---

45. Rochester *Daily Union*, November 6; A. H. Scott to George H. Paul, November 1, Paul Papers; Edward L. Pierce, *The Effect of Proscriptive or Extreme Legislation against Foreigners*, (Boston, 1857), 11. Despite the publicity given to the Turners in the northern press, a Philadelphia Democrat emphasized that many Germans distrusted them as too radical, and their influence was overstated. Stephen S. Remale to Buchanan, July 28, Buchanan Papers.

46. Richardson to Douglas, May 30, 1857, quoted in Johannsen, *Douglas*, 653. Many Protestant Germans were cross-pressured. They disliked slavery and had no wish to see it expand, and they abhorred Catholicism, yet they were repelled by the anti-foreign aspects of nativism, vigorously opposed prohibition, and were deeply suspicious of Know Nothing influence and the presence of so many Maine Law men in the Republican party. See Samuel C. Parks to Trumbull, February 10, Trumbull Papers; Thornbrough, ed., *Fletcher Diary*, v. 5, 533; Carl Schurz, *Reminiscences*, v. 2, 66.

47. Cincinnati *Enquirer*, November 6. German voters in Cincinnati apparently divided about evenly with an estimated third supporting Frémont and another third Buchanan (the remainder failed to vote). The Irish, in contrast, went overwhelmingly Democratic (74 percent).

48. John B. Guthrie to Buchanan, September 8, Buchanan Papers, HSPa; Michigan correspondence signed "Theta," Illinois correspondence signed "Grundy," New York *Evening Post*, September 1, August 28; Koerner, *Memoirs*, v. 2, 21; Louise Taft to Dear Mother, September 30, Taft Papers; John C. Jacobs to Truman Smith, October 10, Edwin D. Morgan Papers; Thomas Quick to Trumbull, July 2, Trumbull Papers. Statewide, the Republicans displayed little strength among the Pennsylvania Dutch, long known for their social conservatism and dislike of radical reform causes. Estimates based on slightly fewer than a third of the state's counties are that 52 percent voted Democratic, 28 percent for Fillmore, and only 1 percent for Frémont (the remainder failed to vote). These figures no doubt unduly minimize Frémont's support among Pennsylvania's German-stock voters but probably accurately reflect their greater support for his opponents. Also note the estimates for Lutheran and German Reform voting in Table 13.28. Apparently, those Pennsylvania Dutch who voted Know Nothing in 1854 for the most part remained loyal to Fillmore in 1856. Some of these voters were German immigrants, but a much larger proportion were native-born citizens, although they still preserved many attributes of German culture. Republicans appear to have been substantially stronger among Germans in Pittsburgh, however. Buffalo *Telegraph* quoted in the New York *Times*, November 25; Holt, *Forging a Majority*, 215–16.

relationship between voting and religion reveals (Tables 13.27 through 13.31). [49] Despite winning some support, Republicans had good reason to be disappointed with their overall share of the German vote. Mutual distrust and dislike between Know Nothings and Germans remained a major problem for the Republican party.

Frustration produced by defeat, coupled with the continuing loyalty of many immigrants to the Democratic party, precipitated scathing denunciations of the foreign-born and especially Catholics in the Republican press and private correspondence. The intensity with which Republicans expressed such criticism starkly confirmed the continuing power of nativism among party members. Irish Catholics were the target for particular abuse and insult. The Irish "pour out on election day in herds and droves, no creature thinking for himself, or acting for himself, but like sheep following their leader, away they go pell mell altogether, just as their own may direct," bristled the Buffalo *Morning Express*. With few exceptions the Irish "marched up to the polls like cattle, and voted the pro-slavery ticket," another Republican paper declared, while the New York *Courier and Enquirer* angrily attributed Frémont's defeat to "Irish bog-trotters, with necks yet raw with a foreign priestly yoke." [50] The Republican state organ in Ohio betrayed a similar attitude when it pronounced Buchanan's victory the result of "a close and perfect combination of two powerful Tyrannies,—that of the slavedrivers, and that of the Roman Catholic church." [51]

In the face of immigrant support for the Democrats, and with cries of fraud in the Pennsylvania and Indiana state elections still reverberating, Republicans called for reform of the voting laws in the wake of Frémont's defeat. Claiming that four-fifths of the state's newly naturalized voters supported Buchanan, a prominent Connecticut Republican advocated a one- or two-year probationary period following naturalization before an immigrant could vote. [52] A number of prominent Republicans supported the idea of a registry law. Senator James Harlan of Iowa, for one, found this idea attractive. Anticipating that the impending construction of major railroad trunk lines would "flood the State with Foreigners," he feared that, unless the legislature passed a registry law, in subsequent elections the Republicans would be swamped at the polls. Even Weed's Albany *Evening Journal*, while hedging on the issue of a registry law, called for some reform of the voting laws in the state's large cities (where, just coincidentally, the Democratic party's power was concentrated). An Indiana Republican, who emphasized the alleged massive fraud in the October election, argued that without a registry law it would be "hopeless [to] attempt to maintain our institutions." After the election even

---

49. Note in particular the inconsistent behavior of Lutheran and German Reform voters in New York, Pennsylvania, Ohio, Indiana, and Illinois (Tables 13.27–13.31).

50. Buffalo *Morning Express*, November 13, 19; Syracuse *Standard* quoted in the Rochester *Daily Union*, November 7; New York *Courier and Enquirer* quoted in the *Chenango American*, November 20; Indianapolis *Daily Journal*, November 5. Other examples from the Republican press are given in the Rochester *Daily Union*, November 8, and the Rochester *Daily American*, November 12. The most prominent Republican journal that joined this chorus of condemnation was the New York *Times*. The Buffalo *Morning Express* was careful to exempt German and Irish Protestants from its criticism.

51. "Slavery and Catholicism—The Two Working Together," *Ohio State Journal*, November 14; Toledo *Blade*, November 7; Address of the Republican State Central Committee of Ohio, New York *Times*, November 17.

52. James M. Bunce to Morgan, November 6, Edwin D. Morgan Papers.

Greeley, despite his well-known hostility to nativism, endorsed both a probationary period after naturalization before voting and a "rigid" registry law.[53]

Several Republicans, on the other hand, criticized such pronouncements. Noting that Republicans in New York City were "getting up a howl for a Registry Law," an upstate party leader denied that any effective law could be devised. Another New York Republican contended that enactment of such a law "would be just what our opponents wish," for it would raise an issue "that would make us trouble." A Sewardite paper argued that ill-tempered denunciation of immigrants by Republicans only reinforced the naturalized voters' loyalty to the Democracy.[54] Cooling tempers and political expediency checked the movement momentarily, but it soon gathered momentum again and before the end of the decade several Republican-controlled states enacted voting reforms—including New York, which passed a registry law, and Massachusetts, where voters approved a two-year probationary period before naturalized citizens could vote.

IV

The Republicans enjoyed some success among immigrant voters, but the nucleus of the party necessarily was native-born voters, a majority of whom in 1856 cast anti-Democratic ballots in the North. In previous elections the American party had won a significant proportion of the native-born, but its share declined sharply in 1856 because of defections to the Republicans, and as a result the Republicans did much better among these voters than did the Americans. Other than in New York, where the Democratic share of the native vote was unusually small, Frémont's advantage over Buchanan among the native-born was not overwhelming, and because of Fillmore's strength among these voters in Indiana, Buchanan's proportion actually slightly exceeded Frémont's in that state (Tables 13.24, 13.25, and 13.26). Obviously, no party could hope to be competitive without winning at least a substantial minority of the native-born, yet there were some important distinctions between those who supported and those who opposed the Republican party.

The deepest political cleavage among native-born voters was between New Englanders, who over several generations had spread throughout extensive areas of the upper North, and southerners, who had migrated northward and occupied a broad belt of counties in the lower North approximately below the forty-first parallel. Cultural differences between Yankees and southerners covered an extraordinary range of customs, attitudes, and institutions ranging from funeral services, the construction of a fence, and diet, to more weighty matters like attitudes towards education, economic development, and moral reform.[55] Over the span of two generations, these groups had come increasingly into

---

53. James Harlan to [William Penn Clarke], December 1, William Penn Clarke Papers; Albany *Evening Journal*, November 8; Thornbrough, ed., *Fletcher Diary*, v. 5, 590–91; Greeley to A. E. Bovay, November 17, Typescript, Greeley Papers, LC; *Ohio State Journal*, November 21; Cincinnati *Commercial*, November 18; James Ashley to Chase, November 27, Chase Papers, LC. While no longer editor of the *Evening Journal*, Weed nevertheless remained the guiding force behind its editorial policy. The Springfield *Republican*, November 8, endorsed the imposition of a literacy requirement for voting as "more practicable" than seeking a change in the naturalization laws and as an especially effective means of "cutting off that class of foreign voters who are most dangerous because most ignorant."

54. E. Peshine Smith to Carey, November 7, Carey Papers; Abijah Beckwith to A. E. Eaton, December 16, Clipping, Abijah Beckwith Journal, Cornell University; Auburn *Daily Advertiser*, November 7.

55. For an excellent discussion of the cultural clash between Yankees and southerners in the Ohio Valley,

contact and conflict, especially in the Ohio River valley, but the emergence of the Republican party greatly intensified this conflict, sharpened its lines of division, and stimulated mutual antagonism.

The Republican party was especially powerful in areas dominated by New Englanders.[56] Not only did Frémont sweep all six New England states, he was also strong in western New York, along Pennsylvania's northern border, and in the northern counties of Ohio, Indiana, Illinois, and Iowa, regions that contained large numbers of Yankees and their descendants (Maps 12 through 16). Previous Democratic Yankee counties joined former Whig Yankee counties in swinging sharply to the Republican party. St. Lawrence County in New York and Tioga County in Pennsylvania, both Democratic strongholds earlier, gave Frémont his highest percentage in each state (74 and 76 percent respectively). Because southern-born voters remained sensitive to the Republicans' animus toward their native section, in regions with a strong southern presence, such as the Ohio River valley and southern Iowa, the party was strikingly weak.[57] In Iowa, where a sizable number of both cultural groups lived, it appears beyond doubt that Republicans won the allegiance of a large majority of Yankee voters and very few of those born in the South (Table 13.26). An Iowa Democrat blamed the party's defeat partly on the presence in the northern part of the state of a large number of New Englanders, who, "educated to all the quisickal & busy body notions of their fathers," were ready "to believe any story any ranting rifle Beecher clergyman may tell them."[58] The split was not as one-sided in Indiana, but nevertheless the general tendency for New Englanders and southerners to vote in opposite directions was clear (Table 13.25). Similarly, in Ohio and Illinois there was a very strong positive relationship between the proportion of Yankees and Frémont's vote, whereas conversely a pronounced negative relationship was evident between the southern-born population and Republican strength (Tables 13.42 and 13.44). New York had few voters who had been born in the South, but former New Englanders backed the Republican party overwhelmingly in that state as they did in Pennsylvania (Tables 13.24 and 13.41).[59] Daniel S. Dickinson traced the Democratic party's defeat in New York primarily to this cause. "Wherever the *New England* people have sway," he groaned to Buchanan, "they came down like an avalanche,—men, women and children,—priest, & people, & church, aggregate, and a train of frightened Buffaloes would be no more deaf to reason or argument."[60]

The Whig party was a national party, and as such it had won many votes from transplanted southerners in the free states. Some of these men now went over to the

---

see Richard Lyle Power, *Planting Corn Belt Culture: The Impress of the Upland Southerner and Yankee in the Old Northwest* (Indianapolis, 1953). Power describes what he aptly terms Yankee cultural imperialism.

56. See the statistics given in Kleppner, *Third Electoral System*, 52–53.

57. The sectional pattern of the 1856 presidential vote is quite apparent in Ohio, Indiana, and Illinois. Frémont's percentage in the northern, central, and southern regions, respectively, of each state were: Ohio, 57.0, 48.5, and 40.6; Indiana 50.6, 49.1, and 22.0; Illinois 64.3, 27.2, and 13.0 (Maps 14, 15, and 16).

58. Amos Harris to John C. Breckinridge, November 22, Breckinridge Family Papers. Not all southern-born voters, of course, were anti-Republican; Lincoln, after all, had been born in Kentucky. Personal considerations and family circumstances weighed heavily in political affiliation. The intensity with which one identified with southern culture was also critical, and, probably for those born in the South, the age at which one migrated.

59. Multiple regression analysis indicates that, independent of other variables, the proportion of Yankees explains 44 percent of the variance of Frémont's vote in New York and 29 percent in Pennsylvania. Even more striking was the situation in Illinois, where together the proportion of Yankees and southerners accounted for no less than 81 percent of the variance of the Republican vote (Tables 13.40, 13.41, 13.44).

60. Daniel S. Dickinson to Buchanan, November 11, Buchanan Papers, HSPa.

Democratic party, but others, unable to bring themselves to join their long-time adversaries and yet fearful of the Republicans' sectionalism, threw away their votes on Fillmore (Tables 13.25 and 13.26). Whereas southern-stock Know Nothings generally rejected the Republicans and remained loyal to their party, the shift already under way among Yankee Know Nothings to the Republican party accelerated in 1856. The Republicans consequently made large gains in former Yankee American strongholds like the Burned Over District in New York and Pennsylvania's northern tier. Manifesting a fervent hostility to rum, Catholics, slavery, and southerners, these men found a congenial place in the Republican ranks. At the same time, the Union issue, more than nativism, accounts for Fillmore's strength among southern-born voters. As they had encountered with conservative businessmen, Republicans in their first national campaign were unable to overcome the fear southern migrants and their descendants harbored of an antislavery, sectional party. Southerners who had moved to the free states often had no particular liking for slavery and no desire to see it expand, but they strongly opposed any outside interference with the institution or anything that threatened its security in states where it already existed. For the large majority, the Republican party smacked of a fanatical abolitionist crusade that would destroy the Union.

Yankee cohesiveness was greater in the West, where Yankees confronted competing cultural groups, than in New England, where they were overwhelmingly dominant. Yankees everywhere, however, nurtured a deep-rooted sense of superiority and mission. Convinced of the moral righteousness of their cause, New Englanders wherever they went were determined to make their values and institutions preeminent, and they had no hesitancy in imposing their will on those in society who did not voluntarily conform to Yankee norms, behavior that accounts in large part for their unpopularity among other groups. A New York paper said of the typical Yankee that he considered himself "a sort of religious, political, industrial, agricultural and commercial missionary."[61] To these dedicated individuals, the Republican party was a party of morality and virtue, of economic and moral progress, of Protestantism and free labor.

Except perhaps in New York, nowhere outside New England were Yankees a majority of the Republican party, but they were highly visible members, often prominent in its most vocal and militant wing, and as such they were instrumental in giving the party an image of intolerant puritanism, especially among its opponents.[62] For cultural groups, both native- and foreign-born, that had come into social conflict with New Englanders, the latter often served as a negative reference group. In New York, where the animosity between Yankees and Yorkers went back well over a century, the socially conservative Yorkers, who were of Dutch heritage and located primarily in the Hudson River valley,

---

61. Kleppner, *Third Electoral System*, 48, 57–58, 72–74, 365; New York *Courier and Enquirer*, [June 1854], quoted in Power, *Planting Corn Belt Culture*, 5.

62. A good example was a speech that Gustave Koerner remembered a prominent German Democrat delivering during the 1856 campaign to a group of his fellow countrymen. The Republicans, according to this speaker, "were made up . . . principally of long-faced, white-livered, hypocritical Yankees, who sold wooden nutmegs and cheated the honest farmers with lightning rods and Yankee clocks. They would not allow a man to cook meals on the Sabbath, or kiss his wife, or take a walk for pleasure. Most of the Republicans were temperance people and hated the Germans because they would drink beer even on Sundays and would sing and dance on the Lord's day." Koerner, *Memoirs*, v. 2, 27. For a discussion of the Republican party's moralistic reputation and its relevance to the sectional crisis, see Joel H. Silbey, "The Surge of Republican Power: Partisan Antipathy, American Social Conflict, and the Coming of the Civil War," Maizlish and Kushma, eds., *American Antebellum Politics*, 199–229.

voted for Fillmore rather than for the more radical Yankee-dominated Republican party (Table 13.27). Likewise in eastern Pennsylvania many groups were repelled by New England antislavery men, and the Republican party was very weak in that part of the state (Maps 12 and 13).[63]

After the election Republicans were quick to draw a connection between this cultural split and voting patterns in 1856. Thus the party's organ in Indiana remarked:

> Northern Indiana and northern Illinois are peopled from the free states by an active, industrious, enterprising and intelligent population, and these portions of both states give large Republican majorities. The southern portion of both these states are peopled from the Slave states, by what is termed in the South "poor white trash"—a slow, lazy, thriftless and ignorant population—and these portions give such heavy Loco-foco [Democratic] majorities as to control the politics of both states.[64]

Focusing on one of New England's most important institutions, the common school, Samuel Bowles wailed, "We are beaten by the ignorance of the people. The excellent common school systems of the New England states and New York," he argued, "have given those states to Fremont." In areas loyal to the Democracy, New England influence and institutions were correspondingly weaker. "Pennsylvania, with no common school system worthy of the name, New Jersey, notoriously . . . behind the times in all matters pertaining to popular education, Indiana with its large settlement from the South of individuals to whom common schools are entire strangers—these have gone for Buchanan."[65] These remarks, which revealed much about the tensions in American politics as well as the Republican party's self-image, represented the culmination of a campaign that had featured to an unprecedented degree unrestrained attacks on the South, its institutions, and its people.

V

In accounting for Frémont's showing, Democrats placed greater emphasis on the influence of the Protestant clergy, particularly Methodists, Baptists, Presbyterians, and Congregationalists, than on any other cause. Franklin Pierce, for example, in a post-election analysis of the Democratic setback in New Hampshire, contended that "the

---

63. New York *Herald*, November 27. Fillmore ran well in the Hudson River valley, where Yorkers were concentrated, and Dutch Reform voters seem to have voted American in 1856 by a decided margin while very few backed Frémont (Table 13.27). In fact, multiple regression analysis establishes that of all socio-economic variables, the proportion of Dutch Reformed had the greatest influence on Fillmore's vote in New York. For a discussion of the cultural clash between these two groups in New York, see Fox, *Yankees and Yorkers*; and David M. Ellis, "Yankee-Dutch Confrontation in the Albany Area,"*NEQ*, v. 45 (June, 1972), 262–70. With the arrival of Irish Catholics after 1845, the hostility between Yankees and Yorkers began to decline, since both groups shared a mutual antagonism to the Irish, but Yorker suspicions of Yankee reformers still lingered.

64. Indianapolis *Weekly State Journal*, November 27, quoted in Harvey Lewis Carter, "A Decade of Hoosier History: Indiana 1850–1860" (unpublished Ph.D. dissertation, University of Wisconsin, 1938), 2. For a spirited attack in the same vein on the northern inhabitants of the state by a paper in southern Illinois, see the Cairo *Weekly Times & Delta*, March 25, 1857, quoted in Hansen, *Third Party System*, 113.

65. Springfield *Republican*, November 8. For similar assertions, see the New York *Times*, November 28; *Ohio State Journal*, November 21; Chicago *Tribune* quoted in the Springfield *Republican*, November 18; Chicago *Democratic Press*, November 19, quoted in Foner, *Free Soil, Free Labor, Free Men*, 34; Truman Smith to John Wilson, November 20, John Wilson Papers.

mastering power which overthrew our party there was a perverted and desecrated pulpit.''
From Wilmot's old district, now a Republican stronghold, a mortified Democrat told
Buchanan:

> We are made up of New England *yankees* here with all the superstitions and prejudices
> of the land of their ancestry. We had all the fanatical methodist & Baptist preachers
> against us hurling their anathemas at us from their pulpits on Sundays and from the
> stump on week days, and also some of all the other denominations and what is still
> worse they are all Know nothings and where that is the case you might as well ''sing
> psalms to a dead horse'' as to attempt to reach their reason.[66]

A number of Democrats complained bitterly of the political activity of Protestant ministers
''in and out of their pulpits'' during the 1856 campaign. ''Preachers of all the Presbyterian
denominations were out fiercely and fanatically against us,'' one Democrat reported after
the election. ''Many of them stood at the polls all day imploring their hearers to vote in
favor of liberty'' and against the Democratic party. It was ''by far the most arduous
contest we ever had.''[67] The Democratic Cleveland *Plain Dealer* attributed the result in
the Western Reserve, which had been settled by New Englanders and had rolled up an
enormous majority for Frémont, to ''those old blue law, blue bellied Presbyterians that
hung the witches and banished the Quakers, [who] are determined to convert the people
of this region into a race of psalm singers, using the degenerate dregs of the old puritans
remaining here to drive the Democrats out.''[68]

As these complaints suggest, the Protestant clergy's support for Frémont was both
vocal and unusual. First galvanized into action in the drive to prevent passage of the
Kansas-Nebraska bill, these ''political parsons,'' as Democrats derided them, entered the
Frémont campaign with great enthusiasm and more than a little self-righteousness. In fact,
Henry Ward Beecher, the most famous Protestant minister in America, stumped actively
for the party's ticket under the direction of the Republican national committee. Aware of
the clergy's influence with some voters, Republicans posed as the defenders of the
pulpit's involvement in politics (while simultaneously condemning the Catholic clergy for
allegedly directing their flock to vote Democratic).[69] ''The '*Lords Elect*' as the preachers
have the impudence to call themselves, are *all against* us,'' muttered an Indiana Democrat
with a mixture of disdain and concern. From New Haven, Dr. Leonard Bacon's daughter
reported that ''all the ministers'' were for Frémont, and an Indiana woman disclosed after
a Presbyterian synod met in her town that there was not one Democrat among the
preachers in attendance. At a Methodist conference in New York, only one of the 200

---

66. Franklin Pierce to Buchanan, November 20, William Patton to Buchanan, November 7, Buchanan
Papers, HSPa.

67. A. Pratt to John C. Breckinridge, September 25, Breckinridge Family Papers; John Graham to
Buchanan, October 17, Buchanan Papers, HSPa; Cincinnati *Enquirer*, June 14, October 9, November 2. For a
strongly worded attack on the political activity of the clergy in New England by the organ of the Democratic
party, see the Washington *Union* quoted in the Hartford *Courant*, November 11.

68. Cleveland *Plain Dealer*, December 3. For other examples, see B. D. Cook to John C. Breckinridge,
August 14, Breckinridge Family Papers; R. McMurdy to Buchanan, October 15, F. W. Fanelly to Buchanan,
November 6, Buchanan Papers, HSPa; Elisha Whitlesey to Littleton Q. Washington, December 31, Littleton Q.
Washington Papers, Duke University.

69. For Republican defenses of clerical involvement in politics, see the *Ashtabula Sentinel*, July 10;
Pittsburgh *Gazette*, August 19; Westfield *Republican*, April 30; *Cortland County Republican*, July 31;
Cincinnati *Gazette*, June 16, 20.

ministers present opposed Frémont.[70] Political sermons became standard fare throughout the summer of 1856, reaching a climax on the Sunday before election day, when, one Massachusetts Democrat sneered, the fanatical clergy "appealed to their deluded followers to vote in such a way as would enable them to give an acceptable account at the Day of Judgment!"[71]

The clergy's active participation helped give the Frémont campaign its strident moral tone. "The present political contest is a religious movement, a revival of religion, 'a great awakening' to be classed among the moral reformations of the world," asserted the approving New York *Observer*, a religious periodical. However the election turned out, rejoiced one minister as the campaign ended, "*the religious feeling through[ou]t the free states is thoroughly aroused* I trust never to sleep again."[72] In one of its last issues before the election, the New York *Independent*, the most influential religious journal of the time, exhorted its readers: "Remember it is for Christ, for the nation, and for the world that you vote at this election! Vote as you pray! Pray as you vote!"[73]

Whether northerners actually voted as they prayed, however, is open to serious question. The overwhelming support for Frémont by the Protestant clergy, especially those of the evangelical denominations, seems not to have been translated into similar behavior at the mass level in many areas (Tables 13.27 through 13.31). Contemporaries were apparently justified in emphasizing the affinity between Congregationalism and Republicanism (as Yankee voting behavior indicated), and Frémont also did well among Presbyterians, especially in Ohio, Pennsylvania, and Illinois. A New York Democrat reported after the election that in his town "not a single Presbyterian" opposed Frémont.[74] In that state Baptists were strongly Republican as well, but elsewhere they displayed no consistent pattern. Methodists, on the other hand, seem not to have backed the Republican cause to any decisive degree. In Pennsylvania, where they had once been strongly Democratic, their partisan allegiance was less one-sided, but many anti-Democratic members supported Fillmore rather than Frémont. The Republican party had still not won the bulk of the Methodists who defected in 1854 from Governor William Bigler, the Democratic incumbent. In addition, there was no strong relationship between Methodism and Frémont's vote in the western states, and Buchanan won many of their votes. Some Democratic Methodists undoubtedly were southern-born, but others were probably long-time Democrats who were unable to break with their traditional party loyalty.[75] Massachusetts Methodists and Baptists, who had long battled against the

---

70. John Law to Joseph Lane, October 2, Joseph Lane Papers, IndU; Theodore Davenport Bacon, *Leonard Bacon* (New Haven, 1931), 421; Mary Niles to Leafie Niles, October 22, John B. Niles Papers, IndU; *Chenango American*, August 28; Cincinnati *Gazette*, June 16, October 14.

71. Nahum Capen to Buchanan, November 4, Buchanan Papers, HSPa.

72. New York *Observer*, October 30, quoted in Richard Carwardine, "The Religious Revival of 1857–8 in the United States," *Studies in Church History*, v. 15 (1978), 402; Calvin Stowe to Harriet Beecher Stowe, November 4, quoted in Harriet Beecher Stowe to the Duke of Sutherland, November 21, Harriet Beecher Stowe Papers, Stowe-Day Foundation.

73. [New York] *Independent*, October 16, quoted in Rhodes, *History of the United States*, v. 2, 167. For the influence of the *Independent* among clergymen, see Oliver Johnson to Sumner, April 24, 1855, Sumner Papers, HU.

74. W. D. Purple to James W. Mandeville, November 16 (quotation), James Mandeville Papers, HEH; George W. Taylor to John H. George, October 28, George Papers. Table 13.27 no doubt understates Frémont's strength among Presbyterians in New York, especially in view of his support among Yankees, although a number (most likely primarily Old School members) apparently remained in the American ranks.

75. Formisano argues that in Michigan, Methodists moved into the Republican party only over a series of elections: *Mass Political Parties*, 261–62, 312–15.

Congregationalists and Unitarians and had formerly been among the strongest Democratic groups in the Commonwealth, appear to have shifted to the Republicans, although Frémont's majorities in pure dissenting towns did not match his overwhelming totals in pure Congregational towns.[76] Throughout the free states, denominational party preferences had shifted since 1852, and Democratic strength among the evangelical denominations had declined. To characterize evangelical voters as constituting anything approaching a voting bloc, or to view the Republican party as simply a vehicle for evangelicalism, however, badly distorts the political reality of the pre-Civil War years. Republicans and Democrats both won votes from all Protestant groups, as well as from the numerous unchurched voters.

The political division between Yankees and southerners, noted earlier, is an important qualification to the interpretation of northern voting before the Civil War along a pietist-nonpietist axis.[77] The evangelical denominations that were strongest among Yankees and often pointed to as the source of Republican strength—the Baptists, Methodists, and Presbyterians—were those churches to which most southern migrants who were church members belonged. Strong opposition to the Republican party among the southern-born precluded any clear connection between evangelical sects and partisanship in the 1856 election.[78]

Although religious divisions were not clear-cut in the 1856 election, the Republican party nevertheless projected an image of morality, Protestantism, middle class respectability, and even self-righteousness. "Never before has a party in Connecticut had enrolled in their ranks such a large proportion of the worth, the intelligence, and the respectability of the community," the Hartford *Courant* boasted of the Republican party. "The great moral issue involved collected together the most orderly, sober and virtuous portion of the voters."[79] The Republican party received the substantial backing of temperance men in Pennsylvania, Iowa, and Illinois, three states where earlier referenda on the liquor question provide a relatively precise measurement of public opinion (Tables 13.32 through 13.34). This solid support is especially noteworthy since Republicans avoided or downplayed the Maine Law issue whenever possible, and it demonstrates the extent to which anti-liquor and antislavery feeling overlapped in the northern electorate, especially among the native-born. Only in Ohio, where the Republican party contained a large contingent of former Democrats and where it received many more naturalized votes than in most states, did the division over drinking not closely parallel partisan lines (Table

---

76. Paul Goodman, "The Politics of Industrialism: Massachusetts, 1830–1870," Richard Bushman et al., eds., *Uprooted Americans: Essays to Honor Oscar Handlin* (Boston, 1979), 183–85.

77. Kleppner, in *Third Electoral System*, attempts unconvincingly to apply his pietist-nonpietist interpretation to the nation as a whole for the period 1853–1892 by stipulating yet another category, salvationist pietists, into which he places southern evangelicals. For a thought-provoking discussion, see Allan J. Lichtman, "Political Realignment and 'Ethnocultural' Voting in late Nineteenth Century America," *Journal of Social History*, v. 16 (Spring, 1983), 55–82.

78. In Ohio, Indiana, and Illinois, controlling for the Yankee and southern population reduces the strength of the relationship between the Baptists, Methodists, and Presbyterians and the Republican vote in 1856; in most cases the resulting regression coefficients are at most only moderately positive. This situation suggests that, in general, religion had less influence on voting behavior than did ethnicity or cultural heritage. Transplanted southerners voted Democratic, in other words, not primarily because they were Baptists, or Methodists, or Presbyterians, but because of their southern background.

79. Hartford *Courant*, November 13. The *Ohio State Journal*, November 14, proclaimed that "the Republican party comprises the great protestant body in America." While these and similar assertions contained more than a kernel of truth, they essentially reflected the party's self-image.

13.35). Almost as many supporters of liquor licenses as opponents voted for Frémont in Ohio. Unlike the American party's lack of success with drys in Iowa and Pennsylvania, in Ohio the party retained the support of a sizable proportion of drys. The anti-liquor impulse had been a vital element in the Know Nothings' initial strength, but by 1856 temperance men had largely abandoned the order for the Republican party. Except in Ohio and Illinois, and there primarily in the southern counties, Fillmore appealed to only a fraction of the supporters of prohibition. Pro-temperance Know Nothings in Pennsylvania, in particular, seem to have voted for Frémont in preference to Fillmore. A Connecticut Democrat felt that Frémont would carry his town "on account that the [residents] are all Maine law & knownothings turned to be Republican[s]."[80] The rise of sectional tensions diverted attention from prohibition, but the issue still had the potential to break apart the fragile Republican coalition. The Republican party's anti-southern crusade, its sense of moral urgency, its identification with anti-Catholicism, and its obvious affinity with anti-liquor sentiment combined to give it a moral and religious quality that transcended its support among evangelical denominations.

VI

A number of political commentators pointed to Frémont's special appeal to young men, who had been mobilized to an unusual extent by the 1856 campaign.[81] Even Democrats asserted that younger voters supported the Republican ticket disproportionately. The Democratic governor of Maine contended that older Democrats, those who had grown up in the party, remained loyal, but that countless young men had gone over to the Republicans. A Republican paper in the same state agreed that "the young men of this State, and in the Free States generally, who have lately come, and are just now coming into the full possession of the elective franchise, are almost in a body in favor of Fremont and freedom."[82] An Illinois correspondent made the same argument concerning German voters. He reported that those Germans who had been in the country a number of years were mostly immune to Republican overtures; rather, it was among recently naturalized Germans, whose identification with the Democratic party was not as long- or well-established, that the Republicans were winning converts.[83]

Political onlookers also claimed that Frémont won support among men who were normally indifferent to political affairs and did not vote on a regular basis, and among the so-called floating vote, that group of electors who were not strongly attached to any party and were thus especially susceptible to short-term forces and the personalities of the candidates. After attending a Republican rally, George Templeton Strong recorded that the Republican party "calls out many who have long eschewed politics," a point also made by several other observers, including William Cullen Bryant, the editor of the

---

80. James G. Patton to Buchanan, September 22, Buchanan Papers, HSPa; Tables 13.32 and 13.34 probably minimize support for the Republican party among anti-prohibition voters in Pennsylvania and Illinois, but the pronounced partisan split on the issue is clear.

81. Adams Diary, November 3, Adams Family Papers. James Ford Rhodes wrote: "It is often remarked that previous to the war the Republican party attracted the great majority of school-boys, and that the first voters were an important factor in its final success." *History of the United States*, v. 1, 285.

82. Portland *Daily Advertiser*, September 4 (quoting Samuel Wells), 16, 22 (quotation). For similar assertions, see the New York *Evening Post*, September 2; William H. Herndon to Sumner, June 20, Sumner Papers, HU; John C. Hamilton to Buchanan, August 12, Buchanan Papers, HSPa.

83. Illinois correspondence signed "Grundy," August 25, New York *Evening Post*, August 28.

Evening Post, who informed his brother that "a very large class of persons who never took any interest in elections before are zealous Fremonters here."[84] The Republican standard bearer's romantic reputation as a heroic man of action, coupled with his relative youth and the fact that he was a fresh new political face, were undeniably great assets and helped produce the "wild, electric enthusiasm" that greeted his nomination. As the Pathfinder, Frémont projected a much more attractive personality than either Buchanan or Fillmore, both of whom were not only aged, shopworn politicians but also dull and colorless individuals without great personal popularity. Witnessing the excitement Frémont's candidacy produced, a western Republican was certain that he would "secure a large portion of that floating vote which is cast for men rather than principles."[85]

The sources of Frémont's vote lend some credence to these assertions. To be sure, Buchanan and Fillmore won many votes from previous non-voters and new voters, and claims about Frémont's overwhelming strength among these groups appear exaggerated. Some (but certainly not all) of Buchanan's support among new voters probably came from recently naturalized immigrants, particularly in states such as Indiana where the foreign-born had largely voted Democratic. Still, if Frémont's support was less sweeping than contemporaries claimed, he did exhibit particular attraction to new voters and less regular participants, especially those who did not vote in 1854 and 1855 (his advantage among non-voters in 1852 was, on the whole, less pronounced). Not all former non-voters were young men, but many were, and reports of Frémont's special magnetism for men just entering the political process, particularly native-born, seem valid (Tables 13.2 through 13.23).[86]

New voters and previously apathetic voters would seem to have been susceptible to the Republican appeal because of their weaker party identities. Older men, with stronger psychological loyalties forged by years of faithful support of a particular party, were much more difficult to dislodge from their traditional political moorings. Young voters with weaker ties to a party, and older men not firmly linked to any party, were much more likely to adopt a different partisan loyalty. The Republican party's crusading enthusiasm particularly attracted young men (as it would do again in the 1860 campaign). In addition, the Know Nothings were disproportionately young men, and the presence of so many former Americans in the Republican ranks in 1856 no doubt also helps account for the party's strength among younger voters. The New York *Herald* noted that for the past few years a number of voters had been politically adrift, and "Know Nothingism afforded a

---

84. Nevins and Thomas, eds. *Strong Diary*, v. 2, 282 (quotation), 285, 307; William Cullen Bryant to John Bryant, October 14, Bryant Family Papers; Portland *Daily Advertiser*, September 22. For an example of a previous non-partisan politicized by the 1856 contest, see Thomas Barlow to Seward, July 11, Seward Papers, UR.

85. New York *Herald*, June 27; George Baldwin to Emily Baldwin, April 17, Baldwin Family Papers. The size of this floating vote can easily be exaggerated for the antebellum period, with its strong partisan loyalties, but this group was generally more a factor in presidential elections, which normally had a higher turnout, than in state contests.

86. Ecological regression estimates for new voters are a more reliable guide to the voting behavior of young men than are multiple regression coefficients for age cohorts. In general, the multiple regression coefficients do not indicate a strong positive relationship between the proportion of men aged twenty-one to twenty-nine and Frémont's vote, but this result basically reflects the lower turnout among young voters rather than their opposition to the Republican party. Indeed, regression coefficients for this age group are generally negative for all parties and positive for the proportion not voting.

temporary lodgement to a vast body of these loose materials;'' many of these voters, in turn, found a place in the Republican party during the Frémont campaign.[87]

Republican strength, as party leaders readily recognized, was centered in rural areas and small towns that dotted the northern countryside. The party was significantly weaker in the large cities.[88] The Republican campaign should not ignore urban centers, one upstate New Yorker advised in 1856, "but our hope is in the *rural districts*; we need to arouse & inspirit the farmers, mechanics,—moral & religious men.'' A prominent New York Democrat warned Buchanan that the party had suffered important losses among farmers, and Republicans claimed to have gained the support of many workingmen as well.[89] In Iowa, a heavily rural state, and also in Maine, the Republicans appear to have done better among farmers than either of the other two parties, although Frémont's margin was not particularly large in the former state (Table 13.36).[90] In Chautauqua County, on the other hand, a heavily Yankee evangelical rural county in the Burned Over District of western New York, Frémont's advantage among farmers was overwhelming and helps account for his receiving more than 64 percent of the vote in that county (Table 13.37).

Among workingmen, skilled workers apparently were much more likely to vote Republican than unskilled workers. In metropolitan areas, if Cincinnati was typical, Buchanan was considerably stronger among laborers (a number of whom were immigrants) than any other occupational group. The American party's support from skilled workers, on the other hand, seems to have all but evaporated by the 1856 election, both in the large cities and small towns, although the party still retained the loyalty of many unskilled workers, who faced the strongest competition from immigrants and had been affected adversely by the economic changes of the era (Tables 13.36 through 13.38). In Cincinnati at least, professionals and merchants decisively backed Fillmore. As the national committee's correspondence documented, Republicans experienced great difficulty attracting the business classes in major cities. Businessmen had formerly been predominantly Whigs, but they feared the sectional Republican party was too radical and a threat to the Union, and hence many refused to contribute to the party's coffers or to vote for its candidates.[91] While some ex-Whig businessmen no doubt supported Buchanan, contemporary observers were probably right in contending that others rejected Frémont for Fillmore, a safe, conservative Union man.[92] Despite the party's subsequent image as

---

87. New York *Herald*, June 27. As has often been true of military candidates, Frémont's candidacy displayed something of a surge effect. Angus Campbell, "Surge and Decline: A Study of Electoral Change," *Public Opinion Quarterly*, v. 24 (Fall, 1960), 397–418.

88. "The Country for Freedom—The Cities for Slavery," *Ohio State Journal*, November 7. Of the six northern cities with a population of more than 100,000 in 1860, Frémont carried only Chicago, and he won less than 24 percent of the combined vote in these cities. Note also the negative coefficients for population per acre in New York, Pennsylvania, and Illinois (Tables 13.40, 13.41, and 13.44).

89. Ovid Miner to Seward, June 16, Seward Papers, UR; Amasa J. Parker to Buchanan, September 14, Buchanan Papers, HSPa; Cincinnati *Commercial*, October 20; Nevins and Thomas, eds., *Strong Diary*, v. 2, 305; Albany *Evening Journal*, October 28, 1857.

90. An estimated 50 percent of the farmers in Maine cast Frémont ballots, compared to 29 percent for Buchanan and less than 1 percent for Fillmore (the remainder did not vote) ($N = 324$ townships).

91. Holt finds in Pittsburgh that businessmen, merchants, and professionals split fairly evenly between Frémont and Buchanan: *Forging a Majority*, 212, 214. In Cleveland, on the other hand, these groups seem to have voted Republican. Kremm, "Republican Party in Cleveland," 211.

92. William Allen Butler to Benjamin F. Butler, August 11, Benjamin F. Butler Papers, NYSL; Nicholas B. Wainwright, ed., *A Philadelphia Perspective: The Diary of Sidney George Fisher Covering the Years*

the party of big business, in its first national campaign Republicanism—both in its electoral support and its energizing spirit—was centered in the rural and small-town middle class, among farmers, skilled workers, and other small independent entrepreneurs who dreamed of rising socially and economically and subscribed to the free labor vision of northern society as one of widespread opportunity and fundamental class harmony.

Wealth was also an important influence on voting behavior. In Cincinnati, Republicans ran behind both competing parties among the poorest segment of society (those with less than $100 in real and personal property), and they won their strongest support proportionally from the middle ranks of the city's population (Table 13.39).[93] Of the states examined, the Republican party was stronger in areas with higher per capita wealth. As in cities, Republican support statewide was probably greatest among those of middle range of wealth rather than those of either extreme.[94] In Pennsylvania, for example, the party was not particularly strong in regions with a high proportion of extremely large farms (more than 1,000 acres) or small farms (less than 100 acres) (Table 13.41). American spokesmen claimed, perhaps accurately, to have the support of the "gentlemen" and "the best men" of the community.[95] Be that as it may, the wealthy classes seem not to have supported the Republican party to any extensive degree. For all its partisanship, Samuel Bowles's assertion shortly before the election that the Republican party was opposed by both "the highest class, aristocratically associated and affiliated, . . . and holding in their hands the sensitive cords of commerce," and by "the lowest class," deceived by the Democratic label and "fed by the rich man's money" had a certain measure of validity.[96]

As is well known, ethnicity, wealth, age, and occupation were not unrelated in nineteenth-century America. By use of multiple regression analysis, it is possible to assess the relative importance of various factors in producing the Republican vote in 1856. Once the effects of other variables are controlled, wealth, ethnicity, place of birth, and religion all independently influenced the Republican vote. As a general rule, ethnicity and place of birth exerted the greatest influence, with the proportion of native- and foreign-born, and Yankees and southerners, especially important (Tables 13.40 through 13.44).[97]

1834–1871 (Philadelphia, 1967), 260; William M. Davis to Henry K. Brown, August 15, William M. Davis Papers, HSPa; incomplete letter from Decatur, dated November 29, Richard Oglesby Papers, IllSHL. There are many letters in the Buchanan Papers, HSPa, discussing Buchanan's support among old-line Whigs, especially in the business community. See, for example, letters from Simeon M. Johnson, September 2, John B. Guthrie, September 8, and Albert C. Ramsey, September 27.

93. Table 13.39 unquestionably exaggerates non-voting among the wealthiest men, although some who were particularly cross-pressured no doubt abstained. Kremm finds a similar pattern in Cleveland, except that the wealthy seem to have voted for Frémont. "Republican Party in Cleveland," 211. Because of the relationship in Pittsburgh of ethnicity to wealth, Holt discovers a somewhat different pattern there for the two poorest categories: *Forging a Majority*, 215n.

94. Results based on average per capita wealth are difficult to interpret, since this average can be badly distorted by a few wealthy individuals in a community. An analysis based on the distribution of wealth in a community is more reliable, but these data are very difficult to come by and generally relate to cities rather than rural districts.

95. William H. Russell to Alphonso Taft, November 5, Taft Papers; Winthrop to Fillmore, September 19, *Private*, Zophar Mills to Fillmore, July 14, *Private*, Fillmore Papers, SUNY.

96. Springfield *Republican*, November 1.

97. Formisano stresses that southerners and Yankees represented different political cultures but they were not separate ethnic groups in the sense that, say, Germans or Scotch-Irish were. The realignment of the 1850s involved both ethnic and cultural factors: *AHR*, v. 82 (June, 1977), 571.

Religion was also a significant factor, although not consistently in every state and with variations among denominations. While less important generally than religion and especially place of birth, wealth nevertheless contributed to the party's support independent of other factors. Occupation, on the other hand, seems to have had less influence once other variables, most notably ethnicity and wealth, are controlled.[98] For the most part Republicans were strongest in areas with a high concentration of native-born, especially New Englanders, and in areas with higher per capita wealth. The relationship with religion was not as consistent, but the Republican party normally did best in communities with the Presbyterian and Congregational churches, and was weak in areas with a high proportion of Catholics, particularly Irish Catholics.

The product of the interaction of a wide variety of political, cultural, socio-economic, and ideological considerations, the Republican party was an amazingly heterogeneous coalition. In 1856 the party brought together orthodox Christians and free-thinking Germans; Maine Law men and anti-prohibitionists; Free Soilers, old Whigs, and former Democrats; Know Nothings and Protestant immigrants; Yankees and those they opposed; farmers and urban workingmen; evangelical Protestants and nothingarians. In assuming the Whigs' position as the major anti-Democratic party, the Republican party did not simply inherit the former Whig voting base. Ethnically the Republican coalition was less homogeneous: While the Republicans had not done as well among the foreign-born as they had hoped, they won a greater share of the immigrant vote, particularly among the Germans, than the Whigs ever had. In addition, a large proportion of Yankee Protestants voted Republican, as Yankee Free Soilers and a number of Yankee Democrats switched parties; at the same time, the Republicans won substantially less support among southern-stock voters in the North than the Whigs had, and the party was weaker among the wealthy and business classes, particularly in large cities. There were some continuities as well, but the changes in voting patterns between the second and third party systems created a fundamentally different anti-Democratic coalition and in the process reduced the Democrats to a minority party in the North.[99]

VII

Factors like religion, wealth, and ethnicity, although they helped shape the voting patterns in the free states, cannot entirely explain either the Republican appeal or the party's strong showing in the 1856 election. Most political commentators agreed that opposition to the South and the Slave Power, particularly as reflected in the Kansas and Sumner issues, propelled the Republicans to their new-found position of strength. The caning of Sumner and the violence in Kansas, Edward Everett told Buchanan, "gave its formidable character & strength to the 'Republican' nomination." The president of the American state council in New York lamented that in the just-concluded campaign the people "acted as if they were bereft of their senses." The incidents in Kansas shocked the moral sense of the country, he asserted, and each new Kansas story drove the wavering back into the

---

98. Iowa is one state for which statistics on wealth, occupation, ethnicity, and religion are all available. Occupation had only a small effect on the Republican vote once these other variables are controlled. Whether the same relationship held true in other states is uncertain, but occupation was probably less important relative to these other factors.

99. Kleppner, *Third Electoral System*, 53, 72, 76; Holt, *Forging a Majority*, 212–14, 216.

Republican ranks.[100] As he helplessly watched Frémont's strength grow, Robert C. Winthrop fumed that "Brooks & Douglas deserve Statues from the Free Soil [Republican] party. The cane of the former & the Kansas Bill of the latter . . . have secured a success to the Agitators which they never could have accomplished without them." Fillmore himself reinforced this sentiment. "Brooks' attack upon Sumner has done more for Freemont [sic] than any 20 of his warmest friends North have been able to accomplish," he grumbled during the campaign. "If Freemont is elected, he will owe his election entirely to the troubles in Kansas, and the martyrdom of Sumner. . . . The Republicans ought to pension Brooks for life."[101]

After the election, one northern Democrat tried to explain the reasons for the remarkable strength of the Republican party. The flood that swept over the North, he declared, arose from feeling rather than judgment. Northerners had become alarmed by the arrogant demands of the slaveholders; they felt that their own rights were in danger; they were disgusted by the brutality that applauded the bludgeon in the Senate; and they were indignant at the events in Kansas. Everywhere one heard nothing but recitals of Kansas outrages and Brooks's assault, "and certain it is, that the Club which broke Mr. Sumner's head, has . . . turned more votes than all other causes that were at work. It admitted neither defence nor palliation . . . and so the feeling grew stronger and stronger until it reached the result we have seen."[102]

Democrats—particularly in the free states—knew how close they had come to being defeated. In his memoirs John W. Forney maintained that only Democratic pledges to do justice to Kansas saved Buchanan. By the time he made this statement, the Pennsylvania editor had broken with Buchanan, but Jesse Bright advanced the same assessment immediately after the election. The Indiana senator explained that in his campaign speeches he tried to separate Buchanan from Pierce's "weak and imbecile" administration by promising that "we would have a new 'shuffle cut and deal'" on Kansas.[103] The new president, as experienced politicians recognized, confronted a major challenge in holding his party together and resolving the territorial controversy, on which the northern and southern wings of his party took increasingly divergent positions. The promises of northern Democrats during the 1856 campaign that Buchanan would deal impartially with Kansas affairs would explode in their faces in 1858, when he attempted to force the proslavery Lecompton constitution through Congress over the strenuous objections of northern Democrats.

While greatly strengthened by the caning of Sumner and the Kansas violence, the Republican party was unable to overcome the handicaps with which it commenced the campaign. Yet what was remarkable was not that Frémont lost the election but that he did so well. "For a *six months old* he has done wonders," a Cincinnati Republican exulted. From the beginning of the campaign, the most prescient Republican leaders had believed that the party had little chance of victory in its first national contest. They had hoped to

100. Edward Everett to Buchanan, December 8, Buchanan Papers, HSPa; Sammons to Fillmore, November 7, Fillmore Papers, SUNY.

101. Robert C. Winthrop to Crittenden, June 3, *Private*, July 18, Private (quotation), Crittenden Papers; Fillmore to William A. Graham, August 9, Hamilton, ed., *Graham Papers*, v. 4, 643–44; Samuel W. Randall to Buchanan, November 10, Buchanan Papers, HSPa; L. Richmond to John W. Geary, October 18, Confidential, Geary Papers.

102. George W. Bethune to Buchanan, November 21, Buchanan Papers, HSPa.

103. Forney, *Anecdotes*, v. 1, 361, v. 2, 240; Jesse D. Bright to Edmund Burke, November 12, Burke Papers.

establish a sound national organization and, by crushing the American party, emerge as the only significant party opposed to the Democrats.[104] These goals had been fulfilled; indeed, the Republicans' performance in the 1856 election exceeded any realistic expectations only six months earlier. Not only did Frémont win a plurality in the North, but the American party had been destroyed as a viable national organization. It was clear in the aftermath of the 1856 election that the Republican party represented the major alternative to the Democrats.

The sectional events of the preceding twelve months were the most important cause of the Know Nothings' decline after two years of considerable potency. Other factors contributed to the erosion of the party's popular strength, however, including the inept record of its elected officials, its inability to preserve national harmony on the slavery issue, and the Republicans' superior leadership.[105] Also important was the muddling of the party's appeal with Fillmore at the head of its ticket. The Know Nothings had risen to power by crusading against old party hacks, calling for political reform, and shrewdly exploiting both anti-Catholic and anti-Nebraska sentiment so pervasive in the North. Fillmore had no interest in any of these issues. To him and the clique of Silver Grey Whigs around him, the major issue of the contest, indeed the great issue since 1850, was the preservation of the Union. In a series of short campaign speeches that he delivered following his return from Europe, Fillmore over and over again stressed the importance of the Union issue while giving only lip service to the nativist sentiments that motivated the party's rank-and-file. "Do you notice that K N-ism already has utterly sunk all discussion of its leading principles?" one Republican asked near the end of the campaign. From a quite different perspective, a New York Know Nothing nonetheless made a similar observation when he complained that the party's speakers "have said too little about the great American principles."[106] Moreover, Fillmore's nomination certainly did not constitute a rejection of old party hacks in favor of new leadership. The Republicans, on the other hand, projected a fresh, vibrant image with a ticket headed by a young, new, and for all intents and purposes non-party man. At the same time, the Republican party very skillfully exploited anti-Catholicism while keeping it secondary to the Kansas issue. The result was the desertion of a large number of American party men—in some states a decisive majority—to the Republicans. Those desertions radically altered the nature of the dying American movement. By confining Fillmore's strength largely to conservatives and diehard nativists, Republicans accomplished their first major objective: They destroyed the American party.

Fillmore men admitted that they were "stunned" by the election's outcome.[107] Some spoke bravely of maintaining the American organization, but Washington Hunt, who

---

104. Richard M. Corwine to Schouler, November 7, Schouler Papers; Adams to Seth M. Gates, September 9 (copy), Adams Family Papers; E. Peshine Smith to Carey, October 26, Carey Papers; New York *Times*, November 6.

105. Holt, *Political Crisis*, 171–75, contains a careful analysis of the decline of Know Nothingism.

106. E. Peshine Smith to Carey, October 31, Carey Papers; D. C. Calvin to Daniel Ullmann, October 13, Ullmann Papers, NYHS; New York *Times*, November 18; New York *Herald*, November 16. Although Fillmore men emphasized the Union issue in the 1856 campaign, nativism undoubtedly held a number of voters in the American camp. Neely, "Richard W. Thompson," correctly points out that not all Union men were indifferent to nativism. Still, the change in the party's electoral support indicates that the masses were sensitive to the shift in the Americans' appeal.

107. J. P. Faurot to Ullmann, November 29, A. G. Hartshorn to Ullmann, November 7, Ullmann Papers, NYHS.

supported Fillmore although he was not a Know Nothing, was more perceptive when he concluded that the order must soon be disbanded. "It has no breadth—no vitality—and ought to be dismissed as soon as we can see what is to become of its forces."[108] Republicans were convinced that the rival American party had been "buried too deep for any resurrection." One of Seward's correspondents chortled that "the Know Nothing party, the meanest, paltriest of all mean & paltry parties, has been killed dead, dead forever, never to rise again." Similarly, the New York *Times* announced with obvious satisfaction that the American organization would never again have such a favorable opportunity to carry a national election, and that "its utter defeat now will give it a staggering blow from which it can never recover."[109]

Republicans predicted that the vindictive American leaders would end up in the Democratic party, but that rank-and-file nativists would for the most part "follow their sympathies into Republicanism."[110] A number of Republicans therefore stressed the need to conciliate the Americans further. Joining them was North American leader Francis H. Ruggles, who told Seward: "The Silver Gray misery, based upon personal jealousy, has been one of the most potent causes of misfortune. This is now broken and dispersed and all of its followers are delivered into our hands." The *Ohio State Journal* was confident that "the great mass of the Fillmore party in Ohio will cleave to the Republican side in the contests hereafter to be fought in the State." Even Fillmore's organ, the Buffalo *Commercial Advertiser*, warned that if Buchanan attempted to force slavery on Kansas or seize Cuba, "Nothing is more certain than the complete consolidation of the American and Republican parties into a compact opposition."[111]

The results of the 1856 presidential election greatly stimulated Republican morale. It was "almost like a victory," a Massachusetts Republican said of Frémont's defeat, an assessment shared by the prominent clergyman William H. Furness, who characterized the result as "a victorious defeat." Disappointed, the New York *Evening Post* took solace in the fact that the Republicans had "laid the basis of a formidable and well-organized party" for the future. Morgan expressed confidence that despite Buchanan's victory, "we have laid the foundation for a party that will defeat his re-election or the election of any body like him." Also hopeful, Preston King predicted that Buchanan would be "the last pro-slavery President this Country will ever see."[112]

Frémont's popular vote left no doubt that the Republicans were victorious in the struggle with the Know Nothings to dominate the anti-Democratic forces in the country. "Henceforth," contended the Albany *Evening Journal*, "there are to be but two National Parties—the Party of Freedom and the Party of Slavery."[113] The climax of an extraordinarily difficult fight for survival, the 1856 campaign marked the emergence of

---

108. Washington Hunt to Samuel B. Ruggles, November 7, Samuel B. Ruggles Papers, NYHS; E. B. Bartlett to Fillmore, November 12, Fillmore Papers, SUNY.

109. James M. Bunce to Morgan, November 6, Edwin D. Morgan Papers; Caleb S. Henry to Seward, November 6, Seward Papers, UR; New York *Times*, November 6; Albany *Evening Journal*, November 6.

110. Albany *Evening Journal*, November 8 (quotation); Edward Rankin to Richard Yates, December 4, Yates Papers; New York *Times*, November 6; Cincinnati *Gazette*, November 5.

111. Francis H. Ruggles to Seward, December 11, quoted in Curran, "New York Know Nothings," 263; *Ohio State Journal*, November 10; Buffalo *Commercial Advertiser*, November 7.

112. James Lawrence to Carey, December 11, Carey Papers; William H. Furness to Sumner, November 9, Sumner Papers, HU; New York *Evening Post*, November 5; Edwin D. Morgan to Welles, November 6, Welles Papers, LC; Preston King to John Bigelow, November 10, quoted in Muller, "Preston King," 581.

113. Albany *Evening Journal*, November 6.

the Republican party as a competitive force in national politics. The annihilation of the political strength of the Know Nothing order, which was a crucial and necessary development in the Republican party's rise to national power, was the single most important triumph that the Republican party in its long history would ever achieve. In losing the 1856 presidential election, Republicans paradoxically also won a great victory.

VIII

"The Republican party was the child of events," George Boutwell asserted as he glanced back on the party's formative years.[114] Certainly the Republican party capitalized adeptly on antislavery sentiment, particularly growing opposition to the political power of the South, that had developed in the North over a number of years and had been stimulated by a series of sectional disputes going back to the Missouri crisis of 1819–1820. In more immediate terms, the Republican movement was a direct response to the Kansas-Nebraska Act. With the passage of that law, one New England paper subsequently explained, "all the anti-slavery seeds which twenty years of toil, sacrifice and patience had disseminated through the public mind burst out into an irrepressible flame."[115] Even in the wake of the anti-Nebraska storm that swept across the North, however, the Republican party faltered and suffered an almost unbroken series of electoral defeats. The party seemed headed for an early death when events in the spring of 1856—particularly the raid on Lawrence by a pro-slavery band and, most important, Preston S. Brooks's assault on Charles Sumner in the Senate chamber—gave it a new lease on life. Republicans entered the 1856 presidential campaign with soaring spirits and revived political momentum, and party leaders shrewdly exploited this opportunity. By rousing sectional feeling to unprecedented heights, they rallied thousands of northerners to the party's cause and were only narrowly defeated. Without these specific events, it is impossible to imagine the Republican party taking shape when it did or winning widespread popular support.

Yet more was involved in the emergence of the Republican party than these specific political events, important as they were. The political realignment of the 1850s involved two distinct phenomena, the collapse of the Jacksonian party system and the death of the Whig party on the one hand, and the rise of the Republican party on the other.[116] Traditionally these developments have been considered products of the same fundamental cause—the Kansas-Nebraska Act and the slavery extension issue. And in fact had the slavery extension issue been all that was involved in the pre-Civil War realignment, the transition from the second to the third party system would have been straightforward and the task confronting Republican organizers immensely simplified. But the antebellum

---

114. George S. Boutwell, *Why I am a Republican* (Hartford, 1884), 22.

115. *Kennebec Journal*, December 29, 1854.

116. The concept of realignment has recently come under heavy criticism. See McCormick, "Realignment Synthesis in American History"; and Lichtman, "End of Realignment Theory?" Both these discussions focus primarily on political change in the 1890s and the 1930s and give little attention to earlier periods. Too much of the discussion concerning realignment theory has simply ignored the upheavals of the 1830s and the 1850s. For a recent example, see Clubb, Flanigan, and Zingale, *Partisan Realignment*, which advances a number of ideas based on developments after the Civil War that are at odds with the reality of the antebellum realignment. Ironically, the theory of realignment, which was originally devised to explain modern political developments, seems a more effective framework for analyzing political change in earlier periods when partisan loyalties were very strong, politics was much less nationally oriented, and parties lacked the institutional structures to foster their continued existence.

realignment was considerably more complex, and the emergence of the Republican party was a much more uneven, drawn-out process.

Beginning at the state and local level rather than the national, the realignment of the 1850s was under way in the North prior to the passage of the Kansas-Nebraska Act in 1854. A number of factors contributed to the onset of realignment, but of particular significance was the rise of ethnocultural issues that cut across traditional partisan lines and thus had unusual potential to disrupt both the Whig and Democratic coalitions. Just when the major parties successfully repulsed the challenge of the Free Soil party following passage of the Compromise of 1850 and a period of sectional calm seemed at hand, ethnocultural issues destroyed the party system. Two issues were especially important in precipitating realignment: temperance, which had been gathering political strength for a decade, and anti-Catholicism and anti-foreignism, which after a brief flurry in the 1840s blazed forth again with increased power in the early 1850s. In a number of states and communities party lines were badly disordered by the beginning of 1854, and everywhere politicians reported that voters' partisan loyalties were weaker than they could ever remember. When at this point Congress approved the fateful Kansas-Nebraska bill, party decomposition in the North rushed to a climax. Thus in 1854 the two issues that would play the dominant roles in realignment—nativism and anti-slavery-extension—came to the forefront of northern politics. The target of a dual onslaught, the Democratic party experienced a string of stunning defeats in the 1854 fall elections. In the party chaos that followed, experienced politicians were at a loss to foretell the ultimate outcome of this revolt. "The political elements are in a state of commotion that baffles all calculation and all foresight," a Maine paper noted accurately in the summer of 1854.[117] Not surprisingly, politicians rowed in many different directions trying to make their way through the swirling political waters.

The immediate beneficiary of these developments was the nativist American or Know Nothing party. Combining nativism, anti-Nebraskaism, and opposition to the existing parties as unresponsive to the public will, the Know Nothings were the most potent force in the 1854 elections. Because these other issues and not just the Nebraska question were central to the 1854 upheaval, the Whig party, despite its opposition in Congress to the repeal of the Missouri Compromise, suffered an even more devastating blow in these elections than did the Democrats. Thousands of rank-and-file nativist Whigs, joined by a number of Democrats and Free Soilers, abandoned the old parties for the new American movement. Battered by first temperance and then nativism, the Whig party abruptly collapsed.

One of the most important third parties in American history, the Know Nothings served as the bridge between the death of the Whig party and the growth of the Republican party. By providing a focus for the forces that destroyed the Jacksonian alignment, the American movement was primarily responsible for the Whig party's demise. The nativist order enjoyed a brief period of ascendancy, but it in turn was destroyed by the sectional forces that produced the Republican party. Different political forces, in other words, were responsible for the disintegration of the second party system on the one hand and the ultimate form and direction that the third party system assumed on the other.

With the Know Nothings riding a crest of popularity, antislavery politicians launched the Republican party. The Republican movement combined Whigs, antislavery Demo-

---

117. *Kennebec Journal*, June 23, 1854.

crats, and Free Soilers who wished to make antislavery the dominant element in northern politics. Some of these groups were adamantly hostile to nativism while others had previously supported the Know Nothings, but, whatever their views on other questions, party members placed greater importance on sectional issues. Still, the party faced major obstacles at its birth. "We were without party history, party pride, or party idols," Lincoln said concerning its beginning. "We were a collection of individuals, but recently in political hostility, one to another; and thus subject to all that distrust, and suspicion, and jealousy could do."[118] But the greatest problem that the new party encountered was the power of the Know Nothings. In most northern states, and particularly in the most populous ones with their sizable electoral votes, the Republican party needed significant nativist support to be victorious. The major task for Republicans was to win over the majority of the northern Know Nothings and displace the nativist society as the Democrats' major adversary.

Over the next two years, the Republican and American parties battled for control of the anti-Democratic forces in the North. Traditionally this struggle has been viewed narrowly as a contest between antislavery and nativism to see which idea would prevail and which one would be shunted aside. This approach, however, erects too rigid a separation between the two movements and describes their relationship incorrectly. In some respects nativism and antislavery competed for political prominence, but in other ways the two movements were closely associated, for clear links existed between them psychologically and in mass support. Except for the Silver Grey Whig element that tried to control the Know Nothing movement and make Unionism its organizing principle, Know Nothings in the free states generally opposed the Kansas-Nebraska Act and the further expansion of slavery. In addition, Americans more often than not favored temperance. There was thus a strong though imperfect affinity among these movements, a situation that greatly complicated the process of realignment in general and the formation of the Republican party in particular.

The results of the 1854 and 1855 state elections demonstrated that together anti-Catholicism and opposition to the expansion of slavery constituted a stronger party program than either sentiment by itself. As long as the Know Nothings continued to exploit both issues, Republicans could not dislodge them from their dominant position with a strictly antislavery platform because of the continuing power of ethnocultural concerns in the electorate. Only in 1856, when the Know Nothings dropped their anti-Nebraska position over the vehement protests of a majority of northern delegates at the national convention, *and* the Republicans explicitly courted nativist support, did the Republicans emerge as the strongest anti-Democratic party in the North. Aided immensely by the events of that year, Republicans capitalized on the growing sectional tensions and made anti-slavery-extension, not nativism, the focus of the anti-Democratic opposition. They reversed priorities from those of the Know Nothings in 1854–1855, but, while stressing antislavery, Republican leaders were careful to reach out to disaffected Americans. They nominated Know Nothings for office, gave them a prominent place in the 1856 campaign, and either endorsed nativist planks in state and local platforms or at least demanded no renunciation of past opinions. In addition, they fashioned a party ideology that united the Slave Power with the Catholic church in an alleged assault on the country's republican heritage. Armed with a more effective appeal that catered to both

---

118. Notes for a Speech at Chicago, February 28, 1857, Basler, ed., *Lincoln Collected Works*, v. 2, 390–91.

antislavery sentiment and anti-Catholicism, Republicans detached substantial numbers of Know Nothings from their previous affiliation and emerged in the 1856 presidential election as the major anti-Democratic party in the country. The American organization, which in the words of one supporter had functioned as "a plough to break ground in the disintegration of the old parties," had been dealt a mortal blow in this election.[119]

In some ways, the realignment of the 1850s resembled the pattern historians and political scientists have ascribed to later party realignments. In particular, Republican strength rested less on the conversion of Democrats than on winning large numbers of newly enfranchised, previously apathetic, and weakly identified voters.[120] The Know Nothings had mobilized these groups, and in displacing them the Republicans won substantial support from these voters in 1856. At the same time, the extent of Democratic defections to the Republican party has often been exaggerated. In a few states ex-Democrats were a major portion of the Republican coalition, but, taking the North as a whole, it is striking how successful Democrats were in holding their traditional loyalists. A large number of Democrats deserted their party in 1854 because of the Nebraska bill, but for many this bolt was merely a protest, and they, along with a smaller proportion of associates who had joined the Know Nothings, soon returned to their regular partisan loyalty. In some states it appears that the majority of Democrats who entered the Republican party did so not through the anti-Nebraska movement but rather via the secret Know Nothing lodges. Know Nothingism was an effective solvent of past party identities, and for many northerners the Know Nothing party was but a temporary sojourn on their way to becoming Republicans.

In more important ways, however, the realignment of the 1850s was significantly different from those that followed. The most obvious difference is that one of the two major parties disappeared and was replaced by a new party. Because the Republican party was not simply the Whig party in new garb, well over half the northern electorate developed a new party identity. The magnitude of this shift in voter loyalties dwarfs that of the 1890s or the 1930s. In addition, the antebellum realignment was much more complex than later ones, since it involved not simply a redistribution of voter loyalties but in the short period of three years nothing less than the death of one party (the Whigs), the rise and fall of another (the Know Nothings), and the emergence as a major party of yet a third (the Republicans). Another critical difference was the extent to which realignment began at the state and local level rather than the national, and the degree to which issues outside Congress were central to the political upheaval.

The realignment of the 1850s began as a mass-based revolt.[121] Politicians did not precipitate realignment, nor were they able at first to control it. The temperance issue was forced into the political arena by reformers outside the established parties, often against the wishes of party leaders. The nativist impulse that swept across the North early in the decade was stimulated by social and economic changes that disrupted people's lives and seemed to threaten their well-being, and was directly a response to the growing political aggressiveness of Catholics and immigrants and the Catholic bishops' demand for tax

---

119. Quoted in the New York *Evening Post*, November 20, 1854.

120. Clubb, Flanigan, and Zingale, *Partisan Realignment*, 22, 133, 214, 257, 267.

121. In this sense the facts of the antebellum realignment generally are in accord with the view of Walter Dean Burnham, who argues that realignments are "constituent acts" that "arise from emergent tensions in society" that are inadequately controlled by the parties and thus "escalate to a flashpoint": *Critical Elections*, 10. Burnham unduly minimizes the role of party leaders once realignment is under way, however.

money for parochial schools. Prominent politicians did not take a leading role in these developments, and in fact were connected with them only to the extent they tried to ignore these problems. As this mass revolt unfolded, party leaders were left behind and had to scurry to catch up with public opinion. In many states, opportunistic professional politicians eventually took control of the American party, but they did not organize the movement and they were not responsible for its initial growth. As a result, many new and obscure men were thrust into power by the Know Nothing movement. From the perspective of many party leaders, political events seemed out of control in 1854 and 1855. "Amid the wild scenes of *fusion* and *confusion* which now reign in the political world," the seasoned political veteran William L. Marcy commented in 1855, "I hardly think any man is potential [*sic*] enough to exercise much controll as to coming events. It sometimes—tho rarely—happens that things get into such an imbroglio that the wisest course is to let them alone."[122]

Nevertheless, the role of party leaders was ultimately crucial in the pre-Civil War realignment. William H. Seward was not entirely accurate when he denied that men determined the issues separating political parties and insisted instead that "it is events which have a stern logic that have marshalled against each other the two opposing masses of citizens in this country."[123] Realignment began with the electorate, but party elites made the critical decisions concerning the formation of the Republican party. Party leaders gave meaning to events, placed them in a larger ideological context, established a party organization, reached out to groups of potential supporters, and presented policy alternatives to the voters. Politicians, of course, were sensitive to the direction of public opinion and sought to harness it to their own ends, but voters responded mainly to the initiatives of leaders. Superior leadership was vital to the success of the Republican party, since the task of uniting such a disparate array of anti-Democratic factions was enormous, and the achievement of Republican managers should not be minimized.

The development of the sectional Republican party as a powerful political movement was ominous for future relations between the North and the South. To an extent unforeseen when Pierce assumed office, sectional animosities had intensified and in each section, suspicion and fear of the other had deepened during his administration. Pointing to recent events as evidence, Republican spokesmen cried that slaveholders and their northern allies were engaged in a conspiracy to destroy liberty and republicanism. Such assertions had been central to American politics since the Revolution, and, however exaggerated, Republican claims about the Slave Power conspiracy won wide acceptance in a northern electorate accustomed to such arguments. In raising this specter, Republican leaders paid little heed to the long-term consequences of such agitation. Convinced that threats of disunion, such as were heard from parts of the South in 1856 should Frémont be elected, were mere bluster, Republicans became more and more strident in their attacks on the South. No doubt a contributing factor was their festering anger over the past behavior of southern politicians: anti-Compromise Whigs' fury over southern Whigs' actions in 1852; the Barnburners' indignation over being displaced in the party of Jackson by a group of men who (in their eyes) placed slavery above the party's true mission; and all groups' resentment over the unexpected repeal of the Missouri Compromise. Having discarded the bond of political fellowship with southerners, Republican leaders were not

---

122. Marcy to Buchanan, September 10, 1855 (Private), Buchanan Papers, HSPa; Preston King to John Bigelow, September 16, 1854, quoted in Muller, "Preston King," 546–47.

123. Seward to John Wilson, December 6, John Wilson Papers.

subject to the restraint imposed by a national party organization, and their sectional rhetoric became increasingly shrill.

Republican propaganda greatly magnified the growing conflict between the North and the South. Yet it would be a mistake to assume that party leaders agitated groundless fears with the aim of merely winning elections. For all its exaggeration, Republican rhetoric exposed a very real fear among a large and growing number of northerners. The Republican argument that there was a conspiracy to destroy liberty gained plausibility with the passage of time, and the events of 1856 especially strengthened its emotional power in the northern electorate. Uncertain where these developments would lead, Republican leaders and voters had ample cause for alarm. Nor was the Republican appeal primarily an unconscious manifestation of internal tensions in northern society. "In spite of old differences, prejudices, and animosities," the party's members, Lincoln declared, "were drawn together by a paramount common danger." That danger, he emphasized, was "the spread, and nationalization of slavery."[124]

The Republican party's remarkable performance in the 1856 presidential election did not mark the end of realignment, only the close of its initial stage.[125] The Whig party had disappeared, the American party was on its deathbed, and the Republican party was the dominant party in the North and the strongest anti-Democratic party in the nation. Republicans had successfully met their first significant challenge: They had displaced the Know Nothings as the second party in the two-party system. But if the party was to survive, it had to win national power. For all their post-election elation, Republican leaders remained keenly aware that Frémont had received only a plurality of the vote in the free states in 1856, and their next objective was to create a northern Republican majority and elect a president in 1860, developments that constituted the second stage of the rise of the Republican party. As they looked ahead to the next presidential election, Republican managers were optimistic that by then they could bring the remaining anti-Democratic groups in the North into the Republican coalition. The poet John Greenleaf Whittier voiced Republicans' confidence when he wrote after Frémont's defeat:

> "If months have well-nigh won the field,
> What may not four years do?"[126]

Events of the next four years would transform the Republican party from the largest party in the North into the strongest party in the nation, and in the process bring the country to the brink of civil war.

---

124. Fragment on the Formation of the Republican Party, [ca. February 28, 1857], Basler, ed., *Lincoln Collected Works*, v. 2, 391.

125. For a discussion of the long-term pattern of flux and stability in the third party system see Kleppner, *Third Electoral System*, 16–47. Baum provides some important corrections concerning this pattern for Massachusetts in his *Civil War Party System*, 8–23.

126. Quoted in Rhodes, *History of the United States*, v. 2, 192.

Bibliography

The following is a selective bibliography. It does not list all the sources I consulted, or even all those cited in the footnotes. Instead, I have noted those works on which I relied most heavily for information, and those that have influenced or challenged my ideas on antebellum politics. Those readers who wish to consult a fuller and more extensively annotated version of this study are referred to my dissertation, "The Origins of the Republican Party, 1852–1856" (University of California, Berkeley, 1980).

Primary Sources

This study rests to a very considerable degree on primary sources. In this section, I have listed in various categories those sources that I found most useful in my research.

Manuscripts

The following list does not include all the manuscript collections I examined in the course of this project but is confined to those collections cited in the footnotes and others that were of value. These collections vary considerably in size and importance, and my footnotes indicate those that were of the greatest significance.

Adams Family Papers, Massachusetts Historical Society
James F. Aldrich Papers, Chicago Historical Society
William Allen Papers, Library of Congress
John Andrews Papers, Massachusetts Historical Society
Appleton Family Papers, Massachusetts Historical Society
Archdiocese of Cincinnati Records, University of Notre Dame
Archdiocese of New Orleans Records, University of Notre Dame
William B. Archer Papers, Illinois State Historical Library
James M. Ashley Memoirs, University of Toledo
David Rice Atchison Papers, University of Missouri
Bacon Family Papers, Yale University
John S. Bagg Papers, Henry E. Huntington Library
Bailhache-Brayman Papers, Illinois State Historical Library
Baldwin Family Papers, Yale University
Bancroft-Bliss Family Papers, Library of Congress
Nathaniel P. Banks, Jr., Papers, Illinois State Historical Library
Nathaniel P. Banks, Jr., Papers, Library of Congress

James D. Barbee Papers, Library of Congress
Samuel L. M. Barlow Papers, Henry E. Huntington Library
Daniel D. Barnard Papers, New York State Library
Hiram Barney Papers, Henry E. Huntington Library
Daniel R. Bearss Papers, Indiana Historical Society
Abijah Beckwith Journal, Cornell University
John Bell Papers, Library of Congress
Thomas Hart Benton Papers, Missouri Historical Society
John Bigelow Papers, New York Public Library
John P. Bigelow Papers, Harvard University
William Bigler Papers, Historical Society of Pennsylvania
Francis W. Bird Papers, Harvard University
James G. Birney Papers, William L. Clements Library, University of Michigan
James Bishop Papers, Rutgers University
William H. Bissell Papers, Missouri Historical Society
Jeremiah S. Black Papers, Library of Congress
James G. Blaine Papers, Library of Congress
Blair Papers, Missouri Historical Society
Blair Family Papers, Library of Congress
Blair-Lee Papers, Princeton University
George Bliss Papers, Massachusetts Historical Society
William C. Bouck Papers, Cornell University
Samuel Bowles Papers, Yale University
Henry M. Brackenridge Papers, University of Pittsburgh
Luther Bradish Papers, New-York Historical Society
John T. Brasee Papers, Ohio Historical Society
Breckinridge Family Papers, Library of Congress
Sidney Breese Papers, Illinois State Historical Library
William H. Brisbane Papers, State Historical Society of Wisconsin
Bryant Family Papers, New York Public Library
Bryant-Godwin Papers, New York Public Library
James Buchanan Papers, Historical Society of Pennsylvania
James Buchanan Papers, Library of Congress
Edward Bumgardner Papers, Kansas State Historical Society
Edmund Burke Papers, Library of Congress
Anson Burlingame Papers, Library of Congress
Benjamin F. Butler Papers, New York State Library
Simon Cameron Papers, Historical Society of Dauphin County
Simon Cameron Papers, Library of Congress
Lewis D. Campbell Papers, Ohio Historical Society
Campbell Family Papers, Duke University
Henry C. Carey Papers, Historical Society of Pennsylvania
Cyrus C. Carpenter Papers, State Historical Society of Iowa
Robert Carter Papers, Harvard University
Shepard Cary Papers, Maine Historical Society
Lewis Cass Papers, Burton Historical Collection, Detroit Public Library
John D. Caton Papers, Library of Congress
Joshua L. Chamberlain Papers, Maine Historical Society
Charles P. Chandler Papers, Maine Historical Society
Zachariah Chandler Papers, Library of Congress
Salmon P. Chase Papers, Cincinnati Historical Society
Salmon P. Chase Papers, Historical Society of Pennsylvania

Salmon P. Chase Papers, Library of Congress
Salmon P. Chase Papers, Ohio Historical Society
George W. Cheever Papers, American Antiquarian Society
Myron H. Clark Papers, New York State Library
William Penn Clarke Papers, Iowa State Department of History and Archives
John M. Clayton Papers, Historical Society of Delaware
John M. Clayton Papers, Library of Congress
C. H. Cleaveland Papers, Ohio Historical Society
John H. Clifford Papers, Massachusetts Historical Society
Ichabod Codding Papers, Swarthmore College
Codding Family Papers, Illinois State Historical Library
Arthur C. Cole Notes, University of Illinois
Cornelius Cole Papers, University of California, Los Angeles
Schuyler Colfax Papers, Indiana Historical Society
Schuyler Colfax Papers, Indiana State Library
Schuyler Colfax Papers, Indiana University
Schuyler Colfax Papers, Library of Congress
Schuyler Colfax Papers, Northern Indiana Historical Society
Thomas Corwin Papers, Library of Congress
Henry H. Crapo Papers, Michigan Historical Collections, University of Michigan
John J. Crittenden Papers, Library of Congress
Dr. Harry Croswell Diary, Yale University
William Cumback Papers, Indiana University
Caleb Cushing Papers, Library of Congress
George M. Dallas Papers, Historical Society of Pennsylvania
Dana Family Papers, Massachusetts Historical Society
David Davis Papers, Chicago Historical Society
David Davis Family Papers, Illinois State Historical Library
John G. Davis Papers, Indiana Historical Society
John G. Davis Papers, State Historical Society of Wisconsin
William M. Davis Papers, Historical Society of Pennsylvania
Henry L. Dawes Papers, Library of Congress
Isaac Dayton Papers, New-York Historical Society
Charles D. Deshler Papers, Rutgers University
Dorothea Dix Papers, Harvard University
John A. Dix Papers, Columbia University
Andrew Jackson Donelson Papers, Library of Congress
James R. Doolittle Papers, State Historical Society of Wisconsin
Stephen A. Douglas Papers, University of Chicago
Stephen A. Douglas Papers, University of Illinois
John Dowling Papers, Indiana Historical Society
Thomas H. Dudley Papers, Henry E. Huntington Library
George G. Dunn Papers, Indiana University
Zebina Eastman Papers, Chicago Historical Society
Edwards Family Papers, Yale University
William H. English Papers, Indiana Historical Society
William H. English Papers, University of Chicago
Jane Andrews Espy Papers, Cincinnati Historical Society
Edward Everett Papers, Massachusetts Historical Society
Thomas Ewing Family Papers, Library of Congress
Erastus Fairbanks Papers, Vermont Historical Society
Alpheus Felch Papers, Burton Historical Collection, Detroit Public Library

Alpheus Felch Papers, Michigan Historical Collections, University of Michigan
Jesse W. Fell Papers, University of Illinois
Fessenden Family Papers, Bowdoin College
William Pitt Fessenden Papers, Library of Congress
William Pitt Fessenden Papers, Western Reserve Historical Society
Millard Fillmore Papers, Buffalo and Erie County Historical Society
Millard Fillmore Papers, State University of New York, Oswego
Hamilton Fish Papers, Library of Congress
Hamilton Fish Papers, University of Virginia
Azariah C. Flagg Papers, Columbia University
Calvin Fletcher Papers, Indiana Historical Society
George G. Fogg Papers, New Hampshire Historical Society
Oran Follett Papers, Cincinnati Historical Society
John C. Frémont Papers, University of California, Berkeley
Benjamin B. French Papers, Library of Congress
J. Alexander Fulton Papers, Pennsylvania Historical and Museum Commission
Samuel Galloway Papers, Ohio Historical Society
William Lloyd Garrison Papers, Boston Public Library
John W. Geary Papers, Beinecke Library, Yale University
John H. George Papers, New Hampshire Historical Society
Joshua R. Giddings Papers, Ohio Historical Society
Giddings-Julian Papers, Library of Congress
Archibald H. Gillespie Papers, University of California, Los Angeles
Joseph Gillespie Papers, Illinois State Historical Library
Robert Goodenow Papers, Maine Historical Society
Francis Granger Papers, Library of Congress
Horace Greeley Papers, Chicago Historical Society
Horace Greeley Papers, Library of Congress
Horace Greeley Papers, New Hampshire Historical Society
Horace Greeley Papers, New York Public Library
Greeley-Colfax Papers, New York Public Library
James W. Grimes Papers, Iowa State Department of History and Archives
Edward Everett Hale Papers, New York State Library
John P. Hale Papers, Dartmouth College
John P. Hale Papers, New Hampshire Historical Society
Murat Halstead Papers, Cincinnati Historical Society
Allen Hamilton Papers, Indiana State Library
Hannibal Hamlin Papers, University of Maine
Gideon Hard Autobiography, New-York Historical Society
John Harper Family Papers, Historical Society of Western Pennsylvania
Benjamin Harrison Papers, Library of Congress
J. Scott Harrison Papers, Library of Congress
Friedrich Hassaurek Papers, Ohio Historical Society
Joseph R. Hawley Papers, Library of Congress
Rutherford B. Hayes Papers, Library of Congress
Rutherford B. Hayes Papers, Rutherford B. Hayes Library
Lucius J. Hendee Papers, Connecticut Historical Society
Herndon-Weik Collection, Library of Congress
Thomas W. Higginson Papers, Harvard University
Thomas W. Higginson Papers, Kansas State Historical Society
Thomas W. Higginson Papers, Library of Congress
Higginson-Burns Collection, Boston Public Library

Richard Hinton Papers, Kansas State Historical Society
Holley Family Papers, Connecticut Historical Society
Joseph Holt Papers, Library of Congress
Mark Howard Papers, Connecticut Historical Society
O. O. Howard Papers, Bowdoin College
William A. Howard Papers, Michigan Historical Collections, University of Michigan
Samuel Gridley Howe Papers, Harvard University
Samuel Gridley Howe Papers, Massachusetts Historical Society
Hubbard Family Papers, Bowdoin College
Archbishop John Hughes Papers, Dunwoodie Archives, St. Joseph's Seminary
Washington Hunt Papers, New York State Library
William Hutchinson Papers, Kansas State Historical Society
Dr. Patrick Henry Jameson Memoirs, Indiana Historical Society
Jay Family Papers, Columbia University
Michael H. Jenks Papers, Bucks County Historical Society
Samuel Johnson Papers, Essex Institute
Frank J. Jones Papers, Cincinnati Historical Society
James F. Joy Papers, Burton Historical Collection, Detroit Public Library
Samuel Judah Papers, Indiana University
Norman B. Judd Papers, Illinois State Historical Library
George W. Julian Papers, Indiana Historical Society
George W. Julian Papers, Indiana State Library
John Pendleton Kennedy Papers, Enoch Pratt Free Library
Elisha W. Keyes Papers, State Historical Society of Wisconsin
Elisha King Diary, Indiana Historical Society
John A. King Papers, New-York Historical Society
John Lyle King Diary, Indiana Historical Society
Samuel J. Kirkwood Papers, Iowa State Department of History and Archives
John T. Klippart Papers, Ohio Historical Society
Henry S. Lane Papers, Indiana Historical Society
Henry S. Lane Papers, Indiana University
Joseph Lane Papers, Indiana University
Charles Lanman Papers, Burton Historical Collection, Detroit Public Library
Charles H. Lanphier Papers, Illinois State Historical Library
Amos A. Lawrence Papers, Massachusetts Historical Society
Joshua Leavitt Papers, Library of Congress
Lewis-Neilson Papers, Historical Society of Pennsylvania
Francis Lieber Papers, Henry E. Huntington Library
Abraham Lincoln Papers, Illinois State Historical Library
Abraham Lincoln Papers, Library of Congress
Alexander Long Papers, Cincinnati Historical Society
Owen Lovejoy Papers, Bureau County Historical Society
Owen Lovejoy Papers, Texas Tech University
McCall Family Papers, Cornell University
Robert McClelland Papers, Library of Congress
John A. McClernand Papers, Illinois State Historical Library
John McLean Papers, Library of Congress
John McLean Papers, Ohio Historical Society
Edward McPherson Papers, Library of Congress
Thomas F. Madigan Collection, New York Public Library
James W. Mandeville Papers, Henry E. Huntington Library
Horace Mann Papers, Massachusetts Historical Society

William L. Marcy Papers, Library of Congress
William L. Marcy Papers, New-York Historical Society
Thomas Marshall Papers, Indiana Historical Society
Charles Mason Papers, Iowa State Department of History and Archives
Sidney D. Maxwell Diary, Cincinnati Historical Society
Charles S. May Papers, Burton Historical Collection, Detroit Public Library
Samuel J. May, Jr., Papers, Boston Public Library
Joseph Medill Papers, Chicago *Tribune* Archives
William Medill Papers, Library of Congress
H. Miles Moore Papers, Kansas State Historical Society
Edwin Barber Morgan Papers, Wells College
Edwin D. Morgan Papers, New York State Library
Justin S. Morrill Papers, Library of Congress
Justin S. Morrill Papers, Vermont Historical Society
Edward Joy Morris Papers, Library of Congress
George Morton Papers, Rutherford B. Hayes Library
Henry A. Muhlenberg Papers, American Philosophical Society
Franklin Muzzy Papers, Maine Historical Society
Elias Nason Papers, American Antiquarian Society
John B. Niles Papers, Indiana University
William Nye Papers, Vermont Historical Society
Richard J. Oglesby Papers, Illinois State Historical Library
Godlove S. Orth Papers, Indiana State Library
John G. Palfrey Papers, Harvard University
John M. Palmer Papers, Illinois State Historical Library
Theodore Parker Papers, Massachusetts Historical Society
Parker-Sumner Scrapbook, Boston Public Library
Lewis B. Parson Papers, Illinois State Historical Library
George W. Patterson Papers, University of Rochester
George H. Paul Papers, State Historical Society of Wisconsin
James A. Pearce Papers, Maryland Historical Society
Philip Phillips Papers, Library of Congress
Willard Phillips Papers, Massachusetts Historical Society
Edward L. Pierce Papers, Harvard University
Edward L. Pierce Papers, Library of Congress
Franklin Pierce Papers, Library of Congress
Franklin Pierce Papers, New Hampshire Historical Society
Austin F. Pike Papers, New Hampshire Historical Society
James Shepherd Pike Papers, Library of Congress
James Shepherd Pike Papers, University of Maine
Samuel C. Pomeroy Papers, Kansas State Historical Society
Fred Porter Journal, Michigan Historical Collections, University of Michigan
John F. Potter Papers, State Historical Society of Wisconsin
Rodman M. Price Papers, Rutgers University
Charles H. Ray Papers, Henry E. Huntington Library
Henry J. Raymond Papers, New York Public Library
Albert G. Riddle Papers, Western Reserve Historical Society
Charles D. Robinson Papers, Kansas State Historical Society
Julius Rockwell Papers, Lenox Public Library
Henry Roedter Papers, University of Illinois
David Rorer Papers, State Historical Society of Iowa
Samuel B. Ruggles Papers, New-York Historical Society

William Salter Papers, Iowa State Department of History and Archives
William Schouler Papers, Massachusetts Historical Society
Carl Schurz Papers, Library of Congress
William H. Seward Papers, New-York Historical Society
William H. Seward Papers, New York Public Library
William H. Seward Papers, University of Rochester
Horatio Seymour Papers, Library of Congress
Horatio Seymour Papers, New-York Historical Society
Horatio Seymour Papers, New York State Library
Thomas H. Seymour Papers, Connecticut Historical Society
John Sherman Papers, Library of Congress
William Tecumseh Sherman Papers, Library of Congress
Joseph Sill Diary, Historical Society of Pennsylvania
Silliman Family Papers, Yale University
Matthew Simpson Papers, Library of Congress
Slifer-Dill Papers, Dickinson College
Smelser Family Papers, Cornell University
Francis O. J. Smith Papers, Maine Historical Society
Gerrit Smith Papers, Syracuse University
Smith Family Papers, New York Public Library
John F. Snyder Papers, Illinois State Historical Library
Henry B. Stanton Papers, New-York Historical Society
Francis Stebbins Papers, Michigan Historical Collections, University of Michigan
Thaddeus Stevens Papers, Library of Congress
William R. Stocking Papers, Burton Historical Collection, Detroit Public Library
Harriet Beecher Stowe Papers, Stowe-Day Memorial Library
Isaac Strohm Papers, Cincinnati Historical Society
Isaac Strohm Papers, Ohio Historical Society
Alexander H. H. Stuart Papers, University of Virginia
Charles Sumner Papers, Boston Public Library
Charles Sumner Papers, Harvard University
Charles Sumner Papers, Henry E. Huntington Library
Charles Sumner Papers, Library of Congress
Charles Sumner Papers, New-York Historical Society
Milton Sutliff Papers, Western Reserve Historical Society
Francis B. Swift Papers, Kansas State Historical Society
William Howard Taft Papers, Library of Congress
Mason W. Tappan Papers, New Hampshire Historical Society
Horace A. Tenney Papers, State Historical Society of Wisconsin
Eli Thayer Papers, Brown University
Jesse B. Thomas Papers, Illinois State Historical Library
Nathan Thomas Papers, Michigan Historical Collections, University of Michigan
Richard W. Thompson Papers, Illinois State Historical Library
Richard W. Thompson Papers, Indiana State Library
Richard W. Thompson Papers, Indiana University
Richard W. Thompson Papers, Lincoln National Life Foundation
Samuel J. Tilden Papers, New York Public Library
Treadwell Family Papers, Michigan Historical Collections, University of Michigan
Samuel Treat Papers, Missouri Historical Society
Allan Trimble Papers, Western Reserve Historical Society
Lyman Trumbull Papers, Library of Congress
Lyman Trumbull Family Papers, Illinois State Historical Library

Daniel Ullmann Papers, Historical Society of Delaware
Daniel Ullmann Papers, New-York Historical Society
John C. Underwood Papers, Library of Congress
Martin Van Buren Papers, Library of Congress
Martin Van Buren Papers, Massachusetts Historical Society
Benjamin F. Wade Papers, Library of Congress
Waldron Family Papers, Michigan State University
Walker-Rockwell Papers, New-York Historical Society
Wallace-Dickey Papers, Illinois State Historical Library
Rev. Henry Dana Ward Diary, New York Public Library
Emory Washburn Papers, Massachusetts Historical Society
Israel Washburn, Jr., Papers, Library of Congress
Israel Washburn, Jr., Papers, Washburn Memorial Library, Norlands Estate
Elihu B. Washburne Papers, Library of Congress
Elihu B. Washburne Papers, Washburn Memorial Library, Norlands Estate
Littleton Q. Washington Papers, Duke University
Francis Wayland Papers, Brown University
James Watson Webb Papers, Yale University
Webb Family Papers, New York Public Library
Daniel Webster Papers, Dartmouth College
Daniel Webster Papers, Harvard University
Daniel Webster Papers, New Hampshire Historical Society
Horatio Nelson Weed Diary, Yale University
Thurlow Weed Papers, Library of Congress
Thurlow Weed Papers, New-York Historical Society
Thurlow Weed Papers, University of Rochester
Gideon Welles Papers, Chicago Historical Society
Gideon Welles Papers, Connecticut Historical Society
Gideon Welles Papers, Library of Congress
Gideon Welles Papers, New York Public Library
John Wentworth Papers, Chicago Historical Society
John Wentworth Papers, Illinois State Historical Library
Whittier-Pickard Papers, Harvard University
Elisha Whittlesey Papers, Western Reserve Historical Society
Henry Wilson Papers, Library of Congress
Joel Wilson Papers, Henry E. Huntington Library
John Wilson Papers, University of California, Berkeley
Robert C. Winthrop Papers, Massachusetts Historical Society
Cyrus Woodman Papers, Maine Historical Society
Hendrick B. Wright Papers, Wyoming Historical and Geological Society
Joseph A. Wright Papers, Indiana State Library
Richard Yates Papers, Illinois State Historical Library
Yates-Pickering Papers, Illinois State Historical Library

Newspapers

Newspapers are an essential source for antebellum politics. Since most were highly partisan, they contain a vast amount of political material, much of it unavailable in other sources. I have made no attempt to list all the newspapers I consulted. Rather, listed below by state are those that were most important for my research. In general, I consulted these papers for the years 1848–1860 for election returns and the years 1852–1856 for political material; some titles were not available for all of these years, in which case I normally used those years available on microfilm.

MAINE
[Augusta] *Kennebec Journal*
Portland *Daily Advertiser*
Portland *Eastern Argus*

NEW HAMPSHIRE
[Concord] *New Hampshire Independent Democrat*
[Concord] *New Hampshire Patriot*

MASSACHUSETTS
Boston *Daily Advertiser*
Boston *Bee*
Springfield *Republican*

CONNECTICUT
Hartford *Courant*
Hartford *Evening Press*
Hartford *Times*

NEW YORK
Albany *Argus*
Albany *Evening Journal*
Albany *Statesman*
Buffalo *Commercial Advertiser*
Buffalo *Morning Express*
Fredonia *Censor*
[Greene] *Chenango American*
Jamestown *Journal*
New York *Evening Post*
New York *Express*
[New York] *Freeman's Journal*
New York *Herald*
New York *Times*
New York *Tribune*

PENNSYLVANIA
[Harrisburg] *Keystone*
Harrisburg *Morning Herald*
Harrisburg *Telegraph*
Pittsburgh *Gazette*
Pittsburgh *Post*
Philadelphia *North American*
Philadelphia *Public Ledger*

OHIO
[Cincinnati] *Catholic Telegraph*
Cincinnati *Commercial*
Cincinnati *Enquirer*
Cincinnati *Gazette*
Cleveland *Plain Dealer*
[Columbus] *Ohio Columbian*
[Columbus] *Ohio State Journal*
[Jefferson] *Ashtabula Sentinel*
Toledo *Blade*

INDIANA
[Indianapolis] *Indiana State Journal*
[Indianapolis] *Indiana State Sentinel*

ILLINOIS
Chicago *Democrat*
[Chicago] *Free West*
Chicago *Tribune*
[Springfield] *Illinois State Journal*
[Springfield] *Illinois State Register*

DISTRICT OF COLUMBIA
[Washington, D.C.] *American Organ*
[Washington, D.C.] *National Era*
[Washington, D.C.] *National Intelligencer*
Washington *Union*

Government Documents

Vital sources for this study are the United States censuses for 1850 and 1860, and the state censuses that were compiled in this decade. I have listed in the Appendix other state documents I used. Also essential was the *Congressional Globe*, which contains many Republican speeches, although in order to understand the workings of Congress it must be supplemented by the dispatches of Washington reporters. Two relevant congressional documents are *House Report*, No. 220, 34th Cong., 1st sess. [*Howard Report*], which details the findings of the Kansas investigating committee in 1856, and *House Report*, No. 182, 34th Cong., 1st sess., which deals with the assault on Charles Sumner by Preston S. Brooks.

Contemporary Books and Pamphlets

Pamphlets were a major means of disseminating political information before the Civil War. Unfortunately, no reasonably complete bibliography of political pamphlets for the antebellum period exists, and locating copies is often difficult. In listing those pamphlets and books that I found most useful I have omitted speeches delivered in Congress.

William E. Robinson, *Franklin Pierce and Catholic Persecution in New Hampshire* (New York, 1852), and Charles O. Gorman, *An Irish Catholic Whig to his Fellow Country Men in the United States* (New York, 1852) are examples of Whig appeals to Catholic voters during the 1852 campaign. Democratic efforts to meet this issue include *The Whig Charge of Intolerance against the New Hampshire Democracy and Pierce* (Boston, 1852) and *The New Hampshire Test* (np, [1852]). Scott's earlier nativist letters and subsequent recantation can be found in *The Political Letters and Writings of General Scott* (np, 1852). *The Proceedings of Two Meetings, Held in Boston . . . to Protest Against the Nomination of Gen. Scott, for the Presidency, and to Recommend Hon. Daniel Webster for that Office* (Boston, 1852) and *Why Southern Whigs should Support the Nominees of the Whig Convention* (Washington, 1852) highlight two problems confronted by the Whig presidential campaign. *The Radical Democracy of New York and the Independent Democracy. Letter from Senator Chase, of Ohio, to Hon. B. F. Butler, of New York* (Washington, 1852) criticizes the Barnburners' decision to return to the regular Democratic organization.

A number of books and pamphlets discuss aspects of the Know Nothing movement. Thomas R. Whitney, *A Defence of the American Policy* (New York, 1856) is especially valuable, since Whitney, who was a Know Nothing congressman, was an insider in the New York order and privy to the secret details of the movement's development. Other defenses of the nativist movement include: Samuel S. Busey, *Immigration: Its Evils and Consequences* (New York, 1969, reprint of 1856 edition); Sam C. Crane, *Facts and Figures for Native-Born Americans* (Ithaca, 1856); John Denig, *The Know Nothing Manual* (Harrisburg, 1855); *Foreignism Fully Exposed* (Washington, 1855); *The Know Nothing Almanac; and True Americans' Manual* (New York, 1854 and 1855); *Startling Facts for Native Americans* (New York, 1855); *Know Nothing Platform: Containing an Account of the Encroachments of the Roman Catholic Hierarchy on the Civil and Religious Liberties of the People* (Philadelphia, 1854?); John Hancock Lee, *The Origin and Progress of the American Party in Politics* (Philadelphia, 1855); and *The Origin, Principles and Purposes of the American Party* (np, nd). These works, along with the American press, amply document the depth of anti-Catholic feeling in the Know Nothing movement. An important speech by a prominent Know Nothing leader that says much about values underpinning the nativist movement is Daniel Ullmann, *The Course of Empire* (New York, 1856).

John W. Forney, *Address on Religious Intolerance and Political Proscription* (Washington, 1855) is a vigorous attack on the Know Nothings by a prominent Pennsylvania Democrat. An exposé of the movement in Pennsylvania is contained in *History of the Rise, Progress & Downfall of Know-Nothingism in Lancaster County* (Lancaster, 1856). Charles Hale, *"Our Houses are our Castles"* (Boston, 1855) excoriates the 1855 Massachusetts legislature's notorious nunnery committee, whose activities helped bring that body into public disrepute.

A number of political pamphlets relate to state matters or state elections. *Speech of Hon. Salmon P. Chase, Delivered at the Republican Mass Meeting in Cincinnati, August 21, 1855* (Columbus, 1855) is an important speech Chase delivered during the 1855 Ohio election. *New York Hards and Softs: Which is the True Democracy?* (New York, 1856) and *The Softs: The True Democracy of the State of New York* (New York, 1856) both rehash the causes of the split in the Democratic party in New York. Two important tracts that deal with the liquor issue in Pennsylvania are *Address of the State Central Prohibitory Committee to the Legislature of Pennsylvania* (Philadelphia, 1854) and *Address of the State Central Prohibitory Committee to the People of Pennsylvania* (Philadelphia, 1855). Speeches attacking the Know Nothings delivered in the New York legislature during the 1855 senatorial contest that resulted in William H. Seward's re-election are collected in *United States Senatorial Question* (Albany, 1855), while the public controversy between Know Nothing legislator and New York *Express* editor Erastus Brooks and Archbishop John Hughes over the state's 1855 anti-Catholic church property law is detailed in *The Controversy between Senator Brooks and "+John," Archbishop of New York* (New York, 1855).

Examples of what Democrats derided as political sermons abound. Typical of these addresses are Rev. R. H. Richardson, *A Discourse Occasioned by the Bill for the Government of Kanzas and*

Nebraska (Chicago, 1854); Rev. J. B. Bittinger, *A Plea for Humanity* (Cleveland, 1854); Rev. Edmund H. Sears, *Revolution or Reform* (Washington, 1856); Rev. Henry C. Fish, *The Voice of Our Brother's Blood* (Newark, 1856); Rev. Noah Porter, *Civil Liberty* (New York, 1856); and Rev. Eden B. Foster, *The North-side View of Slavery* (Concord, N.H., 1856). Indicative of Democratic resentment of clerical meddling in politics is *Letter of Stephen A. Douglas, Vindicating His Character and His Position on the Nebraska Bill against the Assaults . . . of Twenty-five Clergymen of Chicago* (Washington, 1854). These sermons were especially common in 1854, in response to the Kansas-Nebraska Act, and again in 1856, in the wake of the assault on Sumner and the disorder in Kansas, and they continued until the election in November.

The Kansas crisis spawned a number of books and pamphlets. William Phillips, *The Conquest of Kansas, by Missouri and Her Allies* (Boston, 1856) dresses up free-state propaganda in especially colorful prose. *Kansas in 1856* (Washington, 1856) picks up where the congressional investigating committee left off in its catalogue of proslavery "outrages" in the territory. Henry Ward Beecher, *Defence of Kansas* (Washington, 1856) presents the Republican viewpoint by a prominent northern clergyman, while [Jesse D. Bright], *A Review of the Trouble in Kansas* (Washington, 1856) indicts the free-state men and Republicans for the difficulties in the territory. John H. Gihon, *Governor Geary's Administration in Kansas* (Philadelphia, 1857) is a defense by Geary's secretary that gives extracts from much official correspondence. Many of the congressional speeches issued as campaign documents by Republican committees in 1856 focused on the Kansas crisis.

The 1856 presidential campaign produced an abundance of pamphlet literature. *A Sketch of the Events in the Life of George Law, Published in Advance of his Biography* (New York, 1855) is a campaign biography written to promote Law's bid for the American party nomination. Millard Fillmore's speeches upon his return in 1856 from Europe, his only public political statements during the campaign, are contained in *Mr. Fillmore at Home* (np, 1856). James Brooks, *Defence of President Fillmore* (New York, 1856) and Richard W. Thompson, *An Address of the Fillmore State Convention to the People of Indiana* (np, 1856) are endorsements of Fillmore's nomination by prominent American leaders.

Democratic campaign literature includes Mich. W. Clusky, comp., *The Democratic Hand-book* (Washington, 1856); *The Old-Line Whigs for Buchanan!* (Boston, 1856), which prints letters from Rufus Choate and George T. Curtis; *The Fearful Issue to be Decided in November Next!* (np, [1856]), which attacks John C. Frémont and the Republican party as a threat to the Union; and *Short Answers to Reckless Fabrications, Against the Democratic Candidate for President, James Buchanan* (Philadelphia, 1856).

The most important campaign biographies of Frémont are Charles W. Upham, *Life, Explorations, and Public Services of John Charles Fremont* (Boston, 1856); [Horace Greeley], *Life of Col. Fremont* (New York, 1856); and John Bigelow, *Memoir of the Life and Public Services of John Charles Frémont* (New York, 1856), which was written with the assistance of Jessie Frémont.

A number of pamphlets deal with the question of Frémont's religion. Those from the anti-Republican perspective include *Fremont's Romanism Established* (np, 1856); *Col. Fremont's Religious History* (np, [1856]); and *J. C. Fremont's Record. Proof of His Romanism* (np, 1856). Republican denials include *Col. Fremont not a Roman Catholic* (np, [1856]); *Col. Fremont's Religion* (np, [1856]); and *Fremont a Protestant* (np, 1856). Other charges against the Republican nominee are made in *Fremont. Only Seventeen Working Days in the U.S. Senate* (New York, 1856); *John C. Fremont! "Is He Honest? Is He Capable?"* (np, 1856); *John Charles Fremont. A California Statement of His Connexion with Palmer, Cook & Co.* (np, 1856), which accuses him of financial irregularities, as do *Fremont and his Speculations* (Washington, 1856), and *The Accounts of Fremont Examined* (Washington, 1856). *Col. Fremont's Private and Public Character Vindicated by James Buchanan* (New York, 1856) defends him from some of these accusations; the same is true of *Facts and Figures for Fremont and Freedom* (Providence, 1856). Otis P. Lord, *"Fremont's Principles" Exposed* (np, 1856), is a vigorous attack on the Republican party and its standard bearer by a Massachusetts Whig. For an example of Republican charges against Buchanan, see *James Buchanan, His Doctrines and Policy* (New York, 1856).

Francis Preston Blair, Sr., wrote several important campaign pamphlets that sought to link Frémont with the tradition of Jackson and to link the Democratic party in 1856 with that of Calhoun. These include *Gen. Jackson and James Buchanan* (np, 1856); *To My Neighbors* (New York, 1856); and *A Voice from the Grave of Jackson* (Washington, 1856), in which Blair took advantage of his possession of Jackson's papers to quote from Old Hickory's private correspondence. Blair's earlier *Letter to the Republican Association of Washington, D.C.* (Washington, 1855) signalled his imminent departure from the Democratic party.

Gamaliel Bailey, *The Record of Sectionalism* (Washington, 1856) documents the South's control of the offices of the federal government. Bailey's associate, Lewis Clephane, gathered some of the most important Republican documents in *Republican Campaign Documents for 1856* (Washington, 1857). George Weston was an indefatigable party publicist. Among his campaign documents are *The Poor Whites of the South* (Washington, 1856), which emphasizes the oppression of whites in that section; *Who Are Sectional?* (np, 1856), a denial that the Republican party was a sectional organization; *Will the South Dissolve the Union?* (np, 1856), which typified Republican thought by insisting that no threat of secession existed; *Southern Slavery Reduces Northern Wages* (Washington, 1856); and *Who are and Who May be Slaves in the United States* (Washington, 1856). This last document reproduces comments from southern sources on the desirability of enslaving white workers; the same theme is the focus of *The "New" Democratic Doctrine. Slavery not to be Confined to the Negro Race* (New York, 1856).

Important Republican speeches during the campaign include *Speech of David Dudley Field, Delivered at Troy* (np, 1856); Nathaniel P. Banks, Jr., *Address . . . Delivered from the Steps of the Merchants Exchange* (New York, 1856), an appeal to the business community that stresses the party's moderation on slavery; James Watson Webb, *Great Mass Meeting on the Battle Ground of Tippecanoe . . . Speech of General J. Watson Webb* (New York 1856); and George W. Curtis, *The Duty of the American Scholar to Politics and the Times* (New York, 1856). Two important speeches Seward delivered during the campaign that are excluded from his collected works are *Speech of Hon. William H. Seward at Jackson, October 4, 1856* (np, 1856); and *Immigrant White Free Labor, or Imported Black African Slave Labor* (np, nd).

Republicans also diligently circulated letters from prominent politicians of other parties endorsing Frémont. Among the most important are: Hamilton Fish, *Fremont, the Conservative Candidate* (np, 1856); former Kansas governor Andrew H. Reeder, *The Approaching Election of President and the Candidates* (New York, 1856); *Geo. Law & Chauncy Shaffer's Reasons for Repudiating Fillmore and Donelson* (New York, 1856); and Ephraim Marsh, *Reasons for Going for Fremont* (np, 1856). Law, Shaffer, and Marsh were all notable former American party leaders.

In order to assist party spokesmen, political parties traditionally prepared handbooks discussing a wide variety of campaign issues. Republican works of this type include Ichabod Codding, *The Freeman's Manual* (New York, 1856); *Republican Pocket Pistol* (New York, 1856); *The Republican Scrap-Book* (Boston, 1856); and *Republican's Complete Outfit of Facts and Arguments* (New York, 1856).

Because of its critical importance, all three parties lavished special attention on Pennsylvania. Democratic documents include *Address of Senator Bigler, to the Democracy of Philadelphia* (Washington, 1856), and *The Last Appeal to Pennsylvania* (np, 1856). *The Great Fraud by which Pennsylvania is Sought to be Abolitionized* (np, 1856) denounces the Union electoral ticket and urges Fillmore men to support the Fillmore Straight ticket. Future Republican congressman William D. Kelley made several important speeches in Philadelphia that were published, including *Speech of Judge Kelley, Delivered at Spring Garden Hall* (Philadelphia, 1856); *An Address Delivered by Hon. William D. Kelley at the West Philadelphia Hall* (Philadelphia, 1856); and *An Address Delivered by Hon. William D. Kelley at Girard Avenue* (Philadelphia, 1856). A last-minute Republican appeal to the state's American party voters is *The American Party Sold to Buchanan* (Philadelphia, 1856), which publishes correspondence between Fillmore managers and Democratic leaders.

An important early statement of Republican concern for the security of northern civil liberties is

Charles Francis Adams, *What Makes Slavery a Question of National Concern?* (Boston, 1855). Benjamin S. Hedrick, *Are North Carolinians Freemen?* (np, 1856), discusses the author's dismissal from the faculty of the University of North Carolina because of his pro-Frémont sympathies, an incident from which Republicans made political capital in 1856. Charles Sumner, *The Slave Oligarchy and its Usurpations* (Washington, 1855) emphasizes the aggressions of the Slave Power, as does James Watson Webb, *Slavery and its Tendencies* (Washington, 1856), a powerful tract written in response to the Sumner caning.

In a class by itself is Edward L. Pierce, *Effect of Proscriptive or Extreme Legislation Against Foreigners in Massachusetts and New England* (Boston, 1857), which argues on the basis of 1856 voting returns that the foreign-born backed Frémont in the western states. Mention should also be made of *Proceedings of the First Three Republican National Conventions* (Minneapolis, 1893); and *Official Proceedings of the Republican Convention Convened in the City of Pittsburgh, Pennsylvania, on the 22nd of February, 1856* (Washington, 1856).

Published Diaries and Collections of Writings, Speeches, Letters, and Documents

While their importance as well as the quality of editing varies, diaries and collections of writings contain valuable material on antebellum politics. Among the works of Republican leaders, I found the following useful: Theodore C. Pease and James G. Randall, eds., *The Diary of Orville Hickman Browning* (2 vols.: Springfield, 1927–33) presents the thinking of a conservative Whig- Republican. Albert B. Hart, ed., *Diary and Correspondence of Salmon P. Chase, Annual Report* of the AHA, 1902, v. 2, prints selections from a number of Chase letters located in several libraries, but the editing leaves much to be desired, as there are many mistakes and inaccuracies. Much superior in this regard is Robert F. Lucid, ed., *The Journal of Richard Henry Dana, Jr.* (3 vols.: 1968), which contains invaluable material on Massachusetts politics, including the formation of the Republican party. Gayle Thornbrough, Dorothy L. Riker, and Paula Corpuz, eds., *The Diary of Calvin Fletcher* (9 vols.: Indianapolis, 1972–83), which I read in manuscript for the 1850s, is now available in a carefully edited edition. An Indianapolis banker, Methodist, and moral reformer, Fletcher in his diary details life and politics in a western city; it is especially valuable for 1856, when he served as treasurer for the Republican state committee. Particularly important for the light it sheds on Ohio politics is L. Belle Hamlin, ed., "Selections from the Follett Papers," published serially in the Ohio Historical and Philosophical Society *Quarterly Publications*, v. 9–13 (1914–18).

No edition of Horace Greeley's writings has been published, but Joel Benton, ed., *Greeley on Lincoln, with Mr. Greeley's Letters to Charles A. Dana and a Lady Friend* (New York, 1893), prints a number of informative letters from the *Tribune*'s editor concerning affairs in Congress in 1855–56 and Frémont's nomination. Greeley's blunt, colloquial style always makes for entertaining reading, but his observations are often an idiosyncratic mixture of insight and obtuseness. William B. Hesseltine and Rex G. Fisher, eds., *Trimmers, Trucklers & Temporizers: Notes of Murat Halstead from the Political Conventions of 1856* (Madison, 1961) makes conveniently available in slightly abbreviated form the reports of that famous journalist on all the national nominating conventions that year. Halstead's comments, while partisan, are often remarkably shrewd. Also useful are Charles Richard Williams, ed., *Diary and Letters of Rutherford Birchard Hayes* (5 vols.: Columbus, 1922); and George W. Julian, *Speeches on Political Questions* (New York, 1872). Abraham Lincoln's speeches and letters for these years are in Roy P. Basler, Marion Delores Pratt, and Lloyd A. Dunlap, eds., *The Collected Works of Abraham Lincoln* (8 vols.: New Brunswick, 1953–55), with a supplementary volume (Westport, Conn., 1974). An especially valuable collection of letters from Edwin B. Morgan of New York bearing on the speakership struggle in 1855–56 is Temple R. Hollcroft, ed., "A Congressman's Letters on the Speaker Election in the Thirty-fourth Congress," *MVHR*, v. 43 (December, 1956), 444–58. Essential information concerning the Know Nothing party in Indiana is in J. Herman Schauinger, ed., "The Letters of Godlove S. Orth, Hoosier American," *Indiana Magazine of History*, v. 40 (March, 1944), 51–66.

Other works I used include John Weiss, ed., *Life and Correspondence of Theodore Parker* (2 vols.: New York, 1864); George T. Palmer, ed., "A Collection of Letters from Lyman Trumbull to John M. Palmer, 1854–1858," *Journal of the Illinois State Historical Society*, v. 16 (April–July, 1923), 20–41, which makes clear the anti-Nebraska Democrats' uncertainty about the Republican party; and James S. Pike, *First Blows of the Civil War* (New York, 1879), a collection of editorials and columns Pike wrote for the New York *Tribune*. Included in the latter publication are a selection of valuable letters to Pike from prominent Republican politicians, although the published versions contain a number of minor inaccuracies. A major source for these years is Frederick W. Seward's biography of his father, *Seward at Washington as Senator and Secretary of State* (2 vols.: New York, 1891), which prints exerpts from a large number of Seward's letters, some of the originals of which, especially those to his wife, have since disappeared. Unfortunately, the letters are not always dated or fully identified, and they also contain errors and omissions; whenever possible, the printed version should be checked against the original. Most of Seward's important speeches were assembled periodically by George E. Baker and published in *The Works of William H. Seward* (5 vols.: Boston, 1853–84). Also marred by mistakes and substitutions is Rachel S. Thorndike, ed., *The Sherman Letters: Correspondence between General and Senator Sherman from 1837 to 1891* (New York, 1894). One of the best diaries of the nineteenth century is Allan Nevins and Milton Halsey Thomas, eds., *The Diary of George Templeton Strong* (4 vols.: New York, 1952). Strong was an upper-class New Yorker without an intense interest in politics until 1856, when he was swept up in the Frémont campaign and became an active Republican. Selections of Charles Sumner's correspondence are in Edward L. Pierce, *Memoir and Letters of Charles Sumner* (4 vols.: Boston, 1877–93), and many of his speeches are collected in *The Works of Charles Sumner* (10 vols.: Boston, 1870–83). Because Sumner heavily edited his speeches for publication, newspaper accounts or pamphlet editions published immediately after delivery provide a more accurate text.

A few collections of non-Republicans were important for my research. Excerpts from James Buchanan's correspondence are in John B. Moore, ed., *The Works of James Buchanan* (12 vols.: Philadelphia, 1910). Sources for other important Democrats are John R. Dickinson, ed., *Speeches, Correspondence, etc., of the Late Daniel S. Dickinson, of New York* (New York, 1867); Robert W. Johannsen, ed., *The Letters of Stephen A. Douglas* (Urbana, 1961); and John Bigelow, ed., *Letters and Literary Memorials of Samuel J. Tilden* (2 vols.: New York, 1908). Lyon G. Tyler, *Letters and Times of the Tylers* (2 vols.: Richmond, 1885) has some useful material from Robert Tyler on Pennsylvania politics. For conservative Whigs, see Frank H. Severance, ed., *Millard Fillmore Papers* (2 vols.: Buffalo, 1907); Fletcher Webster, ed., *The Writings and Speeches of Daniel Webster* (18 vols.: Boston, 1903), valuable for the 1852 election; and Robert C. Winthrop, *Addresses and Speeches on Various Occasions* (4 vols.: Boston, 1867). Finally, Kirk H. Porter and Donald B. Johnson, comps., *National Party Platforms, 1840–1956* (Urbana, 1956) conveniently brings together widely scattered documents.

Autobiographies, Memoirs, and Reminiscences

While a number of men wrote reminiscences of this period, the quality of these works varies widely. They are all, in some sense, self-serving, although some are more frank and complete than others. Yet such works offer material and insights that cannot be found elsewhere. Those I made use of include: John Bigelow, *Retrospections of an Active Life* (5 vols.: New York, 1910–13); Roeliff Brinkerhoff, *Recollections of a Lifetime* (Cincinnati, 1900); and Lewis Clephane, *Birth of the Republican Party* (Washington, 1889), an invaluable account that focuses on the role of the Republican Association in Washington and has essential material on the Pittsburgh convention. Schuyler Colfax, "Anson Burlingame," *The Independent*, v. 22 (April 7, 1870), although not strictly in the form of a reminiscence, has some vital material on Banks's election as speaker. Charles T. Congdon, *Reminiscences of a Journalist* (Boston, 1880) is very helpful on Massachusetts politics.

Other useful recollections include Frederick N. Dow, ed., *The Reminiscences of Neal Dow*

(Portland, 1898), important for the Maine Law and Maine politics; Shalor W. Eldridge, "Recollections of Early Days in Kansas," *Publications of the Kansas State Historical Society*, v. 2 (1920), which in addition to discussing territorial affairs includes his memories as a delegate to the 1856 Republican convention; Russell Errett, "Formation of the Republican Party in 1856," *Magazine of Western History*, v. 7 (December, 1887), 180–89, and "The Republican Nominating Conventions of 1856 and 1860," *Magazine of Western History*, v. 10 (July, August, 1889), 257–65, 360–65; Maunsell B. Field, *Memories of Many Men and Some Women* (New York, 1875); Oran Follett, "The Coalition of 1855," Alfred E. Lee, ed., *History of the City of Columbus* (2 vols.: New York, 1892), which contains an insider's account of the 1855 Ohio Republican convention and Chase's nomination for governor; and John W. Forney, *Anecdotes of Public Men* (2 vols.: New York, 1873–81), disorganized but with important material scattered throughout it. John C. Frémont, *Memoir of My Life* (Chicago and New York, 1887) goes up only to 1846. A second volume was never published but exists in manuscript form in the Frémont Papers at Berkeley. Frémont's discussion of his nomination and the 1856 campaign is incomplete and not entirely accurate, and so must be used with care. Other useful works are Joshua R. Giddings, *History of the Rebellion* (New York, 1864); Horace Greeley, *Recollections of a Busy Life* (New York, 1868); Peter Harvey, *Reminiscences and Anecdotes of Daniel Webster* (Boston, 1884), important for the 1852 election; George W. Julian, *Political Recollections, 1840–1872* (Chicago, 1884), brief but outspoken; Julian, "The First Republican National Convention," *AHR*, v. 4 (January, 1899), 313–22; and Thomas J. McCormack, ed., *Memoirs of Gustave Koerner, 1809–1896* (2 vols.: Cedar Rapids, 1909), the recollections of an important German leader in Illinois who left the Democratic party for the Republicans.

Alexander K. McClure wrote a series of recollections covering his many years in Pennsylvania politics. The fullest is *Old Time Notes of Pennsylvania* (2 vols.: Philadelphia, 1905), but also useful are *Abraham Lincoln and Men of War-Times*, 4th ed. (Philadelphia, 1892); *Our Presidents and How We Make Them*, 3rd ed. (New York, 1909), which has material on the 1856 presidential campaign; and *Colonel Alexander K. McClure's Recollections of Half a Century* (Salem, Mass., 1902). McClure's writings should be used with extreme caution. He was an inveterate foe of Simon Cameron, and his writings reflect the persistent personal antagonisms that rent the Pennsylvania Republican party, while they exaggerate the degree to which McClure comprehended the meaning of events as they unfolded. Still, his are the only extensive reflections of this era we have by a Republican politician in that key state.

Other reminiscences I used include *Personal Recollections of John M. Palmer* (Cincinnati, 1901), which is disappointingly thin for these years; Donn Piatt, *Memories of the Men Who Saved the Union* (New York, 1887); Mrs. W. S. Robinson, *"Warrington" Pen-Portraits: A Collection of Personal and Political Reminiscences, from 1848 to 1876, from the Writings of William S. Robinson* (Boston, 1877), which has much valuable material on Massachusetts politics; Carl Schurz, *Reminiscences of Carl Schurz* (3 vols.: New York, 1907–08); and Winfield Scott, *Memoirs of Lieut.-General Scott, LL.D., Written by Himself* (2 vols.: New York, 1864), which accurately portrays his difficult personality but says little about his presidential candidacy. Paul Selby, who served as chairman of the Decatur convention in 1856, published several reminiscences of the movement to organize the Republican party in Illinois: "The Genesis of the Republican Party in Illinois," *Illinois State Historical Society Transactions*, v. 11 (1906), 270–83; "Republican State Convention, Springfield, Ill., October 4–5, 1854," *McLean County Historical Society Transactions*, v. 3 (1900), 43–47; and "The Editorial Convention, February 22, 1856," ibid., 30–43. John Sherman's *Recollections of Forty Years* (2 vols.: Chicago, 1895) is, like its subject, dull. Henry B. Stanton, *Random Recollections* (New York, 1887) is brief but informative. Thurlow Weed's *Autobiography of Thurlow Weed*, ed. Harriet A. Weed (Boston, 1883) barely touches on the period of this study. A second volume by his grandson, Thurlow Weed Barnes, *Memoir of Thurlow Weed* (Boston, 1884), prints some correspondence and documents for these years. Henry Wilson, *History of the Rise and Fall of the Slave Power in America* (3 vols.: Boston, 1875–77), while only partly a reminiscence, is useful on national politics, but it downplays Wilson's involvement in the American party.

Secondary Sources

Although this study is based largely on primary sources, a number of secondary works provided me with information as well as influenced my thinking about antebellum politics in general and the beginnings of the Republican party in particular.

The most complete guide to the literature on the coming of the Civil War, of which the rise of the Republican party is an integral part, is Thomas J. Pressly's now dated *Americans Interpret their Civil War* (Princeton, 1954). More recent assessments are David M. Potter, *The South and the Sectional Conflict* (Baton Rouge, 1968); Eric Foner, "The Causes of the American Civil War: Recent Interpretations and New Directions," *CWH*, v. 20 (September, 1974), 197–214, an especially stimulating analysis; and Don E. Fehrenbacher, "The New Political History and the Coming of the Civil War," *Pacific Historical Review*, v. 54 (May, 1985), 117–42, which is a provocative discussion of an important topic.

There are several studies of politics in the decade before the Civil War that have much to say about the early Republican party and the sectional conflict. David M. Potter's *The Impending Crisis, 1848–1861* (New York, 1976), completed and edited by Don Fehrenbacher, is a work of major significance. With an impressive breadth of knowledge, Potter deftly handles many controversial points, and his judgments are fair and even-handed. Despite the book's many insights, however, I am unpersuaded by his overarching argument that the moral issue of slavery was at the center of the sectional conflict. Longer and more inclusive, but with less interpretive insight, is Allan Nevins's *Ordeal of the Union* (2 vols.: New York, 1947). While told in sweeping style, Nevins's account merely reiterates the standard story of the rise of the Republican party. Michael F. Holt, *The Political Crisis of the 1850s* (New York, 1978) is a penetrating analysis of politics during this decade. Holt's volume displays a much greater appreciation of the complexity of the realignment of the 1850s than do most works. Avery Craven, *The Coming of the Civil War*, 2nd ed. rev. (Chicago, 1957) has fallen into disfavor, but I find his emphasis on the role of fear and emotion in both sections an important insight, however much I disagree on the nature and causes of these fears. Over the past two decades Joel H. Silbey has written a number of important articles that have been brought together in *The Partisan Imperative: The Dynamics of American Politics before the Civil War* (New York, 1985). With his main points—that politics in this period involved more than just the slavery issue, and that antebellum party loyalties were remarkably resilient—I am in full agreement. An older but very useful treatment is James Ford Rhodes, *History of the United States from the Compromise of 1850* (7 vols.: New York, 1892-1906). While it is old-fashioned and partisan, Rhodes's history nonetheless is a work of enduring merit.

A landmark in historiography was the publication of Lee Benson's essay, "Research Problems in American Political Historiography," Mirra Komarovsky, ed., *Common Frontiers of the Social Sciences* (Glencoe, Ill., 1957), 113–83. 418–21. In this and subsequent writings, Benson urged historians to study elections over time, to examine the social basis of politics, and to draw upon the theories of other social science disciplines. Much of the recent research on voting patterns and party realignment in the nineteenth century has been stimulated by Benson's path-breaking work and political scientists' studies of the modern electorate. Some familiarity with this latter scholarship is essential for an understanding of the political transformation in the 1850s. The classic work in this regard is V. O. Key, Jr., "A Theory of Critical Elections," *Journal of Politics*, v. 17 (February, 1955), 3–18, which began a reorientation in the way historians and political scientists conceptualized American political development. Since the publication of this article, a number of scholars have refined and modified Key's concepts. Three major works on the process of party realignment are Walter Dean Burnham, *Critical Elections and the Mainsprings of American Politics* (New York, 1970); James L. Sundquist, *Dynamics of the Party System: Alignment and Realignment of Political Parties in the United States*, rev. ed. (Washington, 1983); and Jerome M. Clubb, William H. Flanigan, and Nancy H. Zingale, *Partisan Realignment: Voters, Parties, and Government in American History* (Beverly Hills, 1980). While none of these books is particularly concerned with the pre-Civil War era, their arguments are nevertheless thought-provoking. The major statement of the idea of party systems is William Nisbet Chambers and Walter Dean Burnham, eds., *The American*

Party Systems: Stages of Political Development (New York, 1967). Recently, the theory of realignment has come under attack; see, in particular, Allan J. Lichtman, "The End of Realignment Theory? Toward a New Research Program for American Political History," *Historical Methods*, v. 13 (Summer, 1982), 170–88; and Richard L. McCormick, "The Realignment Synthesis in American History," *Journal of Interdisciplinary History*, v. 13 (Summer, 1982), 85–105. Like the authors of the works they challenge, neither Lichtman nor McCormick devotes much attention to the 1850s.

A major study of modern voter perceptions and behavior is Angus Campbell, Philip E. Converse, Warren E. Miller, and Donald E. Stokes, *The American Voter* (New York, 1960). A more recent work that incorporates the findings of the last two decades is Norman H. Nie, Sidney Verba, and John R. Petrocik, *The Changing American Voter*, enlarged ed. (Cambridge, 1979). Philip E. Converse, "The Nature of Belief Systems in Mass Publics," David Apter, ed., *Ideology and Discontent* (New York, 1964), 206–61, best exemplifies the view that voters' attitudes lack ideological content.

Converse is also the foremost spokesman for the idea of an unchanging American electorate. Most directly in "Change in the American Electorate," Angus Campbell and Philip E. Converse, eds., *The Human Meaning of Social Change* (New York, 1972), 273–337, he posits that the electorate of the previous century was essentially the same as that of the modern era. In making that argument, Converse manifests little understanding of the nature of nineteenth-century voting behavior or acquaintance with the historical sources. For a rebuttal, see Walter Dean Burnham, "Theory and Voting Research," *APSR*, v. 68 (September, 1974), 1002–23. I have presented my view of this and related questions in " 'Politics Seem to Enter into Everything': Political Culture in the North, 1840–1860," Stephen E. Maizlish and John J. Kushma, eds., *Essays on American Antebellum Politics, 1840–1860* (College Station, Texas, 1982), 14–69.

The most ambitious attempt to build on these studies and incorporate the concept of realignment and party systems into an analysis of politics in this period is Paul Kleppner, *The Third Electoral System, 1853–1892: Parties, Voters, and Political Cultures* (Chapel Hill, 1979). This book, which emphasizes religious and ethnic determinants of voting, expands arguments he first developed in *The Cross of Culture: A Social Analysis of Midwestern Politics, 1850–1900* (New York, 1970). Kleppner's analysis of long-term voting cycles is more persuasive than his discussion of mass voting behavior, which lacks adequate statistical documentation. Ronald P. Formisano, *The Birth of Mass Political Parties: Michigan, 1827–1861* (Princeton, 1971) presents a similar general argument. Drawing on these and other works, Robert Kelley, *The Cultural Pattern in American Politics: The First Century* (New York, 1979) is an ambitious synthesis that is good on the linkage between various reform movements and political developments in this decade, although some of his assertions about voting behavior rest on a weak empirical base.

Several scholars have expressed reservations about an ethnocultural model of nineteenth-century voting, or an emphasis on the religious split between evangelicals and pietists as forming the crux of party divisions: Allan J. Lichtman, "Political Realignment and 'Ethnocultural' Voting in Late Nineteenth Century America," *Journal of Social History*, v. 16 (Spring, 1983), 55–82; Richard B. Latner and Peter Levine, "Perspectives in Antebellum Pietistic Politics," *Reviews in American History*, v. 4 (March, 1976), 15–24; J. Morgan Kousser, "The 'New Political History': A Methodological Critique," ibid., 1–14; Richard L. McCormick, "Ethno-Cultural Interpretations of Nineteenth-Century American Voting Behavior," *Political Science Quarterly*, v. 89 (June, 1974), 351–77; and James E. Wright, "The Ethnocultural Model of Voting: A Behavioral and Historical Critique," *American Behavioral Scientist*, v. 16 (May-June, 1973), 653–74. Allan J. Bogue offers a balanced appraisal of this debate in "The New Political History in the 1970's," Michael Kammen, ed., *The Past Before Us* (Ithaca, 1980), 231–51. Also see Don E. Fehrenbacher's article, "The New Political History and the Coming of the Civil War," cited at the beginning of this essay. On the question of religious denominations and politics, see in addition to these works: Philip R. Vandermeer, "Religion, Society, and Politics: A Classification of American Religious Groups," *Social Science History*, v. 5 (Winter, 1981), 3–24; and Charles C. Cole, *The Social Ideas of the Northern Evangelists, 1826–1860* (New York, 1954). The relationship of religion to antebellum society and politics needs much more research. Perceptive pioneering studies of cultural conflict between various groups in American society are Dixon Ryan Fox, *Yankees and Yorkers* (New York, 1940); Richard Lyle Power, *Planting Corn Belt Culture: The Impress of the Upland Southerner and Yankee in the Old Northwest* (Indianapolis, 1953); and Joseph Shafer, ''The Yankee and Teuton in Wisconsin,'' *Wisconsin Magazine of History*, v. 6–7 (December, 1922–December, 1923).

The Jacksonian reform impulse was crucial to the eventual disruption of the Jacksonian party system, but the way in which various reform movements reinforced one another politically has been inadequately explored. A recent overview, which unfortunately neglects nativism entirely, is Ronald G. Walters, *American Reformers, 1815–1860* (New York, 1978). A good account of abolitionism is James Brewer Stewart, *Holy Warriors: The Abolitionists and American Slavery* (New York, 1976), although, like other studies of this subject, it is weaker on the political aspects of the movement. By far the best history of political antislavery is Richard H. Sewell, *Ballots for Freedom: Antislavery Politics in the United States, 1837–1860* (New York, 1976). I disagree with some of its interpretations, but the book is an impressive work based on a wide knowledge of the sources. A study of the Free Soil party is Frederick J. Blue, *The Free Soilers: Third Party Politics, 1848–1854* (Urbana, 1973). For the controversy over the fugitive slave law, one should consult Stanley W. Campbell, *The Slave Catchers: Enforcement of the Fugitive Slave Law, 1850–1860* (Chapel Hill, 1968); Thomas D. Morris, *Free Men All: The Personal Liberty Laws of the North, 1780–1861* (Baltimore, 1974); and Norman L. Rosenberg, ''Personal Liberty Laws and Sectional Crisis: 1850–1861,'' *CWH*, v. 17 (March, 1971), 25–44.

The temperance movement has received inadequate attention, and its political history and its role in the disruption of the second party system have been especially neglected. Frank L. Byrne, *Prophet of Prohibition: Neal Dow and his Crusade* (Madison, 1961) is a capable biography of the architect of the Maine Law. The most complete study of the anti-liquor movement is Ian R. Tyrrell, *Sobering Up: From Temperance to Prohibition in Antebellum America, 1800–1860* (Westport, 1979). Tyrrell makes assertions about the social basis of the movement and its political support, however, that are at odds with voting patterns in northern states. Also useful is Jed Dannenbaum, *Drink and Disorder: Temperance Reform in Cincinnati from the Washingtonian Revival to the WCTU* (Urbana, 1984).

Much work has been done on the educational reform movement, although most of these studies are not explicitly concerned with politics. An excellent recent general discussion is Carl F. Kaestle, *Pillars of the Republic: Common Schools and American Society, 1780–1860* (New York, 1983). Catholic opposition to public schools is examined in Vincent P. Lannie, ''Alienation in America: The Immigrant Catholic and Public Education in Pre-Civil War America,'' *Review of Politics*, v. 32 (October, 1970), 503–21.

The nativist movement is finally commanding the attention it merits, although many questions remain unanswered. Ray A. Billington, *The Protestant Crusade, 1800–1860: A Study of the Origins of American Nativism* (New York, 1938) is an older general history but is not particularly perceptive in its discussion of political nativism, whereas Harry J. Carman and Reinhard H. Luthin, ''Some Aspects of the Know-Nothing Movement Reconsidered,'' *South Atlantic Quarterly*, v. 39 (April, 1940), 213–34, misrepresents both the movement's nature and its significance. In his path-breaking work *Boston's Immigrants, 1790–1865: A Study in Acculturation* (Cambridge, 1941), Oscar Handlin pointed to the need to reevaluate the Know Nothings. Michael F. Holt has written the most important studies of Know Nothingism. In addition to his *Political Crisis of the 1850s*, one should consult ''The Politics of Impatience: The Origins of Know Nothingism,'' *JAH*, v. 55 (September, 1973), 309–31, and ''The Antimasonic and Know Nothing Parties,'' Arthur M. Schlesinger, Jr., ed., *History of U.S. Political Parties* (4 vols.: New York, 1973), 575–737. Holt emphasizes the importance of the Know Nothing revolt in the formation of the Republican coalition, and he recognizes that the American party, much more than the Republican, drew upon the social malaise and economic dislocation of the decade. We still need additional studies of the social bases of the Know Nothing movement, such as George Haynes's pioneering ''A Chapter from the Local History of Knownothingism,'' *New England Magazine*, v. 15 (September, 1896), 82–96. Sister M. Evangeline Thomas, *Nativism in the Old Northwest, 1850–1860* (Washington, D.C., 1936) is weak on analysis but contains some helpful material not readily available. Also useful are Jean Gould Hales, ''The Shaping of Nativist Sentiment,

1848–1860'' (unpublished Ph.D. dissertation, Stanford University, 1973); Richard Carwardine, ''The Know-Nothing Party, the Protestant Evangelical Community and American National Identity,'' *Studies in Church History*, v. 18 (1982), 449–63, a solid treatment of a strangely neglected topic; Robert Francis Hueston, *The Catholic Press and Nativism, 1840–1860* (New York, 1976); and two articles by William G. Bean: ''An Aspect of Know Nothingism—The Immigrant and Slavery,'' *South Atlantic Quarterly*, v. 23 (October, 1924), 319–34; and ''Puritan Versus Celt,'' *NEQ*, v. 7 (March, 1934), 70–89. Stephen E. Maizlish, ''The Meaning of Nativism and the Crisis of the Union: The Know-Nothing Movement in the Antebellum North,'' Maizlish and Kushma, eds., *Essays on American Antebellum Politics*, 166–98, takes a different approach than I do but also sees nativism and antislavery as closely connected. A history of the Know Nothing movement would be an important contribution to the historiography of the 1850s.

We badly need a study of the collapse of the Whig party, a deficiency that will be remedied when Michael F. Holt's book appears. Robert J. Rayback, *Millard Fillmore: Biography of a President* (Buffalo, 1959) is an unimaginative treatment of the last Whig administration. Much better is Robert F. Dalzell, Jr., *Daniel Webster and the Trial of American Nationalism, 1843–1852* (Boston, 1973), which makes clear the growing personal animosities engendered by Webster's and Fillmore's policies. I have analyzed the struggle for the Whigs' 1852 presidential nomination in ''The Whig Party, the Compromise of 1850, and the Nomination of Winfield Scott,'' *Presidential Studies Quarterly*, v. 14 (Summer, 1984), 399–415.

A masterful study of the Pierce administration is Roy F. Nichols, *Franklin Pierce: Young Hickory of the Granite Hills*, 2nd ed., rev. (Philadelphia, 1958). Nichols presents a fuller analysis of the forces that led to Pierce's nomination in *The Democratic Machine, 1850–1854* (New York, 1923). His discussion of the personal rivalries and patronage squabbles that increasingly paralyzed the party is especially helpful. The major event of Pierce's ill-starred presidency, of course, was the Kansas-Nebraska Act. The most convincing explanation of the bill's origins is Nichols, ''The Kansas-Nebraska Act: A Century of Historiography,'' *MVHR*, v. 43 (September, 1956), 187–212. Other important studies include P. Orman Ray, *The Repeal of the Missouri Compromise* (Cleveland, 1909), which stresses the struggle in Missouri politics between Thomas Hart Benton and David Rice Atchison; and Robert W. Johannsen, *Stephen A. Douglas* (New York, 1973), which I think exaggerates Douglas's role in the origins of the repeal of the Missouri Compromise but which provides an exceptionally lucid discussion of the drafting of the bill. Potter's *Impending Crisis* is superb on this, as on so many subjects. Two careful studies of voting patterns in the 1854 session of Congress are Gerald W. Wolff, *The Kansas-Nebraska Bill: Party, Section, and the Coming of the Civil War* (New York, 1977); and Thomas B. Alexander, *Sectional Stress and Party Strength: A Computer Analysis of Roll-Call Voting Patterns in the United States House of Representatives, 1836–1860* (Nashville, 1967), a pioneering study. Facets of public opinion on the Kansas-Nebraska Act are treated in Charles D. Hart, ''The Natural Limits of Slavery Expansion: Kansas-Nebraska, 1854,'' *Kansas Historical Quarterly*, v. 34 (Spring, 1968), 32–50, which focuses on Congress; and Edmund Emmett Lacy, ''Protestant Newspaper Reaction to the Kansas-Nebraska Bill of 1854,'' *Rocky Mountain Social Science Journal*, v. 7 (October, 1970), 61–72.

The resulting disorder in the Kansas territory is discussed in the books already cited by Craven, Nevins, and Potter, but other important works are Paul W. Gates, *Fifty Million Acres: Conflicts over Kansas Land Policy, 1854–1890* (Ithaca, 1954); James Malin's *John Brown and the Legend of Fifty-Six* (Philadelphia, 1942), which is unwieldy and lacks balance; Alice Nichols's popular and not very insightful *Bleeding Kansas* (New York, 1954); and James A. Rawley, *Race & Politics: "Bleeding Kansas" and the Coming of the Civil War* (Philadelphia, 1969). James C. Malin, ''Judge Lecompte and the 'Sack of Lawrence,' May 21, 1856,'' *Kansas Historical Quarterly*, v. 20 (August, November, 1953), 465–94, 558–97, corrects some long-held beliefs concerning the raid on Lawrence. Particularly valuable on Kansas propaganda and northern public opinion is Bernard A. Weisberger, ''The Newspaper Reporter and the Kansas Imbroglio,'' *MVHR*, v. 36 (March, 1950), 633–56. The activities of the New England Emigrant Aid Company are covered in Samuel A. Johnson, *The Battle Cry of Freedom: The New England Emigrant Aid Company in the Kansas Crusade* (Lawrence, Kansas, 1954), a carefully researched, thorough discussion; Horace Andrews,

Jr., "Kansas Crusade: Eli Thayer and the New England Emigrant Aid Company," *NEQ*, v. 35 (December, 1962), 496–514, which takes a more favorable view of Thayer's role in the Kansas movement; and Edgar Langsdorf, "S. C. Pomeroy and the New England Emigrant Aid Company, 1854–1858," *Kansas Historical Quarterly*, v. 7 (August, November, 1938), 227–45, 379–98. Russell K. Hickman deals with some of the controversies during Andrew H. Reeder's territorial governorship in "The Reeder Administration Inaugurated," *Kansas Historical Quarterly*, v. 36 (Autumn, Winter, 1970), 305–40, 424–55. The complexities of Kansas territorial politics are demonstrated by James C. Malin in "The Topeka Statehood Movement Reconsidered: Origins," in *Territorial Kansas: Studies Commemorating the Centennial* (Lawrence, 1954), 33–69.

Many of these works have important implications for the emergence of the Republican party, but relatively few studies of the party's formation have been done. Andrew W. Crandall, *The Early History of the Republican Party, 1854–1856* (Boston, 1930) is thinly researched and fails to satisfactorily answer the important questions raised by the party's development. Brief, traditional treatments can be found in Hans L. Trefousse, "The Republican Party 1854–1864," in Schlesinger, ed., *History of U.S. Political Parties*, v. 2, 1141–72; and the opening chapters of George H. Mayer's pedestrian *The Republican Party, 1854–1966*, 2nd ed. (New York, 1967). Holt's *Political Crisis of the 1850s* manages to say a great deal about this subject in a few pages. There is no satisfactory account of the Republican organizing convention at Pittsburgh, but see the following articles, all in the *Western Pennsylvania Historical Magazine*: Leonard H. Bernstein, "Convention in Pittsburgh: The Story of the National Founding of a New Party," v. 49 (October, 1966), 289–300; Charles W. Dahlinger, "The Republican Party Originated in Pittsburgh," v. 4 (January, 1921), 1–10; and Clarence Edward Macartney, "The First National Republican Convention," v. 20 (June, 1937), 83–100. The actions of Ohio Republicans to organize a national Republican party are described in Robert F. Horowitz, "James M. Ashley and the Presidential Election of 1856," *Ohio History*, v. 83 (Winter, 1974), 4–16. The organizing activities of the group at the *National Era* are sketched in Walter C. Clephane, "Lewis Clephane: A Pioneer Washington Republican," *Records of the Columbia Historical Society*, v. 21 (1918), 263–77.

The nature of the Republican party's appeal before the Civil War has become the subject of renewed historical controversy. In recent years historians have debated the extent of the party's commitment against slavery. Potter, *Impending Crisis*, and particularly Sewell, *Ballots for Freedom*, emphasize the moral dimensions of the slavery question and Republicans' moral opposition to the institution. A number of scholars, on the other hand, insist that racial dislike of blacks explains Republicans' desire to keep slavery out of the territories. Works that make this argument directly include Leon Litwack, *North of Slavery: The Negro in the Free States, 1790–1860* (Chicago, 1961); Eugene H. Berwanger, *The Frontier Against Slavery: Western Anti-Negro Prejudice and the Slavery Expansion Controversy* (Urbana, 1967); and Robert F. Durden, "Ambiguities in the Antislavery Crusade of the Republican Party," Martin Duberman, ed., *The Antislavery Vanguard* (Princeton, 1965), 362–94. Effective rebuttals to this exaggerated interpretation can be found in Eric Foner, *Free Soil, Free Labor, Free Men: The Ideology of the Republican Party before the Civil War* (New York, 1970); Sewell, *Ballots for Freedom*, an especially forceful defense of the Republican party on this matter; and Kenneth M. Stampp, *The Imperiled Union: Essays on the Background of the Civil War* (New York, 1980), 105–35.

Probably the most influential discussion of the ideology of the Republican party is Foner's *Free Soil, Free Labor, Free Men*. Foner recognizes the diverse components of the party's ideology, but he portrays the Republican party as basically a free soil party and emphasizes the desire to protect the North's free labor social system by blocking the expansion of slavery. Despite my disagreement with the general thrust of the book, it has greatly stimulated my thinking about the early Republican party. In a subsequent essay, "Politics, Ideology, and the Origins of the American Civil War," George M. Fredrickson, ed., *A Nation Divided: Problems and Issues of the Civil War and Reconstruction* (Minneapolis, 1975), 15–34, Foner places more emphasis on Republican fears of the Slave Power, an approach that I think more accurately captures the essence of the party's appeal. On the Democratic party, Bruce W. Collins, "The Ideology of Ante-bellum Northern Democrats,"

American Studies, v. 11 (April, 1977), 103–21, is a good discussion with implications beyond its subject.

Given its prominence in Republican rhetoric, surprisingly little has been written about the Republican concept of the Slave Power. Besides an excellent chapter in Foner's book, one should see Russel B. Nye, *Fettered Freedom: Civil Liberties and the Slavery Controversy, 1830–1860*, rev. ed. (East Lansing, 1963); David Brion Davis, *The Slave Power Conspiracy and the Paranoid Style* (Baton Rouge, 1969); and Larry Gara's too brief but nevertheless suggestive "Slavery and the Slave Power: A Crucial Distinction," *CWH*, v. 15 (March, 1969), 5–18. A more extended discussion of my thoughts on this question can be found in "The Republican Party and the Slave Power," Robert H. Abzug and Stephen E. Maizlish, eds., *New Perspectives on Race and Slavery in America* (Lexington, 1986), 57–78.

Scholars are beginning to appreciate the importance of the ideology of republicanism, whose roots go back to the American colonial period, in the first century of the nation's politics. Two excellent historiographic essays by Robert E. Shalhope assess the state of the literature on this subject to 1815: "Toward a Republican Synthesis: The Emergence of an Understanding of Republicanism in American Historiography," *William and Mary Quarterly*, v. 29 (January, 1972), 49–80; and "Republicanism and Early American Historiography," ibid., v. 39 (April, 1982), 334–56. For the period after 1815, the literature is not as rich, but suggestive on this theme are Rush Welter, *The Mind of America, 1820–1860* (New York, 1975); Daniel Walker Howe, *The Political Culture of the American Whigs* (Chicago, 1979); and George B. Forgie, *Patricide in the House Divided: A Psychological Interpretation of Lincoln and His Age* (New York, 1979), which despite a strained psychological interpretation makes clear the importance of the founding fathers to the Civil War generation. Holt, *Political Crises of the 1850s* is the most extended statement of the importance of republicanism in antebellum politics. Holt devotes little attention to the content of republican thought in this decade, but his book better than any other captures the angst that underlay American politics before the Civil War. We very much need studies of the changing nature of the ideologies of republicanism and liberalism in both sections before the Civil War.

There is no monograph on the 1856 election, but several studies deal with important aspects of that contest. Roy F. Nichols and Philip S. Klein provide a brief overview in "The Election of 1856," Arthur M. Schlesinger and Fred L. Israel, eds., *History of American Presidential Elections* (4 vols.: New York, 1971), v. 2, 1007–33. The opening chapters of Roy F. Nichols's authoritative *The Disruption of American Democracy* (New York, 1948) contain a superior analysis of Buchanan's nomination and election from the Democratic perspective. The best account of the caning of Charles Sumner is in David Donald's beautifully written *Charles Sumner and the Coming of the Civil War* (New York, 1960), a first-rate biography. I have discussed the northern response to the caning and its political repercussions in "The Crime against Sumner: The Caning of Charles Sumner and the Rise of the Republican Party," *CWH*, v. 25 (September, 1979), 218–45. There is some important material in Roy F. Nichols, "Some Problems of the First Republican Presidential Campaign,"*AHR*, v. 28 (April, 1923), 492–96; James A. Rawley, *Edwin D. Morgan, 1811–1883: Merchant in Politics* (New York, 1955); Rawley's careful "Financing the Frémont Campaign," *Pennsylvania Magazine of History and Biography*, v. 75 (January, 1951), 25–35; Richard Carwardine, "The Religious Revival of 1857–8 in the United States,"*Studies in Church History*, v. 15 (1978), 393–406, which focuses on a later period but gives some attention to the role of religion in the 1856 election; and Victor B. Howard, "Presbyterians, the Kansas-Nebraska Act, and the Election of 1856," *Journal of Presbyterian History*, v. 49 (Summer, 1971), 133–56. James C. Malin, "Speaker Banks Courts the Free-Soilers: The Frémont-Robinson Letter of 1856," *NEQ*, v. 12 (March, 1939), 103–12, deals with an important aspect of the presidential election, but a better treatment is Fred Harvey Harrington, "The Reception of the Frémont-Robinson Letter: A Note on the 1856 Campaign," *NEQ*, v. 12 (September, 1939), 545–48. Harrington's "Frémont and the North Americans," *AHR*, v. 44 (July, 1939), 842–48, is excellent. Allan Nevins, *Frémont: Pathmarker of the West* (New York, 1955) adequately surveys the Republican nominee's life but is not particularly perceptive in its treatment of Frémont's nomination and presidential candidacy.

More limited in scope but sound is Ruhl J. Bartlett, *John C. Frémont and the Republican Party* (Columbus, 1930). There is no adequate history of the American party in the 1856 election or of Fillmore's candidacy. Some of the party's problems are made clear, however, in Fred Harvey Harrington, " 'The First Northern Victory,' " *JSH*, v. 5 (May, 1939), 186–205, a solid account of Banks's election as speaker. I have discussed over a longer chronological period some of the reasons for the rise of the Republican party and the corresponding decline of the Know Nothings in "Nativism and the Creation of a Republican Majority in the North before the Civil War," *JAH*, v. 72 (December, 1985), 529–59.

Because I have devoted so much attention to state politics, I found state studies particularly valuable. For New England, the following studies were helpful: Richard R. Wescott, "A History of Maine Politics, 1840–1856: The Formation of the Republican Party" (unpublished Ph.D. dissertation, University of Maine, 1966); Harry Draper Hunt, *Hannibal Hamlin of Maine: Lincoln's First Vice President* (Syracuse, 1969); Charles A. Jellison, *Fessenden of Maine: Civil War Senator* (Syracuse, 1962); Thomas R. Bright, "The Anti-Nebraska Coalition and the Emergence of the Republican Party in New Hampshire: 1853–1857," *Historical New Hampshire*, v. 27 (Summer, 1972), 57–88, which is frustratingly vague on key points; Richard H. Sewell, *John P. Hale and the Politics of Abolition* (Cambridge, 1965), a good biography; and Edward Brynn, "Vermont's Political Vacuum of 1845–1856 and the Emergence of the Republican Party," *Vermont History*, v. 28 (Spring, 1970) 113–23. For Connecticut, see Alfred C. O'Connell, "The Birth of the G.O.P. in Connecticut," *Connecticut Historical Society Bulletin*, v. 26 (April, 1961), 33–39, which is of limited value; Robert D. Parmet, "The Know-Nothings in Connecticut" (unpublished Ph.D. dissertation, Columbia University, 1966), a much fuller account but one that ignores some critical questions; and John Niven, *Gideon Welles: Lincoln's Secretary of the Navy* (New York, 1973), a sound treatment of a rather colorless individual. Aspects of Rhode Island's politics are analyzed in Larry A. Rand, "The Know Nothing Party in Rhode Island," *Rhode Island History*, v. 23 (October, 1964), 102–16; and Mario R. DiNunzio and Jan T. Galkowski, "Political Loyalty in Rhode Island—A Computer Study of the 1850's," *Rhode Island History*, v. 36 (August, 1977), 93–95, a superficial discussion.

Massachusetts politics have received a considerable amount of attention. The best work on the state's politics in this decade remains William G. Bean, "Party Transformation in Massachusetts with Special Reference to the Antecedents of Republicanism 1848–1860" (unpublished Ph.D. dissertation, Harvard University, 1922), which unfortunately is not widely distributed. Dale Baum, *The Civil War Party System: The Case of Massachusetts, 1848–1876* (Chapel Hill, 1984) has some useful tables and is significant for its statistical methodology, but it contains only a brief treatment of the period before 1861. Baum fails to address many of the critical questions raised by the rise of the Republican party in the state, and his attempt to downgrade the importance of nativism in the party's formation overlooks or misinterprets essential evidence. The reader will learn more about Massachusetts voting behavior from Paul Goodman's suggestive "The Politics of Industrialism: Massachusetts, 1830–1870," Richard Bushman et al., eds., *Uprooted Americans: Essays to Honor Oscar Handlin* (Boston, 1979), 161–207.

Also helpful in getting through the maze of the state's politics are: Martin Duberman, "Some Notes on the Beginnings of the Republican Party in Massachusetts," *NEQ*, v. 34 (September, 1961), 364–70; Thomas H. O'Connor, *Lords of the Loom: The Cotton Whigs and the Coming of the Civil War* (New York, 1968); George H. Haynes, "The Causes of Know-Nothing Success in Massachusetts," *AHR*, v. 3 (October, 1897), 67–82; John Mulkern, "Western Massachusetts in the Know Nothing Years: An Analysis of Voting Patterns," *Historical Journal of Western Massachusetts*, v. 8 (January, 1980), 14–25; and Kevin Sweeney's superb "Rum, Romanism, Representation, and Reform: Politics in Massachusetts, 1847–1853," *CWH*, v. 22 (June, 1976), 116–37. Good biographies of a number of the state's political leaders are available: Martin B. Duberman, *Charles Francis Adams 1807–1886* (Boston, 1961); Fred Harvey Harrington, *Fighting Politician; Major General N. P. Banks* (Philadelphia, 1948); George S. Merriam, *The Life and Times of Samuel Bowles* (2 vols.: New York, 1885), an old-fashioned biography with generous excerpts from editorials and correspondence; Samuel Shapiro, *Richard Henry Dana, Jr. 1815–1882* (East Lansing, 1961); Frank Otto Gatell, *John Gorham Palfrey and the New England Conscience* (Cambridge, 1963); Donald's biography of Sumner, noted above; and two recent studies of Henry Wilson, Richard H. Abbott, *Cobbler in Congress: Life of Henry Wilson, 1812–1875* (Lexington, 1972), and Ernest McKay, *Henry Wilson: Practical Radical* (Port Washington, 1971). A study of Henry J. Gardner is much needed, but the lack of personal papers makes such an undertaking difficult.

New York has probably been studied more than any other state, and rightfully so. In spite of its title, Mark L. Berger, *The Revolution in the New York Party Systems, 1840–1860* (Port Washington, 1973) focuses only on the years 1854–56 and is brief and thinly researched. A fuller account is Hendrik Booraem V, *The Formation of the Republican Party in New York: Politics and Conscience in the Antebellum North* (New York, 1983), but it, too, concentrates on party leaders and ignores mass voting behavior. Booraem advances no new interpretations of New York politics, but his book contains interesting material on local politics and has a good discussion of the organizational structure of the state's parties. Dale Baum and Dale T. Knobel seek to analyze realignment in the state in "Anatomy of a Realignment: New York Presidential Politics, 1848–1860," *New York History*, v. 65 (January, 1984), 61–81, but if any realignment cannot be understood in terms of presidential elections, it is that of the 1850s.

For the split of the New York Whig party, see Harry J. Carman and Reinhard H. Luthin, "The Seward-Fillmore Feud and the Crisis of 1850" and "The Seward-Fillmore Feud and the Disruption of the Whig Party," *New York History*, v. 24 (April, July, 1943), 163–84, 335–57; and Lee H. Warner, "The Perpetual Crisis of Conservative Whigs: New York's Silver Grays," *New-York Historical Society Quarterly*, v. 57 (July, 1973), 213–36. John A. Krout, "The Maine Law in New York Politics," *New York History*, v. 17 (July, 1936), 260–72, adequately surveys its subject, but William J. Rorabaugh, "Rising Democratic Spirits: Immigrants, Temperance, and Tammany Hall, 1854–1860," *CWH*, v. 22 (June, 1976), 138–57, displays much greater insight. Judah B. Ginsberg, "Barnburners, Free Soilers, and the New York Republican Party," *New York History*, v. 57 (October, 1976), 475–500, deals with a neglected topic but exaggerates Democratic conversions to the Republican party by concentrating on leaders. For the Know Nothing party, see Thomas J. Curran, "Know-Nothings of New York State" (unpublished Ph.D. dissertation, Columbia University, 1963); Curran, "Seward and the Know Nothings," *New-York Historical Society Quarterly*, v. 51 (April, 1967), 141–59, an excellent discussion; and Louis Dow Scisco, *Political Nativism in New York State* (New York, 1901), an early study that still has great value. Joel H. Silbey's essay, " 'The Undisguised Connection': Know Nothings into Republicans: New York as a Test Case," in *The Partisan Imperative* is superior.

Relevant New York biographies include Glyndon G. Van Deusen, *Horace Greeley: Nineteenth Century Crusader* (Philadelphia, 1953), especially good on Greeley's personality; Jeter Isely, *Horace Greeley and the Republican Party 1853–1861* (Princeton, 1947), a first-rate study of the New York *Tribune* editor's political career in this period; Ernest P. Muller, "Preston King: A Political Biography" (unpublished Ph.D. dissertation, Columbia University, 1957), a massive study of an overlooked but important politician; Ivor D. Spencer, *The Victor and the Spoils: A Life of William L. Marcy* (Providence, 1959); Stewart Mitchell, *Horatio Seymour of New York* (Cambridge, 1938); Glyndon G. Van Deusen, *William Henry Seward* (New York, 1967), the best life of this key Republican although less satisfactory on his pre-war career; and Van Deusen, *Thurlow Weed: Wizard of the Lobby* (Boston, 1947).

Pennsylvania's political history in this era has not fared as well as New York's. We very much need a history of the Republican party in the state before the Civil War and a full-scale analysis of voting patterns in the state. John F. Coleman, *The Disruption of the Pennsylvania Democracy* (Harrisburg, 1975) is a competent survey. More stimulating is Michael F. Holt, *Forging a Majority: The Formation of the Republican Party in Pittsburgh, 1848–1860* (New Haven, 1969), a path-breaking work that rekindled historians' interest in the party's beginnings. The lack of a similar study of Philadelphia's politics is unfortunate: William Dusinberre, *Civil War Issues in Philadelphia*

1856–1865 (Philadelphia, 1965), while perceptive and well-argued, eschews voting analysis and is too brief. Other useful studies include C. Maxwell Myers, "The Rise of the Republican Party in Pennsylvania, 1854–1860" (unpublished Ph.D. dissertation, University of Pittsburgh, 1940); Asa Earl Martin, "The Temperance Movement in Pennsylvania Prior to the Civil War," *Pennsylvania Magazine of History and Biography*, v. 49 (July, 1925), 195–230; Erwin S. Bradley, *Simon Cameron, Lincoln's Secretary of War* (Philadelphia, 1966); and Charles B. Going, *David Wilmot, Free-Soiler* (New York, 1924). Warren F. Hewitt, "The Know Nothing Party in Pennsylvania," *Pennsylvania History*, v. 2 (April, 1935), 69–85, is superficial. A history of the Know Nothing party in the state, where the American movement was stronger and exerted influence as a separate organization for a longer time than in most states, would be a major contribution. Roger D. Peterson, "The Reaction to a Heterogeneous Society: A Behavioral and Quantitative Analysis of Northern Voting Behavior 1845–1870, Pennsylvania a Test Case" (unpublished Ph.D. dissertation, University of Pittsburgh, 1970), which deals primarily with the 1854 election, is conceptually limited and unpersuasive in its voting analysis. William A. Gudelunas, Jr., and William G. Shade, *Before the Molly Maguires* (New York, 1976) is a useful analysis of voting in Schuylkill County. For a fuller discussion of the 1854 election, see my article, "Nebraska, Nativism, and Rum: The Failure of Fusion in Pennsylvania, 1854," *Pennsylvania Magazine of History and Biography*, v. 109 (October, 1985), 427–71.

New Jersey politics have received little attention for these years. A capable study is Philip C. Davis, "The Persistence of Partisan Alignment: Issues, Leaders, and Votes in New Jersey, 1840–1860" (unpublished Ph.D. dissertation, Washington University, 1978), which has a great deal of interesting if not easy to extract information.

The best study of Ohio's politics is Stephen E. Maizlish, *The Triumph of Sectionalism: The Transformation of Ohio Politics, 1844–1856* (Kent, 1983), a careful study of elite attitudes and party factionalism, but one that is weakened by a failure to take nativism seriously in the state's politics. This neglect can be partly corrected by reference to two excellent articles: Eugene H. Roseboom, "Salmon P. Chase and the Know-Nothings," *MVHR*, v. 25 (December, 1938), 335–50; and William E. Van Horne, "Lewis D. Campbell and the Know-Nothing Party in Ohio," *Ohio History*, v. 76 (Autumn, 1967), 202–21. I have discussed the 1855 election in more detail in "Salmon P. Chase, Nativism, and the Formation of the Republican Party in Ohio," *Ohio History*, v. 93 (Winter-Spring, 1984), 5–39. John Bennett Weaver, "Nativism and the Birth of the Republican Party in Ohio, 1854–1860" (unpublished Ph.D. dissertation, Ohio State University, 1982) combines evidence of nativism's importance in the Republican party with an interpretation denying its significance. Weaver adopts the distinction between political and cultural nativism advanced by Foner and also endorsed by Baum, a distinction not contained in antebellum sources and one that I find unconvincing. Other useful studies are: Eugene H. Roseboom, *The Civil War Era, 1850–1873* (Columbus, 1944); Victor B. Howard, "The 1856 Election in Ohio: Moral Issues in Politics," *Ohio History*, v. 80 (Winter, 1971), 24–44; and Thomas W. Kremm, "The Old Order Trembles: The Formation of the Republican Party in Ohio," *Cincinnati Historical Society Bulletin*, v. 36 (Fall, 1978), 193–215. Kremm's dissertation, "The Rise of the Republican Party in Cleveland, 1848–1860" (Kent State University, 1974) is a helpful voting analysis. Biographies of two important Republican leaders are Hans L. Trefousse, *Benjamin Franklin Wade: Radical Republican from Ohio* (New York, 1963); and James Brewer Stewart, *Joshua R. Giddings and the Tactics of Radical Politics* (Cleveland, 1970). It is a scandal that there is no good modern biography of Salmon P. Chase. Those available are superficial and uncritical. The scope of Chase's career, his disingenuous personality, and his massive collection of personal papers are a challenge to a biographer. Two articles that deal with Chase's career in the 1850s are Reinhard H. Luthin, "Salmon P. Chase's Political Career before the Civil War," *MVHR*, v. 29 (March, 1943), 517–40; and Frederick J. Blue, "Chase and the Governorship: A Stepping Stone to the Presidency," *Ohio History*, v. 90 (Summer, 1981), 197–220.

The early chapters of Emma Lou Thornbrough, *Indiana in the Civil War Era, 1850–1880* (Indianapolis, 1965) provide a sound outline of the state's politics in this period. Charles

Zimmerman, "The Origin and Rise of the Republican Party in Indiana from 1854 to 1860," *Indiana Magazine of History*, v. 13 (September, December, 1917), 211–69, 349–411, and Carl F. Brand, "The History of the Know Nothing Party in Indiana," ibid., v. 18 (March, June, September, 1922), 47–81, 177–206, 266–306, are early studies based on research in newspapers. More thorough is Roger H. Van Bolt's doctoral dissertation, "The Rise of the Republican Party in Indiana, 1840–1856" (University of Chicago, 1950), the chapters of which appeared in the *Indiana Magazine of History*, v. 47–49 (1951–55). Two useful articles are Walter R. Sharp, "Henry S. Lane and the Formation of the Republican Party in Indiana," *MVHR*, v. 7 (September, 1920), 93–112; and Willard H. Smith, "Schuyler Colfax and the Political Upheaval of 1854–1855," *MVHR*, v. 28 (December, 1941), 383–98. Mark E. Neely, Jr.'s "Richard W. Thompson: The Persistent Know Nothing," *Indiana Magazine of History*, v. 72 (June, 1976), 95–122, is a fine treatment with an important thesis. Two helpful articles by Mildred C. Stoler are "The Democratic Element in the New Republican Party in Indiana," *Indiana Magazine of History*, v. 36 (September, 1940), 185–207; and "Insurgent Democrats of Indiana and Illinois in 1854," ibid., v. 33 (March, 1937), 1–31. These are based on her "Influence of the Democratic Element in the Republican Party of Illinois and Indiana, 1854–1860" (unpublished Ph.D. dissertation, Indiana University, 1938), which is a careful examination of a subject that merits more attention than it has received. Like other historians who concentrate on party leaders, however, Stoler exaggerates both the extent and the permanency of Democratic conversions to the Republican party before the Civil War. Relevant biographies include Ovando J. Hollister, *Life of Schuyler Colfax* (New York, 1886), which prints some important correspondence; Willard H. Smith, *Schuyler Colfax: The Changing Fortunes of a Political Idol* (Indianapolis, 1952); Grace Julian Clarke, *George W. Julian* (Indianapolis, 1923); Patrick W. Riddleberger, *George Washington Julian, Radical Republican* (Indianapolis, 1966); and William D. Foulke, *Life of Oliver P. Morton, Including His Important Speeches* (2 vols.: Indianapolis, 1899).

Much attention has been given to Illinois politics in this period because of the presence of Abraham Lincoln. Arthur C. Cole's *The Era of the Civil War, 1848–1870* (Chicago, 1922) is based on wide research in the state's newspapers and surveys politics in this period. Don E. Fehrenbacher's unpublished doctoral dissertation, "Illinois Political Attitudes 1854–1861" (University of Chicago, 1951), has a good deal of helpful material. The only available study of voting patterns in the state is Stephen L. Hansen, *The Making of the Third Party System: Voters and Parties in Illinois, 1850–1876* (Ann Arbor, 1980), but he strains his statistical results to fit his interpretation. The best account of the early attempts to organize a Republican party in the state is Victor B. Howard, "The Illinois Republican Party," *Journal of the Illinois State Historical Society*, v. 64 (Summer, Autumn, 1973), 125–60, 285–311. Neither Ameda R. King, "The Last Years of the Whig Party in Illinois—1847–1856," Illinois State Historical Society *Transactions*, v. 32 (1925), 108–54, nor John P. Sennig, "The Know-Nothing Movement in Illinois," *Journal of the Illinois State Historical Society*, v. 7 (April, 1914), 7–33, is particularly good. Better are two articles by Thomas M. Keefe: "Chicago's Flirtation with Political Nativism, 1854–1856," *Records of the American Catholic Historical Society*, v. 82 (September, 1971), 131–58; and "The Catholic Issue in the Chicago Tribune before the Civil War," *Mid-America*, v. 57 (October, 1975), 227–45. John M. Rozett, "Racism and Republican Emergence in Illinois, 1848–1860: A Re-evaluation of Republican Negrophobia," *CWH*, v. 22 (June, 1976), 101–15, and James M. Bergquist, "People and Politics in Transition: The Illinois Germans, 1850–60," Frederick C. Luebke, ed., *Ethnic Voters and the Election of Lincoln* (Lincoln, Neb., 1971), 196–226, are capable discussions of controversial questions. For former Democrats in the Republican party, see Mildred C. Stoler's doctoral dissertation, her "Insurgent Democrats of Indiana and Illinois in 1854," both cited above, and her "The Democratic Element in the New Republican Party in Illinois, 1856–1860," *Papers in Illinois History and Transactions for the Year 1942* (1944), 32–71.

Without question the best study of Lincoln's career in this decade is Don E. Fehrenbacher's justly acclaimed *Prelude to Greatness: Lincoln in the 1850's* (Stanford, 1962). Other biographies of Illinois politicians are Don E. Fehrenbacher, *Chicago Giant: A Biography of "Long John"*

Wentworth (Madison, 1957); Willard L. King, *Lincoln's Manager, David Davis* (Cambridge, 1960); and Ralph J. Roske, *His Own Counsel: The Life and Times of Lyman Trumbull* (Reno, 1979), which is better than Mark M. Krug's mediocre *Lyman Trumbull, Conservative Radical* (New York, 1965), although neither does justice to that important politician's pre-war career. The sole contribution of Richard Yates and Catharine Yates Pickering, *Richard Yates, Civil War Governor*, ed. John H. Krenkel (Danville, [1966]) is the correspondence it publishes, but the letters are poorly edited and have countless errors. Johannsen's biography of Douglas, noted above, is excellent on state affairs.

Formisano's *Birth of Mass Political Parties*, cited earlier, is a good analysis of Michigan politics. Richard Current surveys Wisconsin politics in *The Civil War Era, 1848–1873* (Madison, 1976). Useful articles on Wisconsin include Frank L. Byrne, "Maine Law Versus Lager Beer: A Dilemma of Wisconsin's Young Republican Party," *Wisconsin Magazine of History*, v. 52 (Winter, 1958–59), 115–20; and Joseph Schafer, "Know-Nothingism in Wisconsin," *Wisconsin Magazine of History*, v. 8 (September, 1924), 3–21. Ray M. Shortridge's unpublished doctoral dissertation, "Voting Patterns in the American Midwest, 1840–1872" (University of Michigan, 1974), is an exercise in number crunching.

Iowa's politics have attracted unusual attention. A traditional account is Morton M. Rosenberg, *Iowa on the Eve of the Civil War: A Decade of Frontier Politics* (Norman, 1972). Specialized studies include: Louis Pelzer, "The Origin and Organization of the Republican Party in Iowa," *Iowa Journal of History and Politics*, v. 4 (October, 1906), 487–525; two articles by David S. Sparks, "The Birth of the Republican Party in Iowa, 1854–1856," *Iowa Journal of History*, v. 54 (April, 1956), 1–34, and "The Decline of the Democratic Party in Iowa, 1850–1860," ibid., v. 53 (January, 1955), 1–30; and Dan E. Clark, "The History of Liquor Legislation in Iowa, 1846–1861," *Iowa Journal of History and Politics*, v. 6 (January, 1908), 55–87. Robert Swierenga, "The Ethnic Voter and the First Lincoln Election," *CWH*, v. 11 (March, 1965), 27–43, is an important discussion of Dutch voting in this period, a study that has broader implications. William Salter, *Life of James W. Grimes* (New York, 1876) prints some useful correspondence.

As is true today, California's politics before the Civil War were unique and baffling, but insights can be gleaned from John E. Baur, "The Beginnings of the Republican Party," Royce D. Delmatier, Clarence F. McIntosh, and Earl G. Waters, eds., *The Rumble of California Politics: 1848–1970* (New York, 1970), 40–69; Edward A. Dickson, "How the Republican Party was Organized in California," *Historical Society of Southern California Quarterly*, v. 30 (September, 1948), 196–204; Peyton Hurt, "The Rise and Fall of the 'Know Nothings' in California," *California Historical Society Quarterly*, v. 9 (March, June, 1930), 16–49, 99–128; Earl Pomeroy, "California, 1848–1860: Politics of a Representative Frontier State," *California Historical Society Quarterly*, v. 32 (December, 1953), 291–302; and Gerald Stanley, "Slavery and the Origins of the Republican Party in California," *Southern California Quarterly*, v. 60 (Spring, 1978), 1–16; A general history is William H. Ellison, *A Self-Governing Dominion: California, 1849–1860* (Berkeley, 1950).

Southern Republicanism in this period is largely the study of a few individuals. David L. Smiley, *Lion of Whitehall: The Life of Cassius M. Clay* (Madison, 1962) is a biography of a particularly colorful southern Republican. Richard G. Lowe, "The Republican Party in Antebellum Virginia, 1856–1860," *Virginia Magazine of History and Biography*, v. 81 (July, 1973), 259–79, discusses John C. Underwood's activities in 1856. For Francis P. Blair and his sons, there are two good studies: William E. Smith, *The Francis Preston Blair Family in Politics* (2 vols.: New York, 1933); and Elbert B. Smith, *Francis Preston Blair* (New York, 1980), briefer but also a sound treatment.

Statistical Appendix

Mark Twain was fond of quoting a remark attributed to Disraeli that "there are three kinds of lies: lies, damned lies, and statistics." In this study, I have tried to avoid the first two, but I have made extensive use of the statistical analysis of election returns and socioeconomic data to trace the process of party realignment in the 1850s. Some discussion of the nature and limitations of the data and statistical techniques I have employed is appropriate.

Election Returns. I obtained county-level returns for elections of president, governor, and congressman for all northern states from the Inter-university Consortium for Political and Social Research in Ann Arbor. The Consortium's data are readily available in machine-readable form, but several limitations should be noted. First, election returns for minor civil divisions are not included in its archives, which substantially reduces the usefulness of the data so laboriously located and coded. Second, the Consortium's election returns are not complete, and in a few instances I found it necessary to supplement its data for these contests with returns from other sources. The most glaring omission in the Consortium's files, however, is the extremely unfortunate limitation on the offices for which voting returns were collected. Since many crucial contests in the antebellum period occurred in years other than those when a governor or president was elected, I collected additional county-level returns for off-year elections, for referenda, and sometimes for lesser offices in years when there was a gubernatorial contest for all northern states during the period 1848–1860. My basic source for these additional returns was Horace Greeley's *Tribune Almanac* (*Whig Almanac* until 1855), but I also extensively culled newspapers and occasionally consulted state documents and archives in an attempt to locate missing returns. Gaps inevitably remained, but I managed eventually to compile a reasonably complete file of returns, especially for the states I examined most intensively. Counties created after 1850 were excluded from the analysis, and their votes were apportioned to the counties from which they were formed.

In addition to county-level data, I also collected election returns from minor civil divisions for Connecticut, Maine, and Massachusetts, and for thirty-one New York counties (my total sample was 538 townships and city wards), as well as votes by wards for Cincinnati and Philadelphia. Ken Kann allowed me to use his ward returns for Chicago, and Paul Goodman generously made available to me his township returns for Maine and Massachusetts, which I combined with those I had already collected. In addition, Joel H. Silbey kindly sent me township returns for New York that I had been unable to locate.

Eligible Voters. In order to calculate ecological regression coefficients, one must know the number of voters for a given year in a particular electoral unit (county, ward, or township). Six states—Massachusetts, Connecticut, New York, Ohio, Indiana, and Iowa—tabulated the number of voters at some point during the period 1848–1861. The New York state censuses of 1845, 1855, and 1865 recorded the number of voters for each county and township, while the state censuses of 1854 and 1856 did likewise for Iowa. For Ohio, see the auditor's reports for 1855 and 1863. The number of voters in Massachusetts for various years is given in the *Massachusetts Register for the Year 1853*, 322–325; *Manual for the Use of the General Court* (1858), 115–123; and House Document No. 65 (1876), pp. 4–8. Indiana's census of voters (given in the reports of the state auditor for 1850, 1854, and 1866) underenumerated eligible voters in a number of counties. Since the 1851 state constitution allowed aliens to vote, I used instead the number of adult white males in 1850 and 1860 from the federal censuses to calculate the number of voters in each county. The number of voters in 1861 for each Connecticut township is given in the *Connecticut Register* for 1862. To estimate the number of eligible voters for the years before 1861, I multiplied the ratio of voters to polls for each township in 1861 by the number of polls in 1852 and 1854 (given in the *Connecticut Register*, 1853 and 1855). To estimate the number of voters in each Maine township, I multiplied the ratio of adult males to polls for 1841 with the number of polls in 1850 and 1860 (given in the *Maine Register* for 1843 and 1852, and the code of laws for 1860, pp. 342–62). This method fails to take into account the presence of unnaturalized immigrants, but they were not numerous in most of the state's townships. For the city of Portland, which did have a large number of aliens, I used the census of voters given in the Portland *Daily Advertiser*, August 2, 1853. Townships for which the information on polls could not be located were excluded from the analysis. For all these states, I extrapolated linearly for intervening years.

In order to calculate the turnout figures used in this study, I had to estimate the number of eligible voters for the remaining northern states. For Wisconsin I used the number of adult white males (from the 1850 and 1860 federal censuses), since Wisconsin allowed non-citizens to vote. For Rhode Island I used the estimates provided in Chilton Williamson, "Rhode Island Suffrage Since the Dorr War," *NEQ*, v. 28 (March, 1955), 34–50. To estimate the number of voters in the remaining free states, I made use of the information in the 1856 Iowa and 1855 New York state censuses, both of which listed not only the native- and foreign-born population but also the number of native and naturalized voters. Contemporary observers contended uniformly that the ratio of voters to population did not vary widely, so I used the New York ratio (naturalized voters/foreign-born population) to calculate the number of voters in eastern states (Vermont, New Hampshire, Pennsylvania, and New Jersey), and the Iowa ratio for the western states (Michigan, Illinois, and California).

For these states, my method of calculating the estimated size of each state's electorate was as follows. From the federal censuses I obtained the number of adult white males, foreign-born and native inhabitants, in a state. Blacks were included in the estimates for those states (Vermont and New Hampshire) where they were allowed to vote. To calculate the number of naturalized voters I multiplied the foreign-born population by either the New York or Iowa constant. To estimate the number of native voters, I multiplied the percentage of native-born by the total adult white male population. I then added the two figures to get the total number of voters. This procedure overestimates the number of native voters (since adult males were a larger proportion of the immigrant population), and it thus overestimates the total number of voters, but it seemed best to err on the conservative side. As a result, turnout estimates for those northern states for which this estimating procedure was used are too low. In all states for years between censuses, I extrapolated linearly.

This general estimating procedure is imperfect, but it seems justifiable and is certainly superior to using adult males, the most readily available alternative. Of those states whose elections I analyzed intensively, county-level estimates were calculated by this method only for Pennsylvania and Illinois.

Socioeconomic Data. The socioeconomic data used in this study came from a number of widely scattered sources. For most states, the sources for such information were the 1850 and 1860 federal censuses (supplied by the Inter-university Consortium for Political and Social Research). For Iowa and New York, I supplemented the federal data with data from the state censuses (noted above). In addition, for New York, both at the county and township levels, I collected tax assessment figures (primarily from board of supervisors reports published in local newspapers) for the years 1848–1860. Salmon P. Chase diligently collected data on the number of German voters in 1852 for more than half Ohio's counties. This information is in a volume entitled "Vote by Counties— German Voters—1848–1851," which is in the Chase Papers in the Library of Congress. Although the figures are only estimates made by local politicians rather than precise tallies, they have the advantage of referring to voters rather than to the German population as a whole. I also employed Ohio agricultural and tax data by counties, published in the legislative documents for 1854 and 1855. For Indiana, I used the county-level figures for 1850 on place of birth compiled by Joseph E. Layton from census and land records, which are in "Sources of Population in Indiana 1816–1850," *Bulletin of the Indiana State Library*, v. 11 (September, 1916), 3–26. Mark Hornberger, "The Spatial Distribution of Ethnic Groups in Selected Counties in Pennsylvania: A Geographic Interpretation" (unpublished Ph.D. dissertation, Pennsylvania State University, 1974), 38–40, provides estimates of ethnicity for heads of households in eighteen counties. The number of cases is small, but his figures correlate well with those in the federal censuses. Hornberger's statistics pertain to ethnic heritage rather than place of birth and thus provide an index for two particularly important groups in the state that included both native- and foreign-born, the Germans (Pennsylvania Dutch) and the Scotch-Irish. Finally, for the city of Cincinnati, I used the sample drawn by Carl Abbott from the 1860 United States census for place of birth, occupation, and wealth. His study, "Economic Thought and Occupation Structure in Four Middle Western Cities 1850–1860," was made available by the Inter-university Consortium for Political and Social Research (ICPSR Study 7456). None of these individuals nor the consortium bears any responsibility for the interpretations I have drawn from this data.

The socioeconomic data present various difficulties, of which two are especially important. The 1850 and 1860 federal censuses give the number of foreign-born for each county, but they fail to subdivide the population further by place of birth. Both the New York and Iowa state censuses, fortunately, provide more detailed information concerning place of birth. For these two states, I have assumed that the proportion of each ethnic group in the total foreign-born population was the same as among naturalized voters—that is, if Germans were 20 percent of the foreign-born in a county, they were 20 percent of the naturalized voters. I calculated such estimates for New York and Iowa, using the state census for each. For Pennsylvania, Ohio, and Indiana, I used separate estimates (noted above).

The other major problem is religion. New York listed church attendance and membership by county and township for each denomination. Since the New York census did not break down religious data for cities by wards, I used county-level data on attendance in this part of the analysis. For other states outside of New England, I multiplied each denomination's ratio of attendance to church seats (from the New York statistics) times the denomination's accommodations (given in the 1850 and 1860 federal censuses) for each county. I then divided the resulting figure by the county's population to estimate the proportion belonging to a particular church, and I assumed that the proportion of the electorate was the same as that of the general population.

Statistical Techniques. To analyze the data I collected, I used several statistical techniques, including correlations, ecological regression, multiple regression, factor analysis, and two-way analysis of variance. These techniques are becoming increasingly familiar to historians, and books on statistical methods treat most, if not all, of them. Social scientists have held correlations in disfavor since the 1950s, when the idea of the so-called ecological fallacy became canonized. A reaction against this far too extreme attitude has at last begun. A wide literature on this problem is available, but one extremely important article, which convincingly demonstrates the value of aggregate data analysis, is Eric A. Hanushek, John E. Jackson, and John F. Kain, "Model Specification, Use of Aggregate Data, and the Ecological Correlation Fallacy," *Political Methodology*, v. 1 (Winter, 1974), 87–107. The technique of two-way analysis of variance, which is less well known than these other procedures, is described fully in John L. McCarthy and John W. Tukey, "Exploratory Analysis of Aggregate Voting Behavior: Presidential Elections in New Hampshire, 1896–1972," *Social Science History*, v. 2 (Spring, 1978), 292–331. By the manipulation of means and medians, it seeks to isolate year and county effects for a sequence of elections. The method works best on a series of elections over a longer span of time, but it has the important quality that its results are not badly distorted by multi-party elections, and, since so many contests in the 1850s were of this variety, it is valuable in helping sort out year and county trends.

Most of the tables in this study are based on a statistical technique known as ecological regression, which produces estimates of the transition in voting from one election to the next. The proportions in the tables have been rounded to the nearest whole number; rounding sometimes produces sums slightly different from the marginals and, if the denominator is small, can at times produce somewhat misleading impressions of the proportions involved. Consequently, I have based my assertions concerning voting behavior on the actual percentages generated by the regression analysis rather than on the rounded numbers. Missing cases can also cause the marginals to vary slightly from one election to the next and from the true percentages in the state. Because this technique is based on certain assumptions that are in reality rarely completely satisfied, the resulting proportions should be viewed merely as estimates. The regression procedure assumes that the behavior of a particular group is consistent over geographic units (that is; a group votes the same way in, say, a heavily Republican or a heavily Democratic county), or at least that the variation is random and not systematic across units. This assumption is difficult to test and is certainly not always accurate. The closer the assumptions underlying the method are satisfied, the smaller the margin of error in the estimates. Logically impossible estimates of less than zero can, for interpretive purposes, be considered as zero. Such estimates are not uncommon when a group votes overwhelmingly in a certain direction. In addition to this problem, the method works poorly for parties whose support was confined to a few counties (such as the Native American party in Pennsylvania). Because of the wide divergence in population among counties and even townships, I weighted these calculations by number of voters in each county or township according to the procedure outlined in the SPSS (*Statistical Package for the Social Sciences*) regression program. The number of cases is given as N. The "ineligible" category refers to voters enfranchised between the two elections being compared (young men who attained adulthood, and immigrants who were naturalized). Non-voters were eligible to vote in the earlier election but for whatever reason did not participate.

Subject to the errors of rounding, the proportions in the tables added across or down equal the marginals. The rows of the tables indicate how the supporters of a party divided in a subsequent election (in Table 1.1, for example, an estimated 30/38, or approximately 79 percent, of the 1848 Whigs in Connecticut voted for Winfield Scott on the Whig ticket in 1852). The columns give the proportion each group contributed to a party's vote (again in Table 1.1, 1848 Whigs constituted an estimated 3/41, or about 7 percent, of Franklin Pierce's winning coalition in Connecticut in 1852). Party percentages are of the total electorate rather than of the votes cast.

For a full discussion of the technique of ecological regression, see E. Terrence Jones, "Ecological Inference and Electoral Analysis," *Journal of Interdisciplinary History*, v. 2 (Winter, 1972), 249–262; J. Morgan Kousser, "Ecological Regression and the Analysis of Past Politics," ibid., v. 4 (Autumn, 1973), 237–262; Donald E. Stokes, "Cross-Level Inference as a Game Against Nature," in Joseph L. Bernd, ed., *Mathematical Applications in Political Science*, v. 4 (Charlottesville, 1967), 62–83; and W. Phillips Shively, "'Ecological Inference': The Use of Aggregate Data to Study Individuals," *APSR*, v. 63 (December, 1969), 1183–96.

To identify parties' social bases of support, I also utilized multiple regression analysis. Multiple regression measures the influence of each independent variable on the dependent variable (in this case, party vote) while simultaneously controlling for the effects of the other independent variables (religion, place of birth, wealth, and so forth). The sign indicates the direction of the relationship (a positive sign means that as the independent variable increases in strength, so does the dependent variable), and the regression coefficient measures the strength of the relationship. A scrutiny of scatter plots indicated that the relationships in these equations were linear, although other equations could have been used had the relationship been curvilinear. Most of the independent variables are percentages of the population. Except for New York, religion is measured by church accommodations as a ratio of the population, and the figures on place of birth were extrapolated from the 1870 census, adjusted by the proportions of native- and foreign-born for each county given in the 1860 census. For New York, the statistics on church attendance and place of birth in the 1855 state census were used instead. Since the independent variables were not all measured in the same units (church seats, dollars, percentage of the population, and so on) it was necessary to calculate standardized regression coefficients (beta weights). Beta weights indicate the amount of change in standard deviation units in the dependent variable that is produced by a change of one standard deviation unit in an independent variable when the others are controlled. It is thus possible to assess the relative contribution of various independent variables in producing a party's vote in a given election (a variable with a beta coefficient twice as great as that for another variable has twice the influence on a party's vote when the effects of the other independent variables are controlled). Beta weights, unfortunately, are more sensitive to the process of aggregation than are the partial regression coefficients (b), and thus both should be examined. To minimize specification bias, I included in the analysis all variables that had a reasonably high correlation with the dependent variable or with any other independent variable (subject to the limits of multicollinearity discussed below).

When as in this study the units of analysis (counties) have widely varying populations, weighting is necessary in order to apply the usual tests of significance. The regression equations in this study are weighted by the square root of the population in 1860 (1855 for New York). Weighting sometimes produced slight changes in the magnitude of regression coefficients, but for the most part did not alter the direction of the relationship. With only a couple of noted exceptions, the regression coefficients are significant at the .05 level or better, or, in other words, the probability is .95 or better that the true coefficient is not zero (which would mean that there was no relationship between the independent and dependent variable). Most of the coefficients are, in fact, significant at the .001 level or higher. For a fuller discussion of this procedure, see J. Morgan Kousser, ''Making Separate Equal: Integration of Black and White School Funds in Kentucky,'' *Journal of Interdisciplinary History*, v. 10 (Winter, 1980), 399–428, esp. 425–26. The multiple R indicates the strength of the linear relationship between the set of independent variables and the dependent variable, and R^2 indicates the proportion of total variance in the dependent variable explained by the equation. Variables were added to the equation until no additional variable contributed at least one percent to the explained variance. The number of cases (counties) is given as N.

One problem in multiple regression is high correlations between certain independent variables, or multicollinearity, which distorts the resulting regression coefficients. To guard against multicol-linearity, if two variables had a correlation of 0.75 or higher, one was excluded from the analysis. Multicollinearity was a problem particularly with ethnic and religious variables in some states, and with economic indices in most states. Statistical variables available to the historian rarely measure a single quality (since ethnicity, occupation, wealth, religion, and so forth are related), and multiple regression controls for the influence of other variables when calculating the relationship between an independent variable and the dependent variable. On the other hand, regression coefficients and beta weights are not as easy to interpret as the estimates derived by ecological regression.

To illustrate the interpretation of the multiple regressions equations, in Table 13.40 an increase of 1 percent in the Yankee population of a county in New York produces on average an increase (because the sign is positive) of 0.51 percent in John C. Frémont's vote in that county. Conversely, an increase of 1 percent in the Catholic accommodations in a county decreases the Republican vote by 0.9 percent. The proportion of Yankees explains 44 percent of the total variance in the 1856 Republican vote in New York, while the proportion of Catholic accommodations adds another 19 percent. Since these two variables are measured in different units, they are difficult to compare directly. The beta coefficients indicate that for a comparable degree of change the proportion of Catholic accommodations has roughly twice the influence on the Republican vote as the proportion of Yankees (0.33 to 0.14). In some ways, entering various categories of variables (religious variables, ethnic variables, wealth variables, and so on) first into the regression equation is a better way to measure the relative influence of different types of independent variables, but in this study the approach proved unsatisfactory because of the high multicollinearity among almost all the wealth variables and also among some of the ethnic and religious variables. In those states where multicollinearity was a problem, I used per capita wealth as the best and most easily understood index of wealth.

Clear and relatively simple discussions of the technique of step-wise multiple regression can be found in Hubert M. Blalock, Jr., *Social Statistics*, 2nd. ed. rev. (New York, 1979), 451–508; Michael S. Lewis-Beck, *Applied Regression: An Introduction* (Beverly Hills, 1980); and Norman Nie et al., *Statistical Package for the Social Sciences*, 2nd ed. (New York, 1975), 321–42. Particularly important because of their sensitivity to the kinds of data used by historians are Allan J. Lichtman, "Correlation, Regression, and the Ecological Fallacy: A Critique," *Journal of Interdisciplinary History*, v. 4 (Winter, 1974), 417–33; Laura Irwin Langbein and Allan J. Lichtman, "Regression vs. Homogeneous Units: A Specification Analysis," *Social Science History*, v. 2 (Winter, 1978), 172–93; and the same authors' *Ecological Inference* (Beverly Hills, 1978). For a valuable discussion of these and other techniques and their use in analyzing mass voting behavior, see William G. Shade, "'New Political History': Some Statistical Questions Raised," *Social Science History*, v. 5 (Spring, 1981), 171–96; and a response by J. Morgan Kousser and Allan J. Lichtman, "'New Political History': Some Statistical Questions Answered," ibid., v. 7 (Summer, 1983), 321–44.

In an attempt to date the beginning of realignment as well as to trace its general contours, I also factored voting matrixes for my sample states (except Massachusetts). Factor analysis is ideally suited for this purpose, since it seeks to group variables (in this case, elections) that are similar in their distribution. If the party system realigned, therefore, a factor analysis should show the point or points at which distinct breaks occur in the voting alignment. Elections that are closely related to one another align on a particular factor, allowing the researcher to trace chronologically the transition from one party system to another and to distinguish any intervening stages. See the discussion of factor analysis in the SPSS manual, and the references listed therein.

Discussion. Since the proportions obtained from ecological regressions are only estimates, and since they are based on assumptions that do not always hold in reality, I have supplemented my voting analysis with the comments of political observers. In order to improve the estimates for elections in Indiana and Illinois, I divided each state into roughly three equal geographic sections (northern, central, and southern) and ran ecological regressions separately for each section. From the estimates for each section I then computed weighted averages for the state. I followed a similar procedure for several elections in Ohio by generating separate ecological regression estimates for four geographic sections (Western Reserve, northwest, southeast, and southwest) and then calculating weighted statewide estimates. Conducting the analysis by sections improved some of the unreasonable estimates derived by a statewide analysis. In one sense, these results simply verify the observations of contemporaries that voting patterns in these states evidenced basic sectional variations.

I also ran ecological regressions for ethnic and religious data, and in a few instances occupational data. With these variables, the assumptions are somewhat more severe than with election returns and must be noted. In theory, ecological regression should provide good estimates of voting by ethnic, religious, and occupational groups, since these are discrete categories (no voter is a member of two groups simultaneously, since even for men with more than one occupation the census listed only one form of employment) and, combined, they comprise the entire population under study (for religion I included the proportion of the population unaffiliated with any church, the so-called nothingarians). The problem is not knowing the precise relationship between number of voters and size of an ethnic, religious, or occupational group. The assumptions I have made in calculating religious voting patterns are more open to challenge than those for ethnicity, and estimates for church groups should thus be interpreted with even greater caution than usual. Because the occupational statistics in the printed federal censuses were too imprecise for my purposes, I confined this part of my analysis to communities and states for which I had more complete data. I used the tally compiled from the 1850 manuscript census for Chautauqua County, New York, which was published in the Fredonia *Censor*, November 11, 1851, and the figures in the 1856 Iowa state census. Fortunately, such industries as textile factories that traditionally employed females were uncommon in either locality, and to the extent possible I eliminated women from the occupational totals. I then grouped occupations into larger categories according to the findings of a number of studies on social mobility in mid-nineteenth-century America. In this regard, I found Peter R. Knights, *The Plain People of Boston, 1830–1860* (New York, 1971) especially helpful. I assumed that each occupational category's proportion of the total work force was also its proportion of the electorate. Cincinnati posed greater problems because of its large foreign-born population and many factories. For my purposes it was necessary to recombine the data on occupations collected by Carl Abbot in his sample of the 1860 manuscript census (noted above) by eliminating female workers and men under twenty-one from the sample and tallying occupations separately for the native- and foreign-born. I then weighted the proportions by estimates of the number of native and naturalized voters in the city. I also utilized the information on occupations in Maine towns collected by Paul Goodman from the 1850 and 1860 manuscript censuses.

Because my procedure for analyzing the partisanship of denominational groups rests on a number of fragile assumptions, the resulting ecological regression estimates should be interpreted as indicating high, medium, or low support among a church group for a political party rather than as exact proportions. That the estimates generated are, on the whole, consistent with what we know of religion and voting behavior in this period is encouraging. As a further check on these figures, I also calculated multiple regression coefficients for church groups (using the accommodation figures from the federal censuses) and compared the results with the ecological regression estimates. That the results were largely compatible increased my confidence in the ecological regression figures. This check seemed especially important, since the ecological regression estimates are fairly sensitive to the attendance figures employed. In any case, I believe the basic points I make about religion and voting—that church groups voted differently in various states, and that the evangelical vote was not overwhelmingly anti-Democratic—are sound. Better data and further analysis will undoubtedly refine and modify these and other historians' conclusions.

Tables

TABLE 1.1

ESTIMATED RELATIONSHIPS BETWEEN VOTING FOR PRESIDENT
1848 AND PRESIDENT 1852: CONNECTICUT

| | Party in 1852 (President) | | | | |
Party in 1848 (President)	Whig	Democrat	Free Soil	Not Voting	% Electorate 1852
Whig	30	3	1	4	38
Democrat	0	31	0	2	34
Free Soil	2	1	3	−1	6
Ineligible	3	3	0	1	8
Not Voting	2	2	0	11	15
% Electorate 1852	38	41	4	18	

N = 145 townships.

TABLE 1.2

ESTIMATED RELATIONSHIPS BETWEEN VOTING FOR PRESIDENT
1848 AND PRESIDENT 1852: ILLINOIS

| | Party in 1852 (President) | | | | |
Party in 1848 (President)	Whig	Democrat	Free Soil	Not Voting	% Electorate 1852
Whig	22	−2	1	3	23
Democrat	−1	25	0	1	25
Free Soil	0	0	4	3	7
Ineligible	5	6	0	14	25
Not Voting	2	7	0	11	20
% Electorate 1852	28	35	4	32	

N = 99 counties.

TABLE 1.3

ESTIMATED RELATIONSHIPS BETWEEN VOTING FOR PRESIDENT
1848 AND PRESIDENT 1852:   INDIANA

Party in 1848 (President)	Party in 1852 (President)				
	Whig	Democrat	Free Soil	Not Voting	% Electorate 1852
Whig	28	2	1	0	30
Democrat	0	29	0	5	33
Free Soil	1	0	3	0	4
Ineligible	4	6	0	5	15
Not Voting	3	5	0	11	19
% Electorate 1852	35	42	3	20	

N = 91 counties.

TABLE 1.4

ESTIMATED RELATIONSHIPS BETWEEN VOTING FOR PRESIDENT
1848 AND PRESIDENT 1852:   MAINE

Party in 1848 (President)	Party in 1852 (President)				
	Whig	Democrat	Free Soil	Not Voting	% Electorate 1852
Whig	20	1	0	4	25
Democrat	−2	23	1	6	28
Free Soil	1	0	5	3	9
Ineligible	2	4	1	1	7
Not Voting	1	0	−1	30	31
% Electorate 1852	23	29	6	43	

N = 367 townships.

TABLE 1.5

ESTIMATED RELATIONSHIPS BETWEEN VOTING FOR PRESIDENT
1848 AND PRESIDENT 1852: MASSACHUSETTS

Party in 1848 (President)	Party in 1852 (President)				
	Whig	Democrat	Free Soil	Not Voting	% Electorate 1852
Whig	19	5	−2	10	33
Democrat	2	16	0	1	19
Free Soil	4	0	14	3	21
Ineligible	0	0	0	0	1
Not Voting	3	3	3	18	27
% Electorate 1852	29	24	15	32	

N = 302 townships.

TABLE 1.6

ESTIMATED RELATIONSHIPS BETWEEN VOTING FOR PRESIDENT
1848 AND PRESIDENT 1852: NEW YORK

Party in 1848 (President)	Party in 1852 (President)				
	Whig	Democrat	Free Soil	Not Voting	% Electorate 1852
Whig	30	2	−1	4	36
Democrat	−1	20	0	1	20
Free Soil	3	10	3	−2	14
Ineligible	3	4	0	2	9
Not Voting	2	5	0	13	21
% Electorate 1852	38	41	3	18	

N = 473 townships.

TABLE 1.7

ESTIMATED RELATIONSHIPS BETWEEN VOTING FOR PRESIDENT
1848 AND PRESIDENT 1852: OHIO

Party in 1848 (President)	Party in 1852 (President)				
	Whig	Democrat	Free Soil	Not Voting	% Electorate 1852
Whig	33	8	-2	-5	35
Democrat	2	30	2	7	41
Free Soil	3	-3	8	1	9
Ineligible	2	2	0	5	9
Not Voting	0	5	0	2	7
% Electorate 1852	39	43	8	11	

N = 88 counties.

TABLE 1.8

ESTIMATED RELATIONSHIPS BETWEEN VOTING FOR PRESIDENT
1848 AND PRESIDENT 1852: PENNSYLVANIA

Party in 1848 (President)	Party in 1852 (President)				
	Whig	Democrat	Free Soil	Not Voting	% Electorate 1852
Whig	34	-1	0	3	35
Democrat	2	33	0	-2	32
Free Soil	1	1	1	-1	2
Ineligible	-1	4	0	6	9
Not Voting	-2	0	1	22	22
% Electorate 1852	34	37	2	28	

N = 63 counties.

TABLE 1.9

ESTIMATED PERCENTAGES BETWEEN VOTING FOR PRESIDENT 1852 AND NATIVE
AND FOREIGN-BORN VOTERS: NEW YORK, INDIANA, AND IOWA

| | Nativity and Party | | | | |
| | Native-Born | | Foreign-Born | | |
State	Whig	Democrat	Whig	Democrat	N
New York	45 %	40 %	22 %	45 %	360 townships
Indiana	37	41	16	54	91 counties
Iowa	34	32	25	60	47 counties

TABLE 1.10

ESTIMATED PERCENTAGES BETWEEN VOTING FOR PRESIDENT 1852
AND GERMAN AND IRISH VOTERS: NEW YORK, INDIANA, AND IOWA

| | Nativity and Party | | | | |
| | German | | Irish | | |
State	Whig	Democrat	Whig	Democrat	N
New York	17 %	52 %	0 %	57 %	352 townships
Indiana	15	56	19	58	91 counties
Iowa	34	60	17	83	47 counties

TABLE 2.1

ESTIMATED RELATIONSHIPS BETWEEN VOTING FOR PRESIDENT
1852 AND SECRETARY OF STATE 1853: NEW YORK

Party in 1852 (President)	Party in 1853 (Secretary of State)					% Electorate 1853
	Whig	Soft	Hard	Free Democrat	Not Voting	
Whig	24	−7	7	−2	14	37
Democrat	2	23	6	1	10	41
Free Soil	−1	2	−2	3	3	4
Ineligible	1	−1	2	0	1	2
Not Voting	−1	−1	3	0	14	15
% Electorate 1853	25	15	16	2	41	

N = 60 counties.

TABLE 2.2

ESTIMATED RELATIONSHIPS BETWEEN VOTING FOR PRESIDENT
1848 AND SECRETARY OF STATE 1853: NEW YORK

Party in 1848 (President)	Party in 1853 (Secretary of State)					% Electorate 1853
	Whig	Soft	Hard	Free Democrat	Not Voting	
Whig	20	−5	9	−4	13	35
Democrat	3	6	7	1	1	18
Free Soil	4	9	−3	4	5	19
Ineligible	1	0	3	0	5	9
Not Voting	−3	5	−1	1	18	19
% Electorate 1853	25	15	16	2	41	

N = 60 counties.

TABLE 2.3

ESTIMATED RELATIONSHIPS BETWEEN VOTING FOR CANAL COMMISSIONER
1852 AND CANAL COMMISSIONER 1853: PENNSYLVANIA

Party in 1852 (Canal Comm.)	Party in 1853 (Canal Commissioner)				
	Whig	Democrat	Native American	Not Voting	% Electorate 1853
Whig	24	0	0	3	28
Democrat	−4	25	−2	13	31
Ineligible	−1	2	1	1	2
Not Voting	3	1	3	33	39
% Electorate 1853	21	28	1	50	

N = 63 counties.

TABLE 2.4

ESTIMATED PERCENTAGES BETWEEN VOTING ON
PROHIBITION REFERENDA AND PARTY AFFILIATION:
ILLINOIS, IOWA, OHIO, AND PENNSYLVANIA

State and Year	Party and Referendum (Prohibition)									N (Counties)
	Whig			Democrat			Free Soil			
	Yes	No	Not Voting	Yes	No	Not Voting	Yes	No	Not Voting	
Illinois (1855)	65%	4%	31%	2%	98%	0[a]%	67%	0[a]%	33%	99
Iowa (1855)	52	48	0[a]	11	37	52	99	1	0[a]	48
Ohio (1851)	57	31	12	19	62	19	21	0[a]	79	88
Pennsylvania (1854)	34	35	31	27	60	13	69	0[a]	31	63

Party affiliations: Vote in 1852 presidential election.

[a]Percentage set at minimum value and others adjusted.

TABLE 2.5

ESTIMATED RELATIONSHIPS BETWEEN VOTING FOR GOVERNOR
1850 AND GOVERNOR 1852: MAINE

Party in 1850 (Governor)	Party in 1852 (Governor)					
	Whig	Democrat	Free Soil	Wildcat	Not Voting	% Electorate 1852
Whig	16	3	0	−2	4	23
Democrat	1	15	−1	15	−2	29
Free Soil	−1	3	1	2	0	5
Ineligible	0	2	0	1	0	4
Not Voting	4	5	0	0	31	40
% Electorate 1852	20	29	1	15	34	

N = 369 townships.

TABLE 2.6

ESTIMATED RELATIONSHIPS BETWEEN VOTING FOR GOVERNOR
1852 AND GOVERNOR 1853: MAINE

Party in 1852 (Governor)	Party in 1853 (Governor)					
	Whig	Democrat	Free Soil	Morrill	Not Voting	% Electorate 1853
Whig	13	4	−1	−1	4	20
Democrat	1	8	5	8	7	28
Free Soil	0	0	2	0	−1	1
Wildcat	2	10	1	2	1	15
Ineligible	0	1	0	0	1	2
Not Voting	2	1	−1	0	32	34
% Electorate 1853	18	24	6	8	44	

N = 372 townships.

TABLE 2.7

ESTIMATED RELATIONSHIPS BETWEEN VOTING FOR PRESIDENT
1852 AND GOVERNOR 1853: MAINE

| Party in 1852 (President) | Party in 1853 (Governor) | | | | | % Electorate 1853 |
	Whig	Democrat	Free Soil	Morrill	Not Voting	
Whig	17	−2	−1	−2	11	22
Democrat	−1	20	0	7	3	28
Free Soil	0	2	6	1	−4	5
Ineligible	0	0	0	0	2	2
Not Voting	3	4	1	2	32	42
% Electorate 1853	18	24	6	8	44	

N = 372 townships.

TABLE 2.8

PERCENTAGE OF VOTERS SWITCHING PARTIES: MAINE

Year	Whig	Democrat	Free Soil	Not Voting
1848P	0 %	16 %	25 %	24 %
1849	28	14	29	7
1850	8	9	16	20
1852S	23	52	85	23
1852P	27	46	0	15
1853	39	23	39	24

Note: P = Presidential election; S = State election. Percentage switching
for a given election is calculated from the election immediately preceding.
Democratic vote in 1852S, Hubbard; 1853, Pillsbury.

TABLE 2.9

ESTIMATED RELATIONSHIPS BETWEEN VOTING FOR GOVERNOR
1851 AND GOVERNOR 1852: CONNECTICUT

Party in 1851 (Governor)	Party in 1852 (Governor)				
	Whig	Democrat	Free Soil	Not Voting	% Electorate 1852
Whig	28	3	0	4	36
Democrat	2	34	1	1	37
Free Soil	0	1	3	−1	3
Ineligible	2	0	0	0	2
Not Voting	3	1	0	18	22
% Electorate 1852	35	39	4	23	

N = 146 townships.

TABLE 2.10

ESTIMATED RELATIONSHIPS BETWEEN VOTING FOR GOVERNOR
1852 AND GOVERNOR 1853: CONNECTICUT

Party in 1852 (Governor)	Party in 1853 (Governor)				
	Whig	Democrat	Free Soil	Not Voting	% Electorate 1853
Whig	24	6	3	0	34
Democrat	3	30	0	4	38
Free Soil	−1	0	4	0	4
Ineligible	0	0	0	2	3
Not Voting	−2	0	3	21	22
% Electorate 1853	25	37	11	28	

N = 146 townships.

TABLE 2.11

TWO-WAY ANALYSIS OF VARIANCE: CONNECTICUT

Year	Whig Vote Relative to Usual Anti-Democratic Vote	Democratic Vote Relative to Usual Democratic Vote
1848S	+ 1.6 %	-2.0 %
1848P	- 0.1	-4.7
1849	0.	-3.3
1850	- 1.8	+0.2
1851	- 2.2	+0.4
1852S	- 3.8	+2.0
1852P	- 3.9	+2.0
1853	-15.7	+3.2
1854	-14.7	+1.4

S = State election; P = Presidential election.

TABLE 2.12

PARTY DECOMPOSITION: CONNECTICUT 1849-1853

WHIG DECOMPOSITION

Year	Loss From Previous Election	Loss to other Parties	Abstain
1849	16 %	0[a] %	16 %
1850	12	6	6
1851	10	6	4
1852S	22	10	12
1852P	22	22	0[a]
1853	26	9	17

DEMOCRATIC DECOMPOSITION

Year	Loss From Previous Election	Loss to other Parties	Abstain
1849	7 %	7 %	0[a] %
1850	7	7	0[a]
1851	10	7	3
1852S	8	6	2
1852P	20	13	7
1853	21	17	4

S = State election; P = Presidential election.

N = 146 townships.

[a]Percentage set at minimum value and others adjusted.

TABLE 2.13

ESTIMATED RELATIONSHIPS BETWEEN VOTING FOR SUPREME COURT
JUSTICE 1852 AND GOVERNOR 1853:   OHIO

Party in 1852 (Supreme Court)	Party in 1853 (Governor)				
	Whig	Democrat	Free Soil	Not Voting	% Electorate 1853
Whig	24	0	5	4	32
Democrat	-2	32	1	6	36
Free Soil	-1	-1	4	2	6
Ineligible	0	0	-1	4	2
Not Voting	-1	6	4	14	24
% Electorate 1853	21	37	12	30	

N = 88 counties.

TABLE 2.14

ESTIMATED RELATIONSHIPS BETWEEN VOTING ON PROHIBITION
REFERENDUM 1851 AND GOVERNOR 1853:   OHIO

Votes in 1851 (Prohibition Ref.)	Party in 1853 (Governor)				
	Whig	Democrat	Free Soil	Not Voting	% Electorate 1853
Yes	14	9	8	-2	28
No	7	21	-4	2	26
Ineligible	1	2	-2	3	4
Not Voting	-1	5	10	27	41
% Electorate 1853	21	37	12	30	

N = 88 counties.

TABLE 2.15

ESTIMATED RELATIONSHIPS BETWEEN VOTING FOR SUPREME COURT
JUSTICE 1852 AND MAYOR 1853: CINCINNATI

Party in 1852 (Supreme Court)	Party in 1853 (Mayor)					% Electorate 1853
	Inde-pendent Whig	Demo-crat	Free School (Taylor)	Anti-Miami	Not Voting	
Whig	7	-5	24	0	0	26
Democrat	1	25	4	1	-1	29
Free Soil	5	1	-1	0	-3	1
Ineligible	0	-1	-2	-1	7	4
Not Voting	-1	3	-4	4	40	40
% Electorate 1853	11	23	20	4	42	

N = 16 wards.

TABLE 2.16

RISING DEMOCRATIC ASCENDANCY: PARTY DIFFERENTIALS IN CONNECTICUT,
MAINE, NEW YORK, OHIO, AND PENNSYLVANIA, 1848–1853

Year	Connecticut	Maine	New York	Ohio	Pennsylvania
1848S	-3.6 %	9.2 %	--	-0.1 %	-0.1 %
1848P	-5.2	5.6	-23.0 %[a]	4.9	-3.7
1849	-3.9	12.6	-0.6	--	4.1
1850	1.4	11.0	-0.1	4.5	4.9
1851	2.2	--	-1.5	9.3	2.3
1852S	5.4	36.3[b]	--	5.2	5.1
1852P	4.3	11.0	5.2	4.7	5.0
1853	16.8	23.8	9.9[c]	21.8	12.7

Pro-Whig differential shown as negative.

[a]Taylor over Cass. Cass and Van Buren combined 3.6 over Taylor.

[b]Democratic vote combined: 1852, Hubbard and Chandler; 1853, Pillsbury
and Morrill.

[c]Democratic Soft and Hard combined.

TABLE 3.1

ESTIMATED RELATIONSHIPS BETWEEN VOTING FOR GOVERNOR 1853 AND GOVERNOR 1854:   CONNECTICUT

Party in 1853 (Governor)	Party in 1854 (Governor)					% Electorate 1853
	Whig	Democrat	Temperance	Free Soil	Not Voting	
Whig	22	-2	0	2	1	24
Democrat	-1	34	5	-2	0	36
Free Soil	2	0	5	3	1	11
Ineligible	0	0	0	0	3	3
Not Voting	0	1	3	0	23	27
% Electorate 1854	23	33	13	3	29	

N = 146 townships.

TABLE 3.2

ESTIMATED RELATIONSHIPS BETWEEN KNOW NOTHING MEMBERSHIP 1854 AND VOTING ON PROHIBITION REFERENDUM 1851:   OHIO

Referendum in 1851 (Prohibition)	Membership 1854		% Electorate 1854
	Know Nothing	Non-Know Nothing	
Yes	17	11	29
No	7	18	25
Ineligible	2	3	6
Not Voting	-10	50	40
% Electorate 1854	17	83	

N = 49 counties.

TABLE 3.3

ESTIMATED RELATIONSHIPS BETWEEN VOTING FOR SUPREME COURT
JUSTICE 1854 AND PROHIBITION REFERENDUM 1854:   PENNSYLVANIA

| Party in 1854 (Supreme Court) | Referendum in 1854 (Prohibition) | | | % Electorate 1854 |
	Yes	No	Not Voting	
Whig	8	4	1	13
Democrat	−1	30	2	30
American	16	1	5	22
Not Voting	6	−6	35	35
% Electorate 1854	28	29	42	

N = 63 counties.

TABLE 4.1

ESTIMATED RELATIONSHIPS BETWEEN VOTING FOR PRESIDENT
1852 AND SECRETARY OF STATE 1854:   INDIANA

| Party in 1852 (President) | Party in 1854 (Secretary of State) | | | % Electorate 1854 |
	People's	Democrat	Not Voting	
Whig	30	−4	7	33
Democrat	3	37	−2	39
Free Soil	3	−1	1	3
Ineligible	2	2	4	8
Not Voting	2	1	15	18
% Electorate 1854	40	35	25	

N = 91 counties.

TABLE 4.2

ESTIMATED PERCENTAGES BETWEEN PARTISANSHIP IN 1854
AND PLACE OF BIRTH: INDIANA AND IOWA

	Indiana		
	Party in 1854 (Secretary of State)		
Place of Birth 1850	People's	Democrat	Not Voting
Native-born	42 %	34 %	25 %
Foreign-born	19	56	25
German	11	65	24

N = 91 counties.

	Iowa		
	Party in 1854 (Governor)		
Place of Birth 1856	Opposition	Democrat	Not Voting
Native-born	40 %	33 %	27 %
Foreign-born	32	51	17
German	31	49	20

N = 62 counties.

TABLE 4.3

ESTIMATED RELATIONSHIPS BETWEEN VOTING FOR SUPREME COURT
JUSTICE 1852 AND BOARD OF PUBLIC WORKS 1854:   OHIO

| Party in 1852 (Supreme Court) | Party in 1854 (Board of Public Works) | | | |
	People's	Democrat	Not Voting	% Electorate 1854
Whig	25	−1	8	32
Democrat	10	24	2	35
Free Soil	2	0	3	5
Ineligible	0	−2	6	4
Not Voting	7	5	10	23
% Electorate 1854	45	27	29	

N = 88 counties.

TABLE 4.4

ESTIMATED RELATIONSHIPS BETWEEN VOTING ON PROHIBITION
REFERENDUM 1851 AND BOARD OF PUBLIC WORKS 1854:   OHIO

| Referendum in 1851 (Prohibition) | Party in 1854 (Board of Public Works) | | | |
	People's	Democrat	Not Voting	% Electorate 1854
Yes	23	4	1	28
No	11	16	−1	26
Ineligible	2	0	4	6
Not Voting	9	7	24	40
% Electorate 1854	45	27	29	

N = 88 counties.

TABLE 4.5

ESTIMATED RELATIONSHIPS BETWEEN VOTING FOR BOARD OF PUBLIC WORKS 1854 AND KNOW NOTHING MEMBERSHIP 1854: OHIO

Membership 1854	Party in 1854 (Board of Public Works)			% Electorate 1854
	People's	Democrat	Not Voting	
Know Nothing	10	5	2	17
Non-Know Nothing	36	22	25	83
% Electorate 1854	47	26	27	

N = 41 counties.

TABLE 4.6

ESTIMATED RELATIONSHIPS BETWEEN VOTING FOR MAYOR 1853 AND SUPREME COURT JUSTICE 1854: CINCINNATI

Party in 1853 (Mayor)	Party in 1854 (Supreme Court)			% Electorate 1854
	People's	Democrat	Not Voting	
Democrat	4	20	-2	22
Whig	14	1	-5	10
Free School	19	-2	2	19
Anti-Miami	4	0	0	4
Ineligible	-1	2	3	3
Not Voting	1	2	38	41
% Electorate 1854	41	22	36	

N = 16 wards.

Note: Candidates: Whig, Ross; Free School, Taylor; Anti-Miami, Chambers.

501

TABLE 4.7

ESTIMATED RELATIONSHIPS BETWEEN VOTING FOR PRESIDENT
1852 AND GOVERNOR 1854: IOWA

Party in 1852 (President)	Party in 1854 (Governor)			
	Opposition (Grimes)	Democrat	Not Voting	% Electorate 1854
Whig	27	−8	8	28
Democrat	−1	34	−2	31
Free Soil	2	1	0	3
Ineligible	4	3	6	14
Not Voting	6	6	13	25
% Electorate 1854	39	36	25	

N = 48 counties.

TABLE 4.8

ESTIMATED RELATIONSHIPS BETWEEN VOTING FOR PRESIDENT
1852 AND STATE TREASURER 1854: ILLINOIS

Party in 1852 (President)	Party in 1854 (State Treasurer)			
	Anti−Nebraska	Democrat	Not Voting	% Electorate 1854
Whig	18	0	6	24
Democrat	−1	23	8	30
Free Soil	4	−1	0	4
Ineligible	3	5	7	15
Not Voting	0	−2	29	27
% Electorate 1854	24	25	50	

N = 99 counties.

TABLE 4.9

ESTIMATED RELATIONSHIPS BETWEEN VOTING FOR PRESIDENT
1852 AND CONGRESS 1854:   ILLINOIS

Party in 1852 (President)	Party in 1854 (Congress)			% Electorate 1854
	Anti-Nebraska	Democrat	Not Voting	
Whig	18	0	5	24
Democrat	1	24	6	30
Free Soil	4	-1	1	4
Ineligible	4	5	6	15
Not Voting	3	-6	30	27
% Electorate 1854	30	22	48	

N = 99 counties.

Note: Numbers in the Anti-Nebraska column represent the combined vote for all candidates opposed to the regular Democratic nominee.

TABLE 5.1

ESTIMATED RELATIONSHIPS BETWEEN VOTING FOR GOVERNOR
1853 AND GOVERNOR 1854:   MAINE

Party in 1853 (Governor)	Party in 1854 (Governor)					% Electorate 1854
	Whig	Democrat	Morrill	Liberal (Cary)	Not Voting	
Whig	9	-2	10	0	2	18
Democrat	1	18	0	2	2	24
Free Soil	0	-1	6	0	1	6
Morrill	0	1	7	0	1	7
Ineligible	0	1	1	0	0	2
Not Voting	0	1	7	0	34	43
% Electorate 1854	9	19	30	2	40	

N = 380 townships.

503

TABLE 5.2

ESTIMATED RELATIONSHIPS BETWEEN VOTING FOR GOVERNOR
1852 AND GOVERNOR 1854: MAINE

Party in 1854 (Governor)

Party in 1852 (Governor)	Whig	Democrat	Morrill	Liberal (Cary)	Not Voting	% Electorate 1854
Whig	8	2	5	0	4	20
Democrat	0	7	19	−1	3	28
Free Soil	0	0	2	0	0	1
Wildcat	1	8	2	2	2	15
Ineligible	0	1	1	0	2	4
Not Voting	0	1	2	1	29	33
% Electorate 1854	9	19	30	2	40	

N = 372 townships.

TABLE 5.3

ESTIMATED RELATIONSHIPS BETWEEN VOTING FOR PRESIDENT
1852 AND GOVERNOR 1854: MASSACHUSETTS

Party in 1854 (Governor)

Party in 1852 (President)	Whig	Democrat	Free Soil	American	Not Voting	% Electorate 1854
Whig	10	1	0	12	4	27
Democrat	1	6	−1	12	5	23
Free Soil	0	1	3	8	2	15
Ineligible	0	0	0	3	2	5
Not Voting	3	−2	0	6	22	30
% Electorate 1854	14	6	3	41	35	

N = 316 townships.

TABLE 5.4

ESTIMATED RELATIONSHIPS BETWEEN VOTING FOR PRESIDENT
1852 AND SUPREME COURT JUSTICE 1854:   PENNSYLVANIA

| Party in 1852 (President) | Party in 1854 (Supreme Court Justice) | | | | % Electorate 1854 |
	Whig	Democrat	American	Not Voting	
Whig	16	0	10	6	32
Democrat	-2	27	8	3	36
Free Soil	2	0	-1	1	2
Ineligible	-1	2	2	2	4
Not Voting	-1	2	3	23	26
% Electorate	13	30	22	35	

N = 63 counties.

TABLE 5.5

ESTIMATED RELATIONSHIPS BETWEEN VOTING FOR PRESIDENT
1852 AND PROHIBITION REFERENDUM 1854:   PENNSYLVANIA

| Party in 1852 (President) | Referendum in 1854 (Prohibition) | | | % Electorate 1854 |
	Yes	No	Not Voting	
Whig	11	11	10	32
Democrat	10	21	5	36
Free Soil	2	-2	1	2
Ineligible	-1	3	3	4
Not Voting	7	-4	24	26
% Electorate 1854	28	29	42	

N = 63 counties.

TABLE 5.6

ESTIMATED RELATIONSHIPS BETWEEN VOTING FOR SECRETARY OF STATE
1853 AND GOVERNOR 1854: NEW YORK

	Party in 1854 (Governor)					
Party in 1853 (Secretary of State)	Whig	Soft	Hard	American	Not Voting	% Electorate 1854
Whig	17	-3	1	9	-1	24
Soft	1	12	0	1	0	14
Hard	-1	9	4	2	3	17
Ineligible	-1	1	0	1	1	2
Not Voting	6	6	1	7	24	43
% Electorate 1854	22	25	5	20	27	

N = 528 townships.

TABLE 5.7

ESTIMATED RELATIONSHIPS BETWEEN VOTING FOR PRESIDENT
1852 AND GOVERNOR 1854: NEW YORK

	Party in 1854 (Governor)					
Party in 1852 (President)	Whig	Soft	Hard	American	Not Voting	% Electorate 1854
Whig	16	-3	1	15	7	36
Democrat	3	23	3	2	9	40
Free Soil	2	0	0	-1	1	2
Ineligible	0	2	0	2	1	4
Not Voting	0	3	1	3	10	17
% Electorate 1854	22	25	5	20	27	

N = 475 townships.

TABLE 5.8

ESTIMATED PERCENTAGES BETWEEN VOTING FOR GOVERNOR
1854 AND PLACE OF BIRTH 1855: NEW YORK

| Place of Birth 1855 | Party in 1854 (Governor) | | | | |
	Whig	Soft	Hard	American	Not Voting
United States	27 %	15 %	7 %	25 %	27 %
England	55	9	0[a]	36	0[a]
Germany	0[a]	42	0[a]	25	33
Ireland	0[a]	52	7	9	31

N = 351 townships.

[a]Percentage set at minimum value and others adjusted.

TABLE 5.9

ESTIMATED PERCENTAGES BETWEEN RELIGION 1855
AND VOTING FOR GOVERNOR 1854: NEW YORK

| Religion 1855 (Attendance) | Party in 1854 (Governor) | | | | |
	Whig	Soft	Hard	American	Not Voting
Baptist	69 %	18 %	0 %	10 %	0[a]%
Methodist	41	28	21	0	11
Presbyterian	13	0[a]	3	62	21
Congregational	77	22	0[a]	0[a]	0[a]
Lutheran	1	23	36	39	0[a]
Catholic	0[a]	69	10	7	15

N = 60 counties.

[a]Percentage set at minimum value and others adjusted.

TABLE 5.10

ESTIMATED PERCENTAGES BETWEEN RELIGION 1850 AND
VOTING FOR SECRETARY OF STATE 1854:   INDIANA

| Religion 1850 (Attendance) | Party in 1854 (Secretary of State) | | |
	People's	Democrat	Not Voting
Baptist	37 %	35 %	28 %
Methodist	51	49	0[a]
Presbyterian	59	41	0
Lutheran	18	82	0[a]

N = 89 counties.

[a]Percentage set at minimum value and others adjusted.

TABLE 5.11

ESTIMATED PERCENTAGES BETWEEN RELIGION 1850 AND VOTING
FOR SUPREME COURT JUSTICE 1854:   PENNSYLVANIA

| Religion 1850 (Attendance) | Party in 1854 (Supreme Court Justice) | | | |
	Whig	Democrat	American	Not Voting
Baptist	27 %	24 %	49 %	0[a]%
Methodist	0[a]	36	61	2
Presbyterian	56	14	10	20
German Reformed	25	37	38	0[a]
Lutheran	31	61	8	0

N = 62 counties.

[a]Percentage set at minimum value and others adjusted.

TABLE 7.1

ESTIMATED RELATIONSHIPS BETWEEN VOTING FOR GOVERNOR
1855 AND LIEUTENANT GOVERNOR 1855: OHIO

Party in 1855 (Governor)	Party in 1855 (Lieutenant Governor)			
	Republican	Democrat	Not Voting	% Electorate 1855
Republican	36	−1	0	35
Democrat	−1	32	0	31
Trimble	6	0	0	6
Not Voting	0	1	28	28
% Electorate 1855	41	32	28	

N = 88 counties.

TABLE 7.2

ESTIMATED RELATIONSHIPS BETWEEN VOTING FOR SUPREME
COURT JUSTICE 1852 AND GOVERNOR 1855: OHIO

Party in 1852 (Supreme Court)	Party in 1855 (Governor)				
	Republican	Democrat	Trimble	Not Voting	% Electorate 1855
Whig	13	−1	7	12	31
Democrat	14	25	−4	−1	35
Free Soil	4	−1	−1	2	5
Ineligible	−2	0	1	7	6
Not Voting	6	7	2	8	23
% Electorate 1855	35	31	6	28	

N = 88 counties.

TABLE 7.3

ESTIMATED RELATIONSHIPS BETWEEN VOTING FOR BOARD OF
PUBLIC WORKS 1854 AND GOVERNOR 1855: OHIO

| | Party in 1855 (Governor) | | | | |
Party in 1854 (Public Works)	Republican	Democrat	Trimble	Not Voting	% Electorate 1855
People's	20	5	8	10	44
Democrat	6	23	-3	-1	26
Ineligible	-5	1	1	4	2
Not Voting	13	1	0	14	28
% Electorate 1855	35	31	6	28	

N = 88 counties.

TABLE 7.4

ESTIMATED RELATIONSHIPS BETWEEN VOTING FOR BOARD OF
PUBLIC WORKS 1854 AND LIEUTENANT GOVERNOR 1855: OHIO

| | Party in 1855 (Lieutenant Governor) | | | |
Party in 1854 (Public Works)	Republican	Democrat	Not Voting	% Electorate 1855
People's	28	6	10	44
Democrat	3	23	0	26
Ineligible	-4	2	5	2
Not Voting	14	1	13	28
% Electorate 1855	41	32	28	

N = 88 counties.

TABLE 7.5

ESTIMATED RELATIONSHIPS BETWEEN VOTING FOR GOVERNOR AND LIEUTENANT
GOVERNOR 1855 AND KNOW NOTHING MEMBERSHIP 1854: OHIO

| | Party in 1855 (Governor) | | | | |
Membership 1854	Republican	Democrat	Trimble	Not Voting	% Electorate 1855
Know Nothing	7	6	1	2	17
Non-Know Nothing	27	26	5	25	83
% Electorate 1855	35	32	6	27	
(Lieutenant Governor)					
Know Nothing	9	6		2	17
Non-Know Nothing	32	27		25	83
% Electorate 1855	41	32		27	

N = 41 counties.

TABLE 7.6

ESTIMATED RELATIONSHIPS BETWEEN VOTING FOR MAYOR 1853
AND GOVERNOR 1855: CINCINNATI

| | Party in 1855 (Governor) | | | | |
Party in 1853 (Mayor)	Republican	Democrat	Trimble	Not Voting	% Electorate 1855
Independent Whig	4	0	7	-2	10
Democrat	-1	23	0	-1	21
Free School	3	-2	10	7	19
Anti-Miami	5	4	-2	-3	4
Ineligible	1	4	-1	3	7
Not Voting	-2	2	2	37	40
% Electorate 1855	11	31	16	41	

N = 16 wards.

TABLE 7.7

ESTIMATED RELATIONSHIPS BETWEEN VOTING FOR GOVERNOR
1854 AND GOVERNOR 1855: MAINE

| Party in 1854 (Governor) | Party in 1855 (Governor) | | | | |
	Republican	Democrat	Whig	Not Voting	% Electorate 1855
Whig	3	0	7	−1	9
Democrat	4	17	−2	0	18
Morrill	22	7	2	−2	30
Liberal (Cary)	0	2	0	0	2
Ineligible	1	1	−1	0	2
Not Voting	4	5	0	30	39
% Electorate 1855	34	31	7	28	

N = 380 townships.

TABLE 7.8

ESTIMATED RELATIONSHIPS BETWEEN VOTING FOR PRESIDENT
1852 AND GOVERNOR 1855: MAINE

| Party in 1852 (President) | Party in 1855 (Governor) | | | | |
	Republican	Democrat	Whig	Not Voting	% Electorate 1855
Whig	10	−1	9	4	21
Democrat	9	22	−2	−1	27
Free Soil	6	2	0	−3	5
Ineligible	2	2	−1	3	6
Not Voting	7	7	1	26	41
% Electorate 1855	34	31	7	28	

N = 372 townships.

TABLE 7.9

ESTIMATED RELATIONSHIPS BETWEEN VOTING FOR GOVERNOR
1852 AND GOVERNOR 1855: MAINE

Party in 1852 (Governor)	Party in 1855 (Governor)				
	Republican	Democrat	Whig	Not Voting	% Electorate 1855
Whig	7	4	7	1	19
Democrat	16	12	0	-1	27
Free Soil	1	0	0	0	1
Wildcat	4	10	0	1	14
Ineligible	2	2	-1	2	6
Not Voting	4	4	0	25	32
% Electorate 1855	34	31	7	28	

N = 372 townships.

TABLE 7.10

ESTIMATED RELATIONSHIPS BETWEEN VOTING FOR GOVERNOR
1853 AND GOVERNOR 1855: MAINE

Party in 1853 (Governor)	Party in 1855 (Governor)				
	Republican	Democrat	Whig	Not Voting	% Electorate 1855
Whig	11	-1	9	-1	18
Democrat	4	20	-1	0	23
Free Soil	5	1	0	0	6
Morrill	5	2	0	0	7
Ineligible	2	2	-1	1	4
Not Voting	7	8	1	27	42
% Electorate 1855	34	31	7	28	

N = 380 townships.

513

TABLE 7.11

ESTIMATED RELATIONSHIPS BETWEEN VOTING FOR SUPREME COURT
JUSTICE 1854 AND CANAL COMMISSIONER 1855: PENNSYLVANIA

Party in 1855 (Canal Commissioner)

Party in 1854 (Supreme Court)	Fusion	Dem.	Whig	Repub.	Amer.	Nat. Amer.	Not Voting	% Electorate 1855
Whig	7	-1	1	2	0	0	5	13
Democrat	4	23	-2	-3	0	2	5	29
American	13	4	1	0	0	-1	3	21
Ineligible	1	0	0	-1	0	1	1	2
Not Voting	1	2	0	3	0	-1	29	34
% Electorate 1855	27	28	0.4	1	0.1	0.7	43	

N = 63 counties.

TABLE 7.12

ESTIMATED RELATIONSHIPS BETWEEN VOTING FOR GOVERNOR
1854 AND GOVERNOR 1855: MASSACHUSETTS

Party in 1855 (Governor)

Party in 1854 (Governor)	Republican	Democrat	American	Whig	Not Voting	% Electorate 1855
Whig	4	4	1	5	-1	14
Democrat	2	6	-1	-1	0	6
Free Soil	6	-1	-1	0	-1	3
American	8	6	20	0	6	41
Ineligible	-1	0	2	1	1	2
Not Voting	-1	2	4	2	26	34
% Electorate 1855	18	17	26	7	32	

N = 323 townships.

TABLE 7.13

ESTIMATED RELATIONSHIPS BETWEEN VOTING FOR PRESIDENT
1852 AND GOVERNOR 1855: MASSACHUSETTS

Party in 1852 (President)	Party in 1855 (Governor)					% Electorate 1855
	Republican	Democrat	American	Whig	Not Voting	
Whig	11	1	7	2	5	27
Democrat	-1	15	6	0	2	23
Free Soil	10	2	2	0	1	14
Ineligible	-1	0	4	1	3	7
Not Voting	-1	0	6	3	21	29
% Electorate 1855	18	18	26	7	32	

N = 315 townships.

TABLE 7.14

ESTIMATED RELATIONSHIPS BETWEEN VOTING FOR GOVERNOR
1854 AND SECRETARY OF STATE 1855: NEW YORK

Party in 1854 (Governor)	Party in 1855 (Secretary of State)					% Electorate 1855
	Republican	Soft	Hard	American	Not Voting	
Whig	18	0	-6	6	4	22
Soft	-2	15	7	1	3	25
Hard	0	-2	6	1	1	5
American	3	3	-1	12	3	20
Ineligible	-1	0	2	0	2	2
Not Voting	0	-1	4	2	22	27
% Electorate 1855	18	14	11	23	34	

N = 515 townships.

TABLE 7.15

ESTIMATED RELATIONSHIPS BETWEEN VOTING FOR PRESIDENT
1852 AND SECRETARY OF STATE 1855: NEW YORK

| Party in 1852 (President) | Party in 1855 (Secretary of State) | | | | | % Electorate 1855 |
	Republican	Soft	Hard	American	Not Voting	
Whig	15	-1	-4	16	10	35
Democrat	1	15	10	3	10	39
Free Soil	3	0	-1	-1	1	2
Ineligible	0	2	1	1	3	7
Not Voting	-1	-1	5	2	12	17
% Electorate 1855	18	14	12	22	34	

N = 472 townships.

TABLE 7.16

ESTIMATED RELATIONSHIPS BETWEEN VOTING FOR SECRETARY OF STATE
1853 AND SECRETARY OF STATE 1855: NEW YORK

| Party in 1853 (Secretary of State) | Party in 1855 (Secretary of State) | | | | | % Electorate 1855 |
	Republican	Soft	Hard	American	Not Voting	
Whig	16	0	-6	13	1	24
Soft	1	11	0	1	1	14
Hard	-3	1	11	3	4	16
Ineligible	-1	1	1	1	2	4
Not Voting	5	0	4	6	27	42
% Electorate 1855	18	14	11	23	34	

N = 525 townships.

TABLE 7.17

ESTIMATED RELATIONSHIPS BETWEEN VOTING FOR PRESIDENT
1848 AND SECRETARY OF STATE 1855: NEW YORK

	Party in 1855 (Secretary of State)					
Party in 1848 (President)	Republican	Soft	Hard	American	Not Voting	% Electorate 1855
Whig	7	−1	−1	18	10	34
Democrat	2	7	8	−2	4	19
Free Soil	8	5	−3	1	3	14
Ineligible	1	3	2	3	6	15
Not Voting	0	0	4	2	11	19
% Electorate 1855	18	14	11	23	34	

N = 512 townships.

TABLE 7.18

ESTIMATED PERCENTAGES BETWEEN VOTING FOR SECRETARY
OF STATE 1855 AND PLACE OF BIRTH 1855: NEW YORK

	Party in 1855 (Secretary of State)				
Place of Birth 1855	Republican	Soft	Hard	American	Not Voting
United States	27 %	8 %	6 %	23 %	36 %
England	46	0[a]	8	25	22
Germany	0[a]	39	17	13	31
Ireland	0[a]	7	45	17	31

N = 360 townships.

[a]Percentage set at minimum value and others adjusted.

517

TABLE 9.1

ESTIMATED RELATIONSHIPS BETWEEN VOTING FOR GOVERNOR
1854 AND GOVERNOR 1855: CONNECTICUT

| Party in 1854 (Governor) | Party in 1855 (Governor) | | | | |
	Whig	Democrat	American	Not Voting	% Electorate 1855
Whig	9	6	9	−1	22
Democrat	−2	22	11	1	32
Free Soil	1	−3	3	1	3
Temperance	3	2	8	−1	12
Ineligible	0	2	0	0	2
Not Voting	1	2	1	25	28
% Electorate 1855	11	31	32	26	

N = 146 townships.

TABLE 9.2

ESTIMATED RELATIONSHIPS BETWEEN VOTING FOR GOVERNOR
1852 AND GOVERNOR 1855: CONNECTICUT

| Party in 1852 (Governor) | Party in 1855 (Governor) | | | | |
	Whig	Democrat	American	Not Voting	% Electorate 1855
Whig	11	5	15	1	32
Democrat	−2	25	10	2	36
Free Soil	1	−2	3	1	3
Ineligible	0	1	0	6	7
Not Voting	1	1	3	17	21
% Electorate 1855	11	31	32	26	

N = 146 townships.

TABLE 9.3

ESTIMATED RELATIONSHIPS BETWEEN VOTING FOR GOVERNOR
1855 AND GOVERNOR 1856: CONNECTICUT

Party in 1856 (Governor)

Party in 1855 (Governor)	Republican	Democrat	American	Whig	Not Voting	% Electorate 1856
Whig	5	1	3	1	0	10
Democrat	-2	25	5	1	1	30
American	2	8	21	0	0	31
Ineligible	1	0	0	0	1	2
Not Voting	1	1	1	0	23	26
% Electorate 1856	8	36	29	1	25	

N = 146 townships.

TABLE 9.4

ESTIMATED RELATIONSHIPS BETWEEN VOTING FOR GOVERNOR
1854 AND GOVERNOR 1856: CONNECTICUT

Party in 1856 (Governor)

Party in 1854 (Governor)	Republican	Democrat	American	Whig	Not Voting	% Electorate 1856
Whig	1	5	14	2	0	22
Democrat	2	24	7	-1	-1	32
Free Soil	2	-1	1	0	1	3
Temperance	1	4	7	1	-1	12
Ineligible	1	2	0	0	1	4
Not Voting	0	2	1	0	24	28
% Electorate 1856	8	36	29	1	25	

N = 146 townships.

TABLE 9.5

ESTIMATED RELATIONSHIPS BETWEEN VOTING FOR GOVERNOR
1854 AND PROHIBITION REFERENDUM 1855:   IOWA

Party in 1854 (Governor)	Referendum in 1855 (Prohibition)			% Electorate 1855
	Yes	No	Not Voting	
Opposition (Grimes)	25	15	−11	29
Democrat	−1	15	14	27
Ineligible	6	4	14	25
Not Voting	2	−4	20	19
% Electorate 1855	33	30	37	

N = 60 counties.

TABLE 9.6

ESTIMATED RELATIONSHIPS BETWEEN VOTING FOR CONGRESS
1854 AND PROHIBITION REFERENDUM 1855:   ILLINOIS

Party in 1854 (Congress)	Referendum in 1855 (Prohibition)			% Electorate 1855
	Yes	No	Not Voting	
Anti−Nebraska	22	3	2	28
Democrat	2	13	6	21
Ineligible	1	−1	7	7
Not Voting	3	16	25	44
% Electorate 1855	27	32	40	

N = 99 counties.

Note: Numbers in the Anti−Nebraska row represent the combined vote for
all candidates opposed to the regular Democratic nominee.

TABLE 12.1

ESTIMATED RELATIONSHIPS BETWEEN VOTING FOR GOVERNOR
1855 AND GOVERNOR 1856: MAINE

| Party in 1855 (Governor) | Party in 1856 (Governor) | | | | |
	Republican	Democrat	Whig	Not Voting	% Electorate 1856
Republican	36	−2	1	−1	33
Democrat	3	28	−1	1	31
Whig	2	0	4	0	7
Ineligible	0	1	0	1	2
Not Voting	3	2	0	22	27
% Electorate 1856	45	29	4	22	

N = 380 townships.

TABLE 12.2

ESTIMATED RELATIONSHIPS BETWEEN VOTING FOR PRESIDENT
1852 AND GOVERNOR 1856: MAINE

| Party in 1852 (President) | Party in 1856 (Governor) | | | | |
	Republican	Democrat	Whig	Not Voting	% Electorate 1856
Whig	14	−2	6	2	21
Democrat	9	22	−1	−3	27
Free Soil	7	0	0	−2	5
Ineligible	3	2	0	3	7
Not Voting	11	6	0	23	40
% Electorate 1856	45	29	4	22	

N = 372 townships.

TABLE 12.3

ESTIMATED RELATIONSHIPS BETWEEN VOTING FOR GOVERNOR
1852 AND GOVERNOR 1856: MAINE

Party in 1852 (Governor)	Party in 1856 (Governor)				
	Republican	Democrat	Whig	Not Voting	% Electorate 1856
Whig	11	4	5	−1	19
Democrat	20	8	0	−1	27
Free Soil	2	0	0	0	1
Wildcat	4	10	0	1	14
Ineligible	2	3	0	2	7
Not Voting	6	5	0	21	32
% Electorate 1856	45	28	4	22	

N = 372 townships.

TABLE 12.4

ESTIMATED RELATIONSHIPS BETWEEN VOTING FOR GOVERNOR
1853 AND GOVERNOR 1856: MAINE

Party in 1853 (Governor)	Party in 1856 (Governor)				
	Republican	Democrat	Whig	Not Voting	% Electorate 1856
Whig	14	−2	6	−1	17
Democrat	4	20	−1	0	23
Free Soil	7	−1	0	0	6
Morrill	5	1	0	1	7
Ineligible 1853	2	2	0	1	5
Not Voting	12	8	0	21	41
% Electorate 1856	45	29	4	22	

N = 380 townships.

TABLE 12.5

ESTIMATED RELATIONSHIPS BETWEEN VOTING FOR GOVERNOR
1854 AND GOVERNOR 1856: MAINE

Party in 1856 (Governor)

Party in 1854 (Governor)	Republican	Democrat	Whig	Not Voting	% Electorate 1856
Whig	6	0	4	−1	9
Democrat	3	16	−2	0	18
Morrill	26	3	2	−3	29
Liberal (Cary)	0	2	0	0	2
Ineligible	1	1	0	1	4
Not Voting	8	6	0	25	38
% Electorate 1856	45	29	4	22	

N = 380 townships.

TABLE 12.6

ESTIMATED RELATIONSHIPS BETWEEN VOTING FOR GOVERNOR
1855 AND SUPREME COURT JUSTICE 1856: OHIO

Party in 1856 (Supreme Court Justice)

Party in 1855 (Governor)	Republican	Democrat	American	Not Voting	% Electorate 1856
Republican	36	1	−2	−1	34
Democrat	0	36	3	−8	30
Trimble	0	0	4	1	6
Ineligible	2	−2	1	3	3
Not Voting	3	2	1	21	27
% Electorate 1856	41	36	6	17	

N = 88 counties.

TABLE 12.7

ESTIMATED RELATIONSHIPS BETWEEN VOTING FOR PRESIDENT
1852 AND GOVERNOR 1856:   INDIANA

| Party in 1852 (President) | Party in 1856 (Governor) | | | |
	People's	Democrat	Not Voting	% Electorate 1856
Whig	29	−2	3	30
Democrat	−2	36	1	36
Free Soil	4	−1	−1	3
Ineligible	6	7	1	14
Not Voting	3	4	10	17
% Electorate 1856	42	44	14	

N = 91 counties.

TABLE 12.8

ESTIMATED RELATIONSHIPS BETWEEN VOTING FOR SECRETARY
OF STATE 1854 AND GOVERNOR 1856:   INDIANA

| Party in 1854 (Secretary of State) | Party in 1856 (Governor) | | | |
	People's	Democrat	Not Voting	% Electorate 1856
People's	35	2	0	37
Democrat	−2	32	2	33
Ineligible	4	3	0	7
Not Voting	5	6	12	23
% Electorate 1856	42	44	14	

N = 91 counties.

TABLE 12.9

ESTIMATED RELATIONSHIPS BETWEEN VOTING FOR PRESIDENT
1852 AND CANAL COMMISSIONER 1856:   PENNSYLVANIA

| | Party in 1856 (Canal Commissioner) | | | |
Party in 1852 (President)	Union	Democrat	Not Voting	% Electorate 1856
Whig	23	3	5	31
Democrat	5	28	1	34
Free Soil	3	−1	0	1
Ineligible	2	3	4	8
Not Voting	5	4	17	25
% Electorate 1856	36	37	27	

N = 63 counties.

TABLE 12.10

ESTIMATED RELATIONSHIPS BETWEEN VOTING FOR SUPREME COURT
JUSTICE 1854 AND CANAL COMMISSIONER 1856:   PENNSYLVANIA

| | Party in 1856 (Canal Commissioner) | | | |
Party in 1854 (Supreme Court)	Union	Democrat	Not Voting	% Electorate 1856
Whig	14	−1	0	13
Democrat	−3	31	1	29
American	17	4	0	21
Ineligible	1	1	3	4
Not Voting	9	1	24	34
% Electorate 1856	36	37	27	

N = 63 counties.

TABLE 13.1

POPULAR VOTE FOR PRESIDENT 1856: NORTHERN STATES

| State | Frémont | | Buchanan | | Fillmore | |
	No.	%	No.	%	No.	%
California	20,695	18.8	53,368	48.4	36,210	32.8
Connecticut	43,077	53.4	35,028	43.4	2,615	3.2
Illinois	96,158	40.2	105,526	44.1	37,595	15.7
Indiana	94,378	40.1	118,673	50.4	22,405	9.5
Iowa	43,954	49.1	36,170	40.4	9,380	10.5
Maine	67,179	61.3	39,080	35.7	3,325	3.0
Massachusetts	108,190	64.8	39,240	23.5	19,626	11.7
Michigan	71,766	57.2	52,138	41.5	1,660	1.3
New Hampshire	37,473	53.7	31,892	45.7	410	0.6
New Jersey	28,339	28.4	47,446	47.5	24,114	24.1
New York	276,007	46.3	195,878	32.8	124,809	20.9
Ohio	187,497	48.5	170,874	44.2	28,121	7.3
Pennsylvania	147,510	32.0	230,700	50.1	82,176*	17.9
Rhode Island	11,467	57.8	6,680	33.7	1,675	8.5
Vermont	39,561	78.1	10,569	20.9	545	1.1
Wisconsin	66,090	55.3	52,843	44.2	580	0.5
Total North	1,339,341	45.2	1,226,105	41.4	395,246	13.4
Total South	1,196	0.1	606,850	56.0	476,485	43.9
TOTAL	1,340,537	33.1	1,832,955	45.3	871,731	21.6

*Fillmore Union, 55,838; Fillmore Straight, 26,338.

TABLE 13.2

ESTIMATED RELATIONSHIPS BETWEEN VOTING FOR PRESIDENT
1852 AND PRESIDENT 1856: CONNECTICUT

Party in 1852 (President)	Party in 1856 (President)				
	Republican	Democrat	American	Not Voting	% Electorate 1856
Whig	26	7	5	−4	34
Democrat	14	30	−2	−4	37
Free Soil	6	−1	0	−1	4
Ineligible	1	1	0	7	9
Not Voting	1	2	0	13	16
% Electorate 1856	48	39	3	10	

N = 146 townships.

TABLE 13.3

ESTIMATED RELATIONSHIPS BETWEEN VOTING FOR PRESIDENT
1852 AND PRESIDENT 1856: ILLINOIS

Party in 1852 (President)	Party in 1856 (President)				
	Republican	Democrat	American	Not Voting	% Electorate 1856
Whig	15	−2	8	−1	21
Democrat	−9	30	1	4	26
Free Soil	9	−2	−1	−3	3
Ineligible	12	9	3	3	27
Not Voting	4	0	1	19	23
% Electorate 1856	31	34	12	23	

N = 99 counties.

TABLE 13.4

ESTIMATED RELATIONSHIPS BETWEEN VOTING FOR PRESIDENT
1852 AND PRESIDENT 1856: INDIANA

Party in 1852 (President)	Party in 1856 (President)				
	Republican	Democrat	American	Not Voting	% Electorate 1856
Whig	24	−4	8	3	30
Democrat	1	39	−4	0	36
Free Soil	7	−1	−2	−1	3
Ineligible	6	8	0	0	14
Not Voting	−3	3	7	10	17
% Electorate 1856	35	45	8	12	

N = 91 counties.

TABLE 13.5

ESTIMATED RELATIONSHIPS BETWEEN VOTING FOR PRESIDENT
1852 AND PRESIDENT 1856: MAINE

Party in 1852 (President)	Party in 1856 (President)				
	Republican	Democrat	American	Not Voting	% Electorate 1856
Whig	14	1	2	3	21
Democrat	9	20	0	−2	27
Free Soil	7	0	0	−2	5
Ineligible	3	1	0	4	7
Not Voting	10	3	0	26	40
% Electorate 1856	43	25	2	29	

N = 372 townships.

TABLE 13.6

ESTIMATED RELATIONSHIPS BETWEEN VOTING FOR PRESIDENT
1852 AND PRESIDENT 1856: MASSACHUSETTS

Party in 1852 (President)	Party in 1856 (President)				
	Republican	Democrat	American	Not Voting	% Electorate 1856
Whig	22	0	2	3	26
Democrat	8	13	5	−3	22
Free Soil	16	−1	−2	0	14
Ineligible	1	2	2	4	9
Not Voting	5	4	4	16	28
% Electorate 1856	52	17	11	20	

N = 315 townships.

TABLE 13.7

ESTIMATED RELATIONSHIPS BETWEEN VOTING FOR PRESIDENT
1852 AND PRESIDENT 1856: NEW YORK

Party in 1852 (President)	Party in 1856 (President)				
	Republican	Democrat	American	Not Voting	% Electorate 1856
Whig	22	−5	14	4	34
Democrat	8	28	2	0	37
Free Soil	6	−1	−2	0	2
Ineligible	0	5	2	2	10
Not Voting	0	6	4	7	17
% Electorate 1856	35	33	20	12	

N = 480 townships.

TABLE 13.8

ESTIMATED RELATIONSHIPS BETWEEN VOTING FOR PRESIDENT
1852 AND PRESIDENT 1856: OHIO

Party in 1856 (President)

Party in 1852 (President)	Republican	Democrat	American	Not Voting	% Electorate 1856
Whig	20	3	9	3	35
Democrat	11	35	−4	−4	39
Free Soil	11	−1	−2	0	7
Ineligible	4	1	0	5	9
Not Voting	−2	2	3	7	10
% Electorate 1856	43	39	6	11	

N = 88 counties.

TABLE 13.9

ESTIMATED RELATIONSHIPS BETWEEN VOTING FOR PRESIDENT
1852 AND PRESIDENT 1856: PENNSYLVANIA

Party in 1856 (President)

Party in 1852 (President)	Republican	Democrat	Fillmore Union	Fillmore Straight	Not Voting	% Electorate 1856
Whig	13	3	10	1	4	31
Democrat	6	30	1	−2	−1	34
Free Soil	7	−1	−3	−1	−1	1
Ineligible	−3	4	4	1	2	8
Not Voting	2	4	−3	5	17	25
% Electorate 1856	25	40	10	5	21	

N = 63 counties.

530

TABLE 13.10

ESTIMATED RELATIONSHIPS BETWEEN VOTING FOR PRESIDENT
1852 AND GOVERNOR 1856:   ILLINOIS

| Party in 1852 (President) | Party in 1856 (Governor) | | | | |
	Republican	Democrat	American	Not Voting	% Electorate 1856
Whig	19	−2	3	1	21
Democrat	−8	31	0	3	26
Free Soil	8	−2	0	−3	3
Ineligible	12	9	3	2	27
Not Voting	4	−1	0	20	23
% Electorate 1856	36	34	6	23	

N = 99 counties.

TABLE 13.11

ESTIMATED RELATIONSHIPS BETWEEN VOTING FOR GOVERNOR
1855 AND PRESIDENT 1856:   OHIO

| Party in 1855 (Governor) | Party in 1856 (President) | | | | |
	Republican	Democrat	American	Not Voting	% Electorate 1856
Republican	38	1	1	−7	34
Democrat	−5	34	0	1	30
Trimble	1	1	4	−1	6
Ineligible	0	−2	0	5	3
Not Voting	9	6	0	12	27
% Electorate 1856	43	39	6	11	

N = 88 counties.

TABLE 13.12

ESTIMATED RELATIONSHIPS BETWEEN VOTING FOR GOVERNOR
1854 AND PRESIDENT 1856:   NEW YORK

Party in 1854 (Governor)	Party in 1856 (President)				
	Republican	Democrat	American	Not Voting	% Electorate 1856
Whig	28	−8	2	−1	21
Soft	0	23	2	−1	24
Hard	−2	5	2	0	5
American	7	3	9	0	19
Ineligible	−1	3	1	2	5
Not Voting	3	6	4	13	26
% Electorate 1856	35	32	20	12	

N = 515 townships.

TABLE 13.13

ESTIMATED RELATIONSHIPS BETWEEN VOTING FOR SECRETARY
OF STATE 1855 AND PRESIDENT 1856:   NEW YORK

Party in 1855 (Secretary of State)	Party in 1856 (President)				
	Republican	Democrat	American	Not Voting	% Electorate 1856
Republican	24	−2	−3	−2	17
Soft	1	13	1	−1	14
Hard	−2	11	1	0	11
American	2	4	16	1	22
Ineligible	1	1	0	1	3
Not Voting	9	6	5	14	33
% Electorate 1856	35	32	20	12	

N = 512 townships.

TABLE 13.14

ESTIMATED RELATIONSHIPS BETWEEN VOTING FOR GOVERNOR
1856 AND PRESIDENT 1856:   CONNECTICUT

| | Party in 1856 (President) | | | | |
Party in 1856 (Governor)	Republican	Democrat	American	Not Voting	% Electorate 1856
Republican	11	1	0	−4	8
Democrat	1	34	0	1	36
American	32	2	2	−7	29
Whig	2	1	1	−1	1
Not Voting	2	1	1	22	25
% Electorate 1856	48	39	3	10	

N = 146 townships.

TABLE 13.15

ESTIMATED RELATIONSHIPS BETWEEN VOTING FOR GOVERNOR
1854 AND PRESIDENT 1856:   MASSACHUSETTS

| | Party in 1856 (President) | | | | |
Party in 1854 (Governor)	Republican	Democrat	American	Not Voting	% Electorate 1856
Whig	6	3	7	−3	13
Democrat	4	5	−2	−1	6
American	28	5	5	1	40
Free Soil	8	−2	−2	0	3
Ineligible	−1	1	2	2	5
Not Voting	6	5	2	20	33
% Electorate 1856	52	17	11	20	

N = 323 townships.

TABLE 13.16

ESTIMATED RELATIONSHIPS BETWEEN VOTING FOR GOVERNOR
1855 AND PRESIDENT 1856: MASSACHUSETTS

Party in 1855 (Governor)	Party in 1856 (President)				
	Republican	Democrat	American	Not Voting	% Electorate 1856
Republican	22	−2	−2	0	18
Democrat	4	12	3	−3	17
American	18	2	5	0	25
Whig	2	1	5	−1	6
Ineligible	−1	1	1	2	2
Not Voting	6	3	0	22	31
% Electorate 1856	52	17	11	20	

N = 322 townships.

TABLE 13.17

ESTIMATED RELATIONSHIPS BETWEEN VOTING FOR GOVERNOR
1856 AND PRESIDENT 1856: MASSACHUSETTS

Party in 1856 (Governor)	Party in 1856 (President)				
	Republican	Democrat	American	Not Voting	% Electorate 1856
Democrat	2	17	2	−1	20
North American (Gardner)	44	−2	2	0	45
Fillmore American	−1	1	4	1	5
Whig	0	0	4	0	4
Honest Man's Ticket	3	0	0	0	3
Not Voting	4	1	0	20	24
% Electorate 1856	52	17	11	20	

N = 322 townships.

TABLE 13.18

ESTIMATED RELATIONSHIPS BETWEEN VOTING FOR SUPREME COURT
JUSTICE 1854 AND PRESIDENT 1856:   PENNSYLVANIA

Party in 1856 (President)

Party in 1854 (Supreme Court)	Republican	Democrat	Fillmore Union	Straight	Not Voting	% Electorate 1856
Whig	17	−1	0	−1	−2	13
Democrat	−8	33	3	−1	1	29
American	3	4	12	2	1	21
Ineligible	−3	2	3	1	2	4
Not Voting	17	2	−9	3	20	34
% Electorate 1856	25	40	10	5	21	

N = 63 counties.

TABLE 13.19

ESTIMATED RELATIONSHIPS BETWEEN VOTING FOR SECRETARY
OF STATE 1854 AND PRESIDENT 1856:   INDIANA

Party in 1856 (President)

Party in 1854 (Secretary of State)	Republican	Democrat	American	Not Voting	% Electorate 1856
People's	40	0	−2	−1	37
Democrat	−6	34	2	3	33
Ineligible	3	3	1	0	7
Not Voting	−2	7	8	10	23
% Electorate 1856	36	45	8	12	

N = 91 counties.

TABLE 13.20

ESTIMATED RELATIONSHIPS BETWEEN VOTING FOR BOARD OF
PUBLIC WORKS 1854 AND PRESIDENT 1856: OHIO

| Party in 1854 (Public Works) | Party in 1856 (President) | | | | % Electorate 1856 |
	Republican	Democrat	American	Not Voting	
People's	31	8	6	-2	42
Democrat	2	26	-1	-1	25
Ineligible	-7	2	2	9	5
Not Voting	17	4	0	6	27
% Electorate 1856	43	39	6	11	

N = 88 counties.

TABLE 13.21

ESTIMATED RELATIONSHIPS BETWEEN VOTING FOR GOVERNOR
1854 AND PRESIDENT 1856: MAINE

| Party in 1854 (Governor) | Party in 1856 (President) | | | | % Electorate 1856 |
	Republican	Democrat	American	Not Voting	
Whig	6	1	1	0	9
Democrat	4	14	-1	1	18
Morrill	26	3	1	0	29
Liberal (Cary)	0	1	0	1	2
Ineligible	1	2	0	1	4
Not Voting	7	5	1	26	38
% Electorate 1856	43	25	2	29	

N = 380 townships.

TABLE 13.22

ESTIMATED RELATIONSHIPS BETWEEN VOTING FOR GOVERNOR
1854 AND PRESIDENT 1856:   IOWA

	Party in 1856 (President)				
Party in 1854 (Governor)	Republican	Democrat	American	Not Voting	% Electorate 1856
Opposition (Grimes)	31	−5	1	−3	24
Democrat	−14	30	7	−2	22
Ineligible	21	11	0	7	40
Not Voting	6	1	1	8	15
% Electorate 1856	44	37	10	10	

N = 63 counties.

TABLE 13.23

ESTIMATED RELATIONSHIPS BETWEEN VOTING FOR CONGRESS
1854 AND PRESIDENT 1856:   ILLINOIS

	Party in 1856 (President)				
Party in 1854 (Congress)	Republican	Democrat	American	Not Voting	% Electorate 1856
Anti-Nebraska	28	−1	4	−5	26
Democrat	−8	19	7	2	20
Ineligible	6	6	1	1	13
Not Voting	6	10	0	25	41
% Electorate 1856	31	34	12	23	

N = 99 counties.

Anti-Nebraska is the combined vote for all anti-Douglas candidates.

TABLE 13.24

ESTIMATED PERCENTAGES BETWEEN VOTING FOR PRESIDENT
1856 AND PLACE OF BIRTH 1855: NEW YORK

| Place of Birth 1855 | Party in 1856 (President) | | | |
	Republican	Democrat	American	Not Voting
United States	46 %	24 %	19 %	12 %
Foreign-Born	16	56	16	12
New England	100[a]	0[a]	0	0
Rest of U.S.	39	25	22	14
Britain	85	0[a]	15	0[a]
Germany	10	60	14	16
Ireland	0[a]	68	17	14

N = 360 townships. Britain is England, Scotland, and Wales.

[a]Percentage set at maximum or minimum value and others adjusted.

TABLE 13.25

ESTIMATED PERCENTAGES BETWEEN VOTING FOR PRESIDENT
1856 AND PLACE OF BIRTH 1850: INDIANA

| Place of Birth 1850 | Party in 1856 (President) | | | |
	Republican	Democrat	American	Not Voting
United States	42 %	43 %	6 %	9 %
Foreign-Born	0[a]	38	32	29
Yankee	52	29	8	10
Southern U.S.	15	47	22	16
Germany	0[a]	55	21	24

N = 91 counties.

[a]Percentage set at minimum value and others adjusted.

TABLE 13.26

ESTIMATED PERCENTAGES BETWEEN VOTING FOR PRESIDENT
1856 AND PLACE OF BIRTH 1856:   IOWA

| Place of Birth 1856 | Party in 1856 (President) | | | |
	Republican	Democrat	American	Not Voting
United States	49	32	10	9
Foreign-Born	9	68	6	17
Yankee	62	0[a]	0[a]	38
Southern U.S.	0[a]	38	35	28
Germany	0[a]	25	25	50
Britain	42	16	0[a]	42
Ireland	29	71	0[a]	0[a]
Scandinavia	47	0[a]	0[a]	53

N = 63 counties.   Britain is England, Scotland, and Wales.

[a]Percentage set at minimum value and others adjusted.

TABLE 13.27

ESTIMATED PERCENTAGES BETWEEN VOTING FOR PRESIDENT
1856 AND RELIGION 1855: NEW YORK

| Religion 1855 (Attendance) | Party in 1856 (President) | | | |
	Republican	Democrat	American	Not Voting
Baptist	100^a%	0^a%	0^a%	0^a%
Congregational	100^a	0^a	0^a	0^a
Dutch Reform	0^a	26	74	0^a
Episcopal	0^a	50	22	27
Lutheran	0^a	60	40	0^a
Methodist	22	28	8	41
Presbyterian	32	1	67	0^a
Catholic	0^a	70	21	10

N = 60 counties.

^{a}Percentage set at maximum or minimum value and others adjusted.

TABLE 13.28

ESTIMATED PERCENTAGES BETWEEN VOTING FOR PRESIDENT
1856 AND RELIGION 1860: PENNSYLVANIA

| Religion 1860 (Attendance) | Party in 1856 (President) | | | | |
| | Republican | Democrat | Fillmore | | Not Voting |
			Union	Straight	
Baptist	86 %	11 %	2 %	0[a]%	0 %
German Reformed	51	39	0[a]	10	0[a]
Lutheran	0[a]	40	56	0[a]	3
Methodist	48	26	26	0[a]	0[a]
Presbyterian	91	9	0[a]	0[a]	0[a]

N = 63 counties.

[a]Percentage set at minimum value and others adjusted.

TABLE 13.29

ESTIMATED PERCENTAGES BETWEEN VOTING FOR PRESIDENT
1856 AND RELIGION 1860: OHIO

| Religion 1860 (Attendance) | Party in 1856 (President) | | | Not Voting |
	Republican	Democrat	American	
Baptist	82 %	0[a]%	18 %	0[a]%
Congregational	100[a]	0[a]	0[a]	0[a]
German Reformed	98	2	0[a]	0[a]
Lutheran	11	89	0[a]	0[a]
Methodist	28	58	14	0[a]
Presbyterian	76	24	0[a]	0[a]

N = 88 counties.

[a]Percentage set at maximum or minimum value and others adjusted.

TABLE 13.30

ESTIMATED PERCENTAGES BETWEEN VOTING FOR PRESIDENT
1856 AND RELIGION 1860: INDIANA

Religion 1860 (Attendance)	Party in 1856 (President)			
	Republican	Democrat	American	Not Voting
Baptist	0[a]%	46 %	40 %	14 %
Lutheran	30	70	0[a]	0[a]
Methodist	12	52	26	10
Presbyterian	22	44	10	24

N = 90 counties.

[a]Percentage set at minimum value and others adjusted.

TABLE 13.31

ESTIMATED PERCENTAGES BETWEEN VOTING FOR PRESIDENT
1856 AND RELIGION 1860: ILLINOIS

Religion 1860 Attendance	Party in 1856 (President)			
	Republican	Democrat	American	Not Voting
Baptist	0[a]%	48 %	47 %	5 %
Lutheran	54	0[a]	0[a]	46
Methodist	0[a]	64	36	0[a]
Presbyterian	47	12	19	22

N = 97 counties.

[a]Percentage set at minimum value and others adjusted.

TABLE 13.32

ESTIMATED RELATIONSHIPS BETWEEN VOTING ON PROHIBITION
REFERENDUM 1854 AND PRESIDENT 1856: PENNSYLVANIA

Referendum in 1854 (Prohibition)	Party in 1856 (President)					
	Republican	Democrat	Fillmore		Not Voting	% Electorate 1856
			Union	Straight		
Yes	25	7	3	−2	−6	27
No	−2	22	8	0	0	28
Ineligible	−4	3	3	1	1	4
Not Voting	7	7	−5	5	25	40
% Electorate 1856	25	40	10	5	21	

N = 63 counties.

TABLE 13.33

ESTIMATED RELATIONSHIPS BETWEEN VOTING ON PROHIBITION
REFERENDUM 1855 AND PRESIDENT 1856: IOWA

Referendum in 1855 (Prohibition)	Party in 1856 (President)				
	Republican	Democrat	American	Not Voting	% Electorate 1856
Yes	25	−2	0	2	26
No	1	22	7	−5	24
Ineligible	14	3	−3	6	20
Not Voting	3	14	6	7	30
% Electorate 1856	43	37	10	10	

N = 61 counties.

TABLE 13.34

ESTIMATED RELATIONSHIPS BETWEEN VOTING ON PROHIBITION
REFERENDUM 1855 AND PRESIDENT 1856:   ILLINOIS

Referendum in 1855 (Prohibition)	Party in 1856 (President)				
	Republican	Democrat	American	Not Voting	% Electorate 1856
Yes	25	1	5	−5	26
No	0	17	6	7	30
Ineligible	4	3	0	−1	7
Not Voting	2	13	1	21	38
% Electorate 1856	31	34	12	23	

N = 99 counties.

TABLE 13.35

ESTIMATED RELATIONSHIPS BETWEEN VOTING ON PROHIBITION
REFERENDUM 1851 AND PRESIDENT 1856:   OHIO

Referendum 1851 (Prohibition)	Party in 1856 (President)				
	Republican	Democrat	American	Not Voting	% Electorate 1856
Yes	18	4	4	0	26
No	15	19	−6	−5	24
Ineligible	0	1	1	9	11
Not Voting	10	15	7	6	38
% Electorate 1856	43	39	6	11	

N = 88 counties.

TABLE 13.36

ESTIMATED PERCENTAGES BETWEEN VOTING FOR PRESIDENT
1856 AND OCCUPATION 1856:   IOWA

Occupation 1856	Party in 1856 (President)			
	Republican	Democrat	American	Not Voting
Farmer	41 %	37 %	14 %	8 %
Skilled Worker	86	13	0[a]	0
Unskilled Worker	13	18	27	41

N = 63 counties.

[a]Percentage set at minimum value and others adjusted.

TABLE 13.37

ESTIMATED PERCENTAGES BETWEEN VOTING FOR PRESIDENT
1856 AND OCCUPATION 1850:   CHAUTAUQUA COUNTY, NEW YORK

Occupation 1850	Party in 1856 (President)			
	Republican	Democrat	American	Not Voting
Farmer	70 %	13 %	7 %	9 %
Skilled Worker	84	14	2	0[a]
Unskilled Worker	55	9	36	0
Professional–Merchant	95	0[a]	0[a]	5

N = 24 townships.

[a]Percentage set at minimum value and others adjusted.

TABLE 13.38

ESTIMATED PERCENTAGES BETWEEN VOTING FOR PRESIDENT
1856 AND OCCUPATION 1860:   CINCINNATI

| Occupation 1860 | Party in 1856 (President) | | | |
	Republican	Democrat	American	Not Voting
Skilled Worker	31 %	23 %	1 %	45 %
Unskilled Worker	0[a]	74	19	7
Clerk-Sales	15	32	17	36
Professional-Merchant	32	0[a]	68	0[a]

N = 17 wards.

[a]Percentage set at minimum value and others adjusted.

TABLE 13.39

ESTIMATED PERCENTAGES BETWEEN VOTING FOR PRESIDENT
1856 AND WEALTH 1860:   CINCINNATI

| Wealth 1860 | Party in 1856 (President) | | | |
	Republican	Democrat	American	Not Voting
Less than $100	14 %	39 %	27 %	20 %
$100-999	34	21	0[a]	45
$1,000-4,999	48	7	35	10
$5,000-9,999	16	0[a]	84	0[a]
$10,000+	0	40	0[a]	59

N = 17 wards.

[a]Percentage set at minimum value and others adjusted.

TABLE 13.40

INFLUENCE OF EXPLANATORY VARIABLES ON REPUBLICAN VOTE
FOR PRESIDENT 1856: NEW YORK

Explanatory Variable	Regression Coefficient	Standard Error	Beta Coefficient	Change in R^2
Yankee	.51	.03	.14	.44
Catholic	-.90	.03	-.33	.19
Baptist	.70	.03	.13	.06
Universalist	4.39	.16	.16	.03
Blacks	-1.15	.12	-.09	.02
Born in Wales	2.70	.13	.12	.02
Born in Germany	-.54	.03	-.19	.01
Dutch Reform	-.85	.03	-.18	.01
Per Capita Wealth	.02	.00	.19	.01
Episcopal	-2.27	.09	-.23	.02
Unitarian	3.12	.64	.04	.01
Methodist	-.77	.04	-.14	.01
Population/Acre	-.06	.00	-.31	.01

Mult. R = .91

R^2 = .83

N = 60 counties.

TABLE 13.41

INFLUENCE OF EXPLANATORY VARIABLES ON REPUBLICAN VOTE
FOR PRESIDENT 1856:   PENNSYLVANIA

Explanatory Variable	Regression Coefficient	Standard Error	Beta Coefficient	Change in R^2
Yankee	1.08	.01	.50	.29
Presbyterian	.30	.01	.24	.23
Males 21-29	-.72	.08	-.07	.06
Home Manufacturing	2.13	.06	.21	.04
Born in Scotland	8.06	.27	.16	.05
Population/Acre	-2.46	.09	- .33	.03
Farms 1,000+ Acres	-.44	.01	-.36	.03
Per Capita Wealth	.02	.00	.23	.02
Farms 10-100 Acres	-.95	.03	-.33	.02
Dutch Reform	-2.38	.09	-.13	.01
Value Manufactured Products/Employee	-.00	.00	-.11	.01
Value of Slaughtered Animals	-.07	.00	-.16	.00
Born in Ireland	1.19	.07	.23	.00
Catholic	-.52	.02	-.18	.01
Methodist	-.24	.01	-.13	.01

Mult. R = .89

R^2 = .79

N = 63 counties.

TABLE 13.42

INFLUENCE OF EXPLANATORY VARIABLES ON REPUBLICAN VOTE
FOR PRESIDENT 1856: OHIO

Explanatory Variable	Regression Coefficient	Standard Error	Beta Coefficient	Change in R^2
Males 50 and Above	.04*	.05	.01	.32
Yankee	.58	.02	.28	.10
Born in Germany	−.59	.03	−.22	.09
Home Manufacturing	−.50	.06	−.06	.07
Born in South	−.67	.03	−.23	.03
Free Will Baptist	1.42	.04	.20	.03
Other Foreign-Born	−2.84	.06	−.31	.02
German Reform	.76	.02	.19	.01
Lutheran	−.32	.01	−.16	.01
Per Capita Wealth	.02	.00	.19	.00
Methodist	−.03	.01	−.04	.01
Manufacturing Workers	−1.04	.03	−.35	.00
Born in Ireland	1.41	.07	.19	.01

*Not significant at the .05 level.

Mult. R = .84

R^2 = .71

N = 88 counties.

TABLE 13.43

INFLUENCE OF EXPLANATORY VARIABLES ON REPUBLICAN VOTE
FOR PRESIDENT 1856: INDIANA

Explanatory Variable	Regression Coefficient	Standard Error	Beta Coefficient	Change in R^2
Value/Acre	$-.41$	.03	$-.20$	.25
Born in South	$-.60$	.03	$-.20$	.19
Born in Germany	$-.83$	.03	$-.28$	.10
Born in Indiana	$-.78$	.02	$-.42$	.05
Quaker	.62	.02	.20	.03
Born in England–Wales	-12.13	.35	$-.40$	.03
Improved Acreage	.49	.02	.26	.03
Christian Connection	$-.36$	.01	$-.20$	.03
Market Gardening	$-.14$	.01	$-.09$	.01
German Reform	-2.6	.13	$-.12$	.01
Baptist	$-.12$	.01	$-.08$	.01
Value of Slaughtered Animals	$-.04$	.00	$-.07$	.01
Per Capita Wealth	.05	.00	.36	.01

Mult. R = .86

R^2 = .75

N = 88 counties.

550

TABLE 13.44

INFLUENCE OF EXPLANATORY VARIABLES ON REPUBLICAN VOTE
FOR PRESIDENT 1856: ILLINOIS

Explanatory Variable	Regression Coefficient	Standard Error	Beta Coefficient	Change in R^2
Yankee	.54	.01	.22	.76
Born in South	−.79	.01	−.31	.05
Born in Illinois	−.91	.01	−.35	.03
Catholic	−.10	.01	−.03	.02
Males 50 and Above	.78	.05	.09	.02
Congregational	.80	.02	.15	.01
Population/Acre	−69.27	1.85	−.23	.01
Per Capita Wealth	.01	.00	.06	.01

Mult. R = .95

R^2 = .91

N = 89 counties.

Index